HALSBURY'S Laws of England

FIFTH EDITION
2016

Volume 103

This is volume 103 of the Fifth Edition of Halsbury's Laws of England, containing the second part of the title WILLS AND INTESTACY.

The title WILLS AND INTESTACY replaces the WILLS AND INTESTACY title contained in volumes 102 (2010) and 103 (2010). Upon receipt of volumes 102 (2016) and 103 (2016), volumes 102 (2010) and 103 (2010) may be archived.

For a full list of volumes comprised in a current set of Halsbury's Laws of England please see overleaf.

Fifth Edition volumes:

1 (2008), 2 (2008), 3 (2011), 4 (2011), 5 (2013), 6 (2011), 7 (2015), 8 (2015), 9 (2012), 10 (2012), 11 (2015), 12 (2015), 12A (2015), 13 (2009), 14 (2016), 15 (2016), 15A (2016), 16 (2011), 17 (2011), 18 (2009), 19 (2011), 20 (2014), 21 (2016), 22 (2012), 23 (2016), 24 (2010), 25 (2016), 26 (2016), 27 (2015), 28 (2015), 29 (2014), 30 (2012), 31 (2012), 32 (2012), 33 (2013), 34 (2011), 35 (2015), 36 (2015), 37 (2013), 38 (2013), 38A (2013), 39 (2014), 40 (2014), 41 (2014), 41A (2014), 42 (2011), 43 (2011), 44 (2011), 45 (2010), 46 (2010), 47 (2014), 47A (2014), 48 (2015), 49 (2015), 50 (2016), 50A (2016), 51 (2013), 52 (2014), 53 (2014), 54 (2008), 55 (2012), 56 (2011), 57 (2012), 58 (2014), 58A (2014), 59 (2014), 59A (2014), 60 (2011), 61 (2010), 62 (2012), 63 (2012), 64 (2012), 65 (2015), 66 (2015), 67 (2016), 68 (2016), 69 (2009), 70 (2012), 71 (2013), 72 (2015), 73 (2015), 74 (2011), 75 (2013), 76 (2013), 77 (2016), 78 (2010), 79 (2014), 80 (2013), 81 (2010), 82 (2010), 83 (2010), 84 (2013), 84A (2013), 85 (2012), 86 (2013), 87 (2012), 88 (2012), 88A (2013), 89 (2011), 90 (2011), 91 (2012), 92 (2015), 93 (2008), 94 (2008), 95 (2013), 96 (2012), 97 (2015), 97A (2014), 98 (2013), 99 (2012), 100 (2009), 101 (2009), 102 (2016), 103 (2016), 104 (2014)

Consolidated Index and Tables:

2016 Consolidated Index (A–E), 2016 Consolidated Index (F–O), 2016 Consolidated Index (P–Z), 2017 Consolidated Table of Statutes, 2017 Consolidated Table of Statutory Instruments, etc, 2016 Consolidated Table of Cases (A–G), 2016 Consolidated Table of Cases (H–Q), 2016 Consolidated Table of Cases (R–Z, ECJ Cases)

Updating and ancillary materials:

2016 Annual Cumulative Supplement; Monthly Current Service; Annual Abridgments 1974–2015

October 2016

HALSBURY'S
Laws of England

Volume 103

2016

LexisNexis®

Members of the LexisNexis Group worldwide

United Kingdom	RELX (UK) Ltd, trading as LexisNexis, 1–3 Strand, London WC2N 5JR and 9–10 St Andrew Square, Edinburgh EH2 2AF
Australia	Reed International Books Australia Pty Ltd trading as LexisNexis, Chatswood, New South Wales
Austria	LexisNexis Verlag ARD Orac GmbH & Co KG, Vienna
Benelux	LexisNexis Benelux, Amsterdam
Canada	LexisNexis Canada, Markham, Ontario
China	LexisNexis China, Beijing and Shanghai
France	LexisNexis SA, Paris
Germany	LexisNexis GmbH, Dusseldorf
Hong Kong	LexisNexis Hong Kong, Hong Kong
India	LexisNexis India, New Delhi
Italy	Giuffrè Editore, Milan
Japan	LexisNexis Japan, Tokyo
Malaysia	Malayan Law Journal Sdn Bhd, Kuala Lumpur
New Zealand	LexisNexis New Zealand Ltd, Wellington
Singapore	LexisNexis Singapore, Singapore
South Africa	LexisNexis, Durban
USA	LexisNexis, Dayton, Ohio

FIRST EDITION	*Published in 31 volumes between 1907 and 1917*
SECOND EDITION	*Published in 37 volumes between 1931 and 1942*
THIRD EDITION	*Published in 43 volumes between 1952 and 1964*
FOURTH EDITION	*Published in 56 volumes between 1973 and 1987, with reissues between 1988 and 2008*
FIFTH EDITION	*Published between 2008 and 2014, with reissues from 2014*

A CIP Catalogue record for this book is available from the British Library.

ISBN 978-1-4743-0580-8

9 781474 305808

ISBN for the set: 9781405734394

ISBN for this volume: 9781474305808

Typeset by LexisNexis
Printed and bound by CPI Group (UK) Ltd, Croydon, CR0 4YY

Visit LexisNexis at www.lexisnexis.co.uk

HALSBURY ADVISORY BOARD

EDITORS OF THIS VOLUME

RICHARD DEY, BA, LLB, LLM

MOHINI TULLOCH, LLM

FRANCES WARD, LLB,
of the Middle Temple, Barrister

AMANDA WILLIS, LLM

and

AMANDA WRIGHT, LLB

MANAGING EDITOR

HELEN HALVEY, LLB

WILLS AND INTESTACY

Consultant Editor

PROFESSOR LESLEY KING, LLB, Dip Crim,
a Solicitor of the Senior Courts of England and Wales;
Professional Development Consultant, University of Law

The law stated in this volume is in general that in force on 1 September 2016, although subsequent changes have been included wherever possible.

Any future updating material will be found in the Current Service and annual Cumulative Supplement to Halsbury's Laws of England.

TABLE OF CONTENTS

HOW TO USE HALSBURY'S LAWS OF ENGLAND

Volumes

Each text volume of Halsbury's Laws of England contains the law on the titles contained in it as at a date stated at the front of the volume (the operative date).

Information contained in Halsbury's Laws of England may be accessed in several ways.

First, by using the tables of contents.

Each volume contains both a general Table of Contents, and a specific Table of Contents for each title contained in it. From these tables you will be directed to the relevant part of the work.

Readers should note that the current arrangement of titles can be found in the Current Service.

Secondly, by using tables of statutes, statutory instruments, cases or other materials.

If you know the name of the Act, statutory instrument or case with which your research is concerned, you should consult the Consolidated Tables of statutes, cases and so on (published as separate volumes) which will direct you to the relevant volume and paragraph.

(Each individual text volume also includes tables of those materials used as authority in that volume.)

Thirdly, by using the indexes.

If you are uncertain of the general subject area of your research, you should go to the Consolidated Index (published as separate volumes) for reference to the relevant volume(s) and paragraph(s).

(Each individual text volume also includes an index to the material contained therein.)

Updating publications

The text volumes of Halsbury's Laws should be used in conjunction with the annual Cumulative Supplement and the monthly Noter-Up.

The annual Cumulative Supplement

The Supplement gives details of all changes between the operative date of the text volume and the operative date of the Supplement. It is arranged in the same volume, title and paragraph order as the text volumes. Developments affecting particular points of law are noted to the relevant paragraph(s) of the text volumes.

For narrative treatment of material noted in the Cumulative Supplement, go to the Annual Abridgment volume for the relevant year.

Destination Tables

In certain titles in the annual *Cumulative Supplement*, reference is made to Destination Tables showing the destination of consolidated legislation. Those Destination Tables are to be found either at the end of the titles within the annual *Cumulative Supplement*, or in a separate *Destination Tables* booklet provided from time to time with the *Cumulative Supplement*.

The Noter-Up

The Noter-Up is contained in the Current Service Noter-Up booklet, issued monthly and noting changes since the publication of the annual Cumulative Supplement. Also arranged in the same volume, title and paragraph order as the text volumes, the Noter-Up follows the style of the Cumulative Supplement.

For narrative treatment of material noted in the Noter-Up, go to the relevant Monthly Review.

REFERENCES AND ABBREVIATIONS

ACT	Australian Capital Territory
A-G	Attorney General
Admin	Administrative Court
Admlty	Admiralty Court
Adv-Gen	Advocate General
affd	affirmed
affg	affirming
Alta	Alberta
App	Appendix
art	article
Aust	Australia
B	Baron
BC	British Columbia
C	Command Paper (of a series published before 1900)
c	chapter number of an Act
CA	Court of Appeal
CAC	Central Arbitration Committee
CA in Ch	Court of Appeal in Chancery
CB	Chief Baron
CCA	Court of Criminal Appeal
CCR	County Court Rules 1981 (as subsequently amended)
CCR	Court for Crown Cases Reserved
CJEU	Court of Justice of the European Union
C-MAC	Courts-Martial Appeal Court
CO	Crown Office
COD	Crown Office Digest
CPR	Civil Procedure Rules
Can	Canada
Cd	Command Paper (of the series published 1900–18)
Cf	compare
Ch	Chancery Division
ch	chapter
cl	clause
Cm	Command Paper (of the series published 1986 to date)
Cmd	Command Paper (of the series published 1919–56)
Cmnd	Command Paper (of the series published 1956–86)
Comm	Commercial Court

Comr	Commissioner
Court Forms (2nd Edn)	Atkin's Encyclopaedia of Court Forms in Civil Proceedings, 2nd Edn. See note 2 post.
CrimPR	Criminal Procedure Rules
DC	Divisional Court
DPP	Director of Public Prosecutions
EAT	Employment Appeal Tribunal
EC	European Community
ECJ	Court of Justice of the European Community (before the Treaty of Lisbon (OJ C306, 17.12.2007, p 1) came into force on 1 December 2009); European Court of Justice (after the Treaty of Lisbon (OJ C306, 17.12.2007, p 1) came into force on 1 December 2009)
EComHR	European Commission of Human Rights
ECSC	European Coal and Steel Community
ECtHR Rules of Court	Rules of Court of the European Court of Human Rights
EEC	European Economic Community
EFTA	European Free Trade Association
EGC	European General Court
EWCA Civ	Official neutral citation for judgments of the Court of Appeal (Civil Division)
EWCA Crim	Official neutral citation for judgments of the Court of Appeal (Criminal Division)
EWHC	Official neutral citation for judgments of the High Court
Edn	Edition
Euratom	European Atomic Energy Community
EU	European Union
Ex Ch	Court of Exchequer Chamber
ex p	ex parte
Fam	Family Division
Fed	Federal
Forms & Precedents (5th Edn)	Encyclopaedia of Forms and Precedents other than Court Forms, 5th Edn. See note 2 post
GLC	Greater London Council
HC	High Court
HC	House of Commons
HK	Hong Kong
HL	House of Lords
IAT	Immigration Appeal Tribunal
ILM	International Legal Materials
INLR	Immigration and Nationality Law Reports

IRC	Inland Revenue Commissioners
Ind	India
Int Rels	International Relations
Ir	Ireland
J	Justice
JA	Judge of Appeal
Kan	Kansas
LA	Lord Advocate
LC	Lord Chancellor
LCC	London County Council
LCJ	Lord Chief Justice
LJ	Lord Justice of Appeal
LoN	League of Nations
MR	Master of the Rolls
Man	Manitoba
n.	note
NB	New Brunswick
NI	Northern Ireland
NS	Nova Scotia
NSW	New South Wales
NY	New York
NZ	New Zealand
OHIM	Office for Harmonisation in the Internal Market
OJ	The Official Journal of the European Union published by the Publications Office of the European Union
Ont	Ontario
P	President
PC	Judicial Committee of the Privy Council
PEI	Prince Edward Island
Pat	Patents Court
q	question
QB	Queen's Bench Division
QBD	Queen's Bench Division of the High Court
Qld	Queensland
Que	Quebec
r	rule
RDC	Rural District Council
RPC	Restrictive Practices Court
RSC	Rules of the Supreme Court 1965 (as subsequently amended)
reg	regulation
Res	Resolution
revsd	reversed

Rly	Railway
s	section
SA	South Africa
S Aust	South Australia
SC	Supreme Court
SI	Statutory Instruments published by authority
SR & O	Statutory Rules and Orders published by authority
SR & O Rev 1904	Revised Edition comprising all Public and General Statutory Rules and Orders in force on 31 December 1903
SR & O Rev 1948	Revised Edition comprising all Public and General Statutory Rules and Orders and Statutory Instruments in force on 31 December 1948
SRNI	Statutory Rules of Northern Ireland
STI	Simon's Tax Intelligence (1973–1995); Simon's Weekly Tax Intelligence (1996-current)
Sask	Saskatchewan
Sch	Schedule
Sess	Session
Sing	Singapore
TCC	Technology and Construction Court
TS	Treaty Series
Tanz	Tanzania
Tas	Tasmania
UDC	Urban District Council
UKHL	Official neutral citation for judgments of the House of Lords
UKPC	Official neutral citation for judgments of the Privy Council
UN	United Nations
V-C	Vice-Chancellor
Vict	Victoria
W Aust	Western Australia
Zimb	Zimbabwe

NOTE 1. A general list of the abbreviations of law reports and other sources used in this work can be found at the beginning of the Consolidated Table of Cases.

NOTE 2. Where references are made to other publications, the volume number precedes and the page number follows the name of the publication; eg the reference '12 Forms & Precedents (5th Edn) 44' refers to volume 12 of the Encyclopaedia of Forms and Precedents, page 44.

NOTE 3. An English statute is cited by short title or, where there is no short title, by regnal year and chapter number together with the name by which it is commonly known or a description of its subject matter and date. In the case of a foreign statute, the mode of citation generally follows the style of citation in use in the country concerned with the addition, where necessary, of the name of the country in parentheses.

NOTE 4. A statutory instrument is cited by short title, if any, followed by the year and number, or, if unnumbered, the date.

TABLE OF STATUTES

TABLE OF STATUTORY INSTRUMENTS

PARA

Access to Justice Act 1999 (Destination of Appeals) Order 2000, SI 2000/1071
art 1 (2)(a) 890
(c) 890

Administration of Estates (Small Payments) (Increase of Limit) Order 1984, SI 1984/539 663

Administration of Insolvent Estates of Deceased Persons Order 1986, SI 1986/1999
art 3 1104
(1), (2) 981
4 (1)–(3) 981
5 (A1) 981
(1) 981, 1104
(2), (3) 981
Sch 1 1104
Pt II para 12 988
26–28 988
36 988
2 1104

Civil Partnership Act 2004 (Commencement No 2) Order 2005, SI 2005/3175 .... 369, 382

Civil Procedure (Amendment No 2) Rules 2001, SI 2001/1388
r 19 860

Civil Proceedings Fees Order 2008, SI 2008/1053
art 3 (a) 686

Consular Conventions (Arab Republic of Egypt) Order 1986, SI 1986/216 802

Consular Conventions (Czechoslovak Socialist Republic) Order 1976, SI 1976/1216 802

Consular Conventions (Federal Republic of Germany) Order 1957, SI 1957/2052 802

Consular Conventions (French Republic) Order 1953, SI 1953/1455 802

Consular Conventions (Hungarian People's Republic) Order 1971, SI 1971/1845 802

Consular Conventions (Italian Republic) Order 1957, SI 1957/2053 802

Consular Conventions (Japan) Order 1965, SI 1965/1714 802

Consular Conventions (Kingdom of Belgium) Order 1964, SI 1964/1399 802

Consular Conventions (Kingdom of Denmark) Order 1963, SI 1963/370 802

Consular Conventions (Kingdom of Greece) Order 1953, SI 1953/1454 802

Consular Conventions (Kingdom of Norway) Order in Council 1951, SI 1951/1165 802

Consular Conventions (Kingdom of Sweden) Order 1952, SI 1952/1218 802

Consular Conventions (Mongolian People's Republic) Order 1976, SI 1976/1150 802

Consular Conventions (People's Republic of Bulgaria) Order 1968, SI 1968/1861 802

Consular Conventions (Polish People's Republic) Order 1971, SI 1971/1238 802

Consular Conventions (Republic of Austria) Order 1963, SI 1963/1927 802

Consular Conventions (Socialist Federal Republic of Yugoslavia) Order 1966, SI 1966/443 802

Consular Conventions (Spanish State) Order 1963, SI 1963/614 802

Consular Conventions (Union of Soviet Socialist Republics) Order 1968, SI 1968/1378 802

Consular Conventions (United States of Mexico) Order 1955, SI 1955/425 802

County Courts (Interest on Judgment Debts) Order 1991, SI 1991/1184 1187

Court Funds Rules 2011, SI 2011/1734
r 6 (6) 1046
24 (1) 666, 1284
(2), (3) 1284
(4) 666, 1284
(5)–(7) 1284
25 (1), (2) 1284
26 (1), (2) 1284

Estates of Deceased Persons (Forfeiture Rule and Law of Succession) Act 2011 (Commencement) Order 2011, SI 2011/2913
art 2 169

Family Law Reform Act 1969 (Commencement No 1) Order 1969, SI 1969/1140
art 2 167

Family Law Reform Act 1987 (Commencement No 1) Order 1988, SI 1988/425
art 2 358

TABLE OF PROCEDURE

Civil Procedure

Civil Procedure Rules 1998, SI 1998/3132 (CPR)

PARA

Practice Directions supplementing CPR

PARA

TABLE OF EUROPEAN UNION LEGISLATION

Secondary Legislation

Regulations

TABLE OF CONVENTIONS

TABLE OF CASES

PARA

A

PARA

D

PARA

Finucane v Daly [1919] 1 IR 284 384

Firstpost Homes Ltd v Johnson [1995] 4 All ER 355, [1995] 1 WLR 1567, [1995] NPC 135, [1996] 1 EGLR 175, [1995] 28 LS Gaz R 30, [1996] 13 EG 125, 139 Sol Jo LB 187, CA; on appeal [1996] 1 WLR 67, HL 1214

Firth, Re, Loveridge v Firth [1914] 2 Ch 386, 83 LJ Ch 901, 111 LT 332 440

Firth, Re, Sykes v Ball [1938] Ch 517, [1938] 2 All ER 217, 107 LJ Ch 251, 82 Sol Jo 332, 158 LT 489, 54 TLR 633 927

Firth v Fielden (1874) 22 WR 622 346

Fischer v Diffley [2013] EWHC 4567 (Ch), [2014] WTLR 757 899

Fischer v Popham (1875) LR 3 P & D 246, 39 JP 728, 44 LJP & M 47, 23 WR 683, 33 LT 231, P, D and Admlty 69

Fish, Re, Bennett v Bennett [1893] 2 Ch 413, 62 LJ Ch 977, 2 R 467, 69 LT 233, CA 652, 1044

Fish, Re, Ingham v Rayner [1894] 2 Ch 83, 63 LJ Ch 437, 7 R 434, 42 WR 520, 38 Sol Jo 307, 70 LT 825, CA 210, 220, 350

Fisher, Re, Harris v Fisher [1943] Ch 377, [1943] 2 All ER 615, 113 LJ Ch 17, 87 Sol Jo 372, 169 LT 289, 59 TLR 446 .... 496, 1127, 1138

Fisher, Re, Robinson v Eardley [1915] 1 Ch 302, 84 LJ Ch 342, 59 Sol Jo 318, 112 LT 548 .... 320, 393, 449

Fisher v Anderson (1879) 4 SCR 406 393

Fisher v Brierley (No 2) (1861) 30 Beav 267 1130

Fisher v Dixon (1845) 12 Cl & Fin 312, 9 Jur 883, HL 932

Fisher v Fisher (1878) 4 PD 231, 48 LJP 69, P, D and Admlty 913

Fisher v Goode (1875) 23 WR 225, Ct of Ch 1178

Fisher v Hepburn (1851) 14 Beav 626 250

Fisher v Webster (1872) LR 14 Eq 283, 42 LJ Ch 156, 20 WR 765 459

Fisher v Wigg (1701) 2 Eq Cas Abr 535, 1 Com 92, 1 Ld Raym 622, 12 Mod Rep 296, 1 P Wms 14, 1 Salk 391, Holt KB 369 473

Fisher & Sons, Re [1912] 2 KB 491, 81 LJKB 1246, 19 Mans 332, 56 Sol Jo 553, 106 LT 814 1039

Fisher's Goods, Re (1869) 33 JP 503, 20 LT 684 5

Fison's Will Trusts, Re, Fison v Fison [1950] Ch 394, [1950] 1 All ER 501, 94 Sol Jo 238, 66 (pt 1) TLR 475 .... 125–126, 284

Fitchet v Adams (1740) 2 Stra 1128 132

Fittock's Goods, Re (1863) 32 LJPM & A 157, 9 Jur NS 311 754

Fitzgerald, Re (1889) 58 LJ Ch 662, 37 WR 552, 61 LT 221 344

Fitzgerald v Jervoise (1820) 5 Madd 25 1123

Fitzgerald v Ryan [1899] 2 IR 637 .... 148, 212, 414

FitzGibbon v M'Neill [1908] 1 IR 1 231

Fitzhardinge (Lord), Re, Lord Fitzhardinge v Jenkinson (1899) 43 Sol Jo 296, 80 LT 376, 15 TLR 225, CA 1131

Fitzhenry v Bonner (1853) 2 Drew 36, 2 Eq Rep 454, 2 WR 30, 22 LTOS 152 471

Fitzpatrick, Re, Bennett v Bennett [1952] Ch 86, [1951] 2 All ER 949, 95 Sol Jo 744, [1951] 2 TLR 995 .... 1013–1014, 1060

Fitzpatrick, Re, Deane v De Valera (1934) 78 Sol Jo 735 288

Fitzpatrick's Goods, Re (1892) 29 LR Ir 328 .... 628, 1263

Fitzwilliams v Kelly (1852) 10 Hare 266, 22 LJ Ch 1016, 17 Jur 249 1011

Flanders v Clark (1747) 3 Atk 509, 1 Ves Sen 9 637

Flavel's Will Trusts, Re, Coleman v Flavel [1969] 2 All ER 232, [1969] 1 WLR 444, 113 Sol Jo 189 194

Flavell, Re, Murray v Flavell (1883) 25 Ch D 89, 53 LJ Ch 185, 32 WR 102, [1881–5] All ER Rep 267, 49 LT 690, CA 32

Flecher, Re, King v King (1918) 62 Sol Jo 740 .... 1017, 1197

Fleck, Re, Colston v Roberts (1888) 37 Ch D 677, 36 WR 663, sub nom Re Fleck, Colton v Roberts 57 LJ Ch 943, sub nom Re Fleck, Carlton v Roberts 58 LT 624 1008

PARA

PARA

PARA

PARA

PARA

Hodson, Re, ex p Richardson (1818) 3 Madd 138, Buck 202; affd (1819) Buck 421 ... 1036, 1039
Hodson v Micklethwaite (1854) 2 Drew 294, 23 LJ Ch 719, 2 Eq Rep 1157, 2 WR 440 ... 302
Hoff v Atherton [2004] EWCA Civ 1554, [2004] All ER (D) 314 (Nov) ... 48–49, 55, 891
Hogan v Byrne (1862) 13 ICLR 166, 14 Ir Jur 223 ... 36
Hogg v Cook (1863) 32 Beav 641 ... 328
Hogg v Graham (1811) 4 Taunt 135 ... 1291
Hoggins v Paull (1850) 1 Sim NS 92, 20 LJ Ch 75, 15 Jur 5, 16 LTOS 550 ... 370
Hoghton, Re, Hoghton v Fiddey (1874) LR 18 Eq 573, 43 LJ Ch 758, 22 WR 854 ... 1183
Holden, Re (1903) 5 OLR 156, 2 OWR 11, 23 CLT 52 ... 296
Holden, Re, Holden v Smith (1888) 57 LJ Ch 648, 59 LT 358 ... 382
Holden, Re, Isaacson v Holden [1935] WN 52, 179 LT Jo 235 ... 803, 965
Holden v Ramsbottom (1863) 4 Giff 205, 9 Jur NS 350, 1 New Rep 307, 354, 11 WR 302, 66 ER 680, 7 LT 735 ... 296
Holder, Re, National Provincial Bank Ltd v Holder [1953] Ch 468, [1953] 2 All ER 1, [1953] 2 WLR 1079, 97 Sol Jo 353 ... 283
Holder v Holder [1968] Ch 353, [1968] 1 All ER 665, [1968] 2 WLR 237, 112 Sol Jo 17, 205 Estates Gazette 211, CA ... 627, 657
Holder v Howell (1803) 8 Ves 97 ... 96
Holding and Management Ltd v Property Holding and Investment Trust plc [1988] 2 All ER 702, [1988] 1 WLR 644, 132 Sol Jo 626, [1988] 11 LS Gaz R 43; affd [1990] 1 All ER 938, [1989] 1 WLR 1313, 21 HLR 596, 134 Sol Jo 262, [1990] 1 EGLR 65, [1990] 05 EG 75, CA ... 1196
Holford, Re, Holford v Holford [1894] 3 Ch 30, 63 LJ Ch 637, 7 R 304, 42 WR 563, 38 Sol Jo 512, 70 LT 777, 10 TLR 496, CA ... 312
Holford v Wood (1798) 4 Ves 76 ... 402
Holland, Re, Brettell v Holland [1907] 2 Ch 88, 76 LJ Ch 449, 97 LT 49 ... 287
Holland v Allsop (1861) 29 Beav 498, Jur NS 856, 9 WR 683 ... 317
Holland v Clark (1843) 2 Y & C Ch Cas 319, 7 Jur 213 ... 1298
Holland v Hodgson (1872) LR 7 CP 328, 41 LJCP 146, 20 WR 990, [1861–73] All ER Rep 237, 26 LT 709, Ex Ch ... 932
Holland v Wood (1870) LR 11 Eq 91 ... 311, 320
Holland's Estate, Re [1936] 3 All ER 13, 105 LJP 113, 80 Sol Jo 838, 155 LT 417, 53 TLR 3, P, D and Admlty ... 611
Hollebone, Re, Hollebone v Hollebone [1919] 2 Ch 93, 88 LJ Ch 386, [1918–19] All ER Rep 323, 63 Sol Jo 553, 121 LT 116 ... 1127
Holliday, Re [1922] 2 Ch 698, 92 LJ Ch 55, 127 LT 585, 38 TLR 709 ... 556
Holliday, Re, Houghton v Adlard [1947] Ch 402, [1947] 1 All ER 695, [1947] LJR 1086, 91 Sol Jo 278, 76 LT 478, 63 TLR 255 ... 1127
Holliday v Musa [2010] EWCA Civ 335, [2010] All ER (D) 288 (Mar) ... 566
Hollingshead, Re, Hollingshead v Webster (1888) 37 Ch D 651, 57 LJ Ch 400, 36 WR 660, 58 LT 758, 4 TLR 275 ... 977
Hollinrake v Lister (1826) 1 Russ 500 ... 149
Hollis v Smith (1808) 10 East 293 ... 1287
Hollis' Hospital Trustees and Hague's Contract, Re [1899] 2 Ch 540, 68 LJ Ch 673, 47 WR 691, [1895–9] All ER Rep 643, 43 Sol Jo 644, 81 LT 90 ... 143
Holloway, Re, Young v Holloway (1887) 12 PD 167, 56 LJP 81, 35 WR 751, 57 LT 515, 3 TLR 616, sub nom Young v Holloway 56 LJP 81, CA ... 879
Holloway v Clarkson (1843) 2 Hare 521 ... 377
Holloway v Collins (1675) 1 Eq Cas Abr 300, 1 Cas in Ch 245 ... 1073
Holloway v Radcliffe (1857) 23 Beav 163, 26 LJ Ch 401, 5 WR 271, 28 LTOS 301 ... 314, 364

I

J

K

PARA

PARA

M

PARA

McCabe's Goods, Re (1873) LR 3 P & D 94, 38 JP 9, 42 LJP & M 79, 29 LT 250 ... 82, 108
McCalmont, Re, Rooper v McCalmont (1903) 19 TLR 490 ... 286
M'Cann, Re, Donnelly v Moore [1916] 1 IR 255 ... 348
McCarthy, Re, National Bank Ltd v Archbishop of Dublin [1958] IR 311 ... 1087
M'Carthy v M'Carthy (1878) 1 LR Ir 189, 3 LR Ir 317 ... 182
McCausland v Young [1949] NI 49, CA ... 140
McClean v Kennard (1874) 9 Ch App 336, 43 LJ Ch 323, 22 WR 382, 30 LT 186, [1874–80] All ER Rep Ext 2058 ... 1216
M'Cleary, Re, Moffat v M'Cleary [1932] 1 IR 16 ... 139
M'Cleland v Shaw (1805) 2 Sch & Lef 538 ... 1012
McClellan, Re, McClellan v McClellan (1885) 29 Ch D 495, 54 LJ Ch 659, 33 WR 888, 52 LT 741, 1 TLR 400, CA ... 1203
McClement's Trustees v Campbell 1951 SC 167, Ct of Sess ... 278
M'Clure v Evans (or Dawson) (1861) 29 Beav 422, 30 LJ Ch 295, 7 Jur NS 204, 9 WR 428, 3 LT 870 ... 217, 404
McClymont v Hooper (1973) 47 ALJR 222, Aust HC ... 471
McCormick v Grogan (1869) 4 App Cas 82, LR 4 HL 82, 17 WR 961, HL ... 221
McCormick v Simpson [1907] AC 494, 77 LJPC 12, 97 LT 616, PC ... 450
M'Creight v M'Creight (1849) 13 I Eq R 314, 2 Ir Jur 17 ... 37, 1073
Macculloch v Anderson [1904] AC 55, HL ... 236, 308
M'Culloch v Dawes (1826) 5 LJOSKB 56, 9 Dow & Ry KB 40 ... 974, 976
M'Cutcheon v Allen (1880) 5 LR Ir 268 ... 428
M'Dermott v Wallace (1842) 5 Beav 142, 6 Jur 547 ... 395
McDonald, Re (1903) 20 WR 968, 6 OLR 478, 23 CLT 326 ... 387
McDonald, Re (1911) 30 NZLR 896 ... 2, 6
Macdonald, Re, Dick v Fraser [1897] 2 Ch 181, 66 LJ Ch 630, 45 WR 628, 76 LT 713 ... 976–977
Macdonald, Re, McAlpin v Macdonald (1889) 59 LJ Ch 231, 62 LT 541 ... 986
M'Donald v Bryce (1853) 16 Beav 581, 22 LJ Ch 779, 17 Jur 335, 1 WR 261, 21 LTOS 54 ... 318
McDonald v Horn [1995] 1 All ER 961, [1995] ICR 685, [1994] NLJR 1515, CA ... 1196, 1274
Macdonald v Irvine (1878) 8 Ch D 101, 47 LJ Ch 494, 26 WR 381, 38 LT 155, CA ... 114, 156, 1122–1123
Macdonald v Richardson (1858) 1 Giff 81, 5 Jur NS 9, 32 LTOS 237 ... 658
McDonald v Trustees, Executors and Agency Co Ltd (1902) 28 VLR 442 ... 131
M'Donnell v Jebb (1865) 16 I Ch R 359 ... 393
McDonnell v Morrow (1889) 23 LR Ir 591 ... 294
McDonnell v Neil [1951] AC 342, 95 Sol Jo 298, [1951] 1 TLR 642, PC ... 397
M'Donnell v Prendergast (1830) 3 Hag Ecc 212 ... 627
Macduff, Re, Macduff v Macduff [1896] 2 Ch 451, 65 LJ Ch 700, 45 WR 154, [1895–9] All ER Rep 154, 40 Sol Jo 651, 74 LT 706, 12 TLR 452, CA ... 11
McElligott, Re, Grant v McElligott [1944] Ch 216, [1944] 1 All ER 441, 113 LJ Ch 277, 88 Sol Jo 170, 171 LT 10, 60 TLR 246 ... 377, 385
McEuen, Re, McEuen v Phelps [1913] 2 Ch 704, 83 LJ Ch 66, 30 TLR 44, sub nom Re McEwen, McEwen v Phelps [1911–13] All ER Rep 176, 58 Sol Jo 82, 109 LT 701, CA ... 1093, 1118
McEwan v Crombie (1883) 25 Ch D 175, 53 LJ Ch 24, 32 WR 115, 49 LT 499 ... 1201
McFee, Re, McFee v Toner (1910) 79 LJ Ch 676, 103 LT 210 ... 313
McGarrity, Re, Ballance and Benson v McGarrity (1912) 46 ILT 175 ... 408, 435

PARA

PARA

PARA

T

W

WILLS AND INTESTACY

Volume 102

Volume 103

7. FAMILY PROVISION CLAIMS

(1) REQUIREMENT FOR FINANCIAL PROVISION

565. Restrictions on freedom of testamentary disposition. The complete freedom of testamentary disposition which was a characteristic of English law sometimes resulted in a testator disregarding his family obligations and making insufficient provision or no provision for his wife and children. This is prevented in systems of law which are founded on the Roman Civil Law by setting aside for the widow and children definite shares of the estate. The duty of providing maintenance for them is imposed by statute in some Commonwealth jurisdictions. The principle of restriction on freedom of testamentary disposition is reflected in English law by the Inheritance (Provision for Family and Dependants) Act 1975[1]. This Act, which governs applications for provision out of the estates of persons dying on or after 1 April 1976[2], repealed and replaced the Inheritance (Family Provision) Act 1938 and applies whether the deceased made a will or died intestate[3].

1 Ie the Inheritance (Provision for Family and Dependants) Act 1975 see PARA 566 et seq.

2 See the Inheritance (Provision for Family and Dependants) Act 1975 s 26(3). The Inheritance (Provision for Family and Dependants) Act 1975 repealed earlier legislation which, although preserved for deaths before 1 April 1976, is in practice, because of the six-month limit on applications (see PARA 597), defunct, but could still operate where probate has been very much delayed. While cases decided under the Inheritance (Family Provision) Act 1938 represent a continuing body of case law capable of affording guidance to the exercise of the court's powers under the Inheritance (Provision for Family and Dependants) Act 1975, the earlier authorities should be approached with caution because of the substantial changes that have occurred in the legislation itself: *Moody v Stevenson* [1992] Ch 486,[1992] 2 All ER 524, CA per Waite J at 502 and 537.

3 See the Inheritance (Provision for Family and Dependants) Act 1975 s 1(1). The jurisdiction under the Inheritance (Family Provision) Act 1938 could only be exercised where the deceased left a will: see *Re Bidie, Bidie v General Accident Fire and Life Assurance Corpn Ltd* [1949] Ch 121, [1948] 2 All ER 995, CA.

566. Application for financial provision from the deceased's estate. Where after 1 April 1976[1] a person dies domiciled[2] in England and Wales[3], and is survived by any of certain persons[4], that person may apply[5] to the court[6] for an order under the Inheritance (Provision for Family and Dependants) Act 1975[7] on the ground that the disposition of the deceased's estate effected by his will[8] or the law relating to intestacy[9], or the combination of his will and that law, is not such as to make reasonable financial provision[10] for the applicant[11].

Applications under the Inheritance (Provision for Family and Dependants) Act 1975 are not precluded by the forfeiture rule[12].

1 Inheritance (Provision for Family and Dependants) Act 1975 ss 1(1), 27(3).

2 Domicile is distinct from residence: see CONFLICT OF LAWS vol 19 (2011) PARA 336 et seq. The domicile must be proved by the applicant (*Mastaka v Midland Bank Executor and Trustee Co Ltd* [1941] Ch 192, [1941] 1 All ER 236, although it is normally stated in the probate). No one factor is decisive: see *Cyganik v Agulian* [2006] EWCA Civ 129, [2006] All ER (D) 372 (Feb); *Morgan v Cilento* [2004] EWHC 188 (Ch), [2004] WTLR 457; *Holliday v Musa* [2010] EWCA Civ 335, [2010] All ER (D) 288 (Mar). There is no reason in principle why a person whose presence here is unlawful cannot acquire a domicile of choice in this country: *Mark v Mark* [2005] UKHL 42 at [49], [2006] 1 AC 98 at [49], [2005] 3 All ER 912 at [49] per Baroness Hale. See also *Kebbeh v Farmer* [2015] EWHC 3927 (Ch) (overwhelming evidence that the conduct of the deceased was consistent with a settled intention to remain and live indefinitely in Gambia).

3 The Inheritance (Provision for Family and Dependants) Act 1975 does not extend to Scotland or Northern Ireland: s 27(2). In Northern Ireland the Inheritance (Provision for Family and Dependants) (Northern Ireland) Order 1979, SI 1979/924, applies to deaths of individuals domiciled in Northern Ireland on or after 1 September 1979 and is in large part identical to the Inheritance (Provision for Family and Dependants) Act 1975.

4 Ie those persons specified in the Inheritance (Provision for Family and Dependants) Act 1975 s 1(1): see PARA 567.
5 As to the mode of application see PARA 599.
6 'Court', unless the context otherwise requires, means the High Court or where the County Court has jurisdiction by virtue of the County Courts Act 1984 s 25 (see COURTS AND TRIBUNALS vol 24 (2010) PARA 774), the County Court: s 25(1) (definition amended by the Matrimonial and Family Proceedings Act 1984 s 8(2); the Crime and Courts Act 2013 Sch 9 para 92). See also PARA 599. The County Court now has jurisdiction to hear and determine any application for an order under the Inheritance (Provision for Family and Dependants) Act 1975 s 2 (see PARAS 591–592) (including any application for permission to apply for such an order and any application made, in the proceedings on an application for such an order, for an order under any other provision of that Act): County Courts Act 1984 s 25 (amended by SI 1991/724 and the Crime and Courts Act 2013 Sch 9 para 10(1)(a)). See COURTS AND TRIBUNALS vol 24 (2010) PARA 774.
7 Ie under the Inheritance (Provision for Family and Dependants) Act 1975 s 2 (see PARAS 591–592): see s 1(1).
8 'Will' includes codicil: Inheritance (Provision for Family and Dependants) Act 1975 s 25(1).
9 As to the law relating to intestacy see PARA 477 et seq.
10 As to the meaning of reasonable financial provision see PARA 568 et seq.
11 Inheritance (Provision for Family and Dependants) Act 1975 s 1(1).
12 See the Forfeiture Act 1982 s 3(2)(a); and PARAS 39–40. An application brought before that Act came into force by a widow convicted of her husband's manslaughter, as sole beneficiary under his will, failed: *Re Royse, Royse v Royse* [1985] Ch 22, [1984] 3 All ER 339, CA; cf *Re K* [1985] Ch 85, [1985] 1 All ER 403; *Re S* [1996] 1 WLR 235, [1996] 1 FLR 910. See also *Re Land, Land v Land* [2006] EWHC 2069 (Ch), [2007] 1 All ER 324, [2007] 1 WLR 1009 where provision made by will was reasonable but forfeited under forfeiture rule.

567. Persons for whom provision may be made. The Inheritance (Provision for Family and Dependants) Act 1975 enables the court[1] to make an order for a wide variety of relief[2] out of a breadth of property in favour of the following persons[3]:

(1) the spouse or civil partner[4] of the deceased[5];
(2) a former spouse or civil partner of the deceased but not one who has formed a subsequent marriage or civil partnership[6];
(3) a person other than the spouse or former spouse of the deceased[7] who, if the deceased died on or after 1 January 1996, was living in the same household as the deceased as the spouse of the deceased during the whole of the period of two years ending immediately before the date when the deceased died[8];
(4) a person other than a civil partner or former civil partner of the deceased[9] who was living in the same household as the deceased as the civil partner of the deceased during the whole of the period of two years ending immediately before the date when the deceased died[10];
(5) a child[11] of the deceased[12];
(6) any person (not being a child of the deceased) who in relation to any marriage or civil partnership to which the deceased was at any time a party, or otherwise in relation to any family in which the deceased at any time stood in the role of a parent, was treated by the deceased as a child of the family[13]; and
(7) any person, not falling within any other class of applicant, who immediately before the death[14] of the deceased was being maintained, either wholly or partly[15], by the deceased[16].

1 As to the meaning of 'court' see PARA 566 note 6.
2 As to the orders which the court may make see the Inheritance (Provision for Family and Dependants) Act 1975 s 2; and PARA 591.
3 See the Inheritance (Provision for Family and Dependants) Act 1975 s 1(1); and PARA 566. As to the guidelines applicable on the application of particular applicants see PARAS 577–581. Claims under the Inheritance (Provision for Family and Dependants) Act 1975 are personal and do not survive the death of the applicant: *Whytte v Ticehurst* [1986] Fam 64, [1986] 2 All ER 158; *Re Bramwell* [1988] 2 FLR 263. Where an applicant died after the date of the order but before an

appeal could be heard the court allowed her estate to retain a lump sum award: *Smith v Smith (Smith intervening)* [1992] Fam 69, [1991] 2 All ER 306, CA. See also *Barder v Caluori* [1988] AC 20, sub nom *Barder v Barder (Caluori intervening)* [1987] 2 All ER 440, HL.

4 'Spouse' includes a person who is married to a person of the same sex: see Marriage (Same Sex Couples) Act 2013 Sch 3 para 1(1)(c), (2), (3); and MATRIMONIAL AND CIVIL PARTNERSHIP LAW vol 72 (2015) PARAS 1–2. Any reference to a spouse, wife or husband is to be treated as including a reference to a person who, in good faith entered into a void marriage with the deceased unless either:

(1) the marriage of the deceased and that person was dissolved or annulled during the lifetime of the deceased and the dissolution or annulment is recognised by the law of England and Wales; or

(2) that person has during the lifetime of the deceased formed a subsequent marriage or civil partnership: Inheritance (Provision for Family and Dependants) Act 1975 s 25(4) (amended by the Civil Partnership Act 2004 s 71, Sch 4 para 27(1), (4)).

'Wife' also includes the wife of a polygamous marriage: *Re Sehota, Surjit Kaur v Gian Kaur* [1978] 3 All ER 385, [1978] 1 WLR 1506. However a ceremony which does not purport to be of the kind contemplated by the Marriage Acts, produces a non-marriage rather than a void marriage: *A-M v A-M (Divorce: Jurisdiction: Validity of Marriage)* [2001] 2 FLR 6, [2001] Fam Law 495, and the parties will not be eligible to make an application: *Gandhi v Patel* [2002] 1 FLR 603, [2002] Fam Law 262. As to the matters which the court must take into account in considering an application by the spouse of the deceased see PARAS 569, 571–577. Any reference to a civil partner is to be treated as including a reference to a person who in good faith formed a void civil partnership with the deceased unless either:

(a) the civil partnership between the deceased and that person was dissolved or annulled during the lifetime of the deceased and the dissolution or annulment is recognised by the law of England and Wales; or

(b) that person has during the lifetime of the deceased formed a subsequent civil partnership or marriage: Inheritance (Provisions for Family and Dependants) Act 1975 s 25(4A) (added by the Civil Partnership Act 2004 s 71, Sch 4 para 27(5)).

5 Inheritance (Provision for Family and Dependants) Act 1975 s 1(1)(a) (substituted by the Civil Partnership Act 2004 s 71, Sch 4 para 15(1)).

6 Inheritance (Provision for Family and Dependants) Act 1975 s 1(1)(b). 'Former spouse' means a person whose marriage with the deceased was during the lifetime of the deceased either:

(1) dissolved or annulled by a decree of divorce or a decree of nullity of marriage granted under the law of any part of the British Islands; or

(2) dissolved or annulled in any country or territory outside the British Islands by a divorce or annulment which is entitled to be recognised as valid by the law of England and Wales: s 25(1) (substituted by the Matrimonial and Family Proceedings Act 1984 s 25(2); and amended by the Civil Partnership Act 2004 s 71, Sch 4 para 27(2)).

'Former civil partner' means a person whose civil partnership with the deceased was during the lifetime of the deceased either:

(a) dissolved or annulled by an order made under the law of any part of the British Islands; or

(b) dissolved or annulled in any country or territory outside the British Islands by a dissolution or annulment which is entitled to be recognised as valid by the law of England and Wales: Inheritance (Provision for Family and Dependants) Act 1975 s 25(1) (added by the Civil Partnership Act 2004 s 71, Sch 4 para 27(3)).

Any reference to the formation of, or to a person who has formed, a subsequent marriage or civil partnership includes a reference to the formation of, or to a person who has formed, a marriage or civil partnership which is by law void or voidable: Inheritance (Provision for Family and Dependants) Act 1975 s 25(5) (substituted by the Civil Partnership Act 2004 s 71, Sch 4 para 27(5)). The formation of a marriage or civil partnership is to be treated as the formation of a subsequent marriage or civil partnership, in relation to either of the spouses or civil partners, notwithstanding that the previous marriage or civil partnership of that spouse or civil partner was void or voidable: Inheritance (Provision for Family and Dependants) Act 1975 s 25(5A) (substituted by the Civil Partnership Act 2004 s 71, Sch 4 para 27(5)). It is doubtful whether a former spouse who survives the deceased but remarries before an application for financial provision is made is a person qualified to claim: see *Re Collins* [1990] Fam 56, [1990] 2 All ER 47.

Where an order is made on the grant of a decree of divorce, a decree of nullity of marriage or a decree of judicial separation or under the Matrimonial and Family Proceedings Act 1984 s 17 (see MATRIMONIAL AND CIVIL PARTNERSHIP LAW vol 73 (2015) PARA 591), the court, if it considers it just to do so, may, on the application of either party to the marriage, order that the other party to the marriage is not, on the death of the applicant entitled to apply for an order under the Inheritance (Provision for Family and Dependants) Act 1975 s 2 (see PARAS 591–592) and in such a case the court will not subsequently entertain any application for an order under s 2: see ss 15, 15A; and MATRIMONIAL AND CIVIL PARTNERSHIP LAW vol 73 (2015) PARAS 594, 730. Despite the apparent prohibition on the court considering 'any' application where an order has been made, a former spouse who has remarried the deceased or fulfills the requirements of the Inheritance (Provision for Family and Dependants) Act 1975 s 1(1)(ba), (1A) (see the text and note 8) can make an application under s 1(1)(a) or s 1(1)(ba), (1A) as appropriate: see *Chekov v Fryer* [2015] EWHC 1642 (Ch) at [16], 165 NLJ 7668, [2015] All ER (D) 303 (Jun) per Master Matthews.

On making a dissolution order, nullity order, separation order or presumption of death order under the Civil Partnership Act 2004 Pt 2 Chapter 2, or at any time after making such an order, the court, if it considers it just to do so, may, on the application of either of the civil partners, order that the other civil partner is not, on the death of the applicant, entitled to apply for an order under the Inheritance (Provisions for Family and Dependants) Act 1975 s 2 and in such a case the court will not subsequently entertain any application for such an order: see ss 15ZA, 15B; and MATRIMONIAL AND CIVIL PARTNERSHIP LAW vol 73 (2015) PARAS 594, 730. As to the meaning of 'court' see ss 15, 15A, 15ZA, 15B; and MATRIMONIAL AND CIVIL PARTNERSHIP LAW vol 73 (2015) PARAS 594, 730. In the case of a decree of divorce or nullity of marriage, or dissolution or nullity of a civil partnership an order may be made before or after the decree is made absolute, but if it is made before the decree is made absolute it does not take effect unless the decree is made absolute: see ss 15(2), 15ZA(3); and MATRIMONIAL AND CIVIL PARTNERSHIP LAW vol 73 (2015) PARAS 594, 730. As with applications by former spouses, a former civil partner who has entered into a new civil partnership with the deceased or fulfills the requirements of the Inheritance (Provision for Family and Dependants) Act 1975 s 1(1)(ba), (1B) (see the text and note 10), can make an application under s 1(1)(a) or s 1(1)(ba), (1B) as appropriate: see *Chekov v Fryer* [2015] EWHC 1642 (Ch), 165 NLJ 7668, [2015] All ER (D) 303 (Jun).

As to the matters which the court must take into account in considering an application by a former spouse or civil partner of the deceased who has not remarried see PARAS 568–570, 578.

7 Where a former spouse has been excluded from making an application for an order under the Inheritance (Provision for Family and Dependants) Act 1975 s 2 by ss 15, 15A (see note 6) and is therefore not able to apply to the court in that capacity, that person is capable of being a person falling within s 1(1)(ba), (1A) (see the text and note 8): see *Chekov v Fryer* [2015] EWHC 1642 (Ch) at [24], 165 NLJ 7668, [2015] All ER (D) 303 (Jun) per Master Matthews.

8 Inheritance (Provision for Family and Dependants) Act 1975 s 1(1)(ba), (1A) (added by the Law Reform (Succession) Act 1995 s 2(1)–(3)). As to the matters which the court must take into account in considering an application by such a cohabitee see PARAS 570–571, 579. The two persons in question must have lived in the same household for the whole of the two years immediately preceding the death. It is not enough to establish that they did so at some more remote time. As to the meaning of 'immediately before' see note 14. As to divorced couples living together see *Chekov v Fryer* [2015] EWHC 1642 (Ch), 165 NLJ 7668, [2015] All ER (D) 303 (Jun).

As drawn the Inheritance (Provisions for Family and Dependants) Act 1975 s 1(1A) discriminates against same sex couples, contrary to the Convention for the Protection of Human Rights and Fundamental Freedoms (Rome, 4 November 1950; TS 71 (1953); Cmd 8969) art 14 (as set out in the Human Rights Act 1998 Sch 1 Pt 1) and should therefore be construed in accordance with s 3 in a way that does not discriminate on the grounds of sexual orientation; and the Inheritance (Provisions for Family and Dependants) Act 1975 s 1(1A) is therefore to be construed as applying to homosexual couples: *Saunders v Garrett* [2005] WTLR 749. See also *Ghaidan v Godin-Mendoza* [2004] UKHL 30, [2004] 2 AC 557, [2004] 3 All ER 411. However, in the case of deaths occurring on or after 5 December 2005 such interpretation is unnecessary as the Civil Partnership Act 2004 introduced same sex cohabitees as a new category of applicant: see note 4.

The test as to whether a person was living in the same household as the deceased as the spouse of the deceased is objective and should not ignore the multifarious nature of marital relationships: *Re Watson* [1999] 1 FLR 878, [1999] 3 FCR 595. If two people are living in the same household they will not necessarily stop doing so merely because they are temporarily physically separated. The relevant word is 'household' not 'house', and persons remain in the same household if they are tied by their relationship; it is always a question of fact: *Gully v Dix* [2004] EWCA Civ 139 at [24]; [2004] 1WLR 1399 per Ward LJ; *Baynes v Hedger* [2008] EWHC 1587 (Ch) at [121], [2008] 2 FLR 1805; affd on other grounds [2009] EWCA Civ 374, [2009] 2 FLR 767, [2009] All ER (D) 50 (May). There is a distinction between wanting and intending to live in the same household, planning to do so and actually doing so: *Kotke v Saffarini* [2005] EWCA Civ 221, [2005] 2 FLR 517. Retaining a different address is not inconsistent with the claimant living in the household as the wife of the deceased: *Lindop v Agus* [2009] EWHC 1795 (Ch), [2009] WTLR 1175. The nature of the test for financial provision under the Inheritance (Provision for Family and Dependants) Act 1975 s 1(1A) is encapsulated in the following questions: (1) whether there was a settled relationship creating a tie between the parties, evidenced not simply by their living together under the same roof but by the public and private acknowledgement of their mutual society and the mutual protection and support that bound them together; and, if so, (2) whether that relationship had irretrievably broken down or, rather, was merely suspended, with any interruption being transitory: *Kaur v Dhaliwal* [2014] EWHC 1991 (Ch), [2014] Fam Law 1241. The fact that the claimant's residence in England and Wales is unlawful does not prevent the court making reasonable financial provision out of the deceased's estate: *Witkowska v Kaminski* [2006] EWHC 1940 (Ch), [2007] 1 FLR 1547.

9 Where a former civil partner has been excluded from making an application for an order under the Inheritance (Provision for Family and Dependants) Act 1975 s 2 by ss 15ZA, 15B (see note 6) and is therefore not able to apply to the court in that capacity, that person is capable of being a person falling within s 1(1)(ba), (1B): see *Chekov v Fryer* [2015] EWHC 1642 (Ch) at [2], 165 NLJ 7668, [2015] All ER (D) 303 (Jun) per Master Matthews.

10 Inheritance (Provision for Family and Dependants) Act 1975 s 1(1)(ba), (1B) (added by the Civil Partnership Act 2004 s 71, Sch 4 para 15(3)). Unlike the Inheritance (Provision for Family and Dependants) Act 1975 s 1(1A) (see the text and note 6), s 1(1B) does not restrict its application to deaths after a particular date. However 'it is difficult to see how two people could live as civil partners before the concept was invented'. Any difficulty in this respect is capable of being overcome by reading the phrase 'as husband and wife' in s 1(1A) as covering same-sex relationships, as the House of Lords did in *Ghaidan v Godin-Mendoza* [2004] UKHL 30, [2004] 2 AC 557, [2004] 3 All ER 411, and as Master Bowles did in *Saunders v Garrett* [2005] WTLR 749: *Baynes v Hedger* [2008] EWHC 1587 (Ch) at [122], [2008] 2 FLR 1805, [2008] All ER (D) 175 (Jul); affd on other grounds [2009] EWCA Civ 374, [2009] 2 FLR 767, [2009] All ER (D) 50 (May) per Lewison J. As to the matters which the court must take into account in considering an application by such a cohabitee see PARAS 570–571, 579. As to the meaning of 'immediately before' see note 14. Given that both a marriage and a civil partnership are publicly acknowledged relationships it is necessary that the relationship be openly and unequivocally displayed to the outside world: *Lindop v Agus* [2009] EWHC 1795 (Ch), [2009] WTLR 1175; [2010] 1 FLR 631; *Baynes v Hedger* [2008] EWHC 1587 (Ch) at [125], [2008] 2 FLR 1805, [2008] All ER (D) 175 (Jul); affd on other grounds [2009] EWCA Civ 374, [2009] 2 FLR 767, [2009] All ER (D) 50 (May). See also *Baker v Baker* [2008] EWHC 937 (Ch), [2008] 2 FLR 767.

11 'Child' includes an illegitimate child and a child en ventre sa mere at the death of the deceased: Inheritance (Provision for Family and Dependants) Act 1975 s 25(1). An adopted child is a child for the purposes of the Inheritance (Provision for Family and Dependants) Act 1975: see the Adoption Act 1976 s 39(1); and CHILDREN AND YOUNG PERSONS vol 9 (2012) PARA 414. A person who is born a 'child of the deceased' loses his right to claim if he is subsequently adopted before an application for financial provision is made: *Re Collins* [1990] Fam 56, [1990] 2 All ER 47.

12 Inheritance (Provision for Family and Dependants) Act 1975 s 1(1)(c). As to the matters which the court must take into account in considering an application by a child of the deceased see PARAS 570–571, 580.

13 Inheritance (Provision for Family and Dependants) Act 1975 s 1(1)(d) (amended by the Inheritance and Trustees' Powers Act 2014 Sch 2 para 2(2)) The reference in head (6) in the text to a family in which the deceased stood in the role of a parent includes a family of which the deceased was the only member (apart from the applicant): the Inheritance (Provision for Family and Dependants) Act 1975 s 1(2A) (added by the Inheritance and Trustees' Powers Act 2014 Sch 2 para 2(3)). An adult can be a person 'treated by the deceased as a child of the family': *Re Callaghan* [1985] Fam 1, [1984] 3 All ER 790; *Re Leach, Leach v Lindeman* [1986] Ch 226, [1985] 2 All ER 754, CA. A grandchild may be such a person: *Re A (child of the family)* [1998] 1 FLR 347, [1998] 1 FCR 458, CA. As to the matters which the court must take into account in considering an application by a person treated by the deceased as a child of the family see PARAS 570–571, 580.

14 In determining whether a person was maintained 'immediately before' the death of the deceased the court is required to look, not at the de facto state of maintenance existing at the moment of death, but at the settled and enduring basis or arrangement existing at the moment of death: *Re Beaumont, Martin v Midland Bank Trust Co Ltd* [1980] Ch 444, [1980] 1 All ER 266 (a short stay in hospital prior to death is not sufficient to prevent a claim); *Gully v Dix* [2004] EWCA Civ 139, [2004] 1 WLR 1399 (parties living in the same household for the whole of the requisite two year period despite temporary separation resulting from deceased's drinking and violence). See also *Jelley v Iliffe* [1981] Fam 128, [1981] 2 All ER 29, CA. Where the applicant and the deceased had separated on what was likely to be a permanent basis only days before the deceased's death, after ten years of cohabitation, the deceased had abandoned his assumption of responsibility for the applicant and the claim failed: *Kourkgy v Lusher* (1983) 4 FLR 65, 12 Fam Law 86. See also *Layton v Martin* [1986] 2 FLR 227, [1986] Fam Law 212 (the claim could not be pursued where the separation occurred two years before death) and *Ottey v Grundy* [2003] EWCA Civ 1176,

[2003] WTLR 1253, [2003] All ER (D) 05 (Aug) (claim unsuccessful because parties had separated on a permanent basis some months before death and the standing order previously in the applicant's favour had been cancelled). A gift of a capital asset such as a house many years before death cannot amount to maintenance immediately before death even if the claimant still occupies the property: *Baynes v Hedger* [2008] EWHC 1587 (Ch), [2008] 2 FLR 1805, [2008] All ER (D) 175 (Jul); affd on other grounds [2009] EWCA Civ 374, [2009] 2 FLR 767, [2009] All ER (D) 50 (May). The establishment of a trust from which payments are made to the applicant does not amount to maintenance from the deceased even if the deceased is a trustee: *Baynes v Hedger* at [154].

15 'Valuable consideration' does not include marriage or a promise of marriage: Inheritance (Provision for Family and Dependants) Act 1975 s 25(1). In relation to deaths on or after 1 October 2014, a person is to be treated as being maintained by the deceased (either wholly or partly, as the case may be) only if the deceased was making a substantial contribution in money or money's worth towards the reasonable needs of that person, other than a contribution made for full valuable consideration pursuant to an arrangement of a commercial nature: Inheritance (Provision for Family and Dependants) Act 1975 s 1(3) (substituted by the Inheritance and Trustees' Powers Act 2014 Sch 2 para 3).

In relation to deaths before 1 October 2014, 'valuable consideration' was not limited by the words 'pursuant to an arrangement of a commercial nature'. It is therefore necessary in such cases to weigh any services provided against any financial contribution made by the deceased in cases of mutual dependency. Assistance with light household duties is not 'full valuable consideration' (*Re Wilkinson, Neale v Newell* [1978] Fam 22, [1978] 1 All ER 221) but the phrase is not limited to situations where a contractual relationship exists (*Re Beaumont, Martin v Midland Bank Trust Co Ltd* [1980] Ch 444, [1980] 1 All ER 266). If the flow of benefits from the applicant to the deceased is broadly commensurate with the contribution made by the deceased to the applicant, full valuable consideration will be demonstrated, but a caring and devoted applicant is not to be put in a worse position than an uncaring applicant: *Bishop v Plumley* [1991] 1 All ER 236 at 241-242, [1991] 1 WLR 582 at 587-588, CA, per Butler-Sloss LJ. The existence of a tenancy agreement does not preclude an applicant from making an application under the Inheritance (Provision for Family and Dependants) Act 1975 s 1(1)(e) if there was a close friendship within which the deceased wished to make a substantial contribution towards the applicant's maintenance: *Rees v Newbery and Institute of Cancer Research* [1998] 1 FLR 1041. See *Jelley v Iliffe* [1981] Fam 128, [1981] 2 All ER 29, CA; *Re Wilkinson* [1978] Fam 22, [1977] 3 WLR 514. See also *King v Dubrey* [2014] EWHC 2083 (Ch), [2014] WTLR 1411; *Wright-Gordon v Legister* [2014] EWHC 2041 (Ch), [2014] WTLR 1675.

For deaths before 1 October 2014 the wording of the Inheritance (Provision for Family and Dependants) Act 1975 s 3(4) required the deceased to have assumed responsibility for maintenance of the applicant (see PARA 581 note 7): *Re Beaumont, Martin v Midland Bank Trust Co Ltd* [1980] Ch 444, [1980] 1 All ER 266; *Jelley v Iliffe* [1981] Fam 128, [1981] 2 All ER 29, CA; *Baynes v Hedger* [2009] EWCA Civ 374, [2009] 2 FLR 767, [2009] All ER (D) 50 (May). The assumption of responsibility can usually be presumed once actual maintenance is established: *Jelley v Iliffe* [1981] Fam 128, [1981] 2 All ER 29, CA at 137 and 35 per Stephenson LJ.See also *Re B* [2000] Ch 662, [2000] 1 All ER 665.

For deaths on or after 1 October 2014 the Inheritance and Trustees' Powers Act 2014 has amended the Inheritance (Provision for Family and Dependants) Act 1975 s 3(4) to remove the requirement for an assumption of responsibility although it remains a factor for the court to take into account when deciding whether to make an order and, if so, what order to make: see PARA 581 text and notes 13, 14.

16 Inheritance (Provision for Family and Dependants) Act 1975 s 1(1)(e). As to the matters which the court must take into account in considering an application by a dependant of the deceased see PARAS 570–571, 581. The purpose of s 1(1)(e) is to remedy an injustice of a person being put by the deceased in a position of dependency and then deprived of financial support after the deceased's death: *Re Beaumont, Martin v Midland Bank Trust Co Ltd* [1980] Ch 444, [1980] 1 All ER 266; *Jelley v Iliffe* [1981] Fam 128, [1981] 2 All ER 29, CA; *Bishop v Plumley* [1991] 1 All ER 236, [1991] 1 WLR 582, CA. Successful applications have been made by a sister (*Re Wilkinson, Neale v Newell* [1978] Fam 22, [1978] 1 All ER 221); a mistress (*Malone v Harrison* [1979] 1 WLR 1353; *Churchill v Roach* [2004] 2 FLR 989, [2004] 3 FCR 744; a common law husband (*Jelley v Iliffe* above; *Graham v Murphy* [1997] 1 FLR 860, [1997] 2 FCR 441); a common law wife (*Harrington v Gill* (1983) 4 FLR 265, CA; *Bishop v Plumley* [1991] 1 All ER 236, [1991] 1 WLR 582, CA); a friend paying less than the market rent for premises owned by the deceased(*Rees v Newbery and Institute of Cancer Research* [1998] 1 FLR 1041); and a mother who looked after her severely brain-damaged daughter until death (*Re B* [2000] Ch 662, [2000] 1 All ER 665, CA). Homosexual applicants may fall into this category: *Wayling v Jones* [1995] 2 FLR 1029, [1996] 2 FCR 41, CA (where the claim actually succeeded under the doctrine of proprietary estoppel). For a case in which the application failed see eg *Re Beaumont, Martin v*

Midland Bank Trust Co Ltd above. Many of the decisions under the Inheritance (Provision for Family and Dependants) Act 1975 s 1(1)(e) would, in the case of deaths after 1995, be decided under s 1(1)(ba): see the text and note 8.

The burden of proof rests with the applicant, who must prove that he is a person who was being maintained before the court can consider whether reasonable financial provision has been made: *Re Wilkinson, Neale v Newell* above.

Where a claimant has strong ties with another country, the court is entitled to confine the assessment of reasonable maintenance to what, over and above the claimant's own resources, is needed for maintenance in that country: *Witkowska v Kaminski* [2006] EWHC 1940 (Ch) at [30], [2007] 1 FLR 1547 [2006] 3 FCR 250 per Blackburne J.

(2) REASONABLE FINANCIAL PROVISION

568. The test of reasonable financial provision. The test of reasonable financial provision is whether the disposition of the deceased's estate effected by his will[1] or the law relating to intestacy[2], or the combination of his will and that law, is not such as to make reasonable financial provision[3] for the applicant[4]. The language is wholly impersonal and the test is objective[5]. The question is not whether the deceased stands convicted of unreasonableness, but whether the provision in fact made is unreasonable[6].

In exercising its jurisdiction the court is required to follow the statutory directions as to the matters to be considered[7]. The question is answered as at the date of investigation by the court and not as at the date of death[8], and in considering the statutory matters to which the court is required to have regard, the court must take into account the facts as known to it at the date of the hearing[9].

The deceased's reasons for not making any provision for the applicant are relevant but no special significance should be attached to them[10]. The court can override the testamentary wishes of the deceased to the extent permitted by statute[11].

1 As to the meaning of 'will' see PARA 566 note 8.

2 As to the law relating to intestacy see PARA 477 et seq.

3 As to the meaning of 'reasonable financial provision' see the Inheritance (Provision for Family and Dependants) Act 1975 s 1(2); and PARAS 569–570.

4 Inheritance (Provision for Family and Dependants) Act 1975 s 1(1). As to the persons for whom provision may be made see PARAS 567, 577–581.

5 *Re Coventry, Coventry v Coventry* [1980] Ch 461 at 474, [1979] 2 All ER 408 at 418, CA, per Oliver J and at 488–489 and 823 per Goff LJ; *Moody v Stevenson* [1992] Ch 486, [1992] 1 FLR 494, CA; *Jessop v Jessop* [1992] 1 FLR 591, [1992] 1 FCR 253, CA; *Re Jennings* [1994] Ch 286, [1994] 3 All ER 27, CA; *Re Hancock* [1998] 2 FLR 346, [1999] 1 FCR 500, CA; *Rees v Newbery and Institute of Cancer Research* [1998] 1 FLR 1041; *Espinosa v Bourke* [1999] 1 FLR 747, [1999] 3 FCR 76, CA; *H v Mitson* [2009] EWHC 3114 (Fam), sub nom *H v J's Personal Representatives* [2010] Fam Law 343. See also *Re Franks, Franks v Franks* [1948] Ch 62, [1947] 2 All ER 638; *Re Goodwin, Goodwin v Goodwin* [1969] 1 Ch 283, [1968] 3 All ER 12; *Re Gregory, Gregory v Goodenough* [1971] 1 All ER 497 at 502, [1970] 1 WLR 1455 at 1461, CA; *Re Shanahan, De Winter (formerly Shanahan) v Legal Personal Representatives of Shanahan* [1973] Fam 1, [1971] 3 All ER 873. The statutory criteria is to be considered at two stages; the first is a value judgment as to whether or not the deceased's dispositions had made reasonable financial provision and, where the court is satisfied such provision has not been made, the second stage is determining the extent to which the court should exercise its power under the Inheritance (Provision for Family and Dependants) Act 1975: *Ilott v Mitson* [2011] EWCA Civ 346, [2012] 2 FLR 170. See also *Cattle v Evans* [2011] EWHC 945 (Ch), [2011] 2 FLR 843, [2011] All ER (D) 209 (Apr).

Payment of existing debts will not normally amount to maintenance although it may do so if, for example, the payment allows the applicant to carry on a profit-making business or profession: *Re Dennis* [1981] 2 All ER 140 at 146; *Re Abram* [1996] 2 FLR 379 at 396, [1997] 2 FCR 85 at 102; *Baynes v Hedger* [2008] EWHC 1587 (Ch) at [125], [2008] 2 FLR 1805, [2008] All ER (D) 175 (Jul); affd on other grounds [2009] EWCA Civ 374, [2009] 2 FLR 767, [2009] All ER (D) 50 (May).

6 *Re Goodwin, Goodwin v Goodwin* [1969] 1 Ch 283 at 287, [1968] 3 All ER 12 at 15 per Megarry J, approved in *Re Gregory, Gregory v Goodenough* [1971] 1 All ER 497 at 502, [1970] 1 WLR 1455 at 1461, CA, per Winn LJ; *Re Shanahan, De Winter (formerly Shanahan) v Legal Personal Representatives of Shanahan* [1973] Fam 1, [1971] 3 All ER 873; *Millward v Shenton* [1972] 2 All ER 1025, [1972] 1 WLR 711, CA.

7 Ie the matters stated in the Inheritance (Provision for Family and Dependants) Act 1975 s 3: see PARAS 571–581.

8 A lengthy delay between the death and the application or hearing can result in applicants being awarded provision when they would not have succeeded had the application been heard earlier: *Re Hancock* [1998] 2 FLR 346, [1999] 1 FCR 500, CA (where sale of land to a supermarket chain resulted in a six-fold increase in the value of the estate between the grant of probate and the hearing); *Stock v Brown* [1994] 1 FLR 840, [1994] 2 FCR 1125 (where the application was made because interest rates fell some six years after the grant of probate and an extension of time was granted (see PARAS 597–598)). See also *Re Shanahan, De Winter (formerly Shanahan) v Legal Personal Representatives of Shanahan* [1973] Fam 1 at 8, [1971] 3 All ER 873 at 880 per Lord Simon of Glaisdale; *Re Goodwin, Goodwin v Goodwin* [1969] 1 Ch 283 at 289, [1968] 3 All ER 12 at 16 per Megarry J.

9 Inheritance (Provision for Family and Dependants) Act 1975 s 3(5). If re-exercising the discretion conferred by s 2 (see PARAS 591–592), an appellate court must have regard to the facts at the date of the appellate hearing, not at the date of the original hearing: see *Ilott v Mitson* [2015] EWCA Civ 797 at [16], [2016] 1 All ER 932, [2015] 2 FCR 547 per Arden LJ.

10 Evidence of the deceased's reasons, though hearsay, is admissible: see the Civil Evidence Act 1995 s 1; and CIVIL PROCEDURE vol 12 (2015) PARA 870 et seq. The deceased's reasons may be relevant but must be tested by reference to other evidence: *Singer v Isaac* [2001] WTLR 1045; *Re Myers, Myers v Myers* [2004] EWHC 1944 (Fam), [2005] WTLR 851; *Re Gold, Gold v Curtis* [2005] WTLR 673; *H v Mitson* [2009] EWHC 3114 (Fam), sub nom *H v J's Personal Representatives* [2010] Fam Law 343. See also *Re Pugh, Pugh v Pugh* [1943] Ch 387, [1943] 2 All ER 361; *Re Searle, Searle v Siems* [1949] Ch 73, [1948] 2 All ER 426; *Re Smallwood, Smallwood v Martins Bank Ltd* [1951] Ch 369, [1951] 1 All ER 372; *Williams v Johns* [1988] 2 FLR 475; *Robinson v Fernsby* [2003] EWCA Civ 1820, [2004] WTLR 257.

11 Ie to make reasonable provision for the applicant. As to the meaning of 'reasonable financial provision' see PARAS 569, 570. See *Ilott v Mitson* [2015] EWCA Civ 797 at [51], [2016] 1 All ER 932, [2015] 2 FCR 547 per Arden LJ.

569. Meaning of reasonable financial provision in the case of an application by the spouse or civil partner. In the case of an application[1] made by the spouse[2] of the deceased (except where the marriage with the deceased was the subject of a decree of judicial separation and at the date of death the decree was in force and the separation was continuing), or by the civil partner of the deceased (except where, at the date of death, a separation order[3] was in force in relation to the civil partnership and the separation was continuing) reasonable financial provision means such financial provision as it would be reasonable in all the circumstances of the case for a spouse or civil partner to receive, whether or not that provision is required for his maintenance[4].

1 Ie an application for an order under the Inheritance (Provision for Family and Dependants) Act 1975 s 2 (see PARAS 591–592) made by virtue of the Inheritance (Provision for Family and Dependants) Act 1975 s 1(1)(a) in the case of a spouse and s 1(2)(aa) in the case of a civil partner (see PARA 566): see s 1(2)(a), (aa) (s 1(2)(aa) added by the Civil Partnership Act 2004 s 71, Sch 4 para 15(6)).

2 Spouse includes a person who is married to a person of the same sex: see Marriage (Same Sex Couples) Act 2013 Sch 3 para 1(1)(c), (2), (3); and MATRIMONIAL AND CIVIL PARTNERSHIP LAW vol 72 (2015) PARAS 1–2. See further PARAS 567 note 4, 577.

3 Ie a separation order under the Civil Partnership Act 2004 Pt 2 Chapter 2.

4 Inheritance (Provision for Family and Dependants) Act 1975 ss 1(2)(a), (aa), 25(1). On an application by a surviving spouse or civil partner reasonable financial provision is unqualified by what would be reasonable by way of maintenance: see eg *Re Besterman, Besterman v Grusin* [1984] Ch 458, [1984] 2 All ER 656, CA; *Re Bunning, Bunning v Salmon* [1984] Ch 480, [1984] 3 All ER 1; *Jessop v Jessop* [1992] 1 FLR 591, [1992] 1 FCR 253, CA. See also *Moore v Holdsworth* [2010] EWHC 683 (Ch), [2010] All ER (D) 87 (Jun) (such financial provision as was reasonable did not extend to the entire estate absolutely). The special statutory guidelines to be taken into account on applications by spouses and civil partners (see PARA 577) include the provision the applicant might reasonably have expected to receive had the marriage or civil

partnership ended in divorce or dissolution but this is only one of the factors to be considered and the overriding consideration is what is 'reasonable' in all the circumstances: *Re Krubert* [1997] Ch 97, [1996] 3 WLR 959, CA. As to the meaning of 'maintenance' see PARA 570.

570. Meaning of reasonable financial provision in the case of other applicants. In the case of an application[1] made by any applicant other than the surviving husband or wife or civil partner[2] of the deceased, reasonable financial provision means such financial provision as it would be reasonable in all the circumstances of the case for the applicant to receive for his maintenance[3].

There is, for these purposes, no statutory definition of maintenance and the courts have been reluctant to introduce a definition[4]. Maintenance is not limited to the bare necessities of life but is not so broad as to cover anything which may be regarded as desirable for an applicant's benefit or welfare[5] but connotes only payments which, directly or indirectly, enable the applicant in the future to discharge the cost of his daily living at whatever standard of living is appropriate to him but provision need not be by way of income payments if a lump sum is more appropriate[6].

In exceptional cases there can be a failure to make reasonable provision for the maintenance of someone who is not impecunious[7].

1 Ie an application for an order under the Inheritance (Provision for Family and Dependants) Act 1975 s 2 (see PARAS 591–592) made by virtue of s 1(1)(b)–(e) (see PARA 566): see s 1(2)(b). See also PARAS 567, 578–581.

2 As to the meanings of 'husband', 'wife' and 'civil partner' see PARA 567 note 4.

3 Inheritance (Provision for Family and Dependants) Act 1975 ss 1(2)(b), 25(1). Existing means are not conclusive as to the appropriate level at which a claimant is entitled to be maintained: *Ilott v Mitson* [2015] EWCA Civ 797, [2016] 1 All ER 932, [2015] 2 FCR 547 (claimant living in straitened financial circumstances).

4 *Re Dennis, Dennis v Lloyds Bank Ltd* [1981] 2 All ER 140 at 145, 124 Sol Jo 885 per Browne-Wilkinson J.

5 *Re Coventry, Coventry v Coventry* [1980] Ch 461 at 485, [1979] 3 All ER 815 at 819–820, CA, per Goff LJ. See also *Re E, E v E* [1966] 2 All ER 44 at 48, [1966] 1 WLR 709 at 715 per Stamp J (reasonable provision is not limited to keeping a dependant above the bread line); *Millward v Shenton* [1972] 2 All ER 1025 at 1028, [1972] 1 WLR 711 at 715, CA, per Lord Denning MR; *Re Christie, Christie v Keeble* [1979] Ch 168 at 174, [1979] 1 All ER 546 at 550 per Vivian Price QC (reasonable provision refers to no more and no less than the applicant's way of life and well-being, his health, financial security and allied matters such as the well-being, health and financial security of his immediate family for whom he is responsible) (criticised in *Re Coventry, Coventry v Coventry* above). See further *Malone v Harrison* [1979] 1 WLR 1353, 123 Sol Jo 804; *Re Dennis, Dennis v Lloyds Bank Ltd* [1981] 2 All ER 140, 124 Sol Jo 885; *Re Jennings* [1994] Ch 286, [1994] 3 All ER 27, CA; *Re Abram* [1996] 2 FLR 379; *Re Goodchild, Goodchild v Goodchild* [1997] 3 All ER 63, [1997] 1 WLR 1216, CA; *Re Pearce* [1998] 2 FLR 705, [1999] 2 FCR 179, CA; *Churchill v Roach* [2004] 2 FLR 989, [2004] 3 FCR 744; *Negus v Bahouse* [2007] EWHC 2628 (Ch), [2008] 1 FLR 381, [2008] 1 FCR 768; *Webster v Webster* [2008] EWHC 31 (Ch), [2009] 1 FLR 1240.

6 *Re Dennis, Dennis v Lloyds Bank Ltd* [1981] 2 All ER 140 at 145, 124 Sol Jo 885 per Browne-Wilkinson J; approved in *Re Jennings* [1994] Ch 286 at 297, [1994] 3 All ER 27 at 35 per Nourse LJ; and in *Espinosa v Bourke* [1999] 1 FLR 747 at 758, CA, per Butler-Sloss LJ. See *Ilott v Mitson* [2015] EWCA Civ 797, [2016] 1 All ER 932, [2015] 2 FCR 547 in relation to state benefits. As a matter of public policy, the court is not constrained to treat a person's reasonable financial provision as being limited by their exiting state benefits (*Ilott v Mitson* at [69] per Ryder LJ); the court must take into account any loss of state benefits which an award may cause when calculating what order to make (*Ilott v Mitson* at [70] per Sir Colin Rimer). For examples of the kinds of awards made see PARAS 578–581.

7 See *Lewis v Warner* [2016] EWHC 1787 (Ch), [2016] All ER (D) 104 (Jul) (order allowing a financially secure 91 year old to buy at market value the house in which he had been living with the deceased for the last 20 years). The applicant was in poor health and had a support system in place which allowed him to live independently. Newey J held that the recorder was justified in concluding that the deceased's will had failed to make reasonable provision for the applicant; it

was not reasonable financial provision to make no provision for his accommodation so as to lead on her death to sudden eviction from his home.

(3) MATTERS WHICH THE COURT MUST TAKE INTO ACCOUNT

(i) Guidelines Applicable to All Cases

571. The statutory guidelines common to all applicants. Where an application is made for an order under the Inheritance (Provision for Family and Dependants) Act 1975[1], the court[2] must, in determining whether the disposition of the deceased's estate effected by his will[3] or the law relating to intestacy[4], or the combination of his will and that law, is such as to make reasonable financial provision[5] for the applicant[6]. If the court considers that reasonable financial provision has not been made, in determining whether and in what manner it is to exercise its powers to make such an order, the court must have regard to a number of factors[7], including the financial resources and financial needs of the applicant or applicants and the beneficiaries[8], the obligations and responsibilities of the deceased[9], the size and nature of the estate[10], the existence of any physical or mental disability[11] and the conduct of any party[12]. In the case of particular applicants further specific considerations apply[13].

1 Ie an order under the Inheritance (Provision for Family and Dependants) Act 1975 s 2 (see PARAS 591–592): see s 3(1).
2 As to the meaning of 'court' see PARA 566 note 6.
3 As to the meaning of 'will' see PARA 566 note 8.
4 As to the law relating to intestacy see PARA 477 et seq.
5 As to the meaning of 'reasonable financial provision' see PARAS 569–570. As to the test of reasonable financial provision see PARA 568.
6 Inheritance (Provision for Family and Dependants) Act 1975 s 3(1).
7 Inheritance (Provision for Family and Dependants) Act 1975 s 3(1). This provision does not rank the factors to be taken into account: *H v Mitson* [2009] EWHC 3114 (Fam), sub nom *H v J's Personal Representatives* [2010] Fam Law 343.
8 See the Inheritance (Provision for Family and Dependants) Act 1975 s 3(1)(a)–(c); and PARA 572.
9 See the Inheritance (Provision for Family and Dependants) Act 1975 s 3(1)(d); and PARA 573.
10 See the Inheritance (Provision for Family and Dependants) Act 1975 s 3(1)(e); and PARA 574.
11 See the Inheritance (Provision for Family and Dependants) Act 1975 s 3(1)(f); and PARA 575.
12 See the Inheritance (Provision for Family and Dependants) Act 1975 s 3(1)(g); and PARA 576.
13 See PARAS 577–581.

572. Financial resources and financial needs. In making its determination[1] the court[2] is required to have regard to:

(1) the financial resources and financial needs which the applicant has or is likely to have in the foreseeable future[3];
(2) the financial resources and financial needs which any other applicant for an order[4] has or is likely to have in the foreseeable future[5]; and
(3) the financial resources and financial needs which any beneficiary[6] of the estate of the deceased has or is likely to have in the foreseeable future[7].

In considering any person's financial resources for these purposes the court must take into account his earning capacity[8]. The availability of state benefits is also relevant[9]. In considering any person's financial needs the court must take into account his financial obligations and responsibilities[10] and have regard to his needs for the foreseeable future[11].

1 Ie in determining whether the disposition of the deceased's estate is such as to make reasonable financial provision for the applicant and, if reasonable financial provision has not been made,

whether and in what manner the court is to exercise its powers to make an order: see the Inheritance (Provision for Family and Dependants) Act 1975 s 3(1); and PARA 571. As to the meaning of 'reasonable financial provision' see PARAS 569–570. As to the test of reasonable financial provision see PARA 568.

2 As to the meaning of 'court' see PARA 566 note 6.

3 Inheritance (Provision for Family and Dependants) Act 1975 s 3(1)(a).

4 Ie an order under the Inheritance (Provision for Family and Dependants) Act 1975 s 2 (see PARAS 591–592): see s 3(1)(b).

5 Inheritance (Provision for Family and Dependants) Act 1975 s 3(1)(b).

6 'Beneficiary', in relation to the estate of a deceased person, means:

(1) a person who under the will of the deceased or under the law relating to intestacy (see PARA 477 et seq) is beneficially interested in the estate or would be so interested if an order had not been made under the Inheritance (Provision for Family and Dependants) Act 1975; and

(2) a person who has received any sum of money or other property which by virtue of s 8(1) or s 8(2) (see PARAS 583–584) is treated as part of the net estate of the deceased or would have received that sum or other property if an order had not been made under the Act: s 25(1).

As to the net estate see PARA 582.

7 Inheritance (Provision for Family and Dependants) Act 1975 s 3(1)(c). Just as the presence of a needy beneficiary has the potential to weaken an applicant's claim where the estate is limited, so does the absence of any beneficiary with the conventional sort of need have the potential to assist him: see *Ilott v Mitson* [2015] EWCA Civ 797, [2016] 1 All ER 932, [2015] 2 FCR 547. In *Ilott v Mitson*, charities benefiting under a will did not make any case that they had resources and needs to be taken into account.

8 Inheritance (Provision for Family and Dependants) Act 1975 s 3(6). See *Re Ducksbury, Ducksbury v Ducksbury* [1966] 2 All ER 374, [1966] 1 WLR 1226; *Re Bunning, Bunning v Salmon* [1984] Ch 480, [1984] 3 All ER 1 (applicant likely to take part-time employment); *Re Pearson-Gregory* (1957) Times, 11 October (provision made for the applicant under an inter vivos trust); *Jessop v Jessop* [1992] 1 FLR 591, CA (receipt of a pension); *Re Crawford* (1982) 4 FLR 273; *Re Catmull, Catmull v Watts* [1943] Ch 262, [1943] 2 All ER 115; *Re Charman, Charman v Williams* [1951] WN 599, [1951] 2 TLR 1095; *Re Clayton, Clayton v Howell* [1966] 2 All ER 370, [1966] 1 WLR 969; *Re Jennings* [1994] Ch 286, [1994] 3 All ER 27; *Re Gold, Gold v Curtis* [2005] WTLR 673; *Re Myers, Myers v Myers* [2004] EWHC 1944 (Fam), [2005] WTLR 851; *Garland v Morris* [2007] EWHC 2 (Ch), [2007] 2 FLR 528. It may be appropriate to take into account sums already received: *Robinson v Fernsby* [2003] EWCA Civ 1820, [2004] WTLR 257.

9 See *Re Watkins, Hayward v Chatterton* [1949] 1 All ER 695, where Roxburgh J took the view that the testator was entitled to distribute his estate on the footing that his dependant daughter who was a patient in a mental hospital, could and should take advantage of the provisions of the social security legislation; and in *Re Elliott* (1956) Times, 18 May, where Danckwerts J (dissenting from the view expressed by *Re Catmull, Catmull v Watts* [1943] Ch 262 at 268, [1943] 2 All ER 115 at 117 per Uthwatt J) took the view that a testator was not free to dispose of his property elsewhere and make no provision for his widow, merely because she would receive a widow's pension from the state; *Re E, E v E* [1966] 2 All ER 44, [1966] 1 WLR 709 (the availability of state benefits is particularly relevant in the case of small estates). See also *Re Collins* [1990] Fam 56, [1990] 2 All ER 47. See *Ilott v Mitson* [2015] EWCA Civ 797 at [69], [2016] 1 All ER 932, [2015] 2 FCR 547 per Ryder LJ: 'as a matter of public policy, the court is not constrained to treat a person's reasonable financial provision as being limited by their existing state benefits, nor is the court's function substituted for by any assessment of benefits undertaken by the state'. A court must take into account the loss of state benefits when calculating how much to award and in what way to structure it: *Ilott v Mitson* at [60] per Arden LJ. The use of a discretionary trust in such cases is an order within the court's powers under the Inheritance (Provision for Family and Dependants) Act 1975 s 2(1)(d): *Challinor v Challinor* [2009] EWHC 180 (Ch), [2009] WTLR 931; *Hanbury v Hanbury* [1999] 2 FLR 255, [1999] 3 FCR 217.

10 Inheritance (Provision for Family and Dependants) Act 1975 s 3(6).

11 See *Re Ducksbury, Ducksbury v Ducksbury* [1966] 2 All ER 374, [1966] 1 WLR 1226; *Re Clayton, Clayton v Howell* [1966] 2 All ER 370, [1966] 1 WLR 969. The court should take into account any needs that the applicant is reasonably likely to have but it will not normally be appropriate to classify remote or speculative possibilities as specific needs: *Challinor v Challinor* [2009] EWHC 180 (Ch) at [32], [2009] WTLR 931 at [32]. The court will not take into account voluntary expenditure incurred by an applicant with full knowledge of their financial position: *Aston v Aston* [2007] WTLR 1349. In general the reference to 'needs' is to reasonable requirements (*Harrington v Gill* (1983) 4 FLR 265, CA) but provision for a surviving spouse or

civil partner is not limited to what is needed for maintenance: see s 1(2)(a), (aa); and PARA 569. Necessitous circumstances cannot be in themselves the reason to alter the testator's dispositions: *Re Coventry, Coventry v Coventry* [1980] Ch 461, [1979] 2 All ER 408, CA (cited by Butler-Sloss LJ in in *Espinosa v Bourke* [1999] 1 FLR 747, [1999] 3 FCR 76). However, see *Ilott v Mitson* [2011] EWCA Civ 346 at [91], [2011] All ER (D) 37 (Apr), [2012] 2 FLR 170 per Black LJ: 'necessitous circumstances will never actually be the sole factor from amongst the [Inheritance (Provision for Family and Dependants) Act 1975] s 3(1) list to feature in a case'. The size and nature of the estate (Inheritance (Provision for Family and Dependants) Act 1975 s 3(1)(e)) will always be material, as will the situation of any other beneficiary of the estate (s 3(1)(c)). Section 3(1)(g) is drafted in very broad terms and may well draw in other factors, amongst them potentially the views of the deceased, depending on the facts of the individual case.

573. Obligations and responsibilities of the deceased. In making its determination[1] the court[2] is required to have regard to any obligations and responsibilities which the deceased had towards any applicant for an order[3] or towards any beneficiary[4] of the estate of the deceased[5].

As a general rule only those obligations and responsibilities undischarged immediately before death should be considered[6]. In relation to both applicants and beneficiaries, the court considers not only legal obligations and responsibilities but also those which can more loosely be described as moral claims[7], but once an applicant has established that he is a person entitled to apply, in no case is there an invariable prerequisite that a moral obligation or some other special circumstance must be shown[8]. The source of the deceased's estate is a relevant consideration in determining what the obligations and responsibilities of the deceased were and what emphasis should be placed on them[9].

1 Ie in determining whether the disposition of the deceased's estate is such as to make reasonable financial provision for the applicant and, if reasonable financial provision has not been made, whether and in what manner the court is to exercise its powers to make an order: see the Inheritance (Provision for Family and Dependants) Act 1975 s 3(1); and PARA 571. As to the meaning of 'reasonable financial provision' see PARAS 569–570. As to the test of reasonable financial provision see PARA 568.

2 As to the meaning of 'court' see PARA 566 note 6.

3 Ie an order under the Inheritance (Provision for Family and Dependants) Act 1975 s 2 (see PARAS 591–592): see s 3(1)(d).

4 As to the meaning of 'beneficiary' see PARA 572 note 6.

5 Inheritance (Provision for Family and Dependants) Act 1975 s 3(1)(d). For examples of the application of this provision see *Re Joslin, Joslin v Murch* [1941] Ch 200, [1941] 1 All ER 302 (provision made by testator out of very small estate for illegitimate children and their mother, and no provision made for lawful wife: no interference by court); *Re Simson, Simson v National Provincial Bank Ltd* [1950] Ch 38, [1949] 2 All ER 826 (housekeeper beneficiary); *Re Brown, Brown v Knowles* (1955) 105 L Jo 169 (promise made to children of first marriage by testator raising a moral obligation did not oust the court's jurisdiction to entertain application by second wife); *Re Bellman* [1963] P 239, [1963] 1 All ER 513; *Re Ducksbury, Ducksbury v Ducksbury* [1966] 2 All ER 374, [1966] 1 WLR 1226 (conflict between obligations to daughter and second wife); *Sivyer v Sivyer* [1967] 3 All ER 429, [1967] 1 WLR 1482 (conflict between obligations to child and third wife); *Re Fullard, Fullard v King* [1982] Fam 42, [1981] 2 All ER 796, CA (no obligation to former wife); *Re Besterman, Besterman v Grusin* [1984] Ch 458, [1984] 2 All ER 656, CA (obligation to wife stronger than to charity as principal beneficiary); *Re Debenham* [1986] 1 FLR 404 (obligation to 58 year old epileptic daughter); *Rhodes v Dean* [1996] CLY 5555, CA (will left estate to issue making no provision for applicant who took £36,000 contents of joint bank account by survivorship); *Rees v Newbery and Institute of Cancer Research* [1998] 1 FLR 1041 (deceased's 'obligation' to provide friend with low rent tenancy); *Espinosa v Bourke* , [1999] 1 FLR 747, [1999] 3 FCR 76 CA (promise by deceased to adult daughter outweighed relevance of her misbehaviour); *Re Pearce, Pearce v Davis Pearce* [1998] 2 FLR 705, [1999] 2 FCR 179, CA (moral obligation arising from substantial amount of work carried out by deceased's son coupled with promises made by the deceased); *Re Watson* [1999] 1 FLR 878, [1999] 3 FCR 595 (applicant cohabitee has stronger claim than Crown taking estate bona vacantia); *Re Goodchild, Goodchild v Goodchild* [1996] 1 All ER 670, [1996] 1 WLR 694 (agreement between spouses which did not create binding mutual wills nevertheless created a moral obligation); *Challinor v Challinor* [2009] EWHC 180 (Ch), [2009] WTLR 931 (moral obligation to provide for daughter with Down's syndrome).

6 *Re Jennings* [1994] Ch 286, [1994] 3 All ER 27, CA (the Inheritance (Provision for Family and Dependants) Act 1975 does not revive defunct obligations and responsibilities per Nourse LJ at 296 and 34). An application brought by a person who has already been adequately provided for by the deceased will fail if the obligation has been discharged: *Rhodes v Dean* [1996] CLY 5555, CA (deceased left estate to issue but applicant took £36,000 contents of joint bank account by survivorship). See also *Re Talbot, Talbot v Talbot* [1962] 3 All ER 174, [1962] 1 WLR 1113; *Roberts v Roberts* [1964] 3 All ER 503, [1965] 1 WLR 560; *Jessop v Jessop* [1992] 1 FLR 591, [1992] 1 FCR 253, CA.

7 *Re Coventry, Coventry v Coventry* [1980] Ch 461, [1979] 3 All ER 815, CA; *Re Jennings* [1994] Ch 286, [1994] 3 All ER 27, CA; *Re Hancock* [1998] 2 FLR 346, CA; *Re Pearce* [1998] 2 FLR 705, CA; *Espinosa v Bourke* [1999] 1 FLR 747, [1999] 3 FCR 595, CA; *Re Watson* [1999] 1 FLR 878, [1999] 3 FCR 76; *Re Gold, Gold v Curtis* [2005] WTLR 673; *Re Myers, Myers v Myers* [2004] EWHC 1944 (Fam), [2005] WTLR 851; *Garland v Morris* [2007] EWHC 2 (Ch), [2007] 2 FLR 528; *H v Mitson* [2009] EWHC 3114 (Fam), sub nom *H v J's Personal Representatives* [2010] Fam Law 343.

8 *Re Pearce* [1998] 2 FLR 705 at 710, CA, per Nourse LJ; *Re Hancock* [1998] 2 FLR 346, [1999] 1 FCR 500, CA; *Espinosa v Bourke* [1999] 1 FLR 747 at 755, CA, per Butler-Sloss LJ; *Re Watson* [1999] 1 FLR 878, [1999] 3 FCR 595; cf *Re Coventry, Coventry v Coventry* [1980] Ch 461, [1979] 3 All ER 815, CA; *Re Jennings* [1994] Ch 286, [1994] 3 All ER 27, CA. For examples of claims by children which failed where there was no moral obligation see *Re Coventry, Coventry v Coventry* and *Re Jennings*; but see the judgments in *Re Hancock*, *Re Pearce* and *Espinosa v Bourke* which confirm that there is no requirement for such an obligation. See also *Ilott v Mitson* [2015] EWCA Civ 797, [2016] 1 All ER 932, [2015] 2 FCR 547 (ordinary family obligation weighed to some extent in claimant's favour, although as an adult child living independently, the deceased had no responsibility for her). See also *Hope v Knight* [2010] EWHC 3443 (Ch), [2011] WTLR 583 (parent is under no obligation to house an adult child and does not come under such an obligation at death).

9 *Re Styler, Styler v Griffith* [1942] Ch 387, [1942] 2 All ER 201; *Re Brownbridge, Brownbridge v Brownbridge* (1942) 193 LT Jo 185; *Sivyer v Sivyer* [1967] 3 All ER 429, [1967] 1 WLR 1482; *Jelley v Iliffe* [1981] Fam 128, [1981] 2 All ER 29, CA; *Re Callaghan* [1985] Fam 1, [1984] 3 All ER 790; *Re Leach, Leach v Lindeman* [1986] Ch 226, [1985] 2 All ER 754, CA; *Re Goodchild, Goodchild v Goodchild* [1997] 3 All ER 63, [1997] 1 WLR 1216, CA. However, in *Ilott v Mitson* [2015] EWCA Civ 797, [2016] 1 All ER 932, [2015] 2 FCR 547 the court discounted the fact that a significant portion of the estate derived from the father's death benefit paid to his widow many years earlier; it had become part of the general assets of the deceased. That an applicant or beneficiary has assisted the deceased in building up a business is a relevant consideration: *Re Brownbridge, Brownbridge v Brownbridge* above; *Thornley v Palmer* [1969] 3 All ER 31, [1969] 1 WLR 1037; *Re Rowlands* [1984] FLR 813; *Re Abram* [1996] 2 FLR 379, [1996] 2 FLR 379; *Stephanides v Cohen* [2002] EWHC 1869 (Fam), [2002] WTLR 1373; *Wright v Waters* [2014] EWHC 3614 (Ch), [2014] All ER (D) 85 (Nov).

574. The size and nature of the estate. In making its determination[1] the court[2] is required to have regard to the size and nature[3] of the deceased's net estate[4]. Where the estate is large, reasonable financial provision will be judged accordingly and it will not be so important to balance the rights of the applicant against the beneficiaries[5] but a large estate does not of itself justify an award as provision must be reasonable[6]. Applications and appeals in small estates are discouraged by the courts[7] but there is no absolute rule that applications made in small estates must fail[8].

1 Ie in determining whether the disposition of the deceased's estate is such as to make reasonable financial provision for the applicant and, if reasonable financial provision has not been made, whether and in what manner the court is to exercise its powers to make an order: see the Inheritance (Provision for Family and Dependants) Act 1975 s 3(1); and PARA 571. As to the meaning of 'reasonable financial provision' see PARAS 569–570. As to the test of reasonable financial provision see PARA 568.

2 As to the meaning of 'court' see PARA 566 note 6.

3 Where the principal asset of the estate is a property in which the beneficiaries live or from which they make their living the court will have regard to the consequences of ordering provision which results in a premature realisation of that asset but there is no absolute bar to depriving a beneficiary of his home or the like: *Re Brownbridge, Brownbridge v Brownbridge* (1942) 193 LT Jo 185; *Re E, E v E* [1966] 2 All ER 44, [1966] 1 WLR 709; *Thornley v Palmer* [1969] 3 All ER 31, [1969]

1 WLR 1037; *Re Rowlands* [1984] FLR 813, [1984] Fam Law 280; *Re Farrow* [1987] 1 FLR 205; *Baker v Baker* [2008] EWHC 977 (Ch), [2008] 2 FLR 1956. The sale of a business and consequent unlocking of the value of the assets after death is a factor the court can take into account: *McNulty v McNulty* [2002] EWHC 123 (Ch), [2002] WTLR 737. The origin of the deceased's estate is a relevant factor: see the cases cited in PARA 573 note 9.

4 Inheritance (Provision for Family and Dependants) Act 1975 s 3(1)(e). As to the net estate see PARA 582.

5 *Malone v Harrison* [1979] 1 WLR 1353; *Re Inns, Inns v Wallace* [1947] Ch 576, [1947] 2 All ER 308 (applicants only entitled to maintenance should not have awards increased because of size of estate); *Re Borthwick, Borthwick v Beauvais* [1949] Ch 395, [1949] 1 All ER 472 (substantial estate, small provision made by testator for wife, who during the testator's life had been kept in penury: provision increased); *Re Black* (1953) Times, 25 March (large estate: provision for son increased); *Re Besterman, Besterman v Grusin* [1984] Ch 458, [1984] 2 All ER 656, CA; *Re Gold, Gold v Curtis* [2005] WTLR 673; *Re Myers, Myers v Myers* [2004] EWHC 1944 (Fam), [2005] WTLR 851.

6 *Re Coventry, Coventry v Coventry* [1980] Ch 461, [1979] 3 All ER 815, CA; *Re Dennis, Dennis v Lloyds Bank Ltd* [1981] 2 All ER 140, CA. An increase in the value of the estate after death may, however, be a relevant factor in determining whether provision made for the applicant was reasonable: *Re Hancock* [1998] 2 FLR 346, [1999] 1 FCR 500.

7 *Re Coventry, Coventry v Coventry* [1980] Ch 461, [1979] 3 All ER 815, CA; *Re Dawkins, Dawkins v Judd* [1986] 2 FLR 360, [1986] Fam Law 295; *Re Clayton, Clayton v Howell* [1966] 2 All ER 370, [1966] 1 WLR 969. The courts regularly order costs against the claimant in such cases: *Re Vrint, Vrint v Swain* [1940] Ch 920, [1940] 3 All ER 470; *Re E, E v E* [1966] 2 All ER 44, [1966] 1 WLR 709; *Re Fullard, Fullard v King* [1982] Fam 42, [1981] 2 All ER 796, CA; *Brill v Proud* [1984] Fam Law 59, CA.

8 The smallness of the estate neither excludes jurisdiction nor full consideration: *Re Clayton, Clayton v Howell* [1966] 2 All ER 370 at 371, [1966] 1 WLR 969 at 971 per Ungoed-Thomas J. See also eg *Re Vrint, Vrint v Swain* [1940] Ch 920, [1940] 3 All ER 470 (estate too small to provide maintenance); *Re Clayton, Clayton v Howell* (£400 lump sum awarded in place of maintenance from £1,271 estate); *Re Gregory, Gregory v Goodenough* [1971] 1 All ER 497, [1970] 1 WLR 1455, CA (small estate; court slow to deprive testator of his right to dispose of it in his own way); *Re E, E v E* [1966] 2 All ER 44, [1966] 1 WLR 709 (estate too small to provide for deserted wife); and see *Re Joslin, Joslin v Murch* [1941] Ch 200, [1941] 1 All ER 302; *Re Catmull, Catmull v Watts* [1943] Ch 262, [1943] 2 All ER 115; *Re Parry* (1956) Times, 19 April; *Re Parkinson* (1975) Times, 4 October, CA. The availability of state benefits is important in cases where the estate is small: see PARA 572 text and note 9.

575. Physical or mental disability. In making its determination[1] the court[2] is required to have regard to any physical or mental disability of any applicant for an order[3] or any beneficiary[4] of the deceased's estate[5]. The presence of a physical or mental disability does not of itself give rise to or defeat a claim[6] but may affect the obligations or responsibilities which the deceased had towards an applicant or beneficiary[7]. Physical or mental disability may also affect needs and earning capacity[8], and the availability of state aid is often relevant[9].

1 Ie in determining whether the disposition of the deceased's estate is such as to make reasonable financial provision for the applicant and, if reasonable financial provision has not been made, whether and in what manner the court is to exercise its powers to make an order: see the Inheritance (Provision for Family and Dependants) Act 1975 s 3(1); and PARA 571. As to the meaning of 'reasonable financial provision' see PARAS 569–570. As to the test of reasonable financial provision see PARA 568.

2 As to the meaning of 'court' see PARA 566 note 6.

3 Ie an order under the Inheritance (Provision for Family and Dependants) Act 1975 s 2 (see PARAS 591–592): see s 3(1)(f).

4 As to the meaning of 'beneficiary' see PARA 572 note 6.

5 Inheritance (Provision for Family and Dependants) Act 1975 s 3(1)(f).

6 See *Wright v Waters* [2014] EWHC 3614 (Ch), [2014] All ER (D) 85 (Nov) where the claimant's ill health (and necessitous circumstances) were outweighed by the Inheritance (Provision for Family and Dependants) Act 1975 s 3(1)(g) factor, her conduct. As to the effect of conduct see PARA 576.

7 See PARA 573.

8 *Re Clayton, Clayton v Howell* [1966] 2 All ER 370, [1966] 1 WLR 969 (applicant crippled in both legs); *Millward v Shenton* [1972] 2 All ER 1025, [1972] 1 WLR 711, CA (adult child with progressive illness and limited earning capacity); *Re Debenham* [1986] 1 FLR 404; *Re Watson* [1999] 1 FLR 878, [1999] 3 FCR 595 (two-storey house inappropriate for cohabitee applicant with mobility problems); *Robinson v Fernsby* [2003] EWCA Civ 1820, [2004] WTLR 257; *Re Gold, Gold v Curtis* [2005] WTLR 673; *Challinor v Challinor* [2009] EWHC 180 (Ch), [2009] WTLR 931. See also PARA 572.

9 *Re Watkins, Hayward v Chatterton* [1949] 1 All ER 695, [1949] WN 125 (only limited provision necessary where place available in state mental hospital); *Re Wood, Wood v Wood* [1982] LS Gaz R 774 (provision of capital appropriate even where state aid would be reduced as a result); and see *Re E, E v E* [1966] 2 All ER 44, [1966] 1 WLR 709. See also PARA 572 text and note 9.

576. Conduct and other matters. In making its determination[1] the court[2] is required to have regard to any other matter, including the conduct of the applicant or any other person, which in the circumstances of the case the court may consider relevant[3]. This broad guideline refers principally to the conduct of any person[4] (including the deceased[5]) as well as the applicant[6] whether before or after the death[7]. Conduct can be positive as well as negative[8]. The deceased's reasons for not making any provision may be relevant[9].

1 Ie in determining whether the disposition of the deceased's estate is such as to make reasonable financial provision for the applicant and, if reasonable financial provision has not been made, whether and in what manner the court is to exercise its powers to make an order: see the Inheritance (Provision for Family and Dependants) Act 1975 s 3(1); and PARA 571. As to the meaning of 'reasonable financial provision' see PARAS 569–570. As to the test of reasonable financial provision see PARA 568.

2 As to the meaning of 'court' see PARA 566 note 6.

3 Inheritance (Provision for Family and Dependants) Act 1975 s 3(1)(g).

4 Recognition by the persons taking the estate of a continuing moral obligation passing to them, and the ability and willingness to satisfy it, are relevant: *Challinor v Challinor* [2009] EWHC 180 (Ch), [2009] WTLR 931.

5 *Re Borthwick, Borthwick v Beauvais* [1949] Ch 395, [1949] 1 All ER 472 (wife kept in penury by deceased); *Thornley v Palmer* [1969] 3 All ER 31, [1969] 1 WLR 1037 (deceased manic-depressive and violent drunk); *Re W* (1975) 119 Sol Jo 439 (deceased had concealed his financial provision from wife during divorce proceedings).

6 *Mastaka v Midland Bank Executor and Trustee Co Ltd* [1941] Ch 192, [1941] 1 All ER 236 (testatrix's daughter had treated the relationship of mother and daughter as non-existent, and no order was made); *Re Morris* [1967] CLY 4114 (applicant wife who had no intention of assisting in the home); *Re Harker-Thomas* [1969] P 28, [1968] 3 All ER 17, CA (wife concealed her financial position in order to continue to receive maintenance at a higher level than she would have been entitled); *Re Fullard, Fullard v King* [1982] Fam 42, [1981] 2 All ER 796, CA (applicant and deceased were divorced); *Re Snoek* (1983) 13 Fam Law 18 (wife awarded only £5,000 out of estate of £20,000 because of her atrocious and vicious behaviour); *Williams v Johns* [1988] 2 FLR 475 (applicant caused shame and distress to the deceased); *Espinosa v Bourke* [1999] 1 FLR 747, [1999] 3 FCR 76, CA (daughter left deceased to be cared for by grandson and cleaner: *Robinson v Fernsby* [2003] EWCA Civ 1820, [2004] WTLR 257 (dissipation of funds received during deceased's lifetime); *Garland v Morris* [2007] EWHC 2 (Ch), [2007] 2 FLR 528 (no contact between daughter and deceased for many years); *Re Waite, Barron v Woodhead* [2008] EWHC 810 (Ch), [2009] 1 FLR 747, [2009] 2 FCR 631 (alcoholism, allegations of violence on part of both deceased and applicant, evasiveness as to state of finances not relevant to size of award made to surviving spouse); *Ilott v Mitson* [2015] EWCA Civ 797, [2016] 1 All ER 932, [2015] 2 FCR 547 (the fact that mother and daughter were estranged throughout the daughter's adult life did not deprive the daughter of an award, or even substantially diminish it; responsibility for estrangement is difficult to quantify); *Wright v Waters* [2014] EWHC 3614 (Ch), [2015] WTLR 353 (conduct of the claimant outweighed all the factors in her favour and it was held objectively reasonable for the will to make no provision).

7 *Re Hancock* [1998] 2 FLR 346, [1999] 1 FCR 500, CA (delay is a factor which may be taken into account).

8 *Malone v Harrison* [1979] 1 WLR 1353 (conduct of mistress reflected positively); *Stephanides v Cohen* [2002] EWHC 1869 (Fam), [2002] WTLR 1373 (second wife worked hard and revitalised family business, son of first marriage a drug addict). See also *Re Land, Land v Land* [2006] EWHC

2069 (Ch), [2007] 1 All ER 324, [2007] 1 WLR 1009 (claimant's conviction for manslaughter by neglect of deceased did not disqualify him from provision when he had previously faithfully discharged family obligations).

9 See *Ilott v Mitson* [2011] EWCA Civ 346 at [91], [2012] 2 FLR 170 per Black LJ: [the Inheritance (Provision for Family and Dependants) Act 1975] s 3(1)(g) is drafted in very broad terms and may well draw in other factors, amongst them potentially the views of the deceased, depending on the facts of the individual case. As to the relevance of the deceased's reasons see PARA 568 text and note 10.

(ii) Guidelines Applicable to Particular Applicants

577. Guidelines applicable to spouse or civil partner of the deceased. On an application for an order[1] by the deceased's spouse or civil partner[2], in addition to the common statutory guidelines[3], the court[4] must also have regard to[5]:

(1) the applicant's age[6] and the duration of the marriage or civil partnership[7]; and

(2) the contribution made by the applicant to the welfare of the deceased's family, including any contribution made by looking after the home or caring for the family[8].

In the case of an application by the spouse of the deceased, the court must, unless at the date of death a decree of judicial separation was in force and the separation was continuing, also have regard to the provision which the applicant might reasonably have expected to receive if on the day on which the deceased died the marriage, instead of being terminated by death, had been terminated by a decree of divorce[9].

In the case of an application by the civil partner of the deceased, the court must, unless at the date of death a separation order[10] was in force and the separation was continuing, also have regard to the provision which the applicant might reasonably have expected to receive if on the day on which the deceased died the civil partnership, instead of being terminated by death, had been terminated by a dissolution order[11].

1 Ie under the Inheritance (Provision for Family and Dependants) Act 1975 s 2 (see PARA 591): see s 3(2) (amended by the Civil Partnership Act 2004 s 71, Sch 4 para 17(2)).

2 Ie made by virtue of the Inheritance (Provision for Family and Dependants) Act 1975 s 1(1)(a) (see PARA 567): see s 3(2) (as amended: see note 1). Spouse includes a person who is married to a person of the same sex: see Marriage (Same Sex Couples) Act 2013 Sch 3 para 1(1)(c), (2), (3); and MATRIMONIAL AND CIVIL PARTNERSHIP LAW vol 72 (2015) PARAS 1–2.

3 Ie the Inheritance (Provision for Family and Dependants) Act 1975 s 3(1) (see PARAS 571–576): see s 3(2).

4 As to the meaning of 'court' see PARA 566 note 6.

5 Inheritance (Provision for Family and Dependants) Act 1975 s 3(2).

6 Elderly applicants with a limited life expectancy are more likely to be awarded periodical payments or settled property but lump sum awards are not uncommon: see *Re Rowlands* [1984] FLR 813; *Re Bunning, Bunning v Salmon* [1984] Ch 480, [1984] 3 All ER 1; *Stead v Stead* [1985] FLR 16, CA; *Kusminow v Barclays Bank Trust Co Ltd* [1989] Fam Law 66; *Moody v Stevenson* [1992] Ch 486, [1992] 2 All ER 524, CA; *Re Krubert* [1997] Ch 97, [1996] 3 WLR 959, CA; *Re Adams, Adams v Lewis* [2001] All ER (D) 274 (Jan), [2001] WTLR 493; *Baker v Baker* [2008] EWHC 977 (Ch), [2008] 2 FLR 1956. See also *Berger v Berger* [2013] EWCA Civ 1305, [2013] All ER (D) 319 (Oct) (whilst the lower court considered that a life interest was not unreasonable considering the advanced age of the Appellant, the Court of Appeal held that he had failed to give adequate consideration to the divorce position). As to the orders which the court can make see PARA 591.

7 Inheritance (Provision for Family and Dependants) Act 1975 s 3(2)(a) (amended by the Civil Partnership Act 2004 s 71, Sch 4 para 17(3)). Pre-marital co-habitation should not be fully equated with years of marriage but it is a relevant consideration: *Kokosinski v Kokosinski* [1980] Fam 72, [1980] 1 All ER 1106 (a decision under the Matrimonial Causes Act 1973); *Foley v Foley* [1981] Fam 160, [1981] 2 All ER 857, CA (a decision under the Matrimonial Causes Act 1973). Cf *Campbell v Campbell* [1976] Fam 347, [1977] 1 All ER 1 (pre-marital cohabitation does not lengthen marriage); but see *Graham v Murphy* [1997] 1 FLR 860, [1997] 2 FCR 441 (a decision

concerning an applicant under the Inheritance (Provision for Family and Dependants) Act 1975 s 1(1)(e) where the nine years non-dependent cohabitation was taken into account in addition to the nine years of maintenance). See also *Re Rowlands* [1984] FLR 813 (43 years of separation in a marriage of 62 years, applicant widow awarded only £3,000 out of an estate of £100,000).

For examples of awards made to applicants after short marriages see *Moody v Stevenson* [1992] Ch 486, [1992] 2 All ER 524, CA (marriage of 17 years' duration of which the deceased spent the last four in a nursing home; applicant awarded a life interest in the matrimonial home); *Davis v Davis* [1993] 1 FLR 54, [1993] 1 FCR 1002, CA (marriage of seven years' duration; gift of £15,000 to wife shortly before death together with chattels and life interest in remainder of estate not unreasonable provision); *Cunliffe v Fielden* [2005] EWCA Civ 1508, [2006] Ch 361, [2006] 2 All ER 115 (marriage of 13 months; residuary estate to a class of beneficiaries including wife; wife awarded £600,000); *Lilleyman v Lilleyman* [2012] EWHC 821 (Ch), [2013] Ch 1, [2013] 1 All ER 302.

8 Inheritance (Provision for Family and Dependants) Act 1975 s 3(2)(b). See eg *Re Snoek* (1983) 13 Fam Law 18; *Re Rowlands* [1984] FLR 813; *Re Bunning, Bunning v Salmon* [1984] Ch 480, [1984] 3 All ER 1; *Stead v Stead* [1985] FLR 16, CA; *Moody v Stevenson* [1992] Ch 486, [1992] 2 All ER 524, CA; *Davis v Davis* [1993] 1 FLR 54, [1993] 1 FCR 21, CA; *Re Krubert* [1997] Ch 97, [1996] 3 WLR 959, CA. In assessing the contribution made to the welfare of the family of the deceased the court will take into account the conduct of the applicant and the deceased: see *Re Borthwick, Borthwick v Beauvais (No 2)* [1949] Ch 395, [1949] 1 All ER 472; *Thornley v Palmer* [1969] 3 All ER 31, [1969] 1 WLR 1037; *Re Clarke, Clarke v Roberts* [1968] 1 All ER 451, [1968] 1 WLR 415; *Re Gregory, Gregory v Goodenough* [1971] 1 All ER 497, [1970] 1 WLR 1455, CA; *Re Snoek* above; *Stephanides v Cohen* [2002] EWHC 1869 (Fam), [2002] WTLR 1373.

9 But nothing requires the court to treat such provision as setting an upper or lower limit on the provision which may be made by an order under the Inheritance (Provision for Family and Dependants) Act 1975 s 2 (see PARA 591): s 3(2) (amended by the Civil Partnership Act 2004 Sch 30; and the Inheritance and Trustees' Powers Act 2014 Sch 2 para 5(2)). No greater prominence is to be given to this requirement than to any other requirement in the Inheritance (Provision for Family and Dependants) Act 1975 s 3: *Re Krubert* [1997] Ch 97, [1996] 3 WLR 959, CA. In divorce cases, following the House of Lords decision in *White v White* [2001] 1 AC 596, [2001] 1 All ER 1, HL courts apply the statutory provisions to the facts to achieve a result which is fair, and non-discriminatory. There is no presumption of equal division of assets, but as a general guide: 'equality should be departed from only if, and to the extent that, there is good reason for doing so' per Lord Nicholls of Birkenhead at 605 and 9. There is no reason in principle why the same approach should not be applied to proceedings under the Inheritance (Provision for Family and Dependants) Act 1975 but as the deceased is entitled to bequeath his estate to whomsoever he pleases subject to the statutory obligation to make reasonable financial provision for the surviving spouse the concept of equality of division may, depending on the value of the estate, bear little relation to such provision: see *Cunliffe v Fielden* [2005] EWCA Civ 1508 at [19]–[21], [2006] Ch 361, [2006] 2 All ER 115 per Wall LJ. See also *Re Bunning, Bunning v Salmon* [1984] Ch 480, [1984] 3 All ER 1 (award on divorce would be £36,000 but was £60,000 on an application for financial provision); *Re Besterman, Besterman v Grusin* [1984] Ch 458, [1984] 2 All ER 656, CA; *Re Fullard, Fullard v King* [1982] Fam 42, [1981] 2 All ER 796, CA; *Re Farrow* [1987] 1 FLR 205, [1987] Fam Law 14; *Whiting v Whiting* [1988] 2 All ER 275, [1988] 1 WLR 565, CA; *Re Clarke* [1991] Fam Law 364; *Moody v Stevenson* [1992] Ch 486, [1992] 2 All ER 524, CA; *Jessop v Jessop* [1992] 1 FLR 591, CA; *Davis v Davis* [1993] 1 FLR 54, [1993] 1 FCR 1002, CA (a life interest was reasonable although this would not have been ordered on divorce). An exact calculation of the amount payable as ancillary relief is not necessary: *P v G (Family Provision: Relevance of Divorce Provision)* [2004] EWHC 2944 (Fam), [2006] 1 FLR 431 (more than half the estate awarded to surviving spouse). See also *Berger v Berger* [2013] EWCA Civ 1305, [2013] All ER (D) 319 (Oct) (although claim failed due to being out of time court considered the division would have been 50:50). Where a marriage has effectively ended before death despite the fact that there has been no divorce the provision which might have been received on divorce is particularly relevant and where the applicant has already received more than this, no order will be made: *Aston v Aston* [2007] WTLR 1349; *Goenka v Goenka* [2014] EWHC 2966 (Ch), [2016] Ch 267, [2015] 4 All ER 123 (divorce factor carried little weight where the court felt the divorce court would not have given the claimant as much as she enjoyed under the will). See also *Parrish v Sharman* [2001] WTLR 593, CA; *Re Waite, Barron v Woodhead* [2008] EWHC 810 (Ch), [2009] 1 FLR 747, [2009] 2 FCR 631; *Iqbal v Ahmed* [2011] EWCA Civ 900, [2011] 3 FCR 1. A conscious decision not to make any claim for capital provision following a separation agreement while the deceased was alive may make it unjust to seek a capital adjustment after death: see *Hope v Knight* [2010] EWHC 3443 (Ch), [2011] WTLR 583.

10 Ie a separation order made under the Civil Partnership Act 2004 Pt 2 Chapter 2.

11 But nothing requires the court to treat such provision as setting an upper or lower limit on the provision which may be made by an order under the Inheritance (Provision for Family and Dependants) Act 1975 s 2 (see PARAS 591–592): s 3(2) (amended by the Civil Partnership Act 2004 Sch 30; and the Inheritance and Trustees' Powers Act 2014 Sch 2 para 5(2)).

578. Guidelines applicable to former spouse or civil partner of the deceased who has not formed a subsequent marriage or civil partnership. On an application for an order[1] by the deceased's former spouse or civil partner who has not formed a subsequent marriage or civil partnership[2], in addition to the common statutory guidelines[3], the court[4] must also have regard to[5]:

(1) the applicant's age[6] and the duration of the marriage or civil partnership[7]; and

(2) the contribution made by the applicant to the welfare of the deceased's family, including any contribution made by looking after the home or caring for the family[8]. Applications by former spouses or civil partners face particular problems[9].

In general, on an application by such an applicant reasonable financial provision means such financial provision as it would be reasonable in all the circumstances of the case for him to receive for his maintenance[10]. Where, however, within 12 months from the date on which a decree of divorce or nullity of marriage has been made absolute or a decree of judicial separation[11] has been granted, a party to the marriage dies and:

(a) an application for a financial provision order[12] or a property adjustment order[13] under the Matrimonial Causes Act 1973 has not been made by the other party to that marriage[14]; or

(b) such an application has been made but the proceedings on it have not been determined at the time of the death of the deceased[15],

then, if an application for an order under the Inheritance (Provision for Family and Dependants) Act 1975[16] is made by that other party the court, notwithstanding the provisions of that Act[17], has power, if it thinks it just to do so, to treat that party for the purposes of that application as if the decree of divorce or nullity of marriage had not been made absolute or the decree of judicial separation had not been granted, as the case may be[18].

Where within 12 months from the date on which a dissolution order, nullity order, separation order[19] or presumption of death order has been granted, one of the civil partners dies and[20]:

(i) an application for a financial provision order[21] or a property adjustment order[22] under the Civil Partnership Act 2004 has not been made by the other partner[23]; or

(ii) such an application has been made but the proceedings on it have not been determined at the time of the death of the deceased[24],

then, if an application for an order under the Inheritance (Provision for Family and Dependants) Act 1975[25] is made by the surviving civil partner the court, notwithstanding the provisions of that Act[26], has power, if it thinks it just to do so, to treat the surviving civil partner for the purposes of that application as if the dissolution or nullity order had not been made absolute or the separation order or presumption of death order had not been granted, as the case may be[27].

In both such cases reasonable financial provision means such financial provision as it would be reasonable in all the circumstances of the case for a husband or wife or civil partner to receive, whether or not that provision is required for his or her maintenance[28].

1 Ie under the Inheritance (Provision for Family and Dependants) Act 1975 s 2 (see PARA 591): see s 3(2) (amended by the Civil Partnership Act 2004 s 71, Sch 4 para 17(2)).

2 Ie made by virtue of the Inheritance (Provision for Family and Dependants) Act 1975 s 1(1)(b) (see PARA 567): see s 3(2) (as amended: see note 1). As to the meanings of 'former spouse' and 'former civil partner' see PARA 567 note 6. Spouse includes a person who is married to a person of the same

sex: see Marriage (Same Sex Couples) Act 2013 Sch 3 para 1(1)(c), (2), (3); and MATRIMONIAL AND CIVIL PARTNERSHIP LAW vol 72 (2015) PARAS 1–2.

3 Ie the Inheritance (Provision for Family and Dependants) Act 1975 s 3(1) (see PARAS 571–576): see s 3(2).

4 As to the meaning of 'court' see PARA 566 note 6.

5 Inheritance (Provision for Family and Dependants) Act 1975 s 3(2).

6 For relevant case law see PARA 577 note 6. As to the orders which the court can make see PARA 591.

7 Inheritance (Provision for Family and Dependants) Act 1975 s 3(2)(a) (amended by the Civil Partnership Act 2004 s 71, Sch 4 para 17(3)). For relevant case law see PARA 577 note 7.

8 Inheritance (Provision for Family and Dependants) Act 1975 s 3(2)(b). For relevant case law see PARA 577 note 8.

9 Reasonable provision for a former spouse or civil partner is normally nothing, so such applications will rarely be successful: *Re Fullard, Fullard v King* [1982] Fam 42, [1981] 2 All ER 796, CA; *Re O'Rourke, Cameron v Treasury Solicitor* [1996] 2 FLR 716, [1997] FCR 188, CA; *Barrass v Harding* [2001] 1 FLR 138, [2001] 1 FCR 297, CA. For power to order on grant of decrees of divorce, nullity, judicial separation and dissolution of civil partnership that parties are not entitled to make applications under the Inheritance (Provision for Family and Dependants) Act 1975 s 2 see PARA 567 note 6.

10 See the Inheritance (Provision for Family and Dependants) Act 1975 s 1(2)(b); and PARA 570.

11 This provision does not apply in relation to a decree of judicial separation unless at the date of the death of the deceased the decree was in force and the separation was continuing: Inheritance (Provision for Family and Dependants) Act 1975 s 14(2).

12 Ie under the Matrimonial Causes Act 1973 s 23: see the Inheritance (Provision for Family and Dependants) Act 1975 s 14(1)(a). Any reference in the Inheritance (Provision for Family and Dependants) Act 1975 to an order or decree made under the Matrimonial Causes Act 1973 or under any section of that Act is to be construed as including a reference to an order or decree which is deemed to have been made under that Act or under that provision of that Act, as the case may be: Inheritance (Provision for Family and Dependants) Act 1975 s 25(6).

13 Ie under the Matrimonial Causes Act 1973 s 24: see the Inheritance (Provision for Family and Dependants) Act 1975 s 14(1)(a).

14 Inheritance (Provision for Family and Dependants) Act 1975 s 14(1)(a).

15 Inheritance (Provision for Family and Dependants) Act 1975 s 14(1)(b).

16 Ie an order under the Inheritance (Provision for Family and Dependants) Act 1975 s 2 (see PARAS 591–592): see s 14(1).

17 Ie notwithstanding the Inheritance (Provision for Family and Dependants) Act 1975 ss 1, 3 (see PARAS 568–571): see s 14(1).

18 Inheritance (Provision for Family and Dependants) Act 1975 s 14(1).

19 This provision does not apply in relation to a separation order unless at the date of the death of the deceased the separation order was in force and the separation was continuing: Inheritance (Provision for Family and Dependants) Act 1975 s 14A(3) (s 14A added by the Civil Partnership Act 2004 s 71, Sch 4 para 20).

20 See the Inheritance (Provision for Family and Dependants) Act 1975 s 14A(1)(a), (b) (as added: see note 19).

21 Ie under the Civil Partnership Act 2004 Sch 5 Part 1: see the Inheritance (Provision for Family and Dependants) Act 1975 s 14A(1)(c)(i) (as added: see note 19). Any reference in the Inheritance (Provision for Family and Dependants) Act 1975 to an order or decree made under the Civil Partnership Act 2004 or under any provision of that Act is to be construed as including a reference to an order or decree which is deemed to have been made under that Act or under that provision of that Act, as the case may be: Inheritance (Provision for Family and Dependants) Act 1975 s 25(6A) (added by the Civil Partnership Act 2004 s 71, Sch 4 para 27(6)).

22 Ie under the Civil Partnership Act 2004 Sch 5 Part 2: see the Inheritance (Provision for Family and Dependants) Act 1975 s 14A(1)(c)(ii) (as added: see note 19).

23 Inheritance (Provision for Family and Dependants) Act 1975 s 14A(1)(c)(i) (as added: see note 19).

24 Inheritance (Provision for Family and Dependants) Act 1975 s 14A(1)(c)(ii) (as added: see note 19).

25 Ie an order under the Inheritance (Provision for Family and Dependants) Act 1975 s 2 (see PARAS 591–592): see s 14(1).

26 Ie notwithstanding the Inheritance (Provision for Family and Dependants) Act 1975 ss 1, 3 (see PARAS 568–571): see s 14A(2) (as added: see note 19).

27 Inheritance (Provision for Family and Dependants) Act 1975 s 14A(2) (as added: see note 19).

28 See the Inheritance (Provision for Family and Dependants) Act 1975 s 1(2)(a), (aa); and PARA 569.

579. Guidelines applicable to cohabitees. On an application for an order[1] by:

(1) a person other than the spouse[2] or former spouse[3] of the deceased who, if the deceased died on or after 1 January 1996[4], was living in the same household[5] as the deceased as the spouse[6] of the deceased[7]; or

(2) a person other than the civil partner[8] or former civil partner[9] of the deceased who was living in the same household as the deceased as the civil partner of the deceased[10],

during the whole of the period of two years[11] ending immediately before[12] the date when the deceased died, in addition to the common statutory guidelines[13], the court[14] must also have regard to[15]:

(a) the applicant's age[16] and the length of the period during which the applicant lived as the husband or wife or civil partner of the deceased and in the same household as the deceased[17]; and

(b) the contribution made by the applicant to the welfare of the deceased's family, including any contribution made by looking after the home or caring for the family[18].

On an application by such an applicant reasonable financial provision means such financial provision as it would be reasonable in all the circumstances of the case for him to receive for his maintenance[19].

1 Ie under the Inheritance (Provision for Family and Dependants) Act 1975 s 2 (see PARA 591): see s 3(2A) (added by the Law Reform (Succession) Act 1995 s 2(4)).

2 As to applications made by the spouse of the deceased see PARA 577. Spouse includes a person who is married to a person of the same sex: see Marriage (Same Sex Couples) Act 2013 Sch 3 para 1(1)(c), (2), (3); and MATRIMONIAL AND CIVIL PARTNERSHIP LAW vol 72 (2015) PARAS 1–2.

3 As to applications made by the former spouse of the deceased see PARA 578. As to the meaning of 'former spouse' see PARA 567 note 5.

4 See PARA 567 note 8.

5 'Household' has a wider definition than merely residing within the same abode: *Gully v Dix* [2004] EWCA Civ 139, [2004] 1 WLR 1399 (claimant continued to be a part of the 'household' irrespective of the fact that she had spent 3 months living elsewhere). See also *Swetenham v Walkley* [2014] WTLR 845; *Kaur v Dhaliwal* [2014] EWHC 1991 (Ch), [2014] Fam Law 1241; and PARA 366 note 7.

6 As to the meaning of 'living in the same household' see PARA 567 note 8.

7 See the Inheritance (Provision for Family and Dependants) Act 1975 s 1(ba), (1A); and PARA 567.

8 As to applications made by the civil partner of the deceased see PARA 577. As to the meaning of 'civil partner' see PARA 567 note 4.

9 As to applications made by the former civil partner of the deceased see PARA 578. As to the meanings of 'former civil partner' see PARA 567 note 6.

10 See the Inheritance (Provision for Family and Dependants) Act 1975 s 1(ba), (1B); and PARA 567.

11 Applicants who have cohabited in this way for less than two years may satisfy the test of dependency under the Inheritance (Provision for Family and Dependants) Act 1975 s 1(1)(e): see PARAS 567, 581.

12 For examples of the meaning of 'immediately before' see PARA 567 note 14.

13 Ie the Inheritance (Provision for Family and Dependants) Act 1975 s 3(1) (see PARAS 571–576): see s 3(2A) (as added: see note 1).

14 As to the meaning of 'court' see PARA 566 note 6.

15 Inheritance (Provision for Family and Dependants) Act 1975 s 3(2A) (as added: see note 1).

16 See *Re Watson* [1999] 1 FLR 878, [1999] 3 FCR 595 (applicant in her 60s cohabited with the deceased for ten years); *Cattle v Evans* [2011] EWHC 945 (Ch), [2011] 2 FLR 843, [2011] All ER (D) 209 (Apr) (applicant, aged 60, cohabited for 9 years).

17 Inheritance (Provision for Family and Dependants) Act 1975 s 3(2A)(a) (as added (see note 1); and amended by the Civil Partnership Act 2004 s 71, Sch 4 para 18). For examples in the case of applications brought by a spouse or former spouse of the deceased see PARA 577 notes 7–8.

18 Inheritance (Provision for Family and Dependants) Act 1975 s 3(2A)(b) (as added: see note 1). For examples in the case of applications brought by a spouse or former spouse of the deceased see PARA 577 note 8.

19 See the Inheritance (Provision for Family and Dependants) Act 1975 s 1(2)(b); and PARA 570. Maintenance must be assessed in the context of the couple's lifestyle not in the context of the applicant's previous lifestyle: *Negus v Bahouse* [2007] EWHC 2628 (Ch), [2008] 1 FLR 381.

580. A child of the deceased or a person treated as a child of the deceased. On an application for an order[1] by a child of the deceased[2] or a person treated by the deceased as a child of the family[3], in addition to the common statutory guidelines[4], the court[5] must also have regard to the manner in which the applicant was being or in which he might expect to be educated or trained[6].

Where the application is made by a person treated as a child of the family in relation to a death on or after 1 October 2014[7] the court must also have regard to:

(1) whether the deceased maintained the applicant and, if so, to the length of time for which and basis on which the deceased did so, and to the extent of the contribution made by way of maintenance[8];
(2) to whether and, if so, to what extent the deceased assumed responsibility for the maintenance of the applicant[9];
(3) whether in maintaining or assuming responsibility for maintaining the applicant the deceased did so knowing that the applicant was not his own child[10]; and
(4) the liability of any other person to maintain the applicant[11].

Where the application is made by a person treated as a child of the family in relation to a death before 1 October 2014 the court must also have regard to:

(a) whether the deceased had assumed any responsibility for the applicant's maintenance and, if so, to the extent to which and the basis upon which the deceased assumed that responsibility and to the length of time for which the deceased discharged that responsibility[12];
(b) whether in assuming and discharging that responsibility, the deceased did so knowing that the applicant was not his own child[13];
(c) the liability of any other person to maintain the applicant[14].

Whether the child is an adult or a minor[15], in no case is there an invariable prerequisite that the child must show that the deceased had a moral obligation[16] to maintain him or that there is some other special circumstance which entitled him to seek provision[17].

In the case of adult children, while it is not necessary to show that the deceased had such a moral obligation to maintain the applicant, an adult child who is in employment, with an earning capacity for the foreseeable future is unlikely to succeed in his application without some special circumstance[18]. An adult child's knowledge that a parent intends to make no provision for them and consequent lack of expectations may be a factor to be taken into account[19].

On an application by such an applicant reasonable financial provision means such financial provision as it would be reasonable in all the circumstances of the case for him to receive for his maintenance[20].

1 Ie under the Inheritance (Provision for Family and Dependants) Act 1975 s 2 (see PARA 591): see s 3(3).
2 Ie an applicant under the Inheritance (Provision for Family and Dependants) Act 1975 s 1(1)(c) (see PARA 567): see s 3(3). As to the meaning of 'child' see PARA 567 note 11.
3 Ie an applicant under the Inheritance (Provision for Family and Dependants) Act 1975 s 1(1)(d) (see PARA 567): see s 3(3). As to the meaning of a 'person treated by the deceased as a child of the family' see PARA 567 note 13.
4 Ie the Inheritance (Provision for Family and Dependants) Act 1975 s 3(1) (see PARAS 571–576): see s 3(3).
5 As to the meaning of 'court' see PARA 566 note 6.
6 Inheritance (Provision for Family and Dependants) Act 1975 s 3(3).
7 Ie the date on which the Inheritance and Trustees' Powers Act 2014 came into force.

8 Inheritance (Provision for Family and Dependants) Act 1975 s 3(3)(a) (s 3(3)(a) substituted, s 3(3)(aa) added and s 3(3)(b) amended by the Inheritance and Trustees' Powers Act 2014 Sch 2 para 5(3)(a)).
9 Inheritance (Provision for Family and Dependants) Act 1975 s 3(3)(aa) (as added: see note 8).
10 Inheritance (Provision for Family and Dependants) Act 1975 s 3(3)(b) (as amended: see note 8).
11 Inheritance (Provision for Family and Dependants) Act 1975 s 3(3)(c).
12 Inheritance (Provision for Family and Dependants) Act 1975 s 3(3)(a) (as substituted: see note 8).
13 Inheritance (Provision for Family and Dependants) Act 1975 s 3(3)(b).
14 Inheritance (Provision for Family and Dependants) Act 1975 s 3(3)(c).
15 Minor children have a strong claim for financial provision: *Re W (a minor) (claim from deceased's estate)* [1995] 2 FCR 689, sub nom *Re C* [1995] 2 FLR 24; *Robinson v Robinson* [2001] WTLR 267.
16 In the case of minor children the existence of a moral obligation is usually self evident. The decisions relate to adult children see eg *Millward v Shenton* [1972] 2 All ER 1025, [1972] 1 WLR 711, CA (adult child with progressive illness and limited earning capacity); *CA v CC* (1978) Times, 18 November (sub nom *Re McC's Estate* (1979) 9 Fam Law 26); *Re Christie, Christie v Keeble* [1979] Ch 168, [1979] 1 All ER 546 (mother had expressed intention to benefit son and daughter on equal footing, gift of property to son ineffective, adult son successful); *Re Coventry, Coventry v Coventry* [1980] Ch 461, [1979] 3 All ER 815, CA (adult son failed to show moral obligation); *Re Dennis, Dennis v Lloyds Bank Ltd* [1981] 2 All ER 140, 124 Sol Jo 885 (desire for payment of capital sum to creditors was not an application for maintenance, application by adult son failed); *Re Callaghan* [1985] Fam 1, [1984] 3 All ER 790 (adult stepson awarded £15,000 out of estate worth £31,000); *Re Leach, Leach v Lindeman* [1986] Ch 226, [1985] 2 All ER 754, CA (adult stepdaughter who never lived in the deceased's household and was never maintained by the deceased awarded half of the net estate); *Re Debenham* [1986] 1 FLR 404 (moral obligation to 58 year old epileptic daughter rejected by mother since birth; applicant awarded capital sum of £3,000 for immediate needs and income of £4,500 per annum out of estate worth £172,000); *Williams v Johns* [1988] 2 FLR 475 (a physically fit, 43 year old adoptive daughter who was capable of maintaining herself was unable to show that the deceased had any obligation to maintain her; the applicant had not cared for and, in the past, had caused shame and distress to the deceased); *Re Jennings* [1994] Ch 286, [1994] 3 All ER 27, CA (application by adult son failed; mere blood relationship did not give rise to an enduring moral obligation); *Re Goodchild, Goodchild v Goodchild* [1997] 3 All ER 63, [1997] 1 WLR 1216, CA (adult son's application was successful because of moral obligation imposed on deceased by his former wife's mistaken belief that wills were mutually binding); *Re Hancock* [1998] 2 FLR 346, [1999] 1 FCR 500, CA (an adult daughter with no earning capacity who had left home at 19 to live with a man who now had no resources save his pension and disability benefits awarded periodical payments of £3,000 per annum); *Re Pearce* [1998] 2 FLR 705, [1999] 2 FCR 179, CA (an adult son who worked on his father's farm between the ages of 6 and 16 and left only because the deceased could not afford to pay him was awarded a tax free legacy of £85,000 out of an estate worth £285,000); *Espinosa v Bourke* [1999] 1 FLR 747, [1999] 3 FCR 76, CA (55 year old daughter, long out of employment, in financial need and with doubtful earning capacity did not have to show moral obligation; the deceased was under an obligation arising from his promise to leave his wife's portfolio of shares to the daughter).
17 See *Re Pearce* [1998] 2 FLR 705 at 710, CA, per Nourse LJ; and the cases referred to in note 11. See also *Re Hancock* [1998] 2 FLR 346, [1999] 1 FCR 500, CA; *Espinosa v Bourke* [1999] 1 FLR 747 at 755, CA, per Butler-Sloss LJ; *Re Watson* [1999] 1 FLR 878, [1999] 3 FCR 595; cf *Re Coventry, Coventry v Coventry* [1980] Ch 461, [1979] 3 All ER 815, CA; *Re Jennings* [1994] Ch 286, [1994] 3 All ER 27, CA; *Re Myers, Myers v Myers* [2004] EWHC 1944 (Fam), [2005] WTLR 851; *Re Gold, Gold v Curtis* [2005] WTLR 673; *Robinson v Fernsby* [2003] EWCA Civ 1820, [2004] WTLR 257. Long estrangement will reduce a child's chances of success: *Garland v Morris* [2007] EWHC 2 (Ch), [2007] 2 FLR 528, [2007] WTLR 797; *H v Mitson* [2009] EWHC 3114 (Fam), sub nom *H v J's Personal Representatives* [2010] Fam Law 343.
18 *Re Hancock* [1998] 2 FLR 346 at 351, CA, per Butler-Sloss LJ; *Re Pearce* [1998] 2 FLR 705 at 710, CA, per Nourse LJ; *Espinosa v Bourke* [1999] 1 FLR 747 at 755, CA, per Butler-Sloss LJ. Following the decision in *Re Hancock* the moral obligation requirement derived from *Re Coventry, Coventry v Coventry* [1980] Ch 461, [1979] 3 All ER 815, CA is of less rigid application but in many of the successful cases since *Re Coventry, Coventry v Coventry* the applicant has been able to rely on a moral obligation such as a promise made by the deceased to another: see eg *Re Goodchild, Goodchild v Goodchild* [1997] 3 All ER 63, [1997] 1 WLR 1216, CA; *Espinosa v Bourke* above. The older decisions are more eclectic: see eg the cases referred to in note 11.

19 *H v Mitson* [2009] EWHC 3114 (Fam), sub nom *H v J's Personal Representatives* [2010] Fam Law 343. However, in *Ilott v Mitson* [2015] EWCA Civ 797 at [51], [2016] 1 All ER 932, [2015] 2 FCR 547, Arden LJ considered that this factor has little weight on the facts of the case: 'the only beneficiaries are the charities who can have no expectation either: the deceased had no connection with the charities'.

20 See the Inheritance (Provision for Family and Dependants) Act 1975 s 1(2)(b); and PARA570.

581. Guidelines applicable to person being maintained by the deceased. On an application for an order[1] by a person who, immediately before[2] the death of the deceased was being maintained, either wholly or partly, by the deceased[3], in addition to the common statutory guidelines[4], the court[5] must also have regard in relation to deaths before 1 October 2014[6] to the extent to which and the basis upon which the deceased assumed responsibility for the maintenance of the applicant[7] and to the length of time[8] for which the deceased discharged that responsibility[9].

In relation to deaths on or after 1 October 2014 the additional factors the court must have regard to are:

(1) the length of time[10] for which and basis on which the deceased maintained the applicant, and the extent of the contribution[11] made by way of maintenance[12];

(2) whether and, if so, to what extent the deceased assumed responsibility[13] for the maintenance of the applicant[14].

On an application by such an applicant reasonable financial provision means such financial provision as it would be reasonable in all the circumstances of the case for him to receive for his maintenance[15].

1 Ie under the Inheritance (Provision for Family and Dependants) Act 1975 s 2 (see PARA 591).

2 As to the meaning of 'immediately before' see PARA 567 note 14.

3 Ie an applicant under the Inheritance (Provision for Family and Dependants) Act 1975 s 1(1)(e) (see PARA 567) Before the court can consider whether reasonable financial provision has been made for such an applicant, the applicant must satisfy the court that he is a person who was being maintained by the deceased: *Re Wilkinson, Neale v Newell* [1978] Fam 22, [1978] 1 All ER 221. As to what constitutes maintenance see PARA 567 note 14.

4 Ie the matters specifically mentioned in the Inheritance (Provision for Family and Dependants) Act 1975 s 3(1)(a)–(f) (see PARAS 571–576).

5 As to the meaning of 'court' see PARA 566 note 6.

6 Ie the date on which the Inheritance and Trustees' Powers Act 2014 came into force.

7 An assumption of responsibility is necessary but can usually be presumed where the applicant is able to prove actual maintenance: *Jelley v Iliffe* [1981] Fam 128, [1981] 2 All ER 29, CA. Decisions relating to such applicants include eg *Re Wilkinson, Neale v Newell* [1978] Fam 22, [1978] 1 All ER 221 (sister providing free board and lodging); *Malone v Harrison* [1979] 1 WLR 1353 (mistress); *Re Beaumont, Martin v Midland Bank Trust Co Ltd* [1980] Ch 444, [1980] 1 All ER 266 (claim failed; applicant and deceased were two individuals pooling resources without either undertaking any responsibility for maintaining the other); *Jelley v Iliffe* above (provision of rent-free accommodation; common law husband); *Kourkgy v Lusher* (1981) 4 FLR 65, 12 Fam Law 86; *Harrington v Gill* (1983) 4 FLR 265, CA (provision of rent-free accommodation; common law wife); *Williams v Roberts* [1986] 1 FLR 349 (gifts of lump sums, weekly allowance and provision of accommodation; common law wife); *Bishop v Plumley* [1991] 1 All ER 236, [1991] 1 WLR 582, CA (provision of rent-free accommodation; common law wife); *Graham v Murphy* [1997] 1 FLR 860, [1997] 2 FCR 441, (common law husband); *Rees v Newbery and Institute of Cancer Research* [1998] 1 FLR 1041 (friend paying less than market rent); *Re B* [2000] Ch 662, [2000] 1 All ER 665, CA (assumption of responsibility for mother by mentally handicapped daughter); *Baynes v Hedger* [2009] EWCA Civ 374, [2009] 2 FLR 767, [2009] All ER (D) 50 (May), (claim by god-daughter failed because no assumption of responsibility).

8 See *Malone v Harrison* [1979] 1 WLR 1353 (maintenance for 12 years); *Jelley v Iliffe* [1981] Fam 128, [1981] 2 All ER 29, CA (maintenance for eight years); *Harrington v Gill* (1983) 4 FLR 265 (maintenance for eight years); *Williams v Roberts* [1986] 1 FLR 349 (maintenance for nine years); *Bishop v Plumley* [1991] 1 All ER 236, [1991] 1 WLR 582, CA (maintenance for ten years);

Graham v Murphy [1997] 1 FLR 860, [1997] 2 FCR 441 (maintenance for nine years after some nine years non-dependent cohabitation); *Rees v Newbery and Institute of Cancer Research* [1998] 1 FLR 1041 (maintenance for nine years).

9 Inheritance (Provision for Family and Dependants) Act 1975 s 3(4).

10 See note 8.

11 The contribution to the applicant's reasonable needs must be substantial in order for them to be eligible to claim under the Inheritance (Provision for Family and Dependants) Act 1975 s 1(1)(e) (see PARA 567): see s 1(3); and PARA 567 note 15. In *Jelley v Iliffe* [1981] Fam 128, [1981] 2 All ER 29, CA, the provision of free accommodation was regarded as a substantial contribution to the appellant's reasonable needs; in *Ottey v Grundy* [2003] EWCA Civ 1176, [2003] WTLR 1253, [2003] All ER (D) 05 (Aug) the use of a car was not.

12 Inheritance (Provision for Family and Dependants) Act 1975 s 3(4)(a) (s 3(4)(a), (b) substituted by the Inheritance and Trustees' Powers Act 2014 Sch 2 para 5(4)).

13 See note 7.

14 Inheritance (Provision for Family and Dependants) Act 1975 s 3(4)(b) (as substituted: see note 12).

15 See the Inheritance (Provision for Family and Dependants) Act 1975 s 1(2)(b); and PARA 570. Awards include *Harrington v Gill* (1983) 4 FLR 265 (£10,000 for common law wife out of estate of £65,000); *Williams v Roberts* [1986] 1 FLR 349 (£20,000 for common law wife out of estate of £120,000); *Graham v Murphy* [1997] 1 FLR 860, [1997] 2 FCR 441 (£35,000 to enable applicant to purchase smaller property in less expensive area with assistance of a small mortgage); *Rees v Newbery and Institute of Cancer Research* [1998] 1 FLR 1041 (capitalised value of difference between rent payable by applicant and market rent in exchange for applicant surrendering possession of flat held at a low rent without security).

(4) PROPERTY AVAILABLE FOR FINANCIAL PROVISION

(i) Property Always Available

582. Meaning of net estate. In relation to a deceased person, 'net estate'[1] means:

(1) all property[2] of which the deceased had power to dispose by his will[3] (otherwise than by virtue of a special power of appointment) less the amount of his funeral, testamentary and administration expenses, debts and liabilities, including any inheritance tax payable out of his estate on his death[4];

(2) any property in respect of which the deceased held a general power of appointment (not being a power exercisable by will) which has not been exercised[5];

(3) any sum of money or other property which is treated for the purposes of the Inheritance (Provision for Family and Dependants) Act 1975 as part of the deceased's net estate by virtue of the provisions of the Act relating to nominees[6] and gifts mortis causa[7] or by virtue of an order relating to property held on a joint tenancy[8]; and

(4) any sum of money or other property which is, by reason of a disposition or contract made by the deceased, ordered[9] to be provided for the purpose of the making of financial provision under the Act[10].

1 Any reference in the Inheritance (Provision for Family and Dependants) Act 1975 to provision out of the net estate of a deceased person includes a reference to provision extending to the whole of that estate: s 25(3).

2 'Property' includes any chose in action: Inheritance (Provision for Family and Dependants) Act 1975 s 25(1). For these purposes, 'property' does not include property nominated under a pension fund trust deed: *Jessop v Jessop* [1992] 1 FLR 591 at 594, 599, CA, per Nourse J; *Re Cairnes, Howard v Cairnes* (1982) 4 FLR 225. 'Property' is not restricted to property solely within the United Kingdom: *Bheekhun v Williams* [1999] 2 FLR 229, [1999] Fam Law 379, CA.

3 As to the meaning of 'will' see PARA 566 note 8.

4 Inheritance (Provision for Family and Dependants) Act 1975 s 25(1). For this purpose a person who is not of full age and capacity is to be treated as having power to dispose by will of all property of which he would have had power to dispose by will if he had been of full age and capacity: s 25(2).
5 Inheritance (Provision for Family and Dependants) Act 1975 s 25(1).
6 Ie by virtue of the Inheritance (Provision for Family and Dependants) Act 1975 s 8(1) (see PARA 583): see s 25(1).
7 Ie by virtue of the Inheritance (Provision for Family and Dependants) Act 1975 s 8(2) (see PARA 584): see s 25(1).
8 Inheritance (Provision for Family and Dependants) Act 1975 s 25(1). Orders relating to joint tenancies are made under s 9 (see PARA 585): see s 25(1).
9 Ie under the Inheritance (Provision for Family and Dependants) Act 1975 s 10 or s 11 (see PARAS 586–589): see s 25(1).
10 Inheritance (Provision for Family and Dependants) Act 1975 s 25(1).

583. Nomination under statutory enactment. Where a deceased person has in accordance with the provisions of any enactment[1] nominated any person to receive any sum of money or other property[2] on his death and that nomination is in force at the time of his death, that sum of money, after deducting from it any inheritance tax[3] payable in respect of it, or that other property, to the extent of its value at the date of the death of the deceased after deducting from it any inheritance tax so payable, is to be treated for the purposes of the Inheritance (Provision for Family and Dependants) Act 1975 as part of the net estate[4] of the deceased[5].

This provision does not render liable any person who gives effect to a statutory nomination by paying any sum or transferring any other property to the person named in the nomination in accordance with the directions given in the nomination[6].

1 For this purpose 'any enactment' includes secondary legislation: *Goenka v Goenka* [2014] EWHC 2966 (Ch), [2016] Ch 267, [2015] 4 All ER 123 (nomination of NHS death benefit made in accordance with statutory regulations). See also *Rathbone v Bundock* [1962] 2 QB 260, [1962] 2 All ER 257(whether or not statutory regulations constitute an 'enactment' depended upon the context). Hence, the nominated sum is part of the estate. However, nominations made under a private contractual pension scheme are not made in accordance with an enactment: see *Re Cairnes, Howard v Cairnes* (1982) 4 FLR 225. Hence the nominated sum is not part of the estate.
2 As to the meaning of 'property' see PARA 582 note 2.
3 The amount of inheritance tax to be deducted for the purposes of the Inheritance (Provision for Family and Dependants) Act 1975 s 8(1) must not exceed the amount of that tax which has been borne by the person nominated by the deceased: s 8(3). As to inheritance tax see INHERITANCE TAXATION.
4 As to the meaning of 'net estate' see PARA 582.
5 Inheritance (Provision for Family and Dependants) Act 1975 s 8(1).
6 Inheritance (Provision for Family and Dependants) Act 1975 s 8(1). The provisions of the Inheritance (Provision for Family and Dependants) Act 1975 do not render personal representatives liable for having distributed any part of the estate after the end of six months from the date on which representation with respect to the estate of the deceased is first taken out: see s 20(1); and PARA 597.

584. Gifts mortis causa. Where any sum of money or other property[1] is received by any person as a donatio mortis causa[2] made by a deceased person, that sum of money, after deducting from it any inheritance tax[3] payable on it, or that other property, to the extent of its value at the date of the death of the deceased after deducting from it any inheritance tax so payable, is to be treated for the purposes of the Inheritance (Provision for Family and Dependants) Act 1975 as part of the net estate[4] of the deceased[5].

This provision does not render liable a person who gives effect to a donatio mortis causa by paying any sum or transferring any other property[6].

1 As to the meaning of 'property' see PARA 582 note 2.

2 As to gifts mortis causa see generally GIFTS vol 52 (2014) PARA 271 et seq.
3 The amount of inheritance tax to be deducted for the purposes of the Inheritance (Provision for Family and Dependants) Act 1975 s 8(2) must not exceed the amount of that tax which has been borne by the person who has received a sum of money or other property as a donatio mortis causa: s 8(3). As to inheritance tax see INHERITANCE TAXATION.
4 As to the meaning of 'net estate' see PARA 582.
5 Inheritance (Provision for Family and Dependants) Act 1975 s 8(2). A gift made in contemplation of death and conditional upon death is treated as part of the net estate of the deceased whether made with the intention of defeating a claim for family provision or not whereas the property comprising an unconditional gift is only treated as part of the net estate of the deceased if made with an intention to defeat a claim for family provision and the court so orders: see s 10; and PARA 586 et seq.
6 Inheritance (Provision for Family and Dependants) Act 1975 s 8(2).

(ii) Property Available if the Court so Orders

585. Property held on a joint tenancy. Where a deceased person was immediately before his death beneficially entitled to a joint tenancy of any property[1], then, if, an application is made for an order under the Inheritance (Provision for Family and Dependants) Act 1975[2], the court[3] for the purpose of facilitating the making of financial provision for the applicant under the Act may order that the deceased's severable share of that property, must, to such extent as appears to the court to be just in all the circumstances of the case, be treated for the purposes of the Act as part of his net estate[4].

In relation to deaths before October 2014[5] the deceased's severable share of the property can only be treated as part of his net estate if the application is made within six months of the date of the grant[6]. Where such an order is made[7], the deceased's severable share of the property concerned is taken for the purposes of the Inheritance (Provision for Family and Dependants) Act 1975 at its value immediately before death[8].

In relation to deaths on or after 1 October 2014 the bar on the deceased's severable share being included has been removed[9]. The value of the deceased's severable share of the property concerned is taken for the purposes of the Inheritance (Provision for Family and Dependants) Act 1975 to be the value that the share would have had at the date of the hearing of the application for an order[10] had the share been severed immediately before the deceased's death, unless the court orders that the share is to be valued at a different date[11].

In determining the extent to which any severable share is to be treated as part of the net estate of the deceased by virtue of such an order, the court must have regard to any inheritance tax payable in respect of that severable share[12].

1 As to the meaning of 'property' see PARA 582 note 2. For the purposes of this provision there may be a joint tenancy of a chose in action: Inheritance (Provision for Family and Dependants) Act 1975 s 9(4). As to joint tenancies see REAL PROPERTY AND REGISTRATION vol 87 (2012) PARA 198 et seq. As to choses in action see CHOSES IN ACTION. These provisions apply to money held in a joint bank account (*Re Crawford* (1982) 4 FLR 273) and to a policy of insurance and the right to policy monies under it (*Powell v Osbourne* [1993] 1 FLR 1001 at 1004, CA). However, where a policy is taken out in joint names with the intention that the death benefit is payable only to the survivor, there is no joint tenancy: *Murphy v Murphy* [2003] EWCA Civ 1862, [2004] 1 FCR 1.
2 Ie the Inheritance (Provision for Family and Dependants) Act 1975 s 2 (see PARAS 591–592).
3 As to the meaning of 'court' see PARA 566 note 6.
4 Inheritance (Provision for Family and Dependants) Act 1975 s 9(1) (amended and s 9(1A) added by the Inheritance and Trustees' Powers Act 2014 Sch 2 para 7(2)). As to the meaning of 'net estate' see PARA 582. The court has a very broad discretion and no guidelines beyond those contained in the Inheritance (Provision for Family and Dependants) Act 1975 s 9(1): *Re Crawford* (1982) 4 FLR 273 at 280 per Eastham J; *Kourgky v Lusher* (1981) 4 FLR 65. See *Powell v Osbourne* [1993] 1 FLR 1001, [1993] 1 FCR 797, CA (severable share in life policy treated as part

of net estate but its value assessed with regard to the imminence of death so that when the value of the property in question depends upon the death, as with a life policy, the value before death is effectively the same as the value upon death); *Jessop v Jessop* [1992] 1 FLR 591, [1992] 1 FCR 253, CA (severable share in beneficial joint tenancy in house taken partially into account); *Kourgky v Lusher* (severable share in beneficial joint tenancy in matrimonial home not taken into account). See *Lim (a child) v Walia* [2014] EWCA Civ 1076, [2015] Ch 375, [2014] 3 FCR 284 (severable interest in life insurance policy existed immediately prior to deceased's death, but its value was nil as dependent on appropriate claim having been made; no claim having been made, no value to be treated as part of estate). *Hanbury v Hanbury* [1999] 2 FLR 255, [1999] Fam Law 447 (deceased's share of joint bank accounts and investments held in joint names with second wife treated as part of estate to allow provision for disabled daughter).

Where an order is made under the Inheritance (Provision for Family and Dependants) Act 1975 s 9(1) the provisions of s 9 do not render any person liable for anything done by him before the order was made: s 9(3).

5 Ie the date on which the Inheritance and Trustees' Powers Act 2014 came into force.

6 The Inheritance (Provision for Family and Dependants) Act 1975 s 9(1). See text and note 5. The court had no discretion and no power to order that such property be included where it gave leave to apply out of time. The limitation was a trap for the unwary.

7 Ie when an order is made under the Inheritance (Provision for Family and Dependants) Act 1975 s 9(1).

8 Inheritance (Provision for Family and Dependants) Act 1975 s 9(1). See text and note 5. An order may be made many years after death if the application for a grant is delayed: see *Dingmar v Dingmar* [2006] EWCA Civ 942, [2007] Ch 109, [2007] 2 All ER 382. The case revealed shortcomings in the wording of the Inheritance (Provision for Family and Dependants) Act 1975 s 9(1) which on a strict reading would have required the court to value the deceased's interest at the date of the deceased's death many years earlier. The Court of Appeal criticised the drafting of the provision and by a majority judgment held that, instead of valuing the interest at the date of the death, the proportionate share of the property which would have belonged to the deceased had there had been severance was to be treated as the share of the property which the court was empowered to treat as part of the estate.

9 By the Inheritance and Trustees' Powers Act 2014 Sch 2 para 7(2)(a).

10 Ie an order under the Inheritance (Provision for Family and Dependants) Act 1975 s 2 (see PARAS 591–592).

11 Inheritance (Provision for Family and Dependants) Act 1975 s 9(1A) (as added: see note 4). This amendment was introduced to clarify the situation following the Court of Appeal decision in *Dingmar v Dingmar* [2006] EWCA Civ 942, [2007] Ch 109, [2007] 2 All ER 382 (see note 8).

12 Inheritance (Provision for Family and Dependants) Act 1975 s 9(2). As to inheritance tax see INHERITANCE TAXATION.

586. Applications in respect of dispositions intended to defeat applications for financial provision. The court[1] has power to make an order[2] where, on an application for an order for financial provision under the Inheritance (Provision for Family and Dependants) Act 1975[3], the applicant, in the proceedings on that application applies to the court[4], and the court is satisfied that:

(1) less than six years before the date of his death, the deceased, with the intention[5] of defeating an application for financial provision under the Act, made a disposition[6];

(2) full valuable consideration[7] for that disposition was not given by the donee[8] or by any other person[9]; and

(3) the exercise of the powers conferred by this provision would facilitate the making of financial provision for the applicant under the Act[10].

If the court is so satisfied, it may[11], subject to the provisions of the Act[12], order the donee[13] (whether or not at the date of the order he holds any interest in the property[14] disposed of to him or for his benefit by the deceased) to provide, for the purpose of the making of that financial provision, such sum of money or other property as may be specified in the order[15].

Where such an order is made as respects any disposition made by the deceased which consisted of the payment of money to or for the benefit of the donee, the amount of any sum of money or the value of any property so ordered to be provided must not exceed the amount of the payment made by the deceased after deducting from it any inheritance tax borne by the donee in respect of that payment[16].

Where such an order is made as respects any disposition made by the deceased which consisted of the transfer of property (other than a sum of money) to or for the benefit of the donee, the amount of any sum of money or the value of any property so ordered to be provided must not exceed the value at the date of the deceased's death of the property disposed of by him to or for the benefit of the donee, or, if that property has been disposed of by the person to whom it was transferred by the deceased, the value at the date of that disposal, after deducting from it any inheritance tax borne by the donee in respect of the transfer of that property by the deceased[17].

1 As to the meaning of 'court' see PARA 566 note 6.
2 Ie an order under the Inheritance (Provision for Family and Dependants) Act 1975 s 10(2): see s 10(1).
3 Ie under the Inheritance (Provision for Family and Dependants) Act 1975 s 2 (see PARAS 591–592): see s 10(1).
4 Inheritance (Provision for Family and Dependants) Act 1975 s 10(1).
5 This condition is fulfilled if the court is of the opinion that, on a balance of probabilities, the deceased's intention (though not necessarily his sole intention) in making the disposition was to prevent an order for financial provision being made or to reduce the amount of the provision which might otherwise be granted: Inheritance (Provision for Family and Dependants) Act 1975 s 12(1). The requisite intention is subjective: *Re Dawkins, Dawkins v Judd* [1986] 2 FLR 360. See also *Kemmis v Kemmis* [1988] 1 WLR 1307, [1988] 2 FLR 223, CA; *Re Weir* [1993] 2 NIJB 45. The deceased need not have had the existence of the provisions of the Inheritance (Provision for Family and Dependants) Act 1975 present to his mind when making the disposition but must have intended to defeat a claim made after his death against his estate: *Re Kennedy, Kennedy v Official Solicitor to the Supreme Court* [1980] CLY 2820.
6 Inheritance (Provision for Family and Dependants) Act 1975 s 10(2)(a). For these purposes, 'disposition' does not include:
   (1) any provision in a will, any such nomination as is mentioned in s 8(1) (see PARA 583) or any donatio mortis causa (see PARA 584); or
   (2) any appointment of property made, otherwise than by will, in the exercise of a special power of appointment: s 10(7).

   However, subject to these exceptions, 'disposition' includes any payment of money (including the payment of a premium under a policy of assurance) and any conveyance, assurance, appointment or gift of property of any description, whether made by an instrument or otherwise: s 10(7). Section 10 does not apply to any disposition made before 1 April 1976: ss 10(8), 27(3). As to the meaning of 'will' see PARA 566 note 8. A release of a valuable right such as a right to reside in a house for life is a disposition for these purposes: *Clifford v Tanner* [1987] CLY 3881, CA. The service of a notice ending a joint tenancy is not a disposition for the purposes of the Matrimonial Causes Act 1973 s 37 (avoidance of transactions intended to prevent or reduce financial relief): *Bater v Bater, Greenwich London Borough Council v Bater* [1999] 4 All ER 944, CA sub nom *Bater v Greenwich London Borough Council* [1999] 3 FCR 254, CA.
7 As to the meaning of 'valuable consideration' see PARA 567 note 15.
8 'Donee' means the person to whom or for the benefit of whom the disposition was made: Inheritance (Provision for Family and Dependants) Act 1975 s 10(2)(b). Where a disposition is made to a person as a trustee, 'donee' includes the trustee for the time being of the trust in question: s 13(3).
9 Inheritance (Provision for Family and Dependants) Act 1975 s 10(2)(b).
10 Inheritance (Provision for Family and Dependants) Act 1975 s 10(2)(c). See *Hanbury v Hanbury* [1999] 2 FLR 255, [1999] 3 FCR 217 where the court was satisfied that a gift of cash to the deceased's second wife was tainted by the deceased's intention to defeat the claim of his disabled daughter under the Inheritance (Provision for Family and Dependants) Act 1975 but an order under s 10 would not facilitate the making of an order for financial provision, the court exercised its powers under s 9 (see PARA 585) to treat the deceased's severable share of joint property as part of the estate.
11 For the general considerations to which the court must have regard in determining an application under the Inheritance (Provision for Family and Dependants) Act 1975 s 10 see PARA 589.

12 Ie subject to the Inheritance (Provision for Family and Dependants) Act 1975 ss 10, 12, 13 (see the text to notes 13–17; and PARA 587 et seq): see s 10(2).
13 The court's power to order the donee to provide a sum of money or property is exercisable in like manner in relation to the donee's personal representative, but the court has no power to make an order in respect of any property forming part of the donee's estate which has been distributed by the personal representative, who is not to be liable for having distributed any such property before he has notice of the making of an application under the Inheritance (Provision for Family and Dependants) Act 1975 s 10, on the ground that he ought to have taken into account the possibility that such an application would be made: s 12(4). See further PARA 590.
14 As to the meaning of 'property' see PARA 582 note 2.
15 Inheritance (Provision for Family and Dependants) Act 1975 s 10(2). 'Property' includes any chose in action and a policy of insurance and the right to policy monies thereunder: *Powell v Osbourne* [1993] 1 FLR 1001 at 1004, CA. Where the court makes an order under the Inheritance (Provision for Family and Dependants) Act 1975 s 10, it may give such consequential directions as it thinks fit (including directions requiring the making of any payment or the transfer of any property) for giving effect to the order or for receiving a fair adjustment of the rights of the persons affected by it: s 12(3).
16 Inheritance (Provision for Family and Dependants) Act 1975 s 10(3). As to inheritance tax see INHERITANCE TAXATION.
17 Inheritance (Provision for Family and Dependants) Act 1975 s 10(4). Where the power to make the order is exercised in relation to the donee's personal representative (see note 13), the reference in s 10(4) to the disposal of property by the donee includes a reference to disposal by his personal representative: s 12(4)(a). A release of a valuable right such as a right to reside in a house for life is a disposition for these purposes and the value is the amount that a person would pay for its release: *Clifford v Tanner* [1987] CLY 3881, CA.

587. **Subsidiary applications.** Where an original application for an order in respect of a disposition intended to defeat an application for financial provision is made[1] in relation to any disposition, the donee[2] or any applicant for an order for financial provision[3] may make an application on which the court[4] may exercise further special powers[5] if it is satisfied that:

(1) less than six years before the date of the deceased's death, the deceased with the intention[6] of defeating an application for financial provision under the Inheritance (Provision for Family and Dependants) Act 1975 made a disposition other than the disposition which is the subject of the original application[7]; and
(2) full valuable consideration[8] for that other disposition was not given by the person to whom or for whose benefit that other disposition was made or by any other person[9].

If the court is so satisfied, it may exercise in relation to the person to whom or for whose benefit that other disposition was made the powers which it would have had[10] if the original application had been made in respect of that other disposition and the court had been appropriately satisfied[11].

1 Ie an application for an order under the Inheritance (Provision for Family and Dependants) Act 1975 s 10(2) (see PARA 586): see s 10(5).
2 Ie the person to or for whose benefit the disposition was made: see the Inheritance (Provision for Family and Dependants) Act 1975 s 10(2)(b). Where a disposition is made to a person as a trustee, 'donee' includes the trustee for the time being of the trust in question: see s 13(3).
3 Ie under the Inheritance (Provision for Family and Dependants) Act 1975 s 2 (see PARAS 591–592): see s 10(5). Where the power to make the order is exercised in relation to the donee's personal representative, the reference to an application by the donee includes a reference to an application by the personal representative of the donee: s 12(4)(b).
4 As to the meaning of 'court' see PARA 566 note 6.
5 As to the general considerations to which the court must have regard in determining an application under the Inheritance (Provision for Family and Dependants) Act 1975 s 10 see PARA 589.
6 See PARA 586 note 5.
7 Inheritance (Provision for Family and Dependants) Act 1975 s 10(5)(a). As to the meaning of 'disposition' see PARA 586 note 6.
8 As to the meaning of 'valuable consideration' see PARA 567 note 15.

9 Inheritance (Provision for Family and Dependants) Act 1975 s 10(5)(b).
10 Ie under the Inheritance (Provision for Family and Dependants) Act 1975 s 10(2) (see PARA 586): see s 10(5).
11 Inheritance (Provision for Family and Dependants) Act 1975 s 10(5). The court must be satisfied on an original application as to the matters set out in s 10(2)(a), (b), (c) (see PARA 586): see s 10(5). Where an application is made under s 10(5), any reference in s 10 (except in s 10(2)(b)) to the donee includes a reference to the person to whom or for whose benefit that other disposition was made: s 10(5).

588. Applications in respect of contracts to leave property by will intended to defeat applications for financial provision. Where, on an application by the applicant in proceedings on an application for an order for financial provision under the Inheritance (Provision for Family and Dependants) Act 1975[1] the court[2] may make an order if it is satisfied that:

(1) the deceased made a contract[3] by which he agreed to leave by his will[4] a sum of money or other property[5] to any person or by which he agreed that a sum of money or other property would be paid or transferred to any person out of his estate[6];
(2) the deceased made that contract with the intention[7] of defeating an application for financial provision under the Act[8];
(3) when the contract was made full valuable consideration[9] for that contract was not given or promised by the donee[10] or by any other person[11]; and
(4) the exercise of the powers conferred by this provision would facilitate the making of financial provision for the applicant under the Act[12],

the court may[13], subject to the provisions of the Act[14], make certain orders[15].

The court may make any one or more of the following orders[16]:

(a) if any money has been paid or any other property has been transferred to or for the benefit of the donee in accordance with the contract, an order directing him to provide, for the purpose of the making of that financial provision, such sum of money or other property as may be specified in the order[17];
(b) if the money or all the money has not been paid or the property or all the property has not been transferred in accordance with the contract, an order directing the personal representatives not to make any payment or transfer any property, or not to make any further payment or transfer any further property, as the case may be, in accordance with it or directing them only to make such payment or transfer such property as may be specified in the order[18].

Where an order has been made under this provision in relation to any contract, the rights of any person to enforce that contract or to recover damages or to obtain other relief for the breach of it are subject to any adjustment made by the court[19] and survive to such extent only as is consistent with giving effect to the terms of that order[20].

1 Ie under the Inheritance (Provision for Family and Dependants) Act 1975 s 2 (see PARAS 591–592): see s 11(1).
2 As to the meaning of 'court' see PARA 566 note 6.
3 This provision does not apply to a contract made before 1 April 1976: Inheritance (Provision for Family and Dependants) Act 1975 ss 11(6), 27(3). Contract is not defined in the Inheritance (Provision for Family and Dependants) Act 1975 but may include a promise to leave property by will giving rise to an estoppel (*Re Basham* [1987] 1 All ER 405, [1986] 1 WLR 1498), or a promise to leave property by will in consideration of terminating periodical payments (*Soulsbury v Soulsbury* [2007] EWCA Civ 969, [2008] Fam 1, [2008] 1 FLR 90), or an arrangement to leave property by mutual wills (*Re Cleaver, Cleaver v Insley* [1981] 2 All ER 1018, [1981] 1 WLR 939;

Re Dale, Proctor v Dale [1994] Ch 31, [1993] 4 All ER 129; *Re Goodchild, Goodchild v Goodchild* [1996] 1 All ER 670, [1996] 1 WLR 694; *Birmingham v Renfrew* (1936) 57 CLR 666, Aust HC). As to mutual wills see PARA 10.

4 As to the meaning of 'will' see PARA 566 note 8.

5 As to the meaning of 'property' see PARA 582 note 2. 'Property' includes any chose in action and a policy of insurance and the right to policy monies under it: *Powell v Osbourne* [1993] 1 FLR 1001 at 1004, CA, per Dillon LJ.

6 Inheritance (Provision for Family and Dependants) Act 1975 s 11(2)(a). Where the court makes an order under s 11, it may give such consequential directions as it thinks fit (including directions requiring the making of any payment or the transfer of any property) for giving effect to the order or for securing a fair adjustment of the rights of the persons affected by it: s 12(3).

7 This condition is fulfilled if the court is of the opinion that, on a balance of probabilities, the deceased's intention (though not necessarily his sole intention) in making the contract was to prevent an order for financial provision being made or to reduce the amount of the provision which might otherwise be granted by an order: Inheritance (Provision for Family and Dependants) Act 1975 s 12(1). See also PARA 586 note 5.

8 Inheritance (Provision for Family and Dependants) Act 1975 s 11(2)(b).

9 As to the meaning of 'valuable consideration' see PARA 567 note 15. Where an application is made under the Inheritance (Provision for Family and Dependants) Act 1975 s 11 with respect to any contract made by the deceased and no valuable consideration was given or promised by any person for that contract then, notwithstanding anything in s 12(1) (see note 7), it must be presumed, unless the contrary is shown, that the deceased made that contract with the intention of defeating an application for financial provision: s 12(2).

10 'Donee' means the person with whom or for whose benefit the contract was made: Inheritance (Provision for Family and Dependants) Act 1975 s 11(2)(c). Where a payment is made or property is transferred in accordance with a contract to any person as a trustee, 'donee' includes a reference to the trustee or trustees for the time being of the trust in question: s 13(3).

11 Inheritance (Provision for Family and Dependants) Act 1975 s 11(2)(c).

12 Inheritance (Provision for Family and Dependants) Act 1975 s 11(2)(d).

13 As to the general considerations to which the court must have regard in determining an application under the Inheritance (Provision for Family and Dependants) Act 1975 s 11 see PARA 589.

14 Ie subject to the Inheritance (Provision for Family and Dependants) Act 1975 ss 11–13 (see PARAS 586–587, 589): see s 11(2).

15 Inheritance (Provision for Family and Dependants) Act 1975 s 11(2).

16 Notwithstanding anything in the Inheritance (Provision for Family and Dependants) Act 1975 s 11(2), the court may exercise its powers under s 11(2) in relation to any contract made by the deceased only to the extent that it considers that the amount of any sum of money paid or to be paid or the value of any property transferred or to be transferred in accordance with the contract exceeds the value of any valuable consideration given or to be given for that contract, and for this purpose the court must have regard to the value of property at the date of the hearing: s 11(3).

17 Inheritance (Provision for Family and Dependants) Act 1975 s 11(2)(i). This power to order the donee, in relation to any contract, to provide any sum of money or other property is exercisable in like manner in relation to the donee's personal representative, but the court has no power to make an order in respect of any property forming part of the donee's estate which has been distributed by the personal representative, who is not to be liable for having distributed any such property before he has notice of the making of an application under s 11 on the ground that he ought to have taken into account the possibility that such an application would be made: s 12(4). As to the protection of personal representatives see further PARA 590.

18 Inheritance (Provision for Family and Dependants) Act 1975 s 11(2)(ii).

19 Ie under the Inheritance (Provision for Family and Dependants) Act 1975 s 12(3) (see note 6): see s 11(5).

20 Inheritance (Provision for Family and Dependants) Act 1975 s 11(5).

589. General considerations in relation to attempts to defeat application for financial provision. In determining whether and in what manner to exercise any of its powers[1] on an application in respect of a disposition or a contract to leave property by will or other disposition intended[2] to defeat an application for financial provision[3], the court[4] must have regard to the circumstances in which any disposition was made and any valuable consideration[5] which was given for it, the relationship, if any, of the donee[6] to the deceased, the donee's conduct and financial resources and all the other circumstances of the case[7].

1 Ie its powers under the Inheritance (Provision for Family and Dependants) Act 1975 ss 10, 11 (see PARAS 586–588): sees ss 10(6), 11(4).
2 See PARA 586 note 5.
3 Ie under the Inheritance (Provision for Family and Dependants) Act 1975 s 2: see PARAS 591–592.
4 As to the meaning of 'court' see PARA 566 note 6.
5 As to the meaning of 'valuable consideration' see PARA 567 note 15.
6 'Donee' means the person with whom or for whose benefit the contract was made: see the Inheritance (Provision for Family and Dependants) Act 1975 ss 10(2)(b), 11(2)(c). Where a payment is made or property is transferred in accordance with a contract to any person as a trustee, 'donee' includes a reference to the trustee or trustees for the time being of the trust in question: s 13(3).
7 Inheritance (Provision for Family and Dependants) Act 1975 ss 10(6), 11(4).

590. Protection of trustees and personal representatives where application made in relation to attempts to defeat application for financial provision. Where an application is made for an order in respect of a disposition made by the deceased to any person as trustee[1] or in respect of any payment made or property[2] transferred, in accordance with a contract made by the deceased, to any person as trustee[3], the powers of the court[4] to order that trustee to provide a sum of money or other property are subject to certain limitations[5]. The limitations are:

(1) in the case of an application in respect of a disposition which consisted of the payment of money or an application in respect of the payment of money in accordance with a contract, that the amount of any sum of money ordered to be provided must not exceed the aggregate of so much of that money as is at the date of the order in the trustee's hands and the value at that date of any property which represents that money or is derived from it and is at that date in the trustee's hands[6]; and

(2) in the case of an application in respect of a disposition which consisted of the transfer of property (other than a sum of money) or an application in respect of the transfer of property (other than a sum of money) in accordance with a contract, the value of any property ordered to be provided must not exceed the aggregate of the value at the date of the order of so much of the property concerned as is at that date in the trustee's hands and the value at that date of any property which represents the first-mentioned property or is derived from it and is at that date in the trustee's hands[7].

Where any such application is made in respect of a disposition made to any person as a trustee or in respect of any payment made or property transferred in pursuance of a contract to any person as a trustee, the trustee is not liable for having distributed any money or other property on the ground that he ought to have taken into account the possibility that such an application would be made[8].

Where a deceased person entered into a contract by which he agreed to leave by his will[9] any sum of money or other property to any person or by which he agreed that a sum of money, or other property would be paid or transferred to any person out of his estate, then, if the deceased's personal representative has reason to believe that the deceased entered into the contract with the intention of defeating an application for financial provision under the Inheritance (Provision for Family and Dependants) Act 1975, he may, notwithstanding anything in that contract postpone the payment of that sum of money or the transfer of that property until the expiration of the period of six months from the date on which representation with respect to the deceased's estate is first taken out or, if during that period an application is made for an order for financial provision[10], until the determination of the proceedings on that application[11].

1 Inheritance (Provision for Family and Dependants) Act 1975 s 13(1)(a). Such an order is made under s 10 (see PARAS 586–587): see s 13(1)(a). 'Trustee' includes the trustee or trustees for the time being of the trust in question: see s 13(3).
2 As to the meaning of 'property' see PARA 582 note 2.
3 Inheritance (Provision for Family and Dependants) Act 1975 s 13(1)(b). Such an order is made under s 11 (see PARA 588): see s 13(1)(b).
4 Ie under the Inheritance (Provision for Family and Dependants) Act 1975 s 10 or s 11 (see PARAS 586–588): see s 13(1).
5 Inheritance (Provision for Family and Dependants) Act 1975 s 13(1). This is in addition, in the case of an application under s 10, to any provision regarding the deduction of inheritance tax: s 13(1). As to inheritance tax see INHERITANCE TAXATION.
6 Inheritance (Provision for Family and Dependants) Act 1975 s 13(1)(i).
7 Inheritance (Provision for Family and Dependants) Act 1975 s 13(1)(ii).
8 Inheritance (Provision for Family and Dependants) Act 1975 s 13(2).
9 As to the meaning of 'will' see PARA 566 note 8.
10 Ie under the Inheritance (Provision for Family and Dependants) Act 1975 s 2 (see PARAS 591–592): see s 20(3).
11 Inheritance (Provision for Family and Dependants) Act 1975 s 20(3).

(5) ORDER FOR FINANCIAL PROVISION

591. Orders which the court may make. Subject to the provisions of the Inheritance (Provision for Family and Dependants) Act 1975, where an application is made for an order[1], the court[2], if it is satisfied[3] that the disposition of the deceased's estate effected by his will[4] or the law relating to intestacy[5], or the combination of his will and that law, is not such as to make reasonable financial provision[6] for the applicant, may make any one or more of the following orders[7]:

(1) an order for the making to the applicant out of the net estate[8] of the deceased of such periodical payments and for such term as may be specified in the order[9];
(2) an order for the payment to the applicant out of that estate of a lump sum of such amount as may be so specified[10];
(3) an order for the transfer to the applicant of such property[11] comprised in that estate as may be so specified[12];
(4) an order for the settlement for the benefit of the applicant of such property comprised in that estate as may be so specified[13];
(5) an order for the acquisition out of property comprised in that estate of such property as may be so specified and for the transfer of the property so acquired to the applicant or for its settlement for his benefit[14];
(6) an order varying any ante-nuptial or post-nuptial settlement[15] (including such a settlement made by will) made on the parties to a marriage to which the deceased was one of the parties, the variation being for the benefit of the surviving party to that marriage, or any child[16] of that marriage, or any person who was treated by the deceased as a child of the family in relation to that marriage[17];
(7) an order varying any settlement made:
   (a) during the subsistence of a civil partnership formed by the deceased[18]; or
   (b) in anticipation of the formation of a civil partnership by the deceased, on the civil partners (including such a settlement made by will), the variation being for the benefit of the surviving civil

partner, or any child[19] of both the civil partners, or any person who was treated by the deceased as a child of the family in relation to that civil partnership[20];

(8) an order varying for the applicant's benefit the trusts on which the deceased's estate is held (whether arising under the will, or the law relating to intestacy, or both)[21].

An order for the making of periodical payments to the applicant out of the net estate of the deceased may provide for:

(i) payments of such amount as may be specified in the order[22];

(ii) payments equal to the whole of the income of the net estate or of a portion of it as may be so specified[23];

(iii) payments equal to the whole of the income of such part of the net estate as the court may direct to be set aside or appropriated for the purpose[24]; or

(iv) payments determined in any other way[25].

The order may also contain consequential provisions[26].

1 Ie under the Inheritance (Provision for Family and Dependants) Act 1975 s 2: see s 2(1). As to applications see PARA 566. As to who may apply see PARAS 567, 577–581.
2 As to the meaning of 'court' see PARA 566 note 6.
3 As to the matters to which the court must have regard in exercising these powers see PARAS 571–581.
4 As to the meaning of 'will' see PARA 566 note 8.
5 As to the law relating to intestacy see PARA 477 et seq.
6 As to the meaning of 'reasonable financial provision' see PARAS 569–570.
7 Inheritance (Provision for Family and Dependants) Act 1975 s 2(1).
8 As to the meaning of 'net estate' see PARA 582.
9 Inheritance (Provision for Family and Dependants) Act 1975 s 2(1)(a). Where the order provides for the making of payments of an amount specified in the order, the order may direct that such part of the net estate as may be so specified is to be set aside or appropriated for the making out of its income of those payments; but no larger part of the net estate may be so set aside or appropriated than is sufficient, at the date of the order, to produce by its income the amount required for the making of those payments: s 2(3). In assessing for the purposes of an order under s 2 the extent (if any) to which the net estate is reduced by any debts or liabilities (including any inheritance tax paid or payable out of the estate), the court may assume that the order has already been made: s 2(3A) (added by the Inheritance and Trustees' Powers Act 2014 Sch 2 para 4(3)). As to variation etc of orders under the Inheritance (Provision for Family and Dependants) Act 1975 s 2(1)(a) see s 6; and PARA 594. In default of an order payments will be deemed to take effect from the date of the deceased's death: see s 19(1); and PARA 593.

Periodical payments need not be limited to the income of the net estate: *Re Blanch, Blanch v Honhold* [1967] 2 All ER 468, [1967] 1 WLR 987; *Re F* (1965) Times, 26 February. The court has a broad discretion as to the date on which periodical payments should commence. Payments have been ordered to commence from the date of death (*Askew v Askew* [1961] 2 All ER 60, [1961] 1 WLR 725; *Re Goodwin, Goodwin v Goodwin* [1969] 1 Ch 283, [1968] 3 All ER 12; *Stead v Stead* [1985] FLR 16, CA; *Re Farrow* [1987] 1 FLR 205), from the date of the application (*Eyre v Eyre* [1968] 1 All ER 968, [1968] 1 WLR 530), and from the date of judgment (*Re Lecoche, Lecoche v Barclays Bank Ltd* (1967) 111 Sol Jo 136; *Re Debenham* [1986] 1 FLR 404). In determining the date of commencement the court will have regard to the life expectancy of the applicant, the size of the estate, the effect of the order on the administration of the estate and any delay in bringing the application: *Lusternik v Lusternik* [1972] Fam 125, [1972] 1 All ER 592, CA; *Stead v Stead* above; *Re Debenham* above.

10 Inheritance (Provision for Family and Dependants) Act 1975 s 2(1)(b). The order may provide for the payment of the lump sum by instalments of such amount as may be specified in the order: s 7(1). In such a case the court has power, on an application made by the person to whom the lump sum is payable, by the personal representatives of the deceased or by the trustees of the property out of which the lump sum is payable, to vary the order by varying the number of instalments payable, the amount of any instalment and the date on which any instalment becomes payable: s 7(2). A lump sum award may extend to the whole of the net estate: see s 25(3); and PARA 582.

A lump sum order is not equivalent to an order for payment of a debt; it simply puts the applicant in the same position as a beneficiary under a will: *Re Jennery, Jennery v Jennery* [1967]

Ch 280, [1967] 1 All ER 691, CA. A lump sum may be awarded to achieve a specific purpose: *Re Callaghan* [1985] Fam 1, [1984] 3 All ER 790 (purchase of a house); *Re Crawford* (1982) 4 FLR 273 (purchase of annuity). See also *Re Besterman, Besterman v Grusin* [1984] Ch 458, [1984] 2 All ER 656; *Re Bunning, Bunning v Salmon* [1984] Ch 480, [1984] 3 All ER 1; *Stead v Stead* [1985] FLR 16, CA; *Re Debenham* [1986] 1 FLR 404; *Jessop v Jessop* [1992] 1 FLR 591, [1992] 1 FCR 253, CA.

A lump sum is more likely to be awarded where the estate is small and where finality is desirable (*Re Collins* [1990] Fam 56, [1990] 2 All ER 47), where there is a need for a particular asset (*Re Gold, Gold v Curtis* [2005] WTLR 673) or to discharge the debts of a business allowing the applicant to derive an income from it (*Espinosa v Bourke* [1999] 1 FLR 747, [1999] 3 FCR 76, CA).

The quantum of lump sum orders may be assessed on a multiplier and multiplicand basis (*Malone v Harrison* [1979] 1 WLR 1353), on the basis of capitalised periodical payments or on the *Duxbury* basis (see *Duxbury v Duxbury* [1992] Fam 62n, [1990] 2 All ER 77, CA). See also *Re Myers, Myers v Myers* [2004] EWHC 1944 (Fam), [2005] WTLR 851; *Robinson v Fernsby* [2003] EWCA Civ 1820, [2004] WTLR 257.

11 As to the meaning of 'property' see PARA 582 note 2.

12 Inheritance (Provision for Family and Dependants) Act 1975 s 2(1)(c). See *Re Christie, Christie v Keeble* [1979] Ch 168, [1979] 1 All ER 546; *Rajabally v Rajabally* [1987] 2 FLR 390, CA. By analogy with cases of divorce, a contractual tenancy may be property: *Thompson v Thompson* [1976] Fam 25, [1975] 2 All ER 208, CA; *Hale v Hale* [1975] 2 All ER 1090, [1975] 1 WLR 931, CA. In exceptional cases the transfer may be for full consideration: see *Lewis v Warner* [2016] EWHC 1787 (Ch), [2016] All ER (D) 104 (Jul); and PARA 570 note 7.

13 Inheritance (Provision for Family and Dependants) Act 1975 s 2(1)(d). See *Moody v Stevenson* [1992] Ch 486, [1992] 2 All ER 524, CA; *Harrington v Gill* (1983) 4 FLR 265, CA; *Re Mason, Mason v Mason* (1975) 5 Fam Law 124; *Re Abram* [1996] 2 FLR 379, [1997] 2 FCR 85; *Churchill v Roach* [2004] 2 FLR 989, [2004] 3 FCR 744; *Re Myers, Myers v Myers* [2004] EWHC 1944 (Fam), [2005] WTLR 851; *Challinor v Challinor* [2009] EWHC 180 (Ch), [2009] WTLR 931.

14 Inheritance (Provision for Family and Dependants) Act 1975 s 2(1)(e).

15 A pension scheme entered into by one party to a marriage with the intention of providing benefits for both parties may constitute an ante-nuptial or post-nuptial settlement: *Brooks v Brooks* [1996] AC 375, [1995] 3 All ER 257. 'Marriage' includes marriage of a same sex couple: see the Marriage (Same Sex Couples) Act 2013 Sch 3 para 1(1)(a), (2), (3); and MATRIMONIAL AND CIVIL PARTNERSHIP LAW vol 72 (2015) PARAS 1–2.

16 As to the meaning of 'child' see PARA 567 note 11.

17 Inheritance (Provision for Family and Dependants) Act 1975 s 2(1)(f).

18 Inheritance (Provision for Family and Dependants) Act 1975 s 2(1)(g)(i) (added by the Civil Partnership Act 2004 s 71, Sch 4 para 16).

19 As to the meaning of 'child' see PARA 567 note 11.

20 Inheritance (Provision for Family and Dependants) Act 1975 s 2(1)(g)(ii) (as added: see note 18).

21 Inheritance (Provision for Family and Dependants) Act 1975 s 2(1)(h) (added by the Inheritance and Trustees' Powers Act 2014 Sch 2 para 4(2)).

22 Inheritance (Provision for Family and Dependants) Act 1975 s 2(2)(a). As to such orders see head (1) in the text and note 9.

23 Inheritance (Provision for Family and Dependants) Act 1975 s 2(2)(b). See also note 9.

24 Inheritance (Provision for Family and Dependants) Act 1975 s 2(2)(c). See also note 9.

25 Inheritance (Provision for Family and Dependants) Act 1975 s 2(2).

26 See PARA 592.

592. Consequential provisions in order for financial provision. An order for financial provision[1] may contain such consequential and supplemental provisions as the court[2] thinks necessary or expedient for the purpose of giving effect to the order[3] or for the purpose of securing that it operates fairly as between one beneficiary[4] of the deceased's estate and another[5]. The court may, in particular, but without prejudice to the generality of this provision:

(1) order any person who holds any property[6] which forms part of the net estate[7] of the deceased to make such payment or transfer such property as may be specified in the order[8];

(2) vary the disposition of the deceased's estate effected by the will[9] or the law relating to intestacy[10], or by both, in such manner as the court thinks fair and reasonable having regard to the provisions of the order and all the circumstances of the case[11]; and

(3) confer on the trustees of any property which is the subject of an order[12] such powers as appear to the court to be necessary or expedient[13].

Further, the order may provide that any sum paid to the applicant by virtue of an interim order[14] is to be treated to such an extent and in such manner as may be provided by the order as having been paid on account of any payment provided for by the order[15].

1 Ie an order under the Inheritance (Provision for Family and Dependants) Act 1975 s 2 (see PARA 591): see s 2(4).

2 As to the meaning of 'court' see PARA 566 note 6.

3 The court has an unfettered discretion to impose conditions: *Re Preston, Preston v Hoggarth* [1969] 2 All ER 961, [1969] 1 WLR 317. See eg *Re Pointer, Pointer and Shonfield v Edwards* [1941] Ch 60, [1940] 4 All ER 372 (condition that the applicant must inform trustees when her income exceeded a specified limit); *Re Ralphs, Ralphs v District Bank Ltd* [1968] 3 All ER 285, [1968] 1 WLR 1522 (amount paid under interim order to be brought into account against income of legacy); *Barnsley v Ward* (18 January 1980, unreported), CA (condition requiring applicant to use best endeavours to obtain employment imposed during currency of interim award); *Re Doring, Doring v Clark* [1955] 3 All ER 389, [1955] 1 WLR 1217 (annuity payable only in the event of shortfall of income from another source).

4 As to the meaning of 'beneficiary' see PARA 572 note 6.

The Inheritance (Provision for Family and Dependants) Act 1975 does not specify how the diminution of the provisions of the will due to an order for maintenance is to be borne by the persons beneficially interested under the will, but the court's jurisdiction extends to enable it to order an apportionment as between residuary and pecuniary legatees: see eg *Re Westby* (1946) 62 TLR 458 (payment of maintenance out of a pecuniary legacy); *Re Simson, Simson v National Provincial Bank Ltd* [1950] Ch 38, [1949] 2 All ER 826 (payment of maintenance apportioned between legacies and residue); *Re Jackson, Jackson v Nottidge* [1952] WN 352, [1952] 2 TLR 90 (cost of annuity apportioned between legacies and residue); *Re Preston, Preston v Hoggarth* [1969] 2 All ER 961, [1969] 1 WLR 317 (lump sum award borne unequally between beneficiaries of the same class); *Re Bunning, Bunning v Salmon* [1984] Ch 480, [1984] 3 All ER 1 (lump sum award made out of residue); and see *Re Franks, Franks v Franks* [1948] Ch 62, [1947] 2 All ER 638 (application stood over because of uncertainty as to provision required at the date of the hearing).

5 Inheritance (Provision for Family and Dependants) Act 1975 s 2(4).

6 As to the meaning of 'property' see PARA 582 note 2.

7 As to the meaning of 'net estate' see PARA 582.

8 Inheritance (Provision for Family and Dependants) Act 1975 s 2(4)(a). An adjournment will sometimes be necessary to enable such beneficiaries to be separately represented and heard. The applicant's property cannot be settled: *Malone v Harrison* [1979] 1 WLR 1353.

9 As to the meaning of 'will' see PARA 566 note 8.

10 As to the law relating to intestacy see PARA 477 et seq.

11 Inheritance (Provision for Family and Dependants) Act 1975 s 2(4)(b). The court's discretion is unfettered: see note 3. See also *Re Mason, Mason v Mason* (1975) 5 Fam Law 124; *Rajabally v Rajabally* [1987] 2 FLR 390, CA.

12 Ie an order under the Inheritance (Provision for Family and Dependants) Act 1975 s 2: see s 2(4)(c).

13 Inheritance (Provision for Family and Dependants) Act 1975 s 2(4)(c). See *Re Haig, Powers v Haig* [1979] LS Gaz R 476.

14 As to interim orders see the Inheritance (Provision for Family and Dependants) Act 1975 s 5; and PARA 603.

15 Inheritance (Provision for Family and Dependants) Act 1975 s 5(4).

593. Effect of order for financial provision. Where an order is made under the Inheritance (Provision for Family and Dependants) Act 1975[1] then for all purposes, including the purposes of the enactments relating to inheritance tax[2], the will[3] or the law relating to intestacy[4], or both, as the case may be, have effect and are deemed to have had effect as from the deceased's death subject to the provisions of the order[5].

Any such order, or any interim order[6], in favour of an applicant who was:

(1) the former spouse or former civil partner[7] of the deceased[8]; or
(2) an applicant who was the husband or wife[9] of the deceased in a case where the marriage with the deceased was the subject of a decree of judicial separation and at the date of death the decree was in force and the separation was continuing[10]; or
(3) an applicant who was the civil partner[11] of the deceased in a case where, at the date of death, a separation order[12] was in force in relation to their civil partnership and the separation was continuing[13],

in so far as it provides for the making of periodical payments, ceases to have effect on the formation by the applicant of a subsequent marriage or civil partnership[14] except in relation to any arrears due under the order on the date of the formation of the subsequent marriage or civil partnership[15].

1 Ie under the Inheritance (Provision for Family and Dependants) Act 1975 s 2 (see PARAS 591–592): see s 19(1).
2 See INHERITANCE TAXATION.
3 As to the meaning of 'will' see PARA 566 note 8.
4 As to the law relating to intestacy see PARA 477 et seq.
5 Inheritance (Provision for Family and Dependants) Act 1975 s 19(1).
6 Ie any order under the Inheritance (Provision for Family and Dependants) Act 1975 s 5 (see PARA 603): see s 9(2).
7 As to the meanings of 'former spouse' and 'former civil partner' see PARA 567 note 6. As to husbands, wives and civil partners under void marriages and civil partnerships see PARA 567 note 6. 'Spouse' includes a person who is married to a person of the same sex: see Marriage (Same Sex Couples) Act 2013 Sch 3 para 1(1)(c), (2), (3); and MATRIMONIAL AND CIVIL PARTNERSHIP LAW vol 72 (2015) PARAS 1–2.
8 Inheritance (Provision for Family and Dependants) Act 1975 s 19(2)(a) (amended by the Civil Partnership Act 2004 s 71, Sch 4 para 26).
9 As to the meanings of 'husband' and 'wife' see PARA 567 note 4.
10 Inheritance (Provision for Family and Dependants) Act 1975 s 19(2)(b).
11 As to the meaning of 'civil partner' see PARA 567 note 4.
12 Ie an order under the Civil Partnership Act 2004 Pt 2 Chapter 2.
13 Inheritance (Provision for Family and Dependants) Act 1975 s 19(2)(c) (added by the Civil Partnership Act 2004 s 71, Sch 4 para 26).
14 As to formation of subsequent marriage or civil partnership see PARA 567 note 6.
15 Inheritance (Provision for Family and Dependants) Act 1975 s 19(2) (amended by the Civil Partnership Act 2004 s 71, Sch 4 para 26).

594. Variation, discharge, suspension and revival of periodical payment orders. Where the court[1] has made an original order[2] for the making of periodical payments to any person (the 'original recipient'[3]) it has power, on an application[4], by order to vary or discharge the original order or to suspend any provision of it temporarily and to revive the operation of any provision so suspended[5]. Any order made on an application for the variation of the original order may[6]:

(1) provide for the making out of any relevant property[7] of such periodical payments and for such term as may be specified in the order[8] to any person who has applied, or would but for the statutory time limit[9] be entitled to apply, for an order for financial provision[10] (whether or not, in the case of any application, an order was made in favour of the applicant)[11];
(2) provide for the payment out of any relevant property of a lump sum of such amount as may be so specified to the original recipient or to any such person as is mentioned in head (1) above[12]; or

(3) provide for the transfer of the relevant property, or such part of it as may be so specified, to the original recipient or to any such person as is so mentioned[13].

Where the original order provides that any periodical payments payable under it to the original recipient are to cease on the occurrence of an event specified in the order (other than the formation of a subsequent marriage or civil partnership by a former spouse or former civil partner) or on the expiration of a period so specified, then, if, before the end of the period of six months from the date of the occurrence of that event or of the expiration of that period, an application is made for an order under this provision, the court has power to make any order which it would have had power to make if the application had been made before that date (whether in favour of the original recipient or any such person as is mentioned in head (1) above, and whether having effect from that date or from such later date as the court may specify)[14].

In exercising these powers the court must have regard to all the circumstances of the case, including any change in any of the matters to which it was required to have regard when making the order to which the application relates[15]. Where the court makes an order under this provision it may give such consequential directions as it thinks necessary or expedient having regard to the provisions of the order[16].

1 As to the meaning of 'court' see PARA 566 note 6.
2 Ie under the Inheritance (Provision for Family and Dependants) Act 1975 s 2(1)(a) (see PARA 591): see s 6(1). Any reference in s 6 to the original order includes a reference to an order made under s 6: s 6(4).
3 Any reference in the Inheritance (Provision for Family and Dependants) Act 1975 s 6 to the original recipient includes a reference to any person to whom periodical payments are required to be made by virtue of an order under s 6: s 6(4).
4 The application may be made by:
 (1) any person who by virtue of the Inheritance (Provision for Family and Dependants) Act 1975 s 1(1) (see PARA 567) has applied, or would but for s 4 (see PARA 597) be entitled to apply for an order under s 2 (see PARAS 591–592);
 (2) the deceased's personal representatives;
 (3) the trustees of any relevant property (see note 7); and
 (4) any beneficiary of the deceased's estate: s 6(5).
 As to the meaning of 'beneficiary' see PARA 572 note 6.
5 Inheritance (Provision for Family and Dependants) Act 1975 s 6(1), which is expressed to be subject to the provisions of the Act. On an application under s 6 the court may not make any such order as is mentioned in s 2(1)(d), (e) or (f) (see PARA 591), s 9 (see PARA 585), s 10 (see PARAS 586–587) or s 11 (see PARA 588): s 6(9).
6 Inheritance (Provision for Family and Dependants) Act 1975 s 6(2), which is expressed to be without prejudice to the generality of s 6(1).
7 An order under the Inheritance (Provision for Family and Dependants) Act 1975 s 6 may only affect relevant property, namely:
 (1) property the income of which is at the date of the order applicable wholly or in part for the making of periodical payments to any person who has applied for an order under the Inheritance (Provision for Family and Dependants) Act 1975; or
 (2) in the case of an application under s 6(3) in respect of payments which have ceased to be payable on the occurrence of an event or the expiration of a period, property the income of which was so applicable immediately before the occurrence of that event or the expiration of that period, as the case may be: s 6(6).
 See also *Frickler v Personal Representatives of Frickler* (1982) 3 FLR 228.
8 In relation to an order which provides for the making of periodical payments which are to cease on the occurrence of an event specified in the order (other than the formation of a subsequent marriage or civil partnership by a former spouse or former civil partner) or on the expiration of a period so specified, the power to vary an order includes power to provide for the making of periodical payments after the expiration of that period or the occurrence of that event: Inheritance (Provision for Family and Dependants) Act 1975 s 6(10) (amended by Civil Partnership Act 2004 s 71, Sch 4 para 19).

9 Ie but for the Inheritance (Provision for Family and Dependants) Act 1975 s 4 (see PARA 597): see s 6(2)(a). See also *Re Dorgan, Dorgan v Polley* [1948] Ch 366, [1948] 1 All ER 723.
10 Ie under the Inheritance (Provision for Family and Dependants) Act 1975 s 2 (see PARAS 591–592): see s 6(2)(a).
11 Inheritance (Provision for Family and Dependants) Act 1975 s 6(2)(a).
12 Inheritance (Provision for Family and Dependants) Act 1975 s 6(2)(b). Such an order for the payment of a lump sum may provide for the payment of that sum by instalments of such amount as may be specified in the order: s 7(1). In such a case the court has power, on an application by the person to whom the lump sum is payable, by the deceased's personal representatives or by the trustees of the property out of which the lump sum is payable, to vary that order by varying the number of instalments payable, the amount of any instalment and the date on which any instalment becomes payable: s 7(2).
13 Inheritance (Provision for Family and Dependants) Act 1975 s 6(2)(c).
14 Inheritance (Provision for Family and Dependants) Act 1975 s 6(3) (amended by the Civil Partnership Act 2004 s 71, Sch 4 para 19).
15 Inheritance (Provision for Family and Dependants) Act 1975 s 6(7). An accumulation of capital by an applicant may amount to a change of circumstances but need not lead to a variation: *Re Gale, Gale v Gale* [1966] Ch 236, [1966] 1 All ER 945, CA, per Russell LJ.
16 Inheritance (Provision for Family and Dependants) Act 1975 s 6(8).

595. Variation and discharge of orders made in divorce or dissolution proceedings. Where an application for an order for financial provision under the Inheritance (Provision for Family and Dependants) Act 1975[1] is made to the court[2] by any person who was at the time of the death of the deceased entitled to payments from the deceased under a secured periodical payments order made under the Matrimonial Causes Act 1973 or Civil Partnership Act 2004[3], then, in the proceedings on that application, the court has power, on an application made by that person or by the deceased's personal representative, to vary or discharge that periodical payments order or to revive the operation of any provision of it which has been suspended[4]. These powers in relation to an order are exercisable also in relation to any instrument executed in pursuance of the order[5].

In exercising these powers the court must have regard to all the circumstances of the case, including any interim order[6] or order for financial provision[7] which the court proposes to make, and any change (whether resulting from the death of the deceased or otherwise) in any of the matters to which the court was required to have regard when making the secured periodical payments order[8].

1 Ie under the Inheritance (Provision for Family and Dependants) Act 1975 s 2 (see PARAS 591–592): see s 16(1).
2 As to the meaning of 'court' see PARA 566 note 6.
3 As to orders under the Matrimonial Causes Act 1973 see PARA 578 note 12. As to orders under Civil Partnership Act 2004 see PARA 578 note 19.
4 Inheritance (Provision for Family and Dependants) Act 1975 s 16(1). Secured periodical payments orders are suspended under the Matrimonial Causes Act 1973 s 31 or the Civil Partnership Act 2004 Sch 5 Pt 11: see the Inheritance (Provision for Family and Dependants) Act 1975 s 16(1) (amended by the Civil Partnership Act 2004 s 71, Sch 4 para 23). As to the availability of the court's powers under the Inheritance (Provision for Family and Dependants) Act 1975 in applications under the Matrimonial Causes Act 1973 ss 31, 36 see the Inheritance (Provision for Family and Dependants) Act 1975 s 18. As to the availability of the court's powers in applications under Civil Partnership Act 2004 Sch 5 paras 60, 73 see the Inheritance (Provision for Family and Dependants) Act 1975 s 18A.
5 Inheritance (Provision for Family and Dependants) Act 1975 s 16(3).
6 Ie under the Inheritance (Provision for Family and Dependants) Act 1975 s 5 (see PARA 603): see s 16(2).
7 Ie under the Inheritance (Provision for Family and Dependants) Act 1975 s 2 (see PARAS 591–592): see s 16(2).
8 Inheritance (Provision for Family and Dependants) Act 1975 s 16(2).

596. Variation and revocation of maintenance agreements. Where an application for an order for financial provision under the Inheritance (Provision for Family and Dependants) Act 1975[1] is made to the court[2] by any person who was at the time of the death of the deceased entitled to payments from the deceased under a maintenance agreement[3] which provided for the continuation of payments under the agreement after the death of the deceased, then, in the proceedings on that application, the court has power, on an application by that person or by the deceased's personal representative, to vary or revoke that agreement[4]. In exercising these powers the court must have regard to all the circumstances of the case, including any interim order[5] or order for financial provision[6] which the court proposes to make, and any change (whether resulting from the death of the deceased or otherwise) in any of the circumstances in the light of which the agreement was made[7].

If a maintenance agreement is varied by the court under this provision the like consequences ensue as if the variation had been made immediately before the death of the deceased by agreement between the parties and for valuable consideration[8].

1 Ie under the Inheritance (Provision for Family and Dependants) Act 1975 s 2 (see PARAS 591–592): see s 17(1).
2 As to the meaning of 'court' see PARA 566 note 6.
3 In relation to a deceased person, 'maintenance agreement' means any agreement made, whether in writing or not, and whenever made, by the deceased with any person with whom he formed a marriage or civil partnership, being an agreement which contained provisions governing the rights and liabilities towards one another when living separately of the parties to that marriage or civil partnership (whether or not the marriage or civil partnership has been dissolved or annulled) in respect of the making or securing of payments or the disposition or use of any property, including such rights and liabilities with respect to the maintenance or education of any child, whether or not a child of the deceased or a person who was treated by the deceased as a child of the family in relation to that marriage or civil partnership: Inheritance (Provision for Family and Dependants) Act 1975 s 17(4) (amended by the Civil Partnership Act 2004 s 71, Sch 4 para 24). As to the meaning of 'child' see PARA 567 note 11; and as to the meaning of 'property' see PARA 582 note 2. 'Marriage' includes marriage of a same sex couple: see the Marriage (Same Sex Couples) Act 2013 Sch 3 para 1(1)(a), (2), (3); and MATRIMONIAL AND CIVIL PARTNERSHIP LAW vol 72 (2015) PARAS 1–2.
4 Inheritance (Provision for Family and Dependants) Act 1975 s 17(1).
5 Ie under the Inheritance (Provision for Family and Dependants) Act 1975 s 5 (see PARA 603): see s 17(2).
6 Ie under the Inheritance (Provision for Family and Dependants) Act 1975 s 2 (see PARAS 591–592): see s 17(2).
7 Inheritance (Provision for Family and Dependants) Act 1975 s 17(2).
8 Inheritance (Provision for Family and Dependants) Act 1975 s 17(3). As to the meaning of 'valuable consideration' see PARA 567 note 15.

(6) PROCEDURE

597. Time for application. An application for an order under the Inheritance (Provision for Family and Dependants) Act 1975[1] must not, except with the permission of the court[2], be made after the end of the period of six months from the date on which representation with respect to the estate of the deceased is first taken out[3].

In the case of deaths on or after October 2014[4], nothing prevents the making of an application before such representation is first taken out[5]. The following are to be left out of account when considering for the purposes of the Act when representation with respect to the estate of a deceased person was first taken out:

(1) a grant limited to settled land or to trust property[6];
(2) any other grant that does not permit any of the estate to be distributed[7];

(3) a grant limited to real estate or to personal estate, unless a grant limited to the remainder of the estate has previously been made or is made at the same time[8];

(4) a grant, or its equivalent, made outside the United Kingdom[9].

In the case of deaths before 1 October 2014[10], it was generally accepted that an application could not be made before the making of the grant[11]. The following are to be left out of account when considering for the purposes of the Inheritance (Provision for Family and Dependants) Act 1975 when representation with respect to the estate of a deceased person dying before that date was first taken out:

(a) a grant limited to settled land or to trust property;

(b) a grant limited to real estate or to personal estate unless a grant limited to the remainder of the estate has previously been made or is made at the same time[12].

The provisions of the Act do not render the personal representative of a deceased person liable for having distributed any part of the estate, after the end of the period of six months from the date on which representation with respect to the estate of the deceased is first taken out, on the ground that he ought to have taken into account the possibility that:

(i) the court might permit the making of an application for an order under the Act after the end of that period[13]; or

(ii) where such an order has been made, the court might exercise in relation to it its powers[14] to vary, discharge, suspend or revive it[15].

This provision does not, however, prejudice any power to recover, by reason of the making of an order under the Act, any part of the estate so distributed[16].

1 Ie an order under the Inheritance (Provision for Family and Dependants) Act 1975 s 2 (see PARAS 591–592): see s 4.

2 As to the meaning of 'court' see PARA 566 note 6. As to applications for an extension of time see PARA 598.

3 There is no distinction between a person under a disability and any other claimant so time runs against all claimants but disability is a material factor to be considered on an application for an extension of time: *Re W (a minor) (claim from a deceased's estate)* [1995] 2 FCR 689 at 695, sub nom *Re C* [1995] 2 FLR 24 at 28 per Wilson J; *Re Trott, Trott v Miles* [1958] 2 All ER 296, [1958] 1 WLR 604. No further period is initiated if a grant is obtained later in solemn form: *Re Miller, Miller v de Courcey* [1968] 3 All ER 844, [1969] 1 WLR 583. Where a grant is revoked and letters of administration are granted (and vice versa), time runs from the date of the second grant: *Re Freeman* [1984] 3 All ER 906, [1984] 1 WLR 1419; *Re Bidie, Bidie v General Accident Fire and Life Assurance Corpn Ltd* [1949] Ch 121, [1948] 2 All ER 995, CA. As to the correct approach the court should take to an application under the Inheritance (Provision for Family and Dependants) Act 1975 s 4 see *Berger v Berger* [2013] EWCA Civ 1305, [2014] WTLR 35, [2013] All ER (D) 319 (Oct).

4 Ie the date on which the Inheritance and Trustees' Powers Act 2014 came into force.

5 Inheritance (Provision for Family and Dependants) Act 1975 s 4 (amended by the Inheritance and Trustees' Powers Act 2014 Sch 2 para 6).

6 Inheritance (Provision for Family and Dependants) Act 1975 s 23(1)(a) (s 23 substituted by the Inheritance and Trustees' Powers Act 2014 Sch 3 para 2). Where a grant in solemn form confirms a grant in common form, time runs from the date of the grant in common form: *Re Miller, Miller v de Courcey* [1968] 3 All ER 844, [1969] 1 WLR 583. Where a grant is subsequently revoked time only runs from the later valid grant: *Re Freeman* [1984] 3 All ER 906, [1984] 1 WLR 1419; *Re Bidie, Bidie v General Accident Fire and Life Assurance Corpn Ltd* [1949] Ch 121, [1948] 2 All ER 995, CA.

7 Inheritance (Provision for Family and Dependants) Act 1975 s 23(1)(b) (as substituted: see note 6).

8 Inheritance (Provision for Family and Dependants) Act 1975 s 23(1)(c) (as substituted: see note 6).

9 Inheritance (Provision for Family and Dependants) Act 1975 s 23(1)(d) (as substituted: see note 6). A grant sealed under the Colonial Probates Act 1892 s 2 (see PARA 837) counts as a grant made in the United Kingdom for the purposes of the Inheritance (Provision for Family and Dependants) Act 1975 s 23, but is to be taken as dated on the date of sealing: s 23(2) (as so substituted).

10 Ie the date on which the Inheritance and Trustees' Powers Act 2014 came into force.
11 See *Re McBroom* [1992] 2 FLR 49 (the presence of some person entitled to administer the estate of the deceased was necessary). Such an application may be struck out as premature. Cf *Re Searle, Searle v Siems* [1949] Ch 73, [1948] 2 All ER 426 (a decision under the Inheritance (Family Provision) Act 1938 (repealed) and not cited in *Re McBroom;* where a grant of representation had been obtained before trial, the objection was merely procedural and could not be taken at trial).
12 Inheritance (Provision for Family and Dependants) Act 1975 s 23(1). See the text and note 10. A grant limited to pursuing a negligence claim in respect of a road accident in which the deceased had died was not a grant of representation for these purposes: *Re Johnson* [1987] CLY 3882. See also the cases cited in note 3.
13 Inheritance (Provision for Family and Dependants) Act 1975 s 20(1)(a).
14 Ie the court's powers under the Inheritance (Provision for Family and Dependants) Act 1975 s 6 (see PARA 594): see s 20(1)(b).
15 Inheritance (Provision for Family and Dependants) Act 1975 s 20(1)(b).
16 Inheritance (Provision for Family and Dependants) Act 1975 s 20(1).

598. Application for extension of time. The court has an unfettered discretion to permit an application to be made after the end of the period of the period of six months from the date on which representation with respect to the estate of the deceased is first taken out[1]. The discretion is to be exercised judicially[2] and the onus lies on the claimant to make out a substantial case for it being just and proper for the court to exercise its discretion to extend the time[3]. On the hearing of an application it is material to consider:

(1) how promptly and in what circumstances the claimant sought an extension of time (and how promptly the claimant warned the potential defendants of the proposed application)[4];
(2) whether negotiations commenced within the time limit[5];
(3) whether the estate has been distributed before a claim is made or notified[6]; and
(4) whether a refusal to extend time would leave the claimant without redress against anybody[7].

The court will also consider the strength of the applicant's case[8] and any other considerations relevant to the application[9].

In the case of a lengthy delay, it appears to be necessary to show that the application has been provoked by a particular event[10], which may be something for which the respondents were responsible[11] or something extraneous[12].

1 *Re Salmon, Coard v National Westminster Bank Ltd* [1981] Ch 167 at 175, [1980] 3 All ER 532 at 537 per Megarry V-C. An application for an extension of time should be expressly asked for in the claim form and the supporting witness statement or affidavit should set out the reasons why an extension should be granted: see *Practice Direction* [1976] 2 All ER 447, [1976] 1 WLR 418. The application is made when the claim form is issued: see *Re Chittenden, Chittenden v Doe* [1970] 3 All ER 562, [1970] 1 WLR 1618. The application should be the first item of relief claimed: *Re Greaves, Greaves v Greaves* [1954] 2 All ER 109, [1954] 1 WLR 760. Where there is more than one applicant each applicant should apply in time or make an application for an extension of time: *Re Trott, Trott v Miles* [1958] 2 All ER 296, [1958] 1 WLR 604.
2 *Re Salmon, Coard v National Westminster Bank Ltd* [1981] Ch 167 at 175, [1980] 3 All ER 532 at 537 per Megarry V-C; *Re Ruttie, Ruttie v Saul* [1969] 3 All ER 1633, [1970] 1 WLR 89.
3 *Re Salmon, Coard v National Westminster Bank Ltd* [1981] Ch 167 at 175, [1980] 3 All ER 532 at 537 per Megarry V-C; *Stock v Brown* [1994] 1 FLR 840, [1994] 2 FCR 1125; *Re Gonin* [1979] Ch 16, sub nom *Re Gonin, Gonin v Garmeson* [1977] 2 All ER 720; *Re W (a minor) (claim from deceased's estate)* [1995] 2 FCR 689, sub nom *Re C (leave to apply for provision)* [1995] 2 FLR 24.
4 *Re Salmon, Coard v National Westminster Bank Ltd* [1981] Ch 167 at 175, [1980] 3 All ER 532 at 537 per Megarry V-C. Late applications have been allowed in *Re Salmon, Coard v National Westminster Bank Ltd* (five and a half months out of time); *Stock v Brown* [1994] 1 FLR 840, [1994] 2 FCR 1125 (five and a half years out of time); *Re W (a minor) (claim from deceased's estate)* [1995] 2 FCR 689, sub nom *Re C (leave to apply for provision)* [1995] 2 FLR 24 (18 months out of time); *McNulty v McNulty* [2002] EWHC 123 (Ch), [2002] WTLR 737

(three and a half years out of time); but refused in *Re Dennis* [1981] 2 All ER 140 (19 months out of time); and *Re Gonin* [1979] Ch 16, sub nom *Re Gonin, Gonin v Garmeson* [1977] 2 All ER 720 (two and a half years out of time).

5 *Re Salmon, Coard v National Westminster Bank Ltd* [1981] Ch 167 at 175, [1980] 3 All ER 532 at 537 per Megarry V-C; *Re Ruttie, Ruttie v Saul* [1969] 3 All ER 1633, [1970] 1 WLR 89; *Re McNare, McNare v McNare* [1964] 3 All ER 373, [1964] 1 WLR 1255. An extension was granted where the delay was caused by the expectation that the executors would commence proceedings for the construction of the will and that the result of those proceedings might be materially to affect the provision to be made: *Re Bone, Bone v Midland Bank Ltd* [1955] 2 All ER 555, [1955] 1 WLR 703.

6 *Re Salmon, Coard v National Westminster Bank Ltd* [1981] Ch 167 at 175–176, [1980] 3 All ER 532 at 537–538 per Megarry V-C; *Stock v Brown* [1994] 1 FLR 840, [1994] 2 FCR 1125; *Re W (a minor) (claim from deceased's estate)* [1995] 2 FCR 689, sub nom *Re C (leave to apply for provision)* [1995] 2 FLR 24. Distribution alone may not defeat an application if the beneficiaries have not changed their position: *Re Salmon, Coard v National Westminster Bank Ltd* at 176 and 538 per Megarry V-C; *Re Longley, Longley and Longley v Longley* [1981] CLY 2885.

7 *Re Salmon, Coard v National Westminster Bank Ltd* [1981] Ch 167 at 176, [1980] 3 All ER 532 at 538 per Megarry V-C; *Re Gonin* [1979] Ch 16, sub nom *Re Gonin, Gonin v Garmeson* [1977] 2 All ER 720; *Re W (a minor) (claim from deceased's estate)* [1995] 2 FCR 689, sub nom *Re C (leave to apply for provision)* [1995] 2 FLR 24. See also *Re B* [2000] Ch 662, [2000] 1 All ER 665, CA. A prospective claim in negligence against the claimant's own solicitors is not to be totally ignored but is not a factor of any great importance and does not counterbalance other important factors: *Adams v Schofield* [2004] WTLR 1049, CA. A solicitor's ignorance of the limited time in which application might be made was not a circumstance which would justify an extension: *Re Greaves, Greaves v Greaves* [1954] 2 All ER 109, [1954] 1 WLR 760. See also *Re B* [1999] Ch 206, [1999] 2 All ER 425, reversed on other grounds at [2000] Ch 662, [2000] 1 All ER 665; *Re Parnall, Parnall v Hurst* [2003] WTLR 997; *Hannigan v Hannigan* [2006] WTLR 597, [2000] 2 FCR 650, CA; *Nesheim v Kosa* [2006] EWHC 2710 (Ch), [2007] WTLR 149.

8 The applicant must have an arguable case, a case fit to go to trial. The court's approach is similar to that it adopts when considering whether a defendant ought to have leave to defend in proceedings for summary judgment: *Re Dennis, Dennis v Lloyds Bank Ltd* [1981] 2 All ER 140 at 145 per Browne Wilkinson J relying on *Re Stone* (1969) 114 Sol Jo 36, CA. But a strong arguable case may be outweighed by other factors. See *Berger v Berger* [2013] EWCA Civ 1305, [2013] All ER (D) 319 (Oct) where leave was refused despite a strong arguable case (delay of six years from grant with no provoking factor to explain reason for application made it inappropriate to permit application).

9 The factors set out in *Re Salmon, Coard v National Westminster Bank Ltd* [1981] Ch 167, [1980] 3 All ER 532 and dealt with in notes 4–7 above were expressly stated to be non-exhaustive at 176 and 538. The following matters have been taken into account; the claimant had taken legal advice and made a considered decision (*Escrit v Escrit* [1982] 3 FLR 280, distinguished in *Chittock v Stevens* [2000] WTLR 643); those entitled to the deceased's property had been unaware of the fact for a lengthy period due to a mistake as to the ownership of the matrimonial home (*Chittock v Stevens* (a case on rectification but using the same principles)).

10 *Berger v Berger* [2013] EWCA Civ 1305 at [77], [2013] All ER (D) 319 (Oct) per Black LJ.

11 *McNulty v McNulty* [2002] EWHC 123 (Ch), [2002] WTLR 737 (late discovery of the true value of land comprised in the estate which the defendants had concealed).

12 *Stock v Brown* [1994] 1 FLR 840, [1994] 2 FCR 1125 (dramatic fall in interest rates).

599. Mode of application. Both the High Court and the County Court have unlimited jurisdiction in relation to applications under the Inheritance (Provision for Family and Dependants) Act 1975[1]. Furthermore, proceedings may be heard and disposed of by a Master or District Judge[2]. Proceedings are begun by the issue of a claim form[3], appropriately entitled[4]. Claimants must file the written evidence on which they intend to rely with the claim form[5]. The claim form must have exhibited to it an official copy of the grant of probate or letters of administration in respect of the deceased's estate and every testamentary document[6] in respect of which probate or letters of administration were granted[7]. However, where no grant has been obtained, the claimant may make a claim without naming a defendant and may apply for directions as to the representation of the estate[8].

Defendants must file and serve an acknowledgement of service and any written evidence on which they intend to rely within the appropriate time limits[9]. A defendant who is a personal representative and wishes to remain neutral in relation to the claim, and agrees to abide by any decision which the court may make, should state this in Section A of the acknowledgment of service form[10]. In the High Court proceedings may be assigned to the Chancery Division or the Family Division[11].

1 See the County Courts Act 1984 s 25; and COURTS AND TRIBUNALS vol 24 (2010) PARA 774. Procedure in both the High Court and the County Court is governed by CPR 57.14–57.16 and the Practice Direction to that Part. As to the CPR see CIVIL PROCEDURE vol 11 (2015) PARA 6 et seq.
2 See CPR 2.4; CPR PD 2B—*Allocation of cases to Levels of Judiciary*; *Practice Direction* [1999] 3 All ER 192; and CIVIL PROCEDURE vol 11 (2015) PARA 98.
3 CPR 57.16(1). A claim form should be issued under CPR Pt 8: see CPR PD 8A—*Alternative Procedure for Claims*; and CIVIL PROCEDURE vol 11 (2015) PARA 152 et seq. CPR 8.3, 8.5 (see CIVIL PROCEDURE vol 11 (2015) PARAS 154, 321) apply as modified by CPR 57: CPR 57.16(2).
4 Although the general rule for Chancery proceedings is that the title should include only the names of the parties, applications under the Inheritance (Provision for Family and Dependants) Act 1975 should commence 'In the Matter of the Inheritance (Provision for Family and Dependants) Act 1975': *Chancery Guide* (February 2016) para 8.8(iii).
5 CPR 8.5(1); and CIVIL PROCEDURE vol 11 (2015) PARA 154. The claimant's evidence must be served on the defendant with the claim form: CPR 8.5(2); and CIVIL PROCEDURE vol 11 (2015) PARA 154.
6 As to meaning of 'testamentary document' see PARA 870.
7 CPR 57.16(3).
8 CPR 57.16(3A). The written evidence must:
   (1) explain the reasons why it has not been possible for a grant to be obtained (CPR 57.16(3A)(a));
   (2) be accompanied by the original or a copy (if either is available) of the will or other testamentary document in respect of which probate or letters of administration are to be granted (CPR 57.16(3A)(b)); and
   (3) contain the following information, so far as known to the claimant:
      (a) brief details of the property comprised in the estate, with an approximate estimate of its capital value and any income that is received from it (CPR 57.16(3A)(c)(i));
      (b) brief details of the liabilities of the estate (CPR 57.16(3A)(c)(ii));
      (c) the names and addresses of the persons who are in possession of the documents relating to the estate (CPR 57.16(3A)(c)(iii); and
      (d) the names of the beneficiaries and their respective interests in the estate (CPR 57.16(3A)(c)(iv)).

   Where a claim is made in accordance with CPR 57.16(3A) the court may give directions as to the parties to the claim and as to the representation of the estate either on the claimant's application or on its own initiative: CPR 57.16(3B). The Inheritance (Provision for Family and Dependants) Act 1975 s 4 as amended confirms that nothing prevents the making of an application under the Act before representation with respect to the estate of the deceased person is taken out: CPR 57.16(3B).
9 See CPR 57.16(4). The appropriate time limit is 21 days after service of the claim form on the defendant, unless the claim form is served out of the jurisdiction in which case the period is seven days longer than the relevant period specified in CPR 6.35 or CPR PD 6B—*Service out of Jurisdiction*: CPR 57.16(4), (4A). A defendant who is a personal representative of the deceased must file and serve written evidence, which must include the information required by CPR PD 57—*Probate*: CPR 57.16(5).
10 CPR PD 57—*Probate* para 15. This will protect personal representatives from an adverse costs order.
11 CPR 57.15(1). Proceedings, if commenced in the Family Division are subject to the Civil Procedure Rules except that the provisions of the Family Proceedings Rules 1991, SI 1991/1247 relating to the drawing up and service of orders apply instead of the provisions in Part 40 and CPR PD 40B—*Judgments, Orders, Sale of Land etc*: CPR Pt 57.15(2). Transfer between these divisions under CPR 30.5, may be appropriate where there have been previous relevant proceedings in the other division, or where the application involves the taking of complicated accounts (for which special facilities exist in the Chancery Division), or where sufficient grounds can be shown by the parties: *Practice Direction* [1976] 2 All ER 447, [1976] 1 WLR 418.

600. Parties to application. On an application for financial provision the person applying must be the claimant and he should join the personal representatives as necessary defendants[1] together with the beneficiaries[2] most likely to be affected[3]. The court has power at any stage of the proceedings to order that a person be added as a new party[4]. Beneficiaries who have the same interest and unascertained persons may be the subject of a representation order[5].

If a claim is made jointly by two or more claimants and it later appears that any of the claimants have a conflict of interest, any claimant may choose to be represented at the hearing by separate solicitors or counsel or may appear in person; and if the court considers that claimants who are represented by the same solicitors or counsel ought to be separately represented it may adjourn the proceedings until they are[6].

1 *Re Lidington, Lidington v Thomas* [1940] WN 279; *Re Blight* (1946) 96 LJ 233. The personal representatives are required as defendants so that they can give information as to the estate: see CPR PD 57—*Probate* para 16; and PARA 602. If the claimant is a personal representative he should not be a defendant: *Payne v Little* (1851) 13 Beav 114; *Lewis v Nobbs* (1878) 8 ChD 591.

2 As to the meaning of 'beneficiary' under the Inheritance (Provision for Family and Dependants) Act 1975 see PARA 572 note 6. The term is no longer confined to persons benefiting under the will or intestacy.

3 This will normally mean the residuary legatees and/or any major specific legatees or devisees. The claimant may of course be sole executor.

4 Ie under CPR 19.2; CPR PD 19—*Addition and Substitution of Parties* (see CIVIL PROCEDURE vol 11 (2015) PARA 483).

5 See CPR 19.7; and CIVIL PROCEDURE vol 11 (2015) PARA 492 (reversing, in effect, *Re Knowles, Knowles v Birtwell* [1966] Ch 386, [1966] 2 All ER 480n).

6 CPR PD 57—*Probate* para 17. In such a case one of the applicants would strictly have to be made a defendant at that stage.

601. Transfers between courts. An application under the Inheritance (Provision for Family and Dependants) Act 1975 which is pending in either the High Court or the County Court may be transferred to within the County Court and the High Court[1] and between the High Court and the County Court[2].

Where proceedings have been commenced in the High Court, the High Court may order their transfer to a county court[3] or order proceedings in the Royal Courts of Justice or a district registry, or any part of such proceedings, to be transferred from the Royal Courts of Justice to a district registry or from a district registry to the Royal Courts of Justice or to another district registry[4].

Where proceedings have been commenced in the County Court, a court may order proceedings before that court or any part of them, to be transferred to another County Court hearing centre[5]. Proceedings commenced in the County Court can be transferred to the High Court by either the High Court[6] or the County Court[7].

An order made before the transfer of proceedings is not affected by the order to transfer[8].

1 See CPR Pt 30; and CIVIL PROCEDURE vol 11 (2015) PARA 105 et seq. See also COURTS AND TRIBUNALS.

2 See the County Courts Act 1984 ss 40(2), 41(1), 42(2) (see CIVIL PROCEDURE vol 11 (2015) PARA 108); CPR 30.3 (see CIVIL PROCEDURE vol 11 (2015) PARA 105).

3 See the County Courts Act 1984 s 40; and CIVIL PROCEDURE vol 11 (2015) PARA 108. As to the criteria for the transfer of a claim etc see the CPR 30; and CIVIL PROCEDURE vol 11 (2015) PARA 105.

4 See CPR 30.2(4); and CIVIL PROCEDURE vol 11 (2015) PARA 106. A district registry may order proceedings before it for the detailed assessment of costs to be transferred to another district registry: see CPR 30.2(5); and CIVIL PROCEDURE vol 11 (2015) PARA 105. The application should be made to the district registry in which the claim is proceeding: see CPR 30.2(6); and CIVIL PROCEDURE vol 11 (2015) PARA 106.

5 See CPR 30.2(1); and CIVIL PROCEDURE vol 11 (2015) PARA 107. The court may order proceedings before it for the detailed assessment of costs or for the enforcement of a judgment or order to be transferred to another County Court hearing centre if it is satisfied that the proceedings could be more conveniently or fairly taken elsewhere: see CPR 30.2(1); and CIVIL PROCEDURE vol 11 (2015) PARA 107. The application should be made to the County Court hearing centre in which the claim is proceeding: see CPR 30.2(3); and CIVIL PROCEDURE vol 11 (2015) PARA 107.

6 See the County Courts Act 1984 s 41; CPR 30.3; and CIVIL PROCEDURE vol 11 (2015) PARA 108.

7 See the County Courts Act 1984 s 42; CPR 30.3; and CIVIL PROCEDURE vol 11 (2015) PARA 108.

8 CPR 30.4(2); and CIVIL PROCEDURE vol 11 (2015) PARA 106.

602. Procedure subsequent to application for financial provision. A defendant who is a personal representative, and any other defendant who wishes to rely on written evidence, must file with the court written evidence in answer to the application[1] and, at the same time, serve a copy of the evidence on the other parties[2]. Written evidence must be filed with the acknowledgment of service[3]. The written evidence filed by a personal representative must state, to the best of his ability:

(1) full particulars of the value of the deceased's net estate[4];

(2) the person or classes of persons beneficially interested in the estate, giving the names and (in the case of those who are not already parties) the addresses of all living beneficiaries and the value of their interests so far as they are known[5];

(3) whether any living beneficiary is a child or person who lacks capacity[6] (and, if so, naming him)[7]; and

(4) any facts known to the representative which might affect the exercise of the court's statutory powers[8].

The rules as to case management[9], disclosure[10], evidence[11] and offers[12] apply to applications under the Inheritance (Provision for Family and Dependants) Act 1975 in the same way as to other applications. Where there is a dispute as to fact oral evidence will normally be directed so that cross-examination is likely. The evidence admissible is not limited to legal evidence in the strict sense[13], and may cover the deceased's state of mind[14]. The representatives must produce in court at the hearing the original grant of representation[15].

A copy of the order must be sent to the principal registry of the Family Division for entry and filing, and a memorandum of the order must be indorsed on or permanently annexed to the probate or letters of administration under which the estate is being administered[16].

Once an order has been made[17] any subsequent application, whether by a party or by any other person, must be made by the issue of an application notice[18].

1 See CPR 8.5(3), 57.16(5). As to the CPR see further CIVIL PROCEDURE vol 11 (2015) PARA 6 et seq.

2 CPR 8.5(4).

3 See CPR Pt 57.16(4A); and PARA 599.

4 CPR PD 57—*Probate* para 16(1). As to the meaning of 'net estate' see PARA 582 (definition applied by CPR PD 57—*Probate* para 16(1)). In practice it is often impossible to negotiate a compromise until the personal representatives have produced this evidence.

5 CPR PD 57—*Probate* para 16(2).

6 Ie within the meaning of the Mental Capacity Act 2005; see MENTAL HEALTH AND CAPACITY vol 75 (2013) PARA 601.

7 CPR PD 57—*Probate* para 16(3).

8 CPR PD 57—*Probate* para 16(4). Under the earlier Rules of the Supreme Court (see RSC 99(5) confirmed by *Practice Direction* [1976] 2 All ER 447, [1976] 1 WLR 418) personal representatives were required to disclose only those facts known to them; they were not obliged to make inquiries and observations in order to ascertain or confirm other matters. By contrast, CPR PD 57—*Probate*

para 16(4) contains no corresponding limitation; the opening words require personal representatives to provide the required information to the best of their ability so it may be necessary for them to seek additional information.

9 See CPR Pts 3, 26; and CIVIL PROCEDURE vol 11 (2015) PARA 200 et seq; CIVIL PROCEDURE vol 12 (2015) PARA 506.

10 See CPR Pt 31; and CIVIL PROCEDURE vol 12 (2015) PARA 621 et seq.

11 See CPR Pts 32–35; and CIVIL PROCEDURE vol 12 (2015) PARA 689. See also CPR 8.5; and CIVIL PROCEDURE vol 11 (2015) PARA 154.

12 See CPR Pts 36, 37; and CIVIL PROCEDURE vol 12A (2015) PARA 1657 et seq; CIVIL PROCEDURE vol 12A (2015) PARA 1674 et seq.

13 *Re Vrint, Vrint v Swain* [1940] Ch 920, [1940] 3 All ER 470. Earlier wills are admissible.

14 An application under the Inheritance (Provision for Family and Dependants) Act 1975 cannot be used as an indirect way of challenging a will for want of testamentary capacity: *Re Blanch, Blanch v Honhold* [1967] 2 All ER 468, [1967] 1 WLR 987; *Williams v Johns* [1988] 2 FLR 475.

15 CPR PD 57—*Probate* para 18.1. If the court makes an order under the Inheritance (Provision for Family and Dependants) Act 1975, the original grant (together with a sealed copy of the order) must be sent to the Principal Registry of the Family Division for a memorandum of the order to be endorsed on or permanently annexed to the grant in accordance with s 19(3) (see the text to note 16): CPR PD 57—*Probate* para 18.2.

16 Inheritance (Provision for Family and Dependants) Act 1975 s 19(3) (amended by the Administration of Justice Act 1982 s 52; and the Civil Partnership Act 2004 Sch 4 para 26(5)). This does not apply to an order made under the Inheritance (Provision for Family and Dependants) Act 1975 s 15(1) or s 15ZA(1) (see PARA 567): s 19(3) (as so amended). In the case of proceedings in the Family Division the provisions of the Family Procedure Rules 2010, SI 2010/2955 relating to the drawing up and service of orders apply: see CPR 57.15(2).

17 Ie under the Inheritance (Provision for Family and Dependants) Act 1975 s 1 (see PARAS 566–567).

18 As to application notices see CPR Pt 23; and CIVIL PROCEDURE vol 12 (2015) PARA 554 et seq.

603. Interim orders for financial provision. Where on an application for an order under the Inheritance (Provision for Family and Dependants) Act 1975[1] it appears to the court[2]:

(1) that the applicant is in immediate need of financial assistance[3], but it is not yet possible to determine what order, if any, should be made[4]; and

(2) that property forming part of the net estate[5] of the deceased is or can be made available to meet the applicant's needs[6],

the court has power to make an interim order.

It may order that, subject to such conditions or restrictions, if any, as it may impose[7] and to any further order, there is to be paid to the applicant out of the net estate of the deceased such sum or sums and (if more than one) at such intervals as the court thinks reasonable[8]; and it may order that, subject to the provisions of the Act, such payments are to be made until such date as the court may specify, not being later than the date on which the court either makes an order on the original application or decides not to exercise its powers to make an order on that application[9].

Applications for interim awards may be made to cover legal costs where the applicant cannot reasonably procure legal advice and representation by any other means[10].

In determining what interim order, if any, should be made the court must, so far as the urgency of the case admits, have regard to the same matters as those to which it is required to have regard on the principal application[11].

In both the High Court and the county court an application for an interim order need not be specifically made in the claim form[12].

Where the personal representative of a deceased person pays any sum directed by an interim order to be paid out of the deceased's net estate, he is not under any liability by reason of that estate not being sufficient to make the payment, unless at the time of making the payment he has reasonable cause to believe that the estate is not sufficient[13].

1 Ie under the Inheritance (Provision for Family and Dependants) Act 1975 s 2 (see PARAS 591–592): see s 5(1).
2 As to the meaning of 'court' see PARA 566 note 6.
3 Being forced to resort to borrowing and/or state assistance is clear evidence of immediate financial need: *Re Ralphs, Ralphs v District Bank Ltd* [1968] 3 All ER 285, [1968] 1 WLR 1522. See also *Barnsley v Ward* (18 January 1980, unreported), CA (inability to make mortgage repayments evidence of immediate financial need). The need to pay lawyers to conduct litigation challenging a will might be viewed as an immediate financial need, but the need to repay friends' loans which have been left outstanding for many years is not: *Smith v Smith* [2011] EWHC 2133 (Ch), [2011] 3 FCR 614.
4 Inheritance (Provision for Family and Dependants) Act 1975 s 5(1)(a).
5 As to the meaning of 'property' see PARA 582 note 2; and as to the meaning of 'net estate' see PARA 582.
6 Inheritance (Provision for Family and Dependants) Act 1975 s 5(1)(b). Property is available if it is readily saleable even if it might increase in value to the benefit of the estate if retained: *Barnsley v Ward* (18 January 1980, unreported), CA. The income produced by a legacy bequeathed to the applicant is available: *Re Ralphs, Ralphs v District Bank Ltd* [1968] 3 All ER 285, [1968] 1 WLR 1522.
7 See eg *Re Ralphs, Ralphs v District Bank Ltd* [1968] 3 All ER 285, [1968] 1 WLR 1522 (amount paid under interim order to be brought into account against income of legacy); *Barnsley v Ward* (18 January 1980, unreported), CA (condition requiring applicant to use best endeavours to obtain employment).
8 Inheritance (Provision for Family and Dependants) Act 1975 s 5(1). Section 2(2)–(4) (see PARAS 591–592) applies in relation to an interim order as it applies in relation to an order under s 2: s 5(2). For examples of interim orders see *Re Besterman, Besterman v Grusin* [1984] Ch 458, [1984] 2 All ER 656, CA (capital sum of £75,000 and income of £11,500); *Stead v Stead* [1985] FLR 16, CA (periodical payments of £1,500 per annum backdated to date of death); *Re Ralphs, Ralphs v District Bank Ltd* [1968] 3 All ER 285, [1968] 1 WLR 1522 (income from legacy to applicant); *Barnsley v Ward* (18 January 1980, unreported), CA (maintenance of £50 per week). An order under the Inheritance (Provision for Family and Dependants) Act 1975 s 2 may take account of payments made under an interim order: see s 5(4); and PARA 592.
9 Inheritance (Provision for Family and Dependants) Act 1975 s 5(1). As to the effect of the order see s 19(2); and PARA 593.
10 See *R v R* [2014] EWHC 611 (Fam) at [13] where Mostyn J summarised the principles applying to applications under the Legal Aid, Sentencing and Punishment of Offenders Act 2012 ss 49–54 (see MATRIMONIAL AND CIVIL PARTNERSHIP LAW vol 73 (2015) PARAS 512–514, 578) which, in relation to divorce and civil partnership dissolution proceedings, places the powers of the courts to award a costs allowance on a statutory footing. Although the new statutory provisions do not extend to proceedings under the Inheritance (Provision for Family and Dependants) Act 1975, where the application continues to be for an interim order, Mostyn J in *R v R* [2014] EWHC 611 (Fam) expressed the view that the principles set out at [13] ought to apply to such applications.
11 Inheritance (Provision for Family and Dependants) Act 1975 s 5(3). As to these matters see s 3; and PARAS 571–581.
12 An application for an interim order should be made in accordance with CPR Pt 23 supported by evidence of hardship and urgency.
13 Inheritance (Provision for Family and Dependants) Act 1975 s 20(2).

604. Costs in applications for financial provision. Subject to the terms of the Civil Procedure Rules[1], costs are at the discretion of the court[2]. Personal representatives are entitled to have their costs incurred in the capacity of personal representative paid out of the estate on the indemnity basis[3]. In all other cases, as in other forms of contested litigation, the costs of parties generally follow the event[4]. Where a claimant is successful but fails to obtain a judgment more advantageous than an offer to settle which qualifies as a Part 36 offer[5], the defendants are entitled to their costs from the date of the offer, together with interest on those costs from the expiry of the period specified for acceptance, unless the court considers it unjust so to order[6].

Parties may make offers to settle which do not meet the Part 36 requirements, in which case the offer will not have the consequences specified above[7]. The court is required to consider an offer to settle which does not comply with Part 36 when deciding what costs order to make[8].

Applications and appeals in small estates are discouraged, often by the imposition of adverse costs orders against the claimant in such cases[9].

1 See CPR Pts 36, 44–46; and CIVIL PROCEDURE vol 12A (2015) PARA 1653 et seq.

2 See CPR 44.3; and CIVIL PROCEDURE vol 12A (2015) PARAS 1698, 1701.

3 See CPR 46.3; and CIVIL PROCEDURE vol 12A (2015) PARA 1741. The costs of the obligatory witness statement or affidavit in answer should always come out of the estate. See also *Alsop Wilkinson (a firm) v Neary* [1995] 1 All ER 431, [1996] 1 WLR 1220; and the costs order in *Espinosa v Bourke* [1999] 1 FLR 747, [1999] 3 FCR 76, CA, in which the unsuccessful respondent's costs were paid out of the estate.

4 See eg *Millward v Shenton* [1972] 2 All ER 1025, [1972] 1 WLR 711, CA. As in other cases, costs will not necessarily follow the event where there is an interesting point of law involved or the interests of a person under a disability are involved: *Cameron v Treasury Solicitor* [1996] 2 FLR 716, [1997] 1 FCR 188, CA; *Re Watkins, Hayward v Chatterton* [1949] 1 All ER 695.

5 Ie an offer to settle made pursuant to the procedure under CPR Pt 36 (see CIVIL PROCEDURE vol 12A (2015) PARA 1653 et seq).

6 See CPR 36.17; and CIVIL PROCEDURE vol 12A (2015) PARA 1664. For a consideration of circumstances which may make this outcome 'unjust' see *Lilleyman v Lilleyman* [2012] EWHC 1056 (Ch), [2013] 1 Costs LR 25, [2013] 1 All ER 325 (defendants' unrealistic insistence throughout that the will made reasonable provision for the deceased's second wife and the 'no-holds barred' basis upon which they litigated the claim). As Part 36 offers are made without prejudice and therefore not disclosed to the court until the case has been decided, there is the possibility that a carefully calculated award made to a deserving applicant may be substantially eroded by costs: see *Lilleyman v Lilleyman* at [26] where Briggs J expressed, per curiam, 'a real sense of unease at the remarkable disparity between the costs regimes enforced, on the one hand for [Inheritance (Provision for Family and Dependants) Act 1975] cases (whether in the Chancery or Family Divisions) and, on the other hand, in financial relief proceedings arising from divorce. In the latter, my understanding is that the emphasis is all on the making of open offers, and that there is limited scope for costs shifting, so that the court is enabled to make financial provision which properly takes into account the parties' costs liabilities. In sharp contrast, the modern emphasis in [Inheritance (Provision for Family and Dependants) Act 1975] claims, like other ordinary civil litigation, is to encourage without prejudice negotiation and to provide for very substantial costs shifting in favour of the successful party'.

7 See CPR 36.2(2); and CIVIL PROCEDURE vol 12A (2015) PARA 1654.

8 See CPR 44.2; and CIVIL PROCEDURE vol 12A (2015) PARA 1698.

9 See PARA 574 note 7.

8. THE OFFICE OF REPRESENTATIVE

(1) REPRESENTATIVES GENERALLY

605. Origins of representatives. The right to appoint by will an executor to administer the personal estate and chattel interests in land of a testator derives from the earliest period of English law[1]. The right later extended also to real estate[2]. The appointment by the ecclesiastical courts of administrators in cases of intestacy or failure to appoint an executor developed much later[3]. Jurisdiction fell mainly to the ecclesiastical courts where personalty was concerned, to the common law courts where realty was concerned and to the courts of equity in those numerous cases where equity had intervened. The Chancery Division of the High Court now has jurisdiction in all matters concerning the administration and distribution of estates, including contentious probate jurisdiction, while non-contentious probate is assigned to the Family Division[4].

1 Co Litt 111 b note (1) per Hargrave.
2 Ie by virtue of 32 Hen 8 c 1 (Wills) (1540) and 34 & 35 Hen 8 c 5 (Wills) (1542) (both repealed). Until 1897, however, real estate vested in the heir on intestacy: see PARA 945 note 1.
3 See *Hewson v Shelley* [1914] 2 Ch 13 at 39, CA, per Phillimore LJ.
4 See PARA 678. The non-contentious probate jurisdiction of the Family Division is a hangover from the former jurisdiction of the ecclesiastical courts (to which the Family Division is the successor). When it was decided to reorganize the allocation of business in the High Court (by what became the Administration of Justice Act 1970) so that the Chancery Division took over contentious probate from the former Probate Divorce and Admiralty Division (now the Family Division) it was felt that there was little to be gained, and much difficulty would be involved, in transferring non-contentious probate to the Chancery Division as well: 795 HC Official Report (5th series), 4 February 1970, col 447.

606. Meaning of 'executor'. An executor[1] is the person appointed, ordinarily by the testator by his will or codicil[2], to administer the testator's property and to carry into effect the provisions of the will[3]. A special executor may be appointed or is deemed to be appointed in regard to settled land[4].

An executor de son tort is one who takes upon himself the office of an executor, or intermeddles with the goods of a deceased person, without having been appointed an executor by the testator's last valid will or by a codicil to that will[5], or without having obtained a grant of administration from a competent court[6]; and the term is therefore equally applicable in the case of an intestacy as in the case of testacy for there is no such term known to the law as an administrator de son tort[7].

1 An executor is properly described as 'executor of AB' or 'executor of the will of AB' or 'executor of the will and trustee of the estate of AB'.
2 As to the express appointment of an executor by will see PARAS 610–611. As to the appointment of an executor other than by express appointment by the testator see PARAS 610, 612–614.
3 See Shep Touch (7th Edn) p 400; 2 Bl Com 503. See also *Farrington v Knightly* (1719) 1 P Wms 544.
4 See PARA 821 et seq. Such appointment now gives rise to a grant of administration, not probate: see the Non-contentious Probate Rules 1987, SI 1987/2024, r 29; and PARA 822. See also PARA 615. As to executors according to the tenor see PARA 613.
5 The term is not properly applicable to a person appointed as an executor who acts before probate: *Rogers v Frank* (1827) 1 Y & J 409 at 414. As to the liability of an executor de son tort see PARA 1261 et seq.
6 For a definition see Went Off Ex (14th Edn) 320. See also PARA 605. As to the doctrine of relation back after a grant has been obtained see PARA 645 et seq.
7 Godolphin's Orphan's Legacy, Pt II, c 8 s 2.

607. Meaning of 'administrator'. An administrator[1] is a person appointed by a court of competent jurisdiction[2] to administer the property of a deceased person[3].

The office of administrator is said to be dative, because it derives from such a grant[4], whereas the office of executor derives from the will of the deceased person.

1 As to administrators generally see PARA 643 et seq; and as to the forms of grant of letters of administration see PARA 788 et seq. For the purposes of the Administration of Estates Act 1925, 'administration' means, with reference to the real and personal estate of a deceased person, letters of administration, whether general or limited, or with the will annexed or otherwise; and for the purposes of that Act 'administrator' means a person to whom administration is granted: s 55(1)(i), (ii). 'Real estate', save as provided in Pt IV (ss 45–52) (see PARA 485 note 6), means real estate, including chattels real, which by virtue of Pt I (ss 1–3) devolves on the personal representative of a deceased person: s 55(1)(xix). 'Will' includes codicil: s 55(1)(xxviii). An administrator is properly described as 'administrator of the estate of AB'.

2 The court of competent jurisdiction is the High Court, Family Division for non-contentious matters, and the High Court, Chancery Division and the county court in contentious matters: see PARAS 605, 678. Nothing in the Administration of Estates Act 1925 derogates from the powers of the High Court which exist independently of that Act or alters the distribution of business between the several divisions of the High Court, or operates to transfer any jurisdiction from the High Court to any other court: s 53(1). Nothing in that Act affects any unrepealed enactment in a public general Act dispensing with probate or administration as respects personal estate not including chattels real: s 53(2).

3 As to the circumstances in which and the persons to whom grants of administration are made see PARA 754 et seq.

4 See Shep Touch (7th Edn) p 400.

608. Meaning of 'personal representative'. The expression 'personal representative' is used to describe either an executor (whether he has proved the will or not[1]) or an administrator, and is defined by the Administration of Estates Act 1925, for the purposes of that Act, to mean the executor, original or by representation, or administrator for the time being of a deceased person[2]. It includes a special executor[3] and, as regards liability for inheritance tax, an executor de son tort[4]. The personal representatives represent the deceased in regard to his real estate to which he was entitled for an interest not ceasing on his death as well as in regard to his personal estate[5] and are deemed in law to be his heirs and assigns within the meaning of all trusts and powers[6].

1 See *Re Crowhurst Park, Sims-Hilditch v Simmons* [1974] 1 All ER 991 at 1001, [1974] 1 WLR 583 at 593–594 per Goulding J.

2 Administration of Estates Act 1925 s 55(1)(xi). The definitions in the Law of Property Act 1925 s 205(1)(xviii), the Trustee Act 1925 s 68(1) para (9) (see TRUSTS AND POWERS vol 98 (2013) PARA 3), and the Settled Land Act 1925 s 117(1)(xviii) (see SETTLEMENTS vol 91 (2012) PARA 598), are to this extent the same. 'Representation' means the probate of a will and administration, and the expression 'taking out representation' refers to the obtaining of the probate of a will or of the grant of administration: Administration of Estates Act 1925 s 55(1)(xx). As to the meaning of 'will' see PARA 607 note 1; and as to the meaning of 'administration' see PARA 607 note 1.

3 In the definition of 'personal representative', 'executor' includes a person deemed to be appointed executor as respects settled land: Administration of Estates Act 1925 s 55(1)(xi). Cf the Settled Land Act 1925 s 117(1)(xviii). See also PARA 821.

4 In the Inheritance Tax Act 1984, 'personal representative' includes any person by whom or on whose behalf an application for a grant of administration or for the resealing of a grant made outside the United Kingdom is made, and any such person as is mentioned in s 199(4)(a) (ie any person who takes possession of or intermeddles with, or otherwise acts in relation to, property so as to become liable as executor or trustee): see s 272. As to the liability of personal representatives for inheritance tax see ss 200(1)(a), 204(1). See further INHERITANCE TAXATION vol 59A (2014) PARAS 34, 256. As regards any liability for the payment of inheritance tax, 'personal representative' includes any person who takes possession of or intermeddles with the property of a deceased person without the authority of the personal representatives or the court: Administration of Estates Act 1925 s 55(1)(xi). 'Property' includes a thing in action and any interest in real or personal property: s 55(1)(xvii). As to the executor de son tort see PARA 1261 et seq.

5 Administration of Estates Act 1925 s 1(3).

6 Administration of Estates Act 1925 s 1(2). Covenants relating to land of a covenantee are deemed to be made with the covenantee and his successors in title; there is corresponding provision regarding covenants entered into by covenantors: see DEEDS AND OTHER INSTRUMENTS vol 32 (2012) PARA 457.

609. Personal representative as trustee. The expressions 'trust' and 'trustee' in the Trustee Act 1925 extend to the duties incident to the office of a personal representative, and 'trustee', where the context of that Act so admits, includes a personal representative[1]. The Trustee Act 2000 applies in relation to a personal representative administering an estate according to the law as it applies to a trustee carrying out a trust for beneficiaries[2]. The definition in the Trustee Act 1925 also applies for the purposes of the Limitation Act 1980, so that the provisions of that Act concerning trusts and trustees apply to the estates of deceased persons and personal representatives[3]. The administration of the property of a deceased person, whether he dies testate or intestate, is a trust within the meaning of the Judicial Trustees Act 1896[4], so the court may appoint a judicial trustee either to act jointly with or in place of a personal representative[5].

1 See the Trustee Act 1925 s 68(1) para (17); and TRUSTS AND POWERS vol 98 (2013) PARA 1. The Trustee Act 1925 does not, however, apply this definition to a special executor or to an executor de son tort: see s 68(1) para (9); and PARA 642 note 8. As to special executors see PARA 821; and as to the executor de son tort see PARA 1261 et seq.
2 See the Trustee Act 2000 s 35(1); and TRUSTS AND POWERS vol 98 (2013) PARA 1. For this purpose references in the trust instrument are to be read as references to the will: see s 35(2)(a); and TRUSTS AND POWERS vol 98 (2013) PARA 1. As to the meaning of 'trust instrument' see TRUSTS AND POWERS vol 98 (2013) PARA 371. References to a beneficiary or to beneficiaries, apart from the reference to a beneficiary in s 8(1)(b), are to be read as references to a person or the persons interested in the due administration of the estate, and the reference to a beneficiary in s 8(1)(b) is to be read as a reference to a person who under the will of the deceased or under the law relating to intestacy is beneficially interested in the estate: see s 35(2)(b), (c). As to the meaning of 'personal representative' see the Trustee Act 1925; and TRUSTS AND POWERS vol 98 (2013) PARA 3 (definition applied by the Trustee Act 2000 s 39(1)).
3 See the Limitation Act 1980 s 38(1); and LIMITATION PERIODS vol 68 (2016) PARA 916.
4 See the Judicial Trustees Act 1896 s 1(2); and TRUSTS AND POWERS vol 98 (2013) PARA 200. As to the power of the court to substitute or remove personal representatives under the Administration of Justice Act 1985 s 50 see PARA 1165.
5 See the Judicial Trustees Act 1896 s 1(1); and TRUSTS AND POWERS vol 98 (2013) PARA 200. See also *Re Ratcliff* [1898] 2 Ch 352 at 356. As to the transition of office from executorship to trusteeship see PARAS 1148–1150.

(2) THE EXECUTOR

(i) Appointment of Executors

610. Appointment of executors in general. An executor may be appointed:

(1) expressly by the testator in the body of his will[1];
(2) by the exercise of a power of nominating an executor conferred by the testator by his will[2];
(3) by implication from the testator's will, when the executor is known as an executor according to the tenor[3]; or
(4) by virtue of statutory provisions[4].

The executor may accept[5] or renounce[6] the office. Since his title derives from the will, he may in general act before probate has been granted[7].

1 See PARA 611. It was formerly possible to say 'that a will is the only bed where an executor can be begotten or conceived; for where no will is there can be no executor; and this is so conspicuous and evident to every low capacity that it needs no proof or illustration': Went Off Ex (14th Edn) 3.

2 See PARA 612.
3 See PARA 613.
4 See PARAS 614, 775–776, 821.
5 See PARAS 627–629.
6 See PARAS 630–632.
7 See further PARAS 633–636.

611. Express nomination by testator. An express appointment of an executor by the testator must name the appointee and describe him as executor, and must form part of a validly executed will[1]. A testator may appoint any number of executors, but probate may not be granted to more than four persons in respect of the same part of his estate[2].

If a question arises as to the identity of the person appointed, the court may exercise its probate jurisdiction[3] and may admit extrinsic evidence to assist (including evidence of the testator's intention) if the relevant wording of the will is meaningless, or is ambiguous on its face, or if evidence, other than evidence of the testator's intention, shows that the wording is ambiguous in the light of surrounding circumstances[4]. There may be such an uncertainty with regard to the person intended as to render the appointment entirely void[5].

If the court is satisfied that a will is so expressed that it fails to carry out the testator's intentions, in consequence of a clerical error or a failure to understand the testator's instructions, it may order rectification of the will[6].

1 See the Wills Act 1837 s 9; and PARA 60 et seq. In relation to deaths before 1 January 1983, a direction beneath the testator's signature did not form part of the will and could not have effect: *Re Woods* (1868) LR 1 P & D 556; *Re Dallow* (1866) LR 1 P & D 189; *Re Evans* (1923) 128 LT 669. In relation to deaths on or after 1 January 1983, the Wills Act 1837 s 9 (substituted by the Administration of Justice Act 1982 s 17) no longer requires the testator's signature to be at the end of the will: see PARA 66. Where a will, on its face, has been executed in accordance with s 9 and contains an attestation clause reciting that the requirements of that section have been complied with, the presumption of due execution applies and the strongest evidence is required to rebut it: see PARA 895. As to the right to have proved a will which appoints an executor even though there is no property to dispose of see PARA 707.

2 Senior Courts Act 1981 s 114(1). Section 114(1) refers to 'the same part of the estate' whereas the provision it re-enacts (the Supreme Court of Judicature (Consolidation) Act 1925 s 160(1) (repealed)) referred to 'the same property'. The latter words were construed in *Re Holland* [1936] 3 All ER 13 to mean 'the same estate'. In that case the testator appointed four general executors and one literary executor in respect of certain manuscripts, and it was held that one of the five must renounce before probate could be granted. The change in wording almost certainly means that *Re Holland* does not apply to the Senior Courts Act 1981 s 114(1), so that the estate as a whole may be the subject of grants to more than four personal representatives but no individual asset of the estate can be the subject of a grant to more than four. The court will not force an executor to renounce; if he is unwilling to do so, probate will be granted to the permitted number and power reserved to the other or others to prove on a vacancy occurring: see PARA 751. As to renunciation see PARAS 630–632.

3 See *Parkinson v Fawdon* [2009] EWHC 1953 (Ch), [2005] All ER (D) 322 (Jul). This jurisdiction is wider than its jurisdiction as a court of construction: see *Greenough v Martin* (1824) 2 Add 239 and *Methuen v Methuen* (1817) 2 Phillim 416 cited with approval in *Re Resch's Will Trusts, Far West Children's Health Scheme v Perpetual Trustee Co Ltd* [1969] 1 AC 514 at 547, [1967] 3 All ER 915 at 925 per Lord Wilberforce. In *Parkinson v Fawdon* Norris J concluded in relation to a modest estate that this allowed him to take into account:

(1) all the persons and facts known to the deceased at the time when he made his will; and
(2) any document which is substantially contemporaneous with the will and is of an important character and which shows who the testator had in mind and intended by the misdescription,

thereby clarifying the meaning of the will and making an application for rectification under the Administration of Justice Act 1982 s 20 (see note 6) unnecessary.

4 See the Administration of Justice Act 1982 s 21 (which applies where the testator died on or after 1 January 1983); and PARA 219. In relation to the wills of persons who died before 1 January 1983, the court would look at the surrounding circumstances at the date of the making of the will (*Grant v Grant* (1869) LR 2 P & D 8; *Re De Rosaz* (1877) 2 PD 66; *Re Twohill* (1879) 3 LR Ir

21; *Re Brake* (1881) 6 PD 217; *Re O'Reilly* (1873) 43 LJP & M 5). See, however, *Re Jones* (1927) 43 TLR 324, where the holder of an office was appointed executor, not by name, but by reference to the office, and probate was granted to the holder of the office at the death of the testator. The court would not, however, accept evidence of the testator's actual intention (*Re Twohill*; *Re Chappell* [1894] P 98) except where the description was equally applicable in all its parts to two or more persons (*Re Ashton* [1892] P 83; *Re Hubbuck* [1905] P 129; and see also *Charter v Charter* (1874) LR 7 HL 364). Where there was only one individual exactly answering to the name and description the court would not admit evidence to show that some other person was intended: *Re Peel* (1870) LR 2 P & D 46. This is probably still the case in relation to deaths on or after 1 January 1983, subject to the possibility of rectification (see text and note 6).

5 *Re Baylis* (1862) 2 Sw & Tr 613 (appointment of 'any two of my sons' held void for uncertainty); *Re Blackwell* (1877) 2 PD 72 (appointment of 'one of' the testator's sisters held void for uncertainty even though only one of them was living at his death. Cf *Re Horgan* [1971] P 50, [1969] 3 All ER 1570 (appointment of a firm of solicitors 'who may act through any partner or partners of that firm or their successors in business at the date of my death not exceeding two in number' held to be an appointment of all the partners in the firm at the date of the testator's death and not void for uncertainty). As to appointments of partnerships see PARA 623.

6 See the Administration of Justice Act 1982 s 20(1) (which applies where a testator died on or after 1 January 1983); PARA 187. The application for rectification may not, except with the permission of the court, be made after the end of six months from the date of the first grant of representation: see s 20(2); and PARA 187. Rectification will not be necessary if the meaning of the will can be established from evidence: see *Parkinson v Fawdon* [2009] EWHC 1953 (Ch), [2009] All ER (D) 322 (Jul); and note 3.

612. Nomination of executor by person other than testator. By his will a testator may authorise another to nominate an executor, and effect will be given to such nomination[1]. It would appear that the person authorised to nominate the executor may nominate himself[2].

1 *Re Cringan* (1828) 1 Hag Ecc 548; *Re Deichman* (1842) 3 Curt 123. The power to authorise is apparently not affected by the Wills Act 1837: see *Jackson and Gill v Paulet* (1851) 2 Rob Eccl 344.

2 *Re Ryder* (1861) 2 Sw & Tr 127. As to the position of a person empowered to appoint a trustee see TRUSTS AND POWERS vol 98 (2013) PARA 258 et seq.

613. Executor according to the tenor. Where a testator fails to nominate a person in express terms to be his executor, but upon a reasonable construction of his will it appears that a particular person has been appointed to perform the essential duties of an executor, such an appointment is sufficient to constitute that person an executor[1]. The person so appointed is called an 'executor according to the tenor'. Accordingly, a person will be an executor according to the tenor where, being made residuary legatee, he is appointed to discharge all lawful demands against the estate[2]; or where the testator, having directed all his just debts and funeral and testamentary expenses to be duly paid and satisfied as soon as conveniently may be after his decease, gives all his personal estate to a person upon trust to convert into money, get in and receive the same, and to divide the money so produced equally amongst his children[3]; or even where he is simply appointed to pay all the testator's just debts[4].

If a testator employs the word 'trustee' in a loose sense, the person appointed trustee is entitled to obtain probate of the will[5]; but where it cannot be gathered from the will that the person named as trustee is required to pay the testator's debts and generally to administer the estate, he is not entitled to probate[6]. A person may be an executor according to the tenor even in a case where other persons have been expressly appointed executors in the will[7]. The addressee of a testamentary instrument may be an executor according to the tenor[8].

1 *Re Montgomery* (1846) 5 Notes of Cases 99; *Re Collett* (1857) Dea & Sw 274; *Re Adamson* (1875) LR 3 P & D 253 (where the essential duties of an executor were defined to consist of the collection of the deceased's assets, the payment of his funeral expenses and debts and the discharge of the legacies); *Re Brown* (1910) 54 Sol Jo 478.

2 *Grant v Leslie* (1819) 3 Phillim 116. Where a person is appointed universal legatee merely, without any directions, it is not the practice to grant probate to him as executor according to the tenor, but he is entitled to administration with the will annexed: *Re Oliphant* (1860) 1 Sw & Tr 525; *Re Pryse* [1904] P 301, CA. As to administration with the will annexed see PARAS 788–792.
3 *Re Baylis* (1865) LR 1 P & D 21; *Re Drumm* [1931] NI 12. A direction to pay debts is not indispensable: *Re M'Kane* (1887) 21 LR Ir 1; *Re Way* [1901] P 345.
4 *Re Cook* [1902] P 114. See also *Re Manly* (1862) 3 Sw & Tr 56; *Re Bell* (1878) 4 PD 85; *Re Wilkinson* [1892] P 227; *Re Way* [1901] P 345.
5 *Re Earl Leven and Melville* (1889) 15 PD 22; *Re Russell, Re Laird* [1892] P 380; *Re Shaw* (1895) 73 LT 192; *Re Nussey* (1898) 78 LT 169; *Re Kirby* [1902] P 188.
6 *Boddicott and Hamilton v Dalzell* (1756) 2 Lee 294 at 296; *Re Jones* (1861) 2 Sw & Tr 155; *Re Fraser* (1870) LR 2 P & D 183; *Re Punchard* (1872) LR 2 P & D 369; *Re Toomy* (1864) 3 Sw & Tr 562; *Re Lowry* (1874) LR 3 P & D 157; *Re Love* (1881) 7 LR Ir 178; *Re Mackenzie* [1909] P 305.
7 *Grant v Leslie* (1819) 3 Phillim 116; *Re Brown* (1877) 2 PD 110; *Re Lush* (1887) 13 PD 20; *Re Wright* (1908) 25 TLR 15.
8 *Re Manly* (1862) 3 Sw & Tr 56; *Re Stanley* [1916] P 192 (unattested letter held to be a privileged will within the meaning of Wills Act 1837 s 11; see PARA 80).

614. Statutory appointment of executors. The court has statutory power to appoint additional personal representatives in specified cases[1], and special executors are statutorily deemed to have been appointed by the will in relation to settled land in certain circumstances[2].

1 See the Senior Courts Act 1981 s 114(4); and PARAS 775–776.
2 See the Administration of Estates Act 1925 s 22; and PARA 821. Such appointment gives rise to a grant of administration, not probate: see the Non-Contentious Probate Rules 1987, SI 1987/2024, r 29; and PARA 822.

615. General and special executors. In the ordinary course, a person is appointed executor indefinitely and is therefore charged with the administration of the whole will and of all the testator's property[1]. The testator may, however, limit the appointment[2], or executors may be deemed to be appointed by statute for limited purposes or special property, and such an executor is called a special executor[3]. The directions in a will limiting the appointment must be clear[4]. Where special executors are appointed for limited purposes or particular property and other executors are appointed generally for all other purposes and property, those other executors are called the general executors[5].

1 Such an executor has been called a universal executor: *Re Parker's Trusts* [1894] 1 Ch 707 at 720. He has also been called a general executor, but that term is now usually applied to executors who have the general administration of the estate where there are special executors for certain specified property.
2 The usual limitation is in the appointment of special executors of property outside the jurisdiction. The wills of testators who have foreign property often appoint separate executors or trustees of the foreign property. Where it is desired to place particular properties which are within the jurisdiction in the care of particular persons, separate executors may be appointed, for example literary executors or business executors. In such a case, however, it may be preferable to appoint executors for the whole estate, but separate sets of trustees for each particular property. A special grant may be required for settled land: see PARA 821. As to the appointment of different executors for different properties see further PARA 616. As to the application of the statutory limitation of the number of executors where general executors and a special executor are appointed see PARA 611.
3 See PARA 821.
4 *Lynch v Bellew and Fallon* (1820) 3 Phillim 424.
5 Although called general executors, the grant to them will be a 'save and except' one and not a 'general' grant of the whole estate devolving by law on the personal representatives.

616. Different executors for different properties. A testator may appoint different executors for different parts of his estate[1]; he may appoint certain persons executors of his property abroad or of his property in a particular country and others of his property in England[2], and indeed this is commonly done. He may also appoint separate executors of real estate, including real estate vested in him as sole trustee. The High Court may grant probate or administration in respect of any part of the estate of a deceased person, limited in any way the court thinks fit[3]. Where the deceased's estate is known to be insolvent the grant of representation to the estate vested in the deceased beneficially cannot be severed, except as regards a trust estate in which he had no beneficial interest[4]. If special executors are appointed by the will but do not prove and the general executors obtain a grant of probate, the special executors, merely by obtaining a limited grant at a later date, cannot invalidate the acts of general executors done pursuant to the grant to them[5].

An executor appointed solely to administer property abroad is not entitled to probate in this country[6], and a person who is nominated executor only of the property not specified in the will, and who is precluded from dealing with the property disposed of by the will, is similarly disentitled, but he may obtain letters of administration with the will annexed[7].

1 Went Off Ex (14th Edn) 29; *Rose v Bartlett* (1633) Cro Car 292. See also PARA 615 note 2. For the limit on the number of executors to whom a grant may be made see PARA 611.
2 *Re Harris* (1870) LR 2 P & D 83; *Re Cohen's Executors and LCC* [1902] 1 Ch 187.
3 Senior Courts Act 1981 s 113(1). As to applications under s 113 see PARA 819. Probate or administration may be granted where the deceased left no estate: Administration of Justice Act 1932 s 2(1) (repealed, but the Senior Courts Act 1981 s 25 provides that the court has the probate jurisdiction which it had immediately before the commencement of the Senior Courts Act 1981 (see PARA 677)).
4 Senior Courts Act 1981 s 113(2). See note 3.
5 *Re Parker's Trusts* [1894] 1 Ch 707. See also the Administration of Estates Act 1925 s 8; and PARA 629. As to the devolution of real estate see PARA 945. As to special personal representatives for settled land see PARA 821.
6 *Velho v Leite* (1864) 3 Sw & Tr 456.
7 *Re Wakeham* (1872) LR 2 P & D 395. As to administration with the will annexed see PARAS 788–792.

617. Conditional and substituted appointments of executors. A testator may appoint his or her spouse to be executor during the widowhood or widowerhood of the spouse[1], or his son to be his executor upon attaining his majority[2]. He may make the appointment conditional upon the happening of a certain event[3], and he may provide for the determination of the appointment or the substitution of one executor for another upon the happening of a given event[4].

1 Went Off Ex (14th Edn) 29.
2 Went Off Ex (14th Edn) 22–23. As to the appointment of minors see PARA 620.
3 *Re Langford* (1867) LR 1 P & D 458.
4 *Re Lighton* (1828) 1 Hag Ecc 235; *Re Johnson* (1858) 1 Sw & Tr 17; *Re Betts* (1861) 30 LJPM & A 167; *Re Lane* (1864) 33 LJPM & A 185; *Re Foster* (1871) LR 2 P & D 304; *Re Freeman* (1931) 146 LT 143, 75 Sol Jo 764.

618. Failure of appointment of executor as a result of marriage or civil partnership being dissolved or annulled. Where, after a testator has made a will his marriage is dissolved or annulled[1], and he dies on or after 1 January 1996[2], or his civil partnership is dissolved or annulled[3], any provisions of the will appointing executors or trustees which appoint the testator's former spouse or civil partner take effect as if the former spouse or civil partner had died on the date of the dissolution or annulment of the marriage, or civil partnership, except in so far as a contrary intention appears by the will[4].

1 Ie either by a decree of a court of civil jurisdiction in England and Wales, or by a court of some other jurisdiction and the divorce or annulment is recognised in England and Wales: see the Wills Act 1837 s 18A(1); and PARA 178. Marriage includes marriage of a same sex couple; and spouse includes a person who is married to a person of the same sex: see PARAS 24, 87.
2 In relation to testators who died on or after 1 January 1983 but before 1 January 1996, a will which appointed the testator's then spouse as an executor had effect as if that appointment were

omitted, if the marriage had been dissolved or annulled after the will was made, except in so far as a contrary intention appeared by the will: see Wills Act 1837 s 18A(1); and PARA 177.

3 Ie either by a decree of a court of civil jurisdiction in England and Wales, or by a court of some other jurisdiction, and the dissolution or annulment is entitled to recognition in England and Wales by virtue of the Civil Partnership Act 2004 Pt 5 Chapter 3: see the Wills Act 1837 s 18C(1); and PARA 177.

4 See the Wills Act 1837 ss 18A(1), 18C(1); and PARA 177.

(ii) Persons Eligible for Appointment as Executor

619. The choice of executor. No restriction whatever exists upon the choice of an executor. The monarch may be appointed and if appointed will nominate trustees to execute for her and auditors to whom the trustee are to account[1]. An alien may be appointed[2]. A convicted criminal may be appointed[3]; but the fact that the executor is serving a prison sentences may make it impossible for him to administer the estate so that the court may grant administration to others under its discretionary powers[4].

1 Went Off Ex (14th Edn) 39; 4 Co Inst 335; Bac Abr, Prerogative (E) 1; Chitty's Law of the Prerogatives of the Crown p 379. See also CONSTITUTIONAL AND ADMINISTRATIVE LAW vol 20 (2014) PARA 309; CROWN AND CROWN PROCEEDINGS.

2 As to an alien's right to hold property see BRITISH NATIONALITY vol 4 (2011) PARA 411.

3 See eg *Smethurst v Tomlin and Bankes* (1861) 2 Sw & Tr 143 at 147.

4 *Re S* [1968] P 302, [1967] 2 All ER 150. As to the court's discretionary power see PARA 758.

620. Minors as executors. A minor[1] may be appointed executor[2], but he cannot validly exercise the office until he has attained full age[3]. Where a testator by his will[4] appoints a minor to be an executor, the appointment does not operate to vest in the minor the estate[5], or any part of the estate, of the testator, or to constitute him a personal representative for any purpose, unless and until probate is granted to him in accordance with probate rules[6].

Where a person to whom a grant would otherwise be made is a minor[7], administration for his use and benefit, limited until he attains the age of eighteen years, must, unless otherwise directed, be granted to a parent of his with parental responsibility[8], to another person with parental responsibility, to a guardian or special guardian of his, an adoption agency with parental responsibility, a local authority which has or is deemed to have parental responsibility or the residuary beneficiary, or to such other person as the court thinks fit until the minor attains the age of 18[9]. Similarly, if there are several executors and all are minors, administration with the will annexed will be granted to their parents or guardians or special guardians or other persons with parental responsibility, adoption agency with parental responsibility, local authority which has or is deemed to have parental responsibility or the residuary beneficiary, until the first of the co-executors attains that age[10]. The administration will then terminate[11] and the executor who first attains that age will be entitled to probate[12]. If adult executors are appointed jointly with a minor, probate may be granted to the executor or executors not under disability[13] with power reserved to the minor executor, and the minor is entitled to apply for probate on attaining the age of 18[14]. In such a case, no grant of administration for the use and benefit of the minor may be made unless the executors who are not under a disability renounce or, on being cited to accept or refuse a grant, fail to make an effective application for it[15].

1 Ie a person under the age of 18 years: see the Family Law Reform Act 1969 ss 1, 9, 12; and CHILDREN AND YOUNG PERSONS vol 9 (2012) PARAS 1–3.

2 2 Bl Com (14th Edn) 503; 2 Swinburne on Wills (7th Edn) 652; Went Off Ex (14th Edn) 390. An unborn child may be appointed (2 Bl Com (14th Edn) 503; Godolphin's Orphan's Legacy, Pt II, c 9 s 2), and if more than one child is born, all will be admitted executors (Godolphin's Orphan's Legacy (3rd Edn) 102).

3 See the Senior Courts Act 1981 s 118; and the Non-contentious Probate Rules 1987, SI 1987/2024, r 32 (see PARA 795).

4 'Will' includes a nuncupative will and any testamentary document of which probate may be granted: Senior Courts Act 1981 s 128. As to nuncupative wills see PARA 730. See note 3.

5 'Estate' means real and personal estate, and 'real estate' includes:

(1) chattels real and land in possession, remainder or reversion and every interest in or over land to which the deceased person was entitled at the time of his death; and

(2) real estate held on trust or by way of mortgage or security, but not money secured or charged on land (Senior Courts Act 1981 s 128 (definition amended by the Trusts of Land and Appointment of Trustees Act 1996 s 25(2), Sch 4)).

See note 3.

6 Senior Courts Act 1981 s 118. See note 3. 'Probate rules' means rules of court made under s 127 (see PARA 685): s 128. As to the rules of court made under this provision see the Non-Contentious Probate Rules 1987, SI 1987/2024. As to the grant of probate see the text to note 9.

7 Ie where all persons appointed executors are under disability and are or include minors, or where all those persons so appointed who are not under disability renounce or fail to take a grant after being cited to do so: see the Non-contentious Probate Rules 1987, SI 1987/2024, rr 32, 33; and PARAS 795, 798.

8 As to parental responsibility see CHILDREN AND YOUNG PERSONS vol 9 (2012) PARA 150 et seq.

9 See the Non-Contentious Probate Rules 1987, SI 1987/2024, r 32; and PARA 795.

10 See the authorities cited in note 11; and PARA 798.

11 Shep Touch (7th Edn) p 491; Godolphin's Orphan's Legacy, Pt II, c 30 s 6; 4 Burn's Ecclesiastical Law (9th Edn) 384 et seq; Bac Abr, Executors and Administrator (B) 1(3); *Bennet v Baud* (1664) 1 Sid 185; *Taylor v Watts* (1676) Freem KB 425.

12 See the Non-contentious Probate Rules 1987, SI 1987/2024, rr 32, 33; and PARAS 795, 798.

13 *Pigot v Gascoin* (1616) 1 Brownl 46; *Foxwist v Tremain* (1670) 1 Mod Rep 47; *Colborne v Wright* (1678) 2 Lev 239; Bac Abr, Executors and Administrators (B); Com Dig, Administration (B 12). As to the reservation of power to the minor to prove the will at a later date see PARA 798.

14 See the Non-contentious Probate Rules 1987, SI 1987/2024, r 33(1); and PARA 798.

15 See the Non-contentious Probate Rules 1987, SI 1987/2024, r 33(2); and PARA 798.

621. Grants where person appointed as executor lacks mental capacity. If the person appointed executor lacks capacity[1] to manage his affairs, probate will not be granted to him during the period of disability, but if he is sole executor letters of administration with the will annexed will be granted to some person on his behalf[2]. If a person who lacks capacity to manage his affairs is appointed one of several executors, power will be reserved to him to prove after the removal of the disability[3].

1 Ie within the meaning of the Mental Capacity Act 2005; see MENTAL HEALTH AND CAPACITY vol 75 (2013) PARA 601.

2 See the Non-Contentious Probate Rules 1987, SI 1987/2024, r 35; and PARA 804.

3 *Evans v Tyler* (1849) 2 Rob Eccl 128.

622. Corporations as executors. A company or other corporate body may be appointed executor[1], but cannot itself take a grant unless it is a trust corporation[2]. The practice[3] as regards companies or other corporate bodies which are not trust corporations[4] is to grant administration to a nominee, or in the case of a foreign corporation to an attorney, for the use and benefit of the corporation[5]. Where a trust corporation is named in a will[6] as executor, the High Court may grant probate to the corporation either solely or jointly with another person, as the case may require, and the corporation may act as executor accordingly[7]; and, similarly, administration[8] may be granted to a trust corporation either solely or jointly with another person, and the corporation may act as administrator accordingly[9].

1 A corporation sole may also be an executor: Went Off Ex (14th Edn) 39; Godolphin's Orphan's Legacy, Pt II, c 6. For examples of corporations sole see CORPORATIONS

vol 24 (2010) PARA 315. A corporation sole may be granted probate: *Re Haynes* (1842) 3 Curt 75. The appointment of a corporation sole as executor during a vacancy in the office is valid, but may be renounced or disclaimed by the successor in the office: see the Law of Property Act 1925 s 180(3); and CORPORATIONS vol 24 (2010) PARA 448.

The Public Trustee is a corporation sole with power to accept probates or letters of administration of any kind either as principal or as agent for any other person: see the Public Trustee Act 1906 ss 1, 6(1); the Public Trustee Rules 1912, SR & O 1912/348, r 6(c); and TRUSTS AND POWERS vol 98 (2013) PARA 211. However, this provision is overshadowed in relation to the Public Trustee's capacity to act as an executor by the fact that the Public Trustee is also a trust corporation (see note 4). As to administration by the Public Trustee see PARA 784. As to insolvent estates generally see PARA 980 et seq. As to fees see PARA 656. As to the Public Trustee generally see TRUSTS AND POWERS vol 98 (2013) PARA 206 et seq.

2 See the Non-contentious Probate Rules 1987, SI 1987/2024, r 36; and PARA 783. Older authorities state that a corporation aggregate cannot take a grant because it cannot take the oath necessary to probate (Went Off Ex (14th Edn) 39; 1 Bl Com (14th Edn) 476), and it is notable that the Senior Courts Act 1981 s 115(3) expressly enables an authorised officer of a trust corporation to act on behalf of the corporation in the matters of oaths and affidavits (see note 7).

3 It was formerly the practice, where a corporation aggregate was named executor, to appoint a person styled a syndic to receive administration with the will annexed, and the syndic was sworn like any other administrator: see eg *Re Darke* (1859) 1 Sw & Tr 516; *Re Hunt* [1896] P 288. Where a corporation aggregate was appointed together with one or more individual executors a grant could not be made to the syndic unless all those individually appointed renounced probate: *Re Martin* (1904) 90 LT 264. The Administration of Justice Act 1920 s 17 (repealed) gave power to grant probate to a corporation having its principal place of business in the United Kingdom by its corporate name. Section 17 was repealed by the Administration of Estates Act 1925 s 56, Sch 2 Pt II. The effect of the repeal was to restore the former practice of granting administration to a nominee, except in the case of trust corporations.

4 'Trust corporation' means the Public Trustee or a corporation either appointed by the court in any particular case to be a trustee or authorised by rules made under the Public Trustee Act 1906 s 4(3), to act as custodian trustee: Administration of Estates Act 1925 s 55(1)(xxvi); Senior Courts Act 1981 s 128. For the purposes of the Administration of Estates Act 1925 and the Senior Courts Act 1981, the expression 'trust corporation' includes the Treasury Solicitor, the Official Solicitor and any person holding any other official position prescribed by the Lord Chancellor, and, in relation to the property of a bankrupt, includes the trustee in bankruptcy, and, in relation to charitable ecclesiastical and public trusts, also includes any local or public authority so prescribed, and any other corporation constituted under the laws of the United Kingdom or any part of it which satisfies the Lord Chancellor that it undertakes the administration of any such trusts without remuneration, or that by its constitution it is required to apply the whole of its net income after payment of outgoings for charitable ecclesiastical or public purposes, and is prohibited from distributing, directly or indirectly, any part of it by way of profits amongst any of its members, and is authorised by him to act in relation to such trusts as a trust corporation: Law of Property (Amendment) Act 1926 s 3(1) (amended by the Senior Courts Act 1981 s 152(1), Sch 5; and the Deregulation Act 2015 Sch 16 Pt 1 para 2(1), (5)). See note 2.

As to the corporations authorised to act as custodian trustees see the Public Trustee Rules 1912, SR & O 1912/348, r 30; and TRUSTS AND POWERS vol 98 (2013) PARA 234. The Church of England Pensions Board is also included by virtue of the Clergy Pensions Measure 1961 s 31: see ECCLESIASTICAL LAW vol 34 (2011) PARA 537. The expression 'Treasury Solicitor' means the solicitor for the affairs of Her Majesty's Treasury, and includes the solicitor for the affairs of the Duchy of Lancaster: Law of Property (Amendment) Act 1926 s 3(2). As to the meaning of 'United Kingdom' see PARA 4 note 7. As to the Treasury Solicitor see CONSTITUTIONAL AND ADMINISTRATIVE LAW vol 20 (2014) PARA 281. As to the Official Solicitor see COURTS AND TRIBUNALS vol 24 (2010) PARA 755. As to the Lord Chancellor see CONSTITUTIONAL AND ADMINISTRATIVE LAW vol 20 (2014) PARA 255 et seq. As to the solicitor for the Duchy of Lancaster see PARA 782.

For the purposes of the Non-Contentious Probate Rules 1987, SI 1987/2024, 'trust corporation' means a corporation within the meaning of the Senior Courts Act 1981 s 128 as extended by the Law of Property (Amendment) Act 1926 s 3(1): Non-Contentious Probate Rules 1987, SI 1987/2024, r 2(1).

See *Re Skinner* [1958] 3 All ER 273, [1958] 1 WLR 1043 (effect of scheme of arrangement and amalgamation between trust corporation and another company: see PARA 628). See also *Re Bigger* [1977] Fam 203, [1977] 2 All ER 644 (probate can be granted to the Bank of Ireland; distinguishing *Re Barlow* [1933] P 184).

5 See the Non-contentious Probate Rules 1987, SI 1987/2024, r 36(4); and PARA 813. See also *Practice Direction* [1956] 1 All ER 305, [1956] 1 WLR 127.

6 As to the meaning of 'will' see PARA 620 note 4.
7 Senior Courts Act 1981 s 115(1)(a). See note 2. Probate or administration may not be granted to any person as nominee of a trust corporation: s 115(2). Cf note 3. Any officer authorised for the purpose by a trust corporation or its directors or governing body may, on behalf of the corporation, swear affidavits, give security and do any other act which the court may require with a view to the grant to the corporation of probate or administration, and the acts of an officer so authorised are binding on the corporation: s 115(3). See also the Non-Contentious Probate Rules 1987, SI 1987/2024, r 36; and PARA 783.
8 'Administration' includes all letters of administration of the effects of deceased persons, whether with or without a will annexed, and whether granted for general, special or limited purposes: Senior Courts Act 1981 s 128. See note 2.
9 Senior Courts Act 1981 s 115(1)(b). See also note 7.

623. Partnerships as executors. The appointment as executors of an ordinary partnership firm is considered to be an appointment not of the firm collectively, but of the individuals composing the firm[1]. The appointment only extends to the members of the firm at the date of the will[2], unless a contrary intention is there expressed[3]. 'Partner' means profit sharing partner, unless the will states otherwise[4].

Where a firm converts to a limited liability partnership after the date of the will, the appointment takes effect as an appointment of the profit sharing members of the limited liability partnership[5].

1 *Re Fernie* (1849) 6 Notes of Cases 657; *Re Horgan* [1971] P 50, [1969] 3 All ER 1570. As to partnerships generally see PARTNERSHIP.
2 *Re Fernie* (1849) 6 Notes of Cases 657. Accordingly, the dissolution of the firm after the date of the will does not affect the appointment: *Re Fernie*.
3 For a case where a contrary intention was held to exist see *Re Horgan* [1971] P 50, [1969] 3 All ER 1570. If there are more partners than can take a grant, or the testator expresses a wish that not more than a specified number take out a grant, or it is otherwise not appropriate for all of them to do so, power to prove will be reserved to the partners who do not take a grant. As to the statutory limit on numbers see PARA 611. An appointment of eg 'any two of the partners' in a firm would be void for uncertainty: see PARA 611 note 5.

As to the appointment at the testator's death of the partners in a solicitor's firm as executors see further articles by RT Oerton in 64 Law Society's Gazette (1967) 244, 343, and 67 Law Society's Gazette (1970) 46. As to the procedure when a grant is being obtained under such an appointment see PARA 729.
4 *Re Rogers* [2006] EWHC 753 (Ch) at [14], [2006] 2 All ER 792, [2006] 1 WLR 1577 per Lightman J. The oath for executors should, therefore, describe applicants for a grant as 'profit sharing partners'. It is open to a testator to define partner more widely to include salaried partners.
5 See *Re Rogers* [2006] EWHC 753 (Ch) at [14], [2006] 2 All ER 792, [2006] 1 WLR 1577 per Lightman J. The judgment did not address the effect on an appointment of an incorporated practice. However a note circulated from the Leeds District Registry shortly after the decision in *Re Rogers* stated that in the view of the probate registrars such an appointment would take effect as an appointment of the profit sharing members of the company.

624. Insolvent persons as executors. The courts will not accept the disabilities recognised by the canon law on moral or religious grounds[1]; nor will probate be refused solely on the ground of the executor's bankruptcy or insolvency[2]. However, the High Court has a discretion to pass over the person entitled to a grant and appoint another person as administrator, if it appears to be necessary or expedient to do so[3].

The courts of equity have assumed the jurisdiction of restraining a bankrupt executor from acting and of appointing a receiver[4]; if it is necessary to bring an action to recover any part of the estate, the court will compel the executor to allow his name to be used[5]. The jurisdiction is not exercised where the testator himself was at the time of making his will or later aware of the executor's financial position[6]. Where there is a solvent executor willing to act, the court will restrain the bankrupt executor from acting, but will refrain from appointing a receiver[7]. In view of this equitable jurisdiction it is thought that, even before the transfer of contentious probate business to the Chancery Division[8], probate would have been refused in any case where a court of equity would have intervened[9], and that probate would now be refused in such a case[10].

1 *R v Raines* (1698) 1 Ld Raym 361.
2 *Hill v Mills* (1691) 1 Salk 36. See generally BANKRUPTCY AND INDIVIDUAL INSOLVENCY.
3 See the Senior Courts Act 1981 s 116(1); and PARA 759. Any grant of administration under this section may be limited in any way the court thinks fit: s 116(2).
4 As to the appointment of a receiver see CPR Pt 69; and CIVIL PROCEDURE vol 11 (2015) PARA 196.
5 *R v Simpson* (1764) 1 Wm Bl 456; *Utterson v Mair* (1793) 2 Ves 95; *Gladdon v Stoneman* (1808) 1 Madd 143n (cited in *Howard v Papera* (1815) 1 Madd 142); *Re Hopkins, Dowd v Hawtin* (1881) 19 ChD 61, CA.
6 *Stainton v Carron Co* (1854) 18 Beav 146 at 161; *Langley v Hawk* (1820) 5 Madd 46.
7 *Bowen v Phillips* [1897] 1 Ch 174.
8 See PARA 678.
9 This would seem to have been the effect of the transfer to the High Court of the jurisdiction of the former courts of equity and probate by the Judicature Acts (see PARA 677; and COURTS AND TRIBUNALS vol 24 (2010) PARA 699) and of the deference shown to one division of the High Court by another. As to the relationship between the court to which probate jurisdiction is assigned and other divisions of the High Court see also PARAS 669–670, 678, 810, 828.
10 As to the court's discretion to make grants in special circumstances see PARA 759.

625. Debtors as executors. The appointment of a debtor of the testator as executor releases the debt in law because the executor cannot sue himself[1]. The effect is the same where the debtor is jointly, or jointly and severally liable with some other person[2]. If the executor survives the testator but dies before proving the will or is cited to take out probate and does not appear or renounces probate, his rights in respect of the executorship wholly cease and the testator's estate devolves as if he had not been appointed executor[3]. In these cases there can therefore be no release of the debt[4], but in any other case, for example where power is reserved to the executor to prove the will, the debt will be released at law[5].

On the other hand, in equity the executor must account for the debt[6] as assets of the estate available for payment both of creditors and of legatees[7] unless he can prove that the testator clearly[8] and continuously intended in his lifetime, and not by his will[9], to forgive the debt[10]. The requirement by the testator of security for the debt after execution of the will appointing the debtor has been held to negative the intention to forgive[11].

Where the debtor-executor proves the will, he must be taken as having had the amount of the debt in his hands as assets from the testator's death; he cannot accordingly set up the lapse of time between the death and the grant of probate to himself as a bar to the debt, and he is chargeable with interest from the date of death[12].

1 *Nedham's Case* (1610) 8 Co Rep 135a; and see *Re Pink, Pink v Pink* [1912] 2 Ch 528, CA. As to the statutory application of the rules set out in this paragraph on the appointment of a debtor administrator see PARA 643; and as to their statutory application where a debtor becomes his creditor's executor by representation see PARA 641. As to the release of the debt generally see CONTRACT vol 22 (2012) PARA 614 et seq.
2 *Cheetham v Ward* (1797) 1 Bos & P 630; *Freakley v Fox* (1829) 9 B & C 130; *Jenkins v Jenkins* [1928] 2 KB 501; *Nicholson v Revill* (1836) 4 Ad & El 675 at 683; *North v Wakefield* (1849) 13 QB 536.
3 See the Administration of Estates Act 1925 s 5; and PARA 788.
4 The position at common law was otherwise: see *Wankford v Wankford* (1704) 1 Salk 299. See also the Court of Probate Act 1857 s 79; and the Court of Probate Act 1858 s 16 (both repealed, as to deaths after 1925, by the Administration of Estates Act 1925 s 56, Sch 2 Pt I).
5 *Re Applebee, Leveson v Beales* [1891] 3 Ch 422.

6 He must account whether the debt is secured or unsecured: *Re Greg, Fordham v Greg* [1921] 2 Ch 243.
7 *Carey v Goodinge* (1790) 3 Bro CC 110; *Berry v Usher* (1805) 11 Ves 87; *Stamp Duties Comr v Bone* [1977] AC 511, [1976] 2 All ER 354, PC. In equity the debt is discharged by payment at the date of probate: *Jenkins v Jenkins* [1928] 2 KB 501.
8 *Re Pink, Pink v Pink* [1912] 2 Ch 528, CA.
9 *Selwin v Brown* (1735) 3 Bro Parl Cas 607, HL, as explained by Stirling J in *Re Applebee, Leveson v Beales* [1891] 3 Ch 422 at 429–430.
10 *Strong v Bird* (1874) LR 18 Eq 315; *Re Applebee, Leveson v Beales* [1891] 3 Ch 422; *Re Goff, Featherstonhaugh v Murphy* (1914) 111 LT 34. See also *Re Hyslop, Hyslop v Chamberlain* [1894] 3 Ch 522; *Re Greg, Fordham v Greg* [1921] 2 Ch 243.
11 *Re Eiser's Will Trusts, Fogg v Eastwood* [1937] 1 All ER 244. It was also held in this case that the existence of the debt did not prevent the executors making payments for the debtor's maintenance from the income of the residuary estate of the testatrix which they held on discretionary trusts for a class including the debtor.
12 *Ingle v Richards (No 2)* (1860) 28 Beav 366.

626. Effect on incomplete gifts where donee appointed as administrator or executor. The appointment as an executor or administrator[1] of a person to whom the testator has during his lifetime attempted to make an immediate gift[2], whether of real or personal estate[3], which, being incomplete, fails on technical considerations, is sufficient to perfect the gift[4]; but the principle is not to be extended to a case where the testator has merely announced an intention of making a gift at some future time[5], or a case where the intention to make the gift did not continue until the testator's death[6].

1 *Re James, James v James* [1935] Ch 449.
2 *Re Greene, Greene v Greene* [1949] Ch 333, [1949] 1 All ER 167.
3 *Re James, James v James* [1935] Ch 449.
4 *Strong v Bird* (1874) LR 18 Eq 315; *Re Stewart, Stewart v McLaughlin* [1908] 2 Ch 251. See also *Re Stoneham, Stoneham v Stoneham* [1919] 1 Ch 149. As to other types of gift from which such an incomplete gift is to be distinguished see PARA 921.
5 *Vavasseur v Vavasseur* (1909) 25 TLR 250; *Re Innes, Innes v Innes* [1910] 1 Ch 188; *Re Freeland, Jackson v Rodgers* [1952] Ch 110, [1952] 1 All ER 16, CA. As to incomplete gifts see GIFTS vol 52 (2014) PARA 267 et seq.
6 *Re Gonin, Gonin v Garmeson* [1979] Ch 16, [1977] 2 All ER 720.

(iii) Acceptance of the Office of Executor

627. Acceptance of office of executor. The most obvious method of accepting the office of executor is for the person appointed to obtain a grant of probate[1], although the executor may, without applying for probate, do such acts with reference to the testator's estate as constitute an acceptance of the office. Acts which show an intention on the executor's part to take upon himself the office[2] or which would, in the case of a person not appointed executor, render that person liable as an executor de son tort[3], constitute an acceptance. The release of a debt of the testator[4], the application, even though unsuccessful, for the payment of money owing to the testator[5], a statement, in answer to an inquiry by a creditor, that the will has been proved and that the person making the statement is one of the executors[6], have been said to amount to an acceptance.

The mere performance of acts of charity or of necessity[7] does not constitute an acceptance, and the executor may examine the testator's books to determine whether or not he is to accept the office without rendering himself liable to take probate[8]. He may join in opening and operating an executorship account with a bank, allow insurance policies to be indorsed in the joint names of himself and the other executors, join in instructing solicitors, negotiate for a government grant for assets ordered by the testator and carry on the testator's farming business, all apparently without making a later renunciation of executorship ineffective[9].

An application for probate, even if followed by the oath of office, does not prevent the executor from renouncing before the grant has actually passed the seal[10]. A person named as executor may act as the agent for a co-executor who has proved the will without rendering himself liable to account as an executor[11], even though he has not formally renounced[12].

1 A person cannot be compelled to accept the office, even though he has agreed to accept in the testator's lifetime: *Doyle v Blake* (1804) 2 Sch & Lef 231 at 239.
2 Bac Abr, Executors and Administrators (E) 10.
3 *Long and Feaver v Symes and Hannam* (1832) 3 Hag Ecc 771. As to the executor de son tort see PARA 1261 et seq.
4 Went Off Ex (14th Edn) 94; *Pytt v Fendall* (1754) 1 Lee 553.
5 *Re Stevens, Cooke v Stevens* [1897] 1 Ch 422; affd [1898] 1 Ch 162, CA.
6 *Vickers v Bell* (1864) 4 De GJ & Sm 274.
7 Shep Touch (7th Edn) p 466; *Long and Feaver v Symes and Hannam* (1832) 3 Hag Ecc 771. As to what are acts of charity or necessity see PARA 1263.
8 Godolphin's Orphan's Legacy (3rd Edn) Pt II, c 8 s 6. Taking possession of the testator's books of account may be sufficient to show an acceptance: *Clark v Phillips, Bayles v Phillips* (1854) 2 WR 331.
9 See *Holder v Holder* [1968] Ch 353 at 391–392, [1968] 1 All ER 665 at 671–672, CA, per Harman LJ, at 396–397 and 676–677 per Danckwerts LJ, and at 401 and 679–680 per Sachs LJ. In this case it had been conceded on behalf of the executor that his acts debarred him from renouncing, and the judgments of the Court of Appeal were obiter on this point.
10 *Jackson and Wallington v Whitehead* (1821) 3 Phillim 577; *M'Donnell v Prendergast* (1830) 3 Hag Ecc 212; *Mohamidu Mohideen Hadjiar v Pitchey* [1894] AC 437, PC.
11 *Orr v Newton* (1791) 2 Cox Eq Cas 274, PC; *Dove v Everard* (1830) 1 Russ & M 231; *Rayner v Green* (1839) 2 Curt 248.
12 *Stacey v Elph* (1833) 1 My & K 195.

628. Executor who has accepted cannot renounce. An executor who has once so acted as to show an intention of accepting the office cannot afterwards renounce[1]; he may be cited to take probate[2] and be peremptorily ordered to do so[3], but, in the court's discretion[4], he may also be passed over[5]. He cannot discharge himself from his liability to account as executor by renouncing and paying his receipts to the executors who have proved[6], nor can a scheme under the Companies Acts affect the rights, duties or powers of a corporate executor[7].

1 *Rogers v Frank* (1827) 1 Y & J 409; *Long and Feaver v Symes and Hannam* (1832) 3 Hag Ecc 771; *Re Badenach* (1864) 3 Sw & Tr 465; *Re Stevens, Cooke v Stevens* [1897] 1 Ch 422; affd [1898] 1 Ch 162, CA; and see *Re Veiga* (1862) 3 Sw & Tr 13, where the executor had taken a grant. As to acts which amount to acceptance see PARA 627. In *Re Fitzpatrick* (1892) 29 LR Ir 328 it was said that the court may, though perhaps it ought not to, accept the executor's refusal, notwithstanding he has administered; cf the text to notes 4–5. As to actions against an executor before probate see PARA 636.
2 *Re Lister* (1894) 70 LT 812; *Re Coates* (1898) 78 LT 820. Committal will not be ordered against an executor for disobeying such a citation, unless there is served personally on him a copy on which is prominently displayed on the front a warning that disobedience to the order would be a contempt of court punishable by imprisonment (see now CPR 70.2A; and CIVIL PROCEDURE vol 12A (2015) PARA 1298): *Re Bristow* (1891) 66 LT 60; but it is not clear whether such a citation is strictly within the terms of the rule (*Evans v Evans*) (1892) 67 LT 719). In practice the procedure now is to obtain from the registrar on summons an order (which should bear the penal notice) requiring the executor to take a grant or an order for a grant to the citor himself or some other person specified in the summons: see PARA 698.
3 *Mordaunt v Clarke* (1868) LR 1 P & D 592. An executor may be summoned or cited to accept or refuse probate: see PARAS 689, 698, 700.
4 See PARAS 758–759.
5 *Re Biggs* [1966] P 118, [1966] 1 All ER 358.
6 *Read v Truelove* (1762) Amb 417. As to the liability of an executor to account see PARA 1254 et seq.

7 *Re Skinner* [1958] 3 All ER 273, [1958] 1 WLR 1043. See also COMPANIES vol 15A (2016) PARAS 1614, 1616.

629. Effect of acceptance of office of executor. An executor cannot accept in part and refuse in part: he must accept or refuse the office as a whole[1] or, where the appointment is limited, to the full extent of the appointment. In the case of certain settled land the personal representative may, however, before representation has been granted, renounce his office in regard only to the settled land without renouncing it in regard to other property; or he may, after representation has been granted, apply to the court for revocation of the grant in regard to the settled land without applying in regard to other property[2].

An executor of an executor who has accepted the executorship of the later testator cannot renounce the executorship of the earlier[3].

The acceptance of the executorship involves the acceptance of the trusts which the testator himself may have imposed on his executors[4], or which in a court of equity are considered to arise from the office[5].

Where probate is granted to one or some of two or more persons named as executors, whether or not power is reserved to the others or other to prove, all the powers which are by law conferred on the personal representative may be exercised by the proving executor or executors for the time being, and are as effectual as if all the persons named as executors had concurred[6].

1 Shep Touch (7th Edn) p 466.
2 See the Administration of Estates Act 1925 s 23(1); and PARA 828. It would seem that 'settled land' here means land which continues to be settled after the death of the tenant for life: see *Re Bridgett and Hayes' Contract* [1928] Ch 163 at 169. See also PARA 826 note 2. As to special personal representatives in respect of settled land see PARA 821. As to the appointment of special or additional personal representatives in respect of settled land see PARA 828.
3 *Re Perry* (1840) 2 Curt 655; *Brooke v Haymes* (1868) LR 6 Eq 25; *Re Delacour* (1874) 9 IR Eq 86.
4 *Mucklow v Fuller* (1821) Jac 198; *Ward v Butler* (1824) 2 Mol 533; *Stiles v Guy* (1832) 4 Y & C Ex 571 at 575; *Re Sharman's Will Trusts, Public Trustee v Sharman* [1942] Ch 311 at 317, [1942] 2 All ER 74 at 78 (taking out probate involves acceptance of office of trustee of a will imposing trusts). In a loose sense an executor is a trustee for the creditors and beneficiaries, but he is not, as executor, necessarily a trustee (*Re Davis, Re Davis, Evans v Moore* [1891] 3 Ch 119 at 124, CA), although for purposes of administration he has inter alia the powers of trustees of land: see the Administration of Estates Act 1925 s 39; and PARA 1018. As to the principle that, when he has cleared the estate, a personal representative becomes a trustee of property remaining in his hands see PARAS 1148–1150.
5 *Re Marsden, Bowden v Layland, Gibbs v Layland* (1884) 26 ChD 783; *Re Sharman's Will Trusts, Public Trustee v Sharman* [1942] Ch 311, [1942] 2 All ER 74. See also PARA 609.
6 Administration of Estates Act 1925 s 8(1), which applies whenever the testator died: s 8(2). The concurrence of all proving executors is required on a sale of land (both for the contract and the conveyance): see s 2(2); and PARA 1024.

(iv) Renunciation of the Office of Executor

630. Power to renounce office of executor. A person appointed executor who has not acted so as to show an intention of accepting the office[1] and who does not wish to act may renounce the office, either personally or by power of attorney[2], and his renunciation need not be under seal[3]. The renunciation is not final until it is lodged and recorded in the proper court[4]. Therefore it does not become effective until filed[5]. The executor may renounce as soon as the testator is dead, and his renunciation can be filed, provided it is accompanied by the original will[6].

1 As to the rule that an executor who has accepted cannot renounce see PARA 628. As to acts which amount to acceptance see PARA 627. As to the effect of acceptance see PARA 629.

2 Toller's Law of Executors (7th Edn) 42; *Re Rosser* (1864) 3 Sw & Tr 490. As to settled land see PARA 629.
3 *Re Boyle* (1864) 3 Sw & Tr 426.
4 *Re Morant* (1874) LR 3 P & D 151. The instrument of renunciation must be lodged in the principal registry, or a district probate registry.
5 *Re Morant* (1874) LR 3 P & D 151.
6 *Re Fenton* (1825) 3 Add 35. A person entitled to a grant of administration or administration with the will annexed may also renounce, but in such cases the renunciation does not bind the representatives of the renouncing party. An executor to whom power to prove has been reserved may renounce after probate has been granted to a co-executor. See generally Tristram and Coote's Probate Practice (30th Edn) 15.24–15.27.

631. Effect of renunciation of office of executor. Where a person renounces probate his rights in respect of the executorship wholly cease[1] and the representation[2] to the testator, and the administration[3] of the estate, devolve and are to be committed in like manner as if that person had not been appointed executor[4]. Renunciation of probate by an executor does not operate as the renunciation of any right which he may have to a grant of administration in some other capacity unless he expressly renounces such right[5]. Unless a district judge[6] or registrar[7] otherwise directs[8], no person who has renounced administration in one capacity may obtain a grant of it in some other capacity[9], but a form of renunciation of probate by an executor must include renunciation of the right to administration in any other capacity in which he is entitled (for example as residuary legatee in trust) before a grant can be made to a person with a lower title[10]. Renunciation of probate or administration by members of a partnership may be effected[11].

1 He cannot, however, insist on a formal release until the estate has been administered: *Tiger v Barclays Bank Ltd* [1951] 2 KB 556, [1951] 2 All ER 262; affd [1952] 1 All ER 85, CA. As to formal release see PARA 1057.
2 As to the meaning of 'representation' see PARA 608 note 2.
3 As to the meaning of 'administration' see PARA 607 note 1.
4 Administration of Estates Act 1925 s 5(iii), replacing, as to deaths after 1925, the Court of Probate Act 1857 s 79 (repealed, except as to deaths before 1926). A similar statutory cessation of an executor's rights occurs:
   (1) where he survives the testator but dies before proving the will; and
   (2) where he is cited to take probate and does not appear (see PARAS 637, 691).
5 Non-Contentious Probate Rules 1987, SI 1987/2024, r 37(1). See also *Re Gill* (1873) LR 3 P & D 113; *Re Wheelwright* (1878) 3 PD 71; *Re Rayner* (1908) 52 Sol Jo 226; *Re Toscani* [1912] P 1, where a grant of administration de bonis non was made to a person as creditor who had previously renounced probate as an executor.
6 'District judge' means a district judge of the principal registry: Non-Contentious Probate Rules 1987, SI 1987/2024, r 2(1) (definition added by SI 1991/1876).
7 In the Non-Contentious Probate Rules 1987, SI 1987/2024, 'registrar' means the district probate registrar of the district probate registry:
   (1) to which an application for a grant is made or is proposed to be made;
   (2) in rr 26, 40, 41 and 61(2) (see PARAS 701, 776, 841, 854), from which a grant is issued; and
   (3) in rr 46, 47 and 48 (see PARAS 695–700), from which the citation has issued or is proposed to be issued (r 2(1) (definition substituted by SI 1991/1876)).
   'Grant' means a grant of probate or administration and includes, where the context so admits, the resealing of such a grant under the Colonial Probates Acts 1892 and 1927 (see PARA 837): Non-Contentious Probate Rules 1987, SI 1987/2024, r 2(1).
8 A direction may be made either by the registrar of the district probate registry in which the renunciation is filed or by a district judge: Non-Contentious Probate Rules 1987, SI 1987/2024, r 37(4) (amended by SI 1991/1876).
9 Non-Contentious Probate Rules 1987, SI 1987/2024, r 37(2) (amended by SI 1991/1876). See also *Re Rayner* (1908) 52 Sol Jo 226.
10 Cf the Non-Contentious Probate Rules 1987, SI 1987/2024, r 37(1); and the text to note 5.
11 Non-Contentious Probate Rules 1987, SI 1987/2024, r 37(2A) (added by SI 1998/1903).

632. Withdrawal of renunciation of office of executor. A renunciation of probate or administration may be retracted at any time with the leave[1] of a district judge or registrar[2]. After filing, a renunciation cannot be retracted without an order[3], and the renouncing executor must show that the retraction is for the benefit of the estate or of those interested under the will[4]. Retraction will not be allowed merely on the ground that the executor has changed his mind[5]. If a grant has been made to a person entitled in a lower degree, leave to an executor to retract his renunciation of probate may be granted only in exceptional circumstances[6]. Renunciation of probate or administration by members of partnership may be retracted by any two of them with the authority of the others and any such renunciation must recite such authority[7].

An executor who is also the residuary legatee and has renounced in both capacities may, in special circumstances, be permitted to retract his renunciation in the capacity of residuary legatee[8].

Where an executor who has renounced probate has been permitted to retract his renunciation and prove the will[9], the probate takes effect and is deemed always to have taken effect without prejudice to the previous acts and dealings of and notices to any other personal representative[10] who has previously proved the will or taken out letters of administration, and a memorandum of the subsequent probate must be indorsed on the original probate or letters of administration[11].

1 An order giving leave may be made by either by the registrar of a district probate registry where the renunciation is filed or by a district judge: Non-Contentious Probate Rules 1987, SI 1987/2024, r 37(4) (amended by SI 1991/1876). As to the meaning of 'district judge' see PARA 631 note 6; and as to the meaning of 'registrar' see PARA 631 note 7.
2 Non-Contentious Probate Rules 1987, SI 1987/2024, r 37(3) (amended by SI 1991/1876). See also *Re Stiles* [1898] P 12 (proving executor absconded after probate; co-executor allowed to retract renunciation); *Re Thacker* [1900] P 15 (renunciation of right to administration by widow and children of bankrupt intestate; grant to official receiver; debts paid; grant to official receiver revoked; widow and children permitted to retract renunciation and grant made to them); *Re Heathcote* [1913] P 42 (death of wife intestate; renunciation by husband and grant to husband's trustee in bankruptcy; termination of bankruptcy; grant to trustee revoked; grant made to husband); cf *Re Badenach* (1864) 3 Sw & Tr 465 (renunciation held to be invalid). Application for leave to retract is made ex parte: see PARA 703.
3 *Melville v Anketill* (1909) 25 TLR 655, CA.
4 *Re Gill* (1873) LR 3 P & D 113. It seems that an executor will be permitted to retract his renunciation only for the purpose of obtaining a grant: *Re Whitham* (1866) LR 1 P & D 303 at 305.
5 *Re Gill* (1873) LR 3 P & D 113.
6 Non-Contentious Probate Rules 1987, SI 1987/2024, r 37(3) (as amended: see note 2).
7 Non-Contentious Probate Rules 1987, SI 1987/2024, r 37(2A) (added by SI 1988/1093). This is subject to the Non-Contentious Probate Rules 1987, SI 1987/2024, r 37(3).
8 *Re Richardson* (1859) 1 Sw & Tr 515; *Re Morrison* (1861) 2 Sw & Tr 129; *Re Wheelwright* (1878) 3 PD 71. See also PARA 631 text and note 9.
9 As to the meaning of 'will' see PARA 607 note 1.
10 As to the meaning of 'personal representative' see PARA 608.
11 Administration of Estates Act 1925 s 6.

(v) Executor's Acts before Grant

633. Source of executor's title. The executor derives his title under the will[1], if he has been appointed executor by the will[2], but not if he has been appointed by the court under statutory powers[3]. His title under the will is aided in the case of real property by statute[4], and the testator's property vests in him as from the date of death[5] without any interval of time[6]. The probate itself is the authentication of his title[7]; but, if it affects the legal estate in land, it is also a document of title[8].

1 *Comber's Case* (1721) 1 P Wms 766; *Meyappa Chetty v Supramanian Chetty* [1916] 1 AC 603 at 608, PC. In the case of a foreign executor of a foreign domiciled testator where the law of wills and executors is similar to that of England, English law will recognise him as deriving title from the testator's will: see *Redwood Music Ltd v B Feldman & Co Ltd* [1979] RPC 1 (revsd on another point sub nom *Chappell & Co Ltd v Redwood Music Ltd* [1980] 2 All ER 817, HL) where an assignment was recognised as valid where it had been made by beneficiaries deriving title from executors under a Michigan will, the assignment being made before any grant of representation had been obtained in England (a grant in England was still necessary to prove the title, but the assignment was not void for want of entitlement at the time of the assignment).

2 It is not clear whether a special executor appointed or deemed to be appointed for settled land (see the Administration of Estates Act 1925 s 22; and PARA 821) derives any title under the will now that (with effect from 14 October 1991) administration is what is granted to him rather than probate: see the Non-Contentious Probate Rules 1987, SI 1987/2024, r 29; and PARAS 822, 825. As to special executors see PARA 821.

3 For the court's power to appoint see the Senior Courts Act 1981 s 114(2) (see PARA 775); and the Administration of Estates Act 1925 s 23(2) (see PARA 828).

4 See the Administration of Estates Act 1925 ss 1–3 (see PARAS 945–948), which also apply to leaseholds. At common law these vest in the executor by virtue of his appointment: see generally PARAS 942, 945 et seq. By the Law of Property (Amendment) Act 1924 s 9, Sch 9 para 3, a will only operates in equity and therefore an executor does not obtain the legal estate in land under the will, but under the provisions of the Administration of Estates Act 1925 ss 1–3. In practice an executor can only satisfactorily prove his title by production of probate: see the text to note 7; and PARA 659.

As inheritance tax may have to be paid before the grant of probate or administration (see the Senior Courts Act 1981 s 109; and PARA 731) and consequently before the deceased's bank account can be drawn on, the deceased's bank may make a loan for this purpose on the representatives entering upon the required undertaking to be personally responsible. Alternatively the bank may make payment direct to HMRC. As to the payment of inheritance tax generally see INHERITANCE TAXATION vol 59A (2014) PARA 275 et seq.

5 *Woolley v Clark* (1822) 5 B & Ald 744. The estate is automatically divested if the executor renounces probate or survives the testator but dies without having proved the will or is cited to take out probate and does not appear: see PARAS 631, 637, 689. It seems that the contents of an unproved will are not admissible in evidence, but evidence is admissible to show that the will exists without the necessity for proving it in proper form: see *Whitmore v Lambert* [1955] 2 All ER 147, [1955] 1 WLR 495, CA.

6 *Whitehead v Taylor* (1839) 10 Ad & El 210.

7 *Smith v Milles* (1786) 1 Term Rep 475 at 480; *Re Pawley and London and Provincial Bank* [1900] 1 Ch 58. Probate is in general necessary to establish the executor's title: see PARAS 635, 659.

8 This is the effect of the Administration of Estates Act 1925 s 36(5), requiring assents and conveyances by personal representatives to be indorsed on the probate: see *Re Miller and Pickersgill's Contract* [1931] 1 Ch 511; and PARA 1147.

634. Acts done by executor before probate. An executor may generally do before probate all things which pertain to the executorial office[1]. He may pay or release debts[2], get in and receive the testator's estate[3], assent to a legacy[4], and generally intermeddle with the testator's goods[5]. He may distrain for rent[6], demise[7], grant a next presentation[8] or release an action[9]. He may make a conveyance or assignment of personalty[10] or of realty[11]; but although before probate he can give a valid receipt for money payable upon an assignment, he cannot compel a purchaser to complete until after probate has been obtained[12]. He may exercise the statutory power[13] to appoint a new trustee of a trust of which the testator was the last surviving trustee, but his title to exercise the power can only be proved by a proper grant of representation[14].

The acts of an executor who dies without obtaining probate hold good, provided the will is ultimately proved[15].

1 See *Kelsey v Kelsey* (1922) 91 LJ Ch 382.

2 Went Off Ex (14th Edn) 81.

3 *Wills v Rich* (1742) 2 Atk 285.

4 Went Off Ex (14th Edn) 82; *Wankford v Wankford* (1704) 1 Salk 299 at 301; *Johnson v Warwick* (1856) 17 CB 516.
5 *Wankford v Wankford* (1704) 1 Salk 299 at 301. As to intermeddling see PARA 1261 et seq.
6 *Whitehead v Taylor* (1839) 10 Ad & El 210. As to distress generally see LANDLORD AND TENANT vol 62 (2012) PARA 288 et seq.
7 *Roe d Bendall v Summerset* (1770) 2 Wm Bl 692. The power to demise ceases on the executor's assenting to a devise or bequest concerning that property in the will; cf *Doe d Saye and Lord Sele v Guy* (1802) 3 East 120.
8 *Smithley v Chomeley* (1556) 2 Dyer 135a. As to presentation generally see ECCLESIASTICAL LAW vol 34 (2011) PARA 550 et seq.
9 Went Off Ex (14th Edn) 81.
10 *Brazier v Hudson* (1836) 8 Sim 67 at 68.
11 See the Administration of Estates Act 1925 s 2(1) (see PARA 945 note 5), replacing the Land Transfer Act 1897 s 2(2), as respects deaths after 1925.
12 *Newton v Metropolitan Rly Co* (1861) 1 Drew & Sm 583. See also *Re Stevens, Cooke v Stevens* [1897] 1 Ch 422; affd [1898] 1 Ch 162, CA.
13 Ie under Trustee Act 1925 s 36(1): see TRUSTS AND POWERS vol 98 (2013) PARA 275 et seq.
14 *Re Crowhurst Park, Sims-Hilditch v Simmons* [1974] 1 All ER 991, [1974] 1 WLR 583.
15 Went Off Ex (14th Edn) 82; *Brazier v Hudson* (1836) 8 Sim 67; *Wankford v Wankford* (1704) 1 Salk 299 at 308; *Johnson v Warwick* (1856) 17 CB 516. Cf the Administration of Estates Act 1925 s 5(i); and PARA 637.

635. Proceedings taken by executor before probate. As an executor derives his title from the will and not from the grant of probate[1] he may begin an action as executor before probate[2], but he cannot proceed beyond the stage at which it becomes necessary to prove his title[3], as the only evidence of his title is the grant[4]. He may also present a petition in bankruptcy as executor of a deceased creditor[5], or he may petition to wind up a limited company[6] before probate.

Where a debtor does not dispute the debt but requires production of probate before making payment to the executor, the court can and will stay proceedings taken by the executor until production of probate[7].

An executor can also in his personal capacity maintain an action in respect of property of which he has been in actual possession[8], but when the possession is in dispute, he must prove his title as executor[9].

1 *Re Pawley and London and Provincial Bank* [1900] 1 Ch 58.
2 As to proceedings by personal representatives generally see PARA 1273 et seq; and for proceedings against estates in the absence of a grant of probate or administration see PARAS 647, 818.
3 *Wankford v Wankford* (1704) 1 Salk 299 at 303; *Wills v Rich* (1742) 2 Atk 285; *Thompson v Reynolds* (1827) 3 C & P 123; *Meyappa Chetty v Supramanian Chetty* [1916] 1 AC 603, PC; *Re Crowhurst Park, Sims-Hilditch v Simmons* [1974] 1 All ER 991, [1974] 1 WLR 583. See also the Revenue Act 1884 s 11; and PARA 659. The stage at which the executor has to prove his title is as a rule the hearing: *Newton v Metropolitan Rly Co* (1861) 1 Drew & Sm 583; *Re Masonic and General Life Assurance Co* (1885) 32 ChD 373.
4 *R v Netherseal Inhabitants* (1791) 4 Term Rep 258 at 260; *Pinney v Hunt* (1877) 6 ChD 98.
5 *Rogers v James* (1816) 7 Taunt 147; *Re Drakeley, ex p Paddy* (1818) 3 Madd 241. See BANKRUPTCY AND INDIVIDUAL INSOLVENCY vol 5 (2013) PARA 144.
6 *Re Masonic and General Life Assurance Co* (1885) 32 ChD 373.
7 *Tarn v Commercial Bank of Sydney* (1884) 12 QBD 294, following *Webb v Adkins* (1854) 14 CB 401.
8 *Oughton v Seppings* (1830) 1 B & Ad 241.
9 *Pinney v Pinney* (1828) 8 B & C 335.

636. Executor's liability for acts done before probate. If an executor elects to act, he may be sued before probate, and cannot afterwards renounce[1]; but the court will not allow an action to be brought against one appointed executor who has never meant to act, before he has had an opportunity of renouncing[2]; nor will it make an order for general administration in the absence of a duly constituted legal personal representative[3].

1 *Webster v Webster* (1804) 10 Ves 93; *Blewitt v Blewitt* (1832) You 541; *Vickers v Bell* (1864) 4 De GJ & Sm 274; *Re Lovett, Ambler v Lindsay* (1876) 3 ChD 198. See also PARA 628.
2 *Douglas v Forrest* (1828) 4 Bing 686 at 704.
3 *Penny v Watts* (1846) 2 Ph 149 at 152, 154; *Creasor v Robinson* (1851) 14 Beav 589; *Cary v Hills* (1872) LR 15 Eq 79; *Rowsell v Morris* (1873) LR 17 Eq 20 (disapproving *Rayner v Koehler* (1872) LR 14 Eq 262, and *Coote v Whittington* (1873) LR 16 Eq 534). See also *Dowdeswell v Dowdeswell* (1878) 9 ChD 294, CA. As to the appointment of a receiver pending grant see PARA 1166.

(3) THE CHAIN OF REPRESENTATION

(i) Devolution on Death

637. Devolution of office of executor on death. An executorship cannot be assigned at common law because it is an office of personal trust[1]. It can only devolve by operation of law. On the death of one of several representatives, the office, with its incidents, duties and powers, and the estate and interest in all the property vested in the representatives by virtue of their office, devolve upon the survivors or survivor[2].

On the death of a sole executor, or of the last survivor of several executors, the office devolves upon the executor of the sole or last surviving executor[3] who has proved the will[4]; and so long as the chain of representation is unbroken, the last executor in the chain is the executor of every preceding testator[5]. The representation is not transmitted, however, unless the original executor[6] has proved the will of his testator[7], in England and Wales[8], or in Northern Ireland in the case of a person who died domiciled there[9], or the grant of probate by virtue of resealing[10] in England and Wales has the same effect as if made there[11].

On the death of an executor who has survived the testator but never proved the will, the rights of that executor wholly cease and the representation to the testator and the administration of his estate devolve and are to be committed in like manner as if the executor had never been appointed executor[12].

1 See PARA 642.
2 *Flanders v Clarke* (1747) 3 Atk 509; *Eyre v Countess of Shaftsbury* (1725) 2 P Wms 103 at 121. As to banking practice on the death of a trustee see FINANCIAL INSTITUTIONS vol 48 (2015) PARA 167.
3 Administration of Estates Act 1925 s 7(1). Section 7 does not apply on the death of an executor named in a Scottish confirmation recognised in England: see the Administration of Estates Act 1971 s 1(3); and PARA 831.
4 In the text and note 3, 'executor' must be taken to mean an executor who has proved: see the text and notes 6–11.
5 Administration of Estates Act 1925 s 7(2).
6 It was formerly sufficient if the attorney of the original executor obtained a grant with the will (*Re Bayard* (1849) 1 Rob Eccl 768; *Re Murguia* (1884) 9 PD 236), but the wording of the Administration of Estates Act 1925 s 7 does not allow of such an interpretation.
7 Administration of Estates Act 1925 s 7(1).
8 *Re Gaynor* (1869) LR 1 P & D 723; *Twyford v Trail* (1834) 7 Sim 92.
9 See the Administration of Estates Act 1971 s 1(4); and PARA 832.
10 Ie under the Colonial Probates Act 1892 s 2: see PARA 837.
11 See PARA 835.
12 Administration of Estates Act 1925 s 5(i). As to the admission in evidence of the unproved will see PARA 633.

638. Effect on chain of non-proving executor taking grant. Where a number of executors are appointed by the will but they do not all prove, power to prove may be reserved to those who do not then prove[1]. In that case, if the last proving executor dies the office devolves upon the executor of the proving executor, but is divested if and when the non-proving executor later proves the will of the original testator[2]. The non-proving executor may, of course, be cited to take probate, and if he does not appear his rights will cease[3]. If the Public Trustee takes a grant as executor he is considered to continue the chain of executorship[4].

1 As to double grants see PARA 751.
2 Administration of Estates Act 1925 s 7(1).
3 *Re Reid* [1896] P 129, following *Re Noddings* (1860) 2 Sw & Tr 15, as corrected in the Errata and Corrigenda. See also the Administration of Estates Act 1925 ss 5(ii) (see PARA 689), 7(1). As to citations see PARAS 695–700.
4 See President's Instructions, 27 March 1908; and Tristram and Coote's Probate Practice (30th Edn) 9.57.

639. Full executor of limited executor, and vice versa. A full executor of a limited executor sufficiently represents the estate of the original testator[1], but not a limited executor of a full executor[2]. Accordingly where, under the old practice of the Probate Court, a limited grant was made to the estate of a married woman, the chain of representation was broken[3]. The modern practice is, however, to make a general grant[4].

1 *Re Beer* (1851) 2 Rob Eccl 349. As to special or limited executors see PARA 615.
2 *Re Bayne* (1858) 1 Sw & Tr 132; *Re Bridger* (1878) 4 PD 77.
3 *Re Hughes* (1860) 4 Sw & Tr 209; *Re Martin* (1862) 3 Sw & Tr 1; *Re Richards* (1866) LR 1 P & D 156; *Re Bridger* (1878) 4 PD 77.
4 See PARA 753.

640. Break in chain of representation in office of executor. The chain of representation is broken by:

(1) an intestacy;
(2) the failure of a testator to appoint an executor; or
(3) the failure of the executor to obtain probate of a will; but it is not broken by a temporary grant of administration provided probate is subsequently granted[1].

Accordingly the office does not devolve upon the administrator of an executor. On the death of an administrator the office does not devolve and a fresh grant of administration to the unadministered property of the original testator must be obtained[2].

1 Administration of Estates Act 1925 s 7(3). As to temporary grants of administration see PARA 795 et seq. A grant of administration for the use and benefit of an executor during incapacity is equivalent to a grant of probate to him. If a grant for the use and benefit of an executor subject to incapacity is made after the death of his co-executor the executor of the co-executor does not represent the original testator on the death of the executor subject to incapacity: see *Re Frengley* [1915] 2 IR 1.
2 As to administration de bonis non see PARA 793.

641. Powers and liabilities of those in chain of representation. Every person in the chain of representation to a testator:

(1) has the same rights in respect of the testator's estate as the original executor would have had if living[1]; and
(2) to the extent to which the testator' estate has come into his hands, is answerable as if he were an original executor[2].

Where a debtor becomes his deceased creditor's executor by representation[3] his debt[4] is thereupon extinguished[5], but he is accountable for the amount of the debt as part of the creditor's estate in any case where he would be so accountable if he had been appointed as an executor by the creditor's will[6]. This does not apply where the debtor's authority to act as executor is limited to part of the estate which does not include the debt; and a debtor whose debt is extinguished by becoming his creditor's executor by representation is not accountable for its amount where the debt was barred by limitation before he became the executor by representation[7].

1 Administration of Estates Act 1925 s 7(4)(a).
2 Administration of Estates Act 1925 s 7(4)(b).
3 Administration of Estates Act 1925 s 21A(1) (s 21A added by the Limitation Amendment Act 1980 s 10). This provision also applies to administrators: see PARA 643.
4 As to the meaning of 'debt' see PARA 643 note 5.
5 Administration of Estates Act 1925 s 21A(1)(a) (as added: see note 3).
6 Administration of Estates Act 1925 s 21A(1)(b) (as added: see note 3). As to the accountability of a debtor executor see PARA 625.
7 Administration of Estates Act 1925 s 21A(2) (as added: see note 3).

(ii) Devolution Otherwise than on Death

642. Office of executor or administrator not assignable. Neither the office of executor nor that of administrator is assignable at common law[1], but executors and administrators[2] have the statutory powers of a trustee to authorise any person to exercise any or all of their delegable functions[3] as their agents[4] and to appoint any person to act as their nominee[5] or custodian[6] in relation to such assets as they determine[7]. An executor or administrator also has the statutory power of a trustee to delegate by power of attorney the exercise of any trusts, powers or discretions vested in him as such trustee for a period not exceeding 12 months[8]. Any executor who has obtained probate or any administrator who has obtained letters of administration, notwithstanding that he has acted in the administration of the deceased's estate, may, with the consent of the court, after such notice to the persons beneficially interested as the court may direct, transfer the estate to the Public Trustee for administration either solely or jointly with the continuing executors or administrators, if any[9].

On the application of a personal representative or of a beneficiary, the court has power to appoint a person called a judicial trustee to act in the administration of a deceased person's property, and, if sufficient cause is shown, to displace the personal representative[10]. The court also has power to appoint a person to act as personal representative in place of the existing personal representative or representatives or any of them[11].

1 Shep Touch (7th Edn) p 465; 2 Bl Com (14th Edn) 506; *Re Skinner* [1958] 3 All ER 273 at 276, [1958] 1 WLR 1043 at 1046 per Sachs J.
2 For application of the Trustee Act 2000 to personal representatives administering an estate see s 35(1); and PARA 609 note 2. The provisions of the Trustee Act 2000 Pt IV (ss 11–27) apply in relation to a trust with a sole trustee as they apply in relation to other trusts; and trustees (except in ss 12(1), (3), 19(5) (see TRUSTS AND POWERS vol 98 (2013) PARAS 430, 433)) are to be read accordingly: s 25.
3 See the Trustee Act 2000 s 11(1), (2); and TRUSTS AND POWERS vol 98 (2013) PARA 430.
4 See the Trustee Act 2000 s 11(1); and TRUSTS AND POWERS vol 98 (2013) PARA 430. For persons who may act see s 12; and TRUSTS AND POWERS vol 98 (2013) PARA 430.
5 See the Trustee Act 2000 s 16; and TRUSTS AND POWERS vol 98 (2013) PARA 432 et seq.
6 See the Trustee Act 2000 s 17; and TRUSTS AND POWERS vol 98 (2013) PARA 432 et seq.
7 As regards nominees see the Trustee Act 2000 s 16(1)(a). As regards custodians see s 17(1).
8 See the Trustee Act 1925 s 25; and TRUSTS AND POWERS vol 98 (2013) PARA 425. The Trustee Act 1925 s 25 applies to a personal representative as it applies to a trustee, except that s 25(4), which relates to notice of the giving of a power of attorney, applies as if it required the notice there mentioned to be given, in the case of a personal representative, to each of the other personal representatives, if any, except any executor who has renounced probate: see s 25(10)(a); and

TRUSTS AND POWERS vol 98 (2013) PARA 425. Since an executor who has renounced is not normally regarded as an executor, the express exclusion of an executor who has renounced seems to imply that notice should be given to an executor named in the will to whom power to prove the will has been reserved.

In the Trustee Act 1925, 'personal representative' means the executor, original or by representation, or administrator for the time being of a deceased person: s 68(1) para (9). Cf PARA 609 note 1.

9 Public Trustee Act 1906 s 6(2). The court order sanctioning the transfer gives, subject to the provisions of the Public Trustee Act 1906, all the powers of such an executor or administrator to the Public Trustee, and the executor or administrator is not in any way liable in respect of any act or default in reference to the estate subsequent to the date of the order other than the act or default of himself or of persons other than himself for whose conduct he is in law responsible: s 6(2). As to the Public Trustee see TRUSTS AND POWERS vol 98 (2013) PARA 206 et seq.

10 See the Judicial Trustees Act 1896 s 1(1), (2); and TRUSTS AND POWERS vol 98 (2013) PARA 200.

11 Ie under the Administration of Justice Act 1985 s 50: see PARA 1163.

(4) THE ADMINISTRATOR

(i) Administrator's Acts before Grant

643. Source of administrator's title. The administrator derives his title entirely from the grant of letters of administration, and the deceased's property does not vest in him until the grant[1], so he cannot make a lease or other disposition before the grant[2]. After the grant of administration the administrator has, subject to the limitations contained in the grant[3], the same rights and liabilities and is accountable in the same way as if he were the executor of the deceased[4].

Where a debtor becomes his deceased creditor's administrator his debt[5] is then extinguished[6], but he is accountable for the amount of the debt as part of the creditor's estate in any case where he would be so accountable if he had been appointed as an executor by the creditor's will[7]. This does not apply where the debtor's authority to act as administrator is limited to part only of the creditor's estate which does not include the debt; and a debtor whose debt is extinguished by becoming his creditor's administrator is not accountable for its amount where the debt was barred by limitation before he became the administrator[8].

1 *Comber's Case* (1721) 1 P Wms 766; *Woolley v Clark* (1822) 5 B & Ald 744; *Creed v Creed* [1913] 1 IR 48.

2 *Wankford v Wankford* (1704) 1 Salk 299 at 301.

3 As to forms of limited grant see PARA 793 et seq.

4 Administration of Estates Act 1925 s 21. As to the meaning of 'administrator' see PARA 607 note 1. As to the need for a grant whether of probate or administration see PARA 659.

5 'Debt' includes any liability, and 'debtor' and 'creditor' are to be construed accordingly: Administration of Estates Act 1925 s 21A(3) (s 21A added by the Limitation Amendment Act 1980 s 10).

6 Administration of Estates Act 1925 s 21A(1)(a) (as added: see note 5).

7 Administration of Estates Act 1925 s 21A(1)(b) (as added: see note 5). As to the meaning of 'will' see PARA 607 note 1. As to the accountability of a debtor executor see PARA 625. Before s 21A was added, the grant of administration to a debtor of the deceased did not release the debt, even at law; but the running of time was suspended while the debtor was administering the estate, so as to prevent the debt becoming statute-barred: *Seagram v Knight* (1867) 2 Ch App 628, CA.

8 Administration of Estates Act 1925 s 21A(2) (as added: see note 5).

644. Vesting of property pending grant of administration. Where a person dies intestate, his real and personal estate vest in the Public Trustee until the grant of administration[1]. Where a testator dies and at the time of his death there is no executor with power to obtain probate of the will[2], or at any time before probate of the will is granted there ceases to be any executor with power to obtain probate[3], the real and personal estate of which he disposes by the will vests in the Public Trustee until the grant of representation[4]. This vesting of real or personal estate in the Public Trustee does not confer on him any beneficial interest in, or impose on him any duty, obligation or liability in respect of, the property[5]. A notice to quit served on the Public Trustee[6] before a grant or on the persons in occupation as his agents[7] is effective to determine a tenancy.

Any real or personal estate of a person dying before 1 July 1995 vested in the Public Trustee on that date if it was property which was vested in the President of the Family Division immediately before that date, or was not so vested but as at that date there had been no grant of representation in respect of it and there was no executor with power to obtain such a grant[8]. Anything done by or in relation to the President with respect to property vested in him immediately before 1 July 1995 is treated as having been done by or in relation to the Public Trustee[9].

1 Administration of Estates Act 1925 s 9(1) (s 9 substituted by the Law of Property (Miscellaneous Provisions) Act 1994 s 14(1) with effect from 1 July 1995). As to the meaning of 'real estate' see PARA 607 note 1. As to the Public Trustee see TRUSTS AND POWERS vol 98 (2013) PARA 206 et seq. The Administration of Estates Act 1925 s 9 (as originally enacted), in force from 1 January 1926 to 30 June 1995, vested the real and personal estate of a person who died intestate in the President of the Family Division, formerly the Probate, Divorce and Admiralty Division, of the High Court in the same manner and to the same extent as personal estate formerly vested in the Ordinary. Section 9 (as originally enacted) replaced the Court of Probate Act 1858 s 19 (repealed as to deaths after 1925), by virtue of which the personal estate and effects of a person dying intestate became vested in the judge of the Court of Probate for the time being. See also *Re Deans, Westminster Bank Ltd v Official Solicitor* [1954] 1 All ER 496, [1954] 1 WLR 332, where it was held that the President was not a trustee for the purposes of the Trustee Act 1925 and had no duties.

2 Administration of Estates Act 1925 s 9(2)(a) (as substituted: see note 1). As to the meaning of 'will' see PARA 607 note 1.

3 Administration of Estates Act 1925 s 9(2)(b) (as substituted: see note 1).

4 Administration of Estates Act 1925 s 9(2) (as substituted: see note 1).

5 Administration of Estates Act 1925 s 9(3) (as substituted: see note 1). See also *Re Deans, Westminster Bank Ltd v Official Solicitor* [1954] 1 All ER 496, [1954] 1 WLR 332.

6 The Public Trustee may give directions as to the office or offices at which documents may be served on him and must publish such directions in such manner as he considers appropriate: Law of Property (Miscellaneous Provisions) Act 1994 s 19(1). The Lord Chancellor may by regulations make provision with respect to the functions of the Public Trustee in relation to such documents; and the regulations may make different provision in relation to different descriptions of document or different circumstances: s 19(2). The regulations may, in particular, make provision requiring the Public Trustee:

(1) to keep such documents for a specified period and after that period to keep a copy or record of their contents in such form as may be specified (s 19(3)(a));

(2) to keep such documents, copies and records available for inspection at such reasonable hours as may be specified (s 19(3)(b)); and

(3) to supply copies to any person on request (s 19(3)(c)).

'Specified' means specified by or under the regulations: s 19(3). The Public Trustee Act 1906 s 8(5) (payment of expenses out of money provided by Parliament), s 9(1), (3) (provisions as to fees) (see TRUSTS AND POWERS vol 98 (2013) PARA 230), apply in relation to the functions of the Public Trustee in relation to documents to which the Law of Property (Miscellaneous Provisions) Act 1994 s 19 applies as in relation to his functions under the Public Trustee Act 1906: Law of Property (Miscellaneous Provisions) Act 1994 s 19(5) (amended by Public Trustee (Liability and Fees) Act 2002 s 2(4)). As to the Lord Chancellor see CONSTITUTIONAL AND ADMINISTRATIVE LAW vol 20 (2014) PARA 255 et seq.

Such notice will be ineffective where the occupant has acquired statutory protection: see *Moodie v Hosegood* [1952] AC 61, [1951] 2 All ER 582, HL reversing *Smith v Mather* [1948] 2 KB 212, [1948] 1 All ER 704, CA applied by *Fred Long & Son Ltd v Burgess* [1950] 1 KB 115, [1949] 2 All ER 484, CA. See also LANDLORD AND TENANT vol 63 (2012) PARA 743 et seq. The notice to quit should be served direct on the Public Trustee at Public Trust Office, PO Box 3010, London WC2B 6JS: *Practice Direction* [1995] 3 All ER 192, [1995] 1 WLR 1120.

7 *Earl of Harrowby v Snelson* [1951] 1 All ER 140; *Rees d Mears v Perrot* (1830) 4 C & P 230; *Sweeny v Sweeny* (1876) IR 10 CL 375.

8 Law of Property (Miscellaneous Provisions) Act 1994 s 14(2), (3); Law of Property (Miscellaneous Provisions) Act 1994 (Commencement No 2) Order 1995, SI 1995/1317, art 2. Any property so vesting in the Public Trustee is treated as vesting in him under the Administration of Estates Act 1925 s 9(1) if the deceased died intestate, and as vesting under s 9(2) in any other case: Law of Property (Miscellaneous Provisions) Act 1994 s 14(4). As to the vesting of the intestate's estates in the President before 1 July 1995 see note 1.

9 Law of Property (Miscellaneous Provisions) Act 1994 s 14(5). So far as necessary in consequence of the transfer to the Public Trustee of the functions of the Probate Judge any reference in an enactment or instrument to the Probate Judge is to be construed as a reference to the Public Trustee: s 14(6).

(ii) The Doctrine of Relation Back

645. Relation back of administrator's title. In order to prevent injury being done to a deceased person's estate without remedy[1], the courts have adopted the doctrine that on the grant being made the administrator's title relates back to the time of death. This doctrine has been consistently applied in aid of an administrator seeking to recover against a person who has dealt wrongfully[2] with the deceased's chattels or chattels real[3]. It is also applicable against a person dealing wrongfully with the deceased's real estate[4]. It cannot be applied, however, to disturb the interests of other persons validly acquired in the interval, or to give the administrator title to something which has ceased to exist in the interval[5], or to bind the administrator to an agreement made before the grant irrespective of its benefit to the estate[6].

1 *Long v Hebb* (1652) Sty 341; *Waring v Dewberry* (1718) 1 Stra 97; *Mills v Anderson* [1984] QB 704, [1984] 2 All ER 538 distinguished in *Caudle v LD Law Ltd* [2008] EWHC 374 (QB), [2009] 2 All ER 1020, [2008] 1 WLR 1540 (court refused to order delivery of documents which were not required to apply for grant, as copies were obtainable, and recovery was not necessary to safeguard the estate).

2 A person who intermeddles with an intestate estate without a grant may be an executor de son tort, for there is no such term as an administrator de son tort: see PARAS 606, 1261 et seq.

3 *R v Horsley Inhabitants* (1807) 8 East 405; *Tharpe v Stallwood* (1843) 5 Man & G 760; *Foster v Bates* (1843) 12 M & W 226; *Barnett v Earl of Guildford* (1855) 11 Exch 19.

4 *Re Pryse* [1904] P 301, CA.

5 *Fred Long & Son Ltd v Burgess* [1950] 1 KB 115, [1949] 2 All ER 484, CA, where it was held that a tenancy was not revived by this doctrine.

6 *Doe d Hornby v Glenn* (1834) 1 Ad & El 49; *Metters v Brown* (1863) 1 H & C 686; *Mills v Anderson* [1984] QB 704, [1984] 2 All ER 538. See PARA 646.

646. Validation of dispositions made before grant for benefit of estate. The doctrine of relation back[1] is also applied to render valid dispositions of the deceased's property made before the grant when it is shown that those dispositions are for the benefit of the estate[2], or have been made in due course of administration[3]. The disposition need not have been made by the person who ultimately obtains the grant, provided it is ratified by the administrator on obtaining the grant[4]. The doctrine does not apparently justify a distress for rent made before grant[5].

Although, after grant, the administrator may enforce a contract entered into before grant[6], he is not estopped in an action brought after grant from setting up his title of personal representative to defeat his own acts before grant[7].

A promise to pay a debt made to a person assuming to act as administrator and who subsequently obtains letters of administration, will keep the debt alive in favour of the estate[8].

1 See PARA 645.

2 *Morgan v Thomas* (1853) 8 Exch 302 at 307 per Parke B. Whether dispositions made before the grant are for the benefit of the estate is to be judged objectively and in the light of relevant

subsequent events, not subjectively according to what was perceived to be beneficial at the time: *Mills v Anderson* [1984] QB 704, [1984] 2 All ER 538.See also *Caudle v LD Law Ltd* [2008] EWHC 374 (QB), [2009] 2 All ER 1020, [2008] 1 WLR 1540.

3 *Whitehall v Squire* (1703) 1 Salk 295; *Ellis v Ellis* [1905] 1 Ch 613. See also *Hill v Curtis* (1865) LR 1 Eq 90 at 100 per Wood V-C.

4 *Foster v Bates* (1843) 12 M & W 226; *Hill v Curtis* (1865) LR 1 Eq 90. Such ratification may not be necessary where a disposition has been made in pursuance of the duties conferred by the Administration of Estates Act 1925 on an executor de son tort; cf PARA 1266. As to the executor de son tort see PARA 1261 et seq.

5 *Keane v Dee* (1821) Alc & N 496n. However, in the old action of ejectment it allowed a demise to be laid at a period anterior to the grant: *Patten v Patten* (1833) Alc & N 493.

6 *Foster v Bates* (1843) 12 M & W 226.

7 *Doe d Hornby v Glenn* (1834) 1 Ad & El 49; *Metters v Brown* (1863) 1 H & C 686; *Mills v Anderson* [1984] QB 704, [1984] 2 All ER 538.

8 *Bodger v Arch* (1854) 10 Exch 333; *Clark v Hooper* (1834) 10 Bing 480, as explained in *Stamford, Spalding and Boston Banking Co v Smith* [1892] 1 QB 765 at 769, CA.

647. Proceedings begun before grant of administration. The doctrine of the relation back[1] of an administrator's title to the intestate's property to the date of the intestate's death does not render competent a claim which was incompetent when the claim form was issued[2], but where a grant of letters of administration is obtained by the claimant after starting proceedings the court may allow an amendment to the claim form and particulars of claim so as to alter the capacity in which he claims to that of administrator of the intestate's estate[3]. A claim will lie against a person making claims on behalf of the intestate's estate who has not yet obtained a grant of administration[4]. A claim can be brought on behalf of or against the estate of a deceased person where there has been no grant of representation[5]. A creditor or person beneficially interested in an estate may make an application for the appointment of an administrator pending suit[6], and a notice to quit can be validly given to persons in occupation before the issue of a grant, on the ground that those persons are agents of the Public Trustee[7].

The doctrine of relation back also applies for the purposes of the statutory provisions limiting the time for bringing claims to recover land or advowsons; the administrator is deemed to claim as if there had been no interval of time between the death and the grant of administration[8].

1 See PARA 645.

2 See *Ingall v Moran* [1944] KB 160, [1944] 1 All ER 97, CA; *Hilton v Sutton Steam Laundry* [1946] KB 65, [1945] 2 All ER 425, CA; *Finnegan v Cementation Co Ltd* [1953] 1 QB 688, [1953] 1 All ER 1130, CA. See also *Stebbings v Holst & Co Ltd* [1953] 1 All ER 925, [1953] 1 WLR 603; *Bowler v John Mowlem & Co Ltd* [1954] 3 All ER 556, [1954] 1 WLR 1445, CA; *Millburn-Snell v Evans* [2011] EWCA Civ 577, [2012] 1 WLR 41, [2011] All ER (D) 254 (May).

3 Ie by virtue of CPR 17.4(4): see CIVIL PROCEDURE vol 11 (2015) PARA 360. The effect of CPR 17.4 is to remove the effect of *Ingall v Moran* [1944] KB 160, [1944] 1 All ER 97: see *Haq v Singh* [2001] EWCA Civ 957 at [33], [2001] 1 WLR 1594 at [33], [2001] BPIR 1002 at [33] per Arden LJ.

4 *Loudon v Ryder (No 2)* [1953] Ch 423, [1953] 1 All ER 1005.

5 See CPR 19.8; and CIVIL PROCEDURE vol 11 (2015) PARAS 489–490.

6 See PARA 810. As to grants pendente lite see PARA 808.

7 See PARA 644. As to the Public Trustee see TRUSTS AND POWERS vol 98 (2013) PARA 206 et seq.

8 See the Limitation Act 1980 s 26; and LIMITATION PERIODS vol 68 (2016) PARA 923.

(5) PERSONAL REPRESENTATIVES' REMUNERATION

648. General principle governing personal representatives' remuneration. The general principle is that a personal representative must act gratuitously. He is not entitled to any remuneration[1] and he must not make a profit from his office[2]. This principle is subject to three exceptions, namely where the will itself directs remuneration[3], where it is authorised by statute[4] and where the court allows it[5]. Professionally drawn wills normally provide for the remuneration of executors in professional practice[6] and of trust corporations[7]. They may authorise lay trustees to charge for time spent.

1 See PARA 649.
2 See PARA 657.
3 See PARA 652.
4 See PARA 650.
5 See PARA 656.
6 As to the application to executors in professional practice of the general principle that an executor must act gratuitously see PARA 653.
7 See PARA 652. As to the higher standards required of a paid trustee see PARA 1247.

649. No remuneration for time and trouble of personal representative. Apart from the three exceptions previously mentioned[1], the personal representative is not entitled to any allowance for his time and trouble in transacting business as an English personal representative in relation to English estate[2]; he is entitled to his out-of-pocket expenses only[3]. Accordingly, he cannot claim commission for collecting rents[4], or for acting as auctioneer[5] or banker[6], and where he is at once the deceased's partner and executor he cannot claim an allowance for carrying on the business[7].

1 See PARA 648.
2 *Re Northcote's Will Trusts, Northcote v Northcote* [1949] 1 All ER 442. He is not obliged in equity to account for remuneration received in respect of a foreign grant of representation: *Re Northcote's Will Trusts, Northcote v Northcote.*
3 *Robinson v Pett* (1734) 3 P Wms 249; *Brocksopp v Barnes* (1820) 5 Madd 90; *Broughton v Broughton* (1855) 5 De GM & G 160 at 164; *Re Barber, Burgess v Vinicome* (1886) 34 ChD 77 at 81.
4 *Nicholson v Tutin (No 2)* (1857) 3 K & J 159.
5 *Kirkman v Booth* (1848) 11 Beav 273.
6 *Heighington v Grant* (1840) 5 My & Cr 258 at 262. Unless authorised by the will: *Re Waterman's Will Trusts, Lloyds Bank Ltd v Sutton* [1952] 2 All ER 1054.
7 *Burden v Burden* (1813) 1 Ves & B 170; *Stocken v Dawson* (1843) 6 Beav 371. As to when a director who is also a trustee may retain remuneration received by him see eg *Re Llewellin's Will Trusts, Griffiths v Wilcox* [1949] Ch 225, [1949] 1 All ER 487; and TRUSTS AND POWERS vol 98 (2013) PARA 368.

650. Remuneration of professional personal representatives under the Trustee Act 2000 where there is a charging clause in the will. Where a will makes provision for a personal representative[1] to receive payment in respect of services provided by him, a professional[2] personal representative is entitled to receive remuneration[3] in respect of such services, even if they are services which are capable of being provided by a lay personal representative[4].

These provisions substantially amend the common law rules relating to remuneration[5].

1 As to the meaning of 'personal representative' see the Trustee Act 1925; and TRUSTS AND POWERS vol 98 (2013) PARA 3 (definition applied by the Trustee Act 2000 s 39(1)). As to remuneration under the Trustee Act 2000 where there is no charging clause in the will see PARA 651.
2 Ie where the personal representative is either a trust corporation or acting in a professional capacity: see the Trustee Act 2000 s 28(1); and TRUSTS AND POWERS vol 98 (2013) PARA 371. As to when a trustee acts in a professional capacity see the Trustee Act 2000 ss 28(5), 39(2); and TRUSTS AND POWERS vol 98 (2013) PARA 371. As to the meaning of 'trust corporation' see the Trustee Act 1925; and TRUSTS AND POWERS vol 98 (2013) PARA 238 (definition applied by the Trustee Act 2000 s 39(1)).
3 Remuneration to which a personal representative is entitled under the Trustee Act 2000 28 is to be treated remuneration for services and not as a gift for the purposes of the Wills Act 1837 s 15 (gifts to an attesting witness to be void) so that the benefit of a charging clause is not lost if the

personal representative witnesses the will: see the Trustee Act 2000 s 28(4)(a); and TRUSTS AND POWERS vol 98 (2013) PARA 371. Nothing in s 28 is to be treated as affecting the operation of the Wills Act 1837 s 15 in relation to any death occurring before 1 February 2001: Trustee Act 2000 s 33. Remuneration to which a personal representative is entitled under s 28 is to be treated as an administration expense for the purposes of the Administration of Estates Act 1925 s 34(3) (order in which estate to be paid out: see PARA 998) and any provision giving reasonable administration expenses priority over the preferential debts listed in the Insolvency Act 1986 Sch 6 (see BANKRUPTCY AND INDIVIDUAL INSOLVENCY vol 5 (2013) PARAS 592, 594): Trustee Act 2000 s 35(3). Nothing is s 35(3) is to be treated as affecting the operation of the Administration of Estates Act 1925 s 34(3) or the Insolvency Act 1986 Sch 6 in relation to any death occurring before 1 February 2001 (ie the date of commencement of the Trustee Act 2000 s 35): s 35(3), (4); Trustee Act 2000 (Commencement) Order 2001, SI 2001/149, art 2.

4 See the Trustee Act 2000 ss 28(1), (2) (modified by s 35(2)(a)); and TRUSTS AND POWERS vol 98 (2013) PARAS 1, 371. As to the application of s 28 to charitable trusts see s 28(3); and TRUSTS AND POWERS vol 98 (2013) PARA 371. As to when a person acts as a lay trustee see ss 28(6), 39(2); and TRUSTS AND POWERS vol 98 (2013) PARA 371. See also s 33 and TRUSTS AND POWERS vol 98 (2013) PARA 371.

5 As to the common law rules relating to remuneration see PARAS 653–656.

651. Remuneration of personal representative under the Trustee Act 2000 where there is no charging clause in the will. Provided no other provision for remuneration has been made[1], a trust corporation acting as a personal representative[2] is entitled to reasonable remuneration[3] out of the estate for services provided to or on behalf of the estate[4].

A personal representative (who is not a trust corporation, a trustee of a charitable trust or a sole personal representative) and who acts in a professional capacity[5], may likewise be entitled to receive reasonable remuneration out of the estate for any services that he provides to or on behalf of the estate if each other personal representative has agreed in writing that he may be remunerated for the services[6].

A personal representative is entitled to remuneration under the above provisions even if the services in question are capable of being provided by a lay personal representative[7]. The test for determining what is reasonable remuneration is an objective one[8].

1 Ie provided by the will or by any enactment or any provision of subordinate legislation: see the Trustee Act 2000 ss 29(5), 35(2)(a); and TRUSTS AND POWERS vol 98 (2013) PARA 372. As to remuneration under the Trustee Act 2000 where there is a charging clause in the will see PARA 650.

2 The trust corporation must not be a trustee of a charitable trust: see the Trustee Act 2000 s 29(1)(b); and TRUSTS AND POWERS vol 98 (2013) PARA 372. As to the meaning of 'trust corporation' see the Trustee Act 1925; and TRUSTS AND POWERS vol 98 (2013) PARA 238 (definition applied by the Trustee Act 2000 s 39(1)). As to the meaning of 'personal representative' see the Trustee Act 1925; and TRUSTS AND POWERS vol 98 (2013) PARA 3 (definition applied by the Trustee Act 2000 s 39(1)).

3 As to the meaning of 'reasonable remuneration' see the Trustee Act 2000 s 29(3); and TRUSTS AND POWERS vol 98 (2013) PARA 372.

4 See the Trustee Act 2000 ss 29(1), 35(1); and TRUSTS AND POWERS vol 98 (2013) PARA 372.

5 As to a trustee acting in a professional capacity see PARA 650 note 2.

6 See the Trustee Act 2000 ss 29(2), 35(1); and TRUSTS AND POWERS vol 98 (2013) PARA 372.

7 See the Trustee Act 2000 ss 29(4), 35(1). As to when a person acts as a lay trustee see ss 28(6), 39(2); and TRUSTS AND POWERS vol 98 (2013) PARA 371. See also s 33; and TRUSTS AND POWERS vol 98 (2013) PARA 371.

8 See *Pullan v Wilson* [2014] EWHC 126 (Ch), [2014] All ER (D) 108 (Mar). The normal charge-out rate of the trustees is not determinative.

652. Direction in will for remuneration where remuneration is not available under Trustee Act 2000. A testator may of course by his will authorise his executor or the executor's firm to be paid for professional work[1], or for work which an ordinary lay executor could have done in person without the assistance of a professional[2]; but, where remuneration is not available under the Trustee Act

2000[3], to entitle a solicitor to the latter charges there must be clear words in the will[4]: a direction that he should be paid all usual professional charges is not sufficient[5].

For deaths occurring prior to 1 February 2001[6] an authority to a professional executor to make professional charges is a legacy, which will fail if the executor has attested the will[7], and any charges made will be repayable if the will subsequently turns out to be invalid[8]. Such an authority will not be effective where the estate is insolvent[9]. A clause authorising the remuneration of an executor in professional practice has been held to indicate a sufficient intention to remunerate a trust corporation subsequently appointed by codicil[10]. A professional trustee charging clause has been held not to authorise a trust corporation to charge[11].

1 *Re Sherwood* (1840) 3 Beav 338 at 341; *Re Wertheimer, Groves v Read* (1912) 106 LT 590. In *Re Orwell's Will Trusts, Dixon v Blair* [1982] 3 All ER 177, [1982] 1 WLR 1337 it was held in the case of a clause authorising 'any trustee' to charge for work done by him or his firm that it authorised charging for work done by a literary executor and for work done by a private company which was equivalent to a partnership of the literary executor.

2 See *Re Ames, Ames v Taylor* (1883) 25 ChD 72; *Re Fish, Bennett v Bennett* [1893] 2 Ch 413, CA. See also *Willis v Kibble* (1839) 1 Beav 559.

3 For circumstances in which remuneration is available under the Trustee Act 2000 see PARAS 650–651.

4 *Re Chalinder and Herington* [1907] 1 Ch 58. See also *Glenister v Moody* [2003] EWHC 3155 (Ch) at [24]–[25], [2005] WTLR 1205 at [24]–[25] where Judge Reid QC described the words used as clear enough and said that authorities were of limited use; he also considered the point at which a professional who has retired from private practice ceases to be a professional for this purpose.

5 *Re Chapple, Newton v Chapman* (1884) 27 ChD 584. See also *Clarkson v Robinson* [1900] 2 Ch 722, where it was held that an authority to charge for all professional services, whether in the ordinary course of the executor's profession or not, did not authorise a charge for work done outside the executor's profession.

6 Ie the date on which the Trustee Act 2000 came into force.

7 *Re Barber, Burgess v Vinnicome* (1886) 31 ChD 665; *Re Pooley* (1888) 40 ChD 1, CA; *Re Thorley, Thorley v Massam* [1891] 2 Ch 613, CA; *Re Brown, Wace v Smith* [1918] WN 118; *New South Wales Stamp Duties Comr v Pearse* [1954] AC 91 at 113, [1954] 1 All ER 19 at 28, PC. As to legacies to executors see PARA 1068.

8 *Gray v Richards Butler* (1996) 140 Sol Jo LB, (1996) Times, 23 July.

9 *Re White, Pennell v Franklin* [1898] 2 Ch 217, CA; *Re Shuttleworth, Lilley v Moore* (1911) 55 Sol Jo 366; *Re Salmen, Salmen v Bernstein* (1912) 107 LT 108, CA; *Re Worthington, ex p Leighton v MacLeod* [1954] 1 All ER 677.

10 *Re Campbell* [1954] 1 All ER 448, [1954] 1 WLR 516.

11 *Re Cooper, Le Neve-Foster v National Provincial Bank* as reported in (1939) 160 LTR 453. No reasons were given in the decision, and no attention was paid to the Law of Property Act 1925 s 61(b) ('person' in a written instrument includes a corporation unless the context otherwise requires).

653. Position in relation to professional personal representatives where remuneration unavailable under the Trustee Act 2000 or will. Where there is no right to remuneration under the Trustee Act 2000[1] the rule that the representative is not entitled to any allowance for his time and trouble[2] applies in particular to the case of a solicitor representative[3]. In the absence of a special clause[4] in the will authorising him to charge for professional services, he is only entitled to out-of-pocket expenses, and not to profit costs for work done out of court, whether acting for himself or for the body of executors[5].

If a solicitor-representative employs and acts by the firm of which he is a partner, profit costs cannot be allowed[6] even though it is proved to be the firm's practice to arrange that the profit costs should be taken by the members of the firm other than the solicitor-representative[7], or that all the business may have been transacted by such other members[8]. If, however, the solicitor-representative employs, not his firm as such, but the other members of the firm, and there is an express agreement that the solicitor-representative is not to participate in the profits to be derived from the business connected with the estate, profit costs may be allowed to the other members of the firm[9].

Should the representative in disregard of this rule have received any profit costs he must account for them to the estate, even though they were not earned at its expense. Accordingly he must refund the profit costs received by him in preparing a lease, even though the costs were paid by the lessee[10], and he must refund commission received by him on the introduction of business connected with the trust[11].

Although the solicitor-representative is the commonest instance of the executor in professional practice, other professional persons are frequently appointed as executors, and similar principles in relation to charges for services apply to them and to businessmen who are appointed as executors.

1 For circumstances in which remuneration is available under the Trustee Act 2000 see PARAS 650–651.
2 See PARA 649.
3 *Re Worthington, ex p Leighton v MacLeod* [1954] 1 All ER 677, [1954] 1 WLR 526. As regards the inherent jurisdiction to allow remuneration cf PARA 656; as to the duty of a trustee to act gratuitously see TRUSTS AND POWERS vol 98 (2013) PARA 370 et seq; and as to the position and charges of a solicitor-trustee see LEGAL PROFESSIONS vol 66 (2015) PARA 609 et seq.
4 See PARA 652. As to legacies to executors see PARA 1069.
5 *Lincoln v Windsor* (1851) 9 Hare 158; *Broughton v Broughton* (1855) 5 De GM & G 160; *Re Barber, Burgess v Vinicome* (1886) 34 ChD 77; *D'Arcy v O'Kelly* (1921) 55 ILT 48.
6 *Matthison v Clarke* (1854) 3 Drew 3. However, as to costs of litigation see PARA 654 text to note 2.
7 *Re Gates, Arnold v Gates* [1933] Ch 913; and see *Collins v Carey* (1839) 2 Beav 128; *Re Hill, Claremont v Hill* [1934] Ch 623, CA.
8 *Christophers v White* (1847) 10 Beav 523.
9 *Clack v Carlon* (1861) 30 LJ Ch 639; *Re Doody, Fisher v Doody, Hibbert v Lloyd* [1893] 1 Ch 129 at 134, CA; *Re Gates, Arnold v Gates* [1933] Ch 913.
10 *Re Corsellis, Lawton v Elwes* (1887) 34 ChD 675, CA.
11 *Vipont v Butler* [1893] WN 64.

654. Litigation costs where remuneration unavailable under the Trustee Act 2000 or will. The rule that a solicitor-representative is not entitled to an allowance for time and trouble[1] applies where the solicitor does business in court acting for himself as solicitor, whether he is claimant or defendant in the action[2]. There is, however, one exception to this rule: where the solicitor has acted in proceedings, whether of a hostile nature or not, not only on his own behalf but also on behalf of his co-representatives, he will not be prevented from receiving the usual costs, so far as he has not himself added to the expense which would have been incurred if he had appeared only for them[3].

Where a solicitor-executor practises in the provinces and employs a London agent to act in litigation in which the estate is concerned, he is entitled to pay and to be allowed out of the estate his share of the profit costs receivable by the town agent[4].

1 See PARA 649. For circumstances in which remuneration is available under the Trustee Act 2000 see PARAS 650–651.
2 *Re Barber, Burgess v Vinicome* (1886) 34 ChD 77 at 81 per Chitty J.
3 *Craddock v Piper* (1850) 1 Mac & G 664, followed in *Re Barber, Burgess v Vinicome* (1886) 34 ChD 77; *Re Corsellis, Lawton v Elwes* (1887) 34 ChD 675, CA; *Re Doody, Fisher v Doody, Hibbert v Lloyd* [1893] 1 Ch 129 at 138, CA. *Bainbrigge v Blair* (1845) 8 Beav 588 must be treated as overruled: see *Re Barber, Burgess v Vinicome* above at 83 per Chitty J.
4 *Burge v Brutton* (1843) 2 Hare 373.

655. Costs allowed when acting for beneficiary where remuneration unavailable under the Trustee Act 2000. A solicitor-representative, who is not entitled to remuneration under Trustee Act 2000[1], may act as solicitor for a beneficiary in a claim relating to the estate, because that is not part of the business of the trust properly so called, and if his beneficiary obtains his costs out of the estate, the solicitor is not deprived of those costs[2]; but he should not act for a party who occupies an adverse position to the estate, and if he does so he will be disallowed his profit costs[3].

1 For circumstances in which remuneration is available under the Trustee Act 2000 see PARAS 650–651.
2 *Re Barber, Burgess v Vinicome* (1886) 34 ChD 77 at 81.
3 *Re Corsellis, Lawton v Elwes* (1887) 34 ChD 675, CA at 684.

656. Court's power to allow remuneration to personal representatives. The court has statutory jurisdiction to allow remuneration to a personal representative who is a judicial trustee[1], or to a person appointed by the court as a substituted personal representative[2], or on a grant of letters of administration to a trust corporation[3]. There is also an inherent jurisdiction to allow remuneration whether the personal representative or trustee is appointed by the court or not[4], and to allow increased remuneration to a personal representative or trustee who is already authorised to charge[5], but this jurisdiction has been said to be one which is exercised sparingly and only in exceptional cases[6].

Fees are also payable where the Public Trustee acts as personal representative[7].

1 See the Judicial Trustees Act 1896 s 1(5); the Judicial Trustee Rules 1983, SI 1983/370, r 11; *Practice Note* [2003] 3 All ER 974; and TRUSTS AND POWERS vol 98 (2013) PARA 204. See also *Re Ratcliff* [1898] 2 Ch 352.
2 See the Administration of Justice Act 1985 s 50(3); and PARA 1163.
3 See the Trustee Act 1925 ss 42, 68(1) para (17); and TRUSTS AND POWERS vol 98 (2013) PARAS 4, 241. See also *Re Young* (1934) 103 LJP 75.
4 *Re Masters, Coutts & Co v Masters* [1953] 1 All ER 19, [1953] 1 WLR 81; and see *Marshall v Holloway* (1820) 2 Swan 432; *Forster v Ridley* (1864) 4 De GJ & Sm 452; *Re Freeman's Settlement Trusts* (1887) 37 ChD 148. The court's inherent jurisdiction may be exercised so as to allow trustees to retain directors' fees: see *Re Macadam, Dallow v Codd* [1946] Ch 73 at 82–83, [1945] 2 All ER 664 at 672 per Cohen J; *Re Masters, Coutts & Co v Masters* at 20 and 83 per Danckwerts J; *Re Worthington, ex p Leighton v Macleod* [1954] 1 All ER 677 at 679, [1954] 1 WLR 526 at 528 per Upjohn J; *Re Duke of Norfolk's Settlement Trusts, Perth (Earl) v Fitzalan-Howard* [1982] Ch 61, [1981] 3 All ER 220, CA; *Brudenell-Bruce v Moore* [2014] EWHC 3679 (Ch), [2014] All ER (D) 113 (Nov).
5 *Re Duke of Norfolk's Settlement Trusts, Perth (Earl) v Fitzalan-Howard* [1982] Ch 61, [1981] 3 All ER 220, CA.
6 *Re Worthington, ex p Leighton v MacLeod* [1954] 1 All ER 677 at 680, [1954] 1 WLR 526 at 530 per Upjohn J. However, Fox LJ suggested that this was not correct in *Re Duke of Norfolk's Settlement Trusts, Perth (Earl) v Fitzalan-Howard* [1982] Ch 61 at 79, [1981] 3 All ER 220 at 230–231, CA. See also *Re Barbour's Settlement, National Westminster Bank v Barbour* [1974] 1 All ER 1188 at 1192, [1974] 1 WLR 1198 at 1202–1203 per Megarry J (inflation could be a relevant factor even though general rather than exceptional). The court is unlikely to authorise remuneration of a personal representative where the estate is insolvent: *Re White* [1898] 1 Ch 297 (affd [1898] 2 Ch 217, CA); *Re Salmen, Salmen v Bernstein* (1912) 107 LT 108; *Re Duke of Norfolk's Settlement Trusts, Perth (Earl) v Fitzalan-Howard* at 77 and 229 per Fox LJ; or where a trust is short of money: *Brudenell-Bruce v Moore* [2014] EWHC 3679 (Ch), [2014] All ER (D) 113 (Nov). In the latter case, it was suggested at that the jurisdiction should only be exercised where, as in *Foster v Spencer* [1996] 2 All ER 672, (1995) Times, 14 June, work of an exceptional character is performed. See also *Perotti v Watson* [2001] All ER (D) 73 (July) (reversed as to quantum in [2002] EWCA Civ 771, [2002] All ER (D) 247 (Apr)) (remuneration allowed where the solicitor had done a substantial amount of work in relation to the estate even though he had been inept in his conduct of the estate in a number of ways, causing the estate to severely deplete in value).
7 See the Public Trustee Act 1906 s 9; the Public Trustee (Fees) Order 2008, SI 2008/611; and TRUSTS AND POWERS vol 98 (2013) PARA 230.

657. Personal representative may make no profit. It is an imperative rule of the court that a person with fiduciary duties may not derive any pecuniary benefit from his office[1] unless authorised[2] by the trust instrument to do so. Accordingly a personal representative must account to the estate for all profit derived from the trust property or from his office[3] as an English personal representative but not for profit derived from foreign assets received in respect of a foreign grant[4]. If he directly or indirectly purchases trust property the transaction is voidable within a reasonable time[5] at the instance of a beneficiary[6]; and an executor who renews a lease[7], who purchases the reversion of a lease which is renewable by contract or by custom[8], or who purchases the equity of redemption of a mortgage vested in him as executor[9], will be taken to have done so for the benefit of the estate. Similarly, he cannot buy debts due to the estate[10] or legacies[11] at less than their full amount, he cannot as trustee permit the assignment of a tenancy to a company in which he is a director and major shareholder[12], and may not exercise a power of appropriation to appropriate assets of the estate in satisfaction of his own entitlement under a will or intestacy unless the assets are equivalent to cash[13].

The disability to purchase does not extend to an executor who has renounced the executorship[14]. An executor who has acted as such, however, cannot ordinarily[15] avoid the disability by ceasing to act or by retiring from the trusts of the testator's will with a view to enabling himself to purchase[16].

An executor who, in the course of carrying on the testator's business, supplies goods to that business from his own must, in the absence of an express authority in the will, account for all profits made by the transaction[17].

All these transactions may, however, be carried out by order of the court[18], or when they are authorised by the terms of the will if there is one[19], and in practice are commonly carried out without an order if all the beneficiaries, being of full age and free from disability and between them absolutely entitled, concur in the transaction in question[20].

1 *Crosskill v Bower, Bower v Turner* (1863) 32 Beav 86 at 98–99. See TRUSTS AND POWERS vol 98 (2013) PARA 693.

2 'It is an inflexible rule of a court of equity that a person in a fiduciary position . . . is not, unless otherwise expressly provided . . . allowed to put himself in a position where his interest and duty conflict': *Bray v Ford* [1896] AC 44 at 51, [1895–99] All ER Rep 1009 at 1011, HL, per Lord Herschell. See note 19.

3 *Sugden v Crossland* (1856) 3 Sm & G 192, where an executor-trustee who had accepted a sum of money to retire from his office was ordered to refund. See TRUSTS AND POWERS vol 98 (2013) PARA 693.

4 *Re Northcote's Will Trusts, Northcote v Northcote* [1949] 1 All ER 442.

5 See *Re Jarvis, Edge v Jarvis* [1958] 2 All ER 336, [1958] 1 WLR 815 (six years' delay in seeking remedy against executor who carried on testator's business without authority; relief not granted).

6 *Hall v Hallet* (1784) 1 Cox Eq Cas 134; *Holder v Holder* [1968] Ch 353 at 398, [1968] 1 All ER 665 at 677, CA, per Danckwerts LJ.

7 *Keech v Sandford* (1726) Cas *temp* King 61; *Kelly v Kelly* (1874) 8 IR Eq 403; *Re Biss, Biss v Biss* [1903] 2 Ch 40 at 61, CA; *Brady v Brady* [1920] 1 IR 170, CA.

8 See *Phillips v Phillips* (1885) 29 ChD 673, CA. In the absence of fraud the disability does not apply where the lease is not so renewable: *Longton v Wilsby* (1897) 76 LT 770; *Bevan v Webb* [1905] 1 Ch 620. See also *Randall v Russell* (1817) 3 Mer 190. These cases were not cited in *Protheroe v Protheroe* [1968] 1 All ER 1111, [1968] 1 WLR 519, CA.

9 *Fosbrooke v Balguy* (1833) 1 My & K 226.

10 *Anon* (1707) 1 Salk 155; *Ex p James* (1803) 8 Ves 337 at 346.

11 *Barton v Hassard* (1843) 3 Dr & War 461. The purchase will be set aside in favour of the legatees who sold their interests; it will not operate as a release of the estate so as to enure for the benefit of the co-legatees: *Barton v Hassard*.

12 *Re Thompson's Settlement, Thompson v Thompson* [1986] Ch 99, [1985] 2 All ER 720.

13 *Kane v Radley-Kane* [1999] Ch 274, [1998] 3 All ER 753 (applied in *Fazio v Rush* [2002] EWHC 1742 (Ch), [2002] All ER (D) 392 (Jul) in relation to copyrights). As to powers of appropriation

see PARA 1153 et seq. It seems that the rule against self-dealing may also affect the exercise of a power of appointment or other dispositive power where a person who is both an object of the power and a trustee exercises the power in his own favour: see *Re Edward's Will Trusts, Dalgleish v Leighton* [1947] 2 All ER 521 (revsd on other grounds [1948] Ch 440, [1948] 1 All ER 821); *Re Beatty's Will Trusts, Hinves v Brooke* [1990] 3 All ER 844, [1990] 1 WLR 1503; *Re William Makin & Sons Ltd* [1993] BCC 453; *Re Drexel Burnham Lambert UK Pension Plan* [1995] 1 WLR 32; *Edge v Pensions Ombudsman* [1998] Ch 512, [1998] 2 All ER 547 (affd on other grounds [2000] Ch 602, [1999] 4 All ER 546, CA).

14 See PARA 1030.

15 Where, before he purported to renounce, an executor had performed minor and technical acts of intermeddling with the estate but had not afterwards taken any part in administration and the beneficiaries had not relied on him to protect their interests, a purchase by him of property belonging to the estate was held in the special circumstances of the case to be valid, even on the assumption that the renunciation was ineffective: *Holder v Holder* [1968] Ch 353, [1968] 1 All ER 655, CA. See further PARA 627 note 9.

16 See *Ex p James* (1803) 8 Ves 337 at 352; *Re Boles and British Land Co's Contract* [1902] 1 Ch 244 at 246. Where, however, a person had retired from the trusteeship 12 years before the contract it was held that he could purchase trust property: *Re Boles and British Land Co's Contract*. See further TRUSTS AND POWERS vol 98 (2013) PARA 378.

17 *Re Sykes, Sykes v Sykes* [1909] 2 Ch 241, CA, overruling *Smith v Langford* (1840) 2 Beav 362.

18 *Re Drexel Burnham Lambert UK Pension Plan* [1995] 1 WLR 32. As to the High Court's power to make an order approving any sale, purchase, compromise or other transaction by a personal representative see PARA 1169.

19 The authorisation can be express, or implied, for example where a person by being appointed as an executor is put in a position of conflict of interest: *Sargeant v National Westminster Bank plc* (1991) 61 P & CR 518, (1990) EG 62 (CS), CA (the rule that a trustee must not intentionally place himself in a position in which his interest conflicts with his duty does not apply where the trustees have been put in their position by the provisions of the testator's will). See also *Loring v Woodland Trust* [2014] EWCA Civ 1314 at [40], [2015] 1 WLR 3238, [2014] All ER (D) 198 Oct per Lewison LJ ; *Edge v Pensions Ombudsman* [1998] Ch 512, [1998] 2 All ER 547.

20 As to the necessity for independent advice for young persons who have just obtained their majority in order to negative any presumption of undue influence which may arise see eg *Powell v Powell* [1900] 1 Ch 243.

658. Employment of assets in personal representative's own business. A representative who employs assets of the estate in his own business is liable to account[1], at the option of the beneficiaries, either for the profits actually made or for interest on the sum employed[2], unless on its true construction the will authorises the representative to make such profits[3]. Where the representative has mixed the assets with his own money and has employed both in his trade, the beneficiaries, if they elect to take the profits instead of interest, can only insist on the proportionate share attributable to the employment[4].

Where the beneficiaries elect to claim interest, the principle on which the court proceeds is not to visit the representative with compound interest by way of punishment, but to charge him with the interest he has in fact received, or which it is just to say he ought to have received, or which it is so fairly to be presumed that he did receive that he is estopped from saying that he did not receive it[5]. Where the money has been employed in an ordinary trade the court presumes that the party against whom relief is sought has made the amount of profit which persons ordinarily do make in trade, and in that case directs compound interest[6]. In the case of a solicitor's business it is not to be presumed that compound interest could have been made[7]. The ordinary mercantile rate of interest has in the past been taken as 5 per cent[8], but the courts now tend to be guided by the percentages under the rules of court governing interest on judgment debts[9].

1 As to the general liability to account (eg for unauthorised payments or investments etc) see PARA 1254.

2 *Docker v Somes* (1834) 2 My & K 655; *Wedderburn v Wedderburn* (1838) 4 My & Cr 41; *Jones v Foxall* (1852) 15 Beav 388; *Macdonald v Richardson, Richardson v Marten* (1858) 1 Giff 81;

Townend v Townend (1859) 1 Giff 201; *Vyse v Foster* (1872) 8 Ch App 309 at 329 (affd (1874) LR 7 HL 318); *Re Davis, Davis v Davis* [1902] 2 Ch 314.
3 *Re Waterman's Will Trusts, Lloyd Bank Ltd v Sutton* [1952] 2 All ER 1054.
4 *Docker v Somes* (1834) 2 My & K 655; *Wedderburn v Wedderburn* (1838) 4 My & Cr 41.
5 *A-G v Alford* (1855) 4 De GM & G 843 at 851; *Burdick v Garrick* (1870) 5 Ch App 233 at 241. See also *Re Waterman's Will Trusts, Lloyds Bank Ltd v Sutton* [1952] 2 All ER 1054. As to estoppel generally see ESTOPPEL vol 47 (2014) PARA 301 et seq.
6 See *Burdick v Garrick* (1870) 5 Ch App 233 at 242; and *Tebbs v Carpenter* (1816) 1 Madd 290; *Walker v Woodward* (1826) 1 Russ 107; *Jones v Foxall* (1852) 15 Beav 388; *Williams v Powell* (1852) 15 Beav 461; *Walrond v Walrond* (1861) 29 Beav 586; but on the question of yearly rests cf *A-G v Solly* (1829) 2 Sim 518.
7 *Burdick v Garrick* (1870) 5 Ch App 233 at 241.
8 *Vyse v Foster* (1872) 8 Ch App 309 at 329 (on appeal (1874) LR 7 HL 318); *Re Davis, Davis v Davis* [1902] 2 Ch 314; *Re Waterman's Will Trusts, Lloyds Bank Ltd v Sutton* [1952] 2 All ER 1054.
9 See CIVIL PROCEDURE vol 12A (2015) PARA 1235.

(6) THE NEED FOR A GRANT OF PROBATE OR ADMINISTRATION

(i) Need for a Grant Generally

659. Need for grant of probate or administration. In certain cases small amounts of money may be disposed of by nomination or by payment to persons appearing to be entitled to them and no grant of probate or administration is required[1]. In general, however, a grant of probate or letters of administration in the United Kingdom[2] is necessary to enable the personal representatives to make title[3] to the deceased's property and thereafter to administer, collect and protect it for the benefit of the persons interested in the estate, whether as creditors, legatees or next of kin. In particular a grant is essential if the estate comprises real property or securities. A foreign personal representative cannot sue in the United Kingdom in his capacity as such[4]. While an executor who does not obtain a grant in the United Kingdom may validly appoint a trustee of the assets of the estate under the Trustee Act 1925[5], that trustee can only prove his title by reference to a proper grant of representation[6].

No grant is necessary in so far as the deceased has disposed of property by donatio mortis causa[7], because such a gift requires no act by the representative to vest it in the donee[8].

The civil remedy for failure to take out a grant is by citation[9]. If an executor has acted, he can be compelled to take probate[10].

A person who deals with assets of an estate without a grant can be made to account as an executor de son tort[11].

1 See PARA 661. As to funds in court see PARA 666.
2 As to the recognition of Scottish confirmations and Northern Irish grants see PARAS 831–832. As to the resealing of grants under the Colonial Probates Act 1892 see PARA 837. As to the acceptance of probate issued in the Isle of Man or Channel Islands as authority for the transfer of stock registered in the National Savings Stock Register, or the repayment or transfer of savings certificates to the person to whom the grant was made see the National Debt Act 1972 s 7; the National Savings (No 2) Regulations 2015, SI 2015/624; and FINANCIAL INSTRUMENTS AND TRANSACTIONS vol 49 (2015) PARA 151. As to the meaning of 'United Kingdom' see PARA 4 note 7.
3 See the Revenue Act 1884 s 11; the Administration of Estates Act 1925 s 2(1); and PARA 635 notes 3–4. As to an exception in the case of certain life assurance policies see PARA 665. The grant of probate provides conclusive evidence of the executor's appointment and the terms and authenticity of the will: *Griffiths v Hamilton* (1806) 12 Ves 298. See also PARAS 669, 855–856. During the

subsistence of a grant of administration even a validly appointed executor is prevented by statute from acting: see PARA 669 text and note 10. As to the necessity for a grant to maintain proceedings see PARAS 635, 647.

4 See CONFLICT OF LAWS vol 19 (2011) PARA 736. As to foreign domicile grants see PARA 844 et seq.

5 See the Trustee Act 1925 s 36; and TRUSTS AND POWERS vol 98 (2013) PARA 275 et seq.

6 *Re Crowhurst Park, Sims-Hilditch v Simmons* [1974] 1 All ER 991 at 1001–1002, [1974] 1 WLR 583 at 594–595 per Goulding J.

7 Ie a gift conditional on death: see GIFTS vol 52 (2014) PARA 271 et seq.

8 See PARA 921; and GIFTS vol 52 (2014) PARA 271 et seq.

9 See *Re Stevens, Cooke v Stevens* [1897] 1 Ch 422 at 434; on appeal [1898] 1 Ch 162 at 177, CA, per Vaughan Williams LJ. As to citation see PARAS 628, 700. As to the court's power to order production of a will see PARA 680. As to liability to a penalty see PARA 668.

10 See PARA 628. A person who has intermeddled as executor de son tort but has not been appointed executor cannot be compelled to take a grant of administration: *Re Davis* (1860) 4 Sw & Tr 213. As to administration proceedings in such a case see PARA 1168.

11 See PARAS 1263–1272.

(ii) Estates Exempt from Necessity for Grant of Probate or Administration

660. No grant possible in relation to monarch. There is no jurisdiction to make a grant in respect of the estate of a deceased British monarch[1], for to do so would be to contradict the principle of sovereignty and would in substance amount to an impleading of the reigning monarch[2]. Grants are required for the administration of the estates of other members of the royal family. However application can be made to a District Judge or Registrar that a will should not be open to inspection[3].

1 *Re King George III* (1862) 3 Sw & Tr 199.

2 *Re King George III* (1822) 1 Add 255; 4 Co Inst 335; 1 Bl Com (14th Edn) 242 et seq. As to sovereignty see generally CROWN AND CROWN PROCEEDINGS vol 29 (2014) PARA 4.

3 See the Non-Contentious Probate Rules 1987, SI 1987/2024, r 58; PARA 732 note 6; and *Brown v Executors of the Estate of Her Majesty Queen Elizabeth the Queen Mother* [2008] EWCA Civ 56, [2008] 1 WLR 2327 (public inspection of royal will).

661. Miscellaneous statutory exemptions from necessity for grant of probate or administration. In a number of cases provision is made by various enactments[1] authorising the payment of small sums and the disposition of personal effects and investments of small value to persons entitled to them without the necessity of obtaining a grant of probate or administration[2].

1 The enactments and instruments are those listed in the Administration of Estates (Small Payments) Act 1965 s 1, Sch 1, of which:

(1) those listed in Sch Pt I are enactments authorising the disposal of property on death, without the necessity for probate or other proof of title, to persons appearing to be beneficially entitled to it, to relatives or dependants of the deceased or to other persons described in the enactments, but subject to a limit which is in most cases £100 and which does not in any case exceed £100;

(2) those listed in Sch 1 Pt II are enactments giving power to make rules or regulations containing corresponding provisions subject to a limit of £100; and

(3) those listed in Sch 1 Pt III are such rules and regulations as aforesaid and instruments containing corresponding provisions made under other enactments and containing a limit which does not in any case exceed £200 (s 1(1), Sch 1 (amended by the Teachers' Superannuation Act 1965 ss 2(1)(c), 8(1), Sch 3 Pt II; the Trustee Savings Banks Act 1969 s 96(1), Sch 3 Pt I; the Merchant Shipping Act 1970 s 100(3), Sch 5; the Industrial Relations Act 1971 s 169, Sch 9; the National Savings Bank Act 1969, s 28(1), Sch 2; the Friendly Societies Act 1974 s 116(4), Sch 11; the Statute Law (Repeals) Act 1977; the Building Societies Act 1986 s 120(2), Sch 19 Pt I; the Statute Law (Repeals) Act 1993; the Statute Law (Repeals) Act 1998; and the Statute Law (Repeals) Act 2004)).

For the provisions referred to see PARAS 662–664.

2 In the case of deaths on or after 11 May 1984, the limit, subject to the provisions of Administration of Estates (Small Payments) Act 1965 Sch 1, is in each case £5,000 instead of the limit specified in

the enactment or instrument (see note 1); and for references to the said limits in those enactments and instruments there is accordingly substituted references to £5,000: s 1(1) (amended by SI 1984/539).

In addition, in the enactments and instrument listed in the Administration of Estates (Small Payments) Act 1965 s 2, Sch 2 (which enable a person by nomination to dispose of property on his death up to a limit of £100 or, in some cases, £200) the said limit, subject to the provisions of Sch 2, in each case is £5,000 instead of the limit specified in the enactments or instrument; and for references to the said limits in the said enactments and instrument there accordingly is substituted references to £5,000: s 2 (amended by SI 1984/539), Administration of Estates (Small Payments) Act 1965 Sch 2 (amended by the Friendly Societies Act 1974 s 116(4), Sch 11; and by the Statute Law (Repeals) Act 1993).

The Treasury may from time to time by order direct that the Administration of Estates (Small Payments) Act 1965 ss 1, 2, so far as they relate to any enactment have effect as if there were substituted references to such higher amount as may be specified in the order: see s 6(1)(a). Any order under s 6 applies in relation to deaths occurring after the expiration of a period of one month beginning with the date on which the order comes into force: see s 6(2). Any such order may be revoked by a subsequent order and must be made by statutory instrument: s 6(4).

The Treasury may amend or repeal other corresponding or superseded enactments: see s 5 (amended by the National Debt Act 1972 s 6(3); the Friendly Societies Act 1974 s 116(1), Sch 9 para 19; the Trustee Savings Banks Act 1985 ss 4(3), 7(3), Sch 4; and SI 1998/1446). As to the Treasury see CONSTITUTIONAL AND ADMINISTRATIVE LAW vol 20 (2014) PARAS 262–265.

662. Grant unnecessary for personal effects and pensions. Payments and dispositions may be made without obtaining a grant of probate or administration in the case of awards for personal war injuries and damage and other injuries to the effects of marines, pilots and salvage workers[1], personal effects of and arrears of pay, allowances, pensions and other sums due to deceased members of the armed forces[2] and civilian employees in Her Majesty's dockyards and naval establishments[3]; sums due to deceased police pensioners[4]; pensions and awards due to deceased firemen[5]; sums due as salary, wages or emoluments, or superannuation benefits to deceased civil servants[6] and to other persons employed in various public services[7]; superannuation payments due to deceased school teachers[8] and local authority employees[9]; and pensions or refund of pensions contributions of deceased members or office holders of the House of Commons[10].

1 See the Pensions (Navy, Army, Air Force and Mercantile Marine) Act 1939 ss 3–7; the Pensions (Mercantile Marine) Act 1942 ss 1–6, Schedule; and ARMED FORCES vol 3 (2011) PARA 710 et seq. See also the Naval, Military and Air Forces etc (Disablement and Death) Service Pensions Order 2006, SI 2006/606, art 69; and ARMED FORCES vol 3 (2011) PARA 710 et seq.

2 See the Pensions and Yeomanry Pay Act 1884 s 4; the Regimental Debts Act 1893 ss 7, 9; the Navy and Marines (Property of Deceased) Act 1865 ss 6, 8; the Naval Pensions Act 1884 s 2; and the Administration of Estates (Small Payments) Act 1965 s 1, Sch 1 Pts I, II (see PARA 661). In relation to payment generally see the Armed Forces (Pensions and Compensation) Act 2004 s 2(1), (3); and ARMED FORCES vol 3 (2011) PARA 711. See generally ARMED FORCES.

3 See the Navy and Marines (Property of Deceased) Act 1865 s 4; and ARMED FORCES vol 3 (2011) PARA 450.

4 See the Police Pensions Regulations 1987, SI 1987/257, reg L4(3) (amended by SI 2011/3063); and the Police Pensions Regulations 2006, SI 2006/3415, reg 83(4) (amended by SI 2011/3063). As to police pensions generally see POLICE AND INVESTIGATORY POWERS vol 84 (2013) PARA 197 et seq.

5 See the Firefighters' Pension Scheme Order 1992, SI 1992/129, art 2(2), Sch 2 para L5(3); the Firefighters' Pension Scheme Order 2006, SI 2006/3432, art 2, Sch 1, Pt 14, r 6; the Firefighters' Pension Scheme (Wales) Order 2007, SI 2007/1072, art 2, Sch 1, Pt 14, r 6; and FIRE AND RESCUE SERVICES.

6 See the Superannuation Act 1972 s 4; the Administration of Estates (Small Payments) (Increase of Limit) Order 1984, SI 1984/539; and CONSTITUTIONAL AND ADMINISTRATIVE LAW vol 20 (2014) PARA 298.

7 See the Superannuation Act 1972 ss 1(4), 4(3), Sch 1; and CONSTITUTIONAL AND ADMINISTRATIVE LAW vol 20 (2014) PARA 298.

8 See the Teachers' Pensions Regulations 2010, SI 2010/990, reg 113(3). See also EDUCATION vol 36 (2015) PARA 1082.

9 See the Local Government Act 1972 s 119; the Administration of Estates (Small Payments) (Increase of Limit) Order 1984, SI 1984/539; and LOCAL GOVERNMENT vol 69 (2009) PARA 446.
10 See the Parliamentary and other Pensions Act 1972 s 24 (repealed with savings); and the Parliamentary and other Pensions Act 1987 s 2(9), Sch 2; the Administration of Estates (Small Payments) (Increase of Limit) Order 1984, SI 1984/539; and PARLIAMENT vol 78 (2010) PARA 926 et seq.

663. Grant unnecessary for investments and insurances. Payments may also be made, without the need to obtain a grant of probate or administration, in the case of small sums due to deceased holders of government stock and war loans[1], saving certificates[2], and government and savings bank annuities and insurances[3], deceased national savings bank depositors[4], and deceased members of building societies[5], friendly societies[6], industrial and provident societies[7] and trade unions[8].

1 See the National Savings Stock Register (Closure of Register to Gilts) Order 1998, SI 1998/1446, art 27 (see now the National Savings (No 2) Regulations 2015, SI 2015/624); and FINANCIAL INSTRUMENTS AND TRANSACTIONS vol 49 (2015) PARA 134. Where the total value of all holdings of stock entered in the register in the name of a deceased person at the time of his death does not exceed £5,000, and probate of his will, or letters of administration to his estate, or confirmation as executor to the estate is not or are not produced to the Registrar within such time as the Registrar thinks reasonable in the circumstances of the case, the Registrar may, if he thinks fit, transfer the stock or any part of it:
   (1) to a person appearing to the Registrar to be entitled to take out such probate, letters of administration or confirmation; or
   (2) to any other person appearing to the Registrar to be a fit and proper person to receive it (Government Stock Regulations 2004, SI 2004/1611, reg 17(4)).
2 See the Savings Certificates Regulations 1991, SI 1991/1031, reg 15 (see now the National Savings (No 2) Regulations 2015, SI 2015/6240; and FINANCIAL INSTRUMENTS AND TRANSACTIONS vol 49 (2015) PARA 151.
3 See the Government Annuities Act 1929 ss 21, 57 (see FINANCIAL INSTRUMENTS AND TRANSACTIONS vol 49 (2015) PARA 157); the Administration of Estates (Small Payments) Act 1965 s 1, Sch 1 Pt I (see PARA 661); and the Administration of Estates (Small Payments) (Increase of Limit) Order 1984, SI 1984/539.
4 See the National Savings Bank Act 1971 s 9; the National Savings Bank Regulations 1972, SI 1972/764, reg 40 (revoked with savings); the Administration of Estates (Small Payments) (Increase of Limit) Order 1984, SI 1984/539; and FINANCIAL INSTITUTIONS vol 48 (2015) PARA 133. As to the recovery of payments made under invalid nominations see *Pearman v Charlton* (1928) 44 TLR 517.
5 See the Building Societies Act 1986 s 32, Sch 7 para 1; and FINANCIAL INSTITUTIONS vol 48 (2015) PARA 374.
6 See the Friendly Societies Act 1974 ss 66–68; the Administration of Estates (Small Payments) (Increase of Limit) Order 1984, SI 1984/539; and FINANCIAL INSTITUTIONS vol 48 (2015) PARA 702 et seq.
7 See the Co-operative and Community Benefit Societies Act 2014 ss 37–40; and FINANCIAL INSTITUTIONS vol 48 (2015) PARA 992 et seq.
8 See the Trade Union and Labour Relations (Consolidation) Act 1992 ss 17, 18; and EMPLOYMENT vol 41 (2014) PARAS 924–925.

664. Foreign conventions may make grant unnecessary. Where a convention has been concluded with any foreign country, payments and dispositions may be made in respect of deceased nationals of that country under any enactment, rule or regulation authorising payment or delivery of property without representation to consular officers of that country[1].

1 See PARAS 667, 719.

665. Grant unnecessary for life policies effected abroad. Where a policy of life insurance has been effected with an insurance company by a person who dies domiciled elsewhere than in the United Kingdom[1], the production of a grant of representation from a court in the United Kingdom is not necessary to establish the right to receive[2] the policy money[3].

1 As to domicile generally see CONFLICT OF LAWS vol 19 (2011) PARA 336 et seq. As to the meaning of 'United Kingdom' see PARA 4 note 7.

2 The right to receive the policy money includes the right to recover it by legal proceedings: *Haas v Atlas Assurance Co Ltd* [1913] 2 KB 209.

3 See the Revenue Act 1884 s 11 (amended by the Revenue Act 1889 s 19). See also *Re Loir's Policies* [1916] WN 87. Apparently this provision does not affect the liability of the policy money to what is now inheritance tax: see *Haas v Atlas Assurance Co Ltd* [1913] 2 KB 209 at 219. As to life insurance generally see INSURANCE vol 60 (2011) PARA 476 et seq.

666. Grant unnecessary for small amounts held in court. Where the value of the estate is less than £5,000 and the person dies intestate, the Accountant General must pay out the fund in court[1] to the person who claims to have a prior right to a grant of letters of administration if provided with a written request, a written declaration of kinship and a copy of the death certificate of the deceased[2].

1 Ie as a result of a payment into court under CPR Pt 36 (see CIVIL PROCEDURE vol 12A (2015) PARA 1653).

2 See the Court Funds Rules 2011, SI 2011/1734, r 24(1), (4). As to the order of priority to a grant of administration see PARA 768.

667. Powers of consular officers. A consular officer has powers over property:

(1) where a national of a foreign state, to which the statutory provisions have been applied by Order in Council[1], is entitled to payment or delivery in England of any money or property in respect of any interest in the estate of a deceased person, or vesting in possession on the death of any person, or is entitled to payment of any money becoming due on the death of any person[2]; or

(2) where the foreign national is a person to whom any money or property comprised in the estate of a deceased person may be paid or delivered in England, in pursuance of any enactment, rule or regulation (whenever passed or made) authorising payment or delivery of that money or property without representation to the estate of the deceased person being granted[3].

If the foreign national is not resident in England, a consular officer of the state of which he is a national has the same right and power to receive, and give a valid discharge for, the money and property as if he were duly authorised to do so by power of attorney[4]. No person, however, is authorised or required to pay or make delivery to a consular officer if he knows that some other person in England has been expressly authorised to receive the money or property on behalf of the foreign national[5]. An immunity or privilege normally enjoyed by a consular officer does not extend to any act done in the exercise of any power conferred upon him in connection with the estate of a deceased person[6] or any document held by him in connection with it[7].

1 Ie the Consular Conventions Act 1949 s 1: see PARA 802.

2 Consular Conventions Act 1949 s 1(2)(a). As to consular officers see INTERNATIONALRELATIONS LAW vol 61 (2010) PARA 30.

3 Consular Conventions Act 1949 s 1(2)(b).

4 Consular Conventions Act 1949 s 1(2).

5 Consular Conventions Act 1949 s 1(2) proviso.

6 Ie under the Consular Conventions Act 1949 s 1: see s 3.

7 Consular Conventions Act 1949 s 3.

668. Penalty for administering without probate or letters of administration. Any person who takes possession of and in any way administers any part of the estate and effects of any deceased person without obtaining probate of the will or letters of administration of the estate and effects of the deceased within certain time limits[1] is liable to forfeit the sum of £100[2].

1 Ie within six calendar months after the death of the deceased or within two calendar months after the termination of any suit or dispute respecting the will or the right to letters of administration

if there is any such dispute which is not ended within four calendar months after the death: see the Stamp Act 1815 s 37 (as amended: see note 2).

2 Stamp Act 1815 s 37 (amended by the Statute Law Revision Act 1890; and by the Finance Act 1975 ss 52(2), 59(5), Sch 13 Pt I). The Stamp Act 1815 s 37 merely inflicts a penalty for failure to prove the will or take out letters of administration within the specified time; it was not intended that the representative should be prevented from taking out probate or letters of administration after that time: *Bodger v Arch* (1854) 10 Exch 333 at 337 per Parker B. See also *New York Breweries Co v A-G* [1899] AC 62, HL (liability of company which made payments in favour of foreign executors of deceased member, although they had refused to obtain English probate).

Although the penalty is not in terms confined to cases where what is now inheritance tax (see PARA 1266 note 5) is payable, it seems that the penalty will not in fact be exacted where no such tax or duty is payable; cf *Bodger v Arch* at 337, where it was said that the sole object of the Stamp Act 1815 was to secure the payment of duty to the revenue.

(7) EFFECT OF A GRANT OF PROBATE OR LETTERS OF ADMINISTRATION

669. General effect of grant. Probate and letters of administration[1] with a will annexed, while unrevoked, are conclusive evidence of the due execution and validity of the will[2]. Similarly, letters of administration are conclusive of the deceased's intestacy[3]. Probate is also normally conclusive as to the wording of the will[4], unless an application for rectification is made to the Chancery Division[5]. No other division of the High Court will take notice of the right to a grant of representation to the estate of a deceased person[6], and when the probate court has established the right, no other court will permit it to be gainsaid[7]. Where administration[8] has been granted in respect of any real or personal estate[9] of a deceased person, no person can bring any claim or otherwise act as executor of the deceased person in respect of the estate comprised in or affected by the grant until the grant has been recalled or revoked[10]. A grant of probate or letters of administration is not as against a purchaser invalidated on the ground of want of jurisdiction, whether the purchaser has notice of the want or not[11]. A probate claim has been described as in a sense an action in rem[12].

1 As to the indorsement on probates and letters of administration of memoranda of orders made under the enactments relating to family provision see PARA 602.

2 *Whicker v Hume* (1858) 7 HL Cas 124 at 143, 156, 165; *Re Barrance, Barrance v Ellis* [1910] 2 Ch 419; *Re Wernher, Wernher v Beit* [1918] 1 Ch 339 at 350–351 (affd on other grounds [1918] 2 Ch 82, CA). As to the derivation of an executor's title from the will see PARA 633. As to the effect of revocation see PARAS 855–856.

3 *Tourton v Flower* (1735) 3 P Wms 369. As to the relation back of an administrator's title see PARA 645.

4 *Re Bywater, Bywater v Clarke* (1881) 18 ChD 17 at 22, CA, per James CJ. As to the assignment of probate business see PARA 678.

5 As to rectification see the Administration of Justice Act 1982 s 20; and PARA 187.

6 Although other divisions of the High Court have jurisdiction to entertain probate proceedings, they would in fact refrain from exercising it: see PARA 678. As to an executor's powers before probate to begin a claim see PARA 635.

7 See *A-G v Partington* (1864) 3 H & C 193 at 204, Ex Ch (affd sub nom *Partington v A-G* (1869) LR 4 HL 100); and see *Logan v Fairlie* (1825) 2 Sim & St 284 (revsd on another point (1835) 1 My & Cr 59); *Tyler v Bell* (1837) 2 My & Cr 89; *Price v Dewhurst* (1838) 4 My & Cr 76 at 81; *Bond v Graham* (1842) 1 Hare 482; *Whyte v Rose* (1842) 3 QB 493 at 507, Ex Ch; *Lasseur v Tyrconnel* (1846) 10 Beav 28 (decisions before the merger of the former courts of common law, chancery and probate by the Supreme Court of Judicature Act 1873). The case of *M'Mahon v Rawlings* (1848) 16 Sim 429, as reported, appears incapable of explanation. The grant constitutes an order of the court: see PARA 679.

8 As to the meaning of 'administration' see PARA 607 note 1.

9 As to the meaning of 'real estate' see PARA 607 note 1.

10 Administration of Estates Act 1925 s 15. See also *Re West, Barclays Bank Ltd v Handley* [1947] WN 2.
11 See the Law of Property Act 1925 s 204. See also *Re Bridgett and Hayes' Contract* [1928] Ch 163 at 168 (see also PARA 232 note 2); *Hewson v Shelley* [1914] 2 Ch 13, CA.
12 See *Re Langton* [1964] P 163 at 175, [1964] 1 All ER 749 at 757, CA, per Danckwerts LJ. As to the extent to which a judgment in a probate claim is effective against persons who are not parties see PARA 878; and see also PARA 848 note 1.

670. Grant of probate or administration not conclusive as to collateral matters. The judgment of the probate court[1] is conclusive only of the right directly determined and not of any collateral matter[2]. If the testator is in fact dead[3] the grant is the sole[4] and conclusive[5] proof of the personal representative's title, but not of the identity of the person who has obtained it[6], or of the deceased's domicile[7], nor is it strictly even prima facie evidence of death[8]. Where administration has been granted to a person as the next of kin of an intestate, the Chancery Division refuses, except under its probate jurisdiction, to try the question whether in fact the administrator is of kin to him or not[9], and where the decision of the probate court in an administration claim has turned on the question which of the parties is next of kin, that decision is conclusive upon that question in a subsequent claim between the same parties for distribution[10], but would not be so against a person who was neither a party to nor bound by the probate proceedings[11]. A court will, however, decide upon the claims of next of kin additional to those known at the time of the grant if this can be done without in effect revoking or neutralising the grant[12].

The fact that the probate court has admitted a document to probate as forming part of a testator's testamentary provisions does not prevent another court from coming to the conclusion, as a matter of construction, that the document has no operative effect[13].

1 See PARA 678.
2 *Blackham's Case* (1709) 1 Salk 290.
3 *Allen v Dundas* (1789) 3 Term Rep 125.
4 *Pinney v Pinney* (1828) 8 B & C 335; *Pinney v Hunt* (1877) 6 ChD 98; cf *Cox v Allingham* (1822) Jac 514; *Re Ivory, Hankin v Turner* (1878) 10 ChD 372.
5 *Allen v Dundas* (1789) 3 Term Rep 125; cf *Marriot v Marriot* (1725) 1 Stra 666.
6 *Ex p Joliffe* (1845) 8 Beav 168 at 174.
7 *Whicker v Hume* (1858) 7 HL Cas 124 at 144; *Bradford v Young* (1884) 26 ChD 656; *Concha v Concha* (1886) 11 App Cas 541, HL; but see *Vardy v Smith* (1932) 48 TLR 661 (affd 49 TLR 36, CA) where Lord Merrivale P decided the question whether one or the other of two claimants was the deceased's widow by accepting the judgment of a foreign court dissolving the marriage of one of the claimants with the deceased. See also PARA 679. Letters of administration are prima facie evidence of the deceased's domicile: *Eames v Hacon* (1881) 18 ChD 347 at 352, CA. As to domicile generally see CONFLICT OF LAWS vol 19 (2011) PARA 336 et seq.
8 *Moons v De Bernales* (1826) 1 Russ 301 at 307; *Allen v Dundas* (1789) 3 Term Rep 125. Under exceptional circumstances the grant has been admitted as evidence of death: see *French v French* (1755) 1 Dick 268; *Loyd v Finlayson* (1797) 2 Esp 564.
9 *Re Ivory, Hankin v Turner* (1878) 10 ChD 372; *Re Ward, National Westminster Bank Ltd v Ward* [1971] 2 All ER 1249, [1971] 1 WLR 1376.
10 *Barrs v Jackson* (1845) 1 Ph 582.
11 *Mohan v Broughton* [1900] P 56 at 58, CA, per Lindley MR. See also *Long v Wakeling* (1839) 1 Beav 400; and PARA 679.
12 See *Re Ward, National Westminster Bank Ltd v Ward* [1971] 2 All ER 1249 at 1252–1253, [1971] 1 WLR 1376 at 1380–1381 per Plowman J, explaining *Re Ivory, Hankin v Turner* (1878) 10 ChD 372, and *Concha v Concha* (1886) 11 App Cas 541, HL.
13 *Re Hawksley's Settlement, Black v Tidy* [1934] Ch 384 at 396 per Luxmoore J, cited with approval by Lord Neuberger in *Marley v Rawlings* [2014] UKSC 2 at [58], [2015] AC 129, [2014] 1 All ER 807. 'It is true that the will does not make sense, at least if taken at face value, but that is a matter for a 'court of construction'': *Marley v Rawlings* at [59] per Lord Neuberger. See also *Re Resch's Will Trusts, Le Cras v Perpetual Trustee Co Ltd, Far West Children's Health Scheme v Perpetual Trustee Co Ltd* [1969] 1 AC 514 at 547, sub nom *Le Cras v Perpetual Trustee Co Ltd,*

Far West Children's Health Scheme v Perpetual Trustee Co Ltd [1967] 3 All ER 915 at 925, PC (applied in *Parkinson v Fawdon* [2009] EWHC 1953 (Ch), [2009] All ER (D) 322 (Jul)). As to the distinction between the principles applied by a court of probate and those applied by a court of construction see PARA 708.

671. Forgery and fraud in grant of probate. Even after a grant of probate the courts have full jurisdiction to decide that the will is a forgery[1]. Where probate has been obtained by a fraud practised upon the next of kin, a court of equity has jurisdiction to declare the wrongdoer a trustee in respect of the probate[2]. However a court of equity cannot, on the ground of fraud practised upon the testator, set aside a will which has been admitted to probate[3], nor ought it to declare a person who has fraudulently obtained a benefit under the will a trustee for the person defrauded[4]. A probate is conclusive proof of validity until it is recalled[5]. Where administration is granted on concealment of a will which appointed executors, the grant is void from its commencement, and all acts performed by the administrator in that character are equally void, and cannot be made good even though the executor afterwards renounces[6].

1 *R v Gibson* (1802) (cited in Russ & Ry 343n); *R v Buttery and McNamara* (1818) Russ & Ry 342, CCR (overruling *R v Vincent* (1721) 1 Stra 481); *Priestman v Thomas* (1884) 9 PD 210, CA. See also *Allen v Dundas* (1789) 3 Term Rep 125; cf *Gallagher v Kennedy* [1931] NI 207.
2 *Barnesly v Powel* (1748) 1 Ves Sen 119 at 284. See also *Meadows v Duchess of Kingston* (1775) Amb 756 at 762.
3 *Gingell v Horne* (1839) 9 Sim 539; *Allen v M'Pherson* (1847) 1 HL Cas 191; *Meluish v Milton* (1876) 3 ChD 27, CA.
4 See *Meluish v Milton* (1876) 3 ChD 27 at 33, CA, per James LJ. As to revocation of a grant on the ground of fraud see PARA 848.
5 *Allen v M'Pherson* (1847) 1 HL Cas 191; *Meluish v Milton* (1876) 3 ChD 27, CA.
6 *Abram v Cunningham* (1675) 2 Lev 182. It is otherwise if the grant obtained by suppressing the will contains no appointment of executors: *Boxall v Boxall* (1884) 27 ChD 220.

672. Purpose for which court may look at original will. A court of equity has power to look at the original will for the purpose of construing it[1], even though the probate copy is in facsimile[2], but it is not entitled to look at the original will with a view to correcting an inaccuracy in the probate copy[3]. Probate granted of a will and codicil is conclusive of the fact of two instruments, even if written on the same paper[4]. Where, however, a codicil is executed in duplicate and probate is granted of both writings, evidence is admissible to show that they were one and not two instruments[5].

1 *Compton v Bloxham* (1845) 2 Coll 201; *Manning v Purcell* (1855) 7 De GM & G 55; *Re Harrison, Turner v Hellard* (1885) 30 ChD 390, CA. See also *Reeves v Reeves* [1909] 2 IR 521 at 533; *Re Battie-Wrightson, Cecil v Battie-Wrightson* [1920] 2 Ch 330. The court may look at the foreign original, even where only an English translation has been proved: *Re Cliff's Trusts* [1892] 2 Ch 229. In *Sammut v Manzi* [2008] UKPC 58, [2009] 2 All ER 234, the Privy Council declined to attach significance to the formatting achieved by a word processor that may well have been operated by a secretary.
2 *Shea v Boschetti* (1854) 18 Beav 321.
3 *Oppenheim v Henry* (1853) 9 Hare 802n. See also *Havergal v Harrison* (1843) 7 Beav 49; *Gann v Gregory* (1854) 3 De GM & G 777.
4 *Baillie v Butterfield* (1787) 1 Cox Eq Cas 392.
5 *Hubbard v Alexander* (1876) 3 ChD 738; *Whyte v Whyte* (1873) LR 17 Eq 50.

673. Powers of non-proving executors. Probate granted to one of several executors enures for the benefit of all[1]. The application of this principle led to the rule that in actions at law[2] the action was not properly constituted unless all the executors appointed by the will joined as plaintiffs even though some had not proved[3]. It has even been said that on the death of the one who has proved the surviving executor can sue even though he has never proved[4]. It is no longer necessary or proper for non-proving executors to sue or be sued as representing the testator's estate since the proving executors can exercise all the powers conferred by law on the personal representatives[5]. Whether or not it ever was or still is good law that a surviving executor can sue without obtaining probate, it has for a long time been the invariable practice to require the surviving executor to establish his title by obtaining a grant of probate.

1 *Webster v Spencer* (1820) 3 B & Ald 360; *Watkins v Brent* (1835) 7 Sim 512 at 517; on appeal 1 My & Cr 97.
2 The rule apparently did not apply in suits in equity: see *Cummins v Cummins* (1845) 3 Jo & Lat 64 at 92.
3 Selwyn's Nisi Prius (6th Edn) 784; Bullen & Leake's Pleadings (3rd Edn) 153, 472; *Brookes v Stroud* (1702) 7 Mod Rep 39; *Walters v Pfeil* (1829) Mood & M 362; *Cummins v Cummins* (1845) 3 Jo & Lat 64 at 92.
4 See the Irish case of *Cummins v Cummins* (1845) 3 Jo & Lat 64 at 93–94 obiter per Lord Sugden LC. Although this statement was obiter, the whole question of the rights of non-proving executors was carefully considered by the Lord Chancellor in that case at 92–96.
5 See the Administration of Estates Act 1925 s 8; and PARA 629. As to notice on delegation of powers by the proving executor see PARA 642 note 8.

674. Effect of grant of probate or letters of administration upon real estate. All enactments and rules of law relating to the effect of probate or letters of administration as respects chattels real apply to a deceased person's real estate[1].

1 As to deaths on or after 1 January 1898 and before 1 January 1926 see the Land Transfer Act 1897 s 2(2) (repealed as to deaths after 1925), and as to deaths on or after 1 January 1926 see the Administration of Estates Act 1925 s 2(1) (see PARA 945).

As to the meaning of 'real estate' for the purposes of the Land Transfer Act 1897 see s 1(4) (repealed as to deaths after 1925) (see PARA 945), and for its meaning for the purposes of the Administration of Estates Act 1925 see s 3(1) (see PARA 946).

As to the concurrence of all the personal representatives in a contract or conveyance of real estate see PARA 1024.

675. Documents received in evidence without further proof. Every document[1] purporting to be sealed or stamped with the seal or stamp of the Senior Courts or of any office of the Senior Courts is to be received in evidence in all parts of the United Kingdom without further proof[2].

1 An official copy of the whole or any part of a will, or an official certificate of any grant of administration, may be obtained on payment of the prescribed fee: see PARA 732.
2 Senior Courts Act 1981 s 132 (amended by the Constitutional Reform Act 2005 Sch 11 para 26(2)).

As to the meaning of 'United Kingdom' see PARA 4 note 7. As to the reception in one part of the United Kingdom of grants issued in another part see further PARA 830. As to the proof of a will in support of title by virtue of the presumption in favour of documents not less than 20 years old produced from proper custody see CIVIL PROCEDURE vol 12 (2015) PARA 927 et seq. The grant of representation constitutes an order of the court: see PARA 679.

9. THE GRANT OF PROBATE OR ADMINISTRATION

(1) THE HIGH COURT

(i) Jurisdiction

676. Derivation of jurisdiction. The existing jurisdiction to grant and revoke probates and letters of administration dates from 11 January 1858[1], on which date both the voluntary and contentious jurisdiction and authority of all then existing courts[2] and persons in relation to the granting or revocation of probates or letters of administration were absolutely determined[3], and were vested in a court known as the Court of Probate[4].

The Court of Probate was established as a court of record exercising the same powers throughout the whole of England as the Prerogative Court of the Archbishop of Canterbury then exercised in the province of Canterbury in relation to testamentary matters and causes and to the effects of deceased persons within its jurisdiction[5]. The court was given power to require the attendance of witnesses and the production of documents[6], and the practice was to be that of the Prerogative Court of Canterbury[7]. A principal probate registry was established in London, and district registries were set up in the provinces[8]. The Court of Probate was prohibited from entertaining suits for legacies or for the distribution of residues[9].

1 Ie the date of commencement of the Court of Probate Act 1857: see s 1 (repealed).
2 The chief of the existing courts having probate jurisdiction were the ecclesiastical courts. As to the origin and history of ecclesiastical courts see ECCLESIASTICAL LAW vol 34 (2011) PARA 1019 et seq.
3 Court of Probate Act 1857 s 3 (repealed).
4 Court of Probate Act 1857 s 4 (repealed).
5 Court of Probate Act 1857 s 23 (repealed).
6 Court of Probate Act 1857 s 24 (repealed).
7 Court of Probate Act 1857 s 29 (repealed). The present practice is governed in relation to non-contentious business by non-contentious probate rules and in relation to contentious business by the Civil Procedure Rules 1998: see PARAS 685–686.
8 Court of Probate Act 1857 ss 4, 13, Sch A (all repealed). A new scheme of district probate registries was embodied in the Supreme Court of Judicature (Consolidation) Act 1925, Sch 2 (repealed): see PARA 683; and COURTS AND TRIBUNALS vol 24 (2010) PARA 733.
9 Court of Probate Act 1857 s 23 (repealed).

677. Transfer of jurisdiction to High Court. In 1875 the Court of Probate[1] became consolidated with other courts into the Supreme Court of Judicature[2], and its jurisdiction became vested in the High Court of Justice[3]. The High Court has all the powers possessed by the old Court of Probate and those conferred on it by statute since 1875, in respect of both real and personal estate[4].

1 As to the Court of Probate see PARA 676.
2 See the Supreme Court of Judicature Act 1873 s 3 (repealed); and COURTS AND TRIBUNALS vol 24 (2010) PARA 687.
3 Supreme Court of Judicature Act 1873 s 16 (repealed).
4 See the Senior Courts Act 1981 ss 19, 25; and COURTS AND TRIBUNALS vol 24 (2010) PARAS 700, 701. Subject to the provisions of Pt V (ss 105–128) (see PARA 683 et seq), the High Court, in relation to probate and letters of administration, has all jurisdiction as it had immediately before the commencement of the Act (ie 1 January 1982) (see COURTS AND TRIBUNALS vol 24 (2010) PARA 701), and in particular all such contentious and non-contentious jurisdiction as it then had in relation to:
   (1) testamentary causes or matters (s 25(1)(a));
   (2) the grant, amendment or revocation of probate and letters of administration (s 25(1)(b)); and

(3) the real and personal estate of deceased persons (s 25(1)(c)).

Subject to the provisions of Pt V, the High Court performs, in the exercise of its probate jurisdiction, all such duties with respect to the estates of deceased persons as fell to be performed by it immediately before the commencement of the Act: s 25(2).

678. Distribution of probate business between the Family Division and the Chancery Division. Probate business was formerly assigned to the Probate, Divorce and Admiralty Division of the High Court[1]. Although other divisions of the High Court had jurisdiction to entertain probate proceedings[2], they would in fact refrain from exercising such jurisdiction[3].

With effect from 1 October 1971 the Probate, Divorce and Admiralty Division was renamed the Family Division and contentious probate business was transferred to the Chancery Division[4]. Non-contentious or common form probate business[5] remains assigned to the Family Division[6], but all other probate business is assigned to the Chancery Division[7]. References in this title to the 'probate court' are accordingly to the Family Division so far as non-contentious matters are concerned, to the Chancery Division so far as all other probate business is concerned, and to the County Court where that court has probate jurisdiction[8].

References in enactments or documents to the Probate, Divorce and Admiralty Division, the President of that division, the principal probate registry, the principal (or senior) probate registrar and a probate registrar are construed respectively, so far as necessary to preserve the effect of the enactment or document, as references to the Family Division and to the President, principal registry, principal registrar and a registrar of that division[9].

1 See the Supreme Court of Judicature Act 1873 s 34 (repealed); and the Supreme Court of Judicature (Consolidation) Act 1925 s 56(3)(a) (as originally enacted) (repealed). As to the probate jurisdiction of the High Court see PARA 677.

2 See the Supreme Court of Judicature (Consolidated) Act 1925 ss 4(4), 58 (repealed); and the Administration of Justice Act 1928 s 6 (repealed). The Supreme Court of Judicature (Consolidation) Act 1925 s 58(4), by virtue of which a cause or matter could not be assigned to the Probate, Divorce and Admiralty Division unless it fell within the former jurisdiction of the Probate Court or the Court for Divorce and Matrimonial Causes or was within the Admiralty, was repealed by the Administration of Justice Act 1970 s 54(3), Sch 11.

3 See *Pinney v Hunt* (1877) 6 ChD 98 at 101 per Jessel MR; *Bradford v Young* (1884) 26 ChD 656 at 667 per Pearson J; on appeal (1885) 29 ChD 617, CA. The existence of such jurisdiction was denied in *Priestman v Thomas* (1884) 9 PD 70 at 76; on appeal 9 PD 210 at 214, CA, per Cotton LJ.

4 See the Administration of Justice Act 1970 s 1 (as originally enacted); and the Administration of Justice Act 1970 (Commencement No 5) Order 1971, SI 1971/1244.

5 'Non-contentious or common form probate business' means, by virtue of the Senior Courts Act 1981 s 128, the business of obtaining probate and administration where there is no contention as to the right to it, including:

(1) the passing of probates and administrations through the High Court in contentious cases where the contest has been terminated;

(2) all business of a non-contentious nature in matters of testacy and intestacy not being proceedings in any action; and

(3) the business of lodging caveats against the grant of probate or administration.

As to the distinction between non-contentious or common form business and contentious business see PARA 684.

6 Senior Courts Act 1981 s 61(1), Sch 1 para 3(b)(iv). As to the Family Division see generally COURTS AND TRIBUNALS vol 24 (2010) PARA 710.

7 Senior Courts Act 1981 Sch 1 para 1(h). As to the Chancery Division see PARA 865 et seq; and see generally COURTS AND TRIBUNALS vol 24 (2010) PARA 704.

8 As to the contentious probate jurisdiction of the County Court see PARA 866.

9 Administration of Justice Act 1970 s 1(6)(b). The principal probate registry is renamed the principal registry of the Family Division: s 1(1) (repealed).

679. Functions of the probate court. The principal duty of the probate court is to decide whether or not a document is entitled to probate as a testamentary paper[1]; and who is entitled to be constituted the personal representative of the deceased, whether he died testate or intestate. A grant of probate or letters of administration, even though issued in common form out of a probate registry, is an order of the court[2] and cannot therefore as against a purchaser be invalidated on the ground of want of jurisdiction or of any concurrence, consent, notice or service, whether the purchaser has notice of any such want or not[3]. The probate court has no duty to construe a will except in so far as it may be necessary for these purposes[4]. The Chancery Division is the proper court of construction[5]. Nevertheless the probate court may, for the sake of avoiding undue multiplicity of legal proceedings, determine other questions in controversy arising out of the suit[6], but no declaration of legitimacy can be made in a probate action[7].

1 As to what papers are testamentary see PARA 707 note 1. As to the probate court see PARA 678.
2 *Re Bridgett and Hayes' Contract* [1928] Ch 163 at 168.
3 Law of Property Act 1925 s 204(1).
4 See *Re Jones* (1927) 43 TLR 324 (holder of office named as executor; determination that holder at date of testator's death was intended); *Re Gates* [1928] P 128; on appeal [1928] P 178, CA ('all my money'; construction by consent in probate proceedings, varied in Chancery proceedings, *Re Gates, Gates v Cabell* [1929] 2 Ch 420, CA); *Re Dulson* (1929) 45 TLR 228 (grant of administration with will annexed to widow on footing that trusts of will failed); *Re Pesca* (1930) 74 Sol Jo 59 (determination that gift to rector of named church was gift to rector for the time being at testator's death so as to entitle such rector to grant of administration with will annexed; no determination whether gift created valid charitable trust); *Wightman v Cousins* [1931] NI 138; affd [1932] NI 61, CA (trusts of will already administered, not a matter of construction); *Re Hawksley's Settlement, Black v Tidy* [1934] Ch 384 (where opinions as to construction expressed in probate proceedings were treated as obiter in Chancery proceedings); *Re Thomas, Public Trustee v Davies* [1939] 2 All ER 567; *Re Alford* (1939) 83 Sol Jo 566; *Re Fawcett* [1941] P 85, [1941] 2 All ER 341 (cases where it was held in probate proceedings that there is jurisdiction to construe testamentary documents in order to decide which should be admitted to probate). See also PARA 707.
5 *Warren v Kelson* (1859) 1 Sw & Tr 290; cf *Re Tharp* (1878) 3 PD 76, CA. The former Probate, Divorce and Admiralty Division (see PARA 678) would not make a declaration of trust on the footing of contract, as contracts and trusts were outside the matters assigned to it: *Re Heys, Walker v Gaskill* [1914] P 192 at 200 (a case of mutual wills). Cf *Betts v Doughty* (1879) 5 PD 26; *Stone v Hoskins* [1905] P 194. For consideration of the relationship between the court to which probate business is assigned and other divisions of the High Court see PARAS 624, 669–670, 677, 810, 828. As to the effect on problems of jurisdiction of the transfer of contentious probate business to the Chancery Division cf PARA 865.
6 *Re Tharp* (1878) 3 PD 76, CA; *Vardy v Smith* (1932) 48 TLR 661; affd 49 TLR 36, CA (effect of foreign decree of divorce: see PARA 670 note 7); *Re Fawcett* [1941] P 85, [1941] 2 All ER 341.
7 *Warter v Warter* (1890) 15 PD 35. It seems that the restriction applies even though the Family Law Act 1986 s 56 (see CHILDREN AND YOUNG PERSONS vol 9 (2012) PARA 110) confers jurisdiction on the High Court to make declarations of legitimacy, because the proceedings in a probate action will not have been begun by application form as required by the Family Procedure Rules 2010, SI 2010/2955 (see CHILDREN AND YOUNG PERSONS vol 9 (2012) PARA 249): see *Knowles v A-G* [1951] P 54 at 63–64, [1950] 2 All ER 6 at 10–11. An issue of legitimacy may be decided, however, in other proceedings: see CHILDREN AND YOUNG PERSONS vol 9 (2012) PARA 110.

680. Powers over testamentary papers. The court has jurisdiction, where it appears that any person has in his possession, custody or power any document which is or purports to be a testamentary document, whether or not any legal proceedings are pending[1], to issue a witness summons requiring him to bring in the document in such manner as the court may in the summons direct[2]. Alternatively, where it appears that there are reasonable grounds for believing that any person has knowledge of any document which is or purports to be a testamentary document, the High Court may, whether or not any legal proceedings are pending, order him to attend for the purpose of being examined in open court[3]. The court may require any person who is before it in compliance with such an order to answer any question relating to the document concerned[4] and, if appropriate, order him to bring in the document in such manner as the court may direct[5]. Any person who, having been required by the court to do so, fails to attend for examination, answer any question or bring in any document is guilty of contempt of court[6]. The person required to attend for the purpose of being examined is entitled to conduct money[7] and to be represented by counsel[8]. A solicitor holding a will for a client has no privilege in the matter, and may be ordered to bring it in[9]. It is doubtful if a witness summons can issue for service out of the jurisdiction[10]. An order will not be made on application by a person entitled to apply for a grant as an administrator if the document in question is not required before making the application for the grant[11].

A person who dishonestly, with a view to gain to himself or another or with intent to cause loss to another, destroys, defaces or conceals any will or other testamentary document filed or deposited in any court of justice is on conviction on indictment liable to imprisonment for a term not exceeding seven years[12].

1 As to the duty of parties in probate claims to lodge and provide written evidence of testamentary documents see PARA 870.

2 Senior Courts Act 1981 s 123. See also *Re Shepherd* [1891] P 323; and PARA 881 note 4.

An application under the Senior Courts Act 1981 s 123, in a case where there is no probate action pending, for the issue by a district judge or registrar (see PARA 631 note 7) of a witness summons to bring in a will must be supported by an affidavit setting out the grounds of the application, and if any person served with the summons denies that the will is in his possession or control he may file an affidavit to that effect in the registry from which the summons was issued: Non-Contentious Probate Rules 1987, SI 1987/2024, r 50(2) (amended by SI 1991/1876). 'Registry' means the principal registry of the Family Division or a district probate registry: Non-Contentious Probate Rules 1987, SI 1987/2024, r 2(1). As to the meaning of 'district judge' see PARA 631 note 6. See also *Re Emmerson, Rawlings v Emmerson* (1887) 57 LJP 1, CA.

Any application in a probate claim for the issue of a witness summons under the Senior Courts Act 1981 s 123 must be made to a master or district judge: CPR PD 57—*Probate* para 7.3. The application may be made without notice and must be supported by written evidence setting out the grounds of the application: para 7.2. 'Probate claim' means a claim for:

(1) the grant of probate of the will, or letters of administration of the estate, of a deceased person (CPR 57.1(2)(a)(i));

(2) the revocation of such a grant (CPR 57.1(2)(a)(ii)); or

(3) a decree pronouncing for or against the validity of an alleged will (CPR 57.1(2)(a)(iii)),

not being a claim which is non-contentious (or common form) probate business: CPR 57.1(2)(a). As to the meaning of 'non-contentious or common form probate business' see the Senior Courts Act 1981 s 128; and PARA 678 note 5 (definition applied by CPR 57.1(2)(a)). 'Relevant office' means:

(a) in the case of High Court proceedings in a Chancery district registry, that registry (CPR 57.1(2)(b)(i));

(b) in the case of any other High Court proceedings, Chancery Chambers at the Royal Courts of Justice, Strand, London, WC2A 2LL (CPR 57.1(2)(b)(ii)); and

(c) in the case of County Court proceedings, the office of the County Court hearing centre in question (CPR 57.1(2)(b)(iii)),

see also CPR PD 57—*Probate* para 2.2. Any person against whom a witness summons is issued and who denies that the will or other testamentary document referred to in the witness summons is in his possession or under his control may file written evidence to that effect: para 7.4. As to the meaning of 'testamentary document' see PARA 870.

3 Senior Courts Act 1981 s 122(1). An application under s 122 for an order requiring a person to attend for examination may, unless a probate action has been commenced, be made to a district judge or registrar by summons which must be served on every such person: Non-Contentious Probate Rules 1987, SI 1987/2024, r 50(1) (amended by SI 1991/1876). See also *Re Laws* (1872) LR 2 P & D 458; cf *Banfield v Pickard* (1881) 6 PD 33.

Any party applying for an order under the Senior Courts Act 1981 s 122 must serve the application notice on the person against whom the order is sought: see CPR PD 57—*Probate* para 7.1. An application under the Senior Courts Act 1981 s 122 must be made to a master or district judge: CPR PD 57—*Probate* para 7.3.

4 Senior Courts Act 1981 s 122(2)(a).

5 Senior Courts Act 1981 s 122(2)(b).

6 Senior Courts Act 1981 s 122(3). See also *Simmons v Dean* (1858) 27 LJP & M 103; cf *Parkinson v Thornton* (1867) 37 LJP & M 3 (order for attendance in court rather than committal to be made in first instance). As to contempt of court generally see CONTEMPT OF COURT.
7 See *Re Harvey* [1907] P 239, commenting upon *Re Wyatt* [1898] P 15.
8 See *Re Cope* (1867) 36 LJP & M 83.
9 *Re Harvey* [1907] P 239 at 240.
10 See Tristram and Coote's Probate Practice (31st Edn) 27.32. As to the administration of estates involving a conflict of laws see CONFLICT OF LAWS vol 19 (2011) PARA 729 et seq.
11 See *Caudle v LD Law Ltd* [2008] EWHC 374 (QB), [2009] 2 All ER 1020, [2008] 1 WLR 1540 where the claimant did not need the documentation in order to apply for a grant, as copies were obtainable, and he did not need to take possession of the documentation in order to safeguard the estate. For an administrator's acts before grant, see PARAS 643, 644.
12 See the Theft Act 1968 s 20(1); and CRIMINAL LAW vol 25 (2016) PARA 355.

681. Jurisdiction of judges, district judges and masters. Where the rules of court[1] provide for the court to perform any act then, except where an enactment, rule or practice direction provides otherwise, that act may be performed:

(1) in relation to proceedings in the High Court, by any judge, Master or district judge[2] of that Court[3]; and
(2) in relation to proceedings in the County Court, by any judge of the County Court[4].

A district judge may, during the long vacation, exercise all powers exercisable under the non-contentious probate rules[5] by a judge in chambers[6]. An appeal against a decision or requirement of a district judge or registrar is made by summons to a judge[7].

1 Ie the Civil Procedure Rules 1998, SI 1998/3132 (see generally CIVIL PROCEDURE vol 11 (2015) PARA 12 et seq).
2 As to the meaning of 'district judge' see PARA 631 note 6.
3 See CPR 2.4(a); and CIVIL PROCEDURE vol 11 (2015) PARA 97.
4 See CPR 2.4(b); and CIVIL PROCEDURE vol 11 (2015) PARA 97.
5 Ie the Non-Contentious Probate Rules 1987, SI 1987/2024: see r 64.
6 Non-Contentious Probate Rules 1987, SI 1987/2024, r 64 (amended by SI 1991/1876). For instances of applications which are made to the district judge or registrar on summons see PARA 702 et seq.
7 See the Non-Contentious Probate Rules 1987, SI 1987/2024, r 65(1); and PARA 705. As to registrars see PARA 631 note 7. A registrar has no power to set aside the order of another registrar in a co-ordinate jurisdiction: see *Re Mathew* [1984] 2 All ER 396, [1984] 1 WLR 1011.

682. Co-operation between the probate registries and the courts. On the issue of a claim form[1] by which a probate claim[2] is begun, the relevant office[3] will send a notice to Leeds District Probate Registry requesting that all testamentary documents, grants of representation and other relevant documents held at any probate registry are sent to the relevant office[4]. The commencement of a probate claim will, unless a court otherwise directs, prevent any grant of probate or letters of administration being made until the probate claim has been disposed of[5]. A copy of every order made for the rectification of a will[6] must be sent to the principal registry of the family division for filing, and a memorandum of the order must be indorsed on or permanently annexed to, the grant under which the estate is administered[7]. Unless the court orders otherwise, if a testamentary document is held by the court (whether it was lodged by a party or it was previously held at a probate registry) when the claim has been disposed of, the court will send it to Leeds District Probate Registry[8].

1 Under the CPR the claim form is the main method of starting proceedings in the High Court and the county court (in place of the former writ and summons). As to the commencement of proceedings to start a probate claim see CPR Pt 57 and CPR PD 57—*Probate* para 2.1; and see PARA 868 et seq.
2 As to the meaning of 'probate claim' see PARA 680 note 2.

3 As to the meaning of 'relevant office' see PARA 680 note 2.
4 CPR PD 57—*Probate* para 2.3. As to testamentary documents see PARA 870.
5 CPR PD 57—*Probate* para 2.4.
6 See PARA 741.
7 CPR PD 57—*Probate* para 11.
8 CPR PD 57—*Probate* para 3.1.

683. Jurisdiction of district registrars. District probate registries have been established in the provinces[1]. Applications for grants of probate or administration and for the revocation of grants may be made to a district probate registry[2]. Any grant made by a district probate registrar[3] must be made in the name of the High Court under the seal used in the registry[4]. However, a district probate registrar[5] has no power to make a grant in any case in which there is contention until the contention is disposed of[6], or in any case in which it appears to him that a grant ought not to be made without the directions of a judge of the High Court or a district judge[7].

Subject to probate rules[8], no grant in respect of the estate[9], or part of the estate, of a deceased person may be made out of any district probate registry on any application if, at any time before the making of a grant, it appears to the registrar concerned that some other application has been made in respect of that estate or, as the case may be, that part of it, and has not been either refused or withdrawn[10]. Any person aggrieved by a decision or requirement of a registrar may appeal by summons to a judge[11].

1 The Court of Probate Act 1857 s 13, Sch A (repealed) established district registries throughout England. For the present scheme of district registries see the Senior Courts Act 1981 s 104(1)–(3); the District Probate Registries Order 1982, SI 1982/379; and COURTS AND TRIBUNALS vol 24 (2010) PARA 733. A number of sub-registries were established by virtue of the Non-Contentious Probate Rules 1954, SI 1954/796, r 2A (repealed). The functions of a sub-registry are to receive applications for grants (see PARAS 726–727) and search, and record the results of searches, of the index of pending applications maintained by the senior district judge: see the Non-Contentious Probate Rules 1987, SI 1987/2024, r 57 (substituted by SI 1998/1903).
2 Senior Courts Act 1981 s 105(b). See note 1. 'Grant' means a grant of probate or administration: s 128. As to the meaning of 'administration' see PARA 622 note 8.
3 As to the appointment, qualifications, etc of district probate registrars see COURTS AND TRIBUNALS vol 24 (2010) PARAS 739, 747. As to the meanings of 'grant' and 'registrar' see PARA 631 note 7.

A registrar to whom any application is made under the Non-Contentious Probate Rules 1987, SI 1987/2024, may order the transfer of the application to another district judge or registrar having jurisdiction: r 62 (amended by SI 1991/1876). A registrar may hear and dispose of such an application on behalf of any other registrar by whom the application would otherwise have been heard, if that other registrar so requests or an application in that behalf is made by a party making an application under the rules; and where the circumstances require it, the registrar must, without the need for any such request or application, hear and dispose of the application: Non-Contentious Probate Rules 1987, SI 1987/2024, r 62A (added by SI 1998/1903). As to the meaning of 'district judge' see PARA 631 note 6.
4 Senior Courts Act 1981 s 106(1). See note 1.
5 See note 3.
6 Non-Contentious Probate Rules 1987, SI 1987/2024, r 7(1)(a) (amended by SI 1991/1876).
7 Non-Contentious Probate Rules 1987, SI 1987/2024, r 7(1)(b) (amended by SI 1991/1876). As to the meaning of 'district judge' see PARA 631 note 6. In any case in which it appears that a grant ought not to be made without the directions of a judge of the High Court or a district judge, the registrar must send a statement of the matter in question to the principal registry for directions: Non-Contentious Probate Rules 1987, SI 1987/2024, r 7(2) (amended by SI 1991/1876). A district judge may either confirm that the matter be referred to a judge of the High Court and give directions accordingly or may direct the registrar to proceed with the matter in accordance with such instructions as are deemed necessary, which may include a direction to take no further action in relation to the matter: Non-Contentious Probate Rules 1987, SI 1987/2024, r 7(3) (amended by SI 1991/1876).
8 As to the meaning of 'probate rules' see PARA 620 note 6.
9 As to the meaning of 'estate' see PARA 620 note 5.

10 Senior Courts 1981 s 107.
11 See the Non-Contentious Probate Rules 1987, SI 1987/2024, r 65; and PARA 705.

684. Distinction between non-contentious and contentious business. Probate business is divided into non-contentious or common form business, and contentious business. Common form business consists of the obtaining of grants of probate and letters of administration where there is no contention as to the right to obtain them, including the passing of probates and administrations through the court in contentious cases when the contest is terminated, and all business of a non-contentious nature in matters of testacy and intestacy, not being proceedings in any action, and also the business of lodging caveats against the grant of probate or administration[1]. All other business of the court, except the warning of caveats, is contentious[2].

In practice, since the transfer of contentious jurisdiction to the Chancery Division, the criterion is the issue of the claim form. All matters before the issue of a claim form come before the Family Division and all matters after the issue come before the Chancery Division until the contest is terminated by final order or consent[3].

1 See the definition of 'non-contentious, or common form probate business' for the purposes of the Senior Courts Act 1981 Pt V (ss 105–128) set out in s 128 (see PARA 678 note 5); and see Pt V for the provisions of that Act relating to probate causes and matters. The non-contentious jurisdiction remains in the Family Division: see PARA 678. As to the lodging of caveats see PARA 690.
2 Contentious business is assigned to the Chancery Division: see PARAS 678, 865. As to the warning of caveats see PARA 691.
3 See PARA 678.

(ii) Practice and Procedure

685. Probate rules. Probate rules[1] may be made by the Lord Chief Justice, or a judicial office-holder nominated by him, with the agreement of the Lord Chancellor, and prescribing the practice and procedure of the High Court with respect to non-contentious[2] or common form probate business[3].

The Civil Procedure Rules do not apply to non-contentious or common form probate proceedings[4] except to the extent that they are applied to those proceedings by another enactment[5]. The Rules of the Supreme Court 1965[6] apply to non-contentious probate subject to the provisions of the probate rules and any enactment[7].

1 Ie rules of court. The present rules in force are the Non-Contentious Probate Rules 1987, SI 1987/2024. Where the deceased died before 1 January 1926, the person or persons entitled to a grant, subject to the provisions of any enactment, must be determined in accordance with the principles and rules under which the court would have acted at the date of death: r 23. A set of rules to replace the Non-Contentious Probate Rules 1987, SI 1987/2024, were drafted, and a consultation took place: see Consultation on draft rules in relation to non-contentious probate business in England and Wales (closed 29 August 2013). At the date at which this volume states the law no such rules had been made.
2 Non-contentious business remains in the Family Division: see PARA 678. As to the distinction between non-contentious business and contentious business see PARA 684. As to the meaning of 'non-contentious or common form probate business' see PARA 678 note 5.
3 Senior Courts Act 1981 s 127(1) (amended by the Constitutional Reform Act 2005 Sch 1 para 12(2)); Constitutional Reform Act 2005 Sch 1 para 2(1). Probate rules are made in accordance with the Constitutional Reform Act 2005 Sch 1 Pt 1 (see CONSTITUTIONAL AND ADMINISTRATIVE LAW vol 20 (2014) PARA 255): Senior Courts Act 1981 s 127(1) (as so amended). Without prejudice to the generality of the Senior Courts Act 1981 s 127(1), probate rules may make provision for regulating the classes of persons entitled to grants of probate or administration in particular circumstances and the relative priorities of their claims: s 127(2). As to the Lord Chief Justice see CONSTITUTIONAL AND ADMINISTRATIVE LAW vol 20 (2014)

PARA 128; COURTS AND TRIBUNALS vol 24 (2010) PARA 604. As to the Lord Chancellor see CONSTITUTIONAL AND ADMINISTRATIVE LAW vol 20 (2014) PARA 255 et seq.

4 See PARA 684.

5 CPR 2.1(2).

6 Ie as they were in force immediately before 26 April 1999. As from 24 February 2003, CPR Sch 1 RSC Ord 62 (now revoked) does not apply to costs in non-contentious probate matters and CPR Pts 43, 44 (except rr 44.9–44.12), 47, 48 apply to costs in those matters subject to modifications whereby every reference in those parts to a district judge is construed as referring to a district judge of the Principal Registry: see the Non-Contentious Probate Rules 1987, SI 1987/2024, r 60(1), (3) (r 60 substituted by SI 2003/185). See further PARA 687.

7 See the Non-Contentious Probate Rules 1987, SI 1987/2024, r 3(1) (r 3 substituted by SI 1999/1015). However nothing in RSC Ord 3 prevents time from running in the Long Vacation: Non-Contentious Probate Rules 1987, SI 1987/2024, r 3(2) (as so substituted).

686. Fees. Orders have been made[1] laying down the fees which are to be taken in non-contentious[2] and contentious business[3] respectively.

In general, on an application for a grant a fixed fee is payable where the value of the estate exceeds a certain sum[4]. Where the Lord Chancellor is satisfied that there are exceptional circumstances that justify doing so, he may remit a specified fee[5]. If a party satisfies the disposable capital test[6], application may be made for a full or partial remission of the fee[7]. A special fee is prescribed where the estate is exempt from inheritance tax where the deceased was a member of the armed forces and death was on active service[8].

1 Ie under the Courts Act 2003 s 92: see COURTS AND TRIBUNALS vol 24 (2010) PARA 762.

2 See the Non-Contentious Probate Fees Order 2004, SI 2004/3120 (amended by SI 2007/2174; SI 2011/588; SI 2013/2302; SI 2014/513; SI 2014/590; SI 2014/876; and SI 2016/211). As to the fees to be taken in the principal registry of the Family Division and in each district registry see the Non-Contentious Probate Fees Order 2004, SI 2004/3120, art 2, Sch 1 (Sch 1 substituted by SI 2011/588).

3 See the Civil Proceedings Fees Order 2008, SI 2008/1053 (see CIVIL PROCEDURE vol 11 (2015) PARA 68). As to the fees to be taken see art 2, Sch 1; and COURTS AND TRIBUNALS vol 24 (2010) PARA 762. The Order does not apply to non-contentious probate business: art 3(a).

4 On an application for a grant where the value of the estate exceeds £5,000 the fee payable is £155: Non-Contentious Probate Fees Order 2004, SI 2004/3120, Sch 1 Fee 1 (Sch 1 as substituted (see note 2); Sch 1 Fee 1 amended by SI 2014/876). As to proposals to introduce a sliding scale for fees linked to the value of the probate estate see Consultation on proposals to reform fees for grants of probate (closed 1 April 2016). 'Grant' means a grant of probate or letters of administration: Non-Contentious Probate Fees Order 2004, SI 2004/3120, art 1(2)(d). In determining the value of any personal estate there is to be excluded the value of a death gratuity payable under the Judicial Pensions Act 1981 s 17(2) or the Judicial Pensions and Retirement Act 1993 (see COURTS AND TRIBUNALS vol 24 (2010) PARAS 959, 960), or payable to the personal representatives of a deceased civil servant by virtue of a scheme made under the Superannuation Act 1972 s 1 (see CONSTITUTIONAL AND ADMINISTRATIVE LAW vol 20 (2014) PARA 298): Non-Contentious Probate Fees Order 2004, SI 2004/3120, art 3. An additional fee of £60 may be payable on an application for a grant by a personal applicant: see Sch 1 Fee 2 (as so substituted). Where the application is for a duplicate grant or for a second or subsequent grant (including one following a revoked grant) in respect of the same deceased person, other than a grant preceded only by a grant limited to settled land, trust property or part of the estate, a fixed fee of £20 is payable: Sch 1 Fee 3.1 (as so substituted). Where it appears to the Lord Chancellor that an application for a grant is in respect of a death occurring as a result of the earthquake and tsunami in the Indian Ocean on 26 December 2004, he must remit any fee prescribed by the Non-Contentious Probate Fees Order 2004, SI 2004/3120, in that case: Non-Contentious Probate Fees (Indian Ocean Tsunami) Order 2005, SI 2005/266, art 2. Where it appears to the Lord Chancellor that an application for a grant is in respect of a death occurring as a result of another person's detonation of a bomb in London on 7 July 2005, or a death occurring as a result of action taken in a police operation following another person's attempted detonation of a bomb in London on 21 July 2005, he must remit any fee prescribed by the Non-Contentious Probate Fees Order 2004, SI 2004/3120, in that case: Non-Contentious Probate Fees (London Terrorist Bombings) Order 2005, SI 2005/3359, art 2.

5 Non-Contentious Probate Fees Order 2004, SI 2004/3120, art 4, Sch 1A para 16 (art 4 substituted and Sch 1A added by SI 2007/2174; the Non-Contentious Probate Fees Order 2004, SI 2004/3120, Sch 1A substituted by SI 2013/2302). As to the Lord Chancellor see CONSTITUTIONAL AND ADMINISTRATIVE LAW vol 20 (2014) PARA 255 et seq. Where by any convention entered into by

Her Majesty with any foreign power it is provided that no fee is to be required to be paid in respect of any proceedings, the fees specified in the Non-Contentious Probate Fees Order 2004, SI 2004/3120, must not be taken in respect of those proceedings: art 6(1). Where any application for a grant is withdrawn before the issue of a grant, a registrar may reduce or remit a fee: art 6(2).

6 Ie the disposable capital test set out in the Non-Contentious Probate Fees Order 2004, SI 2004/3120, Sch 1A para 3.

7 See the Non-Contentious Probate Fees Order 2004, SI 2004/3120, art 4, Sch 1A paras 2–10 (as substituted and added: see note 5).

8 See the Non-Contentious Probate Fees Order 2004, SI 2004/3120, art 7 (for death occurring before 20th March 2003), and Sch 1 Fee 3.2 (for death occurring on or after 20th March 2003) (Sch 1 as substituted: see note 2). For the exemption from inheritance tax for members of the armed forces where death was on active service etc see Inheritance Tax Act 1984 s 154; and INHERITANCE TAXATION vol 59A (2014) PARA 59.

687. Costs in non-contentious business. A solicitor's costs[1] in respect of all non-contentious[2] business must be fair and reasonable having regard to all the circumstances of the case[3].

There are statutory provisions which provide for the assessment of a solicitor's bill on the application of the client or the solicitor or a person who is liable to either of them to pay the bill or, if a trustee or personal representative is liable to pay the bill, on the application of a person interested in any property out of which the bill is paid or payable[4]. Firms must inform clients of their right to challenge or complain about a bill[5], including the right to complain to the Legal Ombudsman[6].

Where detailed assessment of a bill of costs is ordered, it must be referred:

(1) where the order was made by a district judge[7], to a district judge, a costs judge or an authorised court officer[8]; and

(2) where ordered by a registrar[9] to that registrar, or where this is not possible, in accordance with head (1)[10].

Provision is made for an appeal arising out of a detailed assessment of costs[11].

On any application dealt with by him on summons, the registrar has full power to determine by whom and to what extent the costs are to be paid[12].

Subject to conditions, a solicitor may charge interest on the unpaid amount of his costs plus any paid disbursements and value added tax[13] and a solicitor may take from his client security for the payment of any costs, including the amount of any interest to which the solicitor may become entitled[14].

1 'Solicitor' includes a registered European lawyer within the meaning of the European Communities (Lawyer's Practice) Regulations 2000, SI 2000/1119 (see LEGAL PROFESSIONS vol 66 (2015) PARA 709) who is registered with the Law Society, a body recognised by the Law Society under the Administration of Justice Act 1985 s 9 and a body which holds a licence issued by the Law Society which is in force under the Legal Services Act 2007 Pt 5 (ss 71–111): Solicitors' (Non-Contentious Business) Remuneration Order 2009, SI 2009/1931, art 2 (amended by SI 2012/171). The Solicitors Regulation Authority is the body currently responsible for the regulation of solicitors and to which the powers of the Law Society have been devolved and the Authority is the relevant body in practice: see LEGAL PROFESSIONS vol 65 (2015) PARA 454. 'Costs' means the amount charged in a solicitor's bill, exclusive of disbursements and value added tax: Solicitors' (Non-Contentious Business) Remuneration Order 2009, SI 2009/1931, art 2.

2 As to the distinction between non-contentious business and contentious business see PARA 684. As to legal aid in non-contentious business see PARA 864.

3 See the Solicitors' (Non-Contentious Business) Remuneration Order 2009, SI 2009/1931, art 3; and LEGAL PROFESSIONS vol 66 (2015) PARA 710. See further art 3(a)–(i).

4 Ie the Solicitors Act 1974 ss 70–72: see LEGAL PROFESSIONS vol 66 (2015) PARA 743 et seq.

5 See the Solicitors Regulation Authority Code of Conduct 2016 O(1.14). As to the Solicitors Regulation Authority Code of Conduct see LEGAL PROFESSIONS vol 65 (2015) PARA 293 et seq.

6 See the Solicitors Regulation Authority Code of Conduct 2016 O(1.10). As to the Legal Ombudsman see LEGAL PROFESSIONS vol 65 (2015) PARAS 293 et seq, 315 et seq.

7 As to the meaning of 'district judge' see PARA 631 note 6. In the context of the CPR Pts 43, 44, 47 and 48 'district judge' means only a district judge of the Principal Registry: Non-Contentious Probate Rules 1987, SI 1987/2024, r 60(3) (r 60 substituted by SI 2003/185).

8 Non-Contentious Probate Rules 1987, SI 1987/2024, r 60(2)(a) (as substituted: see note 7). 'Authorised court officer' means any officer of the Family Court, the High Court or the Costs Office, whom the Lord Chancellor has authorised to assess costs: CPR 44.1(1); Non-Contentious Probate Rules 1987, SI 1987/2024, r 60(2)(a), (5) (as so substituted; amended by virtue of SI 2013/262).

9 As to the meaning of registrar see PARA 631 note 7. Note that the definition of 'costs officer' in CPR r 44.1(1) (see note 8) has effect as though it included a district probate registrar: Non-Contentious Probate Rules 1987, SI 1987/2024, r 60(4) (as substituted: see note 7).

10 Non-Contentious Probate Rules 1987, SI 1987/2024, r 60(2)(b) (as substituted: see note 7).

11 As in civil proceedings generally, an appeal against a detailed assessment of costs is dealt with: (1) under CPR 47.21–47.24 (see CIVIL PROCEDURE vol 12A (2015) PARA 1773) where the appeal is against a decision of an authorised costs officer; and (2) under CPR Pt 52 (see CIVIL PROCEDURE vol 12A (2015) PARA 1514 et seq) otherwise: see the Non-Contentious Probate Rules 1987, SI 1987/2024, r 60(8)-(10) (as substituted: see note 7). See also note 8. In either case the appeal is now under the CPR rather than the Rules of the Supreme Court or the County Court Rules: see the Non-Contentious Probate Rules 1987, SI 1987/2024, r 60(11) (as so substituted). Appeals dealt with under CPR Pt 52 lie from a district judge or other officer of the court to a judge of the High Court: see the Non-Contentious Probate Rules, SI 1987/2024, r 60(9) (as so substituted).

12 Non-Contentious Probate Rules 1987, SI 1987/2024, r 63 (amended by SI 1991/1876).

13 See the Solicitors' (Non-Contentious Business) Remuneration Order 2009, SI 2009/1931, art 5; and LEGAL PROFESSIONS vol 66 (2015) PARA 758.

14 See the Solicitors' (Non-Contentious Business) Remuneration Order 2009, SI 2009/1931, art 4; and LEGAL PROFESSIONS vol 66 (2015) PARA 762.

688. Standing searches. Any person who wishes to be notified of the issue of a grant[1] may enter a standing search for the grant by lodging at, or sending by post to any registry[2] or sub-registry, a notice in the prescribed form[3]. A person who has entered a standing search will be sent an office copy of any grant which corresponds with the particulars given on the completed form and which:

(1) issued not more than 12 months before the entry of the standing search[4]; or

(2) issues within a period of six months after the entry of the standing search[5].

1 As to the meaning of 'grant' see PARA 631 note 7.

2 As to the meaning of 'registry' see PARA 680 note 2.

3 Non-Contentious Probate Rules 1987, SI 1987/2024, r 43(1) (substituted by SI 1991/1876). For the prescribed form see the Non-Contentious Probate Rules 1987, SI 1987/2024, r 43(1), Sch 1 Form 2. This procedure is of assistance to persons who wish to take action against an estate or commence proceedings under the Inheritance (Provision for Family and Dependants) Act 1975 (see PARA 565 et seq) or similar legislation when a personal representative is constituted.

In order to facilitate the operation of standing searches and caveats (see PARA 690) and to ensure the accuracy of probate records, it has been directed that in all instances where the deceased died in the United Kingdom and the death has been recorded in the Register of Deaths: (1) the name and dates of birth and death of the deceased as recorded in the register must be included in the oath lodged in support of an application made through a solicitor or probate practitioner for a grant of representation (see PARA 728); (2) the name and date of death of the deceased as recorded in the register must be included in the notice lodged for a standing search or caveat; and (3) in any case where the name by which the deceased was known differs from that recorded in the register, that name must also be included in the oath or notice, as the case may be: *Practice Direction* [1999] 1 All ER 832. The fee on an application for a standing search to be carried out in an estate, for each period of six months including the issue of a copy grant and will, if any, irrespective of the number of pages is £10: Non-Contentious Probate Fees Order 2004, SI 2004/3120, art 2, Sch 1 Fee 5 (Sch 1 substituted by SI 2011/588; Non-Contentious Probate Fees Order 2004, SI 2004/3120, Sch 1 Fee 5 amended by SI 2014/876).

4 Non-Contentious Probate Rules 1987, SI 1987/2024, r 43(2)(a).

5 Non-Contentious Probate Rules 1987, SI 1987/2024, r 43(2)(b). Where an applicant wishes to extend the period of six months, he or his solicitor or probate practitioner may lodge at, or send by post to, the registry or sub-registry at which the standing search was entered, written application for extension: r 43(3)(a) (amended by SI 1991/1876; and SI 1998/1903). An application for extension must be lodged, or received by post, within the last month of the said period of six months, and the standing search is then effective for an additional period of six months from the date on which it was due to expire: Non-Contentious Probate Rules 1987, SI

1987/2024, r 43(3)(b). 'Probate practitioner' means a person who, for the purposes of the Legal Services Act 2007, is an authorised person in relation to an activity which constitutes a probate activity (within the meaning of that Act: see LEGAL PROFESSIONS vol 65 (2015) PARA 352): Non-Contentious Probate Rules 1987, SI 1987/2024, r 2(1) (definition added by SI 1998/1903 and substituted by SI 2009/3348). A standing search which has been extended may be further extended by the filing of a further application for extension subject to the same conditions as set out in the Non-Contentious Probate Rules 1987, SI 1987/2024, r 43(3)(b): r 43(3)(c).

689. Summonses to accept or refuse probate. The High Court has power to summon any person named as executor in a will to prove or renounce probate of the will, and to do such other things concerning the will as the court had power to order such a person to do immediately before 1982[1]. If an executor, without an express renunciation, refrains from appearing to a citation to take probate, his rights in respect of the executorship wholly cease, and the representation devolves as if he had not been appointed executor[2].

1 Senior Courts Act 1981 s 112. Before 1982 the High Court had power to do things concerning the will as were customary before 1926: see the Supreme Court of Judicature (Consolidation) Act 1925 s 159 (repealed). It is immaterial to this power whether or not a claim form has been issued (ie whether the matter is contentious or non-contentious), but the issue of a claim form will affect the jurisdiction in that before the issue of a claim form the power will be exercised by the Family Division and after issue of the claim form by the Chancery Division: see PARA 684.

2 Administration of Estates Act 1925 s 5(ii). As to citations to take probate see further PARA 695 et seq.

690. Caveats. Any person who wishes to show cause against the sealing of a grant[1] may enter a caveat[2] in the principal registry of the Family Division or in any district probate registry or sub-registry[3]. A caveat should only be used to prevent the issue of a grant in respect of a testamentary paper which the caveator contends is not the last will of the deceased[4]. A person, called the caveator, who wishes to enter a caveat, or a solicitor or probate practitioner[5] on his behalf, may effect entry of a caveat[6] by completing the prescribed form[7] in the appropriate book at any registry or sub-registry[8], or by sending by post at his own risk a notice in the prescribed form to any registry or sub-registry and the proper officer must provide an acknowledgment of the entry of the caveat[9]. The caveat must contain the deceased's name and dates of birth and death[10] and late address, the caveator's name (even where the caveat is entered on his behalf by a solicitor or probate practitioner) and an address for service within England and Wales[11].

When a caveat is entered in a district probate registry, the district probate registrar must immediately send a copy to the principal registry of the Family Division to be entered among the caveats in that registry[12]. Except as otherwise provided[13], a caveat remains effective for a period of six months from the date on which it is entered, and where a caveator wishes to extend the period, he or his solicitor or probate practitioner may lodge at, or send by post to, the registry or sub-registry at which the caveat was entered a written application for extension[14]. The district judge or registrar must not allow any grant to be sealed (other than a grant ad colligenda bona[15] or to an administrator pending suit[16]) if he has knowledge of an effective caveat in respect of it[17].

1 As to the meaning of 'grant' see PARA 631 note 7.

2 For the prescribed form of caveat see the Non-Contentious Probate Rules 1987, SI 1987/2024, r 44(2), Sch 1 Form 3 (Sch 1 Form 3 amended by SI 1998/1903). The fee for the entry of a caveat is £20: Non-Contentious Probate Fees Order 2004, SI 2004/3120, art 2, Sch 1 Fee 4 (Sch 1 substituted by SI 2011/588).

3 Senior Courts Act 1981 s 108(1); Non-Contentious Probate Rules 1987, SI 1987/2024, r 44(1) (amended by SI 1991/1876). As to the meaning of 'registry' see PARA 680 note 2. The actual entry of a caveat is merely a ministerial act: *Re Panton* [1901] P 239. The caveat constitutes a direction that no grant should be sealed in the deceased's estate without notice to the caveator.

4 To enter a caveat where the caveator's intention is to make a claim under the Inheritance (Provision for Family and Dependants) Act 1975 (see PARA 565 et seq) is wholly wrong: see *Parnall v Hurst* [2003] WTLR 997.
5 As to the meaning of 'probate practitioner' see PARA 688 note 5.
6 Non-Contentious Probate Rules 1987, SI 1987/2024, r 44(2) (amended by SI 1998/1903).
7 See note 2.
8 Non-Contentious Probate Rules 1987, SI 1987/2024, r 44(2)(a).
9 Non-Contentious Probate Rules 1987, SI 1987/2024, r 44(2)(b).
10 Ie the name and dates of birth and death of the deceased as recorded in the Register of Deaths (where the death is so recorded), and any name by which the deceased was known which differed from that recorded in the register: see *Practice Direction* [1999] 1 All ER 832; and PARA 688 note 3. As to registration of deaths see REGISTRATION CONCERNING THE INDIVIDUAL vol 88 (2012) PARA 277 et seq.
11 See the Non-Contentious Probate Rules 1987, SI 1987/2024, r 49, Sch 1 Form 3 (as amended: see note 2).
12 Senior Courts Act 1981 s 108(2). See note 3. An index of caveats entered in any registry or sub-registry must be maintained and upon receipt of an application for a grant, the registry or sub-registry at which the application is made must cause a search of the index to be made and the appropriate district judge or registrar must be notified of the entry of a caveat against the sealing of a grant for which the application has been made: Non-Contentious Probate Rules 1987, SI 1987/2024, r 44(4) (substituted by SI 1998/1903). As to the meaning of 'district judge' see PARA 631 note 6; and as to the meaning of 'registrar' see PARA 631 note 7. The index is currently maintained at the Leeds District Probate Registry: see *Practice Direction* [1988] 3 All ER 544.
13 Ie by the Non-Contentious Probate Rules 1987, SI 1987/2024, r 44, 45 or 46 (see 3PARA1242 et seq): see r 44(3)(a) (as amended: see note 13).
14 Non-Contentious Probate Rules 1987, SI 1987/2024, r 44(3)(a) (amended by SI 1998/1903). An application for extension must be lodged, or received by post, within the last month of the said period of six months, and the caveat is then effective (save as otherwise provided by the Non-Contentious Probate Rules 1987, SI 1987/2024, r 44) for an additional period of six months from the date on which it was due to expire: r 44(3)(b). A caveat which has been extended may be further extended by the filing of a further application for extension subject to the same conditions as set out in r 44(3)(b): r 44(3)(c). The fee for the extension of a caveat is £20: Non-Contentious Probate Fees Order 2004, SI 2004/3120, art 2, Sch 1 Fee 4 (as amended: see note 2).
15 As to grants ad colligenda bona see PARA 815.
16 Ie under the Senior Courts Act 1981 s 117 (see PARA 808): see the Non-Contentious Probate Rules 1987, SI 1987/2024, r 44(1) (as amended: see note 3).
17 Non-Contentious Probate Rules 1987, SI 1987/2024, r 44(1) (as amended: see note 3). See also *Re Clore* [1982] Fam 113, [1982] 2 WLR 314; approved [1982] Ch 456, [1982] 3 All ER 419, CA. No caveat, however, operates to prevent the sealing of a grant on the day on which the caveat is entered: Non-Contentious Probate Rules 1987, SI 1987/2024, r 44(1) (as so amended).

691. Warnings. If a caveat has been entered[1], any person claiming to have an interest in the estate may cause to be issued from the nominated registry[2] a warning in the prescribed form against the caveat[3].The person warning must state his interest in the estate of the deceased and must require the caveator[4] to give particulars of any contrary interest in the estate[5]. The warning must contain an address for service in England and Wales[6]. The warning or a copy of it must be served on the caveator forthwith[7].

1 See PARA 690.
2 'Nominated registry' means the registry nominated for the purpose of the Non-Contentious Probate Rules 1987, SI 1987/2024, r 44 by the senior district judge or in the absence of any such nomination the Leeds District Probate Registry: r 44(15) (added by SI 1998/1903). 'Senior district judge' means the Senior District Judge of the Family Division or, in his absence, the senior of the district judges in attendance at the principal registry: Non-Contentious Probate Rules 1987, SI 1987/2024, r 2(1) (definition added by SI 1991/1876). As to the meaning of 'registry' see PARA 680 note 2.
3 Non-Contentious Probate Rules 1987, SI 1987/2024, r 44(5) (amended by SI 1998/1903). For the form of warning see the Non-Contentious Probate Rules 1987, SI 1987/2024, r 44(5), Sch 1 Form 4 (Sch 1 Form 4 amended by SI 1991/1876; and SI 1998/1903).
4 As to the caveator see PARA 690.
5 Non-Contentious Probate Rules 1987, SI 1987/2024, r 44(5) (as amended: see note 3).

6 Non-Contentious Probate Rules 1987, SI 1987/2024, r 49.
7 Non-Contentious Probate Rules 1987, SI 1987/2024, r 44(5) (as amended: see note 3).

692. Appearance by caveator. A caveator[1] who has an interest contrary to that of the person warning[2], within eight days of service of the warning on him, inclusive of the day of service, or at any time after that if no affidavit of service has been filed[3], may enter an appearance in the nominated registry[4] by filing the prescribed form of appearance[5], and must forthwith serve[6] on the person warning a copy of the form of appearance sealed with the seal of the court[7]. A caveator who has no contrary interest to that of the person warning but who wishes to show cause against the sealing of a grant[8] to that person may, within the same period, issue and serve a summons for directions[9]. If the caveator finds he has a common interest with the applicant for a grant, he may support the latter's application[10]. On the hearing of the summons for directions, the district judge[11] or registrar[12] may give a direction for the caveat to cease to have effect[13]. Upon being advised by the court concerned of the commencement of a probate action the senior district judge[14] must give notice of the action to the caveator of every caveat then in force, other than a caveat entered by the plaintiff in the action[15], and in respect of any caveat entered subsequent to the commencement of the action, he must give notice to that caveator of the existence of the action[16].

1 As to entry of caveats see PARA 690.
2 As to warnings see PARA 691.
3 Ie under the Non-Contentious Probate Rules 1987, SI 1987/2024, r 44(12) (see PARA 693): see r 44(10) (as amended: see note 7).
4 As to the meaning of 'nominated registry' see PARA 691 note 2.
5 The appearance must set out the caveator's interest, state the date of the will, if any, under which the interest arises and contain an address for service in England and Wales: see the Non-Contentious Probate Rules 1987, SI 1987/2024, rr 44(10), 49, Sch 1 Form 5 (r 44(10) as amended (see note 7); Sch 1 Form 5 amended by SI 1998/1903).
6 As to service see PARA 704.
7 Non-Contentious Probate Rules 1987, SI 1987/2024, r 44(10) (amended by SI 1991/1876; and SI 1998/1903).
8 As to the meaning of 'grant' see PARA 631 note 7.
9 Non-Contentious Probate Rules 1987, SI 1987/2024, r 44(6). The issue of a summons must be notified forthwith to the nominated registry: r 44(9) (amended by SI 1998/1903).
10 *Ingram v Strong* (1815) 2 Phillim 294 at 315.
11 As to the meaning of 'district judge' see PARA 631 note 6.
12 As to the meaning of 'registrar' see PARA 631 note 7.
13 Non-Contentious Probate Rules 1987, SI 1987/2024, r 44(7) (amended by SI 1991/1876).
14 As to the meaning of 'senior district judge' see PARA 691 note 2.
15 Non-Contentious Probate Rules 1987, SI 1987/2024, r 45(1) (amended by SI 1991/1876).
16 Non-Contentious Probate Rules 1987, SI 1987/2024, r 45(2) (amended by SI 1991/1876). It is an abuse of the caveat procedure to enter a caveat where no probate issue arises. For instance, a caveat should not be entered on behalf of a defendant under the family provision legislation where the invalidity of the will is not in issue. As to family provision see PARA 565 et seq.

693. Non-appearance of caveator. A caveator who has not entered an appearance to a warning[1] may at any time withdraw his caveat by giving notice at the registry[2] or sub-registry at which it was entered, and the caveat then ceases to have effect[3]. If it has been withdrawn, the caveator must forthwith give notice of withdrawal to the person warning[4]. If no appearance has been entered by the caveator or no summons has been issued by him[5], the person warning may at any time after eight days of service of the warning on the caveator, inclusive of the day of service, file in the nominated registry[6] an affidavit showing that the warning was duly served and the caveat then ceases to have effect provided there is no pending summons[7].

1 As to appearance to a warning see PARA 692.

2 As to the meaning of 'registry' see PARA 680 note 2.
3 Non-Contentious Probate Rules 1987, SI 1987/2024, r 44(11).
4 Non-Contentious Probate Rules 1987, SI 1987/2024, r 44(11). As to warnings see PARA 691.
5 Ie under the Non-Contentious Probate Rules 1987, SI 1987/2024, r 44(6) (see PARA 692): see r 44(12) (as amended: see note 7).
6 As to the meaning of 'nominated registry' see PARA 691 note 2.
7 Non-Contentious Probate Rules 1987, SI 1987/2024, r 44(12) (amended by SI 1998/1903). A pending summons is made under the Non-Contentious Probate Rules 1987, SI 1987/2024, r 44(6) (see PARA 692): see r 44(12) (as so amended).

694. Subsequent proceedings. Unless a district judge[1] or registrar[2] otherwise directs[3], any caveat in force when a summons for directions is issued remains in force unless withdrawn[4] until the summons has been disposed of[5]. Unless a district judge or, where application to discontinue a caveat is made by consent, a registrar by order made on summons otherwise directs, any caveat in respect of which an appearance to a warning has been entered[6] remains in force until the commencement of a probate action[7]. Unless a district judge by order made on summons otherwise directs, the commencement of a probate action operates to prevent the sealing of a grant[8] (other than a grant to an administrator pending determination of a probate claim[9]) until application for a grant is made by the person shown by the court's decision to be entitled to the grant[10]. If, after appearance, the parties come to terms, a summons on an application to discontinue proceedings may then be taken out, and, on the requisite order being made, the grant will issue in due course[11].

Where a caveat is in force or has ceased to have effect[12] the caveator may not enter further caveats without the leave of a district judge[13].

1 As to the meaning of 'district judge' see PARA 631 note 6.
2 As to the meaning of 'registrar' see PARA 631 note 7.
3 Ie under the Non-Contentious Probate Rules 1987, SI 1987/2024, r 44(7) (see PARA 692): see r 44(8) (as amended: see note 5).
4 Ie under the Non-Contentious Probate Rules 1987, SI 1987/2024, r 44(11) (see PARA 693): see r 44(8) (as amended: see note 5).
5 Non-Contentious Probate Rules 1987, SI 1987/2024, r 44(8) (amended by SI 1991/1876).
6 See PARA 692.
7 Non-Contentious Probate Rules 1987, SI 1987/2024, r 44(13) (amended by SI 1991/1876). For the procedure relating to probate claims generally see CPR Pt 57 and CPR PD 57—*Probate*. See also PARA 868. As to warnings see PARA 691. It is not until a claim form has been issued that there is litigation between the parties: see *Moran v Place* [1896] P 214, CA; *Salter v Salter* [1896] P 291, CA. As to security for costs see PARA 915.
8 As to the meaning of 'grant' see PARA 631 note 7.
9 Ie a grant under the Senior Courts Act 1981 s 117 (see PARA 808 et seq): see the Non-Contentious Probate Rules 1987, SI 1987/2024, r 45(3) (as amended: see note 10). See note 7.
10 Non-Contentious Probate Rules 1987, SI 1987/2024, r 45(3) (amended by SI 1991/1876). Upon such an application for a grant any caveat entered by the plaintiff in the action or in respect of which notice of the action has been given ceases to have effect: Non-Contentious Probate Rules 1987, SI 1987/2024, r 45(4). See also *Palmer v O'Connor* [2006] EWHC 1589 (Ch), [2006] All ER (D) 278 (Mar) where the court allowed an application for a grant to proceed because the caveator had failed to issue proceedings challenging the validity of the will within the time limit previously imposed by a district judge when hearing the initial application for a grant of probate.
11 See Tristram and Coote's Probate Practice (31st Edn) 23.71 et seq.
12 Ie under the Non-Contentious Probate Rules 1987, SI 1987/2024, rr 44(7), (12), 45(4), 46(3) (see PARAS 692–693, 695): see r 44(14) (as amended: see note 13).
13 Non-Contentious Probate Rules 1987, SI 1987/2024, r 44(14) (amended by SI 1991/1876).

695. Citations. A citation[1] is an instrument issuing from, and under the seal of, the principal registry of the Family Division or a district probate registry containing a recital of the reason for its issue and the interest of the party extracting it, and calling upon the party cited to enter an appearance[2] and take the steps specified in it, with an intimation of the nature of the order the court is asked to and may make, unless good cause is shown to the contrary.

A citation is employed only in non-contentious matters[3]: its chief object is to compel all persons having a prior[4] right to a grant to come in and take the grant, or, in default, that administration may be granted to the citor. A citation must be directed to all such persons so that each one has an opportunity to apply for a grant.

Any citation may issue[5] from the principal registry of the Family Division or a district probate registry after the entry of a caveat[6] and is settled by the district judge or registrar[7] before being issued[8]. Every averment in a citation, and such other information as the registrar may require, must be verified by an affidavit sworn by the person issuing the citation (the 'citor'), provided that the district judge or registrar may in special circumstances accept an affidavit sworn by the citor's solicitor or probate practitioner[9]. Every will referred to in a citation must be lodged in a registry before the citation is issued, except where the will is not in the citor's possession and the district judge or registrar is satisfied that it is impracticable to require it to be lodged[10].

1 All citations in non-contentious business must contain an address for service within England and Wales: Non-Contentious Probate Rules 1987, SI 1987/2024, r 49.
2 An appearance is entered by filing in the Non-Contentious Probate Rules 1987, SI 1987/2024, Form 5: r 46(6), Sch 1 Form 5; and see PARA 697.
3 Citations in contentious business have been abolished. As to the present contentious practice where citations would formerly have been used see PARA 877. As to the distinction between non-contentious and contentious business see PARA 684.
4 *Re Harper* [1899] P 59.
5 Application for the issue of a citation may be made by post: *Practice Direction* [1969] 3 All ER 192, [1969] 1 WLR 1283.
6 See the Non-Contentious Probate Rules 1987, SI 1987/2024, r 46(3) (amended by SI 1991/1876). The citor must enter a caveat (see PARA 690) before issuing a citation and, unless a district judge by order made on summons otherwise directs, any caveat in force at the commencement of the citation proceedings, unless withdrawn pursuant to the Non-Contentious Probate Rules 1987, SI 1987/2024, r 44(11) (see PARA 693), remains in force until application for a grant is made by the person shown to be entitled to one by the decision of the court in such proceedings, and upon such application any caveat entered by a party who had notice of the proceedings ceases to have effect: r 46(3) (as so amended). As to the meaning of 'district judge' see PARA 631 note 6. As to the meaning of 'grant' see PARA 631 note 7.
7 As to the meaning of 'registrar' see PARA 631 note 7.
8 Non-Contentious Probate Rules 1987, SI 1987/2024, r 46(1) (amended by SI 1991/1876). The fee for perusing and settling a citation is £12: Non-Contentious Probate Fees Order 2004, SI 2004/3120, art 2, Sch 1 Fee 11 (Sch 1 substituted by SI 2011/588).
9 Non-Contentious Probate Rules 1987, SI 1987/2024, r 46(2) (amended by SI 1991/1876; and SI 1998/1903). Cf *Re Hutley* (1869) LR 1 P & D 596. As to the meaning of 'probate practitioner' see PARA 688 note 5.
10 Non-Contentious Probate Rules 1987, SI 1987/2024, r 46(5) (amended by SI 1991/1876).

696. Service of citation. Every citation must be served personally on the person cited unless on cause shown by affidavit, the district judge[1] or registrar[2] directs some other mode of service, which may include notice by advertisement[3].

Service on a minor should be effected in the presence of one of his parents or guardians, or of the person with whom he resides or in whose care he is[4]. The minor's next of kin should also be served. Where the person cited lacks capacity by reason of an impairment of, or a disturbance in, the functioning of the mind or brain[5] the citation must be served on the person, if any, authorised[6] to conduct in his name or on his behalf the proceedings in connection with which the citation is to be served or, if there is no person so authorised, on the person with whom he resides or in whose care he is[7].

A certificate of service should be indorsed on the citation[8].

1 As to the meaning of 'district judge' see PARA 631 note 6.
2 As to the meaning of 'registrar' see PARA 631 note 7.
3 Non-Contentious Probate Rules 1987, SI 1987/2024, r 46(4) (amended by SI 1991/1876).
4 *Cooper v Green* (1825) 2 Add 454; *Brown v Wildman* (1859) 28 LJP & M 54. There are no special provisions in cases where the citee is a person under a disability but, subject to any enactment, the Rules of the Supreme Court 1965, with any necessary modifications to non-contentious probate matters, apply: Non-Contentious Probate Rules 1987, SI 1987/2024, r 3 (as amended by SI 1999/1015). As to the application of the RSC to non-contentious probate matters see PARA 685. Where both the custodian and the next of kin evaded service, service on the minor was held sufficient: *Lean v Viner* (1864) 3 Sw & Tr 469.
5 Ie within the meaning of the Mental Capacity Act 2005 (see MENTAL HEALTH AND CAPACITY vol 75 (2013) PARA 603). See also note 4 as to a citee who is under a disability.
6 Ie under the Mental Capacity Act 2005 (see note 5) (see MENTAL HEALTH AND CAPACITY vol 75 (2013) PARA 607): see RSC Ord 80 r 16(2)(b) (see note 4). See also Tristram and Coote's Probate Practice (31st Edn) 24.100 et seq; and MENTAL HEALTH AND CAPACITY vol 75 (2013) PARA 995.
7 See RSC Ord 80 r 16(1), (2)(b) (see note 4). See further MENTAL HEALTH AND CAPACITY vol 75 (2013) PARA 558 et seq. See also Tristram and Coote's Probate Practice (31st Edn) 24.100 et seq.
8 *Goodburn v Bainbridge* (1860) 2 Sw & Tr 4; cf *Johnson v Weldy* (1861) 2 Sw & Tr 313 (affidavit of service should show how guardian became guardian).

697. Appearance by person cited. A person who has been cited to appear may enter an appearance[1] within eight days of the service of the citation upon him, inclusive of the day of service, or at any time after then if no application for certain orders[2] has been made by the citor[3].

1 Appearance is effected in the registry from which the citation issued by filing the prescribed form containing inter alia the name, address and interest of the person cited, the date of the will, if any, under which the interest arises and an address for service within England and Wales, and the person appearing must forthwith serve on the citor a copy of the form of appearance sealed with the seal of the registry: see the Non-Contentious Probate Rules 1987, SI 1987/2024, rr 46(6), 49. For the prescribed form of appearance see r 46(6), Sch 1 Form 5. As to the meaning of 'registry' see PARA 680 note 2. As to the meaning of 'citor' see PARA 695 text to note 9. As to default of appearance where the citor is under disability see Tristram and Coote's Probate Practice (31st Edn) 24.102 et seq.
2 Ie orders under the Non-Contentious Probate Rules 1987, SI 1987/2024, rr 47(5), 48(2) (see PARAS 698–700): see r 46(6).
3 Non-Contentious Probate Rules 1987, SI 1987/2024, r 46(6).

698. Citations to accept or refuse a grant. A citation to accept or refuse a grant[1] may be issued at the instance of any person who would himself be entitled to a grant in the event of the person cited renouncing his right[2]. The person cited is compelled by this to accept or refuse a grant. He can accept after entering an appearance by application ex parte by affidavit to a district judge[3] or registrar[4] for an order for a grant to himself[5]. If the person cited has entered an appearance to the citation but has not applied for a grant or has failed to prosecute his application with reasonable diligence the citor[6] may apply by summons to a district judge or registrar for an order for a grant to himself[7]. If the time limited for appearance[8] has expired and the person cited has not entered an appearance, the citor may apply to a district judge or registrar for an order for a grant to himself[9].

Where power to make a grant to an executor has been reserved, a citation calling on him to accept or refuse a grant may be issued at the instance of the executors who have proved the will or the survivor of them or of the executors of the last survivor of deceased executors who have proved[10]. He may then accept by application in the manner described above[11]. If the time limited for appearance[12] has expired and the person cited has not entered an appearance, the citor may apply to a district judge or registrar for an order that a note be made on the grant that the executor in respect of whom power was reserved has been duly cited and has not appeared and that all his rights in respect of the executorship have wholly ceased[13]. If the person cited has entered an appearance but has not applied for a grant or has failed to prosecute his application with reasonable diligence the citor may apply by summons to a district judge or registrar for an order striking out the appearance and for the indorsement on the grant of a similar note[14].

1 As to the meaning of 'grant' see PARA 631 note 7. As to citations generally see PARA 695.
2 Non-Contentious Probate Rules 1987, SI 1987/2024, r 47(1).
3 As to the meaning of 'district judge' see PARA 631 note 6.
4 As to the meaning of 'registrar' see PARA 631 note 7.
5 Non-Contentious Probate Rules 1987, SI 1987/2024, r 47(4) (amended by SI 1991/1876). As to appearance by the person cited see PARA 697.
6 As to the meaning of 'citor' see PARA 695 note 9.
7 Non-Contentious Probate Rules 1987, SI 1987/2024, r 47(7)(a) (amended by SI 1991/1876). The summons must be served on the person cited: Non-Contentious Probate Rules 1987, SI 1987/2024, r 47(7). As to service see PARA 704.
8 See the Non-Contentious Probate Rules 1987, SI 1987/2024, r 46(6); and PARA 697.
9 Non-Contentious Probate Rules 1987, SI 1987/2024, r 47(5)(a) (amended by SI 1991/1876). No summons is necessary in this case (see PARA 703), but the application must be supported by an affidavit showing that the citation was duly served (Non-Contentious Probate Rules 1987, SI 1987/2024, r 47(6)).
10 Non-Contentious Probate Rules 1987, SI 1987/2024, r 47(2).
11 Ie under the Non-Contentious Probate Rules 1987, SI 1987/2024, r 47(4): see the text to note 5.
12 See note 8.
13 Non-Contentious Probate Rules 1987, SI 1987/2024, r 47(5)(b) (amended by SI 1991/1876). No summons is necessary in this case (see PARA 703), but the application must be supported by an affidavit showing that the citation was duly served (Non-Contentious Probate Rules 1987, SI 1987/2024, r 47(6)). As to the cessation of the executor's rights see PARA 689.
14 Non-Contentious Probate Rules 1987, SI 1987/2024, r 47(7)(b) (amended by SI 1991/1876). The summons must be served on the person cited: see the Non-Contentious Probate Rules 1987, SI 1987/2024, r 47(7); and PARA 704.

699. Citation of executor de son tort. A citation calling on an executor who has intermeddled in the estate of the deceased to show cause why he should not be ordered to take a grant[1] may be issued at the instance of any person interested in the estate at any time after the expiration of six months from the death of the deceased, provided that no citation to take a grant may issue while proceedings as to the validity of the will are pending[2]. The person cited, if he is willing to take a grant, may after entering an appearance apply ex parte by affidavit to a district judge[3] or registrar[4] for an order for a grant to himself[5]. If the time limited for appearance has expired[6] and the person cited has not entered an appearance, or after appearance has made no application for a grant[7] or has failed to prosecute his application with reasonable diligence, the citor may apply to a district judge or registrar by summons, which must be served on the person cited, for an order requiring him to take a grant within a specified time, or for a grant to himself or some other person specified in the summons[8].

1 As to the meaning of 'grant' see PARA 631 note 7.
2 Non-Contentious Probate Rules 1987, SI 1987/2024, r 47(3). As to the executor de son tort see PARA 1261 et seq.
3 As to the meaning of 'district judge' see PARA 631 note 6.
4 As to the meaning of 'registrar' see PARA 631 note 7.
5 Non-Contentious Probate Rules 1987, SI 1987/2024, r 47(4) (amended by SI 1991/1876).
6 See the Non-Contentious Probate Rules 1987, SI 1987/2024, r 46(6); and PARA 697.
7 Ie under the Non-Contentious Probate Rules 1987, SI 1987/2024, r 47(4): see r 47(7).
8 Non-Contentious Probate Rules 1987, SI 1987/2024, r 47(5)(c), (7)(c) (amended by SI 1991/1876). In the case of non-appearance the application must be supported by an affidavit showing that the citation was duly served: Non-Contentious Probate Rules 1987, SI 1987/2024, r 47(6).

700. Citation to propound a will. A citation to propound a will may be issued at the instance of any person who has an interest contrary to that of the executors or the persons interested under a will[1]. It must be directed to the executors named in the will and to all the persons interested under it[2], and it compels the executors or the persons interested to propound the will. If the time limited for appearance has expired[3] and no person has entered an appearance, the citor[4] may apply to a district judge[5] or registrar[6] for an order for a grant[7] as if the will were invalid[8]. If the time limited for appearance has expired in the case where no person who has entered an appearance proceeds with reasonable diligence to propound the will, the citor may apply to a district judge or registrar by summons, which must be served on every person cited who has entered an appearance, for an order for a grant as if the will were invalid[9].

1 Non-Contentious Probate Rules 1987, SI 1987/2024, r 48(1). Rule 48 applies only where the will has never been propounded at all: see *Re Jolley, Jolley v Jarvis* [1964] P 262, [1964] 1 All ER 596, CA. As to the procedure where a will has been proved in common form and it is desired to compel proof in solemn form see PARA 863.
2 Non-Contentious Probate Rules 1987, SI 1987/2024, r 48(1).
3 See the Non-Contentious Probate Rules 1987, SI 1987/2024, r 46(6); and PARA 697.
4 As to the meaning of 'citor' see PARA 695 note 9.
5 As to the meaning of 'district judge' see PARA 631 note 6.
6 As to the meaning of 'registrar' see PARA 631 note 7.
7 As to the meaning of 'grant' see PARA 631 note 7.
8 Non-Contentious Probate Rules 1987, SI 1987/2024, r 48(2)(a) (amended by SI 1991/1876). Such application must be supported by an affidavit showing that the citation was duly served: Non-Contentious Probate Rules 1987, SI 1987/2024, r 48(2)(a) (as so amended).
9 Non-Contentious Probate Rules 1987, SI 1987/2024, r 48(2)(b) (amended by SI 1991/1876).

701. Application made by summonses. In non-contentious matters a district judge[1] or registrar[2] may require any application to be made by summons to a district judge or registrar in chambers or a judge in chambers or open court[3]. An application for an inventory and account must be made by summons to a district judge or registrar[4]. A summons for hearing by a district judge or registrar must be issued out of the registry[5] in which it is to be heard[6]. A summons to be heard by a judge must be issued out of the principal registry[7].

1 As to the distinction between non-contentious and contentious business see PARA 684. As to the meaning of 'district judge' see PARA 631 note 6.
2 As to the meaning of 'registrar' see PARA 631 note 7.
3 Non-Contentious Probate Rules 1987, SI 1987/2024, r 61(1) (r 61(1)–(3) amended by SI 1991/1876). For a discussion of the Non-Contentious Probate Rules 1987, SI 1987/2024, r 61(1) and other provisions for notice under the Non-Contentious Probate Rules 1987, SI 1987/2024: see *Ghafoor v Cliff* [2006] EWHC 825 (Ch), [2006] 2 All ER 1079, [2006] 1 WLR 3020.
4 Non-Contentious Probate Rules 1987, SI 1987/2024, r 61(2) (as amended: see note 3). As to the duty of a personal representative to exhibit an inventory and account see PARA 957.
5 As to the meaning of 'registry' see PARA 680 note 2.
6 Non-Contentious Probate Rules 1987, SI 1987/2024, r 61(3) (as amended: see note 3).
7 Non-Contentious Probate Rules 1987, SI 1987/2024, r 61(4).

702. Examples of applications by summons. Applications by summons are made to the district judge[1] or registrar[2] in the following non-contentious matters[3], among others:

(1) where there is a dispute between two or more persons entitled in the same degree as to who is to take a grant[4];
(2) an application for an inventory and account[5];
(3) for an order that an intermeddling executor take a grant of probate[6];
(4) for an order after a citation to accept or refuse a grant or to propound a will when the party cited has entered an appearance but taken no further step[7];

(5) for directions where a caveator who has no interest contrary to that of the person warning wishes to show cause against the sealing of a grant to that person[8]; and

(6) for an order requiring a person to attend for examination[9].

1 As to the meaning of 'district judge' see PARA 631 note 6.
2 As to the meaning of 'registrar' see PARA 631 note 7.
3 As to the distinction between non-contentious and contentious business see PARA 684.
4 See the Non-Contentious Probate Rules 1987, SI 1987/2024, r 27(6); and PARA 774 note 8. As to the meaning of 'grant' see PARA 631 note 7.
5 See the Non-Contentious Probate Rules 1987, SI 1987/2024, r 61(2); and PARA 701. See *CI v NS* [2004] EWHC 659 (Fam), [2004] All ER (D) 30 (Apr); and as to the duty of a personal representative to exhibit an inventory and account see PARA 957.
6 See Non-Contentious Probate Rules 1987, SI 1987/2024, r 47(5)(c), (7)(c); and PARA 699.
7 See Non-Contentious Probate Rules 1987, SI 1987/2024, rr 47(7)(b), 48(2)(b); and PARAS 698, 700.
8 See Non-Contentious Probate Rules 1987, SI 1987/2024, r 44(6); and PARA 692. As to caveats see PARA 690.
9 See Non-Contentious Probate Rules 1987, SI 1987/2024, r 50(1); and PARA 680 note 3.

703. Ex parte applications where application by summons is not required. Where it is necessary to obtain the directions or an order of a district judge[1] or registrar[2] in a non-contentious[3] application for a grant[4], and there is no provision that the matter be brought before him by summons, the application is made ex parte by lodging the necessary affidavits or papers in the registry in which the matter is proceeding[5]. The most usual of such applications are:

(1) for the appointment of a person to obtain administration for the use and benefit of a minor[6];

(2) for the amendment or revocation of grants[7];

(3) for a grant or order after a person cited to accept or refuse a grant or to propound a will has failed to enter an appearance[8];

(4) for the admission to proof of a nuncupative will or a copy or reconstruction of a will[9];

(5) for a grant limited to part of an estate[10];

(6) for a discretionary grant or a grant ad colligenda bona[11];

(7) for leave to swear to death[12];

(8) for leave to withdraw a renunciation of probate or administration[13]; and

(9) for a subpoena to bring in a will[14].

An application to rectify a will may be made to a district judge or registrar unless a probate action has been commenced[15].

1 As to the meaning of 'district judge' see PARA 631 note 6.
2 As to the meaning of 'registrar' see PARA 631 note 7.
3 As to the distinction between non-contentious business and contentious business see PARA 684.
4 As to the meaning of 'grant' see PARA 631 note 7.
5 The district judge or registrar may require any application to be made by summons to a district judge or registrar in chambers or a judge in chambers or open court: see PARA 701. As to applications to be made by summons see PARA 702.
6 See the Non-Contentious Probate Rules 1987, SI 1987/2024, r 32(2); and PARA 795.
7 See the Non-Contentious Probate Rules 1987, SI 1987/2024, r 41; and PARA 854.
8 See the Non-Contentious Probate Rules 1987, SI 1987/2024, rr 47(5)(a), 48(2)(a); and PARAS 698, 700.
9 See the Non-Contentious Probate Rules 1987, SI 1987/2024, r 54; and PARA 730. As to nuncupative wills see PARA 81.
10 See the Non-Contentious Probate Rules 1987, SI 1987/2024, r 51; and PARA 819.
11 See the Non-Contentious Probate Rules 1987, SI 1987/2024, r 52; and PARAS 758, 815.
12 See the Non-Contentious Probate Rules 1987, SI 1987/2024, r 53; and PARA 744.
13 See the Non-Contentious Probate Rules 1987, SI 1987/2024, r 37(3); and PARA 632.

14 See the Non-Contentious Probate Rules 1987, SI 1987/2024, r 50(2); and PARA 680.
15 See the Non-Contentious Probate Rules 1987, SI 1987/2024, r 55(1); and PARA 741.

704. Service of summonses and notices. A judge of the High Court or district judge[1] or, where the application is to be made to a district probate registrar, that registrar[2], may direct that a summons is to be served on such person or persons as the judge, district judge or registrar may direct[3].

Where a summons is required to be served on any person[4], it must be served not less than two clear days before the day appointed for the hearing, unless a judge or district judge or registrar at or before the hearing dispenses with service on such terms, if any, as he may think fit[5].

Unless a district judge or registrar otherwise directs or the non-contentious probate rules[6] otherwise provide, any notice or other document required to be given to or served on any person may be given or served in the prescribed manner[7].

1 As to the meaning of 'district judge' see PARA 631 note 6.
2 As to the meaning of 'registrar' see PARA 631 note 7.
3 Non-Contentious Probate Rules 1987, SI 1987/2024, r 66(1) (amended by SI 1991/1876; and SI 1998/1903). This rule applies if no other provision for service is made by the Non-Contentious Probate Rules 1987, SI 1987/2024: see r 66(1) (as so amended). If either side intends to appear by counsel the summons must be so marked and the other parties notified: *Practice Direction* [1953] 1 WLR 474.
4 Ie required by the Non-Contentious Probate Rules 1987, SI 1987/2024, or by any direction given under r 66(1): see r 66(2) (as amended: see note 5).
5 Non-Contentious Probate Rules 1987, SI 1987/2024, r 66(2) (amended by SI 1991/1876).
6 Ie the Non-Contentious Probate Rules 1987, SI 1987/2024: see r 67 (as amended: see note 7).
7 Non-Contentious Probate Rules 1987, SI 1987/2024, r 67 (amended by SI 1991/1876). Service is prescribed by RSC Ord 65 r 5: see the Non-Contentious Probate Rules 1987, SI 1987/2024, r 67 (as so amended). As to the application of the RSC to non-contentious probate matters see PARA 687 note 11. As to the distinction between non-contentious and contentious business see PARA 684.

705. Non-contentious appeals. An appeal against a decision or requirement of a district judge[1] or registrar[2] is made by summons to a judge[3]. This does not apply to an appeal against a decision in proceedings for the assessment of costs[4].

Where a discretionary jurisdiction is given to the court, the judge is in no way fettered by the previous exercise of the district judge's or registrar's discretion. The judge is entitled to exercise his discretion as though the matter came before him for the first time[5]. An appeal lies to the Court of Appeal from an order made by a judge of the Family or Chancery Division in court[6], whether the matter is contentious or non-contentious[7].

1 As to the meaning of 'district judge' see PARA 631 note 6.
2 As to the meaning of 'registrar' see PARA 631 note 7.
3 Non-Contentious Probate Rules 1987, SI 1987/2024, r 65(1) (r 65(1), (2) amended by SI 1991/1876). If, in an appeal, any person besides the appellant appeared or was represented before the district judge or registrar from whose decision or requirement the appeal is brought, the summons must be issued within seven days for hearing on the first available day and must be served on every such person: Non-Contentious Probate Rules 1987, SI 1987/2024, r 65(2) (as so amended). As to the time for service see PARA 704.
4 Non-Contentious Probate Rules 1987, SI 1987/2024, r 65(3) (added by SI 2003/185). See also the Non-Contentious Probate Rules 1987, SI 1987/2024, r 60; and PARA 687. An appeal arising out of the detailed assessment of costs is dealt with: (1) under CPR 47.21–47.24 (see CIVIL PROCEDURE vol 12A (2015) PARA 1773) if the appeal is against a decision of an authorised costs officer; and (2) under CPR Pt 52 (see CIVIL PROCEDURE vol 12A (2015) PARA 1514 et seq) otherwise: see the Non-Contentious Probate Rules 1987, SI 1987/2024, r 60(8)-(10) (substituted by SI 2003/185). In either case the appeal is made subject to the CPR rather than to the RSC or the County Court Rules. Appeals dealt with under CPR Pt 52 lie from a district judge or other officer of the court to a judge of the High Court. As to the CPR see PARA 647 note 3; and as to

costs in non-contentious business see PARA 687. As to the application of the RSC to non-contentious probate matters see PARA 687 note 11.

5 *Cooper v Cooper* [1936] 2 All ER 542, CA; *Practice Note* [1949] WN 475, CA.

6 See the Senior Courts Act 1981 s 16; and COURTS AND TRIBUNALS vol 24 (2010) PARA 693.

7 *Re Clook* (1890) 15 PD 132, CA. As to the distinction between non-contentious business and contentious business see PARA 684.

706. Evidence of foreign law. Where evidence as to the law of a country or territory outside England and Wales is required on any application for a grant[1], the district judge[2] or registrar[3] may accept[4] an affidavit from any person whom, having regard to the particulars of his knowledge or experience given in the affidavit, he regards as suitably qualified to give expert evidence of the law in question[5] or a certificate by, or act before, a notary practising in the country or territory concerned[6].

Where a will is shown by a properly authenticated copy issued by a notary practising out of England and Wales to have been executed in his presence or that of his predecessor, and recorded in his archives at the time of execution, it may be assumed for the purposes of an uncontested application to prove the will in this country, provided there are no unusual features, that the will is valid as to form by the internal law of the place where it was made[7].

1 As to the meaning of 'grant' see PARA 631 note 7.

2 As to the meaning of 'district judge' see PARA 631 note 6.

3 As to the meaning of 'registrar' see PARA 631 note 7.

4 Non-Contentious Probate Rules 1987, SI 1987/2024, r 19 (amended by SI 1991/1876). As to proof of foreign law see generally CONFLICT OF LAWS vol 19 (2011) PARAS 329-330; CIVIL PROCEDURE vol 12 (2015) PARA 746 et seq.

5 Non-Contentious Probate Rules 1987, SI 1987/2024, r 19(a).

6 Non-Contentious Probate Rules 1987, SI 1987/2024, r 19(b). See also the Civil Evidence Act 1972 s 4(1) (see CIVIL PROCEDURE vol 12 (2015) PARAS 749, 887); and *Practice Direction* [1972] 3 All ER 912, [1972] 1 WLR 1433.

7 *Practice Note* [1972] 3 All ER 1019, [1972] 1 WLR 1539. A will is to be treated as properly executed inter alia if its execution conformed with the internal law in force where it was executed: see the Wills Act 1963 s 1 (see PARA 12); and CONFLICT OF LAWS vol 19 (2011) PARA 748.

(2) INSTRUMENTS ENTITLED TO PROBATE

(i) Wills in England and Wales

707. Instruments of which probate may be granted. In general every instrument purporting to be testamentary[1], or to affect a previous testamentary instrument, and made by a person over the age of 18[2] and of full capacity[3], and executed in accordance with the formal statutory requirements[4], is entitled to probate if it purports to dispose[5] of property[6], whether or not the deceased in fact left any property[7], or contains the appointment of an executor[8] even if the executor renounces probate[9]. A writing which merely revokes a former testamentary disposition without making any disposition of its own ought not to be admitted to probate[10], but the court may grant administration with the writing annexed[11]. A will which merely appoints a guardian ought not to be admitted to probate[12].

1 The primary characteristics of a testamentary instrument are that it is designed to take effect after the testator's death and that it is of its own nature ambulatory and revocable during his life: see Jarman on Wills (8th Edn) 26. See also PARA 1. As to the form see note 4; and PARA 708.

2 See the Wills Act 1837 s 7; and PARA 898. See also PARA 46. As to the exemption from the age requirement in the case of wills of soldiers, sailors and airmen see PARA 79 et seq.

3 See PARA 79 et seq.

4 If it is to be valid in accordance with the internal law of England and Wales a will must normally be in writing, signed by the testator or by some other person in his presence and by his direction; it must appear that the testator intended by his signature to give effect to the will; the signature must be made or acknowledged by the testator in the presence of two or more witnesses present at the same time; and each witness must either attest and sign the will, or acknowledge his signature, in the presence of the testator (but not necessarily in the presence of any other witness), but no form of attestation is necessary: Wills Act 1837 s 9 (substituted, in the case of deaths on or after 1 January 1983, by the Administration of Justice Act 1982 s 17). See also PARA 60 et seq.

A will may be treated as properly executed even though it does not conform to the requirements of the internal law of England and Wales if it complies with a system of law in accordance with which it may validly be executed by virtue of the Wills Act 1963: see PARA 709.

5 Probate of a document which has no dispositive effect will not normally be needed or granted: *Re Thomas, Public Trustee v Davies* [1939] 2 All ER 567 at 577. See, however, the cases cited in note 8.

6 The property of which the instrument purports to dispose may be real or personal: see the Wills Act 1837 s 3; and PARA 26.

7 See the Senior Courts Act 1981 s 25 which confers on the court all such jurisdiction in relation to probates as it had immediately before 1982: see PARA 677 note 4. Before 1982 it had jurisdiction to grant probate notwithstanding that a testator left no estate: see the Administration of Justice Act 1932 s 2(1) (repealed). As to wills disposing solely of property abroad see PARA 722.

8 *Re Leese* (1862) 2 Sw & Tr 442; *Re Jordan* (1868) LR 1 P & D 555; *Re Irvine* [1919] 2 IR 485; *Re Hornbuckle* (1890) 15 PD 149.

9 *Re Jordan* (1868) LR 1 P & D 555.

10 *Re Fraser* (1869) LR 2 P & D 40. See also *Toomer v Sobinska* [1907] P 106; but cf *Re Durance* (1872) LR 2 P & D 406 (provisions of a testamentary nature).

11 *Re Hubbard* (1865) LR 1 P & D 53; *Re Hicks* (1869) LR 1 P & D 683. The present practice is to make a grant of administration without annexing the document. The grant bears a note that a duly attested instrument revoking former wills has been filed. See PARA 791.

12 *Re Morton* (1864) 3 Sw & Tr 422. See also *Gilliat v Gilliat and Hatfield* (1820) 3 Phillim 222.

708. Form of instrument immaterial. The form of the instrument is immaterial. The only requirements are: (1) that it is intended by the testator to operate after his death; and (2) that it is executed in accordance with the statutory requirements[1]. The principles to be applied to the first of these requisites differ from those to be applied on the interpretation of a will in a court of construction. In probate the whole question is one of intention: intention to make a will and intention to revoke a will are completely open to investigation[2]; but in a court of construction, once the validity of the will has been established, the inquiry is restricted to the contents of the instrument itself in order to ascertain the testator's intentions[3]. The intention that it should operate after death need not appear on the face of the instrument, but may be proved by extrinsic evidence[4]. Although on the face of it a document may be testamentary and duly executed, if it is proved that the deceased had no intention that it should operate as a will, it will not be admitted to probate[5]. Conversely, instruments in the form of deeds have been admitted to probate[6].

1 *Habergham v Vincent* (1793) 2 Ves 204 at 231; *Masterman v Maberly* (1829) 2 Hag Ecc 235 at 248; *Cock v Cooke* (1866) LR 1 P & D 241; *Re Coles* (1871) LR 2 P & D 362; *Warwick v Warwick* (1918) 34 TLR 475, CA; *Governors and Guardians of Foundling Hospital v Crane* [1911] 2 KB 367, CA; *Godman v Godman* [1920] P 261, CA (where the cases are reviewed in the judgment of Scrutton LJ); *Re Berger* [1990] Ch 118 at 129, [1989] 1 All ER 591 at 599, CA, per Mustill LJ. See also PARA 60 et seq. As to the statutory requirements see PARA 707 note 4.

2 *Methuen v Methuen* (1817) 2 Phillim 416 at 426; *Re Resch's Will Trusts, Le Cras v Perpetual Trustee Co Ltd, Far West Children's Health Scheme v Perpetual Trustee Co Ltd* [1969] 1 AC 514 at 547, sub nom *Le Cras v Perpetual Trustee Co Ltd, Far West Children's Health Scheme v Perpetual Trustee Co Ltd* [1967] 3 All ER 915 at 925, PC; *Lamothe v Lamothe* [2006] EWHC 1387 (Ch), [2006] All ER (D) 153 (Jun); *Parkinson v Fawdon* [2009] EWHC 1953 (Ch), [2009] All ER (D) 322 (Jul).

3 *Greenough v Martin* (1824) 2 Add 239 at 243; *Re Resch's Will Trusts, Le Cras v Perpetual Trustee Co Ltd, Far West Children's Health Scheme v Perpetual Trustee Co Ltd* [1969] 1 AC 514 at 547, sub nom *Le Cras v Perpetual Trustee Co Ltd, Far West Children's Health Scheme v*

Perpetual Trustee Co Ltd [1967] 3 All ER 915 at 925, PC. As to the probate court's duty to construe a will only for the purpose of proving it see PARA 679. Where the question of what instruments should be admitted to probate is a question of construction, it may be possible to have it determined by construction proceedings instead of by probate proceedings: *Re Finnemore* [1992] 1 All ER 800, [1991] 1 WLR 793. The fact that a document has been admitted to probate does not prevent a court of construction from concluding that it has no operative effect: see PARA 670.

4 *Robertson v Smith* (1870) LR 2 P & D 43; *Re Slinn* (1890) 15 PD 156.

5 *Nichols v Nichols* (1814) 2 Phillim 180; *Ferguson-Davie v Ferguson-Davie* (1890) 15 PD 109; cf *Selwood v Selwood* (1920) 125 LT 26 (soldier's letter not a testamentary paper). See *Corbett v Newey* [1998] Ch 57, [1996] 2 All ER 914, CA (conditionally executed will).

6 *Re Colyer* (1889) 14 PD 48; *Milnes v Foden* (1890) 15 PD 105.

709. Conflict of laws. A will is to be treated as properly executed if it complies with any system of internal law[1] in accordance with which it may be validly executed by virtue of the Wills Act 1963[2].

1 Ie the internal law in force in the territory where the will was executed or in the territory where, at the time of its execution or of the testator's death, he was domiciled or had his habitual residence, or in a state of which, at either of these times, he was a national: see the Wills Act 1963 s 1; and PARA 12; CONFLICT OF LAWS vol 19 (2011) PARA 748. For special provisions as to wills executed on board vessels or aircraft, wills of immovables etc see s 2; and CONFLICT OF LAWS vol 19 (2011) PARA 748.

2 See the Wills Act 1963 s 1; PARA 12; and CONFLICT OF LAWS vol 19 (2011) PARA 748.

710. Proof of soldier's, sailor's or airman's will. In order to prove a soldier's, sailor's or airman's will[1], an affidavit should be sworn showing that at the time of its making the testator was 'in actual military service' or at sea, as the case may be[2] and that he was domiciled in England or Wales[3]. The terms and validity of a privileged will must be established to the district judge's or registrar's satisfaction[4]. Where a testator died domiciled in England and Wales and it appears to the district judge or registrar that there is prima facie evidence that a written will is privileged[5] it may be admitted to proof if he is satisfied that it was signed by the testator or, if unsigned, that it is in the testator's handwriting[6]. If it is signed with the testator's mark, an affidavit must show that he had knowledge of its contents[7]. If the document is unattested, affidavit evidence will be required to prove that the signature is that of the testator[8], and alterations and interlineations by the testator necessitate similar proof[9]. If it is a nuncupative will[10], an application for an order admitting it to proof is governed by special procedure[11].

Where a soldier's will (for example a letter) contains matter in reference to military operations, to the inclusion of which in the probate the military authorities object, the court may grant probate only of the part of the letter which is of a testamentary character without including in the probate the rest of the letter[12].

1 As to the privilege attaching to such wills see PARAS 79–81.

2 See PARAS 79–81.

3 See the Non-Contentious Probate Rules 1987, SI 1987/2024, r 18 (as amended: see note 6). As to domicile generally see CONFLICT OF LAWS vol 19 (2011) PARA 336 et seq.

4 See the Non-Contentious Probate Rules 1987, SI 1987/2024, r 17(2) (amended by SI 1991/1876). Nothing in the Non-Contentious Probate Rules 1987, SI 1987/2024, rr 12–15 (see PARAS 733–734) applies to a privileged will: see r 17(1). As to the meaning of 'district judge' see PARA 631 note 6; and as to the meaning of 'registrar' see PARA 631 note 7.

5 Ie one to which the Wills Act 1837 s 11 (see PARA 79) applies: see the Non-Contentious Probate Rules 1987, SI 1987/2024, r 18 (as amended: see note 6).

6 Non-Contentious Probate Rules 1987, SI 1987/2024, r 18 (amended by SI 1991/1876).

7 *Re Hackett* (1859) 4 Sw & Tr 220; *Re Thorne* (1865) 4 Sw & Tr 36.

8 *Re Hackett* (1859) 4 Sw & Tr 220; *Re Neville* (1859) 4 Sw & Tr 218.

9 See *Re Tweedale* (1874) LR 3 P & D 204.

10 See PARA 81.

11 See PARA 730.

12 *Re Heywood* [1916] P 47.

711. Incorporation of documents. In certain cases documents referred to in a testator's will or codicil, though not themselves duly executed, may be incorporated in the will and included in the probate[1]. Such a document must be strictly identified with the description contained in the will[2]; but extrinsic evidence is admissible for the purpose of identification[3]. The reference must be to a document as an existing document[4] and not to one which is to come into existence at a future date[5]. If the will can be construed as referring equally to an existing or future document, extrinsic evidence is not admissible[6]. The onus of proving the identity of the document and its existence at the date of the will lies upon the party seeking to establish it[7], but the court will draw inferences from the circumstances surrounding the execution of the will[8].

If a document of the kind referred to in the will comes into existence after the date of execution of the will but before the date of execution of a codicil confirming the will, the admissibility of the document to probate depends upon whether it is referred to in the will, treated as speaking at the date of the codicil, as an existing or future document. If the will prima facie refers to the document as an existing document, then, even though it appears from the surrounding circumstances, namely the date of the signing of the document, that it was not in existence at the date when the will was originally executed, the document may nevertheless be admitted to probate, since the will is treated as speaking from the date of its re-execution by the codicil[9]; but if the will, treated as speaking at the date of the codicil, still in terms refers to a future document, the document cannot be admitted to probate even though it was in existence at the date of the codicil[10].

1 *Re Mardon* [1944] P 109 at 112, [1944] 2 All ER 397 at 399. As to the incorporation in a will of the scale fees of a trust corporation see PARA 652. As to the incorporation by reference of standard will forms or clauses as contained in a published document see PARA 736.

2 In such a case the registrar may call for evidence about the incorporation and may require the production of the document: see PARA 736. Where part of a document complies with the description contained in the will, and part does not, the part which complies may be admitted to probate: *Re Osburn* (1969)113 Sol Jo 387, CA.

3 *Allen v Maddock* (1858) 11 Moo PCC 427; *Re Almosnino* (1859) 1 Sw & Tr 508; *Paton v Ormerod* [1892] P 247 at 252; *Re Garnett* [1894] P 90; *Eyre v Eyre* [1903] P 131; *Re Nicholls, Hunter v Nicholls* [1921] 2 Ch 11 (signature and attestation on outside of sealed envelope containing signed will).

4 *Re Mardon* [1944] P 109 at 112, [1944] 2 All ER 397 at 399; *Re Berger* [1990] Ch 118, [1989] 1 All ER 591, CA.

5 *Re Sunderland* (1866) LR 1 P & D 198; *Re Reid* (1868) 38 LJP & M 1; *Durham v Northen* [1895] P 66; *Re Smart* [1902] P 238. Certainty and identification are the very essence of incorporation: *Croker v Marquess of Hertford* (1844) 4 Moo PCC 339 at 366 per Dr Lushington. See also *Re Phillips, Boyle v Thompson* (1918) 34 TLR 256 (reference in will to letter afterwards found deposited in bank); *Re Jones* (1920) 123 LT 202; *Re Saxton, Barclays Bank Ltd v Treasury Solicitor* [1939] 2 All ER 418.

6 *University College of North Wales v Taylor* [1908] P 140, CA.

7 *Singleton v Tomlinson* (1878) 3 App Cas 404, HL.

8 *Re Saxton, Barclays Bank Ltd v Treasury Solicitor* [1939] 2 All ER 418.

9 *Re Lady Truro* (1866) LR 1 P & D 201 ('inventory signed by me and deposited herewith'). See also PARA 1.

10 *Re Smart* [1902] P 238 ('such friends as I may designate in a book or memorandum that will be found with this will'). The decisions in *Re Hunt* (1853) 2 Rob Eccl 622 and *Re Stewart* (1863) 3 Sw & Tr 192, where probate was granted of documents which were referred to as future documents in the will but which came into existence before the date of the codicil, were not based on any principle: see *Re Smart* at 241–242.

712. Probate of codicils. A codicil will be admitted to probate even where the will is not forthcoming[1] or has been revoked by destruction[2], notwithstanding that the codicil may have become unintelligible as a result[3].

1 *Black v Jobling* (1869) LR 1 P & D 685 (commenting on *Clogstoun v Walcott* (1848) 5 Notes of Cases 623, and *Grimwood v Cozens* (1860) 2 Sw & Tr 364); *Gardiner v Courthope* (1886) 12 PD 14; *Re Savage* (1870) LR 2 P & D 78.

2 *Re Turner* (1872) LR 2 P & D 403. See, however, PARA 707.

3 See PARA 100.

713. Several testamentary instruments. Where two testamentary documents are executed[1] on different dates, then, unless the later expressly or by implication revokes the earlier, both should be admitted to probate upon the principle that every document purporting to be testamentary and duly executed ought to be admitted to probate[2]. Where the documents are executed simultaneously, or it cannot be ascertained which was executed first, both are to be admitted to probate if upon any reasonable construction they can be so read as to stand together, but if they cannot be so read, neither is to be admitted to probate[3]. For these purposes the probate court must act as a court of construction[4]. When a final will, not inconsistent with an earlier will, appoints a fresh executor, probate is granted of both instruments to both executors jointly[5].

1 As to separate wills disposing of English property and of foreign property see PARA 723.

2 *Townsend v Moore* [1905] P 66 at 77, CA, per Vaughan Williams LJ; *Re Adams* (1911) 45 ILT 93 (two testamentary papers, the later in date being described as a codicil); *Re Pawle, Winter v Pawle* (1918) 34 TLR 437 (letter as soldier's will and ordinary will both admitted to probate); *Nixon v Prince* (1918) 34 TLR 444; *Deakin v Garvie* (1919) 36 TLR 122, CA.

3 *Phipps v Earl of Anglesey* (1751) 7 Bro Parl Cas 443 at 452, HL; *Townsend v Moore* [1905] P 66 at 77, 84, CA. The court struggles to reconcile dispositions which on the face often might at first sight appear to be somewhat irreconcilable: *Townsend v Moore* at 84–85. As to how far inconsistencies between a later and an earlier instrument amount to a revocation of the earlier see PARA 95 et seq.

Where a testator made a will in favour of two persons and a few days later made further wills, each relating to different property, in favour of those persons and it was shown that he had believed separate wills to be necessary to dispose of separate properties, the inference that he knew and approved of the contents of his wills was held not to apply to printed revocation clauses in the subsequent wills and the wills were admitted to probate without those clauses: *Re Phelan* [1972] Fam 33, [1971] 3 All ER 1256. See also *Re Crannis' Estate, Mansell v Crannis* (1978) 122 Sol Jo 489. As to the presumption of knowledge and approval see PARAS 54–55.

4 *Lemage v Goodban* (1865) LR 1 P & D 57; *Townsend v Moore* [1905] P 66, CA; *Re Hawksley's Settlement, Black v Tidy* [1934] Ch 384. See also PARA 679.

5 *Re Morgan* (1867) LR 1 P & D 323; *Re Strahan* [1907] 2 IR 484.

714. Joint wills. Where two testators make their wills in one and the same instrument, the instrument constitutes a joint will[1]. In practice the whole of a joint will is ordinarily proved on the death of the first of the testators to die[2] as the will of that testator; and it is proved again on the death of the survivor of the testators as his or her will provided the survivor has not revoked it[3]. Wills of two or more persons, for example of husband and wife, made by arrangements between them[4] and conferring reciprocal benefits but contained in separate instruments, are sometimes referred to as joint wills but more usually as mutual wills[5]; so far as grants of probate or administration are concerned, mutual wills are not the subject of any special rule[6].

1 See PARA 9.

2 See Tristram and Coote's Probate Practice (31st Edn) 3.214. The practice, followed in *Re Piazzi-Smyth* [1898] P 7, of proving on the first death only so much of the will as becomes operative on that death is not now followed.

3 See PARA 9.

4 See eg *Re Green, Lindner v Green* [1951] Ch 148, [1950] 2 All ER 913; *Re Goodchild, Goodchild v Goodchild* [1997] 3 All ER 63, [1997] 1 WLR 1216, CA; and *Olins v Waters* [2007] EWCA Civ 1347, [2007] All ER (D) 488 (Oct).
5 As to mutual wills generally see PARA 10.
6 But a person claiming under the doctrine of mutual wills is not a person beneficially interested in the estate under the will of the deceased and so has no basis for making an application under the Administration of Justice Act 1985 s 50 (see PARA 1163): *Thomas and Agnes Carvel Foundation v Carvel* [2007] EWHC 1314 (Ch), [2008] Ch 395, [2007] 4 All ER 81. See further PARA 1163.

715. Duplicate will. Where a will has been made in duplicate and there is a reference in the part produced for probate to execution in duplicate, both parts must be lodged at the registry for a grant, but one part is handed back with the grant after collation[1].

1 See Tristram and Coote's Probate Practice (31st Edn) 3.208. As to the presumption of revocation arising from the destruction of one of the duplicates see PARA 102.

716. Probate of contents of lost will. Where a testamentary instrument has been lost or destroyed in such a way as not to effect a revocation, probate may be granted[1] of its contents upon proof of those contents and of the due execution and attestation of the instrument[2].

A person who wishes to prove an alleged will and is unable to produce it, or any copy or draft of it, or any written evidence of its contents, is bound to prove its contents and its due execution and attestation by evidence which is clear and satisfactory[3]. It seems that the standard of proof required is the ordinary standard of proof in civil cases, namely the establishment of a reasonable balance of probability[4]. If an intention on the part of the alleged testator to do some formal act is established, and the evidence is consistent with that intention having been carried into effect in a proper way, the court may infer the actual observance of all due formalities as a matter of probability[5].

The contents of a lost will may be proved by the evidence of a single witness whose veracity and competency are unimpeached, even if he has an interest[6]. Where an alleged draft of the lost will is produced the court must take the evidence of witnesses side by side with the alleged draft and out of them extract the contents of the will as well as it can[7].

1 As to the special procedure on an application for a grant in respect of nuncupative wills and copies see the Non-Contentious Probate Rules 1987 SI 1987/2024, r 54; and PARA 730. As to the offence of destroying a will see PARA 680 note 12.
2 See the Wills Act 1837 s 20 (intent to revoke necessary); and PARAS 93, 101. See also *Brown v Brown* (1858) 8 E & B 876; *Sugden v Lord St Leonards* (1876) 1 PD 154 at 238–240, CA, per Jessel MR. See further *Allan v Morrison* [1900] AC 604, PC; *Re Crandon* (1901) 84 LT 330; *Re Spain* (1915) 31 TLR 435 (testator, attesting witnesses, and will lost in explosion); *Re Phibbs* [1917] P 93; *Re Queen Marie of Roumania* (1950) 94 Sol Jo 673 (will as embodied in copy of Roumanian 'act de partage' admitted to probate); *Re Webb, Smith v Johnston* [1964] 2 All ER 91, [1964] 1 WLR 509 (will destroyed by enemy action while in solicitor's custody; attestation clause in a completed draft sufficient evidence of due execution). As to revocation of wills see PARA 87 et seq. As to the admissibility of declarations by a testator as evidence by virtue of the Civil Evidence Act 1995 s 1 see CIVIL PROCEDURE vol 12 (2015) PARA 859. As to evidence of execution in proceedings for probate in solemn form see PARA 894 et seq.
3 *Harris v Knight* (1890) 15 PD 170 at 179, CA, per Lindley LJ; *Woodward v Goulstone* (1886) 11 App Cas 469 at 475, HL, per Lord Herschell LC; *Re MacGillivray* [1946] 2 All ER 301, CA.
4 *Wissler v Wipperman* [1955] P 59, [1953] 1 All ER 764; *Re Yelland, Broadbent v Francis* (1975) 119 Sol Jo 562; *Ferneley v Napier* [2010] EWHC 3345 (Ch), [2011] WTLR 1303. In these cases dicta in *Harris v Knight* (1890) 15 PD 170, CA, per Lindley LJ, and in *Woodward v Goulstone* (1886) 11 App Cas 469, HL, per Lord Hershell LC, that proof must be beyond reasonable doubt, were not followed. Evidence of the testator's care or lack of it in relation to paperwork is admissible: see *Wren v Wren* [2006] EWHC 2243 (Ch), 9 ITELR 223, [2006] All ER (D) 30 (Sept).
5 *Harris v Knight* (1890) 15 PD 170, CA.
6 *Sugden v Lord St Leonards* (1876) 1 PD 154, CA; *Re Yelland, Broadbent v Francis* (1975) 119 Sol Jo 562; *Wren v Wren* [2006] EWHC 2243 (Ch), 9 ITELR 223, [2006] All ER (D) 30 (Sept).

7 *Burls v Burls* (1868) LR 1 P & D 472 at 474. The post-testamentary declaration of a testator as to the contents of his will have been admitted by the Court of Appeal (*Sugden v Lord St Leonards* (1876) 1 PD 154, CA, overruling *Quick v Quick and Quick* (1864) 3 Sw & Tr 442; *Gould v Lakes* (1880) 6 PD 1), but the question of their admissibility has been expressly left open by the House of Lords (*Woodward v Goulstone* (1886) 11 App Cas 469, HL). It was held in *Atkinson v Morris* [1897] P 40, CA, that declarations made by a testator after the date of an alleged will were not admissible to prove the execution of a will, following *Doe d Shallcross v Palmer* (1851) 16 QB 747 at 757; *Re Ripley* (1858) 1 Sw & Tr 68; and *Sugden v Lord St Leonards*. See also *Eyre v Eyre* [1903] P 131. Lord Russell of Killowen CJ, however, in *Atkinson v Morris*, admitted the rigour of a rule of evidence which shuts out 'evidence of great cogency and probative force', and it is conceivable that ex post facto declarations by a testator might be admitted as evidence of a testator's intention to have his will duly executed: see *Neal v Denston* (1932) 48 TLR 637; *Clarke v Clarke* (1879) 5 LR Ir 47, CA. Cf *Barkwell v Barkwell* [1928] P 91 at 97 per Lord Merrivale P. See also *Wren v Wren* [2006] EWHC 2243 (Ch), 9 ITELR 223, [2006] All ER (D) 30 (Sept). See also PARAS 895–896.

717. Burnt, faded or torn wills. If the whole or part of a will is destroyed or made illegible by accidental causes such as burning, fading of ink, gnawing by rats or decay of the paper its contents may be proved by parol testimony[1]. Where a torn will is admitted to probate, missing words will not be read into the will by the court, but when proved may be contained in a paper attached to the will[2].

Attempted revocation of a will by burning, tearing, or otherwise destroying and every other circumstance leading to a presumption of revocation by the testator needs to accounted for[3]. Further, where a facsimile copy of the original will is not considered satisfactory for purposes of record, an engrossment suitable for facsimile reproduction may be required[4].

1 See *Re Wright* (1910) 44 ILT 137; *Re Bentley* [1930] IR 445. As to the presumption of revocation arising from intentional destruction or damage see PARA 737; and PARA 106.
2 *Gill v Gill* [1909] P 157; *Re Leigh* [1892] P 82.
3 See the Non-Contentious Probate Rules 1987, SI 1987/2024, r 15; and PARA 737.
4 See the Non-Contentious Probate Rules 1987, SI 1987/2024, r 11(1), (3); and PARA 732. Following a notice issued by Her Majesty's Courts Service with effect from 1 January 2009, two copies of the sworn will and codicils (if applicable) must be supplied in A4 size with every application for a grant lodged by a solicitor or probate practitioner. For applications for grants through solicitors or probate practitioners, see PARA 726; and Tristram and Coote's Probate Practice (31st Edn) 4.232.

(ii) Foreigners' Wills

718. Wills of persons dying domiciled abroad. As a general rule, where a person dies domiciled abroad[1], and it becomes necessary to prove his will in England and Wales, it will be admitted to proof if it is established that the testator was domiciled in the country in question, and that either the foreign court has adopted his will as a valid testament or that his will is valid by the law[2] of that country[3] or if (in the case of deaths in or after 1964) its execution conformed to the internal law in force in the territory where the will was executed or in the territory where, at the time of its execution or of the testator's death, he was domiciled or had his habitual residence, or in a state of which, at either of these times, he was a national[4].

Where the deceased dies domiciled outside England and Wales, probate of any valid will may be granted[5]:

(1) if the will is in the English or Welsh language, to the executor named in it[6]; or

(2) if the will describes the duties of a named person in terms sufficient to constitute him executor according to the tenor of the will[7], to that person[8].

Where the whole or substantially the whole of the estate in England and Wales of such a person consists of immovable property, a grant in respect of the whole estate may be made in accordance with the law which would have been applicable if the deceased had died domiciled in England and Wales[9].

1 As to domicile generally see CONFLICT OF LAWS vol 19 (2011) PARA 336 et seq.
2 However, at common law a will of immovables must comply with the formal requirements as to execution of the lex situs: see CONFLICT OF LAWS vol 19 (2011) PARA 740. This means that, in the case of deaths before 1964, in order to pass immovables situate in England or Wales and be admitted to proof here, a will must have complied with the formal requirements of the Wills Act 1837 (see PARA 707 note 4). As to evidence of foreign law see PARA 706.
3 *Enohin v Wylie* (1862) 10 HL Cas 1; *Re Deshais, Re Countess De Vigny* (1865) 34 LJPM & A 58; *Re Earl* (1867) LR 1 P & D 450; *Miller v James* (1872) LR 3 P & D 4; *Ewing v Orr Ewing* (1885) 10 App Cas 453, HL. 'When a will has been recognised as valid by a court of competent jurisdiction in the country in which the testator was domiciled at the time of his death, it is the established practice of the English court to admit to probate in this country a duly authenticated copy of such will, without further evidence of its validity, as it is presumed that the foreign court has been satisfied on that point': *Re Yahuda* [1956] P 388, [1956] 2 All ER 262 (citing Mortimer On Probate Law And Practice (2nd Edn) p 24). However, see *Re Papillion, Murrin v Matthews* [2006] EWHC 3419 (Ch), [2006] All ER (D) 297 (Dec) where the court refused to recognise the validity of a will admitted to probate by the Superior Court of Canada because of the likelihood that it was not validly executed; it was 'arguable' the deceased was domiciled in Canada but the judge felt he was not bound by the admission of the disputed will to probate in Canada.
4 See the Wills Act 1963 s 1; and PARA 12. As to European Union legislation (not adopted by the United Kingdom) providing that European Union citizens may choose whether the law applicable to their succession should be that of their last habitual residence or that of their nationality and creating a European certificate of succession see PARA 13.
5 Ie without any order under the Non-Contentious Probate Rules 1987, SI 1987/2024, r 30(1) (see PARA 844): r 30(3). As to the procedure for obtaining the grant see PARA 846.
6 Non-Contentious Probate Rules 1987, SI 1987/2024, r 30(3)(a)(i). No expression in a language other than English or Welsh purporting to mean 'executor' will be accepted as constituting by itself an executor: *Practice Direction* [1953] 2 All ER 1154 at 1156, [1953] 1 WLR 1237 at 1239. In a case to which the Non-Contentious Probate Rules 1987, SI 1987/2024, r 30(3)(a) applies, rr 20, 22, 25 and 27 also apply: see r 28(2).
7 See PARA 613.
8 Non-Contentious Probate Rules 1987, SI 1987/2024, r 30(3)(a)(ii).
9 Non-Contentious Probate Rules 1987, SI 1987/2024, r 30(3)(b). See note 6.

719. Grant to consular officers. In certain circumstances, where a foreigner resident abroad is named as executor of a will disposing of property in England or Wales or is otherwise a person to whom a grant of representation to the estate of a deceased person in England or Wales may be made, a grant of representation to the estate is to be made to a consular officer of the state of which the foreign resident is a national[1].

1 See PARA 802. As to the power of a consular officer to give receipts for money or property see PARA 667.

720. Extent to which English grant follows foreign grant. Where probate or its equivalent[1] has been granted by the foreign court to a person whose powers under the will fall short of the powers of an executor according to English law, then unless that person is entitled as executor on one of the grounds previously stated[2], the English grant is not of probate, but of letters of administration[3] with the will annexed[4]. The English court will not make a grant to one who by English law is personally disqualified from taking the grant, for instance a minor[5], notwithstanding that he would be entitled to a grant under the foreign law.

1 There is no equivalent in many foreign countries where the system derives from the civil law: see eg in Germany where the system derives from the civil code (*Bürgerliche Gesetzbuch* (BGB)).
2 See PARA 718.
3 As to the person entitled to the grant see PARA 844.

4 *Re Earl* (1867) LR 1 P & D 450, followed in *Re Humphries* [1934] P 78 (grant to administratrix appointed by foreign court in her capacity as such, without her being obliged to take a grant as next of kin). See *Re Cosnahan* (1866) LR 1 P & D 183; *Re Hill* (1870) LR 2 P & D 89 (grant de bonis non); *Re Briesemann* [1894] P 260; *Re Von Linden* [1896] P 148; *Re Levy (otherwise Benoist)* [1908] P 108 (limited foreign grant, general grant in England); *Re Grewe* (1922) 127 LT 371 (grant of letters of administration requiring security); and see *Practice Direction* [1953] 2 All ER 1154, [1953] 1 WLR 1237. As to the grant of letters of administration see PARA 754 et seq.

5 See *Re Duchess D'Orleans* (1859) 1 Sw & Tr 253; *Re Meatyard* [1903] P 125 at 129. Cf *Re Countess Da Cunha* (1828) 1 Hag Ecc 237 (grant limited to receipt of dividends to which minor was entitled). As to the appointment of a minor as executor see PARA 620.

721. Admission to proof of duly authenticated copy of will. Where a will is not available for proof because it has been retained in the custody of a foreign court[1] or official, a duly authenticated copy of the will may be admitted to proof without the necessity for the making of any order for the purpose[2]. Since the English grant is in general terms, probate will not be given of extracts only of a foreign will dealing with the testator's assets in England or Wales[3]. A person entrusted with administration of the estate by the court of the testator's domicile need not clear off executors when applying for a grant[4].

1 As to the admission to probate in England of a will which has been adopted by a foreign court see PARA 718.

2 Non-Contentious Probate Rules 1987, SI 1987/2024, r 54(2). As to the general necessity for an order for the admission of a copy of a will see PARA 730. As to proof of a copy until the original is proved where the original is detained abroad otherwise than in the custody of a court or official see PARA 750. Where a translation of the original will has been admitted to probate in the foreign country, the English courts decree probate of a translation of such translation: *Re Rule* (1878) 4 PD 76. Cf *Re Lemme* [1892] P 89 (translation of will of British subject registered in French court; probate granted of certified copy of will until original will brought in); *Re Von Linden* [1896] P 148. See *Re Clarke* (1867) 36 LJP & M 72 (Russian probate). Where the testator's English will is lodged with a notary abroad, the notarially certified document lodged may contain a translation into the foreign language and a retranslation into English, in which case, unless the applicant objects, the registry will call for a photographic or duly verified copy of the original will; in any event the registry may require the retranslation to be checked with the original if it appears on the face of the document that the retranslation is or may be inaccurate: *Practice Direction* [1953] 2 All ER 1154 at 1157, [1953] 1 WLR 1237 at 1241.

3 *Re Baroness Von Faber* (1904) 20 TLR 640.

4 *Practice Direction* [1953] 2 All ER 1154, [1953] 1 WLR 1237. As to domicile generally see CONFLICT OF LAWS vol 19 (2011) PARA 336 et seq.

(iii) Wills disposing of Property Abroad

722. Will solely of property abroad. The object of a grant is to enable the executor or administrator to administer property in England and Wales[1]. If there is no such property a grant is normally refused[2], for there is no purpose in making it[3], but the court has power to make a grant where there is no property within the jurisdiction[4].

1 *Re Coode* (1867) LR 1 P & D 449; *Re Tamplin* [1894] P 39; *Re Murray* [1896] P 65. Cf *Stubbings v Clunies-Ross* (1911) 27 TLR 361, where probate was granted of a will disposing of property abroad, some of which, however, had been brought to England; *Re Von Brentano* [1911] P 172. See also note 4.

2 *Re Tucker* (1864) 34 LJPM & A 29; *Aldrich v A-G* [1968] P 281 at 295, [1968] 1 All ER 345 at 351.

3 *Re Thomas, Public Trustee v Davies* [1939] 2 All ER 567.

4 See the Senior Courts Act 1981 s 25(1) (see PARA 677) which preserves the court's jurisdiction in relation to probates as it had immediately before 1982, and so by implication preserves the power conferred by the Administration of Justice Act 1932 s 2(1) (repealed) to make a grant of probate notwithstanding that the testator left no estate in the jurisdiction. Such a grant will only be made when necessary for some collateral purpose, as for example to clothe the applicant with the character of personal representative with a view to legal proceedings abroad: see *Re Coode* (1867) LR 1 P & D 449, where an application for this purpose was refused on the ground that (before the

Administration of Justice Act 1932) the court had no power to grant it; and cf *Re Wayland* [1951] 2 All ER 1041 at 1044 (grant made in respect of Belgian wills not disposing of any English property and of English will).

723. Separate wills of property in England and of property abroad. Where a testator has made two wills, one dealing with his property in England and Wales and the other with his property abroad, probate may be obtained of the former will on the filing of an attested copy of the latter will annexed to an affidavit verifying it[1]. If the two wills are not independent, but the one incorporates the other, probate is granted of both wills as in fact constituting one will[2]. Where it is the testator's intention to keep the different properties separate, probate issues of the English will alone[3], and where a will is left dealing only with property abroad, the court will grant administration of the testator's property in England and Wales to those entitled on intestacy[4].

1 *Re Astor* (1876) 1 PD 150; *Re Callaway* (1890) 15 PD 147; *Re De la Rue* (1890) 15 PD 185; *Re Seaman* [1891] P 253; *Re Fraser* [1891] P 285; *Re Murray* [1896] P 65; *Re Paul, Gilmer v Overman* (1907) 23 TLR 716; and see *Re Bolton* (1887) 12 PD 202 where, with the consent of the Belgian executor, probate was granted of both a Belgian and an English will to the English executor. As to limited probate of copies see PARA 750.

2 *Re Harris* (1870) LR 2 P & D 83; *Re Mercer* (1870) LR 2 P & D 91; *Re De la Saussaye* (1873) LR 3 P & D 42; *Re Lord Howden* (1874) 43 LJP 26; *Re Western* (1898) 78 LT 49; *Re Green* (1899) 79 LT 738; *Re Todd* [1926] P 173 (English and American wills interdependent as to residue both proved, but American will to be handed out to foreign executors, after certified copy made for retention in registry).

3 *Re Schenley* (1903) 20 TLR 127.

4 *Re Mann* [1891] P 293.

(3) PROBATE IN COMMON FORM

(i) How and by whom Obtained

724. Applications for probate or letters of administration. Applications for probate or for letters of administration may be made at the principal registry of the Family Division[1] or any district probate registry[2] or sub-registry[3].

1 Senior Courts Act 1981 s 105(a). As to the practice on obtaining representation where the deceased was a patient within the jurisdiction of the Court of Protection see MENTAL HEALTH AND CAPACITY vol 75 (2013) PARA 720 et seq. As to cases in which money or effects may be disposed of without the necessity of obtaining a grant of representation see PARA 661.

2 Senior Courts Act 1981 s 105(b). As to the powers of district probate registrars see PARA 683. As to fees see PARA 686. See note 1.

3 See PARAS 726–727. As to the establishment of sub-registries see PARA 683.

725. Executor's right to probate. The only person entitled to a grant of probate is the executor[1], whether he is expressly appointed or merely by implication according to the tenor[2]. The application for a grant may be made by the executor in person or through a solicitor or probate practitioner[3]. Where the Crown may be beneficially interested notice must be given to the Treasury Solicitor[4].

1 As to the persons entitled in default of the executor to administration with the will annexed and as to grants to attesting witnesses and their spouses or their civil partners see PARA 790 et seq.

2 *Wankford v Wankford* (1704) 1 Salk 299 at 309; *Re Almosnino* (1859) 1 Sw & Tr 508; *Re Manly* (1862) 3 Sw & Tr 56; *Re Fraser* (1870) LR 2 P & D 183 at 186; *Re Drumm* [1931] NI 12. As to the executor according to the tenor of the will see PARA 613.

3 See PARAS 726–727. As to grants to consular officers where the person entitled to a grant is a non-resident foreigner see PARA 802. As to the meaning of 'probate practitioner' see PARA 688 note 5 and PARA 726 note 2.

4 See PARA 778. As to grants to the Treasury Solicitor see PARA 779. As to the Treasury Solicitor see the Non-Contentious Probate Rules 1987, SI 1987/2024, r 2(1); PARA 769 note 1; and CONSTITUTIONAL AND ADMINISTRATIVE LAW vol 20 (2014) PARA 281.

726. Applications for grants through solicitors or probate practitioners. Application for a grant[1] through a solicitor or probate practitioner[2] may be made at any registry[3] or sub-registry[4]. Every solicitor or probate practitioner through whom an application for a grant is made must give the address of his place of business within England and Wales[5].

1 As to the meaning of 'grant' see PARA 631 note 7.
2 As to the meaning of 'probate practitioner' see PARA 688 note 5.
3 As to the meaning of 'registry' see PARA 680 note 2.
4 See the Non-Contentious Probate Rules 1987, SI 1987/2024, r 4(1) (r 4 amended by SI 1998/1903).
5 Non-Contentious Probate Rules 1987, SI 1987/2024, r 4(2) (as amended: see note 4). As to the inclusion of a solicitor's office reference see PARA 728 note 5. The provision of 'probate activities' is a reserved legal activity for the purposes of the Legal Services Act 2007 see s 12; and LEGAL PROFESSIONS vol 65 (2015) PARA 352.

727. Personal applications. A personal applicant[1] may apply for a grant at any registry[2] or sub-registry[3]. A personal applicant may not apply through an agent, whether paid or unpaid and may not be attended by any person acting or appearing to act as his adviser[4]. No legal advice may be given to a personal applicant by an officer of a registry[5]. A personal applicant must:

(1) produce a certificate of the death of the deceased or such other evidence of the death as the district judge[6] or registrar[7] may approve[8]; and
(2) supply all information necessary to enable the papers leading to the grant to be prepared in the registry[9].

Unless the district judge or registrar otherwise directs, every oath[10] or affidavit required on a personal application must be sworn or executed before an authorised officer[11] by all the deponents[12]. After a will has been deposited in a registry by a personal applicant, it may not be delivered to the applicant or to any other person unless in special circumstances the district judge or registrar so directs[13].

No personal application is to be proceeded with if:

(a) it becomes necessary to bring the matter before the court by action or summons, unless a judge, district judge or registrar so permits[14];
(b) an application has already been made by a solicitor or probate practitioner on behalf of the applicant and has not been withdrawn[15]; or
(c) the district judge or registrar so directs[16].

1 'Personal applicant' means a person other than a trust corporation who seeks to obtain a grant without employing a solicitor or probate practitioner, and 'personal application' has a corresponding meaning: Non-Contentious Probate Rules 1987, SI 1987/2024, r 2(1) (definition amended by SI 1998/1903). As to the meaning of 'trust corporation' see PARA 622 note 4. As to the meaning of 'grant' see PARA 631 note 7. As to the meaning of 'probate practitioner' see PARA 688 note 5.
2 As to the meaning of 'registry' see PARA 680 note 2.
3 Non-Contentious Probate Rules 1987, SI 1987/2024, r 5(1).
4 Non-Contentious Probate Rules 1987, SI 1987/2024, r 5(2). There is an exception on an application for the resealing of a Commonwealth or colonial grant under r 39 (see PARA 841): see r 5(2).
5 Non-Contentious Probate Rules 1987, SI 1987/2024, r 5(8). Every such officer is responsible only for embodying in proper form the applicant's instructions for the grant: r 5(8).
6 As to the meaning of 'district judge' see PARA 631 note 6.
7 As to the meaning of 'registrar' see PARA 631 note 7.
8 Non-Contentious Probate Rules 1987, SI 1987/2024, r 5(5) (amended by SI 1991/1876).

9 Non-Contentious Probate Rules 1987, SI 1987/2024, r 5(6). Where it is necessary for the applicant to produce an original deed or other instrument, it is the practice of the registry to examine the instrument to ensure that it has been properly executed and duly stamped under the Stamp Act 1891: see *Practice Note* [1978] 1 All ER 1046, [1978] 1 WLR 430.

10 As to oaths see PARA 728.

11 'Authorised officer' means any officer of a registry who is for the time being authorised by the President to administer any oath or to take any affidavit required for any purpose connected with his duties: Non-Contentious Probate Rules 1987, SI 1987/2024, r 2(1).

12 Non-Contentious Probate Rules 1987, SI 1987/2024, r 5(7) (amended by SI 1991/1876).

13 Non-Contentious Probate Rules 1987, SI 1987/2024, r 5(4) (amended by SI 1991/1876).

14 Non-Contentious Probate Rules 1987, SI 1987/2024, r 5(3)(a) (amended by SI 1998/1903).

15 Non-Contentious Probate Rules 1987, SI 1987/2024, r 5(3)(b) (amended by SI 1998/1903).

16 Non-Contentious Probate Rules 1987, SI 1987/2024, r 5(3)(c) (amended by SI 1991/1876).

728. Executor's oath. Every application for a grant[1] must be supported by an oath[2] by the applicant in the form applicable to the circumstances of the case, and by such other papers as the district judge[3] or registrar[4] may require[5].

The executor's oath must state that the document of which probate is to be granted is the true and original last will of the deceased and must prove the marking of the will[6], the number of codicils, if any, the name and dates of birth and death[7], the age[8], and last address of the deceased. In the case of names and addresses which appear in the will, any discrepancy between those there given and the true ones must be set out in the oath[9]. The oath must also state whether or not, to the best of the applicant's knowledge, information and belief, there was land vested in the deceased which was settled previously to his death and not by his will and which remained settled notwithstanding his death[10]. Unless a district judge or registrar otherwise directs, the oath must state where the deceased died domiciled[11]. An oath supporting a grant of probate of a privileged will[12] must state the domicile of the deceased at the date of the will and the circumstances on which reliance is placed as constituting the privilege[13]. The oath concludes with a statement of the total value of the estate[14].

Where it is sought to describe the deceased in a grant by some name in addition to his true name, the applicant must depose to the true name of the deceased and specify some part of the estate which was held in the other name, or give any other reason for the inclusion of the other name in the grant[15].

A district judge or registrar may not allow any grant to issue until all inquiries which he may see fit to make have been answered to his satisfaction[16].

1 As to the meaning of 'grant' see PARA 631 note 7.

2 'Oath' means the oath required by the Non-Contentious Probate Rules 1987, SI 1987/2024, r 8 to be sworn by every applicant for a grant: r 2(1). There is an exception for an application for the resealing of a Commonwealth or colonial grant under r 39 (see PARA 841): see r 8(1) (as amended: see note 5). In certain circumstances the applicant may affirm instead of taking an oath: see CIVIL PROCEDURE vol 12 (2015) PARA 826. Every justice of the peace has the power to administer an oath or take an affidavit for the purposes of an application for a grant of probate or letters of administration made in any non-contentious or common form probate business; and must state in the jurat or attestation where and on what date the oath or affidavit is taken or made: see the Courts and Legal Services Act 1990 s 56(1), (2). As to the meaning of 'affidavit' see the Commissioners for Oaths Act 1889 s 11; and CIVIL PROCEDURE vol 12 (2015) PARA 829 (definition applied by the Courts and Legal Services Act 1990 s 56(5)). 'Letters of administration' includes all letters of administration of the effects of deceased persons, whether with or without a will annexed, and whether granted for general, special or limited purposes: s 56(5). As to the meaning of 'non-contentious or common form probate business' see the Senior Courts Act 1981 s 128; and PARA 678 note 5 (definition applied by the Courts and Legal Services Act 1990 s 56(5)). No justice may exercise the powers above in any proceedings in which he is interested: s 56(3). A document purporting to be signed by a justice administering an oath or taking an affidavit must be admitted in evidence without proof of the signature and without proof that he is a justice: s 56(4). As to the appropriate wording to describe the applicant's relationship to the deceased see *Practice Direction* [1988] 2 All ER 308, [1988] 1 WLR 610.

3 As to the meaning of 'district judge' see PARA 631 note 6.

4 As to the meaning of 'registrar' see PARA 631 note 7.
5 Non-Contentious Probate Rules 1987, SI 1987/2024, r 8(1) (amended by SI 1991/1876). As to applications by trust corporations see PARA 783. If a solicitor wishes his office reference to be stated at the foot of the grant following his name this reference should be given following his name at the head of the oath, eg 'Extracted by A B and Company (ref WB) [address]': see *Practice Direction* [1972] 1 All ER 1056, [1972] 1 WLR 401.
6 Every will in respect of which an application for a grant is made:
    (1) must be marked by the signatures of the applicant and the person before whom the oath is sworn (Non-Contentious Probate Rules 1987, SI 1987/2024, r 10(1)(a)); and
    (2) must be exhibited to any affidavit which may be required under the Non-Contentious Probate Rules 1987 as to the validity, terms, condition or date of execution of the will (r 10(1)(b)).

  However, the district judge or registrar may allow a facsimile copy of a will to be marked or exhibited in lieu of the original document: r 10(2) (amended by SI 1991/1876).
7 Ie the name and dates of birth and death as recorded in the Register of Deaths (where the death is so recorded), and any name by which the deceased was known which differed from that recorded in the Register: *Practice Direction* [1999] 1 All ER 832. This information should also be included in a notice lodged for a standing search or caveat: see PARAS 688, 690. As to registration of deaths see REGISTRATION CONCERNING THE INDIVIDUAL vol 88 (2012) PARA 277 et seq.
8 In those cases in which the exact age is not known, the applicant must give the best estimate he can: *Practice Direction* [1981] 2 All ER 832, [1981] 1 WLR 1185.
9 For the requirements where power is to be reserved to executors see PARA 729; and for the appropriate form of oath in such a case see *Practice Direction* [1988] 1 All ER 192, [1988] 1 WLR 195. As to the contents of the oath see generally Tristram and Coote's Probate Practice (31st Edn) 4.91 et seq.
10 Non-Contentious Probate Rules 1987, SI 1987/2024, r 8(3). As to settled land grants see PARA 821 et seq.
11 Non-Contentious Probate Rules 1987, SI 1987/2024, r 8(2) (amended by SI 1991/1876). Where a country has no uniform system of law, the statement of domicile should specify the state, province or other judicial division of the country: *Practice Direction* [1961] 1 All ER 465, [1961] 1 WLR 253. As to domicile generally see CONFLICT OF LAWS vol 19 (2011) PARA 336 et seq.
12 As to privileged wills see PARAS 79–81.
13 *Practice Direction* [1945] WN 120. The statement may be included in a supplementary affidavit: *Practice Direction*. As to special provisions in respect of nuncupative wills see PARA 730. As to nuncupative wills see PARA 81.
14 Where the grant does not extend to the whole estate, the amount stated will be the value of the property to be included in the grant: see *Practice Direction* [1981] 2 All ER 832, [1981] 1 WLR 1185.
15 Non-Contentious Probate Rules 1987, SI 1987/2024, r 9.
16 Non-Contentious Probate Rules 1987, SI 1987/2024, r 6(1) (amended by SI 1991/1876). For example, the district judge or registrar may require proof, in addition to the oath, of the identity of the testator or of the party applying for the grant. Such an affidavit is sometimes needed where the executor is wrongly or imperfectly described in the will: see PARA 738.

729. Power reserved to non-proving executors. Where on an application for probate, power to apply for a like grant is to be reserved to such other of the executors as have not renounced probate[1], notice of the application must be given to the executor or executors to whom power is to be reserved, and unless the district judge[2] or registrar[3] otherwise directs, the oath[4] must state that such notice has been given[5]. However, a district judge or registrar may dispense with the giving of notice if he is satisfied that the giving of such notice is impracticable or would result in unreasonable delay or expense[6]. Where power is to be reserved to executors who are partners[7] in a firm, notice need not be given to them if probate is applied for by another partner in the firm[8].

1 As to renunciation of the office of executor see PARA 630 et seq.
2 As to the meaning of 'district judge' see PARA 631 note 6.
3 As to the meaning of 'registrar' see PARA 631 note 7.
4 As to the meaning of 'oath' see PARA 728 note 2.
5 Non-Contentious Probate Rules 1987, SI 1987/2024, r 27(1) (substituted by SI 1991/1876), which is expressed to be subject to the Non-Contentious Probate Rules 1987, SI 1987/2024, r 27(1A),

(2), (3). Where power is to be reserved to partners of a firm, notice may be given to the partners by sending it to the firm at its principal or last known place of business: r 27(2). As to notices generally see PARA 704.

6 Non-Contentious Probate Rules 1987, SI 1987/2024, r 27(3) (amended by SI 1991/1876).

7 'Partner' means a profit-sharing member of a traditional or limited liability partnership and not a salaried partner or a person merely held out as (but not in fact) a partner: see *Re Rogers* [2006] EWHC 753 (Ch), [2006] 2 All ER 792, [2006] 1 WLR 1577.

8 Non-Contentious Probate Rules 1987, SI 1987/2024, r 27(1A) (added by SI 1991/1876, and amended by SI 1998/1903). See also *Practice Direction* [1990] 2 All ER 576, [1990] 1 WLR 1083, HL.

730. Applications for an order admitting to proof nuncupative wills and copies. An application for an order admitting to proof a nuncupative will[1] or a will contained in a copy, or reconstruction where the original will is not available[2], is made to a district judge[3] or registrar[4]. Where all parties interested are of full age and capacity and consent, ex parte applications for probate in common form of such wills are normally heard by the district judge or registrar[5]. When the estate is small, the court may dispense with the consent of the parties interested in the estate[6]. Where there are minority interests or consent is not forthcoming, or there is no clear evidence that the will was in existence at the time of the testator's death, or of its contents, the application may be directed to be made on summons[7], and, in the case of a will which has been lost or destroyed where there are minority interests or lack of consent, an action for proof in solemn form[8] may be required[9].

The application must be supported by an affidavit setting out the grounds of the application and by such evidence on affidavit as the applicant can adduce[10] as to:

(1) the will's existence after the testator's death, or where there is no such evidence, the facts on which the applicant relies to rebut the presumption that the will has been revoked by destruction[11];

(2) in respect of a nuncupative will, the contents of that will[12]; and

(3) in respect of a reconstruction of a will, the accuracy of that reconstruction[13].

The district judge or registrar may require additional evidence in the circumstances of a particular case as to due execution of the will or as to the accuracy of the copy will, and may direct that notice be given to persons who would be prejudiced by the application[14].

If, in the absence of the original will, there is a true copy or draft of the will in existence, limited probate[15] is granted of that copy or draft[16]; if the contents have to be proved by extrinsic evidence, probate is granted of a reconstruction of the contents of the will as nearly as possible in its original form[17]. Probate may also be granted of a press copy of a copy of the will[18]. Where the contents of a lost will are not completely proved, probate will be granted to the extent to which they are proved[19]. Probate will be decreed to issue of the copy, draft or the substance of the will until the original will or a more authentic copy of it is proved.

1 As to nuncupative wills see PARA 81. As to privileged wills see PARAS 79–81, 728.

2 Cf PARA 716.

3 As to the meaning of 'district judge' see PARA 631 note 6.

4 Non-Contentious Probate Rules 1987, SI 1987/2024, r 54(1) (amended by SI 1991/1876). As to the meaning of 'registrar' see PARA 631 note 7. In any case where a will is not available owing to its being retained in the custody of a foreign court or official, a duly authenticated copy may be admitted to proof without such an order: Non-Contentious Probate Rules 1987, SI 1987/2024, r 54(2). See also PARA 721.

5 See *Re Nuttall* [1955] 2 All ER 921n, [1955] 1 WLR 847 (decided under the Non-Contentious Probate Rules 1954, SI 1954/786 (repealed)). If the district judge or registrar considers that the matter is one which should be dealt with by the court, he has power so to direct under what is now the Non-Contentious Probate Rules 1987, SI 1987/2024, r 61(1) (see PARA 701): see *Re Nuttall*.

6 *Re Apted* [1899] P 272, qualifying *Re Pearson* [1896] P 289. See also *Re Brassington* [1902] P 1.
7 See the Non-Contentious Probate Rules 1987, SI 1987/2024, r 61(1); and PARA 701.
8 See PARA 860 et seq.
9 *Re Barber* (1866) LR 1 P & D 267; *Re Carter* (1908) 52 Sol Jo 600. The claim should allege that the will was never revoked or destroyed by the testator, nor by any person in his presence and by his direction, with the intention of revocation, and that it was valid and subsisting at the time of his death but cannot be found, and set out the substance of the contents: see *Sugden v Lord St Leonards* (1876) 1 PD 154 at 154–158, CA.
10 Non-Contentious Probate Rules 1987, SI 1987/2024, r 54(3).
11 Non-Contentious Probate Rules 1987, SI 1987/2024, r 54(3)(a).
12 Non-Contentious Probate Rules 1987, SI 1987/2024, r 54(3)(b).
13 Non-Contentious Probate Rules 1987, SI 1987/2024, r 54(3)(c).
14 Non-Contentious Probate Rules 1987, SI 1987/2024, r 54(4) (amended by SI 1991/1876).
15 As to grants limited in relation to time see PARA 750.
16 *Re Crofts* (1900) 17 TLR 16; *Re Crandon* (1901) 84 LT 330.
17 *Sugden v Lord St Leonards* (1876) 1 PD 154, CA.
18 *Lafone v Griffin* (1909) 25 TLR 308.
19 *Sugden v Lord St Leonards* (1876) 1 PD 154, CA.

731. Inheritance tax account. Except as otherwise provided[1], the personal representatives of the deceased must deliver to the Commissioners for Her Majesty's Revenue and Customs[2] a full account[3] specifying to the best of their knowledge and belief all appropriate property for the purpose of inheritance tax and the value of that property[4].

In general, no grant[5] may be made, and no grant made outside the United Kingdom[6] may be resealed[7], except on the production of an inheritance tax account[8] showing by means of such receipt or certification as may be prescribed by the Commissioners for Her Majesty's Revenue and Customs[9] either that the inheritance tax payable on the delivery of the account has been paid[10], or that no such tax is so payable[11].

1 Ie except as provided by the Inheritance Tax Act 1984 s 216 or by regulations under s 256: see s 216(1); and INHERITANCE TAXATION vol 59A (2014) PARA 275. Certain small estates ('excepted estates') are exempted from the requirement to deliver a full account: see the Inheritance Tax (Delivery of Accounts) (Excepted Estates) Regulations 2004, SI 2004/2543; and INHERITANCE TAXATION vol 59A (2014) PARA 275. In such cases form IHT 205 must be submitted. For an explanation of the requirements for an excepted estate for deaths before 6 April 2004 see Tristram and Coote's Probate Practice (31st Edn) 8.02 et seq. As to the statement to be included in the oath leading to a grant in respect of such an estate see *Practice Direction* [1981] 2 All ER 832, [1981] 1 WLR 1185.
2 As to the Commissioners for Her Majesty's Revenue and Customs see INCOME TAXATION vol 58 (2014) PARA 33.
3 Ie using IHT 400 or IHT 401.
4 See the Inheritance Tax Act 1984 s 216(1)(a); and INHERITANCE TAXATION vol 59A (2014) PARA 275. In general, where the account is to be delivered by personal representatives, the appropriate property is all property which formed part of the deceased's estate immediately before his death, but where the account is to be delivered by a person who is an executor of the deceased only in respect of settled land in England and Wales the appropriate property is any property to the value of which tax is or would be attributable: see s 216(3), (4); and INHERITANCE TAXATION vol 59A (2014) PARA 275. In certain circumstances a provisional estimate of the value of the property may be delivered; and the Commissioners may from time to time give general or special directions for restricting the property to be specified by any class of personal representatives: see s 216(3)(a), (b); and INHERITANCE TAXATION vol 59A (2014) PARA 275. An account must be delivered before the expiration of the period of 12 months from the end of the month in which the death occurs or, if it expires later, the period of three months beginning with the date on which the personal representatives first act as such: see s 216(6)(a); and INHERITANCE TAXATION vol 59A (2014) PARA 275. For the penalty for failure to deliver an account see s 245(2)(a); and INHERITANCE TAXATION vol 59A (2014) PARA 328.
5 As to the meaning of 'grant' see PARA 631 note 7.
6 As to the meaning of 'United Kingdom' see PARA 4 note 7.
7 As to the resealing of grants see PARA 835 et seq.
8 Ie prepared in pursuance of the Inheritance Tax Act 1984 s 256(1)(aa) (see INHERITANCE TAXATION vol 59A (2014) PARA 275): see the Senior Courts Act 1981 s 109(1).

9 Senior Courts Act 1981 s 109(1) (substituted by the Finance Act 2004 s 294(1)(a)). For the practice in paying inheritance tax according to whether or not a personal application is being made see Tristram and Coote's Probate Practice (31st Edn) 8.02. For personal applications see PARA 727. Corresponding provisions requiring the certification on a grant of the delivery of the Inland Revenue affidavit in the case of persons dying before 13 March 1975 is made by the Customs and Inland Revenue Act 1881 s 30; Finance Act 1894 s 8(17) (both repealed as to deaths on or after that date). See also the Non-Contentious Probate Rules 1987, SI 1987/2024, r 42, Sch 1 Form 1. As to the form of accounts generally see INHERITANCE TAXATION vol 59A (2014) PARA 282.

10 Senior Courts Act 1981 s 109(1)(a) (as substituted: see note 8). See note 7.

11 Senior Courts Act 1981 s 109(1)(b) (as substituted: see note 8). See note 7. Arrangements may be made between the President of the Family Division and the Commissioners of Her Majesty's Revenue and Customs providing for these purposes in such cases as may be specified in the arrangements that the receipt or certification of an account may be dispensed with or that some other document may be substituted for the account required by the Inheritance Tax Act 1984: Senior Courts Act 1981 s 109(2) (amended by the Inheritance Tax Act 1984 ss 274, 276, Sch 8 para 8; and the Finance Act 2004 s 294(1)(b)).

732. Documents and records kept by probate registry. Engrossment of the testamentary documents is not normally required on an application for a grant, though an engrossment must be lodged in certain cases[1]. After the inheritance tax account[2] has if necessary been submitted to and passed by HMRC Inheritance Tax, all the documents, including the original will and codicils, if any, are left at, or sent to, the probate registry or sub-registry, and the form of grant is then filed up at the registry and the record completed[3].

All original wills and other documents which are under the control of the High Court in the principal registry of the Family Division or any district probate registry must be deposited and preserved in such places as may be provided for[4], and such documents are open to inspection, subject to the control of the High Court and to probate rules[5]. An original will or other document will not be open to inspection if, in the opinion of a district judge or registrar, such inspection would be undesirable or otherwise inappropriate[6]. Copies of original wills and certificates of grants of administration may be obtained from probate registries[7].

1 An engrossment suitable for facsimile reproduction may be required where the district judge or registrar considers that a facsimile copy of the original will would not be satisfactory in any particular case for purposes of record: Non-Contentious Probate Rules 1987, SI 1987/2024, r 11(1) (amended by SI 1991/1876). Where a will contains alterations which are not to be admitted to proof, or has been ordered to be rectified by virtue of the Administration of Justice Act 1982 s 20(1) (see PARA 187), an engrossment of the will in the form in which it is to be proved must be lodged: Non-Contentious Probate Rules 1987, SI 1987/2024, r 11(2). Any engrossment lodged must reproduce the punctuation, spacing and division into paragraphs of the will and follow continuously from page to page on both sides of the paper: r 11(3). As an alternative to typewritten engrossments, facsimile copies produced by photography may be used in certain circumstances: see *Practice Direction* [1979] 3 All ER 859. A notice issued by Her Majesty's Courts Service requires that with effect from 1 January 2009 every application for a grant must be supported by two A4 copies of the sworn will and codicils (if applicable); see PARA 728 note 6 for sworn wills and see also Tristram and Coote's Probate Practice (31st Edn) 4.232.

2 An account in respect of inheritance tax must be delivered: see PARA 731. Subject to any arrangements which may from time to time be made between the President of the Family Division and the Commissioners of Her Majesty's Revenue and Customs, the Principal Registry and every district probate registry must, within such period after a grant as the President may direct, deliver to the Commissioners or their proper officer the following documents:

(1) in the case of a grant of probate or of administration with the will annexed, a copy of the will (Senior Courts Act 1981 s 110(a)); and

(2) in every case, such certificate or note of the grant as the Commissioners may require (s 110(b)).

3 Records must be kept of all grants of probate and administration, which are made at the principal registry of the Family Division or in any district probate registry: Senior Courts Act 1981 s 111(1). The records must be in such form and contain such particulars as the President of the Family Division may direct: s 111(2). As from 9 November 1998, records of all such grants of representation must be maintained in the form of a computer record. Annual calendar books will

continue to be prepared and will incorporate the information held on computer. The information must, by virtue of *Practice Direction* [1999] 1 All ER 384, [1998] 1 WLR 1699 revised by *Practice Direction* [2002] 2 All ER 640, comprise:

(1) the full name of the deceased and any alias names;
(2) the last address of the deceased including the postcode if known;
(3) the date of death and domicile of the deceased;
(4) the name(s) and address(es) of the executor(s) or administrator(s);
(5) the type of grant;
(6) the gross and net values of the estate or in the case of an excepted estate the net value of the estate must be stated, rounded up to the next whole thousand, and expressed as 'not exceeding £ . . .';
(7) the name and address of the extracting solicitor (if any) or the fact that the grant was obtained by way of personal application; and
(8) the date of the grant and the issuing registry.

4 Ie provided for in directions given in accordance with the Constitutional Reform Act 2005 Sch 2 Pt 1 (see CIVIL PROCEDURE vol 11 (2015) PARA 9): Senior Courts Act 1981 s 124 (as amended: see note 5).

5 Senior Court Acts 1981 s 124 (amended by the Constitutional Reform Act 2005 Sch 2, Pt 2, para 5). See note 1. The court cannot sanction the taking out of the jurisdiction of an original will admitted to probate: *Re Greer* (1929) 45 TLR 362; cf *Re Guinee* (1929) 73 Sol Jo 569 (Irish Free State's requirement for original will).

6 Non-Contentious Probate Rules 1987, SI 1987/2024, r 58 (amended by SI 1991/1876). As to the meaning of 'district judge' see PARA 631 note 6; and as to the meaning of 'registrar' see PARA 631 note 7. The fee for inspection of a will or other document retained by the registry (in the presence of an officer of the registry) is £20: Non-Contentious Probate Fees Order 2004, SI 2004/3120, art 2, Sch 1 Fee 7 (Sch 1 substituted by SI 2011/588). See *Brown v Executors of the Estate of Her Majesty Queen Elizabeth the Queen Mother* [2008] EWCA Civ 56, [2008] 1 WLR 2327, [2008] All ER (D) 118 (Feb) (public inspection of royal will).

7 An office copy, or a sealed and certified copy, of any will or part of a will open to inspection under the Senior Courts Act 1981 s 124 (see the text to note 5) or of any grant may, on payment of the prescribed fee by an order under the Courts Act 2003 s 92 (see COURTS AND TRIBUNALS vol 24 (2010) PARA 762), be obtained:

(1) from the registry in which in accordance with s 124 the will or documents relating to the grant are preserved (Senior Courts Act 1981 s 125(a) (s 125 amended by the Courts Act 2003 Sch 8 para 262(a));
(2) where in accordance with that provision the will or such documents are preserved in some place other than a registry, from the principal registry of the Family Division (s 125(b) (as so amended)); or
(3) subject to the approval of the Senior Registrar of the Family Division, from the principal registry in any case where the will was proved in or the grant was issued from a district probate registry (s 125(c) (as so amended)).

Where copies are required of original wills or other documents deposited under the Senior Courts Act 1981 s 124, such copies may be facsimile copies sealed with the seal of the court and issued either as office copies or certified under the hand of a district judge or registrar to be true copies: Non-Contentious Probate Rules 1987, SI 1987/2024, r 59 (amended by SI 1991/1876). As to postal and personal applications for copies of wills or grants see *Practice Direction* [1990] 3 All ER 734, [1990] 1 WLR 1510. For fees for copies of documents and for handling postal applications see the Non-Contentious Probate Fees Order 2004, SI 2004/3120, art 2, Sch 1 Fee 8 (Sch 1 as amended (see note 6); Sch 1 Fee 8 amended by SI 2014/876).

733. Proof of due execution. Where the will is perfect on the face of it and there is an attestation clause showing that the statutory requirements[1] have been complied with, probate in common form issues on the oath of the executor alone.

If, however, the will contains no attestation clause, or if the attestation clause is insufficient, or it appears to the district judge[2] or registrar[3] that there is doubt about the due execution of the will, before admitting the will to proof, he must require an affidavit as to due execution from one or more of the attesting witnesses or, if no attesting witness is conveniently available, from any other person who was present when the will was executed[4]. If the district judge or registrar, after considering the evidence, is satisfied that the will was not duly executed, he must refuse probate and mark the will accordingly[5]. If no such affidavit can be obtained, the district judge or registrar may accept affidavit evidence from any person he may think fit to show that the signature on the will is in the deceased's handwriting, or of any other matter which may raise a presumption in favour of the due execution of the will[6]. He may also if he thinks fit require that notice of the application be given to any person who may be prejudiced by the will[7].

Even though there may be no evidence of due execution, a district judge or registrar may accept a will for proof if he is satisfied that the distribution of the estate is not affected[8].

1 As to the statutory requirements see PARA 707 note 4.
2 As to the meaning of 'district judge' see PARA 631 note 6.
3 As to the meaning of 'registrar' see PARA 631 note 7.
4 Non-Contentious Probate Rules 1987, SI 1987/2024, r 12(1) (r 12 amended by SI 1991/1876). The Non-Contentious Probate Rules 1987, SI 1987/2024, rr 12–15 do not apply to any will which it is sought to establish otherwise than by reference to the Wills Act 1837 s 9 (see PARA 60 et seq): Non-Contentious Probate Rules 1987, SI 1987/2024, r 17(1). Such a will may be established on the district judge or registrar being satisfied as to its terms and validity, and includes (without prejudice to the generality of the foregoing):
   (1) any will to which r 18 applies (see PARA 710) (r 17(2)(a) (r 17(2) amended by SI 1991/1876)); and
   (2) any will which, by virtue of the Wills Act 1963, is to be treated as properly executed if executed according to the internal law of the territory or state referred to in s 1 (see PARA 12) (Non-Contentious Probate Rules 1987, SI 1987/2024, r 17(2)(b) (as so amended)).
5 Non-Contentious Probate Rules 1987, SI 1987/2024, r 12(1) (as amended: see note 4).
6 Non-Contentious Probate Rules 1987, SI 1987/2024, r 12(2) (as amended: see note 4). As to the presumption of due execution see PARA 895.
7 Non-Contentious Probate Rules 1987, SI 1987/2024, r 12(2) (as amended: see note 4).
8 Non-Contentious Probate Rules 1987, SI 1987/2024, r 12(3) (as amended: see note 4). As to the presumption of due execution see PARA 895.

734. Proof of wills of blind or illiterate testators. Before admitting to proof a will which appears to have been signed by a blind or illiterate testator or by another person by direction of the testator, or which for any other reason raises doubt as to the testator having had knowledge of the contents of the will at the time of its execution, the district judge[1] or registrar[2] must satisfy himself[3] that the testator had such knowledge[4].

1 As to the meaning of 'district judge' see PARA 631 note 6.
2 As to the meaning of 'registrar' see PARA 631 note 7.
3 A district judge or registrar may require an affidavit from any person he thinks fit for the purpose of satisfying himself as to this matter or to any of the matters referred to in the Non-Contentious Probate Rules 1987, SI 1987/2024, rr 14, 15 (see PARAS 735–737), and in any such affidavit sworn by an attesting witness or other person present at the time of the execution of a will the deponent must depose to the manner in which the will was executed: r 16 (amended by SI 1991/1876).
4 Non-Contentious Probate Rules 1987, SI 1987/2024, r 13 (amended by SI 1991/1876). See also *Edwards v Fincham* (1842) 4 Moo PCC 198.

735. Proof of wills containing obliterations, interlineations and alterations. Where there appears in a will any obliteration, interlineation or other alteration which is not authenticated in the manner prescribed by statute[1], or by the re-execution of the will or by the execution of a codicil, the district judge[2] or registrar[3] must require evidence[4] to show whether the alteration was present at the time the will was executed and must give directions as to the form in which the will is to be proved[5], except where the alteration appears to the district judge or registrar to be of no practical importance[6]. Where necessary the court will allow the use of artificial means to decipher original words or figures[7], but will not resort to physical interference with the document; a magnifying glass may be used, but not chemicals[8]. Writing is not apparent for the purpose of the statutory provisions[9] if it can be read only on the creation of a new document, as for example a photograph taken by infra-red rays[10].

1 See the Wills Act 1837 s 21; and PARA 82.
2 As to the meaning of 'district judge' see PARA 631 note 6.
3 As to the meaning of 'registrar' see PARA 631 note 7.
4 See the Non-Contentious Probate Rules 1987, SI 1987/2024, r 16; and PARA 734 note 3.
5 Non-Contentious Probate Rules 1987, SI 1987/2024, r 14(1) (r 14(1), (2) amended by SI 1991/1876). See, however, the Non-Contentious Probate Rules 1987, SI 1987/2024, r 17; and PARA 733 note 4.
6 Non-Contentious Probate Rules 1987, SI 1987/2024, r 14(2) (as amended: see note 5).
7 *Re Itter, Dedman v Godfrey* [1948] 2 All ER 1052.
8 *Ffinch v Combe* [1894] P 191 at 201 per Sir F Jeune P; *Townley v Watson* (1844) 3 Curt 761. In *Re Gilbert* [1893] P 183, words had been written on the back of the codicil and a piece of blank paper had been pasted over them. The court ordered the blank paper to be removed.
9 Ie for the purposes of the Wills Act 1837 s 21: see PARA 82.
10 *Re Itter, Dedman v Godfrey* [1950] P 130, [1950] 1 All ER 68.

736. Proof of wills with document attached to or incorporated in will. If a will contains any reference to another document in such terms as to suggest that it ought to be incorporated[1] in the will, the district judge[2] or registrar[3] must require the document to be produced and may call for such evidence[4] in regard to the incorporation of the document as he thinks fit[5]. However, when application is made to admit to proof a will which incorporates standard forms or clauses as contained in a published document, production of that document will not be required in any individual case, unless otherwise directed, if the published document containing the standard forms or clauses (together with as many copies as may be required) has been previously lodged with the senior district judge and accepted by him as sufficient lodgment[6].

1 As to incorporation of documents see PARA 711.
2 As to the meaning of 'district judge' see PARA 631 note 6.
3 As to the meaning of 'registrar' see PARA 631 note 7.
4 See the Non-Contentious Probate Rules 1987, SI 1987/2024, r 16; and PARA 734 note 3.
5 Non-Contentious Probate Rules 1987, SI 1987/2024, r 14(3) (amended by SI 1991/1876). See, however, the Non-Contentious Probate Rules 1987, SI 1987/2024, r 17; and PARA 733 note 4. As to the probate registries' practice of examining instruments to ensure that they have been properly and duly stamped under the Stamp Act 1891 see *Practice Direction* [1978] 1 All ER 1046, [1978] 1 WLR 430 (as extended by Secretary's Circular, 10 September 1987).
6 *Practice Direction* [1995] 1 FLR 766.

737. Evidence required where doubt exists as to date or revocation of will. Where there is doubt as to the date on which a will was executed, the district judge[1] or registrar[2] may require such evidence[3] as he thinks necessary to establish the date[4].

Any appearance of attempted revocation of a will by burning, tearing or otherwise destroying and every other circumstance leading to a presumption of revocation by the testator[5] must be accounted for[6] to the district judge's or registrar's satisfaction[7].

1 As to the meaning of 'district judge' see PARA 631 note 6.
2 As to the meaning of 'registrar' see PARA 631 note 7.
3 See the Non-Contentious Probate Rules 1987, SI 1987/2024, r 16; and PARA 734 note 3.
4 Non-Contentious Probate Rules 1987, SI 1987/2024, r 14(4) (amended by SI 1991/1876). See, however, the Non-Contentious Probate Rules 1987, SI 1987/2024, r 17; and PARA 733 note 4.
5 As to revocation see the Wills Act 1837 s 20; and PARA 93.
6 See the Non-Contentious Probate Rules 1987, SI 1987/2024, r 16; and PARA 734 note 3.
7 Non-Contentious Probate Rules 1987, SI 1987/2024, r 15 (amended by SI 1991/1876). See, however, the Non-Contentious Probate Rules 1987, SI 1987/2024, r 17; and PARA 733 note 4.

738. Misdescription of executor. Where the will contains a misdescription or an insufficient description of the person nominated as executor, the grant issues to the person who, according to the evidence, was actually intended by his correct description, with the addition of the description written in the will[1].

1 *Re De Rosaz* (1877) 2 PD 66; *Re Cooper* [1899] P 193; *Re Baskett* (1898) 78 LT 843. See also PARA 728 note 16. The district judge or registrar may, in cases where he considers it necessary, require proof, in addition to an assertion in the executor's oath, of the identity of the party applying for the grant (Non-Contentious Probate Rules 1987, SI 1987/2024, r 6(1) (amended by SI 1991/1876)). This proof may take the form of an additional statement in the oath, or a separate 'affidavit of identity', which must refer to the facts as they were at the date of the will, and must dispose of the possibility of there being another person more nearly approaching the description given in the will. As to executor's oath see PARA 728; and for the practice as regards the description of the executor in the oath and affidavits of identity, see Tristram and Coote's Probate Practice (31st Edn) 4.94 et seq.

739. Exclusion of words from probate. Apart from the court's jurisdiction to rectify the will of a testator who dies after 1983[1], the court has a strictly limited jurisdiction[2] to omit from probate something contained in the will as a result of fraud or inadvertence which is proved not to be part of the testator's will[3]. The jurisdiction, where it exists, is confined to the exclusion of words[4] and does not extend to the insertion of words, since this would run counter to the provisions of the Wills Act 1837[5], nor does it extend to the exclusion of words where the exclusion will alter the sense of what remains, for this would be equivalent to making a new will for the testator[6]. Exclusions have been allowed to remove clerical errors[7] and words inserted as a result of a testator's own mistake[8] or the mistake of his advisers[9]. The court also has power to omit from the probate the signature of a third person at the foot of a will which already bears the signatures of two attesting witnesses, on being satisfied that the third signature was not added with the object of attesting the will[10]. Offensive, scandalous, libellous, blasphemous or undesirable passages having no testamentary relevance[11] may also be omitted from the probate and from any copy of the will subsequently ordered[12], but this is a power to be exercised with great moderation[13], for a testator has the right to explain why he has disposed of his property in a certain way although he has no right to libel anybody in his will by using words which have no direct bearing on the devolution of his property[14]. The court has refused to expunge or strike out the offending words from the original will[15].

1 Ie under the Administration of Justice Act 1982 s 20: see PARAS 741, 186.
2 *Re Horrocks, Taylor v Kershaw* [1939] P 198 at 216, [1939] 1 All ER 579 at 584, CA.
3 *Rhodes v Rhodes* (1882) 7 App Cas 192 at 198, PC. As to the effect of approval by the testator of matter which it is sought to exclude see PARA 906. As to the effect of incapacity (eg delusions), undue influence or fraud as to part only of a will see PARA 892.
4 *Re Schott* [1901] P 190 (overruling *Re Bushell* (1887) 13 PD 7 on this point); *Jane v Jane* (1917) 33 TLR 389 (omission of words in codicil referring by mistake to wrong will); *Re Clark* (1932) 101 LJP 27 (exclusion of misdescription of legatee).
5 *Re Horrocks, Taylor v Kershaw* [1939] P 198 at 216, [1939] 1 All ER 579 at 584, CA.
6 *Re Horrocks, Taylor v Kershaw* [1939] P 198 at 218–219, [1939] 1 All ER 579 at 586, CA.
7 *Re Bushell* (1887) 13 PD 7; *Re Huddleston* (1890) 63 LT 255; *Re Boehm* [1891] P 247.
8 *Re Swords* [1952] P 368, [1952] 2 All ER 281; *Re Phelan* [1972] Fam 33, [1971] 3 All ER 1256.
9 *Re Oswald* (1874) LR 3 P & D 162; *Morrell v Morrell* (1882) 7 PD 68; *Re Moore* [1892] P 378; *Re Boehm* [1891] P 247; *Re Reade* [1902] P 75; *Re Morris* [1971] P 62, [1970] 1 All ER 1057.
10 *Re Sharman* (1869) LR 1 P & D 661; *Re Smith* (1889) 15 PD 2; *Kitcat v King* [1930] P 266 (where two beneficiaries' signatures under the attestation clause were omitted from the probate). As to the effect of superfluous signatures on the avoidance of gifts to attesting witnesses see the Wills Act 1968 s 1; and PARA 44.
11 *Re T* (1961) 105 Sol Jo 325 (testator entitled to give his reasons so long as he does not go too far; part of passage expunged).
12 *Re Wartnaby* (1846) 1 Rob Eccl 423; *Marsh v Marsh* (1860) 1 Sw & Tr 528; *Re White* [1914] P 153; *Re Heywood* [1916] P 47 (part of a soldier's will omitted from probate on representations of

military authorities); *Re Caie* (1927) 43 TLR 697 (views on religious subjects cannot be suppressed because they are disliked); *Re Maxwell* (1929) 140 LT 471; *Re Bowker* [1932] P 93 (words relating to disposal of body).

13 *Re Honywood* (1871) LR 2 P & D 251.

14 *Re Hall* [1943] 2 All ER 159.

15 *Curtis v Curtis* (1825) 3 Add 33; *Re White* [1914] P 153; *Re Maxwell* (1929) 140 LT 471; *Re C* (1960) Times, 28 July ('After five years my wife has shown no sign or wish of returning to me and I must presume her legal desertion': application to expunge refused because, although potentially defamatory, the words gave the version of a testator unable to speak for himself and could be relevant in family provision proceedings).

740. Practice on application for exclusion. A contested application for omission of words from probate[1] must, after the issue of a claim form, be made or referred to the Chancery Division[2]. Other applications are to be made without notice to the district judge or registrar of the registry at which it is proposed to make application for the grant and must be supported by affidavit evidence, exhibiting the will or codicil in question, together with any written consents of persons not under disability who might be prejudiced[3]. A copy of any order made on the application should be lodged with the application for the grant, and will be annexed to the original will[4].

1 See PARA 739.

2 See PARA 678.

3 *Practice Direction* [1968] 2 All ER 592, [1968] 1 WLR 987. If the district judge or registrar is satisfied on the facts and, in the absence of consent, that there is no substantial interest unprotected, he will make the order: see *Practice Direction*. A district judge or registrar may require the application to be made by summons to a district judge or registrar in chambers or a judge in chambers or open court: see PARA 701.

4 *Practice Direction* [1968] 2 All ER 592, [1968] 1 WLR 987. A typewritten copy of the will omitting the words in question should also be lodged for the fiat to be written in the margin before photography: *Practice Direction*; and see PARA 732.

741. Rectification. If a court is satisfied that the will[1] of a testator who dies on or after 1 January 1983[2] is so expressed that it fails to carry out the testator's intentions, in consequence of a clerical error or a failure to understand his instructions, it may order that the will be rectified so as to carry out his intentions[3]. Unless a probate action has been commenced, an application for rectification may be made to a district judge or registrar[4]. The application must be supported by an affidavit, setting out the grounds of the application, together with such evidence as can be adduced as to the testator's intentions, and as to whichever of the following matters are in issue, namely in what respects the testator's intentions were not understood, or the nature of the alleged clerical error[5]. Unless otherwise directed, notice of the application must be given to every person having an interest under the will whose interest might be prejudiced, or such other person who might be prejudiced, by the rectification applied for, and any comments in writing by any such person must be exhibited to the affidavit in support of the application[6]. If the district judge or registrar is satisfied that, subject to any direction to the contrary, notice has been given to every person interested, and that the application is unopposed, he may order that the will be rectified accordingly[7]. Where a will has been ordered to be rectified[8], there must be lodged an engrossment of the will in the form in which it is to be proved[9].

The personal representatives of a deceased person are not liable for having distributed any part of the estate of the deceased, after the end of the period of six months from the date on which representation to the estate of the deceased is first taken out, on the ground that they ought to have taken into account the possibility that the court might permit the making of an application for an order for rectification after the end of that period[10]. This exemption does not, however, prejudice any power to recover, by reason of the making of an order for rectification, any part of the estate so distributed[11].

1 The reference to a will in the Administration of Justice Act 1982 s 20 means any document which is on its face bona fide intended to be a will; it is not limited to a will which complies with the formalities set out in the Wills Act 1837 s 9 (see PARA 60 et seq): *Marley v Rawlings* [2014] UKSC 2, [2015] AC 129, [2014] 1 All ER 807. As to *Marley v Rawlings* and the modern approach to the construction of wills see PARA 188.

2 Ie the date on which the Administration of Justice Act 1982 s 20 came into force: see s 76(11); and PARAS 187, 732.

3 Administration of Justice Act 1982 s 20(1). An application for an order under this provision cannot, except with the permission of the court, be made after the end of the period of six months from the date on which representation with respect to the estate of the deceased was first taken out: see s 20(2). In considering whether to give permission to apply out of time, the court will have regard to the guidelines for similar applications under the Inheritance (Provision for Family and Dependants) Act 1975: see PARA 414; and *Chittock v Stevens* [2000] WTLR 643. See also PARA 187.

4 Non-Contentious Probate Rules 1987, SI 1987/2024, r 55(1) (amended by SI 1991/1876). As to the meaning of 'district judge' see PARA 631 note 6; and as to the meaning of 'registrar' see PARA 631 note 7. Such an application may not be made if a probate action has been commenced: see the Non-Contentious Probate Rules 1987, SI 1987/2024, r 55(1) (as so amended). It is not until a claim form has been issued that there is litigation between the parties: see *Moran v Place* [1896] P 214, CA; *Salter v Salter* [1896] P 291, CA. It has been agreed between the Senior District Judge and the Chief Chancery Master (Secretary's Circular, 24 June 1985) that unopposed applications for rectification of wills may be made to a district judge of the Principal Registry or a registrar of a district probate registry under the authority of the Non-Contentious Probate Rules 1987, SI 1987/2024, r 55, either before or after the issue of the grant. Where rectification is ordered under r 55 after the date of the grant, a memorandum of the order will be annexed to the probate and record copies of the will. Where a question of construction also arises, even if unopposed, the application for rectification should be made to the Chancery Division. As to the procedure in the Chancery Division see PARA 889.

5 Non-Contentious Probate Rules 1987, SI 1987/2024, r 55(2).

6 Non-Contentious Probate Rules 1987, SI 1987/2024, r 55(3) (amended by SI 1998/1903).

7 Non-Contentious Probate Rules 1987, SI 1987/2024, r 55(4) (amended by SI 1991/1876). See also note 3.

8 Ie by virtue of the Administration of Justice Act 1982 s 20(1).

9 Non-Contentious Probate Rules 1987, SI 1987/2024, r 11(2)(b). Any engrossment lodged under this rule shall reproduce the punctuation, spacing and division into paragraphs of the will and shall follow continuously from page to page on both sides of the paper: r 11(3).

10 Administration of Justice Act 1982 s 20(3).

11 Administration of Justice Act 1982 s 20(3). As to such recovery see PARA225 et seq.

742. Time for issuing grant of probate or letters of administration with will annexed. No grant of probate or letters of administration with the will annexed may issue within seven days of the death of the deceased, except with the leave of a district judge or registrar[1]. A district judge or registrar must not allow any grant to issue until all inquiries which he may see fit to make have been answered to his satisfaction[2]. No grant may be made by a registrar in any case in which there is contention, until the contention is disposed of[3], or in any case in which it appears to him that a grant ought not to be made without the directions of a judge or district judge[4], in which case the registrar must send a statement of the matter in question to the principal registry of the Family Division for directions[5]. A district judge may either confirm that the matter be referred to a judge and give directions accordingly or may direct the registrar to proceed with the matter in accordance with such instructions as are deemed necessary, which may include a direction to take no further action in relation to the matter[6].

1 Non-Contentious Probate Rules 1987, SI 1987/2024, r 6(2) (r 6 amended by SI 1991/1876). As to the meaning of 'district judge' see PARA 631 note 6; and as to the meaning of 'registrar' see PARA 631 note 7. As to ordinary grants of administration see PARA 764.

2 Non-Contentious Probate Rules 1987, SI 1987/2024, r 6(1) (as amended: see note 1).

3 Non-Contentious Probate Rules 1987, SI 1987/2024, r 7(1)(a) (r 7 amended by SI 1991/1876).

4 Non-Contentious Probate Rules 1987, SI 1987/2024, r 7(1)(b) (as amended: see note 3). See also *Ghafoor v Cliff* [2006] EWHC 825 (Ch), [2006] 2 All ER 1079, [2006] 1 WLR 3020.
5 Non-Contentious Probate Rules 1987, SI 1987/2024, r 7(2) (as amended: see note 3).
6 Non-Contentious Probate Rules 1987, SI 1987/2024, r 7(3) (as amended: see note 3).

743. Proof of death. The executor's oath specifies the fact and date of the testator's death[1]. A certificate of death or of presumed death issued by the Registrar General from the register kept of births and deaths in civil aircraft[2] may be accepted as sufficient evidence of death on application for a grant of representation[3]. Certain other special certificates of death or presumed death issued by government departments, including the Registrar General of Shipping and Seamen and the service authorities, may be accepted as evidence of death[4].

Where the applicant for a grant is unable to depose to the precise date of death, but the fact of death is certain, the district judge or registrar may make the grant if the applicant swears that the deceased died on the earliest or the latest possible date when death could have occurred, or on some day between the two[5].

1 See *Practice Direction* [1999] 1 All ER 832. See also PARA 728.
2 See AIR LAW vol 2 (2008) PARAS 586–587. As to registration of deaths see REGISTRATION CONCERNING THE INDIVIDUAL vol 88 (2012) PARA 277 et seq.
3 *Practice Note* (1953) 103 L Jo 299.
4 See Tristram and Coote's Probate Practice (31st Edn) 4.158–4.173. See also SHIPPING AND MARITIME LAW vol 94 (2008) PARAS 654–655.
5 *Re Long-Sutton* [1912] P 97 (testator found drowned; no order for leave to swear death necessary).

744. Leave to swear to death. On an application for a grant of probate or administration where there is no direct evidence of death, for example where a person has disappeared and his body has not been found, an application must also be made for leave to swear to the death[1].

An application for leave to swear to the death of a person in whose estate a grant[2] is sought may be made to a district judge or registrar[3]. The application must be supported by an affidavit setting out the grounds of the application and containing particulars of any insurance policies effected on the life of the presumed deceased together with such further evidence as the district judge or registrar may require[4]. The affidavit should generally state:

(1) when and in what circumstances the person who has disappeared was last seen or heard of;
(2) whether any advertisements have been inserted for the purpose of ascertaining his whereabouts, and if so, in what newspapers[5] and with what result;
(3) the applicant's belief that the alleged deceased is dead[6];
(4) whether any letters have been received from him[7];
(5) whether he left any will[8] or died intestate;
(6) those who are entitled on intestacy;
(7) if there is real estate and the death may have occurred before 1926, who is the heir at law[9]; and
(8) particulars of the estate.

The district judge or registrar[10] must be satisfied that all reasonable inquiries have been made[11].

1 The probate court does not find as a fact the death of the deceased; it merely gives the applicant leave to swear to death: see *Re Jackson* (1902) 87 LT 747. The leave and a grant of administration under the court's discretionary power (see PARA 758) may be given simultaneously on the same application if the circumstances so warrant: *Re Lever* (1935) 105 LJP 9. As to the presumption of death see PARA 745.
2 As to the meaning of 'grant' see PARA 631 note 7.

3 Non-Contentious Probate Rules 1987, SI 1987/2024, r 53 (amended by SI 1991/1876). As to the meaning of 'district judge' see PARA 631 note 6; and as to the meaning of 'registrar' see PARA 631 note 7.
4 Non-Contentious Probate Rules 1987, SI 1987/2024, r 53 (as amended: see note 3). See also *Re Saul* [1896] P 151; *Re Barber* (1886) 11 PD 78.
5 Copies of the newspapers should be filed.
6 *Re Hurlston* [1898] P 27; *Re Walker* [1909] P 115.
7 *Re Clarke* [1896] P 287. Any letters received should be filed.
8 Any will should be filed.
9 There may be cases where the heir is interested in the estate even though the death occurs after 1925, for example where a person who was not of testamentary capacity on 1 January 1926 dies intestate without having recovered such capacity. In these cases the name of the heir must be disclosed. As to such cases see PARAS 478, 531 et seq.
10 Cf the Non-Contentious Probate Rules 1987, SI 1987/2024, r 6(1): see PARA 742.
11 *Re Robertson* [1896] P 8, where the court insisted on advertisements although nothing had been heard of the vanished person for 25 years. For a form of affidavit exhibiting a certificate of the Registrar General of Shipping and Seamen in the case of supposed death through the loss of a ship see *Re Dodd* (1897) 77 LT 137 (cf PARA 743 text and note 4).

745. Presumption of death. Until October 2014[1] it was not possible to obtain a decree of presumption of death for all purposes.

If there is no acceptable affirmative evidence that a person was alive at some time during a continuous period of seven years or more, and it can be proved that there are persons who would be likely to have heard of him over that period[2], that those persons have not heard of him, and that all due inquiries have been made appropriate to the circumstances, without result, then the presumption of law is that the person died within the period[3]. Subject to this presumption, the issue whether a person is to be presumed dead is a question of fact[4]. On proof of sufficient inquiries, the court will, however, allow the death of a testator to be sworn after a disappearance of less than seven years[5].

As from October 2014, where a person who is missing is thought to have died or has not been known to be alive for a period of at least seven years, any person[6] may apply to the High Court[7] for a declaration that the missing person is presumed to be dead[8]. Once made, such a declaration is effective against all persons for all purposes[9].

If the courts of a foreign country where the presumed deceased was domiciled have made orders presuming his death and vesting his estate in the persons entitled, his death will be presumed without further evidence, but if there is only an order by the foreign court presuming the death but not vesting the estate, the Family Division requires further evidence to show that he is in fact dead[10].

1 Ie the date on which the Presumption of Death Act 2013 came into force: see the Presumption of Death Act 2013 (Commencement and Transitional and Saving Provision) Order 2014, SI 2014/1810, art 2.
2 See *Re Liebeskind* [1952] CLY 1349 (applicant could not expect to hear from relative if relative behind the Iron Curtain).
3 See *Chard v Chard (otherwise Northcott)* [1956] P 259 at 272, [1955] 3 All ER 721 at 728 per Sachs J. See also CIVIL PROCEDURE vol 12 (2015) PARA 759. There is no presumption that the person died at any particular date during the seven years, or that he died without issue: see CIVIL PROCEDURE vol 12 (2015) PARAS 759–761.
4 See *Chard v Chard (otherwise, Northcott)* [1956] P 259, [1955] 3 All ER 721. See also CIVIL PROCEDURE vol 12 (2015) PARAS 759–761. As to a court order as evidence of death see *Re Rishton* (1921) 90 LJP 374 (see PARA 761 note 2).
5 *Re Matthews* [1898] P 17. See also *Re Winstone* [1898] P 143; *Re Long-Sutton* [1912] P 97; *Greig v Merchant Co of Edinburgh* 1921 SC 76, Ct of Sess.
6 The court may refuse to hear an application under the Presumption of Death Act 2013 s 1 (see text and note 7) if the application is made by someone other than the missing person's spouse, civil partner, parent, child or sibling and the court considers that the applicant does not have a sufficient interest in the determination of the application: s 1(5).

7 Proceedings under the Presumption of Death Act 2013 must be issued in the High Court in either the Chancery Division, or the Family Division: see CPR 57.18(1); and CIVIL PROCEDURE vol 11 (2015) PARA 162 et seq.

8 See the Presumption of Death Act 2013 s 1(1), (2). The High Court has jurisdiction to hear and determine such an application for a declaration of presumed death only if:

(1) the missing person was domiciled in England and Wales on the day on which he or she was last known to be alive (s 1(3)(a));

(2) the missing person had been habitually resident in England and Wales throughout the period of one year ending with that day (s 1(3)(b)); or

(3) the application is made by the spouse or civil partner of the missing person and the applicant either is domiciled in England and Wales on the day on which the application is made, or has been habitually resident in England and Wales throughout the period of one year ending with that day (s 1(3)(c), (4)).

As to declarations of presumed death see CIVIL PROCEDURE vol 11 (2015) PARA 162 et seq. As to domicile generally see CONFLICT OF LAWS vol 19 (2011) PARA 336 et seq; and as to habitual residence generally see CONFLICT OF LAWS vol 19 (2011) PARAS 360–362.

9 See the Presumption of Death Act 2013 s 3(2); and CIVIL PROCEDURE vol 11 (2015) PARA 164. The procedure was used to allow the son of Lord Lucan to succeed to the title of his missing father.

10 *Re Spenceley* [1892] P 255; *Re Schulhof, Re Wolf* [1948] P 66, [1947] 2 All ER 841; *Re Dowds* [1948] P 256.

746. Commorientes after 1925. In cases where, after 31 December 1925, two or more persons have died in circumstances rendering it uncertain[1] which of them survived the other or others, then, subject to any order of the court[2], the deaths must, for all purposes affecting the title to property, be presumed to have occurred in order of seniority, and accordingly the younger is deemed to have survived the elder[3], even if it appears that the deaths were simultaneous[4]. The statutory presumption is, however, excluded by an express contrary provision in a will[5].

Where an intestate died on or after 1 January 1996[6] and the intestate's spouse or civil partner survived the intestate but died before the end of the period of 28 days beginning with the day on which the intestate died, the provisions relating to distribution have effect as respects the intestate as if the spouse or civil partner had not survived the intestate[7].

1 If there is evidence leading to a defined and warranted conclusion that one died before the other, the element of uncertainty is lacking and consequently the presumption never arises: *Re Bate, Chillingworth v Bate* [1947] 2 All ER 418 (applying a dictum of Viscount Simon C in *Hickman v Peacey* [1945] AC 304, [1945] 2 All ER 215, HL). Available evidence should be submitted as soon as possible to a registrar; affidavits from the person who found and the doctor who examined the bodies may be sufficient: see *Practice Direction* [1964] 2 All ER 771, [1964] 1 WLR 1027.

2 These words do not give the court power to disregard the presumption; they enable it to receive evidence in rebuttal but give it no discretion to disregard the presumption on the ground of unfairness or injustice: *Re Lindop, Lee-Barber v Reynolds* [1942] Ch 377 at 382, [1942] 2 All ER 46 at 48 per Bennett J.

3 Law of Property Act 1925 s 184. As to succession on intestacy see PARA 485 et seq.

4 See *Hickman v Peacey* [1945] AC 304, [1945] 2 All ER 215, HL.

5 *Re Guggenheim* (1941) Times, 20 June (declaration by testator that in the event of his wife and himself dying simultaneously or in such circumstances that there be no evidence whether he or his wife died first, his wife should be deemed to have predeceased him); *Re Pringle, Baker v Matheson* [1946] Ch 124, [1946] 1 All ER 88; cf *Re Rowland, Smith v Russell* [1963] Ch 1, [1962] 2 All ER 837, CA. As to the construction of wills see PARA 224 et seq.

6 Ie the date on which the Administration of Estates Act 1925 s 46(2A) was added by the Law Reform (Succession) Act 1995 s 1(1): see s 1(2). See also note 7.

7 See the Administration of Estates Act 1925 s 46(2A); and PARA 485. Prior to 1 October 2014 (ie the date on which the Administration of Estates Act 1925 s 46(3) was repealed by the Inheritance Trustees' Powers Act 2014 Sch 4, para 1(2)) if an intestate and the intestate's spouse or civil partner died, after 31 December 1952, in such circumstances that by virtue of the statutory presumption the spouse or civil partner was deemed to have survived the intestate, the intestate's estate must nevertheless be distributed under the Administration of Estates Act 1925 s 46 (see PARA 485 et seq) as if the spouse or civil partner had not survived: see the Administration of Estates Act 1925 s 46(3) (repealed).

See the definition of 'intestate' in the Administration of Estates Act 1925 s 55(1)(vi); and PARA 1135 note 1. As to the application to a partial intestacy of the statutory provisions for the distribution of intestates' estates see PARAS 479, W514et seq.

(ii) Limited Probates

747. General and limited grants of probate. In a simple case the executors obtain a general grant[1] to the whole estate of the testator, and they alone are his personal representatives and are charged with the administration of all his property. In some cases, however, the testator appoints special executors whose duties are limited to a specific part of the estate[2]. In the case of land settled before the testator's death, and which continues to be settled after his death, special executors are deemed to be appointed by statute[3].

1 This is equally the case where there is a single executor.
2 See PARAS 819–820. The procedure on application for probate limited to part of the estate is the same as for administration so limited: see the Non-Contentious Probate Rules 1987, SI 1987/2024, r 51; and PARA 819.
3 See PARAS 615–616. As to settled land grants see PARA 821 et seq.

748. Types of limited grant of probate. If the special executor[1] obtains his grant (limited to the property or purposes for which he is appointed) first, the subsequent grant made to the other executor is called a caeterorum grant. If that other executor is the first to apply, he obtains a grant save and except the property in respect of which the special executor has been appointed[2].

Where a testator appoints a separate executor for the purpose of carrying into effect the trusts and dispositions of a codicil, probate limited to those trusts and dispositions is granted to that executor. A similar grant is made to a person who is appointed executor for a special purpose or in respect of a specific fund only[3].

1 As to general and special executors see PARA 615.
2 It would appear to be the district judges' or registrars' practice to make a limited and a general grant wherever the special executor is appointed generally. As to the fees payable see PARA 686.
3 See PARA 610 et seq.

749. Grant of administration with will annexed limited to property appointed. Where a testator has made a will which has been revoked by his subsequent marriage or entry into a civil partnership[1] but which contains an exercise of a special power of appointment[2], the court grants administration with the will annexed to the appointee limited to the property appointed[3].

1 For the general rule that a will is revoked by marriage or civil partnership and the exception in the case of a disposition in a will made in exercise of a power of appointment see the Wills Act 1837 s 18; and PARA 87.
2 As to special powers of appointment see TRUSTS AND POWERS vol 98 (2013) PARA 585 et seq.
3 *Re Russell* (1890) 15 PD 111; *Re Poole, Poole v Poole* [1919] P 10 (general grant to widow, with so much of will annexed as related to appointed fund, after revocation of will exercising general power).

750. Grant of probate limited to time. Probate of the contents of a lost will is limited until the original or a more authentic copy is proved[1]. A similar limitation is contained in the probate of a copy of the will of a British subject made abroad when the original is detained in a foreign country[2], unless it is retained in the custody of a foreign court or official[3].

1 As to the procedure see PARA 730. As to proof of contents see PARA 716.
2 *Re Lemme* [1892] P 89; cf *Practice Note* [1942] WN 204. A grant limited as to time is followed by a second or cessate grant: see PARA 752. As to the procedure see PARA 730.
3 See PARA 721.

(iii) Double and Cessate Grants

751. Double grants of probate. Where by reason of their number[1] or otherwise the executors appointed by the will do not all prove, power may be reserved to the non-proving executors to prove at a later date. The second grant will then be known as double probate. It is made in general terms, but the value of the estate is sworn as the value of the assets remaining unadministered at the date of the second grant and not as the original value in the first grant[2].

An inheritance tax account is necessary in every case of a double grant[3].

1 As to the limit on the number of executors to whom probate may be granted see PARA 611.
2 For the practice in the case of a double grant see Tristram and Coote's Probate Practice (31st Edn) 13.127 et seq. See also *Re Griffin* (1910) 54 Sol Jo 378.
3 See the Senior Courts Act 1981 s 109; and PARA 731. As to the form of the inheritance tax account and reporting requirements to Her Majesty's Revenue and Customs see Tristram and Coote's Probate Practice (31st Edn) 8.64 et seq.

752. Cessate grants of probate. Where a testator has directed that in a certain event some other person is to be substituted for his original executor, that other person becomes entitled upon the happening of the event to a grant in his own favour[1]. Such a second grant is known as a cessate grant, and differs from a grant de bonis non administratis[2] by being a re-grant of all the estate remaining, and by being a grant of probate and not of administration with the will annexed. The substituted executor takes the executor's oath, but swears the estate at the value only of what remains undistributed.

A second grant is also required upon the death of a person who has taken a grant for the use and benefit of a person under disability (for example a mentally incapacitated executor), and a cessate grant is made on the removal of a disability, as where a minor attains full age or a mentally incapacitated person recovers his capacity. If an executor becomes unfit to act, there must be a fresh grant[3].

Where a grant has been made of the contents of a lost will, a second grant is made upon the production of the original[4]. Where a codicil is found after probate of a will, a second grant is sometimes made.

An inheritance tax account is necessary in every case of a cessate grant[5].

1 *Re Foster* (1871) LR 2 P & D 304; *Re Freeman* (1931) 146 LT 143 (renunciation of executors; grant to person appointed by codicil to fill any vacancy). As to fees on second or subsequent grants see PARA 686.
2 See PARA 793.
3 *Re Clifton* [1931] P 222.
4 See PARA 750.
5 See the Senior Courts Act 1981 s 109; and PARA 731. As to the form of the inheritance tax account and reporting requirements to Her Majesty's Revenue and Customs see Tristram and Coote's Probate Practice (31st Edn) 8.64 et seq. See also *Re Griffin* (1910) 54 Sol Jo 378.

753. Person obtaining cessate grant may call for account from holder of original grant. A person who obtains a cessate grant[1] or a grant on the revocation of a previous grant may call upon the person in whose favour the original grant was made at any time after the determination of the original grant to exhibit an inventory and account[2]. The order is usually obtained upon summons to a district judge or registrar[3].

1 As to cessate grants see PARA 752.
2 See *Taylor v Newton* (1752) 1 Lee 15; *Re Thomas* [1956] 3 All ER 897n, [1956] 1 WLR 1516 (cases of grants of administration; see further PARAS 797, 855); cf *Re Griffin* (1910) 54 Sol Jo 378 (a case of double probate: see PARA 752). See also the Administration of Estates Act 1925 s 25 (see PARAS 847, 957, 959); and Tristram and Coote's Probate Practice (31st Edn) 19.01 et seq. Every executor in his oath undertakes to render an inventory and account whenever lawfully required to do so.

3 Non-Contentious Probate Rules 1987, SI 1987/2024, r 61(2) (amended by SI 1991/1876). See also PARA 702. As to the meaning of 'district judge' see PARA 631 note 6; and as to the meaning of 'registrar' see PARA 631 note 7.

(4) GENERAL GRANTS OF ADMINISTRATION

754. Foundation of court's jurisdiction to make grant of letters of administration. Where a person dies intestate[1], representation to his estate is obtained by means of a grant of letters of administration[2]. The foundation of the court's jurisdiction[3] to make a grant is the existence of property belonging to the intestate within its jurisdiction to be distributed[4]. It was formerly absolutely essential to show that such property was in England or Wales[5], but where it is necessary to obtain representation for a collateral purpose, administration may now be granted even though the deceased left no estate[6]. Accordingly, for example it may be necessary to constitute a personal representative of the deceased:

(1) to enable legal proceedings in connection with the estate to be begun or defended;

(2) to make title to estate or property vested in the deceased as trustee, and not beneficially; or

(3) to enable a new trustee to be appointed.

A grant of letters of administration may also be necessary in respect of settled land vested in the deceased[7].

1 As to intestacy see PARA 477 et seq. As to the form of grant where there is a testamentary instrument but no effective disposition of any property see PARA 791. As to the right to probate of a document purporting to dispose when there is no existing property see PARA 707.

2 Where there is an alleged will and the parties interested under it have been cited to appear and propound it, but fail to do so, administration is granted as upon an intestacy: *Re Morton, Morton v Thorpe* (1863) 3 Sw & Tr 179; *Re Quick, Quick v Quick* [1899] P 187; *Re Bootle, Heaton v Whalley* (1901) 84 LT 570. See also *Re Dennis* [1899] P 191, following *Crosby v Noton* (1867) 36 LJP & M 55; *Re Gilbert* [1911] 2 IR 36. The grant is an order of the court: see PARA 679.

3 See 13 Edw 1 (Statute of Westminster the Second) (1285) c 19; 31 Edw 3 state 1 c 11 (Administration on Intestacy) (1357); 21 Hen 8 c 5 (1529); Statute of Distribution (1670) (all wholly repealed as regards deaths after 1925); Court of Probate Act 1857; Land Transfer Act 1897 (repealed as regards deaths after 1925); Administration of Estates Act 1925; Supreme Court of Judicature (Consolidation) Act 1925 (repealed); Intestates' Estates Act 1952; and the Senior Courts Act 1981.

4 *Re Tucker* (1864) 3 Sw & Tr 585.

5 *Evans v Burrell* (1859) 28 LJP & M 82; *Re Fittock* (1863) 32 LJPM & A 157.

6 The High Court has all jurisdiction in relation to letters of administration as it had before 1982: see the Senior Courts Act 1981 s 25; and PARAS 677, 707. Before 1982 it had jurisdiction to grant letters of administration where the deceased left no estate: see the Administration of Justice Act 1932 s 2(1) (repealed); and PARA 707. For some years before 1932 the court had, when necessary, made a grant upon a declaration of personal belongings (eg clothes) of nominal amount.

7 As to settled land grants see PARA 821 et seq.

755. Grants on grounds other than intestacy. Letters of administration are granted, not only where the deceased died wholly intestate, but also where, in certain circumstances, he died leaving a will. In such cases letters of administration are granted with the will annexed[1].

1 The grounds on which letters of administration with the will annexed are granted are outlined in PARAS 788–789.

756. No grant of letters of administration to person who unlawfully killed the deceased. Where a person has unlawfully killed the deceased, neither he nor his personal representatives will be granted letters of administration to the estate of the deceased person[1]. Proof of the conviction of a person for an offence by any court in the United Kingdom or by a court martial is sufficient proof, in any civil proceedings where it is relevant, that he committed the offence, unless the contrary is proved[2].

1 *Re Crippen* [1911] P 108; *Re Hall, Hall v Knight and Baxter* [1914] P 1, CA. As to participation in the distribution of the deceased's estate see PARAS 38–40, 480. See also *Scotching v Birch* [2008] EWHC 844 (Ch), [2008] All ER (D) 265 (Mar) ('well established and validated rule' not overridden by any rights claimed by the applicant under the Convention for the Protection of Human Rights and Fundamental Freedoms (Rome, 4 November 1950; TS 71 (1953); Cmd 8969) art 8; and see note 2).

2 See the Civil Evidence Act 1968 s 11; and CIVIL PROCEDURE vol 12A (2015) PARA 1644 et seq. As to the meaning of 'United Kingdom' see PARA 4 note 7. See also *Scotching v Birch* [2008] EWHC 844 (Ch), [2008] All ER (D) 265 (Mar) (mother of the deceased held to lack locus to apply for a grant where she was awaiting trial for murder, having previously admitted manslaughter on grounds of diminished responsibility).

757. Number of administrators. Administration may not be granted to more than four persons in respect of the same part of the estate of a deceased person[1]. Where under an intestacy any beneficiary is a minor or a life interest arises, any grant of administration must be made either to a trust corporation (with or without an individual) or to not less than two individuals, unless it appears to the court to be expedient in all the circumstances to appoint an individual as sole administrator[2].

1 Senior Courts Act 1981 s 114(1). As to the meaning of 'estate' see PARA 620 note 5.

2 Senior Courts Act 1981 s 114(2). See also PARA 775.

758. Court's discretionary power in relation to appointment of administrators. If by reason of any special circumstances it appears to the High Court to be necessary or expedient to appoint as administrator some person other than the person who, but for this provision, would in accordance with probate rules[1] have been entitled to a grant[2], the court may in its discretion appoint as administrator such person as it thinks expedient[3]. Any such grant of administration[4] may be limited in any way the court thinks fit[5].

An application for an order for a grant of administration under the court's discretionary power may be made to a district judge[6] or registrar[7], supported by an affidavit setting out the grounds of the application[8].

1 Ie the Non-Contentious Probate Rules 1987, SI 1987/2024: see the Senior Courts Act 1981 s 116(1).

2 As to the meaning of 'grant' see PARA 683 note 2.

3 Senior Courts Act 1981 s 116(1). See note 1. The exercise of the discretion should not be undertaken lightly; the threshold for establishing the existence of special circumstances is high: *A-B v Dobbs* [2010] EWHC 497 (Fam), [2010] WTLR 931. See also PARA 759.

4 As to the meaning of 'administration' see PARA 622 note 8.

5 Senior Courts Act 1981 s 116(2). See note 1. See also *Re Mathew* [1984] 2 All ER 396, [1984] 1 WLR 1011 (grant with reservation of power of executors to apply for probate); and *Gudavadze v Kay* [2012] EWHC 1683 (Ch), [2012] WTLR 1753 (grant containing term setting aside caveats entered by parties in relation to estate prior to grant).

6 As to the meaning of 'district judge' see PARA 631 note 6.

7 As to the meaning of 'registrar' see PARA 631 note 7.

8 Non-Contentious Probate Rules 1987, SI 1987/2024, r 52(a) (amended by SI 1991/1876). Full disclosure of matters which may be material to the application should be given: see *Shephard v Wheeler* [2000] All ER (D) 19, (2000) Times, 15 February. As to the unsuitability of the non-contentious probate procedure on an application which is likely to be contentious and involve a proliferation of evidence see *Van Hoorn v Van Hoorn* (1978) 123 Sol Jo 65.

759. Special circumstances enabling court to pass over person otherwise entitled to letters of administration. No broad rule of law can be laid down as to what are special circumstances enabling the court to pass over a person otherwise entitled to a grant[1]; each case must be decided upon its own merits[2]. One object which the court keeps in view is the expeditious and economical administration of estates of deceased persons[3]. Special circumstances are not necessarily limited to circumstances in connection with the estate itself or its administration, but can be any other circumstances which make it necessary or expedient to pass over the executor[4]. The mere fact that the next of kin are desirous that the court should make a grant to a nominee, who is a stranger to the estate, is not necessarily regarded as a special circumstance[5]. Where there is a doubt as to the persons claiming as next of kin, and those interested on intestacy are aged and infirm, the court may give effect to an arrangement entered into between the parties that the grant be made to a stranger[6]. The court has also made a joint grant to the next of kin and a person not next of kin, but entitled in distribution[7]. The court may also make a general grant to a receiver appointed by the Chancery Division to get in the intestate's estate[8].

1 As to the court's discretionary power see PARA 758.

2 *Re Chapman* [1903] P 192. See also *Re Stewart (or Stuart)* (1875) LR 3 P & D 244 (will by which a minor was sole beneficiary and was appointed sole executrix, but trustees were appointed for her until she came of age; administration with will annexed granted to trustees until she was of age); *Re Crippen* [1911] P 108 (personal representative of murderer of wife passed over on grant of wife's estate); *Re Byrne* (1910) 44 ILT 98 (grant of estate of deceased employer to nominee of injured workman for purpose of a claim for damages); *Re Hall, Hall v Knight and Baxter* [1914] P 1, CA; *Re Drawmer* (1913) 108 LT 732; *Re S* [1968] P 302, [1967] 2 All ER 150 (both cases where executor in prison passed over); *Re Bowron* (1914) 84 LJP 92 (grant to husband's trustee in bankruptcy; husband not cited); *Re Woolf* (1918) 34 TLR 477 (intestate's son preferred to daughters who had married alien enemies); *Re Ray* (1926) 96 LJP 37 (trust for minor; executor who was unfit and had adverse interest passed over); *Re Potticary* [1927] P 202 (misfeasance of executor); *Re Morgans* (1931) 145 LT 392 (grant to nominees of next of kin who were unable to agree on any one or more of themselves administering the estate); *Re Leguia* [1934] P 80 (grant to creditor on executor and next of kin abstaining from taking a grant where estate was insolvent; but cf the later proceedings by the executor whose citation had been dispensed with (*Re Leguia* (1936) 105 LJP 72)); *Re Simpson* [1936] P 40 (nominee of plaintiff in an action against the estate appointed in lieu of the persons entitled upon the refusal of the latter); *Re Parnall* [1936] P 47 (refusal of persons entitled); *Re Knight* [1939] 3 All ER 928; *Practice Direction* [1965] 1 All ER 923, [1965] 1 WLR 552 (where appropriate, a grant of administration to the estate of a solicitor in practice on his own may be granted to nominees of the Law Society); *Re Biggs* [1966] P 118, [1966] 1 All ER 358 (grant to next of kin passing over an executor who had intermeddled but refused to prove the will); *Re Newsham* [1967] P 230, [1966] 3 All ER 681 (grant passing over widow so as not to prejudice an insurance claim); *Re Clore* [1982] Fam 113, [1982] 2 WLR 314 (approved in *IRC v Stype Investments (Jersey) Ltd, Re Clore* [1982] Ch 456, [1982] 3 All ER 419, CA) (where executors were passed over who had shared responsibility for removing assets from the jurisdiction and opposing the payment of tax found due on the estate); *Scotching v Birch* [2008] EWHC 844 (Ch), [2008] All ER (D) 265 (Mar) (where a father successfully sought to limit the grant of administration to himself on the basis that the child's mother lacked locus to apply for a grant on public policy grounds). See also PARA 756. As to the appointment of criminals as executors see PARA 619. As to grants to the Public Trustee by order or discretion of the court see PARA 785.

Grants have been made in favour of public authorities or their nominees where public expense has been incurred on behalf of poor persons: see eg *Re Hockin* (1895) 73 LT 316; *Re Everley* [1892] P 50; *Re Sharland* (1892) 67 LT 501 (grants to poor law guardians under the Court of Probate Act 1857 s 73 (repealed)). As to the general effect of bankruptcy see PARAS 624, 774.

3 *Re Grundy* (1868) LR 1 P & D 459.

4 *Re Clore* [1982] Fam 113 at 117, [1982] 2 WLR 314 at 318 per Ewbank J (approved in *IRC v Stype Investments (Jersey) Ltd, Re Clore* [1982] Ch 456, [1982] 3 All ER 419, CA); *Buchanan v Milton* [1999] 2 FLR 844. See, however, *Re Edwards-Taylor* [1951] P 24, [1950] 2 All ER 446. See also PARA 956 as to the application of the Senior Courts Act 1981 s 116 in disputes over the disposal of the deceased's body.

5 *Re Richardson* (1871) LR 2 P & D 244; *Teague and Ashdown v Wharton* (1871) LR 2 P & D 360; *Re Hale* (1874) LR 3 P & D 207; *Re Brotherton* [1901] P 139. See, however, *Re Morgans* (1931) 145 LT 392. As to passing over by consent see PARA 760.

6 *Re Hopkins* (1875) LR 3 P & D 235. See also *Re Potter, Potter v Potter* [1899] P 265, where the object in procuring the grant to a stranger was to put an end to litigation between the parties. In the following cases the court considered the circumstances sufficient to justify a special grant to a stranger: *Re Johnson* (1862) 2 Sw & Tr 595; *Re Minshull* (1889) 14 PD 151; *Re Jackson* [1892] P 257; *Re Trigg* [1901] P 42; *Re Barton* [1898] P 11.

7 *Re Grundy* (1868) LR 1 P & D 459; *Re Walsh* [1892] P 230. See also PARA 776.

8 *Re Mayer* (1873) LR 3 P & D 39; *Re Moore* [1892] P 145. As to the appointment of a receiver see PARA 810.

760. Passing over by consent of letters of administration. Although there is authority to the contrary[1], in practice grants are now made to persons not primarily or at all entitled, with the consent of the persons being passed over. Accordingly, where by reason of ill-health an executor is incapable of attending to business or of taking out probate, a grant of administration with the will annexed may be made to his nominee for his use and benefit[2]. Other instances are the grant to a nominee of the Law Society to enable a solicitor's practice to be continued[3], the grant by agreement to a doubtful claimant[4], and the grant to a nominee with no interest in the estate on the agreement of all the persons interested[5].

1 See *Teague and Ashdown v Wharton* (1871) LR 2 P & D 360; and PARA 759 note 5.

2 *Re Davis* [1906] P 330; *Re Roberts* (1858) 1 Sw & Tr 64. As to administration with the will annexed see PARA 788 et seq.

3 See *Practice Direction* [1965] 1 All ER 923, [1965] 1 WLR 552.

4 *Re Minshull* (1889) 14 PD 151 (kinship doubtful; agreement between claimants).

5 *Re Potter, Potter v Potter* [1899] P 265 (auditor of the deceased's accounts appointed); *Re Mathew* [1984] 2 All ER 396, [1984] 1 WLR 1011 (grant to nominees of next of kin who were unable to agree on administration of estate).

761. Person with prior right to letters of administration presumed dead. Where the person who would, if living, be entitled to the grant[1] has been missing for many years, the court may make a grant upon the footing that he is dead, without requiring him to be cited by advertisement[2], but where such person would if alive have a life interest in the estate, a joint grant is necessary[3].

Where the question of the person entitled to the grant depends upon the date of death of a person presumed to have died, the court solves the difficulty by making a grant under its discretionary powers[4]. The court will not under this power make a grant to a person entitled in another capacity[5].

1 As to the order of priority see PARA 768.

2 *Re Reed* (1874) 29 LT 932; *Re Callicott* [1899] P 189; *Re Love* (1901) 17 TLR 721; *Re Chapman* [1903] P 192. It would appear to be sufficient for the applicant to swear to his belief that the absent party is dead (see *Re Chapman*), although the practice is stated to be unsettled: see *Re Jackson* (1902) 87 LT 747, in which case *Re Reed* and *Re Pridham* (1889) 61 LT 302 were considered. Corroborative evidence of the death may be dispensed with: *Re Bowden* (1904) 21 TLR 13. See also *Re Rishton* (1921) 90 LJP 374 (usual affidavits by relatives dispensed with and the court followed an order of the county court which had investigated the question of presumption of death). As to presumption of death see PARA 745.

3 *Re Hall* [1950] P 156, [1950] 1 All ER 718.

4 *Re Peck* (1860) 2 Sw & Tr 506; *Re Harling* [1900] P 59; *Re Parnall* [1936] P 47. As to the court's discretionary power see also PARAS 758–759.

5 *Re Fairweather* (1862) 2 Sw & Tr 588; *Re Smith* (1858) 27 LJP & M 105, where the applicant was only entitled to a limited grant in another capacity.

762. Grant of letters of administration in relation to trust estates. A grant may be made under the court's discretionary power on the application of a beneficiary under a trust of which the deceased was sole surviving trustee[1]. Such a grant will generally be limited to the trust property[2].

1 See generally TRUSTS AND POWERS vol 98 (2013) PARA 1 et seq.

2 The grant is normally made both under the Senior Courts Act 1981 s 113 (see PARA 616), and under s 116 (see PARA 758): see PARA 819. As to the devolution of trust property where there is a duly constituted personal representative see PARA 950 et seq.

763. Notice to parties of discretionary grant. Before making a grant under its discretionary jurisdiction, the court usually requires notice to be given to the parties having a claim to the grant, but it will in special circumstances make the grant without such notice[1].

1 For examples see *Re Hagger* (1863) 3 Sw & Tr 65; *Re Burgess* (1863) 4 Sw & Tr 188; *Re Batterbee* (1889) 14 PD 39; *Re Webb* (1888) 13 PD 71; *Re See* (1879) 4 PD 86; *Re Atherton* [1892] P 104; *Re Moffatt* [1900] P 152; *Re Campion* [1900] P 13; *Re Heerman* [1910] P 357. See also *Re Bailie* (1919) 53 ILT 208 (grant to nephew without citing sister abroad); *Re Leguia* [1934] P 80, where *Re Crawshay* [1893] P 108, and *Re Samson* (1873) LR 3 P & D 48, were cited as precedents.

764. Time for issuing grant of letters of administration. No grant of administration may issue within 14 days of the death of the deceased unless the leave of a district judge or registrar is obtained[1]. Furthermore, a district judge or registrar must not allow any grant to issue until all inquiries he may see fit to make have been satisfactorily answered[2].

1 See the Non-Contentious Probate Rules 1987, SI 1987/2024, r 6(2); and PARA 742. The time limit is only seven days for probate or administration with the will annexed: see r 6(2); and PARA 742. As to the meaning of 'district judge' see PARA 631 note 6; and as to the meaning of 'registrar' see PARA 631 note 7.

2 See the Non-Contentious Probate Rules 1987, SI 1987/2024, r 6(1); and PARA 742. As to the necessity to notify the Treasury Solicitor where the Crown is or may be interested see PARA 778.

765. Evidence required before letters of administration will issue. In addition to evidence of death[1] and the evidence required for the inheritance tax account[2], the person applying[3] for letters of administration must swear an oath[4] in the form applicable to the circumstances of the case[5]. The district judge or registrar may also require other papers in support[6].

On an application for a grant of administration the oath must state in what manner all persons having a prior right to a grant have been cleared off, and whether any minority or life interest arises under the will or intestacy[7]. The oath must also state where the deceased died domiciled[8], and whether or not, to the best of the applicant's knowledge, information and belief, there was land vested in the deceased which was settled previously to his death and which remained settled land notwithstanding his death[9].

1 See PARA 743 et seq.

2 See PARA 731.

3 For the provisions applicable to personal applications and those made through solicitors or probate practitioners see PARA 726 et seq. As to applications by trust corporations see PARA 783; and as to applications by non-trust corporations see PARA 813.

4 See Tristram and Coote's Probate Practice (31st Edn) 6.379. The title of a person to be an administrator is technically called his 'capacity', and a list of 'capacities', being the technical expressions to be used in an oath, is given in the President's Direction 1925: see Tristram and Coote's Probate Practice (31st Edn) 6.390-6.392.

5 See the Non-Contentious Probate Rules 1987, SI 1987/2024, r 8(1); and PARA 728. Where an applicant's right depends upon his legitimation the practice is governed by *Practice Direction* [1965] 2 All ER 560, [1965] 1 WLR 955, which gives the district judge or registrar a discretion in cases where an applicant cannot or cannot without undue hardship obtain a declaration or re-registration. Under intestacies arising on or after 1 January 1970, the Family Law Reform Act 1969 and Family Law Reform Act 1987 give rights to illegitimate relations which makes it necessary in the oath to deal with the claims of any such persons: see note 7.

6 See the Non-Contentious Probate Rules 1987, SI 1987/2024, r 8(1); and PARA 728. As to the meaning of 'district judge' see PARA 631 note 6; and as to the meaning of 'registrar' see PARA 631 note 7.

7 Non-Contentious Probate Rules 1987, SI 1987/2024, r 8(4). See also the Senior Courts Act 1981 s 114(2); and PARA 775. Where the applicant claims to be entitled to share in the estate through

the death of a person who, if alive, would be entitled, the date of that person's death should be stated in the oath. For the wider form of oath necessary on or after 1 January 1970 to clear possible claims by illegitimate relations see *Practice Direction* [1969] 3 All ER 1343, [1969] 1 WLR 1863 and as to clearing off generally, see Tristram and Coote's Probate Practice (31st Edn) 6.388 et seq.

8 See the Non-Contentious Probate Rules 1987, SI 1987/2024, r 8(2); and PARA 728.

9 See the Non-Contentious Probate Rules 1987, SI 1987/2024, r 8(3); and para 728.

766. Guarantees. As a condition of granting administration[1] to any person the High Court may require one or more sureties to guarantee that they will make good, within the limit imposed by the court on the total liability of the surety or sureties, any loss which any person interested in the administration of the estate of the deceased may suffer in consequence of a breach by the administrator of his duties as such[2]. However, the current probate rules[3] make no provision for the taking of guarantees on grants of administration, so for an application for a grant made on or after 1 January 1988[4], a guarantee will not be required. The probate rules do make provision for enforcement of any guarantee that has been given, providing that an application for leave[5] to sue a surety on a guarantee, unless the district judge or registrar otherwise directs[6], is made by summons to a district judge or registrar and notice of the application is served on the administrator, the surety and co-surety[7].

1 As to the meaning of 'administration' see PARA 622 note 8.

2 Senior Courts Act 1981 s 120(1), which is expressed to be subject to s 120(2)–(5) and the probate rules. As to the meaning of 'probate rules' see PARA 620 note 6. The guarantee enures for the benefit of every person interested in the administration of the estate as if contained in a contract under seal made by the surety or sureties with every such person and, where there are two or more sureties, as if they had bound themselves jointly and severally: s 120(2). As to the meaning of 'estate' see PARA 620 note 5. Stamp duty is not chargeable on any such guarantee: s 120(4). Section 120 does not apply where administration is granted to the Treasury Solicitor (see PARA 779), the Official Solicitor (see PARA 805), the Public Trustee (see PARA 784), the Solicitor for the affairs of the Duchy of Lancaster or the Duchy of Cornwall (see PARA 782) or to the consular officer of a foreign state to which the Consular Conventions Act 1949 s 1 applies (see PARA 802), or in such other cases as may be prescribed: Supreme Court Act 1981 s 120(5).

3 Ie the Non-Contentious Probate Rules 1987, SI 1987/2024.

4 Ie the date of the coming into force of the Non-Contentious Probate Rules 1987, SI 1987/2024: see r 1.

5 No action may be brought on any guarantee without the leave of the High Court: Senior Courts Act 1981 s 120(3). See note 2.

6 Ie under the Non-Contentious Probate Rules 1987, SI 1987/2024, r 61, by which a district judge or registrar may require an application to be made by summons to a district judge or registrar in chambers or open court: see PARA 701. As to the meaning of 'district judge' see PARA 631 note 6; and as to the meaning of 'registrar' see PARA 631 note 7.

7 Non-Contentious Probate Rules 1987, SI 1987/2024, r 40 (amended by SI 1991/1876).

(5) ADMINISTRATION SIMPLE

(i) Grants of Administration

767. Grant of letters of administration to foreign representative. Where the intestate dies domiciled abroad leaving property in England, the practice of the English court is to make a grant of letters of administration to the person recognised by the proper court of the country of domicile (including if necessary the foreign state itself if, according to its own law, it claims as successor to the intestate and not as the person entitled to bona vacantia)[1], unless that person is by English law personally disqualified from taking a grant, for instance a minor[2]. Where the person who has obtained the foreign grant is an agent for the party entitled to it, the English court must be satisfied that the agent has authority to make the application in England before making an English grant to him[3].

1 *Re Maldonado, State of Spain v Treasury Solicitor* [1954] P 223, [1953] 2 All ER 1579, CA. As to domicile generally see CONFLICT OF LAWS vol 19 (2011) PARA 336 et seq.
2 See PARA 795 et seq.
3 See *Re Weaver* (1866) 36 LJP & M 41. See also PARA 844 (priority in rights to such a grant and procedure); and PARA 800 et seq (grants to attorneys and consular officers). As to the effect of an English grant of representation see generally CONFLICT OF LAWS vol 19 (2011) PARA 732; and as to the jurisdiction of the English court where it has made such a grant see CONFLICT OF LAWS vol 19 (2011) PARA 738. Personal estate left in England by an intestate who dies domiciled abroad ranks as movable property and is governed by the law of that domicile at the date of the intestate's death; in such case the England court applies the doctrine of total renvoi: see CONFLICT OF LAWS vol 19 (2011) PARA 741.

768. Persons having prior rights to administer. Certain persons are recognised by law as being entitled to administer in priority to others[1], and in the absence of any grounds for the exercise of its discretionary power[2] the court has regard to these rights in making a grant.

In the case of persons dying wholly intestate on or after 1 January 1926[3], the persons having a beneficial interest in the estate are entitled to a grant of administration in the following classes in order of priority[4]:

(1) the surviving spouse or civil partner[5];
(2) the children of the deceased[6] and the issue of any deceased child who died before the deceased[7];
(3) the father and mother of the deceased[8];
(4) brothers and sisters of the whole blood and the issue of any deceased brother or sister of the whole blood who died before the deceased[9];
(5) brothers and sisters of the half blood and the issue of any deceased brother or sister of the half blood who died before the deceased[10];
(6) grandparents[11];
(7) uncles and aunts of the whole blood and the issue of any deceased uncle or aunt of the whole blood who died before the deceased[12]; and
(8) uncles and aunts of the half blood and the issue of any deceased uncle or aunt of the half blood who died before the deceased[13].

For the purpose of determining the person or persons who would be entitled to a grant of representation in respect of the estate of a deceased person who dies on or after 4 April 1988[14], the deceased is presumed, unless the contrary is shown, not to have been survived by:

(a) any person related to him whose father and mother were not married to each other at the time of his birth[15]; or
(b) any person whose relationship with him is deduced through such a person as is mentioned in head (a) above[16].

1 The broad principle upon which a grant is made can be expressed in the following manner: the grant goes according to the interest, live interests are preferred to dead ones, and administration is not granted to minors. An order of sequence is prescribed by the Non-Contentious Probate Rules 1987, SI 1987/2024, r 22: see the text to notes 4–13; and PARA 769. As to the practice where an applicant's right to a grant depends upon legitimation see *Practice Direction* [1965] 2 All ER 560, [1965] 1 WLR 955.
2 See PARA 758.
3 As to the law of intestacy generally see PARA 477 et seq; and for the cases subject to special rules see PARA 531 et seq.
4 Non-Contentious Probate Rules 1987, SI 1987/2024, r 22(1). As to the court's discretionary powers in making a grant see PARA 758.
5 Non-Contentious Probate Rules 1987, SI 1987/2024, r 22(1)(a) (amended by SI 2005/2114). As to the meaning of 'civil partner' see PARA 477.

6 As to the meaning of 'children' see PARA 482; and CHILDREN AND YOUNG PERSONS vol 9 (2012) PARA 3 et seq.
7 Non-Contentious Probate Rules 1987, SI 1987/2024, r 22(1)(b). As to the meaning of 'issue' see PARA 482.
8 Non-Contentious Probate Rules 1987, SI 1987/2024, r 22(1)(c). As to the meaning of 'father and mother of the deceased' see PARAS 482–483. Note that where at the date of death of the deceased on or after 5 April 2005 a person has acquired an alternative gender, his or her relationship to the deceased is described as of the acquired gender but this general rule does not apply to the parents of the deceased where such an acquired gender does not affect his or her status as the father or mother of the child: see the Gender Recognition Act 2004 s 12; PARA 329; and CHILDREN AND YOUNG PERSONS vol 9 (2012) PARA 93. As to the meaning of 'acquired gender' see PARA 329.
9 Non-Contentious Probate Rules 1987, SI 1987/2024, r 22(1)(d).
10 Non-Contentious Probate Rules 1987, SI 1987/2024, r 22(1)(e).
11 Non-Contentious Probate Rules 1987, SI 1987/2024, r 22(1)(f).
12 Non-Contentious Probate Rules 1987, SI 1987/2024, r 22(1)(g).
13 Non-Contentious Probate Rules 1987, SI 1987/2024, r 22(1)(h). Rule 22 does not operate to prevent a grant being made to any person to whom a grant may or may be required to be made under any enactment: r 28(1). Rule 22 also does not apply (except where probate is granted to an executor named, or according to the tenor (see PARA 718), or where the whole estate in England and Wales consists of immovables and a grant is made limited to those (see PARA 844)) where the deceased died domiciled outside England and Wales: r 28(2). As to domicile generally see CONFLICT OF LAWS vol 19 (2011) PARA 336 et seq.
14 See the Family Law Reform Act 1987 s 21(3).
15 Family Law Reform Act 1987 s 21(1)(a). See *Practice Direction* [1988] 2 All ER 308, [1988] 1 WLR 610 for the rebuttal of the presumption and for the appropriate wording to be used in oaths on clearing off those with prior claims and to describe the applicant's relationship to the deceased.
16 Family Law Reform Act 1987 s 21(1)(b). See note 15.

769. Persons entitled in default. In default of any person having a beneficial interest in the estate, the Treasury Solicitor[1] is entitled to a grant of administration if he claims bona vacantia on behalf of the Crown[2]. If all persons entitled to a grant in the case of intestacy[3] have been cleared off, a grant may be made to a creditor of the deceased or to any person who, notwithstanding that he has no immediate beneficial interest in the estate, may have a beneficial interest in the event of an accretion to it[4].

Where all the persons entitled to the estate of the deceased have assigned their whole interest in it to one or more persons, the assignee or assignees replace the assignor in the order of priority for a grant of administration, or, if there are two or more assignors, the assignor with the highest priority[5]. Subject to the rule preferring living persons and persons not under disability where there are two or more persons entitled[6], the personal representative of a person in a class entitled on intestacy[7] or the personal representative of a creditor of the deceased has the same right to a grant as the person whom he represents[8].

1 'Treasury Solicitor' means the solicitor for the affairs of Her Majesty's Treasury and includes the solicitor for the affairs of the Duchy of Lancaster and the solicitor of the Duchy of Cornwall: Non-Contentious Probate Rules 1987, SI 1987/2024, r 2(1). In the Administration of Estates Act 1925 'Treasury Solicitor' means the solicitor for the affairs of Her Majesty's Treasury and includes only the solicitor for the affairs of the Duchy of Lancaster: s 55(1)(xxv). As to grants to the Treasury Solicitor see PARA 779. As to the Treasury Solicitor generally see CONSTITUTIONAL AND ADMINISTRATIVE LAW vol 20 (2014) PARA 281.
2 Non-Contentious Probate Rules 1987, SI 1987/2024, r 22(2). As to the application of r 22 see PARA 768 note 13. The 'Crown' includes the Crown in right of the Duchy of Lancaster and the Duke of Cornwall for the time being: r 2(1).
3 Ie under the Non-Contentious Probate Rules 1987, SI 1987/2024, r 22(1), (2) (see PARA 768; and the text to note 2): see r 22(3).
4 Non-Contentious Probate Rules 1987, SI 1987/2024, r 22(3). See PARA 768 note 4–13. As to grants under the court's discretionary powers to persons other than those enumerated here see PARA 758; and as to limited grants for trust property see PARA 819.
5 Non-Contentious Probate Rules 1987, SI 1987/2024, r 24(1). Where there are two or more assignees, administration may be granted with the consent of the others to any one or more (not

exceeding four) of them: r 24(2). In any case where administration is applied for by an assignee the original instrument of assignment must be produced and a copy of it lodged in the registry: r 24(3). See also PARA 790. As to the meaning of 'registry' see PARA 680 note 2.

6 Ie the Non-Contentious Probate Rules 1987, SI 1987/2024, r 27(5) (see PARA 774): see r 22(4).

7 Ie a person in any of the classes in the Non-Contentious Probate Rules 1987, SI 1987/2024, r 22(1) (see PARA 768 heads (1)–(8)): see r 22(4).

8 Non-Contentious Probate Rules 1987, SI 1987/2024, r 22(4). Where, however, a spouse or civil partner has died without taking a beneficial interest in the whole estate of the deceased as ascertained at the time of the application for the grant, the persons in r 22(1)(b)–(h) (see PARA 768 heads (2)–(8)) are preferred to that spouse's or civil partner's personal representative: r 22(4) (amended by SI 2005/2114).

(ii) Surviving Spouse or Civil Partner

770. Right to grant letters of administration. The surviving spouse or civil partner[1] is primarily entitled to a grant of administration of the estate of a person dying intestate after 1925[2].

The surviving spouse or civil partner is passed over when the marriage or civil partnership was in fact void[3], or where the spouse[4] has obtained a divorce or the civil partner has obtained an order for dissolution or annulment[5] of a civil partnership[6].

If, while a decree of judicial separation or a separation order is in force and the separation is continuing, either of the parties to a marriage or civil partnership dies intestate as respects all or any of his or her property, that property devolves as if the other party had then been dead[7]. Grants which are limited to such property as the deceased acquired since the date of the separation are now appropriate only in the case of deaths before 1 August 1970[8].

Where a surviving spouse or civil partner who is entitled to the whole of the intestate's estate dies without having taken out administration to it, his or her personal representatives have a right to the grant[9].

The surviving spouse's right to a grant is not one which vests in the trustee in bankruptcy, although under its discretionary jurisdiction the court has power to make a grant to the trustee[10].

1 As to the essential requirements of marriage in English law see CONFLICT OF LAWS vol 19 (2011) PARA 517 et seq. 'Marriage' includes marriage of a same sex couple: see the Marriage (Same Sex Couples) Act 2013 Sch 3 para 1(1)(a), (2), (3); and MATRIMONIAL AND CIVIL PARTNERSHIP LAW vol 72 (2015) PARAS 1–2. As regards a death on or after 5 December 2005 the registration of a civil partnership places a surviving civil partner of a deceased person who died intestate in the same position as a lawful spouse of an intestate. Where the intestate's spouse or civil partner survived the intestate but died before the end of the period of 28 days beginning with the day on which the intestate died, the Administration of Estates Act 1925 s 46 has effect as respects the intestate as if the spouse or civil partner had not survived the intestate: Administration of Estates Act 1925 s 46(2A) (added by the Law Reform (Succession) Act 1995 s 1(1); amended by the Civil Partnership Act 2004 Sch 4 para 7). See also PARA 485 note 2. As to beneficial interests arising on intestacy see PARA 485 et seq.

2 See the Non-Contentious Probate Rules 1987, SI 1987/2024, r 22(1)(a); and PARA 768.

3 *Browning v Reane* (1812) 2 Phillim 69 (marriage void for insanity); *Re Hay* (1865) LR 1 P & D 51.

4 *Re Nares* (1888) 13 PD 35; *Re Wallas* [1905] P 326.

5 See the Civil Partnership Act 2004 s 37(1)(a), (b) for the court's power to make dissolution and annulments orders to end a civil partnership. See also PARA 179.

6 As to recognition of foreign divorces, annulments and orders for dissolution of civil partnerships in non-contentious probate applications see PARA 771.

7 Accordingly if, while a decree of judicial separation is in force and the separation is continuing, either of the parties dies intestate, the estate devolves as if the other party to the marriage or civil partnership had then been dead: see the Matrimonial Causes Act 1973 s 18(2); Civil Partnership Act 2004 s 57; and MATRIMONIAL AND CIVIL PARTNERSHIP LAW vol 72 (2015) PARA 257.

8 See the Matrimonial Proceedings and Property Act 1970 ss 40, 43(2) (repealed). For examples of cases applicable in the case of deaths before 1 August 1970 see *Re Jones* (1904) 74 LJP 27; *Re Worman* (1859) 1 Sw & Tr 513; *Re Brighton* (1865) 34 LJPM & A 55. As to where the husband had by the deed of separation resigned all claim to the wife's property acquired after that date see *Allen v Humphrys* (1882) 8 PD 16; *Re Megson* (1899) 80 LT 295.

9 See the Non-Contentious Probate Rules 1987, SI 1987/2024, r 22(4) (amended by SI 2005/2114). But if not so beneficially entitled to the whole estate, the persons in the Non-Contentious Probate Rules 1987, SI 1987/2024, r 22 (1)(b)–(h) are preferred over the spouse or civil partner's personal representatives (see PARA 769 note 8). If the spouse or civil partner has taken out a grant and only partially administered, the grant will be de bonis non. As to grants de bonis non see PARA 793.

10 *Re Turner* (1886) 12 PD 18. See also BANKRUPTCY AND INDIVIDUAL INSOLVENCY vol 5 (2013) PARA 417.

771. Recognition of foreign divorce, annulment or dissolution of civil partnership. In the case of a marriage, the validity of a divorce or annulment obtained by means of judicial or other proceedings is recognised as valid in the United Kingdom[1] if it is effective under the law of the country in which it was obtained, and if at the date of the commencement of the proceedings in which it was obtained either party to the marriage: (1) was habitually resident in the country in which it was obtained; (2) was domiciled in that country; or (3) was a national of that country[2]. As regards a civil partnership, any person may apply to the High Court or the Family Court for a declaration that the validity of a dissolution, annulment or legal separation obtained outside England and Wales in respect of the civil partnership is entitled to recognition in England and Wales[3].

1 As to the meaning of 'United Kingdom' see PARA 4 note 7.

2 See the Family Law Act 1986 ss 45–48; and CONFLICT OF LAWS vol 19 (2011) PARA 537 et seq. As to domicile generally see CONFLICT OF LAWS vol 19 (2011) PARA 336 et seq.

3 See the Civil Partnership Act 2004 s 58(1)(d); and MATRIMONIAL AND CIVIL PARTNERSHIP LAW vol 72 (2015) PARA 463. Additionally, the Civil Partnership (Jurisdiction and Recognition of Judgments) Regulations 2005, SI 2005/3334, allows for the recognition of judgments or orders for dissolution or annulment of civil partnerships and the legal separation of civil partners without any special formalities provided that they were made in the following EU member states: Belgium, Cyprus, Czech Republic, Denmark, Germany, Greece, Spain, Estonia, France, Hungary, Ireland, Italy, Latvia, Lithuania, Luxembourg, Malta, Netherlands, Austria, Poland, Portugal, Slovakia, Slovenia, Finland and Sweden.

772. When grant of letters of administration can be made to surviving spouse or civil partner alone. A grant is made to the surviving spouse or civil partner alone where he or she is the only person beneficially entitled under the intestacy[1], or where there is no life interest arising[2] and no minor is contingently entitled[3] under the intestacy. Where a life interest arises or a minor is contingently entitled, the grant is usually a joint one[4].

1 As to the circumstances in which the surviving spouse or civil partner is the only person entitled see PARA 485.

2 No life interest can arise in the case of deaths on or after 1 October 2014: see PARA 488. As to the only circumstances in which a life interest arises in the case of a death on or after 1 January 1953 see PARA 486.

3 As to the circumstances in which, in the case of a death on or after 1 January 1953, a minor may be contingently entitled see PARAS 500–499, 511. As to deaths on or after 1 January 1926 but before 1 January 1953 see PARA 525.

4 See PARA 775.

(iii) Next of Kin

773. Rights of next of kin among themselves to grant letters of administration. Where there is a contest between persons equally entitled to a grant of administration[1], certain rules of preference have been recognised:

(1) preference is given to the next of kin[2] who has the support of the greatest interest[3];
(2) preference is given to the one who comes first for the grant[4];
(3) primogeniture gives no right[5], but if other things are precisely equal the fact of being the elder sibling may incline the balance[6];
(4) other things being equal, an individual accustomed to business is preferred[7].

A grant can always be made to any person the court thinks fit, even to a stranger, under its discretionary power and this may be the preferred course if those entitled to the grant cannot agree amongst themselves who should act[8].

1 For the order of priority see PARA 768. If a question arises as to the relative suitability of parties equally entitled to administration, application may be made to a district judge or registrar of the district probate registry where the grant application is being made, or is proposed to be made, on summons supported by affidavits setting out the interest of each party and the grounds upon which the claims to the grant are based and opposed: see the Non-Contentious Probate Rules 1987, SI 1987/2024, r 61(3); and see also r 27(6) and PARA 774 note 8.
2 In speaking of deaths after 1925, 'next of kin' must be taken to refer only to such relatives entitled under the statutory rules for distribution of an intestate's estate (see PARA 485 et seq).
3 *Elwes v Elwes* (1728) 2 Lee 573; *Budd v Silver* (1813) 2 Phillim 115.
4 *Cordeux v Trasler* (1865) 34 LJPM & A 127.
5 *Warwick v Greville* (1809) 1 Phillim 123 at 125.
6 *Coppin v Dillon* (1832) 4 Hag Ecc 361 at 376.
7 *Williams v Wilkins* (1812) 2 Phillim 100.
8 *Re Morgans* (1931) 145 LT 392. For the discretionary power to appoint an administrator see PARA 758.

774. Circumstances affecting right of preference. Unless a district judge[1] or registrar[2] otherwise directs, administration must be granted to a person of full age in preference to the guardian of a minor, and to a living person in preference to the personal representative of a deceased person[3]. The bankruptcy of one of two persons in equal degree of relationship is a reason for giving the preference to the other[4]. The fact that one of the next of kin is also a creditor is a reason against his being preferred in a contest for administration[5]. A person having an original interest is preferred to one with a derivative interest[6], but the court may make the grant to the latter, even without requiring the former to be cited[7].

A grant of administration may be made to any person entitled to it without notice to other persons entitled in the same degree[8].

1 As to the meaning of 'district judge' see PARA 631 note 6.
2 As to the meaning of 'registrar' see PARA 631 note 7.
3 Non-Contentious Probate Rules 1987, SI 1987/2024, r 27(5) (amended by SI 1991/1876). See also note 8.
4 *Bell v Timiswood* (1812) 2 Phillim 22; *Iredale v Ford and Bramworth* (1859) 1 Sw & Tr 305. As to disqualification by reason of bankruptcy see PARA 624; and as to other circumstances taken into account see PARA 759.
5 *Webb v Needham* (1823) 1 Add 494; *Re Toole* [1913] 2 IR 188. As to the rights of creditors see PARA 786.
6 *Re Carr* (1867) LR 1 P & D 291 at 292 per Sir JP Wilde.
7 *Re Kinchella* [1894] P 264. See also the Non-Contentious Probate Rules 1987, SI 1987/2024, r 27(4); and the text to note 8.
8 Non-Contentious Probate Rules 1987, SI 1987/2024, r 27(4). For useful guidance on when notices should be given see *Ghafoor v Cliff* [2006] EWHC 825 (Ch), [2006] 2 All ER 1079, [2006] 1 WLR 3020. Disputes between persons entitled to a grant in the same degree must be brought by summons before a district judge or registrar: Non-Contentious Probate Rules 1987, SI 1987/2024, r 27(6) (amended by SI 1991/1876). The issue of such a summons must be noted immediately in the index of pending grant applications: Non-Contentious Probate Rules 1987, SI 1987/2024, r 27(7) (substituted by SI 1998/1903). If the issue of such a summons is known to the district judge or registrar he must not allow any grant to be sealed until the summons is finally disposed of: Non-Contentious Probate Rules 1987, SI 1987/2024, r 27(8) (amended by SI 1991/1876). The

Non-Contentious Probate Rules 1987, SI 1987/2024, r 27 does not operate to prevent a grant being made to any person to whom a grant may or may be required to be made under any enactment: r 28(1). Rule 27 also does not apply (except where probate is granted to an executor named, or according to the tenor (see PARA 718), or where the whole estate in England and Wales consists of immovables and a grant is made limited to those (see PARA 844)) where the deceased died domiciled outside England and Wales: r 28(2). As to domicile generally see CONFLICT OF LAWS vol 19 (2011) PARA 336 et seq.

775. **Joint grants.** Where under a will[1] or intestacy any beneficiary is a minor or a life interest arises, any grant of administration[2] by the High Court must be made either to a trust corporation[3] (with or without an individual), or to a consular officer of a foreign state[4], or to not less than two individuals, unless it appears to the court to be expedient in all the circumstances to appoint an individual as sole administrator[5]. The purpose is to protect the interest of the minor or remainderman, and for this reason it seems that if after grant to one administrator the value of the estate is or becomes such that a previously unexpected minority or remainder arises the proper course is for him to apply for the appointment of a second administrator[6]. The court may appoint a single administrator where the estate is insolvent[7], and where an administrator pending suit is appointed[8].

If at any time during the minority of a beneficiary or the subsistence of a life interest under a will or intestacy there is only one personal representative (not being a trust corporation), the court may, on the application of any person interested or the guardian or receiver of any such person, and in accordance with probate rules[9], appoint one or more additional personal representatives to act while the minority or life interest subsists and until the estate is fully administered[10].

The appointment of such an additional personal representative does not have the effect of including him in any chain of representation[11].

1 As to the meaning of 'will' see PARA 620 note 4.
2 As to the meaning of 'administration' see PARA 622 note 8.
3 As to the meaning of 'trust corporation' see PARA 622 note 4.
4 See PARA 802 and note 10.
5 Senior Courts Act 1981 s 114(2). As to the only circumstances in which a life interest arises see PARA 301. On an application for a grant of administration the oath supporting the grant (see PARA 765) must state whether any minority or life interest so arises and the court may act on such evidence: see the Non-Contentious Probate Rules 1987, SI 1987/2024, r 8(4); Senior Courts Act 1981 s 114(3). Where an applicant desires to be appointed as sole administrator, he should state in the oath to lead to the grant or in a separate affidavit the reasons for which the court is asked to make such a grant: *Practice Direction* [1982] 3 FLR 185.
6 As to the court's power to appoint an additional administrator see the text to note 10. After administration is complete the same situation may arise, but in this case it is a simple matter to appoint an additional trustee.
7 See *Re Herbert* [1926] P 109. Cf *Re White* [1928] P 75, CA, and *Re Hall* [1950] P 156, [1950] 1 All ER 718, in which cases the correctness of the decision in *Re Herbert* was not directly in issue. As to grants to creditors see PARA 786.
8 See the Senior Courts Act 1981 s 117; and PARA 808. See also *Re Lindley, Lindley v Lindley* [1953] P 203, [1953] 2 All ER 319; *Re Haslip* [1958] 2 All ER 275n, [1958] 1 WLR 583.
9 Ie in accordance with the Non-Contentious Probate Rules 1987, SI 1987/2024: see the Senior Courts Act 1981 s 114(4). See note 5.
10 Senior Courts Act 1981 s 114(4). This provision does not apply where the existing personal representative is a consular officer of a foreign state appointed under the Consular Conventions Act 1949: see s 1(4); and PARAS 719, 802. See note 5.
11 Senior Courts Act 1981 s 114(5). As to the chain of representation see PARA 637 et seq. See note 5.

776. **Procedure on application for appointment of more than one administrator.** The application to add a personal representative[1] must be made to a district judge[2] or registrar[3] and must be supported by an affidavit by the applicant, the consent of the proposed additional personal representative and such other evidence as the

district judge or registrar may require[4]. On the application the district judge or registrar may direct that a note be made on the original grant of the addition of a further personal representative, or he may impound or revoke the grant or make such other order as the circumstances of the case may require[5].

A person entitled in priority to a grant of administration may, without leave, apply for a grant with a person entitled in a lower degree, provided that there is no other person entitled in a higher degree to the person to be joined, unless every other such person has renounced[6]. An application for leave to join with a person entitled in priority to a grant of administration a person having no right or no immediate right to a grant must be made to a district judge or registrar, and must be supported by an affidavit by the person entitled in priority, the consent of the person proposed to be joined as administrator and such other evidence as the district judge or registrar may direct[7]. Unless a district judge or registrar otherwise directs, there may, without any such application, be joined with a person entitled in priority to administration[8] any nominated person[9] or a trust corporation[10].

1 Ie under the Senior Courts Act 1981 s 114(4) (see PARA 775): see the Non-Contentious Probate Rules 1987, SI 1987/2024, r 26(1) (as amended: see note 4).
2 As to the meaning of 'district judge' see PARA 631 note 6.
3 As to the meaning of 'registrar' see PARA 631 note 7.
4 Non-Contentious Probate Rules 1987, SI 1987/2024, r 26(1) (r 26 amended by SI 1991/1876).
5 Non-Contentious Probate Rules 1987, SI 1987/2024, r 26(2) (as amended: see note 4).
6 Non-Contentious Probate Rules 1987, SI 1987/2024, r 25(1). Rule 25 does not operate to prevent a grant being made to any person to whom a grant may or may be required to be made under any enactment: r 28(1). Rule 25 also does not apply (except where probate is granted to an executor named, or according to the tenor (see PARA 718), or where the whole estate in England and Wales consists of immovables and a grant is made limited to those (see PARA 844)) where the deceased died domiciled outside England and Wales: r 28(2).
7 Non-Contentious Probate Rules 1987, SI 1987/2024, r 25(2) (r 25(2), (3) amended by SI 1991/1876).
8 Non-Contentious Probate Rules 1987, SI 1987/2024, r 25(3) (as amended: see note 7). As to the order of priority see PARA 768.
9 Non-Contentious Probate Rules 1987, SI 1987/2024, r 25(3)(a). A person is nominated under r 32(3) (see PARA 795) or r 35(3) (see PARA 805): see r 25(3)(a).
10 Non-Contentious Probate Rules 1987, SI 1987/2024, r 25(3)(b). As to the meaning of 'trust corporation' see PARA 622 note 4.

777. Disputes as to who is next of kin. Where there is a dispute as to who is in fact the next of kin of an intestate, the question is tried as an interest action (sometimes called an interest cause), the practice in which is similar to that in actions for proving a will in solemn form[1]. The claim form must contain a statement of the nature of the interest in the estate of the claimant and of each defendant[2]. If a party disputes another party's interest he must state this in his statement of case and set out his reasons[3]. The unsuccessful party in an interest action is ordered to pay the costs unless the circumstances are exceptional[4].

1 See PARA 860 et seq.
2 See CPR 57.7(1). The decision in an interest action may involve an issue of pedigree or of legitimacy but a prayer for a declaration of legitimacy can only be made by petition and not in probate proceedings: *Warter v Warter* (1890) 15 PD 35. See also the Family Law Act 1986 ss 56, 58(4); and CHILDREN AND YOUNG PERSONS vol 9 (2012) PARA 110.
3 See CPR 57.7(2).
4 *Wiseman v Wiseman* (1866) LR 1 P & D 351.

(iv) The Crown and the Duchies

778. The Crown's right to take letters of administration. Where a person dies intestate after 31 December 1925 leaving no person entitled to share in his estate under the provisions relating to distribution on intestacy[1], the intestate's residuary estate belongs to the Crown[2] as bona vacantia in lieu of any right to escheat[3]. Administration is granted to the Treasury Solicitor[4] on behalf of the Crown[5]. The administrator's duty is to get in the estate, pay the debts and account for the balance to the use of the Crown[6]. In the case of partial intestacy only, the Treasury Solicitor is entitled, not to a general grant, but to a grant limited to the property undisposed of by the will[7]. Where administration was decreed to the Crown but not taken out, a creditor was allowed to come in and take a grant[8]. In any case in which it appears that the Crown is or may be beneficially interested in the estate of a deceased person, notice of intended application for a grant must be given by the applicant to the Treasury Solicitor, and the district judge or registrar may direct that no grant is to issue within 28 days after the notice has been given[9].

1 As to intestacy see PARA 477 et seq. As to deaths on or after 1 January 1953 see PARA 485 et seq; and as to deaths on or after 1 January 1926 but before 1 January 1953 see PARA 521 et seq.
2 Alternatively the intestate's residuary estate belongs to the Duchy of Lancaster or the Duke of Cornwall, as the case may be: see PARA 782.
3 Administration of Estates Act 1925 s 46(1)(vi). See PARAS 512–513, 527. As to the rights of a foreign state in the case of a foreigner dying abroad see PARA 513. As to escheat and bona vacantia see CROWN AND CROWN PROCEEDINGS vol 29 (2014) PARA 145 et seq.
4 As to the meaning of 'Treasury Solicitor' see PARA 769 note 1. As to grants to the Treasury Solicitor see PARA 779. As to the Treasury Solicitor generally see CONSTITUTIONAL AND ADMINISTRATIVE LAW vol 20 (2014) PARA 281.
5 See the Non-Contentious Probate Rules 1987, SI 1987/2024, r 22(2); and PARA 769. As to the meaning of the 'Crown' see PARA 769 note 2.
6 *Megit v Johnson* (1780) 2 Doug KB 542. See also *R v Sutton* (1670) 1 Wms Saund 271b note 1.
7 *Re Rhoades* (1866) LR 1 P & D 119. However, in *Jones v Treasury Solicitor* (1932) 48 TLR 615; affd 49 TLR 75, CA, the court made a general grant of administration to the Treasury Solicitor with the will annexed. This point does not appear to have been taken.
8 *Re Steinorth* (1856) Dea & Sw 270. See also *Re Ball* (1902) 47 Sol Jo 129.
9 Non-Contentious Probate Rules 1987, SI 1987/2024, r 38 (amended by SI 1991/1876). As to the meaning of 'district judge' see PARA 631 note 6; and as to the meaning of 'registrar' see PARA 631 note 7.

779. Grant of letters of administration to the Treasury Solicitor. The Treasury Solicitor[1] deals with the property in accordance with certain statutory provisions and rules[2]. He is not required to deliver any affidavit, statutory declaration, account, certificate or other statement verified on oath; in lieu of this he delivers a signed account or particulars of the estate of the deceased[3]. Upon any change in the holder of the office, the letters of administration, with all their incidents, vest in the Treasury Solicitor for the time being without further grant[4]. The court has power to revoke the grant[5].

1 As to the Treasury Solicitor see PARA 769 note 1; and CONSTITUTIONAL AND ADMINISTRATIVE LAW vol 20 (2014) PARA 281.
2 See the Treasury Solicitor Act 1876 s 4 (amended by the Statute Law Revision Act 1963); the Treasury Solicitor Act 1876 s 5 (amended by the Statute Law (Repeals) Act 1986); the Administration of Estates Act 1925 s 30(4) (amended by the Statute Law (Repeals) Act 1981); and the Treasury Solicitor (Crown's Nominee) Rules 1997, SI 1997/2870. The Treasury Solicitor maintains with the Paymaster General at the Bank of England the Crown's Nominee Account into which all moneys received by or vested in the Treasury Solicitor under any administration are paid: r 3(1); Treasury Solicitor Act 1876 s 4(1). All sums payable by the Treasury Solicitor are to be paid out of this account by authorised orders of the Paymaster General: Treasury Solicitor (Crown's Nominee) Rules 1997, SI 1997/2870, r 3(2).
3 Administration of Estates Act 1925 s 30(3) (amended by the Administration of Justice Act 1970 s 54(3), Sch 11).
4 See the Treasury Solicitor Act 1876 s 2.
5 See the Treasury Solicitor Act 1876 s 2.

780. Proceedings by or against the Treasury Solicitor. Where the administration of the real and personal estate of any deceased person has been granted to the Treasury Solicitor[1] proceedings by or against him for the recovery of the real or personal estate or any part or share of it are of the same character and are instituted and carried on in the same manner and are subject to the same rules of law and equity (including in general the rules of limitation under the statutes of limitation[2] or otherwise) as if the administration had been granted to him as one of the persons interested in the deceased's estate[3].

Accordingly, if the Treasury Solicitor hands over assets of the intestate to the Crown, and next of kin subsequently establish their claim in time, he must account for the assets so parted with, together with interest[4]. If the monarch to whom the property is handed over is dead before the claim is established, the next of kin's right is against his successor[5].

1 See PARA 779. As to the Treasury Solicitor see CONSTITUTIONAL AND ADMINISTRATIVE LAW vol 20 (2014) PARA 281.

2 See especially the Limitation Act 1980; and LIMITATION PERIODS vol 68 (2016) PARA 901 et seq.

3 Administration of Estates Act 1925 s 30(1). Proceedings by or against the Crown in respect of real and personal estate are not to be instituted except subject to the same rules of law and equity subject to which a proceeding for the like purposes might be instituted by or against a subject: s 30(2) (amended by the Limitation Act 1939 s 34(4), Schedule). As to the periods of limitation applicable to actions claiming the real or personal estate of a deceased person, and for special provisions relating to the recovery of trust property see LIMITATION PERIODS vol 68 (2016) PARA 1138 et seq. As to the application of the Limitation Act 1980 to proceedings by or against the Crown see CROWN AND CROWN PROCEEDINGS vol 29 (2014) PARA 88; LIMITATION PERIODS vol 68 (2016) PARA 903. As to proceedings by or against the Crown generally see CROWN AND CROWN PROCEEDINGS vol 29 (2014) PARA 90 et seq. The Crown does not take an intestate's estate as trustee where it has been found that there are no next of kin: *Re Mason* [1929] 1 Ch 1, CA; *Re Blake, Re Minahan's Petition of Right* [1932] 1 Ch 54. See also *Re Diplock, Diplock v Wintle* [1948] Ch 465, [1948] 2 All ER 318, CA; on appeal sub nom *Ministry of Health v Simpson* [1951] AC 251, [1950] 2 All ER 1137, HL.

4 *A-G v Köhler* (1861) 9 HL Cas 654; *Partington v A-G* (1869) LR 4 HL 100; *Re Dewell, Edgar v Reynolds* (1858) 4 Drew 269. Where executors under an order in an action had paid certain personal estate to the Treasury Solicitor, who had not taken out administration, the Crown was not charged with interest: *Re Gosman* (1881) 17 ChD 771, CA.

5 *Re Mason* [1928] Ch 385 (affd on another point [1929] 1 Ch 1, CA), not following dicta in *A-G v Köhler* (1861) 9 HL Cas 654 at 672.

781. Proceedings against personal representative who hands property to the Crown. Where an estate is administered by an executor or administrator who hands over the balance to the Crown because he cannot discover any next of kin to the deceased, the next of kin are entitled to treat this as a breach of trust, and to proceed against him and make him responsible, but their right is against the executor or administrator personally, and not against the Treasury Solicitor unless the latter makes himself personally responsible[1].

1 See *Re Mason* [1928] Ch 385 at 399; affd [1939] 1 Ch 1, CA; *A-G v Köhler* (1861) 9 HL Cas 654 at 672. As to grants to and actions against the Treasury Solicitor see PARAS 779–780. As to the Treasury Solicitor see CONSTITUTIONAL AND ADMINISTRATIVE LAW vol 20 (2014) PARA 281.

782. Grant of letters of administration to solicitors of the Duchies of Lancaster and Cornwall. The duchies' right[1] to a grant was originally confined to bona vacantia situate within the duchy[2], but was extended in 1926 to the intestate's residuary estate as bona vacantia and in lieu of any right to escheat[3], but there is no provision entitling the duchies to property outside the confines of the duchy, whether real or personal, of an intestate dying resident within the duchy[4]. In such a case (and where the converse applies), separate grants to the

Treasury Solicitor and to the solicitor to the duchy would be appropriate, but the need for this is in practice obviated by agreement between the authorities in question[5].

The solicitor for the affairs of the Duchy of Lancaster[6], when applying for or obtaining administration of the estate of a deceased person, is not required to deliver any affidavit, statutory declaration, account, certificate or other statement verified on oath; in lieu of this he delivers a signed account or particulars of the estate of the deceased[7]. Upon any change in the holder of the office, the letters of administration, with all their incidents, vest in the Duchy solicitor for the time being without further grant[8]. The court has power to revoke the grant[9].

The solicitor of the Duchy of Cornwall is not exempted on applying for or obtaining administration from the requirement to deliver an affidavit, statutory declaration, account, certificate or other statement verified on oath as are the Treasury Solicitor and the solicitor for the affairs of the Duchy of Lancaster[10]. A new grant is required when the office of solicitor to the Duchy of Cornwall becomes vacant because he is not a corporation sole[11].

1 In the Non-Contentious Probate Rules 1987, SI 1987/2024, the 'Crown' includes the Crown in right of the Duchy of Lancaster and the Duke of Cornwall, and 'Treasury Solicitor' includes the solicitor for the affairs of the Duchy of Lancaster and the solicitor of the Duchy of Cornwall: see r 2(1); and PARA 769 notes 1–2. In the Administration of Estates Act 1925, 'Treasury Solicitor' includes only the solicitor for the affairs of the Duchy of Lancaster: see s 55(1)(xxv); and PARA 769 note 1. As to the Duchy of Lancaster see CROWN AND CROWN PROCEEDINGS vol 29 (2014) PARA 214 et seq; and as to the Duchy of Cornwall see CROWN AND CROWN PROCEEDINGS vol 29 (2014) PARA 232 et seq. As to grants to and actions against the Treasury Solicitor see PARAS 779–780.

2 The analogy is with the foreshore, felons' goods and treasure trove: *Dyke v Walford* (1846) 5 Moo PCC 434 at 480–481. As to bona vacantia see CROWN AND CROWN PROCEEDINGS vol 29 (2014) PARA 149 et seq.

3 Administration of Estates Act 1925 s 46(1)(vi). See also PARA 512; and CROWN AND CROWN PROCEEDINGS vol 29 (2014) PARAS 150–151, 154.

4 It is doubtful whether the concept of 'domicile' may be applied to any unit less than a sovereign state: see CONFLICT OF LAWS vol 19 (2011) PARA 336 et seq.

5 Such agreement also covers the case of duchy manors lying outside the confines of Cornwall, which are nevertheless strictly part of the Duchy of Cornwall: see CROWN AND CROWN PROCEEDINGS vol 29 (2014) PARA 245.

6 See the Duchy of Lancaster Act 1920 s 3(3); and the Administration of Estates Act 1925 s 30(4) (both amended by the Statute Law (Repeals) Act 1981). See also note 1.

7 See the Administration of Estates Act 1925 ss 30(3), 55(1)(xxv) (s 30(3) amended by the Administration of Justice Act 1970 s 54(3), Sch 11).

8 See the Treasury Solicitor Act 1876 s 2; applied by the Duchy of Lancaster Act 1920 s 3(3) (as amended: see note 6).

9 See the Treasury Solicitor Act 1876 s 2; applied by the Duchy of Lancaster Act 1920 s 3(3) (as amended: see note 6).

10 In the Administration of Justice Act 1925, the solicitor to the Duchy of Cornwall is not included in the definition of 'Treasury Solicitor': see note 1.

11 See Ing's Bona Vacantia 26.

(v) Trust Corporations and the Public Trustee

783. Grant of letters of administration to trust corporations. An application for a grant[1] to a trust corporation[2] must be made through one of its officers, who must depose in the oath[3] that the corporation is a statutory trust corporation[4] and that it has power to accept a grant[5]. Where the trust corporation is the holder of an official position[6], any officer whose name is included on a list filed with the senior district judge[7] of persons authorised to make affidavits and sign documents on behalf of the office holder may act as the officer through whom the holder of that official position applies for the grant[8]. In all other cases a certified copy of the resolution of the trust corporation authorising the officer to make the application must be lodged, or it must be deposed in the oath that such certified copy has been filed with the senior district judge, that the officer is identified in it by the position he holds, and that such resolution is still in force[9].

Where a trust corporation applies for a grant of administration otherwise than as a beneficiary or the attorney of some person, the consents of all persons entitled to a grant and of all persons interested in the deceased's residuary estate must be lodged with the application, unless the district judge[10] or registrar[11] directs that these consents be dispensed with on such terms, if any, as he thinks fit[12].

1 As to the meaning of 'grant' see PARA 631 note 7.
2 As to the meaning of 'trust corporation' see PARA 622 note 4. As to corporations other than trust corporations see PARA 622.
3 As to the meaning of 'oath' see PARA 728 note 2.
4 Ie a trust corporation within the meaning of the Senior Courts Act 1981 s 128 (as extended by the Law of Property (Amendment) Act 1926) (see PARA 622 note 4): see the Non-Contentious Probate Rules 1987, SI 1987/2024, rr 2(1), 36(1).
5 Non-Contentious Probate Rules 1987, SI 1987/2024, r 36(1). Where a trust corporation has been appointed as executor on terms and conditions specifically referred to as being in existence at the date of the will or of its republication as the case may be, provided that the oath contains a statement to the effect that nothing in these terms or conditions limits the corporation's power to take a full grant, it will not normally be necessary to produce them on the application: *Practice Direction* [1981] 2 All ER 1104. It is not necessary for the oath or grant to account for any change, following re-registration under the Companies Act 1980 (repealed: see now the Companies Act 2006 s 58; and COMPANIES vol 14 (2016) PARA 199), in the suffix to the name of the corporation, and evidence will not normally be required that the corporation has registered or re-registered under that Act: *Practice Direction* [1982] 1 All ER 384, [1982] 1 WLR 214.
6 For examples of official positions see PARA 622.
7 As to the meaning of 'senior district judge' see PARA 691 note 2.
8 Non-Contentious Probate Rules 1987, SI 1987/2024, r 36(2)(a) (r 36(2) amended by SI 1991/1876).
9 Non-Contentious Probate Rules 1987, SI 1987/2024, r 36(2)(b) (as amended: see note 8). See also PARA 622.
10 As to the meaning of 'district judge' see PARA 631 note 6.
11 As to the meaning of 'registrar' see PARA 631 note 7.
12 Non-Contentious Probate Rules 1987, SI 1987/2024, r 36(3) (amended by SI 1991/1876).

784. Grant of letters of administration to the Public Trustee. The Public Trustee[1] is equally entitled with any other person or class of persons to a grant of administration, whether general, or with the will annexed, or limited as to time or otherwise[2], but as between the Public Trustee and the surviving spouse or next of kin of the deceased, the latter are to be preferred, unless for good cause shown to the contrary[3]. The consent or citation of the Public Trustee is not required for the grant to any other person[4]. The Public Trustee is not required to give security[5].

The Public Trustee is entitled to apply for administration as a trust corporation[6], and may act as attorney for any person where the execution of any trust is involved[7]. Any executor or administrator who has obtained a grant of probate or letters of administration may, with the sanction of the court, transfer his powers to the Public Trustee[8].

1 The Public Trustee is a corporation sole with perpetual succession and an official seal, constituted by the Public Trustee Act 1906 s 1(2): see TRUSTS AND POWERS vol 98 (2013) PARA 207. In the wording of the grant the 'Public Trustee' should be so described. When the Public Trustee applies he must clear off executors in the usual manner and give notice to the residuary legatees and devisees or their representatives or to other persons entitled in priority: Instruction by Sir Gorell Barnes P, 27 March 1908. As to the Public Trustee generally see TRUSTS AND POWERS vol 98 (2013) PARA 206 et seq.

2 See the Public Trustee Act 1906 ss 6(1), 15; and TRUSTS AND POWERS vol 98 (2013) PARA 211. The Public Trustee is authorised to accept probate of letters of administration of any kind: see the Public Trustee Rules 1912, SR & O 1912/348, r 6(c); and TRUSTS AND POWERS vol 98 (2013) PARA 211.
3 See the Public Trustee Act 1906 s 6(1); and TRUSTS AND POWERS vol 98 (2013) PARA 211.
4 See the Public Trustee Act 1906 s 6(1); and TRUSTS AND POWERS vol 98 (2013) PARA 211.
5 See the Public Trustee Act 1906 s 11(4) (amended by the Administration of Estates Act 1971 s 12(2), (4), Sch 2 Pt II). He is subject, however, to the same liabilities and duties as if he had given security: see the Public Trustee Act 1906 s 11(4) (as so amended).
6 See the Senior Courts Act 1981 s 128; and PARAS 622, 783.
7 See the Public Trustee Rules 1912, SR & O 1912/348, r 6(b); and TRUSTS AND POWERS vol 98 (2013) PARA 209.
8 See the Public Trustee Act 1906 s 6(2); and TRUSTS AND POWERS vol 98 (2013) PARA 211.

785. Limitation of Public Trustee's powers. It is generally accepted that the Public Trustee cannot act as executor of a person domiciled abroad except in respect of a will of English land[1]. As regards his power to act as trustee the test is whether the trust is by declaration or implication an English trust[2].

Grants of administration have been made by order of the court, particularly in time of war, limited to collecting and preserving an estate; and also under the court's discretionary power[3], with wider powers; but in practice the Public Trustee is seldom willing to take a grant of representation where the deceased has died domiciled out of England[4].

1 As to the Public Trustee generally see TRUSTS AND POWERS vol 98 (2013) PARA 206 et seq. As to domicile generally see CONFLICT OF LAWS vol 19 (2011) PARA 336 et seq.
2 *Re Hewitt's Settlement, Hewitt v Hewitt* [1915] 1 Ch 228, where it was held that the Public Trustee has no power to accept the trusteeship of a foreign settlement. See also the Recognition of Trusts Act 1987; and CONFLICT OF LAWS vol 19 (2011) PARA 721 et seq.
3 See PARA 758.
4 See Tristram and Coote's Probate Practice (31st Edn) 9.73.

(vi) Creditors

786. Creditor's right to grant of letters of administration. If all persons entitled to a grant in priority[1] have been cleared off, a grant may be made to a creditor[2]. A creditor can only obtain a grant on the renunciation of the Treasury Solicitor[3].

Where there is a minority or a life interest, the grant must be made either to a trust corporation, with an individual, or to not less than two individuals[4], unless the estate is insolvent or the grant is made pending suit[5].

A creditor may be preferred to persons entitled to share in the estate by reason of insolvency or other special circumstances[6].

1 As to the order of priority see PARAS 768–769. See also PARA 787.
2 See the Non-Contentious Probate Rules 1987, SI 1987/2024, r 22(3); and PARA 769. See also PARA 790. Such a grant may be revoked if the creditor failed to make full disclosure of matters material to his application for a grant: see *Shephard v Wheeler* [2000] All ER (D) 19, (2000) Times, 15 February. As to the meaning of 'creditor' see PARA 787 and for the position where there is a grant with will annexed see PARA 790.
3 See the Non-Contentious Probate Rules 1987, SI 1987/2024, r 22(2), (3); and PARA 769. See also *Re Heerman* [1910] P 357. As to grants to the Treasury Solicitor see PARA 779.
4 See the Senior Courts Act 1981 s 114(2); and PARA 775. As to grants to corporations see PARAS 622, 783, 813.
5 As to these two exceptions or possible exceptions see PARA 775. As to insolvent estates generally see PARA 981 et seq.
6 See the Senior Courts Act 1981 s 116(1); and PARA 758. See note 2.

787. Meaning of 'creditor'. For the purpose of obtaining a grant a secured creditor[1], a surety who has paid off his deceased principal's debt[2] and the personal representative of a deceased creditor[3] are creditors. A creditor whose debt is statute-barred may have a grant[4]. It is not the practice to make a grant to a purchaser of a debt after the death[5], but a grant may be made to the trustee in bankruptcy of a creditor[6], or to the assignee of the trustee[7], or to the person who has paid the intestate's funeral expenses[8]. In a proper case an undertaker who pays expenses may take a grant as creditor[9], although he is not normally regarded as a creditor of the deceased[10].

1 *Roxburgh v Lambert* (1829) 2 Hag Ecc 557; *Re Godfrey* (1861) 2 Sw & Tr 133; *Re Lowe* (1898) 78 LT 566. As to a grant to a nominee of a company as creditor in respect of unpaid calls on shares see COMPANIES vol 15A (2016) PARA 1334.

2 *Williams v Jukes* (1864) 34 LJPM & A 60.

3 See the Non-Contentious Probate Rules 1987, SI 1987/2024, r 22(4); and PARA 769. See, however, PARAS 768, 790.

4 *Coombs v Coombs* (1866) LR 1 P & D 288. See also LIMITATION PERIODS vol 68 (2016) PARA 945.

5 *Baynes v Harrison* (1856) Dea & Sw 15; *Day v Thompson, Re Frampton* (1863) 3 Sw & Tr 169; *Re Coles, Macnin v Coles* (1863) 3 Sw & Tr 181. Cf *Re Cosh* (1909) 25 TLR 785.

6 *Downward v Dickinson, Re Chune* (1864) 3 Sw & Tr 564.

7 *Re Burdett* (1876) 1 PD 427.

8 *Newcombe v Beloe* (1867) LR 1 P & D 314; *Re Percy, Fairland v Percy* (1875) LR 3 P & D 217 at 222; *Re Fowler* (1852) 16 Jur 894.

9 See note 8.

10 An undertaker is a creditor of the personal representatives in their capacity as such and is therefore in a different position from a creditor to whom the deceased owed a debt in his lifetime. An undertaker cannot cite those entitled to take a grant as he is not next entitled in priority to take the grant. If the person entitled to apply for the grant refuses or neglects to apply, the undertaker may apply for a discretionary order under the Senior Courts Act 1981 s 116; see PARA 758 et seq.

(6) ADMINISTRATION WITH THE WILL ANNEXED

788. When grant will be made with will annexed. Administration with the will annexed[1] is granted in the following cases:

(1) where no executor has been appointed or the appointment is void for uncertainty[2], or the persons appointed executors predecease the testator;

(2) where the executors survive the testator but die before taking out probate[3];

(3) where the executors are cited to take out probate and do not appear to the citation[4];

(4) where the executors renounce probate of the will[5]; and

(5) where the court exercises its discretion by passing over an executor[6].

Where a sole or last surviving executor dies intestate without having fully administered, administration is granted with the will annexed de bonis non. Special considerations apply to this form of grant[7].

1 Subject to and in accordance with the probate rules (see PARA 620 note 6) administration with the will annexed continues to be granted in every case in which the High Court had power to make such a grant before 1982: Senior Courts Act 1981 s 119(1). Where administration with the will annexed is granted, the will is to be performed and observed in the same manner as if probate of it had been granted to an executor: s 119(2). As to the meaning of 'administration' see PARA 622 note 8; and as to the meaning of 'will' see PARA 620 note 4. For the provisions of the Administration of Estates Act 1925 ss 22, 23 relating to special executors in the case of settled land see PARAS 629, 821 et seq. As to special cases see PARA 789.

Administration with the will annexed is sometimes called 'administration cum testamento annexo'.

2 See PARA 611.

3 Administration of Estates Act 1925 s 5(i).

4 Administration of Estates Act 1925 s 5(ii). An executor cannot appear to a citation and consent to a grant to another of administration with the will annexed; he must withdraw his appearance: *Garrard v Garrard* (1871) LR 2 P & D 238. Where the executor is believed to be living, but has disappeared, a grant may be made to a beneficiary without citation of or notice to the executor: *Re Crawshay* [1893] P 108; *Re Massey* [1899] P 270; *Re Wright* (1898) 79 LT 473; *Re Williams* [1918] P 122 (absconding executor not cited; grant to legatee); *Re Leguia* [1934] P 80 (grant despite non-citation of executor, who failed to act in regard to insolvent).

5 Administration of Estates Act 1925 s 5(iii).

6 See the Senior Courts Act 1981 s 116; and PARA 758. A grant of administration with the will annexed may also be made where the executor is a minor, or suffering from mental disorder, or out of the jurisdiction, but it is usual to make a grant for his use and benefit: see PARA 795 et seq.

7 As to administration de bonis non see PARA 793 et seq.

789. Special cases requiring letters of administration with will annexed. In certain special cases it may also be necessary to make a grant with the will annexed, as where the appointment of his executor is directed by the testator not to take effect until after an interval of time[1], or where there is a will containing a valid execution of a power, but not made in conformity with the laws of the testator's domicile[2].

1 *Graysbrook v Fox* (1564) 1 Plowd 275 at 279. As to conditional appointments see PARA 617.

2 *Re Huber* [1896] P 209; *Re Vannini* [1901] P 330, explaining *Re Hallyburton* (1866) LR 1 P & D 90; *Re Tréfond* [1899] P 247. See also *Re Poole, Poole v Poole* [1919] P 10 (grant where will was avoided except as to exercise of power). As to domicile generally see CONFLICT OF LAWS vol 19 (2011) PARA 336 et seq.

790. Persons to whom grant made with will annexed. The persons entitled to a grant[1] in respect of a will are determined in accordance with the following order of priority[2]:

(1) the executor[3];

(2) any residuary legatee or devisee holding in trust for any other person[4];

(3) any other residuary legatee or devisee (including one for life) or where the residue is not wholly disposed of by the will, any person entitled to share in the undisposed of residue (including the Treasury Solicitor when claiming bona vacantia on behalf of the Crown)[5];

(4) the personal representative of any residuary legatee or devisee (but not one for life, or one holding in trust for any other person), or of any person entitled to share in any residue not disposed of by the will[6];

(5) any other legatee or devisee (including one for life or one holding in trust for any other person) or any creditor of the deceased[7]; and

(6) the personal representative of any other legatee or devisee (but not one for life or one holding in trust for any other person) or of any creditor of the deceased[8].

Provision is made for cases where two or more persons are entitled in the same degree[9]. Where all the persons entitled to the estate (whether under a will or on intestacy) have assigned their whole interest to one or more persons, the assignees replace, in the order of priority for a grant, the assignor or, if there are two or more assignors, the assignor with the highest priority[10]. A copy of the instrument of assignment must be lodged[11]. Where a gift to any person fails because the donee or his or her spouse or civil partner is an attesting witness[12] such person has no right to a grant as a beneficiary named in the will, without prejudice to his right to a grant in any other capacity[13].

1 As to the meaning of 'grant' see PARA 631 note 7. As to probate grants see PARA 724 et seq. This applies where the deceased died on or after 1 January 1926: see the Non-Contentious Probate Rules 1987, SI 1987/2024, r 20.

2 See the Non-Contentious Probate Rules 1987, SI 1987/2024, r 20. Rule 20 does not operate to prevent a grant being made to any person to whom a grant may or may be required to be made

under any enactment: r 28(1). Rule 20 also does not apply (except where probate is granted to an executor named, or according to the tenor (see PARA 718)), or where the whole estate in England and Wales consists of immovables and a grant is made limited to those (see PARA 844)) where the deceased died domiciled outside England and Wales: r 28(2). As to settled land grants see PARA 821 et seq.

3 Non-Contentious Probate Rules 1987, SI 1987/2024, r 20(a), which is expressed to be subject to r 36(4)(d) (see PARA 813). As to executors' rights to probate see PARA 725.

4 Non-Contentious Probate Rules 1987, SI 1987/2024, r 20(b).

5 Non-Contentious Probate Rules 1987, SI 1987/2024, r 20(c). However, unless a district judge or registrar otherwise directs, a residuary legatee or devisee whose legacy or devise is vested in interest is preferred to one entitled on the happening of a contingency: r 20(c) proviso (i) (amended by SI 1991/1876). In addition, where the residue is not in terms wholly disposed of, the district judge or registrar may, if satisfied that the testator has nevertheless disposed of the whole or substantially the whole of the known estate, allow a grant to be made to any legatee or devisee entitled to, or to a share in, the estate so disposed of, without regard to the persons entitled to share in any residue not disposed of by the will: Non-Contentious Probate Rules 1987, SI 1987/2024, r 20(c) proviso (ii). As to the meaning of 'district judge' see PARA 631 note 6; and as to the meaning of 'registrar' see PARA 631 note 7. As to the Treasury Solicitor see PARA 778 et seq.

6 Non-Contentious Probate Rules 1987, SI 1987/2024, r 20(d).

7 Non-Contentious Probate Rules 1987, SI 1987/2024, r 20(e). However, unless a district judge or registrar otherwise directs, a legatee or devisee whose legacy or devise is vested in interest is preferred to one entitled on the happening of a contingency: r 20(e) proviso (amended by SI 1991/1876). As to creditors see PARA 786 et seq.

8 Non-Contentious Probate Rules 1987, SI 1987/2024, r 20(f).

9 See the Non-Contentious Probate Rules 1987, SI 1987/2024, r 27; and PARA 774. As to joint grants see PARA 775.

10 See the Non-Contentious Probate Rules 1987, SI 1987/2024, r 24(1); and PARA 769. Where there are two or more assignees, the grant may, with the others' consent, be made to any one or more (not exceeding four) of them: see r 24(2); and PARA 769.

11 See the Non-Contentious Probate Rules 1987, SI 1987/2024, r 24(3); and PARA 769.

12 Ie under the Wills Act 1837 s 15 (see PARA 41): see the Non-Contentious Probate Rules 1987, SI 1987/2024, r 21.

13 Non-Contentious Probate Rules 1987, SI 1987/2024, r 21; Civil Partnership Act 2004 Sch 4, paras 1, 3.

791. Testamentary instrument merely revoking prior will. Where a testator has revoked his will by a duly executed testamentary paper, and has died without making any disposition of his property, the grant will normally go as on an intestacy without annexing any testamentary paper[1].

1 *Toomer v Sobinska* [1907] P 106, departing from the form of grant in *Re Durance* (1872) LR 2 P & D 406. See also *Re Irvine* [1919] 2 IR 485; and PARA 707.

792. Necessity for second grant. A second grant of administration is necessary where a grant has been made with the will annexed for the benefit of a mentally incapable executor[1] and the executor dies, or where it has been made to the attorney of two executors and one of them dies[2]. In the latter case, before a grant is made to the attorney of any surviving executor, notice must, unless dispensed with by the district judge or registrar, be given to any surviving co-executors[3]. The grant is made for the use and benefit of the executor and is limited until further representation is granted or in such other way as the district judge or registrar directs[4].

1 See PARA 804.

2 See the Non-Contentious Probate Rules 1987, SI 1987/2024, r 31; and PARA 800. The death of a joint principal normally terminates the power: see eg *Graham v Jackson* (1845) 6 QB 811; *Life Association of Scotland v Douglas* (1886) 13 R 910, Ct of Sess; but see the Powers of Attorney Act 1971 s 5(1); (in relation to lasting powers of attorney) the Mental Capacity Act 2005 s 14(5); and AGENCY vol 1 (2008) PARA 193. It seems that where a grant of representation has been obtained on the authority of the power, the effect of the death will depend on the terms of the grant. Accordingly, a grant to the attorney of named principals 'as their lawful attorney' would cease to have effect upon the death of one of them. See also *Re Dinshaw* [1930] P 180, where the surviving

executor appointed fresh attorneys and the court revoked the original grant and made a fresh grant to the fresh attorneys. See further Tristram and Coote's Probate Practice (31st Edn) 11.86.

3 See the Non-Contentious Probate Rules 1987, SI 1987/2024, r 31(2); and PARA 800. As to the meaning of 'district judge' see PARA 631 note 6; and as to the meaning of 'registrar' see PARA 631 note 7. Where the attorney administrator of one of two persons equally entitled to a grant has died the attorney of the other will be appointed on proof of notice to the person whose attorney has died: *Re Barton* [1898] P 11.

4 See the Non-Contentious Probate Rules 1987, SI 1987/2024, r 31(1); and PARA 800.

(7) SPECIAL AND LIMITED GRANTS OF ADMINISTRATION

(i) Unadministered Estate

793. Grant de bonis non. Where a sole or last surviving executor or administrator to whom a grant has been made dies without having fully administered the deceased's estate and the chain of representation does not apply[1], it is accordingly necessary to appoint, under a second grant, an administrator to administer the property of the original deceased left unadministered[2]. This second grant is a grant of administration de bonis non administratis (that is, 'for unadministered goods')[3]. If the original deceased left a will, such that the first grant was either of probate or with will annexed, the second grant is referred to as cum testamento annexe de bonis non administratis.

Where the will of the original testator has been proved abroad and the executor dies without proving it in England, the latter's executor, even though he proves his own testator's will in England, does not then become the representative of the original testator; he must obtain a grant of administration in respect of the original testator's estate in England[4]. Where an executor has acted and dies intestate without having obtained probate, the grant of administration made to the testator's estate is a first simple grant with the will annexed[5] and not a grant de bonis non[6].

A de bonis non grant will also be made where a sole or last surviving executor or administrator becomes incapable of acting[7]. The court also has power to appoint an administrator for unadministered estate where the original administrator has disappeared[8].

The applicant for administration de bonis non must prepare the usual inheritance tax account and take the oath[9].

1 As to the chain of representation see PARA 637 et seq. Administration is complete only after debts and legacies have been paid, accounts prepared and any land or other assets remaining in the estate have been vested in those beneficially entitled by means of assents. As to payment of debts see PARA 966 et seq; as to payment of legacies and distribution of assets generally see PARA 118 et seq; and as to assents see PARA 1139 et seq.

2 See 2 Bl Com (14th Edn) 506. A de bonis non grant cannot be made following the death of one of a number of executors or administrators to whom a grant has been made, nor is it necessary, because the survivors have full power to complete the administration. Where, after advertisement without result, the sole or surviving executor has paid the unclaimed residue of an estate to the Crown as bona vacantia this residue does not form part of the unadministered estate and the administrator de bonis non has as such no title to it: *Re Aldhous, Noble v Treasury Solicitor* [1955] 2 All ER 80, [1955] 1 WLR 459. As to the Crown's right to bona vacantia see PARA 778.

3 The phrase 'de bonis non' is not strictly accurate since the grant covers land as well as goods. The phrase 'unadministered estate' may be more appropriate and is here used interchangeably with the more colloquial 'de bonis non'. A de bonis non grant differs from a cessate (or second grant) in that although the latter is also only necessary where part of the estate is still unadministered, the latter is a re-grant to the whole estate whereas the former is a grant to that part which is unadministered. See PARA 752.

4 *Re Gaynor* (1869) LR 1 P & D 723.

5 See PARA 788.
6 *Wankford v Wankford* (1704) 1 Salk 299 at 308.
7 Ie no longer has capacity within the meaning of the Mental Capacity Act 2005: see MENTAL HEALTH AND CAPACITY vol 75 (2013) PARA 601. In this case, the original grant is not revoked and the new grant will be a grant de bonis non for the use and benefit of the incapable grantee, limited during his incapacity except that if the new grantee is an executor to whom power has been reserved, an ordinary grant of double probate will issue with a note referring to the incapacity of the other proving, or sole surviving proving, executor. As to 'power reserved' see PARA 729 and as to 'double probate' see PARA 751. See also PARA 807. As to where one of several proving executors or administrators loses the mental capacity to act see PARA 850 note 1.
8 *Re Saker* [1909] P 233; *Re French* [1910] P 169.
9 See the Senior Courts Act 1981 s 109(1); and PARA 731. The estate is sworn at the value of what remains unadministered at the time. Where inheritance tax in respect of the full value of the estate was paid in the first instance, no further tax is payable. See Tristram and Coote's Probate Practice (31st Edn) 13.59–13.80; and INHERITANCE TAXATION vol 59A (2014) PARA 275.

794. Rights of preference observed. In making a grant for unadministered estate[1] the court has regard to the same rights of preference by which an original grant is regulated, and accordingly follows the general practice of making the grant to those who have the greatest interest[2].

A grant for the unadministered estate (with the will annexed if appropriate) is made to the person entitled in the order of priority previously explained[3], and the court may at its discretion dispense with formal notice to an executor who has expressed his intention not to act further[4]. A de bonis non grant will not be made to the legal personal representative of a minor or other beneficiary under the statutory trusts in respect of any undisposed of property, unless the beneficiary has attained an absolutely vested interest[5].

1 See PARA 793 notes 1, 3.
2 *Savage v Blythe* (1796) 2 Hag Ecc App 150; *Almes v Almes* (1796) 2 Hag Ecc App 155; *Re Carr* (1867) LR 1 P & D 291; *Re Griffiths, Morgan v Stephens* [1917] P 59 (interest suit). See also PARAS 768, 790.
3 See PARA 768 for the order where the original deceased died intestate and PARA 790 for the order where the original deceased left a will.
4 *Re Campion* [1900] P 13.
5 Ie by reaching 18, or marrying or entering into a civil partnership before the age of 18: see PARA 499.

(ii) Administration during Minority of Person Entitled

795. Grants on behalf of minors. Where the person to whom a grant[1] would otherwise be made[2] is a minor, administration for his use and benefit limited until he attains the age of 18[3] must[4], unless otherwise directed, and subject to the overriding power set out below[5] and to the right of a residuary beneficiary[6] be granted[7] to:

(1) a parent of the minor who has or is deemed to have parental responsibility for him[8];
(2) a person who has or is deemed to have parental responsibility for the minor[9];
(3) a step parent of the minor who has parental responsibility for him[10];
(4) a guardian of the minor[11];
(5) a special guardian of the minor who has been so appointed[12];
(6) an adoption agency which has parental responsibility[13]; or
(7) a local authority which has or is deemed to have parental responsibility for the minor[14].

Where the minor is sole executor and has no interest in the residuary estate of the deceased, administration for the use and benefit of the minor limited until he attains the age of 18, unless a district judge[15] or registrar[16] otherwise directs, must be granted to the person entitled to the residuary estate[17]. A district judge or registrar has, however, an overriding power to order the appointment of a person to obtain administration for the use and benefit of the minor, limited until he attains the age of 18, in default of, or jointly with, or to the exclusion of, any person mentioned in heads (1) to (7) above[18]. Where there is only one person competent and willing to take a grant[19], such person may, unless a district judge or registrar otherwise directs, nominate any fit and proper person to act jointly with him in taking the grant[20].

The right of a minor executor to probate on attaining the age of 18 years may not be renounced by any person on his behalf[21]. The right of a minor to administration may be renounced only by a person appointed and authorised to renounce on behalf of the minor by a district judge or registrar[22].

1 As to the meaning of 'grant' see PARA 631 note 7.
2 Ie either as sole executor or as administrator. For the statutory provisions as to administration during the minority of an executor see PARA 620. For the principle that an adult has a prior right where more than one person is entitled see PARA 774.
3 An executor who is a minor is entitled to probate when he comes of age: see PARA 620.
4 It seems that this provision is subject to the court's discretionary power to appoint some person other than the person by law entitled: see PARA 758; and cf *Re Stewart (or Stuart)* (1875) LR 3 P & D 244, where administration was granted to persons who by a will were appointed trustees on behalf of an executor who was a minor and a beneficiary.
5 Ie subject to the Non-Contentious Probate Rules 1987, SI 1987/2024, r 32(2) (see note 15): see r 32(1).
6 Ie subject to the Non-Contentious Probate Rules 1987, SI 1987/2024, r 32(1) proviso: see note 14.
7 Non-Contentious Probate Rules 1987, SI 1987/2024, r 32(1). For the evidence required in support of an application for a grant on behalf of a minor see *Practice Direction* [1991] 4 All ER 562, [1991] 1 WLR 1069.
8 Non-Contentious Probate Rules 1987, SI 1987/2024, r 32(1)(a) (substituted by SI 1991/1876). A parent has, or is deemed to have, parental responsibility in accordance with the Children Act 1989 s 2(1), 2(1A), 2(2), 2(2A), or 4 or 4ZA, s 108(6), Sch 14 para 4 or 6, or an adoption order within the meaning of the Adoption Act 1976 s 12(1) or the Adoption and Children Act 2002 s 46(1): Non-Contentious Probate Rules 1987, SI 1987/2024, r 32(1)(a) (as so substituted; and amended by SI 2005/3504; SI 2009/1893). As to parental responsibility see CHILDREN AND YOUNG PERSONS vol 9 (2012) PARA 150 et seq.
9 Non-Contentious Probate Rules 1987, SI 1987/2024, r 32(1)(aa) (added by SI 1998/1903). A person has parental responsibility by virtue of the Children Act 1989 s 12(2) where the court has made a child arrangements order under s 8 which names that person as a person with whom the minor is to live (see CHILDREN AND YOUNG PERSONS vol 9 (2012) PARA 287): see the Non-Contentious Probate Rules 1987, SI 1987/2024, r 32(1)(aa) (as so added; amended by SI 2014/852).
10 Non-Contentious Probate Rules 1987, SI 1987/2024, r 32(1)(ab) (added by SI 2005/3504). This applies to a step parent who has parental responsibility in accordance with the Children Act 1989 s 4A (see CHILDREN AND YOUNG PERSONS vol 9 (2012) PARA 158): see the Non-Contentious Probate Rules 1987, SI 1987/2024, r 32(1)(ab) (as so added).
11 Non-Contentious Probate Rules 1987, SI 1987/2024, r 32(1)(b) (substituted by SI 1991/1876; and amended by SI 1998/1903). This applies to a guardian who is appointed or deemed to have been appointed in accordance with the Children Act 1989 s 5 or Sch 14 para 12, 13 or 14 (see CHILDREN AND YOUNG PERSONS vol 9 (2012) PARA 162 et seq): see the Non-Contentious Probate Rules 1987, SI 1987/2024, r 32(1)(b) (as so substituted and amended).
12 Non-Contentious Probate Rules 1987, SI 1987/2024, r 32(1)(ba) (added by SI 2005/3504). This applies to a special guardian who is appointed in accordance with the Children Act 1989 s 14A (see CHILDREN AND YOUNG PERSONS vol 9 (2012) PARA 305): see the Non-Contentious Probate Rules 1987, SI 1987/2024. r 32(1)(ba) (as so added).
13 Non-Contentious Probate Rules 1987, SI 1987/2024, r 32(1)(bb) (added by SI 2005/3504). This applies to an adoption agency which has parental responsibility by virtue of the Adoption and Children Act 2002 s 25(2) (see CHILDREN AND YOUNG PERSONS vol 9 (2012) PARA 371): see the Non-Contentious Probate Rules 1987, SI 1987/2024, r 32(1)(bb) (as so added).
14 Non-Contentious Probate Rules 1987, SI 1987/2024, r 32(1)(c) (added by SI 1998/1903). A local authority has parental responsibility by virtue of the Children Act 1989 s 33(3) where the court has

made a care order under s 31(1)(a) in respect of the minor and that local authority is designated in that order (see CHILDREN AND YOUNG PERSONS vol 9 (2012) PARA 318 et seq): see the Non-Contentious Probate Rules 1987, SI 1987/2024, r 32(1)(c) (as so added).

15 As to the meaning of 'district judge' see PARA 631 note 6.

16 As to the meaning of 'registrar' see PARA 631 note 7.

17 Non-Contentious Probate Rules 1987, SI 1987/2024, r 32(1) proviso (amended by SI 1991/1876).

18 Non-Contentious Probate Rules 1987, SI 1987/2024, r 32(2) (substituted by SI 1991/1876). Application for such an order may be made ex parte (see PARA 703) by the intended appointee, who must file a supporting affidavit: see the Non-Contentious Probate Rules 1987, SI 1987/2024, r 32(2) (as so substituted). The right of a minor to administration may be renounced only by a person appointed under r 32(2) and authorised by the district judge or registrar to renounce on behalf of the minor: r 34(2) (amended by SI 1991/1876).

19 Ie under the Non-Contentious Probate Rules 1987, SI 1987/2024, r 32: see r 32(3) (as amended: see note 20).

20 Non-Contentious Probate Rules 1987, SI 1987/2024, r 32(3) (amended by SI 1991/1876).

21 Non-Contentious Probate Rules 1987, SI 1987/2024, r 34(1). As to the appointment of a minor as co-executor see PARA 798.

22 Non-Contentious Probate Rules 1987, SI 1987/2024, r 34(2) (amended by SI 1991/1876). The person so authorised must be appointed under the Non-Contentious Probate Rules 1987, SI 1987/2024, r 32(2): see note 18.

796. Limit of grant. The administration during minority determines upon the coming of age of the minor or of any one of several minors for whose use and benefit the grant was made[1]. It does not determine upon the death of one of several minors[2], but if the guardian dies during their minority a second grant becomes necessary[3]. Except in point of time there is no other limit to the administration[4].

1 See PARAS 795–798.

2 *Jones v Earl of Strafford* (1730) 3 P Wms 79 at 89. A fresh grant is necessary on the coming of age of the minor. As to cessate grants see PARA 752. If all the minors for the use and benefit of whom the grant has been made die before reaching the age of 18 the grant ceases, and a grant of administration de bonis non becomes necessary. As to grants de bonis non see PARA 793.

3 See PARA 752.

4 *Re Cope, Cope v Cope* (1880) 16 ChD 49; *Monsell v Armstrong* (1872) LR 14 Eq 423; *Re Thompson and M'Williams' Contract* [1896] 1 IR 356.

797. Administrator's liability to account. On his coming of age the minor is entitled to call for an account from the administrator, even though his administration may previously have been revoked and his successor in office may have released him[1]. If the minor renounces on coming of age, the person who is then appointed administrator is in a position to call for an account[2]. During his term of office a judgment for administration may be made against an administrator during minority[3].

1 1 Roll Abr 910, Executor (M), pl 3. As to revocation see PARA 847 et seq.

2 *Taylor v Newton* (1752) 1 Lee 15.

3 *Re Taylor, Sewell v Ransford* (1873) 21 WR 244. See PARA 1162 et seq.

798. Minor appointed co-executor with adult. Where a minor is appointed executor jointly with one or more other executors, probate may be granted to the executor or executors not under disability, with power reserved to the minor executor and the minor executor is entitled to apply for probate on attaining the age of 18 years[1]. Administration for the use and benefit of a minor executor until he attains the age of 18 years may be granted[2] if, and only if, the executors who are not under disability renounce or, on being cited to accept or refuse a grant, fail to make an effective application for it[3]. The right of a minor executor to probate on attaining the age of 18 may not be renounced by any person on his behalf[4]. A minor executor to whom power is reserved will not be liable for the acts of his co-executors until he takes out probate[5].

1 Non-Contentious Probate Rules 1987, SI 1987/2024, r 33(1).

2 Ie under the Non-Contentious Probate Rules 1987, SI 1987/2024, r 32 (see PARAS 795–799): see r 33(2).
3 Non-Contentious Probate Rules 1987, SI 1987/2024, r 33(2).
4 Non-Contentious Probate Rules 1987, SI 1987/2024, r 34(1).
5 *Russel's Case* (1584) 5 Co Rep 27a; *Whitmore v Weld* (1685) 1 Vern 326 at 328; *Cummins v Cummins* (1845) 3 Jo & Lat 64.

799. Necessity for two administrators. Where two administrators are necessary because of a minority or life interest[1] and there is only one person competent and willing to take a grant during minority, he may nominate a fit and proper person as his co-administrator and, unless a district judge or registrar otherwise directs, joint administration will be granted to them[2].

1 Ie by virtue of the Senior Courts Act 1981 s 114(2): see PARA 775.
2 See the Non-Contentious Probate Rules 1987, SI 1987/2024, r 32(3) (amended by SI 1991/1876); and PARA 795. A summons is not normally needed in this case: see PARA 776. As to the meaning of 'district judge' see PARA 631 note 6; and as to the meaning of 'registrar' see PARA 631 note 7.

(iii) Administration by Attorneys and Consular Officers

800. Grants to attorneys. The lawfully constituted attorney of a person entitled to a grant[1] may apply for administration for the use and benefit of the donor, and such grant is limited until further representation is granted, or in such other way as the district judge[2] or registrar[3] may direct[4]. Where the donor is an executor, notice of the application must be given to any other executor unless such notice is dispensed with by the district judge or registrar[5]. Where the donor lacks mental capacity[6] and the attorney is acting under an enduring power of attorney or a lasting power of attorney, provision is made for an application by the attorney[7].

Where an attorney administrator seeks a concurrent grant in another estate in his capacity of personal representative, this further grant will not be issued without inspection of the power of attorney. A power in general terms appointing the attorney for all purposes will be accepted as establishing his right to apply for the further grant; but if the power is a limited one confined to obtaining the first grant, a further power extending the attorney's duties to obtaining the further grant will be required[8].

1 As to the meaning of 'grant' see PARA 631 note 7.
2 As to the meaning of 'district judge' see PARA 631 note 6.
3 As to the meaning of 'registrar' see PARA 631 note 7.
4 Non-Contentious Probate Rules 1987, SI 1987/2024, r 31(1) (amended by SI 1991/1876). A substituted attorney will be accepted, if substitution is authorised by the power, or by the laws of the domicile of the creator of the power: *Re Abdul Hamid Bey* (1898) 67 LJP 59. A general power executed during the testator's lifetime has been held sufficient: *Re Barker* [1891] P 251; cf *Re Cassidy* (1832) 4 Hag Ecc 360. It does not exclude the claims of other persons entitled: *Anstruther v Chalmer* (1826) 2 Sim 1. See also *Re Rendell, Wood v Rendell* [1901] 1 Ch 230; *Re Boyd* (1912) 46 ILT 294. Where a grant has been made to the attorney of a person entrusted with administration of the estate or entitled to administer the estate of a person who has died domiciled abroad and the donor of the power of attorney subsequently applies for a grant to himself, a further order is necessary, and it must be shown by affidavit that he is the person at that time entrusted with the administration by the foreign court, or that he is still entitled by the law of the foreign country to administer the estate: *Practice Direction* [1953] 2 All ER 1154, [1953] 1 WLR 1237.
5 Non-Contentious Probate Rules 1987, SI 1987/2024, r 31(2) (amended by SI 1991/1876).
6 Ie within the meaning of the Mental Capacity Act 2005 Pt 1; see PARA 804 note 4.
7 Non-Contentious Probate Rules 1987, SI 1987/2024, r 31(3) (substituted by SI 2007/1898). Provision is made under the Non-Contentious Probate Rules 1987, SI 1987/2024, r 35 (see PARAS 804–805): see r 31(3) (as so substituted). The Mental Capacity Act 2005 replaced enduring powers of attorney with lasting powers of attorney with effect from 1 October 2007: see MENTAL HEALTH AND CAPACITY vol 75 (2013) PARA 618. However, such enduring powers of attorney

that were executed before that date may be registered after that date: see Sch 4; and AGENCY vol 1 (2008) PARA 194 et seq. The oath should confirm that the donor remains mentally capable or is not mentally incapable and that the Public Guardian has not registered the power: see Tristram and Coote's Probate Practice (31st Edn) 11.42. If the power has been registered the application for the grant must be made under Non-Contentious Probate Rules 1987, SI 1987/2024, r 35 (see PARAS 804–805). On or after 1 October 2007 a donor may execute an instrument intended to create a property and affairs lasting power of attorney or/and an instrument intended to create a personal welfare lasting power of attorney: see Tristram and Coote's Probate Practice (31st Edn) 11.44. Of these, only a lasting power of attorney in respect of property and (financial) affairs may be used for the purpose of obtaining a grant for the use and benefit of the donor: see Tristram and Coote's Probate Practice (31st Edn) 11.44. A lasting power of attorney is not created and therefore unusable until the Public Guardian registers it irrespective of whether the donor lacks capacity within the meaning of the Mental Capacity Act 2005 or not (see note 6): see Tristram and Coote's Probate Practice (31st Edn) 11.44. An application that relies upon a registered lasting power of attorney should include a statement in the oath that the donor does not lack capacity within the meaning of the Mental Capacity Act 2005 to manage his property and affairs and that the registered lasting power of attorney has not been revoked nor has the donee disclaimed his appointment: see Tristram and Coote's Probate Practice (31st Edn) 11.44. For meaning of 'oath' see PARA 728 note 2. As to enduring powers of attorney and lasting powers of attorney generally see AGENCY vol 1 (2008) PARAS 194–238.

8 *Practice Direction* [1957] 1 All ER 602, [1957] 1 WLR 464.

801. Requirements for grant to attorney administrators. The attorney need not necessarily be resident in England and Wales[1], and residence abroad may be accepted[2]. An informal document clearly purporting to authorise the applicant to apply for the grant may be accepted[3]. If the original is a general power of attorney it may be withdrawn from the registry after grant provided an examined copy is lodged before withdrawal.

A grant cannot be made to a single person as attorney if there is a minority, or if a life interest arises under the will or intestacy, even though a sole executor as such would be entitled to probate[4]. In all such cases two attorneys or a trust corporation, with or without an individual in addition, must be appointed to obtain the grant[5].

If the grant is made to the attorneys of one only of several executors, it is limited until the principal or any one of the other executors applies for probate[6]. On the death of the principal, or on any other event which would operate as a revocation of the power of attorney, such a grant ceases to be effective[7]. For this reason an administrator under such a grant has been held to be unable to make a title to property such as a purchaser was bound to accept[8].

1 *Re Leeson* (1859) 1 Sw & Tr 463.

2 *Re Reed* (1864) 3 Sw & Tr 439; *Re Ballingall* (1863) 3 Sw & Tr 441n.

3 *Re Elderton* (1832) 4 Hag Ecc 210 (memorandum); *Re Ormond* (1828) 1 Hag Ecc 145; *Re Boyle* (1864) 3 Sw & Tr 426 per Lord Penzance. The Powers of Attorney Act 1971 s 1 provides that, without prejudice to any requirement in, or having effect under, any other Act as to the witnessing of instruments creating powers of attorney, an instrument creating a power of attorney must be executed as a deed by the donor of the power: see the Powers of Attorney Act 1971 s 1(1), (3); AGENCY vol 1 (2008) PARA 16; and Tristram and Coote's Probate Practice (31st Edn) 11.45. If signed by another person on behalf of the donor two other persons must be present as witnesses and must attest the instrument: see the Law of Property (Miscellaneous Provisions) Act 1989 s 1(3); AGENCY vol 1 (2008) PARA 15; and Tristram and Coote's Probate Practice (31st Edn) 11.45. As to the requirements for a valid enduring power of attorney or lasting power of attorney see PARA 800 note 7 and Tristram and Coote's Probate Practice (31st Edn) at 11.42 et seq.

4 See the Senior Courts Act 1981 s 114(2); and PARA 775.

5 Ie under the Senior Courts Act 1981 s 114(2): see PARA 775.

6 *Re Black* (1887) 13 PD 5. No grant will be made without notice to the other executors, but the district judge or registrar may dispense with such notice: see PARA 800.

7 *Webb v Kirby* (1856) 7 De GM & G 376.

8 *Webb v Kirby* (1856) 7 De GM & G 376 (a grant de bonis non then becomes necessary: see PARA 793); *Taynton v Hannay* (1802) 3 Bos & P 26. As to the effect of the death of one of joint

principals see PARA 792 note 2. Persons dealing with such an administrator can, it seems, take advantage of the provisions of the Powers of Attorney Act 1971 s 5: see AGENCY vol 1 (2008) PARA 193.

802. Grant to consular officer as if to attorney. In cases in which a national of a foreign state to which the statutory provisions[1] have been applied by Order in Council[2] is named as executor in the will of a deceased person disposing of property in England, or is otherwise a person to whom a grant of representation to the estate in England of a deceased person may be made, then if the court is satisfied, on the application of a consular officer of the foreign state, that the foreign national is not resident in England and, if no application for a grant of representation is made by a person duly authorised by power of attorney to act for him in that behalf, the court must make to the applicant consular officer any such grant of representation to the estate of the deceased as would be made to the consular officer if he were duly authorised by power of attorney to apply for it[3]. The court, however, if it thinks fit, may postpone the making of the grant during such period as it considers appropriate having regard to the circumstances of the case[4]. Such a grant of representation may be made to the consular officer alone notwithstanding that a minority or life interest may be involved[5], and sureties are not required[6]. The grant may be made to the consular officer by his official title and to his successors in office; and in such a case all the office of administrator and all the estate, rights, duties and liabilities of the administrator are vested in and imposed on the person for the time being holding the office[7].

No fresh grant can be required by reason only of the death or vacation of office of the person to whom the grant was made or in whom it is vested[8], but this provision does not affect any limitation contained in the grant, or any power of the court to revoke the grant[9].

1 Ie the Consular Conventions Act 1949 s 1: see the text to notes 3–9; and PARA 667.
2 The following Consular Conventions Orders applying the Consular Conventions Act 1949 s 1 have been made under s 6 (which allows s 1 to be applied by order to any foreign state with which a consular convention providing for matters for which provision is made by s 1 has been concluded): the Consular Conventions (Kingdom of Norway) Order in Council 1951, SI 1951/1165; the Consular Conventions (Kingdom of Sweden) Order 1952, SI 1952/1218; the Consular Conventions (Kingdom of Greece) Order 1953, SI 1953/1454; the Consular Conventions (French Republic) Order 1953, SI 1953/1455; the Consular Conventions (United States of Mexico) Order 1955, SI 1955/425; the Consular Conventions (Federal Republic of Germany) Order 1957, SI 1957/2052; the Consular Conventions (Italian Republic) Order 1957, SI 1957/2053; the Consular Conventions (Kingdom of Denmark) Order 1963, SI 1963/370; the Consular Conventions (Spanish State) Order 1963, SI 1963/614; the Consular Conventions (Republic of Austria) Order 1963, SI 1963/1927; the Consular Conventions (Kingdom of Belgium) Order 1964, SI 1964/1399; the Consular Conventions (Japan) Order 1965, SI 1965/1714; the Consular Conventions (Socialist Federal Republic of Yugoslavia) Order 1966, SI 1966/443; the Consular Conventions (Union of Soviet Socialist Republics) Order 1968, SI 1968/1378; the Consular Conventions (People's Republic of Bulgaria) Order 1968, SI 1968/1861; the Consular Conventions (Polish People's Republic) Order 1971, SI 1971/1238; the Consular Conventions (Hungarian People's Republic) Order 1971, SI 1971/1845; the Consular Conventions (Mongolian People's Republic) Order 1976, SI 1976/1150; the Consular Conventions (Czechoslovak Socialist Republic) Order 1976, SI 1976/1216; and the Consular Conventions (Arab Republic of Egypt) Order 1986, SI 1986/216.
Any such order may be revoked by a subsequent order: Consular Conventions Act 1949 s 6(2).
3 Consular Conventions Act 1949 s 1(1). As to grants to attorneys see PARAS 800–801.
4 Consular Conventions Act 1949 s 1(1) proviso.
5 See the Consular Conventions Act 1949 s 1(4) (amended by the Senior Courts Act 1981 Sch 5), excluding the application of the Senior Courts Act 1981 s 114(2) (see PARAS 757, 775).
6 See the Senior Courts Act 1981 s 120(5); and PARA 766.
7 Consular Conventions Act 1949 s 1(3) (amended by the Administration of Estates Act 1971 s 12, Sch 2 Pt II).

8 Consular Conventions Act 1949 s 1(3) (as amended: see note 7).
9 Consular Conventions Act 1949 s 1(3) proviso.

803. Attorney's position. A person acting under a power of attorney has the same status as the donor of the power would have if applying personally[1], except that a chain of executorship is not constituted through the attorney, though it is not finally broken. The chain revives if and when the executor obtains probate of his testator's will[2]. As regards the claims of third parties, an attorney administrator is liable to be sued by the parties beneficially interested in the estate[3]. An attorney administrator may be directed to obtain the protection of the Trustee Act 1925[4] by advertisement for foreign claims[5], and it has been held that if, before being sued, he pays over money to the principal on whose behalf he has obtained the grant, he gets a good discharge[6]. He cannot, however, get a good discharge from a principal who has not obtained representation in any country[7].

An attorney administrator for a foreign principal who either is an executor or according to the law of the domicile stands in the place of an executor, may be authorised to hand over any surplus after satisfaction of English liabilities and foreign liabilities of which he has notice, to his foreign principal[8], but the fact that he is so authorised or justified does not necessarily imply that he is under any duty to do so, and since the court has a duty to see that the persons charged with the administration of the estate in England carry the dispositions contained in an English will into effect the court may order distribution accordingly[9].

1 See *Re Dewell, Edgar v Reynolds* (1858) 4 Drew 269 at 272; *Re Rendell, Wood v Rendell* [1901] 1 Ch 230.
2 For the chain of executorship see PARA 637 et seq.
3 *Chambers v Bicknell* (1843) 2 Hare 536. As to the liabilities of a personal representative on which he may be sued see PARA 1239 et seq.
4 See the Trustee Act 1925 s 27; PARA 964; and TRUSTS AND POWERS vol 98 (2013) PARA 355.
5 *Re Holden, Isaacson v Holden* [1935] WN 52.
6 *De Viesca v Lubbock* (1840) 10 Sim 629; *Eames v Hacon* (1881) 18 ChD 347, CA.
7 *Re Rendell, Wood v Rendell* [1901] 1 Ch 230.
8 *Re Achillopoulos, Johnson v Mavromichali* [1928] Ch 433; *Re Weiss* [1962] P 136, [1962] 1 All ER 308.
9 *Re Manifold, Slater v Chryssaffinis* [1962] Ch 1, [1961] All ER 710; *Re Lorillard, Griffiths v Catforth* [1922] 2 Ch 638, CA.

(iv) Administration during Incapacity of Person Entitled

804. Grant where person entitled to grant lacks capacity to manage affairs. Where a district judge[1] or registrar[2] is satisfied that a person entitled to a grant[3] lacks capacity[4] to manage his affairs, administration for his use and benefit, limited until further representation be granted or in such other way as the district judge or registrar may direct, may be granted[5]. The grant is not made unless all persons entitled in the same degree as the person incapable have been cleared off, but a district judge or registrar may otherwise direct[6]. In the case of such mental incapacity, notice of intended application for a grant durante dementia[7] must be given to the Court of Protection[8], except where the applicant is the person authorised by the Court of Protection to apply for the grant[9].

1 As to the meaning of 'district judge' see PARA 631 note 6.
2 As to the meaning of 'registrar' see PARA 631 note 7.
3 As to the meaning of 'grant' see PARA 631 note 7.
4 Ie within the meaning of the Mental Capacity Act 2005 (see MENTAL HEALTH AND CAPACITY vol 75 (2013) PARA 597). See also MENTAL HEALTH AND CAPACITY vol 75 (2013) PARA 599 et seq.

5 Non-Contentious Probate Rules 1987, SI 1987/2024, r 35(2) (amended by SI 1991/1876 and SI 2007/1898). In this case the grant is called a grant durante dementia. As to the order of priority for such a grant see PARA 805. As to the revocation of a grant on these grounds see PARA 850.

6 Non-Contentious Probate Rules 1987, SI 1987/2024, r 35(1) (amended by SI 1991/1876 and SI 2007/1898). This rule will apply, for example, if there is another executor willing and competent to take probate.

7 See note 5.

8 As to the Court of Protection see MENTAL HEALTH AND CAPACITY vol 75 (2013) PARA 720. The notice is given informally by letter. Under the Mental Capacity Act 2005 s 16, the Court of Protection may appoint a deputy to make decisions for a person who lacks capacity in relation to a matter or matters concerning his personal welfare or his property and affairs: see MENTAL HEALTH AND CAPACITY vol 75 (2013) PARA 724.

9 Non-Contentious Probate Rules 1987, SI 1987/2024, r 35(5) (amended by SI 1998/1903). As to the person authorised by the Court of Protection see note 8.

805. Person to whom the grant is made where person entitled lacks capacity to manage his affairs. Where the person entitled to take the grant lacks capacity to manage his affairs[1], the grant[2] may be made to the person authorised by the Court of Protection to apply for the grant[3]. Where there is no person so authorised, the grant may be made to the lawful attorney of the person lacking mental capacity acting under a registered enduring power of attorney or a lasting power of attorney[4]. Where there is no such attorney entitled to act, or if the attorney renounces administration for the use and benefit of the person lacking mental capacity, the grant may be made to the person entitled to the residuary estate of the deceased[5]. Where a grant is required to be made to not less than two administrators[6], and there is only one person competent and willing to take a grant, administration may, unless a district judge[7] or registrar[8] otherwise directs, be granted to such person jointly with any other person nominated by him[9]. Notwithstanding the foregoing, administration for the use and benefit of the person lacking mental capacity may be granted to such other person as the district judge or registrar may by order direct[10].

If the person lacking mental capacity, although having the prior right to administer, is not the only person entitled on distribution, the grant may in a suitable case be made to another of the persons entitled in distribution on his own behalf[11].

1 See PARA 804 note 4.

2 As to the meaning of 'grant' see PARA 631 note 7.

3 See the Non-Contentious Probate Rules 1987, SI 1987/2024, r 35(2)(a) (amended by SI 2007/1898). See also MENTAL HEALTH AND CAPACITY vol 75 (2013) PARA 720 et seq. As to the person authorised by the Court of Protection, see PARA 805 note 8.

4 Non-Contentious Probate Rules 1987, SI 1987/2024, r 35(2)(b) (amended by SI 2007/1898). As to the requirements on such an application see *Practice Direction* [1986] 2 All ER 41, [1986] 1 WLR 419. A lasting power of attorney must give the donee powers to deal with the property and affairs (which include finance) of the donor: Tristram and Coote's Probate Practice (31st Edn) 11.278. A power limited to making decisions about the donor's personal affairs, or that does not include specific power to obtain a grant or general power to deal with property and affairs, is not acceptable: Tristram and Coote's Probate Practice (31st Edn) 11.278. A medical certificate confirming the donor's lack of capacity within the meaning of the Mental Capacity Act 2005 must be filed with the application because a lasting power of attorney may have been registered with the Public Guardian before the donor lacked capacity within the meaning of that Act: Tristram and Coote's Probate Practice (31st Edn) 11.279. As to enduring powers of attorney and lasting powers of attorney generally see AGENCY vol 1 (2008) PARA 194 et seq. See also PARA 800 note 7.

5 Non-Contentious Probate Rules 1987, SI 1987/2024, r 35(2)(c) (amended by SI 2007/1898).

6 See PARA 775.

7 As to the meaning of 'district judge' see PARA 631 note 6.

8 As to the meaning of 'registrar' see PARA 631 note 7.

9 Non-Contentious Probate Rules 1987, SI 1987/2024, r 35(3) (amended by SI 1991/1876).

10 Non-Contentious Probate Rules 1987, SI 1987/2024, r 35(4) (amended by SI 1991/1876; SI 1998/1903; and SI 2007/1898). See also *Re Hastings* (1877) 4 PD 73.

11 *Re Williams* (1830) 3 Hag Ecc 217. This will in practice be done only in exceptional circumstances, and would be by means of an order under the court's discretionary powers: see PARA 758.

806. Grant to stranger or creditor where person entitled lacks capacity to manage his affairs. If all persons interested in the estate of an intestate renounce and consent, the court will make a grant to a creditor for the use and benefit of the person lacking mental capacity[1] or to a stranger for the like use[2].

Before a creditor or other person with an inferior title can obtain a grant where the person first entitled is a person lacking mental capacity, the latter and his next of kin should be cited[3].

1 *Re Penny* (1846) 1 Rob Eccl 426.

2 *Re Burrell* (1858) 1 Sw & Tr 64 (stepmother); *Re Eccles* (1889) 15 PD 1.

3 *Re Sharland, Windeatt v Sharland* (1871) LR 2 P & D 266.

807. Representative losing capacity to manage his affairs after grant. Where a sole representative loses capacity to manage his affairs after having obtained a grant, the practice is, without revoking the old grant, to make a new grant:

(1) if there is a person authorised by the Court of Protection to apply for the grant, to that person[1]; or

(2) if there is none, to the residuary legatee or devisee, in the case of testacy, and in the case of intestacy to another of the persons entitled to share in the estate[2].

A new grant may also be made to the representative's attorney acting under an enduring power of attorney or lasting power of attorney[3]. The new grant is for the use and benefit of the person mentally incapacitated during his incapacity; it is usually a general grant, but may be limited[4]. In the case of a foreigner, the new grant may be made to the foreign curator[5].

In the case of one of several proving executors or administrators who later lose mental capacity, the old grant is revoked and a new grant made to the other representatives[6].

Where a grant has been issued to an attorney of a donor for the use and benefit of that donor and the donor later loses mental capacity, the attorney will be able to continue with the administration, provided that the donor has also appointed the same attorney under a sufficient enduring power of attorney or lasting power of attorney, either of which has been registered with the Court of Protection, even if the power of attorney used on the grant application was a different power of attorney and it has been revoked by the donor's loss of mental capacity[7].

1 See PARA 805.

2 *Re Crump* (1821) 3 Phillim 497. See MENTAL HEALTH AND CAPACITY vol 75 (2013) PARA 564.

3 See *Practice Direction* [1986] 2 All ER 41, [1986] 1 WLR 419; and PARA 805. An attorney under an enduring power of attorney is not able to continue the administration on behalf of the grantee in reliance on the power of attorney: see *Practice Direction* (and presumably the same is true of a lasting power of attorney). As to enduring powers of attorney and lasting powers of attorney see AGENCY vol 1 (2008) PARA 194 et seq.

4 See *Re Crump* (1821) 3 Phillim 497.

5 *Re Goldschmidt* (1898) 78 LT 763.

6 *Re Shaw* [1905] P 92; *Re Newton* (1843) 3 Curt 428. See also *Re Clifton* [1931] P 222. See also *Practice Direction* [1986] 2 All ER 41, [1986] 1 WLR 419. As to attorneys acting under an enduring power of attorney or lasting power of attorney see note 3. See also Tristram and Coote's Probate Practice (31st Edn) 11.40 et seq, 11.243 et seq. As to revocation in cases of lack of capacity see PARA 850.

7 See *Practice Direction* [1986] 2 All ER 41, [1986] 1 WLR 419.

(v) Administration pending Determination of a Probate Claim

808. Grant pending determination of a probate claim. Where any legal proceedings concerning the validity of the will[1] of a deceased person, or for obtaining, recalling or revoking any grant[2] are pending, the High Court may grant administration[3] of the estate[4] of the deceased person in question to an administrator pending determination of the probate claim, who has all the rights, duties and powers of a general administrator[5]. An administrator pending determination of a probate claim is, like a receiver[6], an officer of the court and subject to its immediate control and must act under its direction; and, except in such circumstances as may be prescribed[7], no distribution of the estate, or any part of the estate, of the deceased person in question may be made by such an administrator without the leave of the court[8]. The court may, out of the estate of the deceased, assign an administrator pending determination of a probate claim such reasonable remuneration as it thinks fit[9]. The court is not bound in this case to appoint two such administrators where a life or minority interest arises[10].

1 As to the meaning of 'will' see PARA 620 note 4. See also *Re Miesegaes, Misegaes v Misegaes* [1950] WN 232.
2 As to the meaning of 'grant' see PARA 683 note 2.
3 As to the meaning of 'administration' see PARA 622 note 8. Formerly this particular grant was known as a grant 'pendente lite' or 'pending suit' but under the Civil Procedure Rules is called 'administration pending determination of a probate claim'. As to the meaning of 'probate claim' see CPR 57.1(2); and CIVIL PROCEDURE vol 11 (2015) PARA 161.
4 As to the meaning of 'estate' see PARA 620 note 5.
5 Senior Courts Act 1981 s 117(1), which is expressed to be subject to s 117(2) (see the text to notes 7–8).
6 Ie a receiver under the CPR Pt 69 (see rr 69.4–69.7) will apply: see PARA 810 note 3.
7 'Prescribed' means prescribed by rules of court: Senior Courts Act 1981 s 151(1). The application is made by application notice under CPR Pt 23 in the probate claim: see CPR PD 57—*Probate* para 8.1; and PARA 810.
8 Senior Courts Act 1981 s 117(2). See note 5.
9 Senior Courts Act 1981 s 117(3).
10 See *Re Lindley, Lindley v Lindley* [1953] P 203, [1953] 2 All ER 319; *Re Haslip* [1958] 2 All ER 275n, [1958] 1 WLR 583. See also PARA 775.

809. Exercise of jurisdiction. To found the jurisdiction to make a grant pending determination of a probate claim there must be a probate claim actually pending in the Chancery Division[1]. Proceedings on a caveat do not constitute a claim[2]. The application may be made by any person, whether or not a party to the pending action, as, for instance, a creditor[3]; but the court has no power to order the administrator to pay the creditor's debt[4]. The jurisdiction is not exercised where there is a person legally entitled to represent or take possession of the property, as in the case of a surviving partner[5], but it is not confined to cases of necessity[6].

1 As to grants and appointments of representatives ad litem for the purpose of other proceedings see PARA 817. As to the jurisdiction of the Chancery Division see PARA 678. As to the meaning of 'probate claim' see PARA 808 note 3.
2 See *Salter v Salter* [1896] P 291, CA.
3 See *Tichborne v Tichborne, ex p Norris* (1869) LR 1 P & D 730; *Re Evans, Evans v Evans* (1890) 15 PD 215; *Re Cleaver* [1905] P 319.
4 *Re Evans, Evans v Evans* (1890) 15 PD 215. Except with the consent of all interested parties, the court cannot pay maintenance out of the estate to a residuary legatee: *Whittle v Keats* (1866) 35 LJP & M 54; cf *Re Harver, Harver v Harver* (1889) 14 PD 81.
5 *Horrell v Witts and Plumley* (1866) LR 1 P & D 103. See also *Mortimer v Paull and Paull* (1870) LR 2 P & D 85 where an executor was appointed under a will and a codicil was in dispute which did not affect his appointment. In small estates expense may be saved by an undertaking given to the court by the personal representatives in lieu of the appointment of an administrator pending determination of a probate claim: see *Re Day* [1940] 2 All ER 544.

6 *Bellew v Bellew* (1865) 34 LJPM & A 125, where Sir J P Wilde said that he would not follow the established practice of requiring a case of necessity to be made out before making the grant, but would adopt the practice of the Chancery courts, and make the grant wherever a Chancery court would appoint a receiver. The same principle was followed in *Re Bevan, Bevan v Houldsworth* [1948] 1 All ER 271, CA.

810. Procedure for application for grant of administration. An application[1] for an order for the grant of administration is made by application notice in the probate claim in question[2]. If an order is made an application for the grant of letters of administration should be made at the Principal Registry of the Family Division[3]. It is not the practice, except by consent, to appoint a party to the claim either as administrator or as receiver[4], although, where it is clearly desirable, a party to the claim may be appointed[5]. If the parties will not agree, the appointment of a neutral administrator is left to the master or district judge[6]. Every application relating to the conduct of the administration must be made by application notice in the probate claim in question[7].

1 Ie under the Senior Courts Act 1981 s 117 (see PARA 808).
2 CPR PD 57—*Probate* para 8.1. As to the content of the application notice and procedure see Tristram and Coote's Probate Practice (31st Edn) 38.01 et seq.
3 CPR PD 57—*Probate* PD 57 para 8.4. The order may be made by a master or district judge: para 8.3. Where an order for a grant of administration is made under the Senior Courts Act 1981 s 117, CPR 69.4–69.7 apply as if the administrator were a receiver appointed by the court and if the court allows the administrator remuneration under r 69.7 it may make an order under the Senior Courts Act 1981 s 117 (3) assigning the remuneration out of the estate of the deceased: see CPR PD 57—*Probate* para 8.2(1), (2). See note 1.
4 *Stratton v Ford* (1754) 2 Lee 49 at 50; *Northey v Cock* (1822) 1 Add 326 at 330 per Sir J Nicholl; *Young (otherwise Mearing) v Brown* (1827) 1 Hag Ecc 53; *De Chatelain v Pontigny* (1858) 1 Sw & Tr 34; *Re Shorter, Shorter v Shorter* [1911] P 184 (executor not appointed).
5 *Re Griffin, Griffin v Ackroyd* [1925] P 38.
6 *Whittle v Keats* (1866) 35 LJP & M 54; *Re Bevan, Bevan v Houldsworth* [1948] 1 All ER 271 at 274, CA.
7 CPR PD 57—*Probate* para 8.2(3).

811. Determination of appointment of administrator. The appointment of an administrator to whom letters of administration are granted following an order[1] ceases automatically when a final order in the probate claim is made but continues pending any appeal[2]. The administrator may, however, in certain cases be entitled to retain money received by him until his accounts have been brought in and passed[3].

1 Ie an order under the Senior Courts Act 1981 s 117 (see PARA 808).
2 CPR PD 57—*Probate* para 8.5.
3 *Re Wieland, Wieland v Bird* [1894] P 262. As to the court's current practice regarding the administrator's accounts see Tristram and Coote's Probate Practice (31st Edn) 38.12.

812. Administrator's liability. While his functions continue, an administrator pending determination of a probate claim is liable to be sued by a creditor without leave of the court, in the same way as a general administrator[1], and there is no special jurisdiction to stay proceedings against him[2].

1 *Re Toleman, Westwood v Booker* [1897] 1 Ch 866. See also *Tichborne v Tichborne* (1870) LR 2 P & D 41. As to the liability of a general administrator see PARA 643.
2 *Martin v Toleman* (1897) 77 LT 138.

(vi) Miscellaneous Limited Grants

813. Grant to non-trust corporation. Where a corporate body other than a trust corporation[1] would, if an individual, be entitled to a grant[2], administration for its use and benefit, limited until further representation is granted, may be granted to its nominee[3] or to its lawfully constituted attorney[4]. The nominee or attorney must depose in the oath that the corporate body is not a trust corporation[5]. A copy of the resolution[6] appointing the nominee or, as the case may be, the power of attorney, sealed by the corporate body or otherwise authenticated to the district judge's[7] or registrar's[8] satisfaction, must be lodged with the application[9]. Such administration may not be granted where a corporate body is appointed executor jointly with an individual unless the right of the individual has been cleared off[10].

1 As to the meaning of 'trust corporation' see PARA 622 note 4. As to trust corporations see PARA 783.

2 As to the meaning of 'grant' see PARA 631 note 7.

3 Where a corporation is entitled as executor it must be established that it has power under its constitution to take a grant through its nominee: see *Practice Direction* [1956] 1 All ER 305, [1956] 1 WLR 127. As to the former practice in appointing a syndic see PARA 622 note 3.

4 Non-Contentious Probate Rules 1987, SI 1987/2024, r 36(4)(a). See also PARA 622. A foreign corporation appointed executor may appoint an attorney to take a grant for its use and benefit until further representation is granted, it being immaterial whether or not the will has been proved in the court of the domicile unless there is some other person entrusted by the foreign court who has applied in England: *Practice Direction* [1953] 2 All ER 1154 at 1156, [1953] 1 WLR 1237 at 1240. A solicitor's firm which has become a limited liability partnership under the Limited Liability Partnership Act 2000 and so is a 'recognised body' by virtue of the Administration of Justice Act 1985 s 9 (see LEGAL PROFESSIONS vol 65 (2015) PARA 496 et seq), is not a partnership within the meaning of the Partnership Act 1890 s 1(2)(b) but has a corporate identity: see the Limited Liability Partnership Act 2000 s 1(5); andLEGAL PROFESSIONS vol 65 (2015) PARA 496 et seq; PARTNERSHIP vol 79 (2014) PARA 243. In *Re Rogers* [2006] EWHC 753 (Ch), [2006] 2 All ER 792, [2006] 1 WLR 1577 the court took a practical and common sense view in giving effect to the intentions of the testatrix that on a true construction a grant of probate should be made to profit-sharing members of the limited liability partnership (they being the equivalent of partners in the previous partnership). Lightman J held that just as a partner in a partnership was a profit-sharing partner, the appointment could only apply to profit-sharing members unless a contrary intention is established in the will. Following *Re Rogers* similar considerations should apply to an incorporated practice recognised by the Solicitors Regulation Authority so that it is treated as a successor firm for the purpose of construing the usual succession clause to a partnership firm. In this case (profit-sharing or share-owning) directors or members replace partners who may apply for a grant of probate as executors. See further LEGAL PROFESSIONS vol 65 (2015) PARA 499. See also PARA 623.

5 Non-Contentious Probate Rules 1987, SI 1987/2024, r 36(4)(c).

6 A duly authenticated copy of a resolution passed by the committee or other body most completely representing a corporation, association or public, charitable or private body of persons entitled as beneficiary or creditor is sufficient: *Practice Direction* [1956] 1 All ER 305, [1956] 1 WLR 127.

7 As to the meaning of 'district judge' see PARA 631 note 6.

8 As to the meaning of 'registrar' see PARA 631 note 7.

9 Non-Contentious Probate Rules 1987, SI 1987/2024, r 36(4)(b) (amended by SI 1991/1876). See also PARA 622.

10 Non-Contentious Probate Rules 1987, SI 1987/2024, r 36(4)(d).

814. Grants to unincorporated bodies. Where an unincorporated body of persons or association is entitled as beneficiary or creditor, it obtains a grant through its nominee, who must produce an authenticated copy of a resolution appointing him passed by the committee or other body most completely representing it[1].

1 *Practice Direction* [1956] 1 All ER 305, [1956] 1 WLR 127. As to unincorporated bodies generally see CORPORATIONS vol 24 (2010) PARA 301.

815. Grant ad colligenda bona. A grant (known as a grant ad colligenda bona) for getting in and preserving the assets of a deceased person may be made where delay in obtaining the full grant might prove detrimental to the estate[1]. The grant may be made even to a stranger connected as an agent or otherwise with the deceased's affairs[2]. Application for an order for a grant of administration ad colligenda bona may be made to a district judge[3] or registrar[4] usually without notice and must be supported by an affidavit setting out the grounds of the application[5].

The grant is usually limited to the collection and preservation of the estate, the giving of discharges for debts due to the estate, and the preservation of the assets collected either by investment or by payment into court[6]. The grant may authorise the administrator to renew a lease[7], to let farms and other portions of the real estate, with power to sell farm stock and implements of husbandry[8], or the goodwill of a business[9], to reimburse solicitors for tax and costs, to pay debts and funeral expenses and to pay income in respect of a life interest[10].

1 *Re Clarkington* (1861) 2 Sw & Tr 380; *Re Wyckoff* (1862) 3 Sw & Tr 20; *Re Clore* [1982] Fam 113, [1982] 2 WLR 314; approved in *IRC v Stype Investments (Jersey) Ltd, Re Clore* [1982] Ch 456, [1982] 3 All ER 419, CA(where a grant was made to the Official Solicitor on an application by the Commissioners of Inland Revenue where executors had delayed in applying for probate). Grants ad colligenda bona are to a great extent avoided by application being made under the Senior Courts Act 1981 s 116: see PARA 758. A grant ad colligenda bona is always one of administration and if the deceased died testate, the will is not proved or annexed to the grant.

2 *Re Radnall* (1824) 2 Add 232; *Re Gudolle* (1835), cited in *Re Wyckoff* (1862) 3 Sw & Tr 20 at 22.

3 As to the meaning of 'district judge' see PARA 631 note 6.

4 As to the meaning of 'registrar' see PARA 631 note 7.

5 See the Non-Contentious Probate Rules 1987, SI 1987/2024, r 52(b) (amended by SI 1991/1876). The district judge or registrar may require the application to be made on summons to a judge, district judge or registrar particularly where there are, or may be, active competing interests (Non-Contentious Probate Rules 1987, SI 1987/2024, r 61(1) (amended by SI 1991/1876)). As to 'notice' see *Ghafoor v Cliff* [2006] EWHC 825 (Ch), [2006] 2 All ER 1079, [2006] 1 WLR 3020. See also Tristram and Coote's Probate Practice (31st Edn) 25.180 et seq.

6 The powers conferred on an administrator ad colligenda bona may be extended so as to include, for instance, a power to sell chattels real. As to the administrator's liability for rent in such a case see *Whitehead v Palmer* [1908] 1 KB 151.

7 *Re Clarkington* (1861) 2 Sw & Tr 380.

8 *Re Roberts* [1898] P 149.

9 *Re Schwerdtfeger* (1876) 1 PD 424; *Re Bolton* [1899] P 186.

10 *Re Sanpietro, Re Van Tuyll Van Serooskerken* [1941] P 16, [1940] 4 All ER 482.

816. Grant where will is abroad or mislaid. A grant may be made in a case where the will of a testator is in a foreign country[1], or where there is believed to have been a will which has been accidentally mislaid or destroyed[2]. The grant is limited in time until the original will or an authenticated copy of it is brought into the registry[3].

1 *Re Metcalfe* (1822) 1 Add 343; *Re Brown* (1899) 80 LT 360. See PARA 730 note 4 where the will is in the custody of a foreign court.

2 *Re Campbell* (1829) 2 Hag Ecc 555; *Re Wright* [1893] P 21.

3 *Re Wright* [1893] P 21; *Re Greig* (1866) LR 1 P & D 72. In *Re Campbell* (1829) 2 Hag Ecc 555, the grant was not so limited.

817. Grant limited to beginning or carrying on proceedings. Administration may be granted limited to an action[1] with a view to beginning[2] or carrying on proceedings[3] whether on behalf of the estate or against it[4]. The administrator under such a grant sufficiently represents the estate for the purpose of the proceedings, where it is merely desired to bind the estate of a person who, if alive, would have been a necessary party[5]. Where the object of Chancery proceedings is to administer the estate in respect of which a grant limited to an action has been obtained, or to obtain relief involving general accounts and inquiries in respect of the estate, a general administrator is a necessary party to the proceedings[6].

1 This grant was formerly called a grant 'ad litem' but is usually now known as a grant 'limited to an action'. For an alternative method of bringing proceedings where a cause of action has survived the death but no personal representative has been constituted see PARA 818.
2 *Woolley and Gordon v Green* (1820) 3 Phillim 314.
3 *Re Dodgson* (1859) 1 Sw & Tr 259; *Day v Thompson, Re Frampton* (1863) 3 Sw & Tr 169. See *Re Byrne* (1910) 44 ILT 98. See also *Re Simpson's Estate, Re Gunning's Estate* [1936] P 40; *Re Knight's Goods* [1939] 3 All ER 928 (motion), appointment of an administrator ad litem, on the application by the plaintiff to appoint a defendant. As to administration pending determination of a claim for the purpose of probate proceedings see PARA 808.
4 If someone wishes to bring a claim against an estate for reasonable financial provision under the Inheritance (Provision for Family and Dependants) Act 1975 and there is no person either entitled or, if entitled, willing to apply for a grant, the Official Solicitor has intimated in a circular dated 11 November 1976 that he will usually be willing to obtain a grant. As to the procedure to be followed for financial provision claims under the Inheritance (Provision for Family and Dependants) Act 1975 see PARA 597 et seq.
5 *Faulkner v Daniel* (1843) 3 Hare 199; *Davis v Chanter* (1848) 2 Ph 545; *Groves v Lane* (1852) 16 Jur 1061; cf *Williams v Allen* (1862) 4 De GF & J 71.
6 *Groves v Lane* (1852) 16 Jur 1061; *Dowdeswell v Dowdeswell* (1878) 9 ChD 294, CA.

818. Procedure when person with interest in litigation dies. Where a person who had an interest in a claim has died and that person has no personal representative, the court[1] may order[2]:

(1) the claim to proceed in the absence of a person representing the estate of the deceased[3]; or

(2) a person to be appointed to represent the estate of the deceased[4].

Where a defendant[5] against whom a claim could have been brought has died and a grant of probate or administration has been made, the claim must be brought against the persons who are the personal representatives of the deceased[6]. Where, however, such a grant has not been made, the claim must be brought against 'the estate of' the deceased[7] and the claimant[8] must apply to the court for an order[9] appointing a person to represent the estate of the deceased in the claim[10]. Where any order has been made under the foregoing provisions, any judgment or order made or given in the claim is binding on the estate of the deceased[11].

It has been held that this practice is not appropriate where the estate to which it is desired to appoint a representative is itself the subject of the dispute[12] and also that there is no power to appoint a person as a representative against his will[13].

The jurisdiction may be exercised in proceedings by mortgagees[14], but not with a view to making a foreclosure order against a sole defendant's estate[15], nor generally to bind the estate of a deceased person who was the only person liable in the action[16]. The court may, however, appoint a person to represent the estate of a sole claimant who has died insolvent, to enable the defendant to have someone against whom he may move for dismissal of the action[17]. The power to appoint a representative is not confined to representation of the estate of a deceased party to the litigation[18]. Money will not be paid out of court to a person appointed to represent the estate, but will be carried over to a separate account[19].

1 As to the meaning of 'court' see CIVIL PROCEDURE vol 11 (2015) PARA 119. The court's power is now contained in CPR 19.8 (see CIVIL PROCEDURE vol 11 (2015) PARAS 489–490).
2 Before making such an order, the court may direct notice of the application to be given to any other person with an interest in the claim: CPR 19.8(4).
3 CPR 19.8(1)(a).
4 CPR 19.8(1)(b). See note 9 regarding notice.
5 As to the meaning of 'defendant' see CIVIL PROCEDURE vol 11 (2015) PARA 117.
6 CPR 19.8(2)(a).

7 CPR 19.8(2)(b)(i). A claim is treated as having been brought against 'the estate of' the deceased in accordance with CPR 19.8(2)(b)(i) where:
   (1) the claim is brought against the 'personal representatives' of the deceased but a grant of probate or administration has not been made (CPR 19.8(3)(a)); or
   (2) the person against whom the claim was brought was dead when the claim was started (CPR 19.8(3)(b)).

8 As to the meaning of 'claimant' see CIVIL PROCEDURE vol 11 (2015) PARA 117.

9 Before making an order under CPR 19.8, the court may direct notice of the application to be given to any other person with an interest in the claim: CPR 19.8(4). As to the meaning of 'court' see note 1. When appointed to represent the deceased defendant, the Official Solicitor is entitled to substitute himself for the solicitors on the record as acting for the deceased: *Watts v Official Solicitor* [1936] 1 All ER 249, CA.

10 CPR 19.8(2)(b)(ii). Where a claimant fails to apply for an order to appoint a personal representative, the action is not duly constituted and the proceedings may be discontinued: *Piggott v Aulton* [2003] EWCA Civ 24, [2003] RTR 540.

11 CPR 19.8(5).

12 *Silver v Stein* (1852) 1 Drew 295, decided under the repealed Court of Chancery Procedure Act 1852 s 44, which RSC Ord 15 r 15 replaced and which is itself now replaced by CPR 19.8 (see note 1).

13 *Pratt v London Passenger Transport Board* [1937] 1 All ER 473, CA (Official Solicitor). See also *Re Curtis and Betts* [1887] WN 126, CA; *Prince of Wales etc Association Co v Palmer* (1858) 25 Beav 605 at 606; *Hill v Bonner* (1858) 26 Beav 372; *Re Raphael, Warburg v Raphael* (1916) 61 Sol Jo 99 (Public Trustee unwilling). Cf *Re Deans, Westminster Bank Ltd v Official Solicitor* [1954] 1 All ER 496, [1954] 1 WLR 332 (plaintiffs seeking to enforce guarantee against intestate's estate; estate vested in the President (see PARA 644); application for appointment of Official Solicitor (see COURTS AND TRIBUNALS vol 24 (2010) PARA 755) to represent the estate and for vesting order in respect of property subject to guarantee in favour of the Official Solicitor: the President is not a trustee, and in any event the court would not press the Official Solicitor to consent, as the plaintiffs could apply for a grant of representation of the deceased's estate). In addition to the power conferred by CPR 19.8, the court under its discretionary powers (see PARA 758) may grant letters of administration to the Official Solicitor limited to his defending a proposed action against the estate of a deceased person: *Re Knight* [1939] 3 All ER 928.

14 *Curtius v Caledonian Fire and Life Insurance Co* (1881) 19 ChD 534, CA; *Peat v Gott* [1885] WN 46; *Neal v Barrett* [1887] WN 88; *Scott v Streatham and General Estates Co Ltd* [1891] WN 153. See also MORTGAGE vol 77 (2016) PARA 534 et seq.

15 *Aylward v Lewis* [1891] 2 Ch 81.

16 *Re Curtis and Betts* [1887] WN 126, CA.

17 *Wingrove v Thompson* (1879) 11 ChD 419.

18 See *Lean v Alston* [1947] KB 467, [1947] 1 All ER 261, CA, when in a personal injury action it was desired to serve a third party notice on the representative of the estate of a deceased person, the court had power to make an appointment under CPR Sch 1 RSC Ord 15 r 15 (now replaced by CPR 19.8: see note 1), even though the deceased was not a party to the original action.

19 *Rawlins v McMahon* (1852) 1 Drew 225; *Byam v Sutton* (1855) 19 Beav 646.

819. Grant limited to specific property. A grant may be made to a beneficiary limited to the trust fund where the trustee in whose name the fund stands is dead and without a personal representative[1]. If the trustee died testate his will should be annexed to the grant[2]. An application for a grant of administration or probate[3] limited to part of the estate may be made to a district judge[4] or registrar[5] and must be supported by an affidavit setting out the grounds of the application[6], and:

(1) stating whether the deceased's estate is known to be insolvent[7]; and
(2) showing how any person entitled to a grant in respect of the whole estate in priority to the applicant has been cleared off[8].

Where several persons are interested in the trust fund the grant is limited to the applicant's interest unless the others consent to the grant extending to their respective interests[9]. The person entitled to administer the trust fund should be cited[10].

1 *Re Ratcliffe* [1899] P 110; *Re Agnese* [1900] P 60; *Murray v Champernowne* [1901] 2 IR 232. For the power to grant representation in respect of any part of the estate of a deceased person, limited

in any way the court thinks fit see the Senior Courts Act 1981 s 113; and PARA 616. See further *Re Newsham* [1967] P 230, [1966] 3 All ER 681. See also PARA 820.
2 *Re Butler* [1898] P 9.
3 As to limited probates see PARA 747 et seq.
4 As to the meaning of 'district judge' see PARA 631 note 6.
5 As to the meaning of 'registrar' see PARA 631 note 7.
6 Non-Contentious Probate Rules 1987, SI 1987/2024, r 51 (amended by SI 1991/1876). The application is made ex parte: see PARA 703.
7 Non-Contentious Probate Rules 1987, SI 1987/2024, r 51(a).
8 Non-Contentious Probate Rules 1987, SI 1987/2024, r 51(b).
9 *Pegg v Chamberlain* (1860) 1 Sw & Tr 527.
10 *Pegg v Chamberlain* (1860) 1 Sw & Tr 527; *Re Kingwell* (1899) 81 LT 461.

820. Examples of limited grant. A grant may be made limited to a legacy[1], to a fund appropriated for the payment of a legacy[2], to property the subject of a mortgage[3], to the appointment of a new trustee and the vesting of the trust property in him[4], and to bringing particular actions[5].

A limited grant should not, however, be made to a person entitled to a general grant unless a very strong reason is given, and cannot be made except under the court's discretion[6]. Although the court may, by statute, grant probate or administration in respect of the real estate or any part of it either separately or together with probate or administration of the personal estate[7], this does not allow a separate grant of part only of the personal estate[8] to be made to a person entitled to a general grant. It seems that such a person, if unwilling to take a general grant, will be passed over under the discretionary power[9].

1 *Re Steadman* (1828) 2 Hag Ecc 59; *Re Baldwin* [1903] P 61.
2 *Re Biou, Indigent Blind School and Westminster Hospital v Flack* (1843) 3 Curt 739.
3 *Re Lowe* (1898) 78 LT 566; *Re Kingwell* (1899) 81 LT 461.
4 *Re Berry* [1907] 2 IR 209.
5 *Re Williams* (1859) 23 JP 519; *Re Winstone* [1898] P 143; *Re Byrne* (1910) 44 ILT 98.
6 *Re Lady Somerset* (1867) LR 1 P & D 350; *Re Watts* (1860) 1 Sw & Tr 538.
7 Ie under the Senior Courts Act 1981 s 113: see PARA 616.
8 *Re Newsham* [1967] P 230, [1966] 3 All ER 681 (court's inherent jurisdiction was not argued and the position under the statute was conceded, so the decision appears to be obiter on an ex parte application).
9 See *Re Newsham* [1967] P 230 at 233, [1966] 3 All ER 681 at 682 per Karminski J. As to the court's discretionary power see PARA 758.

(8) SETTLED LAND GRANTS

821. Special executors. A testator may appoint, and in default of express appointment is deemed to have appointed[1], as his special executors in regard to settled land[2] the persons, if any, who are at his death the trustees of the settlement[3], and probate may be granted to such trustees specially limited to the settled land[4]. The testator may appoint other persons, either with or without such trustees or any of them, to be his general executors in regard to his other property and assets[5].

1 As to the derivation of the title of an executor so deemed to have been appointed see PARA 633.
2 For this purpose, 'settled land' means land vested in the testator which was settled previously to his death and not by his will: Administration of Estates Act 1925 s 22(1). In general in that Act 'settled land' has the same meaning as in the Settled Land Act 1925 (see SETTLEMENTS vol 91 (2012) PARA 581): Administration of Estates Act 1925 s 55(1)(xxiv). As to the meaning of 'will' see PARA 607 note 1. Subject to certain exceptions, new settlements created on or after 1 January 1997 are not settlements for the purposes of the Settled Land Act 1925: see the Trusts of Land and Appointment of Trustees Act 1996 s 2; and REAL PROPERTY AND REGISTRATION vol 87 (2012) PARA 104; SETTLEMENTS vol 91 (2012) PARA 577.

Where the deceased dies wholly intestate, administration is to be granted, as regards land settled before his death, to the trustees, if any, of the settlement if willing to act: see PARA 825.

3 'Trustees of the settlement' has the same meaning as in the Settled Land Act 1925 (see SETTLEMENTS vol 91 (2012) PARA 651): Administration of Estates Act 1925 s 55(1)(xxiv).

4 Administration of Estates Act 1925 s 22(1). However, as from 14 October 1991, the special executors can obtain only a grant of administration, rather than probate: see the Non-Contentious Probate Rules 1987, SI 1987/2024, r 29; and PARA 822. As a result all grants issued on or after that date in respect of settled land are grants of administration, are silent as to whether the deceased died testate or intestate and are issued only as separate grants limited to settled land.

5 Administration of Estates Act 1925 s 22(2). As to the meaning of 'property' see PARA 608 note 4. Section 22, with its special definition of 'settled land' in s 22(1) (see note 2), does not apply where, on the death of the tenant for life, the settlement comes to an end: *Re Bridgett and Hayes' Contract* [1928] Ch 163. See also the definition of 'settled land' in the Non-Contentious Probate Rules 1987, SI 1987/2024, r 29(1); and PARA 822 note 1.

822. Grants in respect of settled land. The order of priority for a grant of administration limited to settled land[1] is as follows:

(1) the special executors[2];

(2) the trustees of the settlement at the time of the application for the grant[3]; and

(3) the personal representatives of the deceased[4].

Where there is settled land and a grant is made in respect of the free estate only, the grant must expressly exclude the settled land[5].

1 In the Non-Contentious Probate Rules 1987, SI 1987/2024, r 29, 'settled land' means land vested in the deceased which was settled prior to his death and not by his will and which remained settled land notwithstanding his death: r 29(1) (r 29 substituted by SI 1991/1876). See also PARA 821 note 2. As to settled land generally see SETTLEMENTS vol 91 (2012) PARA 576 et seq.

2 Non-Contentious Probate Rules 1987, SI 1987/2024, r 29(2)(i) (as substituted: see note 1). The special executors are those in regard to settled land constituted by the Administration of Estates Act 1925 s 22 (see PARA 821): see the Non-Contentious Probate Rules 1987, SI 1987/2024, r 29(2)(i) (as so substituted).

3 Non-Contentious Probate Rules 1987, SI 1987/2024, r 29(2)(ii) (as substituted: see note 1).

4 Non-Contentious Probate Rules 1987, SI 1987/2024, r 29(2)(iii) (as substituted: see note 1). 'Deceased' refers to the person in whom the settled land is vested: see PARA 823.

5 Non-Contentious Probate Rules 1987, SI 1987/2024, r 29(3) (as substituted: see note 1).

823. Devolution of legal estate in settled land. In a properly constituted settlement of land[1], the legal estate is vested in the person or persons entitled by statute to exercise the powers of a tenant for life[2]. Where there is more than one such person, the legal estate on the death of one passes by survivorship to the survivor or survivors without any grant of representation[3]. On the death of a sole or last survivor, the legal estate is held by his personal representatives on trust to convey it, if and when required to do so to the person next entitled and if more than one, as joint tenants[4].

There is no absolute necessity that a settlement should be properly constituted. The legal estate may be outstanding in a settlor[5] or a personal representative, and in such cases, on the settlor's death, it will pass to his personal representative or on the death of a personal representative it will pass according to the chain of representation or be made the subject of a grant de bonis non[6].

1 See the Settled Land Act 1925 ss 4, 6; and SETTLEMENTS vol 91 (2012) PARA 589 et seq. See also PARA 821 note 2.

2 As to these persons see the Settled Land Act 1925 ss 19–26; and SETTLEMENTS vol 91 (2012) PARA 662 et seq.

3 See the Administration of Estates Act 1925 s 3(4); and PARA 948.

4 See the Settled Land Act 1925 s 7(1); and SETTLEMENTS vol 91 (2012) PARA 599.

5 This might be the case in a settlement constituted by deed or declaration of trust: see SETTLEMENTS vol 91 (2012) PARA 513.

6 As to the chain of representation see PARA 637 et seq. As to grants de bonis non see PARA 793.

824. When a settled land grant is necessary. The necessity for a settled land grant only arises when the legal estate was vested in a sole or sole surviving tenant for life[1], and in such cases only when the land continues to be settled land after his death[2]. Where the land ceases to be settled land on the death of the tenant for life[3] it passes under the ordinary general grant of the free estate to the general personal representative[4].

1 See PARA 823 note 2.
2 It was originally thought that the land remained technically settled land until vested in absolute owners or trustees for sale. It was held, however, in *Re Bridgett and Hayes' Contract* [1928] Ch 163, that it ceased to be such on the death of the tenant for life. This point is only the subject of a dictum in *Re Bridgett and Hayes' Contract*, but the dictum was adopted in *Re Bordass* [1929] P 107, and has always been acted on by the probate registry. Where, however, after ceasing to be settled land under one settlement, the property immediately becomes settled land under another settlement, a settled land grant is necessary: *Re Taylor* [1929] P 260.
3 As to the duration of settlements see the Settled Land Act 1925 s 3; and SETTLEMENTS vol 91 (2012) PARA 609.
4 *Re Bridgett and Hayes' Contract* [1928] Ch 163.

825. Settled land grants on death of tenant for life. Several possibilities arise where, after the death of the tenant for life, land continues to be settled land. If the tenant for life dies wholly intestate he is not deemed to have appointed special executors[1] and a limited grant of administration is made to the trustees of the settlement, if willing to act[2], who may have been appointed trustees before or after the death, under the court's discretionary power[3].

If the tenant for life dies testate[4] he will have appointed or will be deemed to have appointed as his special executors the persons, if any, who are at his death the trustees of the settlement[5] and a limited grant of administration is made to these trustees[6]. It is not clear how far a testator is deemed to have appointed a sole trustee as special executor, but assuming that he is so deemed there is no objection to a grant (being one of administration) to one trustee[7]. If there are no trustees of the settlement at the testator's death and if the settlement was originally created by will or arose on intestacy, then the settlor's personal representative is by statute[8] a trustee of the settled land and is entitled to a grant of limited administration[9]. If he is a sole personal representative not being a trust corporation he must appoint an additional trustee to act with him[10].

Trustees appointed after the death of the tenant for life are not special executors under the Settled Land Act 1925[11], but may apply for a grant of administration, either jointly with any special executors or without[12]. If applying without the special executors, the prior right[13] of the special executors must be cleared off.

1 The Administration of Estates Act 1925 s 22(1) refers only to a testator, but it seems that for this purpose any provable will is sufficient, even if the appointment fails or is renounced. The term has no statutory definition. See PARA 821.
2 See the Senior Courts Act 1981 s 113; and PARA 616.
3 See PARA 758. See also the Non-Contentious Probate Rules 1987, SI 1987/2024, r 29(3); and PARA 822.
4 See note 1.
5 See the Administration of Estates Act 1925 s 22(1); and PARA 821. As to the meaning of 'trustees of the settlement' see PARA 821 note 3. For this provision to operate there must be a will, and trustees of the settlement at the death of the tenant for life, and the settled land must have been vested in the tenant for life. Where settled land is outstanding in a personal representative or a settlor, it falls to be dealt with on the death of those persons and not on the death of the tenant for life. Where the settlor is the tenant for life and no vesting deed has been executed, it is conceived that s 22 applies, and a special grant or the clearing off of the persons entitled to such grant is required. A similar position arises if land subject to an annuity is vested in the person beneficially entitled to the land subject to the annuity, and it is conceived that the rule as to a special grant

applies and the position is not altered by the Law of Property (Amendment) Act 1926 s 1 (see SETTLEMENTS vol 91 (2012) PARA 604). See also PARA 821.

6 As to limited grants see PARA 813 et seq.

7 Where there are different trustees of different settlements of which the deceased was the tenant for life, the grant to each set of trustees is limited to the land included in the particular settlement.

8 Ie by virtue of the Settled Land Act 1925 s 30(3): see SETTLEMENTS vol 91 (2012) PARA 652.

9 *Re Gibbings* [1928] P 28.

10 See the Settled Land Act 1925 s 30(3); and SETTLEMENTS vol 91 (2012) PARA 652. Subsequent appointments and discharges are made under the Trustee Act 1925 s 36, by virtue of s 64(1): *Re Dark, Glover v Dark* [1954] Ch 291, [1954] 1 All ER 681.

11 Such trustees could not be deemed to be appointed by the tenant for life as special executors within the meaning of the Administration of Estates Act 1925 s 22(1): see PARA 821 note 1.

12 See Tristram and Coote's Probate Practice (31st Edn) 10.89.

13 See notes 2–3.

826. General grants including settled land. It is no longer the practice to issue grants including settled land[1]. Separate grants are required in respect of the settled land and the general free estate, even where the persons entitled to the settled land grant are the same as those entitled to the general grant, or the special personal representatives have either been cleared off or renounced[2].

1 That is since 14 October 1991: see Tristram and Coote's Probate Practice (31st Edn) 4.64.

2 Such renunciation is provided for: see the Administration of Estates Act 1925 s 23(1); and PARA 828.

827. Limited grants where the land ceases to be settled. Where settled land ceases to be such on the death of the tenant for life and the Treasury Solicitor is entitled to a general grant of representation to the estate[1], the court may except the land from the general grant and make a limited grant to the remainderman[2] or other person beneficially entitled[3]. Similar grants have been made after citation[4] and without citation of the next of kin[5], or where the persons otherwise entitled to a grant are cleared off by renunciation[6].

1 Ie under the Non-Contentious Probate Rules 1987, SI 1987/2024, r 22(2): see PARAS 769, 778. See also *Re Mortifee* [1948] P 274. As to the Treasury Solicitor see CONSTITUTIONAL AND ADMINISTRATIVE LAW vol 20 (2014) PARA 281.

2 *Re Dalley* (1926) 136 LT 223 (a case decided before the ruling in *Re Bridgett and Hayes' Contract* [1928] Ch 163 (see PARA 824)). As to limited grants see PARA 813 et seq.

3 *Re Mortifee* [1948] P 274.

4 See *Re Bordass* [1929] P 107. As to citations see PARA 695.

5 See *Re Birch* [1929] P 164.

6 As to renunciation see PARA 828.

828. Renunciation and revocation of grants in relation to settled land. Where settled land[1] becomes vested in a personal representative[2], not being a trustee of the settlement[3], upon trust to convey the land[4] to or assent to the vesting of it in the tenant for life or statutory owner[5] in order to give effect to a settlement[6] created before the death of the deceased and not by his will[7], or would on the grant of representation[8] to him, have become so vested, such representative may[9]:

(1) before representation has been granted, renounce his office in regard only to the settled land without renouncing it in regard to other property[10]; or

(2) after representation has been granted, apply to the court for revocation of the grant in regard to the settled land without applying in regard to other property[11].

Whether such renunciation or revocation is made or not, the trustees of the settlement, or any person beneficially interested under it, may apply to the High Court for an order appointing a special or additional personal representative in respect of the settled land[12]. When so appointed, any such personal representative is in the same position as if representation had originally been granted to him alone in place of any original personal representative, or to him jointly with the original personal representative, as the case may be, limited to the settled land, but without prejudice to any previous acts and dealings of the personal representative originally constituted or the effect of notices given to him[13].

The court may make such an order subject to such security, if any, being given by or on behalf of the special or additional personal representative, as the court may direct, and must, unless the court considers that special considerations apply, appoint such persons as may be necessary to secure that the persons to act as representatives in respect of the settled land, if willing to act, are the same persons as are the trustees of the settlement[14]. Rules of court may be made for prescribing for all matters required for giving effect to the above provisions[15].

The grant may be limited in any way the court thinks fit[16].

1 As to the meaning of 'settled land' see PARA 821 note 2.
2 As to the meaning of 'personal representative' see PARA 608.
3 As to the meaning of 'trustee of the settlement' see PARA 821 note 3.
4 As to the meaning of 'land' see PARA 946 note 1.
5 'Tenant for life' and 'statutory owner' have the same meanings as in the Settled Land Act 1925 (see SETTLEMENTS vol 91 (2012) PARAS 572, 667): Administration of Estates Act 1925 s 55(1)(xxiv).
6 'Settlement' has the same meaning as in the Settled Land Act 1925 (see SETTLEMENTS vol 91 (2012) PARA 579): Administration of Estates Act 1925 s 55(1)(xxiv).
7 As to the meaning of 'will' see PARA 607 note 1.
8 As to the meaning of 'representation' see PARA 608 note 2.
9 Administration of Estates Act 1925 s 23(1).
10 Administration of Estates Act 1925 s 23(1)(a). See also PARAS 629, 847. As to the meaning of 'property' see PARA 608 note 4.
11 Administration of Estates Act 1925 s 23(1)(b).
12 Administration of Estates Act 1925 s 23(2). In *Re Clifton* [1931] P 222, one of two special executors became mentally disordered, and the court revoked the grant and made a new grant to the same executor with power to the other to come in, and appointed a special additional personal representative. It is not clear why the additional personal representative was appointed, as the sole executor could have acted alone. Note that after 14 October 1991, any new grant can only be one of administration and not probate: see Tristram and Coote's Probate Practice (31st Edn) 10.96 et seq.

The representative appointed may be ordered to give security: see the Administration of Estates Act 1925 s 23(3) (see the text and note 14). The person applying for the appointment of a special or additional personal representative must give notice of the application to the principal registry of the Family Division of the High Court in the manner prescribed: s 23(4) (amended by the Administration of Justice Act 1970 s 1(6), Sch 2 para 3). This occurs after application in Chancery Chambers: see *Practice Direction* [1928] WN 225. As to the prescribed manner see the Non-Contentious Probate Rules 1987, SI 1987/2024, r 67; and PARA 704.
13 Administration of Estates Act 1925 s 23(2).
14 Administration of Estates Act 1925 s 23(3) (amended by the Administration of Justice Act 1970 Sch 2 para 3). An office copy of the order when made must be furnished to the principal registry of the Family Division of the High Court for entry, and a memorandum of the order must be indorsed on the probate or administration: Administration of Estates Act 1925 s 23(3) (as so amended).
15 Administration of Estates Act 1925 s 23(5). In particular, rules may be made for:
(1) notice of any application being given to the proper officer (s 23(5)(a));
(2) production of orders, probates, and administration to the registry (s 23(5)(b));
(3) the indorsement on a probate or administration of a memorandum of an order, subject or not to any exceptions (s 23(5)(c));
(4) the manner in which the costs are to be borne (s 23(5)(d);
(5) protecting purchasers and trustees and other persons in a fiduciary position, dealing in good faith with or giving notices to a personal representative before notice of any order has been indorsed on the probate or administration or a pending action has been registered in respect of the proceedings (s 23(5)(e)).

For the rules of court see the Non-Contentious Probate Rules 1987, SI 1987/2024.
16 See the Senior Courts Act 1981 s 113; and PARA 616.

829. Disposing of settled land. The special personal representatives[1] may dispose of the settled land without the concurrence of the general personal representatives, who may likewise dispose of the other property[2] and assets of the deceased without the concurrence of the special personal representatives[3].

1 For these purposes, the expression 'special personal representatives' means the representatives appointed to act for the purposes of settled land and includes any original personal representative who is to act with an additional personal representative for those purposes: Administration of Estates Act 1925 s 24(2). As to the meaning of 'settled land' see PARA 821 note 2. As to the meaning of 'personal representative' see PARA 608. As to the appointment of special executors see PARA 821.
2 As to the meaning of 'property' see PARA 608 note 4.
3 Administration of Estates Act 1925 s 24(1).

(9) RECOGNITION AND RESEALING

(i) Scottish Confirmations and Northern Irish Grants

830. Recognition and evidence. Statutory provision has been made for the mutual recognition of grants between the courts of England and Wales, and of Scotland and Northern Ireland[1]. A document purporting to be a confirmation, additional confirmation or certificate of confirmation given under the seal of office of any commissariat in Scotland, and a document purporting to be a grant of probate or of letters of administration issued under the seal of the High Court in Northern Ireland or of the principal or district probate registry there, are, except where the contrary is proved, to be taken to be such without further proof[2]. Duplicates and copies are similarly admissible if they purport to be sealed[3]. There is similar provision for the admission in Scotland and Northern Ireland of English grants[4].

1 See the Administration of Estates Act 1971 ss 1–3; and PARAS 830–834. A grant should normally be extracted in that part of the United Kingdom in which the deceased was domiciled and it will then (unless any special limitation is included) make title to the whole of the United Kingdom assets, but if the circumstances make it necessary application may be made for a grant in England and Wales although the deceased died domiciled in Scotland or Northern Ireland: see *Practice Direction* [1971] 1 WLR 1790 and Tristram and Coote's Probate Practice (31st Edn) 12.23. As to domicile generally see CONFLICT OF LAWS vol 19 (2011) PARA 336 et seq.
2 Administration of Estates Act 1971 s 4(1)(a), (2)(a).
3 See the Administration of Estates Act 1971 s 4(1)(b), (2)(b).
4 See the Administration of Estates Act 1971 s 4(3).

831. Scottish confirmations. Where a person dies domiciled in Scotland, a confirmation[1] granted in respect of all or part of his estate and noting his Scottish domicile[2], and a certificate of confirmation noting his Scottish domicile and relating to one or more items of his estate[3] are treated, without being resealed, for the purposes of English law as a grant of representation to the executors named in the confirmation or certificate in respect of the property of the deceased of which according to the terms of the confirmation they are executors or, as the case may be, in respect of the items specified in the certificate of confirmation[4]. Such confirmation or certificate of confirmation is treated as a grant of probate where it appears from the confirmation or certificate that the executors named in it are executors nominate[5], and, in any other case, as a grant of administration[6], but the provisions as to the devolution of the office of executor constituting the chain of representation do not apply in either case[7]. It may contain or have appended to it, signed by the sheriff clerk, a note or statement of property in England and Wales or Northern Ireland held by the deceased in trust, being a note or statement which has been set forth in any inventory recorded in the books of the court[8]. Property specified in the note or statement is then treated in English law in the same way as property comprised in the confirmation or certificate[9]. Real estate in England or Wales may be included in the inventory of the estate of a person who dies domiciled in Scotland[10].

1 A 'confirmation' is in Scottish law equivalent to a grant whether of probate or administration. 'Confirmation' includes an additional confirmation; and 'executors' in relation to a confirmation or certificate of confirmation is to be construed according to Scottish law: Administration of Estates Act 1971 s 1(7).
2 Administration of Estates Act 1971 s 1(1)(a). As to domicile generally see CONFLICT OF LAWS vol 19 (2011) PARA 336 et seq.
3 Administration of Estates Act 1971 s 1(1)(b).
4 Administration of Estates Act 1971 s 1(1). As to the reciprocal arrangement whereby English and Northern Irish grants are recognised in Scotland see s 3; and PARA 833.
5 Administration of Estates Act 1971 s 1(2)(a).
6 Administration of Estates Act 1971 s 1(2)(b).
7 See the Administration of Estates Act 1971 s 1(3). As to the chain of representation see PARA 637 et seq.
8 See the Administration of Estates Act 1971 s 5(1).
9 See the Administration of Estates Act 1971 s 5(2).
10 See the Administration of Estates Act 1971 s 6.

832. Northern Irish grants. Where a person dies domiciled in Northern Ireland a grant of probate of his will, or letters of administration in respect of his estate (or any part of it) made by the High Court in Northern Ireland and noting his domicile there is treated in English law, without being resealed, as if it had been originally made by the High Court in England and Wales[1].

1 Administration of Estates Act 1971 s 1(4). The High Court in Northern Ireland has all the jurisdiction formerly exercised by the High Court of Justice of Ireland, which included probate jurisdiction: *Re Gault* [1922] P 195. As to the reciprocal arrangement by which English grants and Scottish confirmations are recognised in Northern Ireland see the Administration of Estates Act 1971 s 2; and PARA 833. As to domicile generally see CONFLICT OF LAWS vol 19 (2011) PARA 336 et seq.

833. English grants. Where the deceased died domiciled in England and Wales, a grant of probate of his will or letters of administration in respect of his estate (or any part of it) made by the High Court in England and Wales, and noting his domicile there, is, without being resealed, of the same force and effect in relation to property in Scotland as a Scottish confirmation given to the executor or administrator[1], and is treated for the purposes of the law of Northern Ireland as if it had been made by the High Court in Northern Ireland[2].

1 Administration of Estates Act 1971 s 3(1). In the case of a person who died domiciled in Northern Ireland, the same applies to a Northern Irish grant: see s 3(1). As to domicile generally see CONFLICT OF LAWS vol 19 (2011) PARA 336 et seq. As to the meaning of 'confirmation' see PARA 831 note 1.
2 Administration of Estates Act 1971 s 2(1). In the case of a person who died domiciled in Scotland, a Scottish confirmation or certificate of confirmation is treated as being a grant of probate where it appears that the executors are executors nominate, and in any other case as a grant of letters of administration, for the purposes of the law of Northern Ireland: see s 2(2), (3).

834. Effect of recognition. The foregoing provisions for the recognition of confirmations and grants[1] apply after 1 January 1972 to confirmations and grants made before that date so that resealing is no longer necessary in such cases even where the confirmation or grant was made many years before the Administration of Estates Act 1971[2]. In such cases the relevant provision has effect as if it had come into force immediately before the grant was made[3]. However, a person who is a personal representative according to English law only by virtue of that Act may not be required to deliver up his grant to the High Court[4].

1 See PARAS 830–833. As to the meaning of 'confirmation' see PARA 831 note 1.
2 See the Administration of Estates Act 1971 ss 1(6), 2(5), 3(2).
3 See the Administration of Estates Act 1971 s 1(6); but cf ss 2(5), 3(2).
4 Administration of Estates Act 1971 s 1(5), excluding the application of the Administration of Estates Act 1925 s 25(c) (see PARA 847).

(ii) Sealing of Commonwealth and Colonial Grants

835. General effect of resealing. The resealing in the English court of grants of probate or letters of administration issued in the Republic of Ireland (but only in respect of grants issued before 1 April 1923)[1], and of grants issued in many Commonwealth countries[2], is to give them the similar force and effect and the same operation in England as though they were originally granted there, but the date of the grant for purposes of English law is the date of resealing and not the date of the original grant[3].

1 See PARA 836.
2 See PARA 837. As to changes of title and cessation of dominion status see COMMONWEALTH vol 13 (2009) PARA 701 et seq.
3 *Burns v Campbell* [1952] 1 KB 15, [1951] 2 All ER 965, CA. As to the duties imposed on the grantee see PARA 839.

836. Grants from the Republic of Ireland. Grants issued in the Republic of Ireland on or after 1 April 1923 may not be resealed in England, even if the death occurred before that date; and grants issued in England on or after that date may not be transmitted to the Republic of Ireland for resealing there, even if the death occurred before that date[1].

There is no exclusive jurisdiction as to probate in the case of a deceased person leaving property in two or more states, and the English court may make an original grant in respect of property situate in England if the relative Irish grant made in respect of property in Ireland has not already been resealed here[2].

1 President's Direction, 17 March 1925. The Republic of Ireland ceased on 18 April 1949 to be part of the Crown's dominions: see COMMONWEALTH vol 13 (2009) PARA 728.
2 *Re Millar, Irwin v Caruth* [1916] P 23.

837. Commonwealth and colonial grants. Only grants issued in the territories to which the Colonial Probates Act 1892 has been applied by Order in Council under the power conferred by the Act and the Colonial Probates (Protected States and Mandated Territories) Act 1927 may be resealed in England. The Colonial Probates Act 1892 provides for the resealing by the English court[1] of grants[2] (including grants de bonis non)[3] made by the court of any British possession[4] not forming part of the United Kingdom, to which the Act has been applied by Order in Council[5].

The Colonial Probates Act 1892 also applies to grants made by any British court having jurisdiction in any foreign country in pursuance of an Order in Council whether made under any Act or otherwise[6]. If a grant made by a court in such a country is produced to, and a copy of it is deposited with, the English court, the grant may be sealed with the seal of the English court and then has the same force and effect as if granted by that court[7].

1 As to the practice see PARA 841. Formerly the grantee of probate in a colony where the deceased was domiciled had to obtain a grant in England with the will annexed: *Re Earl* (1867) LR 1 P & D 450.

2 Ie any instrument having in a British possession the same effect which under English law is given to probate and letters of administration. As to the practice on the resealing of an election to administer (eg as obtained in New Zealand) or similar document having the same effect as a grant see *Practice Direction* (1982) 126 Sol Jo 176.

3 *Re Smith* [1904] P 114. As to grants de bonis non see PARA 793.

4 The Colonial Probates Act 1892 has been extended so as to be applicable by Order in Council to protected and trust territories: see the Colonial Probates (Protected States and Mandated Territories) Act 1927 s 1. It applies in relation to the Hong Kong Special Administrative Region of the People's Republic of China, following the reversion of Hong Kong to Chinese rule: see the Colonial Probates Act 1892 s 1A (added by SI 1997/1572).

5 See the Colonial Probates Act 1892 ss 1, 4. As to the territories to which the Act has been applied see PARA 838.

6 See the Colonial Probates Act 1892 ss 3, 6. The Act may also be extended by Order in Council to foreign countries in which for the time being Her Majesty has jurisdiction, by the joint effect of the Foreign Jurisdiction Act 1890 s 5, Sch 1, and the Foreign Jurisdiction Act 1913 s 1.

7 Colonial Probates Act 1892 s 2(1) (amended by the Finance Act 1975 s 52(1), Sch 12 paras 2,4; and by the Senior Courts Act 1981 ss 152(1), 153(4), Sch 5), which is expressed to be subject to the Senior Courts Act 1981 s 109 (see PARA 731). As to requirements for resealing see PARA 840 and as to the practice and procedure see PARA 841. Rules of court may be made for regulating the procedure and practice, including fees and costs, in courts of the United Kingdom, on and incidental to an application for sealing a probate or letters of administration granted in a British possession to which the Colonial Probates Act 1892 applies: s 2(5).

838. Countries to which the Colonial Probates Act 1892 applies. The Colonial Probates Act 1892 was originally applied by a series of Orders in Council which have been consolidated in the Colonial Probates Act Application Order 1965[1]. Grants may be resealed by the English court if made in the following countries and territories: Aden[2], Alberta, Antigua, Australian Capital Territory, Bahamas, Barbados, Belize[3], Bermuda, Botswana[4], British Antarctic Territory, British Columbia, British Solomon Islands Protectorate, British Sovereign Base Areas in Cyprus, Brunei, Cayman Islands, Christmas Island (Australian), Cocos (Keeling) Islands, Cyprus (Republic)[5], Dominica, Falkland Islands Colony, Falkland Islands Dependencies, Fiji, Gambia, Ghana, Gibraltar, Grenada, Guyana[6], Hong Kong[7], Jamaica, Kenya, Kiribati[8], Lesotho[9], Malawi, Malaysia[10], Manitoba, Montserrat, New Brunswick, New Guinea (Trust Territory), New South Wales, New Zealand, Newfoundland, Nigeria, Norfolk Island, Northern Territory of Australia, North-West Territories of Canada, Nova Scotia, Ontario, Papua, Prince Edward Island, Queensland, St Christopher, Nevis and Anguilla, St Helena, St Lucia, St Vincent, Saskatchewan, Seychelles, Sierra Leone, Singapore[11], South Africa[12], South Australia, Sri Lanka[13], Swaziland, Tanzania, Tasmania, Tortola[14], Trinidad and Tobago, Turks and Caicos Islands, Tuvalu[15], Uganda, Vanuatu[16], Victoria, Western Australia, Zambia and Zimbabwe[17].

1 Ie the Colonial Probates Act Application Order 1965, SI 1965/1530. For additional orders see notes 7, 16. See also PARA 837 note 6.

2 Grants made after November 1967 (when Aden ceased to be part of Her Majesty's dominions: see COMMONWEALTH vol 13 (2009) PARA 732) cannot be resealed.

3 Formerly British Honduras: see COMMONWEALTH vol 13 (2009) PARA 741.

4 Formerly Bechuanaland Protectorate: see COMMONWEALTH vol 13 (2009) PARA 742.

5 Only grants issued by the courts under the jurisdiction of the recognised government of Cyprus may be resealed. Any document purporting to be a grant issued by a court of the 'Turkish Republic of Northern Cyprus', having only de facto jurisdiction, may not be resealed although such a document may be used to support an application for an order under the Non-Contentious Probate Rules 1987, SI 1987/1024, r 30(1)(c) (see Tristram and Coote's Probate Practice (31st Edn) 12.110–12.115).

6 Formerly British Guiana: see COMMONWEALTH vol 13 (2009) PARA 754.

7 As to the application of the Colonial Probates Act 1892 to the Hong Kong Special Administrative Region of the People's Republic of China following the reversion of Hong Kong to Chinese rule on

1 July 1997 see PARA 837 note 4. The Colonial Probates Act Application Order 1965, SI 1965/1530, in relation to that region, continues in force accordingly: see the Colonial Probates Act 1892 s 1A (added by SI 1997/1572).

8 Formerly the Gilbert Islands: see COMMONWEALTH vol 13 (2009) PARA 758.

9 Formerly Basutoland: see COMMONWEALTH vol 13 (2009) PARA 759.

10 The Colonial Probates Act 1892 continues, by virtue of the Singapore Act 1966, to apply to Singapore after its secession from the Federation of Malaysia on 9 August 1965: see COMMONWEALTH vol 13 (2009) PARA 778.

11 See note 10.

12 South Africa Act 1962 s 2(1), Sch 2 para 1. As to obtaining a copy of the will in the case of an executor testamentary for the purposes of the Non-Contentious Probate Rules 1987, SI 1987/2024, r 39(5) (see PARA 841) see Tristram and Coote's Probate Practice (31st Edn) 18.59–18.60. The term 'executor testamentary' to describe the grantee indicates that the deceased died testate.

13 Formerly Ceylon: see COMMONWEALTH vol 13 (2009) PARA 781.

14 Ie the British Virgin Islands: see COMMONWEALTH vol 13 (2009) PARA 866.

15 Formerly the Ellice Islands: see COMMONWEALTH vol 13 (2009) PARA 786.

16 Ie by virtue of the Colonial Probates Act (Application to the New Hebrides) Order 1976, SI 1976/579. Vanuatu was formerly known as the New Hebrides: see COMMONWEALTH vol 13 (2009) PARA 788.

17 Formerly Southern Rhodesia: see COMMONWEALTH vol 13 (2009) PARA 734. See also *Practice Direction* [1980] 2 All ER 324, [1980] 1 WLR 553.

839. Effect of sealing on estate in England and Wales. A person to whom letters of administration have been granted in a country or territory to which the Colonial Probates Act 1892 applies[1] has, on their being sealed by the High Court[2], the same duties with respect to the estate of the deceased in England and Wales and the debts which fall to be paid there, as are imposed by statute[3] on a person granted administration by the High Court[4].

1 See PARA 838.

2 Ie under the Colonial Probates Act 1892 s 2 (see PARA 837): see the Administration of Estates Act 1971 s 11(2).

3 Ie under the Administration of Estates Act 1925 s 25(a), (b) (getting in and administering the estate (see PARA 959 et seq), exhibiting on oath an inventory of it (see PARA 957) and rendering accounts (see PARA 1254)): see the Administration of Estates Act 1971 s 11(2).

4 Administration of Estates Act 1925 s 11(2). As to the general effect of resealing see PARA 835.

840. Requirements for resealing. As a condition of sealing letters of administration granted in a country or territory to which the Colonial Probates Act 1892 applies[1], the High Court may, in certain cases[2] require one or more sureties, in such amount as the court thinks fit, to guarantee that they will make good, within any limit imposed by the court on the total liability of the surety or sureties, any loss which any person interested in the administration of the estate of the deceased in England and Wales may suffer in consequence of a breach by the administrator of his duties in administering it there[3].

A guarantee given in pursuance of any such requirement enures for the benefit of every person interested in the administration of the estate in England and Wales as if contained in a contract under seal made by the surety or sureties with every such person and, where there are two or more sureties, as if they had bound themselves jointly or severally[4]. No claim may be brought on any such guarantee without the leave of the High Court[5]. Stamp duty is not chargeable on any such guarantee[6].

The above provisions apply to the sealing by the High Court in England and Wales of letters of administration granted by a British court in a foreign country as they apply to the sealing of letters of administration granted in a country or territory to which the Colonial Probates Act 1892 applies[7].

Before sealing a probate or letters of administration, the court may require such evidence, if any, as it thinks fit of the domicile of the deceased[8].

1 See PARA 838.
2 Ie cases to which the Senior Courts Act 1981 s 120 (power to require administrators to produce sureties) (see PARA 766) applies and subject to the Administration of Estates Act 1971 s 11(4)–(8) and subject to and in accordance with probate rules: see s 11(3) (as amended: see note 3). 'Probate rules' means rules of court made under the Senior Courts Act 1981 s 127: Administration of Estates Act 1971 s 11(8) (definition substituted by the Senior Courts Act 1981 s 152(1), Sch 5). As to the probate rules see the Non-Contentious Probate Rules 1987, SI 1987/2024; and PARA 841. Under the Non-Contentious Probate Rules 1987, SI 1987/2024, there is no longer provision for the giving of guarantees as a condition of resealing colonial or Commonwealth grants: see PARA 841.
3 Administration of Estates Act 1971 s 11(3) (amended by the Senior Courts Act 1981 s 152(1), (4), Schs 5, 7). The provision applies in lieu of the Colonial Probates Act 1892 s 2 (see PARA 837 et seq): Administration of Estates Act 1971 s 11(1).
4 Administration of Estates Act 1971 s 11(4).
5 Administration of Estates Act 1971 s 11(5). See PARA 841 and notes 19–21 thereto.
6 Administration of Estates Act 1971 s 11(6).
7 Administration of Estates Act 1971 s 11(7). See also PARAS 837–838.
8 Colonial Probates Act 1892 s 2(2). No oath is required on an application for resealing and the statement as to domicile given in the account (see PARA 841 note 14) is normally accepted.

841. Practice and procedure. A sealed duplicate or certified copy of the Commonwealth or colonial grant may be resealed in England[1]. If the deceased died domiciled in the place where the grant was made, and the grant was not such as would be made in England, the grant may nonetheless be resealed here[2]. Where the deceased did not die domiciled in such a place and there is a minority or life interest under English law, the statutory provisions as to the number of personal representatives must be observed[3]. A limited or temporary Commonwealth or colonial grant may be resealed in England only by leave of a district judge or registrar[4].

Except by leave of a district judge or registrar, a Commonwealth or colonial grant may not be resealed unless it was made to[5]:

(1) a person entrusted with the administration of the estate by the court having jurisdiction at the place where the deceased died domiciled[6];
(2) where there is no person so entrusted, to the person beneficially entitled to the estate by the law of the place where the deceased died domiciled or, if there is more than one person so entitled, to such of them as the district judge or registrar may direct[7];
(3) the executor named in the will (if it is in the English or Welsh language)[8]; or
(4) if the will describes the duties of a named person in terms sufficient to constitute him executor according to the tenor of the will, to that person[9].

The application may be made by the person to whom the grant was made or by any person authorised in writing to apply on his behalf[10]. It must be accompanied by:

(a) the grant[11];
(b) a copy of the grant[12];
(c) a copy of any will to which the grant relates[13]; and
(d) Her Majesty's Customs and Excise affidavit or account[14].

The district judge or registrar must send notice of the resealing to the court which made the grant[15].

The present probate rules[16] do not provide for the giving of guarantees as a condition of resealing colonial or Commonwealth grants[17], so where an application for a grant is made on or after 1 January 1988[18], a guarantee will not be required. The rules do make provision for enforcement of any guarantee, providing that an application for leave[19] to sue a surety on a guarantee, unless the district judge or registrar otherwise directs[20], is made by summons to a district judge or registrar and notice of the application is served on the administrator, the surety and any co-surety[21].

1 See the Colonial Probates Act 1892 s 2(4).
2 *Re McLaughlin* [1922] P 235. See also the Non-Contentious Probate Rules 1987, SI 1987/2024, r 30(1), applied by r 39(3); and the text to notes 6–7. As to domicile generally see CONFLICT OF LAWS vol 19 (2011) PARA 336 et seq.
3 See the Senior Courts Act 1981 s 114(2); and PARA 775.
4 Non-Contentious Probate Rules 1987, SI 1987/2024, r 39(4) (amended by SI 1991/1876). As to the meaning of 'district judge' see PARA 631 note 6; and as to the meaning of 'registrar' see PARA 631 note 7. See also *Re Smith* [1904] P 114. In *Re Sanders* [1900] P 292 a colonial grant was allowed to be resealed, although the deceased left no assets in England and Wales; however, there was under the will of a third person a legacy due to the deceased's representatives.
5 Non-Contentious Probate Rules 1987, SI 1987/2024, r 39(3) (amended by SI 1991/1876).
6 Non-Contentious Probate Rules 1987, SI 1987/2024, rr 30(1)(a), 39(3) (r 39(3) as amended: see note 5).
7 Non-Contentious Probate Rules 1987, SI 1987/2024, rr 30(1)(b), 39(3) (both amended by SI 1991/1876).
8 Non-Contentious Probate Rules 1987, SI 1987/2024, rr 30(3)(a)(i), 39(3) (r 39(3) as amended: see note 5).
9 Non-Contentious Probate Rules 1987, SI 1987/2024, rr 30(3)(a)(ii), 39(3) (r 39(3) as amended: see note 5). As to executorship according to the tenor see PARA 613.
10 Non-Contentious Probate Rules 1987, SI 1987/2024, r 39(1). Application may be made by post: *Practice Direction* [1975] 2 All ER 280, [1975] 1 WLR 662.
11 See PARA 837.
12 See the Colonial Probates Act 1892 s 2(1); and PARA 837.
13 Non-Contentious Probate Rules 1987, SI 1987/2024, r 39(5). The grant must include a copy of any such will or be accompanied by a copy of it certified as correct by or under the authority of the court by which the grant was made and, where the copy of the grant to be deposited (see PARA 837) does not include a copy of the will, a copy of it must also be deposited: r 39(5).
14 Non-Contentious Probate Rules 1987, SI 1987/2024, r 39(2). An affidavit (as opposed to an account) is required only where the deceased died before 13 March 1975. See PARA 731. Her Majesty's Customs and Excise was integrated with Inland Revenue to become Her Majesty's Revenue and Customs; see CUSTOMS AND EXCISE vol 31 (2012) PARA 921 et seq.
15 Non-Contentious Probate Rules 1987, SI 1987/2024, r 39(6) (amended by SI 1991/1876). The fee for resealing the grant is £155: see the Non-Contentious Probate Fees Order 2004, SI 2004/3120, Sch 1 Fee 1 (Sch 1 substituted by SI 2011/588; the Non-Contentious Probate Fees Order 2004, SI 2004/3120, Sch 1 Fee 1 amended by SI 2014/876).
16 Ie the Non-Contentious Probate Rules 1987, SI 1987/2024.
17 Ie under the Administration of Estates Act 1971 s 11(3): see PARA 840.
18 Ie the date of the coming into force of the Non-Contentious Probate Rules 1987, SI 1987/2024: see r 1.
19 No action can be brought on a guarantee without the leave of the High Court: see the Administration of Estates Act 1971 s 11(5); and PARA 840.
20 Ie under the Non-Contentious Probate Rules 1987, SI 1987/2024, r 61(1), by which a district judge or registrar may require an application to be made by summons to a district judge or registrar in chambers or open court: see PARA 701.
21 Non-Contentious Probate Rules 1987, SI 1987/2024, r 40 (amended by SI 1991/1876).

842. Resealing English grants in the Commonwealth. The foregoing provisions for resealing grants in England[1] are not applied to any place unless the legislature of that place has made adequate provision for the recognition there of grants made by the courts of the United Kingdom[2]. Where notice is received in the principal registry of the Family Division of the resealing of an English grant, notice of any amendment or revocation of the grant must be sent to the court by which it was resealed[3].

1 See PARAS 835–841.

2 See the Colonial Probates Act 1892 s 1. As to the countries to which those provisions apply see PARA 838.
3 Non-Contentious Probate Rules 1987, SI 1987/2024, r 39(7).

843. Cancellation of resealing. Where it appears to the High Court that a grant resealed under the Colonial Probates Acts 1892 and 1927 ought not to have been resealed, the court may call in the relevant document[1] and, if satisfied that the resealing would be cancelled at the instance of a party interested, may cancel the resealing[2].

1 'Relevant document' means the original grant or, where some other document was sealed by the court under those Acts, that document: Senior Courts Act 1981 s 121(3). As to the meaning of 'grant' see PARA 683 note 2.
2 Senior Courts Act 1981 s 121(3). A resealing may be cancelled without the relevant document being called in, if it cannot be called in: s 121(4).

(10) FOREIGN DOMICILE GRANTS

844. Right to grant. Where the deceased dies domiciled outside England and Wales, a grant[1] may be made by order of the district judge or registrar[2], limited in such way as he may direct to any of the following persons[3]:

(1) to the person entrusted with the administration of the estate by the court having jurisdiction at the place where the deceased died domiciled[4];

(2) where there is no person so entrusted, to the person beneficially entitled to the estate by the law of the place where the deceased died domiciled or, if there is more than one person so entitled, to such of them as the district judge or registrar may direct[5]; or

(3) if in the district judge's or registrar's opinion, the circumstances so require, to such person as he may direct[6].

A grant made under head (1) or head (2) above may be issued jointly with such person as the district judge or registrar may direct if the grant is required to be made to not less than two administrators[7].

Except in certain cases[8], the general rules as to priority for a grant[9] do not apply where the deceased died domiciled outside England and Wales[10].

When it is necessary to decide whether an English grant should be obtained, consideration should be given to the question whether a grant has already been extracted and, if so, to the alternative of obtaining the resealing of that grant[11].

1 As to the meaning of 'grant' see PARA 631 note 7.
2 As to the meaning of 'district judge' see PARA 631 note 6; and as to the meaning of 'registrar' see PARA 631 note 7.
3 Non-Contentious Probate Rules 1987, SI 1987/2024, r 30(1) (amended by SI 1991/1876). As to the special provisions as to probate see the Non-Contentious Probate Rules 1987, SI 1987/2024, r 30(3); and PARA 718. As to the practice regarding grants in cases concerning foreign domiciles see Tristram and Coote's Probate Practice (31st Edn) 12.17 et seq. As to the rights of a foreign state see PARA 767. As to domicile generally see CONFLICT OF LAWS vol 19 (2011) PARA 336 et seq.
4 Non-Contentious Probate Rules 1987, SI 1987/2024, r 30(1)(a).
5 Non-Contentious Probate Rules 1987, SI 1987/2024, r 30(1)(b) (amended by SI 1991/1876).
6 Non-Contentious Probate Rules 1987, SI 1987/2024, r 30(1)(c) (amended by SI 1991/1876).
7 Non-Contentious Probate Rules 1987, SI 1987/2024, r 30(2) (amended by SI 1991/1876). A grant may be required to be made to not less than two administrators by virtue of the Senior Courts Act 1981 s 114(2) where a minority or life interest arises: see PARA 775.
8 Ie except in a case to which the Non-Contentious Probate Rules 1987, SI 1987/2024, r 30(3) applies (see PARA 718): see r 28(2).
9 Ie the Non-Contentious Probate Rules 1987, SI 1987/2024, r 20 (see PARA 790), r 22 (see PARAS 768–769), r 25 (see PARA 776), and r 27 (see PARAS 729, 774): see r 28(2).
10 Non-Contentious Probate Rules 1987, SI 1987/2024, r 28(2).
11 As to the resealing of grants see PARA 830 et seq.

845. Foreign administrator. Although, in the absence of special circumstances, where the deceased died domiciled abroad an English grant of administration will be made to the person[1] entrusted with the administration by the court of the deceased's domicile[2], the English courts will not follow the grant of administration made by the courts of the country of the deceased's domicile where to do so would be to act in contradiction of English law[3]. Accordingly, a grant will not normally be made to a minor domiciled abroad, since his minority would prevent him from exercising in England the authority given him[4].

1 If a grant should be made to not less than two administrators, according to English law a person may be appointed to act jointly with the foreign administrator: see the Non-Contentious Probate Rules 1987, SI 1987/2024, r 30(2); and PARA 844.

2 See the Non-Contentious Probate Rules 1987, SI 1987/2024, r 30(1)(a); and PARA 844. See also *Enohin v Wylie* (1862) 10 HL Cas 1; *Re Earl* (1867) LR 1 P & D 450 at 452; *Re Briesemann* [1894] P 260 at 261; *Re Humphries* [1934] P 78; *Procedure Direction* [1951] WN 167; *Re Kaufman* [1952] P 325, [1952] 2 All ER 261. Where the whole or substantially the whole of the estate in England and Wales is immovable property, a grant in respect of the whole estate may be made in accordance with the law applicable if the deceased died domiciled in England and Wales: see the Non-Contentious Probate Rules 1987, SI 1987/2024, r 30(3)(b); and PARA 718. Cf *Duncan v Lawson* (1889) 41 ChD 394 at 397 per Kay J, where it was suggested that the administrator should be appointed in relation to leaseholds in England belonging to a domiciled Scotsman according to English law. See also *Pepin v Bruyère* [1902] 1 Ch 24, CA. *Duncan v Lawson* was distinguished in *Re Kaufman* [1952] P 325 at 330, [1952] 2 All ER 261 at 263. As to domicile generally see CONFLICT OF LAWS vol 19 (2011) PARA 336 et seq.

3 *Re Duchess D'Orleans* (1859) 1 Sw & Tr 253. See also *Re Papillon, Murrin v Matthews* [2006] EWHC 3419 (Ch), [2006] All ER (D) 297 (Dec); and PARA 718 note 3.

4 *Re Duchess D'Orleans* (1859) 1 Sw & Tr 253. Cf *Re Meatyard* [1903] P 125. Where a grant is of a very limited nature it will sometimes be made even to a minor domiciled abroad: *Re Countess Da Cunha* (1828) 1 Hag Ecc 237 (grant limited to receipt of dividends to which the minor was entitled).

846. Procedure to obtain grant. Unless otherwise directed by a district judge or registrar, the domicile at the date of death must be sworn to in the oath[1] and is usually recited in the grant[2]. Where evidence as to the law of any country or territory outside England and Wales is required the district judge or registrar may accept an affidavit from any person whom, having regard to the particulars of his knowledge or experience given in the affidavit, the district judge or registrar regards as suitably qualified to give expert evidence of the law in question or a certificate by or an act before a notary practising in the country or territory concerned[3]. Any affidavit of law should refer to the facts and state the law applicable, but there must be proper supporting evidence of the facts themselves[4]. Affidavits of law made by a person qualified[5] to give evidence must set out particulars of the knowledge and experience claimed by the deponent to make him competent to give expert evidence of the law of the country in question[6]. An application for a grant to the person entrusted or entitled will not be accepted in the Personal Application Department[7].

1 See the Non-Contentious Probate Rules 1987, SI 1987/2024, r 8(2); and PARA 728. As to the meaning of 'district judge' see PARA 631 note 6; and as to the meaning of 'registrar' see PARA 631 note 7. As to resealing grants where the deceased died domiciled outside England and Wales see generally PARA 830 et seq. As to domicile generally see CONFLICT OF LAWS vol 19 (2011) PARA 336 et seq.

2 See *Practice Direction* [1953] 2 All ER 1154 at 1156, [1953] 1 WLR 1237 at 1239. As to Spanish wills see *Practice Direction* [1953] 1 WLR 459 (affidavit of law normally conclusive).

3 See the Non-Contentious Probate Rules 1987, SI 1987/2024, r 19; and PARA 706. See also the Civil Evidence Act 1972 s 4(1) (see CIVIL PROCEDURE vol 12 (2015) PARAS 749, 887); and *Practice Direction* [1972] 3 All ER 912, [1972] 1 WLR 1433.

4 See *Practice Direction* [1957] 1 All ER 576, [1957] 1 WLR 462.

5 Ie under the Civil Evidence Act 1972 s 4(1): see CIVIL PROCEDURE vol 12 (2015) PARAS 749, 887.

6 See the Non-Contentious Probate Rules 1987, SI 1987/2024, r 19 (as amended by SI 1991/1876). It appears there may no longer be an automatic bar on the acceptance of an affidavit of the law made by the person claiming to be entitled to the grant, his attorney, or the spouse of either as was stated to be the case in *Practice Direction* [1972] 3 All ER 912, [1972] 1 WLR 1433. See Tristram and Coote's Probate Practice (31st Edn) 12.25–12.26.
7 *Practice Direction* [1953] 2 All ER 1154 at 1157, [1953] 1 WLR 1237 at 1241.

(11) REVOCATION OF GRANTS

(i) When and How a Grant may be Revoked

847. Jurisdiction to revoke grants. Jurisdiction to revoke a grant lies with the Chancery Division of the High Court or the County Court if the matter is contentious, and with the Family Division if it is non-contentious[1]. The power to revoke[2] includes power of the court's own motion to call in the grant and revoke or to revoke if necessary without calling in[3]. In a contentious matter revocation is ordered by judgment in a probate claim[4] in the Chancery Division or the County Court[5]. In a non-contentious matter if a district judge or registrar is satisfied that a grant should be amended or revoked he may so order[6], although, except in special circumstances, no grant may be so amended or revoked except on the application or with the consent of the person to whom it was made[7]. There is no jurisdiction for a district judge or registrar to set aside or vary a previous order to revoke[8].

1 See PARA 678. As to the distinction between non-contentious and contentious business see PARA 684.
2 See the Senior Courts Act 1981 s 121(1); and PARA 851.
3 See the Senior Courts Act 1981 s 121(2); and see PARA 851. A similar power enables the court to 'cancel' (as opposed to 'revoke') a grant resealed under the Colonial Probate Acts 1892 and 1927: see the Senior Courts Act 1981 s 121(3), (4); and PARA 843. As to resealing see PARA 835 et seq.
4 See CPR rr 57.1(2)(a)(ii), 57.6.
5 As to the procedure see CPR PD 57—*Probate*; and PARA 888.
6 See the Non-Contentious Probate Rules 1987, SI 1987/2024, r 41(1); and PARA 854. As to the meaning of 'district judge' see PARA 631 note 6; and as to the meaning of 'registrar' see PARA 631 note 7. As to the meaning of 'grant' see PARA 631 note 7. It is the duty of a personal representative to deliver up to the High Court the grant of probate or administration when required to do so by that court: Administration of Estates Act 1925 s 25(c) (substituted by the Administration of Estates Act 1971 s 9).
7 See the Non-Contentious Probate Rules 1987, SI 1987/2024, r 41(2); and PARA 854.
8 *Re Mathew* [1984] 2 All ER 396, [1984] 1 WLR 1011.

848. Revocation on ground of false suggestion. A grant may be revoked where it has been obtained upon a false suggestion, whether made fraudulently[1] or in ignorance where the false suggestion obscures a defect in the title to the grant[2]; it may also be revoked where it subsequently becomes inoperative or useless, or where if allowed to subsist it would prevent the due administration of the estate.

Accordingly, a grant may be revoked if it was obtained on the false suggestion that the person entitled to it is dead[3], or while an action is pending in another competent court as to the validity of a will[4], or by a woman claiming to be the relict of the deceased, but who was not, in fact, legally married to him[5], or by impostors[6], or by the elected guardian of a minor where there is a testamentary guardian[7], or by a minor on the erroneous understanding that he is of age[8], or by the next of kin where there is a valid residuary bequest[9]. A grant of probate of the will of a living person will be revoked[10].

Revocation will not be granted where the applicant's only complaint is such as to constitute a prima facie case for an order for an inventory and account[11]. It is not necessary for a grant based on the erroneous statement that certain persons are 'the only persons entitled to share in the estate' to be revoked in order to give other beneficiaries the share to which they were legally entitled[12].

1 The general rule that a judgment obtained by fraud can be set aside only as against the person who committed or procured the fraud does not apply to an action to set aside a judgment granting probate of a will inasmuch as the will must be either good or bad as against all the world: *Birch v Birch* [1902] P 130, CA. See also PARA 669; and CIVIL PROCEDURE vol 12A (2015) PARA 1225.
2 *Re Cope* [1954] 1 All ER 698, [1954] 1 WLR 608.
3 *Harrison v Weldon* (1731) 2 Stra 911.
4 *Lord Trimlestown v Lady Trimlestown* (1830) 3 Hag Ecc 243.
5 *Re Moore* (1845) 3 Notes of Cases 601; *Re Langley* (1851) 2 Rob Eccl 407.
6 *Re Bergman* (1842) 2 Notes of Cases 22.
7 *Re Morris* (1862) 2 Sw & Tr 360.
8 No minor may act as executor during his minority: *Re Stewart (or Stuart)* (1875) LR 3 P & D 244. Before the Administration of Estates Act 1798 s 6 (repealed, except as to deaths before 1926), a minor could act as executor after the age of 17. The age is now 18: see the Senior Courts Act 1981 s 118; the Family Law Reform Act 1969 s 1; and PARA 620.
9 *Warren v Kelson* (1859) 1 Sw & Tr 290.
10 *Re Napier* (1809) 1 Phillim 83.
11 *Re Cope* [1954] 1 All ER 698, [1954] 1 WLR 608. As to the inventory see further PARA 957.
12 *Re Ward, National Westminster Bank Ltd v Ward* [1971] 2 All ER 1249, [1971] 1 WLR 1376.

849. Revocation on discovery of subsequent will or want of due execution. Where a will has been discovered after a grant of letters of administration or a later will after a grant of probate, or where the grant has been made pending a caveat[1], the original grant may be revoked. A codicil discovered after a grant of probate, if it does not vary the appointment of executors, may be proved alone; if it does vary the appointment, the original grant must be revoked. Where a codicil is discovered after a grant of administration with the will annexed, the original grant must be revoked[2].

A grant made per incuriam must be revoked, and a grant may be revoked or merely amended if the name of the deceased is wrongly stated[3].

Where it is discovered after the issue of a grant that a will proved in common form was not duly executed, application should be made for revocation of the grant[4].

1 *Offley v Best* (1666) 1 Lev 186. As to caveats see PARA 690.
2 See *Re Byrne (No 2)* (1910) 44 ILT 192, where a will was found after a limited administrator had acted on his grant, and the court impounded the limited grant and granted probate to the executrix named in the will. As to administration with the will annexed see PARA 788 et seq. As to limited grants see PARA 813 et seq.
3 Tristram and Coote's Probate Practice (31st Edn) 17.33.
4 Tristram and Coote's Probate Practice (31st Edn) 17.29. See also *Barrett v Bem* [2009] EWHC 2597 (Ch), [2009] All ER (D) 157 (Oct) (court ordered revocation of the grant of probate of the will and a decree pronouncing against its validity on being satisfied that it had been impossible for the deceased to have signed the will and that on the evidence of a handwriting expert, the signature on the will was not that of the deceased) (will subsequently held validly executed at a retrial following new evidence, although that decision was reversed on appeal: [2011] EWHC 1247 (Ch), [2012] Ch 573, [2011] 3 WLR 1193; rvsd [2012] EWCA Civ 52, [2012] Ch 573, [2012] 2 All ER 920, [2012] 3 WLR 330) and *Court v Despallieres* [2009] EWHC 3340 (Ch), [2010] 2 All ER 451, [2010] Fam Law 251 (revocation of grant because testator had entered into a civil partnership subsequent to execution of the will, thereby revoking it).

850. Revocation for purpose of better administration. A grant may be revoked where one of two or more of the executors or administrators becomes incapable of acting by reason of loss of mental capacity or physical ill-health[1], where a creditor administrator has disappeared[2], or wishes to retire[3] after completely settling his own debt, or where the administrator, whether creditor, widow or next of kin, has disappeared[4], for the real object which the court always keeps in view is the due and proper administration of the estate and the interest of the parties beneficially entitled to it[5].

A general grant of administration with the will annexed ought not to be revoked on the application of an administrator who has intermeddled with the estate and applies for revocation and a grant to some other next of kin[6], and only on strong grounds where he has not intermeddled[7]. In the above cases the grant may be revoked at the instance of a creditor[8].

A district judge or registrar may, inter alia, revoke a grant on an application to add a personal representative[9].

Under the present practice, a further grant following a revoked grant will be a general grant to all the estate and not a grant de bonis non[10].

1 See *Re Galbraith* [1951] P 422, [1951] 2 All ER 470n (although this was a case where both surviving executors lacked the ability to act). Usually, if a sole or last surviving grantee subsequently loses capacity to act, the grant is not revoked; see PARA 793 note 7. As to an executor or administrator lacking capacity within the meaning of the Mental Capacity Act 2005 see PARA 804.
2 *Re Jenkins* (1819) 3 Phillim 33; *Re Bradshaw* (1887) 13 PD 18.
3 *Re Hoare* (1833) cited in 2 Sw & Tr 361n.
4 *Re Covell* (1889) 15 PD 8; *Re Loveday* [1900] P 154; *Re Colclough* [1902] 2 IR 499; *Re Thomas* [1912] P 177; *Re Boyd* (1912) 46 ILT 294. Cf *Re Dye* (1850) 2 Rob Eccl 342; *Re Ferrier* (1828) 1 Hag Ecc 241; *Re Hoare* (1833) cited in 2 Sw & Tr 361n; *Re Thacker* [1900] P 15.
5 *Re Loveday* [1900] P 154 at 156. See also Tristram and Coote's Probate Practice (31st Edn) 17.13–17.26, 17.64–17.65.
6 *Re Reid* (1886) 11 PD 70, CA. As to intermeddling see PARA 1261 et seq.
7 *Re Heslop* (1846) 1 Rob Eccl 457. In a special case probate was revoked on the application of the grantee, a married woman, on the ground of difficulties in transferring stock: *Meek and Donald v Curtis* (1827) 1 Hag Ecc 127 at 129.
8 *Re French* [1910] P 169.
9 See the Non-Contentious Probate Rules 1987, SI 1987/2024, r 26(2); and PARA 776. As to the power to appoint an additional personal representative see PARAS 775–776. As to the meaning of 'district judge' see PARA 631 note 6; as to the meaning of 'registrar' see PARA 631 note 7; and as to the meaning of 'personal representative' see PARA 608.
10 See Tristram and Coote's Probate Practice (31st Edn) 17.27. As to 'de bonis non' see PARA 793.

851. Revocation at the instance of the court. Where it appears to the High Court that a grant of probate or administration ought not to have been granted or that it contains an error, the court may call in the grant and revoke if it is satisfied that the grant would be revoked at the instance of a party interested[1]. If the grant cannot be called in the court may nevertheless revoke it[2].

1 Senior Courts Act 1981 s 121(1). See also *Re Davies, Panton v Jones* (1978) Times, 22 May (where letters of administration were revoked on an irregularity).
2 See the Senior Courts Act 1981 s 121(2). See note 1.

852. Revocation of limited grants. A limited grant may be revoked in favour of the assignee of the interest to which the grant was limited[1]. A grant limited to carrying on proceedings in Chancery ought not, while still in force, to be revoked in order that a general grant may issue; it should be supplemented by a caeterorum grant[2].

1 *Re Ferrier* (1828) 1 Hag Ecc 241. As to limited grants see PARA 813 et seq.
2 *Re Brown* (1872) LR 2 P & D 455; *Re Byrne (No 2)* (1910) 44 ILT 192. Cf PARA 849 note 2. As to caeterorum grants see PARA 748.

853. Executor ought not to apply for revocation. An executor who has obtained probate in common form[1] is not entitled to take steps to have the grant revoked, or to cite the persons interested under the will to propound it in solemn form[2]. He may propound it himself in solemn form, and then give notice to the legatees or devisees that it is to be opposed, and that he does not intend to take steps to support it unless he is guaranteed his costs[3]. An executor who is also next of kin and has obtained probate, even with full knowledge of the facts, may, however, on a reasonable explanation, take proceedings for revocation[4].

Probate in common form granted by consent cannot afterwards be revoked on proof that the conditions on which it was granted have not been complied with, unless it was procured by fraud or circumvention[5].

1 As to probate in common form see PARA 724 et seq.
2 As to the object of citations see PARA 695; and as to the former procedure by citation and intervention see *Re Langton* [1964] P 163, [1964] 1 All ER 749, CA. As to probate in solemn form see PARA 860 et seq.
3 *Re Chamberlain* (1867) LR 1 P & D 316.
4 *Re Williams, Williams v Evans* [1911] P 175 (action by executor next of kin for revocation of probate). See PARA 862.
5 *Nicol v Askew* (1837) 2 Moo PCC 88 (Privy Council appeal from Jamaica).

854. Procedure for revocation: non-contentious matter. A district judge[1] or registrar[2] may, in a non-contentious matter, if satisfied that a grant[3] should be revoked or amended order accordingly[4]. However, unless there are special circumstances he may do so only on the application or with the consent of the person to whom the grant was made[5]. Evidence is filed by affidavit setting out the circumstances, and if the registrar is for any reason not satisfied the matter is referred to a judge[6].

A revoked grant must be produced and delivered to the district judge or registrar at the time of its revocation, so that it may be cancelled in the registry[7].

1 As to the meaning of 'district judge' see PARA 631 note 6.
2 As to the meaning of 'registrar' see PARA 631 note 7.
3 As to the meaning of 'grant' see PARA 631 note 7.
4 Non-Contentious Probate Rules 1987, SI 1987/2024, r 41(1) (amended by SI 1991/1876). Application is made ex parte: see PARA 703. As to the procedure in relation to contentious revocation see PARA 888. As to the distinction between non-contentious and contentious business see PARA 684.
5 Non-Contentious Probate Rules 1987, SI 1987/2024, r 41(2). If the consent is not forthcoming, the district judge or registrar may direct the application be made on summons see r 61; and PARA 701.
6 See *Re Bergman* (1842) 2 Notes of Cases 22.
7 As to the calling in of a grant where it is revoked at the instance of the court itself, however, see PARA 851.

(ii) Effect of Revocation

855. Effect of revocation generally. All payments and dispositions[1] made in good faith to a personal representative[2] under a representation[3] which is subsequently revoked are a valid discharge to the person making the same[4]. The personal representative who acted under the revoked representation may retain and reimburse himself in respect of any payments or dispositions made by him which the person to whom representation is afterwards granted might have properly made[5]. However, he remains liable to account, in the same way as an original administrator is liable to account after a cessate grant to another administrator[6].

1 As to the meaning of 'disposition' see PARA 969 note 7.
2 As to the meaning of 'personal representative' see PARA 608.
3 As to the meaning of 'representation' see PARA 608 note 2.
4 Administration of Estates Act 1925 s 27(2).
5 Administration of Estates Act 1925 s 27(2).
6 See PARA 753.

856. Right to indemnity where payments made in good faith upon grant. Persons and corporations making or permitting to be made any payment or disposition[1] in good faith under a representation[2] are entitled to be indemnified and protected in so doing, notwithstanding any defect or circumstance whatsoever affecting the validity of the representation[3].

1 As to the meaning of 'disposition' see PARA 969 note 7.
2 As to the meaning of 'representation' see PARA 608 note 2.
3 Administration of Estates Act 1925 s 27(1). See *Allen v Dundas* (1789) 3 Term Rep 125.

857. Effect of revocation upon legal proceedings. If, while any legal proceeding is pending in any court[1] by or against an administrator[2] to whom a temporary administration[3] has been granted, that administration is revoked, that court may order that the proceeding be continued by or against the new personal representative[4] in like manner as if it had been originally commenced by or against him, but subject to such conditions and variations, if any, as that court directs[5].

1 Including the County Court: see the Administration of Estates Act 1925 s 17(2) (added by the County Courts Act 1984 s 148(1), Sch 2 Pt III para 11).
2 As to the meaning of 'administrator' see PARA 607 note 1.
3 As to the meaning of 'administration' see PARA 607 note 1.
4 As to the meaning of 'personal representative' see PARA 608.
5 Administration of Estates Act 1925 s 17(1) (numbered as such by the County Courts Act 1984 Sch 2 Pt III para 11).

858. Validity of conveyance not affected by revocation of grant of representation. All conveyances[1] of any interest in real[2] or personal estate made[3] to a purchaser[4] by a person to whom probate or letters of administration have been granted are valid, notwithstanding any subsequent revocation or variation of the probate or administration[5].

Accordingly, the former distinction between cases where the grant was voidable only[6] and void ab initio[7] no longer prevails.

1 'Conveyance' includes a mortgage, charge by way of legal mortgage, lease, assent, vesting, declaration, vesting instrument, disclaimer, release and every other assurance of property or of an interest in it by any instrument, except a will, and 'convey' has a corresponding meaning: Administration of Estates Act 1925 s 55(1)(iii). As to the meaning of 'will' see PARA 607 note 1.
2 As to the meaning of 'real estate' see PARA 607 note 1.
3 Ie made before 1926 or after 1925: see the Administration of Estates Act 1925 s 37(1).
4 'Purchaser' means a lessee, mortgagee, or other person who in good faith acquires an interest in property for valuable consideration, also an intending purchaser and 'valuable consideration' includes marriage and formation of a civil partnership, but does not include a nominal consideration in money: Administration of Estates Act 1925 s 55(1)(xviii) (amended by the Civil Partnership Act 2004 Sch 4 para 12).
5 Administration of Estates Act 1925 s 37(1). This provision is without prejudice to any court order made before 1926 and applies whether the testator or intestate died before 1926 or after 1925: s 37(2). Section 37 gives statutory effect to *Hewson v Shelley* [1914] 2 Ch 13, CA (cited in note 7) (which overruled *Ellis v Ellis* [1905] 1 Ch 613, and *Abraham v Conyngham* (1676) 2 Lev 182). See also *Re Bridgett and Hayes' Contract* [1928] Ch 163; *Creed v Creed* [1913] 1 IR 48; *Dooley v Dooley* [1927] IR 190, CA; *McParland v Conlon* [1930] NI 138, CA, following *Hewson v Shelley*.
6 Where a grant of administration was obtained by the suppression of a will not appointing executors, a sale of leaseholds by the administratrix was upheld: *Boxall v Boxall* (1884) 27 ChD 220. See also *Packman's Case* (1596) 6 Co Rep 18b; *Blackborough v Davis* (1701) 1 P Wms 41 at 43; *Woolley v Clark* (1822) 5 B & Ald 744; *Craster v Thomas* [1909] 2 Ch 348, CA (revoked Indian grant).
7 Where a grant of administration was obtained by suppressing a will appointing executors, the grant was held to be void ab initio, and any dealings by the administrator were void (*Graysbrook v Fox* (1564) 1 Plowd 275; *Abraham v Conyngham* (1676) 2 Lev 182; *Ellis v Ellis* [1905] 1 Ch 613), until the principle now made statutory was pronounced in *Hewson v Shelley* [1914] 2 Ch 13, CA, where the deceased's widow was granted letters of administration as if on intestacy and conveyed to a purchaser part of the real estate; a will appointing executors was afterwards found,

and the executors, after obtaining probate, sued the widow for recovery of the sold realty. The Court of Appeal held that the purchaser retained a good title.

859. Stay of proceedings after revocation. Where an administration judgment or order has been made in a claim brought by a person whose grant is subsequently revoked, an order may be obtained to stay all further proceedings in the action[1], or on appeal the claim may be dismissed or the order or judgment may be reversed[2].

1 *Houseman v Houseman* (1876) 1 ChD 535, CA.
2 *Re Dean, Dean v Wright* (1882) 21 ChD 581, CA.

10. CONTENTIOUS PROBATE

(1) WHEN PROBATE IN SOLEMN FORM IS NECESSARY

860. Proof in solemn form. If there is any doubt as to the validity of a will or any apprehension that there may be opposition to it, or proof of it in common form has been prevented by a caveat and the entry of an appearance to the warning of that caveat[1], it is open to the executor or any person with a beneficial interest under the will[2] to prove it in solemn form. To obtain such proof he must begin a probate claim[3], making the persons interested in opposing the will, whether under another will or on intestacy, defendants[4]. All persons whose interest may be adversely affected by the outcome of the claim must be either joined as parties or served with notice of proceedings[5] so that such persons will be bound by the order of the court[6]. Where there are a large number of persons who might be affected, it is not always convenient to join them all as parties and in such circumstances the court may direct that they are served, so allowing them to become parties and in any event binding them to the result of the claim[7]. In certain cases it may be appropriate to apply for a representation order, either where parties have the same interest or to represent the interest of parties who are unborn or cannot be found or ascertained[8].

Anyone intending to make a probate claim should, before commencing proceedings, observe any relevant pre-action protocol[9].

1 See PARAS 690–694.
2 See also PARA 863 for others who may call for proof in solemn form.
3 The procedure is now governed by the CPR Pt 57. CPR Pt 57 section I deals with probate claims and is supplemented by *Practice Direction—Probate* PD 57. As to the meaning of 'probate claim' see PARA 680 note 2. As to the CPR generally see CIVIL PROCEDURE vol 11 (2015) PARA 12 et seq. Where a probate claim was issued before 15 October 2001, the rules in force immediately before that date apply, rather than Part 57: see the Civil Procedure (Amendment No 2) Rules 2001, SI 2001/1388, r 19. As well as probate claims, Part 57 and its Practice Direction cover claims for rectification of wills in Section II (see PARA 889), claims and applications to substitute or remove a personal representative in Section III (see PARA 1163) and claims under the Inheritance (Provision for Family and Dependants) Act 1975 in Section IV (see PARA 597).
4 Where a legatee will take the same amount whatever the outcome under another will or on intestacy, he is not a person interested and need not be joined.
5 See PARAS 878, 885.
6 See Tristram and Coote's Probate Practice (30th Edn) 26.06, 26.07. An order obtained by consent or default does not normally found res judicata: see *Pople v Evans* [1969] 2 Ch 255, [1968] 2 All ER 743; *Re Barraclough* [1967] P 1, [1965] 2 All ER 311. As to the court's power to approve a compromise and bind absent persons see PARA 885. The court may, under CPR 39.3(3) (see CIVIL PROCEDURE vol 12 (2015) PARA 1069), set aside an order in a probate claim in appropriate circumstances, eg if a defendant is by unavoidable accident prevented from appearing at the trial: see *Re Barraclough* at 11 and 316 per Payne J. See also CPR 39.3(5) (see CIVIL PROCEDURE vol 12 (2015) PARA 1069) which provides that the application to set aside may only be granted if the applicant acted promptly when he found out about the court's order, had a good reason for not attending the trial, and has a reasonable prospect of success. See also *Hackney London Borough Council v Driscoll* [2003] EWCA Civ 1037, [2003] 4 All ER 1205, [2003] 1 WLR 2602 where a defendant had notice of the proceedings but no notice of the trial but was still required to show a reasonable prospect of success.
7 See CPR 19.8A; and CIVIL PROCEDURE vol 11 (2015) PARA 495. If a person is served with notice of a claim and files an acknowledgment of service within 14 days, he becomes a party to the claim but if he does not, he is bound by any judgment given in the claim as if he was a party: see CPR 19.8A (6); and CIVIL PROCEDURE vol 11 (2015) PARA 495. As to acknowledgment of service see PARA 869. See also PARA 878.
8 See CPR 19.7; and CIVIL PROCEDURE vol 11 (2015) PARA 492. See also PARA 878.
9 Pre-action protocols are statements of best practice about pre-action conduct which have been approved by the Head of Civil Justice and are listed in *Practice Direction—Pre-Action Conduct*: see para 18 for the protocols in force. Before commencing proceedings, the court will expect the

parties to have exchanged sufficient information to understand each other's position; make decisions about how to proceed; try to settle the issues without proceedings; consider a form of alternative dispute resolution to assist with settlement; support the efficient management of those proceedings; and reduce the costs of resolving the dispute: *Practice Direction—Pre-Action Conduct* para 3. Currently there is no official protocol specific to contentious probate, but the court will expect the parties to potential probate proceedings, in accordance with the overriding objective as set out in CPR Pt 1 (see CIVIL PROCEDURE vol 12 (2015) PARA 504), to act reasonably in exchanging information and documents relevant to the claim and generally in trying to avoid the necessity for the start of proceedings and, unless the circumstances make it inappropriate, before starting proceedings the parties should:

(1) exchange sufficient information about the matter to allow them to understand each other's position and make informed decisions about settlement and how to proceed;

(2) make appropriate attempts to resolve the matter without starting proceedings, and in particular consider the use of an appropriate form of alternative dispute resolution in order to do so.

A form of pre-action protocol has been devised by the Association of Contentious Trust and Probate Practitioners ('ACTAPS') called 'The ACTAPS Practice Guidance Notes for the Resolution of Trust and Probate Disputes'. Apart from the protocols, in will disputes every effort should be made by executors to avoid costly litigation and full information should be given to those attacking the will as to how the will was made, including in appropriate cases the circumstances in which the instructions for it were given and all the surrounding circumstances leading up to the preparation and making of the will. In this respect a solicitor involved in taking instructions and execution of the will is a potential witness and can be called upon to provide a statement to any interested party about the circumstances: *Larke v Nugus* (1979) 123 Sol Jo 337, [2000] WTLR 1033 and see Law Society Practice Note *Disputed Wills* (16 April 2009). In addition, the conduct of the parties, before as well as during the proceedings, and the efforts made, if any, before and during the proceedings in order to try to resolve the dispute, are to be taken into account by the court in assessing the amount of costs to be recoverable by one party from another: see CPR 44.4(3)(a); PARA 908; and CIVIL PROCEDURE vol 12A (2015) PARA 1707. As to the court's power to obtain evidence about testamentary documents before proceedings are commenced see the Senior Courts Act 1981 ss 122, 123; and PARA 680. As to the court's power to order disclosure of documents before proceedings are started see PARA 880.

861. When an executor need not prove. An executor is not obliged to propound a will, and may be condemned in costs if he sets up a document unjustifiably[1]. If he has not intermeddled with the estate he may renounce probate[2], or he may fail to appear to a citation to propound the will, and if it is pronounced for in solemn form may still accept probate[3].

1 See *Re Speke, Speke v Deakin* (1913) 109 LT 719; and PARA 910.

2 See PARA 630.

3 *Bewsher v Williams and Ball* (1861) 3 Sw & Tr 62. If, however, he failed to appear to a citation to take out probate his rights in respect of the executorship would wholly cease: see PARA 689.

862. Procedure where validity of codicil in doubt. An executor who doubts the validity of a codicil should not cite the persons interested under it to propound it, but should proceed to prove the will in solemn form[1]. A bare executor who has proved a will in common form cannot, as executor, take proceedings to call in question the validity of that will[2], but if the executor has a personal interest in the estate and has taken out probate in common form he may be entitled to revocation of probate if he offers an adequate explanation[3].

1 *Re Benbow* (1862) 2 Sw & Tr 488; *Re Muirhead* [1971] P 263, [1971] 1 All ER 609.

2 *Re Chamberlain* (1867) LR 1 P & D 316.

3 *Re Williams, Williams v Evans* [1911] P 175 (executor next of kin); cf *Dooley v Dooley* [1927] IR 190, CA. See also PARA 853.

863. Persons entitled to call for proof in solemn form. The persons entitled on intestacy are entitled to call for proof in solemn form, whether or not probate has been granted in common form; and so may a legatee or devisee whose legacy or devise has been omitted from the probate, and an executor, legatee, or devisee named in any other testamentary instrument of the deceased whose interest is adversely affected by the will in question[1]. Where, however, probate has been granted in common form, the person concerned to compel proof in solemn form must proceed for revocation of the grant unless the executors themselves decide to propound the will in solemn form[2]. A potential applicant for reasonable financial provision also has a sufficient interest to start a claim[3].

The mere acquiescence of one of the persons entitled on intestacy in probate being granted in common form is no bar to the exercise of this right by him, even though he has received a legacy under the will[4], but he must bring into court the amount of his legacy[5] unless he is a minor[6]. Long acquiescence may prove a bar unless the party can account satisfactorily for the delay[7].

The following may also claim proof of a will in solemn form:

(1) the Treasury Solicitor where on intestacy the estate would pass to the Crown as bona vacantia because there is no known person capable of taking an absolute interest in his estate under the statutory provisions relating to distribution on intestacy[8];
(2) the solicitors for the duchies of Cornwall or Lancaster where the estate would on intestacy pass as bona vacantia[9] and the deceased died domiciled in, or, if he died abroad, possessed property in, either of the duchies[10];
(3) a creditor or other appointee to whom administration has actually been granted if a will is said to have been found and proceedings are taken to revoke the grant[11]; and
(4) a creditor of a beneficiary of an estate where the creditor stood to gain if the beneficiary inherited more on intestacy if the will in the her favour was invalid[12].

1 See Tristram and Coote's Probate Practice (30th Edn) 27.02 et seq.
2 *Re Jolley, Jolley v Jarvis* [1964] P 262 at 271, [1964] 1 All ER 596 at 599, CA, per Wilmer LJ, and at 275 and 602 per Danckwerts LJ. As to probate in common form see PARA 724 et seq.
3 See *O'Brien v Seagrave* [2007] EWHC 1247 (Ch), [2007] 3 All ER 633, [2007] 1 WLR 2002 where the applicant's motivation for bringing a probate claim was that the claim for reasonable financial provision under the Inheritance (Provision for Family and Dependants) Act 1975 (see PARA 565 et seq) was more likely to succeed on intestacy than under a will.
4 *Bell v Armstrong* (1822) 1 Add 365; *Core v Spencer* (1796) cited in 1 Add 374; *Merryweather v Turner* (1844) 3 Curt 802.
5 *Bell v Armstrong* (1822) 1 Add 365 at 374; *Braham v Burchell* (1826) 3 Add 243 at 256.
6 *Goddard v Norton* (1846) 5 Notes of Cases 76.
7 *Newell v Weeks* (1814) 2 Phillim 224 at 232.
8 See PARAS 778–779. As to the Treasury Solicitor see CONSTITUTIONAL AND ADMINISTRATIVE LAW vol 20 (2014) PARA 281.
9 As to the circumstances in which the estate of a deceased person passes as bona vacantia see PARAS 512–513. As to distribution on intestacy see generally PARA 477 et seq.
10 As to the rights of the Duchy of Lancaster and the Duke of Cornwall to bona vacantia see PARA 512. As to domicile generally see CONFLICT OF LAWS vol 19 (2011) PARA 336 et seq.
11 *Menzies v Pulbrook and Ker* (1841) 2 Curt 845; *Dabbs v Chisman, Jennens v Lord Beauchamp* (1810) 1 Phillim 155, but a mere creditor of an estate who has not taken a grant does not have sufficient 'interest'.
12 *Randall v Randall* [2016] EWCA Civ 494, (2016) Times, 28 June (if there had been any doubt whether the creditor would have had an interest before the introduction of the civil procedure rules ('CPR'), that was resolved by the CPR's requirement to give effect to the overriding objective: justice required the husband to be able to bring the claim).

864. Legal aid. The Legal Aid, Sentencing and Punishment of Offenders Act 2012[1] makes provision for a new legal aid system[2]. The Act makes no provision for legal aid in contentious probate cases[3].

1 Legal Aid, Sentencing and Punishment of Offenders Act 2012 Pt 1 (ss 1–43).

2 See LEGAL AID vol 65 (2015) PARA 1 et seq. See also PARA 1275. The Legal Services Commission is abolished and replaced by the Legal Aid Agency (see LEGAL AID vol 65 (2015) PARA 156) and overall responsibility for legal aid now lies with the Lord Chancellor (see the Legal Aid, Sentencing and Punishment of Offenders Act 2012 s 1).

3 See the Legal Aid, Sentencing and Punishment of Offenders Act 2012 s 9, Sch 1 Pt 1.

(2) JURISDICTION

865. Jurisdiction of the High Court. The High Court has unlimited jurisdiction over contentious probate business[1], and the Chancery Division is the division of the High Court to which such business is assigned[2]. As a result of the transfer of the jurisdiction in contentious probate to the Chancery Division[3], construction of wills and administration of estates is merged in one division reducing some of the problems of jurisdiction which have arisen in the past[4]. The Chancery Division is also concerned, as before, with the supervision of the administration and distribution of the estate[5], the interpretation of the will[6] and the guidance of the personal representatives[7].

1 See the Senior Courts Act 1981 s 25; and PARA 677. As to the meaning of contentious probate business see PARA 684; and as to the functions of the probate court see PARA 679.

2 See the Senior Courts Act 1981 s 61(1), Sch 1 para 1(h); and CPR 57.2(2). As to the history of the probate jurisdiction, which was originally that of the ecclesiastical courts, see PARAS 676–678. Probate proceedings may only be carried on at the Royal Courts of Justice or in a Chancery District Registry: see PARA 868.

Probate claims designated by CPR 57.2 must be started in a designated County Court hearing centre: CPR PD 2C—*Starting Proceedings in the County Court* para 3.1(3). See further the County Court Directory set out in that Practice Direction. As to probate claims in the County Court see CPR 57.2(3); and PARA 866.

3 Ie from the then Probate, Divorce and Admiralty Division (now the Family Division), with effect from 1 October 1971: see PARA 678.

4 See PARA 679. Where a question of validity of a will is purely one of the construction of testamentary documents, it is now possible to have it resolved in proceedings for a declaration instead of propounding the will in solemn form: see eg *Re Finnemore* [1992] 1 All ER 800, [1991] 1 WLR 793.

5 The court must see that the personal representatives carry the will into effect so far as they are able to do so (*Re Manifold, Slater v Chryssaffinis* [1962] Ch 1 at 18, [1961] 1 All ER 710 at 719), and will if necessary retain the administration under its control (*Re Lorillard, Griffiths v Catforth* [1922] 2 Ch 638, CA).

6 See PARA 679. See also PARA 185 et seq.

7 See PARA 1168.

866. Jurisdiction of the County Court. Where an application for the grant or revocation of probate or administration is made through the principal registry of the Family Division or a district probate registry[1] and it is shown to the satisfaction of the County Court that the value of the deceased's net estate at the date of death does not exceed the County Court limit[2], the County Court has jurisdiction in respect of any contentious probate matter arising in connection with an application for the grant or revocation of probate or administration[3].

Probate claims in the County Court must only be started by sending the claim to, or making the claim at a County Court hearing centre where there is also a Chancery district registry; or the County Court at Central London[4]. If these preconditions are not fulfilled, jurisdiction cannot be conferred on the County Court by the consent of the parties[5].

1 Ie under the Senior Courts Act 1981 s 105 (see PARA 724).

2 At the date at which this volume states the law the county court limit is £30,000: see the High Court and County Courts Jurisdiction Order 1991, SI 1991/724, art 2(7B) (added by SI 2005/587); the County Court Jurisdiction Order 2014, SI 2014/503, art 3; and COURTS AND TRIBUNALS vol 24 (2010) PARA 767.

3 High Court and County Courts Jurisdiction Order 1991, SI 1991/724, art 2(7B) (as added: see note 2).

4 CPR 57.2(3).

5 The County Courts Act 1984 ss 18, 24 (see COURTS AND TRIBUNALS vol 24 (2010) PARAS 767, 776), which enable jurisdiction in many types of case to be conferred by consent, do not apply to probate proceedings. As to the power of the High Court to transfer proceedings to the county court see PARA 867.

867. Transfer of proceedings. The High Court may order the transfer of any proceedings before it to the County Court, either on its own motion or on the application of any party[1]. The High Court has no power to grant a new trial or to make any order or give directions as to the mode of trial in the County Court[2] or to make any order as to costs[3]. After transfer, any application as to the mode of trial must be made to the County Court[4].

If probate proceedings which are before the County Court are outside the County Court jurisdiction the County Court must either transfer them to the High Court or strike them out[5]. In addition, the County Court or the High Court may order transfer to the High Court of probate proceedings which are in the County Court[6]. The County Court may transfer proceedings before it, or any part of those proceedings, to another County Court hearing centre[7], and the High Court may transfer proceedings, or any part of them, which are before the High Court, from the Royal Courts of Justice to a Chancery district registry, or from a Chancery district registry to the Royal Courts of Justice or another Chancery district registry[8].

In considering whether to exercise any of its discretionary powers of transfer[9] the court is to have regard to:

(1) the financial value of the claim, and the amount in dispute (if different)[10];
(2) whether it would be more convenient or fair for hearings to be held in some other court within the County Court[11];
(3) the availability of a judge specialising in the type of claim in question[12];
(4) whether the facts, legal issues, remedies or procedures involved are simple or complex[13];
(5) the importance of the outcome of the claim to the public in general[14];
(6) the facilities available at the court where the claim is being dealt with and whether they may be inadequate because of any disabilities of a party or potential witness[15];
(7) whether the making of a declaration of incompatibility under the Human Rights Act 1998[16] has arisen or may arise[17]; and
(8) in the case of civil proceedings by or against the Crown[18], the location of the relevant government department or officers of the Crown and, where appropriate, any relevant public interest that the matter should be tried in London[19].

1 See the County Courts Act 1984 s 40(2), (3); and CIVIL PROCEDURE vol 11 (2015) PARA 108. The transfer of proceedings under s 40 does not affect any right of appeal from the order directing the transfer: see s 40(5); and CIVIL PROCEDURE vol 11 (2015) PARA 108. As to the criteria to which the court is to have regard in considering whether to exercise any of its discretionary powers of transfer see the text and note 10.

2 *Zealley v Veryard* (1866) LR 1 P & D 195.

3 *Macleur v Macleur* (1868) LR 1 P & D 604.

4 See *Norris v Allen* (1862) 32 LJPM & A 3.

5 See the County Courts Act 1984 s 42(1), (7); and CIVIL PROCEDURE vol 11 (2015) PARA 108. Striking out is to occur if the claimant knew or ought to have known that the proceedings were outside the county court jurisdiction: see s 42(1)(b); and CIVIL PROCEDURE vol 11 (2015) PARA 108.

6 See the County Court Act 1984 ss 41, 42(2); and CIVIL PROCEDURE vol 11 (2015) PARA 108; CIVIL PROCEDURE vol 12A (2015) PARA 1271. The transfer of proceedings under s 42 does not affect any right of appeal from the order directing the transfer: see s 42(4); and CIVIL PROCEDURE vol 11 (2015) PARA 108. For the criteria to which the court is to have regard see the text and notes 10–18.
7 See CPR 30.2(1); and CIVIL PROCEDURE vol 11 (2015) PARA 107. For the criteria to which the court is to have regard see the text and notes 10–17.
8 See CPR 30.2(4), (8); and CIVIL PROCEDURE vol 11 (2015) PARA 106. For the criteria to which the court is to have regard see the text and notes 10–18. As to the Chancery district registries see PARA 868 note 5.
9 Ie the County Courts Act 1984 ss 40(2), 41(1) or 42(2) and CPR 30.2(1), (4) (see the text to notes 1, 6–8): see CPR 30.3(1). Contentious probate proceedings are among the exceptions to the general rule that claims in the High Court in London with an estimated value of less than £100,000 should be transferred to the county court, and are expressed to be suitable for trial in the High Court in London: *Practice Direction—the Multi-Track* PD 29 paras 2.2, 2.6. Transfer of proceedings are usually dealt with at a case management conference: see PARA 877.
10 CPR 30.3(2)(a). See also CIVIL PROCEDURE vol 11 (2015) PARA 105.
11 CPR 30.3(2)(b). See also CIVIL PROCEDURE vol 11 (2015) PARA 105.
12 CPR 30.3(2)(c). See also CIVIL PROCEDURE vol 11 (2015) PARA 105.
13 CPR 30.3(2)(d). See also CIVIL PROCEDURE vol 11 (2015) PARA 105.
14 CPR 30.3(2)(e). See also CIVIL PROCEDURE vol 11 (2015) PARA 105.
15 CPR 30.3(2)(f). See also CIVIL PROCEDURE vol 11 (2015) PARA 105.
16 Ie under the Human Rights Act 1998 s 4: see RIGHTS AND FREEDOMS vol 88A (2013) PARA 18.
17 CPR 30.3(2)(g). See also CIVIL PROCEDURE vol 11 (2015) PARA 105.
18 As to the meaning of 'civil proceedings' see CPR 66.1(2); and CIVIL PROCEDURE vol 12A (2015) PARA 1310 (definition applied by CPR 30.3(2)(h)).
19 CPR 30.3(2)(h). See also CIVIL PROCEDURE vol 11 (2015) PARA 105.

(3) PROCEDURE

868. Claim form. A probate claim[1] in solemn form must be begun by the issue of a claim form[2] containing a statement of the nature of the interest of the claimant and of each defendant in the estate of the deceased to which the claim relates[3]. The claim form and all subsequent court documents relating to a probate claim must be marked at the top 'In the estate of [name] deceased (Probate)'[4]. If the claim is to be commenced in the High Court, the claim form must be issued out of Chancery Chambers at the Royal Courts of Justice or one of the Chancery district registries[5]. If a probate claim is suitable to be heard in the County Court, the claim form must be issued at a County Court hearing centre in a place where there is also a Chancery district registry or the Central London County Court[6]. The commencement of a probate claim will, unless a court otherwise directs, prevent a grant of probate or letters of administration being made until the probate claim has been disposed of[7]. A claim form may with the permission of the court be served out of the jurisdiction[8]. A claim form must either contain or have served with it particulars of claim, or else contain a statement that particulars of claim are to follow[9].

In a probate claim which seeks the revocation of a grant of probate or letters of administration every person who is entitled, or claims to be entitled, to administer the estate under that grant must be made a party to the claim[10].

The service of the claim form and acknowledgment of service are governed by the general Civil Procedure Rules[11].

1 As to the meaning of 'probate claim' see PARA 680 note 2.
2 The form must be issued in the relevant office using the procedure in the CPR Pt 7: see CPR 57.3; and CIVIL PROCEDURE vol 11 (2015) PARA 135. For the general rules concerning claim forms see

CPR Pt 7; *Practice Direction—How to Start Proceedings: the Claim Form* PD 7A. As to the meaning of 'claim form' see CIVIL PROCEDURE vol 11 (2015) PARA 244. See also CIVIL PROCEDURE vol 11 (2015) PARA 139 et seq.

3 See CPR 57.7(1); and CIVIL PROCEDURE vol 11 (2015) PARA 161. If a party disputes another party's interest in the estate he must state this in his statement of case and set out his reasons: see CPR 57.7(2); and CIVIL PROCEDURE vol 11 (2015) PARA 161. See also PARA 777. As to those with an interest in the estate see PARA 863. As to statements of case see PARA 875. For the steps to be taken before commencing proceedings and notification of persons who may be affected by the claim but are not joined as parties see PARAS 860, 878. As to the practice in claims for revocation of a grant see PARA 888.

4 *Practice Direction—Probate* PD 57 para 2.1.

5 See CPR 57.3(a); and *Practice Direction—Probate* PD 57 para 2.2. The Chancery district registries are at Birmingham, Bristol, Caernarfon, Cardiff, Leeds, Liverpool, Manchester, Mold, Newcastle upon Tyne, and Preston: PD 57 para 2.2.

6 See CPR 57.3; and *Practice Direction—Probate* PD 57 para 2.2. As to the jurisdiction of the County Court see PARA 866.

7 *Practice Direction—Probate* PD 57 para 2.4. See also caveats (PARA 690 et seq) and grants of letters of administration pending the determination of a probate claim (PARA 808 et seq and PARA 870 note 3). All probate claims are allocated to the multi-track: CPR 57.2.(4). As to the multi-track see CIVIL PROCEDURE vol 11 (2015) PARA 233 et seq.

8 As to service in Scotland and Northern Ireland see CPR 6.32; and CIVIL PROCEDURE vol 11 (2015) PARA 265; as to service outside the UK where the permission of the court is not required see CPR 6.33; and CIVIL PROCEDURE vol 11 (2015) PARA 266; as to service out of the jurisdiction where the permission of the court is required see CPR 6.36; *Practice Direction—Service out of the Jurisdiction* PD 6B para 3.1(14); and CIVIL PROCEDURE vol 11 (2015) PARA 267. Proceedings concerning wills and succession are excluded from the scope of the Convention on Jurisdiction and Enforcement of Judgments in Civil and Commercial Matters (Brussels, 27 September 1968, OJ C027, 26.1.98, p 1) and the Convention on Jurisdiction and Enforcement of Judgments in Civil and Commercial Matters (Lugano, 16 September 1988, OJ L319, 25.11.88, p 9) by art 1 of the Brussels Convention (see the Civil Jurisdiction and Judgments Act 1982 ss 2(2), 3A(2), Sch 1, Sch 3C; and CONFLICT OF LAWS vol 19 (2011) PARA 375), and so probate proceedings may not be served in EC or EFTA countries without the permission of the court under CPR 6.36: see CONFLICT OF LAWS vol 19 (2011) PARA 372. The court may grant such permission retrospectively: *Kosa v Nesheim* [2006] EWHC 2710 (Ch), [2007] Fam Law 1132, [2006] All ER (D) 40 (Oct).

9 See CPR 16.2(2); and CIVIL PROCEDURE vol 11 (2015) PARA 343. For particulars of claim see PARA 872.

10 See CPR 57.6(1).

11 For the rules governing service and acknowledgment of service see CPR Pts 6, 10; and CIVIL PROCEDURE vol 11 (2015) PARAS 244, 311. As to the requirement of and time limit for acknowledgment of service and as to failure to acknowledge service see PARA 869.

869. Failure to acknowledge service of claim form. A defendant on whom a probate claim form is served must file an acknowledgment of service[1]. Subject to the longer periods allowed where service is out of the jurisdiction[2], the period for filing an acknowledgment of service is:

(1) if the defendant is served with a claim form which states that particulars of claim are to follow, 28 days after service of the particulars of claim; and

(2) in any other case, 28 days after service of the claim form[3]. Even if no acknowledgment of service is filed, the claimant is unable to seek default judgment[4].

Where any of several defendants to a probate claim fails to acknowledge service of the claim form, the claimant may, after the time for acknowledging service has expired and upon filing written evidence of service of the claim form and (if no particulars of claim were contained in or served with the claim form) the particulars of claim on that defendant proceed with the probate claim as if that defendant had acknowledged service[5]. Where no defendant acknowledges service or files a defence[6] then, unless on the application of the claimant the court orders the claim to be discontinued, the claimant may, after the time for acknowledging service or filing a defence (as the case may be) has expired[7], apply to the court for an order that the claim is to proceed to trial[8]. When applying for such an order the claimant must file written evidence of service of the claim form and (if no particulars of claim were contained in or served with the claim form) the particulars of claim on each of the defendants[9]. Where the court grants an order for trial, it may direct the claim to be tried on written evidence[10].

1 CPR 57.4(1). As to the meaning of 'probate claim' see PARA 680 note 2; and as to the meaning of 'claim form' see CIVIL PROCEDURE vol 11 (2015) PARA 244. As to acknowledgment of service generally see CPR Pt 10; and CIVIL PROCEDURE vol 11 (2015) PARA 311 et seq.

2 If the claim form is served out of the jurisdiction under CPR 6.32 or 6.33, the period for filing an acknowledgment of service is 14 days longer than the relevant period specified in CPR 6.35 or Practice Direction B supplementing CPR Pt 6: CPR 57.4(3). Where the court gives permission to serve out of the jurisdiction under CPR 6.36 it will specify the period within which the defendant may acknowledge service: see CPR 6.37(5)(a)(i); and CIVIL PROCEDURE vol 11 (2015) PARA 287. As to service of the claim form outside the jurisdiction see PARA 868.

3 CPR 57.4(2). This is expressed to be subject to CPR 57.4(3) (see note 2). Note that a longer period is given for acknowledging service in a probate claim than in other claims (the usual period is 14 days) to allow for the fact that when he acknowledges service, the defendant must at the same time file his written evidence about testamentary documents and lodge those documents (see PARA 870).

4 CPR 57.10(1). CPR 10.2 and Pt 12 do not apply. Note that an application can still be made for an order that the claim proceed to trial on written evidence: see the text and note 10.

5 CPR 57.10(2).

6 As to the filing of a defence see PARA 873.

7 See the text to note 2.

8 CPR 57.10(3). As to discontinuance see PARA 883.

9 CPR 57.10(4).

10 CPR 57.10(5). As to trial on written evidence cf PARA 876. For the rules as to written evidence see CPR Pt 32; *Practice Direction—Evidence* PD 32; and CIVIL PROCEDURE vol 12 (2015) PARAS 689, 710–711, 771 et seq.

870. Testamentary documents. A testamentary document is a will or draft will, written instructions for a will made by or at the request or under the instructions of the testator and any document purporting to be evidence of the contents or to be a copy of a will which is alleged to have been lost or destroyed[1]. In a probate claim[2] any testamentary document of the deceased person in the possession or control of any party must be lodged with the court[3]. Unless the court directs otherwise, the testamentary documents must be lodged in the relevant office[4] by the claimant when the claim form is issued[5] and by a defendant when he acknowledges service[6].

The claimant and every defendant who acknowledges service of the claim form must in written evidence[7]:

(1) describe any testamentary document of which he has any knowledge or, if he does not know of any such testamentary document, state that fact[8]; and

(2) if any testamentary document of which he has knowledge is not in his possession or under his control, give the name and address of the person in whose possession or under whose control it is or, if he does not know the name and address of that person, state that fact[9].

Unless the court directs otherwise, any such written evidence must be filed in the relevant office by the claimant, when the claim form is issued and by a defendant when he acknowledges service[10]. Except with the permission of the court, a party to a probate claim is not allowed to inspect the testamentary documents or written evidence lodged or filed by any other party until he himself has lodged his testamentary documents and filed his evidence[11]. Supplementary written evidence may be ordered[12], or may be voluntarily filed.

A party desiring that a testamentary document be examined by an expert should apply to the court[13].

1 CPR 57.1(2)(c). 'Will' includes a codicil: CPR 57.1(2)(d).
2 As to the meaning of 'probate claim' see PARA 680 note 2.
3 See CPR 57.5(1). As to the marking of the will and any other original documents and the front sheet to be attached to them see the Chancery Guide (2016) para 29.48. It is important that testamentary documents should not be marked, stapled or folded. Accordingly a testamentary document should be described in, but not made an exhibit to, the written evidence (see text and note 7). In a case in which there is urgent need to commence a probate claim (for example, in order to be able to apply immediately for the appointment of an administrator pending the determination of the claim) and it is not possible for the claimant to lodge the testamentary documents or to file the evidence about testamentary documents in the relevant office at the same time as the claim form is to be issued, the court may direct that the claimant is allowed to issue the claim form upon his giving an undertaking to the court to lodge the documents and file the evidence within such time as the court shall specify: *Practice Direction—Probate* PD 57 para 3.3. As to the appointment of an administrator pending determination of a claim see PARA 808 et seq. For the powers of the court to order a person to attend for examination about a testamentary document or to bring it in, see PARA 680. See also PARA 871 regarding transmission of testamentary documents.
4 As to the meaning of 'relevant office' see PARA 680 note 2.
5 CPR 57.5(2)(a). As to the meaning of 'claim form' see CIVIL PROCEDURE vol 11 (2015) PARA 244.
6 CPR 57.5(2)(b). As to the time for a defendant to acknowledge service see PARA 869.
7 CPR 57.5(3). See further *Practice Direction—Probate* PD 57 para 3.2 and the annex to the Practice Direction for the form of the written evidence which must be signed by the party personally and not by his solicitor or other representative (except if a party is a child or a protected party the written evidence must be signed by his litigation friend). The testamentary documents should be described but not exhibited: see note 3.
8 CPR 57.5(3)(a).
9 CPR 57.5(3)(b).
10 CPR 57.5(4).
11 CPR 57.5(5). As to lodging of testamentary documents see text and notes 5, 6. As to filing of written evidence see text and notes 8, 9.
12 See *Peacock v Lowe* (1867) LR 1 P & D 311; subsequent proceedings at 478n.
13 See CIVIL PROCEDURE vol 12 (2015) PARA 901. As to expert witnesses generally see CIVIL PROCEDURE vol 12 (2015) PARA 888.

871. Transmission of testamentary documents and verification. When the claim form[1] is issued, the relevant office[2] will send a notice to Leeds District Probate Registry requesting that all testamentary documents[3], grants of representation and other relevant documents currently held at any probate registry are sent to the relevant office[4].

When a probate claim is listed for trial outside London the solicitor for the party responsible for preparing the court bundle must write to the Chancery Registry to request in writing that the testamentary documents be forwarded to the appropriate district registry[5].

Where an attesting witness is unable to attend the Rolls Building or the appropriate District Registry in order to sign his or her witness statement or swear his or her affidavit in the presence of an officer of the court, the solicitor concerned may request from Masters' Appointments or from the District Registry, a photographic copy of the will or codicil in question[6].

1 As to the meaning of 'claim form' see CIVIL PROCEDURE vol 11 (2015) PARA 244.
2 As to the meaning of 'relevant office' see PARA 680 note 2.
3 As to the meaning of 'testamentary document' see PARA 870.
4 See *Practice Direction—Probate* 57 para 2.3. When the claim has been disposed of, unless the court orders otherwise, if a testamentary document is held by the court (whether it was lodged by a party or it was previously held at a probate registry), the court will send it to the Leeds District Probate Registry: para 3.1.

5 See the Chancery Guide (2016) para 29.56. Reference should also be made to the Chancery Guide for the practice as regards bundles of documents and procedure generally in probate claims.

6 See the Chancery Guide (2016) para 29.55. When the court orders trial on written evidence it is normally necessary for an attesting witness to sign a witness statement or swear an affidavit of due execution of the will or codicil sought to be admitted to probate. Either the attesting witness can attend at the court and sign or swear his evidence before an officer of the court or, if unable to do so, his solicitor may request from the court a photocopy of the will or codicil. The will or codicil will be certified as authentic by the court and may be exhibited to the witness statement or affidavit of due execution in lieu of the original. The witness statement or affidavit must in that case state that the exhibited document is an authenticated copy of the document signed in the witness' presence: see the Chancery Guide (2016) para 29.55.

872. Particulars of claim. Particulars of claim must include a concise statement of the facts on which the claimant relies[1] and must be contained in or served with the claim form[2], or served on the defendant by the claimant within 14 days after service of the claim form[3] provided that they must be served on the defendant no later than the latest time for serving a claim form[4]. If the particulars of claim are not included in or served with the claim form, the claim form must include a statement that particulars of claim will follow[5]. If the particulars of claim are not included in the claim form, they must be verified by a statement of truth[6].

1 See CPR 16.4 and CIVIL PROCEDURE vol 11 (2015) PARA 345. As to what facts must be stated and included in the claimant's statement of case see PARA 875. See also PARA 868 note 3. As to the CPR see generally CIVIL PROCEDURE vol 11 (2015) PARA 12 et seq.

2 See CPR 7.4(1)(a); and CIVIL PROCEDURE vol 11 (2015) PARA 145. As to the meaning of 'claim form' see CIVIL PROCEDURE vol 11 (2015) PARA 244.

3 See CPR 7.4(1)(b); and CIVIL PROCEDURE vol 11 (2015) PARA 145.

4 See CPR 7.4(2); and CIVIL PROCEDURE vol 11 (2015) PARAS 145, 345. The latest time for serving the particulars of claim is four months after the date of issue of the claim or six months thereafter where the claim form is to be served out of the jurisdiction: see CPR 7.5(1), (2); and CIVIL PROCEDURE vol 11 (2015) PARAS 144, 345. As to service of the claim form out of the jurisdiction see PARA 868 note 8.

5 See CPR 16.2(2); and CIVIL PROCEDURE vol 11 (2015) PARA 345.

6 See CPR 22.1; and CIVIL PROCEDURE vol 11 (2015) PARA 363. See also *Practice Direction—Statement of Case* PD 16 para 3.4; and CIVIL PROCEDURE vol 11 (2015) PARA 345.

873. Defence, counterclaim and reply. A defence must, subject to certain exceptions[1], be filed within 14 days after service of the particulars of claim[2] or, if the defendant files an acknowledgment of service, 28 days after service of the particulars of claim[3]. A defendant to a probate claim[4] who contends he has any claim or is entitled to any remedy relating to the grant of probate of the will, or letters of administration of the estate, of the deceased person must serve a counterclaim making that contention[5]. If the claimant fails to serve particulars of claim within the time allowed, a defendant may, with the permission of the court, serve a counterclaim and the probate claim then continue as if the counterclaim were the particulars of claim[6].

Any reply must be served and filed at the time when the claimant files his destinations questionnaire[7]. Any defence to counterclaim should be included in the same document as the reply and should follow on from it[8].

A probate counterclaim[9] must contain a statement of the nature of the interest of each of the parties in the estate of the deceased to which the probate counterclaim relates[10]. Unless within seven days after the service of a probate counterclaim an application is made for an order[11] for the probate counterclaim to be dealt with in separate proceedings or struck out and the application is granted, the court must order the transfer of the proceedings to either the Chancery Division (if it is not already assigned to that Division) and to either the Royal Courts of Justice or a Chancery district registry (if it is not already proceeding in one of those places) or, if the County Court has jurisdiction, to a County Court hearing centre where there is also a Chancery district registry or the Central London County Court[12].

1 The exceptions are where different limits apply under the provisions referred to in CPR 15.4(2). These include:
   (1) CPR 6.35 (which specifies how the period for filing a defence is calculated where the claim form is served out of the jurisdiction); and
   (2) CPR Pt 11 (which provides that, where the defendant makes an application disputing the court's jurisdiction, he need not file a defence before the hearing) (see CPR 15.4(2); and CIVIL PROCEDURE vol 11 (2015) PARA 315).
2 See CPR 15.4(1); and CIVIL PROCEDURE vol 11 (2015) PARA 345 et seq. As to particulars of claim see PARA 872.
3 See CPR 57.4(2). The general rule for filing a defence under CPR 15.4 applies subject to the words 'under Part 10' being omitted from CPR 15.4(1)(b): CPR 57.4(4). As to acknowledgment of service see PARA 869. In his defence, the defendant must state which of the allegations in the particulars of claim he denies; which he is unable to admit or deny, but which he requires the claimant to prove; and which he admits: see CPR 16.5(1); and CIVIL PROCEDURE vol 11 (2015) PARA 352. Where the defendant denies an allegation, he must state his reasons for doing so and if he intends to put forward a different version of events from that given by the claimant, he must state his own version: see CPR 16.5(2); and CIVIL PROCEDURE vol 11 (2015) PARA 352. See also PARA 875. A defence may be confined to requiring the claimant to prove the will in solemn form, and this provides certain advantages in terms of costs if it fails: see PARA 874.
4 As to the meaning of 'probate claim' see PARA 680 note 2.
5 CPR 57.8(1). In general, where a defendant to a claim serves a counterclaim under CPR Pt 20, the defence and counterclaim should normally form one document with the counterclaim following on from the defence: see *Practice Direction—Defence and Reply* PD 15 para 3.1; and CIVIL PROCEDURE vol 11 (2015) PARA 338.
6 CPR 57.8(2). As to the defences available see PARA 891 et seq.
7 See CPR 15.8; and CIVIL PROCEDURE vol 11 (2015) PARA 356. As to the directions questionnaire see CPR 26.3; and CIVIL PROCEDURE vol 11 (2015) PARA 204. The time for filing the directions questionnaire is set by the court but is at least 14 days after deemed service of it and it is not served until at least one defendant has served a defence: see CPR 26.3(1), (2), (6); and CIVIL PROCEDURE vol 11 (2015) PARA 204.
8 See *Practice Direction—Defence and Reply* PD 15 para 3.2.
9 'Probate counterclaim' means a counterclaim in any claim other than a probate claim by which the defendant claims any such remedy as is mentioned in CPR 57.1(2)(a): CPR 57.9(1). As to CPR 57.1(2)(a) see PARA 860. Subject to CPR 57.9(3)–(5), CPR 57 applies with the necessary modifications to a probate counterclaim as it applies to a probate claim: CPR 57.9(2).
10 CPR 57.9(3).
11 Ie under CPR 3.1(2)(e) or 3.4 (see CIVIL PROCEDURE vol 11 (2015) PARAS 241, 487; CIVIL PROCEDURE vol 12 (2015) PARAS 516, 530): CPR 57.9(4).
12 CPR 57.9(4). If an order is made for a probate counterclaim to be dealt with in separate proceedings, the order must order transfer of the probate counterclaim as required under CPR 57.9(4): CPR 57.9(5). As to the Chancery district registries see PARA 868 note 5. As to transfer of proceedings see PARA 867.

874. Limitation of costs on notice of intention to cross-examine only. A defendant may give notice in his defence that he will raise no positive case but will insist on the will being proved in solemn form, and, for that purpose, will cross-examine the witnesses who attested the will[1]. In such a case the court will not make an order for costs against the defendant unless it considers that there was no reasonable ground for opposing the will[2]. It does not follow because a defendant fails that there was no reasonable ground[3]. A person seeking to call in and obtain revocation of a probate[4], or a party alleging in his statement of case undue influence or fraud, has no right to give such a notice but questions may be asked as to testamentary capacity and knowledge and approval[5].

1 CPR 57.7(5)(a). See also CIVIL PROCEDURE vol 11 (2015) PARA 161. Any application by the claimant for summary judgment is subject to the right of the defendant to require witnesses to attend for cross examination: *Practice Direction—Probate* PD 57 para 5.2. As to summary judgment see PARA 884.

2 CPR 57.7(5)(b). For a recent example of a defendant ordered to pay costs because of lack of reasonable grounds see *Elliott v Simmonds* [2016] EWHC 962 (Ch). However, costs were ordered only from the date on which the defendant had sufficient material on which to form a view about whether there was any reasonable ground to oppose the will. Where a party unsuccessfully opposes a will, it is possible that he may not be ordered to pay the successful party's costs even though he did not give such a notice in his defence: see PARA 911. As to costs generally see PARA 908 et seq.

3 *Davies v Jones* [1899] P 161. In *Re Spicer, Spicer v Spicer* [1899] P 38, and *Perry v Dixon* (1899) 80 LT 297, the defendants were ordered to pay the costs.

4 *Tomalin v Smart* [1904] P 141. See also *Patrick v Hevercroft* (1920) 123 LT 201. As to revocation see PARA 847 et seq.

5 *Ireland v Rendall* (1866) LR 1 P & D 194; *Cleare v Cleare* (1869) LR 1 P & D 655; *Harrington v Bowyer* (1871) LR 2 P & D 264.

875. Contents of statements of case. In a probate claim[1], the claim form[2] must contain a statement of the nature of the interest of the claimant and of each defendant in the estate[3]. Further, if a party disputes another party's interest in the estate he must state this in his statement of case[4] and set out his reasons[5]. Additionally, any party who contends that at the time when a will was executed the testator did not know of and approve its contents must give particulars of the facts and matters relied on[6] and any party who wishes to contend that:

(1) a will was not duly executed;
(2) at the time of the execution of the will the testator lacked testamentary capacity; or
(3) the execution of the will was obtained by undue influence or fraud, must set out the contentions specifically and give particulars of the facts and matters relied on[7].

A statement of case should make clear the general nature of the case of the party whose statement it is, and should be a concise statement of the facts on which he relies[8]. It must be verified by a statement of truth[9], and may refer to points of law, give the names of witnesses, and have served with it copies of documents[10]. A claimant or counterclaiming defendant must specifically set out in his particulars of claim, among other things, any allegation of fraud, and any details of unsoundness of mind or undue influence where he wishes to rely on them in support of his claim[11].

1 As to the meaning of 'probate claim' see PARA 680 note 2.

2 As to the meaning of 'claim form' see CIVIL PROCEDURE vol 11 (2015) PARA 244.

3 CPR 57.7(1). See also CIVIL PROCEDURE vol 11 (2015) PARA 139. See also *O'Brien v Seagrave* [2007] EWHC 788 (Ch), [2007] 3 All ER 633, [2007] 1 WLR 2002; *Randall v Randall* [2016] EWCA Civ 494, (2016) Times, 28 June.

4 'Statement of case':

(1) means a claim form, particulars of claim where these are not included in a claim form, defence, CPR Pt 20 claim, or reply to defence; and
(2) includes any further information given in relation to them voluntarily or by court order under rule 18.1 (CPR 2.3(1)).

5 CPR 57.7(2). See also the cases in note 3.

6 CPR 57.7(3). As to the allegation of want of knowledge and approval see PARA 901 et seq.

7 CPR 57.7(4). As to want of due execution see PARA 894 et seq. As to want of testamentary capacity see PARA 48 et seq. As to undue influence and fraud see PARA 56 et seq. For instances where undue influence or fraud has not been alleged in a statement of case and those challenging a will for want of knowledge and approval want to raise it see *Re Stott, Klouda v Lloyds Bank Ltd* [1980] 1 All ER 259, [1980] 1 WLR 246; and *Couwenbergh v Valkova* [2008] EWHC 2451 (Ch), [2008] All ER (D) 264 (Oct). See also *Wintle v Nye* [1959] 1 All ER 552 at 560, [1959] 1 WLR 284 at 294, HL, per Viscount Simonds, who made the point that a charge of fraud must be proved affirmatively, as opposed to merely putting the respondent to proof of knowledge and approval. In *Re Fuld (No 3), Hartley v Fuld* as reported in [1968] P 675 at 722, Scarman J suggested that it would be preferable that allegations of fraud and undue influence should feature less in probate statements of case since the decision in *Wintle v Nye*. See also *Brennan v Prior* [2015] EWHC 3082 (Ch), [2015] All ER (D) 119 (Nov) (clarification of an order that, given the aggressive way in

which the claimant had advanced her unsuccessful challenge to the will (which included unsubstantiated claims of undue influence) she should pay the costs of the executors and the beneficiaries).

8 See CPR 16.2(1)(a); and *McPhilemy v Times Newspapers Ltd* [1999] 3 All ER 775 at 793, CA, per Lord Woolf MR. The need for extensive statements of case including particulars is reduced by the requirement that witness statements are exchanged (see PARA 882), and the purpose of statements of case is to identify the issues and the extent of the dispute between the parties: *McPhilemy v Times Newspapers Ltd* at 792–793 per Lord Woolf MR. For the detailed rules concerning statements of case see CPR Pt 16 and *Practice Direction—Statements of Case* PD 16; and for amendments to them see CPR Pt 17 and *Practice Direction—Amendments to Statements of Case* PD 17. See also CIVIL PROCEDURE vol 11 (2015) PARAS 357–360.

9 See CPR 22.1(1)(a). In a statement of case a statement of truth is a statement that the party whose case it is (or that party's litigation friend) believes the facts stated to be true, and it may be signed either by the party whose case it is (or that party's litigation friend), or by the party's legal representative on behalf of that party (or litigation friend): see CPR 22.1(4)–(6).

10 See *Practice Direction—Statements of Case* PD 16 para 13.3. Documents relied on should be referred to in the statement of case and copies supplied, rather than set out extensively in the statement of case, and if an extract from a document has to be included it should be placed in a schedule: *Chancery Guide* (2016) para 10.16.

11 See *Practice Direction—Statements of Case* PD 16 para 8.2 which applies subject to the specific provisions of CPR 57.7(1)-(4) (see text and notes 3, 5–7).

876. Judgment in default not available in probate claims. The rules which ordinarily apply to allow a claimant to obtain a default judgment against a defendant who has failed to serve an acknowledgment of service or defence[1] do not apply to a probate claim[2]. Where the defendant fails to serve an acknowledgment of service or defence when required[3], the claimant may apply for an order for trial of the probate claim[4]. If an order is made the court may direct the probate claim to be tried on written evidence[5]. If the court orders trial on written evidence in such a case or there is an application for summary judgment for an order pronouncing for a will in solemn form[6], an attesting witness has to make a witness statement or swear an affidavit of due execution[7] of any will or codicil sought to be admitted to probate[8].

1 See CPR Pt 12. See also CIVIL PROCEDURE vol 12 (2015) PARA 535.

2 See CPR 57.10(1) which disapplies CPR 10.2 and Pt 12. As to the meaning of 'probate claim' see PARA 680 note 2.

3 Ie required by CPR 57.10(3). See PARA 869. As to the time for filing an acknowledgment of service and defence see CPR 57.4 and PARAS 869, 873.

4 See CPR 57.10(3), (4); and PARA 869.

5 CPR 57.10(5); and see PARA 869.

6 See *Practice Direction—Probate* PD 57 para 5.1 and as to summary judgment see PARA 884.

7 As to affidavits of due execution see PARAS 733, 894.

8 See *Practice Direction—Probate* PD 57 para 5.1. As to the practical issues that arise see also PARA 871 note 6.

877. Case management in contentious probate cases. After the service of the defence[1], the court will serve a directions questionnaire on each party[2]. When the completed questionnaires have been filed by the parties[3], or the period for doing so has expired, whichever is the sooner, the court will allocate the claim to the multi-track[4]. The court will then either issue directions and a timetable for the steps to be taken before the trial, or fix a case management conference or a pre-trial review, or both, and give such other directions as it sees fit[5]. In giving directions in a probate claim[6], the court will give consideration to the questions:

(1) whether any person who may be affected by the claim and who is not joined as a party should be joined as a party or given notice of the claim[7]; and

(2) whether to make a representation order[8].

The court will fix a date or period for the trial to take place as soon as practicable[9], and will, after the time fixed by the timetable or directions for the parties to return the pre-trial checklist[10], set a timetable for the trial[11].

Apart from the special power to order the production of testamentary papers[12], and the requirement that the parties sign witness statements or swear affidavits of testamentary documents[13], the steps to be taken before trial in a probate claim on the multi-track are much the same as in other proceedings[14].

1 Where there are two or more defendants and at least one of them serves a defence, the allocation questionnaire is served when they have all served a defence or the period for the filing of the last defence has expired: see CPR 26.3(2). See also CIVIL PROCEDURE vol 11 (2015) PARA 204.

2 See CPR 26.3(1); and CIVIL PROCEDURE vol 11 (2015) PARA 204. The court can dispense with the need for a questionnaire: see CPR 26.3(1)(b); and CIVIL PROCEDURE vol 11 (2015) PARA 204.

3 On filing the completed questionnaire a party may make a written request for a stay of proceedings while the parties try to settle the case by alternative dispute resolution or other means, and if all parties request such a stay or the court considers it appropriate, a stay of one month (with the possibility of subsequent extensions) will be directed: see CPR 26.4; and CIVIL PROCEDURE vol 11 (2015) PARA 206.

4 See CPR 26.5 notwithstanding that all probate claims are directed to be allocated to the multi-track irrespective of the value of the claim: see CPR 57.2(4). As to the factors relevant to transfer of proceedings see PARA 867.

5 See CPR 29.2(1); and CIVIL PROCEDURE vol 11 (2015) PARA 234. At this stage the court's first concern is to ensure that the issues between the parties are identified and that the necessary evidence is prepared and disclosed: see *Practice Direction—the Multi-track* PD 29 para 4.3. The parties are encouraged to agree directions where possible (see para 4.6), but these must be approved by the court and satisfy the requirements of paras 4.7, 4.8 which include agreeing a date or period for the trial. See also CPR 29.4. As to directions concerning further information see PARA 879; as to disclosure of documents see PARA 880; and as to evidence see PARA 882.

6 As to the meaning of 'probate claim' see PARA 680 note 2.

7 Ie given notice of the claim under CPR 19.8A or otherwise. See PARA 878.

8 *Practice Direction—Probate* PD 57 para 4. A representation order referred to in the text is a representation order under CPR 19.6 or 19.7 (see CIVIL PROCEDURE vol 11 (2015) PARAS 491–492). It is submitted that the reference to CPR 19.6 is wrong because CPR 19.6(5) provides that CPR 19.6 does not apply to a claim to which CPR 19.7 applies. See PARA 878 notes 5, 6.

9 See CPR 29.2(2).

10 Ie under CPR 29.6. The pre-trial checklist is sometimes referred to by its former name of listing questionnaire.

11 See CPR 29.8. For further details of case management on the multi-track see CPR Pt 29; *Practice Direction—the Multi-track* PD 29. As to directions concerning evidence see PARAS 882, 886.

12 See PARA 680.

13 See PARA 870.

14 See CPR Pts 29–35; and CIVIL PROCEDURE vol 11 (2015) PARA 233 et seq.

878. Parties and notice to non-parties. All persons who may be adversely affected by the outcome of a probate claim[1] must be either joined as parties or served with notice of proceedings[2] so that such persons will be bound by the order of the court[3]. Where there are a large number of persons who might be affected, the court may direct that they are served, so allowing them to become parties and in any event binding them to the result of the claim[4]. In certain cases it may be appropriate to apply for a representation order[5], for instance to represent the interest of parties who cannot be ascertained or where parties have the same interest[6]. If the person successfully propounding the will gives notice of the proceedings to interested parties, without obtaining such an order of the court, they should still be bound by an order pronouncing for or against the will in solemn form unless new facts come to light[7].

1 As to the meaning of 'probate claim' see PARA 680 note 2.

2 Any number of claimants or defendants may be joined as parties to a claim: see CPR 19.1; and CIVIL PROCEDURE vol 11 (2015) PARA 480. However the rule in CPR 19.3(1) that all persons

jointly entitled to a remedy must be joined as parties and the rule in CPR 19.3(2) that a person who does not agree to be a claimant must be joined as a defendant, do not apply to a probate claim: see CPR 19.3(3); and CIVIL PROCEDURE vol 11 (2015) PARA 495. Note that in a claim for revocation of a grant, every person who is or claims to be entitled to administer the estate under that grant must be made a party to the claim: CPR 57.6(1). See also PARA 888.

3 See Tristram and Coote's Probate Practice (30th Edn) 26.06, 26.07; and PARA 860.

4 See CPR 19.8A; and CIVIL PROCEDURE vol 11 (2015) PARA 495. If a person is served with notice of a claim and files an acknowledgment of service within 14 days, he becomes a party to the claim but if he does not, he is bound by any judgment given in the claim as if he was a party: see CPR 19.8A(5), (6); and CIVIL PROCEDURE vol 11 (2015) PARA 495. As to acknowledgment of service see PARA 869. See also PARA 885.

5 CPR 19.7 applies to representation orders in claims regarding the estate of a deceased person: see CPR 19.7(1)(a); and CIVIL PROCEDURE vol 11 (2015) PARA 492. Consequently, the usual rule dealing with representation orders in CPR 19.6 is not applicable to probate claims: see CPR 19.6(5); and CIVIL PROCEDURE vol 11 (2015) PARA 491. An order under CPR 19.7 may be applied for by any person who seeks to be so appointed or by any party to the claim and the order may be made at any time before or after the claim has started: see CPR 19.7(4); and CIVIL PROCEDURE vol 11 (2015) PARA 492. See also note 6. As to approval of compromises after a representation order has been made see PARA 885.

6 See CPR 19.7; and CIVIL PROCEDURE vol 11 (2015) PARA 492. The court may make an order appointing a person to represent any other person or persons in the claim where the person or persons to be represented:
(1) are unborn;
(2) cannot be found;
(3) cannot easily be ascertained; or
(4) are a class of persons who have the same interest in a claim and one or more members of that class are within head (1), (2) or (3) above; or to appoint a representative would further the overriding objective (see CPR 19.7(2); and CIVIL PROCEDURE vol 11 (2015) PARA 492).

As to the overriding objective see PARA 647 note 3. See also note 5. Representation orders may be made at a case management conference: see PARA 877.

7 See PARAS 860, 887.

879. Court may order further information about execution of will. In a claim concerning the validity of a will it may be appropriate for the court to order a party to give additional information about the execution of the will and the surrounding circumstances[1]. Otherwise the practice as to ordering a party to clarify any matter which is in dispute in the proceedings or to give additional information in relation to such a matter is no different in probate matters from the practice in other forms of litigation[2]. Personal representatives[3] and any person who may have a claim arising out of a patient's death have a statutory right of access to information in health records[4].

1 See *Re Holloway, Young v Holloway* (1887) 12 PD 167, CA (allegation of exercise of undue influence by executors and universal legatee; a request for further information, then called interrogatories, allowed as to benefits received by them from deceased in his lifetime, as to the agreement between them in his lifetime, as to the division of his property, and as to the making over of property by the legatee to the executor). The current procedure for exchange of witness statements (see PARA 882) will reduce, but not in all cases eliminate completely, the need for requests for further information.

2 See CPR Pt 18; and CIVIL PROCEDURE vol 11 (2015) PARA 361. Orders for clarification and additional information under CPR Pt 18 replace the former interrogatories and requests for further and better particulars.

3 As to the meaning of 'personal representative' see PARA 608.

4 See the Access to Health Records Act 1990 s 3(1)(f); and CONFIDENCE AND INFORMATIONAL PRIVACY vol 19 (2011) PARA 66; MEDICAL PROFESSIONS vol 74 (2011) PARA 42. As to the obligations of a solicitor to provide information about the preparation and execution of a will see PARAS 860, 882.

880. Disclosure of documents. The court has power to order standard disclosure[1] and specific disclosure[2] of documents, and will consider whether to order, and normally will order, standard disclosure[3] as part of giving directions after allocation of a case to the multi-track[4]. The court also has power to order disclosure before proceedings start[5] and power to order disclosure against a person who is not a party to the claim[6].

In probate claims disclosure may be ordered more widely than in other claims. Where testamentary capacity is in issue, inquiry may extend to the whole life of the testator and to anything in his handwriting[7]. The same may apply, though to a lesser extent, where the issue raised is the exercise of undue influence or of fraud[8], or where the allegation is that the deceased did not know or approve of the contents of the will in question.

1 An order to give disclosure is an order to give standard disclosure unless the court otherwise directs, but the court or the parties by written agreement may dispense with or limit standard disclosure: see CPR 31.5; and CIVIL PROCEDURE vol 12 (2015) PARA 623. A party to a claim discloses a document by stating that the document exists or has existed: CPR 31.2. 'Document' means anything in which information of any description is recorded: CPR 31.4. Standard disclosure is disclosure by a party of the documents which are or have been in his control on which he relies, or which adversely affect his own case, adversely affect another party's case, or support another party's case and the documents which he is required to disclose by a relevant practice direction: see CPR 31.6, 31.8; CIVIL PROCEDURE vol 12 (2015) PARAS 621, 623. The disclosing party must make a reasonable search for documents (see CPR 31.7; and CIVIL PROCEDURE vol 12 (2015) PARA 624), and disclosure is effected by providing a list and a disclosure statement (see CPR 31.10; and CIVIL PROCEDURE vol 12 (2015) PARA 627). As to the right to inspect and claims to withhold from inspection see PARA 881.

2 As to specific disclosure see CPR 31.12; and CIVIL PROCEDURE vol 12 (2015) PARA 630. See also note 1.

3 As to standard disclosure see CPR 31.6; and CIVIL PROCEDURE vol 12 (2015) PARA 623.

4 See CPR 29.2; *Practice Direction—Disclosure and Inspection of Documents* PD 31A para 1.1; and CIVIL PROCEDURE vol 11 (2015) PARA 234. For the rules as to disclosure see CPR Pt 31; *Practice Direction—Disclosure and Inspection of Documents* PD 31A; and CIVIL PROCEDURE vol 12 (2015) PARA 623 et seq. As to the right of any person who may have a claim arising out of a deceased person's death to access to that person's health records see the Access to Health Records Act 1990 s 3; and CONFIDENCE AND INFORMATIONAL PRIVACY vol 19 (2011) PARA 66; MEDICAL PROFESSIONS vol 74 (2011) PARA 42. As to case management on the multi-track see PARA 877. As to the requirement that all parties give written evidence of testamentary documents see PARA 870.

5 Ie under the Senior Courts Act 1981 s 33(2); and the County Courts Act 1984 s 52(2). For the procedure see CPR 31.16.

6 Ie under the Senior Courts Act 1981 s 34(2) (see note 4); and the County Courts Act 1984 s 53. For the procedure see CPR 31.17. See also PARA 881 note 3.

7 *Austin v Collett* (1907) Times, 7 December per Bargrave Deane J. A countervailing factor is the overriding objective and in particular the principle of proportionality: see CPR Pt 1; and PARA 860 note 9.

8 As to the defences of undue influence or fraud see PARA 56 et seq.

881. Right to inspection. A party to whom a document has been disclosed has a right to inspect the document, except where the party disclosing it no longer controls it, has a right or duty to withhold it, or considers that inspection would be disproportionate to the issues in the case[1]. A party may also inspect a document mentioned in a statement of case, a witness statement, a witness summary, or an affidavit[2]. A party may also apply for an order for inspection of any document mentioned in an expert's report which has not already been disclosed in the proceedings[3]. Under the special power of the court to order the production of an instrument purporting to be testamentary the court may, whether or not any legal proceedings are pending, order any person in whose possession or control the instrument is to bring it into court in such manner as the court may direct[4].

In one case inspection of a coffin buried in consecrated ground has been obtained[5].

1 See CPR 31.3; and CIVIL PROCEDURE vol 12 (2015) PARA 628. The disclosure list must list the documents withheld, and give the reasons for claiming to withhold them (see CPR 31.3(2),

31.10(4), 31.19(3), (4)), and the claim can be challenged under CPR 31.12 or 31.19(5). As to the grounds upon which production must be resisted see PARA 882. See also CIVIL PROCEDURE vol 12 (2015) PARA 621 et seq.

2 See CPR 31.14(1); CIVIL PROCEDURE vol 12 (2015) PARA 632.

3 See CPR 31.14(2) (CIVIL PROCEDURE vol 12 (2015) PARA 632) which is expressed to be subject to CPR 35.10(4) which makes provision in relation to instructions referred to in an expert's report.

4 Ie under the Senior Courts Act 1981 s 123: see PARA 680. See also *Re Shepherd* [1891] P 323, where the executor and solicitor of a deceased testatrix were ordered to deposit in the registry all wills and testamentary papers of hers which were in their possession, and the applicant was given liberty to take copies. As to the court's general power to order disclosure of documents before proceedings have started see PARA 880.

5 See *Druce v Young* [1899] P 84; *R v Tristram* [1898] 2 QB 371, DC (both cases are episodes in the same litigation, where revocation of a grant of probate was claimed on the grounds that the deceased was still living for some time after his officially recorded death).

882. Evidence and privilege. The court may control the evidence by giving directions as to the issues on which evidence is required, the nature of the evidence required to decide those issues, and the way in which it is to be placed before the court[1]. The court will order a party to serve on the other parties any witness statement[2] of the oral evidence which the party serving the statement intends to rely on in relation to issues of fact to be decided at the trial[3]. Hearsay evidence is admissible subject to procedural rules for giving advance notice of reliance on it, and to the court's power to control the evidence[4].

Difficulties can arise in a probate claim as to the evidence of a testator's advisers, especially solicitors with whom there was a privileged relationship during his lifetime[5]. The death of a client does not end the privilege, which can be claimed by successors in title[6]. As between such successors in title, however, the privilege cannot be claimed, for the privilege belongs equally to all who derive title under the testator, whether personal representatives, beneficiaries or, presumably, creditors[7]. If the privilege was shared with some other person or persons during the testator's lifetime, it seems that the solicitor is bound not to make any disclosure even to the testator's successors in title unless he has the consent of the other person or persons entitled to the privilege[8].

A solicitor who is not a party to probate proceedings cannot be required to answer requests for information, but he can be ordered by the court to disclose documents[9], and he can be summoned to give evidence or produce documents[10]. If there is any claim to privilege for his potential evidence he should refuse disclosure to anyone until compelled upon by witness summons to answer questions after argument on the claim to privilege. Subject to this qualification a solicitor should, if there is a genuine dispute, make available a statement of his evidence about the execution of the will and the circumstances surrounding it to any person who asks him for such a statement, whether or not the solicitor is acting for persons propounding any will of the testator[11]. A failure to do so which leads to unnecessary litigation may mean that those challenging the will are not ordered to pay the costs of the challenge even though the will is found to be valid[12].

1 See CPR 32.1(1); and CIVIL PROCEDURE vol 12 (2015) PARA 510; CIVIL PROCEDURE vol 12 (2015) PARA 1063. The court may use this power to exclude evidence that would otherwise be admissible and to limit cross-examination: see CPR 32.1(2), (3); and CIVIL PROCEDURE vol 12 (2015) PARAS 510, 685, 845; CIVIL PROCEDURE vol 12 (2015) PARA 1063. There are no express limitations on the exercise of this power, although it must be exercised in support of dealing justly with the case: *Grobelaar v News Group Newspapers Ltd* (1999) Times, 12 August, CA. As to the overriding objective when exercising such powers see CPR Pt 1.

2 A witness statement is a written statement signed by a person which contains the evidence which that person would be allowed to give orally: CPR 32.4(1). It must be verified by a statement of truth (see CPR 22.1(1); and CIVIL PROCEDURE vol 11 (2015) PARA 363), and contempt of court proceedings may be brought in respect of dishonest false statements in a witness statement (see

CPR 32.14; and CIVIL PROCEDURE vol 12 (2015) PARA 778). For the formal requirements see *Practice Direction—Evidence* PD 32; and CIVIL PROCEDURE vol 12 (2015) PARA 768. The witness must still be called to give oral evidence at the trial: see CPR 32.5(1); and CIVIL PROCEDURE vol 12 (2015) PARAS 694, 773, 841. For the other rules concerning witness statements see CPR Pt 32; and CIVIL PROCEDURE vol 12 (2015) PARA 768 et seq.

3 See CPR 32.4(2); and CIVIL PROCEDURE vol 12 (2015) PARA 772. The order will normally be made on allocation of the claim to the multi-track (see PARA 877) and will normally be for simultaneous exchange of witness statements by a specified date: see *Practice Direction—the Multi-track* PD 29 para 4.10(3); and CIVIL PROCEDURE vol 11 (2015) PARA 236. If a witness statement cannot be obtained, an application should be made to the court for permission to serve a witness summary: see CPR 32.9; and CIVIL PROCEDURE vol 12 (2015) PARA 776. If a witness statement or a witness summary for use at trial is not served in respect of an intended witness within the time specified by the court, then the witness may not be called to give oral evidence unless the court gives permission: CPR 32.10. As to hearsay evidence see the text and note 4; as to compelling witnesses who refuse to give evidence voluntarily see CPR Pt 34 and note 10; and as to adducing expert evidence see CPR Pt 35. Directions as to evidence at the trial will be given by the court on listing of the claim for trial: see CPR 29.8; *Practice Direction—the Multi-track* PD 29 para 9.2; and CIVIL PROCEDURE vol 11 (2015) PARA 239. See also PARA 886.

4 See the Civil Evidence Act 1995 s 1; and CIVIL PROCEDURE vol 12 (2015) PARA 859 et seq. For the procedural requirements see s 2; CPR 33.1–33.5; and CIVIL PROCEDURE vol 12 (2015) PARA 859 et seq. The requirement to give notice does not apply to a statement which a party to a probate claim wishes to put in evidence and which is alleged to have been made by the person whose estate is the subject of the proceedings: CPR 33.3(b). As to the court's overriding power to control the evidence see the text and note 1.

5 As to the confidentiality of communications between solicitor and client see CONFIDENCE AND INFORMATIONAL PRIVACY vol 19 (2011) PARA 36; LEGAL PROFESSIONS vol 65 (2015) PARAS 538-539.

6 There is no privilege for documents in so far as they relate to the attestation and execution of a will: see PARA 894.

7 See *Russell v Jackson* (1851) 9 Hare 387; *Bullivant v A-G for Victoria* [1901] AC 196 at 206, HL, per Lindley LJ although Lindley LJ does not specifically state the privilege belongs 'equally' to those deriving title under the testator and so it may be that privilege passes to the personal representatives in the first instance. As to privilege in rectification claims see PARA 889.

8 See *Rochefoucauld v Boustead* (1896) 65 LJ Ch 794; revsd on another point [1897] 1 Ch 196, CA.

9 See PARA 880.

10 See CPR 34.2, 34.3; and CIVIL PROCEDURE vol 12 (2015) PARAS 807, 808, 815. A summons to produce documents can order their production on the date fixed for the hearing or some other date (see CPR 34.2(4)), and a party to the claim may apply for an order for the examination of a witness before the hearing: see CPR 34.2(4), 34.8; and CIVIL PROCEDURE vol 12 (2015) PARA 782.

11 Advice on disclosure by a solicitor following a request for information about the execution of a will and the circumstances surrounding its preparation was issued by the Council of the Law Society in September 1959. The tenor of the advice was that the knowledge of the solicitor makes him a material witness and so he should make available a statement of his evidence regarding the execution of the will and the circumstances surrounding it to anyone concerned in proving or challenging the will, whether or not the solicitor acted for those propounding the will. This advice was confirmed by the Court of Appeal in *Larke v Nugus* (1979) 123 Sol Jo 337 and later reported in [2000] WTLR 1033. The Law Society has since updated its advice to provide supplementary information: see the Law Society Practice Note *Disputed Wills* (6 Oct 2011); and see also PARA 860 note 7.

12 See *Larke v Nugus* (1979) 123 Sol Jo 337, [2000] WTLR 1033. However, this was described by Nugee QC sitting as deputy judge in *Mausner v Mincher* [2006] EWHC 1283 (Ch) at [9], [2006] All ER (D) 240 (Apr) as an 'exceptional case': the signature of the testatrix, an elderly woman was wobbly, the will contained a gift to persons on whom the testatrix was dependent and the executor, who was a solicitor who had been responsible for drawing up the will 'had taken the bizarre view that the defendants were not entitled to a copy of it or to any explanation of the circumstances in which it had been drawn up'.

883. Discontinuance and dismissal. The rules which apply generally[1] to the withdrawal and discontinuance of proceedings do not apply to a probate claim[2]. At any stage of a probate claim the court may, on the application of the claimant or of any defendant who has acknowledged service of the claim form[3], order the claim to be discontinued or dismissed on such terms as to costs or otherwise as it thinks just and may further order that a grant of probate of the will or letters of administration of the estate of the deceased person be made to the person entitled to it[4]. An order for the discontinuance or dismissal of a probate claim will normally lead to a grant of probate or of letters of administration in common form[5].

1 See CPR Pt 38 and note 4. See also CIVIL PROCEDURE vol 12 (2015) PARA 1033.
2 See CPR 57.11(1) which states that CPR Pt 38 does not apply to a probate claim. As to the meaning of 'probate claim' see PARA 680 note 2.
3 As to the meaning of 'claim form' see CIVIL PROCEDURE vol 11 (2015) PARA 244; and see PARA 869 for acknowledgment of service.
4 CPR 57.11(2). The difference is that whilst ordinarily under Pt 38 (see note 1) a claimant may, subject to exceptions, discontinue at any time (see CPR 38.1(1)–(3)), in a probate claim, the court's permission must always be obtained to discontinue. Permission to discontinue may be refused if the circumstances warrant it, ie where serious issues have been raised over the validity of the will (see *Green v Briscoe* [2005] All ER (D) 96 (May)) and on an application for discontinuance of a claim challenging a will, the application was granted since, when viewed objectively, there was no serious issue to be resolved as regards the will but no order for costs was made against the claimant because there was no evidence to show that the claimant had acted unreasonably or in bad faith in challenging the will in the first place (*Re Jean Wylde, Wylde v Culver* [2006] EWHC 923 (Ch), [2006] 4 All ER 345, [2006] 1 WLR 2674). As to the award of costs in a discontinuance see also *Kay v Tibbs* [2007] All ER (D) 31 (Feb) and *Smith v Springford* [2008] All ER (D) 59 (Feb). For costs in probate claims generally see PARA 908 et seq.
5 *Practice Direction—Probate* PD 57 para 6.1(2). For the procedure on applying for an order of discontinuance: see Tristram and Coote's Probate Practice (30th Edn) 38.04.

884. **Striking-out and summary judgment.** The court may strike out the whole or part of a statement of case[1] if it appears to disclose no reasonable grounds for bringing or defending the claim, or to be an abuse of the court's process or otherwise likely to obstruct the just disposal of the proceedings, or if it appears that there has been a failure to comply with a rule, practice direction or court order[2]. If the court strikes out a claimant's statement of case and it considers that the claim is totally without merit, the court's order must record that fact and the court must at the same time consider whether it is appropriate to make a civil restraint order[3].

In addition the court in probate proceedings has an inherent jurisdiction[4], in common with the courts in other civil proceedings, to stay proceedings which are frivolous and vexatious or an abuse of the process of the court[5], but this jurisdiction is sparingly exercised and then only in exceptional and clear cases[6]. The court will consider for this purpose whether the claimant can by his action obtain any real or material advantage for himself or for others and whether at a later stage in proceedings the statutory rules on limitation or laches would be a conclusive defence[7].

The court may give summary judgment against a claimant or a defendant in a probate claim on the whole of the claim, or on a particular issue, if it considers that the claimant has no real prospect of succeeding on the claim or issue or the defendant has no real prospect of successfully defending the claim or issue and, in either case, there is no other compelling reason why the case or issue should be disposed of at a trial[8].

1 As to statements of case see PARA 875.
2 See CPR 3.4(1), (2); and CIVIL PROCEDURE vol 11 (2015) PARAS 487; CIVIL PROCEDURE vol 12 (2015) PARA 530. For the possible consequences of such an order and relief see CPR 3.4–3.9; and for the procedure see *Practice Direction—Striking out a Statement of Case* PD 3A. See also CIVIL PROCEDURE vol 12 (2015) PARAS 516–534. The authorities tend to support the view that the court will never strike out a claim to revoke a grant of probate or letters of administration on the mere ground of delay in instituting it, unless it is satisfied that the claim is otherwise frivolous or vexatious or is for other reasons an abuse of the process of the court: see *Re Flynn, Flynn v Flynn* [1982] 1 All ER 882, [1982] 1 WLR 310, distinguishing *Re Hassan* [1981]

78 LS Gaz R 842. As to abuse of process by relitigating a probate claim see *Re Langton* [1964] P 163 at 179, [1964] 1 All ER 749 at 759, CA, per Diplock LJ.

3 See CPR 3.4(6); and CIVIL PROCEDURE vol 12 (2015) PARA 523. As to the meaning of 'civil restraint order' see PARA 1175.

4 See the Senior Courts Act 1981 s 49(3); CPR 3.4(5); and CIVIL PROCEDURE vol 12 (2015) PARA 1043.

5 *Willis v Earl Beauchamp* (1886) 11 PD 59, CA. See also *Mohan v Broughton* [1899] P 211 (affd [1900] P 56, CA); *Mahon v Quinn* [1904] 2 IR 267; *Birch v Birch* [1902] P 130, CA. Cf *Peters v Tilly* (1886) 11 PD 145. See also CIVIL PROCEDURE vol 12 (2015) PARAS 1043–1044.

6 *Re Coghlan, Briscoe v Broughton* [1948] 2 All ER 68 at 73, CA, per Tucker LJ. See also *Re Flynn, Flynn v Flynn* [1982] 1 All ER 882; and note 2.

7 *Willis v Earl Beauchamp* (1886) 11 PD 59, CA; *Re Coghlan, Briscoe v Broughton* [1948] 2 All ER 68 at 74, CA, per Evershed LJ. The exercise of the jurisdiction is described as a 'drastic step': see *Re Coghlan, Briscoe v Broughton* at 76 per Hodson J. As to limitation generally see LIMITATION PERIODS. See also note 1.

8 See CPR 24.2, 24.3(1), (2); and CIVIL PROCEDURE vol 12 (2015) PARA 549. See also *Martin v Browne* [2008] EWCA Civ 712, [2008] All ER (D) 82 (Jul). Where an order pronouncing for a will in solemn form is sought on an application for summary judgment, the evidence in support of the application must include written evidence proving due execution of the will: *Practice Direction—Probate* PD 57 para 5.1. For the practice and procedure in summary judgment applications see CPR Pt 24; *Practice Direction—the Summary Disposal of Claims* PD 24; and CIVIL PROCEDURE vol 12 (2015) PARA 550. As to written evidence see PARA 882 ; and see also PARA 874 as regards the right of a defendant to require witnesses to the will to attend for cross-examination under CPR 57.7(5).

885. Compromise or settlement of probate claims. Where, on a compromise of a probate action[1] in the High Court:

(1) the court is invited to pronounce for the validity of one or more wills, or against the validity of one or more wills, or for the validity of one or more wills and against the validity of one or more other wills[2]; and

(2) the court is satisfied that consent to the making of the pronouncement or, as the case may be, each of the pronouncements in question has been given by or on behalf of every relevant beneficiary[3], the court may without more pronounce accordingly[4]. Alternatively, where the parties to a claim agree to settle, the court may either order the trial of the claim on written evidence which will lead to a grant in solemn form[5], or order that the claim be discontinued or dismissed which will lead to a grant in common form[6].

Where all those who are interested are of full age and capacity and consent to a compromise, they may agree to any terms, subject to the legal requirements for proper proof or disproof of the validity of the testamentary document in any case where the statutory procedure[7] for dispensing this is not available. If unascertained charities may be affected, the Attorney General must be made a party[8].

The court may approve a compromise on behalf of minors, but it has no power to force one upon them against the opinion of their advisers[9], and it will only approve such a compromise when proceedings have been commenced, and on proper evidence that the compromise is for their benefit[10].

The court's approval is required to settle a claim in which an order has been made[11] appointing a person to represent any other person or persons in the claim who are unborn, or cannot be found, or cannot easily be ascertained or who are persons within a class who have the same interest in a claim[12]. The court may approve a settlement where it is satisfied that the settlement is for the benefit of all the represented persons[13]. Unless the court otherwise directs, any judgment or order given in a claim in which a party is acting as a representative is binding on all persons represented in the claim[14] but may only be enforced by or against a party to the claim with the permission of the court[15].

Where the court has at any time directed that notice of any judgment or order given in the claim is served on a person who is not a party but who may be affected by it[16], then such person is bound by the judgment or order as if he had been a party to the claim but he may, provided he acknowledges service, within 28 days after the notice is served on him, apply to the court to set aside or vary the judgment or order, and take part in any proceedings relating to the judgment or order[17].

1 'Probate action' means an action for a grant of probate of the will, or letters of administration of the estate, of a deceased person or for the revocation of such a grant, or for a decree pronouncing for or against the validity of an alleged will, not being an action which is non-contentious or common form probate business: Administration of Justice Act 1985 s 49(2). 'Action' means any civil proceedings commenced by writ or in any other manner prescribed by rules of court: s 56. Since the enactment of the CPR, an action is now known as a claim and proceedings are commenced by claim form: see PARA 647 note 3. See also CIVIL PROCEDURE vol 11 (2015) PARA 139. 'Will' includes a nuncupative will and any testamentary document of which probate may be granted: Administration of Justice Act 1985 s 56. As to the distinction between non-contentious and contentious business see PARA 684.
2 Administration of Justice Act 1985 s 49(1)(a).
3 Administration of Justice Act 1985 s 49(1)(b). 'Relevant beneficiary', in relation to a pronouncement relating to any will or wills of a deceased person, means:
(1) a person who under any such will is beneficially interested in the deceased's estate; and
(2) where the effect of the pronouncement would be to cause the estate to devolve as on an intestacy (or partial intestacy), or to prevent it from so devolving, a person who under the law relating to intestacy is beneficially interested in the estate (s 49(2)).
As to the persons entitled on intestacy see PARA 477 et seq.
4 Administration of Justice Act 1985 s 49(1). This permits a probate claim to be compromised without a trial with the court making an order for or against the validity of the will in solemn form if every 'relevant beneficiary' (see note 3) has consented to the proposed order. It is available only in the High Court. Applications under s 49 may be heard by a master or district judge and must be supported by written evidence identifying the relevant beneficiaries (see note 3) and exhibiting the consents of each of them; written evidence of testamentary documents (see PARA 870) will still be necessary: *Practice Direction—Probate* PD 57 para 6.1, 6.2.
5 *Practice Direction—Probate* PD 57 para 6.1(1). Such evidence remains necessary because the court itself has to be satisfied on some evidence even if the parties agree. The action is in a sense an action in rem: see PARA 887 note 1. As to trials on written evidence see PARA 876.
6 *Practice Direction—Probate* PD 57 para 6.1(2). As to discontinuance and dismissal see PARA 883. When a probate action is settled without pronouncing in solemn form, it is usual to order the grant to issue to X 'if entitled thereto'; and see Tristram and Coote's Probate Practice (30th Edn) 38.07.
7 See the text and notes 1–6.
8 *Boughey v Minor* [1893] P 181; *Re King, Jackson v A-G* [1917] 2 Ch 420. See also CHARITIES vol 8 (2015) PARAS 603, 605.
9 Cf *Re Birchall, Wilson v Birchall* (1880) 16 ChD 41, CA.
10 *Norman v Strains* (1880) 6 PD 219. See also Tristram and Coote's Probate Practice (30th Edn) 38.07.
11 Ie an order under CPR 19.7(2). See PARA 878 note 6.
12 See CPR 19.7(2), (5); and CIVIL PROCEDURE vol 11 (2015) PARA 492.
13 See CPR 19.7(6); and CIVIL PROCEDURE vol 11 (2015) PARA 492.
14 See CPR 19.7(7)(a); and CIVIL PROCEDURE vol 11 (2015) PARA 492.
15 See CPR 19.7(7)(b); and CIVIL PROCEDURE vol 11 (2015) PARA 492.
16 Ie under CPR 19.8A(2). See PARA 878 note 5.
17 See CPR 19.8A(8); and CIVIL PROCEDURE vol 11 (2015) PARA 495. As to the application of the rules on acknowledgment of service see CPR 19.8A(9); and CIVIL PROCEDURE vol 11 (2015) PARA 495.

886. Trial of probate claim. The trial of a probate claim follows a similar course to any other civil claim[1]. Jury trial of a probate claim is not available in the High Court[2], but is possible in the County Court if fraud by a party to the proceedings is in issue[3]. The witnesses to the execution of the will are the court's witnesses and may be cross-examined by the party calling them[4].

1 See CPR 32.1–32.5; Pt 39; *Practice Direction—the Multi-track* PD 29 paras 9, 10; *Practice Direction—Miscellaneous Provisions Relating to Hearings* PD 39A. See also CIVIL PROCEDURE vol 11 (2015) PARA 215. A witness statement will be treated as the witness's evidence in chief unless the court orders otherwise: see CPR 32.5(2); and CIVIL PROCEDURE vol 12 (2015) PARA 773. A witness giving oral evidence at trial may with the permission of the court amplify his witness statement and give evidence in relation to new matters which have arisen since service of his witness statement, but the court will give permission to do this only if it considers that there is good reason not to confine the witness's evidence to his witness statement: CPR 32.5(3), (4); and CIVIL PROCEDURE vol 12 (2015) PARA 773. As to the court's powers to control evidence and as to witness statements see PARA 882. The hearing will be in public unless there are reasons for holding it in private: CPR 39.2(1), 39.2(3)(c), (f); and see also *Practice Direction—Miscellaneous Provisions Relating to Hearings* PD 39A para 1.5.

2 The Senior Courts Act 1981 s 69 (see CIVIL PROCEDURE vol 12 (2015) PARA 1072) governing jury trial in the High Court only applies to the Queen's Bench Division, while contentious probate is assigned to the Chancery Division: see PARA 865.

3 See the County Courts Act 1984 s 66(3)(a); and CIVIL PROCEDURE vol 12 (2015) PARA 1072. Jury trial can only be ordered if the party accused of fraud makes the application for such a trial, and it can still be refused if the court thinks that the trial requires prolonged examination of documents or accounts, or any scientific or local investigation, which cannot conveniently be made with a jury: see s 66(3); and CIVIL PROCEDURE vol 12 (2015) PARA 1072.

4 See PARA 894.

887. Effect of judgment in probate proceedings. A judgment in probate proceedings is binding not only on the parties to the claim, but on every person who has had notice of the claim, and has a right to intervene[1]. Where, upon the facts then known, he has no such right, he is not bound if other facts subsequently come to light[2]. The court has power to order service of copies of the proceedings on non-parties in such a way that they are bound by the court's judgment if they do not become parties[3], and to order that persons not parties to a claim be bound by a compromise[4].

1 *Newell v Weeks* (1814) 2 Phillim 224; *Ratcliffe v Barnes* (1862) 2 Sw & Tr 486; *Mecredy v Brown* [1906] 2 IR 437, CA; *Re Langton* [1964] P 163, [1964] 1 All ER 749, CA. See also *Dansereau v Berget* [1954] AC 1 at 8, [1953] 2 All ER 1058 at 1059, PC (grant of probate in England conclusive between contestants). A probate action has been said to be in a sense an action in rem: *Re Langton* at 175 and 757 per Danckwerts LJ. See also PARAS 860, 878, 885.

2 *Young v Holloway* [1895] P 87; *Re Langton* [1964] P 163 at 179, [1964] 1 All ER 749 at 759, CA, per Diplock LJ. As to the effect of fraud see PARAS 58–59; and CIVIL PROCEDURE vol 12A (2015) PARA 1643.

3 See PARA 878.

4 See PARA 885.

888. Claims for revocation of grant of probate or letters of administration. If revocation of a grant of probate or letters of administration is disputed the procedure is by probate claim[1] and the grant must, if not already lodged in court[2], be lodged in the relevant office[3]. If the person to whom the grant was made is a claimant he must lodge the probate or letters of administration in the relevant office when the claim form is issued[4]. If any defendant has the grant under his control, he must lodge it in the relevant office when he acknowledges service[5].

The claimant must allege as the ground for revoking the grant the invalidity of the will or the defendant's want of interest[6]. Any claim for revocation which is groundless and vexatious may be stayed[7], but it seems doubtful if the court would stay such a claim merely on the ground that the existence of laches would be likely to defeat subsequent proceedings to recover property[8].

Every person entitled or claiming to be entitled to administer the estate of a deceased person under an unrevoked grant must be made a party to any probate claim seeking revocation of the grant[9].

1 As to the contentious jurisdiction and procedure see PARA 865 et seq. As to the meaning of 'probate claim' see PARA 680 note 2. For the grounds for, and the effect of, revocation of a grant see PARA 847 et seq.
2 'Court' includes the principal registry of the Family Division or a district probate registry: CPR 57.6(4). As to the transmission of documents see PARAS 682, 871.
3 As to the meaning of 'relevant office' see PARA 680 note 2.
4 CPR 57.6(2).
5 CPR 57.6(3).
6 The claimant in revocation proceedings cannot limit his costs by the notice procedure: see PARA 874.
7 *Willis v Earl Beauchamp* (1886) 11 PD 59, CA; *Mohan v Broughton* [1900] P 56, CA; *Mohan v Quinn* [1904] 2 IR 267; cf *Peters v Tilly* (1886) 11 PD 145; *Young v Holloway* [1895] P 87; *Re Coghlan, Briscoe v Broughton* [1948] 2 All ER 68, CA (applications for dismissals of actions on this ground rejected); *Re Langton* [1964] P 163, [1964] 1 All ER 749, CA. See also PARA 884; and CIVIL PROCEDURE vol 12 (2015) PARAS 527, 1039 et seq.
8 See *Re Coghlan, Briscoe v Broughton* [1948] 2 All ER 68, CA.
9 See CPR 57.6(1).

889. Procedure on application to rectify. Where an application is made for the rectification of a will[1] every personal representative of the estate must be joined as a party[2]. If the claimant is the person to whom the grant was made in respect of the will of which rectification is sought, he must, unless the court orders otherwise, lodge the grant with the court when the claim form is issued[3]. If the defendant has the grant in his possession or under his control, he must, unless the court orders otherwise, lodge it in the relevant office within 14 days after the service of the claim form on him[4]. A copy of every order made for the rectification of a will must be sent to the principal registry of the Family Division for filing, and a memorandum of the order must be endorsed on, or permanently annexed to, the grant under which the estate is administered[5].

1 Ie an application under the Administration of Justice Act 1982 s 20: see PARA 741; and PARA 187. Such an application does not fall within the definition of 'probate claim' in CPR 57.1(2)(a) (see PARA 680 note 2), although it would be possible to combine it with a probate claim. As to the procedure for obtaining rectification of a will in the Family Division where there is no dispute see PARA 741.
2 CPR 57.12(2). As to the meaning of 'personal representative' see PARA 608.
3 *Practice Direction—Probate* PD 57 para 10.1. The corresponding provision in a claim for revocation is contained in CPR 57.6(2) and requires the claimant to lodge the grant in the 'relevant office' rather than 'court' (see PARA 888 note 4). It is submitted that *Practice Direction—Probate* PD 57 para 10.1 should say 'relevant office' so as to be consistent with the rule for revocation and the corresponding rule for rectification as regards the defendant (see text and note 4). As to the meaning of 'claim form' see CIVIL PROCEDURE vol 11 (2015) PARA 244 and for 'relevant office' see PARA 680 note 2. There is no requirement in CPR 57 or *Practice Direction—Probate* PD 57 that in a rectification claim the personal representatives must also file written evidence of any facts that might affect the exercise of the court's powers, as is the case if a claim is made under the Inheritance (Provision for Family and Dependants) Act 1975: see CPR 57.16(5); and *Practice Direction—Probate* PD 57 para 16(4). However, asserting privilege over testamentary documents may, following the analogy with other probate actions, be viewed as being inconsistent with the neutral role of personal representatives and the overriding objective of the CPR; see PARA 882 note 11. As to the Inheritance (Provision for Family and Dependants) Act 1975 see PARA 565 et seq. As to privilege see PARA 882. As to testamentary documents see PARA 870. As to the meaning of 'overriding objective' see PARA 647 note 3.
4 See *Practice Direction—Probate* PD 57 para 10.2.
5 See *Practice Direction—Probate* PD 57 para 11.

890. Appeals in probate claims. In probate claims, the route of an appeal is determined by the type of decision from which an appeal is sought, the court which made the decision and the person who made the decision[1]. Where the decision to be appealed is a final decision[2], the appeal lies to the Court of Appeal irrespective of the court of first instance[3]. Similarly, where the decision to be appealed was itself an appeal, an appeal lies from that decision to the Court of Appeal and not to any other court[4]. In both these cases, the identity of the court making the decision against which the appeal is sought and the person who ordered it is immaterial.

Subject thereto, an appeal from a decision[5] of:

(1) the High Court lies to the Court of Appeal[6] but lies to a judge of the High Court[7] where such decision to be appealed is made by:
    (a) a person holding office under certain provisions of the Senior Courts Act 1981[8];
    (b) a district judge of the High Court[9]; or
    (c) a person appointed to act as a deputy for any person holding such an office as is referred to in head (a) or (b) above or to act as a temporary additional officer in such office[10]; and
(2) the County Court lies to the High Court[11] unless the decision to be appealed is made by a district judge or deputy district judge of the County Court, in which case an appeal lies to a judge of the County Court[12].

Permission is required for every appeal from a decision of a judge[13] in the County Court or the High Court, subject to certain exceptions, including an appeal against a committal order[14].

Every appeal is limited to a review of the decision of the lower court unless a practice direction makes different provision, or the court considers that, in the circumstances of an individual appeal, it would be in the interests of justice to hold a rehearing[15]. Where an appeal which is to be heard by the County Court or the High Court would raise an important point of principle or practice or there is some other compelling reason for the Court of Appeal to hear it, the appeal may be transferred to the Court of Appeal[16].

An order or judgment of the Court of Appeal in civil proceedings lies to the Supreme Court but only with the leave of the Court of Appeal or of the Supreme Court[17]. In certain circumstances an appeal may be brought direct from the High Court to the Supreme Court where a point of law of general public importance is involved[18]. There is no appeal from the decision of the Court of Appeal on any appeal from the County Court in proceedings in respect of any contentious matter arising with any grant, or revocation, of probate or administration that[19] has been applied for through the principal registry of the Family Division or a district probate registry[20].

1 See the Access to Justice Act 1999 (Destination of Appeals) Order 2000, SI 2000/1071; and CIVIL PROCEDURE vol 12A (2015) PARA 1515. As to security of costs in appeals see PARA 915.

2 'Final decision' means a decision of a court that would finally determine, subject to any possible appeal or detailed assessment of costs, the entire proceedings whichever way the court decided the issues before it: Access to Justice Act 1999 (Destination of Appeals) Order 2000, SI 2000/1071, art 1(2)(c). A decision of a court is treated as a final decision where it:
   (1) is made at the conclusion of part of a hearing or trial which has been split into parts; and
   (2) would, if made at the conclusion of that hearing or trial, be a final decision under art 1(2)(c) (see art 1(3); and CIVIL PROCEDURE vol 12A (2015) PARA 1515).

3 An appeal lies to the Court of Appeal where the decision to be appealed is a final decision in a claim made under CPR Pt 7 and allocated to the multi-track or made in proceedings to which CPR Pt 57 Section I, II, or III applies: see the Access to Justice Act 1999 (Destination of Appeals) Order 2000, SI 2000/1071, art 4; and CIVIL PROCEDURE vol 12A (2015) PARA 1515. As to CPR 57 Sections II and III see PARA 860.

4 For instances where an appeal is made to the County Court or the High Court (other than from the decision of an officer of the court authorised to assess costs by the Lord Chancellor) and on

hearing the appeal the court makes a decision, see the Access to Justice Act 1999 (Destination of Appeals) Order 2000, SI 2000/1071, art 5; and CIVIL PROCEDURE vol 12A (2015) PARA 1515.

5 'Decision' (as opposed to 'final decision' see note 2) includes any judgment, order or direction of the High Court or the County Court: Access to Justice Act 1999 (Destination of Appeals) Order 2000, SI 2000/1071, art 1(2)(a).

6 See the Senior Courts Act 1981 s 16(1); and COURTS AND TRIBUNALS vol 24 (2010) PARA 693.

7 See the Access to Justice Act 1999 (Destination of Appeals) Order 2000, SI 2000/1071, art 2; and CIVIL PROCEDURE vol 12A (2015) PARA 1515.

8 See the Access to Justice Act 1999 (Destination of Appeals) Order 2000, SI 2000/1071, art 2(a); and CIVIL PROCEDURE vol 12A (2015) PARA 1515. A person mentioned in head (a) in the text is a person holding office referred to in the Senior Courts Act 1981 Sch 2 Pt II: see the Access to Justice Act 1999 (Destination of Appeals) Order 2000, SI 2000/1071, art 2(a) (amended by the Constitutional Reform Act 2005 s 59(5), Sch 11 para 1(2)).

9 See the Access to Justice Act 1999 (Destination of Appeals) Order 2000, SI 2000/1071, art 2(b); and CIVIL PROCEDURE vol 12A (2015) PARA 1515.

10 See the Access to Justice Act 1999 (Destination of Appeals) Order 2000, SI 2000/1071, art 2(c); and CIVIL PROCEDURE vol 12A (2015) PARA 1515.

11 See the Access to Justice Act 1999 (Destination of Appeals) Order 2000, SI 2000/1071, art 3(1); and CIVIL PROCEDURE vol 12A (2015) PARA 1515.

12 See the Access to Justice Act 1999 (Destination of Appeals) Order 2000, SI 2000/1071, art 3(2); and CIVIL PROCEDURE vol 12A (2015) PARA 1515.

13 'Judge' means, unless the context otherwise requires, a judge, master or district judge or a person authorised to act as such: CPR 2.3(1).

14 See CPR 52.3(1)(a); and CIVIL PROCEDURE vol 12A (2015) PARA 1517. Such permission may be obtained from the lower court or from the appeal court (see CPR 52.3(2); and CIVIL PROCEDURE vol 12A (2015) PARA 1517), save where the appeal is to the Court of Appeal from the County Court or High Court decision which was itself made on appeal, in which case permission is required from the Court of Appeal (see CPR 52.13(1); and CIVIL PROCEDURE vol 12A (2015) PARA 1542). 'Lower court' means the court, tribunal or other person or body from whose decision an appeal is brought; and 'appeal court' means the court to which an appeal is made: CPR 52.1(3)(b), (c). The Court of Appeal will not give permission unless it considers that the appeal would raise an important point of principle or practice, or there is some other compelling reason for the Court of Appeal to hear it: see CPR 52.13(2); and CIVIL PROCEDURE vol 12A (2015) PARA 1542. For the general procedure for permission to appeal see CIVIL PROCEDURE vol 12A (2015) PARA 1517. For the procedure for obtaining permission see CPR 52.4, 52.5; *Practice Direction—Appeals to the Court of Appeal* PD 52C; and CIVIL PROCEDURE vol 12A (2015) PARA 1517 et seq.

15 See CPR 52.11(1); and CIVIL PROCEDURE vol 12A (2015) PARA 1531. As to the hearing of appeals see CPR 52.11; and CIVIL PROCEDURE vol 12A (2015) PARAS 1530, 1579. For the powers of the appeal court, which include all those of the lower court, see CPR 52.10; and CIVIL PROCEDURE vol 12A (2015) PARA 1529. See also *Sherrington v Sherrington* [2005] EWCA Civ 326 at [33], [2005] All ER (D) 359 (Mar) where, in explaining the appropriate approach of the Court of Appeal to the issues, so far as they are appeals on fact, Lord Justice Peter Gibson giving judgment said: 'If this court is convinced that the judge was plainly wrong, then it is its duty to interfere'. In *Sharp v Adam* [2006] EWCA Civ 449 at [95], 10 ITELR 419 at [95], [2006] All ER (D) 277 (Apr) at [95], Lord Justice May said: 'We [the Court of Appeal] are not a court of first instance. Our task is to review the deputy judge's decision. His decision was in the end a decision of fact based upon all the evidence he heard. We can only allow on appeal if we are satisfied he was wrong. We are not so satisfied'.

16 See CPR 52.14; and CIVIL PROCEDURE vol 12A (2015) PARA 1538. The court from or to which an appeal is made or from which permission to appeal is sought can order the appeal to be transferred to the Court of Appeal. The Master of the Rolls has the power to direct that an appeal which would be heard by the County Court or the High Court should be heard instead by the Court of Appeal: see the Access to Justice Act 1999 s 57; and CIVIL PROCEDURE vol 12A (2015) PARA 1566.

17 See the Constitutional Reform Act 2005 s 40; and COURTS AND TRIBUNALS vol 24 (2010) PARAS 657, 658.

18 See the Administration of Justice Act 1969 ss 12, 13; and COURTS AND TRIBUNALS vol 24 (2010) PARA 659.

19 Ie under the Senior Courts Act 1981 s 105: see PARA 724.

20 See the County Courts Act 1984 s 82 (amended by the Crime and Courts Act 2013 Sch 9 Pt 1 paras 1, 10(1)(b), (32)). See also CIVIL PROCEDURE vol 12A (2015) PARA 1566.

(4) GROUNDS FOR OPPOSING PROBATE

(i) In General

891. Grounds available for opposing probate. Express provision is made for statements of case in probate claims for a party[1] to contend want of due execution[2], want of testamentary capacity[3], want of knowledge and approval[4], undue influence[5] and fraud[6]. A party is not, however, limited to these five grounds, and he may, for example, contend that the alleged will was not a testamentary document[7], that it was revoked[8], that the claimant is estopped, for example by a previous judgment[9] from setting up the will, or that the deceased was a minor[10] at the time the will purports to have been executed.

These contentions may often overlap, but they should be separately stated[11]. In particular the contention that there was want of knowledge and approval will be a normal concomitant of the contention that there was want of testamentary capacity because if the latter contention is proved it will follow that there was want of knowledge and approval as well. However, someone possessing testamentary capacity may be shown not to know and approve the will when the volition is affected by undue influence or fraud[12].

1 See PARA 875. As to counterclaims see PARA 873; and as to default of statement of case see PARA 876. A party opposing probate by making contentions may be either the claimant, for example if seeking the revocation of a grant, or the defendant where, for an example, another person is making a claim for a grant or to propound a will.
2 See CPR 57.7(4)(a); and PARAS 894–896.
3 See CPR 57.7(4)(b); and PARAS 48–53. As to burden of proof see PARA 897 et seq.
4 See CPR 57.7(3); and PARAS 54, 901–907.
5 See CPR 57.7(4)(c); and PARAS 56–57.
6 See CPR 57.7(4)(c); and PARAS 58–59.
7 See eg *Re Berger* [1990] Ch 118, [1989] 1 All ER 591, CA; *Corbett v Newey* [1998] Ch 57, [1996] 2 All ER 914, CA. See also PARA 54.
8 See for example *Court v Despallieres, Re Ikin* [2009] EWHC 3340 (Ch), [2010] 2 All ER 451, [2010] Fam Law 251. As to the requisites for revocation see PARA 87 et seq.
9 As to the effect of a judgment see PARAS 878, 887.
10 As to the general requirement that a testator must be of full age see PARAS 46, 707. As to privileged wills see PARA 79 et seq.
11 See PARA 875. The requirements of testamentary capacity and knowledge and approval are conceptually distinct: see *Hoff v Atherton* [2004] EWCA Civ 1554, [2005] WTLR 99; *Westendorp v Warwick* [2006] EWHC 915 (Ch), [2006] All ER (D) 248 (Apr).
12 See PARA 57.

892. Part of will may be excluded. If the court is satisfied that only part of a will was obtained by undue influence or fraud[1], or that the testator did not have a sound disposing mind in regard to a particular part of a will[2], it may reject the part and pronounce for the rest of the will[3]. The converse is in general true if want of knowledge and approval is established[4], but there are cases where part of a will may be excluded on grounds generally amounting merely to clerical error or inadvertence[5].

1 *Barton v Robins* (1769) 3 Phillim 455n; *Billinghurst v Vickers (formerly Leonard)* (1810) 1 Phillim 187 at 199; *Allen v M'Pherson* (1847) 1 HL Cas 191; *Fulton v Andrews* (1875) LR 7 HL 448; *Farrelly v Corrigan* [1899] AC 563, PC.
2 Cf *Parker v Felgate* (1883) 8 PD 171 per Sir J Hannen P. As to want of sound disposing mind see PARA 897 et seq.
3 See *Rhodes v Rhodes* (1882) 7 App Cas 192, PC; *Sarat Kumari Debi v Sakhi Chand* (1928) LR 56 Ind App 62, PC. As to the exclusion of words from probate see also PARA 739. A court should not pronounce against part of a will as a means of expressing its disapproval of the propounder of the will: *Fuller v Strum* [2001] EWCA Civ 1879, [2002] 2 All ER 87, [2002] 1 WLR 1097.

4 See PARA 906. As to delusions see PARA 52.
5 See PARAS 739, 906. As to rectification in these circumstances see PARAS 65, 741.

893. Medical evidence as to testamentary capacity. The value and function of medical evidence on the issues affecting testamentary capacity are sometimes difficult to assess. The personal medical knowledge of the testator's own doctor, or of a psychiatrist who has had the opportunity of examining the testator at the time of his will[1], must normally carry great weight. It is important in cases of doubt to try to have the proposed testator medically examined after some legal explanation of the criteria discussed in the paragraphs which follow[2]. There is no specific diagnosis which necessarily denotes incapacity[3], but while the world at large can only contrast the doubtful cases with the sane, the physician has at hand the alternative contrast with the insane[4].

1 See PARA 49 note 2. Foreign law and medical knowledge on testamentary capacity are discussed in *Banks v Goodfellow* (1870) LR 5 QB 549 at 561 et seq. In *Caton v Goddard* [2007] All ER (D) 370 (Oct) the court held that, on the balance of probabilities, the evidence produced by a medical expert commissioned after the death was to be preferred to the evidence of the solicitor who had attended the testatrix and drafted the will. In *Key v Key* [2010] EWHC 408 (Ch), [2010] All ER (D) 155 (Apr) evidence was given by two medical experts; the claimant's expert had the advantage of carrying out an assessment of the deceased during his lifetime which outweighed what would have been the greater weight attributed to the defendant's more experienced expert. See also *Boycott v Mollekin* [2005] All ER (D) 433 (Jul) where a decision of the Court of Protection revoking an enduring power of attorney made on the same day as the will was held to be clear evidence of lack of capacity to make the will. However, capacity is issue and time specific so a person may have sufficient capacity to contract a valid marriage but not to manage his own affairs; and may have capacity to make a valid will at some times but not others: see *A, B and C, X, Y and Z* [2012] EWHC 2400 (COP), [2013] WTLR 187.

2 See generally PARAS 48–53. As to the burden of proof see PARAS 897, 899, 900.

3 All diagnoses are matters of degree, and persons suffering from any one of such diagnoses may still be competent to make a will: *Smith v Tebbitt* (1867) LR 1 P & D 398 at 402, 421. Further the possession of an imperfect memory is not be equated with an absence of testamentary capacity: *Banks v Goodfellow* (1870) LR 5 QB 549; *Simon v Byford* [2014] EWHC Civ 280 at [40], [2014] WTLR 1097, 17 ITELR 536 per Lewison LJ. In modern cases the courts have commented that medical examinations are often directed towards matters not at the heart of the issue of capacity to make a will: see *Scammell v Farmer* [2008] EWHC 1100 (Ch) at [94], [2008] All ER (D) 296 (May) at [94] (the tests administered were directed at assessing a different capability than the capacity to make a will and were largely directed at memory and the deceased's powers of recall; ability to recollect the names of immediate family or ability to comprehend the extent of her estate); and *Re Ritchie, Ritchie v Joslin* [2009] EWHC 709 (Ch), [2009] All ER (D) 59 (Apr) (doctor based his opinion on a medical examination five weeks earlier on an unrelated medical matter and on the deceased's ability to answer questions appropriately and his ability to make an assessment of her circumstances and orientation; doctor was not aware that the deceased's will cut out her children and he did not carry out any formal assessment). However, in *Plowright v Smith* [2006] All ER (D) 234 (Jul) the court found the testator had lacked testamentary capacity on the strength of a report from a psychiatrist who had not examined the testator but who stated the effect that a constant infusion of diamorphine would have had on the mind of someone suffering from terminal cancer; whilst there had been evidence from the witnesses to the execution of the will that the testator had been of sound mind, there was no expert medical evidence to refute the claims in the psychiatrist's report. See also *Sharp and Bryson v Adam* [2006] EWCA Civ 449, 10 ITELR 419, [2006] All ER (D) 277 (Apr) (where impairment of cognitive functions caused by multiple sclerosis led to the testator lacking the capacity to arrive at a rational judgment and 'the expert evidence as a whole was capable of outweighing contemporary observations'); *Ledger v Wootton* [2007] EWHC 90 (Ch), [2007] All ER (D) 99 (Oct); and PARA 52 note 5. As to good practice concerning professional records, formal reports and certificates of capacity see the Mental Capacity Act 2005 ss 42, 43; the Mental Capacity Act 2005 Code of Practice (23 April 2007) paras 4.61, 4.62; and MENTAL HEALTH AND CAPACITY vol 75 (2013) PARA 602. As to the availability of medical records in support of a claim arising out of a patient's death see PARA 879.

4 *Smith v Tebbitt* (1867) LR 1 P & D 398 at 404. An apparently extravagant version of this proposition was doubted in *Banks v Goodfellow* (1870) LR 5 QB 549 at 556, where the earlier cases are reviewed.

(ii) Want of Due Execution

894. Evidence of execution. Probate of a will may be opposed on the ground that the statutory requirements[1] for due execution have not been complied with. The evidence of one of the attesting witnesses, if he deposes to the due execution, is sufficient[2]. It has been held that, if he fails to prove the due execution, the other attesting witness must be called, even though he may be an adverse witness[3]. The party calling an attesting witness is entitled to cross-examine him[4], because the witness is a witness of the court and not the witness of one of the parties[5]. It follows that the court is entitled if it thinks fit to see documents which would otherwise under the general law be clearly entitled to privilege[6]. The court will not exclude further relevant evidence to rebut that of the attesting witnesses, for the purpose of the statutory requirements is the prevention of fraud, and the exclusion of such evidence would increase the possibility of fraud[7]. If neither of the attesting witnesses can be found, or both are dead, any person who in fact saw the execution may be called[8], and the court is entitled to read the affidavit of one of the attesting witnesses previously made upon the application for a grant in common form[9].

Where the witnesses are dead, evidence may be admitted[10] of persons who were told by one of the witnesses that she had witnessed the will[11].

The burden of proving due execution, whether by presumption[12] or by positive evidence, rests on the person setting up the will[13].

1 As to the statutory requirements see PARA 707 note 4, 60 et seq.
2 *Belbin v Skeats* (1858) 1 Sw & Tr 148; *Forster v Forster* (1864) 33 LJPM & A 113.
3 *Coles v Coles and Brown* (1866) LR 1 P & D 70; cf *Bowman v Hodgson* (1867) LR 1 P & D 362. In *Neal v Denston* (1932) 147 LT 460 the first of the attesting witnesses failed to satisfy the court that he had any useful recollection of the transaction, and the second attesting witness, who proved adverse to due execution, was called for the defence.
4 *Re Brock, Jones v Jones* (1908) 24 TLR 839; *Oakes v Uzzell* [1932] P 19. Cross-examination is not confined to the issue of due execution: see *Re Webster, Webster v Webster* [1974] 3 All ER 822n, [1974] 1 WLR 1641.
5 *Re Fuld, Hartley v Fuld* [1965] P 405 at 409–410, sub nom *Re Fuld (No 2), Hartley v Fuld* [1965] 2 All ER 657 at 658–659 per Scarman J. The court has an inquisitorial capacity: *Re Fuld, Hartley v Fuld* at 410 and 659. As to professional privilege see PARA 882. The witnesses may be cross-examined as to their veracity even where undue influence or fraud are not raised in the statements of case: see *Wintle v Nye* [1959] 1 All ER 552 at 560, [1959] 1 WLR 284 at 294, HL. As to the contents of statements of case see PARA 875.
6 See *Re Fuld, Hartley v Fuld* [1965] P 405, sub nom *Re Fuld (No 2), Hartley v Fuld* [1965] 2 All ER 657; and note 5.
7 *Re Vere-Wardale, Vere-Wardale v Johnson* [1949] P 395, [1949] 2 All ER 250. See also *Barrett v Bem* [2009] All ER (D) 157 (Oct) (evidence of handwriting expert established that it had been impossible for the deceased to have signed the will).
8 *Mackay v Rawlinson* (1919) 35 TLR 223.
9 *Gornall v Mason* (1887) 12 PD 142; cf *Hayes v Willis* (1906) 75 LJP 86; *Mackay v Rawlinson* (1919) 35 TLR 223 (undefended suit). Cf the Non-Contentious Probate Rules 1987, SI 1987/2024, r 12(1) (see PARA 733).
10 Ie hearsay evidence under the Civil Evidence Act 1995: see CIVIL PROCEDURE vol 12 (2015) PARA 859 et seq.
11 *Re Yelland, Broadbent v Francis* (1975) 119 Sol Jo 562. Cf PARA 716.
12 As to the presumption of due execution see PARA 895.
13 *Clery v Barry* (1887) 21 LR Ir 152 at 155n, CA. Proof that the will was duly executed and that the testator knew and approved its contents may be assisted by the presumption: *Re Musgrove, Davis v Mayhew* [1927] P 264, CA.

895. Presumption of due execution. The principle omnia praesumuntur rite esse acta[1] applies where the will is regular on the face of it, with an attestation clause and the signatures of the testator and witnesses in their proper places[2]. This presumption of due execution applies where there is a proper attestation clause, even though the witnesses have no recollection of having witnessed the will[3], and even though the attestation clause appears only on the completed draft of a last will[4]. It applies where the testator's name has been affixed by his direction just as where he has himself written his name[5]. It may be rebutted by evidence of the attesting witnesses or otherwise, but the evidence as to some defect in execution must be clear, positive and reliable[6], since the court ought to have the strongest evidence before it believes that a will, with a perfect attestation clause and signed by the testator, was not duly executed[7]. Where there is only an incomplete attesting clause it seems that the presumption applies, but with less force than where the attestation clause is in proper form[8]. Where both the attesting witnesses are dead and the will is in regular form the principle is applicable on proof of the handwriting[9].

1 Ie the principle that all things are presumed to have been done rightly.

2 *Vinnicombe v Butler* (1864) 3 Sw & Tr 580 at 582 per Sir J Wilde; *Lloyd v Roberts* (1858) 12 Moo PCC 158; *Wright v Sanderson* (1884) 9 PD 149, CA; and see *Harris v Knight* (1890) 15 PD 170, CA; *Re Musgrove, Davis v Mayhew* [1927] P 264, CA (no step taken to prove will for 20 years); *Scarff v Scarff* [1927] 1 IR 13, CA. In *Otuka v Alozie* [2006] EWHC 3493 (Ch), [2005] All ER (D) 265 (Dec) the court said that the presumption of due execution increases in force where the will contained a 'perfect attestation' clause. As to proof of due execution see also PARA 733.

3 *Woodhouse v Balfour* (1887) 13 PD 2; *Byles v Cox* (1896) 74 LT 222; *Re Webb, Smith v Johnston* [1964] 2 All ER 91, [1964] 1 WLR 509.

4 *Re Webb, Smith v Johnston* [1964] 2 All ER 91, [1964] 1 WLR 509. See also *Re Yelland, Broadbent v Francis* (1975) 119 Sol Jo 562; *Re Phibbs* [1917] P 93. As to lost wills see further PARA 716.

5 *Clery v Barry* (1887) 21 LR Ir 152, CA.

6 *Croft v Croft* (1865) 4 Sw & Tr 10; *Glover v Smith* (1886) 57 LT 60; *Wyatt v Berry* [1893] P 5; *Pilkington v Gray* [1899] AC 401, PC; *Re Moore* [1901] P 44. In *Dayman v Dayman* (1894) 71 LT 699 the presumption prevailed against the testimony of both the attesting witnesses, and in *Wilson v Beddard* (1841) 12 Sim 28 at 34 Shadwell V-C suggested that the evidence of witnesses denying a solemn act which they had attested ought to receive the slightest possible attention, a suggestion cited apparently with approval by Lord Brougham in *M'Gregor v Topham* (1850) 3 HL Cas 132 at 156. In *Neal v Denston* (1932) 147 LT 460 the presumption prevailed where the recollection of the attesting witnesses was doubted; see further PARA 896. On public policy grounds, the Court of Appeal has stated that a court should have the strongest evidence before accepting that a will with a perfect attestation clause was not properly executed: per Peter Gibson LJ in *Sherrington v Sherrington* [2005] EWCA Civ 326, [2005] All ER (D) 359 (Mar), [2005] WTLR 587, citing Lord Penzance in *Wright v Rogers* (1869) LR 1 P & D 678 at 682, who, however, continued that, where both witnesses swear that the will was not duly executed and there is no evidence the other way, there is no footing for the court to affirm that the will was duly executed.

The need for 'the strongest evidence' was confirmed by Neuberger LJ in *Channon v Perkins* [2005] EWCA Civ 1808 at [7], [2006] WTLR 425 for two reasons, one practical (oral testimony as to the way in which a document was executed many years ago is not likely to be inherently particularly reliable on most occasions) and one of principle (by setting aside a will on extraneous evidence, one is declining to implement the wishes of the testator following his death). Arden LJ suggested at [45] that there is a sliding scale according to which evidence will constitute the 'strongest evidence' in one case but not in another. What constitutes the 'strongest evidence' in any particular case will depend on totality of the relevant facts of that case, and the court's evaluation of the probabilities. The more probable it is, from the circumstances, that the will was properly attested, the greater will be the burden on those seeking to displace the presumption. Lack of recollection on its own may not be sufficient to satisfy the court, but evidence from both witnesses that they were nowhere near the place of execution stated in the attestation clause on the particular date would be likely to carry more weight. For recent examples where the presumption has been rebutted see *Re Singh* [2011] EWHC 2907 (Ch); [2012] WTLR 1 (first witness maintained that he had never spoken to or met the second witness, a traditional Sikh who had a turban and beard, that he had never had a traditional Sikh man in his house, and he had not been to the second witness' house); *Re Whelan* [2015] EWHC 3301 (Ch) (evidence showed that the witnesses had not been present together when the will was witnessed and the testatrix had not been present at the time). See also *Re Parslow, Parslow v Parslow* (1959) Times, 3 December (evidence from a handwriting expert that the attestation was forged by the testatrix).

7 *Wright v Rogers* (1869) LR 1 P & D 678 at 682; *O'Meagher v O'Meagher* (1883) 11 LR Ir 117; *Whiting v Turner* (1903) 89 LT 71; and see *Goodisson v Goodisson* [1913] 1 IR 31 (on appeal [1913] 1 IR 218, CA); *Dubourdieu v Patterson* (1919) 54 ILT 23 (evidence that witnesses did not see testatrix sign; will not set aside); *Weatherhill v Pearce* [1995] 2 All ER 492, [1995] 1 WLR 592 (will upheld despite evidence from witnesses casting some doubt on validity of attestation); *Re Chapman, National Trust for Places of Historic Interest and National Beauty v Royal National Institute for the Blind* (1999) 1 ITELR 863, [1999] All ER (D) 81 (presumption applied in the absence of an attestation clause where the evidence of the surviving witness cast some doubt on the validity of the execution of the will but not enough to rebut it). See also PARAS 77, 896.

8 *Vinnicombe v Butler* (1864) 3 Sw & Tr 580 at 582; *Re Rees* (1865) 34 LJPM & A 56; see also *Clarke v Clarke* (1879) 5 LR Ir 47, CA (attestation by marks); *Burgoyne v Showler* (1844) 1 Rob Eccl 5: *Byles v Cox* (1896) 74 LT 222 (no attestation clause; presumption applied on proof of signature of testator and one witness and some other affirmative evidence). See also *Otuka v Alozie* [2006] EWHC 3493 (Ch), [2005] All ER (D) 265 (Dec).

9 *Burgoyne v Showler* (1844) 1 Rob Eccl 5; *Re Thomas* (1859) 1 Sw & Tr 255; *Re Rees* (1865) 34 LJPM & A 56; *Re Spain* (1915) 31 TLR 435.

896. Faulty memory or death of witness. In a contested claim the court will scrutinise the evidence of an attesting witness which tends to prove absence of due execution with great care, and, if his recollection is faulty or negative, or if he shows any hostile animus, will be disposed to put his evidence aside and act on the presumption that the will is good[1].

The presumption of due execution may be applied where there is no attestation clause and the attesting witnesses are dead[2], but this is only done in case of a failure of evidence as to circumstances of the signing and attestation[3].

1 *Blake v Knight* (1843) 3 Curt 547; *Burgoyne v Showler* (1844) 1 Rob Eccl 5 at 11 per Dr Lushington; *Thomson v Hall* (1852) 2 Rob Eccl 426; *Gwillim v Gwillim* (1859) 3 Sw & Tr 200; *Re Gunstan, Blake v Blake* (1882) 7 PD 102 at 115, CA, per Holker LJ; *Wright v Sanderson* (1884) 9 PD 149 at 160, CA, per Lord Selborne; *Woodhouse v Balfour* (1887) 13 PD 2; *Re Moore* [1901] P 44; *Neal v Denston* (1932) 147 LT 460. See also *Cooper v Bockett* (1846) 4 Moo PCC 419; *Lloyd v Roberts* (1858) 12 Moo PCC 158; *Re Benjamin* (1934) 150 LT 417; *Weatherhill v Pearce* [1995] 2 All ER 492, [1995] 1 WLR 592; and see cases cited at PARA 895 note 6.

2 *Re Peverett* [1902] P 205; *Trott v Skidmore* (1860) 2 Sw & Tr 12; *Re Malins* (1887) 19 LR Ir 231. See also *Re Denning, Harnett v Elliott* [1958] 2 All ER 1, [1958] 1 WLR 462, where two unexplained names on the back of the document were inferred to be there for purposes of attestation.

3 See *Re Strong, Strong v Hadden* [1915] P 211; *Rolleston v Sinclair* [1924] 2 IR 157, CA; *Scarff v Scarff* [1927] 1 IR 13, CA. A will which has been lost or accidentally destroyed may be admitted to probate if it is established that there was a proper attestation clause, and that the will purported to be attested by two witnesses, although there is no evidence as to who they were: *Re Phibbs* [1917] P 93. See also PARAS 716, 894–895.

(iii) Want of Sound Disposing Mind

A. TESTAMENTARY CAPACITY IN GENERAL

897. Burden of proof of testamentary capacity The burden of proving testamentary capacity falls on the person propounding the will, but this burden is satisfied prima facie in the case of a rational will by proving that it was validly executed[1]. A person[2] of full age and sound mind may make a valid will and there is today no restriction on the testamentary capacity of persons convicted of crimes[3] and virtually no restriction on the capacity of aliens as such[4]. It is in general not nationality but, in the case of immovables, the lex situs, and in the case of movables, the law of the deceased's domicile, that governs testamentary capacity in the case of a will with a foreign element[5].

1 *Symes v Green* (1859) 1 Sw & Tr 401; *Sutton v Sadler* (1856–57) 5 WR 880. As to a description of a shifting burden of proof see *Key v Key* [2010] EWHC 408 (Ch), [2010] All ER (D) 155 (Apr). See also *Ledger v Wootton* [2007] EWHC 90 (Ch) at [97], [2007] All ER (D) 99 (Oct) per Alistair

Norris QC. As to general burden of proof see PARA 899. Any contention of want of the testator's capacity must be pleaded specifically: see PARA 875. As to the date at which capacity must exist see PARA 50.

2 Former incapacities of married women were abolished by the Law Reform (Married Women and Tortfeasors) Act 1935 ss 1, 2(1) (as originally enacted).

3 See *Re Crippen* [1911] P 108. There seems never to have been any personal incapacity to prevent a convicted person making a will.

4 See the Status of Aliens Act 1914 s 17; and BRITISH NATIONALITY vol 4 (2011) PARA 411. An alien's freedom of testamentary disposition does not, however, extend to any interest in real or personal property to which any person has or may become entitled by reason of any disposition made on death occurring before 12 May 1870: see s 17 proviso (5); and BRITISH NATIONALITY vol 4 (2011) PARA 411.

5 See CONFLICT OF LAWS vol 19 (2011) PARA 746 et seq.

898. Immaturity and testamentary capacity. A minor who is a soldier, sailor or airman may in certain circumstances make a valid will[1], but otherwise a minor cannot[2] make a valid will[3].

Whether an adult with learning difficulties has the capacity to make a will falls to be decided by applying the ordinary criteria for testamentary capacity and each case will be decided on its own facts[4].

1 See PARAS 79–81.

2 Ie where his capacity to make a will is governed by English domestic law: see the enactments cited in note 3. As to capacity in the case of a will where there is a foreign element see PARA 897. The age of majority in English law is 18, and is attained on the commencement of the eighteenth anniversary of a person's birth: see the Family Law Reform Act 1969 ss 1(1), 9(1); and CHILDREN AND YOUNG PERSONS vol 9 (2012) PARAS 1–2.

3 See the Wills Act 1837 s 7, by which no will made by a person under the age of 18 is valid; and PARA 46. The monarch is in legal contemplation never a minor (see CROWN AND CROWN PROCEEDINGS vol 29 (2014) PARA 16), but no grant is in any case made to the estate of a deceased British monarch: see PARA 660. As to the capacity of a minor to be a witness to the execution of a will see PARA 78.

4 As to the need for a sound disposing mind and testamentary capacity see PARA 899.

B. NECESSITY FOR SOUND DISPOSING MIND

899. Presumption of testamentary capacity. Generally speaking, the law presumes capacity, and no evidence is required to prove the testator's sanity, if it is not impeached[1]. A will, rational on the face of it and shown to have been signed and attested in the manner prescribed by law, is presumed, in the absence of any evidence to the contrary, to have been made by a person of competent understanding. However, it is the duty of the executors or any other person setting up a will to show that it is the act of a competent testator, and therefore, where any dispute or doubt exists as to the capacity of the testator, his testamentary capacity must be established and proved affirmatively[2]. The issue of capacity is one of fact[3]. The burden of proof of sanity is considerably increased when it appears that the testator had been subject to previous unsoundness of mind[4]. The justice or injustice of the disposition may throw some light upon the question of the testator's capacity[5]. The testator's suicide shortly after making the will raises no presumption of insanity if there is no other evidence of insanity[6]. The court will not reject a will merely because it 'sounds to folly' without evidence of insanity[7]. Parole or documentary evidence will be admitted to show that the will expresses the testator's deliberate intention; all statements of his, whether oral or written, preparatory to making his will, and his conduct generally in relation to it, are of importance to show whether in fact he was aware of the character of the act which he was performing[8]. A rational act rationally done affords strong evidence of his capacity to make a will[9].

1 *Steed v Calley* (1836) 1 Keen 620 at 635. The common law presumption that a person has capacity until the contrary is proved now has statutory force: see the Mental Capacity Act 2005 s 1(2); and MENTAL HEALTH AND CAPACITY vol 75 (2013) PARA 601. However, this provision refers to the presumption applying for the purposes of decisions under the Mental Capacity Act 2005. There are differing decisions as to the relevance and application of the Mental Capacity Act 2005 to the determination of testamentary capacity, but the weight of decision is that the Act has no application in relation to testamentary capacity: see *Scammell v Farmer* [2008] EWHC 1100 (Ch), [2008] All ER (D) 296 (May); *Walker v Badmin* [2014] EWHC 71 (Ch), [2014] All ER (D) 258 (Nov); *Kicks v Leigh* [2014] EWHC 3926 (Ch), [2015], 4 All ER 329 and also the Mental Capacity Act 2005 Code of Practice (23 April 2007) paras 4.31–4.33. But cf *Fischer v Diffley* [2013] EWHC 4567 (Ch), [2014] WTLR 757. See also PARA 45.

2 *Sutton v Sadler* (1857) 5 WR 880; *Symes v Green* (1859) 1 Sw & Tr 401 at 402; *Smith v Tebbitt* (1867) LR 1 P & D 398 at 436; *Keays v M'Donnell* (1872) IR 6 Eq 611; *Smee v Smee* (1879) 5 PD 84 at 91; and see *Harris v Ingledew* (1730) 3 P Wms 91 at 93; *Wallis v Hodgeson* (1740) 2 Atk 56; *Waring v Waring* (1848) 6 Moo PCC 341 at 355; *Cleare v Cleare* (1869) LR 1 P & D 655 at 657; *Earl of Longford v Purdon* (1877) 1 LR Ir 75. For recent application of this principle see *Ledger v Wootton* [2007] EWHC 90 (Ch), [2007] All ER (D) 99 (Oct) and *Devas v Mackay* [2009] EWHC 1951 (Ch), [2009] All ER (D) 09 (Aug). As to an attesting witness impeaching the will see PARAS 894–895.

3 *Earl of Longford v Purdon* (1877) 1 LR Ir 75 at 79; *Sutton v Sadler* (1857) 5 WR 880.

4 *Smee v Smee* (1879) 5 PD 84; *Groom v Thomas* (1829) 2 Hag Ecc 433; *Re Watts* (1837) 1 Curt 594; *Snook v Watts* (1848) 11 Beav 105; *Bannatyne v Bannatyne* (1852) 2 Rob Eccl 472 at 447. As to the burden of proof where the will is made in a lucid interval see PARA 900.

5 *Harwood v Baker* (1840) 3 Moo PCC 282 at 291. See also *Sharpe v Adam* [2006] EWCA Civ 449, [2006] WTLR 1059, (2007–08) 10 ITELR 419.

6 *Burrows v Burrows* (1827) 1 Hag Ecc 109.

7 *Arbery v Ashe* (1828) 1 Hag Ecc 214.

8 *Wheeler and Batsford v Alderson* (1831) 3 Hag Ecc 574; *Butlin v Barry* (1837) 1 Curt 614 at 629; *Durling and Parker v Loveland* (1839) 2 Curt 225; and see *Levy v Lindo* (1817) 3 Mer 81 at 85.

9 *Cartwright v Cartwright* (1793) 1 Phillim 90 at 100; and see *Clarke v Lear and Scarwell* (1791) cited in 1 Phillim at 119; *Williams v Goude* (1828) 1 Hag Ecc 577; *Rutherford v Maule* (1832) 4 Hag Ecc 213 at 226.

900. Burden of proof where will made in lucid interval. It has been held that once incapacity before the date of the will has been established, the burden lies on the party propounding the will to show that it was made after recovery or during a lucid interval and is therefore valid[1]. This presumption of a continuing mental state is no longer so important[2]. A person challenging a will on the basis of lack of testamentary capacity must provide sufficient evidence to raise a doubt. Once this is done the person propounding the will must prove capacity[3].

1 *Groom v Thomas* (1829) 2 Hag Ecc 433; *Re Watts* (1837) 1 Curt 594; *Bannatyne v Bannatyne* (1852) 2 Rob Eccl 472 at 477; *Nichols and Freeman v Binns* (1858) 1 Sw & Tr 239; *Smee v Smee* (1879) 5 PD 84; *Re Walker, Watson v Treasury Solicitor* (1912) 28 TLR 466. In such a case the will should be regarded with great distrust, and every presumption should, in the first instance be made against it, especially where the will is one in which natural affection and claims of near relationship have been disregarded: *Banks v Goodfellow* (1870) LR 5 QB 549 at 570. It is not, however, necessary in order to constitute a lucid interval that the testator should be restored to as vigorous or active a state of intellect as he enjoyed before his incapacity: *Ex p Holyland* (1805) 11 Ves 10 at 11; *Creagh v Blood* (1845) 8 I Eq R 434 at 439.

2 Following the Court of Appeal's decision in *Masterman-Lister v Brutton & Co, Masterman-Lister v Jewell* [2002] EWCA Civ 1889, [2003] 3 All ER 162, [2003] 1 WLR 1511 which decided that adults must be presumed competent to manage their property and affairs until the contrary is proved. See also the statutory presumption in the Mental Capacity Act 2005 s 1(2) which, although probably not directly relevant to the determination of testamentary capacity (as to which see PARA 899 note 1), tends to inform the court's approach.

3 See *Key v Key* [2010] EWHC 408 (Ch) at [97], [2010] All ER (D) 155 (Apr) per Alistair Norris QC. This task will be easier if there is either clear evidence of incapacity for a lengthy period or evidence of incapacity in other areas at the time the will was made.

(iv) Want of Knowledge and Approval

901. Knowledge and approval essential in regard to will. Probate of a will may also be opposed on the ground of the testator's want of knowledge and approval by evidence of circumstances attending or at least relevant to the preparation and execution of the will[1]. Such a contention must be made in the statement of case[2]. The standard of proof required is satisfaction on the preponderance (or balance) of probability[3]. The court must consider the inherent probabilities and where the testator has an opportunity to read the will, particularly where the will is short, it is likely to refuse to find lack of knowledge and approval in the absence of any clear or cogent evidence to the contrary[4].

Although the concepts of testamentary capacity and knowledge and approval are conceptually distinct, it seems a similar rule applies as to the time when knowledge and approval must be shown to have existed[5].

1 *Re Musgrove, Davis v Mayhew* [1927] P 264 at 280, CA; *Re R* [1951] P 10 at 17, [1950] 2 All ER 117 at 121. See further PARAS 54, 902 et seq.

2 See CPR 57.7(3). As to statements of case see PARA 875. See also *Franks v Sinclair* [2006] EWHC 3365 (Ch) at [61], [2006] All ER (D) 340 (Dec) at [61].

3 See *Fuller v Strum* [2001] EWCA Civ 1879; [2002] 1 WLR 1097, [2002] 2 All ER 87, [2002] 1 WLR 1097 per Chadwick LJ at [72].; and *Devas v Mackay* [2009] EWHC 1951 (Ch), [2009] All ER (D) 09 (Aug). See also PARA 54.

4 Sherrington v Sherrington [2005] EWCA Civ 326; [2005] 3 F.C.R. 538at [96]. See also Fuller v Strum [2001] EWCA Civ 1879; [2002] 1 WLR 1097, [2002] 2 All ER 87; [2001] W.T.L.R. 527 [2001] W.T.L.R. 527.

5 *Perrins v Holland* [2010] EWCA Civ 840, [2010] All ER (D) 210 (Jul) (affg *Re Perrins, Perrins v Holland, Perrins v Dooney* [2009] EWHC 1945 (Ch), [2009] WTLR 1387) ('In my judgment, therefore, in a case in which the principle in *Parker v Felgate* is applied it is not necessary to prove knowledge and approval of the will, provided that the testator believes that it gives effect to his instructions; and it does in fact do so' at [52] per Lewison J)). As to the principle in *Parker v Felgate* (1883) 80 PD 171 see PARA 50.

902. Presumption of knowledge and approval in regard to will. Although it has been laid down as a general rule[1] that in the absence of fraud, the fact that his will has been duly read over to a capable testator on the occasion of its execution, or that its contents have been brought to his notice in any other way, should when coupled with his execution of the will be held conclusive evidence that he knew and approved of its contents, the rigidity of the rule has been progressively eroded[2]. There is, now, no conclusive presumption that a testator who executes his will after having it read to him must be held to have known and approved of the contents; it is open to the tribunal before which the question arises to find as a fact that the will had not been read to him in such a way as to convey to his mind a due appreciation of its contents[3]. However, the presumption of knowledge and approval stated above must be rebutted by the clearest evidence[4].

Traditionally, the court has approached the question of knowledge and approval on a two-stage basis, asking first whether the opponent of the will has established a prima facie case that the testator did not in fact know of and approve the contents of the will; and secondly, whether or not those suspicions were allayed by the propounder of the will[5]. However, where a judge has heard evidence of fact and expert opinion over a period of many days relating to the character, state of mind and likely desires of the testator and the circumstances in which the will was drafted and executed, it is preferable for the court to consider all the relevant evidence and then, drawing such inferences as it can from the totality of the material, decide whether or not those propounding the will have discharged the burden of establishing that the testator knew and approved of the contents of the alleged will[6].

1 *Guardhouse v Blackburn* (1866) LR 1 P & D 109 at 116 per Sir JP Wilde (the judge restated the same proposition in slightly different terms in his charge to the jury in *Atter v Atkinson* (1869) LR 1 P & D 665 at 670).
2 See *Re Morris* [1971] P 62 at 76, 77, [1970] 1 All ER 1057 per Latey J, citing *Fulton v Andrew* (1875) LR 7 HL 448 where Lord Cairns LC said at 460–461 that he would 'greatly deprecate the introduction or creation of fixed and unyielding rules of law which are not imposed by Act of Parliament'.
3 *Fulton v Andrew* (1875) LR 7 HL 448, commenting on *Atter v Atkinson* (1869) LR 1 P & D 665; *Garnett-Botfield v Garnett-Botfield* [1901] P 335; *Re Morris* [1971] P 62, [1970] 1 All ER 1057. See also *Re Phelan* [1972] Fam 33, [1971] 3 All ER 1256; *Beamish v Beamish* [1894] 1 IR 7. See also *Franks v Sinclair* [2006] EWHC 3365 (Ch), [2006] All ER (D) 340 (Dec) where knowledge and approval could not be presumed just because the will was read out to the testatrix just before execution.
4 *Gregson v Taylor* [1917] P 256 (misdescription of legatee included in probate).
5 See Parke J's analysis in *Barry v Butlin* (1838) 2 Moo PCC 480, quoted by Lindley LJ in *Tyrell v Painton* [1894] P 151.
6 *Gill v Woodalll* [2010] EWCA 1430 at [21], [2011] Ch 380, [2011] 3 WLR 85 per Lord Neuberger citing Sachs J in *Re Creror* (unreported) but see (1956) 106 LJ 694, 695, cited and followed by Latey J in *Re Morris* [1971] P 62 at 78, [1970] 1 All ER 1057 and applied in *Wharton v Bancroft* [2011] EWHC 3250 (Ch), [2012] WTLR 693; *Simon v Byford* [2014] EWHC Civ 280, [2014] WTLR 1097, 17 ITELR 536; *Sharp v Hutchins* [2015] EWHC 1240 (Ch); [2015] WTLR 1269.

903. Circumstances rebutting presumption of knowledge and approval of contents of will. Whenever the circumstances under which a will is prepared raise a well-grounded suspicion that it does not express the testator's mind, the court ought not to pronounce in favour of it unless the suspicion is removed[1], even though those opposing the will do not raise any positive case but merely insist that the will is proved in solemn form[2]. Accordingly, where a person propounds a will prepared by himself or on his instructions, under which he benefits, the onus is on him to prove the righteousness of the transaction[3] and that the testator knew and approved of it[4]. A similar onus is raised where there is some weakness in the testator which, although it does not amount to incapacity, renders him liable to be made the instrument of those around him[5]; or where the testator is of extreme age[6]; or where knowledge of the contents of the will is not brought home to him[7]; or where the will was prepared on verbal instructions only[8], or was made by interrogating the testator[9]; or where there was any concealment or misrepresentation[10]; or where the will is at variance with the testator's known affections[11], or previous declarations[12], or dispositions in former wills[13], or there is a general sense of impropriety[14].

1 *Tyrrell v Painton* [1894] P 151 at 159, CA, per Davey LJ; *Donnelly v Broughton* [1891] AC 435, PC; *Paske v Ollat* (1815) 2 Phillim 323. As to the interpretation of separate wills see PARA 713. A will need not originate from the testator: see *Constable v Tufnell* (1833) 4 Hag Ecc 465 at 485; see also *Tanner v Public Trustee* [1973] 1 NZLR 68, Wellington CA, applying *Barry v Butlin* (1838) 2 Moo PCC 480. See also PARA 54.
2 See remarks in *Knight v Edonya* [2009] EWHC 2181 (Ch), [2009] All ER (D) 207 (Aug) at [13] although in that case the circumstances were held such as not to excite suspicion.
3 See *Fuller v Strum* [2001] EWCA Civ 1879 at [65], [2002] 2 All ER 87, [2002] 1 WLR 1097 per Chadwick LJ who said that the expression is not to be taken as a licence by the court to refuse probate to a document of which it disapproves. The question is whether the contents of the will do truly represent the testator's testamentary intentions.
4 *Barry v Butlin* (1838) 2 Moo PCC 480 at 482; *Fulton v Andrew* (1875) LR 7 HL 448 at 471; *Re Liver, Scott v Woods* (1955) 106 LJo 75. Cf *Tyrrell v Painton* [1894] P 151, CA; *Wintle v Nye* [1959] 1 All ER 552, [1959] 1 WLR 284, HL. The Law Society (ie the body responsible for the regulation of solicitors: see now the Solicitors Regulation Authority) demands a high standard of solicitors who benefit under wills they have prepared: *Re a Solicitor* [1975] QB 475, [1974] 3 All ER 853. In *Franks v Sinclair* [2006] EWHC 3365 (Ch), [2006] All ER (D) 340 (Dec), the

court found lack of knowledge and approval by rejecting the evidence of a solicitor who had prepared a will for his mother and attended her at its execution. Under the will, he was a beneficiary as to half the residuary estate. See also PARA 905. Simply initiating the process of drawing up a will under which the propounder benefited (but not being present at the taking of instructions or execution) did not excite the suspicion or concern of the court; nor that the will was made just before the testator's death when he had shown no previous inclination to make one: *Knight v Edonya* [2009] EWHC 2181 (Ch), [2009] All ER (D) 207 (Aug). However, the element of suspicion arising from the circumstances, although by no means overpowering, is sufficient to call for affirmative proof of knowledge and approval, beyond that constituted by the due execution of a rational will: *Key v Key* [2010] EWHC 408 (Ch), [2010] All ER (D) 155 (Apr) (following the death of his wife, the testator was left in the sole care of his eldest daughter and was so placed in a position of extreme vulnerability to any suggestion to change his will, which had previously been favourable to his two sons, in favour of her and her sister). See also *Barrett v Bem* [2012] EWCA Civ 52, [2012] Ch 573, [2012] 2 All ER 920 (testator's sister signed will on his behalf); *Bennett v Petit* [2013] EWHC 955 (Ch), [2013] All ER (D) 37 (May); and PARA 64.

5 *Ingram v Wyatt* (1828) 1 Hag Ecc 384 (revsd on the facts sub nom *Wyatt v Ingram* (1831) 3 Hag Ecc 466); *Mountain v Bennet* (1787) 1 Cox Eq Cas 353; *Harwood v Baker* (1840) 3 Moo PCC 282. See also *Re Heinke, Westminster Bank Ltd v Massey* (1959) Times, 21 January (effect of alcohol may be such as to impair knowledge and approval of testator, but not his capacity). As to what constitutes undue influence see PARA 56.

6 See *Kinleside v Harrison* (1818) 2 Phillim 449; *Griffiths v Robins* (1818) 3 Madd 191 (deed).

7 *Paske v Ollat* (1815) 2 Phillim 323.

8 *Middleton v Forbes* (1787) cited in 1 Hag Ecc at 395, 398; *Mackenzie v Handasyde* (1829) 2 Hag Ecc 211.

9 *Green v Skipworth* (1809) 1 Phillim 53 at 58.

10 *Segrave v Kirwan* (1828) Beat 157; *Allen v M'Pherson* (1847) 1 HL Cas 191 at 207; *Paske v Ollat* (1815) 2 Phillim 323. As to fraud see PARA 58.

11 *King v Farley* (1828) 1 Hag Ecc 502; *Brydges v King* (1828) 1 Hag Ecc 256.

12 *Baker v Batt* (1838) 2 Moo PCC 317; *Brydges v King* (1828) 1 Hag Ecc 256.

13 *Marsh v Tyrrell and Harding* (1828) 2 Hag Ecc 84 (revsd by consent (1832) 3 Hag Ecc 471); *Mynn v Robinson* (1828) 2 Hag Ecc 169 at 179; *Brydges v King* (1828) 1 Hag Ecc 256; *Harwood v Baker* (1840) 3 Moo PCC 282.

14 *Butlin v Barry* (1837) 1 Curt 614; *Durling and Parker v Loveland* (1839) 2 Curt 225. In *Gill v Woodall* [2010] EWCA Civ 1430, [2011] Ch 380, [2011] 3 WLR 85 (severe agrophobia meant that the testatrix was unlikely to understand the contents of a will read to her in a solicitor's office; there was no evidence that she was present when her husband gave instructions for the couple's wills or that she ever saw the draft wills sent for approval).

904. Fiduciary relationship between testator and beneficiary. While the mere proof of the existence of a fiduciary relationship does not raise a presumption of undue influence of itself sufficient to vitiate a gift by will[1], the existence of a fiduciary relationship between the testator and a beneficiary raises a suspicion of impropriety and renders it necessary to prove that the testator knew and approved the contents of the will he has made[2]; still stricter proof is required where the will has been prepared or obtained by such a beneficiary[3]. The medical practitioner[4], the spiritual adviser[5] and especially the legal adviser[6] are each in a fiduciary position to those who come to them for advice.

1 *Parfitt v Lawless* (1872) LR 2 P & D 462. See PARA 57. See also GIFTS vol 52 (2014) PARA 214; MISREPRESENTATION vol 76 (2013) PARA 836 et seq.

2 *Butlin v Barry* (1837) 1 Curt 614 (affd sub nom *Barry v Butlin* (1838) 2 Moo PCC 480); *Durling and Parker v Loveland* (1839) 2 Curt 225; *Atter v Atkinson* (1869) LR 1 P & D 665 at 668; *Fulton v Andrew* (1875) LR 7 HL 448 at 463; *Wintle v Nye* [1959] 1 All ER 552, [1959] 1 WLR 284, HL.

3 *Huguenin v Baseley* (1807) 14 Ves 273; *Popham v Brooke* (1828) 5 Russ 8; *Segrave v Kirwan* (1828) Beat 157; *Ingram v Wyatt* (1828) 1 Hag Ecc 384 (revsd on the facts sub nom *Wyatt v Ingram* (1831) 3 Hag Ecc 466); *Middleton v Sherburne* (1841) 4 Y & C Ex 358; *Wintle v Nye* [1959] 1 All ER 552, [1959] 1 WLR 284, HL.

4 *Popham v Brooke* (1828) 5 Russ 8; *Dent v Bennett* (1839) 4 My & Cr 269; *Greville v Tylee* (1851) 7 Moo PCC 320.

5 *Parfitt v Lawless* (1872) LR 2 P & D 462; *Middleton v Sherburne* (1841) 4 Y & C Ex 358; *Huguenin v Baseley* (1807) 14 Ves 273.

6 *Seagrave v Kirwan* (1828) Beat 157; *Ingram v Wyatt* (1828) 1 Hag Ecc 384 (revsd on the facts sub nom *Wyatt v Ingram* (1831) 3 Hag Ecc 466); *Maccabe v Hussey* (1831) 2 Dow & Cl 440, HL; *Raworth v Marriott* (1833) 1 My & K 643; *Dufaur v Croft* (1840) 3 Moo PCC 136; *Powell v Powell* [1900] 1 Ch 243; *Willis v Barron* [1902] AC 271, HL; *Wright v Carter* [1903] 1 Ch 27, CA; *Wintle v Nye* [1959] 1 All ER 552, [1959] 1 WLR 284, HL. See also *Franks v Sinclair* [2006] EWHC 3365 (Ch), [2006] All ER (D) 340 (Dec) where, although the propounder of the will was a solicitor, the suspicion arose because he was a substantial beneficiary who had prepared the will (see PARA 903 note 4).

905. Will prepared by a person in his own favour. Where a person has prepared a will in his own favour it is his duty to bring to the testator's mind the effect of his testamentary act, and failure to do so may amount to fraud[1]. Those who take for their own benefit after having been instrumental in preparing or obtaining a will have thrown upon them the onus of showing the righteousness of the transaction[2]. This means that, if no evidence is given by the party on whom the burden is cast, the issue must be found against him[3], but if evidence is given on which the court can come to a determinate conclusion the onus need not be considered. On the other hand, if the evidence is so evenly balanced that no determinate conclusion can be reached, the onus becomes the determining factor of the whole case[4]. It is a circumstance that ought generally to excite suspicion and call for vigilant and jealous examination of the evidence in support of the instrument[5]. It rests upon the person who has procured a will under which he takes a large benefit to show that the will does really express the testator's mind and intention[6]. The mere circumstance that the person who prepared a will takes an interest under it does not vitiate the will, and the principles must not be used to raise a cloud of unjustifiable suspicion[7].

An analogous principle applies in equity by which an executor who has prepared a will in his own favour may not be allowed to benefit[8].

1 *Fulton v Andrew* (1875) LR 7 HL 448 at 463 per Lord Cairns LC.
2 *Fulton v Andrew* (1875) LR 7 HL 448 at 471 per Lord Hatherley. It was this phrase, 'righteousness of the transaction', which gave rise to a form of pleading which places on the opposing party the onus of removing any grounds of suspicion. It is a plea often used where undue influence cannot be proved, and is sometimes applicable where the person preparing the will has some close link of kinship, affection, or interest with the beneficiary: cf *Tyrrell v Painton* [1894] P 151, CA. However, the phrase is not to be taken by the court as a licence to refuse probate to a document of which it disapproves, whether the disapproval stems from the circumstances in which the document has been executed or from its contents: see *Fuller v Strum* [2001] EWCA Civ 1879, [2002] 2 All ER 87, [2002] 1 WLR 1097. See also *Knight v Edonya* [2009] EWHC 2181 (Ch), [2009] All ER (D) 207 (Aug). See also PARA 903.
3 *Barry v Butlin* (1838) 2 Moo PCC 480; *Harmes v Hinkson* [1946] WN 118, PC.
4 *Harmes v Hinkson* [1946] WN 118, PC; and *Stark v Dennison* [1973] 1 WWR 368, Alta CA, following *Robins v National Trust Co* [1927] AC 515 at 520, PC. See also CIVIL PROCEDURE vol 12 (2015) PARA 703. As to the right to begin proceedings see PARA 56 note 2.
5 *Barry v Butlin* (1838) 2 Moo PCC 480 at 482 per Parke B; *Brown v Fisher* (1890) 63 LT 465; *Tyrrell v Painton* [1894] P 151 at 157, CA, per Lindley LJ; *Re Liver, Scott v Woods* (1956) 106 L Jo 75; *Stark v Dennison* [1973] 1 WWR 368, Alta CA. As to the right of a solicitor to take a benefit under a client's will see LEGAL PROFESSIONS vol 66 (2015) PARA 608. See also PARA 903 note 4. See also *Franks v Sinclair* [2006] EWHC 4465, [2006] All ER (D) 340 (Dec).
6 *Brown v Fisher* (1890) 63 LT 465; *Finny v Govett* (1908) 25 TLR 186, CA.
7 *Low v Guthrie* [1909] AC 278 at 283, HL; *Harmes v Hinkson* [1946] WN 118, PC. Cf *Spiers v English* [1907] P 122 at 124 per Sir G Barnes.
8 See *Re Pugh's Will Trusts, Marten v Pugh* [1967] 3 All ER 337, [1967] 1 WLR 1262; and TRUSTS AND POWERS vol 98 (2013) PARA 153.

906. Partial exclusion of words from will. Where the testator is shown to have known and approved of a particular word or clause, it cannot be excepted from the grant, even though it produces an effect contrary to his real intention, or may have been inserted by a slip on the part of the draughtsman[1]. The remedy in such cases lies with the court construing the will or, in the case of deaths after 1 January 1983[2], with the remedy of rectification[3]. The court will refuse probate of a document executed by mistake[4] and may omit words from the probated will where they were included by mistake[5].

1 *Harter v Harter* (1873) LR 3 P & D 11; *Collins v Elstone* [1893] P 1; *Rhodes v Rhodes* (1882) 7 App Cas 192, PC; *Gregson v Taylor* [1917] P 256; *Re Beech, Beech v Public Trustee* [1923] P 46, CA. See also *Fuller v Strum* [2001] EWCA Civ 1879, [2002] 2 All ER 87, [2002] 1 WLR 1097. As to the limited jurisdiction to exclude words from probate in certain cases see PARAS 739, 892; and as to the court's power to rectify mistakes in wills see PARAS 187, 741.
2 Ie the date on which the Administration of Justice Act 1982 came into effect.
3 As to the court's power to rectify mistakes in wills see PARAS 187, 741.
4 *Re Meyer* [1908] P 353. As to mistake generally see MISTAKE vol 77 (2016) PARA 12 et seq.
5 See PARAS 739, 892.

907. Issue of want of knowledge and approval to be raised in probate court. Questions of want of knowledge or approval must be raised in the probate court[1], but where that court holds the will to be valid equity may impose a trust on the bequest. For example a legal adviser cannot benefit from his own ignorance or negligence and, if he takes a benefit under a will to the prejudice of other persons as a result, he may be held to be a trustee for those persons[2].

1 *Nelson v Oldfield* (1688) 2 Vern 76; *Allen v M'Pherson* (1847) 1 HL Cas 191; *Meluish v Milton* (1876) 3 ChD 27, CA. As to the construction of references to the probate court see PARA 678.
2 *Segrave v Kirwan* (1828) Beat 157 at 166; *Bulkley v Wilford* (1834) 8 Bli NS 111, HL. See also PARAS 59 text and note 4, 58 note 5.

(5) COST OF PROBATE PROCEEDINGS

908. Costs of probate proceedings generally. The costs of probate proceedings are in the discretion of the court[1], and if the court decides to make an order about costs the general rule is that the unsuccessful party will be ordered to pay the costs of the successful party[2]. This is subject to the court's power to make a different order[3], and the exception for probate proceedings in the Court of Appeal[4].

In deciding what order, if any, to make about costs the court must have regard to all the circumstances, including the conduct of all the parties[5], whether a party has succeeded on part of his case, even if he has not been wholly successful, and any admissible offer to settle[6].

Costs should be asked for at the trial[7], and the bill served at the commencement of detailed assessment must include at one and the same time all the costs to which the order entitles the litigant[8].

1 See the Senior Courts Act 1981 s 51 (see CIVIL PROCEDURE vol 12A (2015) PARA 1684); and CPR 44.2(1) (which provides that the court has discretion as to whether costs are payable by one party to another, the amount of those costs, and when they are to be paid). For the different orders as to the amount of costs which may be made see CPR 44.2(6); and CIVIL PROCEDURE vol 12A (2015) PARA 1702. As to costs on discontinuance of a claim see PARA 883. See also CIVIL PROCEDURE vol 12 (2015) PARA 1037.
2 See CPR 44.2(2)(a); *Page v Williamson* (1902) 87 LT 146. See also *Twist v Tye* [1902] P 92 at 93; *Spiers v English* [1907] P 122 at 123, the principal authority on this point, approved in *Re Cutcliffe's Estate, Le Duc v Veness* [1959] P 6, [1958] 3 All ER 642, CA and see also *Kostic v Chaplin* [2007] EWHC 2909 (Ch), [2008] 2 Costs LR 271, [2007] All ER (D) 119 (Dec). See also *Morris v Davies* [2012] EWHC 1981 (Ch), [2012] WTLR 1569, [2012] All ER (D) 275 (Jul).
3 See CPR 44.2(2)(b); and CIVIL PROCEDURE vol 12A (2015) PARA 1698. In addition the court has a general discretion as to whether costs are payable by one party to another before the general rule becomes applicable: see CPR 44.2(1)(a); and CIVIL PROCEDURE vol 12A (2015) PARA 1698. See also PARAS 909–911.
4 The general rule does not apply to proceedings in the Court of Appeal from a judgment, direction, decision or order given or made in probate proceedings: CPR 44.2(3)(b).

5 The conduct of the parties includes:
(1) conduct before, as well as during, the proceedings, and in particular the extent to which the parties followed the *Practice Direction—Pre-Action Conduct* or any relevant pre-action protocol (see PARA 860 note 6);
(2) whether it was reasonable for a party to raise, pursue or contest a particular allegation or issue;
(3) the manner in which a party has pursued or defended his case or a particular allegation or issue; and
(4) whether a claimant who has succeeded in his claim, in whole or in part, exaggerated his claim (CPR 44.2(5)).
See also *Morris v Davies* [2012] EWHC 1981 (Ch), [2012] WTLR 1569, [2012] All ER (D) 275 (Jul); and note 2.

6 See CPR 44.2(4); and CIVIL PROCEDURE vol 12A (2015) PARA 1701. As to the overriding objective see PARA 647 note 3. The CPR provides one specific exception to the general rule which relates to probate claims, ie where the defence is confined to requiring the will to be proved in solemn form and cross-examining the witnesses to the will (see PARA 874): see CPR 57.7(5); and PARA 878. Before the CPR came into force on 26 April 1999 there were established principles which the court followed with respect to the costs of probate proceedings by which in certain circumstances the unsuccessful party was not ordered to pay the costs of the successful party: see PARAS 909–911. The CPR neither exclude nor expressly indorse these principles, but they continue to be followed. See *Kostic v Chaplin* [2007] EWHC 2909 (Ch), [2008] 2 Costs LR 271, [2007] All ER (D) 119 (Dec). As to costs and offers to settle see the Court of Appeal decision in *Mitchell v James* [2002] EWCA Civ 997, [2003] 2 All ER 1064, [2004] 1 WLR 158, CA which held that terms as to costs do not fall within the scope of an offer made under CPR Pt 36. A term as to costs can be included in an offer outside CPR Pt 36 and the court will have regard to any such offer in exercising its discretion as to costs at the end of the case. As to offers under CPR Pt 36 see CIVIL PROCEDURE vol 12A (2015) PARA 1653 et seq. As to the court's discretion as to who should pay costs see now generally CPR 44.2.

7 *Re Elmsley, Dyke v Williams* (1871) LR 2 P & D 239; cf *Bewsher v Williams and Ball* (1861) 3 Sw & Tr 62 (costs refused at trial but allowed on motion subsequently).

8 *Re Segalov, Hyman and Teff v Segalov* [1952] P 241, [1952] 2 All ER 107. As to failing to include costs of previous solicitors see *Harris v Moat Housing Group South Ltd* [2007] EWHC 3092 (QB), [2008] 1 WLR 1578.

909. Costs of successful parties. As a general rule, an executor who proves a will in solemn form, whether he has done so of his own motion or has been put to proof, is entitled to have his costs[1] as between solicitor and client out of the estate without a court order[2]. A beneficiary who successfully propounds a will in solemn form is entitled to an order for his costs and expenses out of the estate[3]. A person entitled under an intestacy[4] or to a grant of probate under a prior will who successfully contests the validity of a later will is also entitled to an order for his costs out of the estate, so far as an unsuccessful party who is ordered to pay his costs fails to pay them. If, however, the successful party is not entitled to a grant as a personal representative of the deceased, and the order for costs is confined to being an order against another party, then it seems that the successful party can only recover his costs (if at all) from the other party[5]. Where there is sufficient divergence of interest between defendants, they are justified in appearing by separate counsel[6].

1 *Re Price, Williams v Jenkins* (1886) 31 ChD 485; *Graham v M'Cashin* [1901] 1 IR 404, CA.

2 *Re Plant, Wild v Plant* [1926] P 139, CA; *Headington v Holloway* (1830) 3 Hag Ecc 280 at 282; *Re Fuld, Hartley v Fuld (No 3)* [1968] P 675 at 720, [1965] 3 All ER 776 at 783 per Scarman J. For exceptions to the rule see PARA 910. Cf CPR 46.3, which provides that where a person is or has been a party to any proceedings in the capacity of trustee or personal representative (and CPR 44.5 does not apply), the general rule is that that person is entitled to be paid the costs of those proceedings, insofar as they are not recovered from or paid by any other person, out of the relevant trust fund or estate, and where that person is entitled to be paid any of those costs out of the fund or estate, those costs will be assessed on the indemnity basis.See also PARA 908 note 6. As to indemnity basis and scale of costs generally see Tristram and Coote's Probate Practice (30th Edn) 40.10. See also CIVIL PROCEDURE vol 12A (2015) PARA 1704.

3 *Sutton v Drax* (1815) 2 Phillim 323; *Wilkinson v Corfield* (1881) 6 PD 27. The unsuccessful party is not always ordered to pay the successful party's costs: see PARA 911.

4 *Critchell v Critchell* (1863) 3 Sw & Tr 41; *Bewsher v Williams and Ball* (1861) 3 Sw & Tr 62.

5 *Nash v Yelloly* (1862) 3 Sw & Tr 59; but cf *Cross v Cross* (1864) 3 Sw & Tr 292. Failure of the successful party to obtain his costs out of the estate could prevent any claim being brought to recover the costs (so far as not recovered from the unsuccessful party) as damages for professional negligence against the solicitor who prepared the will which has been pronounced against, since such a claim is the estate's rather than a beneficiary's: see *Worby v Rosser* (1999) Times, 9 June, [1999] All ER (D) 571, CA. However 'if a solicitor does fail to take instructions from the proposed testator, does take them from a third party and does not check to see he has understood his instructions properly and moreover, as alleged in this case, does not keep a proper note of his instructions, it is reasonably foreseeable that a challenge to whatever wills are executed as a result will in turn ensue and the costs thereby incurred are also foreseeable': *Sifri v Clough & Willis* [2007] EWHC 985 (Ch) at [17] [2007] WTLR 1453 at [17] per Judge Roger Kaye QC where two wills were prepared by a solicitor who took his instructions through a third party; following a successful probate action to set aside the wills but in which no order for costs was made, the claimant brought a negligence action against the solicitor who had drafted the two wills; the claimant was awarded 40% of the costs incurred in the earlier probate action but failed in her claim for damages resulting from the delay to the administration of the estate caused by the probate action. In *Re Fuld, Hartley v Fuld (No 3)* [1968] P 675, [1965] 3 All ER 776 the costs of the successful parties were ordered to be paid out of the estate and the unsuccessful party was ordered to contribute to the costs borne by the estate.

6 *Bagshaw v Pimm* [1900] P 148, CA.

910. When executor is liable for costs. Although, as already stated, an executor, whether as claimant or defendant, is prima facie justified in propounding a will and generally entitled to his costs out of the estate, he may be refused his costs or condemned in the costs if it is proved that he must have known that he was propounding a document which could not be supported[1]. He is not obliged to propound a will[2], and may by unreasonable conduct not only disentitle himself to costs but render himself liable to pay the costs of the successful parties[3], especially if he himself takes a large benefit under the will which he seeks to propound[4].

If one of two executors is held to have exercised undue influence, and the other to have been free from blame, costs may be ordered against both[5].

1 *Boughton v Knight* (1873) LR 3 P & D 64; *Rogers v Le Cocq* (1896) 65 LJP 68; *Page v Williamson* (1902) 87 LT 146. See also PARA 861. See also *Smith v Springford* [2008] All ER (D) 59 (Feb) as to executor's liability for costs on discontinuance once he becomes aware that the document cannot be supported. See also PARA 883.

2 *Rennie v Massie* (1866) LR 1 P & D 118 at 119.

3 The practice was fully discussed in *Re Plant, Wild v Plant* [1926] P 139, CA, where it was held that when an executor propounded a will and codicil, and the will was admitted to probate and the codicil pronounced against, he was entitled to costs out of the estate unless he had acted unreasonably. See also PARA 909 text and note 2.

4 *Re Speke, Speke v Deakin* (1913) 109 LT 719; *Re Osment, Child and Jarvis v Osment* [1914] P 129 (costs of all parties ordered to come out of legacies bequeathed to the executor, whose conduct had been the cause of the litigation); *Thomas v Jones* [1928] P 162 (solicitor, personally interested, disregarded client's testamentary capacity and was ordered to pay part of increased costs); *Re Austin* (1929) 73 Sol Jo 545 (solicitor's benefit under will he prepared). An executor has a right to costs out of the estate unless, as said of a trustee by Sir G Jessel MR in *Turner v Hancock* (1882) 20 ChD 303 at 305, CA, it is 'lost or curtailed by such inequitable conduct . . . as may amount to a violation or culpable neglect of his duty'; cited in *Thomas v Jones* at 165 per Lord Merrivale P. See also *Baker v Batt* (1838) 2 Moo PCC 317; *Burls v Burls* (1868) LR 1 P & D 472 (will lost or destroyed through executor's negligence); *Re Scott, Huggett v Reichman* (1966) 110 Sol Jo 852; *Re Persse's Estate, O'Donnell v Bruce and Dawson* (1962) 106 Sol Jo 432.

5 *Re Barlow, Haydon v Pring* [1919] P 131, CA; *Re Jeffries, Hill v Jeffries* (1916) 33 TLR 80, CA. See also *Kelly v O'Connor* [1917] 1 IR 312 (donatio mortis causa held not to be assets for payment of costs); *Selwood v Selwood* (1920) 125 LT 26 (unsuccessful attempt to obtain probate of soldier's letter).

911. Unsuccessful parties: costs. Subject to the overriding consideration that costs are a matter of discretion[1], two general principles have been laid down as to unsuccessful parties[2]:

(1) where the cause of litigation takes its origin in the fault of the testator[3] or of those interested in the residuary estate[4], the costs of the unsuccessful party are allowed out of the estate; and

(2) the unsuccessful party will not be ordered to pay costs if there is a sufficient and reasonable ground, looking to his knowledge and means of knowledge, to question the execution of the will or the testator's capacity, or his knowledge and approval of the will[5].

The court will not make an order for costs against a defendant who gives notice in his defence that he does not raise any positive case but insists that the will be proved in solemn form and for that purpose is to cross-examine the witnesses who attested the will[6], unless the court considers that there was no reasonable ground for opposing the will[7].

A party unsuccessfully seeking to revoke a grant must pay the costs, unless he has reasonable grounds for raising the question[8]. The probability is that if a party unsuccessfully makes charges of undue influence and fraud he will be condemned in the costs not only of those charges but of the whole action[9].

1 See PARA 908.
2 *Mitchell and Mitchell v Gard and Kingwell* (1863) 3 Sw & Tr 275 at 278 per Sir JP Wilde; *Spiers v English* [1907] P 122; *Re Cutcliffe's Estate, Le Duc v Veness* [1959] P 6, [1958] 3 All ER 642, CA; *Kostic v Chaplin* [2007] EWHC 2909 (Ch), [2008] 2 Costs LR 271, [2007] All ER (D) 119 (Dec).
3 Eg where the testator left his testamentary papers in a confused or disorderly state: *Mitchell and Mitchell v Gard and Kingwell* (1863) 3 Sw & Tr 275; *Lemage v Goodban* (1865) LR 1 P & D 57 at 63; *Davies v Gregory* (1873) LR 3 P & D 28; *Jenner v Ffinch* (1879) 5 PD 106; *Re Hall-Dare, Le Marchant v Lee Warner* [1916] 1 Ch 272; *Rowe v Clarke* [2006] EWHC 1292 (Ch), [2006] All ER (D) 124 (May). Similarly where the testator's conduct had been the cause of the litigation: see *Re Ritchie, Ritchie v Joslin* [2009] All ER (D) 78 (Apr) applying *Spiers v English* [1907] P 122; and *Kostic v Chaplin* [2007] EWHC 2909 (Ch), [2008] 2 Costs LR 271, [2007] All ER (D) 119 (Dec).
4 See *Smith v Smith* (1865) 4 Sw & Tr 3; *Orton v Smith* (1873) LR 3 P & D 23. See also *Re Birkby* (1929) 73 Sol Jo 556 (lost will).
5 See eg *Ferrey v King* (1861) 3 Sw & Tr 51; *Bramley v Bramley* (1864) 3 Sw & Tr 430; *Tippett v Tippett* (1865) LR 1 P & D 54; *Aylwin v Aylwin* [1902] P 203; *Tyrrell v Painton* [1894] P 151, CA; *Walters v Smee* [2008] EWHC 2902 (Ch), [2008] All ER (D) 30 (Dec) (court not accepting unsuccessful party's plea to depart from normal rule); *Perrins v Holland (as executor of the estate of Perrins)* [2009] EWHC 2558 (Ch), [2009] All ER (D) 124 (Nov). As to limitation of costs by notice in a defence that the defendant whose defence it is will raise no positive case but insist on the will being proved in solemn form, and cross-examine only, see PARA 874. See also *Re Fanshawe, Harari v Rollo* (1983) Times, 17 November, CA (allegations of want of knowledge and approval rejected by the judge after an 11 day trial; held a proper exercise of the judge's discretion to make no order for costs where he held it was reasonable to insist on proof of the will in solemn form but the unsuccessful party had conducted the case as straight hostile litigation).
6 Ie under CPR 57.7(5)(a) (see PARA 874).
7 See CPR 57.7(5)(b); and PARA 874. See *Elliott v Simmonds* [2016] EWHC 962 (Ch) for an example of a costs order made against a challenger of the will from the date at which she and her advisers had sufficient material on which to form a view on whether there were reasonable grounds to challenge the will.
8 *Spiers v English* [1907] P 122, commenting on *Wilson v Bassil* [1903] P 239; *Levy v Leo* (1909) 25 TLR 717; *Oldcorn v Tenniswood* (1909) 25 TLR 825; *Re Cutcliffe's Estate, Le Duc v Veness* [1959] P 6, [1958] 3 All ER 642, CA.
9 *Re Cutcliffe's Estate, Le Duc v Veness* [1959] P 6 at 21, [1959] 3 All ER 642 at 648–649, CA, per Hodson LJ. See also, however, *Larke v Nugus* (1979) 123 Sol Jo 337, [2000] WTLR 1033, CA (allegations of undue influence and want of knowledge and approval withdrawn by the defendants; the trial judge took the view that the costs of the former should be paid out of the estate and of the latter by the defendants, but that the allegations were based on similar facts, and so made no order for costs). As to the factors relevant to alleging in a statement of case want of knowledge and approval alone or together with undue influence or fraud see PARA 875.

912. Default of defence: costs. The challenge raised by a defaulting defendant can in general necessitate a full trial despite the failure to acknowledge service or serve a defence[1], because the claimant may need to obtain declarations or other relief not obtainable under a default judgment[2]. In such cases it has been held that the claimant is entitled to his costs[3], and the same principle that he should obtain his costs against such a defendant would seem to apply where a claimant is driven to a probate trial by a defaulting defendant.

1 As to default of acknowledgment of service see PARA 869; and as to default of statements of case see PARA 876.
2 Ie under CPR Pt 12. However, a default judgment is not available in probate proceedings although the claimant may, in default of acknowledgment of service or defence, apply for trial on written evidence: see CPR 57.10 (1), (3)-(5); and PARAS 869, 876. As to the principles governing declarations by the court see *Wallersteiner v Moir* [1974] 3 All ER 217 at 251, [1974] 1 WLR 991 at 1028–1029, CA, per Buckley LJ.
3 *Grant v Knaresborough UDC* [1928] Ch 310. As to limitation of costs by notice to cross-examine only see PARA 874.

913. Costs allowable on assessment. It has been held that where an unsuccessful party has been ordered to pay costs, he must bear the additional costs[1] thrown on the estate by the appointment of an administrator pending determination of a probate claim, but it has also been held that this will not include the cost of the work done by the administrator which would have been necessary in any event, and that there must be an apportionment[2]. The allowance on detailed assessment of costs resulting from the retention of leading counsel is a matter for the court's discretion, but it has been held that where a compromise had been agreed through leading counsel on both sides it was inconsistent with the agreement to object to the allowance of such costs on assessment[3].

1 *Fisher v Fisher* (1878) 4 PD 231; see also that case as reported in 48 LJP 69.
2 *Re Howlett, Howlett v Howlett* [1950] P 177, [1950] 1 All ER 485. See also *Kostic v Chaplin* [2007] EWHC 2909 (Ch) at [43], [2008] 2 Costs LR 271 at [43], [2007] All ER (D) 119 (Dec) at [43]. As to administration pending determination of a probate claim see PARA 808 et seq. As to limitation of costs by notice to cross-examine only see PARA 874.
3 *Re Bond, Osborne v Cresswell* [1952] WN 534, CA.

914. Payment of costs out of certain portions of the estate. Where an order is made in a probate claim that costs are to be paid out of the estate, the judge making the order may direct out of what portion of the estate they are to be paid and in what proportions[1]. Where they are directed generally to be paid out of the estate they are payable out of the entirety of the estate in due order of administration[2]. Where the order in probate proceedings for payment of costs is not made until after an order has been made for the administration of the estate, the order in the probate proceedings can only operate upon what remains after payment of the costs of administration[3].

1 *Dean v Bulmer* [1905] P 1; *Harrington v Butt* [1905] P 3n; *Re Osment, Child and Jarvis v Osment* [1914] P 129 (see PARA 910 note 4). Such power is now derived from the general discretion conferred on the court by the Senior Courts Act 1981 s 51 (see PARA 908). As to the court's power to order a legal or other representative to pay wasted costs, see the Senior Courts Act 1981 s 51(6), (7), (7A), (12A), (13); CPR 44.11.
2 *Re Vickerstaff, Vickerstaff v Chadwick* [1906] 1 Ch 762; and see *Brisco v Baillie and Hamilton* [1902] P 234 at 238. The ground upon which *Re Shaw, Bridges v Shaw* [1894] 3 Ch 615 was based has disappeared.
3 *Re Mayhew, Rowles v Mayhew* (1877) 5 ChD 596, CA; *Major v Major* (1854) 2 Drew 281.

915. Security for costs. A defendant may apply for security for his costs of the proceedings from the claimant and the court may make an order[1] if satisfied, having regard to all the circumstances of the case, that it is just to make such an order and provided certain conditions are satisfied[2]. The defendant may also seek an order against someone other than the claimant, again, if certain conditions are satisfied[3]. A caveator is not held to have instituted the proceedings and cannot be ordered to give security[4]. The court may order security for costs of an appeal against an appellant, or a respondent who also appeals, on the same grounds as it may order security for costs against a claimant[5].

1 See CPR 25.12; and CIVIL PROCEDURE vol 12 (2015) PARA 617. As to a trustee or personal representative's entitlement to the costs of proceedings out of the relevant fund or estate see CPR 46.3; and PARA 909 note 2.

2 See CPR 25.13; and CIVIL PROCEDURE vol 12 (2015) PARA 618.

3 See CPR 25.14; and CIVIL PROCEDURE vol 12 (2015) PARA 619.

4 *Re Emery, Emery v Emery* [1923] P 184 (in which the only parties were the executor as plaintiff and the caveator as defendant); *Rose v Epstein* [1974] 2 All ER 1065, [1974] 1 WLR 1565 (affd [1974] 3 All ER 745, [1974] 1 WLR 1565 at 1572, CA). The substance of the matter has to be considered both as to the substantive proceedings and the role (offensive or defensive) of the parties in the proceedings in question. As to caveators see PARA 690 et seq.

5 See CPR 25.15; and CIVIL PROCEDURE vol 12 (2015) PARA 620.

11. DEVOLUTION ON THE REPRESENTATIVE

(1) PROPERTY WHICH DEVOLVES

916. Meaning of 'devolution'. 'Devolution' is the passing of property from a person dying to a person living[1], and in this title the word is confined to the passing of property from a deceased person to his personal representative[2].

1 *Parr v Parr* (1833) 1 My & K 647 at 648 per Leech MR; *Earl of Zetland v Lord Advocate* (1878) 3 App Cas 505 at 520, HL, per Lord Selborne.

2 As to the meaning of 'personal representative' see PARA 608.

917. Devolution of property on death. All property[1], whether personal or real[2], to which a deceased person was entitled for an interest not ceasing on his death[3] now devolves on his personal representative[4]. 'Real estate' is a term of art; a technical term well understood[5]. Except in so far as is expressly provided by statute, it does not include leasehold interests or other chattels real[6]. For the purpose, however, of the statutory provisions which relate to the devolution of real estate in the case of death occurring after 1925[7], 'real estate' includes chattels real as well as land in possession, remainder or reversion[8]. It comprises all interests in land[9], whether corporeal or incorporeal[10] and includes manors[11] and advowsons[12]. The devolution of real estate is considered in detail elsewhere in this title[13].

'Personal estate'[14] includes money, share of government and other funds, securities for money (not being real estate), debts[15], choses (or things) in action[16], rights[17], credits, goods[18] and all other property (not being real estate) which by law devolves on the executor or administrator, and any share or interest in such property[19].

Personal property which does not pass to the personal representative of a deceased person includes personal property passing by the exercise by the deceased's will of a general power of appointment[20], an interest in a joint tenancy where another joint tenant survives[21] and the interest of a corporator sole in corporation property[22].

1 As to the meaning of 'property' see PARAS 608 note 4, 943 note 1. Certain rights of the deceased are not regarded as property but as a dignity, eg a title or the right to bear arms: see *Manchester Corpn v Manchester Palace of Varieties Ltd* [1955] P 133, [1955] 1 All ER 387.

2 Real property in England and Wales devolves on a personal representative under the Administration of Estates Act 1925 ss 1–3: see PARA 945. Personal property vests in the personal representative at common law. Chattels real so vest at common law and are also included within the operation of ss 1–3: see PARAS 942, 945. Except as otherwise expressly provided, the Administration of Estates Act 1925 does not apply in any case where the death occurred before 1 January 1926: see s 54. As to the devolution of real estate before 1926 see PARA 945.

In general, the devolution of immovable property is governed by the law of the place where it is situated and succession to movable property is governed by the law of the deceased's domicile: see CONFLICT OF LAWS vol 19 (2011) PARA 676 et seq.

3 The interest of a deceased joint tenant if another joint tenant survives him and the interest of a corporation sole in the corporate property are interests which cease on death: see PARAS 943, 948.

4 As to vesting of an intestate's estate in the President of the Family Division until grant see PARA 644. As to the meaning of 'personal representative' see PARA 608.

5 *Butler v Butler* (1884) 28 ChD 66 at 71 per Chitty J. Hence the general principle, that a testator who uses a technical term is presumed to use the technical term in its technical sense, applies.

6 Leaseholds apart from statute are personal estate because it was formerly considered that a lease was merely a contract for the enjoyment of the land demised. If the tenant was wrongly dispossessed he had no right of action at law to recover the land itself, but could only bring an action against the lessor for damages for breach of the covenant for quiet enjoyment (3 Bl Com (14th Edn) 157–158): see PERSONAL PROPERTY vol 80 (2013) PARA 804; REAL PROPERTY AND REGISTRATION vol 87 (2012) PARAS 1–2.

7 Ie the Administration of Estates Act 1925 Pt I (ss 1–3).
8 See the Administration of Estates Act 1925 s 3(1)(i); and PARA 946. As to the meaning of 'real estate' for the purposes of the Administration of Estates Act 1925 generally see PARA 607 note 1.
9 As to the meaning of 'land' see PARA 946 note 1. See eg the Wills Act 1837 s 1 (which defines 'real estate' for the purposes of that Act (see PARA 282)); and cf the definition of 'land' in the Settled Land Act 1925 s 117(1)(ix) (see SETTLEMENTS vol 91 (2012) PARA 581). See also REAL PROPERTY AND REGISTRATION. The distinction between real estate and personalty has become immaterial in most cases for the purposes of the distribution of estates of intestates who die after 31 December 1925 since real and personal property are now constituted into one blended fund and distributed together: see PARA 1135.
10 As to the distinction between corporeal and incorporeal hereditaments see REAL PROPERTY AND REGISTRATION vol 87 (2012) PARA 8.
11 As to the nature of manors see CUSTOM AND USAGE vol 32 (2012) PARA 95 et seq.
12 As to advowsons see ECCLESIASTICAL LAW vol 34 (2011) PARA 550.
13 See PARA 945 et seq. As to partnership property see PARA 919. As to property the subject of a general power of appointment see PARAS 948, 954–955, 969. As to chattels real see PARAS 942, 945. As to trust and mortgage property see PARA 950 et seq. As to settled land see PARA 821 et seq.
14 As to the meaning of 'personal chattels' for the purposes of the Administration of Estates Act 1925 see PARA 488 note 4.
15 Ie including debts created by statute, as for instance the right to recover overpayment of rent under rent restrictions legislation: *Dean v Wiesengrund* [1955] 2 QB 120, [1955] 2 All ER 432, CA; *Rickless v United Artists Corpn* [1988] QB 40, [1987] 1 All ER 679, CA.
16 As to the devolution of choses (or things) in action see PARA 934 et seq.
17 Eg performer's rights: see *Rickless v United Artists Corpn* [1988] QB 40, [1987] 1 All ER 679, CA; *Experience Hendrix LLC v Purple Haze Records Ltd* [2007] EWCA Civ 501, [2007] FSR 769, [2007] All ER (D) 430 (May).
18 As to the devolution of chattels see PARA 928 et seq.
19 See eg the Wills Act 1837 s 1 (which defines 'personal estate' for the purposes of that Act: see PARA 284). See also PERSONAL PROPERTY vol 80 (2013) PARA 805. As to leasehold estates see note 6. In some cases objects of property may be either real or personal, according to the surrounding circumstances: see PARA 928.
20 *O'Grady v Wilmot* [1916] 2 AC 231, HL. The rule is different in the case of real estate (including chattels real): see PARA 954. Personal estate disposed of in pursuance of a general power of appointment is assets for the payment of debts and the personal representatives are the persons entitled to receive it: see PARAS 948, 954–955, 969.
21 See the Administration of Estates Act 1925 s 3(4), considered in relation to real estate in PARA 948. See also *Southcote v Hoare* (1810) 3 Taunt 87. As to the right of survivorship in the case of a joint tenancy of personalty see PERSONAL PROPERTY vol 80 (2013) PARA 829. An apparent beneficial joint owner may in fact be entitled to the whole fund enabling his personal representatives to claim it as belonging to the estate: *Sillett v Meek* [2007] EWHC 1169 (Ch), 10 ITELR 617, [2007] All ER (D) 248 (May). As to partnership property see PARA 919.
22 See the Administration of Estates Act 1925 s 3(5), considered in relation to real estate in PARA 948.

918. Constructive conversion. Except in the case of a trust created by the will of a testator dying before 1 January 1997, where land is held by trustees subject to a trust for sale, land is no longer regarded as personal property[1]. In the case of wills of testators dying before 1 January 1997 the equitable doctrine of conversion continues to apply under which real estate may be treated as converted into personalty, or personalty into real estate, and may devolve beneficially as so converted[2]. Real estate may continue to be treated as converted[3] where at the deceased's death there existed a contract for the sale of the real estate[4], where the court has ordered a sale[5], or where there is a contract giving an option of purchase and the option is not exercised until after the death of the person granting the option[6].

1 See the Trusts of Land and Appointment of Trustees Act 1996 s 3; and REAL PROPERTY AND REGISTRATION vol 87 (2012) PARA 7. The doctrine of conversion was abolished with effect from 1 January 1997: see s 3; and REAL PROPERTY AND REGISTRATION vol 87 (2012) PARA 7.
2 As to the equitable doctrine of conversion see EQUITABLE JURISDICTION vol 47 (2014) PARA 138 et seq. As to its effect on the devolution of the beneficial interest under a will or on an intestacy see EQUITABLE JURISDICTION vol 47 (2014) PARAS 143, 149. As to the ademption of

a demise by the notional conversion of the subject matter see EQUITABLE JURISDICTION vol 47 (2014) PARA 143. As to notional reconversion on the failure of the purpose of conversion see EQUITABLE JURISDICTION vol 47 (2014) PARA 147.

3 See Pettit 'Demise of Trusts for Sale and the Doctrine of Conversion?' [1997] 113 LQR 207–211.

4 See EQUITABLE JURISDICTION vol 47 (2014) PARA 150.

5 See EQUITABLE JURISDICTION vol 47 (2014) PARA 152. See also *Steed v Preece* (1874) LR 18 Eq 192.

6 See EQUITABLE JURISDICTION vol 47 (2014) PARA 151.

919. Partnership property. Subject to the terms of the partnership agreement, the personal representatives of a partner who has died are entitled in equity[1] to the deceased's interest in the partnership property[2]. This interest devolves as personalty[3]. Subject to any agreement between the partners, a partnership is dissolved as regards all the partners by the death of any partner[4]. Mutual covenants by partners that they and their respective executors and administrators are to continue as partners cannot be specifically enforced against the representatives of a deceased partner, and if they refuse to continue the partnership it will be dissolved as from the death of their testator, but his estate may be liable for damages in respect of the breach of contract[5].

In the absence of any agreement between the partners, the personal representatives of a deceased partner are entitled to have the partnership business wound up and disposed of, and may apply to the court to enforce this right[6].

1 The legal estate in land passes by survivorship at law (see the Law of Property Act 1925 ss 34, 36, 39(4), Sch 1 Pt IV; and PARA 948) to the surviving partners who hold it on trust for the benefit of the persons entitled in equity (see *Green v Whitehead* [1930] 1 Ch 38, CA; *Re Fuller's Contract* [1933] Ch 652; Partnership Act 1890 s 20(2)). See PARTNERSHIP vol 79 (2014) PARA 118. As to the meaning of 'personal representative' see PARA 608.

2 See the Partnership Act 1890 s 20(1); and PARTNERSHIP vol 79 (2014) PARA 118. The rule that a partner has no right to take the interest of a deceased partner by survivorship is of long standing: see Co Litt 182a; *Jeffereys v Small* (1683) 1 Vern 217. Formerly the right of survivorship was excluded both at law and in equity (*R v Collector of Customs, Liverpool* (1813) 2 M & S 223), but as to the passing of the legal estate in land by survivorship since 1926 see note 1.

3 *Re Bourne, Bourne v Bourne* [1906] 2 Ch 427 at 432, CA, per Romer LJ. Land held subject to a trust for sale is not to be regarded as personal property (see the Trusts of Land and Appointment of Trustees Act 1996 s 3; and REAL PROPERTY AND REGISTRATION vol 87 (2012) PARA 7); but there is for this purpose no distinction at common law and in equity between real and personal estate of the partnership: *Waterer v Waterer* (1873) LR 15 Eq 402; Pettit 'Demise of Trusts for Sale and the Doctrine of Conversion?' [1997] 113 LQR 207–211; cf *A-G v Hubbuck* (1884) 13 QBD 275, CA. See PARTNERSHIP vol 79 (2014) PARAS 115–116. As to the liability of the estate of a deceased partner for partnership debts see PARA 1232.

4 See the Partnership Act 1890 s 33(1); and PARTNERSHIP vol 79 (2014) PARA 175. The estate of the deceased partner is not liable for debts contracted after the date of death: see s 36(3). Death of a limited partner does not operate as a dissolution of a limited partnership: see the Limited Partnerships Act 1907 s 6(2); and PARTNERSHIP vol 79 (2014) PARA 226. As to the death of a member of a limited liability partnership incorporated under the Limited Liability Partnership Act 2000 see PARTNERSHIP vol 79 (2014) PARA 238.

5 *Downs v Collins* (1848) 6 Hare 418.

6 See the Partnership Act 1890 s 39; and PARTNERSHIP vol 79 (2014) PARA 205. As to the rights of the representative where the partnership business is carried on without settling accounts, and the accountability of partners for private profits see PARA 1035; and PARTNERSHIP vol 79 (2014) PARAS 205–208. As to the representative's rights following the death of a member of a limited liability partnership see the Limited Liability Partnerships Act 2000 s 7(1)(a), (2), (3); and PARTNERSHIP vol 79 (2014) PARA 238.

920. Personal representatives' lien on surplus partnership assets. Unless there is something in the partnership articles to the contrary, the surviving partner has not only the right but also the duty to realise the partnership property, and for the purposes of that realisation to carry on the business if it is necessary to do so[1]. The representatives of a deceased partner have a general lien on the surplus assets of the partnership in respect of their deceased partner's interest in the partnership, but they have no lien on any specific asset, whether personalty or realty, such as would fetter its realisation or conversion into money by the surviving partner[2].

Subject to any agreement between the partners, the amount due from the surviving partners to the representatives of a deceased partner in respect of the deceased partner's share is a debt accruing at the date of death[3].

1 *Re Bourne, Bourne v Bourne* [1906] 2 Ch 427, CA.

2 *Re Bourne, Bourne v Bourne* [1906] 2 Ch 427 at 432, CA, per Romer LJ, and at 434 per Fletcher Moulton LJ. See also *Re Langmead's Trusts* (1855) 20 Beav 20 (affd on appeal 7 De GM & G 353); *Payne v Hornby* (1858) 25 Beav 280; and PARTNERSHIP vol 79 (2014) PARAS 141–142. As to the devolution of goodwill see PARTNERSHIP vol 79 (2014) PARAS 212–216. As to lien generally see LIEN.

3 See the Partnership Act 1890 s 43; and PARTNERSHIP vol 79 (2014) PARA 211. Rules which, subject to any agreement, are to be observed in settling accounts between partners after a dissolution are contained in s 44: see PARTNERSHIP vol 79 (2014) PARA 211. As to proof in the bankruptcy of surviving partners see BANKRUPTCY AND INDIVIDUAL INSOLVENCY.

921. Gifts mortis causa. A donatio mortis causa is a gift inter vivos by which the donee is to have the absolute title to the subject of the gift, not at once, but if the donor dies[1]. The donee's title becomes absolute at the moment of the donor's death so that the property given never vests in the donor's personal representative[2], who is obliged if necessary to lend his name or give his indorsement to assist the donee in completing his title[3].

1 *Re Beaumont, Beaumont v Ewbank* [1902] 1 Ch 889 at 892 per Buckley J. If the donor recovers, the donee is a trustee for him: *Staniland v Willott* (1852) 3 Mac & G 664. As to donationes mortis causa see generally GIFTS vol 52 (2014) PARA 271 et seq. As to establishing a donation mortis causa (and per curiam: considerable caution is required and the courts should not permit any further expansion of the doctrine) see *King v Dubrey* [2015] EWCA Civ 581, [2016] Ch 221, [2016] 2 WLR 1. Donationes mortis causa are treated as part of the deceased's estate for the purposes of liability to inheritance tax (see the Inheritance Tax Act 1984 ss 4(1), 5(1)) and may be subject to claims under the Inheritance (Provision for Family and Dependants) Act 1975 (see PARA 584).

2 *Tate v Hilbert* (1793) 2 Ves 111. As to the meaning of 'personal representative' see PARA 608.

3 *Re Beaumont, Beaumont v Ewbank* [1902] 1 Ch 889 at 894 per Buckley J. See also *Duffield v Elwes* (1827) 1 Bli NS 497, HL; *Re Dillon, Duffin v Duffin* (1890) 44 ChD 76 at 83, CA, per Cotton LJ; *Re Richards, Jones v Rebbeck* [1921] 1 Ch 513; and GIFTS vol 52 (2014) PARA 271. As to the liability of the donee of a donatio mortis causa for the donor's debts see *Tate v Leithead* (1854) Kay 658. As to the payment of inheritance tax see the Inheritance Tax Act 1984 s 211(3); and *Re Hudson, Spencer v Turner* [1911] 1 Ch 206. See also GIFTS vol 52 (2014) PARA 278.

(2) PERSONAL REPRESENTATIVES' INTEREST IN DEVOLVED PROPERTY

922. Nature of the personal representatives' and the beneficiaries' interests. The property which devolves on the personal representative is held by him in right of the deceased and not in his own right[1]. The entire ownership of the property comprised in the estate of a deceased person, both legal and equitable, which remains unadministered is in the deceased's legal personal representative for the purposes of administration[2]. He has full control of all the items making up the estate and can give a good title to them[3]. The beneficiaries have no specific interest in any of the property comprising the residue until the residue has been ascertained in due course of administration[4], but they do have a general title to residue, and this general title constitutes a transmissible interest[5] which is not affected by the completion of the administration, so that their interests remain the same before and after the administration is complete[6]. A beneficiary in possession is not a trespasser, but has no answer to the personal representative's claim for possession for the purposes of the administration; he must give possession on receipt of a notice to quit, but is not liable for mesne profits until after the notice has expired[7].

1 *Re Davis, Re Davis, Evans v Moore* [1891] 3 Ch 119 at 124, CA. As to the meaning of 'personal representative' see PARA 608.
2 *Stamp Duties Comr (Queensland) v Livingston* [1965] AC 694, [1964] 3 All ER 692, PC; *Re Leigh's Will Trusts, Handyside v Durbridge* [1970] Ch 277 at 281, [1969] 3 All ER 432 at 434; *Marshall (Inspector of Taxes) v Kerr* [1995] 1 AC 148 at 157, [1994] 3 All ER 106 at 112, HL, per Lord Templeman. See also *Bernstein v Jacobson* [2008] EWHC 3454 (Ch).
3 *Attenborough v Solomon* [1913] AC 76, HL. As to the rights, duties and liabilities of personal representatives in due course of administration see PARAS 956 et seq, 1212 et seq.
4 *Stamp Duties Comr (Queensland) v Livingston* [1965] AC 694, [1964] 3 All ER 692, PC (criticising dicta of Lord Cairns LC in *Cooper v Cooper* (1874) as reported in LR 7 HL 53 at 65–66); *Re Leigh's Will Trusts, Handyside v Durbridge* [1970] Ch 277 at 281, [1969] 3 All ER 432 at 434 per Buckley J; *Marshall (Inspector of Taxes) v Kerr* [1995] 1 AC 148, [1994] 3 All ER 106, HL. See also *Lord Sudeley v A-G* [1897] AC 11, HL; *Vanneck v Benham* [1917] 1 Ch 60; *Barnardo's Homes v Income Tax Special Comrs* [1921] 2 AC 1, HL; *IRC v Smith* [1930] 1 KB 713, CA; *Corbett v IRC* [1938] 1 KB 567, [1937] 4 All ER 700, CA; *Re Cunliffe-Owen, Mountain v IRC* [1953] Ch 545 at 553–555, [1953] 2 All ER 196 at 200–201, CA, per Evershed MR. See further *Re Holmes, Villiers v Holmes* [1917] 1 IR 165. As to the special legislation governing liability to income tax during the administration of an estate see INCOME TAXATION vol 59 (2014) PARA 2075 et seq. As to the rights of a trustee in bankruptcy of a residuary beneficiary see *Re Hemming, Raymond Saul & Co (a firm) v Holden* [2008] EWHC 2731 (Ch), [2009] Ch 313, [2009] 2 WLR 1257; and PARA 1219.
5 *Re Leigh's Will Trusts, Handyside v Durbridge* [1970] Ch 277, [1969] 3 All ER 432. Beneficiaries also have interests which are held 'on trusts' by the personal representatives for the purpose of the Variation of Trusts Act 1958 s 1(1): see *Bernstein v Jacobson* [2008] EWHC 3454 (Ch); and TRUSTS AND POWERS vol 98 (2013) PARA 1 et seq.
6 *Re Gibbs, Midland Bank Executor and Trustee Co Ltd v IRC* [1951] Ch 933 at 940, [1951] 2 All ER 63 at 68; *Re Cunliffe-Owen, Mountain v IRC* [1953] Ch 545 at 555, 560–561, [1953] 2 All ER 196 at 201, 204, CA, per Evershed MR, and at 565 and 207 per Romer LJ. See also *Re Hemming, Raymond Saul & Co (a firm) v Holden* [2008] EWHC 2731 (Ch), [2009] Ch 313, [2009] 2 WLR 1257.
7 *Williams v Holland* [1965] 2 All ER 157, [1965] 1 WLR 739, CA. As to the power to assent subject to a mortgage see PARA 1145.

923. Effect of personal representative's bankruptcy. On the bankruptcy of the personal representative[1], the deceased's property does not pass to the trustee in bankruptcy[2], but the creditors of the testator or intestate, by their conduct in permitting the representative to employ the assets in his business, may preclude themselves from claiming them as against the representative's creditors[3]. Where the representative is also residuary legatee, the court will assist his trustee in bankruptcy to get in the deceased's assets[4].

A lease which contains a provision for forfeiture upon the bankruptcy of the lessee, his executors, administrators or assigns is liable to forfeiture upon the bankruptcy of the lessee's representative[5].

1 As to the meaning of 'personal representative' see PARA 608.
2 See the Insolvency Act 1986 s 283(3)(a); and BANKRUPTCY AND INDIVIDUAL INSOLVENCY vol 5 (2013) PARA 441. See also *Kitchen v Ibbetson* (1873) LR 17 Eq 46.
3 *Fox v Fisher* (1819) 3 B & Ald 135; *Kitchen v Ibbetson* (1873) LR 17 Eq 46. See also *Re Thomas* (1842) 1 Ph 159; and BANKRUPTCY AND INDIVIDUAL INSOLVENCY vol 5 (2013) PARA 397.
4 *Ex p Butler* (1749) 1 Atk 210 at 213.
5 *Doe d Bridgman v David* (1834) 1 Cr M & R 405. See generally BANKRUPTCY AND INDIVIDUAL INSOLVENCY vol 5 (2013) PARAS 425–427; LANDLORD AND TENANT vol 63 (2012) PARA 751.

924. Right of personal representative's judgment creditor. The property of a testator or intestate is not liable to be taken in execution under a judgment against his representative personally[1] unless the representative has converted the assets to his own use[2] or unless, from lapse of time and an enjoyment of the assets inconsistent with the trusts of the will, an inference may be raised of a gift of the property by the deceased's creditors or beneficiaries to the representative[3].

1 *Farr v Newman* (1792) 4 Term Rep 621; *M'Leod v Drummond* (1810) 17 Ves 152 at 168 per Lord Eldon LC; *Gaskell v Marshall* (1831) 1 Mood & R 132; *Kinderley v Jervis* (1856) 22 Beav 1 at 23 per Romilly MR.

2 *Quick v Staines* (1798) 1 Bos & P 293, distinguished in *Gaskell v Marshall* (1831) 1 Mood & R 132.

3 *Ray v Ray* (1851) Coop G 264, distinguished in *Re Morgan, Pillgrem v Pillgrem* (1881) 18 ChD 93, CA. As to the meaning of 'personal representative' see PARA 608.

925. Merger of estates. Inasmuch as the personal representative holds the assets not in his own right but in a fiduciary capacity, there is no merger of an estate held by the representative as such in an estate which he holds in his own right[1].

1 2 Bl Com (14th Edn) 177; *Re Radcliffe, Radcliffe v Bewes* [1892] 1 Ch 227, CA. See EQUITABLE JURISDICTION vol 47 (2014) PARA 202. As to the meaning of 'personal representative' see PARA 608.

926. Joint representation. A joint representative is regarded as a single person[1]. Accordingly, one of several executors may give a good discharge for a debt due to the estate[2], and settle an account with a person accountable to the estate, even, it would appear, against the dissent of his co-executor[3]; and it seems that the same principle applies to joint administrators[4]. A conveyance of real estate requires the concurrence of all proving executors or all administrators or an order of the court[5]. If one of two personal representatives contracts to sell real estate expressly on behalf of both, he seems to have authority to bind the other personal representative, but if in fact that express authority is lacking he will not obtain specific performance of the contract because a contract purporting to be made by two executors jointly cannot be enforced as if it were a contract by one executor severally; conversely, however, a contract may be specifically enforced if one of two executors contracts alone without expressly purporting to bind the other[6].

Where several executors have been registered as the holders of stock or shares in a company incorporated under the Companies Clauses Acts, a transfer by some or one only is invalid[7]; and in the case of stock registered at the Bank of England the bank may decline to give effect to a transfer unless the instrument of transfer is executed by all the representatives[8]. The share or interest of a member in a company regulated by the Companies Act 2006 is transferable in the manner provided by the articles of the company[9]. As between themselves and the company, executors registered as the holders of shares are joint holders in their individual capacity, and any transfer of those shares must be executed by all of them[10].

1 Bac Abr, Executors and Administrators (D) 1.

2 *Charlton v Earl of Durham* (1869) 4 Ch App 433.

3 *Smith v Everett* (1859) 27 Beav 446, considered in *Fountain Forestry Ltd v Edwards* [1975] Ch 1 at 13–14, [1974] 2 All ER 280 at 285 per Brightman J. In *Lepard v Vernon* (1813) 2 Ves & B 51 it was held that a court of equity would not assist such a settlement. As to one executor bringing foreclosure proceedings, the other having absconded see *Drage v Hartopp* (1885) 28 ChD 414.

4 See *Jacomb v Harwood* (1751) 2 Ves Sen 265; *Smith v Everett* (1859) as reported in 29 LJ Ch 236 at 239–240 per Romilly MR; *Fountain Forestry Ltd v Edwards* [1975] Ch 1 at 14, [1974] 2 All ER 280 at 285 per Brightman J. Cf *Hudson v Hudson* (1737) 1 Atk 460; *Warwick v Greville* (1809) 1 Phillim 123 at 126; *Stanley v Bernes* (1828) 1 Hag Ecc 221 at 221–222.

In so far as the principle still exists that denial by a lessee of his landlord's title will give rise to a forfeiture, it seems that a denial by one of several representatives may give rise to a forfeiture: see *Warner v Sampson* [1958] 1 QB 404, [1958] 1 All ER 44 (revsd on other grounds [1959] 1 QB 297, [1959] 1 All ER 120, CA); *WG Clark (Properties) Ltd v Dupre Properties Ltd* [1992] Ch 297, [1992] 1 All ER 596. See further LANDLORD AND TENANT vol 63 (2012) PARAS 753, 774.

As to payment of a statute-barred debt by one of several personal representatives see PARA 974. As to an acknowledgement by one of several personal representatives see PARA 976.

5 See PARA 1024.

6 *Sneesby v Thorne* (1855) 7 De GM & G 399; *Fountain Forestry Ltd v Edwards* [1975] Ch 1, [1974] 2 All ER 280. As to the liability of a joint contractor's personal representatives see PARA 1023. See also 124 NLJ 749 (8 August 1974).

7 *Barton v North Staffordshire Rly Co* (1888) 38 ChD 458; *Barton v London and North Western Rly Co* (1889) 24 QBD 77, CA. See COMPANIES vol 15A (2016) PARAS 1858–1890.

8 See the Government Stock Regulations 2004, SI 2004/1611, reg 17(2); and FINANCIAL INSTRUMENTS AND TRANSACTIONS vol 49 (2015) PARA 126.

9 See the Companies Act 2006 ss 541, 544(1), (2); and PARA 929. In the case of the death of a member, the survivor or survivors where the deceased was a joint holder, and the legal personal representatives of the deceased where he was a sole holder, are the only persons recognised by the company as having any title to his interest in the shares; but nothing in this provision releases the estate of a deceased joint holder from any liability in respect of any share which had been jointly held by him with other persons: see the Companies (Tables A to F) Regulations 1985, SI 1985/805, Schedule Table A, art 29; and COMPANIES vol 14 (2016) PARAS 277, 344; COMPANIES vol 15A (2016) PARA 1332.

10 See COMPANIES vol 15A (2016) PARA 1890.

927. Apportionment of income. All rents[1], annuities[2], dividends[3] and other periodical payments[4] in the nature of income are considered as accruing from day to day[5]. Accordingly, unless the instrument in question provides to the contrary[6], the personal representative of a person entitled to a life interest is entitled to the apportioned part of all such payments made after the death[7] of the deceased in so far as they relate to any period before the death[8]. Where the investments or other property yielding the income so apportionable have been appropriated or transferred to other persons absolutely entitled before the payment has been made, the personal representative is entitled to recover the apportioned part from the trustees or from the persons to whom they have been transferred, as the case may be[9]. Where, however, such investments have been sold cum dividend, the personal representative has no right, except in special circumstances, to any apportioned part of the proceeds of sale[10], for it is not practicable to calculate such an apportionment[11].

1 'Rents' includes rent service, rentcharge and rent seck and also tithes and all periodical payments or renderings in lieu of or in the nature of rent or tithes: Apportionment Act 1870 s 5. Cf the Administration of Estates Act 1925, for the purposes of which 'rent' includes a rent service or a rentcharge or other rent, toll, duty or annual or periodical payment in money or money's worth issuing out of or charged upon land, but does not include mortgage interest; and 'rentcharge' includes a fee farm rent: s 55(1)(xxi).

2 'Annuities' includes salaries and pensions: Apportionment Act 1870 s 5.

3 'Dividends' includes (besides dividends strictly so called) all payments made by the name of dividend, bonus or otherwise out of the revenue of trading or other public companies, divisible between all or any of the members of such companies, whether such payments are usually made or declared at any fixed times or otherwise; and all such divisible revenue is, for the purposes of the Apportionment Act 1870, deemed to have accrued by equal daily increment during and within the period for or in respect of which the payment of the revenue is declared or expressed to be made, but 'dividend' does not include payments in the nature of a return or reimbursement of capital: s 5.

4 Annual sums payable under insurance policies are not apportionable: Apportionment Act 1870 s 6.

5 Apportionment Act 1870 s 2 (amended by the Statute Law Revision (No 2) Act 1983). Any entitlement to income under a new trust (see TRUSTS AND POWERS vol 98 (2013) PARA 172) is to income as it arises, and accordingly the Apportionment Act 1870 s 2 does not apply in relation to the trust, subject to any contrary intention that appears in any trust instrument of the trust and in any power under which the trust is created or arises: see the Trusts (Capital and Income) Act 2013 s 1(1), (4).

6 The effect of the Apportionment Act 1870 can be excluded by express stipulation: s 7.

7 If a landlord dies on the day when payment is due, the rents when received are income of the estate since the rent is not due until the end of that day: *Re Aspinall, Aspinall v Aspinall* [1961] Ch 526, [1961] 2 All ER 751. See also LANDLORD AND TENANT vol 62 (2012) PARA 259.

8 See the Apportionment Act 1870 s 4. See also *Re Muirhead, Muirhead v Hill* [1916] 2 Ch 181; *Re Henderson, Public Trustee v Reddie* [1940] Ch 368, [1940] 1 All ER 623. Payments made or accrued due before death are treated as capital and are not apportionable: *Re Aspinall, Aspinall v Aspinall* [1961] Ch 526, [1961] 2 All ER 751.
9 *Re Henderson, Public Trustee v Reddie* [1940] Ch 368, [1940] 1 All ER 623.
10 *Bulkeley v Stephens* [1896] 2 Ch 241; *Re Walker, Walker v Patterson* [1934] WN 104; *Re Firth, Sykes v Hall* [1938] Ch 517, [1938] 2 All ER 217; *Re Winterstoke's Will Trust, Gunn v Richardson* [1938] Ch 158, [1937] 4 All ER 63; *Re Henderson, Public Trustee v Reddie* [1940] Ch 368, [1940] 1 All ER 623.
11 *Re Henderson, Public Trustee v Reddie* [1940] Ch 368, [1940] 1 All ER 623.

(3) DEVOLUTION OF CHATTELS

928. Devolution of chattels generally. All movable chattels have always devolved as personal property[1]; but certain chattels are so closely annexed to the inheritance that they accompany the land as realty, and accordingly at the time when land did not vest in the personal representative[2] they passed direct to the heir or devisee. Deer in a park, unless reclaimed and confined[3], or fish in a pond are chattels of such a nature[4].

The same applies to heirlooms which accompany the inheritance, whether they pass by special custom, such as the best bed or the like, or whether they savour of the inheritance. In the latter class are included title deeds and the chest or box in which they are usually kept, the patent creating a dignity[5], the garter and collar of a knight[6], an ancient horn where the tenure is by cornage[7], and the ancient jewels of the Crown[8].

The right of an undischarged bankrupt to hold goods acquired after bankruptcy until the intervention of the trustee in bankruptcy is a right which is transmissible to his personal representative[9].

1 Godolphin's Orphan's Legacy, Pt I c 13.
2 As to the devolution of real estate see PARA 944. As to the meaning of 'personal representative' see PARA 608.
3 *Morgan v Earl of Abergavenny* (1849) 8 CB 768; *Ford v Tynte* (1861) 2 John & H 150; *Inglewood Investment Co Ltd v Forestry Commission* [1988] 1 All ER 783, [1988] 1 WLR 1278. See also ANIMALS vol 2 (2008) PARAS 712, 974.
4 2 Bl Com (14th Edn) 427–428.
5 The provisions of the Law of Property Act 1925 do not affect the limitation of, or authorise any disposition to be made of, any title or dignity of honour which in its nature is inalienable: s 201(2). See also PARA 917.
6 *Earl of Northumberland's Case* (1584) Owen 124.
7 *Pusey v Pusey* (1684) 1 Vern 273.
8 *Viscount Hill v Dowager Viscountess Hill* [1897] 1 QB 483 at 494, CA, per Chitty LJ; Co Litt 18b. See also REAL PROPERTY AND REGISTRATION vol 87 (2012) PARA 17.
9 *Fyson v Chambers* (1842) 9 M & W 460. As to after acquired property see BANKRUPTCY AND INDIVIDUAL INSOLVENCY vol 5 (2013) PARAS 458–461, 489.

929. Devolution of shares in a company. Whatever the nature of a company's assets[1], the shares or other interest of any member are personal estate, transferable[2] in the manner provided by the articles of the company (or by a stock transfer) and not of the nature of real estate[3]. On the death of a sole[4] holder of shares the title to his shares devolves on his personal representatives[5].

1 As to the power to hold land see COMPANIES vol 14 (2016) PARA 319.
2 As to methods of transfer see COMPANIES vol 14 (2016) PARA 400 et seq. As to the rights of a survivor under a joint holding of shares see PARA 926.
3 See the Companies Act 2006 s 773; and COMPANIES vol 14 (2016) PARA 409.
4 As to the position on the death of a joint holder see PARA 926.

5 See COMPANIES vol 15A (2016) PARA 1334. As to the meaning of 'personal representative' see PARA 608.

930. Devolution of crops and emblements. Certain produce of the soil passes as personal estate. Where the occupier of land, who has an estate determining with his own life, has sown or planted the soil with a view to raising a crop, and dies before harvest time, his personal representatives as against the remainderman are entitled to the profits of the crop as compensation for the labour and expense of tilling, manuring and sowing the land[1]. Such profits are called emblements[2].

The estate of a life tenant is not entitled against a remainderman or a subsequent tenant for life if the crop was sown not by the deceased life tenant but by the settlor[3].

If an owner of an estate of inheritance in the land sowed a crop and then died before harvest time, then under the former law[4] the crop devolved as personal estate upon his personal representatives as against his heir[5], but did not so devolve as against a devisee of the land under his will[6] unless the will showed an intention that the crops should be excepted out of the devise[7]. Under the present law the crops will in any case vest in the owner's personal representatives on his death, but it seems that the authorities under the former law as to the effect of a devise and of exception out of the devise will still apply in relation to the equitable interest in growing crops[8].

1 2 Bl Com (14th Edn) 122; *Lawton v Lawton* (1743) 3 Atk 13 at 16; *Re De Falbe, Ward v Taylor* [1901] 1 Ch 523, CA. As to the meaning of 'personal representative' see PARA 608.
2 As to emblements see generally AGRICULTURAL LAND vol 1 (2008) PARA 369.
3 *Anon* (1608) Godb 159; *Grantham v Hawley* (1615) Hob 132.
4 As to the difference which formerly existed between the devolution of personal property and real property see PARA 917.
5 2 Bl Com (14th Edn) 403–404; *Lawton v Lawton* (1743) 3 Atk 13 at 16.
6 *Cooper v Woolfitt* (1857) 2 H & N 122.
7 *West v Moore* (1807) 8 East 339; *Cox v Godsalve* (1699) 6 East 604n. A gift of stock upon a farm is sufficient to pass crops as emblements: see *Re Roose, Evans v Williamson* (1880) 17 ChD 696, following *West v Moore*, and *Cox v Godsalve*, and disapproving *Vaisey v Reynolds* (1828) 5 Russ 12.
8 See PARA 291.

931. Devolution of natural products of the soil. The natural products of the soil devolve with the land unless they have been actually severed in the lifetime of the deceased owner, or have been granted to him separately from the land[1]. To cut down ornamental trees or timber, except in the case of estates which are cultivated merely for the produce of saleable timber and where the timber is cut periodically[2], or except in accordance with a prevailing local usage[3], is an act of waste on the part of a limited owner, such as a tenant for life. Accordingly, on the death of the owner the beneficial interest in the trees or timber, whether cut down or blown down in his lifetime[4], or the proceeds of their sale, devolved upon the owner of the first estate of inheritance, or passed upon the trusts of the settlement[5]. Where the limited owner dies after 1925 the legal title to it appears to vest in his special personal representatives (if any)[6].

1 Went Off Ex (14th Edn) 147; *Re Ainslie, Swinburn v Ainslie* (1885) 30 ChD 485, CA.
2 *Honywood v Honywood* (1874) LR 18 Eq 306 at 309.
3 *Dashwood v Magniac* [1891] 3 Ch 306 at 357, CA.
4 *Herlakenden's Case* (1589) 4 Co Rep 62a at 63b.
5 *Bewick v Whitfield* (1734) 3 P Wms 267; *Marquis of Ormond v Kynnersley* (1830) cited in 15 Beav 10; *Lushington v Boldero* (1851) 15 Beav 1.
6 As to the devolution of settled land see PARA 949.

932. Devolution of ornamental and trade fixtures. The general maxim of the law is that whatever is annexed to land becomes part of the land[1], but upon this maxim certain exceptions have been engrafted in respect of both ornamental and trade fixtures[2]. These exceptions become of importance in cases where the person who has annexed the chattel had only a life interest in the property to which the chattel has been annexed.

The personal representative[3] of a tenant for life who has affixed a chattel to the freehold is entitled to remove it[4] where, from the nature of the chattel, it is evident that it has been attached to the freehold for the purpose of ornamentation and for its better enjoyment as a chattel[5], or has been affixed as machinery[6] to the freehold for the purpose of trade. The degree and object of attachment must be considered for this purpose. There need not be an inquiry into the motive of the person who affixed the chattel but the object and purpose are to be inferred from the circumstances of the case[7]. On the death of an owner in fee simple or of a term of years[8], however, chattels, whether fixed for trade purposes[9] or for the purpose of ornamentation[10], pass with the land to which they are fixed[11].

1 *Holland v Hodgson* (1872) LR 7 CP 328 at 334, Ex Ch, per Blackburn J. The question whether or not a chattel has been annexed depends partly on the degree of physical fixation and partly on the intent to be inferred from the circumstances. Absence of fixation does not prevent a chattel from being annexed, nor does physical fixation prevent it from remaining a chattel if the intent as derived from the circumstances so decrees. Framed paintings, however affixed, remain chattels: see *Berkley v Poulett* [1977] 1 EGLR 86 at 95 per Stamp LJ followed in *Brudenell-Bruce, Earl of Cardigan v Moore* [2012] EWHC 1024 (Ch), [2012] All ER (D) 108 (Apr). See also *Elitestone Ltd v Morris* [1997] 2 All ER 513, [1997] 1 WLR 687, HL; *Chelsea Yacht and Boat Club Ltd v Pope* [2001] 2 All ER 409, [2000] 1 WLR 1941, CA; and the cases cited in note 7.

2 *Elliott v Bishop* (1854) 10 Exch 496 at 507–508 per Martin B; *Lord Dudley v Lord Warde* (1751) Amb 113; *Lawton v Lawton* (1743) 3 Atk 13. See also LANDLORD AND TENANT vol 62 (2012) PARAS 179–180.

3 As to the meaning of 'personal representative' see PARA 608.

4 *Re Hulse, Beattie v Hulse* [1905] 1 Ch 406.

5 *Re De Falbe, Ward v Taylor* [1901] 1 Ch 523, CA (disapproving *D'Eyncourt v Gregory* (1866) LR 3 Eq 382, and explaining *Norton v Dashwood* [1896] 2 Ch 497); affd sub nom *Leigh v Taylor* [1902] AC 157, HL. See also *Viscount Hill v Bullock* [1897] 2 Ch 482, CA; and cf *Bulkeley v Lyne Stephens, Re Lyne Stephens, Lyne Stephens v Lubbock* (1895) 11 TLR 564.

6 *Lawton v Lawton* (1743) 3 Atk 13; *Lord Dudley v Lord Warde* (1751) Amb 113; *Lawton v Salmon* (1782) 1 Hy Bl 260n; *Re Hulse, Beattie v Hulse* [1905] 1 Ch 406.

7 *Re De Falbe, Ward v Taylor* [1901] 1 Ch 523 at 535, CA, per Vaughan Williams LJ; affd sub nom *Leigh v Taylor* [1902] AC 157, HL.

8 *Finney v Grice* (1878) 10 ChD 13; but cf *Re Seton-Smith, Burnand v Waite* [1902] 1 Ch 717.

9 *Bain v Brand* (1876) 1 App Cas 762, HL.

10 *Re Whaley, Whaley v Roehrich* [1908] 1 Ch 615; *Re Scott, Scott v Scott* [1914] 1 Ch 847.

11 *Re Lord Chesterfield's Settled Estates* [1911] 1 Ch 237; *Norton v Dashwood* [1896] 2 Ch 497; *Lawton v Salmon* (1782) 1 Hy Bl 260n; *Fisher v Dixon* (1845) 12 Cl & Fin 312, HL.

933. Exercise of deceased's power of election. Where a person at his death was entitled out of several chattels to take his choice of one or more for his own use under a grant which conferred an immediate interest, and did not do so, his personal representative[1] might claim by election[2], but if no interest passed to the deceased person in his lifetime, his representative could not claim to elect[3]. Similarly, where there was a lease to a person of several acres, out of a parcel of a large number of acres, and the lessee died before making an election, his representative might make it[4].

1 As to the meaning of 'personal representative' see PARA 608.

2 Toller's Law of Executors (7th Edn) 173. Where a condition not personal to the legatee gives an option to the legatee to perform one of two or more things within a particular period previously to the vesting of the bequest, the right of election may be exercised by his representatives: see Roper's Legacies (4th Edn) 777; *Re Goodwin, Ainslie v Goodwin* [1924] 2 Ch 26.

3 Toller's Law of Executors (7th Edn) 173; Co Litt 145a; Com Dig, Election (B).

4 *Jones v Cherney* (1680) Freem KB 530.

(4) DEVOLUTION OF CHOSES IN ACTION

934. Devolution of choses (or things) in action generally. On the death of any person, choses (or things) in action to which he was entitled are in general included in the property which passes to his personal representative[1]. An interest in a chose in action which the deceased had jointly with another person who survives him will, however, pass not to the deceased's personal representatives but by survivorship to the other person[2]; where a contract is founded upon personal consideration, the death of either party puts an end to it[3]; and property (including any thing in action) vested in a corporation sole passes to the successors of the corporation sole[4].

A covenant relating to land of the covenantee made after 1925 is deemed to be made with the covenantee and his successors in title[5].

The survival of causes of action in favour of, or against, personal representatives is considered elsewhere in this title[6].

1 Went Off Ex (14th Edn) 159; cf the definition of 'personal estate' in the Wills Act 1837 s 1 (by which 'personal estate' for the purposes of the Act extends to chattels real); and PARA 917. As to choses (or things) in action generally see CHOSES IN ACTION. As to the meaning of 'personal representative' see PARA 608.
2 *Southcote v Hoare* (1810) 3 Taunt 87 (benefit of covenant made with joint covenantor). As to the construction of such a covenant if made after 1925 see DEEDS AND OTHER INSTRUMENTS vol 32 (2012) PARA 462 et seq. Cf the Administration of Estates Act 1925 s 3(4) (see PARA 948). As to the special rule applicable to partnership property see PARA 919.
3 See PARA 1213; and CONTRACT vol 22 (2012) PARA 639.
4 See the Law of Property Act 1925 s 180(1) (cited in relation to chattels real in PARA 942); and CORPORATIONS vol 24 (2010) PARAS 450, 473.
5 See DEEDS AND OTHER INSTRUMENTSvol32 (2012) PARA 457.
6 See PARA 1277.

935. Devolution of bills of exchange. The title to bills of exchange, cheques and promissory notes passes on the death of the holder to his personal representatives[1], who may sue on the instrument or negotiate it[2].

1 As to the meaning of 'personal representative' see PARA 608.
2 See FINANCIAL INSTRUMENTS AND TRANSACTIONS vol 49 (2015) PARA 391.

936. Right to exercise option to take shares. The personal representatives[1] of a member of a limited company, being entitled to the privileges as well as to the burdens of membership, may, so long as the name of the deceased member remains on the register, claim to avail themselves of an offer of new shares made to the members of the company during the lifetime of the deceased member[2].

1 As to the meaning of 'personal representative' see PARA 608.
2 *James v Buena Ventura Nitrate Grounds Syndicate Ltd* [1896] 1 Ch 456, CA. See also COMPANIES vol 14 (2016) PARA 445.

937. Compensation charged. Under the statutory provisions relating to agricultural holdings[1] and business premises[2] the personal representatives[3] of a landlord tenant for life who have been compelled to pay compensation to a tenant are entitled to a charge upon the holding in respect of the amount which they have so paid[4].

Interests qualifying for compensation for depreciation of the value of land caused by the use of public works[5], or for compensation in the form of basic loss payments or occupiers' loss payments[6] may be acquired by inheritance. A personal representative may serve a blight notice[7].

When a person has been convicted of a criminal offence and when subsequently his conviction has been reversed or he has been pardoned on the ground that a new or newly discovered fact shows beyond reasonable doubt that there has been a miscarriage of justice, the Secretary of State must pay compensation for the miscarriage of justice to the person who has suffered punishment as a result of such conviction or, if he is dead, to his personal representatives, unless the non-disclosure of the unknown fact was wholly or partly attributable to the person convicted[8].

1 See the Agricultural Holdings Act 1986 s 86; and AGRICULTURAL LAND vol 1 (2008) PARA 474 et seq.
2 See the Landlord and Tenant Act 1927 s 12, Sch; and LANDLORD AND TENANT vol 63 (2012) PARA 917.
3 As to the meaning of 'personal representative' see PARA 608.
4 *Re Agricultural Holdings (England) Act 1883, Gough v Gough* [1891] 2 QB 665, CA.
5 See the Land Compensation Act 1973 s 11; and COMPULSORY ACQUISITION OF LAND vol 18 (2009) PARA 886.
6 See the Land Compensation Act 1973 s 33G; and COMPULSORY ACQUISITION OF LAND vol 18 (2009) PARA 835.
7 See the Town and Country Planning Act 1990 s 161(1); and COMPULSORY ACQUISITION OF LAND vol 18 (2009) PARA 547; PLANNING vol 83 (2010) PARAS 1164 et seq, 1168 et seq.
8 See the Criminal Justice Act 1988 s 133.

938. Insurance policies and payments to representatives. The exclusive right of a personal representative to receive and give a discharge for money due upon policies effected by the deceased upon the life of the deceased is subject to the terms of the contract of insurance[1].

An insurance effected on his or her life by one spouse or civil partner and expressed to be for the benefit of the other or of their children creates a trust so that the money payable does not form part of the insured's estate; if trustees have been appointed, the money is payable to them, but in default of such appointment it is payable to the insured's personal representatives in trust for the beneficiaries[2].

1 *O'Reilly v Prudential Assurance Co Ltd* [1934] Ch 519, CA, where policies were provided for payment to the insured's executor or administrator, subject to a proviso that a receipt for the policy money by any relation of the insured should discharge the insurers and be conclusive evidence of payment to the person lawfully entitled; the insurers, in ignorance of the existence of a grant of administration to the insured's estate, paid the policy money to a relation of the insured, and took a receipt from her, and a claim against them by the insured's administratrix failed. See also *Da Costa v Prudential Assurance Co* (1918) 120 LT 353, CA. It is, however, doubtful whether the insurers could rely on such a proviso if at the time of payment they knew of the existence of a personal representative of the insured or that his estate was liable to estate duty: *O'Reilly v Prudential Assurance Co Ltd* at 534 per Romer LJ, and at 535 per Maugham LJ. As to the meaning of 'personal representative' see PARA 608.
2 See the Married Women's Property Act 1882 s 11; the Civil Partnership Act 2004 s 70; and INSURANCE vol 60 (2011) PARA 509.

939. Patents and copyright and related devolution of rights. Where, in respect of patents granted and applications made before 1 June 1978, a person claiming to be the inventor of an invention died without making application for a patent, the application could be made by, and the patent granted to, his legal personal representative[1]. On or after 1 June 1978 a patent may be granted to the successor or successors in title of the inventor[2].

The rules of law applicable to the devolution of personal property generally apply to patents[3]. Special provisions apply to patents held in co-ownership[4] but such provisions do not affect the rights or obligations of the trustees or personal representatives of a deceased person[5].

Copyright is transmissible by testamentary disposition as personal or movable property[6].

1 See the Patents Act 1949 s 1(3); the Patents Act 1977 s 127, Sch 1. The last of such patents expired in 1998: see the Patents Act 1949 s 22(3); and the Patents Act 1977 Sch 1 para 4. See further PATENTS AND REGISTERED DESIGNS vol 79 (2014) PARAS 302, 304.

2 See the Patents Act 1977 s 7(2); and PATENTS AND REGISTERED DESIGNS vol 79 (2014) PARA 306.

3 As to the devolution of personal property see PARA 917.

4 See the Patents Act 1977 s 36; and PATENTS AND REGISTERED DESIGNS vol 79 (2014) PARA 371. As to patents granted before 1 June 1978 see the Patents Act 1949 s 55; and PATENTS AND REGISTERED DESIGNS vol 79 (2014) PARAS 302, 304.

5 See the Patents Act 1977 s 36; and PATENTS AND REGISTERED DESIGNS vol 79 (2014) PARA 371. No directions in relation to patents may be made so as to affect the rights or obligations of the trustees or personal representatives of a deceased person: see s 8(8); and PATENTS AND REGISTERED DESIGNS vol 79 (2014) PARA 361.

6 See the Copyright, Designs and Patents Act 1988 s 90(1); and COPYRIGHT vol 23 (2016) PARA 653. As to the transmission and creation of interests in copyright generally see COPYRIGHT vol 23 (2016) PARA 639. See also the Artist's Resale Right Regulations 2006, SI 2006/346 (amended by SI 2009/2792) which create a transmissible entitlement to a royalty on certain sales of graphic or plastic art: see PARA 27 note 23: and COPYRIGHT vol 23 (2016) PARA 696 et seq.

940. Survival of causes of action. Causes of action vested in a person at the time of his death survive for the benefit of his estate. This subject and the qualifications of this principle are considered subsequently[1].

1 See PARA 1277 et seq.

941. Digital assets. There is no definitive meaning of the term 'digital assets' but it is normally used in relation to items which are accessed on-line. Some such items[1] may only be enjoyed on licence by the licensee and so cannot be transferred on death. Others types of digital asset are not assets in the usual sense because they have no intrinsic value and cannot normally be transferred[2]. Different again are bank and other accounts which are accessed online[3]; the underlying balance is a conventional asset (or liability) which can be transferred. Bitcoin[4] is an example of an asset which exists only in electronic form but which has real value.

Online facilities or platforms which offer file and document storage may, or may not, hold something of value to a third party, such as intellectual property rights or commercially sensitive information[5]. Ownership of a domain name or website is another form of digital asset which may have a commercial value. The terms on which the facility was bought or licensed will govern whether or not it can be transferred.

Those digital assets which are capable of transmission will vest in the personal representative, although ascertaining the existence of such assets and of accessing them may prove difficult[6].

1 Eg items such as downloaded music or films.

2 Eg social media and email accounts.

3 Eg online bank accounts and investment accounts; accounts used for online gambling or auction selling and store cards which may have a credit (or debit) balance which can be transferred in the same way as conventional accounts. As to electronic money see FINANCIAL INSTRUMENTS AND TRANSACTIONS vol 49 (2015) PARA 29 et seq. As to online gambling see INFORMATION TECHNOLOGY LAW vol 57 (2012) PARAS 601–605. As to online auctions see AUCTION vol 4 (2011) PARA 57; INFORMATION TECHNOLOGY LAW vol 57 (2012) PARA 599.

4 Ie a digital asset and payment system.

5 As to intellectual property rights held online see INFORMATION TECHNOLOGY LAW vol 57 (2012) PARA 513 et seq. As to informational privacy see CONFIDENCE AND INFORMATIONAL PRIVACY vol 19 (2011) PARA 1 et seq; INFORMATION TECHNOLOGY LAW vol 57 (2012) PARA 671 et seq.

6 Bitcoins, for example, are held in a virtual wallet which is accessed by a private key. If the private key is lost, the bitcoin network will not recognise any other evidence of ownership; the coins are then unusable, and thus effectively lost.

(5) DEVOLUTION OF LEASES AND OTHER CHATTELS REAL

942. Devolution of leaseholds. The vesting of a term of years[1] in the deceased's personal representative is by operation of law[2]. The executor who accepts the office cannot waive the terms[3], and is bound by covenants contained in a lease[4]. The vesting, being a conclusion of law, is not an assignment within a clause in a lease restraining assignment[5].

A yearly tenant's interest is transmissible to the deceased's personal representative[6], and notice to quit must be given to him[7]. The interest of a statutory tenant under the rent restriction and security of tenure legislation is a personal right which cannot be transmitted by will[8] and which does not vest in the tenant's personal representative[9].

1 As to the legislation affecting leaseholds generally see LANDLORD AND TENANT. The Landlord and Tenant Act 1954 s 41 contains special provisions for the protection of beneficiaries where a business tenancy is held on trust: see LANDLORD AND TENANT vol 63 (2012) PARA 880. 'Term of years absolute' has the same meaning in the Administration of Estates Act 1925 as it has in the Settled Land Act 1925 (see SETTLEMENTS vol 91 (2012) PARA 579): see the Administration of Estates Act 1925 s 55(1)(xxiv).

2 *Ackland v Pring* (1841) 2 Man & G 937 at 952. See the Administration of Estates Act 1925 ss 1, 3(1); and PARAS 608, 945–946. As to the liability of the representative for rent see LANDLORD AND TENANT vol 63 (2012) PARA 744. As to the right to enfranchise leaseholds see LANDLORD AND TENANT vol 64 (2012) PARA 1505 et seq.

3 *Billinghurst v Speerman* (1695) 1 Salk 297.

4 *Lloyds Bank Ltd v Jones* [1955] 2 QB 298, [1955] 2 All ER 409, CA. However by complying with the terms of Trustee Act 1925 s 26 the personal representative can escape personal liability in respect of any subsequent claim under the lease: see PARA 989. See also PARA 1224.

5 *Seers v Hind* (1791) 1 Ves 294. As to such clauses generally see LANDLORD AND TENANT vol 62 (2012) PARA 630 et seq.

6 *Doe d Shore v Porter* (1789) 3 Term Rep 13; *James v Dean* (1805) 11 Ves 383 at 393. As to the meaning of 'personal representative' see PARA 608.

7 *Parker d Walker v Constable* (1769) 3 Wils 25.

8 *John Lovibond & Sons Ltd v Vincent* [1929] 1 KB 687, CA. As to statutory tenancies see LANDLORD AND TENANT vol 63 (2012) PARA 944 et seq.

9 *Skinner v Geary* [1931] 2 KB 546, CA; *Drury v Johnston* [1928] NI 25. As to the protection afforded to members of a statutory (or assured) tenant's family after his death see the Rent Act 1977 s 2, Sch I Pt I; the Housing Act 1988 s 17; and LANDLORD AND TENANT vol 63 (2012) PARAS 953 et seq, 1096, 1170.

943. Devolution of lease to corporation sole. Any property[1] or any interest in it which, at any time, is or has been vested in a corporation sole (including the Crown), unless and until otherwise disposed of by the corporation, passes and devolves to and vests in, and is deemed always to have passed and devolved to or vested in, the successors from time to time of the corporation[2].

1 'Property' includes a thing in action and any interest in real or personal property: Law of Property Act 1925 s 205(1)(xx).

2 Law of Property Act 1925 s 180(1). See also the Administration of Estates Act 1925 s 3(5); and PARA 948. See further CORPORATIONS vol 24 (2010) PARA 450. Before 1926 a lease for years made to a corporation sole and his successors passed to the personal representative and not to the successors of the corporation sole: Co Litt 49b. As to the meaning of 'personal representative' see PARA 608.

944. Next presentations of benefice. Where a benefice becomes vacant and either:

(1) the registered patron who would have been entitled to present upon the vacancy is dead and the person to whom the right of patronage is to be transferred has not before the vacancy occurs been registered as a patron of that benefice; or

(2) the registered patron dies during the vacancy,

then the right of presentation to that benefice upon that vacancy is exercisable by that patron's personal representatives[1].

1 Patronage (Benefices) Measures 1986 s 21. The same was true under the former law: see *R v Fane* (1589) 4 Leon 107 at 109. The principle did not previously apply to donative benefices, the right of donation of which passed to the heir (*Repington v Governors of Tamworth School* (1763) 2 Wils 150), but all donated benefices have long since become presentative: see ECCLESIASTICAL LAW vol 34 (2011) PARA 550. As to restrictions on the exercise of patronage see ECCLESIASTICAL LAW vol 34 (2011) PARA 600 et seq. As to the meaning of 'personal representative' see PARA 608.

(6) DEVOLUTION OF REAL ESTATE

945. Statutory devolution of real estate on personal representative. On a death after 1925[1] real estate[2] to which the deceased was entitled for an interest not ceasing on his death[3] devolves from time to time, notwithstanding any testamentary disposition of it, on his personal representative in like manner as before 1926[4] chattels real devolved on the personal representative from time to time of a deceased person[5].

1 On the death intestate before 1 January 1898 of a beneficial owner, real estate devolved immediately upon his heir, subject (in cases where such rights attached) to rights of dower, freebench and curtesy (see REAL PROPERTY AND REGISTRATION vol 87 (2012) PARA 39), and subject also, after 1 September 1890, to the widow's right under the Intestates' Estates Act 1890 in cases where that Act applied.

If the deceased died between 1 January 1898 and 31 December 1925, such of his real estate as was vested in him without a right in any other person to take by survivorship (other than land of copyhold tenure or customary freehold in any case in which an admission or any act by the lord of the manor was necessary to perfect the title of a purchaser from the customary tenant) vested in his personal representative or representatives from time to time as if it were a chattel real, to be held with and subject to the powers, rights, duties and liabilities mentioned in the Land Transfer Act 1897 in trust for the persons by law beneficially entitled to it; and such persons had the same power of requiring a transfer of the real estate as persons beneficially entitled to personal estate had of requiring a transfer of such personal estate. As to the meaning of 'personal representative' see PARA 608.

2 As to the meaning of 'real estate' see PARA 946. As to partnership property see PARA 919; as to chattels real see PARA 942; as to trust and mortgage estates see PARA 950 et seq; and as to settled land see PARA 949.

3 See PARA 948.

4 Before 1926, the legal estate vested in all the executors irrespective of the question whether they had obtained probate or not, inasmuch as an executor derives his title from the will and not from probate; but it seems that the estate was divested by the executor renouncing probate: see *Re Pawley and London and Provincial Bank* [1900] 1 Ch 58. In case of an intestacy, inasmuch as an administrator derived his title from the grant of letters of administration, it was held that until administration was taken out the legal estate in the intestate's land devolved on his heir at law: see *Wankford v Wankford* (1704) 1 Salk 299; *John v John* [1898] 2 Ch 573; *Re Griggs, ex p London School Board* [1914] 2 Ch 547, CA.

5 Administration of Estates Act 1925 s 1(1). Subject to the provisions of that Act, all enactments and rules of law, and all jurisdiction of any court with respect to the appointment of administrators or to probate or letters of administration, or to dealings before probate in the case of chattels real, and with respect to costs and other matters in the administration of personal estate, in force before 1 January 1926, and all powers, duties, rights, equities, obligations and liabilities of a personal representative in force on that date with respect to chattels real, apply and attach to the personal representative and have effect with respect to real estate vested in him, and in particular all such powers of disposition and dealing as were before 1926 exercisable as respects chattels real by the survivor or survivors of two or more personal representatives, as well as by a single personal

representative, or by all the personal representatives together, are exercisable by the personal representative or representative of the deceased with respect to his real estate: s 2(1). As to the general necessity for the concurrence in a conveyance of all the personal representatives who have taken a grant see s 2(2); and PARA 1024. Without prejudice to the rights and powers of personal representatives, the appointment of a personal representative in regard to real estate does not, save as in that Act provided, affect:

(1) any rule as to marshalling or as to administration of assets;
(2) the beneficial interest in real estate under any testamentary disposition;
(3) any mode of dealing with any beneficial interest in real estate or the proceeds of sale of it; or
(4) the right of any person claiming to be interested in real estate to take proceedings for its protection or recovery against any person other than the personal representative (s 2(3)).

On a death intestate after 1925 the real estate vests, pending a grant of administration, in the President of the Family Division: see PARA 644. Equitable interests can be disposed of subject and without prejudice to the estate and powers of a personal representative: see the Wills Act 1837; and PARA 74.

946. Meaning of 'real estate' for devolution purposes. For the purpose of the statutory provisions as to devolution, 'real estate' includes:

(1) chattels real, and land[1] in possession, remainder or reversion, and every interest in or over land to which a deceased person was entitled at the time of his death[2]; and
(2) real estate held on trust[3] (including settled land)[4] or by way of mortgage or security but not money charged on land[5].

1 'Land' has the same meaning as in the Law of Property Act 1925 (see REAL PROPERTY AND REGISTRATION vol 87 (2012) PARA 7): Administration of Estates Act 1925 s 55(1)(via) (definition added by the Trusts of Land and Appointment of Trustees Act 1996 s 25(1), Sch 3 para 6(1), (5)). Prior to 1 January 1997, land was defined in accordance with the Settled Land Act 1925 s 117(1)(ix) (see SETTLEMENTS vol 91 (2012) PARA 581): see the Administration of Estates Act 1925 s 55(1)(xxiv) (as originally enacted); and PARA 823.
2 Administration of Estates Act 1925 s 3(1)(i).
3 Property held in trust by two or more persons falls within the exception mentioned in PARA 948 text and note 5, and passes by survivorship. As to devolution on the death of a sole trustee see further PARA 950.
4 As to the devolution of the legal estate in settled land see PARA 949.
5 Administration of Estates Act 1925 s 3(1)(ii) (amended by the Trusts of Land and Appointment of Trustees Act 1996 s 25(2), Sch 4).

947. Vesting of real estate in the personal representative for devolution purposes. For the purpose of the statutory provisions as to devolution, 'personal representative' means the executor, original or by representation, or administrator for the time being of the deceased[1]. Accordingly, the real estate vests in all the executors named in the will, whether they have proved the will or not, with the exception of those who have survived the testator but have died without having taken out probate, or have renounced probate or have failed to appear to a citation to take probate[2]; but the proving executors can sell without the concurrence of any who do not prove[3]. Where, however, a person appoints special executors of his property abroad, and general executors, his real estate in England and Wales vests in the latter to the exclusion of the former, and the general executors can make good title to it[4].

1 See PARA 608.
2 See the Administration of Estates Act 1925 s 5; and PARAS 631, 637 et seq. As to the effect of renunciation and failure to appear to a citation to take probate see PARAS 631, 698 et seq.
3 See the Administration of Estates Act 1925 s 2(2); and PARA 1024. The practical effect of this is that it is safe to deal with all such personal representatives as have taken a grant.
4 *Re Cohen's Executors and LCC* [1902] 1 Ch 187. As to the power of special personal representatives and general personal representatives to dispose of settled land and free estate respectively see PARA 829.

948. Deeming provisions in relation to real estate. A testator is deemed to have been entitled at his death to any interest in real estate[1] passing under any gift contained in his will which operates as an appointment under a general power to appoint by will or operates under the testamentary power conferred by statute[2] to dispose of an entailed interest[3]. Unless disposed of under the statutory power, an entailed interest of a deceased person is deemed an interest ceasing on his death[4]. The interest of a deceased person under a joint tenancy where another tenant survives the deceased is an interest ceasing on his death[5]. On the death of a corporation sole his interest in the corporation's real and personal estate is deemed to be an interest ceasing on his death and devolving on his successor[6].

1 As to the meaning of 'real estate' see PARA 946.

2 See the Law of Property Act 1925 s 176; REAL PROPERTY AND REGISTRATION vol 87 (2012) PARA 135; and PARA 948.

3 Administration of Estates Act 1925 s 3(2). See further PARA 954. As to entailed interests see REAL PROPERTY AND REGISTRATION vol 87 (2012) PARA 114.

4 Administration of Estates Act 1925 s 3(3). Any further or other interest of the deceased in the same property in remainder or reversion which is capable of being disposed of by his will is not, however, deemed to be an interest so ceasing: s 3(3).

5 Administration of Estates Act 1925 s 3(4). In the case of beneficial joint tenants, both the legal estate and the beneficial interest pass by survivorship. Despite the statutory provision by which land limited to joint tenants is held in trust, a surviving joint tenant who is solely and beneficially interested may deal with his legal estate as if it were not held in trust: see the Law of Property Act 1925 s 36(2); and REAL PROPERTY AND REGISTRATION vol 87 (2012) PARA 214. Where only the legal estate is held jointly (ie where there is a beneficial tenancy in common: see the Law of Property Act 1925 ss 34, 39(4), Sch 1 Pt IV; and REAL PROPERTY AND REGISTRATION vol 87 (2012) PARA 56 et seq), only the legal estate passes by survivorship, and any interest of the deceased which does not cease on his death passes to his personal representative. As to the meaning of 'personal representative' see PARA 608. As to the beneficial interest in partnership property see PARA 919.

6 Administration of Estates Act 1925 s 3(5). This provision applies on the demise of the Crown as regards all property, real and personal, vested in the Crown as a corporation sole: s 3(5). See also the Law of Property Act 1925 s 180(1) (see PARA 943); and CORPORATIONS vol 24 (2010) PARA 450.

949. Devolution of settled land. A legal estate in settled land[1] vested in a person as tenant for life[2], where the settlement ceases on his death, devolves upon his general personal representative[3]. Where in such a case the settlement does not so cease, the land may devolve upon the trustees of the settlement either under a special limited grant or under a general grant including settled land[4]; where the trustees of the settlement are cleared off, the tenant for life's general personal representatives may obtain a grant in respect of the settled land[5]. Upon the death of a tenant pur autre vie[6] the legal estate devolves in the same manner as settled land; the beneficial interest of the tenant, which is an equitable interest only, passes to his personal representative as being an interest not ceasing on his death[7].

1 Except in the case of a settlement created on the occasion of an alteration in any interest in, or of a person becoming entitled under, a settlement which was in existence on 1 January 1997 or derives from a settlement in existence on that date, from 1 January 1997 no settlement for the purposes of the Settled Land Act 1925 can be created and no settlement is deemed to be a settlement under that Act: see the Trusts of Land and Appointment of Trustees Act 1996 s 2(1), (2); and SETTLEMENTS vol 91 (2012) PARA 506. A settlement for the purposes of the Settled Land Act 1925 will permanently cease where, at any time after 1 January 1997, there is no land or personal chattels to which the Settled Land Act 1925 s 67(1) (heirlooms) applies subject to the settlement: see the Trusts of Land and Appointment of Trustees Act 1996 s 2(4); and SETTLEMENTS vol 91 (2012) PARA 506.

2 See the Settled Land Act 1925 ss 1, 2, 19, 20. After 1925, the legal estate in fee simple or other the whole legal estate subject to the settlement is vested in the tenant for life or in the trustees of the settlement as statutory owners: see SETTLEMENTS.

3 *Re Bridgett and Hayes' Contract* [1928] Ch 163; *Re Bordass* [1929] P 107. On the death of the deceased, land may cease to be settled land under one settlement and immediately become settled under another, and will not then so vest in the general personal representative: *Re Taylor* [1929] P 260. As to the meaning of 'personal representative' see PARA 608.
4 As to the circumstances in which a general grant expressly including settled land may be made see the Non-Contentious Probate Rules 1987, SI 1987/2024, r 29; and PARA 822. A grant in respect of the free estate only, where there is also settled land, expressly excludes settled land: see r 29(3); and PARA 822.
5 See the Non-Contentious Probate Rules 1987, SI 1987/2024, r 29(2)(iii); and PARA 822.
6 On the death of a tenant pur autre vie after 1897 and before 1926, the legal estate which his heir would formerly have taken as special occupant passed to the deceased tenant's personal representative: see the Land Transfer Act 1897 s 1 (repealed).
7 See the Administration of Estates Act 1925 s 1(1); and PARA 945.

(7) DEVOLUTION OF TRUST AND MORTGAGE ESTATES

950. Devolution of personalty held on trust. Personal estate vested in a sole or a last surviving or continuing trustee devolves upon his personal representatives[1], who have power to appoint new trustees in the place of the deceased trustee, whether he was the last survivor of several trustees or the sole trustee[2], where there is no person nominated by the instrument creating the trust for the purpose of appointing new trustees, or where there is no person so nominated able and willing to act[3].

1 As to the meaning of 'personal representative' see PARA 608. As to the appointment of separate executors for this purpose and the effect of an unlimited grant to general executors in spite of such an appointment see PARA 616.
2 See *Re Shafto's Trusts* (1885) 29 ChD 247. See also the Trustee Act 1925 s 18(2); and TRUSTS AND POWERS vol 98 (2013) PARA 268. The personal representative's powers cease on the appointment of new trustees, so that if the personal representative is to continue as one of the trustees he must be re-appointed: see s 36(1); *Re Sampson* [1906] 1 Ch 435.
3 Trustee Act 1925 s 36(1). As to the appointment of new trustees generally, and the court's powers to make a vesting order, see TRUSTS AND POWERS vol 98 (2013) PARA 275 et seq.

951. Devolution of realty held on trust. Real estate and chattels real vested in any person solely on any trust devolve on his death on his personal representative[1], who has the same power of disposing of the realty as if it were a chattel real, and is deemed in law the trustee's heir and assign within the meaning of all trusts and powers[2].

Since 1881, therefore, the personal representative has accordingly been substituted for the trustee's heir or assign, but at first he had no powers additional to those which the heir or assign formerly had[3]. Now, however, the proving personal representative of a sole or last surviving or continuing trustee has all the powers of such trustee or other the trustees or trustee for the time being of the trust[4].

Notwithstanding that the trust estate vests in the personal representative of the sole or last surviving trustee, a power of appointing new trustees can be validly exercised by the person in whom the power is vested under the trust; and the appointment operates to oust the personal representative from the trust[5].

1 See the Administration of Estates Act 1925 ss 1(1), 3(1)(ii) (see PARAS 945–946) which, as to trust and mortgage estates, replace the repealed Conveyancing Act 1881 s 30. In the absence of a personal representative the legal estate vests in the President of the Family Division (see PARA 644); but before 1926 real estate held by a sole surviving trustee apparently vested on his death intestate, while no personal representative was constituted, in the heir (see *Re Pilling's Trusts* (1884) 26 ChD 432; and cf PARA 644 note 1). As to the meaning of 'personal representative' see PARA 608. As to the appointment of separate executors for this purpose and the effect of an unlimited grant to general executors in spite of such appointment see PARA 616.

Before statute provided for the devolution on personal representatives, on the death intestate without heirs of a trustee or mortgagee the estate escheated to the Crown or lord (see *A-G v Duke of Leeds* (1833) 2 My & K 343) unless the lord had admitted the trustee or mortgagee on a surrender which gave him notice of the trust, in which case he was bound by it (*Weaver v Maule* (1830) 2 Russ & M 97).

2 See the Administration of Estates Act 1925 ss 1(2), 2; and PARA 945.

3 *Re Ingleby and Boak and Norwich Union Insurance Co* (1883) 13 LR Ir 326; *Re Crunden and Meux's Contract* [1909] 1 Ch 690.

4 See the Trustee Act 1925 s 18(2); and TRUSTS AND POWERS vol 98 (2013) PARA 257.

5 *Re Routledge's Trusts, Routledge v Saul* [1909] 1 Ch 280. See TRUSTS AND POWERS vol 98 (2013) PARA 257 et seq.

952. Exercise of powers on death of sole or last continuing trustee. Until the appointment of new trustees, the personal representatives[1] or representative for the time being of a sole trustee, or, where there were two or more trustees, of the last surviving or continuing trustee, are capable of exercising or performing any power or trust which was given to, or capable of being exercised by, the sole or last surviving or continuing trustee, or other the trustees or trustee for the time being of the trust[2]. The representatives may, however, decline to act in the trusts[3], and they are under no obligation to appoint new trustees[4].

1 As to the meaning of 'personal representative' see PARA 608.

2 Administration of Estates Act 1925 s 1(2); Trustee Act 1925 s 18(2). Cf the Settled Land Act 1925 s 30(3) (see SETTLEMENTS vol 91 (2012) PARA 652). The personal representatives only have the powers of a sole surviving trustee. The latter cannot give a receipt for capital money unless a trust corporation, but apparently the Trustee Act 1925 s 18(3) implies that two personal representatives can. Section 18 has been so construed in practice.

3 *Legg v Mackrell* (1860) 2 De GF & J 551; *Re Ridley, Ridley v Ridley* [1904] 2 Ch 774; *Re Benett, Ward v Benett* [1906] 1 Ch 216, CA.

4 *Re Knight's Will* (1884) 26 ChD 82, CA.

953. Mortgage estates for devolution purposes. Real estate, including chattels real[1], held by way of mortgage by any person solely, devolves upon his personal representatives[2]. They are entitled to receive and give a good discharge for the mortgage money, and may accordingly exercise the statutory power of sale[3]. In the case of several mortgagees or of several transferees[4], where the money is expressed to have been advanced on a joint account, the personal representatives of the last survivor may, so far as no intention to the contrary is expressed, give a good discharge for the mortgage money, notwithstanding any notice to the payer of a severance of the joint account[5], and are, therefore, also in a position to exercise the statutory power of sale.

1 As to the meaning of 'real estate' see PARA 946. A mortgage can only be effected at law either by a demise or a subdemise for a term of years absolute or by a legal charge: see the Law of Property Act 1925 ss 85, 86; and MORTGAGE vol 77 (2016) PARA 161 et seq.

2 See the Administration of Estates Act 1925 ss 1(1), 3(1), replacing the repealed Conveyancing Act 1881 s 30. The case of copyholds before 1925 formed an exception. Where the legal estate was in trustees, the equitable estate descended according to the custom of the manor regulating the descent of the legal estate provided the trusts were executed; but if the trusts were executory, the equitable estate descended according to the general rules of inheritance: *Trash v Wood* (1839) 4 My & Cr 324; applied in *Re Hudson, Cassels v Hudson* [1908] 1 Ch 655 (resulting trust). Under the Administration of Estates Act 1925 ss 1, 3(1)(ii), enfranchised copyholds devolved upon the personal representatives. As to land formerly copyhold see REAL PROPERTY AND REGISTRATION vol 87 (2012) PARA 36 et seq.

As to the meaning of 'personal representative' see PARA 608. As to the appointment of separate executors for trust or mortgage estates and the effect of an unlimited grant to general executors in spite of such appointment see PARA 616.

3 See the Law of Property Act 1925 s 106(1); and MORTGAGE vol 77 (2016) PARA 454 et seq. The statutory power of sale only applies to a case of a mortgage made by deed: see s 101(1); and MORTGAGE vol 77 (2016) PARA 446.

4 This applies where the mortgage or transfer was executed since 31 December 1881.
5 See the Law of Property Act 1925 s 111; and MORTGAGE vol 77 (2016) PARAS 186, 644.

(8) DEVOLUTION OF PROPERTY SUBJECT TO A GENERAL POWER OF APPOINTMENT

954. Real estate's devolution. Real estate[1], including chattels real, disposed of by a will which operates as an appointment under a general power to appoint by will or operates under the testamentary power conferred by statute to dispose of an entailed interest[2] is deemed to be the property of the testator which vests in his personal representative[3].

1 As to the meaning of 'real estate' see PARA 946.
2 For the statutory power to dispose of an entailed estate by will see the Law of Property Act 1925 s 176; and REAL PROPERTY AND REGISTRATION vol 87 (2012) PARA 136.
3 See the Administration of Estates Act 1925 ss 1(1), 3(1), (2); and PARA 948. As to the meaning of 'personal representative' see PARA 608.

955. Personal estate's devolution. All property, whether real or personal, disposed of in exercise of a general power of appointment (including the statutory power to dispose of entailed interests) constitutes assets for the payment of debts[1]. For inheritance tax purposes, a person who has a general power[2] which enables him, or would if he were sui juris enable him, to dispose of any property other than settled property, or to charge money on any property other than settled property, is treated as beneficially entitled to the property or money[3]. The personal representative is, however, the only person entitled to receive personal estate so appointed[4], and he might give a valid receipt for it to the trustee of the settlement[5].

References to the estate of a deceased person in the Administration of Estates Act 1925 include property over which the deceased exercises a general power of appointment (including the statutory power to dispose of entailed interest) by will[6].

1 See PARA 969.
2 For these purposes, 'general power' means a power or authority enabling the person by whom it is exercisable to appoint or dispose of property as he thinks fit: Inheritance Tax Act 1984 s 5(2).
3 Inheritance Tax Act 1984 s 5(2). See *O'Grady v Wilmot* [1916] 2 AC 231 at 250–251, HL (for estate duty purposes, personal estate excluding leaseholds, over which a general power of appointment had been exercised, was property which did not pass to the executor as such); and INHERITANCE TAXATION vol 59A (2014) PARA 264.
4 *Re Hoskin's Trusts* (1877) 6 ChD 281, CA; *O'Grady v Wilmot* [1916] 2 AC 231 at 250–251, HL; and see *Re Guedalla, Lee v Guedalla's Trustees* [1905] 2 Ch 331. As to the meaning of 'personal representative' see PARA 608.
5 *Re Hoskin's Trusts* (1877) 6 ChD 281, CA; *O'Grady v Wilmot* [1916] 2 AC 231 at 250–251, HL; *Re Peacock's Settlement, Kelcey v Harrison* [1902] 1 Ch 552 (administrator with will annexed).
6 Administration of Estates Act 1925 s 55(3).

12. THE ADMINISTRATION OF ASSETS

(1) THE REPRESENTATIVE'S FIRST DUTIES

(i) Funeral and Inventory

956. Duties in relation to disposal of the body. Where a person appoints executors they are prima facie entitled to the possession, and are responsible for the disposal, of the dead body[1]. In the absence of an executor, it must be asked who has the best claim to be appointed administrator[2]. The deceased's directions as to the nature of his funeral specifying where burial or cremation is to be carried out are not legally binding[3]. However, by statute, a direction for the anatomical examination of a person's body after death and the removal of parts of it for medical purposes may in certain cases be effective[4].

1 See *Dobson v North Tyneside Health Authority* [1996] 4 All ER 474, [1997] 1 FLR 598, CA. As to duties as to burial and as to cremation see CREMATION AND BURIAL vol 24 (2010) PARAS 1102–1103. It is a criminal offence to prevent a proper burial: *R v Hunter* [1974] QB 95, [1973] 2 All ER 286, CA; *R v Skidmore* [2008] EWCA Crim 1464, [2009] Crim LR 42, [2008] All ER (D) 146 (Jul). Where a mother and father were in dispute as to the disposal of the ashes of their minor daughter it was held that division of the ashes would not be appropriate and they should be scattered in Nuneaton where the entire family had a focus and not in Wales where the child died: *Fessi v Whitmore* [1999] 1 FLR 767. See also *Hartshorne v Gardner* [2008] 2 FLR 1681, [2008] Fam Law 985, where the factors that were relevant in determining the form or place of the funeral or interment were the deceased's own wishes and the reasonable wishes and requirements of family and friends who were left. The place with which the deceased had the closest connection was relevant as to the ultimate resting place.

2 Ie under the Non-Contentious Probate Rules 1987, SI 1987/2024, r 22: see PARA 768. Where there was a dispute over burial arrangements, Hale J was prepared to accept that in an appropriate case a person with no prior entitlement to the grant could use the Senior Courts Act 1981 s 116 (see PARA 758) to obtain the grant and hence the right to decide funeral arrangements: see *Buchanan v Milton* [1999] 2 FLR 844; applied in *Ibuna v Arroyo* [2012] EWHC 428 (Ch), [2012] WTLR 827, [2012] All ER (D) 36 (Mar); and *Anstey v Mundle* [2016] EWHC 1073 (Ch), [2016] All ER (D) 285 (Feb). See also *Burrows v HM Coroner for Preston* [2008] EWHC 1387 (QB), [2008] 2 FLR 1225, [2008] All ER (D) 201 (May), where the court gave guidance on whether it should exercise its discretion to vary the Non-Contentious Probate Rules 1987, SI 1987/2024, r 22 and concluded in that case that it was necessary for the natural mother's rights, as the person prima facie entitled, to be displaced. See also *Scotching v Birch* [2008] EWHC 844 (Ch), [2008] All ER (D) 265 (Mar); *Lewisham Hospital NHS Trust v Hamuth* [2006] EWHC 1609 (Ch), [2006] All ER (D) 145 (Jan); and PARA 31.

3 *Williams v Williams* (1882) 20 ChD 659. In *Burrows v HM Coroner for Preston* [2008] EWHC 1387 (QB), [2008] 2 FLR 1225, [2008] All ER (D) 201 (May), the court considered that the deceased's wishes as to funeral arrangements were one of the special circumstances to be taken into account in deciding whether or not to exercise its discretion to vary the Non-Contentious Probate Rules 1987, SI 1987/2024, r 22 (see note 2); this being consistent with art 8 of the Convention for the Protection of Human Rights and Fundamental Freedoms (Rome, 4 November 1950; TS 71 (1953); Cmd 8969) (commonly referred to as the 'European Convention on Human Rights') (see RIGHTS AND FREEDOMS vol 88A (2013) PARA 88). However Peter Smith J doubted the relevance of the Convention to the disposal of a body in *Ibuna v Arroyo* [2012] EWHC 428 (Ch) at [50], [2012] WTLR 827, [2012] All ER (D) 36 (Mar).

4 See the Human Tissue Act 2004 Pt 1 (ss 1–12); and CREMATION AND BURIAL vol 24 (2010) PARA 1102; MEDICAL PROFESSIONS vol 74 (2011) PARA 54 et seq.

957. Duty to produce inventory. The personal representatives[1] of a deceased person are under a duty, when required to do so by the court[2], to exhibit on oath in the court a full inventory of the estate and when so required render an account of the administration of the estate to the court[3].

Any interest in the estate of a testator or intestate is sufficient to support an application for an inventory[4], and mere lapse of time is no bar to the right[5]; but the court has a discretion to refuse the application[6]. The duty to exhibit an inventory is not confined to the original representatives, but may be enforced against the representatives of an administrator with the will annexed[7], or against the executor of one of several executors, even if there is an executor of the original testator still surviving[8].

Under this statutory jurisdiction the court can only require that the property of which the deceased died possessed should be included in the inventory; it cannot call for an account of the subsequent profits of his business[9].

1 As to the meaning of 'personal representative' see PARA 608.
2 'Court' means the High Court and also the County Court where that court has jurisdiction: Administration of Estates Act 1925 s 55(1)(iv) (definition amended by the Courts Act 1971 s 56(4), Sch 11 Pt II). See also PARA 847. Only the High Court can require the grant to be delivered up: see the Administration of Estates Act 1925 s 25(c); and PARA 847. The application is by application notice: see PARA 702. Making such an application does not constitute starting an administration action: *CI v NS* [2004] EWHC 659 (Fam), [2004] All ER (D) 30 (Apr).
3 Administration of Estates Act 1925 s 25(b) (s 25 substituted by the Administration of Estates Act 1971 s 9). As to the long-standing practice, apart from statute, for personal representatives to exhibit an inventory only when required to do so see *Phillips v Bignell* (1811) 1 Phillim 239 at 240 per Sir John Nicholl. See also PARA 1254.
4 *Myddleton v Rushout* (1797) 1 Phillim 244.
5 *Jickling v Bircham* (1843) 2 Notes of Cases 463; *Scurrah v Scurrah* (1841) 2 Curt 919 at 921.
6 *Burgess v Marriott* (1843) 3 Curt 424 at 426; *Ritchie v Rees and Rees* (1822) 1 Add 144; *Bowles v Harvey* (1832) 4 Hag Ecc 241; *Scurrah v Scurrah* (1841) 2 Curt 919.
7 *Ritchie v Rees and Rees* (1822) 1 Add 144 at 158. As to administration with the will annexed see PARAS 788–792.
8 *Gale v Luttrell* (1824) 2 Add 234.
9 See *Pitt v Woodham* (1828) 1 Hag Ecc 247 at 250.

958. Power to enter deceased's house. The representative may enter into the testator's house and remove his personal effects if he can do so without violence[1]. The power extends to the case of a deceased tenant for life or tenant in tail[2].

1 Went Off Ex (14th Edn) 202.
2 *Stodden v Harvey* (1608) Cro Jac 204.

(ii) Getting in and Investing the Property

959. Duty to get in the estate. The personal representatives[1] of a deceased person are under a duty to collect and get in the deceased's real and personal estate[2] and administer it according to law[3]. A personal representative should get in as speedily as possible all money of his testator outstanding upon personal security only[4], and call in any balance due from a co-executor[5]. He is not required, however, to make good the loss if he has done all he can to obtain payment, even though his efforts have not proved successful; and even if he has taken no steps to obtain payment but it appears, or there is reasonable ground for believing, that such steps would have been ineffectual he is exonerated from liability[6]. In such a case the burden of proving the grounds of his belief rests upon him[7].

In the case of money outstanding on real security, there is no duty upon the personal representatives to realise a mortgage created by the deceased himself where the realisation is not required for any testamentary purpose, and the security itself is not in any peril[8]. There is no obligation to sell non-income-bearing assets in order to increase sums due under an agreement to pay maintenance on the dissolution of a marriage[9]. Where the deceased is a shareholder in a company and the company's articles provide that the company is to purchase the shareholding of the deceased upon valuation, then the deceased's personal representatives are obliged to sell the shareholding to the company[10].

1 As to the meaning of 'personal representative' see PARA 608.

2 As to the meaning of 'real estate' see PARA 607 note 1.
3 Administration of Estates Act 1925 s 25(a) (s 25 substituted by the Administration of Estates Act 1971 s 9).
4 *Lowson v Copeland* (1787) 2 Bro CC 156; *Powell v Evans* (1801) 5 Ves 839; *Tebbs v Carpenter* (1816) 1 Madd 290; *A-G v Higham* (1843) 2 Y & C Ch Cas 634; *Caney v Bond* (1843) 6 Beav 486; *Gardner v Gardner* (1837) 1 Jur 402; *Evans v Flight* (1838) 2 Jur 818.
5 *Stiles v Guy* (1849) 1 H & Tw 523.
6 *Clack v Holland* (1854) 19 Beav 262 at 271 per Romilly MR; *Re Roberts, Knight v Roberts* (1897) 76 LT 479, CA.
7 *Re Brogden, Billing v Brogden* (1888) 38 ChD 546, CA; *Re Greenwood, Greenwood v Firth* (1911) 105 LT 509.
8 *Re Chapman, Cocks v Chapman* [1896] 2 Ch 763 at 778, CA, per Lopes LJ. In relation to loans made before 1 February 2001, where the security has fallen in value below the two-thirds limit under the Trustee Act 1925 s 8(1) (repealed in relation to loans made after that date: see the Trustee Act 2000 Sch 3 paras 2, 3; and the Trustee Act 2000 (Commencement) Order 2001, SI 2001/49), it is not the personal representatives' absolute duty at once to call in the mortgage, but they have a discretion, which they must exercise as practical persons with due regard to all the circumstances of the case: *Re Medland, Eland v Medland* (1889) 41 ChD 476, CA; and see TRUSTS AND POWERS vol 98 (2013) PARA 453 et seq. As to the rules on lending money on mortgage see TRUSTS AND POWERS vol 98 (2013) PARA 469 et seq.
9 *Re Korda* (1958) Times, 19 July, CA.
10 *Dashfield v Davidson* [2008] EWHC 486 (Ch), [2009] 1 BCLC 220, [2008] All ER (D) 258 (Mar).

960. Duty in relation to foreign assets. Once a grant of representation has issued, it is the personal representative's duty to administer the assets in accordance with the lex loci of the assets[1]. He must, therefore, get in the assets situated in the country in which the grant was made, pay the deceased's debts and liabilities and distribute the balance to those entitled. An English court may judicially administer English and foreign assets together by acting on the person of the representative[2].

1 *Re Lorillard, Griffiths v Catforth* [1922] 2 Ch 638, CA. However, the English courts will not always compel an English administrator to hand the assets to a foreign administrator: *Re Lorillard, Griffiths v Catforth*. See also *Re Manifold, Slater v Chryssaffinis* [1962] Ch 1, [1961] 1 All ER 710; *Re Weiss's Estate* [1962] P136, [1962] 1 All ER 308. See also CONFLICT OF LAWS vol 19 (2011) PARA 729 et seq.
2 *Stirling-Maxwell v Cartwright* (1878) 9 ChD 173; *Ewing v Orr-Ewing* (1883) 9 App Cas 34, HL. See also *Chellaram v Chellaram* [1985] Ch 409, [1985] 1 All ER 1043.

961. The executor's year. The general rule is that a year[1] from the date of death is a reasonable time within which a personal representative should realise investments which it is not proper to retain[2]. The rule has been described as a prima facie and not a fixed rule[3], and where personal representatives acting in the honest exercise of their discretion postpone the sale beyond the end of the first year they will not be liable for any loss occasioned by the postponement[4].

A direction contained in the will that the executors should sell with all convenient speed does not render it obligatory upon them to sell at any particular time; they are still entitled to exercise a reasonable discretion[5]. Where the will contains such a direction, executors should, however, dispose of shares in an unlimited company as soon as possible[6]. They may be charged with a loss occasioned by their refusing an advantageous offer[7].

Where executors are given a discretion under the will as to the retention or the postponement of the conversion of existing securities, they are not liable for mere errors of judgment if they act honestly and with ordinary prudence[8], even though the securities retained are shares in an unlimited company[9].

1 The executor's year can be viewed from two aspects: (1) whether the executor is under a duty to pay the testator's debts within that time; or (2) whether the executor is under a duty to get in assets

and realise unauthorised investments within that time. As regards the former aspect, there is no rule of law that it is the executor's duty to pay the testator's debts within a year from his death: see PARA 966 text and note 8.

2 *Hiddingh (Heirs) v De Villiers Denyssen, Hiddingh v Denyssen, Denyssen v Hiddingh* (1887) 12 App Cas 624 at 631, PC. The personal representatives are not bound to distribute the deceased's estate until the expiration of one year from death; this is called the power to postpone distribution: Administration of Estates Act 1925 s 44. As to the meaning of 'personal representative' see PARA 608.

3 *Grayburn v Clarkson* (1868) 3 Ch App 605 at 606 per Page Wood LJ. See also *Hughes v Empson* (1856) 22 Beav 181.

4 *Buxton v Buxton* (1835) 1 My & Cr 80; *Marsden v Kent* (1877) 5 ChD 598, CA; *Re Chapman, Cocks v Chapman* [1896] 2 Ch 763 at 782, CA, per Rigby LJ.

5 *Grayburn v Clarkson* (1868) 3 Ch App 605 at 608 per Selwyn LJ.

6 *Grayburn v Clarkson* (1868) 3 Ch App 605; *Sculthorpe v Tipper* (1871) LR 13 Eq 232.

7 *Taylor v Tabrum* (1833) 6 Sim 281; *Fry v Fry* (1859) 27 Beav 144.

8 *Re Chapman, Cocks v Chapman* (1896) 2 Ch 763, CA; *Re Smith, Smith v Thompson* [1896] 1 Ch 71. As to the rights as between tenant for life and remainderman in respect of wasting or reversionary property see PARA 1122 et seq.

9 *Re Norrington, Brindley v Partridge* (1879) 13 ChD 654, CA.

962. Duty in relation to investment of cash. Where the executor is not directed by the will to invest his testator's money he incurs no liability by leaving it in the bank[1], but he must keep it in a separate account and not mix it with other money[2]. Where he is under an obligation to invest he must not allow money to remain at the bank for an unnecessarily long period[3], although he may leave a considerable sum there for the purposes of administration[4], or until an investment is found[5]. If he leaves money with his bank to be invested he should see that the investment is made[6].

1 *Johnson v Newton* (1853) 11 Hare 160; *Re Marcon's Estate, Finch v Marcon* (1871) 40 LJ Ch 537. Where, however, the executor is a bank the question whether the executor is liable to pay interest on money deposited with itself may depend on the charging clause in the will being such as to exclude that liability: see *Re Waterman's Will Trusts, Lloyds Bank Ltd v Sutton* [1952] 2 All ER 1054. In this connection it may be material whether the corporate executor is the same legal person as the bank.

2 *Wilks v Groom* (1856) 25 LJ Ch 724 at 729 per Kindersley V-C. As to the liability to account for profits made out of estate money and the duty to act gratuitously see PARA 648 et seq.

3 *Moyle v Moyle* (1831) 2 Russ & M 710; *Fletcher v Walker* (1818) 3 Madd 73.

4 *Dawson v Massey* (1809) 1 Ball & B 219 at 231; *Swinfen v Swinfen (No 5)* (1860) 29 Beav 211.

5 *Fenwicke v Clarke* (1862) 4 De GF & J 240; *Re Hurst, Addison v Topp* (1892) 67 LT 96, CA. As to trust investments generally see TRUSTS AND POWERS vol 98 (2013) PARA 446 et seq.

6 *Challen v Shippam* (1845) 4 Hare 555.

963. Lending money on personal security. In the absence of express authority the personal representatives[1] ought not to lend on personal security[2], even if given by several persons[3]. Even where there is authority to lend on personal security, representatives ought not to lend to one of themselves[4]; nor, without authority, should they lend upon second[5] or contributory mortgages[6].

1 As to the meaning of 'personal representative' see PARA 608.

2 *Walker v Symonds* (1818) 3 Swan 1 at 63. As to powers to lend on personal security see also TRUSTS AND POWERS vol 98 (2013) PARA 451.

3 *Holmes v Dring* (1788) 2 Cox Eq Cas 1.

4 —*v Walker* (1828) 5 Russ 7; *Stickney v Sewell* (1835) 1 My & Cr 8.

5 *Norris v Wright* (1851) 14 Beav 291 at 308; *Drosier v Brereton* (1851) 15 Beav 221 at 226; *Lockhart v Reilly* (1857) 1 De G & J 464 at 476; *Re Roberson, Campkin v Barton* [1883] WN 110.

6 *Webb v Jonas* (1888) 39 ChD 660. As to trust investments generally see TRUSTS AND POWERS vol 98 (2013) PARA 446 et seq.

(iii) Notices for Claims

964. Issue of advertisements for claims against estate. In order to safeguard himself a personal representative[1] should issue advertisements requiring any person interested to send him within the time, not being less than two months, fixed in the notice, particulars of his claim[2] in respect of the property to which the notice relates[3]. The advertisement should be inserted in the London Gazette, and, as regards land, in a newspaper circulating in the district in which the land is situated[4]; but there is no absolute rule requiring it to be inserted in any other London newspaper, that must depend upon the circumstances of each case[5]. Where the deceased's residence was outside London an advertisement should be inserted in a newspaper in the neighbourhood[6]. In the absence of special circumstances there is no reason why the advertisement should be inserted more than once[7].

Where advertisement is impossible the court may give leave to distribute upon the footing that all the debts and liabilities of the estate have been ascertained. Such leave only operates to protect the personal representative, and does not prevent the missing beneficiary or absent creditor from following the assets[8].

Where a beneficiary is presumed dead, it is open to the personal representative to take out missing beneficiary insurance as an alternative to bringing proceedings before the court, notwithstanding that the personal representative is a beneficiary of the estate[9].

1 As to the meaning of 'personal representative' see PARA 608.
2 The words 'claims against the estate', which are commonly used in such advertisements, have been held to include the claims of persons beneficially interested under the will or intestacy as well as the claims of creditors (*Newton v Sherry* (1876) 1 CPD 246), but such a form of words is misleading and advertisements ought to follow more closely the wording of the Trustee Act 1925 s 27: *Re Aldhous, Noble v Treasury Solicitor* [1955] 2 All ER 80, [1955] 1 WLR 459. In certain newspapers, advertisements by personal representatives will be inserted in the form of a schedule under a common heading, in order to save space and expense and avoid repetition of formal words: see [1948] WN Misc 47.
3 See the Trustee Act 1925 s 27(1) (amended by the Law of Property (Amendment) Act 1926 ss 7, 8(2), Schedule; and the Trusts of Land and Appointment of Trustees Act 1996 s 25(1), Sch 3 para3(7)); and TRUSTS AND POWERS vol 98 (2013) PARA 355. As to the time within which personal representatives should advertise see *Re Kay, Mosley v Kay* [1897] 2 Ch 518. The Trustee Act 1925 s 27 applies notwithstanding anything to the contrary in the will: s 27(3).
4 See the Trustee Act 1925 s 27(1) (as amended: see note 3). See also *R v Westminster Betting and Licensing Committee, ex p Peabody Donation Fund* [1963] 2 QB 750, sub nom *R v Westminster Betting and Licensing Committee, ex p Peabody Donation Fund (Governors)* [1963] 2 All ER 544.
5 *Re Bracken, Doughty v Townson* (1889) 43 ChD 1 at 9, CA, per Cotton LJ.
6 *Wood v Weightman* (1872) LR 13 Eq 434.
7 *Re Bracken, Doughty v Townson* (1889) 43 ChD 1 at 7, CA, per North J.
8 *Re Gess, Gess v Royal Exchange Assurance* [1942] Ch 37. See also PARA 1106. As to the following of property see PARA 1095 et seq.
9 *Re Evans, Evans v Westcombe* [1999] 2 All ER 777.

965. Effect of advertising. After the time specified in the advertisement for sending in claims[1] the personal representative is at liberty to distribute the assets, having regard to those claims of which he has notice[2], but he is under no liability in respect of those assets to any person of whose claim he has had no notice whatever[3]. He is entitled to the same protection as if he had administered the estate under a judgment of the court[4], but the property distributed or any property representing it may be followed into the hands of any person other than a purchaser who may have received it[5]. He is not, however, free from liabilities of which he has notice, even though no claim in respect of them has been sent in answer to his advertisement[6]; nor is he free from any obligation to make searches or obtain official certificates of search similar to those which an intending purchaser would be advised to make or obtain[7].

1 The representative must give not less than two months' notice from the date of the last notice, where more than one notice is given: see the Trustee Act 1925 s 27(1); PARA 964; and TRUSTS AND POWERS vol 98 (2013) PARA 355. It is usual to give rather longer than two months' notice, as the appearance of the advertisement may be delayed. As to the meaning of 'personal representative' see PARA 608.

2 See *MCP Pension Trustees Ltd v AON Pension Trustees Ltd* [2009] EWHC 1351 (Ch), [2010] 1 All ER (Comm) 323, [2009] All ER (D) 222 (Jul) (requirement under the Trustee Act 1927 s 27(2) for personal representatives to have 'notice' rather than 'knowledge').

3 See the Trustee Act 1925 s 27(2); and TRUSTS AND POWERS vol 98 (2013) PARA 355. See also *Re Burke, King v Terry* (1919) 54 LJo 430. In special circumstances an inquiry will be directed as to what advertisements are necessary to enable the personal representatives to obtain the protection of this provision: *Re Letherbrow, Hopp v Dean* [1935] WN 34 at 48; *Re Holden, Isaacson v Holden* [1935] WN 52. The protection afforded by the Trustee Act 1925 s 27(2) does not extend to claims under the Inheritance (Provision for Family and Dependants) Act 1975 (see PARA 590); nor to claims resulting from rectification of the will under the Administration of Justice Act 1982 s 20 (see PARA 741).

4 *Clegg v Rowland* (1866) LR 3 Eq 368.

5 See the Trustee Act 1925 s 27(2)(a); and TRUSTS AND POWERS vol 98 (2013) PARA 355. As to the effect of this provision see PARA 1106; and as to following assets see PARA 1095 et seq.

6 *Re Land Credit Co of Ireland, Markwell's Case* (1872) 21 WR 135; *Guardian Trust and Executors Co of New Zealand Ltd v Public Trustee of New Zealand* [1942] AC 115, [1942] 1 All ER 598, PC (executor not entitled to disregard notice of claim because he believed it to be invalid).

7 See the Trustee Act 1925 s 27(2)(b); and TRUSTS AND POWERS vol 98 (2013) PARA 355. As to the searches which an intending purchaser should make see CONVEYANCING vol 23 (2016) PARA 84 et seq.

(2) PAYMENT OF DEBTS PRESENTLY DUE

(i) Solvent Estates

966. Duty to pay debts. Apart from any provisions contained in the will of a testator which expressly or impliedly deal with the payment of debts, it is the duty of the personal representatives[1], as a matter of the due administration of a solvent[2] estate, to pay their testator's debts, including unpaid income tax[3], capital gains tax[4], and inheritance tax[5], with due diligence having regard to the assets in their hands properly applicable for that purpose.

In determining whether due diligence has been shown regard must be had to all the circumstances of the case[6]. This duty is owed not only to creditors but also to beneficiaries, whether or not the debt bears interest[7]. There is no rule of law that the debts must be paid within a year from the testator's death, but due diligence must be shown, and if debts are not paid within the year the onus is thrown on the personal representatives to justify the delay[8].

1 As to the meaning of 'personal representative' see PARA 608.

2 As to insolvent estates see PARA 981. It seems that where there is serious doubt about the solvency of the estate administration should proceed on the basis of insolvency: cf *George Lee & Sons (Builders) Ltd v Olink* [1972] 1 All ER 359, [1972] 1 WLR 214, CA.

3 As to the liability of personal representatives for unpaid income tax see the Taxes Management Act 1970 s 74; and INCOME TAXATION vol 59 (2014) PARA 1763. As to the effect of a trust to pay debts see PARA 980.

4 No chargeable gain arises on death: see the Taxation of Chargeable Gains Act 1992 s 62(1); and CAPITAL GAINS TAXATION vol 6 (2011) PARA 699. The personal representatives are, however, liable for capital gains tax incurred before death where the liability has not been settled by the deceased before his death.

5 See the Inheritance Tax Act 1984 s 200; and INHERITANCE TAXATION vol 59A (2014) PARA 256. As to the duty to submit to Her Majesty's Revenue and Customs an affidavit or account see PARA 731. As to the personal representatives' liabilities for inheritance tax see PARAS 1217, 1255.

6 *Re Tankard, Tankard v Midland Bank Executor and Trustee Co Ltd* [1942] Ch 69 at 72, [1941] 3 All ER 458 at 463 per Uthwatt J.

7 *Re Tankard, Tankard v Midland Bank Executor and Trustee Co Ltd* [1942] Ch 69 at 72, [1941] 3 All ER 458 at 463 per Uthwatt J. See also *Hall v Hallet* (1784) 1 Cox Eq Cas 134.

8 *Re Tankard, Tankard v Midland Bank Executor and Trustee Co Ltd* [1942] Ch 69 at 74, [1941] 3 All ER 458 at 464 per Uthwatt J, explaining and approving *Grayburn v Clarkson* (1868) 3 Ch App 605. As to the executor's year see PARA 961.

967. Debt payable in foreign currency. An English court may give judgment for a sum of money expressed in foreign currency or the sterling equivalent at some determinable[1] date where there is a contractual obligation to pay in foreign currency under a contract the proper law of which is that of a foreign country or of England[2] and where the money of account and payment is that of that country or possibly of some other country but not of the United Kingdom[3]. The date of any conversion into sterling is in general the date of payment or enforcement[4]. For the purpose of proving a debt in a liquidation or administration the amount in question is to be converted into sterling at the rate prevailing on the date of the order for the winding up or administration of the company[5]. Where a person dies leaving assets which are insufficient to meet their liabilities, the date of death of the debtor is the date at which foreign currency debts are converted into sterling[6].

1 See the text to notes 4–5.

2 *Barclays Bank International Ltd v Levin Bros (Bradford) Ltd* [1977] QB 270, [1976] 3 All ER 900.

3 *Miliangos v George Frank (Textiles) Ltd* [1975] 3 All ER 801 at 813, [1975] 3 WLR 758 at 771, HL, per Lord Wilberforce. See further FINANCIAL INSTRUMENTS AND TRANSACTIONS vol 49 (2015) PARA 28.

4 *Miliangos v George Frank (Textiles) Ltd* [1975] 3 All ER 801 at 814, [1975] 3 WLR 758 at 772, HL, per Lord Wilberforce, at 838 and 799 per Lord Cross of Chelsea, and at 841 and 802 per Lord Fraser of Tullybelton.

5 See the Insolvency Rules 1986, SI 1986/1925, r 2.86(1), r 4.91; and COMPANY AND PARTNERSHIP INSOLVENCY vol 16 (2011) PARA 284. But see *Re Lehman Bros International (Europe) (in administration) (No 4)* [2015] EWCA Civ 485, [2016] Ch 50 where the Court of Appeal held (Lewison J dissenting) that the conversion was for the purposes of proof only and did not prevent creditors claiming against that company for any currency losses suffered as a result of a decline in the value of sterling between the date of the commencement of the administration and the date or dates of payment. See also *Re Dynamics Corporation of America* [1976] 2 All ER 669, [1976] 1 WLR 757; *Re Lines Bros Ltd* [1983] Ch 1, [1982] 2 All ER 183, [1982] 2 WLR 1010, CA.

6 See the Insolvency Act 1986 s 382, the Insolvency Rules 1986, SI 1986/1925, r 6.111; and BANKRUPTCY AND INDIVIDUAL INSOLVENCY vol 5 (2013) PARAS 508, 557. David Richards J explained in *Re Estate of Platon Elenin (aka Boris Abramovich Berezovsky), Lockston Group Inc v Wood* [2015] EWHC 2962 (Ch), [2016] 1 WLR 2091, [2016] BPIR 94, [2015] All ER (D) 231 (Oct) that there had to be a single date for the ascertainment of liabilities and the effect of the provisions was that the date of death was to be taken for quantification and identification of debts, conversion into sterling of debts denominated in foreign currencies; interest on interest-bearing debts was provable up to but not after that date and interest after that date was payable on all proved debts out of any surplus.

968. Foreign assets; equality of payment. In the administration of assets in England a creditor of whatever nationality is entitled to be paid equally with English creditors in the same class[1], although in a case in which the foreign assets were distributed so as to give the foreign creditors, as such, priority, the court would, in distributing the English assets, be astute to equalise the payments, and take care that no foreign creditor should come in and receive anything until the English creditors had been paid a proportionate amount[2]. Where there are creditors whose claims are statute barred by English law but still enforceable according to the law of the deceased's domicile the English court may, in the exercise of its discretion, refuse to order the payment of any balance left after the discharge of debts enforceable in England to the administrator in the country of the domicile, and may itself undertake the distribution of the balance to the persons beneficially entitled[3].

1 *Re Kloebe, Kannreuther v Geiselbrecht* (1884) 28 ChD 175 (reviewing *Cook v Gregson* (1854) 2 Drew 286); *Eames v Hacon* (1881) 18 ChD 347, CA; *Blackwood v R* (1882) 8 App Cas 82, PC.
2 *Re Kloebe, Kannreuther v Geiselbrecht* (1884) 28 ChD 175 at 177.
3 *Re Lorillard, Griffiths v Catforth* [1922] 2 Ch 638, CA.

969. Assets properly applicable for payment of debts. A deceased[1] person's legal and equitable[2] real and personal estate[3], to the extent of his beneficial interest in it, and the real and personal estate of which he disposes by will[4] in pursuance of any general power (including the statutory power to dispose of entailed interests[5]), are assets for payment of his debts (whether by specialty or simple contract) and liabilities[6]. Any disposition[7] by will inconsistent with this rule is void as against the creditors, and the court must, if necessary, administer the property for the purpose of the payment of the debts and liabilities; but this rule takes effect without prejudice to the rights of incumbrancers[8]. If a creditor desires administration of the estate by the court it is not necessary for him to sue on behalf of other creditors as well as on his own behalf[9].

The testator cannot by his will create a charge as against his general creditors upon the fund in favour of a particular creditor[10], although he may have contracted to do so.

1 This applies to persons dying after 1925.
2 'Legal estates' mean the estates charges and interests in or over land (subsisting or created at law) which are by statute authorised to subsist or to be created at law; and 'equitable interests' mean all other interests and charges in or over land: Administration of Estates Act 1925 s 55(1)(vii) (definition amended by the Trusts of Land and Appointment of Trustees Act 1996 s 25(2), Sch 4). For practical purposes legal estates may be considered to consist of the fee simple, the term of years absolute and perpetual rentcharges.
3 As to the meaning of 'real estate' see PARA 607 note 1.
4 As to the meaning of 'will' see PARA 607 note 1.
5 See PARA 954 note 1.
6 Administration of Estates Act 1925 s 32(1). As to the liability for debts of property forming the subject of a donatio mortis causa see eg *Tate v Leithead* (1854) Kay 658 at 659; and GIFTS vol 52 (2014) PARA 271 et seq. As to the availability of the deceased's severable share of a joint tenancy see PARA 988 note 6.
7 'Disposition' includes a conveyance and also a devise, bequest and an appointment of property contained in a will, and 'dispose of' has a corresponding meaning: Administration of Estates Act 1925 s 55(1)(iii). As to the meaning of 'conveyance' see PARA 858 note 1.
8 Administration of Estates Act 1925 s 32(1).
9 *Re James, James v Jones* [1911] 2 Ch 348.
10 *Beyfus v Lawley* [1903] AC 411, HL.

970. Creditor's statutory rights against beneficiary. In addition to the right considered above[1] the creditor has certain statutory rights against a beneficiary of his debtor's real or personal estate.

If any person to whom any beneficial interest in the real or personal estate[2] devolves or is given, or in whom any such interest vests, disposes of it in good faith before a claim is brought or process is sued out against him, he is personally liable for the value of the interest so disposed of by him, but the interest is not liable to be taken in execution in the action or under the process[3]. Accordingly, the property cannot be followed[4] into the hands of a purchaser just because he has notice of a debt, and he is not bound to see that his purchase money is applied in payment thereof[5]. However, an assent, or conveyance[6] by a personal representative[7] to a person other than a purchaser[8] does not prejudice the rights of any person to follow the property to which the assent or conveyance relates, or any property representing it, into the hands of the person in whom it is vested by the assent or conveyance, or of any other person, not being a purchaser, who may have received it or in whom it may be vested[9].

Notwithstanding any such assent or conveyance the court[10] may, on the application of any creditor or other person interested[11]:

(1) order a sale, exchange, mortgage, charge, lease, payment, transfer or other transaction to be carried out which the court considers requisite for the purpose of giving effect to the rights of the persons interested[12];

(2) declare that the person, not being such a purchaser as is mentioned above, in whom the property is vested is a trustee for those purposes[13];

(3) give directions respecting the preparation and execution of any conveyance or other instrument or as to any other matter required for giving effect to the order[14]; or

(4) make any vesting order, or appoint a person to convey in accordance with the statutory provisions[15] to that effect[16].

1 See PARA 969.
2 As to the meaning of 'real estate' see PARA 607 note 1.
3 Administration of Estates Act 1925 s 32(2).
4 As to following property see PARA 1095 et seq.
5 *Jones v Noyes and Allen* (1858) 28 LJ Ch 47.
6 As to the meaning of 'conveyance' see PARA 858 note 1. As to assents see PARA 1139 et seq.
7 As to the meaning of 'personal representative' see PARA 608.
8 As to the meaning of 'purchaser' see PARA 858 note 4.
9 Administration of Estates Act 1925 s 38(1). It has been held, under the Debts Recovery Act 1830 (repealed except as to deaths before 1926), that a conveyance in good faith for value by an equitable tenant for life protected the interest from creditors: see *Re Atkinson, Proctor v Atkinson* [1908] 2 Ch 307, CA, adopting dictum of Lord Chelmsford LC in *Coope v Cresswell* (1866) 2 Ch App 112 at 122, and applying *British Mutual Investment Co v Smart* (1875) 10 Ch App 567, and *Re Hedgely, Small v Hedgely* (1886) 34 ChD 379.
10 The County Court has jurisdiction where the estate does not exceed in amount or value the county court limit: Administration of Estates Act 1925 ss 38(4), 55(1)(iiiA) (both added by the County Courts Act 1984 s 148(1), Sch 2 Pt III paras 12, 15). As to the county court limit see PARA 866 note 2. Where the estate exceeds the limit the county court can be given jurisdiction by agreement: see the County Courts Act 1984 s 24(2)(d); and COURTS AND TRIBUNALS vol 24 (2010) PARA 767.
11 Administration of Estates Act 1925 s 38(2). Section 38 does not prejudice the rights of a purchaser or person deriving title under him, and applies whether the testator or intestate died before or after 1 January 1926: s 38(3). See also *Re Illidge, Davidsons v Illidge* (1884) 27 ChD 478 at 482, CA, per Cotton LJ; *Worthington & Co Ltd v Abbott* [1910] 1 Ch 588.
12 Administration of Estates Act 1925 s 38(2)(a).
13 Administration of Estates Act 1925 s 38(2)(b).
14 Administration of Estates Act 1925 s 38(2)(c).
15 Ie under the Trustee Act 1925 ss 44–56 (see TRUSTS AND POWERS vol 98 (2013) PARA 315 et seq): see the Administration of Estates Act 1925 s 38(2)(d).
16 Administration of Estates Act 1925 s 38(2)(d).

971. Effect of registration of administration action. The registration by the creditor as a pending action[1] of an action for administration sufficiently indicating the real estate sought to be charged is sufficient, before final judgment, to entitle the creditor to priority over a purchaser or mortgagee from any defendant entitled to real estate under the will, except where the defendant is in such a position that the purchaser or mortgagee has a right to suppose that he is selling or mortgaging for the purpose of paying the testator's debts[2].

1 As to the registration of pending actions see the Land Charges Act 1972 s 5; the Land Registration Act 2002 s 87; and REAL PROPERTY AND REGISTRATION vol 87 (2012) PARAS 537–538.
2 *Price v Price* (1887) 35 ChD 297.

972. Effect of registration of judgment. A judgment entered up against the devisee or person entitled on intestacy of the deceased for the devisee's or successor's personal debts does not defeat the rights of the deceased's creditors against the land devised or descended[1], and the devisee or successor takes no beneficial interest in it except subject to and after payment of the deceased's debts[2].

1 *Kinderley v Jervis* (1856) 22 Beav 1.
2 *Kinderley v Jervis* (1856) 22 Beav 1. See also the Administration of Estates Act 1925 s 32(1) (see PARA 969), s 33(2) (see PARA 1135).

973. Statutory preferences. There are certain statutory preferences which extend to all the assets, and have priority over all other debts. The preference of these claims is not affected by the fact that the estate may be in course of administration under the bankruptcy laws[1].

The personal representatives[2] of an officer of a registered friendly society or branch, having in his possession by virtue of his office[3] any money or property belonging to the society or branch, must, on his death, upon demand, pay the money and deliver over the property to the trustees of the society or branch in preference to any other debt or claim against the estate[4]. It is immaterial that the money of the society cannot be specifically traced[5].

Where a voluntary arrangement[6] has been succeeded by the bankruptcy of the debtor on the petition of the supervisor or a person bound by the voluntary arrangement, any expenses properly incurred as expenses of the administration of the voluntary arrangement are a first charge on the debtor's estate[7].

1 See the Insolvency Act 1986 s 328(2); and BANKRUPTCY AND INDIVIDUAL INSOLVENCY vol 5 (2013) PARA 591. It is not clear whether these categories of debt have preference over the funeral and testamentary expenses; these are now only given express preference over the preferential debts set out in s 386, Sch 6 (see BANKRUPTCY AND INDIVIDUAL INSOLVENCY vol 5 (2013) PARA 591 et seq): see PARA 981.
2 As to the meaning of 'personal representative' see PARA 608.
3 To ensure preference, the receipt must have been strictly by virtue of his office: *Re Jardine, ex p Fleet* (1850) 4 De G & Sm 52; *Re Aberdein* (1896) 13 TLR 7. The preference applies even though the deceased had ceased to be an officer of the society or branch before the date of his death: *Re Eilbeck, ex p Good Intent Lodge No 987 of the Grand United Order of Oddfellows Trustees* [1910] 1 KB 136.
4 See the Friendly Societies Act 1974 s 59(1)(a), (2); and FINANCIAL INSTITUTIONS vol 48 (2015) PARA 648.
5 *Moors v Marriott* (1878) 7 ChD 543; *Re Atkins, ex p Edmonds* (1882) 46 LT 240; *Re Miller, ex p Official Receiver* [1893] 1 QB 327.
6 As to voluntary arrangements see BANKRUPTCY AND INDIVIDUAL INSOLVENCY vol 5 (2013) PARA 43 et seq.
7 See the Insolvency Act 1986 s 276(2); and BANKRUPTCY AND INDIVIDUAL INSOLVENCY vol 5 (2013) PARA 589.

974. Statute-barred debts. A personal representative has a right to pay a debt barred by statute[1], but he may not pay such a debt after it has been judicially declared by a court of competent jurisdiction to be so barred[2], or if the estate is insolvent[3].

After an order has been made for the administration of the estate, any creditor or legatee has the right to set up the statute, notwithstanding the representative's refusal to do so, against a creditor who comes in under the order to prove his debt[4], but not against the claimant in a creditor's administration claim[5].

Where none of the parties wishes to set up the statute, the court will not set it up on behalf of an absent beneficiary[6]. Where a claim form has been issued by the executors for the determination, without administration of the estate, of the question whether a defendant is a creditor[7], the parties must be treated as standing in the same position as if an administration order had been made, and the residuary legatee is accordingly entitled to insist upon the statute being set up[8].

The right of one of several representatives to pay a statute-barred debt against the wishes of his co-representatives has never been judicially determined[9].

1 Ie barred by the Limitation Act 1980: see LIMITATION PERIODS vol 68 (2016) PARA 901 et seq. See *Stahlschmidt v Lett* (1853) 1 Sm & G 415; *Hill v Walker* (1858) 4 K & J 166, disapproving of a dictum of Bayley J in *M'Culloch v Dawes* (1826) 9 Dow & Ry KB 40 at 43; and cf *Re Carey, Carey v Carey* (1915) 49 ILT 226. As to the meaning of 'personal representative' see PARA 608.
2 *Re Midgley, Midgley v Midgley* [1893] 3 Ch 282, CA.
3 Statute-barred debts are not provable in an insolvency (see BANKRUPTCY AND INDIVIDUAL INSOLVENCY vol 5 (2013) PARA 518), and the insolvency rules apply to the administration of an insolvent estate: see PARA 981.
4 *Shewen v Vanderhorst* (1831) 1 Russ & M 347; *Moodie v Bannister* (1859) 4 Drew 432.
5 See *Briggs v Wilson* (1854) 5 De GM & G 12; *Fuller v Redman (No 2)* (1859) 26 Beav 614.
6 *Re Alston, Alston v Trollope* (1866) LR 2 Eq 205.
7 Ie under CPR 64.2(a) (see CIVIL PROCEDURE vol 11 (2015) PARA 188).
8 *Re Wenham, Hunt v Wenham* [1892] 3 Ch 59. See also *Re Turner, Klaftenberger v Groombridge* [1917] 1 Ch 422.
9 See *Re Midgley, Midgley v Midgley* [1893] 3 Ch 282 at 297, CA, where Lindley LJ expressed his opinion that it was the law that a representative might pay such a debt with knowledge that his co-representative objected to the payment; the point was, however, left open at 301 per Lopes LJ. See also *Astbury v Astbury* [1898] 2 Ch 111 at 115 per Stirling J. As to joint representation see PARA 926.

975. Debts barred by the Statute of Frauds. The right to pay a debt barred by the Limitation Act 1980[1] is an exception to the general rule that it is a devastavit for a personal representative to pay that which need not be paid, and is not to be extended to a debt to which the Statute of Frauds[2] affords a good defence[3].

1 See PARA 974; and LIMITATION PERIODS vol 68 (2016) PARA 901 et seq.
2 Ie the Statute of Frauds (1677) s 4 (see FINANCIAL INSTRUMENTS AND TRANSACTIONS vol 49 (2015) PARA 677), which renders certain contracts unenforceable unless evidenced by a memorandum in writing. Section 4 has been in part repealed by the Law Reform (Enforcement of Contracts) Act 1954, and now applies only to a promise to answer for the debt, default or miscarriage of another. As to what constitutes such a promise see FINANCIAL INSTRUMENTS AND TRANSACTIONS vol 49 (2015) PARA 677. As to the disapplication of the Statute of Frauds (1677) s 4 in relation to financial collateral arrangements see the Financial Collateral Arrangements (No 2) Regulations 2003, SI 2003/3226, reg 4(1).
3 *Re Rownson, Field v White* (1885) 29 ChD 358, CA. In this case *Re Garratt's Trust* (1870) 18 WR 684, to the contrary effect, was not cited. As to liability on a devastavit see PARA 1244 et seq.

976. Acknowledgment of debts. The inclusion of a debt by the personal representative in the account for probate is not a sufficient acknowledgment to take the debt out of the operation of the Limitation Act 1980[1].

Where a partner is executor of his late partner and makes payments of principal or interest on account of a partnership debt, these payments will, in the absence of proof to the contrary, be taken to have no reference to his executorial character, and will not keep the debt alive against his testator's estate[2].

If a claim is brought by the creditor against two representatives, and one admits the debt while the other pleads the statute, the court accepts the latter's plea as being most for the benefit of the estate[3]. An acknowledgment by one of several personal representatives of any claim to the personal estate of a deceased person or to any share or interest in it binds the estate of the deceased person[4]. An acknowledgment of a debt by a person binds successors but not any other person[5].

1 See *Re Beavan, Davies, Banks & Co v Beavan* [1912] 1 Ch 196 (followed in *Lloyd v Coote and Ball* [1915] 1 KB 242; *Bowring-Hanbury's Trustee v Bowring-Hanbury* [1943] Ch 104, [1943] 1 All ER 48, CA), not following *Smith v Poole* (1841) 12 Sim 17 (inclusion in an inventory exhibited in the probate court held to be sufficient acknowledgment), and questioning *Re Emmett,*

Jenkins v Emmett (1906) 95 LT 755 (inclusion in Inland Revenue affidavit held to be sufficient acknowledgment). In *Spollan v Magan* (1851) 1 ICLR 691 at 700, inclusion in an account filed in administration proceedings in Chancery was held to be sufficient acknowledgment; and see *Read v Price* [1909] 1 KB 577; affd [1909] 2 KB 724, CA. For formal provisions as to acknowledgments see the Limitation Act 1980 s 30; and LIMITATION PERIODS vol 68 (2016) PARA 1183.

2 *Thompson v Waithman* (1856) 3 Drew 628; *Brown v Gordon* (1852) 16 Beav 302; *Re Tucker, Tucker v Tucker* [1894] 3 Ch 429, CA.

3 *Chaffe v Kelland* (1637) 1 Roll Abr 929; *Re Midgley, Midgley v Midgley* [1893] 3 Ch 282 at 302, CA, per Lopes LJ.

4 See the Limitation Act 1980 s 31(8); and LIMITATION PERIODS vol 68 (2016) PARA 1213. For the earlier case law see *Atkins v Tredgold* (1823) 2 B & C 23; *M'Culloch v Dawes* (1826) 9 Dow & Ry KB 40; *Tullock v Dunn* (1826) Ry & M 416; *Scholey v Walton* (1844) 12 M & W 510; *Re Macdonald, Dick v Fraser* [1897] 2 Ch 181. As to joint representation see also PARA 926.

5 See the Limitation Act 1980 s 31(6). A 'successor' includes a personal representative (see s 31(9)) but not a surety (see *UCB Corporate Services Ltd v Kohli* [2004] EWHC 1126 (Ch), [2004] 2 All ER (Comm) 422, [2004] All ER (D) 205 (May)). See also LIMITATION PERIODS vol 68 (2016) PARA 1211. As to the meaning of 'personal representative' see PARA 608.

977. Effect of part payment of debt. Part payment of principal or interest differs in effect from an acknowledgment or promise, as such payment enures to the benefit of all persons liable to the debt, while the effect of an acknowledgment is confined to the person who makes it[1].

At common law a personal representative[2] does not either by his acknowledgment or promise to pay or by part payment of principal or interest render his co-representative personally chargeable with the debt; and the latter will not be liable for a devastavit if, without knowledge of the debt having been kept alive, he pays away the assets[3]; but by statute an acknowledgment or payment by one of several personal representatives in respect of any claim to the personal estate of a deceased person binds the estate[4].

1 *Coope v Cresswell* (1866) 2 Ch App 112 at 124 per Lord Chelmsford LC. See also *UCB Corporate Services Ltd v Kohli* [2004] EWHC 1126 (Ch), [2004] 2 All ER (Comm) 422, [2004] All ER (D) 205 (May). As to acknowledgment see PARA 976.

2 As to the meaning of 'personal representative' see PARA 608.

3 *Re Macdonald, Dick v Fraser* [1897] 2 Ch 181 at 188 per Stirling J; *Re Hollingshead, Hollingshead v Webster* (1888) 37 ChD 651 at 658 per Chitty J. As to liability on a devastavit see PARA 1244 et seq.

4 See the Limitation Act 1980 s 31(8); and LIMITATION PERIODS vol 68 (2016) PARA 1213.

978. When time runs against a creditor. Time runs against a creditor whose cause of action accrued during the life of the deceased debtor, even though administration to the estate has not been taken out, and there has been no personal representative who can be sued[1]. As there can be no complete cause of action, however, until there is somebody who can be sued[2], time does not begin to run against a creditor whose debt becomes due after the debtor's death until administration has been taken out to his estate[3], or until the executor before obtaining probate, has so meddled with the estate as to render himself liable to be sued for the debts owing by the estate[4].

1 *Boatwright v Boatwright* (1873) LR 17 Eq 71. An acknowledgment by the deceased may bind persons other than his personal representatives: see the Limitation Act 1980 s 31; and LIMITATION PERIODS vol 68 (2016) PARA 1207 et seq. As to the meaning of 'personal representative' see PARA 608.

2 *Douglas v Forrest* (1828) 4 Bing 686 at 704 per Best CJ.

3 See *Jolliffe v Pitt* (1715) 2 Vern 694.

4 See *Webster v Webster* (1804) 10 Ves 93; *Flood v Patterson* (1861) 29 Beav 295. As to the right to sue an executor who has acted before obtaining probate see *Re Lovett, Ambler v Lindsay* (1876) 3 ChD 198. As to a claim based on a devastavit see PARA 1244 et seq.

979. Charge for payment of debts. Before 1926 a charge by a testator of debts upon his personal estate did not affect the running of time[1], but a charge by a testator of debts upon realty, or a blended fund of real and personal estate, enlarged the period of limitation to 12 years where the testator had left real estate[2]. Since 1925 personal and real estate are equally applicable for payment of debts[3] and since 1939 there has been a 12 year limitation period for debts charged on personalty as well as ones charged on realty[4].

1 This was because the charge was nugatory, the debts being payable out of personalty anyway: *Scott v Jones* (1838) 4 Cl & Fin 382, HL. See also *Re Hepburn, ex p Smith* (1884) 14 QBD 394.

2 *Re Stephens, Warburton v Stephens* (1889) 43 ChD 39; *Re Raggi, Brass v H Young & Co Ltd* [1913] 2 Ch 206.

3 See PARAS 969, 998. Accordingly it could be argued that where a charge of debts on realty or a mixed fund makes no difference to the order of applications of assets to pay debts, the limitation period may be unaffected (see notes 1–2). The Land Transfer Act 1897 made real estate subject to the payment of debts, but it was held that an express charge of debts on real estate by a testator dying after it came into force still extended the limitation period: *Re Balls, Trewby v Balls* [1909] 1 Ch 791. See also LIMITATION PERIODS vol 68 (2016) PARA 1103 et seq. The Administration of Estates Act 1925 s 32 (see PARA 969) in providing that the real and personal estate of a deceased person are assets for the payment of debts does not impose a charge: see *Re Moon, Holmes v Holmes* [1907] 2 Ch 304; *Re Welch, Mitchell v Willders* [1916] 1 Ch 375.

4 See the Limitation Act 1980 s 20(1) (see LIMITATION PERIODS vol 68 (2016) PARA 1103), which applies to money charged on pure personalty as well as money charged on realty.

980. Trust for payment of debts. If a testator creates an express trust for payment of his debts the creditors, as beneficiaries, may be in a more advantageous position than mere creditors[1].

If there is a devise in trust for payment of debts generally, this does not revive a debt which had become barred before the testator's death[2].

1 See the Limitation Act 1980 s 21, under which the limitation period is only six years; but no period applies in the case of any fraud or fraudulent breach of trust to which the trustee was a party or privy or to the recovery of trust property from the trustee: see LIMITATION PERIODS vol 68 (2016) PARA 1139. It seems that the words imposing the trust might also create a charge within s 20(1): see PARA 979; and LIMITATION PERIODS vol 68 (2016) PARA 1103.

2 *Burke v Jones* (1813) 2 Ves & B 275.

(ii) Insolvent Estates

981. Application of bankruptcy rules. If the estate of a deceased person is insolvent, and being administered otherwise than in bankruptcy[1], then, subject to the payment of reasonable funeral[2], testamentary and administration expenses[3], which have priority over the preferential debts[4], and payment of the statutory preferences[5], the same provisions[6] as may be in force for the time being under the law of bankruptcy with respect to the assets of individuals made bankrupt apply to the administration of the estate with respect to the respective rights of secured and unsecured creditors[7], to debts and liabilities provable[8], to the valuation of future and contingent liabilities[9], and to the priorities[10] of debts and other payments[11].

Certain specified provisions of the Insolvency Act 1986[12] apply, with modifications[13], to the insolvent estates of deceased persons dying before the making of a bankruptcy application or presentation of a bankruptcy petition[14].

If a debtor dies after making a bankruptcy application, the proceedings will continue as if the deceased debtor were alive[15]. If a debtor against whom a bankruptcy petition has been presented dies, the proceedings in the matter, unless the court otherwise orders, continue as if he were alive[16]. The reasonable funeral and testamentary expenses have priority over the preferential debts[17]. If a debtor dies after presentation of a bankruptcy petition but before service, the court may order service to be effected on his personal representatives or such other person as it thinks fit[18].

1 As to the administration in bankruptcy of the insolvent estate of a deceased person under an insolvency administration order see the Insolvency Act 1986 s 421; the Administration of Insolvent Estates of Deceased Persons Order 1986, SI 1986/1999; and BANKRUPTCY AND INDIVIDUAL INSOLVENCY vol 5 (2013) PARA 830 et seq. For the purposes of Insolvency Act 1986 s 421, the estate of a deceased person is insolvent if, when realised, it will be insufficient to meet in full all the debts and other liabilities to which it is subject: see s 421(4).

2 As to funeral expenses see CREMATION AND BURIAL vol 24 (2010) PARA 1137.

3 As to testamentary and administration expenses see PARA 1013 et seq. See also note 4.

4 Ie the preferential debts listed in the Insolvency Act 1986 s 386, Sch 6 (see BANKRUPTCY AND INDIVIDUAL INSOLVENCY vol 5 (2013) PARA 591 et seq): see the Administration of Insolvent Estates of Deceased Persons Order 1986, SI 1986/1999, art 4(2). Where the petition is presented after the debtor's death, in the exercise of his functions under the Insolvency Act 1986 s 305 (see BANKRUPTCY AND INDIVIDUAL INSOLVENCY vol 5 (2013) PARA 473) where an insolvency administration order has been made, the trustee must have regard to any claim by the personal representative to payment of reasonable funeral, testamentary and administration expenses incurred by him in respect of the deceased debtor's estate or, if there is no such personal representative, to any claim by any other person to payment of any such expenses incurred by him in respect of the estate provided that the trustee has sufficient funds in hand for the purpose, and such claims have priority over the preferential debts listed in Sch 6: s 305(5) (added as a modification to s 305 by SI 1986/1999); art 3(1), Sch 1 Pt II para 20. As regards payment of professional charges, remuneration to which a personal representative is entitled under the Trustee Act 2000 s 28 (statutory power: see TRUSTS AND POWERS vol 98 (2013) PARA 371) or s 29 (express power: see TRUSTS AND POWERS vol 98 (2013) PARA 372) is now treated as an administration expense for the purposes of:

(1) the Administration of Estates Act 1925 s 34(3) (order in which estate to be paid out: see PARA 998 et seq) (Trustee Act 2000 s 35(3)(a)); and

(2) any provision giving reasonable administration expenses priority over the preferential debts listed in the Insolvency Act 1986 Sch 6 (Trustee Act 2000 s 35(3)(b)).

Where an insolvency administration order is made, any payments made by the personal representatives between the date of death and the making of the order are void unless ratified by the court: see the Insolvency Act 1986 s 284 (as modified by SI 1986/1999); and *Re Vos, Dick v Kendall Freeman* [2006] BPIR 348, [2005] WTLR 1619. See also Tolley's Administration of Estates at G6.1.

5 See PARA 973.

6 These apply to all classes of administration of insolvent estates, whether in or out of court: *A-G v Jackson* [1932] AC 365 at 484, HL.

7 For the rules as to secured and unsecured creditors see BANKRUPTCY AND INDIVIDUAL INSOLVENCY vol 5 (2013) PARAS 538, 574 et seq. See also PARA 987.

8 For the rules as to debts and liabilities provable see BANKRUPTCY AND INDIVIDUAL INSOLVENCY vol 5 (2013) PARA 507 et seq. As to the interpretation of 'provable' in relation to an insolvent estate see *Berry v Child Support Agency* [2016] EWHC 1418 (Ch) at [148] per Judge McCahill QC: the reference to provable debts and liabilities had to be read as referring to the system of submitting proofs and not to the distinction between provable and non-provable debts which exists in the case of the bankruptcy of a living person.

In the event of the insolvency of an estate against which proceedings are maintainable by virtue of the Law Reform (Miscellaneous Provisions) Act 1934 s 1 (see PARA 1278 et seq), any liability in respect of the cause of action in respect of which the proceedings are maintainable is deemed to be a debt provable in the administration of the estate, notwithstanding that it is a demand in the nature of unliquidated damages arising otherwise than by a contract, promise or breach of trust: s 1(6).

9 For the rules as to the valuation of future and contingent liabilities see BANKRUPTCY AND INDIVIDUAL INSOLVENCY vol 5 (2013) PARAS 510, 519, 554, 560.

10 For the rules as to priority of debts see the Insolvency Act 1986 Sch 6; and BANKRUPTCY AND INDIVIDUAL INSOLVENCY vol 5 (2013) PARA 587 et seq. See also *Re Whitaker, Whitaker v Palmer* [1901] 1 Ch 9, CA (voluntary creditors to be paid pari passu with creditors for value).

11 Administration of Insolvent Estates of Deceased Persons Order 1986, SI 1986/1999, art 4(1), (2) (art 4(1) amended by SI 2016/481). See *Re Pink, Elvin v Nightingale* [1927] 1 Ch 237 at 241; *Re Bush, B Lipton Ltd v Mackintosh* [1930] 2 Ch 202 at 207–208; *A-G v Jackson* [1932] AC 365 at 384, HL (decided under the Administration of Estates Act 1925 s 34(1), Sch 1 Pt Ipara2 (repealed); which contained similar provisions to the Administration of Insolvent Estates of Deceased Persons Order 1986, SI 1986/1999). The relevant provisions of the Insolvency Act 1986 bind the Crown:

see s 434 (see BANKRUPTCY AND INDIVIDUAL INSOLVENCY vol 5 (2013) PARA 3); cf *A-G v Jackson; Re Mitchell, Hatton v Jones* [1954] Ch 525 at 529, [1954] 2 All ER 246 at 248. The requirement that a trustee in bankruptcy must be a qualified insolvency practitioner (see the Insolvency Act 1986 s 292(2); and BANKRUPTCY AND INDIVIDUAL INSOLVENCY vol 5 (2013) PARA 314) does not apply in relation to a personal representative who administers an insolvent estate otherwise than in bankruptcy: see the Administration of Insolvent Estates of Deceased Persons Order 1986, SI 1986/1999, art 4(3).

12 Ie the provisions of the Insolvency Act 1986 specified in the Administration of Insolvent Estates of Deceased Persons Order 1986, SI 1986/1999, art 3(1), Sch 1 Pts II, III: see art 3(1).

13 Ie as modified by the Administration of Insolvent Estates of Deceased Persons Order 1986, SI 1986/1999, Sch 1 Pts I, II and with any further such modifications as may be necessary to render them applicable to the estate of a deceased person: see art 3(1). There can be problems establishing how much of the insolvency code dealing with a living bankrupt is carried over into the case of an deceased insolvent person, where there has been no formal bankruptcy process: see *Berry v Child Support Agency* [2016] EWHC 1418 (Ch) at [143] per Judge McCahill QC.

14 Administration of Insolvent Estates of Deceased Persons Order 1986, SI 1986/1999, art 3(1) (amended by SI 2016/841). The provisions of the Insolvency Rules 1986, SI 1986/1925, and any order made under the Insolvency Act 1986 s 415 (fees and deposits) (see BANKRUPTCY AND INDIVIDUAL INSOLVENCY vol 5 (2013) PARA 825) also apply accordingly: see the Administration of Insolvent Estates of Deceased Persons Order 1986, SI 1986/1999, art 3(1). In the case of any conflict between any provision of the Insolvency Rules 1986, SI 1986/1925, and any provision of the Administration of Insolvent Estates of Deceased Persons Order 1986, SI 1986/1999, the provisions of the latter prevail: art 3(2).

15 Administration of Insolvent Estates of Deceased Persons Order 1986, SI 1986/1999, art 5(A1) (added by SI 2016/481). In such case the modifications specified in art 5(A1), Sch 2 apply: art 5(A1) (as so added).

16 Administration of Insolvent Estates of Deceased Persons Order 1986, SI 1986/1999, art 5(1) (amended by SI 2016/481). In such case the modifications specified in art 5(1), Sch 2 apply: art 5(1).

17 Administration of Insolvent Estates of Deceased Persons Order 1986, SI 1986/1999, art 5(2). The preferential debts are those listed in the Insolvency Act 1986 Sch 6: see the Administration of Insolvent Estates of Deceased Persons Order 1986, SI 1986/1999, art 5(2).

18 Administration of Insolvent Estates of Deceased Persons Order 1986, SI 1986/1999, art 5(3).

982. Cases of doubtful solvency. The rules referred to in the preceding paragraph also prevail where there is sufficient reason to believe that the estate will turn out insolvent[1], and to an estate which, though sufficient for payment in full of the deceased's debts and liabilities apart from the costs of administration, becomes insufficient by reason of those costs[2], and to an estate which, although otherwise solvent, is shown to be insolvent when the capitalised value of an annuity which the testator was under an obligation to pay is taken into account[3]. The court may direct an inquiry whether the estate is insolvent[4].

1 *Re Hopkins, Williams v Hopkins* (1881) 18 ChD 370 at 377, CA, per Jessel MR. Although the language of the Administration of Insolvent Estates of Deceased Persons Order 1986, SI 1986/1999, art 4(1) (see PARA 981) is not quite the same as that of the Supreme Court of Judicature Act 1875 s 10 (repealed) ('may prove to be' insolvent), the problem is the same, and it is a question of fact whether there is good ground for believing that the estate will turn out to be insolvent: *Re Pink, Elvin v Nightingale* [1927] 1 Ch 237 at 241. In *National Westminster Bank plc v Lucas; Re Estate of Jimmy Savile* [2014] EWHC 653 (Ch), [2014] BPIR 551, [2014] WTLR 637, because of claims made against the estate, there was a real risk the estate may prove insolvent. The bank's scheme designed to facilitate the speedy and inexpensive resolution of personal injury claims was approved and the application to remove the bank as executor was dismissed. See TRUSTS AND POWERS vol 98 (2013) PARA 340. See also PARA 981 note 11. As to the statutory protection of a personal representative who pays a debt in full when he had no reason to believe the estate was insolvent see PARA 983; as to protection against contingent liabilities see PARAS 990–991; and as to the risks and problems for personal representatives in cases of doubtful solvency see *Re Vos, Dick v Kendall Freeman* [2006] BPIR 348, [2005] WTLR 1619. See also Tolley's Administration of Estates at G6.1.

2 *Re Leng, Tarn v Emmerson* [1895] 1 Ch 652, CA.

3 *Re Pink, Elvin v Nightingale* [1927] 1 Ch 237.

4 *Re Smith, Green v Smith* (1883) 22 ChD 586. It is not the proper practice to insert in the administration order a direction that the bankruptcy rules are to apply: *Re Murray, Woods v*

Greenwell (1882) 45 LT 707, not following *Re Hildick, Hipkins v Hildick* (1881) 44 LT 547. As to administration in bankruptcy see BANKRUPTCY AND INDIVIDUAL INSOLVENCY vol 5 (2013) PARA 830 et seq.

983. Protection of personal representatives paying debts in full. A personal representative is not liable to account to a creditor of the same degree as a paid creditor on the insolvency of the estate[1], provided that either:

(1) the debt was paid to a creditor of the estate (including the personal representative himself so long as he has not obtained the grant solely by reason of his being a creditor) in good faith and at a time when he has no reason to believe that the estate is insolvent[2]; or

(2) being an administrator who has obtained the grant solely by reason of his being a creditor he has in good faith paid the debt of a creditor other than himself at a time when he has no reason to believe that the estate is insolvent[3].

1 Administration of Estates Act 1971 s 10(2). As to the meaning of 'personal representative' see PARA 608.

2 Administration of Estates Act 1971 s 10(2)(a).

3 Administration of Estates Act 1971 s 10(2)(b). These provisions were enacted in connection with the abolition (by s 10(1)) in relation to the estates of persons dying on or after 1 January 1972 (see ss 12(6), 14(2)) of the former right of a personal representative to retain out of the assets of the estate sufficient to meet a debt owing to himself as against creditors of equal or lower degree, and his former right to prefer creditors of the same class. For observations on the effect of the abolition see JHG Sunnucks 'Debts–Preference and Retainer' [1972] 122 NLJ 26.

984. Interest on debts. Where an insolvent estate subsequently realises sufficient to pay the principal of all the debts[1], the bankruptcy rule[2] as to pari passu payment of interest[3] upon all debts, whether by law carrying interest or not, applies.

1 See eg *Leeder v Ellis* [1953] AC 52, [1952] 2 All ER 814, PC.

2 See the Insolvency Act 1986 s 328(4), (5) (modified by SI 1986/1999); and BANKRUPTCY AND INDIVIDUAL INSOLVENCY vol 5 (2013) PARAS 591, 596.

3 In the case of an insolvent estate of a deceased person the interest is paid from the date of death of the deceased debtor at whichever is the greater of the rate specified in the Judgments Act 1838 s 17 at the date of death of the deceased debtor or the rate applicable to the debt apart from the bankruptcy: Insolvency Act 1986 s 328(4), (5) (modified by SI 1986/1999).

985. Time for proving debt. A creditor may come in at any time so long as there are assets remaining undistributed[1], provided he has not been guilty of wilful default in not sending in his claim previously[2]. He is, however, put upon the terms of paying the costs occasioned by his application, and is not allowed to disturb prior distributions or to delay the payment of dividends to the other creditors. A similar practice prevails in bankruptcy[3].

1 *Lashley v Hogg* (1805) 11 Ves 602; *Angell v Haddon* (1816) 1 Madd 529; *David v Frowd* (1833) 1 My & K 200 at 209; *Brown v Lake* (1847) 1 De G & Sm 144; *Brett v Carmichael* (1866) 35 Beav 340; *Re Metcalf, Hicks v May* (1879) 13 ChD 236, CA; *Harrison v Kirk* [1904] AC 1, HL.

2 *Hull v Falkoner* (1865) 5 New Rep 266.

3 *Re McMurdo, Penfield v McMurdo* [1902] 2 Ch 684 at 699, CA, per Vaughan Williams LJ. See also the Insolvency Act 1986 s 325 (rights of creditor who proves after one or more dividends have been declared), s 330(4) (effect of final dividend); the Insolvency Rules 1986, SI 1986/1925, r 11.8 (proof altered after payment of dividend); and BANKRUPTCY AND INDIVIDUAL INSOLVENCY vol 5 (2013) PARAS 609, 615.

986. Creditors who have disappeared. Where funds subsequently fall in, but some of the creditors whose proofs have been allowed have disappeared, the court does not divide the entire fund among the creditors who can be traced, but retains a sum to meet the claims of those who have disappeared[1].

1 *Re Macdonald, McAlpin v Macdonald* (1889) 59 LJ Ch 231; *Ashley v Ashley* (1877) 4 ChD 757, CA.

987. Secured creditors. A secured creditor[1] cannot prove for the whole of his debt and rely upon his security for any balance which, owing to the deficiency of assets, might remain unpaid. Under the insolvency rules the secured creditor who wishes to prove against the estate must do one of three things:

(1) he may realise his security and prove for the balance[2];

(2) he may surrender his security for the general benefit of creditors, and prove for his whole debt, as if it were unsecured[3]; or

(3) he may assess the value of his security and prove for the balance due to him after deducting the assessed value[4].

So long as there are assets remaining undistributed he may, however, with the agreement of the trustee in bankruptcy or the permission of the court[5] alter the value which he has put on his security in his proof[6], or prove for the first time after one or more dividends have been declared[7].

A secured creditor who chooses to rest upon his security without adopting any one of the above courses has no debt provable in respect of which any reserve is to be made on a declaration of a dividend[8]. A creditor of two estates for the same debt receives dividends on the whole of his debts from both estates until satisfied[9].

1 A creditor has a secured debt for the purpose of the insolvency rules to the extent that the he holds any security for the debt (whether a mortgage, charge, lien or other security) over any property of the debtor, other than a lien on books, papers or other records (except to the extent that they consist of documents of title to property and are held as such): see the Insolvency Act 1986 s 383(2), (4); and BANKRUPTCY AND INDIVIDUAL INSOLVENCY vol 5 (2013) PARA 574.
2 Insolvency Rules 1986, SI 1986/1925, r 6.109(1).
3 Insolvency Rules 1986, SI 1986/1925, r 6.109(2).
4 See the Insolvency Rules 1986, SI 1986/1925, rr 6.96, 6.98(1)(e) (as substituted by SI 2004/1070), Insolvency Rules 1986, SI 1986/1925, rr 6.115–6.118.
5 If he is the petitioner and it is a value he has put in the petition, or he has voted in respect of the unsecured balance, he can only revalue the security with the permission of the court: Insolvency Rules 1986, SI 1986/1925, r 6.115(2) (amended by SI 2010/686).
6 Insolvency Rules 1986, SI 1986/1925, r 6.115(1) (amended by SI 2010/686). If the revaluation increases the amount of the debt which is unsecured, it will not disturb dividends already declared but will entitle the creditor to payment of any missed dividends (if there are sufficient assets remaining) before any further dividends are paid: see r 11.9(3). The trustee in bankruptcy has a right to redeem a security at the value put on it in the creditor's proof, subject to the creditor having an opportunity to apply to revalue it (see r 6.117), and a right to require a sale of the security (see r 6.118). See further BANKRUPTCY AND INDIVIDUAL INSOLVENCY vol 5 (2013) PARA 574 et seq.
7 See the Insolvency Act 1986 s 325(1); and BANKRUPTCY AND INDIVIDUAL INSOLVENCY vol 5 (2013) PARA 609. Cf under the former law *Re McMurdo, Penfield v McMurdo* [1902] 2 Ch 684, CA; *Re Becher* [1944] Ch 78.
8 See *Re Lee, ex p Good* (1880) 14 ChD 82, CA.
9 *Bonser v Cox* (1842) 6 Beav 84.

988. Assets available for creditors on insolvency. In contrast to the previous law[1], where the insolvent estate of a deceased person is being administered in bankruptcy, the provisions of the bankruptcy legislation for setting aside transactions at an undervalue or preferences[2], rendering dispositions void[3], and restricting proceedings and the rights of creditors under execution or attachment[4], apply.

Whether or not such an estate is being administered in bankruptcy, an application can be made for an order nullifying the effect of a transaction defrauding creditors[5].

Where an insolvency administration order has been made in respect of the insolvent estate of a deceased person and the petition for the order was presented after 2 April 2001[6] and within the period of five years beginning with the day on which he died, and immediately before his death he was beneficially entitled to an interest in any property as joint tenant, then for the purpose of securing that debts and other liabilities to which the estate is subject are met, the court may, on an application by the trustee appointed pursuant to the insolvency administration order, make an order[7] requiring the survivor to pay to the trustee an amount not exceeding the value lost to the estate[8]. In determining whether to make such an order, and determining its terms, the court must have regard to all the circumstances of the case, including the interests of the deceased's creditors and of the survivor[9]; but, unless the circumstances are exceptional, the court must assume that the interests of the deceased's creditors outweigh all other considerations[10].

1 Ie before the Insolvency Act 1986 replaced the Bankruptcy Act 1914 with effect from 29 December 1986. See *Re Gould, ex p Official Receiver* (1887) 19 QBD 92, CA, which held that the bankruptcy provisions for setting aside voluntary settlements did not apply to the administration of insolvent estates of deceased persons in bankruptcy; *Re Eichholz, Eichholz's Trustee v Eichholz* [1959] Ch 708.

2 See the Insolvency Act 1986 ss 339–342 (applied to the insolvent estate of a deceased person by the Administration of Insolvent Estates of Deceased Persons Order 1986, SI 1986/1999, Sch 1 Pt II paras 26–28). The provisions for setting aside extortionate credit transactions (see the Insolvency Act 1986 s 343) and for the avoidance of general assignments of book debts unregistered under the Bills of Sale Act 1878 (see the Insolvency Act 1986 s 344) also apply: see the Administration of Insolvent Estates of Deceased Persons Order 1986, SI 1986/1999, Sch 1 Pt II para 28; and BANKRUPTCY AND INDIVIDUAL INSOLVENCY vol 5 (2013) PARAS 697–702.

3 See the Insolvency Act 1986 s 284 (applied to the insolvent estate of a deceased person by the Administration of Insolvent Estates of Deceased Persons Order 1986, SI 1986/1999, Sch 1 Pt II para 12) which renders void any disposition or payment made after the death of the debtor unless made with the consent of the court or subsequently ratified by it.

4 See the Insolvency Act 1986 s 285 (applied to the insolvent estate of a deceased person by the Administration of Insolvent Estates of Deceased Persons Order 1986, SI 1986/1999, Sch 1 Pt II para 12) which restrains obtaining any remedy or (except with the leave of the court) commencing any legal proceedings after the debtor's death. See also the Insolvency Act 1986 s 346 (restrictions on enforcement procedures after bankruptcy order) and s 347 (distress for rent) which apply after the making of an insolvency administration order by virtue of the Administration of Insolvent Estates of Deceased Persons Order 1986, SI 1986/1999, Sch 1 Pt II para 28. See BANKRUPTCY AND INDIVIDUAL INSOLVENCY vol 5 (2013) PARAS 703, 711 et seq, 752.

5 See the Insolvency Act 1986 ss 423–425; applied by the Administration of Insolvent Estates of Deceased Persons Order 1986, SI 1986/1999, Sch 1 Pt II para 36. If an insolvent administration order has been made only the official receiver or the trustee in bankruptcy can apply for an order under the Insolvency Act 1986 ss 423–425, but if no insolvent administration order has been made only a victim of the transaction can do so (see s 424). If such a transaction is set aside by a victim of the transaction the assets recovered fall into the estate: see ss 423(2)(a), 424(2), 425(1)(a); and *Richardson v Smallwood* (1822) Jac 552. See BANKRUPTCY AND INDIVIDUAL INSOLVENCY vol 5 (2013) PARA 688 et seq. An administration order can be made after a grant has been issued; it relates back to the date of death, making all payments made by the personal representatives void unless ratified by the court: see PARA 981 note 4.

6 See the Insolvency Act 2000 (Commencement No 1 and Transitional Provisions) Order 2001, SI 2001/766, art 2(1)(b).

7 Ie under the Insolvency Act 1986 s 421A: see note 8.

8 Insolvency Act 1986 s 421A(1), (2) (s 421A added by the Insolvency Act 2000 s 12(1)). 'Value lost to the estate' means the amount which, if paid to the trustee, would in the court's opinion restore the position to what it would have been if the deceased had been adjudged bankrupt immediately before his death: Insolvency Act 1986 s 421A(9) (as so added). Any sums required to be paid to the trustee in accordance with such an order are to be comprised in the estate: s 421A(5) (as so added).

In *Re Palmer (a debtor)* [1994] Ch 316, [1994] 3 All ER 835, CA, it was held that the severable share under a joint tenancy which the deceased owned was not available for his creditors although the position might be otherwise if bankruptcy proceedings were sufficiently far advanced before the debtor's death to sever the joint tenancy: see *Re Palmer (A Debtor)* at 341, 839 per Balcombe LJ. The effect of this decision was reversed by the introduction of the Insolvency Act 1986 s 421A to enable the trustee of a deceased insolvent to make application for the recovery of the value of the deceased's former interest in a joint tenancy from the survivor for the benefit of the estate: see the text and notes 6–7. As to the availability to pay the deceased's debts out of assets over which a general power has been exercised see PARA 969.

9 'Survivor' means the person who, immediately before the death, was beneficially entitled as joint tenant with the deceased or, if the person who was so entitled dies after the making of the insolvency administration order, his personal representatives: Insolvency Act 1986 s 421A(7) (as added: see note 8). If there is more than one survivor an order under s 421A may be made against all or any of them, but no survivor is required to pay more than so much of the value lost to the estate as is properly attributable to him: s 421A(8) (as so added). 'Insolvency administration order' has the same meaning as in any order under s 421 having effect for the time being (see BANKRUPTCY AND INDIVIDUAL INSOLVENCY vol 5 (2013) PARA 840): s 421A(9) (as so added).

10 Insolvency Act 1986 s 421A(3) (as added: see note 8). The order may be made on such terms and conditions as the court thinks fit: s 421A(4), (6) (as so added).

(3) DISCHARGE OF LIABILITIES NOT PRESENTLY DUE

989. Treatment of contingent liabilities where estate insolvent. Where the estate is insolvent, contingent liabilities are provided for in accordance with the rules applicable in bankruptcy[1]. Where the estate is solvent the personal representative is not entitled as against creditors to make provision for contingent liabilities because such liabilities do not constitute a debt until the contingency has arisen[2], and accordingly a creditor, even of inferior degree, is entitled to be paid in full without regard to the contingency that the liability may ripen into a debt[3].

A personal representative, however, can only distribute the assets among the beneficiaries without regard to contingent liabilities at his peril[4]. Accordingly, if the estate comprises shares in a joint stock company not fully paid up, and the executor pays a legacy, and a call is subsequently made upon the shares, the representative is liable to pay the amount of the legacy toward satisfaction of the call[5].

1 See PARA 981.

2 See *Re Hargreaves, Dicks v Hare* (1890) 44 ChD 236, CA. As to the meaning of 'personal representative' see PARA 608.

3 *Eeles v Lambert* (1648) 2 Vern 101n; *Read v Blunt* (1832) 5 Sim 567.

4 As to the protection of the personal representative by application to the court for permission to distribute see PARA 991. As to the lien of a personal representative or trustee over the estate or trust fund for liabilities which may be incurred under a statute not yet in force see *X v A* [2000] 1 All ER 490.

5 *Taylor v Taylor* (1870) LR 10 Eq 477. See also COMPANIES vol 15A (2016) PARA 1134. As to the personal representative's right to have the payment refunded by the legatee see PARA 1096.

990. Protection for personal representatives in regard to leaseholds, etc. Statutory protection is given to a personal representative or trustee[1] who as such:

(1) is liable for any rent, covenant or agreement reserved by or contained in any lease[2];

(2) is liable for any rent, covenant or agreement payable under or contained in any grant[3] made in consideration of a rentcharge[4];

(3) is liable for any indemnity given in respect of any such rent, covenant or agreement[5]; or

(4) has entered into or may be required to enter into an authorised guarantee agreement[6] with respect to any lease comprised in the deceased's estate or the trust estate[7].

In relation to the first three categories, the protection is available where the personal representative or trustee satisfies all liabilities under the lease or grant which may have accrued, and been claimed, up to the date of the conveyance or transfer of the property in question, and, where necessary, sets apart a sufficient fund to answer any future claim in respect of any fixed and ascertained sum which the lessee or grantee[8] agreed to lay out on the property demised or granted, even though the period for laying it out may not have arrived[9]; in any such case the personal representative or trustee may convey or transfer the property to a purchaser[10], legatee, devisee or other person entitled to call for a conveyance or transfer of it[11].

In relation to the fourth category, the statutory protection is available without more in the case of a potential liability to enter into an authorised guarantee agreement, and in the case of such an agreement already entered into it is available where the personal representative or trustee satisfies all liabilities under the agreement which may have accrued and been claimed up to the date of distribution[12]. Thereafter he may distribute the residuary real and personal estate of the deceased testator or intestate, or, as the case may be, the trust estate (other than the fund, if any, set apart to answer a future claim to a fixed and ascertained sum), to or among the persons entitled, without appropriating any part, or any further part, as the case may be, of the estate to meet any future liability under the lease or grant[13], or under any authorised guarantee agreement, or any potential liability to enter into any authorised guarantee agreement[14], and, notwithstanding such distribution, he will not be personally liable in respect of any subsequent claim under the lease or grant[15] or under any authorised guarantee agreement[16]. However, the right of the lessor or grantor or the persons deriving title under him to follow the assets or trust property into the hands of the persons among whom they have been distributed[17] is not prejudiced, and these provisions apply notwithstanding anything to the contrary in the will or other instrument, if any, creating the trust[18].

This statutory protection does not, however, extend to protect an executor who by entering into possession of his testator's leaseholds has incurred in addition to his liability as an executor the personal liability of an assignee of the term[19].

1 As to the liability under a lease of the personal representative of the original lessee see also PARA 1222. As to the meaning of 'personal representative' see PARA 608.
2 Trustee Act 1925 s 26(1)(a). 'Lease' includes an underlease and an agreement for a lease or underlease and any instrument giving any such indemnity as is mentioned in s 26(1) or varying the liabilities under the lease: s 26(3).
3 'Grant' applies to a grant whether the rent is created by limitation, grant, reservation or otherwise, and includes an agreement for a grant and any instrument giving any such indemnity as is mentioned in the Trustee Act 1925 s 26(1), or varying the liabilities under the grant: s 26(3).
4 Trustee Act 1925 s 26(1)(b).
5 Trustee Act 1925 s 26(1)(c).
6 'Authorised guarantee agreement' has the same meaning as in Landlord and Tenant (Covenants) Act 1995 (see LANDLORD AND TENANT vol 63 (2012) PARA 741): Trustee Act 1925 s 26(1A) (added by the Landlord and Tenant (Covenants) Act 1995 s 30(1), Sch 1 para 1). It can only relate to a lease granted after 31 December 1995: see LANDLORD AND TENANT vol 63 (2012) PARA 741.
7 Trustee Act 1925 s 26(1A) (as added: see note 6).
8 'Lessee' and 'grantee' include persons respectively deriving title under them: Trustee Act 1925 s 26(3).
9 Trustee Act 1925 s 26(1) (amended by the Law of Property (Amendment) Act 1926 ss 7, 8(2), Schedule).
10 In the Law of Property (Amendment) Act 1859 s 27 (repealed) (which these provisions replace), 'purchaser' meant a person who bought the lease and paid a price in money for it; it did not include

an assignee who was paid money for taking over the lease and indemnifying the executor: *Re Lawley, Jackson v Leighton* [1911] 2 Ch 530.
11 Trustee Act 1925 s 26(1) (as amended: see note 9).
12 Trustee Act 1925 s 26(1A) (as added: see note 6).
13 Trustee Act 1925 s 26(1)(i). See also *Millar v Sinclair* [1903] 1 IR 150.
14 Trustee Act 1925 s 26(1A)(a) (as added: see note 6).
15 Trustee Act 1925 s 26(1A)(ii).
16 Trustee Act 1925 s 26(1A)(b) (as added: see note 6).
17 See PARA 1105. As to the right to follow assets see PARA 1095 et seq.
18 Trustee Act 1925 s 26(2).
19 *Re Owers, Public Trustee v Death* [1941] Ch 389, [1941] 2 All ER 589. See also PARA 991.

991. Protection for personal representatives distributing estate under court order. Where the estate is subject to contingent liabilities not within the statutory protection[1] a personal representative[2] ought not to distribute the assets amongst the beneficiaries without the sanction of the court. Provided the personal representative keeps back nothing which ought to be disclosed to the court, the court order authorising distribution is a complete indemnity to him in respect of the consequent application of the assets[3], and it is therefore unnecessary for the court to retain funds in court for his protection[4], or, it is conceived, to direct the beneficiaries to indemnify him[5]. The court will, however, order the retention of sufficient sums in court where the contingent liability of the estate is dependent only on the survivorship of annuitants[6]. Where the personal representative, by remaining in possession of the deceased's leaseholds, renders himself liable to be sued in his personal character as assignee of the term[7], he is entitled to be secured against the lessor's claims by retention of assets or by a proper indemnity from the beneficiaries[8], unless he has already executed an assent in respect of those leaseholds[9].

Where a sum has been retained in court to meet a contingent debt it will be paid out to the beneficiaries on the expiration of the period after which the creditor's action would be statute-barred[10].

A contingent creditor of the estate may not be entitled to an order for administration[11].

1 See PARA 990.
2 As to the meaning of 'personal representative' see PARA 608.
3 *Dean v Allen* (1855) 20 Beav 1; *Waller v Barrett* (1857) 24 Beav 413; *Smith v Smith* (1861) 1 Drew & Sm 384; *Re King, Mellor v South Australian Land Mortgage and Agency Co* [1907] 1 Ch 72. See also *Re Yorke, Stone v Chataway* [1997] 4 All ER 907, where it was held that it is advisable for the personal representatives of a deceased Lloyd's name protected by Equitas reinsurance to seek the protection of the court before distributing the deceased's assets if there is a risk of future claims being made against the estate. Where the only, or only substantial, reason for delaying distribution is the possibility of personal liability to Lloyd's creditors, there is a streamlined form of application which will be heard by a master rather than a judge: see *Practice Note* [2001] 3 All ER 765. See also *Re K* [2007] EWHC 622 (Ch), [2007] WTLR 1007, where the court gave guidance on its approach to applications for protection in cases where the cause of concern was a series of disputed and stale claims against the estate.
4 *Re King, Mellor v South Australian Land Mortgage and Agency Co* [1907] 1 Ch 72, in which the judgment of Neville J reviews the prior authorities, among which there was some conflict of opinion. In *Fletcher v Stevenson* (1844) 3 Hare 360, it was held that the covenantee had an equity to have a fund set aside to meet a contingent claim. In *King v Malcott* (1852) 9 Hare 692; *Smith v Smith* (1861) 1 Drew & Sm 384; *Dodson v Sammell* (1861) 1 Drew & Sm 575, it was held that he had no such equity.
5 *Re Nixon, Gray v Bell* [1904] 1 Ch 638; *Re King, Mellor v South Australian Land Mortgage and Agency Co* [1907] 1 Ch 72. For a form of order see *Re Sales, Powsland v Roberts* [1920] WN 54; *Re Johnson, Johnson v King Edward Hospital Fund for London* [1940] WN 195.
6 *Re Arnold, Calvert v Whelen* [1942] Ch 272, [1942] 1 All ER 501. It appears from this case that this question is now a matter of degree in the remoteness or otherwise of the contingency.
7 As to the extent of his liability see PARA 1223.

8 *Re Nixon, Gray v Bell* [1904] 1 Ch 638; *Re Owers, Public Trustee v Death* [1941] Ch 389, [1941] 2 All ER 589.
9 *Re Bennett, Midland Bank Executor and Trustee Co Ltd v Fletcher* [1943] 1 All ER 467.
10 *Re Lewis, Jennings v Hemsley* [1939] Ch 232, [1939] 3 All ER 269. See generally LIMITATION PERIODS vol 68 (2016) PARA 901 et seq.
11 *Re Hargreaves, Dicks v Hare* (1890) 44 ChD 236, CA. As to the requirements for making a claim see further PARA 1174.

(4) ORDER OF APPLICATION OF ASSETS IN ADMINISTRATION

(i) General Rules for Order of Application of Assets

992. Statutory order of application of assets. Subject to the directions of the will, the order in which assets are to be applied in the discharge of the debts and liabilities is based upon the presumed intentions of the testator, and these have been given statutory form[1].

1 See the Administration of Estates Act 1925 s 34(3), Sch 1 Pt II (which applies in the case of persons dying after 31 December 1925); and PARAS 998–1005. As to the extent, if any, to which the statutory order applies to the discharge of legacies see PARA 1107.

993. Exclusion of statutory order by creation of mixed fund. When an estate is insolvent, the contest is between the creditors among themselves as to the priority in which their debts are to be paid[1]. When an estate is solvent, the creditors are paid in full and the contest is between the beneficiaries among themselves: (1) as to the order in which resort is had to the various parts of the estate for payment of the debts and liabilities; and (2) what parts of the estate are charged with payment of the pecuniary legacies and in what order. Both these matters which arise in the administration and distribution of a solvent estate are to be determined primarily[2] by the directions, if any, contained in the will, and the statutory order of application of assets[3] takes effect subject to those directions[4].

Accordingly, where a testator combines his real and personal estate in one general fund, and directs the whole of that fund to be applied for the payment of debts or legacies, the creation of the mixed fund excludes the statutory order of application of assets[5], and the real and personal estate must be applied in the discharge of the debts or legacies rateably according to their respective values[6]. A gift of real and personal estate together, coupled with a direction to sell and to pay debts or legacies out of the proceeds, creates a mixed fund[7]; a direction that the real estate is to be sold and that the proceeds of sale are to be considered as part of the personal estate will have the same effect[8]. It is not necessary that there should be an absolute conversion directed by the will; a power of sale may be sufficient if, from the terms of the will as a whole, it can be gathered that the testator had the intention of creating a mixed fund[9]. The mere gift of real and personal estate together, coupled with a direction to pay debts or legacies, or a trust for the payment of debts or legacies, is not by itself sufficient to constitute a mixed fund in the absence of words in the will showing an intention on the testator's part that his real estate should be sold for the purpose of meeting the debts or legacies[10].

1 As to insolvent estates see PARA 981 et seq.
2 Ie subject to any variation which may be made by an order under the Inheritance (Provision for Family and Dependants) Act 1975 (see PARA 565 et seq). As to the danger of distribution without regard to the possibility of such an order see PARA 1064.

3 See PARA 998 et seq.
4 Administration of Estates Act 1925 s 34(3), Sch 1 Pt II para 8(a). See *Re Petty, Holliday v Petty* [1929] 1 Ch 726; *Re Kempthorne, Charles v Kempthorne* [1930] 1 Ch 268, CA; *Re Martin, Midland Bank Executor and Trustee Co Ltd v Marfleet* [1955] 1 All ER 865; *Re Berrey's Will Trusts, Greening v Warner* [1959] 1 All ER 15, [1959] 1 WLR 30; *Re Feis, Guillaume v Ritz-Remorf* [1964] Ch 106 at 117, [1963] 3 All ER 303 at 310; *Re Wilson, Wilson v Mackay* [1967] Ch 53 at 66, [1966] 2 All ER 867 at 871; *Re Eleanor Taylor's Estate and Will Trusts, Re Jane Taylor's Estate and Will Trusts, Taylor v Taylor* [1969] 2 Ch 245, [1969] 1 All ER 113. Where a question arises as to the property on which a charge of debts is to operate, the court inclines to a construction which gives the creditors a charge on the larger amount of property: *Noel v Weston* (1813) 2 Ves & B 269 at 274.
5 *Re Petty, Holliday v Petty* [1929] 1 Ch 726 (statutory order varied so far as it provided for payment primarily out of lapsed share of residue as property undisposed of; cf PARA 998 head (1)).
6 *Roberts v Walker* (1830) 1 Russ & M 752; *Simmons v Rose* (1856) 6 De GM & G 411.
7 *Roberts v Walker* (1830) 1 Russ & M 752; *Stocker v Harbin* (1841) 3 Beav 479; *Salt v Chattaway* (1841) 3 Beav 576; *Dunk v Fenner* (1831) 2 Russ & M 557; *Fourdrin v Gowdey* (1834) 3 My & K 383; *Tatlock v Jenkins* (1854) Kay 654; *Bedford v Bedford* (1865) 35 Beav 584.
8 *Kidney v Coussmaker* (1797) 7 Bro Parl Cas 573, HL; *Bright v Larcher* (1858) 3 De G & J 148; *Simmons v Rose* (1856) 6 De GM & G 411.
9 *Allan v Gott* (1872) 7 Ch App 439; *Re Timson, Harper v Timson* [1953] 2 All ER 1252, [1953] 1 WLR 1361.
10 *Boughton v Boughton, Boughton v James* (1848) 1 HL Cas 406; *Tench v Cheese* (1855) 6 De GM & G 453; *Wells v Row* (1879) 48 LJ Ch 476; *Luckcraft v Pridham* (1879) 48 LJ Ch 636; *Re Smith, Smith v Smith* [1913] 2 Ch 216 at 223; and see *Re Cowell, Temple v Temple* (1920) 150 LT Jo 296.

994. Other ways in which statutory order for payment of debts may be displaced. The creation of a mixed fund is not the only way by which the statutory order for the payment of funeral, testamentary and administration expenses, debts and liabilities[1], can be displaced. Accordingly, a direction for payment of such expenses out of the proceeds of the conversion of the testator's personal estate[2], or a gift of residue subject to the payment of such expenses[3], is sufficient to exclude the statutory order so far as it provides primarily for payment out of property undisposed of by will[4]; but a mere direction to pay such expenses, followed by a gift of residue[5], or a gift of residue followed by a direction to pay duty[6], will not exclude the statutory order. Again, an express charge of such expenses on specific bequests, followed by a gift of residue to a legatee other than the legatees of the specific property, excludes the statutory order and renders such expenses primarily payable out of the specific bequests to the exoneration of residue[7], whereas a charge of such expenses on a legacy, the residue being undisposed of, is insufficient to exclude the statutory order so as to make the legacy the primary fund for payment in place of the undisposed of estate[8].

1 See PARA 998 et seq. As to mixed funds see PARA 993.
2 *Re Atkinson, Webster v Walter* [1930] 1 Ch 47; *Re Martin, Midland Bank Executor and Trustee Co Ltd v Marfleet* [1955] Ch 698, [1955] 1 All ER 865 (payment primarily out of proceeds of conversion and not out of undisposed of realty, as provided by statute; cf PARA 999).
3 *Re Kempthorne, Charles v Kempthorne* [1930] 1 Ch 268, CA; *Re Harland-Peck, Hercy v Mayglothing* [1941] Ch 182, [1940] 4 All ER 347, CA (payment out of entire residue, not out of lapsed share; cf PARA 999).
4 See PARA 999.
5 *Re Lamb, Vipond v Lamb* [1929] 1 Ch 722 (payment out of lapsed share of residue); criticised in *Re Cruse, Gass v Ingham* [1930] WN 206; *Re Kempthorne, Charles v Kempthorne* [1930] 1 Ch 268 at 298, CA; but approved and applied in *Re Tong, Hilton v Bradbury* [1931] 1 Ch 202, CA (payment out of lapsed share of income of residue); *Re Worthington, Nichols v Hart* [1933] Ch 771, CA (payment out of lapsed share of residue).
6 *Re Sanger, Taylor v North* [1939] Ch 238, [1938] 4 All ER 417 (payment out of lapsed share of residue).
7 *Re Littlewood, Clark v Littlewood* [1931] 1 Ch 443; *Re James, Lloyds Bank Ltd v Atkins* [1947] Ch 256, [1947] 1 All ER 402; *Re Meldrum, Swinson v Meldrum* [1952] Ch 208, [1952] 1 All ER

274 (in effect varying the order contained in the Administration of Estates Act 1925 s 34(3), Sch 1 Pt II paras 2, 3 (see PARAS 1000–1001)). See also *Re Ridley, Nicholson v Nicholson* [1950] Ch 415, [1950] 2 All ER 1 (general devise of realty 'free of all death duties' followed by bequest of pecuniary legacies and residuary gift; intention shown that realty should not be resorted to until personalty exhausted; devise of realty a specific and not a residuary disposition).

8 *Re Gordon, Watts v Rationalist Press Association Ltd* [1940] Ch 769, [1940] 3 All ER 205, where it was held, following a dictum of Maugham J in *Re Kempthorne, Charles v Kempthorne* [1930] 1 Ch 268 at 278, CA, that such a charge could not in itself be sufficient to displace the statutory order in view of the fact that property so charged and property given for the payment of debts are expressly allocated places in the statutory order after property undisposed of (see PARAS 999, 1001–1002; see also *Re Meldrum, Swinson v Meldrum* [1952] Ch 208 at 213–214, [1952] 1 All ER 274 at 277, where it was pointed out that it is a question purely of construction of each will whether or not the testator has varied the statutory order).

995. Where exonerated gift lapses. The right to exoneration does not enure for the benefit of a person who becomes entitled to a lapsed gift, whether the fund appropriated to the exoneration is one of realty[1] or of specific personal assets[2], the right to the benefit of the exoneration being, in fact, a part of the legacy which has failed[3].

1 *Dacre v Patrickson* (1860) 1 Drew & Sm 182.

2 *Re Meere, Kilford v Blaney* (1885) 31 ChD 56, CA, overruling on this point *Browne v Groombridge* (1819) 4 Madd 495.

3 *Re Meere, Kilford v Blaney* (1885) 31 ChD 56 at 66, CA.

996. Secured and unsecured debts. The statutory order of application[1] applies to the discharge of unsecured debts, whereas secured debts are primarily payable out of the property on which they are charged[2]. In accordance with this principle, where a person has contracted to purchase property and dies before paying the purchase money, the property contracted to be purchased is primarily liable for the unpaid purchase money, unless by his will or deed or other document he has signified a contrary intention, and a devisee or successor is not entitled to have the unpaid purchase money discharged or satisfied out of any other part of the testator's estate[3].

1 See PARA 992.

2 See the Administration of Estates Act 1925 s 35; and PARA 1006 et seq.

3 See the Administration of Estates Act 1925 s 35, replacing, as regards estates of persons dying after 1925, the Real Estate Charges Act 1854, the Real Estate Charges Act 1867, and the Real Estate Charges Act 1877, a series of statutes which are known as Locke King's Acts and are repealed as respects deaths after 1925. See also *Re Cockcroft, Broadbent v Groves* (1883) 24 ChD 94; *Re Birmingham, Savage v Stannard* [1959] Ch 523, [1958] 2 All ER 397; following *Lysaght v Edwards* (1876) 2 ChD 499; *Re Kidd, Brooman v Withall* [1894] 3 Ch 558; and cf *Re Coxen, MacCullum v Coxen* [1948] 2 All ER 492 at 496. See also PARAS 1006 text and note 6, 1008 text and note 7.

997. Marshalling. The principle of marshalling in the administration of assets is a process of adjustment directed to ensuring that assets are ultimately applied in accordance with their proper order of liability, notwithstanding that in the actual course of administration assets more remotely liable have been used in priority to those more immediately liable[1]. Accordingly, where debts are charged on real estate, but are in fact paid out of personalty, with the result that pecuniary legatees are disappointed, the legatees have an equitable right to compensation[2], and to have the assets marshalled so as to render the real estate charged with debts available for their legacies[3]. The doctrine of marshalling in this connection is considered elsewhere in this work[4].

1 *Re Townley, Public Trustee v Allder* [1922] 1 Ch 154 at 159, a case of marshalling in favour of specific and pecuniary legacies to the prejudice of residue. For a modern example see *Re Ross* [2013] EWHC 2724 (Ch), [2014] WTLR 321, [2013] All ER (D) 221 (Sep).

2 *Re Cohen, National Provincial Bank Ltd v Katz* [1960] Ch 179 at 190, [1959] 3 All ER 740 at 745; *Re Matthews' Will Trusts, Bristow v Matthews* [1961] 3 All ER 869 at 873, [1961] 1 WLR 1415 at 1419. See also *Re Ross, Petterson v Ross* [2013] EWHC 2724 (Ch), [2013] All ER (D) 221 (Sep).

3 *Re Stokes, Parsons v Miller* (1892) 67 LT 223; *Re Salt, Brothwood v Keeling* [1895] 2 Ch 203; *Re Roberts, Roberts v Roberts* [1902] 2 Ch 834; *Re Kempster, Kempster v Kempster* [1906] 1 Ch 446; *Re Bate, Bate v Bate* (1890) 43 ChD 600, contra, is overruled.

4 See EQUITABLE JURISDICTION vol 47 (2014) PARA 195 et seq.

(ii) Order in Payment of Debts and Liabilities

998. Order of application since 1925. In the case of death after 1925[1] the statutory order of application applies[2]. Subject to rules of court and the statutory provisions as to charges on the deceased's property, and to any provisions contained in his will[3], the deceased's real and personal estate[4] is applicable towards the discharge of the funeral, testamentary and administration expenses[5], debts and liabilities payable out of it in the following order[6]:

(1) property undisposed of by will[7];
(2) property included in a residuary gift[8];
(3) property the subject of specific gifts[9];
(4) property charged with the payment of debts[10];
(5) the fund for pecuniary legacies[11];
(6) property specifically devised or bequeathed[12]; and
(7) property appointed under a general power[13].

The statutory order deals only with the ultimate adjustment of the burden as between the parties becoming entitled to the testator's estate[14].

1 Where the will was made before 31 December 1925, although in administering the estate the provisions in the text relating to the order of application of assets must be applied, yet in construing the will regard must be had to the law in force at the time of its execution, ie before the alterations in the law were made: *Re Atkinson, Webster v Walter* [1930] 1 Ch 47 at 50; *Re Littlewood, Clark v Littlewood* [1931] 1 Ch 443 at 445; and see PARA 1012. As to the distinction between the payment of debts and liabilities in administering an estate on the one hand and the incidence of legacies and other questions of priority arising on distribution see PARA 1107.

As to the position where the estate is insolvent see PARA 981. As to the distinction between legal and equitable assets formerly prevailing in relation to the order of payment of debts see EQUITABLE JURISDICTION vol 47 (2014) PARA 61.

2 Ie by the Administration of Estates Act 1925 s 34(3), Sch 1 Pt II.

3 See PARA 993. As to the meaning of 'will' see PARA 607 note 1.

4 As to the meaning of 'real estate' see PARA 607 note 1. Where, by reason of an election to take under an instrument, property has been set free to pass under an instrument, that property becomes subject to all the incidents to which it would have been subject had it been throughout the property of the testator: *Re Williams, Cunliffe v Williams* [1915] 1 Ch 450 at 456.

5 As to the meaning of 'funeral expenses' see CREMATION AND BURIAL vol 24 (2010) PARA 1137. As to testamentary and administration expenses see PARA 1013 et seq. As to the order of application of assets in the payment of legacies see PARA 1107.

6 See the Administration of Estates Act 1925 s 34(3), Sch 1 Pt II. The court has no discretion and must apply the statutory rules: see *Re Ross* [2013] EWHC 2724 (Ch), [2014] WTLR 321, [2013] All ER (D) 221 (Sep).

7 See PARA 999.

8 See PARA 1000.

9 See PARA 1001.

10 See PARA 1002.

11 See PARA 1003.

12 See PARA 1004.

13 See PARA 1005.

14 *Re Tong, Hilton v Bradbury* [1931] 1 Ch 202 at 212, CA.

999. Property undisposed of by will. If there is property[1] of the deceased undisposed of by will[2], and if as a matter of construction the will does not otherwise provide[3], this undisposed of property is first applicable in payment of debts and liabilities, but subject to the retention out of it of a fund sufficient to meet any pecuniary legacies[4]. Included in property undisposed of by will are a lapsed share of residue[5] or of income[6] and a lapsed devise of real estate[7].

1 As to the meaning of 'property' see PARA 608 note 4. See also PARA 998 note 4.
2 As to the meaning of 'will' see PARA 607 note 1.
3 *Re Feis, Guillaume v Ritz-Remorf* [1964] Ch 106, [1963] 3 All ER 303. See PARA 993.
4 Administration of Estates Act 1925 s 34(3), Sch 1 Pt II para 1. See also the cases cited in PARA 994 notes 2–6. As to restrictions on the disposition of the matrimonial home if one spouse dies intestate leaving the other surviving see PARA 490. As to the meaning of 'pecuniary legacy' see PARA 1003.
5 *Re Lamb, Vipond v Lamb* [1929] 1 Ch 722; *Re Petty, Holliday v Petty* [1929] 1 Ch 726; *Re Worthington, Nichols v Hart* [1933] Ch 771, CA; *Re Sanger, Taylor v North* [1939] Ch 238, [1938] 4 All ER 417.
6 *Re Tong, Hilton v Bradbury* [1931] 1 Ch 202 at 212, CA.
7 *Re Atkinson, Webster v Walter* [1930] 1 Ch 47.

1000. Property included in residuary gift. The second class of property applicable in payment of debts and liabilities[1] is property[2] of the deceased not specifically devised or bequeathed but included, either by a specific or by a general description, in a residuary gift[3] subject to the retention out of such property of a fund sufficient to meet any pecuniary legacies[4], so far as not provided for under the preceding paragraph[5].

Accordingly, a fund must be set aside out of residue to satisfy pecuniary legacies, and since pecuniary legacies are still primarily payable out of personalty it will be set aside primarily out of personalty in the absence of a contrary intention[6]. The residue is divided notionally into two separate funds, the first to meet pecuniary legacies, and a second fund consisting of the balance of the residue. The second fund must be exhausted before the first is touched, so that the old rule by which debts and testamentary expenses were a first charge on the residuary personalty is displaced[7].

1 See PARA 998.
2 As to the meaning of 'property' see PARA 608 note 4.
3 Although all devises used to be regarded as specific, a general or universal gift of real estate is 'residuary' for this purpose: see *Re Wilson, Wilson v Mackay* [1967] Ch 53 at 68, [1966] 2 All ER 867 at 871 per Pennycuick J; and PARA 119.
4 As to the meaning of 'pecuniary legacy' see PARA 1003.
5 Administration of Estates Act 1925 s 34(3), Sch 1 Pt II para 2. For decisions as to the effect of this provision see PARA 994 text and note 7.
6 See PARAS 1107–1112. The creation of a mixed fund of realty and personalty out of which the legacies are to be paid can be an expression of a contrary intention: see PARA 1111.
7 *Re Anstead, Gurney v Anstead* [1943] Ch 161 at 164, [1943] 1 All ER 522 at 524 per Uthwatt J; *Re Wilson, Wilson v Mackay* [1967] Ch 53 at 71, [1966] 2 All ER 867 at 873–874 per Pennycuick J.

1001. Property the subject of specific gifts. The third class of property applicable in payment of debts and liabilities[1] is property[2] of the deceased specifically appropriated or devised or bequeathed, either by a specific or by a general description, for the payment of debts[3]. This must be read as referring to property other than property included in a residuary gift[4].

1 See PARA 998.
2 As to the meaning of 'property' see PARA 608 note 4.
3 Administration of Estates Act 1925 s 34(3), Sch 1 Pt II para 3.
4 *Re Kempthorne, Charles v Kempthorne* [1930] 1 Ch 268 at 300, CA; and see PARA 1000.

1002. Property charged with payment of debts. The fourth class of property applicable in payment of debts and liabilities[1] is property[2] of the deceased charged with[3] or devised or bequeathed, either by a specific or by a general description, subject to a charge for the payment of debts[4]. This must be read as referring to property other than property included in a residuary gift[5].

1 See PARA 998.
2 As to the meaning of 'property' see PARA 608 note 4.
3 The effect for this purpose of a charge of debts is preserved, notwithstanding that under the Administration of Estates Act 1925 s 32(1) (see PARA 969), the charge is no longer necessary: *Re Kempster, Kempster v Kempster* [1906] 1 Ch 446.
4 Administration of Estates Act 1925 s 34(3), Sch 1 Pt II para 4. The statutory provision appears to be in accordance with the former law that if the personalty was exhausted legatees could come on the real estate charged with the payment of debts, whether expressly or by inference: see *Re Salt, Brothwood v Keeling* [1895] 2 Ch 203; *Re Roberts, Roberts v Roberts* [1902] 2 Ch 834, holding that *Re Bate, Bate v Bate* (1890) 43 ChD 600 was overruled.
5 *Re Kempthorne, Charles v Kempthorne* [1930] 1 Ch 268 at 300, CA; and see PARA 1000.

1003. Fund for pecuniary legacies. The fifth class of property applicable in payment of debts and liabilities[1] is the fund, if any, retained to meet pecuniary legacies[2]. 'Pecuniary legacy' includes an annuity, a general legacy, a demonstrative legacy so far as not discharged out of the designated property[3] and any general direction by the testator for the payment of money, including all inheritance tax free from which any devise, bequest or payment is made to take effect[4].

1 See PARA 998.
2 Administration of Estates Act 1925 s 34(3), Sch 1 Pt II para 5. Formerly, where the general personal estate was insufficient for the payment of debts and legacies, pecuniary legatees had no right to make the residuary devisee contribute rateably: see *Collins v Lewis* (1869) LR 8 Eq 708; *Dugdale v Dugdale* (1872) LR 14 Eq 234; *Tomkins v Colthurst* (1875) 1 ChD 626; *Farquharson v Floyer* (1876) 3 ChD 109.
3 As to the meaning of 'property' see PARA 608 note 4.
4 Administration of Estates Act 1925 s 55(1)(ix); Inheritance Tax Act 1984 s 273, Sch 6para1; Finance Act 1986 s 100(1).

1004. Property specifically devised or bequeathed. The sixth class of property applicable in payment of debts and liabilities[1] is property[2] specifically devised or bequeathed[3], rateably according to value[4]; but neither portions[5] nor legacies[6] charged on real estate are liable to contribute with the real estate or specific legacies. The value of the property is the value to the testator, and therefore, where real estate is devised subject to a mortgage and to the payment of legacies, the mortgage may be deducted from the value but not the legacies[7].

1 See PARA 998.
2 As to the meaning of 'property' see PARA 608 note 4.
3 If a testator confers upon a beneficiary an option to purchase shares forming part of the estate at a price below market value, but does not make a distinct bequest of the beneficial interest represented by the difference between the option price and the market value, the beneficial interest in question is not property specifically bequeathed and has no place in the statutory order of application of assets; in such a case the property subject to the option is, it seems, the last to be available for the payment of debts: *Re Eve, National Provincial Bank Ltd v Eve* [1956] Ch 479, [1956] 2 All ER 321.
4 Administration of Estates Act 1925 s 34(3), Sch 1 Pt II para 6. As to specific legacies see PARA 118. As to demonstrative legacies see PARA 120.
5 *Raikes v Boulton* (1860) 29 Beav 41; *Re Saunders-Davies, Saunders-Davies v Saunders-Davies* (1887) 34 ChD 482.
6 *Re John, Jones v John* [1933] Ch 370; *Re Bawden, National Provincial Bank of England v Cresswell, Bawden v Cresswell* [1894] 1 Ch 693.
7 See *Raikes v Boulton* (1860) 29 Beav 41; *Re Saunders-Davies, Saunders-Davies v Saunders-Davies* (1887) 34 ChD 482. The respective values must be ascertained as at the date of the testator's death: *Fielding v Preston* (1857) 1 De G & J 438; *Re Cohen, National Provincial Bank Ltd v Katz* [1960] Ch 179, [1959] 3 All ER 740: *Re Ross* [2013] EWHC 2724 (Ch), [2014] WTLR 321, [2013] All ER (D) 221 (Sep). Where real estate subject to an incumbrance was specifically devised free from incumbrances so as to exclude the operation of Locke King's Acts (see PARA 996 note

3), a pecuniary legatee was entitled to have recourse against the devised realty to the extent to which the incumbrance had been discharged out of the personal estate: *Re Smith, Smith v Smith* [1899] 1 Ch 365.

1005. Property appointed. The seventh class of property applicable in payment of debts and liabilities[1] is property[2] appointed by will[3] under a general power[4], including the statutory power to dispose of entailed interests[5], rateably according to value[6]. For such property to be available for payment of debts and liabilities the power must be actually exercised[7].

1 See PARA 998.
2 As to the meaning of 'property' see PARA 608 note 4.
3 As to the meaning of 'will' see PARA 607 note 1.
4 See *Fleming v Buchanan* (1853) 3 De GM & G 976 at 980; *Beyfus v Lawley* [1903] AC 411, HL. See also PARAS 954–955. As to the exercise of a general power by will see PARA 1114; and TRUSTS AND POWERS vol 98 (2013) PARA 577 et seq.
5 See the Law of Property Act 1925 s 176; and REAL PROPERTY AND REGISTRATION vol 87 (2012) PARA 136. Although the creation of new entailed interests on or after 1 January 1997 is prohibited (see the Trusts of Land and Appointment of Trustees Act 1996 s 2(6), Sch 1para5; and REAL PROPERTY AND REGISTRATION vol 87 (2012) PARA 114; SETTLEMENTS vol 91 (2012) PARA 578), this power continues to be exercisable in relation to existing entails.
6 Administration of Estates Act 1925 s 34(3), Sch 1 Pt II para 7. This preserves the old rule as to property expressly appointed by will which applied before 1926: see eg *Fleming v Buchanan* (1853) 3 De GM & G 976; *Beyfus v Lawley* [1903] AC 411, HL; *Williams v Williams, Re Hartley, Williams v Jones* [1900] 1 Ch 152.
7 *Holmes v Coghill* (1802) 7 Ves 499; on appeal (1806) 12 Ves 206. As to powers generally see TRUSTS AND POWERS.

1006. Interests charged with the payment of debts. Where a person dies possessed of or entitled to, or, under a general power of appointment (including the statutory power to dispose of entailed interests[1]), by his will[2] disposes of, an interest in property[3] which, at the time of his death, is charged with the payment of money, whether by way of legal mortgage, equitable charge[4] or otherwise[5], including a lien for unpaid purchase money[6], and the deceased has not by will, deed or other document signified a contrary or other intention[7], the interest so charged is, as between the different persons claiming through the deceased, primarily liable for the payment of the charge, and every part of the interest bears, according to its value, a proportionate part of the charge on the whole[8].

As this provision applies only to disputes between different persons claiming through the deceased, it is not applicable at the instance of a residuary legatee against a specific devisee, where the devised estate has been mortgaged to secure a partnership debt, and the partnership assets are sufficient to repay the advance[9], or where the property specifically bequeathed has been charged with a debt and the testator is merely a surety for payment of the debt which is paid off by the principal debtor after the testator's death[10], or to charges affecting an estate which descends to a tenant in tail under a settlement not made by the deceased[11].

1 See PARAS 954, 1005.
2 As to the meaning of 'will' see PARA 607 note 1.
3 As to the meaning of 'property' see PARA 608 note 4. Personalty did not come within the repealed enactments now replaced by the Administration of Estates Act 1925 s 35, and a legatee of personal estate of a testator subject to a mortgage was entitled, in the absence of a contrary intention, to have the mortgage debt discharged out of other parts of the estate: see *Knight v Davis* (1833) 3 My & K 358; *Bothamley v Sherson* (1875) LR 20 Eq 304; *Re Butler, Le Bas v Herbert* [1894] 3 Ch 250; *Re Chantrell, Sutleffe v Von Liverhoff* [1907] WN 213; *Re Williams, Cunliffe v Williams* [1915] 1 Ch 450.
4 *Re Turner, Tennant v Turner* [1938] Ch 593, [1938] 2 All ER 560.
5 See eg *Re Riddell, Public Trustee v Riddell* [1936] Ch 747, [1936] 2 All ER 1600.
6 *Re Cockcroft, Broadbent v Groves* (1883) 24 ChD 94. See also PARA 996.
7 As to what constitutes a contrary intention see PARA 1008.

8 Administration of Estates Act 1925 s 35(1). Nothing in s 35 affects the right of a person entitled to the charge to obtain payment or satisfaction of it either out of the other assets of the deceased or otherwise: s 35(3). As to the enactments replaced by this provision see PARA 996 note 3. The enactments replaced applied equally to next of kin as to legatees (*Re Fraser, Lowther v Fraser* [1904] 1 Ch 726, CA), but did not impose any personal liability on the devisee (*Syer v Gladstone* (1885) 30 ChD 614 at 616).

9 *Re Ritson, Ritson v Ritson* [1899] 1 Ch 128, CA.

10 *Re Hawkes, Reeve v Hawkes* [1912] 2 Ch 251.

11 *Re Anthony, Anthony v Anthony* [1893] 3 Ch 498. As to settlements see generally SETTLEMENTS.

1007. What constitutes a charge for payment of debts. The statutory provisions as to interests charged with the payment of debts[1] apply to a statutory charge for inheritance tax[2], a collateral mortgage[3], and formerly applied to a charge on land taken in execution under a writ of elegit[4], but a general charge upon the real estate in aid of the personal estate to pay legacies or debts, or both, is not a charge within the enactment, as the object and intention of the provisions is not, in such a case, to alter the administration of assets or to make the real estate primarily liable to the exoneration of the general estate[5].

1 See PARA 998.

2 Or the taxes which preceded inheritance tax (ie estate duty or capital transfer tax: see PARAS 1266 note 5, 1128 note 2). See *Re Bowerman, Porter v Bowerman* [1908] 2 Ch 340. For the statutory charge for inheritance tax see the Inheritance Tax Act 1984 s 237; and INHERITANCE TAXATION vol 59A (2014) PARA 303 et seq. What is referred to here is a charge for one of these taxes which arises before the deceased's death.

3 *Coleby v Coleby* (1866) LR 2 Eq 803.

4 *Re Anthony, Anthony v Anthony* [1892] 1 Ch 450. The writ of elegit has been abolished.

5 *Hepworth v Hill* (1862) 30 Beav 476 at 483 per Romilly MR.

1008. What constitutes a contrary intention. A charge of or general direction for payment of debts upon or out of a testator's personal estate, or his residuary real and personal estate[1], or his residuary real estate is not a sufficient signification of a contrary or other intention[2]; the intention must be further signified by words expressly or by necessary implication referring to all or some part of the charge[3]. Accordingly, a direction to pay debts, except mortgage debts on Blackacre, out of the residue, is sufficient indication of an intention to throw on the residue a mortgage debt on Whiteacre[4]; the realty will also be exonerated if, in the direction to pay debts, a debt is included by a description sufficient to identify it as being a debt which happens to be secured by mortgage[5]; and a contrary intention is expressed by a direction to pay debts out of a special fund, not being one of the funds referred to above[6]. However, where a testator devises property which he has contracted to buy, a direction to pay out of residue 'sums of money secured on mortgage' does not throw on the residue the unpaid balances of the purchase money in respect of which the vendor has a lien on the property comprised in the contract for sale[7]. The contrary intention need not appear in the will; it may be gathered from the mortgage deeds themselves[8], or from some other document[9]. It is not fatal to a claim of contrary intention that the arrangements made by the testator pre-dated the will[10].

1 As to the meaning of 'real estate' see PARA 607 note 1.

2 Administration of Estates Act 1925 s 35(2)(a), (b), substantially reproducing the Real Estate Charges Act 1877 s 1 (repealed as respects deaths after 1925).

3 Administration of Estates Act 1925 s 35(2), substantially reproducing the Real Estate Charges Act 1867 s 1 (repealed as respects deaths after 1925). See also *Re Major, Taylor v Major* [1914] 1 Ch 278. As to the construction of the will see PARA 993 note 4. For a recent example of a will making separate gifts of two properties subject to a charge, one expressed to be free of mortgage and one not, see *Re Ross* [2013] EWHC 2724 (Ch), [2014] WTLR 321, [2013] All ER (D) 221 (Sep).

4 *Re Valpy, Valpy v Valpy* [1906] 1 Ch 531. A direction to pay the mortgage debt on Whiteacre out of the proceeds of sale of Blackacre does not enable the devisees of Whiteacre to go against the

general estate for any deficiency: *Re Birch, Hunt v Thorn* [1909] 1 Ch 787, explaining *Allen v Allen* (1862) 30 Beav 395 at 403; and see *Re Fegan, Fegan v Fegan* [1928] Ch 45.

5 *Re Fleck, Colston v Roberts* (1888) 37 ChD 677.

6 *Re Fegan, Fegan v Fegan* [1928] Ch 45. If the special fund is insufficient, the property charged is not exonerated so as to throw the balance of the mortgage debt on the general personal estate: *Re Fegan, Fegan v Fegan*.

7 *Re Beirnstein, Barnett v Beirnstein* [1925] Ch 12; *Re Birmingham, Savage v Stannard* [1959] Ch 523 at 530, [1958] 2 All ER 397 at 401. See also PARA 996.

8 See the Administration of Estates Act 1925 s 35(1) (see PARA 1006), substantially reproducing the Real Estate Charges Act 1854 s 1 (repealed as respects deaths after 1925); and *Re Campbell, Campbell v Campbell* [1893] 2 Ch 206.

9 A letter giving notice on the testator's part to pay off a mortgage in six months' time merely shows an intention by him to pay off the mortgage in his lifetime, and shows no intention that the debt should not be borne by the specific devisee: *Re Nicholson, Nicholson v Boulton* [1923] WN 251. A letter by the testator enclosing a cheque for the completion of a purchase shows merely his intention to pay the balance of the purchase money in his lifetime, and, if the testator dies before completion, the devisee takes the property subject to the vendor's lien: *Re Wakefield, Gordon v Wakefield* [1943] 2 All ER 29, CA. As to the vendor's lien see LIEN vol 68 (2016) PARA 859 et seq.

10 *Ross v Perrin-Hughes* [2004] EWHC 2559 (Ch), 7 ITELR 405, [2004] All ER (D) 159 (Nov). If there is written evidence that the testator has so structured his affairs that it is clear that he always intended that the charge should be repaid from the proceeds of a specific insurance policy or fund in the event of his death, that is sufficient to provide a 'contrary or other intention'; and in this context, in referring to common lending arrangements as described by the Court of Appeal in *Smith v Clerical Medical and General Life Assurance Society* [1993] 1 FLR 47, [1992] 1 FCR 262, the court must recognise the widespread use of endowment mortgages in property transactions: see *Ross v Perrin-Hughes* at [19]–[22].

1009. Several properties comprised in one charge left to different beneficiaries. Where several properties are comprised in one mortgage or charge and are devised or bequeathed to different persons, those persons must bear the debt rateably unless the will shows a contrary intention[1]. The use of the word 'collateral' or the fact that one property was brought into charge subsequently on the occasion of a further advance does not indicate a contrary intention[2]; nor does the fact that property devised is subject to a conditional option for a third party to purchase at a price below the proportionate amount of the sum due[3]. Similarly a contrary intention is not indicated even after 1925[4] by the fact that one of the properties passes under a residuary devise and one under a specific devise, although a specific devise now takes priority over a residuary devise[5]. A contrary intention may also be gathered from the language of the documents or the nature of the transaction if these indicate that one property was intended to form a primary security and the other a secondary security[6].

1 See the Administration of Estates Act 1925 s 35(1) (see PARA 1006), substantially reproducing the Real Estate Charges Act 1854 s 1 (repealed as respects deaths after 1925). See also *Re Newmarch, Newmarch v Storr* (1878) 9 ChD 12 at 17, CA; *Re Major, Taylor v Major* [1914] 1 Ch 278. The same rule applies where freeholds and leaseholds and pure personalty are comprised in one mortgage: *Trestrail v Mason* (1878) 7 ChD 655; *Leonino v Leonino* (1879) 10 ChD 460. The rule applied before 1926 as between heir at law and next of kin in the case of intestacy: *Evans v Wyatt* (1862) 31 Beav 217. As to cases where the old rules of descent still apply see PARA 478.

2 *Re Athill, Athill v Athill* (1880) 16 ChD 211 at 225–226, CA, per Cotton LJ.

3 *Re Biss, Heasman v Biss* [1956] Ch 243, [1956] 1 All ER 89.

4 *Re Neeld, Carpenter v Inigo-Jones* [1962] Ch 643 at 692, [1962] 2 All ER 335 at 361, CA, per Upjohn LJ; overruling on this point *Re Biss, Heasman v Biss* [1956] Ch 243, [1956] 1 All ER 89; and *Re Cohen, National Provincial Bank Ltd v Katz* [1960] Ch 179, [1959] 3 All ER 740.

5 See the Administration of Estates Act 1925 s 34(3), Sch 1 Pt II paras 2, 3; and PARAS 1000–1001.

6 Such an intention was found in *Lipscomb v Lipscomb* (1868) LR 7 Eq 501; *De Rochefort v Dawes* (1871) LR 12 Eq 540, but was not found in *Leonino v Leonino* (1879) 10 ChD 460; *Re Athill, Athill v Athill* (1880) 16 ChD 211, CA.

1010. Several properties comprised in separate mortgages. Where several properties are comprised in separate mortgages, and the mortgage on one of the properties exceeds in amount the value of that property, the amount of the deficiency must be discharged out of the testator's general estate and not out of the surplus value of the other mortgaged properties[1]; but a collective devise of lands of any tenure to the same set of persons prima facie throws the aggregate charges on to the aggregate lands in exoneration of the testator's general estate[2].

1 *Re Holt, Holt v Holt* (1916) 85 LJ Ch 779.
2 *Re Baron Kensington, Earl of Longford v Baron Kensington* [1902] 1 Ch 203.

1011. Liabilities incident to particular property. At common law a liability which is naturally incident to any particular form of property must be borne by that property[1]. Accordingly, a fine, incident to the preservation of a lease, must be paid by the person to whom the term is bequeathed[2]; and it has been held that the legatee of leasehold property which is out of repair is not entitled to have it put into repair at the expense of the testator's general estate[3]. Calls made subsequent to the death upon partly paid shares must be paid by the legatee of the shares[4]. Before 1926 liabilities accrued due at the date of death, whether in respect of rent[5] or in respect of calls made before death[6], were payable, like other debts, out of the general personal estate[7]; but after 1925 the burden of liabilities in any way charged upon the particular property[8] accrued due at the date of death must, subject to the terms of the will, be borne by the particular property to which the liabilities is naturally incident[9].

1 See *Halliwell v Tanner* (1830) 1 Russ & M 633; *Re Butler, Le Bas v Herbert* [1894] 3 Ch 250.
2 *Fitzwilliams v Kelly* (1852) 10 Hare 266.
3 *Hickling v Boyer* (1851) 3 Mac & G 635; doubted in *Harris v Poyner* (1852) 1 Drew 174.
4 *Armstrong v Burnet* (1855) 20 Beav 424; *Addams v Ferick* (1859) 26 Beav 384. Distinguish from the ordinary case of partly paid shares such cases as *Blount v Hipkins* (1834) 7 Sim 43 at 51; *Jaques v Chambers* (1846) 16 LJ Ch 243; *Clive v Clive* (1854) Kay 600.
5 *Barry v Harding* (1844) 1 Jo & Lat 475.
6 *Addams v Ferick* (1859) 26 Beav 384.
7 *Re Timberlake, Archer v Timberlake* (1919) 63 Sol Jo 286; *Re Beecham, Woolley v Beecham* (1919) 63 Sol Jo 430.
8 Eg arrears of interest in a mortgage or calls upon shares where the articles give the company a lien for unpaid calls.
9 See the Administration of Estates Act 1925 s 35; and PARA 1006 et seq.

1012. Wills made before 31 December 1925. Where the will was made before 31 December 1925, although in administering the estate the provisions of the Administration of Estates Act 1925 relating to the order of application of assets[1] must be applied, yet in construing the will regard must be had to the law in force at the time of its execution[2].

In the case of death before 1926 the personal estate of a deceased person was the primary fund for the payment of his debts[3], but where a testator appropriated a specific portion of his personal estate for the payment of his debts, that portion was the primary fund for payment unless the residuary personal estate was undisposed of[4], and a testator might, of course, make his realty the primary fund for payment of his debts, or create a mixed fund for payment of his debts[5].

In order to make the realty the primary fund, it was necessary for a testator before 1926 to use language which showed a manifest intention that his personal estate should be exonerated[6]. An express charge of debts upon his realty[7], or an express devise of his realty in trust for payment of debts[8], was in itself insufficient to displace the ordinary rule that the personal estate was the primary fund; the charge or trust was treated as the constitution merely of an auxiliary fund for payment of debts, and the ordinary rule was only displaced where from the rest of the will it could be clearly gathered that the testator intended to exonerate his personal estate[9].

1 Ie the Administration of Estates Act 1925 s 34(3), Sch 1 Pt II: see PARA 998 et seq.
2 Ie before the alterations in the law were made: *Re Atkinson, Webster v Walter* [1930] 1 Ch 47 at 50; *Re Littlewood, Clark v Littlewood* [1931] 1 Ch 443 at 445.
3 *Walker v Jackson* (1743) 2 Atk 624; *Duke of Ancaster v Mayer* (1785) 1 Bro CC 454. The order of abatement was as follows:
(1) the general or residuary personalty, not exonerated or exempted (see eg *Manning v Spooner* (1796) 3 Ves 114 at 117; *Harmood v Oglander* (1803) 8 Ves 106 at 124 (where a share of the residuary personalty lapsed, the debts were not payable primarily out of the lapsed share (see eg *Blann v Bell* (1877) 7 ChD 382)));
(2) real estate specifically appropriated to or devised in trust for payment of debts (see eg *Milnes v Slater* (1803) 8 Ves 295 at 304; *Stead v Hardaker* (1873) LR 15 Eq 175);
(3) real estate descended (see eg *Barber v Wood* (1877) 4 ChD 885);
(4) real estate devised, charged with the payment of debts (*Aldrich v Cooper* (1803) 8 Ves 382 at 396; *Re Stokes, Parsons v Miller* (1892) 67 LT 223; and see PARA 1003 note 2 (where a share of realty charged with payment of debts lapsed, the lapsed share bore only its rateable proportion of the debts (*Ryves v Ryves* (1871) LR 11 Eq 539)));
(5) general pecuniary legacies rateably (see PARA 1003 note 2);
(6) real estate devised, whether specifically or as residue, and personal estate specifically bequeathed rateably (see eg *Powell v Riley* (1871) LR 12 Eq 175; *Jackson v Pease* (1874) LR 19 Eq 96; and see the cases cited in PARA 1004 notes 5–7);
(7) real and personal property expressly appointed by will in exercise of a general power of appointment (see eg *Fleming v Buchanan* (1853) 3 De GM & G 976; *Beyfus v Lawley* [1903] AC 411, HL (where the power was executed by reason of a bequest of the testator's personal estate, or of any bequest of personal property described in a general manner, personal property the subject of the general power was included in the bequest (see the Wills Act 1837 s 27); it formed part of the testator's personal estate, and therefore went in exactly the same way as his other personal estate, and was not necessarily postponed, as a fund liable for the payment of his debts, to other assets of the testator (*Williams v Williams, Re Hartley, Williams v Jones* [1900] 1 Ch 152); see also PARA 1005 note 7)).
4 *Browne v Groombridge* (1819) 4 Madd 495; *Choat v Yeats* (1819) 1 Jac & W 102; *Hewett v Snare* (1847) 1 De G & Sm 333; *Lomax v Lomax* (1849) 12 Beav 285; *Newbegin v Bell* (1857) 23 Beav 386; *Trott v Buchanan* (1885) 28 ChD 446; *Re Smith, Smith v Smith* [1913] 2 Ch 216 at 223; *Re Littlewood, Clark v Littlewood* [1931] 1 Ch 443 at 445.
5 See PARA 993.
6 *Bootle v Blundell* (1815) 1 Mer 193 at 219–220 per Lord Eldon LC; *Bickham v Cruttwell* (1838) 3 My & Cr 763; *Forrest v Prescott* (1870) LR 10 Eq 545 at 549 per Malins V-C; *Re Meere, Kilford v Blaney* (1885) 31 ChD 56 at 62, CA, per Lord Halsbury LC; *Re Smith, Smith v Smith* [1913] 2 Ch 216; *Re Littlewood, Clark v Littlewood* [1931] 1 Ch 443. As to the presumption in favour of giving creditors a charge on the larger amount of property see PARA 993 note 4.
7 *Tait v Lord Northwick* (1799) 4 Ves 816 at 823; *Re Banks, Banks v Busbridge* [1905] 1 Ch 547.
8 *M'Cleland v Shaw* (1805) 2 Sch & Lef 538; *Rhodes v Rudge* (1826) 1 Sim 79.
9 For cases in which the personal estate was held to be exonerated see *Burton v Knowlton* (1796) 3 Ves 107; *Bootle v Blundell* (1815) 1 Mer 193; *Greene v Greene* (1819) 4 Madd 148; *Michell v Michell* (1820) 5 Madd 69; *Lance v Aglionby* (1859) 27 Beav 65; *Gilbertson v Gibertson* (1865) 34 Beav 354; *Forrest v Prescott* (1870) LR 10 Eq 545; *Re Meere, Kilford v Blaney* (1885) 31 ChD 56, CA; *Duffy v Duffy* [1920] 1 IR 122. For cases in which the personal estate was held not to be exonerated see *French v Chichester* (1706) 2 Vern 568; *Haslewood v Pope* (1734) 3 P Wms 322; *Duke of Ancaster v Mayer* (1785) 1 Bro CC 454; *Tait v Lord Northwick* (1799) 4 Ves 816; *M'Cleland v Shaw* (1805) 2 Sch & Lef 538; *Brummel v Prothero* (1796) 3 Ves 111; *Aldridge v Lord Wallscourt* (1810) 1 Ball & B 312; *Tower v Lord Rous* (1811) 18 Ves 132; *Rhodes v Rudge* (1826) 1 Sim 79; *Trott v Buchanan* (1885) 28 ChD 446; *Re Banks, Banks v Busbridge* [1905] 1 Ch 547; *Walker v M'Kay* [1917] 1 IR 278, CA.

(iii) Testamentary and Administration Expenses

1013. General principle deciding whether costs and expenses are payable from the general estate. It is often important to decide whether costs and expenses incurred by a personal representative are properly payable out of the estate as testamentary and administration expenses[1] or should be borne by the legatees or devisees or persons entitled on intestacy out of their respective interests. The general principle is that the estate must bear the expenses incident to the proper performance of the duties of the personal representative[2] as personal representative but not the expenses involved in the execution of trusts which arise after the estate has been administered or an assent given[3], or the expenses of clearing the property comprised in a gift so as to make it available by way of assent in favour of the donee[4].

1 See PARA 998. As to the meaning of 'personal representative' see PARA 608.
2 *Sharp v Lush* (1879) 10 ChD 468, where it was said that 'executorship expenses' and 'testamentary expenses' meant the same thing; *Re Clemow, Yeo v Clemow* [1900] 2 Ch 182 at 190.
3 *Re Fitzpatrick, Bennett v Bennett* [1952] Ch 86, [1951] 2 All ER 949; cf *Lord Brougham v Lord Poulett* (1855) 19 Beav 119, where a fund was directed to be set aside to pay debts, legacies, funeral expenses, expenses of proving the will 'and the execution of the trusts thereof', and it was held that in the context the last-mentioned expenses were limited to expenses properly payable by the executors as such. See also *Re Evans, Evans v Westcombe* [1999] 2 All ER 777, where expenses incurred in respect of a missing beneficiary policy were allowed as an administration expense. As to assents see also PARA 1148.
4 *Re Matthews' Will Trusts, Bristow v Mathews* [1961] 3 All ER 869 at 876, [1961] 1 WLR 1415 at 1422 per Pennycuick J.

1014. General costs of administration. The general costs of administering the estate are testamentary expenses, for this term is not confined to expenses connected with the will, and indeed it applies to an intestacy[1]. The estate must therefore bear the cost of obtaining the grant[2], collecting and preserving the assets, discharging the debts and distributing the balance[3]. The insurance premium for a missing beneficiary policy can be a proper testamentary expense[4]. It seems that the cost of moving and storing objects specifically bequeathed before and after the executor assents to the bequest is borne by the legatee[5].

1 *Sharp v Lush* (1879) 10 ChD 468; *Re Clemow, Yeo v Clemow* [1900] 2 Ch 182. As to professional charges see PARA 981 note 4.
2 *Re Elementary Education Acts 1870 and 1873* [1909] 1 Ch 55, CA.
3 *Sharp v Lush* (1879) 10 ChD 468. The cost of distribution may include the cost of obtaining legal advice, without commencing proceedings, as to the proper distribution of the estate: *Sharp v Lush* at 471.
4 *Re Evans, Evans v Westcombe* [1999] 2 All ER 777.
5 *Re De Sommery, Coelenbier v De Sommery* [1912] 2 Ch 622; *Re Pearce, Crutchley v Wells* [1909] 1 Ch 819; *Re Grosvenor, Grosvenor v Grosvenor* [1916] 2 Ch 375; *Re Sivewright, Law v Fenwick* [1922] WN 338; *Re Leach, Milne v Daubeny* [1923] 1 Ch 161; *Re Scott, Scott v Scott* [1915] 1 Ch 592, CA; *Re Fitzpatrick, Bennett v Bennett* [1952] Ch 86, [1951] 2 All ER 949. See also PARA 1060 text and notes 4–5. The expenses of preserving chattels pending exercise of a right of selection are a testamentary expense, however: *Re Collins Settlement Trusts, Donne v Hewetson* [1971] 1 All ER 283, [1971] 1 WLR 37.

1015. Fees of the Public Trustee and trust corporations. The acceptance and withdrawal fees of the Public Trustee[1] or trust corporations in respect of an annuity are borne by the estate where the residue of the estate has been given subject to payment of the annuity[2], but where funds are set aside to secure annuities and do not then fall into residue the withdrawal fee must be borne by those funds and not by residue[3]. Similarly the acceptance fee in respect of a settled legacy is paid by the estate but the withdrawal fee is paid out of the legacy[4]. Income fees are payable out of income[5] and must be borne by the income of a settled legacy[6] or, in case of an annuity, out of the funds set aside to secure the annuity[7] or the residuary estate[8] as the case may be.

1 As to the Public Trustee see TRUSTS AND POWERS vol 98 (2013) PARA 206 et seq.

2 *Re Hulton, Midland Bank Executor and Trustee Co Ltd v Thompson* [1936] Ch 536, [1936] 2 All ER 207; *Re Riddell, Public Trustee v Riddell* [1936] Ch 747, [1936] 2 All ER 1600; cf *Re Bentley, Public Trustee v Bentley* [1914] 2 Ch 456.
3 *Re Godwin, Coutts & Co v Godwin* [1938] Ch 341, [1938] 1 All ER 287; *Re Evans' Will Trusts, Public Trustee v Gausby* [1948] Ch 185, [1948] 1 All ER 381.
4 *Re Roberts' Will Trusts, Younger v Lewins* [1937] Ch 274, [1937] 1 All ER 518.
5 *Re Hicklin, Public Trustee v Hoare* [1917] 2 Ch 278; *Re Riddell, Public Trustee v Riddell* [1936] Ch 747, [1936] 2 All ER 1600.
6 *Re Roberts' Will Trusts, Younger v Lewins* [1937] Ch 274, [1937] 1 All ER 518.
7 *Re Godwin, Coutts & Co v Godwin* [1938] Ch 341, [1938] 1 All ER 287; *Re Evans' Will Trusts, Public Trustee v Gausby* [1948] Ch 185, [1948] 1 All ER 381.
8 *Re Hulton, Midland Bank Executor and Trustee Co Ltd v Thompson* [1936] Ch 536, [1936] 2 All ER 207.

1016. Inheritance tax and capital gains tax. Inheritance tax payable in respect of the deceased person's death on property situated in the United Kingdom[1] which vests in the personal representatives[2] is treated as a testamentary expense[3], unless the deceased showed a contrary intention in his will[4].

There is no capital gains tax on death[5]. Capital gains tax due from the deceased during his lifetime would be payable as an ordinary debt or liability of his estate.

1 Foreign death duties or taxes are not normally a testamentary expense, and are usually borne by specific legatees of the property subject to them: *Re Scott, Scott v Scott* [1915] 1 Ch 592, CA; *Re Brewster, Butler v Southam* [1908] 2 Ch 365; *Re De Sommery, Coelenbier v De Sommery* [1912] 2 Ch 622; *Shelley v New South Wales Institution for Deaf and Dumb and Blind* [1919] AC 650, PC; *Re Matthews' Will Trusts, Bristow v Matthews* [1961] 3 All ER 869 at 876, [1961] 1 WLR 1415 at 1422 per Pennycuick J. See, however, *Re Sebba, Lloyd's Bank Ltd v Hutson* [1959] Ch 166, [1958] 3 All ER 393, where certain Canadian duties were held to be payable out of residue without the pecuniary legacies being subject to them, and where the double tax relief was allocated to the beneficiaries who bore the United Kingdom estate duty on the assets entitled to the relief. United Kingdom inheritance tax on property situated outside the United Kingdom is not treated as a testamentary expense (see the Inheritance Tax Act 1984 s 211(1); and INHERITANCE TAXATION vol 59A (2014) PARA 271) and is borne by that property: *Re Scull, Scott v Morris* (1917) 87 LJCh 59, CA; *Re Sebba, Lloyd's Bank Ltd v Hutson*. See also *Scarfe v Matthews* [2012] EWHC 3071 (Ch), [2012] STC 2487 (adopted children of deceased who were acting contrary to his will by exercising their rights under French law were not entitled to have their tax liability discharged by executors of deceased's will). As to the incidence of inheritance tax see also PARA 1128 et seq.
2 Ie other than property comprised in a settlement immediately before the deceased's death (see the Inheritance Tax Act 1984 s 211(1)), so that, for example, the inheritance tax on settled land or on settled property subject to a general power exercised by the deceased would not be treated as a testamentary expense, even though such property became vested in the personal representatives. See also INHERITANCE TAXATION vol 59A (2014) PARA 271. As to the meaning of 'personal representative' see PARA 608.
3 See the Inheritance Tax Act 1984 s 211(1); and INHERITANCE TAXATION vol 59A (2014) PARA 271. Where any amount of inheritance tax paid by personal representatives does not fall to be borne as part of the testamentary expenses of the estate, that amount, where occasion requires, is to be repaid to them by the person in whom the property to which the tax is attributable is vested: see s 211(3); and INHERITANCE TAXATION vol 59A (2014) PARA 271.
4 Inheritance Tax Act 1984 s 211(2). A direction freeing from inheritance tax property which would otherwise bear its own inheritance tax is treated as a pecuniary legacy by the Administration of Estates Act 1925: see PARA 1003.
5 See the Taxation of Chargeable Gains Act 1992 s 62(1); and CAPITAL GAINS TAXATION vol 6 (2011) PARA 699.

1017. Costs of proceedings. Costs of proceedings are in the discretion of the court[1], but the discretion is a judicial one exercised on the following principles. The executor's costs of probate proceedings are testamentary expenses and therefore payable out of the estate[2], and the costs of other parties may be, but are not necessarily also allowed[3]. The executor's costs of proceedings for directions or the construction of the will or administration of the estate by the court are testamentary expenses and, if the fault is the testator's, the costs of all necessary parties[4] will be payable out of the estate[5], even if only one particular fund is concerned[6].

1 See PARAS 908, 1196. See also *Corbett v Bond Pearce (a firm)* [2006] EWCH 909 (Ch), [2006] All ER (D) 01 (May), where the personal representative claimed for recovery of the losses suffered by the testatrix's estate as a result of proceedings over the preparation and execution of a later will which was found to be invalid on account of admitted negligence in its preparation and execution by the testatrix's solicitors, and in respect of which the costs of all parties to the probate action were ordered to be paid out of the testatrix's estate.
2 See PARAS 909–910.
3 See PARAS 909, 911.
4 As to unnecessary parties or parties whose claims are without merit see *Re Amory, Westminster Bank Ltd v British Sailors' Society Inc at Home and Abroad* [1951] 2 All ER 947n; *Re Daysh, Dale v Duke of Richmond* [1951] 1 TLR 257; *Re Preston, Raby v Port of Hull Society's Sailors' Orphans Homes* [1951] Ch 878, [1951] 2 All ER 421.
5 *Re Buckton, Buckton v Buckton* [1907] 2 Ch 406; *Morrell v Fisher* (1851) 4 De G & Sm 422; *Harloe v Harloe* (1875) LR 20 Eq 471; *Re Clarke, Clarke v St Mary's Convalescent Home* (1907) 97 LT 707; *Miles v Harrison* (1874) 9 Ch App 316; *Re Young, Young v Dolman* (1881) 44 LT 499, CA; *Penny v Penny* (1879) 11 ChD 440; *Re Groom, Booty v Groom* [1897] 2 Ch 407; *Re Vincent, Rohde v Palin* [1909] 1 Ch 810; *Re Hall-Dare, Le Marchant v Lee Warner* [1916] 1 Ch 272.
6 *Re Flecher, King v King* (1918) 62 Sol Jo 740. As to the costs of administration proceedings see further PARA 1196 et seq.

1018. Right of indemnity. The personal representative is entitled to be reimbursed from the estate, or may pay out of the estate, expenses properly incurred by him when acting on behalf of the estate, without any special provision to that effect[1]. This right of indemnity is a first charge as well upon the income as upon the capital of the estate, and the expenses may be retained out of the income until provision can be made for raising them out of the capital[2]. The charges and expenses include the costs of probate proceedings[3], and of claims relating to the estate, which were brought or defended with the leave of the court, or which, though no leave had been obtained, it was proper to bring or defend[4]. Should the representative desire to have his costs assessed by a costs judge against the estate, he should obtain an express direction to that effect in the order for the detailed assessment of his costs, charges and expenses[5].

A personal representative who has improperly brought or defended proceedings will be disallowed as against the estate both his solicitor's bill of costs in the proceedings and the costs he has had to pay to his opponent[6].

1 See the Trustee Act 2000 ss 31(1), (1A), (2), 35(1); and TRUSTS AND POWERS vol 98 (2013) PARA 348. See also *A-G v Norwich Corpn* (1837) 2 My & Cr 406 at 424; and PARA 609. As to the right to indemnity for loss occasioned by co-representatives see PARA 1252; and as to costs see PARA 1196 et seq. As to the right to reimburse agents, nominees and custodians see the Trustee Act 2000 s 32; and PARA 1049. As to the meaning of 'personal representative' see PARA 608.
2 *Stott v Milne* (1884) 25 ChD 710, CA.
3 *Re Price, Williams v Jenkins* (1886) 31 ChD 485; *Graham v M'Cashin* [1901] 1 IR 404, CA. As to costs of probate proceedings generally see PARA 908 et seq.
4 *Re Beddoe, Downes v Cottam* [1893] 1 Ch 547, CA; *Re England's Settlement Trusts, Dobb v England* [1918] 1 Ch 24. See PARA 1196. As to notices for claims see PARA 964. See also *Evans v Evans* [1985] 3 All ER 289, [1986] 1 WLR 101, CA (distinguishing *Re Dallaway* [1982] 3 All ER 118, [1982] 1 WLR 756), which held that it is not appropriate for the personal representative to be indemnified out of the estate against the costs of defending a claim to beneficial entitlement to the whole estate, where all the beneficiaries are of full age and capacity.
5 See *Payne v Little* (1859) 27 Beav 83.
6 *Chambers v Smith* (1846) 2 Coll 742; varied on another point sub nom *Smith v Chambers* (1847) 2 Ph 221. As to the right of the personal representative to the court's guidance see PARA 1168; and as to the expediency of obtaining such guidance in bringing or defending hostile actions see PARAS 1196, 1274.

(5) TRUSTS AND POWERS OF THE REPRESENTATIVE

(i) Trusts and Powers Generally

1019. Statutory powers. With effect from 1 January 1997, in addition to any powers and discretions conferred by the will, the personal representatives[1] of a person whatever his date of death[2], in dealing with his real and personal estate[3], for purposes of administration[4], or during a minority of any beneficiary or the subsistence or any life interest, or until the period of distribution arrives[5], have:

(1) as respects the personal estate, the same powers and discretions, including power to raise money by mortgage or charge (whether or not by deposit of documents), as a personal representative had before 1926 with respect to personal estate vested in him[6]; and

(2) as respects the real estate, all the functions conferred on them by Part I of the Trusts of Land and Appointment of Trustees Act 1996[7].

These powers are without prejudice to the powers conferred on personal representatives by the Trustee Act 2000[8]. In the exercise of his powers a personal representative or trustee is expected to act gratuitously unless the will or the court or statute makes provision for his remuneration[9].

1 As to the meaning of 'personal representative' see PARA 608.
2 Administration of Estates Act 1925 s 39(3).
3 As to the meaning of 'real estate' see PARA 607 note 1.
4 As to the meaning of 'administration' see PARA 607 note 1.
5 Administration of Estates Act 1925 s 39(1). See *Re Trollope's Will Trusts, Public Trustee v Trollope* [1927] 1 Ch 596 at 605; and PARA 1149.
6 Administration of Estates Act 1925 s 39(1)(i) (amended by the Trusts of Land and Appointment of Trustees Act 1996 s 25, Sch 3para6, Sch 4). As to these powers see PARA 1021 et seq.
7 Administration of Estates Act 1925 s 39(1)(ii) (substituted by Trusts of Land and Appointment of Trustees Act 1996 Sch 3para6). As to the trust which arises on an intestacy see PARA 1135 et seq. For restrictions on the disposition of the matrimonial home if one spouse dies intestate leaving the other surviving see PARA 489. The functions under the Trusts of Land and Appointment of Trustees Act 1996 include all the powers of an absolute owner: see ss 6(1), 18; and TRUSTS AND POWERS vol 98 (2013) PARA 476. The other functions conferred by Pt I (ss 1–18) on personal representatives are: power to postpone sale where there is a trust for sale (see s 4(1) and TRUSTS AND POWERS vol 98 (2013) PARA 407), power to convey land to beneficiaries of full age and capacity who are absolutely entitled to it (see s 6(2) and TRUSTS AND POWERS vol 98 (2013) PARA 476), power to purchase a legal estate in any land in England and Wales for investment, occupation by a beneficiary, or for any other reason (see ss 6(3), 17 and TRUSTS AND POWERS vol 98 (2013) PARA 476, 479), power to partition land among beneficiaries of full age and absolutely entitled (see s 7) power to delegate functions to beneficiaries by power of attorney (see s 9), and regulation of the rights of occupation of beneficiaries (see s 13 and TRUSTS AND POWERS vol 98 (2013) PARA 166): see s 18; and TRUSTS AND POWERS vol 98 (2013) PARA 474. If the administration of the estate is followed by trusteeship (see PARAS 1149–1150) these functions will continue and s 10 (consents to exercise of functions by trustees: see TRUSTS AND POWERS vol 98 (2013) PARA 477) and s 14 (powers of court: see TRUSTS AND POWERS vol 98 (2013) PARA 479) will then apply, as will also s 11 (duty to consult beneficiaries: see TRUSTS AND POWERS vol 98 (2013) PARA 477) in certain circumstances: see PARA 1020 note 5. As to the personal representatives' duties in exercising their powers see PARA 1020.

Before 1 January 1997, in relation to real estate personal representatives had all the powers, discretions and duties conferred or imposed by law and by statute on trustees holding land upon an effectual trust for sale: see the Administration of Estates Act 1925 s 39(1)(ii), (iii) (as originally enacted) (with effect from 1 January 1926). The statutory powers of trustees for sale were all the powers of a tenant for life and the trustees of a settlement under the Settled Land Act 1925: see the Law of Property Act 1925 s 28(1) (repealed with effect from 1 January 1997 by the Trusts of Land and Appointment of Trustees Act 1996 Sch 4). As to this provision, and as to the powers so applied and the powers of trustees for sale in general see REAL PROPERTY AND REGISTRATION vol 87 (2012) PARA 106; SETTLEMENTS vol 91 (2012) PARA 510.

8 Administration of Estates Act 1925 s 39(1A) (added by the Trustee Act 2000 s 40(1), Sch 2 Pt 2 para28). The Trustee Act 2000 applies in relation to a personal representative administering an estate according to the law as it applies to a trustee carrying out a trust for beneficiaries: s 35(1). As to powers under the Trustee Act 2000 see PARA 1033 (the power to insure), PARA 1049 (power to employ agents). Additionally, personal representatives have the same statutory powers as trustees (subject to any contrary intention in the will) contained in the Trustee Act 1925 Pt II (ss 12–33): see s 68(1) paras (9), (17), s 69(1), (2). As to powers of trustees generally see TRUSTS AND POWERS vol 98 (2013) PARA 1 et seq.

9 See PARA 648 et seq.

1020. Personal representatives' duties in exercising powers. At common law it is the duty of personal representatives to hold an even hand between all the beneficiaries of the estate[1]. On the one hand they must not unduly delay the payment or provision of any of the legacies, but on the other they ought not to sacrifice the interests of persons entitled in remainder by realising the estate for the benefit of a pecuniary legatee at an inopportune time when the value of securities is low. They must act prudently and properly in the management of the estate as a whole[2]. Accordingly, it is not the duty of an executor to agree a valuation for inheritance tax at the highest price which might be obtained so as to make a beneficiary who had an option to purchase at that valuation pay the highest price[3]. The court will not in general interfere with the exercise of a discretion[4], but may do so when beneficiaries are absolutely entitled between them, to ensure that their unanimous wishes are complied with[5].

By statute there is a single duty of care[6] which applies to a personal representative such that whenever the duty applies[7], he must exercise such care and skill as is reasonable in the circumstances, having regard in particular:

(1) to any special knowledge or experience that he has or holds himself out as having[8]; and

(2) if he acts as personal representative in the course of a business or profession, to any special knowledge or experience that it is reasonable to expect of a person acting in the course of that kind of business or profession[9].

1 This includes persons entitled or potentially entitled as statutory beneficiaries under the family provision legislation: see PARA 567. Where there is land in the estate, in exercising the powers conferred by the Trusts of Land and Appointment of Trustees Act 1996 s 6 (see PARA 1019 note 7) personal representatives and trustees are to have regard to the rights of the beneficiaries: see s 6(5). See also note 5. As to the duty of personal representatives to hold a fair balance between capital and income in defraying expenditure in cases (before 1 January 1997) where by virtue of Law of Property Act 1925 s 28 (repealed with effect from 1 January 1997 by the Trusts of Land and Appointment of Trustees Act 1996 Sch 4), and the Administration of Estates Act 1925 s 39(1) (as originally enacted), the powers both of a tenant for life and of the trustees of a settlement were vested in them see *Re Lord Boston's Will Trusts, Inglis v Lord Boston* [1956] Ch 395, [1956] 1 All ER 593; and PARA 1019 note 7. As to the self-dealing rule and exercise of powers see PARA 1030.

2 See *Re Lepine, Dowsett v Culver* [1892] 1 Ch 210 at 219, CA; *Re Charteris, Charteris v Biddulph* [1917] 2 Ch 379 at 388, 397, CA.

3 *Re Hayes' Will Trusts, Pattinson v Hayes* [1971] 2 All ER 341, [1971] 1 WLR 758 (an estate duty case).

4 *Re Whichelow, Bradshaw v Orpen* [1953] 2 All ER 1558, [1954] 1 WLR 5.

5 *Butt v Kelson* [1952] Ch 197, [1952] 1 All ER 167, CA. If the administration of the estate is followed by trusteeship (see PARAS 1149–1150) the trustees must in exercise of any function relating to land, so far as practicable, consult the beneficiaries of full age with interests in possession in the land, and must, so far as consistent with the general interest of the trust, give effect to their wishes or the wishes of the majority, according to the value of their combined interests: Trusts of Land and Appointment of Trustees Act 1996 s 11(1). This duty, however, only applies if the trust arises by statute (eg under an intestacy or statutory joint tenancy or tenancy in common) or under a will made on or after 1 January 1997 which does not exclude it: s 11(2). For the powers of beneficiaries who are together absolutely entitled to the trust property to substitute new trustees see ss 19–21; and TRUSTS AND POWERS vol 98 (2013) PARAS 285–286, 337.

6 See the Trustee Act 2000 s 1(2); and TRUSTS AND POWERS vol 98 (2013) PARA 389.
7 The Trustee Act 2000 ss 2, 35(1), Sch 1 provides that the duty of care applies to a personal representative:
(1) when exercising the general power of investment or any other power of investment, however conferred (see TRUSTS AND POWERS vol 98 (2013) PARAS 390, 453) (Sch 1 para 1(a));
(2) when carrying out a duty to which he is subject under s 4 or s 5 (duties relating to the exercise of a power of investment or to the review of investments: see TRUSTS AND POWERS vol 98 (2013) PARAS 454, 455) (Sch 1 para 1(b));
(3) when exercising the power under s 8 to acquire land (see TRUSTS AND POWERS vol 98 (2013) PARA PARAS 390, 475) (Sch 1 para 2(a));
(4) when exercising any other power to acquire land, however conferred (see TRUSTS AND POWERS vol 98 (2013) PARA 476) (Sch 1 para 2(b));
(5) when exercising any power in relation to land acquired under a power mentioned in head (3) or (4) (Sch 1 para 2(c));
(6) when entering into arrangements under which a person is authorised under s 11 to exercise functions as an agent (see PARA 1049; and TRUSTS AND POWERS vol 98 (2013) PARAS 390, 430) (Sch 1 para 3(1)(a));
(7) when entering into arrangements under which a person is appointed under s 16 to act as a nominee (see PARA 1049; and TRUSTS AND POWERS vol 98 (2013) PARA 432) (Sch 1 para 3(1)(b));
(8) when entering into arrangements under which a person is appointed under s 17 or 18 to act as a custodian (see PARA 1049; and TRUSTS AND POWERS vol 98 (2013) PARA 432) (Sch 1 para 3(1)(c));
(9) when entering into arrangements under which, under any other power, however conferred, a person is authorised to exercise functions as an agent or is appointed to act as a nominee or custodian (see PARA 1049; and TRUSTS AND POWERS vol 98 (2013) PARA 433) (Sch 1 para 3(1)(d));
(10) when carrying out his duties under s 22 (review of agent, nominee or custodian, etc: see TRUSTS AND POWERS vol 98 (2013) PARA 436) (Sch 1 para 3(1)(e));
(11) when exercising the power under the Trustee Act 1925 s 15 to do any of the things referred to in that section, and when exercising any corresponding power, however conferred (see PARA 1043; and TRUSTS AND POWERS vol 98 (2013) PARAS 390, 431) (Trustee Act 2000 Sch 1 para 4);
(12) when exercising the power under the Trustee Act 1925 s 19 to insure property, and when exercising any corresponding power, however conferred (see PARA 1033; and TRUSTS AND POWERS vol 98 (2013) PARAS 390, 513, 514) (Trustee Act 2000 Sch 1 para 5);
(13) when exercising the power under the Trustee Act 1925 s 22(1) or s 22(3) to do any of the things referred to there, and when exercising any corresponding power, however conferred (see TRUSTS AND POWERS vol 98 (2013) PARA 436) (Trustee Act 2000 Sch 1 para 6).

For the purposes of heads (6)–(10), entering into arrangements under which a person is authorised to exercise functions or is appointed to act as a nominee or custodian includes, in particular:
(a) selecting the person who is to act (Sch 1 para 3(2)(a));
(b) determining any terms on which he is to act (Sch 1 para 3(2)(b)); and
(c) if the person is being authorised to exercise asset management functions, the preparation of a policy statement under s 15 (Sch 1 para 3(2)(c)).

The duty of care does not apply if or in so far as it appears from the trust instrument (ie the will, in the case of personal representatives) that the duty is not meant to apply: see Sch 1 para 7.
8 Trustee Act 2000 s 1(1)(a).
9 Trustee Act 2000 s 1(1)(b).

(ii) Power to Alienate and Charge

1021. Particular powers. The powers of the personal representative[1] which have already been generally stated[2] include, for the purposes previously stated[3], in particular the power on intestacy to charge the assets or sell leaseholds for the purpose of paying to one of the next of kin his share in the estate[4]; the statutory power of sale of any real or personal estate as to which the deceased died intestate[5]; in relation to the personal estate, the same power to raise money by mortgage or charge, whether or not by deposit of documents, as a personal representative had before 1926[6] with respect to personal estate vested in him[7]; the power by a conveyance of a legal estate in land to a purchaser for money or money's worth to overreach equitable interests and powers[8]; and all the powers necessary so that every contract entered into by a personal representative is binding on and enforceable against and by the personal representative for the time being of the deceased and may be carried into effect or be varied or rescinded by him, and in the case of a contract entered into by a predecessor as if it had been entered into by himself[9].

1 'Personal representative' does not include trustees in the ordinary sense: *Re Trollope's Will Trusts, Public Trustee v Trollope* [1927] 1 Ch 596 at 603. As to the meaning of 'personal representative' see PARA 608.
2 See PARA 1019.
3 See PARA 1019.
4 *Re O'Donnell* [1905] 1 IR 406, CA; *Re Norwood and Blake's Contract* [1917] 1 IR 172.
5 See the Administration of Estates Act 1925 s 33(1) (substituted by the Trusts of Land and Appointment of Trustees Act 1996 s 5(1), Sch 2para5). As to the meaning of 'real estate' see PARA 607 note 1. As to the meaning of 'intestate' see PARA 1135 note 1. Before 1 January 1997, the Administration of Estates Act 1925 s 33(1) (as originally enacted) provided for a trust for sale of an intestate estate with power to postpone sale.
6 See PARAS 1023–1024.
7 See the Administration of Estates Act 1925 s 39(1)(i) (amended by the Trusts of Land and Appointment of Trustees Act 1996 s 25, Sch 3para6, Sch 4); and PARA 1019.
8 See the Law of Property Act 1925 s 2(1)(iii); and REAL PROPERTY AND REGISTRATION vol 87 (2012) PARA 263.
9 Administration of Estates Act 1925 s 39(1)(iii) (amended by the Trusts of Land and Appointment of Trustees Act 1996 Sch 3 para6). Nothing in the Administration of Estates Act 1925 s 39 affects the right of any person to require an assent or conveyance to be made: s 39(2). As to the meaning of 'conveyance' see PARA 858 note 1. As to assents see PARA 1139 et seq. As to the contract for the sale of, and conveyance or transfer of, real estate where there are two or more representatives see s 2(2); and PARA 1024.

1022. Additional powers allowing personal representatives to alienate or charge assets. In addition to the powers stated previously[1], the personal representative has the following powers:

(1) with respect to real estate vested in him[2], he has the same powers of alienation as a personal representative had at common law with respect to chattels real[3];

(2) for the purpose of paying inheritance tax for which he is liable[4], or raising the amount of it when paid, and whether or not the property to which the tax is attributable is vested in him, to raise the amount of the tax by sale or mortgage of, or a terminable charge on, that property or any part of it[5];

(3) for giving effect to beneficial interests, he may limit or demise land for a term of years absolute, with or without impeachment for waste, to trustees on usual trusts for raising or securing any principal sum and interest on it for which the land, or any part of it, is liable, and may limit or grant a rentcharge for giving effect to any annual or periodical sum for which the land or its income, or any part of it, is liable[6];

(4) where he is authorised to pay or apply capital money subject to a trust for any purpose or in any manner, he has power to raise the money required by sale, conversion, calling in or mortgage of all or any part of the trust property for the time being in possession[7];

(5) before giving an assent or making a conveyance in favour of any person entitled, he may permit that person to take possession[8] of the land, and such possession does not prejudicially affect the representative's right to

take or resume possession, nor his power to convey the land as if he were in possession of it but subject to the interest of any lessee, tenant or occupier in possession or in actual occupation of the land[9].

1 See PARA 1021.
2 As to what real estate devolves on the personal representative see the Administration of Estates Act 1925 ss 1(1), 3(1), (2); and PARA 945. 'Real estate' for this purpose includes leaseholds: see PARA 946. As to the meaning of 'personal representative' see PARA 608.
3 See the Administration of Estates Act 1925 s 2(1); and PARA 945.
4 As to the personal representatives' liability for inheritance tax see PARAS 1217, 1255.
5 See the Inheritance Tax Act 1984 s 212(1); and INHERITANCE TAXATION vol 59A (2014) PARA 272.
6 Administration of Estates Act 1925 s 40(1). This provision applies whenever the testator or intestate died: s 40(2). As to limited legal estates and their conversion in 1925 see the Law of Property Act 1925 s 39, Sch 1 Pt I; and REAL PROPERTY AND REGISTRATION vol 87 (2012) PARA 51.
7 See the Trustee Act 1925 s 16(1); and TRUSTS AND POWERS vol 98 (2013) PARA 521. This provision applies notwithstanding anything to the contrary contained in the instrument, if any, creating the trust: see s 16(2).
8 'Possession' includes the receipt of rents and profits or the right to receive the same if any: Administration of Estates Act 1925 s 55(1)(xii).
9 Administration of Estates Act 1925 s 43(1). This provision applies whatever the date of death of the testator or intestate: s 43(3).

1023. Power to alienate personalty. The personal representative[1] has and always had a complete and absolute control over the deceased's personal property, and, at any time before he has assented, he can dispose of the effects, whether they are legal or equitable[2], by mortgage or pledge as well as by sale[3], notwithstanding that the property disposed of is specifically bequeathed[4] or limited in trust by the will[5]. He may give the mortgagee a power of sale over the mortgaged assets[6].

One of several personal representatives[7] can enter into a binding contract for sale of personalty forming part of the deceased's estate[8]. If the representative who entered into the contract purported to do so not only on his own behalf but also on behalf of his co-representative and his co-representative did not authorise him to do so and has not subsequently ratified his act, the court may refuse to enforce the contract[9]. It appears, however, that the court may enforce the contract, even if the co-representative dissents, where the representative who entered into the contract in terms contracted solely on his own behalf without purporting to act with the concurrence of the co-representative[10].

1 As to the meaning of 'personal representative' see PARA 608.
2 *Nugent v Gifford* (1738) 1 Atk 463 at 464. An instrument of transfer of the share or other interest of a deceased member of a company (1) may be made by his personal representative although the personal representative is not himself a member of the company; and (2) is as effective as if the personal representative had been such a member at the time of the execution of the instrument: see the Companies Act 2006 s 773; and COMPANIES vol 14 (2016) PARAS 409, 445. As to the power of an attorney administrator to make title to property see PARA 800.
3 *Mead v Lord Orrery* (1745) 3 Atk 235 at 240; *Scott v Tyler* (1788) 2 Dick 712 at 725; *M'Leod v Drummond* (1810) 17 Ves 152 at 154; *Earl Vane v Rigden* (1870) 5 Ch App 663.
4 *Ewer v Corbet* (1723) 2 P Wms 148; *Langley v Earl of Oxford* (1748) Amb 795; *Andrew v Wrigley* (1792) 4 Bro CC 125.
5 *M'Leod v Drummond* (1810) 17 Ves 152.
6 *Russell v Plaice* (1854) 18 Beav 21; *Cruikshank v Duffin* (1872) LR 13 Eq 555. See also *Thorne v Thorne* [1893] 3 Ch 196.
7 Apart from statute a single executor has power to dispose of the deceased's personal estate: see *Jacomb v Harwood* (1751) 2 Ves Sen 265 at 267; *Simpson v Gutteridge* (1816) 1 Madd 609 at 617; *Fountain Forestry Ltd v Edwards* [1975] Ch 1 at 11, [1974] 2 All ER 280 at 283 per Brightman J; cf *Turner v Hardey* (1842) 9 M & W 770. In *Fountain Forestry Ltd v Edwards* at 14 and 285, Brightman J thought that there was no decisive authority on the question whether an administrator acting without his co-administrator had the same power of disposition as an executor acting without his co-executor, but, having regard to dicta of Romilly MR in *Smith v*

Everett (1859) as reported in 29 LJ Ch 236 at 239–240, in favour of a single administrator, he was content to assume for the purposes of the case before him that a single administrator had such power; see also PARA 926 text and note 4.

8 *Fountain Forestry Ltd v Edwards* [1975] Ch 1, [1974] 2 All ER 280. The case concerned a contract for the sale of land before the amendment of the Administration of Estates Act 1925 s 2(2) by the Law of Property (Miscellaneous Provisions) 1994 s 16, with effect from 1 July 1995, required all personal representatives to join in a contract to sell land (see PARA 1024), but it remains relevant to personal estate.

9 *Sneesby v Thorne* (1855) 7 De GM & G 399; *Fountain Forestry Ltd v Edwards* [1975] Ch 1, [1974] 2 All ER 280.

10 *Fountain Forestry Ltd v Edwards* [1975] Ch 1 at 15, [1974] 2 All ER 280 at 286 per Brightman J. See also 124 NLJ 749 (8 August 1974).

1024. Alienation of land. Where there are two or more personal representatives[1] a conveyance[2] of real estate[3], devolving under the provisions relating to the devolution of real estate[4], or a contract for such a conveyance, may not be made without the concurrence of all the personal representatives or a court order[5]. If, however, probate is granted to one or some of two or more persons named as executors, whether or not power is reserved to the other or others to prove, any conveyance of the real estate or contract for such a conveyance may be made by the proving executor or executors for the time being, without a court order, and is as effectual as if all the persons named as executors had concurred in it[6].

Apart from statute, where an executor is selling or mortgaging real estate devised to himself and charged with the payment of legacies only, the assignee is bound to see to the application of the purchase money[7]. Where, however, the real estate is charged with payment of debts as well as of legacies, the assignee is under no such obligation, even though there are, to his knowledge, no debts of the testator existing[8], or though the purchase money is expressed to be raised for the payment of legacies only[9].

1 As to the meaning of 'personal representative' see PARA 608.

2 As to the meaning of 'conveyance' see PARA 858 note 1.

3 As to the meaning of 'real estate' see PARA 946.

4 Ie under the Administration of Estates Act 1925 Pt I (ss 1–3): see PARA 945 et seq.

5 Administration of Estates Act 1925 s 2(2) (amended by the Law of Property (Miscellaneous Provisions) Act 1994 s 16(1), 21(2), Sch 2). See also *Johnson v Clarke* [1928] Ch 847. As to joint representation see generally PARA 926. Before the amendment of Administration of Estates Act 1925 s 2(2), with effect from 1 July 1995, the concurrence of all the personal representatives was needed for a conveyance of real estate, but, as in the case of personal estate (see PARA 1023), not for a contract to convey it.

6 Administration of Estates Act 1925 s 2(2) (as amended: see note 5).

7 *Horn v Horn* (1825) 2 Sim & St 448; *Johnson v Kennett* (1835) 3 My & K 624 at 630 per Lord Lyndhurst LC; *Re Rebbeck, Bennett v Rebbeck* (1894) 42 WR 473. For statutory protection see PARA 1026 et seq.

8 *Johnson v Kennett* (1835) 3 My & K 624; *Page v Adam* (1841) 4 Beav 269; *Forbes v Peacock* (1846) 1 Ph 717 at 721; *Stroughill v Anstey* (1852) 1 De GM & G 635 at 653. In *Eland v Eland* (1839) 4 My & Cr 420 the liability of the assignee to see to the payment of the legacies was not disputed.

9 *Re Henson, Chester v Henson* [1908] 2 Ch 356. See also *Parker v Judkin* [1931] 1 Ch 475, CA.

1025. Purchaser's common law protection. A mortgagee or purchaser from a personal representative[1] has the right to infer that the representative is acting fairly in the execution of his duty, and is not bound to inquire as to the debts or legacies[2] or the application of the money[3]. The property alienated cannot be followed into his hands by either creditor[4] or legatee[5]. The alienee's title will not be affected by the fact that, in a transaction in which the representative is known to be acting as such[6], the alienation does not purport to be made for administrative purposes[7] or to be executed by the representative in his character as such[8].

At common law a purchase or mortgage for valuable consideration from an executor, who is also residuary legatee, of an asset of the testator by a person who has no notice of the existence of unsatisfied debts of the testator, is valid against the unsatisfied creditors, whether the assignee acquires a legal or an equitable interest in the asset[9]. The same principle applies to the case of a specific legacy assigned by an executor who is the specific legatee[10]; but where legacies are charged upon the property bequeathed to the executor, the assignee takes the property subject to the legacies charged upon it[11].

1 As to the meaning of 'personal representative' see PARA 608.
2 *Watkins v Cheek* (1825) 2 Sim & St 199 at 205 per Leach V-C.
3 *Corser v Cartwright* (1875) LR 7 HL 731; and see *Keane v Robarts* (1819) 4 Madd 332 at 359; *Parker v Judkin* [1931] 1 Ch 475, CA. See also PARA 1026.
4 *Nugent v Gifford* (1738) 1 Atk 463; *Elliot v Merriman* (1740) 2 Atk 41.
5 *Ewer v Corbet* (1723) 2 P Wms 148; *Whale v Booth* (1784) 4 Term Rep 625n. See also the Administration of Estates Act 1925 ss 36(9), 38; and PARAS 970, 1147.
6 *Solomon v Attenborough* [1912] 1 Ch 451 at 456, 459, CA; on appeal sub nom *Attenborough v Solomon* [1913] AC 76, HL.
7 See *Colyer v Finch* (1856) 5 HL Cas 905 at 923; *Corser v Cartwright* (1875) LR 7 HL 731.
8 *Re Venn and Furze's Contract* [1894] 2 Ch 101; *Re Henson, Chester v Henson* [1908] 2 Ch 356 at 364.
9 *Graham v Drummond* [1896] 1 Ch 968, following the principles laid down in *Nugent v Gifford* (1738) 1 Atk 463; *Mead v Lord Orrery* (1745) 3 Atk 235; *Taylor v Hawkins* (1803) 8 Ves 209; *Whale v Booth* (1784) 4 Term Rep 625n; *Storry v Walsh* (1854) 18 Beav 559; *Scott v Tyler* (1788) 2 Dick 712; and *M'Leod v Drummond* (1807) 14 Ves 353 at 360 (on appeal (1810) 17 Ves 152).
10 *Hall v Andrews* (1872) 27 LT 195.
11 *Bank of Bombay v Suleman Somji* (1908) 99 LT 532, PC, distinguishing *Graham v Drummond* [1896] 1 Ch 968. It seems that this would not now be the case with respect to freeholds and leaseholds where the executor conveys or assigns as such. As to the over-reaching effect of a conveyance by personal representatives see PARA 1021.

1026. Purchaser's statutory protection: notice and receipt. A conveyance of a legal estate[1] made by a personal representative[2] to a purchaser for money or money's worth is not invalidated by reason only that the purchaser may have notice that all the deceased's debts, liabilities, funeral and testamentary or administration expenses, duties and legacies have been discharged or provided for[3].

No purchaser or mortgagee dealing with the representative is concerned to see that the money paid on the sale or advanced on the mortgage is wanted, or that no more than is wanted is raised, or otherwise as to its application[4].

The written receipt of a representative for any money payable to him is a sufficient discharge to the person paying the money, and effectually exonerates him from seeing to the application or being answerable for any loss or misapplication of it[5].

1 As to the meaning of 'conveyance' see PARA 858 note 1; and as to the meaning of 'legal estate' see PARA 969 note 2.
2 As to the meaning of 'personal representative' see PARA 608.
3 Administration of Estates Act 1925 s 36(8), (11). Section 36 is applicable to assents and conveyances made on or after 1 January 1926, whether the testator or intestate died before or after that date: see s 36(12). See also *Re Spencer and Hauser's Contract* [1928] Ch 598 at 605. Apart from s 36 doubts might have been raised as to whether the personal representative should not make title as trustee: see PARA 1150.
4 Trustee Act 1925 ss 17, 68(1)para (17).
5 See the Trustee Act 1925 ss 14(1), 68(1)para(17); and TRUSTS AND POWERS vol 98 (2013) PARA 517. This provision (which re-enacts with slight variation of language the Trustee Act 1893 s 20(1) (repealed)), applies notwithstanding anything to the contrary in the will: see the Trustee Act 1925 s 14(3).

1027. Purchaser's statutory protection: statements, revocation etc. A statement in writing by a personal representative[1] that he has not given or made an assent or conveyance[2] in respect of a legal estate[3] in land is, in favour of a purchaser for money or money's worth[4], but without prejudice to any previous disposition[5] made in favour of another purchaser deriving title mediately or immediately under the personal representative, sufficient evidence[6] that an assent or conveyance has not been given or made in respect of the legal estate to which the statement relates, unless notice of a previous assent or conveyance affecting that estate has been placed on or annexed to the probate or letters of administration[7]. A conveyance of a legal estate by a personal representative to a purchaser accepted on the faith of such a statement operates, without prejudice as aforesaid and unless notice of a previous assent or conveyance affecting that estate has been placed on or annexed to the probate or letters of administration, to transfer or create the legal estate expressed to be conveyed in like manner as if no previous assent or conveyance had been made by the personal representative[8].

All conveyances of any interest in real and personal estate[9] made to a purchaser by a person to whom probate or letters of administration have been granted are valid, notwithstanding any subsequent revocation, or variation, of the probate or letters of administration[10]. Where a representation is revoked, all payments and dispositions made in good faith to a personal representative under the representation are a valid discharge to the person making the same[11].

1 As to the meaning of 'personal representative' see PARA 608.
2 This provision applies to assents and conveyances made after 31 December 1925, whether the testator or intestate died before or after that date: Administration of Estates Act 1925 s 36(12). As to assents in relation to land generally see PARA 1143 et seq. As to the meaning of 'conveyance' see PARA 858 note 1.
3 As to the meaning of 'legal estate' see PARA 969 note 2.
4 Administration of Estates Act 1925 s 36(11). As to the meaning of 'purchaser' in the Administration of Estates Act 1925 generally see PARA 858 note 4.
5 As to the meaning of 'disposition' see PARA 969 note 7.
6 As to what is sufficient evidence cf PARA 1149 note 5.
7 Administration of Estates Act 1925 s 36(6). The saving clause in this provision deprives it of most of its value as a protection. As to the placing of notice on the probate or letters of administration see PARA 1147.
8 Administration of Estates Act 1925 s 36(6). Since the conveyance must be accepted on the faith of the statement the omission to make such a statement (in practice usually made by a recital in the conveyance) cannot be remedied subsequently. A personal representative making a false statement is liable as if the statement had been contained in a statutory declaration: s 36(6). See also CRIMINAL LAW vol 26 (2016) PARA 782. As to the effect of an assent see generally PARA 1146 et seq.
9 As to the meaning of 'real estate' see PARA 607 note 1.
10 See the Administration of Estates Act 1925 s 37(1); and PARA 858.
11 See the Administration of Estates Act 1925 s 27(2); and PARA 855.

1028. When transaction is impeachable. If the nature of the transaction not affecting a legal estate[1] affords intrinsic evidence that the personal representative is not acting in the execution of his duty, but is committing a breach of trust, the purchaser or mortgagee holds the property subject to the claims of creditors and beneficiaries[2]. It rests, however, upon the person seeking to impeach the validity of the transaction to prove that the purchaser or mortgagee had notice of the true state of facts[3]; the mere fact that an executor who is also a devisee includes property of his own in the security[4], or gives a security for an originally unsecured advance[5], is not sufficient to rebut the ordinary presumption that the money has been raised for administrative purposes; but where the representative has, either expressly or informally[6], assented to the dispositions of the will[7], the effect of the assent is to strip the representative of his title as such and to clothe him with a title as trustee, and if after that, merely because he has physical possession of personal property, he purports to deal with it as the representative the disposition may be set aside[8].

The title of a person who lends money to another, not known by the lender to be, but who is in fact, an executor, for his private purposes, upon an equitable mortgage of what is really the testator's property, is postponed to the prior equity of the persons beneficially interested in the property[9]. Fraud or collusion on the part of the lender will, of course, vitiate the transaction[10].

1 As to transactions in the case of a legal estate see the Administration of Estates Act 1925 s 36(7); and PARAS 1026; 1147. As to the meaning of 'personal representative' see PARA 608.
2 *Watkins v Cheek* (1825) 2 Sim & St 199 at 205; *Hill v Simpson* (1802) 7 Ves 152; *Ricketts v Lewis* (1882) 20 ChD 745; *Re Verrell's Contract* [1903] 1 Ch 65; and see *Wilson v Moore* (1834) 1 My & K 337; *Walker v Taylor* (1861) 4 LT 845, HL. The Administration of Estates Act 1925 s 36(8) applies only to legal estates in real estate, including chattels real: see PARA 1026.
3 *Corser v Cartwright* (1875) LR 7 HL 731. Where knowledge of facts from which the existence of a certain state of things is reasonably to be inferred is proved, actual notice exists: *Wise v Whitburn* [1924] 1 Ch 460 (notice arising out of requisition), explaining the dictum of Warrington LJ in *Re Kemnal and Still's Contract* [1923] 1 Ch 293 at 310, CA.
4 *Barrow v Griffith, Barrow v Newman* (1864) 11 Jur NS 6.
5 *Miles v Durnford* (1852) 2 De GM & G 641.
6 Since 1 January 1926 an assent to the vesting of a legal estate in real estate, including chattels real, is required to be in writing: see the Administration of Estates Act 1925 s 36(4); and PARA 1144.
7 As to the mode and effect of assents generally see PARA 1139 et seq.
8 *Solomon v Attenborough* [1912] 1 Ch 451 at 458, CA (affd sub nom *Attenborough v Solomon* [1913] AC 76 at 82, HL); *Wise v Whitburn* [1924] 1 Ch 460.
9 *Re Morgan, Pillgrem v Pillgrem* (1881) 18 ChD 93, CA.
10 *Earl Vane v Rigden* (1870) 5 Ch App 663 at 668; *Rice v Gordon* (1848) 11 Beav 265; *Scott v Tyler* (1788) 2 Dick 712 at 725; *Ewer v Corbet* (1723) 2 P Wms 148; *Mead v Lord Orrery* (1745) 3 Atk 235 at 240; *Whale v Booth* (1784) 4 Term Rep 625n. See also the definition of 'purchaser' in the Administration of Estates Act 1925 s 55(1)(xviii); and PARA 858 note 4.

1029. Sale to creditor or surviving partner. A personal representative may sell part of the assets to a creditor at a fixed price in discharge of his debt[1], and there is no objection to the representative of a partner selling the share of the deceased partner to the surviving partners[2].

1 *Hepworth v Heslop* (1849) 6 Hare 561 at 569; *Earl Vane v Rigden* (1870) 5 Ch App 663 at 668; *Re Jones, Peak v Jones* [1914] 1 Ch 742 at 747. As to the meaning of 'personal representative' see PARA 608.
2 *Chambers v Howell* (1847) 11 Beav 6.

1030. Personal representative may not sell to himself without authority. Personal representatives may not, without the sanction of the court[1], or authorisation by the will[2], sell to one of themselves either directly or indirectly[3], although a sale may be made to one who has renounced the executorship[4], and a sale cannot be impeached merely on the ground that when it was entered upon the purchaser might have proved the will, even though in fact he subsequently renounced probate[5]. Such a sale is voidable at the instance of the beneficiaries no matter how fair the price[6]. Where there has been a contractual relationship between the deceased and the personal representative the subsequent fiduciary relationship does not preclude the representative from asserting his rights under the pre-existing contract[7], although there may be reasons for watching narrowly the course he takes in the fulfilment of the contract[8].

1 The procedure is by CPR Pt 8 claim form under CPR 64.2. See also CPR PD 64A—*Estates, Trusts and Charities* para 1(2)(b). An order approving the purchase may be made on application without a hearing: see CPR PD 64A para 1A. If the court considers that an oral hearing is required it will give appropriate directions: CPR PD 64A para 1A.5.

2 *Sargeant v National Westminster Bank plc* (1990) 61 P & CR 518, CA. It is not clear whether such authorisation would be binding on creditors of an estate.
3 *Hall v Hallet* (1784) 1 Cox Eq Cas 134; *Cook v Collingridge* (1823) Jac 607; *Re Norrington, Brindley v Partridge* (1879) 13 ChD 654, CA; *Re Harvey, Harvey v Lambert* (1888) 58 LT 449. This rule does not prevent a surviving husband or wife who is also one of the personal representatives of an intestate from purchasing out of the intestate's estate an interest in the matrimonial home (see PARA 489 note 9) but does prevent an appropriation of assets under the Administration of Estates Act 1925 s 41 in satisfaction of an entitlement under a will or intestacy see PARA 657 note 13. For other examples of the rule which prohibits self-dealing by personal representatives and trustees (and its exceptions) see PARA 657.
4 *Mackintosh v Barber* (1822) 1 Bing 50.
5 *Clark v Clark* (1884) 9 App Cas 733, PC.
6 *Tito v Waddell (No 2), Tito v A-G* [1977] Ch. 106 at 225, [1977] 2 WLR 496 at 605 per Megarry VC.
7 *Vyse v Foster* (1874) LR 7 HL 318; *Hordern v Hordern* [1910] AC 465, PC; *Re Lewis, Lewis v Lewis* (1910) 103 LT 495; *Re MacAdam, Dallow v Codd* [1946] Ch 73, [1945] 2 All ER 664; *Re Mulholland's Will Trusts, Bryan v Westminster Bank Ltd* [1949] 1 All ER 460; *Sargeant v National Westminster Bank plc* (1990) 61 P & CR 518, CA.
8 *Vyse v Foster* (1874) LR 7 HL 318 at 332.

1031. Manner of sale. Where a personal representative[1] has a duty or power to sell property he has, in the absence of a direction to the contrary, power to sell, or concur with any other person in selling, all or any part of the property, either subject to prior charges or not, either together or in lots, by public auction or private contract, subject to such conditions of sale as he may think fit, with power to buy in at an auction, or to vary or rescind a contract for sale, and to resell, without being answerable for any loss[2]. Before 1926 it had ultimately been decided that the power to sell all or any part of the property would justify a sale of minerals[3] apart from the land, without the sanction of the court[4]. Since 1 January 1926 power to sell or dispose of land includes power to sell or dispose of part of it, whether the division is horizontal, vertical or made in any other way[5]. The personal representative has in any case in relation to land the powers of an absolute owner[6].

1 As to the meaning of 'personal representative' see PARA 608.
2 Trustee Act 1925 ss 12(1), 69(1), (2) (s 12(1) amended by the Trusts of Land and Appointment of Trustees Act 1996 s 25(1), Sch 3para3(2)). The Trustee Act 1925 s 12(1) and those provisions relating to trustees set out in the text and note 5, and in PARAS 1032–1033, are applied to personal representatives by the Trustee Act 1925 s 68(1)para(17) (see PARA 609). See also the Administration of Estates Act 1925 s 39(1), (1A) (see PARA 1019); and TRUSTS AND POWERS vol 98 (2013) PARAS 4, 476.
3 In the case of timber (a very doubtful analogy: see *Re Chaplin and Staffordshire Potteries Waterworks Co's Contract* [1922] 2 Ch 824 at 847, CA), it was held in *Cholmeley v Paxton* (1825) 3 Bing 207 (affd sub nom *Cockerell v Cholmeley* (1830) 10 B & C 564), that trustees could not sell land without the timber, or the timber without the land.
4 *Re Chaplin and Staffordshire Potteries Waterworks Co's Contract* [1922] 2 Ch 824, CA, where the earlier conflicting authorities were considered and explained.
5 Trustee Act 1925 s 12(2) (amended by the Trusts of Land and Appointment of Trustees Act 1996 Sch 3para 3(2)). See TRUSTS AND POWERS vol 98 (2013) PARA 481.
6 See the Trusts of Land and Appointment of Trustees Act 1996 ss 6(1), 18; and PARA 1019.

1032. Depreciatory conditions. A sale by a personal representative[1] cannot be impeached by a beneficiary upon the ground that any of the conditions of sale were unnecessarily depreciatory, unless it also appears that the consideration for the sale was rendered inadequate as a result[2]. After execution of the conveyance, in order to impeach the sale for unnecessarily depreciatory conditions, it must be shown that the purchaser was acting in collusion with the representative at the time when the contract for sale was made[3].

The personal representative has a statutory power of giving a valid discharge for money, securities, investments or other personal property or effects payable, transferable or deliverable to him under any trust or power[4].

1 As to the meaning of 'personal representative' see PARA 608.
2 Trustee Act 1925 s 13(1).
3 Trustee Act 1925 s 13(2). Section 13 applies to sales made before or after 1 January 1926: s 13(4).
4 Trustee Act 1925 s 14(1) (amended by the Trustee Act 2000 s 40(1), Sch 2 para 19). See also PARA 1019. The restriction by virtue of which a sole trustee (other than a trust corporation) cannot give a valid receipt for the proceeds of sale of land or other capital money arising under a trust of land (see the Trustee Act 1925 s 14(2); and TRUSTS AND POWERS vol 98 (2013) PARA 517) does not apply to a sole personal representative: see the Law of Property Act 1925 s 27(2) (substituted by the Law of Property (Amendment) Act 1926 s 7, Schedule; and amended by the Trusts of Land and Appointment of Trustees Act 1996 s 25(1), Sch 3para4); and the Administration of Estates Act 1925 s 2(1) (see PARA 945).

1033. Power to insure. A personal representative[1] may insure any property which is subject to the trust against risks of loss or damage due to any event[2], and may pay the premiums out of the trust funds[3] (that is any income or capital funds of the trust)[4]. In the case of property held on a bare trust[5], the power to insure is subject to any direction given by the beneficiary or each of the beneficiaries:

(1) that any property specified in the direction is not to be insured[6]; and
(2) that any property specified in the direction is not to be insured except on such conditions as may be so specified[7].

The statutory duty of care applies to the excercise of the power to insure[8].

1 As to the meaning of 'personal representative' see PARA 608. A personal representative has in relation to land all the powers of an absolute owner: see the Trusts of Land and Appointment of Trustees Act 1996 ss 6(1), 18; and PARA 1019.
2 Trustee Act 1925 ss 19(1)(a), 68(1) para (17), 69(1) (s 19 substituted by the Trustee Act 2000 s 34(1)).
3 Trustee Act 1925 s 19(1)(b) (as substituted: see note 2).
4 Trustee Act 1925 s 19(5) (as substituted: see note 2); and see TRUSTS AND POWERS vol 98 (2013) PARA 513.
5 Property is held on a bare trust if it is held on trust for:
 (1) a beneficiary who is of full age and capacity and absolutely entitled to the property subject to the trust (Trustee Act 1925 s 19(3)(a) (as substituted: see note 2); or
 (2) beneficiaries each of whom is of full age and capacity and who (taken together) are absolutely entitled to the property subject to the trust: (s 19(3)(b) (as so substituted)).
6 Trustee Act 1925 s 19(2)(a) (as substituted: see note 2). If a direction under s 19(2) is given, the power to insure, so far as it is subject to the direction, ceases to be a delegable function for the purposes of the Trustee Act 2000 s 11 (power to employ agents: see PARA 1049): Trustee Act 1925 s 19(4) (as so substituted).
7 Trustee Act 1925 s 19(2)(b) (as substituted: see note 2). See note 6.
8 See PARA 1020; and TRUSTS AND POWERS vol 98 (2013) PARA 513.

1034. Power to recover rent. To recover rent due or accruing to the deceased, a personal representative[1] may exercise specified powers for commercial rent arrears recovery[2] that would have been exercisable by the deceased if he had still been living[3].

1 As to the meaning of 'personal representative' see PARA 608.
2 The text refers to the exercise of any powers under the Tribunals, Courts and Enforcement Act 2007 s 72(1) (commercial rent arrears recovery: see LANDLORD AND TENANT vol 62 (2012) PARA 419) or 81 (right to rent from sub-tenant: LANDLORD AND TENANT vol 62 (2012) PARA 428): Administration of Estates Act 1925 s 26(4) (substituted by the Tribunals, Courts and Enforcement Act 2007 Sch 14 para 28).
3 Administration of Estates Act 1925 s 26(4).

(iii) Power to Carry on the Deceased's Business

1035. Necessity for express power to carry on business. An executor had formerly no power, in the absence of a direction contained in his testator's will, to carry on the testator's business[1], whether carried on in partnership or by the testator alone, except for the purpose of winding it up[2]. A general power to postpone the conversion of a testator's estate bequeathed upon trust for sale is sufficient authority to an executor to carry on the business for a reasonable period with a view to selling it as a going concern[3], and may be sufficient to authorise the business to be carried on during any period of postponement until the date for actual distribution arrives, if the power to postpone is properly exercised[4]. A power to postpone the sale of land is implied in every trust of land[5].

Although, however, the executor may have no authority to continue the business, it is his duty, as it is also that of an administrator, to do whatever may be required to be done to preserve the business as an asset[6], and if he acts in good faith and to the best of his judgment he is not liable for a breach of trust in continuing it for some years[7].

A power to an executor to carry on his testator's business may not upon his renouncing empower an administrator with the will annexed to do so[8]; nor will the court normally authorise an administrator to carry on an intestate's trade where the parties interested are not sui juris[9].

1 *Kirkman v Booth* (1848) 11 Beav 273. As to the meaning of 'executor' see PARA 606.
2 *Collinson v Lister* (1855) 20 Beav 356; affd 7 De GM & G 634. As to the personal representative's right to have a partnership business wound up see PARA 919. As to the meaning of 'personal representative' see PARA 608.
3 *Re Chancellor, Chancellor v Brown* (1884) 26 ChD 42, CA; *Re Smith, Arnold v Smith* [1896] 1 Ch 171. As to the power of a personal representative to apply for an interim authority notice to temporarily carry on the business of the holder of a licence to sell intoxicating liquor see the Licensing Act 2003 s 47; and LEISURE AND ENTERTAINMENT vol 67 (2016) PARA 116.
4 *Re Crowther, Midgley v Crowther* [1895] 2 Ch 56. See also *Re Smith, Arnold v Smith* [1896] 1 Ch 171 at 174 per North J; *Re Ball, Jones v Jones* (1930) 74 Sol Jo 298; as considered in *Re Rooke, Rooke v Rooke* [1953] Ch 716 at 723, sub nom *Re Rooke's Will Trusts, Taylor v Rooke* [1953] 2 All ER 110 at 113–114.
5 As to trusts of land see the Trusts of Land and Appointment of Trustees Act 1996 s 1(1); and as to the general powers trustees have in relation to land subject to the trust see s 6; and TRUSTS AND POWERS vol 98 (2013) PARA 1 et seq. If there is a disposition on trust for sale of land, whenever made, there will be implied, despite any provision to the contrary made by the disposition, a power for the trustees to postpone sale of the land: see s 4(1).
6 *Strickland v Symons* (1883) 22 ChD 666 at 671 per Pollock B; on appeal (1884) 26 ChD 245, CA. See also *Marshall v Broadhurst* (1831) 1 Cr & J 403. As to the personal representative's duty to act gratuitously see PARA 648. It has been held in Canada that a depreciation allowance may be charged against income payable to the tenant for life: *Re Stekl* (1973) 40 DLR (3d) 407, BC SC. In making decisions as to the conduct of the business the court's guidance may be obtained under CPR 64.2, and CPR PD 64A—*Estates, Trusts and Charities* para 1: see PARA 1168 et seq.
7 *Garrett v Noble* (1834) 6 Sim 504.
8 In *Lambert v Rendle* (1863) 3 New Rep 247, the will appointed separate persons as executors and trustees and conferred power to carry on the business on the executors only, and was held not to authorise the administrators to do so. See also PARA 1052.
9 *Land v Land* (1874) 43 LJ Ch 311.

1036. What funds may be employed in testator's business. An executor who is authorised to carry on the testator's business is not entitled to employ in the business any of the general assets of his testator beyond the fund directed to be so employed[1]. Where the testator has not authorised the employment of any of his general assets the executor is only entitled to employ the assets already embarked in the business[2].

1 *Re Ballman, ex p Garland* (1804) 10 Ves 110; *Cutbush v Cutbush* (1839) 1 Beav 184; *Fraser v Murdoch* (1881) 6 App Cases 855, HL. As to the meaning of 'executor' see PARA 606.
2 *Re Hodson, ex p Richardson* (1818) 3 Madd 138 (affd (1819) Buck 421); *Fraser v Murdoch* (1881) 6 App Cases 855, HL.

1037. Borrowing powers in relation to testator's business. If the executor finds it impossible to carry on the testator's business with the assets already engaged in it or authorised by his testator, he should apply to the court for its directions[1]. He has no power to borrow money for the purpose and charge his testator's assets outside the business with repayment of the loan[2], although he can give a valid charge upon the assets already engaged in the business[3]. Where the personal representative has express authority to increase the business, he is entitled to borrow money and secure the loan by mortgage of assets outside the business[4].

1 *M'Neillie v Acton* (1853) 4 De GM & G 744. As to the procedure see PARA 1168 et seq. As to the meaning of 'executor' see PARA 606.
2 *M'Neillie v Acton* (1853) 4 De GM & G 744.
3 *Devitt v Kearney* (1883) 13 LR Ir 45, CA.
4 See *Re Dimmock, Dimmock v Dimmock* (1885) 52 LT 494. As to the meaning of 'personal representative' see PARA 608.

1038. Conversion of testator's business into limited company. It has been held in Scotland that a power given to an executor to carry on the testator's business authorises the conversion of the business into a private limited company with the same capital and under the same control as before[1].

The necessary power is frequently given by express clauses in wills, and where these are lacking the court will supply the omission in appropriate cases.

1 *MacKechnie's Trustees v Macadam* 1912 SC 1059. As to the meaning of 'executor' see PARA 606.

1039. Personal representative's liability and right to indemnity when carrying on testator's business. The personal representative is personally liable upon all contracts into which he enters and for all debts which he incurs in carrying on the deceased's business[1], notwithstanding that he avowedly contracts as representative[2]; but he is entitled to be indemnified out of the assets in respect of all liabilities properly incurred in carrying on a business, even in priority to the claims of the deceased's creditors, where he has carried it on for such reasonable time as is necessary to enable him to sell it as a going concern[3]. It rests upon the representative to prove that he has acted with a view to selling the business as a going concern[4].

1 *Re Ballman, ex p Garland* (1804) 10 Ves 110; *Re Hodson, ex p Richardson* (1818) 3 Madd 138; *Owen v Delamere* (1872) LR 15 Eq 134; *Re Percy, Fairland v Percy* (1875) LR 3 P & D 217; *Re Morgan, Pillgrem v Pillgrem* (1881) 18 ChD 93 at 99, CA; *Re Evans, Evans v Evans* (1887) 34 ChD 597, CA; *Fraser v Murdoch* (1881) 6 App Cas 855, HL. The executor may be made bankrupt (*Re Ballman, ex p Garland*), but executors carrying on their testator's business cannot be adjudicated bankrupt on the footing that they are partners. They may be joint debtors and liable to be made bankrupt individually: *Re Fisher & Sons* [1912] 2 KB 491. As to the duty of a personal representative to act gratuitously see PARA 648. As to the meaning of 'personal representative' see PARA 608.
2 *Labouchere v Tupper* (1857) 11 Moo PCC 198; *Liverpool Borough Bank v Walker* (1859) 4 De G & J 24.
3 *Dowse v Gorton* [1891] AC 190 at 199, HL, per Lord Herschell.
4 *Re Millard, ex p Yates* (1895) 72 LT 823, CA.

1040. Extent of personal representative's indemnity when carrying on testator's business. A direction contained in the will for the continuance of the testator's business is binding upon the beneficiaries, so that, as against them, the executor is entitled to resort to the assets authorised to be employed in the business to indemnify himself against liabilities incurred in carrying it on[1]. The direction is not, however, binding upon the testator's creditors, and the executor cannot by reason only of such authority maintain a claim to indemnity as against them[2].

Where, however, those creditors have agreed to the continuance of the business, the personal representative is entitled to be indemnified out of the estate in priority to their claims[3], and the indemnity is not to be limited to that portion of the assets which has come into existence, or changed its form since the death[4]. The creditors' agreement must be a consent to the carrying on of the business for them or for the estate of which they are creditors and against which they have a right to claim. Whether such consent has been given or not is a question of fact, but consent is not to be implied merely from the creditors' conduct in not interfering with the business[5]. In the case of consent by a testator's creditors the right to an indemnity exists independently of any authority by the testator to continue the business[6]. A receiver or manager appointed in an administration action in succession to an executor is entitled to be indemnified on the same principles as the executor[7].

1 *Re Ballman, ex p Garland* (1804) 10 Ves 110; *Re Beater, ex p Edmonds* (1862) 4 De GF & J 488 at 498. As to the meaning of 'executor' see PARA 606.
2 *Dowse v Gorton* [1891] AC 190 at 199, HL, per Lord Herschell; *Re Millard, ex p Yates* (1895) 72 LT 823, CA; *Lucas v Williams (No 2)* (1862) 4 De GF & J 439; *Re East, London County and Westminster Banking Co Ltd v East* (1914) 111 LT 101, CA.
3 Questions of this nature will generally arise when the estate is insolvent, and then, as there is nothing for the beneficiaries, the creditors are really masters of the situation. As to insolvent estates see PARA 981 et seq. As to the meaning of 'personal representative' see PARA 608.
4 *Dowse v Gorton* [1891] AC 190, HL.
5 *Re Oxley, John Hornby & Sons v Oxley* [1914] 1 Ch 604, CA, disapproving on this point dicta in *Re Brooke, Brooke v Brooke* [1894] 2 Ch 600 at 607; *Re Hodges, Hodges v Hodges* [1899] 1 IR 480 at 484.
6 *Re Brooke, Brooke v Brooke* [1894] 2 Ch 600.
7 *Re Brooke, Brooke v Brooke* [1894] 2 Ch 600; *O'Neill v McGrorty* [1915] 1 IR 1.

1041. Personal representative's creditors' right of subrogation. The remedy of a creditor for a debt contracted after the death is against the personal representative and not against the estate[1]; but the creditor is in equity entitled to stand in the place of the personal representative and to claim the benefit of his right to an indemnity[2]. Accordingly, where the business has been continued by the representative with the consent of the deceased's creditors, the representative's creditors are entitled to payment in priority to the deceased's creditors[3].

This right is, however, strictly confined to the assets to which the representative himself could have resorted for an indemnity[4]. Accordingly, where the representative has lost his right to an indemnity because he is in default to the estate, the creditors are in no better position, and are not entitled to have their debts paid out of the specific assets unless the default is made good[5]. Where there are several representatives, one of whom is in default to the trust estate, but the others can show clear accounts, the creditors can claim the benefit of the indemnity to which the representatives with the clear accounts are entitled[6]. A mere default in rendering accounts is not sufficient to destroy the indemnity; there must be an indebtedness to the estate on the part of the representatives[7].

1 *Farhall v Farhall* (1871) 7 Ch App 123; *Owen v Delamere* (1872) LR 15 Eq 134. As to the meaning of 'personal representative' see PARA 608.

2 *Re Beater, ex p Edmonds* (1862) 4 De GF & J 488 at 498; *Re Johnson, Shearman v Robinson* (1880) 15 ChD 548; *Re Evans, Evans v Evans* (1887) 34 ChD 597, CA; *Moore v M'Glynn* [1904] 1 IR 334. As to the right of subrogation see EQUITABLE JURISDICTION vol 47 (2014) PARA 207 et seq.

3 *Re Hodges, Hodges v Hodges* [1899] 1 IR 480. The same rule applies where the executor has continued the business under an administration order (*Tinkler v Hindmarsh* (1840) 2 Beav 348), but not where a legatee has carried on the business with the acquiescence of the executors (*Re O'Kelly, Burke v Whelan* [1920] 1 IR 200).

4 *Re Johnson, Shearman v Robinson* (1880) 15 ChD 548; *Re Morris* (1889) 23 LR Ir 333.

5 *Re Johnson, Shearman v Robinson* (1880) 15 ChD 548.

6 *Re Frith, Newton v Rolfe* [1902] 1 Ch 342.

7 *Re Kidd, Kidd v Kidd* (1894) 70 LT 648.

1042. Right of creditor to obtain administration order. The right of a trade creditor to the benefit of the personal representative's indemnity entitles him to an order for the administration of the deceased's estate[1]. As between the representative and his trade creditors, the representative's right to an indemnity out of the assets for his costs and expenses prevails over the creditor's right to be paid out of those assets[2]. Where an administration order has been made the representative's trade creditors are entitled to interest on their debts from the date when the master has certified the debts[3]. A representative who has advanced his own money to pay debts incurred in carrying on the business is entitled to interest on the balance due to him at the end of each year[4].

1 *Re Shorey, Smith v Shorey* (1898) 79 LT 349.

2 *Re Owen, Frisby, Dyke & Co v Owen* (1892) 66 LT 718.

3 *Re Bracey, Hull v Johns* [1936] Ch 690, [1936] 2 All ER 767.

4 See *Finch v Pescott* (1874) LR 17 Eq 554; and PARA 1258.

(iv) Power to Compromise

1043. Compromise of claims generally. A personal representative has extensive powers to compromise claims[1] in external disputes[2]. It is a wide power under which the terms of the compromise may include, where the other party to the compromise is a beneficiary, the other party giving up his or her beneficial interest[3]. In cases of difficulty the personal representative may apply to the court, surrender his discretion, and ask the court to exercise it[4]. The only question to be considered in the case of a compromise effected by a personal representative under these powers is whether the representative has acted in good faith or not. Any one of several representatives may settle an account, and the settlement is binding upon the others[5].

A personal representative has no power, without the consent of, or approval of the court on behalf of[6], all parties interested in the estate, to compromise a question involving the validity of the will, and consequently his own position as executor[7], or a family provision claim[8], or any internal dispute[9] such as the interpretation of the will.

1 *Re Houghton, Hawley v Blake* [1904] 1 Ch 622 at 625 per Kekewich J. The statutory power under the Trustee Act 1925 s 15 is subject to the discharge of the duty of care set out in the Trustee Act 2000 s 1(1): see PARA 1020; and TRUSTS AND POWERS vol 98 (2013) PARA 518. As to the meaning of 'personal representative' see PARA 608.

2 Ie cases in which there is some issue between the trustees or personal representatives on behalf of the trust or estate as a whole, and the outside world: see *Re Earl of Strafford, Royal Bank of Scotland Ltd v Byng* [1980] Ch 28 at 32, [1978] 3 All ER 18 at 20 per Sir Robert Megarry V-C; affd [1980] Ch 28, [1979] 1 All ER 513, CA.

3 *Re Earl of Strafford, Royal Bank of Scotland Ltd v Byng* [1980] Ch 28, [1979] 1 All ER 513, CA.

4 See *Re Ezekiel's Settlement Trusts, National Provincial Bank Ltd v Hyam* [1942] Ch 230, CA (where the court approved a compromise despite the opposition of the adult beneficiaries); *Re Earl of Strafford, Royal Bank of Scotland Ltd v Byng* [1980] Ch 28, [1979] 1 All ER 513, CA. As to the procedure see PARA 1168 et seq.
5 *Smith v Everett* (1859) 27 Beav 446 at 454; *Fountain Forestry Ltd v Edwards* [1975] Ch 1, [1974] 2 All ER 280.
6 As to the court's powers to approve compromises on behalf of children and protected parties (ie a party, or intended party, who lacks capacity to conduct proceedings) see CPR 21.10; and *Practice Direction—Children and Protected Parties* PD 21. As to the court's powers, in proceedings concerning estates of deceased persons, to approve compromises on behalf of persons who are not parties to the proceedings, including unborn or unascertained persons see PARA 885; and CIVIL PROCEDURE vol 11 (2015) PARAS 490, 492.
7 *Graham v M'Cashin* [1901] 1 IR 404 at 413, CA. As to compromise in contentious probate proceedings see PARA 885.
8 Such a claim is in the nature of a claim to a beneficial interest in the estate. As to family provision claims see PARA 565 et seq.
9 Ie where one beneficiary under the trusts is at issue with another beneficiary under the trusts: see *Re Earl of Strafford, Royal Bank of Scotland Ltd v Byng* [1980] Ch 28 at 32–33, [1978] 3 All ER 18 at 20 per Sir Robert Megarry V-C; affd [1980] Ch 28, [1979] 1 All ER 513, CA. However, in *Re Warren, Weedon v Reading* (1884) 53 LJ Ch 1016 (a decision upon a provision in 23 & 24 Vict c 145 (Powers of Trustees, Mortgagees, etc) (1860) s 30 (repealed), which was similar in wording to the Trustee Act 1925 s 15(f)) it was stated that the power extended to a compromise where the estate had been distributed to certain relatives of the testator, there was then a claim by persons not previously known to the executors, and the executors compromised the claims of the latter by paying agreed sums out of the executors' own pockets.

1044. Compromise of co-executor's claim. It has been held that one of two executors may, in a proper case, compromise a claim of his co-executor against the estate[1]. The position is, however, a delicate one, and the executor would do well to apply to the court for its directions[2]. Where the compromise is shown to be injurious to the estate it will not be upheld[3]; nor can a settlement of accounts between a body of trustees and one of their number bar the right of the beneficiaries to investigate and challenge the accounts[4].

1 *Re Houghton, Hawley v Blake* [1904] 1 Ch 622. As to the meaning of 'executor' see PARA 606.
2 *Re Houghton, Hawley v Blake* [1904] 1 Ch 622 at 626. As to such applications see PARA 1168 et seq.
3 *De Cordova v De Cordova* (1879) 4 App Cas 692, PC.
4 *Re Fish, Bennett v Bennett* [1893] 2 Ch 413, CA.

(v) Power to Pay into Court

1045. Statutory right to pay into court. Personal representatives have a statutory right to pay money or securities belonging to their trust into court[1] and they may indeed be forced to do so by the court on application by a person interested[2]. The receipt or certificate of the proper officer is a sufficient discharge[3]. Where the majority are desirous of making the payment in, the court may order the payment in to be made without the concurrence of the minority[4]; and when the money or securities are deposited with any bank, broker or other depository, may order payment or delivery to the majority for the purpose of payment into court[5].

A judgment creditor of a creditor of the deceased cannot obtain a third party debt order against funds paid into court by the deceased's representatives[6].

1 Trustee Act 1925 ss 63(1), 68(1)para(17) (s 63(1) amended by the Administration of Justice Act 1965 s 36(4), Sch 3). See also TRUSTS AND POWERS vol 98 (2013) PARA 357.
2 The application is by claim form under CPR Pt 8: see CPR PD 8A—*Alternative Procedure for Claims* para 3.3; and CIVIL PROCEDURE vol 11 (2015) PARA 150 et seq.
3 See the Trustee Act 1925 s 63(2); and TRUSTS AND POWERS vol 98 (2013) PARA 357. See also *Re Salaman, De Pass v Sonnenthal* [1907] 2 Ch 46; revsd on another point [1908] 1 Ch 4, CA.
4 See the Trustee Act 1925 s 63(3); and TRUSTS AND POWERS vol 98 (2013) PARA 357.

5 See the Trustee Act 1925 s 63(4); and TRUSTS AND POWERS vol 98 (2013) PARA 357. As to County Court jurisdiction see PARA 866.
6 *Stevens v Phelips* (1875) 10 Ch App 417 (a case concerning a garnishee order). A garnishee order is now called a third party debt order: see CIVIL PROCEDURE vol 12A (2015) PARA 1406.

1046. Practice in paying in. When a deposit is made under the Trustee Act 1925, the personal representative[1] must make and file a witness statement or affidavit[2], and on receipt of a deposit schedule[3] and a copy of the witness statement or affidavit[4], the Accountant General will accept the deposit[5]. The Accountant General will also accept the deposit if a written request[6] and a sealed copy of the court order authorising the deposit is provided[7].

If the personal representative pays money or securities into court, unless the court orders otherwise, he must immediately serve notice of the payment into court on every person interested in or entitled to the money or securities[8]. Where the County Court has jurisdiction[9] payment will be to the county court[10].

1 As to the meaning of 'personal representative' see PARA 608.
2 As to the contents of the witness statement or affidavit see CPR PD 37—*Miscellaneous Provisions About Payments Into Court* para 6.1. As to where it must be filed see CPR PD 37 para 6.2. The application is made on CFO 103 '*Request for Deposit (Trustee Act 1925 with affidavit or witness statement)*'. If the amount to be deposited is under £500 in value, the Chief Chancery Master must approve the deposit by endorsement on CFO 103: see Notes on CFO 103. See also TRUSTS AND POWERS vol 98 (2013) PARA 360.
3 'Deposit schedule' means a schedule to an order directing that a fund be deposited in court: Court Funds Rules 2011, SI 2011/1734. As to the application see CFO 101 '*Deposit Schedule*'.
4 Ie filed in accordance with CPR 37.4 (see CIVIL PROCEDURE vol 12A (2015) PARA 1679): Court Funds Rules 2011, SI 2011/1734, r 6(6)(a)(ii).
5 See the Court Funds Rules 2011, SI 2011/1734, r 6(6)(a); and CIVIL PROCEDURE vol 11 (2015) PARA 72.
6 'Written request' means a request made on a form approved by the Accountant General to: (1) deposit funds in court; (2) deal with a fund in court; or (3) receive payment from a fund in court: see the Court Funds Rules 2011, SI 2011/1734, r 3(2). As to the form see CFO 100 Request for Deposit. As to the meaning of 'fund in court' see and CIVIL PROCEDURE vol 11 (2015) PARA 71.
7 See the Court Funds Rules 2011, SI 2011/1734, r 6(6)(b).
8 CPR PD 37—*Miscellaneous Provisions About Payments Into Court* para6.3.
9 See the Trustee Act 1925 s 63A(3)(d) (s 63A added by the County Courts Act 1984 s 148(1), Sch 2 Pt I para 1). The matter must be one of those set out in the Trustee Act 1925 s 63A and be within the county court limit. As to the county court limit see PARA 866 note 2.
10 As to the manner of paying funds into the County Court see Court Funds Rules 2011, SI 2011/1734, r 6(6), (7), r 8; and CIVIL PROCEDURE vol 11 (2015) PARA 73.

1047. When a deposit is justifiable. Personal representatives are justified in paying a fund into court where there is a reasonable doubt as to the person entitled to it[1], and the only question arising cannot readily be settled by means of an application to the court[2]. They are also justified in doing so where there is difficulty in obtaining their discharge[3] by reason of the minority[4] or physical[5] or mental[6] incapacity of the person entitled, or because he is abroad and they are uncertain, for example, whether he is alive or dead[7]. They ought not to do so for the mere purpose of escaping liability when there is no reasonable doubt as to the performance of their trust[8], nor merely to avoid threatened proceedings[9], or to escape their responsibilities in contesting unfounded claims[10] or in discovering whether or not a power has been exercised[11]. The beneficiaries' refusal to execute a release is not of itself a sufficient reason for representatives to pay money into court[12].

A representative who pays a fund into court loses any discretionary powers he may have with regard to the application of the fund[13], but he remains a trustee[14].

1 *Re Wylly's Trust* (1860) 28 Beav 458; *Re Jones* (1857) 3 Drew 679; *Re Davies' Trusts* (1914) 59 Sol Jo 234. As to the meaning of 'personal representative' see PARA 608.

2 *Re Giles* (1886) 55 LJ Ch 695. The power to advertise and other protection given by the Trustee Act 1925 ss 26–30 (see TRUSTS AND POWERS vol 98 (2013) PARAS 354–355) have since 1925 resulted in less use being made of the power to pay into court. Abuse of the power may result in the personal representative being deprived of his costs: *Re Giles* at 696 per Kay J.
3 *Re Parker's Will* (1888) as reported in 58 LJ Ch 23 at 25, CA, per Fry LJ. As to the discharge of personal representatives see PARA 1057.
4 *Re Hodges* (1855) 4 De GM & G 491; *Re Richards* (1869) LR 8 Eq 119. However, a parent or guardian with parental responsibility for a minor now has a right to receive in his own name, for the benefit of the minor, property which the minor is entitled to receive: see the Children Act 1989 s 3(3); and CHILDREN AND YOUNG PERSONS vol 9 (2012) PARAS 40, 152.
5 *Re Biddulph's Trusts, Re Poole's Trusts* (1852) 5 De G & Sm 469.
6 *Re Parker's Will* (1888) 39 ChD 303, CA.
7 *Re Elliot's Trusts* (1873) LR 15 Eq 194 at 197.
8 *Re Elliot's Trusts* (1873) LR 15 Eq 194.
9 *Re Fagg's Trust* (1850) 19 LJ Ch 175.
10 *Re Thakeham Sequestration Moneys* (1871) LR 12 Eq 494.
11 *Re Cull's Trusts* (1875) LR 20 Eq 561.
12 *Re Cater's Trusts (No 2)* (1858) 25 Beav 366; *Re Roberts' Trusts* (1869) 38 LJ Ch 708.
13 *Re Murphy's Trusts* [1900] 1 IR 145, following *Re Williams' Settlement* (1858) 4 K & J 87; *Re Coe's Trust* (1858) 4 K & J 199, and dissenting from *Re Landon's Trusts* (1871) 40 LJ Ch 370.
14 *Thompson v Tomkins* (1862) 2 Drew & Sm 8; *Barker v Peile* (1865) 2 Drew & Sm 340; cf *Re Poplar and Blackwall Free School* (1878) 8 ChD 543; *Re Bailey's Trust* (1854) 3 WR 31.

1048. Costs of payment into court. The personal representative[1] may deduct the reasonable costs of the payment into court where no dispute has arisen, or is likely to arise, as to the deduction[2], but the better course is for him to pay in the whole fund, leaving it for the court to settle the amount of costs to which he is entitled upon the application for payment out[3]. The court's jurisdiction on applications relating to the fund is limited to the fund actually paid into court, and does not extend to sums which have been deducted before payment in; if the beneficiaries desire to question the deductions, they must bring a separate action[4].

1 As to the meaning of 'personal representative' see PARA 608.
2 *Beaty v Curson* (1868) LR 7 Eq 194.
3 *Re Parker's Will* (1888) 39 ChD 303, CA.
4 *Re Bloye's Trust* (1849) 1 Mac & G 488 at 504; *Re Barber's Will* (1849) 32 LJ Ch 709; *Re Parker's Will* (1888) 39 ChD 303, CA.

(vi) Power to Employ Agents, Nominees and Custodians

1049. Power to employ and pay agents, nominees and custodians. Under their statutory powers[1], personal representatives[2] may authorise any person to exercise any or all of their delegable functions as their agent[3]. Other than in the case of a charitable trust[4], their delegable functions consist of any function other than: (1) any function relating to whether or in what way any assets should be distributed; (2) any power to decide whether any fees or other payment due to be made out of the trust funds should be made out of income or capital; or (3) any power conferred by any other enactment or under the will which permits delegation of their functions or to appoint a person to act as a nominee or custodian[5].

The persons whom the personal representatives may so authorise to exercise functions as their agent include one or more of their number[6] subject to the personal representatives not being able to authorise two (or more) persons to exercise the same function unless they are to exercise the function jointly[7]. Personal representatives may not authorise a beneficiary to exercise any function as their agent (even if the beneficiary is also a trustee)[8]. The personal representatives may authorise a person to exercise functions as their agent even though he is also appointed to act as their nominee or custodian[9]. The personal representatives may authorise a person to exercise functions as their agent on such terms as to remuneration and other matters as they may determine[10] but terms permitting the agent to appoint a substitute, or restricting the liability of the agent or his substitute, or permitting the agent to act in circumstances capable of giving rise to a conflict of interest are permitted only if reasonably necessary[11]. Personal representatives may not authorise a person to exercise any of their asset management functions as their agent except by an agreement which is in writing or evidenced in writing[12]. The personal representatives must supply the agent with a policy statement giving guidance as to how the asset management functions should be exercised and the agreement must require the agent to comply with the policy statement or any replacement[13]. Personal representatives may appoint a nominee to hold assets[14] and may also appoint a custodian to undertake the safe custody of assets[15]. If they retain or invest in securities payable to bearer, they must appoint a person to act as a custodian of the securities[16].

Obligations are placed on personal representatives to keep under review the arrangements under which the agent, nominee or custodian acts and how those arrangements are put into effect and, if circumstances make it appropriate to do so, must consider whether there is any need to exercise any power of intervention[17] that they have and if they consider that there is a need to exercise such a power, must do so[18]. A personal representative is not liable for any act or default of the agent, nominee or custodian unless he has failed to comply with the duty of care[19] when entering into the arrangements under which the person acts as agent, nominee or custodian or when carrying out his duties[20].

1 The statutory powers are now in Trustee Act 2000 Pt IV (ss 11–27) (see TRUSTS AND POWERS vol 98 (2013) PARA 429 et seq) which replaced the more limited powers in Trustee Act 1925 s 23 with effect from 1 February 2001: see the Trustee Act 2000 s 40(1), (3), Sch 2 Pt II para 23, Sch 4 Pt II; and the Trustee Act 2000 (Commencement) Order 2001, SI 2001/49. The provisions of the Trustee Act 2000 apply in relation to a personal representative administering an estate according to the law as they apply to a trustee carrying out a trust for beneficiaries: s 35. The powers under the Trustee Act 2000 Pt IV apply regardless of the date of the will except they do not affect the operation of an appointment before 1 February 2001: see the Trustee Act 2000 s 40(2), Sch 3 para 6; and the Trustee Act 2000 (Commencement) Order 2001, SI 2001/49, SI 2001/49, art 2. Under the former powers, trustees, instead of acting personally, had power to employ and pay an agent, whether a solicitor, banker, stockbroker or other person, to transact any business or do any act required to be transacted or done in the execution of the trust, including the receipt and payment of money, and were entitled to be allowed and paid all charges and expenses so incurred, and were not responsible for the default of any such agent if employed in good faith: see the Trustee Act 1925 s 23(1) (repealed); and TRUSTS AND POWERS vol 98 (2013) PARA 439 et seq. As to a discussion on whether trustees had delegated to an impermissible extent see *Daniel v Tee* [2016] EWHC 1538 (Ch), [2016] 4 WLR 115.

As to the statutory power of personal representatives to delegate by means of a power of attorney see the Trustee Act 1925 s 25; and PARA 642. A direction contained in a testator's will that his executors should employ a particular person as solicitor is not binding upon the executors, and does not confer any right on the person named to be employed as solicitor: *Finden v Stephens* (1846) 2 Ph 142; *Shaw v Lawless* (1838) 5 Cl & Fin 129, HL; *Foster v Elsley* (1881) 19 ChD 518. As to the appointment and functions of overseers of a will see Went Off Ex (14th Edn) 2.

2 As to the meaning of 'personal representative' see PARA 608.

3 See the Trustee Act 2000 s 11(1); and TRUSTS AND POWERS vol 98 (2013) PARA 430. A person authorised under this provision to exercise a function is (whatever the terms of the agency) subject to any specific duties or restrictions attached to the function: see s 13; and TRUSTS AND POWERS vol 98 (2013) PARA 430.

4 As to delegable functions in the case of a charitable trust see the Trustee Act 2000 s 11(3)–(5); and TRUSTS AND POWERS vol 98 (2013) PARA 430.

5 See the Trustee Act 2000 s 11(2); and TRUSTS AND POWERS vol 98 (2013) PARA 430.

6 Trustee Act 2000 s 12(1).

7 Trustee Act 2000 s 12(2).

8 Trustee Act 2000 s 12(3).

9 Trustee Act 2000 s 12(4). This is so whether appointed under the Trustee Act 2000 s 16–18 (see TRUSTS AND POWERS vol 98 (2013) PARA 432) or under any other power: see s 12(4).

10 See the Trustee Act 2000 s 14(1); and TRUSTS AND POWERS vol 98 (2013) PARA 431.

11 See the Trustee Act 2000 s 14(2), (3); and TRUSTS AND POWERS vol 98 (2013) PARA 431. These limitations can be further restricted, modified or excluded by appropriate provision in the will since the powers conferred by Trustee Act 2000 Pt IV are in addition to powers conferred otherwise than by the Act but are subject to any restriction or exclusion imposed by the will or by any enactment or any provision of subordinate legislation: see the Trustee Act 2000 s 26; and TRUSTS AND POWERS vol 98 (2013) PARA 429.

12 Trustee Act 2000 s 15(1); and see TRUSTS AND POWERS vol 98 (2013) PARA 431. As to asset management see ss 5, 39(1); and TRUSTS AND POWERS vol 98 (2013) PARAS 430–431.

13 See the Trustee Act 2000 s 15(2) and TRUSTS AND POWERS vol 98 (2013) PARA 431. The personal representatives must formulate any guidance given in the policy statement with a view to ensuring that the functions will be exercised in the best interests of the estate and the policy statement must be in, or evidenced in writing: see s 15(3), (4); and TRUSTS AND POWERS vol 98 (2013) PARA 431.

14 See the Trustee Act 2000 s 16; and TRUSTS AND POWERS vol 98 (2013) PARA 430. As to the persons who may be appointed as nominees see s 19 (see TRUSTS AND POWERS vol 98 (2013) PARA 433); and as to the terms of such appointment see s 20 (see TRUSTS AND POWERS vol 98 (2013) PARA 434).

15 See the Trustee Act 2000 s 17; and TRUSTS AND POWERS vol 98 (2013) PARA 432. As to the persons who may be appointed as custodians see s 19 (see TRUSTS AND POWERS vol 98 (2013) PARA 433); and as to the terms of such appointment see s 20 (see TRUSTS AND POWERS vol 98 (2013) PARA 434).

16 See the Trustee Act 2000 s 18; and TRUSTS AND POWERS vol 98 (2013) PARA 432.

17 The power of intervention includes a power to give directions to the agent, nominee or custodian and a power to revoke the authorisation or appointment: see the Trustee Act 2000 s 22(4); and TRUSTS AND POWERS vol 98 (2013) PARA 436.

18 See the Trustee Act 2000 s 22(1); and TRUSTS AND POWERS vol 98 (2013) PARA 436. This also applies in a case where personal representatives appoint agents, nominees or custodians under any power conferred on them by the will or any enactment or any provision in subordinate legislation except where such application is inconsistent with the terms of the will or the enactment or provision of subordinate legislation: see s 21(2), (3).

19 Ie the duty of care under the Trustee Act 2000 s 1, Sch 1para3: see PARA 1020.

20 Trustee Act 2000 s 23(1); and see TRUSTS AND POWERS vol 98 (2013) PARA 437. The 'duties' referred to in the text are those relating to the obligations under s 22 (see the text and note 17). If the personal representative has agreed a term under which the agent, nominee or custodian is permitted to appoint a substitute, the personal representative is not liable for any act or default of the substitute unless he has failed to comply with the duty of care when agreeing that term, or when carrying out his duties under s 22 in so far as they relate to the use of the substitute: s 23(2).

1050. Personal representative's liability in relation to employment of agents. A personal representative[1] who employs an agent does not by doing so divest himself of his duties as a personal representative[2]. He is personally liable in contract to the agent[3], but is entitled to be indemnified out of the estate to the extent that the contract is a proper one in the circumstances[4]. He may accordingly make payments in respect of the contract of agency directly from the trust estate[5].

1 As to the meaning of 'personal representative' see PARA 608.

2 *Re Weall, Andrews v Weall* (1889) 42 ChD 674. See also TRUSTS AND POWERS vol 98 (2013) PARA 445. As to the appointment of agents, nominees and custodians see PARA 1049. As to agency generally see AGENCY.

3 *Staniar v Evans* (1886) 34 ChD 470 at 476; *Re Blundell, Blundell v Blundell* (1888) 40 ChD 370 at 376.

4 *Staniar v Evans* (1886) 34 ChD 470. As to the personal representative's duty himself to act gratuitously see PARA 648.

5 *Re Blundell, Blundell v Blundell* (1888) 40 ChD 370 at 377.

(vii) Survivorship of Powers

1051. Statutory provision allowing surviving trustees to exercise powers conferred jointly. There is statutory provision, in the absence of a contrary direction in the will[1], for the survivor or survivors to exercise powers or trusts given to or imposed on two or more personal representatives jointly[2].

1 See the Trustee Act 1925 s 69(2), by which the powers conferred by that Act, unless otherwise stated, apply only so far as a contrary intention is not expressed in the trust instrument. See TRUSTS AND POWERS vol 98 (2013) PARA 4.

2 See the Trustee Act 1925 ss 18(1), 68(1)para (17), 69(1); and TRUSTS AND POWERS vol 98 (2013) PARA 424. As to the exercise of powers and trusts by the personal representative of a sole or last surviving or continuing trustee see PARA 952.

1052. Whether powers are personal or annexed to office. The question whether a power is intended to be personal to the individuals to whom it is given, or whether it is intended to be annexed to their office, is one of construction[1].

The presumption is that every power given to trustees which enables them to deal with or affect the trust property is prima facie given to them ex officio as an incident of their office and passes with the office to the holders or holder for the time being[2]. The mere fact that the power is one requiring the exercise of a wide personal discretion is not enough to exclude the prima facie presumption. The testator's reliance on the individuals to the exclusion of the holders of the office must be expressed in clear and apt language[3]. The fact that the power is expressed to be given to 'my executors herein named'[4] or 'to my trustees in whom I place complete confidence'[5] is not sufficient to indicate that there is a confidence reposed in the individuals apart from their official capacity. Where the power is annexed to the office, an executor who renounces probate is incapable of exercising it[6].

1 See TRUSTS AND POWERS vol 98 (2013) PARAS 104 et seq, 528–529.

2 *Re Smith, Eastick v Smith* [1904] 1 Ch 139; *Re De Sommery, Coelenbier v De Sommery* [1912] 2 Ch 622.

3 *Re Smith, Eastick v Smith* [1904] 1 Ch 139 at 144 per Farwell J, commenting upon the dictum of Sir W Grant MR in *Cole v Wade* (1807) 16 Ves 27 at 44, 'that wherever the power is of a kind that indicates a personal confidence, it must prima facie be understood to be confined to the individual to whom it is given; and will not, except by express words, pass to others, to whom by legal transmission the same character may happen to belong'.

4 *Re Mainwaring, Crawford v Forshaw* [1891] 2 Ch 261, CA. See also *Re Bacon, Toovey v Turner* [1907] 1 Ch 475.

5 *Re Symm's Will Trusts, Public Trustee v Shaw* [1936] 3 All ER 236.

6 *Re Mainwaring, Crawford v Forshaw* [1891] 2 Ch 261, CA. See also *Keates v Burton* (1808) 14 Ves 434; *A-G v Fletcher* (1835) 5 LJ Ch 75. A power to an executor to carry on the testator's business may not, upon the executor renouncing, be exercisable by an administrator: see PARA 1035.

13. THE DISTRIBUTION OF ASSETS

(1) LEGACIES AND ANNUITIES

(i) Obligation to Distribute to those Entitled

1053. Obligation to distribute to those entitled. The ultimate object of the administration of an estate is to place the beneficiaries in possession of their interest[1] and accordingly, subject to the terms of the will if any, the personal representative[2] owes the beneficiaries a duty to pay the debts and to ascertain the residuary estate with due diligence[3]. The residuary legatee is not entitled to any particular asset of the testator's estate; his right is to have the clear residue ascertained and to have his share of it paid over[4]. However, subject to the terms of the will if any, the actual residue should be conveyed to the beneficiaries in its unconverted state unless conversion is necessary in the course of administration[5] or special circumstances apply[6].

1 *Re Tankard, Tankard v Midland Bank Executor and Trustee Co Ltd* [1942] Ch 69 at 72, [1941] 3 All ER 458 at 463 per Uthwatt J.
2 As to the meaning of 'personal representative' see PARA 608.
3 The duty to pay debts with due diligence is also owed to the creditors: *Tankard v Midland Bank Executor and Trustee Co Ltd* [1942] Ch 69, [1941] 3 All ER 458. As to the residuary legatee's right to have the residue ascertained see PARA 1116.
4 *Lord Sudley v A-G* [1897] AC 11; *Vanneck v Benham* [1917] 1 Ch 60; *Dr Barnardo's Homes v Special Commissioners of Income Tax* [1921] 2 AC 1. See also *Re Hemming's Estate, Raymond Saul & Co v Holden* [2008] EWHC 2731 (Ch) at [52], [2009] Ch 313 at [52], [2009] 2 WLR 1257 at [52] where Richard Snowden QC describes the right of the residuary legatee as a composite right to have the estate properly administered and to have the residue paid to him as and when the administration is complete.
5 *Cooper v Cooper* (1874) LR 7 HL 53; *Wightwick v Lord* (1857) 6 HL Cas 217; *Blake v Bayne* [1908] AC 371.
6 *Re Marshall, Marshall v Marshall* [1914] 1 Ch 192; *Re Sandeman's Will Trusts, Sandeman v Hayne* [1937] 1 All ER 368; *Re Weiner's Will Trusts, Wyner v Braithwaite* [1956] 2 All ER 482, [1956] 1 WLR 579; *Lloyds Bank plc v Duker* [1987] 3 All ER 193 [1987] 1 WLR 1324 (directing that, although as a general rule a person entitled to an aliquot share of an estate was entitled to insist on a corresponding part of the estate property being distributed to him intact if it was readily divisible, the executors were bound in that case to sell a majority shareholding and to distribute the proceeds in order to make a proportionate distribution by value). See also *Stephenson (Inspector of Taxes) v Barclays Bank Trust Co Ltd* [1975] 1 All ER 625 at 637-638 per Walton J; *Crowe v Appleby (Inspector of Taxes)* [1975] 3 All ER 529 (realty).

1054. Distribution within the executor's year. In general a personal representative[1] is not bound to distribute the deceased's estate before the expiration of one year from the death[2].

The personal representative has a year within which fully to inform himself of the state of the testator's property[3], and during that period he cannot be required to pay any legacies, even though they are expressly directed by the testator to be payable within the year[4]; he is entitled to pay them within the year if he chooses[5].

1 As to the meaning of 'personal representative' see PARA 608.
2 Administration of Estates Act 1925 s 44. See also PARA 961.
3 See *Cancer Research Campaign v Ernest Brown & Co* [1998] PNLR 592 at 613, [1997] STC 1425 at 1441 per Harman J. As to the payment of debts cf PARA 966.
4 *Pearson v Pearson* (1802) 1 Sch & Lef 10; *Wood v Penoyre* (1807) 13 Ves 325 at 333; *Benson v Maude* (1821) 6 Madd 15. See also *Re Smith, Dowzer v Dowzer* (1914) 48 ILT 236; *Re Lord Llangattock, Johnson v Church of England Central Board of Finance* (1918) 34 TLR 341.
5 *Garthshore v Chalie* (1804) 10 Ves 1 at 13; *Angerstein v Martin* (1823) Turn & R 232 at 241. As to the ascertainment of residue see PARA 1116.

1055. No duty to notify beneficiaries. Unlike a trustee[1], it would appear that a personal representative is under no obligation to give notice to a legatee of his legacy or of conditions attached to his legacy unless there are special reasons[2].

1 The trustee of an express trust is under a duty to inform a beneficiary that he has an interest under the terms of the trust but is not obliged to go to the length of giving legal advice as to the nature of the interest: *Hawksley v May* [1956] 1 QB 304, [1955] 3 All ER 353. See also *Brittlebank v Goodwin* (1868) LR 5 Eq 545 (duty of the trustee's administrator); *Burrows v Walls* (1855) 5 De GM & G 233. See also TRUSTS AND POWERS vol 98 (2013) PARA 402. As to when a personal representative becomes a trustee see PARA 1149.

2 *Chauncy v Graydon* (1743) 2 Atk 616; *Re Lewis, Lewis v Lewis* [1904] 2 Ch 656, CA; *Re Mackay, Mackay v Gould* [1906] 1 Ch 25; *Hawksley v May* [1956] 1 QB 304 at 322, [1955] 3 All ER 353 at 362 per Havers J. See also *Cancer Research Campaign v Ernest Brown & Co* [1998] PNLR 592, [1997] STC 1425. But see *Wroe v Seed* (1863) 4 Giff 425 at 429; *Brittlebank v Goodwin* (1868) LR 5 Eq 545.

(ii) Payment of Legacies

1056. Receipts and machinery of payment. A personal representative is entitled to a receipt on payment of a legacy, and this is a sufficient discharge, so that he is only in exceptional circumstances entitled to a formal deed of release[1].

The currency in which a legacy should be paid is decided by the testator's intention[2].

1 *Re Roberts' Trusts* (1869) 38 LJ Ch 708; *Munro v Fitzgerald* (1844) 3 LTOS 3. As to release by deed see PARA 1057; and TRUSTS AND POWERS vol 98 (2013) PARA 365. A foreign consular officer may in certain cases give a valid discharge on behalf of a foreign national resident abroad: see the Consular Conventions Act 1949 s 1(2); and PARA 802.

2 As to the testator's intention see PARA 224 et seq.

1057. Formal deed of release. Personal representatives are only entitled to be discharged upon the distribution of the residuary estate and not before[1]. It is usual in a complicated case for a formal deed of release containing proper recitals to be executed by the persons entitled to the residue, although in simple cases they merely sign the residuary accounts. Where the personal representatives are required to deal with the property otherwise than in accordance with the will or the rights of the beneficiaries they can legally demand from beneficiaries a deed of release[2]. Where personal representatives or trustees are entitled to receive the residue, a receipt under seal cannot be demanded[3].

1 *Tiger v Barclays Bank Ltd* [1951] 2 KB 556, [1951] 2 All ER 262; affd [1952] 1 All ER 85, CA. As to the residuary estate under a will see PARA 298.

2 *King v Mullins* (1852) 1 Drew 308; *Chadwick v Heatley* (1845) 2 Coll 137. See also PARA 1056 text and note 1.

3 *Re Cater's Trusts (No 2)* (1858) 25 Beav 366 at 367; *Re Hoskin's Trusts* (1877) 5 ChD 229 at 234.

1058. Rights of annuitants. An annuity given by will prima facie runs from the testator's death[1], but in the absence of a direction to the contrary[2], the first instalment does not become due until the expiration of the year, nor does a sum of money directed to be invested in the purchase of an annuity carry interest before the expiration of the year[3].

An annuitant is not entitled to have the residuary estate kept in hand to meet his annuity; he is only entitled to such security as will make it practically certain that his annuity will be paid in full[4].

Money bequeathed to be invested in the purchase of an annuity for the legatee's life is a vested legacy, and the legatee may either take the sum or have it laid out in an annuity. Should the legatee survive the testator but die before the money is laid out, or even before the fund is available (for example during the life of a person after whose death the investment is to be made)[5] it is still a vested legacy, and may be claimed by his personal representatives[6]. The same principle applies to a direction to purchase an annuity of a particular amount. The right to take its value in cash instead of the annual payment vests in the annuitant on the testator's death, and, should the annuitant die before the annuity is purchased, his personal representatives are entitled to such a sum as would, at the testator's death, have purchased the annuity[7].

1 *Gibson v Bott* (1802) 7 Ves 89 at 96; *Stamper v Pickering* (1838) 9 Sim 176. As to annuities generally see PERSONAL AND OCCUPATIONAL PENSIONS vol 80 (2013) PARA 675 et seq.
2 *Houghton v Franklin* (1823) 1 Sim & St 390; *Irvin v Ironmonger* (1831) 2 Russ & M 531.
3 *Re Friend, Friend v Young (No 2)* (1898) 78 LT 222.
4 *Re Parry, Scott v Leak* (1889) 42 ChD 570; see also *Harbin v Masterman* [1896] 1 Ch 351, CA. As to whether an annuity is charged on capital as well as income see PERSONAL AND OCCUPATIONAL PENSIONS vol 80 (2013) PARA 675 et seq.
5 *Bayley v Bishop* (1803) 9 Ves 6.
6 *Yates v Compton* (1725) 2 P Wms 308; *Barnes v Rowley* (1797) 3 Ves 305; *Palmer v Craufurd* (1819) 3 Swan 483. The setting aside by the court of a fund to meet annuities or legacies charged on residuary estate is an act of administration only, and does not release the residue from the charge: *Re Evans and Bettell's Contract* [1910] 2 Ch 438. As to vesting see PARA 412 et seq.
7 *Dawson v Hearn* (1831) 1 Russ & M 606; *Re Robbins, Robbins v Legge* [1907] 2 Ch 8, CA; *Brown's Trustees v Thom* (1915) 53 SLR 59. When the annuitant dies before the purchase of the annuity, but after payment to him of instalments of the annuity, his representatives are entitled to such a sum as would have purchased the annuity on the date of the payment of the last instalment, together with interest on that sum from that date, even though the date falls within a year of the testator's death: *Re Brunning, Gammon v Dale* [1909] 1 Ch 276. See further PERSONAL AND OCCUPATIONAL PENSIONS vol 80 (2013) PARA 687.

1059. Rights of contingent legatees. The right of a contingent legatee[1] is limited in a manner similar to that of an annuitant[2]. His only right is to have security for the payment of his legacy if the contingency arises[3]. If a personal representative, without going to the court, can prove that he has acted reasonably, and that he has set apart an ample sum to answer the legacy and has invested it, and has then proceeded to distribute the residue, he will not be held personally liable to make good the loss if it should turn out that the sum so retained is not sufficient to answer the contingent legacy[4].

1 As to contingent legatees see PARA 1083.
2 As to annuitants see PARA 1058.
3 *Webber v Webber* (1823) 1 Sim & St 311; *King v Malcott* (1852) 9 Hare 692.
4 *Re Hall, Foster v Metcalfe* [1903] 2 Ch 226 at 233, CA, per Romer LJ (where the legatee was entitled to recover the balance of the legacy from the residuary estate); *Re Oswald, Oswald v Oswald* (1919) 64 Sol Jo 242.

1060. Preservation of specific legacies. A personal representative should, so far as possible, preserve articles specifically bequeathed and, unless compelled, he ought not to apply them in payment of debts[1]. The cost of getting in a legacy specifically bequeathed ought to be borne by the general estate[2], but the personal representative should not incur the costs of litigation to recover such an article from a third party[3]. Sums paid after assent in the discharge of foreign taxes and costs incurred in connection with them[4], and the cost of warehousing and preserving, pending an assent, articles specifically bequeathed, in the absence of a direction to the contrary, ought to be borne by the specific legatee[5]. Similarly, the costs of inquiries to ascertain the person entitled to a legacy or otherwise incurred in relation to the legacy are borne by that legacy unless the court otherwise directs[6]; but the general estate will bear costs occasioned by difficulties of interpretation of the will[7].

1 *Clarke v Earl of Ormonde* (1821) Jac 108. Subject to the payment of debts the specific legatee is entitled to call upon the personal representatives to pay or transfer to him the subject matter of the legacy in due course of administration: *Re Stratton's Disclaimer* [1958] Ch 42 at 54perJenkins LJ. See also *IRC v Hawley* [1928] 1 KB 578; *Re Parsons, Parsons v A-G* [1943] Ch 12, [1942] 2 All ER 496; *Re Neeld, Carpenter v Inigo-Jones* [1962] Ch 643, [1962] 2 All ER 335, CA; *Kavanagh v Best* [1971] NI 89. See also PARA 1146 et seq.

2 *Perry v Meddowcroft* (1841) 4 Beav 197, 204. As to the provision for relief from duty and value added tax in respect of imported legacies see the Customs and Excise Duties (General Reliefs) Act 1979 s 7; and CUSTOMS AND EXCISE vol 31 (2012) PARA 886.

3 The executor should rather vest the asset in the beneficiary by way of an assent and execute an assignment to him of any relevant cause of action: *Re Clough-Taylor, Coutts & Co v Banks* [2003] WTLR 15.

4 *Re De Sommery, Coelenbier v De Sommery* [1912] 2 Ch 622.

5 *Re Rooke, Jeans v Gatehouse* [1933] Ch 970 (following *Re Pearce, Crutchley v Wells* [1909] 1 Ch 819; not following *Sharp v Lush* (1879) 10 ChD 468); and see *Re Wilson, Wilson v Mackay* [1967] Ch 53 at 65, [1966] 2 All ER 867 at 870 per Pennycuick J. The costs of putting a specific legatee in possession of his specific legacy, such as the cost of packing and transporting to England chattels situated abroad, or the cost of transferring shares or mortgages, should, it would seem, be borne by the legatee: see *Re Scott, Scott v Scott* [1915] 1 Ch 592, CA; *Re Grosvenor, Grosvenor v Grosvenor* [1916] 2 Ch 375; *Re Fitzpatrick, Bennett v Bennett* [1952] Ch 86, [1951] 2 All ER 949; but see *Re Hewett, Eldridge v Hewett* (1920) 90 LJ Ch 126; *Re Sivewright, Law v Fenwick* (1922) 128 LT 416; *Re Leach, Milne v Daubeny* [1923] 1 Ch 161 (the two last-cited cases being cases where the estate was insufficient to pay the pecuniary legacies in full). Where the will enabled beneficiaries to select items, the cost of storing and insuring those items before selection fell on income arising from residue and not on the beneficiaries: *Re Collins's Settlement Trusts, Donne v Hewetson* [1971] 1 All ER 283, sub nom *Re Collins' Will Trusts, Donne v Hewetson* [1971] 1 WLR 37. As to the costs after an assent see PARA 1013.

6 As to the reasons for which such a direction may be given see *Re Whitaker, Denison-Pender v Evans* [1911] 1 Ch 214; *Re Townend, Knowles v Jessop* [1914] WN 145; *Re Vincent, Rohde v Palin* [1909] 1 Ch 810.

7 *Re Hall-Dare, Le Marchant v Lee Warner* [1916] 1 Ch 272; *Cheung v Worldcup Investments Inc* (2008) 11 ITELR 449.

1061. Absolute bequest with directions as to application. Where there is a bequest of money to or in trust for a legatee absolutely, but with a direction for the enjoyment or application of the money in a particular mode, for example towards purchasing a house in the country, the legatee is entitled to receive the money regardless of the particular mode directed for its enjoyment or application[1].

1 *Knox v Lord Hotham* (1845) 15 Sim 82; *Lassence v Tierney* (1849) 1 Mac & G 551; *Re Skinner's Trusts* (1860) 1 John & H 102; *Moryoseph v Moryoseph* [1920] 2 Ch 33 (rule in *Lassence v Tierney* extended to realty). See also *Barlow v Grant* (1684) 1 Vern 255; *Nevill v Nevill* (1701) 2 Vern 431; *Re Osoba, Osoba v Osoba* [1979] 2 All ER 393. As to the right of a minor to a sum directed to be applied in placing him out as an apprentice see *Barton v Cooke* (1800) 5 Ves 461 at 463.

1062. Payment of vested gift not to be postponed. Where a legatee takes an absolute vested[1] interest in a sum of money on attaining the age of majority, a direction that the sum is not to be paid to him[2], or is to be accumulated[3] until a subsequent period, is to be disregarded, unless during the interval the property is given to another. The principle is equally applicable where the legatee is a charity, corporate or unincorporate[4].

1 As to vesting see PARA 412 et seq.

2 *Curtis v Lukin* (1842) 5 Beav 147 at 155; *Rocke v Rocke* (1845) 9 Beav 66; *Re Johnston, Mills v Johnston* [1894] 3 Ch 204; *Re Couturier, Couturier v Shea* [1907] 1 Ch 470.

3 *Josselyn v Josselyn* (1837) 9 Sim 63; *Saunders v Vautier* (1841) 4 Beav 115; *Gosling v Gosling* (1859) John 265. In *Re Marshall, Marshall v Marshall* [1914] 1 Ch 192, CA, it was held that the

right of a legatee absolutely entitled to a share of residue to have a transfer of his share ought, in the absence of special circumstances, to prevail over the discretion of trustees to postpone conversion. See also PARA 1053 note 6.

4 *Harbin v Masterman* [1894] 2 Ch 184, CA; affd sub nom *Wharton v Masterman* [1895] AC 186, HL. See also CHARITIES vol 8 (2015) PARA 439.

1063. Personal representatives have no duty to inquire as to adoption, illegitimacy or parental orders in favour of a gamete donor. A personal representative is not under a duty, by virtue of the law relating to the administration of estates, to inquire, before conveying or distributing any property, whether:

(1) any adoption[1] has been effected or revoked[2];

(2) any parental order[3] has been made or revoked[4]; or

(3) any person is illegitimate, or is adopted by one of his natural parents, and could be legitimated[5] (or if deceased be treated as legitimated)[6],

if that fact could affect entitlement to property[7]. Nor is a personal representative liable to any person by reason of a conveyance or distribution of the property made without regard to any such fact if he has not received notice of the fact before the conveyance or distribution[8].

These provisions, which apply from 1 January 1988[9] in the case of adoption, 6 April 2010[10] in the case of parental orders and 22 August 1976[11] in the case of legitimacy, do not prejudice the right of a person to follow the property, or any property representing it, into the hands of another person, other than a purchaser, who has received it[12]. Nor does the repeal of the former law[13] on those dates affect the application of that law in relation to a disposition of property effected by an existing[14] instrument[15].

1 As to the meaning of 'adoption' see the Adoption Act 1976 s 38(1); the Adoption and Children Act 2002 s 66(1); and CHILDREN AND YOUNG PERSONS vol 9 (2012) PARA 413. References to adoption in the Adoption and Children Act 2002 ss 66-76 do not include adoptions effected before that chapter came into force on 30 December 2005: see the Adoption and Children Act (Commencement No 9) Order 2005, SI 2005/2213; and CHILDREN AND YOUNG PERSONS vol 9 (2012) PARA 413. Adoptions before that date are those defined in and governed by the Adoption Act 1976 ss 38–49. As to adoption see generally CHILDREN AND YOUNG PERSONS vol 9 (2012) PARA 360 et seq.

2 See the Adoption Act 1976 s 45(1); the Adoption and Children Act 2002 s 72(1); and CHILDREN AND YOUNG PERSONS vol 9 (2012) PARA 416.

3 Ie a parental order under the Human Fertilisation and Embryology Act 2008 s 54 (see CHILDREN AND YOUNG PERSONS vol 9 (2012) PARA 129).

4 See the Adoption and Children Act 2002 s 72(1) and the Human Fertilisation and Embryology (Parental Orders) Regulations 2010, SI 2010/985, reg 2, Sch 1; and CHILDREN AND YOUNG PERSONS vol 9 (2012) PARA 416.

5 As to the meaning of 'legitimated person' see the Legitimacy Act 1976 s 10(1); and CHILDREN AND YOUNG PERSONS vol 9 (2012) PARA 142.

6 See the Legitimacy Act 1976 s 7(1); and CHILDREN AND YOUNG PERSONS vol 9 (2012) PARA 148.

7 See the Adoption Act 1976 s 45(1); the Legitimacy Act 1976 s 7(1); the Adoption and Children Act 2002 s 72(1); and the Human Fertilisation and Embryology (Parental Orders) Regulations 2010, SI 2010/985, reg 2, Sch 1. See also CHILDREN AND YOUNG PERSONS vol 9 (2012) PARAS 116, 148, 416.

8 See the Adoption Act 1976 s 45(2); the Legitimacy Act 1976 s 7(2); the Adoption and Children Act 2002 s 72(2); and CHILDREN AND YOUNG PERSONS vol 9 (2012) PARA 416.

9 See the Adoption Act 1976 s 74(2); and the Adoption Act (Commencement No 2) Order 1987, SI 1987/1242. The equivalent provisions in the Adoption and Children Act 2002 take effect on 30 December 2005; see note 1.

10 See the Human Fertilisation and Embryology (Parental Orders) Regulations 2010, SI 2010/985, reg 1(1).

11 See the Legitimacy Act 1976 s 12(2).

12 See the Adoption Act 1976 s 45(3); Legitimacy Act 1976 s 7(3); Adoption and Children Act 2002 s 72(3); and CHILDREN AND YOUNG PERSONS vol 9 (2012) PARAS 148, 416. As to following assets see EQUITABLE JURISDICTION vol 47 (2014) PARA 238 et seq.

13 As to the former law see the Adoption Act 1958 s 17(3); and the Adoption Act 1964 s 1(1) (both repealed by the Children Act 1975 s 108(1)(b), Sch 4) under which a personal representative could convey or distribute property to or among the people entitled to it without having ascertained that no adoption order had been made by virtue of which some other person might be entitled to an interest in the property, and was not liable to any person so entitled if he had no notice of the claim at the time of the conveyance or distribution.

14 For these purposes, 'existing' means made before 1 January 1976: Adoption Act 1976 s 72(1); Legitimacy Act 1976 s 10(1). See also CHILDREN AND YOUNG PERSONS vol 9 (2012) PARA 417. For these purposes:

(1) a will or codicil is regarded as being made at the date of the testator's death (Legitimacy Act 1976 s 10(3)(a); Adoption Act 1976 s 46(3); Adoption and Children Act 2002 s 73(4); and Human Fertilisation and Embryology (Parental Orders) Regulations 2010, SI 2010/985, reg 2, Sch 1);

(2) an oral disposition of property is deemed to be contained in an instrument made when the disposition was made (Legitimacy Act 1976 s 10(3)(b); Adoption Act 1976 s 46(2); Adoption and Children Act 2002 s 73(3); and Human Fertilisation and Embryology (Parental Orders) Regulations 2010, SI 2010/985, reg 2, Sch 1); and

(3) provisions of the law of intestate succession applicable to the estate of a deceased person must be treated as if contained in an instrument executed by him (while of full capacity) immediately before his death (Legitimacy Act 1976 s 5(2); Adoption Act 1976 s 46(4); Adoption and Children Act 2002 s 73(5); and Human Fertilisation and Embryology (Parental Orders) Regulations 2010, SI 2010/985, reg 2, Sch 1).

As to the meaning of 'disposition' see Adoption Act 1976 s 46(1); Adoption and Children Act 2002 s 73(2); and Human Fertilisation and Embryology (Parental Orders) Regulations 2010, SI 2010/985, reg 2, Sch 1; and CHILDREN AND YOUNG PERSONS vol 9 (2012) PARA 417.

15 Legitimacy Act 1976 s 5(1); Adoption Act 1976 s 42(1). See also CHILDREN AND YOUNG PERSONS vol 9 (2012) PARA 417.

1064. Pending proceedings for family provision. A personal representative distributes the estate at his own risk[1] if proceedings are pending for family provision or otherwise[2] or if the period of six months from the grant of representation, during which an application for family provision must normally be made[3], is not yet expired and there is any possibility or expectation that an application may be made[4].

1 A personal representative should form his own view as to payments which can properly be made and if he is not prepared to make payments on his own responsibility, he should obtain the consent of the parties who might conceivably be affected and if consent is not forthcoming he can apply to the court for leave to make the payments: *Re Ralphs, Ralphs v District Bank Ltd* [1968] 3 All ER 285 at 288 per Cross J.

2 Ie under the Inheritance (Provision for Family and Dependants) Act 1975: see PARA 565 et seq.

3 See PARA 597.

4 See *Re Simson, Simson v National Provincial Bank Ltd* [1950] Ch 38 at 42–43, [1949] 2 All ER 826 at 829 per Vaisey J. Personal representatives are not, however, liable for having distributed any part of the estate of the deceased after the expiration of the six month period on the ground that they ought to have taken into account the possibility that the court might exercise its power (see PARAS 597–598) to extend the period or vary its order, but this provision is without prejudice to any power to recover any part of the estate so distributed arising by virtue of the making of an order under the Inheritance (Provision for Family and Dependants) Act 1975: see s 20(1); and PARAS 583, 597. As to the right to follow assets see PARA 1095 et seq. For restrictions on the disposal of a matrimonial home in the case of an intestacy see PARA 490.

1065. Payment of legacy to bankrupt or person under disability. Where a legatee has become bankrupt in the testator's lifetime, payment of a legacy to him without notice of his bankruptcy before the trustee in bankruptcy has intervened has been held to be good[1]. However, the case law on this issue was decided before the current legislation[2] was enacted and may be unreliable.

Payment of a legacy cannot safely be made to a person who is known to the personal representative to lack capacity[3] to manage his affairs, but a personal representative can obtain a good receipt from a deputy appointed by the Court of

Protection or donee of a lasting power of attorney with the appropriate authority[4]. A legacy should not be paid to a minor[5].

1 *Re Ball* [1899] 2 IR 313, CA; *Cohen v Mitchell* (1890) 25 QBD 262, CA. But see text and note 2. As to the position where the bankruptcy is subsequent to the date of death see PARA 1219. As to the powers of the trustee in bankruptcy to intervene see the Insolvency Act 1986 s 307; and BANKRUPTCY AND INDIVIDUAL INSOLVENCY vol 5 (2013) PARA 458.

2 The Insolvency Act 1986 s 307(4) provides that a trustee in bankruptcy has no remedy against a person who acquires property in good faith, for value and without notice of the bankruptcy: see BANKRUPTCY AND INDIVIDUAL INSOLVENCY vol 5 (2013) PARA 459. The provision does not protect the personal representatives, who have not 'acquired' the relevant property; they have transferred it to the beneficiary. The transfer by the personal representatives is not made for value, but under a purported legal obligation to the beneficiary. In the absence of protection from s 307(4), personal representatives who wrongly transfer property to a bankrupt beneficiary will not obtain a good receipt: see BANKRUPTCY AND INDIVIDUAL INSOLVENCY vol 5 (2013) PARAS 458–459.

3 Ie within the meaning of the Mental Capacity Act 2005 s 2 (see MENTAL HEALTH AND CAPACITY vol 75 (2013) PARA 599 et seq). The personal representative may obtain a good discharge by payment into court in the Chancery Division: *Re Parker's Will* (1888) 39 ChD 303, CA. See also PARA 1045; and TRUSTS AND POWERS vol 98 (2013) PARA 357. If the personal representatives properly and honestly appropriate and set apart the legacy and invest and accumulate the dividends after appropriation they are free from responsibility in the case of an adult legatee suffering from mental disorder: *Pothecary v Pothecary* (1848) 2 De G & Sm 738.

4 As to the appointment of deputies by the Court of Protection see the Mental Capacity Act 2005 s 19 and as to donees of lasting powers of attorney see s 9. See also MENTAL HEALTH AND CAPACITY vol 75 (2013) PARAS 619 et seq, 735.

5 See PARA 1072 et seq.

1066. Limitation of proceedings for recovery. Subject to special provisions relating to actions in respect of trust property[1], no action in respect of any claim to the personal estate of a deceased person or to any share or interest in any such estate (whether under a will or on intestacy) may be brought after the expiration of 12 years from the date when the right accrued[2].

1 Ie subject to the Limitation Act 1980 s 21(1), (2): see LIMITATION PERIODS vol 68 (2016) PARA 1138.

2 See the Limitation Act 1980 s 22; and LIMITATION PERIODS vol 68 (2016) PARA 1159.

(iii) Legacies to Debtors

1067. General legatee must bring debt into account. Where the legatee of a general legacy[1] or share of residue[2] is a debtor to the estate, he is not entitled to receive his legacy without bringing his debt into account[3].

This principle is not applicable in the case of a specific devisee or of a specific legatee of leaseholds or chattels[4], but is applicable where the specific legacy is represented by a sum of money in the hands of the personal representative[5]. It is not applicable to a legacy which has been appropriated by the personal representative for the legatee[6].

It applies even though the legacy has been incumbered[7], or the debt is statute-barred[8]. It does not apply where the legacy is, but the debt is not, immediately payable[9], or where the legatee is the executor and residuary legatee of a person indebted to the testator on a statute-barred debt[10].

The principle is equally applicable in the case of a debtor claiming a distributive share of the estate under an intestacy[11].

1 As to general legacies see PARA 119.

2 As to the residuary estate see PARA 1113 et seq.

3 See *Cherry v Boultbee* (1839) 4 My & Cr 442; *Re Akerman, Akerman v Akerman* [1891] 3 Ch 212. For a wider application of the principle see *Re Rhodesia Goldfields Ltd, Partridge v Rhodesia Goldfields Ltd* [1910] 1 Ch 239 at 246; *Re Dacre, Whitaker v Dacre* [1916] 1 Ch 344 at 347, CA;

Selangor United Rubber Estates Ltd v Cradock (No 4) [1969] 3 All ER 965 at 972, [1969] 1 WLR 1773 at 1778 per Ungoed-Thomas J. The principle does not apply where the debt is owing by a partnership firm of which the legatee is a member (*Turner v Turner* [1911] 1 Ch 716, CA), nor, as a general rule, where the debt is owing not to the testator, but to a firm in which the testator was a partner (*Jackson v Yates* [1912] 1 IR 267). As to the nature of the principle see BANKRUPTCY AND INDIVIDUAL INSOLVENCY vol 5 (2013) PARA 573. As to equitable set-off see EQUITABLE JURISDICTION vol 47 (2014) PARAS 244–248; and as to set-off generally see CIVIL PROCEDURE vol 11 (2015) PARA 382 et seq. As to satisfaction of debts by legacies see EQUITABLE JURISDICTION vol 47 (2014) PARAS 188–190. As to retainer by a trustee against a beneficiary see TRUSTS AND POWERS vol 98 (2013) PARA 363.

4 *Re Akerman, Akerman v Akerman* [1891] 3 Ch 212. For the executor's right of retainer to apply there must be money in the shape of a debt on the one side and money on the other side: see *Re Savage, Cull v Howard* [1918] 2 Ch 146 at 149 per Sargant J. As to specific legacies see PARA 118.

5 *Re Taylor, Taylor v Wade* [1894] 1 Ch 671.

6 *Ballard v Marsden* (1880) 14 ChD 374.

7 *Re Knapman, Knapman v Wreford* (1881) 18 ChD 300, CA.

8 The statute only barred the remedy, not the debt, so that the executors remained entitled to exercise their right of retainer: *Courtnay v Williams* (1846) 15 LJ Ch 204; *Coates v Coates* (1864) 33 Beav 249; *Gee v Liddell (No 2)* (1866) 35 Beav 629; *Re Cordwell's Estate, White v Cordwell* (1875) LR 20 Eq 644. See also *Dingle v Coppen, Coppen v Dingle* [1899] 1 Ch 726.

9 *Re Rees, Rees v Rees* (1889) 60 LT 260 (debt not accruing due until after time for payment of legacy); *Re Abrahams, Abrahams v Abrahams* [1908] 2 Ch 69 (debt payable by instalments due at one year after death).

10 *Re Bruce, Lawford v Bruce* [1908] 2 Ch 682, CA.

11 *Re Cordwell's Estate, White v Cordwell* (1875) LR 20 Eq 644. The principle was not, however, applicable to the case of a debtor who was his creditor's heir: *Re Milnes, Milnes v Sherwin* (1885) 53 LT 534. As to distribution on intestacy see PARA 477 et seq.

1068. Effect of legatee's bankruptcy. Where the legatee has become bankrupt in the testator's lifetime the right to have debts brought into account[1] cannot be exercised by the personal representative, except to the extent of a dividend or composition payable in the bankruptcy[2]. Where the legatee's bankruptcy is subsequent to the testator's death, the right can be exercised in full unless the personal representative has chosen to prove in the bankruptcy[3].

1 See *Cherry v Boultbee* (1839) 4 My & Cr 442; *Re Hodgson, Hodgson v Fox* (1878) 9 ChD 673; and PARA 1067.

2 See *Re Watson, Turner v Watson* [1896] 1 Ch 925; and BANKRUPTCY AND INDIVIDUAL INSOLVENCY vol 5 (2013) PARA 573.

3 See *Re Watson, Turner v Watson* [1896] 1 Ch 925; *Stammers v Elliott* (1868) 3 Ch App 195; *Armstrong v Armstrong* (1871) LR 12 Eq 614; and BANKRUPTCY AND INDIVIDUAL INSOLVENCY vol 5 (2013) PARA 575.

(iv) Legacies to Executors

1069. Presumption that legacy is given to executor as such. The presumption is that a legacy to a person appointed executor is given to him in that character, and it is on him to show something in the nature of the legacy, or other circumstances arising on the will, to repel that presumption[1], if he does not act as executor and yet claims the legacy[2]. Where in the gift the testator has designated the executor-legatee as a friend[3] or as a relation[4], or where the legacy is expressed to be given as a mark of respect[5] or as a remembrance[6], the presumption is rebutted. It is also rebutted where the legacy is one of residue[7], or is given to the executor after the death of the tenant for life under the will[8]; but a difference either in the nature or amount of the legacy given to one executor as compared with those given to other executors is not as a general rule of itself sufficient to show that the gift is not attached to the office[9].

If a gift is made to an executor to be disposed of in accordance with a separate memorandum, but not so as to create any trust, the question whether the executor takes absolutely and beneficially is one of construction[10].

1 Williams and Mortimer on Executors 31, approved in *Re Appleton, Barber v Tebbit* (1885) 29 ChD 893 at 895, CA, per Cotton LJ. In *Re Appleton, Barber v Tebbit* at 895, Cotton LJ added that he thought parol evidence was admissible to rebut the presumption, but Fry LJ at 898 expressly abstained from concurring in that view. In the cases of *Piggott v Green* (1833) 6 Sim 72 and *Calvert v Sebbon* (1841) 4 Beav 222 the legacy was held to be annexed to the office. In *Wildes v Davies* (1853) 1 Sm & G 475; *Brand v Chaddock* (1871) 24 LT 347; and *Re Bunbury's Trusts* (1876) 10 IR Eq 408, the legacy was held to be not so attached. A request that a handsome gratuity should be given to the executor is void for uncertainty: *Jubber v Jubber* (1839) 9 Sim 503. As to the rights of an executor on a partial intestacy see PARA 517.
2 See the text to notes 3–10. As to executors in professional practice see PARA 653.
3 *Re Denby* (1861) 3 De GF & J 350. It is easier to infer an intention that a sole trustee is to take than that two or more trustees are to do so: *Re Pugh's Will Trusts, Marten v Pugh* [1967] 3 All ER 337 at 341, [1967] 1 WLR 1262 at 1267 per Pennycuick J.
4 *Compton v Bloxham* (1845) 2 Coll 201 at 203; *Dix v Reed* (1823) 1 Sim & St 237.
5 *Burgess v Burgess* (1844) 1 Coll 367.
6 *Bubb v Yelverton* (1871) LR 13 Eq 131.
7 *Re Maxwell, Eivers v Curry* [1906] 1 IR 386, CA, following *Griffiths v Pruen* (1840) 11 Sim 202.
8 *Re Reeve's Trusts* (1877) 4 ChD 841, cf *Slaney v Watney* (1866) LR 2 Eq 418 (where the executor and trustee never acted so were not entitled to share in bequest of stock).
9 *Re Appleton, Barber v Tebbit* (1885) 29 ChD 893 at 896, CA, per Cotton LJ, commenting upon *Jewis v Lawrence* (1869) LR 8 Eq 345.
10 *Re Stirling, Union Bank of Scotland Ltd v Stirling* [1954] 2 All ER 113, [1954] 1 WLR 763, following *Re Falkiner, Mead v Smith* [1924] 1 Ch 88. See also PARA 370. If the executor is a solicitor who has prepared the will there must be a strong presumption against his taking beneficially: *Re Rees's Will Trusts, Williams v Hopkins* [1950] Ch 204, [1949] 2 All ER 1003, CA; *Re Pugh's Will Trusts, Marten v Pugh* [1967] 3 All ER 337, [1967] 1 WLR 1262.

1070. When executor is entitled to a legacy. Where a legacy is attached to the office, an executor who does not act is not entitled to the benefit[1], even though he is prevented from acting by age or infirmity[2]. It is sufficient if the executor has in fact done something showing an intention to act as executor, even though he dies before proving the will[3]; and where an executor who has proved the will and acted in the administration of the estate renounces the trusteeship after administration he is nevertheless entitled to a legacy given on condition that he proves the will and accepts the trusteeship[4]. An annuity given to an executor for his trouble does not cease by reason of the institution of administration proceedings[5].

A legacy to an executor, although attached to the office, stands upon the same footing as ordinary legacies; it was subject to legacy duty[6] before that duty was abolished, and is liable to abatement[7].

1 *Abbot v Massie* (1796) 3 Ves 148 at 149; *Slaney v Watney* (1866) LR 2 Eq 418. Where the legacy is attached to the office, a revocation by codicil of the appointment of the executor also revokes the legacy: *Re Russell, Public Trustee v Campbell* (1912) 56 Sol Jo 651.
2 *Hanbury v Spooner* (1843) 5 Beav 630; *Re Hawkin's Trusts* (1864) 33 Beav 570.
3 *Harrison v Rowley* (1798) 4 Ves 212; *Lewis v Mathews* (1869) LR 8 Eq 277. Conversely, an executor who proves without any intention of acting may be disallowed the legacy: *Harford v Browning* (1787) 1 Cox Eq Cas 302.
4 *Re Sharman's Will Trusts, Public Trustee v Sharman* [1942] Ch 311, [1942] 2 All ER 74. For the construction of a condition that the executor must 'act in the trusts hereof' see *Re Parry, Dalton v Cooke* [1969] 2 All ER 512, [1969] 1 WLR 614.
5 *Baker v Martin* (1836) 8 Sim 25. As to administration proceedings see PARA 1162 et seq.
6 *Re Thorley, Thorley v Massam* [1891] 2 Ch 613, CA.
7 *Fretwell v Stacy* (1702) 2 Vern 434; *Duncan v Watts* (1852) 16 Beav 204; *Debney v Eckett* (1858) 4 Jur NS 805. As to abatement see PARA 1087 et seq. As to the authority to make professional charges see PARA 652.

1071. Lien on defaulting executor's interest. Where an executor who is also a beneficiary is in default to his testator's estate, the estate is entitled to a lien on his beneficial interest[1]. This lien is good not only against the executor himself but against his assignee[2] even though the wasting of the assets took place subsequently to the assignment[3]; and it applies not only to the beneficial interest taken by the executor directly under the will but to any interest to which he may have become entitled derivatively, for example as being one of the next of kin of a beneficiary who has died intestate[4]. An unpaid beneficiary has, however, no lien upon a specific legacy given to an executor[5], and the lien will be discharged by the acceptance of a composition in the bankruptcy of the defaulting executor[6].

1 *Barnett v Sheffield* (1852) 1 De GM & G 371; *Cole v Muddle* (1852) 10 Hare 186; *Re Carew, Carew v Carew* [1896] 1 Ch 527; affd [1896] 2 Ch 311, CA. As to lien generally see LIEN vol 68 (2016) PARA 801 et seq.
2 *Irby v Irby (No 3)* (1858) 25 Beav 632.
3 *Morris v Livie* (1842) 1 Y & C Ch Cas 380.
4 *Jacubs v Rylance* (1874) LR 17 Eq 341; *Doering v Doering* (1889) 42 ChD 203; *Re Dacre, Whitaker v Dacre* [1916] 1 Ch 344, CA. As to intestacy see PARA 477 et seq.
5 *Geary v Beaumont* (1817) 3 Mer 431. As to specific legacies see PARA 118.
6 *Re Sewell, White v Sewell* [1909] 1 Ch 806. As to compositions in bankruptcy see BANKRUPTCY AND INDIVIDUAL INSOLVENCY vol 5 (2013) PARA 856.

(v) Legacies to Minors

1072. Payment of legacy to minor. In the absence of an express direction in the will a personal representative cannot safely pay a legacy to a minor until the minor attains his majority[1]. A married minor may give a valid receipt for income and accumulations of income[2], but trustees still have a discretion to withhold payment until a married minor attains his majority if withholding is for the minor's benefit[3].

A legacy bequeathed by a testator who dies domiciled in England may be paid to the legatee on his own receipt if he is of full age by the law of his domicile even though still a minor by English law[4], and if he is under age according to both laws it will be paid to him when he comes of age according to either law, whichever happens first[5]. The court will not, however, pay a legacy to the father of a minor domiciled abroad as a matter of right and without evidence as to its application for his benefit, even if by the lex loci the father is entitled to receive the money as legal guardian[6].

1 Toller's Law of Executors (7th Edn) 314. The age of majority is now 18: see the Family Law Reform Act 1969 s 1; and CHILDREN AND YOUNG PERSONS vol 9 (2012) PARAS 1, 40.
2 See the Law of Property Act 1925 s 21; and CHILDREN AND YOUNG PERSONS vol 9 (2012) PARA 40.
3 *Re Somech, Westminster Bank Ltd v Phillips* [1957] Ch 165, [1956] 3 All ER 523.
4 *Re Hellmann's Will* (1866) LR 2 Eq 363; *Re Schnapper* [1928] Ch 420; *Donohoe v Donohoe* (1887) 19 LR Ir 349. As to domicile see CONFLICTOFLAWS vol 19 (2011) PARA 336 et seq.
5 *Re Hellmann's Will* (1866) LR 2 Eq 363. Accordingly, neither law is held exclusive. In some cases it may be proper for the trustees to pay the legacy into court under the Trustee Act 1925 s 63: see PARA 1045; and TRUSTS AND POWERS vol 98 (2013) PARA 357 et seq.
6 *Re Chatard's Settlement* [1899] 1 Ch 712, explaining *Re Crichton's Trust* (1855) 24 LTOS 267; *Re Ferguson's Trust* (1874) 22 WR 762; *Re Brown's Trust* (1865) 12 LT 488.

1073. Payment to parents and guardians. At common law a personal representative cannot obtain a valid receipt from the minor's father[1]. If, however, the minor, after attaining his majority, ratifies a payment made to his father, he cannot afterwards sue the personal representative[2].

A parent with parental responsibility[3] or a properly appointed guardian[4] can give a valid receipt for a legacy for a minor[5].

1 *Holloway v Collins* (1675) 1 Cas in Ch 245, 1 Eq Cas Abr 300 (executor ordered to make payment to plaintiff on attaining his majority having previously paid the father who then died insolvent); *Dagley v Tolferry* (1715) 1 P Wms 285 (executor ordered to pay legacy to legatee's creditors having previously paid the father); *Rotherham v Fanshaw* (1748) 3 Atk 628 at 629. If, however, on a true construction of the legacy it is payable to the father to be divided by him among his family including his minor child, the payment to the father is good: *Cooper v Thornton* (1790) 3 Bro CC 96; affd 3 Bro CC 186.

2 *Cooper v Thornton* (1790) 3 Bro CC 96; affd 3 Bro CC 186.

3 As to the meaning of 'parental responsibility' see the Children Act 1989 s 3; and CHILDREN AND YOUNG PERSONS vol 9 (2012) PARA 151.

4 Ie by a guardian appointed by the court or, on the death of a parent with parental responsibility for the minor, by that parent, or by an existing guardian of the minor: see the Children Act 1989 s 5(1)–(4); and CHILDREN AND YOUNG PERSONS vol 9 (2012) PARA 162 et seq. Where the appointment is made other than by the court it must be made in writing and signed and dated: see s 5(5). See also CHILDREN AND YOUNG PERSONS vol 9 (2012) PARA 166.

5 See the Children Act 1989 s 3(2), (3); and CHILDREN AND YOUNG PERSONS vol 9 (2012) PARAS 40, 152; *M'Creight v M'Creight* (1849) 13 I Eq R 314 at 327 per Brady LC; *Bedell v Constable* (1668) Vaugh 177; *Re Cresswell* (1881) 45 LT 468. See further Waterworth 'Minor Solutions: Receipt Clauses under the Regime of the Children Act 1989' [1997] Private Client Business 37.

1074. Discharge of personal representatives for legacy to minor. Personal representatives[1] are discharged if they obtain a valid receipt in respect of a legacy[2], but if that is not possible they may exercise their statutory power to pay the legacy into court[3], or to appropriate any part of the real or personal estate[4] of the testator in satisfaction of the legacy[5]. After exercising their power to appropriate, the personal representatives hold the assets appropriated as trustees[6]. On an appointment of trustees during a minority[7], the personal representatives as such are discharged from all further liability in respect of the devise, legacy, residue or share, which may be retained in its existing condition or state of investment, or may be converted into money, and the money may be invested in any authorised investment[8].

1 Ie personal representatives in their capacity as trustees: see the Trustee Act 1925 s 68(1) para (17); and PARA 609. As to the meaning of 'personal representative' see s 68(1) para (9); and TRUSTS AND POWERS vol 98 (2013) PARA 3.

2 See PARA 1056.

3 See the Trustee Act 1925 s 63(1), (2); and TRUSTS AND POWERS vol 98 (2013) PARA 357. As to the jurisdiction of the county court see s 63A(3)(d); and PARA 1046. See also TRUSTS AND POWERS vol 98 (2013) PARA 56. Payment in may give no better discharge than is otherwise available: *Re Elliot's Trusts* (1873) LR 15 Eq 194. If the payment in is unnecessary because other remedies are available the personal representatives will not necessarily be entitled to recover their costs out of the estate: *Re Hemings' Trusts* (1856) 3 K & J 40.

4 As to the meaning of 'real estate' see PARA 607 note 1.

5 See the Administration of Estates Act 1925 s 41(1); and PARAS 1153–1154. Executors exercising this power are not liable for a subsequent devaluation of the appropriated share whereas prior to 1926 if an executor, wishing to distribute the residue, set aside and invested in proper securities an ample sum to answer an infant's legacy, he was nevertheless personally liable for any loss if the investment proved insufficient when the infant attained his majority: *Re Salomons, Public Trustee v Wortley* [1920] 1 Ch 290. See PARA 1153 et seq.

6 *Re Smith, Henderson-Roe v Hitchins* (1889) 42 ChD 302; *Re Adams, Verrier v Haskins* [1906] WN 220; *Re Gompertz Estate, Parker v Gompertz* (1910) 55 Sol Jo 76; *Re Ponder, Ponder v Ponder* [1921] 2 Ch 59; *Re Cockburn's Will Trusts, Cockburn v Lewis* [1957] Ch 438, sub nom *Re Cockburn Cockburn v Lewis* [1957] 2 All ER 522.

7 See PARA 1075.

8 See the Administration of Estates Act 1925 s 42(1). The Trustee Act 1925 s 36 may also be available to personal representatives: see *Re Cockburn's Will Trusts, Cockburn v Lewis* [1957] Ch 438, sub nom *Re Cockburn Cockburn v Lewis* [1957] 2 All ER 522.

1075. Appointment of trustees to hold legacy for minor. Where a minor is absolutely entitled, under the will[1] or on the intestacy[2] of a person, whenever that person died, to a devise or legacy, or to the residue of the deceased's estate, or any share in it, and that devise, legacy, residue or share is not under the deceased's will, if any, devised or bequeathed to trustees for the minor, the deceased's personal representatives[3] may appoint a trust corporation[4] or two or more individuals not exceeding four (whether or not including the personal representatives or one or more of them) to be the trustee or trustees of the devise, legacy, residue or share for the minor, and to be trustees of any land[5] devised or any land being or forming part of that residue or share for the purposes of the Settled Land Act 1925, and of the statutory provisions relating to the management of land during a minority[6], and may execute or do any assurance or thing requisite for vesting the devise, legacy, residue or share in the trustee or trustees so appointed[7].

1 As to the meaning of 'will' see PARA 607 note 1.
2 See note 7.
3 As to the meaning of 'personal representative' see PARA 608.
4 As to the meaning of 'trust corporation' see PARA 622 note 4.
5 As to the meaning of 'land' see PARA 946 note 1.
6 Ie the Settled Land Act 1925 s 102: see SETTLEMENTS vol 91 (2012) PARAS 566–567; CHILDREN AND YOUNG PERSONS vol 9 (2012) PARAS 54–55.
7 Administration of Estates Act 1925 s 42(1). This provision does not apply on an intestacy unless the minor is entitled to an absolute vested interest (*Re Yerburgh, Yerburgh v Yerburgh* [1928] WN 208); and under an intestacy where the devolution of the intestate's estate is governed by English law it is no longer possible for a minor to become entitled to such an interest except on marriage (*Re Wilks, Keefer v Wilks* [1935] Ch 645 at 650; and see PARAS 499, 511). However, this provision also applies to estates regulated by foreign law and therefore applies if under foreign law a minor takes such an interest: *Re Kehr, Martin v Foges* [1952] Ch 26, [1951] 2 All ER 812; and see *Chellaram v Chellaram* [1985] Ch 409, [1985] 1 All ER 1043.
As to the liability of a personal representative who before 1926 retained or sold any such devise, legacy, residue or share see the Administration of Estates Act 1925 s 42(2).

1076. Entitlement to maintenance out of income of legacy where testator is the parent or person in loco parentis. The practice of the Chancery Division whereby a minor is entitled to maintenance during his minority out of the income of a legacy to which he is entitled contingently on his attaining his majority[1] applies where four conditions are satisfied:

(1) where the testator is the parent or stands in loco parentis to the child[2];
(2) the legacy is for the child not to trustees upon trust for the child[3];
(3) the legacy is contingent on attaining majority or marrying under that age[4];
(4) the testator has not provided another fund for the maintenance of the child[5].

The legacy in such a case carries interest from the testator's death[6] if the income available is sufficient and subject to any rules of court to the contrary[7].

1 *Re Bowlby, Bowlby v Bowlby* [1904] 2 Ch 685, CA (where the whole law on this subject is discussed and the practice is said to be based on the father's presumed intention to provide for the maintenance of his child, at 698 per Vaughan Williams LJ). The practice applies notwithstanding that the conditions as to the vesting or payment of the legacy are such that if he were in a different relation to the testator he would not be entitled to the income until attaining full age or the happening of some other event upon which the legacy was to become vested or payable: see *Re Bowlby, Bowlby v Bowlby* [1904] 2 Ch 685, CA at 698.
2 *Green v Belchier* (1737) 1 Atk 505 at 507; *Beckford v Tobin* (1749) 1 Ves Sen 308 at 310; *Cavendish v Mercer* (1776) 5 Ves 195n, LC; *Re George* (1877) 5 ChD 837 at 843, CA, per James LJ. The father is the only parent with reference to whom the first alternative of the proposition is true and a mother is not in loco parentis, even to her own child, unless she is actually supporting the child: *Re Eyre, Johnson v Williams* [1971] 1 Ch 351 at 356 per Younger J.

3 *Re Medlock, Ruffle v Medlock* (1886) 55 LJ Ch 738; *Re Pollock, Pugsley v Pollock* [1943] Ch 338; see also PARA 1081. In such circumstances the legacy will be set apart and as such will generally carry interest from one year after the testator's death: see PARA 1083 text and note 4.

4 The allowance of income on a contingent legacy is an exception to the general rule: see PARA 1083. The court may in a proper case draw from the terms of the will an inference that income is to be allowed on a legacy to a child contingent on the attainment of an age greater than the legal age of majority: *Re Jones, Meacock v Jones* [1932] 1 Ch 642 (discussing *Re Abrahams, Abrahams v Bendon* [1911] 1 Ch 108).

Otherwise, where the contingency extends beyond attaining the age of majority, the consent of the remainderman may be required (*Fendall v Nash* (1779) 5 Ves 197n, LC; *Fairman v Green* (1804) 10 Ves 45; *Cannings v Flower* (1835) 7 Sim 523); or no interest may be payable (see *Re Abrahams, Abrahams v Bendon* [1911] 1 Ch 108).

5 *Re George* (1877) 5 ChD 837 at 843, CA, per James LJ (in these circumstances the income of the legacy is supposed not to be required for maintenance); *Re Rouse's Estate* (1852) 9 Hare 649; *Re West, Westhead v Aspland* [1913] 2 Ch 345; *Re Stewart, Stewart v Bosanquet* (1913) 57 Sol Jo 646; *Beckford v Tobin* (1749) 1 Ves Sen 308 at 310; *Donovan v Needham* (1846) 9 Beav 164; *Re Moody, Woodroffe v Moody* [1895] 1 Ch 101 at 106 et seq; *Re Abrahams, Abrahams v Bendon* [1911] 1 Ch 108. The rule nevertheless applies if the court can find an intention that the testator intended to provide maintenance, eg where he authorised his trustees to provide a home for his children: *Re Jones, Meacock v Jones* [1932] 1 Ch 642; and see *Re Stokes, Bowen v Davidson* [1928] Ch 716. Where a father bequeathed a legacy to his daughter in case she should attain full age, and made no provision for her maintenance between marriage under age and attainment of full age, interest was allowed on the legacy between the time of her marrying under age and attaining full age: *Chambers v Goldwin* (1805) 11 Ves 1. The statutory power of maintenance out of a share of residue given to a minor contingently upon his attaining his majority does not disentitle him to maintenance out of the income of a pecuniary legacy given upon the same contingency: *Re Moody, Woodroffe v Moody* [1895] 1 Ch 101. As to the statutory power of maintenance see PARA 1078; and CHILDREN AND YOUNG PERSONS vol 9 (2012) PARAS 63–66.

6 *Wilson v Maddison* (1843) 2 Y & C Ch Cas 372; *Re Stokes, Bowen v Davidson* [1928] Ch 716. See also the cases cited in PARA 1077 note 3.

7 See the Trustee Act 1925 s 31(3) (which provision sets the rate of interest at 5% per annum); and CHILDREN AND YOUNG PERSONS vol 9 (2012) PARA 66.

1077. Legacy to minor who is not the testator's child. If the minor is not the child of the testator or one to whom the testator stood in loco parentis, a legacy given contingently upon his attaining his majority stands upon the same footing as an ordinary contingent legacy; it does not (save as otherwise provided by statute) carry the intermediate income unless there is a direction in the will that it should be set apart[1].

Where the income of a legacy is given for the maintenance or education[2] of a minor, the legacy carries interest from the testator's death[3] even if the minor is not a child of the testator[4]. Where the income is given to an adult subject to an obligation to maintain minors, the legacy does not carry interest from the death[5], but if income is given to an adult to enable him to maintain his children the legacy may carry interest from the death if such an intention can be gathered from the will[6].

1 See PARA 1083; and *Re Dickson, Hill v Grant* (1885) 29 ChD 331, CA; *Re Reade-Revell, Crellin v Melling* [1930] 1 Ch 52.

2 *Re Selby-Walker, Public Trustee v Selby-Walker* [1949] 2 All ER 178.

3 *Harvey v Harvey* (1722) 2 P Wms 21; *Haughton v Harrison* (1742) 2 Atk 329 at 330 per Lord Hardwicke LC; *Beckford v Tobin* (1749) 1 Ves Sen 308 at 310 per Lord Hardwicke LC; *Crickett v Dolby* (1795) 3 Ves 10 at 13 per Arden MR; *Hill v Hill* (1814) 3 Ves & B 183; *Pett v Fellows* (1733) 1 Swan 561n. A posthumous child is only entitled to interest from his birth: *Rawlins v Rawlins* (1796) 2 Cox Eq Cas 425.

4 *Pett v Fellows* (1733) 1 Swan 561n; *Leslie v Leslie* (1835) L & G *temp* Sugd 1; *Re Richards* (1869) LR 8 Eq 119; *Re Churchill, Hiscock v Lodder* [1909] 2 Ch 431; *Re Stokes, Bowen v Davidson* [1928] Ch 716.

5 *Re Crane, Adams v Crane* [1908] 1 Ch 379 (income given to daughter-in-law to maintain herself and testator's grandchildren).

6 *Re Ramsay, Thorpe v Ramsay* [1917] 2 Ch 64 (income given to widow to maintain herself and testator's children). See also *Raven v Waite* (1818) 1 Swan 553 at 559 (sum given to provide maintenance for separated wife of testator's nephew with separate allowance on condition of maintaining her children).

1078. Entitlement to income not applied in maintenance. The entitlement of a minor to maintenance out of the income of a legacy[1] does not mean that in the case of a general legacy or a specific legacy under a will coming into operation before 1926[2] the minor acquires a vested interest in the income. If he dies under the age of majority the surplus income not applied for maintenance does not pass to his representatives[3]. Where a share of residue is given absolutely to a minor contingently on his attaining his majority, the minor will be entitled to both capital and arrears of income on attaining his majority[4].

Subject to any contrary intention expressed in the will, where the will comes into operation after 1925 the right to the surplus income is in most cases[5] governed by the Trustee Act 1925[6].

1 See PARAS 1076–1077.
2 As a general rule contingent specific gifts under wills coming into operation after 1925 carry the intermediate income but contingent specific gifts before that date and contingent general legacies do not: see PARA 1083.
3 *Re Bowlby, Bowlby v Bowlby* [1904] 2 Ch 685; *Re Ferguson, Curry v Bell* (1915) 49 ILT 110. See CHILDREN AND YOUNG PERSONS vol 9 (2012) PARA 62.
4 See *Re Bowlby, Bowlby v Bowlby* [1904] 2 Ch 685 at 711, CA, per Cozens-Hardy LJ.
5 For possible exceptions see CHILDREN AND YOUNG PERSONS vol 9 (2012) PARA 58.
6 See the Trustee Act 1925 s 31(2); and CHILDREN AND YOUNG PERSONS vol 9 (2012) PARA 65.

1079. Application of statutory power of maintenance. Once the estate has been cleared and the residue ascertained, both executors[1] and administrators[2] who hold property belonging to a minor are trustees[3] for the purpose of exercising the statutory powers of trustees relating to the maintenance of minors[4].

1 *Re Smith, Henderson-Roe v Hitchins* (1889) 42 ChD 302.
2 *Re Adams, Verrier v Haskins* [1906] WN 220.
3 As to the meaning of 'trustee' see the Trustee Act 1925 s 68(1) para (17); and PARA 609.
4 See the Trustee Act 1925 s 31(1) (amended for trusts created or arising on or after 1 October 2014 by the Inheritance and Trustees' Powers Act 2014 and replacing, as respects instruments coming into operation after 1925, the Conveyancing Act 1881 s 43 (repealed)); and CHILDREN AND YOUNG PERSONS vol 9 (2012) PARAS 61–66. As to the application of the statutory power of maintenance where a minor is entitled to a contingent interest under an intestacy see the Administration of Estates Act 1925 s 47(1)(ii); and PARA 502. See also CHILDREN AND YOUNG PERSONS vol 9 (2012) PARA 63.

(vi) Interest and Accretions

1080. General principles in relation to interest and accretions. Where an account of legacies[1] is directed by any judgment then, subject to any directions contained in the codicil or will in question and to any order made by the court, interest is to be allowed on each legacy at the basic rate payable for the time being on funds in court or at such other rate as the court directs, beginning at the expiration of one year from the testator's death[2], even if expressly made payable out of a particular fund which does not fall in until after a longer period[3]. It is generally accepted that the interest rate applicable on an account of legacies should be followed in administering an estate out of court, unless the will provides otherwise.

The legatee's right to interest on a non-residuary legacy arises as a matter of administration to prevent the injustice of the residuary legatees receiving something which otherwise they could not have, merely because there has been a delay in distribution. The interest is not therefore a part of the legacy itself and must not be so regarded in determining questions of abatement[4].

No action to recover arrears of interest in respect of a legacy may normally be brought after six years from the date when the interest became due[5].

A true residuary legacy comprises all that is left after the prior gifts have been satisfied, so no question of interest on such a gift can arise, but if a testator expressly defers the date for payment of a residuary gift the surplus income arising during the period of postponement may be undisposed of and pass on intestacy[6].

1 As to the liability to account see PARA 1254 et seq. As to the remedy of account generally see EQUITABLE JURISDICTION vol 47 (2014) PARA 49.

2 CPR PD 40A—*Accounts, Inquiries etc* para 15. The current basic rate of interest on funds in court is 0.1% with effect from 6 June 2016. The rate was previously 0.3% with effect from 1 July 2009, 1% with effect from 1 June 2009, 2% with effect from 1 February 2009 and 4% with effect from 1 February 2002. As to court fund rates generally see the Government website. Prior to 2 December 2002 the rate was 6% with effect from 1 October 1983; substituted for the previous rate of 5% which applied with effect from 1 October 1982: see CPR Sch 1 RSC Ord 44 r 10 (revoked). The alternative to the court funds rate of 'such other rate as the court shall direct' indicates that the executors may apply to the court in appropriate circumstances for a different rate: see *Re Allen, Lewis v Vincent* (2007) 10 ITELR 506 (High Court of New Zealand awarded a rate lower than the statutory rate). As to the rate of interest payable on statutory legacies on intestacy see PARA 485 note 23.

There is a wide discretion to award interest on debts or damages in respect of any sum for which judgment is given or payment is made before judgment: see the Senior Courts Act 1981 s 35A; the County Courts Act 1984 s 69; and COURTS AND TRIBUNALS vol 24 (2010) PARA 701. Older decisions as to the permitted rate of interest vary: see *Re Burley, Tatham v Welch* [1917] WN 115; *Re Brinton, Brinton v Preen* [1923] WN 195 (interest at 5% on the specific legacies allowed on realisation of the residuary estate); *Re Hall, Barclays Bank Ltd v Hall* [1951] 1 All ER 1073, [1951] 1 TLR 850 (interest at 4% on a general legacy of shares in a company where dividends accrued during the period between the expiration of a year after the testator's death and the satisfaction of the legacy). It has been held that interest is not allowed at a higher rate (except in the cases set out in PARA 1076) even though the residuary estate has been producing interest at a higher rate: *Re Campbell, Campbell v Campbell* [1893] 3 Ch 468; *Sitwell v Bernard* (1801) 6 Ves 520.

3 *Re Lord's Estate, Lord v Lord* (1867) 2 Ch App 782 at 789 per Lord Cairns LJ; *Re Whiteley, Whiteley v Bishop of London* (1909) 26 TLR 16, CA; *Re Yates, Throckmorton v Pike* (1907) 96 LT 758, CA; *Walford v Walford* [1912] AC 658, HL. As to interest on contingent legacies to minors for maintenance by parents or persons in loco parentis see PARA 1076 text and note 4.

4 *Re Wyles, Foster v Wyles* [1938] Ch 313, [1938] 1 All ER 347. As to abatement see PARA 1087 et seq.

5 See the Limitation Act 1980 s 22; and LIMITATION PERIODS vol 68 (2016) PARA 1159.

6 *Re Oliver, Watkins v Fitton* [1947] 2 All ER 162, 177 LT 308; *Re Gillett's Will Trusts, Barclays Bank Ltd v Gillett* [1950] Ch 102, [1949] 2 All ER 893; *Re Geering, Gulliver v Geering* [1964] Ch 136, [1962] 3 All ER 1043. As to the residuary estate see PARA 1113 et seq. As to the intermediate income on contingent gifts of residue see PARA 1083.

1081. Date from which interest payable. An immediate general legacy[1] carries interest only from the expiration of a year after the testator's death[2], even though it is directed to be paid as soon as possible[3], and even though it is in favour of the testator's adult child[4] or of the testator's wife[5] or of trustees contingently for a child of the testator who is a minor[6]. A legacy made payable out of the proceeds of sale of real estate also carries interest only from the expiration of a year after the testator's death[7].

A legacy given to a minor as executor does not carry interest until he attains his majority and agrees to act[8].

Interest will be payable as from the date of death where it is directed by the will to be paid immediately after the testator's death[9], where it amounts to satisfaction of a debt[10] and where the legacy is charged on land and no time is fixed for payment[11].

1 As to general legacies see PARA 119.

2 *Sitwell v Bernard* (1801) 6 Ves 520; *Wood v Penoyre* (1807) 13 Ves 325 at 333–334; *Re Palfreeman, Public Trustee v Palfreeman* [1914] 1 Ch 877.
3 *Webster v Hale* (1803) 8 Ves 410 at 413; *Benson v Maude* (1821) 6 Madd 15.
4 *Wall v Wall* (1847) 15 Sim 513. See also *Raven v Waite* (1818) 1 Swan 553. As to interest on legacies to minor children see PARA 1076.
5 *Stent v Robinson* (1806) 12 Ves 461, disagreeing with the dictum of Arden MR in *Crickett v Dolby* (1795) 3 Ves 10 at 17; *Re Whittaker, Whittaker v Whittaker* (1882) 21 ChD 657.
6 *Re Pollock, Pugsley v Pollock* [1943] Ch 338, [1943] 2 All ER 443. As to legacies to minors see PARA 1072 et seq.
7 *Turner v Buck* (1874) LR 18 Eq 301.
8 *Re Gardner, Long v Gardner* (1892) 41 WR 203. Where the executor is an adult interest must not commence before he proves the will: *Angermann v Ford* (1861) 29 Beav 349.
9 *Re Riddell, Public Trustee v Riddell* [1936] Ch 747, [1936] 2 All ER 1600; *Re Pollock, Pugsley v Pollock* [1943] Ch 338, [1943] 2 All ER 443.
10 *Clark v Sewell* (1744) 3 Atk 96 at 99. As to satisfaction of debts by legacy see EQUITABLE JURISDICTION vol 47 (2014) PARAS 188–190.
11 *Pearson v Pearson* (1802) 1 Sch & Lef 10; *Shirt v Westby* (1808) 16 Ves 393. See also *Re Waters, Waters v Boxer* (1889) 42 ChD 517.

1082. Interest on legacies payable at a future date. Legacies payable at a future date carry interest from that date[1] and not before[2]. Where they are made payable within a particular period exceeding one year from the testator's death they carry interest from the end of the year, if the discretion to postpone payment is merely for the convenience of the estate, and there are sufficient assets within the period to pay them[3]; but not until the expiration of the period specified if the discretion to postpone is given for the residuary legatee's personal benefit[4].

The interest on a vested legacy liable to be divested on the happening or non-happening of a particular event belongs to the legatee and carries interest until the happening of the defeasance[5], but, in the absence of testamentary direction, a future vested legacy liable to be divested does not carry the intermediate income[6].

1 *Re Gyles, Gibbon v Chaytor* [1907] 1 IR 65; *Re White, White v Shenton* (1909) 101 LT 780.
2 *Donovan v Needham* (1846) 9 Beav 164 (interest on legacies is given for delay of payment and until the day of payment arrives no interest is generally demandable); *Re McGeorge, Ratcliff v McGeorge* [1963] Ch 544, [1963] 1 All ER 519, distinguishing *Bickersteth v Shanu* [1936] AC 290, [1936] 1 All ER 227, PC.
3 *Varley v Winn* (1856) 2 K & J 700; *Re Olive, Olive v Westerman* (1884) 53 LJ Ch 525.
4 *Thomas v A-G* (1837) 2 Y & C Ex 525.
5 *Re Buckley's Trusts* (1883) 22 ChD 583. As to conditional gifts see PARA 128 et seq.
6 *Re Gillett's Will Trusts, Barclays Bank Ltd v Gillett* [1950] Ch 102, [1949] 2 All ER 893. As to those legacies which carry the intermediate income see PARA 1083.

1083. Interest on contingent legacies. A contingent or future specific devise or bequest[1] of property, whether real or personal, and a contingent residuary devise of freehold land, and a specific or residuary devise of freehold land to trustees upon trust for persons whose interests are contingent or executory, subject to the statutory provisions relating to accumulations[2], carry the intermediate income of that property from the testator's death, except so far as that income or any part of it may be otherwise expressly disposed of[3]. A contingent general legacy does not, as a rule, carry interest until the happening of the contingency. Where, however, a contingent general legacy is directed to be severed from the rest of the estate for the benefit of the legatee it carries the intermediate income[4], but not where the severance is directed merely for the convenience of administering the estate[5]. A contingent gift of residuary personalty, or of a blended fund of real and personal estate, carries the intermediate income[6] even if the donee is not yet in being[7].

The above rules apply in respect of wills coming into operation after 1925[8]. A contingent specific legacy[9] and a contingent gift of residuary realty[10] under a will which came into operation before 1926 does not carry with it the intermediate income unless it has been directed to be set apart[11].

1 See note 3.
2 As to accumulations see the Law of Property Act 1925 ss 164–166 (in relation to wills executed before 6 April 2010); the Perpetuities and Accumulations Act 2009 (in relation to wills executed after 6 April 2010); and PERPETUITIES AND ACCUMULATIONS vol 80 (2013) PARA 129 et seq.
3 Law of Property Act 1925 s 175(1). A pecuniary legacy to a minor upon attaining his majority is not a specific bequest within the meaning of this provision so as to carry the intermediate income, and the intermediate income cannot be applied for his maintenance except in a case falling within the principles stated in PARA 1076, since the statutory powers relating to the maintenance of minors (see PARA 1079) apply in general in the case of a contingent interest only if it carries the intermediate income: see the Trustee Act 1925 s 31(3); CHILDREN AND YOUNG PERSONS vol 9 (2012) PARA 66; and *Re Raine, Tyerman v Stanfield* [1929] 1 Ch 716. Where this provision does apply it may be necessary to accumulate intermediate income until the person ultimately entitled can be ascertained: see *Re McGeorge, Ratcliffe v McGeorge* [1963] Ch 544, [1963] 1 All ER 519. As to the meaning of 'property' see REAL PROPERTY AND REGISTRATION vol 87 (2012) PARA 1; As to the meaning of 'land' see REAL PROPERTY AND REGISTRATION vol 87 (2012) PARA 7; and as to the meaning of 'income' see REAL PROPERTY AND REGISTRATION vol 87 (2012) PARA 1151.
4 *Dundas v Wolfe Murray* (1863) 1 Hem & M 425; *Kidman v Kidman* (1871) 40 LJ Ch 359; *Re Medlock, Ruffle v Medlock* (1886) 55 LJ Ch 738; *Re Inman, Inman v Rolls* [1893] 3 Ch 518; *Re Clements, Clements v Pearsall* [1894] 1 Ch 665; *Re Woodin, Woodin v Glass* [1895] 2 Ch 309, CA.
5 *Re Judkin's Trusts* (1884) 25 ChD 743.
6 *Green v Ekins* (1742) 2 Atk 473; *Genery v Fitzgerald* (1822) Jac 468; *Re Dumble, Williams v Murrell* (1883) 23 ChD 360; *Re Burton's Will, Banks v Heaven* [1892] 2 Ch 38; *Re Taylor, Smart v Taylor* [1901] 2 Ch 134. See also *Re Mellor, Alvarez v Dodgson* [1922] 1 Ch 312, CA.
7 *Bective v Hodgson* (1864) 10 HL Cas 656.
8 Law of Property Act 1925 s 175(2). As to the payment of interest, apart from statute, on a contingent legacy to a minor by his parent see PARA 1076.
9 *Guthrie v Walrond* (1883) 22 ChD 573; *Re Eyre, Johnson v Williams* [1917] 1 Ch 351. For an exception in the case of a minor see PARA 1077.
10 *Hodgson v Earl Bective* (1863) 1 Hem & M 376; affd sub nom *Bective v Hodgson* (1864) 10 HL Cas 656.
11 *Re Woodin, Woodin v Glass* [1895] 2 Ch 309, CA.

1084. Arrears of annuities. Arrears of annuities do not generally carry interest[1], even though the annuity is intended as a provision for a wife or child[2], or is charged on corpus as well as on income[3].

1 *Re Hiscoe, Hiscoe v Waite* (1902) 71 LJ Ch 347. For exceptions to the general rule see *Torre v Browne* (1855) 5 HL Cas 555 at 578. As to annuities see PERSONAL AND OCCUPATIONAL PENSIONS vol 80 (2013) PARA 675 et seq.
2 *Torre v Browne* (1855) 5 HL Cas 555 at 577; *Re Earl of Berkeley, Inglis v Countess Berkeley* [1968] Ch 744 at 761, [1968] 3 All ER 364 at 374, CA, per Harman LJ.
3 *Wheatly v Davies* (1876) 35 LT 306.

1085. Dividends and rents. All accretions from the date of death are carried with a specific legacy[1], whether vested[2] or contingent[3].

Where there is a general legacy[4] of shares in a company the legatees are not entitled to dividends which accrue during the period between the expiration of a year after the testator's death and the satisfaction of the legacies; they are entitled only to interest for that period[5].

The dividends on a specific legacy[6], the rents on a specific devise[7] and the income of residue in a case where the beneficiary is entitled to the whole income from the testator's death[8] must be apportioned[9], as between the testator's estate and the beneficiary, up to the date of the testator's death unless there is an express direction to the contrary[10].

1 As to specific legacies see PARA 118.
2 *Sleech v Thorington* (1754) 2 Ves Sen 560 at 563; *Re Jeffery's Trusts* (1866) LR 2 Eq 68; *Re Marten, Shaw v Marten* [1901] 1 Ch 370; and see *Re Jacob, M'Coy v Jacob* [1919] 1 IR 134. The specific legatee is entitled to the income from the death of the testator where the specific legacy is vested but enjoyment is postponed: *Long v Ovenden* (1881) 16 ChD 691; *Guthrie v Walrond* (1883) 22 ChD 573.
3 *Re Buxton, Buxton v Buxton* [1930] 1 Ch 648.
4 As to general legacies see PARA 119.
5 *Re Hall, Barclays Bank Ltd v Hall* [1951] 1 All ER 1073, [1951] 1 TLR 850. As to the rate of interest see PARA 1080.
6 *Pollock v Pollock* (1874) LR 18 Eq 329.
7 *Hasluck v Pedley* (1874) LR 19 Eq 271; *Constable v Constable* (1879) 11 ChD 681.
8 Ie entitled under the Apportionment Act 1870 s 2: see LANDLORDANDTENANT vol 62 (2012) PARA 279; PERSONAL AND OCCUPATIONAL PENSIONS vol 80 (2013) PARA 716; SETTLEMENTS vol 91 (2012) PARAS 858–859. The Apportionment Act 1870 s 2 does not apply in relation to new trusts in certain circumstances: see the Trusts (Capital and Income) Act 2013 s 1; and PARA 927.
9 *Re Bate, Public Trustee v Bate* [1938] 4 All ER 218, a case where the rule in *Howe v Earl of Dartmouth* (see PARA 1122) was excluded.
10 See the Apportionment Act 1870 s 7; and *Re Bate, Public Trustee v Bate* [1938] 4 All ER 218.

1086. Appropriation of payments to principal or interest. Subject to any direction in the will or order of the court to the contrary, where a legacy cannot be satisfied when due, a payment is made on account of principal and interest of a legacy and the legatee may appropriate the payment first to interest and then to principal[1].

1 *Re Prince, Hardman v Willis* (1935) 51 TLR 526; *Thomas v Montgomery* (1830) 1 Russ & M 729; *Re Morley's Estate* [1937] Ch 491, [1937] 3 All ER 204. As to the deduction of income tax from such payments where attributable to interest see INCOME TAXATION.

(vii) Abatement of Legacies and Annuities

1087. Abatement of general legacies. If an estate is insufficient to pay all the legacies in full, the general legacies[1] (which in this context include annuities[2]) must, in the absence of a contrary direction by the testator[3], abate in equal proportions[4]. The onus of proving that his legacy was intended by the testator to be paid in priority lies on the party seeking priority, and the proof must be clear and conclusive[5] on the language of the will. Near relationship to the testator does not of itself give a legatee priority over other legatees[6]. A mere direction to pay a legacy immediately, or within one month, or within three months after a testator's death, is no evidence of any intention on the testator's part to give priority to that particular legacy in case of a deficiency in the estate[7]. A legacy given to a testator's widow to be paid immediately after his death for her immediate wants is liable to abatement with the other legacies[8]. A legacy to an executor is not entitled to any priority[9].

Inheritance tax on lifetime gifts or on assets which do not vest in the personal representatives is not a testamentary expense[10] and a direction in the will to pay such tax will be treated as a legacy, for the purposes of abatement, to the person who would otherwise pay and would, therefore, be similarly liable to abatement. 'Pecuniary legacy' is defined[11] to include all death duties free from which any devise, bequest, or payment is made to take effect; so a direction in a will to pay tax on foreign assets which would otherwise be paid by the beneficiary will be liable to abatement.

1 As to general legacies see PARA 119. The reference to legacies in the text includes those contained in, or substituted by, a codicil: *Re MacCarthy, National Bank Ltd v Archbishop of Dublin* [1958] IR 311.
2 As to annuities see generally REAL PROPERTY AND REGISTRATION vol 87 (2012) PARA 1104 et seq.
3 *Marsh v Evans* (1720) 1 P Wms 668; *Lewin v Lewin* (1752) 2 Ves Sen 415.
4 2 Bl Com (14th Edn) 512. See also *Re Whitehead, Whitehead v Street* [1913] 2 Ch 56; *Re Bosanquet, Unwin v Petre* (1915) 85 LJ Ch 14; *Re Daniels, London City and Midland Executor and Trustee Co Ltd v Daniels* (1918) 87 LJ Ch 661.
5 *Miller v Huddlestone* (1851) 3 Mac & G 513 at 523 per Lord Truro LC. As to priority of payment of legacies see *Re Harris, Harris v Harris* [1912] 2 Ch 241; *Thwaites v Foreman* (1844) 1 Coll 409 at 414 (on appeal (1846) 15 LJ Ch 397); *Re Leach, Milne v Daubeny* [1923] 1 Ch 161.
6 *Re Schweder's Estate, Oppenheim v Schweder* [1891] 3 Ch 44. Where before 1926 a legacy was bequeathed to the testator's widow in satisfaction of her right to dower she was regarded as a purchaser of the legacy, and if she elected to take it in lieu of dower the legacy had priority over other legacies, notwithstanding that it might greatly exceed the amount of the dower (*Burridge v Bradyl* (1710) 1 P Wms 127; *Blower v Morret* (1752) 2 Ves Sen 420; *Davenhill v Fletcher* (1754) Amb 244; *Heath v Dendy* (1826) 1 Russ 543; *Roper v Roper* (1876) 3 ChD 714 at 719). The widow was not entitled to priority where the testator left no real estate to which the right to dower could attach, or where he had barred her right to dower by any mode in which dower could be barred, including a disposition of his real estate by will (*Re Greenwood, Greenwood v Greenwood* [1892] 2 Ch 295; *Re Whitehead, Whitehead v Street* [1913] 2 Ch 56). As to dower see REAL PROPERTY AND REGISTRATION vol 87 (2012) PARA 156.
7 *Re Schweder's Estate, Oppenheim v Schweder* [1891] 3 Ch 44 at 45 per Chitty J, following *Blower v Morret* (1752) 2 Ves Sen 420, and dissenting from *Re Hardy, Wells v Borwick* (1881) 17 ChD 798. See also *Brown v Allen* (1681) 1 Vern 31; *Beeston v Booth* (1819) 4 Madd 161.
8 *Cazenove v Cazenove* (1889) 61 LT 115.
9 *Duncan v Watts* (1852) 16 Beav 204; *O'Higgins v Walsh* [1918] 1 IR 126; *Re Brown, Wace v Smith* (1918) 62 Sol Jo 487; *Re Leach, Milne v Daubeny* [1923] 1 Ch 161.
10 See the Inheritance Tax Act 1984 s 211; PARA 1128; and INHERITANCE TAXATION vol 59A (2014) PARA 271.
11 See the Administration of Estates Act 1925 s 55(1)(ix); and PARA 1003. Abatement was also required where a legacy was given free of the former legacy duty: see *Re Turnbull, Skipper v Wade* [1905] 1 Ch 726; *Re Leach, Milne v Daubeny* [1923] 1 Ch 161. As to the abolition of legacy duty see INHERITANCE TAXATION vol 59A (2014) PARA 1.

1088. Abatement of demonstrative legacies and specific legacies. Demonstrative legacies[1] do not abate with general legacies[2] except so far as the fund provided is insufficient for their payment[3]. When the fund provided is exhausted demonstrative legacies abate proportionately with the other general legacies[4].

Specific legacies[5] do not abate with general legacies, but where the general estate is insufficient to pay all the debts, they must abate rateably among themselves[6]. The rule applies to a gift of a specific fund in aliquot proportions[7], but where fixed sums are given out of a particular fund and the balance is disposed of as residue, and not as an aliquot proportion, the residue must first be exhausted[8].

1 As to demonstrative legacies see PARA 120.
2 As to general legacies see PARA 119.
3 *Roberts v Pocock* (1798) 4 Ves 150 at 160; *Mann v Copland* (1817) 2 Madd 223; *Fowler v Willoughby* (1825) 2 Sim & St 354; *Mullins v Smith* (1860) 1 Drew & Sm 204.
4 *Paget v Huish* (1863) 1 Hem & M 663; *Mullins v Smith* (1860) 1 Drew & Sm 204 at 210.
5 As to specific legacies see PARA 118.
6 *Brown v Allen* (1681) 1 Vern 31; *Duke of Devon v Atkins* (1726) 2 P Wms 381. See also *Re Compton, Vaughan v Smith* [1914] 2 Ch 119; *Re Cohen, National Provincial Bank Ltd v Katz* [1960] Ch 179, [1959] 3 All ER 740. See also the Administration of Estates Act 1925 s 34(3), Sch 1 Pt II; and PARA 998 et seq.
7 *Page v Leapingwell* (1812) 18 Ves 463.

8 *Petre v Petre* (1851) 14 Beav 197. See also *De Lisle v Hodges* (1874) LR 17 Eq 440; *Re Tunno, Raikes v Raikes* (1890) 45 ChD 66.

1089. Abatement of legacy in satisfaction of debt. There appears to be some doubt whether a legacy given in satisfaction of a debt abates with legacies given to volunteers[1]. In a case where the debt was an ascertained debt and the legatee had elected to take under the will a legacy far in excess of his debt, it was held that his legacy must abate rateably with the other pecuniary legacies[2], but there are statements to be found that legacies to creditors are not liable to abatement with legacies to volunteers[3]. A creditor with whom the testator has compounded cannot be treated as a purchaser of his legacy[4].

1 As to legacies given in satisfaction of debt see EQUITABLE JURISDICTION vol 47 (2014) PARAS 188–190.
2 *Re Wedmore, Wedmore v Wedmore* [1907] 2 Ch 277; *Re Whitehead, Whitehead v Street* [1913] 2 Ch 56 (legacy conditional on release under settlement).
3 See *Davies v Bush* (1831) You 341 at 343 per Lord Lyndhurst LCB; *Re Lawley, Zaiser v Lawley* [1902] 2 Ch 799 at 807, CA, per Cozens-Hardy LJ; on appeal sub nom *Beyfus v Lawley* [1903] AC 411, HL.
4 *Coppin v Coppin* (1725) 2 P Wms 291 at 296. As to compositions see BANKRUPTCY AND INDIVIDUAL INSOLVENCY vol 5 (2013) PARA 856.

1090. Abatement of annuities. Where annuities[1] are given by will and abatement is necessary in accordance with the rules[2], the annuities must be valued and abated proportionately and (subject to what is stated below) the abated sum must be paid to the annuitant[3] or to his personal representatives if he has died after the sum has been ascertained[4]. The sums paid in respect of annuities abated in this way are capital sums and are not taxable for income tax purposes[5].

This rule of administration yields to a contrary intention expressed by the testator, and it is accordingly necessary first to ascertain from the will whether the testator has in fact provided for the deficiency which has occurred[6]. Moreover, cases may occur where, although the annual income is insufficient to provide for the annuities, it is apparent, having regard to the age of the annuitants and other circumstances, that the capital and income together must be amply sufficient to satisfy the annuities in full. In those circumstances it may work great hardship on the residuary legatee if capital sums are paid to the annuitants. Accordingly in cases of this kind the annuitants are not entitled to demand capital sums in lieu of their annuities[7].

1 As to annuities see generally REAL PROPERTY AND REGISTRATION vol 87 (2012) PARA 1104 et seq.
2 As to these rules see PARAS 1087–1088.
3 *Long v Hughes* (1831) 1 De G & Sm 364; *Wright v Callender* (1852) 2 De GM & G 652; *Wroughton v Colquhoun* (1847) 1 De G & Sm 357; *Innes v Mitchell* (1847) 2 Ph 346; *Re Cottrell, Buckland v Bedingfield* [1910] 1 Ch 402; *Re Richardson, Richardson v Richardson* [1915] 1 Ch 353; *Re Dempster, Borthwick v Lovell* [1915] 1 Ch 795; *Miller v Huddlestone* (1851) 3 Mac & G 513; *Daniell v Daniell* (1849) 3 De G & Sm 337 at 342.
4 See *Re Ross, Ashton v Ross* [1900] 1 Ch 162.
5 *IRC v Lady Castlemaine* [1943] 2 All ER 471. This principle extends to payments made as income payments before the deficiency is discovered: see INCOME TAXATION vol 58 (2014) PARA 550. If annuities were given free of legacy duty, the duty was treated as an additional legacy for the purposes of valuation: *Re Turnbull, Skipper v Wade* [1905] 1 Ch 726. As to the abolition of legacy duty see INHERITANCE TAXATION vol 59A (2014) PARA 1. As to the valuation of annuities for the purposes of inheritance tax see INHERITANCE TAXATION vol 59A (2014) PARA 242.
6 *Re De Chassiron, Lloyds Bank Ltd v Sharpe* [1939] Ch 934, [1939] 3 All ER 321.
7 *Re Hill, Westminster Bank v Wilson* [1944] Ch 270, [1944] 1 All ER 502, CA. These principles can be applied by the personal representatives in the course of administration without a court order: *Re Brouncker, Mairis v Mandeville* [1938] WN 147; *Re Bradberry, National Provincial Bank Ltd v Bradberry* [1943] Ch 35, [1942] 2 All ER 629.

1091. Defeasible annuities. Where the annuity[1] is defeasible upon the happening of an event in the lifetime of the annuitant he is not entitled to have the capital sum paid over to him, but that sum should be applied in the purchase of an annuity, and the annuity so purchased should be paid to the annuitant until the event occurs or the annuitant dies[2].

1 As to annuities see generally REAL PROPERTY AND REGISTRATION vol 87 (2012) PARA 1104 et seq.

2 *Carr v Ingleby* (1831) 1 De G & Sm 362; *Gratrix v Chambers* (1860) 2 Giff 321; *Re Richardson, Mahony v Treacy* [1915] 1 IR 39; *Re Dempster, Borthwick v Lovell* [1915] 1 Ch 795. If, however, the annuity is payable by virtue of a covenant entered into by the testator during his life and not by virtue of a gift in his will, and, his estate being insufficient to pay the annuity in full, the annuity has been valued in an administration action and is represented by a fund in court, the fund must be paid to the annuitant: *Re Sinclair, Allen v Sinclair, Hodgkins v Sinclair* [1897] 1 Ch 921, distinguished in *Re Dempster, Borthwick v Lovell* at 800.

1092. Gift over of annuity fund after annuitant's death. Complications occur where a fund is directed to be appropriated to answer an annuity[1] and there is a gift over of the appropriated fund after the annuitant's death. In such a case the contest is not merely between those interested in the fund on the one hand and the other legatees on the other hand but also between those interested in the fund among themselves. In cases of this kind, it is a matter of construction whether the annuitant or those entitled under the gift over is or are entitled to priority. If the rights of the annuitant are paramount, the capital value of the annuity, abated if necessary, is paid to the annuitant[2]. If the rights of those entitled under the gift over are paramount, a sum is ascertained and invested in a manner which will, with all reasonable certainty, produce the annuity, and the annuitant is entitled to the income produced by this sum, abated if necessary[3]. Finally, a third method may be adopted by which the capital value of the annuity, abated if necessary, is ascertained, and the annuitant is paid the full amount of his annuity, resort being had to the capital of the fund, until the fund is exhausted. Any surplus left when the annuitant dies is paid to those entitled under the gift over[4].

1 As to annuities see generally REAL PROPERTY AND REGISTRATION vol 87 (2012) PARA 1104 et seq.

2 *Re Farmer, Nightingale v Whybrow* [1939] Ch 573, [1939] 1 All ER 319; *Re Wilson* [1940] Ch 966, [1940] 4 All ER 57.

3 *Re Carew, Channer v Franklyn* [1939] Ch 794, [1939] 3 All ER 200.

4 *Re Nicholson, Chadwyck-Healey v Crawford* [1938] 3 All ER 270; *Re Thomas, Public Trustee v Falconer* [1946] Ch 36, [1945] 2 All ER 586.

1093. Valuation of annuities. The valuation of annuities[1] is a matter in which it is desirable that there should be a uniform practice although alternative methods may be resorted to when the circumstances are unusual[2]. The valuation should be an actuarial valuation, and facts, such as the health of the annuitant or the risks attendant to his vocation, must be disregarded[3]. When the valuation is made by the court, every relevant fact known at the date of the hearing will be taken into account[4]. Therefore, if an annuitant has died since the testator, the value of his annuity is taken to be the actual amount of the arrears to which he was entitled up to the date of his death according to the tenor of the will[5]; and where a considerable period has elapsed since the testator's death, and the annuitant is still living, the proper method of valuation is to calculate the capital value of the annuity at the time of the valuation and add the arrears to the sum so ascertained[6]. In ordinary cases, however, where there has been no material change in the circumstances since the date of the testator's death, it is convenient and right to take that date as the date for any valuations which have to be made[7].

When an annuity given free of income tax[8] has to be valued, the rate of tax to be taken into account is the rate ruling at the date when the valuation has to be made[9].

It is competent for the personal representatives themselves to make any necessary valuations without recourse to the court, but it is proper for them to seek the court's directions if they are uncertain about the course they ought to pursue[10].

Annuitants in possession are not bound, as between themselves and reversionary annuitants, to bring past payments into hotchpot[11].

1 As to annuities see generally REAL PROPERTY AND REGISTRATION vol 87 (2012) PARA 1104 et seq. As to the valuation of annuities for inheritance tax purposes see INHERITANCE TAXATION vol 59A (2014) PARA 242.
2 *Re Bradberry, National Provincial Bank Ltd v Bradberry* [1943] Ch 35 at 40, [1942] 2 All ER 629 at 633 per Uthwatt J; *Re McEuen, McEuen v Phelps* [1913] 2 Ch 704, CA.
3 *Ex p Thistlewood* (1812) 19 Ves 236. The sum which the particular annuity might realise if sold is therefore irrelevant and the valuation should be made by reference to the sum required to purchase a government annuity of the amount specified: *Re Bradberry, National Provincial Bank Ltd v Bradberry* [1943] Ch 35 at 40, [1942] 2 All ER 629 at 634 per Uthwatt J. The Finance Act 1962 terminated the power to grant annuities under the Government Annuities Act 1929 except in special cases but retained the Government Annuity tables used primarily to calculate these annuities: see the Finance Act 1962 s 33; and FINANCIAL INSTRUMENTS AND TRANSACTIONS vol 49 (2015) PARA 154; PERSONAL AND OCCUPATIONAL PENSIONS vol 80 (2013) PARA 687. The sum is now to be determined by reference to the Government Annuity Table Order 1963, SI 1963/1178: see PERSONAL AND OCCUPATIONAL PENSIONS vol 80 (2013) PARA 687.
4 *Potts v Smith* (1869) LR 8 Eq 683 at 686 per James V-C; *Re Bradberry, National Provincial Bank Ltd v Bradberry* [1943] Ch 35, [1942] 2 All ER 629.
5 *Re Bradberry, National Provincial Bank Ltd v Bradberry* [1943] Ch 35, [1942] 2 All ER 629; *Todd v Bielby* (1850) 27 Beav 353; *Re Ellis, Nettleton v Crimmins* [1935] Ch 193; *Re Ball, Lucas v Ball* [1940] 4 All ER 245; *Re Cox, Public Trustee v Eve* [1938] Ch 556, [1937] 1 All ER 661; *Re Twiss* [1941] Ch 141, [1941] 1 All ER 93.
6 *Heath v Nugent* (1860) 29 Beav 226; *Re Wilkins, Wilkins v Rotherham* (1884) 27 ChD 703; *Delves v Newington* (1885) 52 LT 512; *Re Bradberry, National Provincial Bank Ltd v Bradberry* [1943] Ch 35 at 46, [1942] 2 All ER 629 at 636 per Uthwatt J.
7 *Re Bradberry, National Provincial Bank Ltd v Bradberry* [1943] Ch 35 at 46, [1942] 2 All ER 629 at 636 per Uthwatt J.
8 As to income tax see INCOME TAXATION.
9 *Re Ball, Lucas v Ball* [1940] 4 All ER 245; *Re Twiss* [1941] Ch 141, [1941] 1 All ER 93; *Re Viscount Rothermere, Mellors, Basden & Co v Coutts & Co* [1945] Ch 72, [1944] 2 All ER 593.
10 *Re Bradberry, National Provincial Bank Ltd v Bradberry* [1943] Ch 35 at 39, [1942] 2 All ER 629 at 631 per Uthwatt J; *Re Brouncker, Mairis v Mandeville* [1938] WN 147.
11 *Re Metcalf, Metcalf v Blencowe* [1903] 2 Ch 424. The direction to the contrary appearing in the order in *Potts v Smith* (1869) LR 8 Eq 683 is inconsistent with the judgment in that case: *Re Metcalf, Metcalf v Blencowe* at 428 per Farwell J. As to hotchpot see PARA 515.

1094. Valuation of reversionary annuities. Where a testator bequeaths a reversionary annuity[1] and also immediate pecuniary legacies, and his estate is ascertained at his death to be insufficient, the court values the annuity on the basis of its being a reversionary interest, and this valuation abates rateably with the immediate legacies[2]. Again, where in the case of a bequest of a reversionary annuity the estate is only ascertained at some point of time after the testator's death to be insufficient, and before that point of time the reversionary annuity has fallen into possession, the value of the reversionary annuity must be ascertained by adding the amount of the arrears accrued since the annuity fell into possession to the then present value of the future payments[3].

Where a testator bequeaths two annuities, one immediate and the other reversionary, and the immediate annuity is for some time paid in full, but the estate is subsequently found to be insufficient, and that annuity remains for some time unpaid, then, in the division between the immediate and reversionary annuitants of the funds ultimately available, the immediate annuitant is not bound to bring into hotchpot his early payments in full[4].

1 As to annuities see REAL PROPERTY AND REGISTRATION vol 87 (2012) PARA 1104 et seq.
2 *Re Metcalf, Metcalf v Blencowe* [1903] 2 Ch 424 at 428; *Innes v Mitchell* (1846) 1 Ph 710 at 716.
3 *Potts v Smith* (1869) LR 8 Eq 683 at 687. If the reversionary interest has not fallen into possession at the time when the estate is ascertained to be insufficient, it would seem that the annuity should be valued as at that time on the basis of its being a reversionary interest, but this rule is not settled.
4 *Re Metcalf, Metcalf v Blencowe* [1903] 2 Ch 424. As to hotchpot see PARA 515.

(viii) Refunding

1095. Right to follow assets. The principle that trust property may be followed[1], the effect of a mixing of trust funds with other funds[2], the limitation period applicable to proceedings to recover assets from persons who have been wrongly paid or overpaid[3], and the classes of persons who are entitled to exercise the right and call for a refund[4] are considered elsewhere in this work.

1 See EQUITABLE JURISDICTION vol 47 (2014) PARA 238.
2 See EQUITABLE JURISDICTION vol 47 (2014) PARA 240.
3 See EQUITABLE JURISDICTION vol 47 (2014) PARA 243.
4 See EQUITABLE JURISDICTION vol 47 (2014) PARA 243.

1096. Refunding between personal representative and legatee. A personal representative who has voluntarily paid a legacy cannot call upon the legatee to refund[1]. It is otherwise where there is a deficiency of assets and the personal representative has made payment of a legacy under compulsion of an action[2].

An executor-trustee who has severed a portion of the estate in favour of a particular legatee is not entitled to have recourse to the severed portion to indemnify himself against a liability which he has been called upon to discharge in respect of another portion of the estate[3].

1 *Hilliard v Fulford* (1876) 4 ChD 389; *Herbert v Badgery* (1894) 10 WN 128. The voluntary payment in full of a legacy by an executor amounts to an admission by him of assets sufficient for all, so he will be compelled, if solvent, to pay all other legacies in full whatever the state of the assets: *Orr v Kaines* (1750) 2 Ves Sen 194; approved *Re Diplock, Diplock v Wintle* [1948] Ch 465 at 487–488, [1948] 2 All ER 318 at 329, CA, per Lord Greene MR (affd on appeal sub nom *Ministry of Health v Simpson* [1951] AC 251 at 267, [1950] 2 All ER 1137 at 1141–1142, HL, per Lord Simonds). As to the admission of assets see PARA 1298 et seq. As to the rights of the unpaid or underpaid legatee against overpaid persons see PARA 1099. As to the personal representative's right against strangers (ie persons who are not beneficiaries of the estate) paid under a mistake of fact or law see PARA 1097 note 3 and PARA 1099 note 1. See also PARA 1207.
2 See *Newman v Barton* (1690) 2 Vern 205; and EQUITABLE JURISDICTION vol 47 (2014) PARA 243.
3 *Fraser v Murdoch* (1881) 6 App Cas 855, HL; *Re Craven, Watson v Craven* [1914] 1 Ch 358. As to appropriation see PARA 1153 et seq.

1097. Refunding between personal representative and residuary legatee. A personal representative cannot recover from a residuary legatee a payment made with notice of a debt[1]; but where the personal representative has parted with the residue to the residuary legatee under a mistake he can call on that legatee to refund whether the payment is made under a mistake of fact[2] or under a mistake of law[3]. The personal representative's right to recover is subject to the defences available in the law of restitution[4]. The question whether a personal representative can recover interest from an overpaid legatee or whether he must restrict himself to recovering the capital paid to the legatee without interest is open to doubt[5].

1 *Jervis v Wolferstan* (1874) LR 18 Eq 18 at 25 per Sir G Jessel MR.

2 Eg where he has parted with the residue without knowledge of anything that interferes with the right of the residuary legatee to receive it and debts are subsequently discovered which he is obliged to pay. Notice at the time of distribution of a mere liability which does not constitute a debt does not prevent him from subsequently calling upon the residuary legatee: see *Jervis v Wolferstan* (1874) LR 18 Eq 18; *Whittaker v Kershaw* (1890) 45 Ch D 320, CA.

3 The former rule precluding recovery of money paid under a mistake of law has been abolished: *Kleinwort Benson Ltd v Lincoln City Council* [1999] 2 AC 349, [1998] 4 All ER 513, HL. Therefore, it is no longer safe to follow older decisions such as *Coppin v Coppin* (1725) 2 P Wms 291; *Orr v Kaines* (1750) 2 Ves Sen 194; *Bate v Hooper* (1855) 5 De GM & G 338; *Downes v Bullock* (1858) 25 Beav 54; *Jervis v Wolferstan* (1874) LR 18 Eq 18 at 25 per Jessel MR; *Re Bird, Evans, Dodd v Evans* [1901] 1 Ch 916; *Re Diplock, Diplock v Wintle* [1948] Ch 465. A personal representative may also have recourse to restitutionary remedies against strangers (ie persons who are not beneficiaries of the estate) paid under a mistake of fact or law: see PARA 1099 note 1; and see *Fea v Roberts* [2006] WTLR 255 (mistaken identity); *Re Clapham, Barraclough v Mell* [2005] EWHC 3387 (Ch), [2006] WTLR 203 (misconstruction of a will).

4 *Kleinwort Benson Ltd v Lincoln City Council* [1999] 2 AC 349 at 372, [1998] 4 All ER 513 at 530, HL, per Lord Goff. The probable defences include, but may not be limited to change of position(*Ministry of Health v Simpson* [1951] AC 251, [1950] 2 All ER 1137, HL; *Lipkin Gorman v Karpnale Ltd* [1991] 2 AC 548, [1992] 4 All ER 512, HL), estoppel and compromise. See further RESTITUTION vol 88 (2012) PARA 565 et seq.

5 The presently accepted rule is that, in recalling a payment to an overpaid legatee the court is not to demand interest (*Jervis v Wolferstan* (1874) LR 18 Eq 18 at 27) although, if the legatee is entitled to another fund making interest in the hands of the court, there ought to be a recoupment out of his share (*Gittins v Steele* (1818) 1 Swan 199). The position is now uncertain following the award of interest in *Westdeutsche Landesbank Girozentrale v Islington London Borough Council* [1996] AC 669, [1996] 2 All ER 961, HL.

1098. Right to equalise out of future payments. An executor-trustee who has overpaid one beneficiary is entitled in the future administration of the trusts to equalise the payments at the expense of the overpaid beneficiary[1]; and there is no general rule that he cannot claim such an adjustment in his own favour where he is the person responsible for the mistake which has been made[2].

1 *Livesey v Livesey* (1827) 3 Russ 287; *Dibbs v Goren* (1849) 11 Beav 483.

2 *Re Ainsworth, Finch v Smith* [1915] 2 Ch 96; *Re Reading, Edmonds v Reading* (1916) 60 Sol Jo 655. In special circumstances, however, an executor may be unable to claim an adjustment: *Re Horne, Wilson v Cox Sinclair* [1905] 1 Ch 76.

1099. Refunding at the instance of legatees. Equity[1] will not allow one person to retain what is really and legally applicable to the payment of another[2]. Accordingly, where a legacy has been wrongly paid or overpaid under a mistake of law or fact and without the approval of the other beneficiaries[3], then, notwithstanding any contrary former practice of the ecclesiastical courts[4], the court will compel the wrongly paid or overpaid legatee to refund[5] normally without interest[6], whether the person properly entitled is a creditor[7] or another legatee[8]. The right of an underpaid legatee to claim directly against an overpaid legatee is, however, subject to the qualification that the underpaid legatee must first exhaust his remedy against the personal representative who has made the wrongful payment[9] and is not available where the deficiency of assets has arisen since the date of payment by reason of acts of waste by the personal representative or otherwise[10]. A residuary legatee who institutes administration proceedings can be compelled in those proceedings to refund, for the purpose of paying legacies, money paid to him by the personal representative before the claim[11].

Where one of several residuary legatees has received his share of the estate the other cannot call upon him to refund if the estate is subsequently wasted, but they can do so if the wasting has taken place before the share was received[12]. It lies upon the person requiring the money to be refunded to show that the payment was made in excess[13].

1 Recourse may also be had to restitutionary remedies: see *Lipkin Gorman v Karpnale Ltd* [1991] 2 AC 548, [1992] 4 All ER 512, HL; *Kleinwort Benson Ltd v Lincoln City Council* [1999] 2 AC 349, [1998] 4 All ER 513, HL. See also RESTITUTION vol 88 (2012) PARA 401 et seq.
2 *Harrison v Kirk* [1904] AC 1 at 7, HL, per Lord Davey. As to refunding between creditors and legatees see PARA 1101.
3 *Rogers v Ingham* (1876) 3 ChD 351, CA.
4 See *Ministry of Health v Simpson* [1951] AC 251 at 267, [1950] 2 All ER 1137 at 1141, HL, per Lord Simonds.
5 *Noel v Robinson* (1682) 1 Vern 90; *Nelthrop v Hill* (1669) 1 Cas in Ch 135; *Grove v Banson* (1669) 1 Cas in Ch 148; *Chamberlain v Chamberlain* (1675) 1 Cas in Ch 256; *Anon* (1683) 1 Vern 162; *Newman v Barton* (1690) 2 Vern 205; *Walcott v Hall* (1788) 2 Bro CC 305; *Peterson v Peterson* (1866) LR 3 Eq 111; *Re Rivers, Pullen v Rivers* [1920] 1 Ch 320.
6 See EQUITABLE JURISDICTION vol 47 (2014) PARA 243.
7 *Harrison v Kirk* [1904] AC 1, HL.
8 *David v Frowd* (1833) 1 My & K 200.
9 *Ministry of Health v Simpson* [1951] AC 251, [1950] 2 All ER 1137, HL. See PARA 1096 note 1; and EQUITABLE JURISDICTION vol 47 (2014) PARA 242.
10 *Re Diplock, Diplock v Wintle* [1948] Ch 465 at 487–488, [1948] 2 All ER 318 at 329, CA, per Lord Greene MR (affd sub nom *Ministry of Health v Simpson* [1951] AC 251, [1950] 2 All ER 1137, HL); *Anon* (1718) 1 P Wms 495; *Walcott v Hall* (1788) 2 Bro CC 305; *Fenwick v Clarke* (1862) 4 De GF & J 240.
11 *Prowse v Spurgin* (1868) LR 5 Eq 99.
12 *Peterson v Peterson* (1866) LR 3 Eq 111; *Re Winslow, Frere v Winslow* (1890) 45 ChD 249. See also EQUITABLE JURISDICTION vol 47 (2014) PARA 243. In *Re Rivers, Pullen v Rivers* [1920] 1 Ch 320, where residuary legatees had been paid but a sum set aside in administration proceedings to pay an annuity proved insufficient to pay the legacy left to the annuitant's children after the death, it was held that the residuary legatees were liable to refund the amount of the deficiency to the children.
13 *Peterson v Peterson* (1866) LR 3 Eq 111 at 114.

1100. Refunding on intestacy. Where an intestate's estate has been distributed among the presumed next of kin[1], and another person subsequently establishes his title to be next of kin, he can compel the persons among whom the estate has been distributed to refund what has been paid to them in excess of their shares[2].

If the estate of a testator has been distributed on the footing that an invalid residuary disposition was valid, then, subject to the qualification that they have first exhausted their remedies against the personal representatives[3], the next of kin may claim directly against the persons to whom the residuary estate has been wrongly distributed[4].

1 As to distribution of an intestate's estate see PARAS 1135–1138.
2 *David v Frowd* (1833) 1 My & K 200; *Sawyer v Birchmore* (1837) 2 My & Cr 611. The question whether the distribution was in pursuance of a court order is immaterial, except that where distribution was in pursuance of an order, an unpaid creditor is not required to bring a further action against the personal representative before proceeding against the persons wrongfully paid: *Re Diplock, Diplock v Wintle* [1948] Ch 465 at 489–490, [1948] 2 All ER 318 at 330, CA, per Lord Greene MR; on appeal sub nom *Ministry of Health v Simpson* [1951] AC 251 at 268, [1950] 2 All ER 1137 at 1142, HL, per Lord Simonds. See also see PARA 1106.
3 See PARAS 1096–1099.
4 *Ministry of Health v Simpson* [1951] AC 251, [1950] 2 All ER 1137, HL.

1101. Refunding between creditor and legatees. A creditor has no legal right to recover payment of his debt against a legatee, but, in order to do justice and to avoid the evil of allowing one person to retain what is really and legally applicable to the payment of another, the court has devised a remedy by which, where the estate has been distributed either out of court or in court without regard to the rights of a creditor, it has allowed the creditor to recover back what has been paid to the beneficiaries or to the next of kin[1]. The creditor's right being, however, purely equitable, it may be met by any answer which affords a good equitable defence[2], such as laches, acquiescence or other conduct which would render it unjust for the court to allow him to assert any right against the legatee[3].

1 *Harrison v Kirk* [1904] AC 1 at 7, HL, per Lord Davey; *Noel v Robinson* (1681) 1 Vern 90 at 94; *March v Russell* (1837) 3 My & Cr 31; *National Assurance Co v Scott* [1909] 1 IR 325. As to the extent to which it is material whether the distribution was in court or out of court see PARA 1100 note 2.

2 *Harrison v Kirk* [1904] AC 1 at 7, HL; *March v Russell* (1837) 3 My & Cr 31; *National Assurance Co v Scott* [1909] 1 IR 325; *Blake v Gale* (1886) 32 ChD 571, CA.

3 *Ridgway v Newstead* (1860) 2 Giff 492 at 501 per Stuart V-C; on appeal (1861) 3 De GF & J 474. See also *Re Eustace, Lee v McMillan* [1912] 1 Ch 561, where delay did not amount to laches. As to equitable defences generally see EQUITABLE JURISDICTION vol 47 (2014) PARA 244 et seq.

1102. Creditor's right against fund in court. Where the estate is being administered by the court the creditor can at any time, upon such terms as the court may think fit to impose, come in and claim against a fund in court standing to the general credit of the administration proceedings[1].

As against a fund which has been carried to a separate account in administration proceedings, the creditor whose claim has not been previously established has no right to have the whole of the debt paid out of the fund, but only such proportion of it as the fund bears to the whole of the assets distributed by the court[2].

1 *Beattie v Cordner* [1903] 1 IR 1, CA; affd sub nom *Harrison v Kirk* [1904] AC 1, HL. See also *Browne v Browne* [1919] 1 IR 251. The court may require a creditor to pay the costs of the application: see *Harrison v Kirk* at 6 per Lord Davey; *Gillespie v Alexander* (1827) 3 Russ 130 at 136 per Lord Eldon LC.

2 *Gillespie v Alexander* (1827) 3 Russ 130; *Greig v Somerville* (1830) 1 Russ & M 338. The fact that funds have been carried to separate credits does not of itself free them from liabilities which could attach to funds standing to a general credit: *O'Neill v M'Grorty* [1915] 1 IR 1.

1103. Creditor's right when the estate has been administered out of court. Where the estate has been administered out of court the creditor is entitled to proceed against a legatee for the whole of the debt, and not merely for a proportionate part[1], notwithstanding that the legatee has received payment of his legacy in entire ignorance of the creditor's claim[2]. He is entitled to attack any legatee whom he chooses, and the person attacked is entitled to a contribution from his co-legatees[3].

1 *Davies v Nicolson* (1858) 2 De G & J 693.

2 *March v Russell* (1837) 3 My & Cr 31.

3 *Davies v Nicolson* (1858) 2 De G & J 693, where the order was that the specific legatee was liable to pay the creditor, without prejudice to any question between himself, the executor and the residuary legatee.

1104. Contribution where one or more beneficiaries insolvent. Where the court has directed contribution among the beneficiaries for payment of debts and costs, and one of the beneficiaries is insolvent, it will direct an additional contribution among the solvent beneficiaries[1].

If a debtor[2] by or against whom a bankruptcy petition has been presented dies, the proceedings in the matter are, subject to any order to the contrary, continued as if he were alive[3].

1 *Conolly v Farrell* (1846) 10 Beav 142; *Re Peerless, Peerless v Smith* (1901) 45 Sol Jo 670.

2 Ie being a beneficiary who is under an obligation to contribute.

3 Administration of Insolvent Estates of Deceased Persons Order 1986, SI 1986/1999, art 5(1), Sch 2. Where the estate of a deceased person is insolvent and is being administered otherwise than in bankruptcy the administration is subject to various provisions of the Insolvency Act 1986 as

provided for in the Administration of Insolvent Estates of Deceased Persons Order 1986, SI 1986/1999, art 3, Sch 1. See PARA 981; and BANKRUPTCY AND INDIVIDUAL INSOLVENCY vol 5 (2013) PARA 830 et seq.

1105. Rights of creditors against purchasers. Unsatisfied creditors have a right to follow a legacy against volunteers claiming through the legatee, but they have no such right against a purchaser in good faith from the legatee[1]. Where the personal representative has not parted with control over the assets, or where the legacy is represented by a fund in court, the purchaser from the legatee takes subject to the rights of unsatisfied creditors, even if their claims are established after the purchase[2].

1 *Dilkes v Broadmead* (1860) 2 Giff 113 (on appeal 2 De GF & J 566); *Spackman v Timbrell* (1837) 8 Sim 253. See also the Administration of Estates Act 1925 s 32(2); and PARA 970.
2 *Noble v Brett* (1858) 24 Beav 499; *Hooper v Smart, Piper v Piper, Bailey v Piper* (1875) 1 ChD 90.

1106. Effect of order or enactment protecting representative. Even if personal representatives have distributed the estate under the protection of a court order, the right of a beneficiary or creditor to follow assets is not affected[1]. The right to follow assets is similarly preserved, subject in certain cases to provisions for the protection of purchasers, by the enactments which relate to the protection of personal representatives against liability in respect of rents and covenants[2] against claims of which they have not received notice within the time fixed in the statutory advertisements[3], and against certain claims by persons for whom reasonable provision has not been made[4] and by the enactments which relate to the effect of an assent or conveyance by personal representatives[5] against claims by or through adopted or illegitimate children of which they had no notice at the time of conveyance or distribution of the estate[6]. Where the personal representative is protected against claims, the person seeking to follow the assets into the hands of beneficiaries may take proceedings to follow the assets without previously taking proceedings against, or joining, the personal representatives[7].

1 *Re Gess, Gess v Royal Exchange Assurance* [1942] Ch 37. See also *Re Benjamin, Neville v Benjamin* [1902] 1 Ch 723. The effect of distributing under the protection of a court order is to protect the personal representatives but the right of a creditor or beneficiary remains. In the case of small estates the personal representatives may take out missing beneficiary insurance instead: *Re Evans, Evans v Westcombe* [1999] 2 All ER 777. As to following assets see EQUITABLE JURISDICTION vol 47 (2014) PARA 238 et seq. See also PARA 1194.
2 See PARA 990.
3 See PARA 965.
4 See PARA 1064 note 3.
5 See PARA 970.
6 See PARA 1063.
7 *Clegg v Rowland* (1866) LR 3 Eq 368; *Hunter v Young* (1879) 4 ExD 256, CA; *Re Frewen, Frewen v Frewen* (1889) 60 LT 953. See also PARA 1100 note 2.

(2) ORDER OF APPLICATION OF ASSETS ON PAYMENT OF PECUNIARY LEGACIES

1107. Difficulties of statutory interpretation. The duty of identifying which parts of the estate are charged with the payment of pecuniary legacies[1], and in what order, is a problem of distribution and is altogether distinct from the administrative question of the order in which the assets are to be applied in payment of the debts and liabilities[2], although the distinction has not been uniformly observed. The Administration of Estates Act 1925 directs that the estate of a person dying after 1925, if solvent, is to be applied towards the discharge of funeral, testamentary and administration expenses, debts and liabilities, in the statutory order of application of assets[3], but makes no mention of legacies. Legacies are, however, referred to in the provisions which set out the statutory order[4]. This has caused difficulty in interpreting the statutory provisions, and the authorities are contradictory and confused, but it is submitted that the law is as stated in the ensuing paragraphs.

1 As to the meaning of 'pecuniary legacy' see the Administration of Estates Act 1925 s 55(1)(ix). See also PARA 118 et seq.
2 As to the order of payment of debts and liabilities see PARA 998 et seq.
3 See the Administration of Estates Act 1925 s 34(3); and PARA 998 et seq.
4 See the Administration of Estates Act 1925 s 34(3), Sch 1 Pt II paras 1, 2, 5; and PARAS 999–1000.

1108. The first fund for payment. Subject to any contrary provisions of the will[1], the first fund for payment of pecuniary legacies, in the case of all deaths after 1925, is any property of the deceased otherwise undisposed of by will[2]. With this one exception the legislation of 1925 has not directly[3] altered the previous law on this subject, and accordingly the presumption must be that Parliament did not intend to alter the rules[4] which regulated the matter before 1926 and that these continue to apply[5].

1 See the Administration of Estates Act 1925 s 33(7); and PARA 1135 et seq. As to the meaning of 'will' see PARA 607 note 1.
2 See the Administration of Estates Act 1925 ss 33(2), 34(3), Sch 1 Pt II para 1 (s 33(2) amended by the Trusts of Land and Appointment of Trustees Act 1996 s 5(1), Sch 2 para 5(1), (3)). Both the Administration of Estates Act 1925 s 33(2) and Sch 1 Pt II para 1 require a fund to be set aside, out of property otherwise undisposed of by the will, to provide for pecuniary legacies, and from this the necessary implication arises that the fund should be applied for that purpose: see *Re Worthington, Nichols v Hart* [1933] Ch 771, CA; *Re Sanger, Taylor v North* [1939] Ch 238, [1938] 3 All ER 417; *Re Gillett's Will Trusts, Barclays Bank Ltd v Gillett* [1950] Ch 102, [1949] 2 All ER 893; *Re Martin, Midland Bank Executor Trustee Co Ltd v Marfleet* [1955] Ch 698, [1955] 1 All ER 865; *Re Midgley, Barclays Bank Ltd v Midgley* [1955] Ch 576, [1955] 2 All ER 625. For decisions to the contrary see *Re Taylor's Estate and Will Trusts* [1969] 2 Ch 245, [1969] 1 All ER 113; *Re Beaumont's Will Trusts, Walker v Lawson* [1950] Ch 462, [1950] 1 All ER 802 (criticised in *Re Midgley, Barclays Bank Ltd v Midgley*); *Re Berrey's Will Trusts, Greening v Waters* [1959] 1 All ER 15, [1959] 1 WLR 30. See also *Re Wilson, Wilson v Mackay* [1967] Ch 53, [1966] 2 All ER 867; and PARA 993.
3 For the effect of the provision by which the payment of debts and liabilities out of residue is made subject to the retention of a fund to meet pecuniary legacies see PARA 1000.
4 As to these rules see PARAS 1109–1112.
5 *Re Thompson, Public Trustee v Husband* [1936] Ch 676, [1936] 2 All ER 141; *Re Rowe* [1941] Ch 343, [1941] 2 All ER 330.

1109. General rules on payment of pecuniary legacies before 1926. Before 1926 the general rule was that, in the absence of a sufficient indication of a contrary intention, pecuniary legacies were payable out of the personal estate not specifically bequeathed[1].

Where there was a bequest of pecuniary legacies, and a gift of the residue of the testator's real and personal estate in one mass, it was a general rule of construction that the residuary real estate was charged with the payment of the legacies in aid of the personal estate[2]. For the application of this rule it was not necessary that the testator should use the word 'residue', and a gift of realty and personalty in terms which substantially amount to a residuary gift was sufficient[3]; the rule applied whether the legacies were given before or after the gift of residue[4]. Where there was simply a charge of legacies upon real estate, that charge was nothing more than ancillary to the personal estate, and could not be enforced against the real estate where the personal estate was sufficient to pay all the legacies[5].

If the personal estate was sufficient at the time the legacy became payable, a subsequent wasting of the assets before the legacy was actually paid would not throw the legacy upon the real estate[6], except where the personal representative and the devisee were the same person[7].

1 *Robertson v Broadbent* (1883) 8 App Cas 812, HL. See also *Re Fowler, Fowler v Wittingham* (1915) 139 LT Jo 183; *Re Thompson, Public Trustee v Husband* [1936] Ch 676, [1936] 2 All ER 141; *Re Rowe* [1941] Ch 343, [1941] 2 All ER 330; *Re Beaumont's Will Trusts, Walker v Lawson* [1950] Ch 462, [1950] 1 All ER 802 (criticised, so far as it relates to the law after 1925, in *Re Midgley, Barclays Bank Ltd v Midgley* [1955] Ch 576, [1955] 2 All ER 625). For the effect of the provision contained in the Administration of Estates Act 1925 by which the payment of debts and liabilities out of residue is made subject to the retention of a fund to meet pecuniary legacies see PARA 1000.
2 *Greville v Browne* (1859) 7 HL Cas 689; *Re Brooke, Brooke v Rooke* (1876) 3 ChD 630.
3 *Re Bawden, National Provincial Bank of England v Cresswell, Bawden v Cresswell* [1894] 1 Ch 693; *Re Smith, Smith v Smith* [1899] 1 Ch 365; *Re Balls, Trewby v Balls* [1909] 1 Ch 791. See also *Re Cowell, Temple v Temple* (1920) 150 LT Jo 296.
4 *Re Balls, Trewby v Balls* [1909] 1 Ch 791.
5 *Re Ovey, Broadbent v Barrow* (1885) 31 ChD 113 at 118 per Pearson J. As to where land is specifically devised see PARA 1110.
6 *Richardson v Morton* (1871) LR 13 Eq 123.
7 *Howard v Chaffers, Howard v Robinson* (1863) 2 Drew & Sm 236; *Humble v Humble* (1838) 2 Jur 696.

1110. Payment of pecuniary legacies where land is specifically devised. The presumption is against an intention to charge land specifically devised, and a mere charge on all the testator's land is not sufficient to rebut the presumption[1]. However, the question must always be one of intention[2].

1 *Conron v Conron* (1858) 7 HL Cas 168 at 190 per Lord Cranworth; *Spong v Spong* (1829) 3 Bli NS 84, HL; *Re Chester, Ryan v Chester* (1914) 49 ILT 97.
2 *Bank of Ireland v McCarthy* [1898] AC 181, HL.

1111. Payment of pecuniary legacies from a mixed fund. Where the testator's real and personal property has been so blended together as to form a mixed fund for the payment of legacies, the legacies must be borne by the real and personal estate rateably[1]. The rule, however, as to rateable payment out of a mixed fund does not extend beyond the things which the testator has expressly directed to be paid out of the fund[2], and it may accordingly occur that the realty comprised in the fund may be charged rateably with the payment of debts, but only in aid of the personalty in discharge of the legacies[3].

1 *Re Spencer Cooper, Poë v Spencer Cooper* [1908] 1 Ch 130; *Re Owers, Public Trustee v Death* [1941] Ch 17, [1940] 4 All ER 225, CA. As to mixed funds for payment of debts and legacies see PARA 993.
2 *Elliott v Dearsley* (1880) 16 ChD 322 at 329, CA, per James LJ.
3 *Elliott v Dearsley* (1880) 16 ChD 322, CA; *Re Boards, Knight v Knight* [1895] 1 Ch 499 (overruling dictum of Jessel MR in *Gainsford v Dunn* (1874) LR 17 Eq 405 at 408); *Re Thompson, Public Trustee v Husband* [1936] Ch 676, [1936] 2 All ER 141.

1112. Realty may be the primary or exclusive fund for legacies. A testator may make his real estate the primary fund for the payment of legacies. He may also make it the exclusive fund, and questions occasionally arise as to whether the legatee can have recourse to the personalty. Where the testator shows a separate and independent intention that the money is to be paid to the legatee in any event, the intention will not be held to be controlled merely by a direction in the will that the money is to be raised in a particular way or out of a particular fund[1], and in such a case recourse may be had to the personal estate if the real estate proves deficient[2]. Where, however, the testator simply charges his real estate with a sum of money, and then bequeaths the money so charged, the real estate alone is liable to the payment[3].

1 *Dickin v Edwards* (1844) 4 Hare 273 at 276 per Wigram V-C.
2 As to those cases in which real estate has been held to be the primary fund see *Savile v Blacket* (1722) 1 P Wms 777 at 778; *Welby v Rockcliffe* (1830) 1 Russ & M 571; *Williams v Hughes* (1857) 24 Beav 474.
3 *Dickin v Edwards* (1844) 4 Hare 273 at 276 per Wigram V-C. See also *Spurway v Glynn* (1804) 9 Ves 483.

(3) THE RESIDUARY ESTATE UNDER A WILL

(i) Residuary Estate Given Absolutely

1113. What a residuary gift comprises. A general residuary gift passes everything not disposed of, whether the testator has not attempted to dispose of it or whether the disposition fails by lapse or any other event[1]. In order to exclude from such a gift a particular property belonging to the testator and not otherwise disposed of by will it is necessary to find a plain and unequivocal intention on his part not to include that property in the residuary gift; the mere fact that he is under the erroneous impression that the particular property is not his to dispose of does not exclude the property from the residue[2].

1 See *Re Bagot, Paton v Ormerod* [1893] 3 Ch 348 at 359, CA, per Lopes LJ; *Easum v Appleford* (1840) 5 My & Cr 56 at 61; *Bernard v Minshull* (1859) John 276; *Re Blight, Blight v Hartnoll* (1883) 23 ChD 218, CA; *Craw's Trustees v Blacklock* 1920 SC 22, Ct of Sess; *Re Barnes' Will Trusts, Prior v Barnes* [1972] 2 All ER 639, [1972] 1 WLR 587. As to the effect of a residuary devise see the Wills Act 1837 s 25; and PARA 183. Where a testator is dealing with a definite ascertained sum, the word 'residue' only refers to the exact amount remaining after prior amounts are taken out, and will not catch a share which has failed: *Bagge v Bagge* [1921] 1 IR 213. As to the distinction between a gift of residuary estate and a gift of the residue of residuary estate and the application of lapse see *Re Whitrod, Burrows v Base* [1926] Ch 118. As to the tax treatment of the income of the residuary estate see the Income Tax (Trading and Other Income) Act 2005 Pt 5 Ch 6 (ie ss 649–682A) and the Corporation Tax Act 2009 Pt 10 Ch 3 (ie ss 934–967); and INCOME TAXATION vol 59 (2014) PARAS 2079–2091. As to the dangers of distribution within six months of the date of the grant see PARA 1064.
2 *Re Bagot, Paton v Ormerod* [1893] 3 Ch 348 at 359, CA, commenting on the earlier decisions in *Circuitt v Perry* (1856) 23 Beav 275; *Harris v Harris* (1869) 17 WR 790; *Hawks v Longridge* (1873) 29 LT 449; and *Clibborn v Clibborn* (1857) 2 Ir Jur 386.

1114. Property subject to general power of appointment may pass under a general gift. A general devise of the testator's real estate or a general bequest of his personal estate is to be construed as including any real or personal estate, as the case may be, which the testator may have power to appoint in any way he may think proper, and is to operate as an execution of that power in the absence of a contrary intention[1].

1 See the Wills Act 1837 s 27; PARA 170; and TRUSTS AND POWERS vol 98 (2013) PARA 577. The instrument creating the power may be so framed as to exclude from the operation of s 27 any particular kinds of will: *Phillips v Cayley* (1889) 43 ChD 222 at 233, CA, per Bowen LJ; *Re Davies, Davies v Davies* [1892] 3 Ch 63. A person preparing a will who is aware that the testator has a general power of appointment is under a duty to remind the testator of the existence of the power, to ascertain whether he wishes to exercise it and if so in whose favour: see *Gibbons v Nelsons* (2000) Times, 21 April, [2000] All ER (D) 479. As to the effect of an appointment being limited to an extent necessary to pay debts and legacies see *Hawthorn v Shedden* (1856) 3 Sm & G 293; *Re Seabrook, Gray v Baddeley* [1911] 1 Ch 151; *Re Jarrett, Re Vrenegroor, Bird v Green* [1919] 1 Ch 366. As to the exercise of powers by will see TRUSTS AND POWERS vol 98 (2013) PARA 577 et seq. As to construction of wills see PARA 185 et seq. References in the Administration of Estates Act 1925 to a deceased person's estate include property over which he exercises a general

power of appointment: see the Administration of Estates Act 1925 ss 1(1), 3(1), (3); and PARA 954. As to the meanings of 'real estate' and 'personal estate' see the Wills Act 1837 s 1; and PARA 282 notes 3, 4.

1115. Failure of share of residue. Where a gift of part of the residue fails, the lapsed share does not fall into residue, but goes as undisposed of[1]. A direction, however, that a revoked[2] or lapsed share[3] is to fall into residue amounts to a gift of that share to the other residuary legatees.

If a legacy given out of a share of residue fails, it goes to the next of kin as undisposed of[4]. Where, however, the will contains a gift over operating upon the share of residue as a whole, the gift of the remaining part of that share carries such a legacy in the event of its failure[5].

Where part of residue is given to an attesting witness the gift is null and void[6] and the will must be treated, so far as conferring any beneficial interest on such person, as though it did not contain the offending disposition[7].

1 *Re Wood's Will* (1861) 29 Beav 236; *Sykes v Sykes* (1868) 3 Ch App 301; *Re Forrest, Carr v Forrest* [1931] 1 Ch 162. See also *Re Bentley, Podmore v Smith* (1914) 110 LT 623; *Re Whitrod, Burrows v Base* [1926] Ch 118.

2 *Re Palmer, Palmer v Answorth* [1893] 3 Ch 369, CA, overruling *Humble v Shore* (1847) 7 Hare 247. See also *Re Forrest, Carr v Forrest* [1931] 1 Ch 162.

3 *Re Allan, Dow v Cassaigne* [1903] 1 Ch 276, CA.

4 *Lloyd v Lloyd* (1841) 4 Beav 231, applied in *Green v Pertwee* (1846) 5 Hare 249 but doubted in *Re Judkin's Trusts* (1884) 25 ChD 743 at 750 per Kay J.

5 *Re Parker, Stephenson v Parker* [1901] 1 Ch 408, doubting *Skrymsher v Northcote* (1818) 1 Swan 566.

6 See the Wills Act 1837 s 15; and PARAS 41, 78.

7 *Re Doland's Will Trusts, Westminster Bank Ltd v Phillips* [1970] Ch 267; [1969] 3 All ER 713 (a proviso 'if the trusts of any of the shares aforesaid of my residuary estate shall fail' was ineffective in those circumstances and the relevant share was undisposed of and passed on intestacy); *Aplin v Stone* [1904] 1 Ch 543; *Jull v Jacobs* (1876) 3 ChD 703.

1116. Residuary legatee's right to have residue ascertained. A residuary legatee has a right to insist that the personal representative pay the debts, legacies and funeral and testamentary expenses with due diligence, so that the clear residue may be ascertained and paid over to him, or, if he has only a life interest in it, may be duly secured for the benefit of the persons successively entitled[1]; but the effect of the bequest is not to vest in him any particular asset of the testator[2].

1 *Wightwick v Lord* (1857) 6 HL Cas 217 at 226. As to the personal representative's duty to pay debts see PARA 966 et seq. As to the personal representative's duty in respect of legacies see PARA 1054.

2 See PARA 922.

1117. Valuation of estate for purposes of hotchpot. Where a testator has provided that advances made to beneficiaries in his lifetime are to be brought into account against their shares in his residuary estate, or where hotchpot otherwise applies[1], the general rule is, it seems, that in the absence of a contrary direction in the will, the estate and the beneficiaries' interests in it[2] are to be valued at the date of distribution and not at the date of the testator's death[3].

The date of valuation must control not only the division of the capital but also the mode of dealing with the individual income[4]. Two methods can be adopted, but there is a conflict of authority as to which method is prima facie applicable where there is nothing in the context to show the testator's intention[5]. The first method is to value the distributable fund at death and add to that the sum to be brought into hotchpot, and then ascertain the fractions which are to be applied to the distribution of intermediate income and capital when it falls to be distributed[6]. The second method is to deal with the income by adding interest at the legacy rate[7] on the amount of the advances to the income actually received between the date of death and the date of actual distribution, and then divide the resulting income among the beneficiaries, debiting the advanced beneficiary with interest on the advances. On distribution of the capital the amount of the advances is then added to the sum of money to be divided which is actually in the trustees' hands. The gross sums are then divided between the beneficiaries and the advanced beneficiary is debited with the advance[8].

1 Eg under the rule against double portions: see EQUITABLE JURISDICTION vol 47 (2014) PARA 182. As to hotchpot see PARA 515.
2 Life interests are actuarially valued: *Re Morton, Morton v Warham* [1956] Ch 644, [1956] 3 All ER 259.
3 *Re Hillas-Drake, National Provincial Bank Ltd v Liddell* [1944] Ch 235, [1944] 1 All ER 375; *Re Slee, Midland Bank Executor and Trustee Co Ltd v Slee* [1962] 1 All ER 542, [1962] 1 WLR 496, not following *Re Gunther's Will Trusts, Alexander v Gunther* [1939] Ch 985, [1939] 3 All ER 291; *Re Oram, Oram v Oram* [1940] Ch 1001, [1940] 4 All ER 161. The question is, however, not resolved: see the text and notes 5–7; and PARA 405.
4 *Re Slee, Midland Bank Executor and Trustee Co Ltd v Slee* [1962] 1 All ER 542 at 549, [1962] 1 WLR 496 at 506 per Cross J.
5 *Re Slee, Midland Bank Executor and Trustee Co Ltd v Slee* [1962] 1 All ER 542 at 549, [1962] 1 WLR 496 at 506–507 per Cross J (where the court considered that it was free to adopt whichever of the two methods seemed the more appropriate, but Cross J held that prima facie the second method ought to be adopted). In *Re Hillas-Drake, National Provincial Bank Ltd v Liddell* [1944] Ch 235, [1944] 1 All ER 375, Simonds J held that the second method should be adopted where there is no express direction in the will to the contrary. See PARA 405.
6 *Re Mansel, Smith v Mansel* [1930] 1 Ch 352.
7 See PARA 1080.
8 *Re Wills, Dulverton v Macleod* [1939] Ch 705, [1939] 2 All ER 775; *Re Hillas-Drake, National Provincial Bank Ltd v Liddell* [1944] Ch 235, [1944] 1 All ER 375; *Re Slee, Midland Bank Executor and Trustee Co Ltd v Slee* [1962] 1 All ER 542 at 549, [1962] 1 WLR 496 at 506 per Cross J. On a division of funds the values at the date of distribution should be adjusted by adding the amounts paid for inheritance tax because the division should be considered as made before payment of that tax: see *Re Slee, Midland Bank Executor and Trustee Co Ltd v Slee* [1962] 1 All ER 542, [1962] 1 WLR 496 (where the advance itself was not liable to estate duty and the residuary estate bore its own duty), applying *Re Tollemache, Forbes v Public Trustee* [1930] WN 138. But see *Re Turner's Will Trusts, Westminster Bank Ltd v Turner* [1968] 1 All ER 321, [1968] 1 WLR 227. As to the burden of inheritance tax on death see PARA 1128; and INHERITANCE TAXATION vol 59A (2014) PARA 58 et seq.

(ii) Residuary Estate Settled

1118. Ascertaining the income of the residue: the rule in *Allhusen v Whittell*. The tenant for life of the residuary estate is normally entitled to the income of that estate from the date of death[1]. He is not, however, entitled to the whole of the income actually derived from the estate and he is not entitled to the income arising from what is wanted for payment of debts or legacies, unless the will expressly provides to the contrary[2], because that never becomes residue in any way whatever. Accordingly, although personal representatives are at liberty, as between themselves and the persons interested in the residue, to have recourse to any funds they please in order to pay debts and legacies, yet in adjusting accounts between the tenant for life and the remainderman the rule is that they must be treated as having paid the debts and legacies (other than contingent legacies[3]) not out of capital only, nor out of income only, but with such portion of the capital as, together with the income of that portion[4], is sufficient for the purpose[5]. The apportionment under the rule is to be made by ascertaining what portion of capital, together with interest on it from the death to the date of payment of each debt or legacy, was necessary to discharge the debt or legacy[6]. The rule does not apply in relation to a new trust[7] (subject to any contrary intention that appears in any trust instrument of the trust and in any power under which the trust is created or arises)[8].

1 See eg *Angerstein v Martin* (1823) Turn & R 232; *Hewitt v Morris* (1824) Turn & R 241; *La Terriere v Bulmer* (1827) 2 Sim 18. As to apportionment on the death of a tenant for life see *Re Henderson, Public Trustee v Reddie* [1940] Ch 368, [1940] 1 All ER 623; and SETTLEMENTS vol 91 (2012) PARAS 858–861.

2 See *Re Ullswater, Barclays Bank Ltd v Lowther* [1952] Ch 105, [1951] 2 All ER 989.

3 The rule stated in the text applies to contingent debts (see *Re Perkins, Brown v Perkins* [1907] 2 Ch 596; *Re Poyser, Landon v Poyser* [1910] 2 Ch 444; *Re Berkeley, Inglis v Berkeley (Countess)* [1968] Ch 744, [1968] 3 All ER 364); but does not apply to contingent legacies (see *Allhusen v Whittell* (1867) LR 4 Eq 295 at 303; *Re Fenwick's Will Trusts, Fenwick v Stewart* [1936] Ch 720, [1936] 2 All ER 1096).

4 As to the taxation consequences of the rule and limited interest in residue see the Income Tax (Trading and Other Income) Act 2005 s 650(2), Corporation Tax Act 2009 s 935(2); and INCOME TAXATION vol 59 (2014) PARA 2079.

5 *Allhusen v Whittell* (1867) LR 4 Eq 295. The rule in *Allhusen v Whittell* As to the application of the rule to sums paid by executors in respect of rents and outgoings under short leases and sums paid by them to assignees of the leases in consideration of their relieving the estate from liability under such leases see *Re Shee, Taylor v Stoger* [1934] Ch 345. In applying the rule the income of the estate is the net income after deduction of tax: *Re Oldham, Oldham v Myles* (1927) 71 Sol Jo 491. The rule applies not only to payments made during the first year, but to payments made during subsequent years: *Re Wills, Wills v Hamilton* [1915] 1 Ch 769. The average rate of interest earned in each year should be adopted for the purpose of calculation: *Re Wills, Wills v Hamilton*; *Re Shee, Taylor v Stoger*.

6 The rule applies to debts, legacies, administration and funeral expenses and death duties payable out of residue: *Re McEuen, McEuen v Phelps* [1913] 2 Ch 704, CA; *Re Wills, Wills v Hamilton* [1915] 1 Ch 769. It is established by these cases, however, that the rule in *Allhusen v Whittell* (1867) LR 4 Eq 295 is not universal, but that the court, in adjusting accounts, will deal equitably between the tenant for life and the remainderman.

7 'New trust' means a trust created or arising on or after 1 October 2013 (and includes a trust created or arising on or after 1 October 2013 under a power conferred before that date): Trusts (Capital and Income) Act 2013 s 1(5).

8 See the Trusts (Capital and Income) Act 2013 s 1(2)(d), (4); and TRUSTS AND POWERS vol 98 (2013) PARAS 172.

1119. Interest on legacies. Where a testator's residuary estate bequeathed in trust for a beneficiary for life and remaindermen yields an income of an average below the rate of interest payable on pecuniary legacies bequeathed by the will[1], the difference between the legacy rate and the interest actually produced by the amounts of the estate representing those legacies must be deducted from the capital of the estate as from the testator's death instead of being paid as against the tenant for life out of the income of the rest of the estate[2].

1 See CPR PD 40A—*Accounts, Inquiries etc* para 15; and PARA 1080.

2 *Massy v Gahan* (1889) 23 LR Ir 518. See also *Allhusen v Whittell* (1867) LR 4 Eq 295. See also PARA 1080.

1120. Real estate charged with debts. Where real estate is charged with debts and recourse is had to the real estate, then, as from the testator's death, the tenant for life must keep down the interest upon all the debts bearing interest, for payment of which recourse is had to the real estate[1].

1 *Marshall v Crowther* (1874) 2 ChD 199 (that is to say that the interest on the debts is payable from the income not the capital).

1121. Liability to pay annuity created before death. Where the testator was liable as a debtor to pay an annuity created before his death either of two courses may, it seems, in general be adopted. The successive instalments of the annuity may be borne by income and capital in proportion to the actuarial values of the life estate and reversion at the testator's death[1], or the sum required for the payment of each instalment may be apportioned by calculating what sum set aside at the testator's death and accumulated at simple interest would have met the particular payment, the sum so ascertained to be attributed to capital, and the accumulated interest to income[2].

Special circumstances may suggest or require other methods, for example where the annuity had been given in consideration of a loan to avoid the laws against usury it was treated as an ordinary mortgage, the tenant for life being only liable to keep down the interest[3]; and where the testator's estate was liable for a periodic payment of uncertain amount which was compromised after his death for payment of a lump sum, this was treated as an ordinary debt of the estate[4]; but in such cases it would seem that there ought to be an apportionment between capital and income[5]. The rate of interest to be employed in the calculation depends on the rate for the time being produced by the estate[6].

The rule does not apply to contingent legacies as opposed to contingent debts[7].

If neither the testator nor his estate were liable in respect of the annuity, but it is merely a charge on the property, it must be borne entirely by the tenant for life[8].

1 *Yates v Yates* (1860) 28 Beav 637; *Re Dawson, Arathoon v Dawson* [1906] 2 Ch 211.

2 *Re Earl of Berkeley, Inglis v Countess of Berkeley* [1968] Ch 744 at 754, [1968] 3 All ER 364 at 369, CA, per Harman LJ; *Re Perkins, Brown v Perkins* [1907] 2 Ch 596, where the gift of the life estate was contingent and, in the calculation, the date taken for setting aside the sum was not the testator's death but the day on which the gift of the life estate vested. The above principle was adopted in *Re Thompson, Thompson v Watkins* [1908] WN 195; *Re Poyser, Landon v Poyser* [1910] 2 Ch 444. See also *Re Darby, Russell v MacGregor* [1939] Ch 905 at 914–915, [1939] 3 All ER 6 at 12, CA, per Sir Wilfrid Greene MR. As to the rate of interest see the text and note 6. It is thought that in view of the above cases the earlier decisions in *Re Muffett, Jones v Mason* (1888) 39 ChD 534 (explained and followed in *Re Bacon, Grissel v Leathes* (1893) 62 LJ Ch 445. See also Seton's Judgments and Orders (7th Edn) 1567); *Re Harrison, Townson v Harrison* (1889) 43 ChD 55; and (except so far as it would be regarded as an exercise of the court's discretion in special circumstances) *Re Henry, Gordon v Gordon* [1907] 1 Ch 30 (where the tenant for life was recouped out of capital, or held entitled to a charge upon capital, for all payments of the annuity) would not now be followed.

3 *Bulwer v Astley* (1844) 1 Ph 422.

4 *Re Henry, Gordon v Gordon* [1907] 1 Ch 30.

5 Cf *Re Shee, Taylor v Stoger* [1934] Ch 345 (sums paid by executors in respect of liabilities under leases held to be apportionable on the principle recognised in *Allhusen v Whittell* (1874) LR 4 Eq 295 (see PARA 1118)).

6 See the cases cited on this point in PARA 1118 note 5. Where the estate was invested in consols different rates have been adopted: see *Re Perkins, Brown v Perkins* [1907] 2 Ch 596 (3%); *Re Poyser, Landon v Poyser* [1910] 2 Ch 444 (3.5%). See also PARA 1085.

7 *Re Fenwick's Will Trusts, Fenwick v Stewart* [1936] Ch 720, [1936] 2 All ER 1096.

8 *Re Popham, Butler v Popham* (1914) 111 LT 524; *Re Darby, Russell v MacGregor* [1939] Ch 905, [1939] 3 All ER 6, CA, overruling on this point *Re Thompson, Thompson v Watkins* [1908] WN 195.

1122. The rule in *Howe v Earl of Dartmouth*. Where the residuary personal estate[1] is settled, in the absence of any evidence of a contrary intention[2], it is to be assumed that the testator intended that his legatees should enjoy the same thing in succession. In order, accordingly, to give effect to his intention, the rule is that such parts of the estate as are of a wasting or reversionary character, or are represented by securities of a hazardous nature, ought, as between the tenant for life and the remainderman, to be converted and invested in permanent investments of a recognised character[3]. The same principle applies where the testator bequeaths life annuities out of wasting property; the property should be sold and a permanent fund created for payment of the annuities[4]. The rule[5] is commonly excluded but there is a wealth of authority on when it applies. The rules concerning its application are complex and technical[6]. The rule does not apply in relation to a new trust[7] (subject to any contrary intention that appears in any trust instrument of the trust and in any power under which the trust is created or arises)[8]. However, trustees have power to sell any property which before the removal of the rule they would have been under a duty to sell[9].

1 The rule does not, and never did, apply to real estate: see PARA 1123.
2 See eg *Re Scholfield's Wills Trusts, Scholfield v Scholfield* [1949] Ch 341, [1949] 1 All ER 490, where the testator intended that benefits payable out of the income from his leaseholds should expire with the leaseholds. War damage compensation was ordered to be invested in annuities to produce a similar result.
3 *Howe v Earl of Dartmouth, Howe v Countess of Aylesbury* (1802) 7 Ves 137; *Pickering v Pickering* (1839) 4 My & Cr 289; *Cafe v Bent* (1845) 5 Hare 24 at 35; *Pickup v Atkinson* (1846) 4 Hare 624 at 628; *Macdonald v Irvine* (1878) 8 ChD 101 at 112, CA; *Re Van Straubenzee, Boustead v Cooper* [1901] 2 Ch 779 at 782; *Re Bates, Hodgson v Bates* [1907] 1 Ch 22 at 26. See also TRUSTS AND POWERS vol 98 (2013) PARAS 172–173.
4 *Fryer v Buttar* (1837) 8 Sim 442; *Wightwick v Lord* (1857) 6 HL Cas 217.
5 Strictly the rule in *Howe v Earl of Dartmouth* only applies where there is no trust for conversion. The analogous rule where there is such a trust is sometimes referred to as the rule in *Dimes v Scott* (1828) 4 Russ 195, or the rule in *Gibson v Bott* (1802) 7 Ves 89, but it is a common practice to refer to both rules under the single name. See also *Re Berry, Lloyds Bank Ltd v Berry* [1962] Ch 97 at 106, [1961] 1 All ER 529 at 535 per Pennycuick J. There is a third rule, also referred to under the same name, in *Re Chesterfield's Trusts* (1883) 24 ChD 643 which applies to reversions or other non-income yielding property apportioned retrospectively partially to income when they fall in or are sold. A clause in a will excluding the rule in *Howe v Earl of Dartmouth* also excludes the rule in *Re Chesterfield's Trusts*: *Re Hey's Settlement Trusts, Hey v Nickell-Lean* [1945] 1 All ER 618 at 627 per Cohen J.
6 See PARA 1123 et seq.
7 'New trust' means a trust created or arising on or after 1 October 2013 (and includes a trust created or arising on or after 1 October 2013 under a power conferred before that date): Trusts (Capital and Income) Act 2013 s 1(5).
8 See the Trusts (Capital and Income) Act 2013 s 1(2)(a), (4); and TRUSTS AND POWERS vol 98 (2013) PARA 172.
9 See the Trusts (Capital and Income) Act 2013 s 1(3), (4).

1123. Exceptions to rule in *Howe v Earl of Dartmouth*. The rule in *Howe v Earl of Dartmouth*[1] does not, and never did, apply to real estate[2] nor does it apply to leaseholds with an unexpired term of more than 60 years treated as settled land[3] or after 1925 to leaseholds held upon trust for sale[4], or, it seems, to property as to which a person dies wholly or partially intestate after 1925[5], but it continues to apply to pure personalty[6]. The rule does not apply to a contingent legacy[7].

The rule is not to be applied in cases in which there is an indication of an intention that the property should be enjoyed in specie; but, although small indications of such an intention may be sufficient, the burden of showing the intention is upon those who desire to exclude the operation of the rule[8]. The rule does not apply in the case of immovables situated in a foreign country[9].

A discretionary power to postpone sale, now implied into all trusts for sale of land[10], may also be sufficient to exclude the application of the rule[11].

The rule does not apply in relation to a new trust[12] (subject to any contrary intention that appears in any trust instrument of the trust and in any power under which the trust is created or arises)[13].

1 See PARA 1122.
2 *Re Woodhouse* [1941] Ch 332 at 335, [1941] 2 All ER 265 at 267 per Simonds J. See also *Re Searle, Searle v Baker* [1900] 2 Ch 829; *Re Earl Darnley, Clifton v Darnley* [1907] 1 Ch 159; *Hope v d'Hedouville* [1893] 2 Ch 361; *Casamajor v Strode* (1809) 19 Ves 390n; *Fitzgerald v Jervoise* (1820) 5 Madd 25; *Yates v Yates* (1860) 28 Beav 637; *Re Oliver, Wilson v Oliver* [1908] 2 Ch 74 (where there were mixed funds in which cases the tenant for life was held entitled to the income of real estate pending conversion under a trust for sale; conversely, where money is directed to be invested in real estate, the beneficiary for life is entitled to the income until the investment is made); *Sitwell v Bernard* (1801) 6 Ves 520; *Kilvington v Gray* (1825) 2 Sim & St 396; *Tucker v Boswell* (1843) 5 Beav 607; *Macpherson v Macpherson* (1852) 19 LTOS 221, HL.

3 *Re Gough, Phillips v Simpson* [1957] Ch 323, [1957] 2 All ER 193.
4 The rule was excluded by statute in respect of a trust for sale of land coming into operation before or after 1925 (see the Law of Property Act 1925 s 28(2) (repealed); and REAL PROPERTY AND REGISTRATION vol 87 (2012) PARA 106) whether the trust was expressly created by the will or by statute: see *Re Brooker, Brooker v Brooker* (1926) 70 Sol Jo 526; *Re Berton, Vandyk v Berton* [1939] Ch 200, [1938] 4 All ER 286.
5 *Re Thornber, Crabtree v Thornber* [1937] Ch 29, [1936] 2 All ER 1594, CA. See also PARA 477.
6 *Re Trollope's Will Trusts, Public Trustee v Trollope* [1927] 1 Ch 596.
7 *Re Fenwick's Will Trusts, Fenwick v Stewart* [1936] Ch 720, [1936] 2 All ER 1096.
8 *Morgan v Morgan* (1851) 14 Beav 72 at 82; *Macdonald v Irvine* (1878) 8 ChD 101 at 124, CA; *Re Eaton, Danies v Eaton* (1894) 70 LT 761; *Stanier v Hodgkinson* (1903) 73 LJ Ch 179; *Re Inman, Inman v Inman* [1915] 1 Ch 187; *Re Slater, Slater v Jonas* (1915) 85 LJ Ch 432; *Re Aste, Mossop v Macdonald* (1918) 87 LJ Ch 660; *Re Grant, Grant v Grant* (1920) 150 LT Jo 296; *Re Corelli* (1925) 69 Sol Jo 525; *Re Barratt, National Provincial Bank v Barratt* [1925] Ch 550. In the following cases the language was not considered sufficiently strong to exclude the rule: *Re Hubbuck, Hart v Stone* [1896] 1 Ch 754, CA; *Re Game, Game v Young* [1897] 1 Ch 881; *Re Wareham, Wareham v Brewin* [1912] 2 Ch 312, CA; *Re Evans' Will Trusts, Pickering v Evans* [1921] 2 Ch 309. See also TRUSTS AND POWERS vol 98 (2013) PARA 173.
9 *Re Moses, Moses v Valentine* [1908] 2 Ch 235.
10 Since 1 January 1997 in the case of every trust for sale of land created by a disposition whether before or after that date there is implied a power for the trustees to postpone sale of the land: see the Trusts of Land and Appointment of Trustees Act 1996 s 4(1), (2); and REAL PROPERTY AND REGISTRATION vol 87 (2012) PARA 105.
11 *Simpson v Lester* (1858) 4 Jur NS 1269; *Re Pitcairn, Brandreth v Colvin* [1896] 2 Ch 199; *Re Bentham, Pearce v Bentham* (1906) 94 LT 307. Cf *Yates v Yates* (1860) 28 Beav 637; *Re Llewellyn's Trusts* (1861) 29 Beav 171; *Brown v Gellatly* (1867) 2 Ch App 751. See also PARA 1125.
12 'New trust' means a trust created or arising on or after 1 October 2013 (and includes a trust created or arising on or after 1 October 2013 under a power conferred before that date): Trusts (Capital and Income) Act 2013 s 1(5).
13 See the Trusts (Capital and Income) Act 2013 s 1(2)(a), (b), (3), (4); and TRUSTS AND POWERS vol 98 (2013) PARA 172.

1124. Effect of trust for conversion. On 1 January 1997 the doctrine of conversion was abolished in relation to trusts for sale of land, and in relation to trusts to invest personalty in the purchase of land except in relation to trusts for sale created by will where the testator died before that date[1]. An interest under a trust for sale of land will now pass under a gift of residuary realty and the rule in *Howe v Earl of Dartmouth*[2], which never applied to realty, will not therefore apply to such property[3]. Subject to that, the rule applies where there is a trust for conversion[4], even though there is a discretionary power to postpone conversion, or to retain existing securities[5], unless the power amounts to a power to postpone or retain permanently for the benefit of the tenant for life[6], or unless there is a gift to the tenant for life of the actual income derived from the estate pending the conversion[7]. In the last mentioned case, however, the discretion does not go so far as to enable the executor to alter the parties' rights, except in so far as he may do so by postponing the conversion of one portion of the estate rather than another as a matter of management[8].

1 See the Trusts of Land and Appointment of Trustees Act 1996 s 3(1), (2); and REAL PROPERTY AND REGISTRATION vol 87 (2012) PARA 7; SETTLEMENTS vol 91 (2012) PARA 798. Subject to the exception referred to in the text, these provisions take effect whether the trust is created or arises before or after 1 January 1997: see s 3(3).
2 See PARA 1122.
3 See the Trusts of Land and Appointment of Trustees Act 1996 s 3(1); and REAL PROPERTY AND REGISTRATION vol 87 (2012) PARA 7; SETTLEMENTS vol 91 (2012) PARA 798.
4 See *Dimes v Scott* (1828) 4 Russ 195; *Gibson v Bott* (1802) 7 Ves 89 at 98; *Caldecott v Caldecott* (1842) 1 Y & C Ch Cas 312; *Brown v Gellatly* (1867) 2 Ch App 751; *Furley v Hyder* (1873) 42 LJ Ch 626; *Wentworth v Wentworth* [1900] AC 163, PC.

5 *Re Carter* (1892) 41 WR 140; *Re Woods, Gabellini v Woods* [1904] 2 Ch 4; *Re Chaytor, Chaytor v Horn* [1905] 1 Ch 233; *Re Parry, Brown v Parry* [1947] Ch 23, [1946] 2 All ER 412; *Re Berry, Lloyds Bank Ltd v Berry* [1962] Ch 97, [1961] 1 All ER 529.

6 *Re Inman, Inman v Inman* [1915] 1 Ch 187; *Re Rogers, Public Trustee v Rogers* [1915] 2 Ch 437. In the case of all trusts for sale of land created by a devise or bequest or an appointment of property contained in a will there is implied, despite any provision to the contrary made in the disposition, a power for the trustees to postpone sale of the land: see the Trusts of Land and Appointment of Trustees Act 1996 s 4(1), (2); the Law of Property Act 1925 s 205(1)(ii); and REAL PROPERTY AND REGISTRATION vol 87 (2012) PARA 105.

7 *Wrey v Smith* (1844) 14 Sim 202; *Mackie v Mackie* (1845) 5 Hare 70; *Re Chancellor, Chancellor v Brown* (1884) 26 ChD 42 at 46, CA; *Re Thomas, Wood v Thomas* [1891] 3 Ch 482; *Re Elford, Elford v Elford* [1910] 1 Ch 814; *Re Sherry, Sherry v Sherry* [1913] 2 Ch 508; *Re Godfree, Godfree v Godfree* [1914] 2 Ch 110; *Re Slater, Slater v Jonas* (1915) 85 LJ Ch 432.

8 *Rowlls v Bebb, Re Rowlls, Walters v Treasury Solicitor* [1900] 2 Ch 107 at 117, CA, per Lindley MR; and see *Re Hey's Settlement Trusts, Hey v Nickell-Lean* [1945] Ch 294, [1945] 1 All ER 618.

1125. Where there is no trust for conversion. The mere absence of a direction to convert is not sufficient to exclude the operation of the rule in *Howe v Earl of Dartmouth*[1]; but, where there is no trust for conversion, an express power to retain existing investments is sufficient to exclude it[2], and for this purpose there is no distinction between unauthorised securities of a wasting and those of a permanent nature[3].

1 *Morgan v Morgan* (1851) 14 Beav 72. See also *Taylor v Clark* (1841) 1 Hare 161; *Meyer v Simonsen* (1852) 5 De G & Sm 723 at 727; *Porter v Baddeley* (1877) 5 ChD 542; *Re Eaton, Daines v Eaton* [1894] WN 95. As to the rule in *Howe v Earl of Dartmouth* see PARA 1122.

2 *Gray v Siggers* (1880) 15 ChD 74; *Re Sheldon, Nixon v Sheldon* (1888) 39 ChD 50; *Re Bates, Hodgson v Bates* [1907] 1 Ch 22; *Re Nicholson, Eade v Nicholson* [1909] 2 Ch 111, disapproving *Porter v Baddeley* (1877) 5 ChD 542.

3 *Re Nicholson, Eade v Nicholson* [1909] 2 Ch 111, setting at rest the doubt raised by North J in *Re Sheldon, Nixon v Sheldon* (1888) 39 ChD 50, and by Kekewich J in *Re Bates, Hodgson v Bates* [1907] 1 Ch 22 as to whether such a distinction ought to be made.

1126. Adjustment where income-producing property is retained. Where income-producing property which ought to have been converted by the personal representative is in fact retained, the rights of the tenant for life and remainderman are adjusted upon the following basis. Where there is a direction to convert but no express power to postpone[1], or the duty to convert is implied under the rule in *Howe v Earl of Dartmouth*[2], the property is valued as at the expiration of one year after the testator's death; where there is a direction to convert coupled with an express power to postpone conversion, the date of valuation is the death of the testator[3]. In either case the tenant for life is allowed interest upon the ascertained value[4], and the balance of the income actually produced is capitalised. The tenant for life is entitled to the income derived from the investments of the capitalised income[5]. If the income is insufficient to pay the interest, the tenant for life can be recouped from capital when the investments are sold[6]. As to the rate of interest, the traditional rate allowed is 4 per cent[7], but this is not a hard and fast rule and the rate can be changed by the court if conditions as to rates of interest generally justify an alteration[8]. There is no need for adjustment in relation to a new trust[9] (subject to any contrary intention that appears in any trust instrument of the trust and in any power under which the trust is created or arises)[10].

1 *Re Fawcett* [1940] Ch 402. See also *Dimes v Scott* (1828) 4 Russ 195; *Mehrtens v Andrews* (1839) 3 Beav 72; *Taylor v Clark* (1841) 1 Hare 161; *Wilkinson v Duncan* (1857) 23 Beav 469. Cf *Johnson v Routh* (1857) 27 LJ Ch 305; *Hume v Richardson* (1862) 4 De GF & J 29; *Jackson v Jackson* (1869) 17 WR 547; *Re Hazeldine, Public Trustee v Hazeldine* [1918] 1 Ch 433.

2 *Morgan v Morgan* (1851) 14 Beav 72; *Re Wareham, Wareham v Brewin* [1912] 2 Ch 312, CA; *Re Evans' Will Trusts, Pickering v Evans* [1921] 2 Ch 309; *Yates v Yates* (1860) 28 Beav 637 (power of sale). As to the rule see PARA 1122.

3 *Re Parry, Brown v Parry* [1947] Ch 23, [1946] 2 All ER 412. See also *Allhusen v Whittell* (1867) LR 4 Eq 295; *Furley v Hyder* (1873) 42 LJ Ch 626; *Re Woods, Gabellini v Woods* [1904] 2 Ch 4; *Re Chaytor, Chaytor v Horn* [1905] 1 Ch 233; *Re Owen, Slater v Owen* [1912] 1 Ch 519; *Re Beech, Saint v Beech* [1920] 1 Ch 40; *Re Baker, Baker v Public Trustee* [1924] 2 Ch 271. Cf *Re Lynch Blosse, Richards v Lynch Blosse* [1899] WN 27; *Re Llewellyn's Trusts* (1861) 29 Beav 171 (power to sell and retain).

4 Interest is allowed on the investments valued en bloc, not on the value of each investment separately: *Re Owen, Slater v Owen* [1912] 1 Ch 519; *Re Fawcett* [1940] Ch 402. As to interest rates see PARA 1080; and note 2.

5 *Brown v Gellatly* (1867) 2 Ch App 751; *Re Beech, Saint v Beech* [1920] 1 Ch 40; *Re Fawcett* [1940] Ch 402. As to where conversion is expressly postponed see *Green v Britten* (1863) 1 De GJ & Sm 649; *Re Lambert, Lambert v Lambert* (1892) 36 Sol Jo 327. As to the position where a tenant for life has received the income of an unauthorised investment made by the trustees of a settlement see *Re Hoyles, Row v Jagg (No 2)* [1912] 1 Ch 67; and TRUSTS AND POWERS vol 98 (2013) PARA 687. As to the rights of beneficiaries for life and in remainder in the case of a compulsory sale of property see COMPULSORYACQUISITIONOFLAND vol 18 (2009) PARAS 682–683.

6 *Re Fawcett* [1940] Ch 402.

7 *Re Fawcett* [1940] Ch 402; *Re Parry, Brown v Parry* [1947] Ch 23, [1946] 2 All ER 412. See also *Brown v Gellatly* (1867) 2 Ch App 751; *Re Beech, Saint v Beech* [1920] 1 Ch 40; *Meyer v Simonsen* (1852) 5 De G & Sm 723 at 727. Cf *Re Woods, Gabellini v Woods* [1904] 2 Ch 4 at 13; *Re Chaytor, Chaytor v Horn* [1905] 1 Ch 233 at 241 (where 3% was fixed); and PARA 1127 note 1. It is submitted that the prescribed legacy rate would now be an appropriate starting point: see CPR PD 40A—*Accounts, Inquiries etc* para 15; and PARA 1080.

8 *Re Parry, Brown v Parry* [1947] Ch 23, [1946] 2 All ER 412. In general interest rates of 8 and 9% have been applied at times of high general rates. Presumably lower rates would be applied in times of low interest.

9 As to the meaning of 'new trust' see PARA 1122 note 7.

10 See the Trusts (Capital and Income) Act 2013 s 1(2)(b), (4); and TRUSTS AND POWERS vol 98 (2013) PARA 172.

1127. Adjustment where reversionary property is retained. Where the property which ought to have been sold consists of personal estate which eventually falls in some years after the testator's death, the apportionment is made by ascertaining what sum put out at interest traditionally at 4 per cent[1] on the day of the testator's death, and accumulated at compound interest with a deduction for income tax, would, with the accumulations of interest, have produced at the day of receipt the amount actually received; the sum so ascertained is to be treated as capital, and the residue as income[2]. This principle applies not only to reversions[3] but generally to property which is outstanding, for example, policies on the life of a third person[4], capital money payable by instalments[5], compensation payable under the town and country planning legislation[6], royalties[7], monthly sums payable under a policy[8], sums payable under a service agreement for a period after the death[9], or any portions of the estate upon which the income is for any reason not paid in due course[10]. The principle does not apply to property in which the testator's interest was an immediate absolute interest subject only to a charge on income[11]. There is no need for adjustment in relation to a new trust[12] (subject to any contrary intention that appears in any trust instrument of the trust and in any power under which the trust is created or arises)[13].

1 The rate of interest allowed has usually been 4% (*Turner v Newport* (1846) 2 Ph 14 at 18; *Re Earl of Chesterfield's Trusts* (1883) 24 ChD 643 at 653–654), but in some cases only 3% has been allowed (*Re Hengler, Frowde v Hengler* [1893] 1 Ch 586; *Rowlls v Bebb, Re Rowlls, Walters v Treasury Solicitor* [1900] 2 Ch 107, CA; *Re Duke of Cleveland's Estate, Hay v Wolmer* [1895] 2 Ch 542; and see *Re Goodenough, Marland v Williams* [1895] 2 Ch 537; *Re Davy, Hollingsworth v Davy* [1908] 1 Ch 61 at 64–65, CA, per Cozens-Hardy MR); but the rate generally allowed is 4% (*Re Evans' Will Trusts, Pickering v Evans* [1921] 2 Ch 309; *Re Baker, Baker v Public Trustee* [1924] 2 Ch 271). See also PARA 1126. The court has a discretion to direct payment at a higher rate and could well do so where there would otherwise be a discrepancy between this and other comparable rates.

2 *Re Earl of Chesterfield's Trusts* (1883) 24 ChD 643; *Re Hollebone, Hollebone v Hollebone* [1919] 2 Ch 93. The rule laid down in these cases has no application to real estate: *Re Woodhouse* [1941] Ch 332, [1941] 2 All ER 265. The rule in *Re Earl of Chesterfield's Trusts* was cited and applied by Wilberforce J in *Re Chance's Will Trusts, Westminster Bank v Chance* [1962] Ch 593 at 608, [1962] 1 All ER 942 at 949. The rule in *Re Earl of Chesterfield's Trusts* does not apply in relation to a new trust (see TRUSTS AND POWERS vol 98 (2013) PARA 172) subject to any contrary intention appearing in any trust instrument of the trust and in any power under which the trust is created or arises: Trusts (Capital and Income) Act 2013 s 1(2)(c), (4). 'New trust' means a trust created or arising on or after 1 October 2013 (and includes a trust created or arising on or after 1 October 2013 under a power conferred before that date): s 1(5).

3 See eg *Wilkinson v Duncan* (1857) 23 Beav 469; *Wright v Lambert* (1877) 6 ChD 649; *Rowles v Bebb, Re Rowlls, Walters v Treasury Solicitor* [1900] 2 Ch 107, CA. See also *Re Hobson, Walker v Appach* (1885) 55 LJ Ch 422.

4 *Re Morley, Morley v Haig* [1895] 2 Ch 738; *Re Earl of Chesterfield's Trusts* (1883) 24 ChD 643.

5 *Re Hollebone, Hollebone v Hollebone* [1919] 2 Ch 93; *Re Guinness's Settlement, Guinness v SG Warburg (Executor and Trustee) Ltd* [1966] 2 All ER 497, [1966] 1 WLR 1355, following *Re Hey's Settlement Trusts* [1945] Ch 294.

6 *Re Chance's Will Trusts, Westminster Bank v Chance* [1962] Ch 593, [1962] 1 All ER 942. As to town and country planning legislation see generally PLANNING.

7 *Re Evans' Will Trusts, Pickering v Evans* [1921] 2 Ch 309.

8 *Re Fisher, Harris and Fisher v Fisher* [1943] Ch 377, [1943] 2 All ER 615.

9 *Re Payne, Westminster Bank Ltd v Payne* [1943] 2 All ER 675.

10 See *Turner v Newport* (1846) 2 Ph 14 (bond debt); *Beavan v Beavan* (1869) 24 ChD 649n (mortgage debt with arrears of interest; arrears of annuity and interest); *Re Earl of Chesterfield's Trusts* (1883) 24 ChD 643 (mortgage debt with arrears of interest). See also *Re Duke of Cleveland's Estate, Hay v Wolmer* [1895] 2 Ch 542 (money paid away from testator's estate but afterwards recovered); *Delves v Newington* (1885) 52 LT 512.

11 *Re Holliday, Houghton v Adlard* [1947] Ch 402, [1947] 1 All ER 695.

12 As to the meaning of 'new trust' see PARA 1122 note 7.

13 See the Trusts (Capital and Income) Act 2013 s 1(2)(c), (4); and TRUSTS AND POWERS vol 98 (2013) PARA 172.

(iii) Incidence of Death Duties

1128. Burden of inheritance tax on death. Subject to any contrary intention shown by a testator in his will[1], inheritance tax[2] including any interest on that tax[3] payable by the deceased's personal representatives[4] is treated as part of the general testamentary and administration expenses of the estate[5] but only so far as it is attributable to the value of property in the United Kingdom which:

(1) vests in the deceased's personal representatives[6]; and

(2) was not immediately before the death comprised in a settlement[7].

Accordingly, inheritance tax payable in respect of property appointed by will under a general power of appointment[8], property comprised in a donatio mortis causa[9], property situated outside the United Kingdom[10] and property subject to a joint tenancy immediately before the death is not generally a testamentary expense[11].

Where any amount of inheritance tax paid by the personal representatives does not fall to be borne as part of the general testamentary and administration expenses of the estate, that amount must, where occasion requires, be repaid to them by the person in whom the property to the value of which the tax and interest is attributable is vested[12].

1 See the Inheritance Tax Act 1984 s 211(2); and INHERITANCE TAXATION vol 59A (2014) PARA 271. As to when a testator shows a contrary intention in his will see PARA 1129.

2 Inheritance tax is payable on the value transferred by a chargeable transfer deemed to have been made on death: see the Inheritance Tax Act 1984 ss 1, 4(1); and INHERITANCE TAXATION vol 59A (2014) PARAS 8–10. Inheritance tax is an amended and renamed version of capital transfer tax, the amendments being effective for deaths and other chargeable events on or after 18 March 1986 and the renaming being effective for deaths and other chargeable events occurring

on or after 25 July 1986: see INHERITANCE TAXATION vol 59A (2014) PARA 3. Capital transfer tax replaced estate duty and was leviable on deaths after 12 March 1975: see INHERITANCE TAXATION vol 59A (2014) PARA 2. Estate duty remains chargeable on deaths occurring before 13 March 1975 and the transitional provisions applicable to deaths occurring between 12 November 1974 and 13 March 1975 are still in force: see the Finance Act 1975 s 49; and INHERITANCE TAXATION vol 59A (2014) PARA 2, 4. Certain other obsolete death duties were also finally abolished by s 50: see INHERITANCE TAXATION vol 59A (2014) PARA 1; and PARAS 1133, 1135.

3 See the Inheritance Tax Act 1984 s 211(4); and INHERITANCE TAXATION vol 59A (2014) PARA 271.

4 As to the meaning of 'personal representative' see the Inheritance Tax Act 1984 s 272; and INHERITANCE TAXATION vol 59A (2014) PARA 34. The personal representative is liable for the inheritance tax on the value transferred by a chargeable transfer made on the death of any person so far as the tax is attributable to the value of property which either: (1) was not immediately before the death comprised in a settlement; or (2) was so comprised and consists of land in the United Kingdom which devolves or vests in him: see s 200(1)(a); and INHERITANCE TAXATION vol 59A (2014) PARA 264. For these purposes a person who takes possession of or intermeddles with, or otherwise acts in relation to, property so as to become liable as executor or trustee, and any person to whom the management of property is entrusted on behalf of a person not of full legal capacity is treated as a person in whom the property is vested: see ss 199(4), 200(4); and INHERITANCE TAXATION vol 59A (2014) PARA 253. As to the meaning of 'United Kingdom' see PARA 4 note 7.

5 The tax and any interest on it will be payable out of the assets of the estate in the order of priority prescribed by the Administration of Estates Act 1925 s 34(3), Sch 1 Pt II: see PARA 992 et seq.

6 See the Inheritance Tax Act 1984 s 211(1)(a); and INHERITANCE TAXATION vol 59A (2014) PARA 271.

7 See the Inheritance Tax Act 1984 s 211(1)(b); and INHERITANCE TAXATION vol 59A (2014) PARA 271.

8 *O'Grady v Wilmot* [1916] 2 AC 231.

9 *Re Hudson, Spencer v Turner* [1911] 1 Ch 206.

10 See the Inheritance Tax Act 1984 s 211(1); and INHERITANCE TAXATION vol 59A (2014) PARA 271.

11 The interest of a joint tenant accrues automatically to the surviving joint tenant(s) on his death and thus does not vest in his personal representatives: see PARAS 29, 33 note 9.

12 See the Inheritance Tax Act 1984 s 211(3); and INHERITANCE TAXATION vol 59A (2014) PARA 271.

1129. Free of duty provisions. Except where prohibited by statute[1], a testator may by his will effectually alter the normal rules for the incidence of inheritance tax[2] and may thus prescribe the manner in which as between the beneficiaries any duties are to be borne[3]. A testator's intention to exonerate parts of his estate from the liability to inheritance tax[4] which they would otherwise bear must be inferred as a matter of construction[5] from the terms of the will.

So far as any provision in any document, whenever executed, refers to estate duty or death duties it is to have effect, as far as may be, as if the reference included a reference to inheritance tax[6]. In the following paragraphs notes of cases referring to estate duty and other duties are included as they may be of assistance in construing testamentary instruments containing gifts free of tax.

1 See the Inheritance Tax Act 1984 s 41 (none of the tax attributable to a non-exempt share of residue is to fall on an exempt share nor is any tax on the value transferred to fall on any exempt specific gift); and PARA 1134.

2 As to the burden of inheritance tax on death see PARA 1128.

3 See the Inheritance Tax Act 1984 s 211(2); and INHERITANCE TAXATION vol 59A (2014) PARA 271. See also PARA 1128.

4 On the construction of the particular will 'duty' may refer only to legacy duty: see eg *Re McNeill, Royal Bank of Scotland v MacPherson* [1958] Ch 259, [1957] 3 All ER 508, CA.

5 *Gude v Mumford* (1837) 2 Y & C Ex 445. As to the normal rules of construction see PARA 185 et seq.

6 See the Inheritance Tax Act 1984 s 273, Sch 6 para 1. See also the Finance Act 1986 s 100; and INHERITANCE TAXATION vol 59A (2014) PARAS 2–3.

1130. Presumptions as to burden of tax. Wills commonly provide that specified dispositions of property are to be free of tax or that tax and duties generally are to be paid out of a specified fund. The cases all refer to 'duty' and not to 'tax' but may nonetheless be of assistance in construing testamentary instruments made free of tax.

Where the will creates a life interest it may also make provision for the payment of the further tax payable on the death of the tenant for life but there is a strong presumption to the contrary[1]. Complications also arise as to whether a testator intended by his will to affect additional taxes imposed by statute after his death relating to the death of a life tenant[2].

There is a presumption that a testator intends to provide only for such taxes as are payable on his death[3].

A reference to tax will normally be construed as a reference to tax payable only on dispositions made by the will[4] and payable under English law and not to duty payable under foreign law[5], unless, as in the case of foreign immovables, only foreign taxes are payable[6]. A clause in the will exonerating from tax dispositions contained in the will, will normally[7] but not necessarily[8] be construed as extending to similar dispositions or variations[9] made by codicil[10] or by the testamentary exercise of a special power of appointment[11].

An intention that a legacy should be tax-free cannot be implied from the fact that if tax were deducted the sum left would not be sufficient for some purpose specified in the will[12]. It has also been held that a direction for payment of duty on gifts made during the testator's lifetime cannot extend to amorphous rights in a joint account[13], nor will a specific devise be exonerated unless the will in effect gives the devisee an additional legacy of the tax in question[14].

Subject to the presumption stated above, each will must be construed by the normal canons, and no general statement of the meaning of particular words in other wills is conclusive[15].

1 *Re Wedgwood, Allen v Public Trustee* [1921] 1 Ch 601, CA; *Re Laidlaw, Wilkinson v Lyde* [1930] 2 Ch 392 at 396; *Re Shepherd, Public Trustee v Henderson* [1949] Ch 116, [1948] 2 All ER 932; *Re Howell, Drury v Fletcher* [1952] Ch 264, [1952] 1 All ER 363. See also *Re Palmer, Palmer v Palmer* [1916] 2 Ch 391 at 401, CA; *Re Paterson's Will Trusts, Lawson v Page* [1963] 1 All ER 114, [1963] 1 WLR 623; *Re Embleton's Will Trusts, Sodeau v Nelson* [1965] 1 All ER 771, [1965] 1 WLR 840.

2 In the following cases the expressions used in wills made before the passing of the Finance Act 1914, which abolished certain relief in respect of settled property (see s 14 (repealed); and INHERITANCE TAXATION vol 59A (2014) PARA 1), were held to cover the estate duty chargeable on a death subsequent to that of the testator: *Re Brown, Turnbull v Royal National Lifeboat Institution* (1916) 60 Sol Jo 353 ('every bequest to be free and clear of duties', the expression being contrasted with the terms of another gift by the will to A for life and then 'subject to any duty' to B); *Re Hatch, Hatch v Hatch* (1916) 115 LT 472 (direction to pay the 'duties payable in respect of all and every the benefits given by this my will'); *Re Stoddart, Bird v Grainger* [1916] 2 Ch 444 ('legacies (whether settled or otherwise) . . . to be paid and enjoyed free of all death duties', with a direction to the trustee 'to pay or provide for . . . the duties thereon'); *Re Tinkler, Loyd v Allen* [1917] 1 Ch 242 ('all duties payable in respect of the said sum . . . shall be paid out of and be a charge upon my residuary estate'); *Re Eve, Hall v Eve* [1917] 1 Ch 562 ('all the foregoing gifts, bequests, and legacies shall be free of duty,' the words 'gifts', etc being construed as applying to the successive beneficial interests); *Dunn's Trustees v Dunn* 1924 SC 613, Ct of Sess ('free of legacy or other duty'). Cf *Re Lomer, Public Trustee v Victoria Hospital for Children* [1929] 1 Ch 731 (legacies payable, after deaths of life tenants, in a certain order of 'priority'; the earlier legacies held to be payable in full so that the estate duty would fall on the later legacies).

In the following cases the expressions used in wills made before the Finance Act 1914 were held not to cover the estate duty chargeable on a death subsequent to that of the testator: *Re Snape, Elam v Phillips* [1915] 2 Ch 179 ('free of all duty'); *Re Palmer, Palmer v Palmer* [1916] 2 Ch 391, CA (legacies to be 'handed over or paid free of all duties or deductions in respect of duties (other than income tax)' and trustees to 'make provision' for duties); *Re Gunn, Harvey v Gunn* [1916] WN 283 (direction to pay the estate duty 'in respect of my estate or any part thereof'); *Re D'Oyly, Vertue v D'Oyly* [1917] 1 Ch 556 ('free of duty', with a direction to pay 'the duties on the . . .

legacies'); *Re Wedgwood, Allen v Public Trustee* [1921] 1 Ch 601, CA ('free of all death duties', with a direction to 'pay and provide for . . . the duties'); *Re Duke of Sutherland, Chaplin v Leveson-Gower* [1922] 2 Ch 782 ('all the legacies and annuities and all other gifts, bequests, and devises' to be 'free from all death duties'); *Re Fenwick, Lloyds Bank Ltd v Fenwick* [1922] 2 Ch 775 (provision for payment of 'all duties of every description . . . to which my estate . . . shall be liable'); *Re Sarson, Public Trustee v Sarson* [1925] Ch 31 (direction that 'all legacies, devises and bequests shall be free of all duties, and that all estate, settlement, succession, legacy and other duties, in respect of any of my property . . . shall be paid out of my residuary estate'); *Re Laidlaw, Wilkinson v Lyde* [1930] 2 Ch 392 (legacies to be 'satisfied paid and enjoyed free of death duties').

In the following cases the expressions used in wills made after the passing of the Finance Act 1914 were held to cover the estate duty chargeable on a death subsequent to that of the testator: *Re Parker, White v Stewart* (1917) 86 LJ Ch 766, CA ('free of . . . settlement estate duty and all other death duties'); *Re Northcliffe, Arnholz v Hudson* [1929] 1 Ch 327 (every benefit given by the will to be 'free of all death duties whatsoever').

In the following cases the expressions used, in wills made after the passing of the Finance Act 1914, were held not to cover the estate duty chargeable on a death subsequent to that of the testator: *Re Beecham, Woolley v Beecham* (1923) 130 LT 558, CA (direction to pay 'all death duties of every kind on every part of my estate . . . so that this direction shall operate to exonerate any part of my estate which otherwise would or might be charged with or liable for any death duties'); *Re Jones, Lambert v Colbourn* [1928] WN 227 at 228 (direction to pay 'all duties . . . incidental to the execution of the trusts'); *Re Trimble, Wilson v Turton* [1931] 1 Ch 369 ('free of all duties'); *Re Hicks, Bach v Cockburn* [1933] 1 Ch 335 ('free from all death duties . . . whether presently or presumptively or prospectively payable', the words having been taken from a pre-1914 precedent).

3 See the cases cited in note 1.

4 See *Re Walley, National Westminster Bank Ltd v Williams* [1972] 1 All ER 222, [1972] 1 WLR 257, where in exceptional circumstances the phrase 'funeral and testamentary expenses and debts and all death duties' was held to extend to gifts which only became fully effective on the death, although not to other gifts inter vivos. See also PARA 1016; and *Re Hudson, Spencer v Turner* [1911] 1 Ch 206, not cited in *Re Walley, National Westminster Bank Ltd v Williams*.

5 *Re Norbury, Norbury v Fanland* [1939] Ch 528, [1939] 2 All ER 625; *Re Cunliffe-Owen, Mountain v Comber* [1951] Ch 964, [1951] 2 All ER 220; *Re Goetze, National Provincial Bank Ltd v Mond* [1953] Ch 96, [1953] 1 All ER 76; *Re Blake, Lynch v Lombard* [1955] IR 89; *Re Sebba, Lloyds Bank Ltd v Hutson* [1959] Ch 166, [1958] 3 All ER 393. As to the right of legatees to share in credits allowed under a double taxation relief agreement see *Re Goetze, National Provincial Bank Ltd v Mond*; and INHERITANCE TAXATION vol 59A (2014) PARAS 227–229.

6 *Re Quirk, Public Trustee v Quirk* [1941] Ch 46.

7 *Byne v Currey* (1834) 2 Cr & M 603; *M'Alpine v Studholme* (1883) 10 R 837, Ct of Sess; *Re Sealy, Tomkins v Tucker* (1901) 85 LT 451.

8 *Re King, Barclays Bank Ltd v King* [1942] Ch 413, [1942] 2 All ER 182, CA; *Early v Benbow* (1846) 2 Coll 342; *Early v Benbow* (1846) 2 Coll 354; *Brown's Trustees v Gow* (1902) 5 F 127, Ct of Sess; but cf *Williams v Hughes* (1857) 24 Beav 474 at 482.

9 *Fisher v Brierley (No 2)* (1861) 30 Beav 267.

10 Similarly a direction in a codicil will apply to dispositions in a later codicil: *Re Dresden, Lindo v London Hospital* (1910) Times, 22 July. Where a legacy or annuity is given by will free of duty, and, by a codicil, another legacy or annuity is substituted for it, the latter gift is to be paid free of duty (*Cooper v Day* (1817) 3 Mer 154; *Earl of Shaftesbury v Duke of Marlborough* (1835) 7 Sim 237; *Re Trinder, Sheppard v Prance* (1911) 56 Sol Jo 74), but not where the gift is to a different legatee by reason of the death of the legatee named in the will (*Chatteris v Young* (1827) 2 Russ 183) or where, although the gift is primarily to the same legatee, its character has been so altered that it is to be regarded as a separate and distinct gift (*Burrows v Cottrell* (1830) 3 Sim 375), as for example where a settled legacy is given in place of an absolute legacy (*Re Trinder, Sheppard v Prance*).

11 *Re Edwards, Lloyds Bank Ltd v Worthington* [1946] 2 All ER 408; *Re Marquis of Bath's Settlement, Thynne v Stewart* (1914) 111 LT 153; *Muir (or Williams) v Muir* [1943] AC 468 at 483, HL. Testamentary expenses do not include estate duty on property appointed by will under a general power of appointment: *O'Grady v Wilmot* [1916] 2 AC 231, HL.

12 *Re De Rosaz, Rymer v De Rosaz* (1886) 2 TLR 871.

13 *Re Figgis, Roberts v MacLaren* [1969] 1 Ch 123 at 150, [1968] 1 All ER 999 at 1014 per Megarry J.

14 *Re Phuler's Will Trusts, Midland Bank Executor and Trustee Co Ltd v Logan* [1964] 2 All ER 948, [1965] 1 WLR 68; *Re Neeld, Carpenter v Inigo-Jones* [1964] 2 All ER 952n, [1965] 1 WLR 73n, CA. See also *Re Williams, Williams and Glyn's Trust Co Ltd v Williams* [1974] 1 All ER 787, [1974] 1 WLR 754.

15 As to the normal rules of construction see PARA 224 et seq.

1131. Words affecting the incidence of duty. In particular cases the following words or phrases have been construed as affecting the incidence of duty: 'without any deduction whatsoever except in respect of income tax'[1]; 'free from all taxes and deductions except property tax and legacy or succession duty'[2]; 'my . . . duties'[3]; 'clear amount or value'[4]; 'all expenses . . . including the estate duty'[5]; 'clear money'[6]; 'free of any incumbrances'[7]; 'clear of all charges and outgoings'[8]; 'clear of property tax and all expenses whatsoever attending the same'[9]; 'free from all expense'[10]; 'to be paid clear'[11]; 'free from any charge or liability in respect thereof'[12]; 'free of all outgoings and payments except the annual and other rent'[13]; 'clear value'[14]; 'net sum'[15]; and 'free of duty'[16].

1 *Re Parker-Jervis, Salt v Locker* [1898] 2 Ch 643. For similar wording see also *Re Maryon-Wilson, Wilson v Maryon-Wilson* [1900] 1 Ch 565, CA; *Smith v Anderson* (1828) 4 Russ 352; *Re Rayer, Rayer v Rayer* [1903] 1 Ch 685; *Floyer v Bankes* (1863) 3 De GJ & Sm 306; *Barksdale v Gilliat* (1818) 1 Swan 562; *Ferguson v Ogilby* (1862) 12 I Ch R 411; *Re Smith-Bosanquet, Smith v Smith-Bosanquet* [1940] Ch 954, [1940] 3 All ER 519. See also *Re Keele Estates (No 2), Aveling v Sneyd* [1952] Ch 603, [1952] 2 All ER 164.

2 *Re Lord Fitzhardinge, Lord Fitzhardinge v Jenkinson* (1899) 80 LT 376, CA; *Re Previté, Sturges v Previté* [1931] 1 Ch 447; *Re Lonsdale Will Trusts, Lowther v Lowther* [1960] Ch 288 at 308, [1959] 3 All ER 679 at 689, CA, per Lord Evershed MR. The same result follows where the words are simply 'free from all deductions': *Re Earl of Egmont's Settled Estates, Lefroy v Egmont* [1912] 1 Ch 251. Where a testator bequeathed a sum to make up, with the income of a settled fund, 'a clear annual income' of £1,500, without 'deduction . . . for the legacy tax or any other matter, cause, or thing' it seems that the annuitant was entitled to be indemnified out of the testator's estate against succession duty under the settlement (*Peareth v Marriott* (1882) 22 ChD 182, CA), but where the deceased covenanted to pay during his life or within 12 months of his death a certain sum, 'free from all deductions whatsoever', and the sum was paid by his executor, the covenantees could not recover from the executor the succession duty payable by them (*Re Higgins, Day v Turnell* (1885) 31 ChD 142, CA; *Re Williams, Williams and Glyn's Trust Co Ltd v Williams* [1974] 1 All ER 787, [1974] 1 WLR 754).

3 *Re Pimm, Sharpe v Hodgson* [1904] 2 Ch 345, distinguished in *Re Briggs, Richardson v Bantoft* [1914] 2 Ch 413. See also PARA 1133 note 1.

4 *Re Coxwell's Trusts, Kinloch-Cooke v Public Trustee* [1910] 1 Ch 63. The word 'net' has been construed as meaning 'clear': *Re Saunders, Saunders v Gore* [1898] 1 Ch 17, CA.

5 These words were held to cover additional estate duty, imposed by an Act passed after the testator's death: *Re Briscoe, Royds v Briscoe* (1910) 55 Sol Jo 93. See also *Re Palmer, Palmer v Palmer* [1916] 2 Ch 391, CA; *Re Walley, National Westminster Bank Ltd v Williams* [1972] 1 All ER 222, [1972] 1 WLR 257. See also PARA 1130 note 4.

6 *Re Palmer, Leventhorpe v Palmer* (1912) 106 LT 319, CA.

7 *Re Nesfield, Barber v Cooper* (1914) 110 LT 970.

8 *Re Earl Cadogan Settlements, Richmond v Lambton* (1911) 56 Sol Jo 11.

9 *Courtoy v Vincent* (1823) Turn & R 433.

10 *Gosden v Dotterill* (1832) 1 My & K 56 at 60.

11 *Ford v Ruxton* (1844) 1 Coll 403.

12 *Warbrick v Varley* (1861) 30 Beav 241.

13 *Re Taber, Arnold v Kayess* (1882) 46 LT 805.

14 *Re Currie, Bjorkman v Lord Kimberley* (1888) 57 LJ Ch 743.

15 *Re Grant, Nevinson v United Kingdom Temperance and General Provident Institution* (1915) 85 LJ Ch 31.

16 *Re Dawson's Will Trusts, National Provincial Bank Ltd v National Council of the YMCA Inc* [1957] 1 All ER 177, [1957] 1 WLR 391. This direction was held to include an inter vivos gift.

1132. Words which do not affect the incidence of duty. In the following cases the expressions used did not affect the incidence of the duty: 'necessary expenses'[1];

'cash value of £6,000'[2]; a direction to raise probate duty which was held not to apply to estate duty[3]; 'testamentary expenses'[4]; and 'all death duties'[5].

An appointment under a power of the sum required to provide for death duties on a specific property carries only the sum appointed, the duty on the appointed sum being payable out of it[6].

A direction contained in a will made after the abolition of legacy duty that the duty on pecuniary legacies was to be paid by the legatees was construed as inserted under a misapprehension as to the continued existence of legacy duty or similar duty, and not intended to render the legatees liable to pay a proportionate part of estate duty[7].

1 *Michie's Executors v Michie* (1905) 7 F 509, Ct of Sess. In the following cases also the expressions used were held not to affect the incidence of estate duty: *Re Baxter, Baxter v Baxter* (1898) 42 Sol Jo 611 (direction to pay 'all estate and other duties' held not to cover a gift inter vivos); *Berry v Gaukroger* [1903] 2 Ch 116, CA ('legacy' payable in part out of real estate); *Michie's Executors v Michie* ('necessary expenses' in a Scottish will); *Kekewich v Kekewich* (1909) 101 LT 887 ('cash value of £6,000'); *Re Boxer, Morris v Woore* [1910] 2 Ch 69 (direction to raise probate duty held not to apply to estate duty); *Re Briggs, Richardson v Bantoft* [1914] 2 Ch 413 (direction to pay 'all death duties' held not to cover a sum covenanted to be paid to trustees and secured on the testator's real estate), distinguishing *Re Pimm, Sharpe v Hodgson* [1904] 2 Ch 345; *Re Brown, Turnbull v Royal National Lifeboat Institution* (1916) 60 Sol Jo 353 (bequests of personalty 'subject to any duty' not required to bear any estate duty); cf *Fraser v Croft* (1898) 25 R 496, Ct of Sess (power for liferentrix of heritable property, who was also sole residuary legatee, to 'raise such sums as may be required to pay all death and succession duties which may fall upon her' did not entitle her to throw upon the heritage the estate duty in respect of the movable property).

2 *Kekewich v Kekewich* (1909) 101 LT 887.

3 *Re Boxer, Morris v Woore* [1910] 2 Ch 69.

4 Death duties which, by virtue of the fact that the property does not pass to the executor as such, are a first charge on the property are not testamentary expenses: *Re Jolley, Neal v Jolley* (1901) 17 TLR 244; *Re Sharman, Wright v Sharman* [1901] 2 Ch 280; *Re Spencer-Cooper, Poë v Spencer-Cooper* [1908] 1 Ch 130; *Re Rosenthal, Schwarz v Bernstein* [1972] 3 All ER 552, [1972] 1 WLR 1273 (trustees who paid out of residue estate duty on a specifically devised house risked personal liability if they could not recover the duty from the devisee). See also PARA 1245; and INHERITANCE TAXATION vol 59A (2014) PARA 265. It has been held that 'testamentary expenses, including death duties' include only such estate duty as is normally a testamentary expense: *Re Massey, Ram v Massey* (1920) 122 LT 676. The incorporation of the Statutory Will Forms 1925, SR & O 1925/780, Form 8, does not alter the incidence of duty on real estate: *Re Previté, Sturges v Previté* [1931] 1 Ch 447.

Certain objects of national etc interest were subject to exemption from estate duty until sale, under the Finance Act 1930 s 4 (repealed), and are now exempt from inheritance tax under certain circumstances: see the Inheritance Tax Act 1984 ss 30, 31; and INHERITANCE TAXATION vol 59A (2014) PARA 148 et seq. As to the application of 'free of duty' provisions to such objects see *Re Lord Leconfield, Wyndham v Lord Leconfield* (1904) 90 LT 399, CA; *Re Lord Swaythling, Samuel v Swaythling* (1912) 29 TLR 88; *Re Scott, Scott v Scott* [1916] 2 Ch 268, CA (applied in *Re Oppenheimer, Tyser v Oppenheimer* [1948] Ch 721; *Re Bedford, Russell v Bedford* [1960] 3 All ER 756, [1960] 1 WLR 1331).

5 *Re Phuler's Will Trusts, Midland Bank Executor and Trustee Co Ltd v Logan* [1964] 2 All ER 948, [1965] 1 WLR 68; *Re Neeld, Carpenter v Inigo-Jones* [1964] 2 All ER 952n, [1965] 1 WLR 73n, CA (if the testator has already made a distinction between gifts free of duty and gifts not free of duty even the word 'all' may refer only to the gifts made free of duty).

6 *Re Constantine, Willan v Constantine* (1926) 70th Report of Inland Revenue Commissioners (Cmd 2989) 13.

7 *Re Rumball, Sherlock v Allan* [1956] Ch 105, [1955] 3 All ER 71, CA.

1133. Annuities and burden of duty. In the case of an annuity the following expressions have affected the burden of duty: 'clear of all deductions'[1]; 'clear of all taxes and outgoings'[2]; 'without any deduction or abatement out of the same'[3]; 'clear of all taxes and deductions whatsoever'[4]; 'one annuity or clear yearly sum'[5]; 'free yearly annuity'[6]; 'tax free and without any deduction'[7].

1 *Dawkins v Tatham* (1829) 2 Sim 492; *Re Coles' Will* (1869) LR 8 Eq 271.

2 *Louch v Peters* (1834) 1 My & K 489.

3 *Smith v Anderson* (1828) 4 Russ 352.
4 *Stow v Davenport* (1833) 5 B & Ad 359 at 366.
5 *Gude v Mumford* (1837) 2 Y & C Ex 445; *Re Dyet, Morgan v Dyet* (1902) 87 LT 744.
6 *Bulloch v Beaton* (1853) 15 Dunl 373, Ct of Sess. For similar wording see also *Wilks v Groom* (1856) 4 WR 697; *Baily v Boult* (1851) 14 Beav 595; *Haynes v Haynes* (1853) 3 De GM & G 590; *Re Robins, Nelson v Robins* (1888) 58 LT 382.
7 *Re Lord Fermoy* (1890) MacCarthy's Leading Cases in Land Purchase Law 55. See also *Re Cayley, Awdry v Cayley* [1904] 2 Ch 781 (direction to pay 'the death duties payable out of my estate'), distinguishing *Re Lewis, Lewis v Smith* [1900] 2 Ch 176; *Re Turnbull, Skipper v Wade* [1905] 1 Ch 726 ('free from duty'); *Re Waller, Margarison v Waller* [1916] 1 Ch 153 ('net income'). In the following cases the expressions used were held not to affect the incidence of settlement estate duty: *Re Lewis, Lewis v Smith* (direction to pay 'all duties payable by law out of my estate'); *Dundas's Trustees v Dundas's Trustees* 1912 SC 375 (covenant to pay a sum which would with other funds 'make up the sum of £30,000').

1134. Burden of tax on partially exempt residue. Notwithstanding the terms of the will, none of the tax attributable to the value of the property comprised in residue is allowed to fall on any gift of a share of residue if or to the extent that the transfer is exempt with respect to the gift[1].

A problem arises in calculating shares of residue where one or more shares are exempt from inheritance tax and one or more shares are not exempt. It is a question of construction of the will as to whether the shares are to be calculated after providing for the debts, funeral and testamentary expenses but before payment of the inheritance tax on the non-exempt shares, the gross division approach, or after deduction of the appropriate amount of inheritance tax, the net division approach[2]. In the gross division approach the non-exempt beneficiaries receive less of the net estate, through having suffered inheritance tax on their shares, than the exempt beneficiaries. The consequences, in terms of tax payable[3] and the amounts of residue to which the two classes of beneficiary are entitled, can be strikingly different[4].

1 Inheritance Tax Act 1984 s 41(b); and see INHERITANCE TAXATION vol 59A (2014) PARA 147.
2 *Re Ratcliffe, Holmes v McMullan* [1999] STC 262 (applying the gross division approach where a standard trust for sale and conversion of the real and personal estate not otherwise disposed of was followed by an instruction to stand possessed of the residue 'after payment thereout of my debts funeral and testamentary expenses' in specified shares). See also *Re Benham's Will Trusts, Lockhart v Harker* [1995] STC 210 (applying the net division approach).
3 The net division approach requires a grossing up calculation for tax purposes to prevent non-exempt beneficiaries benefiting from an exemption to which they are not entitled: see the Inheritance Tax Act 1984 s 41(b); and INHERITANCE TAXATION vol 59A (2014) PARA 147.
4 *Re Ratcliffe, Holmes v McMullan* [1999] STC 262 at 265 per Blackburne J (where a net division would have increased the inheritance tax payable by approximately £100,000).

(4) THE RESIDUARY ESTATE ON INTESTACY

1135. Payment of debts, liabilities etc held on trust under intestacy rules. On the death of a person intestate[1] after 31 December 1925[2] as to any real or personal estate, that estate is held in trust by his personal representatives with the power to sell it[3].

The personal representatives must pay out of the ready money of the deceased (so far as not disposed of by his will, if any[4]) and any net money arising from disposing of any other part of his estate (after payment of costs[5]) all such funeral[6], testamentary and administration expenses[7], debts and other liabilities as are properly payable out of it[8]. From the residue the personal representative must set aside a fund sufficient to provide for any pecuniary legacies[9] bequeathed by the deceased's will, if any[10].

1 'Intestate' includes a person who leaves a will but dies intestate as to some beneficial interest in his real or personal estate: Administration of Estates Act 1925 s 55(1)(vi). Where the deceased leaves a will, s 33 has effect subject to the provisions contained in the will: s 33(7). As to the respective application to cases of partial intestacy of s 33 and s 49 see PARA 516.
2 These provisions apply only to deaths after 31 December 1925: Administration of Estates Act 1925 s 54.
3 Administration of Estates Act 1925 s 33(1) (substituted by the Trusts of Land and Appointment of Trustees Act 1996 s 5(1), Sch 2 para 5(2)). As to the meaning of 'real estate' see PARA 607 note 1.
4 Administration of Estates Act 1925 s 33(2)(a) (s 33(2) amended by the Trusts of Land and Appointment of Trustees Act 1996 Sch 2 para 5(3)).
5 Administration of Estates Act 1925 s 33(2)(b) (as amended: see note 4).
6 As to funeral expenses see CREMATIONANDBURIAL vol 24 (2010) PARA 1136 et seq.
7 As to testamentary and administration expenses see PARA 1013 et seq.
8 Administration of Estates Act 1925 s 33(2) (as amended: see note 4).
9 As to the meaning of 'pecuniary legacy' for this purpose see PARA 1003.
10 Administration of Estates Act 1925 s 33(2) (as amended: see note 4). Nothing in s 33 affects the rights of any creditor of the deceased (as to which see PARA 966 et seq) or the rights of the Crown in respect of death duties: s 33(6). As to the incidence of death duties see PARAS 1128–1134.

1136. Powers of investment where estate held on trust under intestacy rules. During the minority of any beneficiary or the subsistence of any life interest, and pending the distribution of the whole or any part of the deceased's estate, the personal representatives[1] may invest the residue of the money, or so much of it as may not have been distributed, under the Trustee Act 2000[2].

1 As to the meaning of 'personal representative' see PARA 608.
2 Administration of Estates Act 1925 s 33(3) (amended by the Trustee Act 2000 Sch 2 para 27). As to the investment of trust money see TRUSTS AND POWERS vol 98 (2013) PARA 446 et seq.

1137. Distribution of residuary estate under intestacy rules. The money left in the hands of the personal representative[1] and any investments for the time being representing it, and any part of the estate of the deceased which remains unsold and is not required for administration purposes, is referred to as 'the residuary estate of the intestate'[2], which is to be distributed in the manner or held upon the trusts prescribed by statute[3].

1 As to the meaning of 'personal representative' see PARA 608.
2 Administration of Estates Act 1925 s 33(4) (amended by the Trusts of Land and Appointment of Trustees Act 1996 s 5(1), Sch 2 para 5(4)). For the purposes of the Administration of Estates Act 1925 s 33(4) (although not for the purposes of s 46(1)) the residuary estate of the intestate includes assets which do not fall for purposes of succession to be regulated by English law: *Re Collens, Royal Bank of Canada (London) Ltd v Krogh* [1986] Ch 505, [1986] 1 All ER 611.
3 See PARA 485 et seq.

1138. Income pending distribution under intestacy rules. The income, including net rents and profits[1] of real estate[2] and chattels real after payment of rates, taxes, rent, costs of insurance, repairs and other outgoings properly attributable to income, of so much of the deceased's real and personal estate as may not be disposed of by his will, if any, or may not be required for administration purposes, may, however that estate is invested, as from the deceased's death, be treated and applied as income, and for that purpose any necessary apportionment may be made between the tenant for life and the remainderman[3].

1 As to the meaning of 'rent' see the Administration of Estates Act 1925 s 55(1)(xxi); and PARA 927 note 1. 'Income' includes rents and profits: s 55(1)(v).
2 As to the meaning of 'real estate' see PARA 607 note 1.
3 Administration of Estates Act 1925 s 33(5). This provision has been held to exclude the rule in *Howe v Earl of Dartmouth* (see PARA 1122) with regard to the property as to which the deceased

died intestate (*Re Sullivan, Dunkley v Sullivan* [1930] 1 Ch 84; but see *Re Fisher, Harris and Fisher v Harris* [1943] Ch 377, [1943] 2 All ER 615). See also PARA 496 note 4. As to the apportionment of income between the tenant for life and the remainderman see PARA 1118 et seq. As to the special provisions for the incidence of income tax on the income of the residuary estate see INCOME TAXATION vol 59 (2014) PARA 2075 et seq.

(5) ASSENTS

(i) Personal Estate

1139. Necessity for assent of personalty. The bequest of a legacy, whether general[1] or specific[2], transfers only an inchoate property to the legatee: the executor's assent[3] is necessary to render it complete and perfect[4]. The right is one which devolves on the legatee's personal representatives should he die before the assent is given[5]. In the case of a release of a debt by will[6] the executor's assent is necessary, as the release in effect amounts to a legacy of the debt[7].

The necessity for assent by an executor applies to residuary bequests[8], and to interests arising under a partial intestacy[9], and an executor may assent to part of a residuary gift without assenting to the whole[10].

The assent of one of several representatives to a bequest of pure personalty is sufficient[11], even though the bequest is to himself[12].

An executor may assent before probate[13], and the assent will not be affected by his dying without having obtained probate, provided the will is subsequently proved[14].

An executor may be compelled by the legatee to assent, should he refuse to do so without just cause[15].

1 As to general legacies see PARAS 119.
2 As to specific legacies see PARAS 118.
3 As to evidence of assent see PARA 1143 et seq.
4 An administrator cannot assent in favour of a person entitled on intestacy in respect of pure personalty: see PARA 1143 note 1.
5 *Re Leigh's Will Trusts* [1970] Ch 277, [1969] 3 All ER 432.
6 As to the release of a debt by will see PARA 297.
7 *Sibthorp v Moxton* (1747) 1 Ves Sen 49 at 50 per Lord Hardwicke LC.
8 As to residuary bequests see PARA 1113 et seq.
9 As to partial intestacy see PARA 514 et seq.
10 *Austin v Beddoe* (1893) 41 WR 619; but see *Elliott v Elliott* (1841) 9 M & W 23 at 27 per Parke B. The doctrine which always applied to chattels real was extended by the Land Transfer Act 1897 s 3(1) (repealed as respects deaths after 1925) to devises of real estate vesting in the personal representative.
11 Went Off Ex (14th Edn) 413.
12 *Townson v Tickell* (1819) 3 B & Ald 31 at 40.
13 *Johnson v Warwick* (1856) 17 CB 516. See also PARAS 633–634. An administrator derives his title from the grant, so a person entitled to administer cannot assent before grant: see PARA 643.
14 *Brazier v Hudson* (1836) 8 Sim 67. As to an executor's liability to be sued see PARAS 636, 1146; and as to actions by and against representatives see PARA 1271 et seq.
15 Went Off Ex (14th Edn) 70.

1140. When a condition may be attached to assent of personalty. A personal representative has no power to attach as a condition to his assent the performance of some subsequent act by the legatee or other person entitled, although he may apparently agree to give his assent upon the performance of a condition precedent[1].

1 Went Off Ex (14th Edn) 429. As to security for duties etc as a condition of giving an assent see PARA 1145.

1141. Assent of personalty by implication. An assent to the vesting of personal estate or of an equitable interest in real estate[1] may be express or implied. It need not be in writing[2], nor need it be given in any particular form. Informal expressions, if sufficiently clear to indicate intention, may amount to an assent[3]. The assent may also be implied from the executor's conduct. Thus the application, in the maintenance of minors, of rents of leaseholds bequeathed to the executor in trust for maintaining them during minority and afterwards in trust for the legatee on attaining his majority[4]; allowing a legatee of a term to receive the income[5]; the payment by the executor of rent, coupled with the charging of the legatee with the payments in account[6]; or the payment of a charge subject to which a legacy is given[7], would amount to an assent to the bequest. However, an executor may and often does make general payments to a legatee without binding himself to an assent, and the court will not infer an assent in such circumstances unless there is evidence that the executor intended to assent as, for instance, by representations to that effect or by special payments out of or on account of rents to which the legatee would be entitled after assent[8].

In case of dispute, the question whether there has been an assent or not is generally one of fact[9]; but an expression which is ambiguous and applies equally to either view is no evidence of an assent[10].

An assent to a life interest is an assent to the interest in remainder, and conversely an assent to an interest in remainder enures for the benefit of the tenant for life[11].

1 As to an assent to the vesting of a legal estate see PARA 1144.
2 Cf the Administration of Estates Act 1925 s 36(4): see PARA 1144.
3 See eg *Doe d Sturges v Tatchell* (1832) 3 B & Ad 675; *Barnard v Pumfrett* (1841) 5 My & Cr 63; and Com Dig, Administration (C6). The carrying in of the residuary account does not raise any implication that the duties of the executors are completed: see *Attenborough v Solomon* [1913] AC 76, HL; *IRC v Smith* [1930] 1 KB 713, CA.

If legal title to property (eg shares in companies) is to pass, the appropriate transfer will be needed to vest the legal right in the beneficiary; in the case of savings certificates an encashment is not necessary, but they can be transferred: *Note: Inherited National Savings* [1954] 1 All ER 519n.
4 *Paramour v Yardley* (1579) 2 Plowd 539.
5 Went Off Ex (14th Edn) 414. However, cf *Wise v Whitburn* [1924] 1 Ch 460. As to the position where, since 1925, a personal representative permits possession of land to be taken by a person entitled see the Administration of Estates Act 1925 s 43(1); and PARA 1022.
6 *Doe d Mabberley v Mabberley* (1833) 6 C & P 126.
7 *Young v Holmes* (1717) 1 Stra 70.
8 *Thorne v Thorne* [1893] 3 Ch 196.
9 *Elliott v Elliott* (1841) 9 M & W 23 at 27; *Mason v Farnell* (1844) 12 M & W 674. In *IRC v Smith* [1930] 1 KB 713, CA, it was held that whether the residue had been ascertained and a bequest assented to was a question of fact, which, for the purpose of super tax, was to be determined by the commissioners; and further that the existence of an outstanding mortgage did not of itself prevent the implication of an assent, though the contrary conclusion had been reached in *Daw v IRC* (1928) 14 TC 58.
10 *Doe d Chidgey v Harris* (1847) 16 M & W 517 at 520 per Alderson B.
11 *Stevenson v Liverpool Corpn* (1874) LR 10 QB 81; *Adams v Peirce* (1724) 3 P Wms 11. See also *Wise v Whitburn* [1924] 1 Ch 460.

1142. Gift of personalty to executor. In the case of a gift to the executor, assent (which may be express or implied) is equally necessary[1]. If the executor in his manner of administering the property does any act which shows that he regards himself as owning it beneficially, that is to be taken as evidence of his assent; but if his acts are referable to his character of executor, they are not evidence of assent[2].

Even before 1926, if a term was bequeathed to an executor for his life, mere entry into possession was not sufficient to amount to an assent[3], since such an assent would amount to an assent to the bequest in remainder[4], which would prevent the executor from availing himself of the estate in remainder for the purpose of paying debts or legacies[5]. A similar rule applies to a gift to an executor of a life interest in furniture[6].

1 Toller's Law of Executors (7th Edn) 345. As to the requirement for an assent in writing in the case of legal estates in land see PARA 1144.
2 *Doe d Hayes v Sturges* (1816) 7 Taunt 217 at 223 per Gibbs CJ. In *Fenton v Clegg* (1854) 9 Exch 680, an entry by an executor into possession of a leasehold, and a disposition of it by his will, were held to amount to an assent to the bequest to himself.
3 *Doe d Hayes v Sturges* (1816) 7 Taunt 217; *Doe d Sturges v Tatchell* (1832) 3 B & Ad 675 at 680.
4 See PARA 1141; and *Trail v Bull* (1853) 22 LJ Ch 1082 at 1083 per Lord Cranworth.
5 *Doe d Hayes v Sturges* (1816) 7 Taunt 217 at 221; *A-G v Potter* (1842) 5 Beav 164.
6 *Richards v Browne* (1837) 3 Bing NC 493.

(ii) Real Estate

1143. Power to assent of real estate. Since 1 January 1926 a personal representative[1] may assent[2] to the vesting, in any person who may be entitled to it, of any estate or interest in real estate[3] to which the testator or intestate was entitled or over which he exercised a general power of appointment by his will, including the statutory power to dispose of entailed interests[4], and which devolved upon the personal representative[5].

The persons in whose favour the assent may be executed are those entitled by devise, bequest, devolution, appropriation[6] or otherwise[7]. They may be entitled beneficially or as trustees or personal representatives[8].

An assent in relation to real estate must be made by all executors who have proved the will or by all the administrators, as the case may be[9].

Where, on the death of the testator or intestate, real estate is comprised in a settlement[10], the deceased's personal representatives may vest it by means of a vesting assent in the tenant for life or statutory owners[11].

Any person who against the personal representatives claims to be entitled to have real estate vested in him by an assent may apply to the court for a vesting order[12].

1 Ie an executor or administrator: see PARA 608. An administrator can still not assent in favour of a person entitled on an intestacy to pure personalty, but in most cases of this nature either delivery is sufficient or formal transfer is necessary.
2 As to the form of an assent see PARA 1144; and as to the effect of an assent see PARA 1146 et seq.
3 As to the meaning of 'real estate', which includes chattels real, see PARA 607 note 1.
4 See the Law of Property Act 1925 s 176; and PARA 954. See also REAL PROPERTY AND REGISTRATION vol 87 (2012) PARA 112 et seq.
5 See the Administration of Estates Act 1925 s 36(1). The power has existed since 1 January 1926. An assent may be made whether the testator or intestate died before or after that date: s 36(12). In the case of deaths before 1926 it was necessary that the estate had not been fully administered on that date. As to property devolving on the personal representative see PARA 917. As it is a condition that the property should be property to which the deceased was entitled and which devolved upon the personal representative, there is doubt whether an assent is applicable in the case of property which falls into the deceased's estate after his death and is conveyed to the personal representative to hold as a part of his estate. In these circumstances a conveyance may be the safest course of action: see *Re Stirrup's Contract, Stirrup v Foel Agricultural Co-operative Society* [1961] 1 All ER 805, [1961] 1 WLR 449.
6 As to appropriation see PARA 1153 et seq.
7 See the Administration of Estates Act 1925 s 36(1). Whatever meaning may be attached to the word 'otherwise' it is in practice undesirable that an assent should be given except in favour of persons entitled by devise, bequest, devolution or appropriation. For an example of an assent giving effect to a contract of sale made by the testator see *GHR Co v IRC* [1943] KB 303, [1943] 1 All ER 424.
8 See the Administration of Estates Act 1925 s 36(1).

9 See the Administration of Estates Act 1925 s 2(2); and PARA 1024. See also PARA 1146 note 2.
10 As to what constitutes a settlement see the Settled Land Act 1925 s 1; and SETTLEMENTS vol 91 (2012) PARA 579.
11 See the Settled Land Act 1925 ss 6–8; and SETTLEMENTS vol 91 (2012) PARAS 598–599.
12 See the Administration of Estates Act 1925 s 43(2). The County Court has jurisdiction under this provision where the estate in respect of which the application is made does not exceed in amount or value the County Court limit: s 43(4) (added by the County Courts Act 1984 s 148(1), Sch 2 Pt III para 14). As to the County Court limit see PARA 866 note 2. As to the County Court see COURTS AND TRIBUNALS vol 24 (2010) PARA 758 et seq. Any such application will normally be brought under CPR Pt 8 procedure: see CPR Pt 8; CPR PD 8A—*Alternative procedure for claims.* See also CIVIL PROCEDURE vol 11 (2015) PARA 150 et seq.

1144. Form of assent of real estate. An assent to the vesting of a legal estate[1] in land is required to be in writing[2]. It must be signed by the personal representative[3] and name the person in whose favour it is given; an assent in this form[4] operates to vest in that person the legal estate to which it relates[5]. An assent not in writing or not in favour of a named person is not effectual to pass a legal estate[6].

It follows that an assent to the vesting in the person entitled to it of any equitable interest in real estate need not be in writing[7].

The statutory covenants as to title implied by a person being expressed to convey as personal representative are implied in an assent in writing made before 1 July 1995 as in a conveyance by deed made before that date[8]. In an assent in writing made on or after 1 July 1995 there are implied the same covenants as in any other instrument effecting or purporting to effect a disposition of property with limited title guarantee from that date onwards[9].

If the form of an assent is used where a conveyance is necessary to carry the legal estate[10], this will be valid as a conveyance if it is executed as a deed and the intention is clear[11], as preference is given to intent over technical import and form[12].

1 As to the meaning of 'legal estates' see PARA 969 note 2.
2 Administration of Estates Act 1925 s 36(4).
3 As to the meaning of 'personal representative' see PARA 608.
4 An assent is not required to be by deed: see the Law of Property Act 1925 s 52(2)(a). In practice, the forms prescribed by the Land Registration Rules 2003, SI 2003/1417, r 206, Sch 1 require execution as a deed but their use is optional on first registration. Dispositions of registered land are required to be completed by registration: see the Land Registration Act 2002 s 27(2). In the case of unregistered land, compulsory first registration applies on the transfer of a qualifying estate by means of an assent: see the Land Registration Act 2002 s 4(1)(a)(ii). For this purpose a qualifying estate is an unregistered legal estate which is a freehold estate or a leasehold estate for a term which, at the time of the transfer, grant or creation has more than seven years to run: s 4(2). As to the procedure and prescribed forms for registration see REAL PROPERTY AND REGISTRATION vol 87 (2012) PARA 232 et seq. It was held under the Land Transfer Act 1897 s 3 (repealed as regards deaths after 1925), that an executor was not bound to describe the land in more precise terms than those contained in the will: *Re Pix, Plomley v Stileman* [1901] WN 165. In practice the description is often taken from the last conveyance, since the assent may ultimately become a root of title. As to stamp duty see PARA 1151.
5 Administration of Estates Act 1925 s 36(4).
6 Administration of Estates Act 1925 s 36(4). *Re Edwards' Will Trusts, Edwards v Edwards* [1982] Ch 30, [1981] 2 All ER 941, CA. It is desirable that a personal representative who is a trustee or devisee should, after the administration has been completed, execute an assent in writing in his own favour, in order to show that his duties as personal representative have ceased, and that he now holds the property as trustee or devisee: *Re Yerburgh, Yerburgh v Yerburgh* [1928] WN 208. If he dies without having executed an assent in his own favour it is in practice necessary on a sale of land to obtain a grant of administration de bonis non to his estate for the protection of the purchaser (see PARA 793); but since there is no question of a legal estate 'passing', it may not be strictly necessary: see *Re Pitt, Pitt v Mann* (1928) 44 TLR 371; *Re Hodge, Hodge v Griffiths* [1940] Ch 260; *Harris v Harris* [1942] LJNCCR 119. It was held in *Re King's Will Trusts, Assheton v Boyne* [1964] Ch 542, [1964] 1 All ER 833, that a personal representative who is a trustee or devisee must execute an assent in his own favour, but the relevant case law was not all before the court. In *Re Edwards's Will Trusts, Edwards v Edwards*, it was held that, although the

legal estate might not pass on the death of an administrator beneficially entitled who had failed to execute a written assent, the equitable beneficial interest in the property did vest and accordingly formed part of his estate on his death. See also *Re Cockburn's Will Trusts, Cockburn v Lewis* [1957] Ch 438, [1957] 2 All ER 522, applying *Re Ponder, Ponder v Ponder* [1921] 2 Ch 59, and distinguishing *Harvell v Foster* [1954] 2 QB 367, [1954] 2 All ER 736, CA. As to when a personal representative becomes a trustee see PARA 1150.

7 *Re Edwards' Will Trusts, Edwards v Edwards* [1982] Ch 30, [1981] 2 All ER 941, CA. As to assent by implication see PARA 1141. A personal representative may let a beneficiary into possession of land before giving an assent, however, without prejudice to his power to retake possession or dispose of the land: see the Administration of Estates Act 1925 s 43(1); and PARA 1022.

8 See the Administration of Estates Act 1925 s 36(3) (repealed); Law of Property Act 1925 s 76(1)(F), Sch 2 Pt VI (both repealed as regards dispositions made on or after 1 July 1995); and CONVEYANCING vol 23 (2016) PARA 182.

9 See the Law of Property (Miscellaneous Provisions) Act 1994 s 12(3). As to the covenants implied in an instrument effecting or purporting to effect a disposition of property with limited title guarantee see ss 2, 3(3), 4, 5; and CONVEYANCING vol 23 (2016) PARA 182.

10 Ie where the statutory provisions for assenting are not relevant because the transferee is not entitled by devise, bequest, devolution, appropriation or otherwise: see PARA 1143.

11 *Re Stirrup's Contract, Stirrup v Foel Agricultural Co-operative Society* [1961] 1 All ER 805, [1961] 1 WLR 449 (assent by deed valid as a conveyance).

12 *Marquis Cholmondeley v Lord Clinton* (1821) 2 Jac & W 1 at 91.

1145. Security for duties, debts or liabilities as a condition of giving an assent. A personal representative[1] may, as a condition of giving an assent or making a conveyance, require security for the discharge of any such duties, debt or liability to which the estate or interest is subject, but is not entitled to postpone the giving of an assent merely by reason of the subsistence of any such duties, debt or liability if reasonable arrangements have been made for discharging the same[2].

An assent may be given subject to any legal estate or charge by way of legal mortgage[3], but no beneficiary is entitled to compel an executor to exercise this power[4].

1 As to the meaning of 'personal representative' see PARA 608.

2 Administration of Estates Act 1925 s 36(10). This provision replaced the Land Transfer Act 1897 s 3(1) (repealed as regards deaths after 1925) by which the personal representatives might assent or convey subject to a charge for the payment of any money which they were liable to pay. The charge did not extend to debts for which, prior to the Act, the personal representatives of the debtor would not have been liable if they had parted with the whole personal estate, and therefore, where the personal representatives had given the usual statutory notices to the creditor, the charge did not apply to debts of which they had no notice at the date of the conveyance to the devisees: *Re Cary and Lott's Contract* [1901] 2 Ch 463. Although the assent or conveyance does not mention the charge, the land remains subject to it where the grantee has notice: *Parker v Judkin* [1931] 1 Ch 475, CA.

3 Administration of Estates Act 1925 s 36(10).

4 *Williams v Holland* [1965] 2 All ER 157, [1965] 1 WLR 739, CA. As to the interest of a beneficiary in an unadministered estate see PARA 922.

(iii) Effect of Assent; Stamp Duties and Costs

1146. Irrevocability of assent and relation back. The assent once given is irrevocable[1]. An assent in relation to real estate operates to vest in any person entitled to it the estate or interest to which the assent relates[2]. The title to a legacy vests immediately upon the assent in the legatee[3] so as to enable him to bring an action at law against the personal representative or any other person in possession of the bequest[4]. An assent in relation to real estate relates back to the deceased's death unless a contrary intention appears[5], and the legatee of a specific legacy has the right to recover the intermediate profits of the thing bequeathed[6].

Where executors who are also trustees under the will have assented they cease to hold the property as executors and from then on hold it as trustees[7].

1 *Noel v Robinson* (1681) 2 Vent 358.
2 Administration of Estates Act 1925 s 36(2). An assent is a 'conveyance' for the purposes of the Act: see s 55(1)(iii); and PARA 858 note 1. As to the effect of an assent executed as a deed where a conveyance proper was required see PARA 1144.
3 Ie in the person who is the rightful legatee and not necessarily in the person in whom the assent purports to vest the property: see *Re West, West v Roberts* [1909] 2 Ch 180, where a codicil was found, some years after the assent, altering a bequest of shares and giving them to another legatee. As to the effect of an assent in relation to real estate see PARA 1147 note 5.
4 *Saunder's Case* (1599) 5 Co Rep 12a; *Williams v Lee* (1745) 3 Atk 223; *Doe d Lord Saye and Sele v Guy* (1802) 3 East 120; *Re Culverhouse, Cook v Culverhouse* [1896] 2 Ch 251. An action at law cannot be brought against an executor upon a promise to pay a general legacy: *Jones v Tanner* (1827) 7 B & C 542. As to actions against personal representatives see PARA 1271 et seq.
5 Administration of Estates Act 1925 s 36(2).
6 *Re West, West v Roberts* [1909] 2 Ch 180; *IRC v Hawley* [1928] 1 KB 578. See PARA 1085.
7 *Attenborough v Solomon* [1913] AC 76, HL; but cf *Wise v Whitburn* [1924] 1 Ch 460. As to when a personal representative becomes a trustee see further PARA 1149.

1147. Protection of purchaser following assent or conveyance. If no notice of a previous assent or conveyance affecting the legal estate has been placed on or annexed to the probate or letters of administration, an assent or conveyance[1] by a personal representative[2] in respect of that legal estate[3] must be taken in favour of a purchaser[4] as sufficient evidence[5] that the person in whose favour the assent or conveyance is given or made is the person entitled to have the legal estate conveyed to him and upon the proper trusts, if any[6]. The assent or conveyance does not otherwise prejudicially affect the claim of any person rightfully entitled to the estate vested or conveyed or any charge on it[7]. An assent or conveyance given or made by a personal representative does not, except in favour of a purchaser of a legal estate, prejudice the right of the personal representative or any other person to recover the estate or interest to which it relates, or to be indemnified out of the estate or interest against any duties, debt or liability to which the estate or interest would have been subject if there had not been any assent or conveyance[8].

Any person in whose favour an assent or conveyance of a legal estate is made by a personal representative may require that notice of the assent or conveyance be written or indorsed on or permanently annexed to the probate or letters of administration, at the cost of the estate, and that the probate or letters of administration be produced, at the like cost, to prove that the notice has been placed on it or annexed to it[9].

1 As to the meaning of 'conveyance' see PARA 858 note 1.
2 As to the meaning of 'personal representative' see PARA 608.
3 As to the meaning of 'legal estates' see PARA 969 note 2.
4 For these purposes, 'purchaser' means a purchaser for money or money's worth: Administration of Estates Act 1925 s 36(11). Cf the extended definition of 'purchaser' in s 55(1)(xviii): see PARA 858 note 4.
5 The assent is not 'conclusive' evidence, but a purchaser may accept it unless or until, on a proper investigation of the vendor's title, facts come to his knowledge which indicate the contrary: *Re Duce and Boots Cash Chemists (Southern) Ltd's Contract* [1937] Ch 642, [1937] 3 All ER 788.
6 Administration of Estates Act 1925 s 36(7). It will be noted that by s 36(4) an assent is to operate to vest a legal estate in a named person: see PARA 1144. Apparently this provision is not the absolute provision it appears to be, for, if it were, there would be no need for s 36(7). The reason appears to be that s 36(4) is governed by s 36(1), (2), and an assent can only operate to vest an estate or interest in the person if he is in fact entitled to it.
7 Administration of Estates Act 1925 s 36(7).
8 Administration of Estates Act 1925 s 36(9).
9 Administration of Estates Act 1925 s 36(5). A purchaser from a personal representative can insist on an acknowledgement for production and delivery of copies of the probate or letters of

administration (*Re Miller and Pickersgill's Contract* [1931] 1 Ch 511), but a subsequent purchaser will generally be debarred from objecting to the absence of such an acknowledgement: see the Law of Property Act 1925 s 45(7); and CONVEYANCING vol 23 (2016) PARA 116. As to the effect of a statement in writing by the personal representative that he has not given or made an assent or conveyance in respect of the legal estate see the Administration of Estates Act 1925 s 36(6); and PARA 1027.

1148. Assents in relation to trusteeship. The power to assent is confined to personal representatives[1], and difficulties can arise as to whether a personal representative who may have fully administered and become a trustee still has power to assent and whether he needs to assent in his own favour as trustee[2]. The capacities of personal representative and trustee are not mutually exclusive, and a personal representative who has fully administered the estate and holds the residue as a trustee is not thus necessarily and automatically discharged from his obligations as personal representative, or, in particular, from the obligations of any bond which he may have entered into for the due administration of the estate[3]. A personal representative retains his character as such (as distinct from his statutory powers of management[4]) for all time or, in the case of a grant of administration for a limited period, until the termination of the period of the grant[5].

1 See PARAS 1139, 1143.
2 See PARA 1150.
3 *Harvell v Foster* [1954] 2 QB 367, at 379–380, 383, [1954] 2 All ER 736 at 743, 745, CA, per Sir R Evershed MR (criticising statements in *Re Ponder, Ponder v Ponder* [1921] 2 Ch 59). See also *Re Cockburn's Will Trusts, Cockburn v Lewis* [1957] Ch 438, [1957] 2 All ER 522, distinguishing *Harvell v Foster*; and following *Re Ponder, Ponder v Ponder*. As to the principle that taking out probate may involve the acceptance of the office of trustee see PARA 629.
4 As to such statutory powers see PARA 1150.
5 *Re Timmis, Nixon v Smith* [1902] 1 Ch 176 at 183; *Harvell v Foster* [1954] 2 QB 367 at 383, [1954] 2 All ER 736 at 745, CA, per Sir R Evershed MR. The representative retains, for example, the capacity to represent the estate in legal proceedings: *Harvell v Foster*.

1149. When a personal representative becomes a trustee. If property is specifically devised or bequeathed to an executor upon trust he becomes trustee of it when he has assented[1] or severed the property from the rest of the estate[2] or has executed a declaration of trust[3]. As regards residue, the major change in character from representation to trusteeship occurs when the estate has been fully administered in the sense that all debts and liabilities have been discharged and the residue ascertained[4]. When the trusts affecting the residue are designed to continue after completion of the administration, the personal representative should then execute an assent to the vesting of the residue in himself as trustee[5].

1 *Dix v Burford* (1854) 19 Beav 409; *Clegg v Rowland* (1866) LR 3 Eq 368 at 373. See also *Attenborough v Solomon* [1913] AC 76 at 82–83, HL; *Byrchall v Bradford* (1822) 6 Madd 235 at 240–241; *Wise v Whitburn* [1924] 1 Ch 460. For the circumstances in which an assent is required to be in writing see PARA 1144.
2 *Ex p Dover* (1834) 5 Sim 560; *Phillipo v Munnings* (1837) 2 My & Cr 309; *O'Reilly v Walsh* (1872) 6 IR Eq 555 (affd 7 IR Eq 167); *Re Cockburn's Will Trusts, Cockburn v Lewis* [1957] Ch 438, [1957] 2 All ER 522.
3 *Re Rowe, Jacobs v Hind* (1889) 58 LJ Ch 703, CA.
4 *Re Smith, Henderson-Roe v Hitchins* (1889) 42 ChD 302 at 304; *Re Earl of Stamford, Payne v Stamford* [1896] 1 Ch 288 at 296; *Re Timmis, Nixon v Smith* [1902] 1 Ch 176 at 182–183; *Re Gompertz Estate, Parker v Gompertz* (1910) 55 Sol Jo 76 (executor); *Harvell v Foster* [1954] 2 QB 367 at 379–380, 383, [1954] 2 All ER 736 at 745, CA, per Sir R Evershed MR (administrator); *Charlton v Earl of Durham* (1869) 4 Ch App 433 at 439; *Re Willey* [1890] WN 1, CA; *Eaton v Daines* [1894] WN 32 (executor); *Re Ponder, Ponder v Ponder* [1921] 2 Ch 59 (administrator). As to statutory trusts applicable on an intestacy see PARA 1135 et seq. As to the principle that the acceptance of an executorship involves acceptance of the trusts imposed by the will see PARA 629.

5 *Re Yerburgh, Yerburgh v Yerburgh* [1928] WN 208 (administrator). Before 1926 an administrator could not assent. Since 1 January 1926 an assent must be in writing in order to pass a legal estate in land: see PARA 1144. Although it has been stated in certain cases that an executor becomes a trustee (see eg *Attenborough v Solomon* [1913] AC 76 at 83–84, HL; *Re Trollope's Will Trusts, Public Trustee v Trollope* [1927] 1 Ch 596 at 605; *Re Gibbs, Midland Bank Executor and Trustee Co Ltd v IRC* [1951] Ch 933 at 938, [1951] 2 All ER 63 at 67 per Danckwerts J), it seems that the execution of an assent in his favour is not strictly necessary in order to clothe a personal representative with the character of a trustee: see PARA 1144 note 6.

1150. Effect of personal representative becoming a trustee. When after administration a personal representative holds as trustee on trusts imposed by statute on the death of a person intestate[1] he may continue to exercise the special powers of management conferred upon a personal representative by the Administration of Estates Act 1925[2] so long as any beneficiary is a minor or any life interest is subsisting[3]. If, however, the personal representative, having completed the administration, holds on trusts declared by the will, those special powers of management are no longer available to him, notwithstanding the minority of a beneficiary or the subsistence of a life interest[4]. In either case, being a trustee he is entitled to exercise the statutory power of appointing new or additional trustees[5], or to apply to the court[6] for the appointment of new trustees[7].

The question whether a personal representative has become a trustee is also important in the following instances:

(1) when considering the application of the Limitation Act 1980[8];
(2) when considering the form of proceedings against him, whether for devastavit[9] or breach of trust[10]; and
(3) to determine whether or not he can as sole personal representative or trustee give a good receipt for capital money[11].

1 See the Administration of Estates Act 1925 s 33; and PARA 1135 et seq.
2 See the Administration of Estates Act 1925 s 39; and PARA 1019.
3 *Re Trollope's Will Trusts, Public Trustee v Trollope* [1927] 1 Ch 596; cf *Re Wilks, Keefer v Wilks* [1935] Ch 645, where infants were beneficially interested under the law of the domicile of a deceased person who died intestate as to property in this country.
4 *Re Trollope's Will Trusts, Public Trustee v Trollope* [1927] 1 Ch 596.
5 See the Trustee Act 1925 s 36; *Re Cockburn's Will Trusts, Cockburn v Lewis* [1957] Ch 438, [1957] 2 All ER 522; and TRUSTS AND POWERS vol 98 (2013) PARAS 275–276. As to the special powers of personal representatives to appoint trustees of minors' property see PARA 1075.
6 See the Trustee Act 1925 s 41; and TRUSTS AND POWERS vol 98 (2013) PARA 289 et seq. Section 41(4) prohibits the appointment of an executor or administrator as distinct from a trustee: see TRUSTS AND POWERS vol 98 (2013) PARA 297.
7 *Re Willey* [1890] WN 1, CA (application to court by executors for appointment of new trustee); *Eaton v Daines* [1894] WN 32 (appointment by executors who had become trustees held good); *Re Ponder, Ponder v Ponder* [1921] 2 Ch 59 (new trustee appointed by court to act with administratrix who had cleared estate); *Re Pitt, Pitt v Mann* (1828) 44 TLR 371 (appointment by administratrix who had cleared estate; appointment held good). For comment on *Re Ponder, Ponder v Ponder*, and *Re Pitt, Pitt v Mann*, see *Harvell v Foster* [1954] 2 QB 367 at 382–383, [1954] 2 All ER 736 at 745, CA, per Sir R Evershed MR.
8 Once the administration of the estate is complete, actions in relation to will trusts are subject to the same limitation period as lifetime trusts: see trusts created by a will *Davies v Sharples* [2006] EWHC 362 (Ch); [2006] WTLR 839. If the will imposes no duties to be performed by the personal representative as trustee, the limitation period for trust property will not normally apply: *Re Richardson, Pole v Pattenden* [1920] 1 Ch 423, CA; see also *Re Davis, Evans v Moore* [1891] 3 Ch 119, CA; *Re Barker, Buxton v Campbell* [1892] 2 Ch 491. If, on the other hand, trusts arise under the will or intestacy it may be clear, by reason of the lapse of time or otherwise, that the estate has been administered and that the property in question is held by the personal representative as trustee: *Re Oliver, Theobald v Oliver* [1927] 2 Ch 323. See also eg *Re Swain, Swain v Bringeman* [1891] 3 Ch 233; *Re Page, Jones v Morgan* [1893] 1 Ch 304; *Re Timmis, Nixon v Smith* [1902] 1 Ch 176; *Davies v Sharples* [2006] EWHC 362 (Ch), [2006] WTLR 839. See the Limitation Act 1980 ss 21, 22; and LIMITATION PERIODS vol 68 (2016) PARA 1138 et seq.

9 See the Limitation Act 1980 s 23; and LIMITATION PERIODS vol 68 (2016) PARA 1008. See also *Charlton v Low* (1734) 3 P Wms 328 at 331. As to devastavit see PARA 1244 et seq.
10 See PARA 1244.
11 See PARA 1032 note 4.

1151. Stamp duties. Stamp duty was abolished, except in relation to instruments relating to stock or marketable securities and the acquisition of certain partnership interests, by the Finance Act 2003[1]. In relation to land transactions it was replaced by stamp duty land tax with effect from 1 December 2003[2]. The acquisition of property by a person in or towards satisfaction of his entitlement under a will or on an intestacy is exempt from charge to stamp duty land tax[3] unless the person acquiring the property gives any consideration for it other than the assumption of secured debt[4]. Thus a simple assent of land whether under hand or executed as a deed attracts no stamp duty land tax.

An assent to give effect to a contract of sale entered into in the lifetime of the deceased formerly attracted ad valorem stamp duty as a conveyance on sale[5].

An assent which vests property appropriated in satisfaction of a general legacy of money or in satisfaction of any interest of a surviving spouse or civil partner in an intestate's estate is not subject to ad valorem duty as a conveyance on sale[6], nor is any fixed duty payable[7].

1 See the Finance Act 2003 s 125, Schs 15, 20. As to stamp duties generally see STAMP TAXES.
2 See the Finance Act 2003 Part 4 (ss 42–124, Schs 3–19); the Stamp Duty Land Tax (Appointment of the Implementation Date) Order 2003, SI 2003/2899, art 2. Unlike its predecessor, stamp duty land tax is chargeable on land transactions whether or not there is any instrument effecting the transaction: see the Finance Act 2003 s 42. As to stamp duty land tax see STAMP TAXES.
3 Finance Act 2003 Sch 3 para 3A(1) (added by the Finance Act 2004 s 300).
4 Finance Act 2003 Sch 3 para 3A(2) (as added: see note 3). For this purpose 'secured debt' means an obligation, whether certain or contingent, to pay a sum of money either immediately or at a future date which, immediately after the death of the deceased is secured on the property: Finance Act 2003 Sch 3 para 3A(4) (as so added). If the person acquiring the property gives any consideration the chargeable consideration is determined in accordance with Sch 4 para 8A(1) (see STAMP TAXES vol 96 (2012) PARA 434: Sch 3 PARA 3A(3) (as so added).
5 *GHR Co v IRC* [1943] KB 303, [1943] 1 All ER 424. See STAMP TAXES. Stamp duty itself is now limited in application: see text and note 1. In relation to a contract for the sale of land the relevant tax is now stamp duty land tax: see note 2. An assent cannot of course be used to give effect to a sale by the personal representatives: see PARA 1143 note 7.
6 See the Finance Act 1985 s 84(4), (5); and STAMP TAXES vol 96 (2012) PARA 361. Formerly an assent executed in favour of a pecuniary legatee in pursuance of a power of appropriation under which the beneficiary's consent was required, being contractual in substance, was required to be stamped as a conveyance on sale: *Jopling v IRC* [1940] 2 KB 282, [1940] 3 All ER 279. Such consent is in general a prerequisite of the power of appropriation conferred by the Administration of Estates Act 1925 s 41: see PARA 1153 et seq. Assents giving effect to appropriations in favour of residuary legatees, where the legatees received no more than their entitlement under the will, were it seems, accepted by the Inland Revenue as being outside the scope of the ad valorem charge but fixed duty was payable: Stamp Act 1891 s 62, Sch 1 (repealed by the Finance Act 1999 Sch 20 Pt V para 2 with effect to instruments executed on or after 1 October 1999).
7 Fixed duty was abolished for instruments falling within Finance Act 1985 s 84(4), (5) and executed on or after 13 March 2008, except in relation to instruments effecting a land transaction: Finance Act 2008 s 99, Sch 32. Prior to that date it was generally possible to certify the instrument as exempt from stamp duty in accordance with the Stamp Duty (Exempt Instruments) Regulations 1987, SI 1987/516.

1152. Costs of assent and transfer. Where personal representatives assent to specific legacies, the costs of transfer are payable by the legatees[1], but the costs of assent in relation to settled land are payable out of the trust estate[2].

1 *Re Grosvenor, Grosvenor v Grosvenor* [1916] 2 Ch 375. See also PARAS 1013–1014, 1060 text and note 5.

2 See the Settled Land Act 1925 s 8(2); and SETTLEMENTS vol 91 (2012) PARA 599. This is so both in the case of land that ceased to be settled on the death of the deceased and where it continues to be settled: see ss 7(5), 8(2); and SETTLEMENTS vol 91 (2012) PARA 599.

(6) APPROPRIATION

(i) Statutory Power

1153. Statutory power of appropriation. A personal representative[1] has a statutory power of appropriation, whether the deceased died intestate[2] or not and whenever he died[3] subject, generally, to certain consents[4].

The personal representative may appropriate any part of the real or personal estate[5], including things in action, in their actual condition or state of investment at the time of appropriation, in or towards satisfaction of any legacy bequeathed by the deceased or of any other interest or share in his property[6], whether settled or not[7], as to the personal representative may seem just and reasonable[8], according to the respective rights of the persons interested in the property[9]. The power extends to property over which a testator has exercised a general power of appointment, including the statutory power[10] to dispose of entailed interests[11].

The statutory power of appropriation authorises the setting apart of a fund to answer an annuity by means of the income[12] of that fund or otherwise[13]; but it is not to be exercised so as to affect prejudicially any specific devise or bequest[14]; and it does not prejudice any other power of appropriation conferred by law[15] or by the will[16], if any, of the deceased[17]. It takes effect with any extended powers conferred by that will, if any[18].

1 As to the meaning of 'personal representative' see PARA 608.
2 As to the meaning of 'intestate' see PARA 1135 note 1.
3 See the Administration of Estates Act 1925 s 41(1), (9). As to the power of the surviving spouse or civil partner of an intestate to require the intestate's personal representative to appropriate a dwelling house comprised in the estate towards his or her interest under the intestacy see PARA 489. See also *Re Phelps, Well v Phelps* [1980] Ch 275, [1979] 3 All ER 373.
4 See PARAS 1154–1155.
5 As to the meaning of 'real estate' see PARA 607 note 1.
6 As to the meaning of 'property' see PARA 608 note 4.
7 See PARA 1155 note 2. As to settled property see SETTLEMENTS. The personal representative can appropriate in his own favour as beneficiary but such an appropriation would be invalid if made without the consent of the beneficiaries or the sanction of the court. The self-dealing rule that a disposition of trust property to a trustee was automatically voidable at the suit of a beneficiary also applies to personal representatives, who are not exempted from that rule by the Administration of Estates Act 1925 s 41: *Kane v Radley-Kane* [1999] Ch 274, [1998] 3 All ER 753. See also *Re Thompson's Settlement* [1986] Ch 99, [1985] 2 All ER 720. Cf *Re Richardson, Morgan v Richardson* [1896] 1 Ch 512. As to the self-dealing rule see TRUSTS AND POWERS vol 98 (2013) PARA 378.
8 As to the valuation of the deceased's property see PARA 1157.
9 Administration of Estates Act 1925 s 41(1). The personal representative must have regard to the rights of any person who may afterwards come into existence or who cannot be found or ascertained at the time of appropriation and of any other person whose consent is not required under the provisions as to consents (as to which see PARAS 1154–1155): s 41(5). However, nothing in s 41 prevents the personal representative from giving effect to the statutory right of the surviving spouse of an intestate as to the appropriation of the matrimonial home: see PARA 489.
10 See PARA 954.
11 Administration of Estates Act 1925 s 41(9). As to entailed interests see REAL PROPERTY AND REGISTRATION vol 87 (2012) PARA 112 et seq.
12 As to the meaning of 'income' see PARA 1138 note 1.
13 Administration of Estates Act 1925 s 41(9).
14 Administration of Estates Act 1925 s 41(1) proviso (i).
15 See PARA 1158.

16 As to the meaning of 'will' see PARA 607 note 1.

17 Administration of Estates Act 1925 s 41(6) (amended by the Trusts of Land and Appointment of Trustees Act 1996 s 25(1), Sch 3 para 6(1), (3)).

18 Administration of Estates Act 1925 s 41(6) (as amended: see note 17).

1154. Consents required for statutory appropriation: absolute interests. Save as otherwise provided by the will[1] of the deceased[2], the exercise of the statutory power of appropriation requires certain consents[3].

If the appropriation is for the benefit of a person of full age and capacity absolutely and beneficially entitled in possession[4], the consent of that person is necessary[5].

If the person whose consent is so required is a minor[6] or lacks capacity[7] to give consent, the consent must be given on his behalf by his parents or parent, testamentary or other guardian or a person appointed as deputy for him by the Court of Protection[8], or if, in the case of a minor, there is no such parent or guardian, by the court on the application of his litigation friend[9].

If no deputy is appointed for a person who lacks capacity to consent, then, if the appropriation is of an investment authorised by law or by the will, if any, of the deceased for the investment of money subject to the trust, no consent is required on behalf of such person[10].

1 As to the meaning of 'will' see PARA 607 note 1.

2 See the Administration of Estates Act 1925 s 41(6); and PARA 1153.

3 See the Administration of Estates Act 1925 s 41(1) proviso (ii) (as amended: see note 9).

4 As to the meaning of 'possession' see PARA 1022 note 8.

5 Administration of Estates Act 1925 s 41(1) proviso (ii)(a).

6 From 1 January 1997, where a person purports to convey a legal estate in land to a minor or minors alone, the conveyance is not effective to pass the legal estate but operates as a declaration that the land is held in trust for the minor or minors (or if he purports to convey it to the minor or minors in trust for any persons, for those persons): see the Trusts of Land and Appointment of Trustees Act 1996 s 2(6), Sch 1 para 1(1); and SETTLEMENTS vol 91 (2012) PARA 578. Prior to 1 January 1997, where a minor became beneficially entitled in possession to land for an estate in fee simple or for a term of years absolute, his interest was deemed to be comprised in a settlement: see the Settled Land Act 1925 s 1(1)(ii)(d); and SETTLEMENTS vol 91 (2012) PARA 578.

7 Ie within the meaning of the Mental Capacity Act 2005 (see MENTAL HEALTH AND CAPACITY vol 75 (2013) PARA 601).

8 As to the Court of Protection see MENTAL HEALTH AND CAPACITY vol 75 (2013) PARA 720 et seq.

9 Administration of Estates Act 1925 s 41(1) proviso (ii) (amended by the Mental Health Act 1959 s 149(1), Sch 7 Pt I; and the Mental Capacity Act 2005 s 67(1), Sch 6 para 5(1), (2)(a)(i)). As to the appointment of a litigation friend see CPR Pt 21; and CIVIL PROCEDURE vol 11 (2015) PARA 475.

10 Administration of Estates Act 1925 s 41(1) proviso (iv) (amended by the Mental Health Act 1959 Sch 7 Pt I; and the Mental Capacity Act 2005 s 67(1), Sch 6 para 5(1), (2)(b)).

1155. Consents required for statutory appropriation: settled legacies. An appropriation of property[1] made in respect of a settled legacy, share or interest[2] requires the consent of either the trustee, if any (not being also the personal representative), or of the person who may for the time being be entitled to the income[3].

If the person entitled to the income is a minor or a person who lacks capacity[4] to give consent, an appropriation for his benefit requires the consent of his parent or parents, testamentary or other guardian or a person appointed as deputy for him by the Court of Protection[5].

If, independently of the personal representative[6], there is no trustee of a settled legacy, share or interest, and no person of full age and capacity entitled to its income[7], no consent is required to the appropriation, provided the appropriation is of an investment authorised by law or by the will, if any, of the deceased for the investment of money subject to the trust[8].

No consent, save that of a trustee, if any, of a settled legacy, share or interest, is required on behalf of a person who may come into existence after the time of appropriation, or who cannot be found or ascertained at that time[9].

1 As to the meaning of 'property' see PARA 608 note 4.
2 'Settled legacy, share or interest' includes any legacy, share or interest to which a person is not absolutely entitled in possession at the date of the appropriation, and includes an annuity: Administration of Estates Act 1925 s 41(8). As to the meaning of 'possession' for these purposes see PARA 1022 note 8. As to settlements see generally SETTLEMENTS.
3 Administration of Estates Act 1925 s 41(1) proviso (ii)(b). As to the meaning of 'income' see PARA 1138 note 1.
4 Ie within the meaning of the Mental Capacity Act 2005 (see MENTAL HEALTH AND CAPACITY vol 75 (2013) PARA 601).
5 Administration of Estates Act 1925 s 41(1) proviso (ii) (amended by the Mental Health Act 1959 s 149(1), Sch 7 Pt I; and the Mental Capacity Act 2005 s 67(1) Sch 6 para 5(1), (2)(a)(i)). If no deputy has been appointed for a person who lacks capacity to consent, then, if the appropriation is of an investment authorised by law or by the will, if any, of the deceased for the investment of money subject to the trust, no consent is required on behalf of such a person: Administration of Estates Act 1925 s 41(1)(iv) (amended by the Mental Health Act 1959 Sch 7 Pt I and the Mental Capacity Act 2005 s 67(1) Sch 6 para 5(1), (2)(b)). The County Court has jurisdiction under the Administration of Estates Act 1925 s 41(1) proviso (ii) where the estate in respect of which the application is made does not exceed in amount or value the County Court limit: s 41(1A) (added by the County Courts Act 1984 s 148(1), Sch 2 Pt III para 13). As to the County Court limit see PARA 866 note 2.
6 As to the meaning of 'personal representative' see PARA 608.
7 As to the meaning of 'income' see PARA 1138 note 1.
8 Administration of Estates Act 1925 s 41(1) proviso (v).
9 Administration of Estates Act 1925 s 41(1) proviso (iii).

1156. Effect of appropriation under statutory power. Any property[1] duly appropriated under the statutory power of appropriation is from then on to be treated as an authorised investment and may be retained or dealt with accordingly[2].

The appropriation binds all persons interested in the property of the deceased whose consent is not requisite to the appropriation[3].

Where an appropriation is made in respect of a settled legacy, share or interest[4], the property appropriated remains subject to all trusts and powers of leasing, disposition and management or varying investments which would have been applicable to it or to the legacy, share or interest in respect of which the appropriation is made, if no such appropriation had been made[5].

If after any real estate has been appropriated in purported exercise of the foregoing statutory powers[6] the person to whom it was conveyed disposes of it or any interest in it, then, in favour of a purchaser[7], the appropriation is deemed to have been made in accordance with the statutory power and after all requisite consents, if any, had been given[8].

The personal representative[9] may give effect to an appropriation by any conveyance[10] including an assent[11].

1 As to the meaning of 'property' see PARA 608 note 4.
2 Administration of Estates Act 1925 s 41(2). As to authorised investments for trust funds see TRUSTS AND POWERS vol 98 (2013) PARA 1 et seq.
3 Administration of Estates Act 1925 s 41(4). As to the consents required see PARAS 1154–1155.
4 As to the meaning of 'settled legacy, share or interest' see PARA 1155 note 2.
5 Administration of Estates Act 1925 s 41(6) (amended by the Trusts of Land and Appointment of Trustees Act 1996 s 25(1), Sch 3 para 6(1), (3)).
6 Ie the powers conferred by the Administration of Estates Act 1925 s 41 (see PARAS 1153–1155): see s 41(7).

7 As to the meaning of 'purchaser' for these purposes see PARA 858 note 4.
8 Administration of Estates Act 1925 s 41(7).
9 As to the meaning of 'personal representative' see PARA 608.
10 As to the meaning of 'conveyance' see PARA 858 note 1.
11 Administration of Estates Act 1925 s 41(3). As to stamp duties on an assent giving effect to an appropriation see PARA 1151.

1157. Valuation for purposes of statutory appropriation. For the purposes of the statutory power of appropriation the personal representative[1] may ascertain and fix the value of the respective parts of the deceased's real and personal estate[2] and liabilities as he may think fit, and must employ a duly qualified valuer when necessary[3]. The value of assets appropriated should be the value as at the date of appropriation and not as at the date of death[4].

1 As to the meaning of 'personal representative' see PARA 608.
2 As to the meaning of 'real estate' see PARA 607 note 1.
3 Administration of Estates Act 1925 s 41(3). In *Re Brookes, Brookes v Taylor* [1914] 1 Ch 558 an appropriation of property by a trustee without ascertaining the value of the property at the time of appropriation was held to be a breach of trust. As to stamp duty see PARA 1151. As to valuers see BUILDING CONTRACTS vol 6 (2011) PARA 489 et seq.
4 *Re Charteris, Charteris v Biddulph* [1917] 2 Ch 379 at 386, CA; *Robinson v Collins* [1975] 1 All ER 321, sub nom *Re Collins, Robinson v Collins* [1975] 1 WLR 309. See also PARA 489.

(ii) Common Law Powers

1158. Vested legacies. Apart from statute[1], an appropriation in the strict sense of the word by a personal representative of a specific portion of the assets to answer a vested absolute legacy may, in the absence of a power of appropriation contained in the will, only be made with the consent of a legatee who is sui juris[2]. Where a share of residue is immediately payable the personal representative may enter into an arrangement with the legatee to take over a particular asset in satisfaction of his legacy either in whole or pro tanto without obtaining the consent of the other residuary legatees; and if the transaction is a fair one, and the legatee does not receive more than his share of the assets, the appropriation is unimpeachable[3]. A sole personal representative can appropriate in his own favour as beneficiary but such an appropriation would be invalid if made without the consent of the other beneficiaries or the sanction of the court[4].

Where a legacy is presently vested, but payable in future, the legatee has an absolute right to require the amount of the legacy to be invested by the personal representative; where that is done it amounts to an appropriation in the strict sense of the word[5]. Where there has been a partial distribution of specific assets by way of appropriation this is regarded as equivalent to a distribution of cash of the same value as those assets at the date of distribution[6].

1 For the statutory powers of appropriation see PARA 1153 et seq.
2 *Re Salaman, De Pass v Sonnenthal* [1907] 2 Ch 46; *Re Salomons, Public Trustee v Wortley* [1920] 1 Ch 290. As to vested absolute legacies see PARA 375 et seq.
3 *Re Lepine, Dowsett v Culver* [1892] 1 Ch 210, CA.
4 *Kane v Radley-Kane* [1999] Ch 274, [1998] 3 All ER 753; *Re Bythway, Gough v Dames* (1911) 80 LJ Ch 246 (a sole executor who is one of the beneficiaries cannot appropriate at his own price in satisfaction of a legacy bequeathed to him shares or securities which have no ascertained market value); cf *Re Richardson, Morgan v Richardson* [1896] 1 Ch 512.
5 *Re Hall, Foster v Metcalfe* [1903] 2 Ch 226 at 231, CA. See also *Phipps v Annesley* (1740) 2 Atk 57 at 58; *Johnson v Mills* (1749) 1 Ves Sen 282.
6 *Re Richardson, Morgan v Richardson* [1896] 1 Ch 512 at 516; *Re Gollin's Declaration of Trust, Turner v Williams* [1969] 3 All ER 1591, [1969] 1 WLR 1858.

1159. Contingent legacies. Where a legacy is contingent[1], and by the will part of the income arising from the legacy is to go to the legatee before the happening of the contingency, it may be properly inferred that the testator intended a fund to be set apart and invested to answer the legacy. The personal representative has, in such a case, power to set apart and invest a sum of money to carry out his testator's intentions[2]. Where, however, no interest is directed to be paid on it in the meantime, the executor has no power to appropriate a fund to satisfy the legacy[3] in the absence of a direction in the will to appropriate and set aside a fund[4], nor can the legatee require such an appropriation to be made[5]. The personal representative may, however, set aside a sum amply sufficient to answer the legacy, invest it, and then proceed to distribute the residue without rendering himself personally liable to make good the loss if it should subsequently turn out that the sum so retained was not sufficient to answer the legacy[6].

1 As to contingent legacies after 1925 see PARA 1083. See also TRUSTS AND POWERS vol 98 (2013) PARA 174.
2 *Re Hall, Foster v Metcalfe* [1903] 2 Ch 226 at 233, CA. See also *Green v Pigot* (1781) 1 Bro CC 103.
3 *Re Hall, Foster v Metcalfe* [1903] 2 Ch 226 at 233, CA. See also *Green v Pigot* (1781) 1 Bro CC 103.
4 See *Re Oswald, Oswald v Oswald* (1919) 64 Sol Jo 242.
5 *Re Hall, Foster v Metcalfe* [1903] 2 Ch 226 at 235, CA. See also *Webber v Webber* (1823) 1 Sim & St 311; *King v Malcott* (1852) 9 Hare 692 at 696.
6 *Re Hall, Foster v Metcalfe* [1903] 2 Ch 226 at 233, CA. In *Re Rivers, Pullen v Rivers* [1920] 1 Ch 320 a sum invested and set aside by order of the court to provide for an annuity proved insufficient to pay a legacy payable on the death of the annuitant. The residuary legatees, who had obtained payment of various sums under court orders of which the pecuniary legatee had not had notice, were held liable to make good the deficiency in the sum available for the pecuniary legatee.

1160. Settled legacies. Personal representatives who are also trustees of settled shares of residue may appropriate specific assets, provided they are investments of an authorised nature, to the settled shares[1]. They may appropriate to one share without making a corresponding appropriation to the other shares[2]. A power in a will to retain property forming part of the deceased's estate unconverted throughout the trust is equivalent to a power to invest in that class of property, and constitutes that class of property an authorised investment for the purpose of appropriation to a settled share[3]. In the case of a trust created by the will of a person dying before 1 January 1997 a mere power to postpone conversion[4] following a trust for sale[5] does not have that effect[6].

1 *Re Waters, Preston v Waters* [1889] WN 39; *Re Richardson, Morgan v Richardson* [1896] 1 Ch 512. As to settlements see generally SETTLEMENTS.
2 *Re Nickels, Nickels v Nickels* [1898] 1 Ch 630.
3 *Fraser v Murdock* (1881) 6 App Cas 855, HL (stocks and shares); *Re Brooks, Coles v Davis* (1897) 76 LT 771 (shares); *Re Cooke's Settlement, Tarry v Cooke* [1913] 2 Ch 661 (leaseholds)'; *Re Wragg, Wragg v Palmer* [1919] 2 Ch 58 (freeholds).
4 The doctrine of conversion has been largely abolished (see the Trusts of Land and Appointment of Trustees Act 1996 s 3(1); and PARA 918) except in the case of a trust created by the will of a person dying before 1 January 1997: see s 3(2); and PARA 288. In respect of a trust created or arising before or after that date, where land is held by trustees subject to a trust for sale, the land is no longer regarded as personal property; and where personal property is subject to a trust for sale in order that the trustees may acquire land, the personal property is not regarded as land: s 3(1). See also REAL PROPERTY AND REGISTRATION vol 87 (2012) PARA 7.
5 In the case of every trust for sale of land created by a disposition, whenever the trust is created or arises, there is to be implied, despite any provision to the contrary made by the disposition, a power for the trustees to postpone sale of the land: see the Trusts of Land and Appointment of Trustees Act 1996 s 4(1), (2).
6 *Re Craven, Watson v Craven* [1914] 1 Ch 358; *Re Beverly, Watson v Watson* [1901] 1 Ch 681 at 688.

1161. Extent and effect of power. The power of appropriation extends to pure personalty of whatever nature[1], to chattels real[2] and appears to have applied, in the case of a trust created by the will of a person dying before 1 January 1997 to real estate where there is a trust for sale[3] and conversion[4].

Where an appropriation in the strict sense of the word has been made, all profit or loss, as the case may be, in respect of the appropriated fund goes to or falls upon the legatee[5]. A simple appropriation without payment of equality money will not attract any stamp duties[6].

1 See *Elliott v Kemp* (1840) 7 M & W 306 at 313 (furniture); *Barclay v Owen* (1889) 60 LT 220; *Re Lepine, Dowsett v Culver* [1892] 1 Ch 210, CA (mortgage debt); *Re Richardson, Morgan v Richardson* [1896] 1 Ch 512; *Re Brooks, Coles v Davis* (1897) 76 LT 771 (shares in a brewery company); *Re Nickels, Nickels v Nickels* [1898] 1 Ch 630 (stock); *Re Waters, Preston v Waters* [1889] WN 39 (mortgages and other securities).

2 *Re Beverly, Watson v Watson* [1901] 1 Ch 681.

3 See PARA 1160 note 5.

4 *Re Beverly, Watson v Watson* [1901] 1 Ch 681 at 686. As to the abolition of conversion see PARAS 918, 1162 note 4.

5 *Burgess v Robinson* (1817) 3 Mer 7 at 9; *Rock v Hardman* (1819) 4 Madd 253; *Kimberley v Tew* (1843) 4 Dr & War 139, 149; *Re Hall, Foster v Metcalfe* [1903] 2 Ch 226, CA.

6 As to stamp duties on assents giving effect to appropriations see PARA 1151.

14. THE ROLE OF THE COURT

(1) ADMINISTRATION AND OTHER REMEDIES

1162. Jurisdiction of court in relation to administration of estates and execution of trusts. In the administration of estates and the execution of trusts (including the distribution of fully administered estates)[1] the Chancery Division of the High Court[2] exercises a supervisory jurisdiction. Applications can be made to the Chancery Division for:

(1) the court to determine any question arising in the administration of the estate of a deceased person, or the execution of a trust[3]; or

(2) an order for the administration of the estate of a deceased person, or the execution of a trust, to be carried out under the direction of the court (an 'administration order')[4].

The court will only make an administration order if it considers that the issues between the parties cannot properly be resolved in any other way[5].

The County Court has concurrent jurisdiction with the High Court where the estate sought to be administered does not exceed in amount or value the County Court limit[6]. Where the value exceeds that sum jurisdiction may be conferred on the County Court by agreement in writing[7]. Subject to any provision requiring proceedings to be in the County Court, the High Court may, on the application of any party or on the court's own motion[8], order the transfer of any proceedings before it to the County Court[9].

1 As to the distinction between administration and distribution see PARA 1107. As to the distinction between executorship and trusteeship see PARA 1148.

2 As to the statutory assignment of these jurisdictions to the Chancery Division see the Senior Courts Act 1981 s 61, Sch 1para1(c), (d); and COURTS AND TRIBUNALS vol 24 (2010) PARA 704.

3 CPR 64.2(a). See note 4.

4 CPR 64.2(b). As to applications to court for an administration order see PARA 1166. As to the determination of questions without administration see PARA 1169.

Appeal lies from the High Court to the Court of Appeal in accordance with the rules generally applicable to such appeals: see CIVIL PROCEDURE vol 12A (2015) PARA 1557.

5 CPR PD 64A—*Estates, Trusts and Charities* para 3.1. See also PARAS 1168–1169.

6 See the County Courts Act 1984 s 23(a); and COURTS AND TRIBUNALS vol 24 (2010) PARA 776. As to the County Court limit see PARA 866 note 2.

7 See the County Courts Act 1984 s 24; and COURTS AND TRIBUNALS vol 24 (2010) PARA 776.

8 See the County Courts Act 1984 s 40(3); and CIVIL PROCEDURE vol 11 (2015) PARA 108.

9 See the County Courts Act 1984 s 40(1), (2); CPR 30.2; and CIVIL PROCEDURE vol 11 (2015) PARA 108. Proceedings transferred under the County Courts Act 1984 s 40 are to be transferred to the County Court as the High Court considers appropriate, having taken into account the convenience of the parties and that of any other persons likely to be affected and the state of business in the courts concerned: County Courts Act 1984 s 40(4) (substituted by the Courts and Legal Services Act 1990 s 2(1); and amended by the Crime and Courts Act 2013 Sch 9 para 10); and CIVIL PROCEDURE vol 11 (2015) PARA 108. As to the matters to which the court is to have regard see CPR 30.3; and PARA 867. See also *Chancery Guide* (2016) para 14.15 et seq.

1163. Power of the High Court to substitute or remove personal representatives. Where an application relating to the estate of a deceased person is made to the High Court[1] by or on behalf of a personal representative of the deceased or a beneficiary[2] of the estate, the court may in its discretion[3]:

(1) appoint a person (a 'substituted personal representative') to act as personal representative of the deceased in place of the existing personal representative or representatives or any of them[4]; or

(2) if there are two or more existing personal representatives of the deceased, terminate the appointment of one or more, but not all, of those persons[5].

Where the court appoints a person to act as a substituted personal representative of a deceased person[6], then if that person is appointed to act with an executor or executors, the appointment constitutes him executor as from the date of the appointment, except for the purpose of including him in any chain of representation[7]; and, in any other case, the appointment constitutes that person administrator as from the date of appointment[8].

When exercising its discretion the court is governed by the same principles that govern the removal of trustees[9]. The overriding considerations are whether the trusts are being properly executed and the welfare of the beneficiaries[10].

Just as time does not run against a beneficiary in an administration action, it does not run against a beneficiary who is merely seeking the removal of a personal representative[11].

The court may authorise a person appointed as a substituted personal representative to charge remuneration for his services, on such terms as the court thinks fit, whether or not involving the submission of bills of costs for detailed assessment by the court[12].

1 Ie under the Administration of Justice Act 1985 s 50(1). For revocation of a grant of probate or administration for the purpose of better administration of the estate see PARA 850. Claims must be brought in the High Court and are assigned to the Chancery Division: CPR 57.13(2). Every personal representative of the estate must be made a party: CPR 57.13(3). As to the meaning of 'personal representative' see PARA 608.

2 For these purposes, 'beneficiary', in relation to the estate of a deceased person, means a person who is beneficially interested in the estate under the will of the deceased person or under the law relating to intestacy: Administration of Justice Act 1985 s 50(5). A person who claims under the doctrine of mutual wills is not a person beneficially interested in the estate under the will of the deceased and so is not entitled to make an application under s 50(1); such a person is a beneficiary of a trust which arises as a result of the agreement between two testators not to revoke their wills unilaterally. However, as the beneficiary of a trust it is possible to make an application under the Judicial Trustees Act 1896 s 1 for the removal of a trustee: *Thomas and Agnes Carvel Foundation v Carvel* [2007] EWHC 1314 (Ch), [2008] Ch 395, [2007] 4 All ER 81. As to judicial trustees see TRUSTS AND POWERS vol 98 (2013) PARA 197 et seq. As to mutual wills see PARA 10.

3 Administration of Justice Act 1985 s 50(1). Friction or hostility is not of itself a reason for removal, although it should not be disregarded: *Letterstedt v Broers* (1884) 9 App Cas 371; applied in *Kershaw v Micklethwaite* [2010] EWHC 506 (Ch).

4 Administration of Justice Act 1985 s 50(1)(a).

5 Administration of Justice Act 1985 s 50(1)(b). Where an application relating to the estate of a deceased person is made under s 50(1), the court may, if it thinks fit, proceed as if the application were, or included, an application for the appointment of a judicial trustee in relation to that estate under the Judicial Trustees Act 1896: Administration of Justice Act 1985 s 50(4); and see note 2. The Administration of Justice Act 1985 s 50 is applicable in a case of a person named as an executor but who has not been granted probate: see *Goodman v Goodman* [2013] All ER (D) 118 (Jan).

As to the procedure governing an application under the Administration of Justice Act 1985 s 50 see CPR 57.13; CPR PD 57—*Probate* paras 12–14. If substitution or removal of a personal representative is sought by application in existing proceedings, CPR 57.13 applies with references to claims being read as if they referred to applications: CPR 57.13(5).

6 Administration of Justice Act 1985 s 50(2).

7 Administration of Justice Act 1985 s 50(2)(a). As to the chain of representation see PARA 637 et seq.

8 Administration of Justice Act 1985 s 50(2)(b).

9 See *Thomas and Agnes Carvel Foundation v Carvel* [2007] EWHC 1314 (Ch), [2008] Ch 395, [2007] 4 All ER 81.

10 *Letterstedt v Broers* (1884) 9 App Cas 371 (friction or hostility between trustees and beneficiaries is not of itself a reason for the removal of the trustees, but where the hostility is grounded on the mode in which the trust has been administered, it is not to be disregarded). See *Thomas and Agnes Carvel Foundation v Carvel* [2007] EWHC 1314 (Ch), [2008] Ch 395, [2007] 4 All ER 81; *Re Loftus, Green v Gaul* [2006] EWCA Civ 1124, [2006] 4 All ER 1110, [2007] 1 WLR 591; *Heyman v Dobson* [2007] EWHC 3503 (Ch), [2007] All ER (D) 275 (Dec); *Alkin v Raymond* [2010] All ER (D) 48 (May); *Brudenell-Bruce v Moore* [2014] EWHC 3679 (Ch), [2014] All ER

(D) 113 (Nov). The power to remove and replace personal representatives is not limited to cases of misconduct: see *Angus v Emmott* [2010] EWHC 154 (Ch), [2010] All ER (D) 70 (Feb) (application to remove executors based on their hostile relationship). As to guidance on what the court would view as serious enough to justify the removal of personal representatives under the Administration of Justice Act 1985 s 50 see Harris *v Earwicker* [2015] EWHC 1915 (Ch). See *also National Westminster Bank plc v Lucas; Re Estate of Jimmy Savile* [2014] EWHC 653 (Ch), [2014] BPIR 551, [2014] All ER (D) 92 (Mar); and PARA 982.

11 *Re Loftus, Green v Gaul* [2006] EWCA Civ 1124 at [29], [2006] 4 All ER 1110 at [29], [2007] 1 WLR 591 at [29] per Chadwick LJ. The primary remedy of a beneficiary who complains of an unjustified delay in the administration of an estate is an administration action. The power to appoint a judicial trustee under Judicial Trustees Act 1896 and the later power conferred by Administration of Justice Act 1985 s 50(1) were introduced to offer a remedy where the administration of the estate had broken down and it was not desired to put the estate to the cost of a full administration.

12 Administration of Justice Act 1985 s 50(3). Section 50(3) refers to 'taxation by the court'; this is now termed 'assessment' under the CPR: see CIVIL PROCEDURE vol 12A (2015) PARA 1749 et seq.

1164. Power of the Public Trustee to administer solvent small estates. Provision is made for the administration of solvent small estates to be undertaken by the Public Trustee in place of the existing executor or administrator[1]. Any person who in the opinion of the Public Trustee would be entitled to apply to the court[2] for an order for the administration by the court of an estate, the gross capital value of which is proved to the satisfaction of the Public Trustee to be less than £1,000[3], may apply to the Public Trustee to administer the estate, and, where any such application is made and it appears to the Public Trustee that the persons beneficially entitled are persons of small means, the Public Trustee must administer the estate, unless he sees good reason for refusing to do so[4].

1 See the Public Trustee Act 1906 s 2(1)(a), (4); and TRUSTS AND POWERS vol 98 (2013) PARA 207. As to grants of administration to the Public Trustee see PARA 784. As to the Public Trustee's fees see PARA 656. As to the Public Trustee generally see TRUSTS AND POWERS vol 98 (2013) PARA 206 et seq.

2 As to where proceedings have already been commenced see PARA 1165.

3 The limit has been £1,000 since 1906. As a result of inflation this provision has ceased to have any practical utility. The Public Trustee may not accept the administration of any estate which he knows or believes to be insolvent: see the Public Trustee Act 1906 s 2(4); *Re Devereux, Toovey v Public Trustee* [1911] 2 Ch 545 at 549 per Eve J; and TRUSTS AND POWERS vol 98 (2013) PARA 207. An estate which had been reduced by partial distribution from £1,200 to £500 at the date of the application was held to be a small estate: *Re Devereux, Toovey v Public Trustee.*

4 Public Trustee Act 1906 s 3(1). See also TRUSTS AND POWERS vol 98 (2013) PARA 212. Government policy is that the Public Trustee should be a trustee of last resort. There are circumstances where the role of trustee can adequately be carried out by individuals in the private sector. As to the effect of the Public Trustee undertaking administration see TRUSTS AND POWERS vol 98 (2013) PARA 212. As to where a legal representative has not already been constituted see PARA 1165 note 2.

1165. Administration by the Public Trustee. Where proceedings have been instituted in any court for the administration of an estate, and by reason of its small value the court considers that the estate can be more economically administered by the Public Trustee or that for any other reason it is expedient that it should be administered by the Public Trustee instead of by the court[1], the court may order that it be administered by him in like manner, subject to any special directions by the court, as if the administration of the estate had been undertaken by him upon an application to him for the purpose[2].

1 As to applications to the Public Trustee to administer the estate see PARA 1164.

2 Public Trustee Act 1906 s 3(5). See also TRUSTS AND POWERS vol 98 (2013) PARA 215. It seems that neither s 3(1) (see PARA 1162) nor s 3(5) can apply unless a legal personal representative has already been constituted, for this condition must be fulfilled before any proceedings can be instituted for the administration of an estate by the court: see *Dowdeswell v Dowdeswell* (1878) 9 ChD 294, CA; *Rowsell v Morris* (1873) LR 17 Eq 20. As to grants of administration to the Public

Trustee see PARA 784. For the power of a personal representative who has obtained a grant to transfer the administration of the estate to the Public Trustee see the Public Trustee Act 1906 s 6(2) (see TRUSTS AND POWERS vol 98 (2013) PARA 57. As to the right to apply to the Public Trustee for an audit of a trust or estate see TRUSTS AND POWERS vol 98 (2013) PARA 217 et seq.

1166. Applications to court for an administration order. Application can be made to the court to determine any question arising in the administration of an estate or for an order that the administration of the estate be carried out under the direction of the court[1]. The court will only make an administration order if it considers that the issues between the parties cannot properly be resolved in any other way[2].

Claims must be made using the alternative procedure[3] and all personal representatives[4] must be made parties[5]. In any claim the court has jurisdiction to appoint a receiver[6].

1 See CPR 64.2(a), (b); and PARAS 1162, 1169.

2 CPR PD 64A—*Estates, Trusts and Charities* para 3.1. If, in a claim for an administration order, the claimant alleges that the personal representatives have not provided proper accounts, the court may: (1) stay the proceedings for a specified period, and order them to file and serve proper accounts within that period; or (2) if necessary to prevent proceedings by other creditors or persons claiming to be entitled to the estate, make an administration order and include in it an order that no such proceedings are to be taken without the court's permission: CPR PD 64A para 3.2. Where a claim is made against the estate by any person who is not a party to the proceedings no party other than the personal representatives may take part in any proceedings relating to the claim without the permission of the court and the court may impose on that party such terms as to costs or otherwise as it thinks fit: CPR PD 64A para 3.3. See *Aeroflot v Berezovsky* [2013] EWHC 4348 (Ch), [2014] All ER (D) 166 (Jan) (order relating to disclosure and inspection of documents refused on ground of cost).

3 Ie under CPR Pt 8 (see CIVIL PROCEDURE vol 11 (2015) PARA 150 et seq): CPR 64.3. For the procedural rules relating to the conduct of claims generally see further CIVIL PROCEDURE vol 11 (2015) PARA 150 et seq.

4 All references within CPR Pt 64 and its Practice Directions to trustees include executors and administrators: CPR 64.1(2). As to the meaning of 'personal representative' see PARA 608.

5 CPR 64.4(1)(a). Any personal representative who does not consent to being a claimant must be made a defendant: CPR 64.4(1)(b). The claimant may make parties to the claim any persons with an interest in or claim against the estate who it is appropriate to make parties having regard to the nature of the order sought: CPR 64.4(1)(c).

6 See CPR 69.2; and CIVIL PROCEDURE vol 11 (2015) PARA 196.

1167. Service of documents out of jurisdiction. The claimant may serve a claim form out of the jurisdiction with the permission of the court[1] where a claim is made for any remedy which might be obtained in proceedings for the administration of the estate of a person who died domiciled within the jurisdiction[2].

The court will not give permission unless satisfied that England and Wales are the proper place in which to bring the claim[3]. In particular, where the application is for permission to serve a claim form in Scotland or Northern Ireland and it appears to the court that the claimant may also be entitled to a remedy in Scotland or Northern Ireland, the court, in deciding whether to give permission, will compare the cost and convenience of proceeding there or in the jurisdiction; and, where relevant have regard to the powers and jurisdiction of the Sheriff court in Scotland or the county courts or courts of summary jurisdiction in Northern Ireland[4].

1 Ie under CPR 6.36: see CIVIL PROCEDURE vol 11 (2015) PARA 267.

2 CPR PD 6B—*Service Out of the Jurisdiction* para 3.1(13). For documents to be filed see CPR PD 6Bpara4.1; and CIVIL PROCEDURE vol 11 (2015) PARA 267. As to domicile generally see CONFLICT OF LAWS vol 19 (2011) PARA 336 et seq.

3 CPR 6.37(3).
4 CPR 6.37(4).

(2) DETERMINATION OF QUESTIONS

1168. Personal representatives' right to the court's guidance. Where questions of difficulty arise in the administration or distribution of an estate, the personal representatives[1], like trustees, are entitled to have those questions determined by the court[2] unless all the persons concerned, being of full legal capacity and between them absolutely entitled, determine the matter by agreement. The costs of such an application to the court are normally payable out of the estate[3]. The court's jurisdiction to determine such questions cannot be excluded by the terms of the will or otherwise[4].

The Civil Procedure Rules provide that a claim may be issued for the determination of any question arising in the administration of a deceased person[5].

1 As to the meaning of 'personal representative' see PARA 608.
2 In giving directions on a personal representative's or trustee's application the court is engaged solely in determining what should be done in the best interests of the estate and not in determining the rights of the parties: *Marley v Mutual Security Merchant Bank and Trust Co Ltd* [1991] 3 All ER 198, PC. Where an application to the court involves the surrender of a discretion to the court by personal representatives or trustees the court may adjourn the question for an inquiry: see *Re Somech, Westminster Bank Ltd v Phillips* [1957] Ch 165, [1956] 3 All ER 523. As to the procedure in the County Court see the County Courts Act 1984 s 76; CPR Sch 2 CCR Ord 1 r 6; and COURTS AND TRIBUNALS vol 24 (2010) PARA 859.
3 As to costs see PARA 1196 et seq.
4 See *Re Wynn's Will Trusts, Public Trustee v Newborough* [1952] Ch 271, [1952] 1 All ER 341; and PARA 137.
5 See CPR 64.2(a); and PARA 1169.

1169. Determination of questions without administration. Personal representatives may ask the court to determine any question arising in the administration of an estate[1]. The claim must be made using the alternative procedure[2]. The following are examples of the types of claim which may be made:

(1) a claim for the determination of any of the following questions:
  (a) any question as to who is included in any class of persons having a claim against the estate of a deceased person or a beneficial interest in the estate of such a person[3];
  (b) any question as to the rights or interests of any person claiming to be a creditor of the estate of a deceased person or entitled under a will or on the intestacy of a deceased person[4];
(2) a claim for any of the following remedies:
  (a) an order requiring a trustee (including an executor or administrator)[5] to provide and, if necessary, verify accounts, to pay into court money which he holds in that capacity or to do or not to do any particular act[6];
  (b) an order approving any sale, purchase, compromise or other transaction by a trustee[7]; or
  (c) an order directing any act to be done which the court could order to be done if the estate in question were being administered under the direction of the court[8].

Personal representatives may request the court to determine a claim for approval of a sale, purchase, compromise or other transaction under head (2)(b) without a hearing[9]. The court will always consider whether it is possible to deal with the application on paper without a hearing[10].

Where an order is made for the sale of any property vested in trustees, those persons have the conduct of the sale unless the court directs otherwise[11].

1 CPR 64.2(a); and see PARA 1162. As to the meaning of 'personal representative' see PARA 608.
2 Ie under CPR Pt 8 (see CIVIL PROCEDURE vol 11 (2015) PARA 150 et seq): see CPR 64.3.
3 See CPR PD 64A—*Estates, Trusts and Charities* para 1(1)(a).
4 See CPR PD 64A—*Estates, Trusts and Charities* para 1(1)(b).
5 CPR Pt 64 and its Practice Directions refer to 'trustees'; all references to trustees include executors and administrators: CPR 64.1(2).
6 See CPR PD 64A—*Estates, Trusts and Charities* para 1(2)(a).
7 See CPR PD 64A—*Estates, Trusts and Charities* para 1(2)(b). See note 5.
8 See CPR PD 64A—*Estates, Trusts and Charities* para 1(2)(c).
9 See CPR PD 64A—*Estates, Trusts and Charities* para 1A.1. The procedure is set out inPD 64A para 1A: see TRUSTS AND POWERS vol 98 (2013) PARAS 659–664. If the court considers that an oral hearing is unnecessary, it will consider the claim on the papers. If it considers that an oral hearing is required, it will give appropriate directions. The claim form for these applications may be issued without naming a defendant: see CPR 8.2A; and CIVIL PROCEDURE vol 11 (2015) PARA 153.
10 *Chancery Guide* (2016) para 29.13. Cases in which the directions can be given without a hearing include those where personal representatives apply to be allowed to distribute the estate of a deceased Lloyd's name, following the decision in *Re Yorke, Stone v Chataway* [1997] 4 All ER 907. See PARA 1170.
11 See CPR PD 64A—*Estates, Trusts and Charities* para3.4.

1170. Directions in relation to estates of deceased Lloyd's Names. Personal representatives who wish to apply to the court for permission to distribute the estate of a deceased Lloyd's Name, or trustees who wish to administer any will trusts arising in such an estate, may adopt a special procedure[1], where appropriate[2].

Personal representatives (and, if applicable, trustees) may apply by a claim form issued under the alternative procedure[3] for permission to distribute the estate (and, if applicable, to administer the will trusts) on the footing that no or no further provision need be made for Lloyd's creditors. Ordinarily, the claim form need not name any other party[4].

If the amount of costs has been agreed with the residuary beneficiaries (or, if the costs are not to be taken from residue, with the beneficiaries affected) their signed consent to those costs should also be submitted[5]. If the claimants are inviting the court to make a summary assessment they should submit a statement of costs[6].

The application will be considered in the first instance by the Master who, if satisfied that the order should be made, may make the order without requiring the attendance of the applicants, and the court will send it to them. If not so satisfied, the Master may give directions for the further disposal of the application[7].

1 The procedure concerning the estates of deceased Lloyd's names was introduced as a result of *Re Yorke, Stone v Chataway* [1997] 4 All ER 907, and is governed by *Practice Statement* [2001] 3 All ER 765.
2 The procedure will be appropriate where (1) the only, or only substantial, reason for delaying distribution of the estate is the possibility of personal liability to Lloyd's creditors; and (2) all liabilities of the estate in respect of syndicates of which the Name was a member have for the years 1992 and earlier (if any) been reinsured (whether directly or indirectly) into the Equitas group; and (3) all liabilities of the estate in respect of syndicates of which the Name was a member have for the years 1993 and later (if any) arise in respect of syndicates which have closed by reinsurance in the usual way or are protected by the terms of an Estate Protection Plan issued by Centrewrite Ltd or are protected by the terms of EXEAT insurance cover provided by Centrewrite Ltd: Practice Statement [2001] 3 All ER 765.

As from 30 June 2009 all 1992 and prior year non-life business underwritten at Lloyd's by open and closed year Names together with the benefit of substantial reinsurance was transferred to a company to be called Equitas Insurance Ltd under the insurance business transfer provisions contained in the Financial Services and Markets Act 2000 Pt VII (ss 104–117): see FINANCIAL SERVICES REGULATION vol 50A (2016) PARA 826 et seq. The transfer binds all policyholders as a matter of UK law and will automatically be recognised under the law throughout the European Economic Area ('EEA'). However, the extent to which the Pt VII transfer will be recognised by courts of overseas jurisdictions in the event that a claim is brought against a Name in their jurisdiction after the transfer takes effect is uncertain.

3 Ie under CPR Pt 8: see CIVIL PROCEDURE vol 11 (2015) PARA 150 et seq.

4 It may be issued in this form without a separate application for permission under CPR 8.2A: *Practice Statement* [2001] 3 All ER 765. The claim should be supported by a witness statement or an affidavit substantially in the form set out in Appendix 11 adapted as necessary to the particular circumstances and accompanied by a draft of the desired order substantially in the form also set out in Schedule 1 to the *Practice Statement* [2001] 3 All ER 765.

5 *Practice Statement* [2001] 3 All ER 765.

6 Ie in the form specified in CPR PD 44—*General Rules about Costs*. If in his discretion the Master (or outside London, the District Judge) thinks fit, he will summarily assess the costs but with permission for the paying party to apply within 14 days of service of the order on him to vary or discharge the summary assessment. Subject to the foregoing, the order will provide for a detailed assessment unless subsequently agreed: *Practice Statement* [2001] 3 All ER 765.

7 *Practice Statement* [2001] 3 All ER 765.

(3) PARTIES

1171. Who may institute proceedings. An administration claim may be instituted by either the personal representatives[1] or the creditors or the beneficiaries[2]. Where in a claim brought by the beneficiaries the estate is found to be insolvent, the proceedings will be reconstituted with the creditors as claimants and the personal representatives and beneficiaries as defendants. The beneficiaries will only continue as parties to the claim to enable them to be before the court when the question of costs is determined[3].

1 A personal representative cannot bring an administration claim against a single creditor as sole defendant: *Mandeville v Mandeville* (1888) 23 LR Ir 339, CA; *Re Roe, Roe v Squire* (1911) 45 ILT 144; *Re Bradley, Bradley v Barclays Bank Ltd* [1956] Ch 615, [1956] 3 All ER 113. The proper procedure is for the personal representative to persuade a friendly creditor to make a claim, on behalf of himself and all other creditors (*Mandeville v Mandeville*), or to present a petition for the administration of the estate as an insolvent estate: see the Insolvency Act 1986 s 421; the Administration of Insolvent Estates of Deceased Persons Order 1986, SI 1986/1999; and BANKRUPTCY AND INDIVIDUAL INSOLVENCY vol 5 (2013) PARA 830 et seq. As to the administration of insolvent estates see PARA 981 et seq.

2 As to the administration of small estates by the Public Trustee see PARAS 1164–1165.

3 *Re Van Oppen, Roberts v Gray* [1935] WN 51. Beneficiaries should not normally be made defendants in an administration claim brought by creditors: see PARA 1173.

1172. Parties to applications to court. The general rule in administration claims[1] or claims for the determination of questions without administration[2] is that all the executors or administrators of the estate or trustees of the trust, as the case may be, to which the claim relates, must be parties to the proceedings[3]. Where the proceedings are brought by executors, administrators or trustees, any of them who do not consent to being joined as a claimant must be made a defendant[4]. An executor who has not proved should not be made a party[5] unless he has acted as executor[6] or intermeddled with the assets[7]. A judgment for general administration will not be made in the presence only of an administrator ad litem[8] or of an executor de son tort[9].

The claimant may make parties to the claim any persons with an interest in or claim against the estate, or an interest under the trust, who it is appropriate to make parties having regard to the nature of the order sought[10]. A claim may be brought by or against trustees, executors or administrators in that capacity without adding as parties any persons who have a beneficial interest in the trust or estate[11]. Where an administration order has been made in relation to the estate of a deceased person and a claim is made against the estate by any person who is not a party to the proceedings, no party other than the executors or administrators of the estate may take part in any proceedings relating to the claim without the permission of the court; and the court may direct or permit any other party to take part in the proceedings, on such terms as to costs or otherwise as it thinks fit[12].

In relation to any claim relating to the estate of a deceased person[13], the court may at any time direct that notice of the claim or any judgment or order given in the claim be served on any person who is not a party but who is or may be affected by it[14]. Any person served with a notice of a judgment or order is bound by the judgment or order as if he had been a party to the claim; but may, provided he acknowledges service:

(1) within 28 days after the notice is served on him, apply to the court to set aside or vary the judgment or order; and
(2) take part in any proceedings relating to the judgment or order[15].

1 As to the meaning of 'administration claim' see PARA 1162.
2 See PARA 1169.
3 CPR 64.4(1)(a).
4 CPR 64.4(1)(b). See also *Latch v Latch* (1875) 10 Ch App 464. See further *Re Dracup, Field v Dracup* (1892) 36 Sol Jo 327; *Lacons v Warmoll* [1907] 2 KB 350 at 368, CA, per Buckley LJ; *M'Sweeney v Murphy* [1919] 1 IR 16. The court has a general power to order a person to be added as a new party: see CPR 19.2(2). As to the court's power to make representation orders see CPR 19.6–7A; and PARAS 818, 885, 1271–1272. See also CIVIL PROCEDURE vol 12A (2015) PARA 1220. Where the claim relates to the internal affairs of the estate it may be appropriate for at least some of the beneficiaries to be parties; if need be, the court may make representation orders in certain cases: see *Chancery Guide* (2016) para 29.14.
5 *Dyson v Morris* (1842) 1 Hare 413; *Strickland v Strickland* (1842) 12 Sim 463.
6 *Vickers v Bell* (1864) 4 De GJ & Sm 274.
7 *Re Lovett, Ambler v Lindsay* (1876) 3 ChD 198.
8 *Dowdeswell v Dowdeswell* (1878) 9 ChD 294, CA.
9 *Rowsell v Morris* (1873) LR 17 Eq 20. As to the executor de son tort see PARA 1261 et seq.
10 CPR 64.4(1)(c). Hence it is not necessary for all persons having a beneficial interest in or claim against the estate to be parties to the claim notwithstanding CPR 19.3 and without prejudice to the court's powers under CPR Pt 19. A legatee's action is taken to be for himself and the other legatees whether so expressed or not: *Re Greaves, Bray v Tofield* (1881) 18 ChD 551 at 554.
11 CPR 19.7A(1). Any judgment or order given or made in the claim is binding on the beneficiaries unless the court orders otherwise in the same or other proceedings: CPR 19.7A(2).
12 CPR PD 64A—*Estates, Trusts and Charities* para 3.3.
13 CPR 19.8A(1).
14 CPR 19.8A(2).
15 CPR 19.8A(8).

1173. Creditor's right to take proceedings for the administration of the estate. A creditor may take proceedings for the administration of the personal estate either on his own behalf alone or on behalf of himself and all other creditors[1]. Where the creditor desires to have the realty administered as well as the personalty, he may claim as against such assets on his own behalf alone[2].

In a claim brought by a creditor, the personal representative completely represents the estate[3] and the residuary legatee should not be made a party[4]. Until judgment, the creditor, although claiming on behalf of himself and all other creditors, has the control of the claim, and, subject to the court's direction, may deal with the claim as he pleases[5]. However, the judgment enures for the benefit of all creditors[6] and the claimant creditor cannot subsequently accept payment of his debt and allow the claim to be dismissed[7]. Even with the consent of the creditor, a legatee cannot avail himself of the creditor's claim; he must begin a fresh claim[8].

1 *Re Blount, Nayler v Blount* (1879) 27 WR 865; *Re Greaves, Bray v Tofield* (1881) 18 ChD 551 at 554.
2 Where a creditor is claiming in a representative capacity, this fact ought to be shown on the face of the claim form: see *Re Tottenham, Tottenham v Tottenham* [1896] 1 Ch 628. It was formerly held that he must bring a claim on behalf of himself and all other creditors (*Worraker v Pryer* (1876) 2 ChD 109, dissenting from *Cooper v Blissett* (1876) 1 ChD 691; *Re Royle, Fryer v Royle* (1877) 5 ChD 540; *Re Greaves, Bray v Tofield* (1881) 18 ChD 551); except where the realty was devised to trustees who had power to sell and give receipts (*Re McKeown* (1874) 22 WR 292; *Wooldridge v Norris* (1868) LR 6 Eq 410).
3 The personal representative is normally the only proper party to attend and oppose claims brought against the estate: *Re Watts, Smith v Watts* (1882) 22 ChD 5, CA. As to the meaning of 'personal representative' see PARA 608.
4 *Re Youngs, Doggett v Revett, Re Youngs Vollum v Revett* (1885) 30 ChD 421, CA; *Re Ward, Bemment v Balls* (1878) 47 LJ Ch 781. For an instance where a beneficiary should be made an additional defendant see PARA 1171.
5 *Woodgate v Field* (1842) 2 Hare 211 at 214; *Wood v Westall* (1831) You 305.
6 *Re Greaves, Bray v Tofield* (1881) 18 ChD 551 at 552–553.
7 *Handford v Storie* (1825) 2 Sim & St 196.
8 *Re Ainsworth, Cockcroft v Sanderson* [1895] WN 153.

1174. Requirements for making a claim. To enable a person to maintain a claim he must have an existing interest in the property. The interest may be vested or contingent, future or remote, but it must be an existing interest; a mere possibility is insufficient[1]. Accordingly, a member of a class of possible next of kin of a living person cannot maintain an administration claim[2], nor need the class be served with the judgment[3]; but a member of a contingent class, for example surviving brothers and sisters of a person who will take if that person dies without leaving issue, has a sufficient interest[4]. A person whose claim against the estate would not support a claim at law against the personal representative, for example a person claiming under an annuity granted by the deceased in his lifetime in respect of which there are no arrears[5], or a person claiming arrears under an order for the payment of maintenance[6], is not entitled to an administration order. A claim for costs due in pursuance of an order of a competent court creates a debt which can be enforced against the debtor's estate, and upon which an administration claim can be founded[7]; and where the testator's business has been carried on by the personal representative, an administration claim may be maintained by a creditor of the business, although there were no creditors of the testator, or of the estate, prior to his death[8].

1 *Davis v Angel* (1862) 4 De GF & J 524; *Clowes v Hilliard* (1876) 4 ChD 413. It is submitted that persons interested under a discretionary trust have a sufficient interest to maintain a claim; cf *Re Beckett's Settlement, Re Beckett, Eden v Von Stutterheim* [1940] Ch 279 at 285; *A-G v Farrell* [1931] 1 KB 81, CA.
2 *Clowes v Hilliard* (1876) 4 ChD 413, commenting upon *Roberts v Roberts* (1848) 2 Ph 534; *Fussell v Dowding* (1884) 27 ChD 237.
3 *Fowler v James* (1847) 1 Ph 803.
4 *Peacock v Colling* (1885) 54 LJ Ch 743, CA.
5 *Re Hargreaves, Dicks v Hare* (1890) 44 ChD 236, CA. As to claims maintainable against the personal representative see PARA 1183 et seq. As to the meaning of 'personal representative' see PARA 608.
6 *Re Woolgar, Woolgar v Hopkins* [1942] Ch 318, [1942] 1 All ER 583.
7 *Re Naters, Ainger v Naters* (1919) 88 LJ Ch 521 (order of consistory court, followed by a monition to pay which was never obeyed by the deceased).
8 *Re Bach, Walker v Bach, Lloyds Bank v Bach* [1892] WN 108; *Re Shorey, Smith v Shorey* (1898) 79 LT 349. See also PARA 1041.

(4) CONSOLIDATION AND TRANSFER

1175. Consolidation and conduct of claim. Where several claims are pending for the administration of the same estate, the court may on an application[1] made before judgment in any of the claims, or on its own initiative[2], have them consolidated[3]. After the order to consolidate, the claims proceed as one claim, and one judgment is pronounced in the consolidated claim[4].

If the court of its own initiative strikes out a statement of case or dismisses an application, and it considers that the claim or application is totally without merit, the court's order must record that fact and it must at the same time consider whether it is appropriate to make a civil restraint order[5].

1 See CPR 3.3(1). The application should be made by application notice: see CPR Pt 23; and CIVIL PROCEDURE vol 12 (2015) PARA 554 et seq.
2 See CPR 3.3(1). Where the court proposes an order of its own initiative it may give any person likely to be affected by the order an opportunity to make representations (see CPR 3.3(2)(a)) but where it does not do so a party affected may apply to have the order set aside, varied or stayed (see CPR 3.3(5)(a)).
3 See CPR 3.1(2)(g).
4 The conduct of the consolidated claims should, as a rule, be given to the party who has the greatest interest in keeping down the costs of the proceedings: see *Re Prime's Estate* (1883) 48 LT 208 at 210. Therefore, a residuary legatee will be preferred to a creditor or executor: see *Penny v Francis* (1860) 7 Jur NS 248; *Kelk v Archer, Archer v Kelk* (1852) 16 Jur 605.
5 CPR 3.3(7). As to civil restraint orders see CPR 2.3(1); and CIVIL PROCEDURE vol 12 (2015) PARA 523.

1176. Transfer after administration order. Where an order for the administration under the court's direction of the estate of a deceased person is made in the High Court the court may order proceedings in the Royal Courts of Justice or a district registry, or any part of such proceedings to be transferred from the Royal Courts of Justice to a district registry or from a district registry to the Royal Courts of Justice or to another district registry[1] and the High Court may order proceedings in any division to be transferred to another division[2].

An application for a transfer must, if the claim is proceeding in a district registry, be made to that registry[3] and an application for the transfer of proceedings to or from a specialist list must be made to a judge dealing with claims in that list[4]. The application for the transfer may be made without notice[5]. However, where the court orders proceedings to be transferred, the court from which they are to be transferred must give notice of the transfer to all the parties[6].

The rule was formerly not applied to an action against the representative personally[7], nor would the court restrain a creditor who had, prior to the administration order, recovered judgment against the representative from pursuing his remedy on the judgment against the representative personally[8], but the fact that an action against a representative includes a claim against him personally does not prevent the action being transferred or stayed so far as it seeks to enforce a claim against the defendant as representative[9].

1 See CPR 30.2(4); and PARA 867. The court is required to have regard to the criteria set out at CPR 30.3: see PARA 867. See further CIVIL PROCEDURE vol 11 (2015) PARA 106.
2 See CPR 30.5(1).
3 See CPR 30.2(6).
4 See CPR 30.5(3).
5 *Field v Field* [1877] WN 98; *Whitaker v Robinson* [1877] WN 201; *Re United Kingdom Electric Telegraph Co* (1881) 29 WR 332; *Re Sharpe, Scott v Sharpe* [1884] WN 28; *Re Capelovitch Estate and Will Trusts, Sandelson v Capelovitch* [1957] 1 All ER 33, [1957] 1 WLR 102. As to the form of the application see CPR Pt 23; and CIVIL PROCEDURE vol 12 (2015) PARA 554 et seq.
6 CPR 30.4(1).

7 Ie prior to the commencement of the CPR on 26 April 1999 (seeCIVIL PROCEDURE vol 12 (2015) PARA 504). See *Chapman v Mason* (1879) 40 LT 678.
8 See *Re Womersley, Etheridge v Womersley* (1885) 29 ChD 557; *Haly v Barry* (1868) 3 Ch App 452 at 457 per Page Wood LJ.
9 See *Re Pimm, Malkin v Pimm, Steward v Sharpe (No 2)* [1916] WN 202, CA. It is likely that these principles remain applicable notwithstanding the introduction of the CPR: see CIVIL PROCEDURE vol 11 (2015) PARA 12 et seq.

1177. Stay of proceedings after judgment in concurrent claim. Where several claims are commenced for the administration of the same estate and they are not consolidated before judgment is pronounced in one of them, the court may on an application[1] or on its own initiative[2] stay the whole or part of any proceedings or judgment either generally or until a specified date or event[3]. The general practice is that the costs of the proceedings which are stayed are made costs in the other claim[4] but this practice will be departed from where the judgment has been unfairly obtained[5], or where the relief sought by and obtainable in the other claims is more comprehensive than that in the claim in which the judgment has been made[6], although in the latter case the judgment may be allowed to proceed on the undertaking of the parties to submit to the additional accounts and inquiries[7]. Where two claims are brought on behalf of claimants who are minors, the one that will be proceeded with is that which is more for their benefit[8].

1 See CPR 3.3(1). The application should be made by application notice: see CPR Pt 23; and CIVIL PROCEDURE vol 12 (2015) PARA 554 et seq.
2 See CPR 3.3(1). As to where the court proposes an order of its own initiative see PARA 1175 note 2.
3 See CPR 3.1(2)(f). See also *Taylor v Southgate* (1839) 4 My & Cr 203; *Wynne v Hughes* (1859) 26 Beav 377 at 382; *Harvey v Coxwell, Wilson v Coxwell* (1875) 32 LT 52. As to claims against the representative personally see PARA 1176.
4 *Gwyer v Peterson, Peterson v Peterson* (1858) 26 Beav 83; *Taylor v Southgate* (1839) 4 My & Cr 203; *Kenyon v Kenyon* (1866) 35 Beav 300. The costs are payable in due course of administration: *Re Clark, Cumberland v Clark* (1869) 4 Ch App 412.
5 *Harris v Gandy, Wills v Gandy* (1859) 1 De GF & J 13; *Rhodes v Barret, ex p Singleton* (1871) LR 12 Eq 479.
6 *Pickford v Hunter* (1831) 5 Sim 122; *Rigby v Strangways* (1846) 2 Ph 175; *Underwood v Jee* (1849) 1 Mac & G 276; *Hoskins v Campbell, Gibbon v Campbell* (1864) 2 Hem & M 43; *Zambaco v Cassavetti* (1871) LR 11 Eq 439.
7 *Gwyer v Peterson, Peterson v Peterson* (1858) 26 Beav 83; *Matthews v Palmer, Pritchard v Palmer* (1863) 11 WR 610; and see *Vanrenen v Piffard, Piffard v Vanrenen* (1865) 13 WR 425.
8 *Virtue v Miller* (1871) 19 WR 406. See also *Harris v Lightfoot, Harris v Harris* (1861) 10 WR 31.

1178. Conduct of proceedings after stay. If a claim is stayed by reason of a judgment in another claim having been first obtained, the general rule is to give the conduct of the proceedings to the claimant in the first claim[1]. The court has a discretion[2], and will depart from the rule where the relief sought in the stayed claim is imperfect[3], or the claim is defective[4], or where the claim of the claimant whose claim was first instituted is disputed in good faith[5].

The court has power to deprive a claimant of the conduct of the proceedings on account of delay[6]. As a general rule the person so deprived will not be allowed his costs of attending the taking of the accounts subsequent to his removal[7], but he will be allowed his costs of appearing on further consideration to ask for costs up to his removal[8].

1 *Frost v Ward* (1864) 2 De GJ & Sm 70; *Belcher v Belcher* (1865) 2 Drew & Sm 444; *Zambaco v Cassavetti* (1871) LR 11 Eq 439; *Rhodes v Barret, ex p Singleton* (1871) LR 12 Eq 479; *Matthews v Matthews, Willyams v Matthews* (1876) 45 LJ Ch 711 (conduct given to plaintiffs in first action, which was stayed, as being persons mainly interested in the estate); *Hawkes v Barrett* (1820) 5 Madd 17. The rule applied where the first action was in the Palatine Court (see COURTS

AND TRIBUNALS vol 24 (2010) PARA 699) and the second, in which the decree was obtained, in the High Court: *Re Swire, Mellor v Swire* (1882) 21 ChD 647, CA. See also *Townsend v Townsend* (1883) 23 ChD 100, CA.

2 See *Re Swire, Mellor v Swire* (1882) 21 ChD 647, CA.

3 *Re Smith's Estate, McMurray v Mathew, Mathew v Mathew* (1876) 33 LT 804.

4 *Re McRae, Forster v Davis, Norden v McRae* (1883) 25 ChD 16, CA.

5 *Re Ross, Wingfield v Blair* [1907] 1 Ch 482.

6 *Sims v Ridge* (1817) 3 Mer 458 at 467; *Bennett v Baxter* (1840) 10 Sim 417; *Cook v Bolton* (1828) 5 Russ 282.

7 *Armstrong v Armstrong* (1871) LR 12 Eq 614.

8 *Joseph v Goode, Fisher v Goode* (1875) 23 WR 225. As to costs see PARA 1196 et seq.

(5) THE JUDGMENT OR ORDER

1179. Court's discretion to make order. The court will only make an administration order if it considers that the issues between the parties cannot properly be resolved in any other way[1]. An order may be refused even though the claimant is a minor[2], or though the testator has directed his executors to take proceedings to have the estate administered by the court[3].

1 CPR PD 64A—*Estates, Trusts and Charities* para 3.1. As to the exercise of this discretion see *Re Wilson, Alexander v Calder* (1885) 28 ChD 457; *Re Gyhon, Allen v Taylor* (1885) 29 ChD 834, CA; *Campbell v Gillespie* [1900] 1 Ch 225; *De Quetteville v De Quetteville* (1902) 19 TLR 109; order varied on appeal (1903) 19 TLR 383, CA. See also CIVIL PROCEDURE vol 12A (2015) PARA 1426.

2 *Re Blake, Jones v Blake* (1885) 29 ChD 913, CA.

3 *Re Stocken, Jones v Hawkins* (1888) 38 ChD 319, CA.

1180. Chancery Masters' or District Judges' powers. Where, in relation to proceedings in the Chancery Division, the Civil Procedure Rules provide for the court to perform any act then, except where an enactment, rule or practice direction provides otherwise, that act may be performed by any Master or District Judge of that division[1].

A District Judge of the Chancery Division may not without the consent of the Supervising Judge for the region in which the District Judge is sitting, or without the consent of their nominee[2]:

(1) approve a compromise[3]:
  (a) on behalf of a person under a disability where that person's interest in a fund, or if there is no fund, the amount of the claim, exceeds the prescribed maximum[4] or any larger sum specified by the Chancellor of the High Court; and
  (b) on behalf of absent, unborn and unascertained persons[5];

(2) make final orders[6] except for the removal of protective trusts where the interest of the principal beneficiary has not failed or determined[7];

(3) give permission to executors, administrators and trustees to bring or defend proceedings or to continue the prosecution or defence of proceedings, and granting an indemnity for costs out of the trust estate[8].

A master may also grant permission to distribute the estate of a deceased Lloyd's Name whose liabilities have been reinsured into Equitas without requiring the attendance of the applicants[9].

1 See CPR 2.4; and CIVIL PROCEDURE vol 11 (2015) PARAS 97, 99.

2 CPR PD 2B—*Allocation of Cases to Levels of Judiciary* para 7B.2. As to other proceedings in the Chancery Division in which the consent of the Supervising Judge is required see CPR PD 2B—Allocation of Cases to Levels of Judiciary para 7B.2(d)–(f).

3 CPR PD 2B—*Allocation of Cases to Levels of Judiciary* para 7B.2(a). This provision does not apply to applications under the Inheritance (Provision for Family and Dependants) Act 1975 (see PARA 565 et seq): see CPR PD 2B—*Allocation of Cases to Levels of Judiciary* para 7B.2(a).
4 CPR PD 2B—*Allocation of Cases to Levels of Judiciary* para 7B.2(a)(i). The prescribed maximum is £100,000: see CPR PD 2B para 7B.2(a).
5 CPR PD 2B—*Allocation of Cases to Levels of Judiciary* para 7B.2(a)(ii).
6 Ie under the Variation of Trusts Act 1958 s 1(1): see CPR PD 2B—*Allocation of Cases to Levels of Judiciary* para 7B.2(b).
7 CPR PD 2B—*Allocation of Cases to Levels of Judiciary* para 7B.2(b).
8 CPR PD 2B—*Allocation of Cases to Levels of Judiciary* para 7B.2(c).
9 See Practice Statement [2001] 3 All ER 765; *Re Yorke, Stone v Chataway* [1997] 4 All ER 907; and PARA 1170.

1181. Order for accounts. If, in a claim for an administration order[1], the claimant alleges that the personal representatives have not provided proper accounts, the court may:

(1) stay the proceedings for a specified period, and order them to file and serve proper accounts within that period[2]; or
(2) if necessary to prevent proceedings by other creditors or persons claiming to be entitled to the estate or fund, make an administration order and include in it an order that no such proceedings are to be taken without the court's permission[3].

Nothing short of an order for administration will prevent a creditor from bringing a claim against the representatives[4].

1 As to the meaning of 'administration order' see PARA 1162.
2 CPR PD 64A—*Estates, Trusts and Charities* para 3.2(1). As to the meaning of 'personal representative' see PARA 608.
3 CPR PD 64A—*Estates, Trusts and Charities* para 3.2(2).
4 *Re Barrett, Whitaker v Barrett* (1889) 43 ChD 70; *Re Mills, Mills v Mills* [1884] WN 21.

1182. Order not limited to assets within the jurisdiction. The judgment for the administration of a deceased's personal estate is not limited to assets within the jurisdiction, even where he died domiciled abroad[1].

1 *Re Maxwell, Stirling-Maxwell v Cartwright* (1879) 11 ChD 522, CA. As to domicile generally see CONFLICT OF LAWS vol 19 (2011) PARA 336 et seq.

1183. Order for account on footing of wilful default. In appropriate cases the court may order an account of what the personal representatives might have received but for their wilful neglect and default[1]. Once one act of wilful default has been proved, the court has jurisdiction to make an order for an account on the footing of wilful default in respect of the whole estate[2]. In taking the account under a judgment based on the footing of wilful default it is open to the claimant to go into other instances, and in this respect a wilful default claim differs from a claim brought in respect of active breaches of trust[3].

Where, however, a claimant has obtained a common administration judgment against a representative he cannot, in taking the accounts, charge him with wilful default, nor can he maintain a subsequent claim against him charging him with wilful default without the permission of the court[4]. Where, however, in his statement of case he has made an allegation of wilful default, and the claim to relief in respect of it has not been dismissed, the court may, even after a common administration judgment, at any subsequent stage of the proceedings, if evidence of wilful default is adduced, direct further accounts to be taken on that footing[5]. An application for account on this basis is a hostile act and should not be brought until all other options have been explored[6].

1 Where the court orders any account to be taken or any inquiry to be made, it may, by the same or a subsequent order, give directions as to the manner in which the account is to be taken and

verified or the inquiry is to be conducted: CPR PD 40A—*Accounts, Inquiries etc* para 1.1; CPR Pt 40; and CIVIL PROCEDURE vol 12A (2015) PARAS 1256, 1257. See, for example, *Walker v Walker* [2007] EWHC 597 (Ch), [2007] All ER (D) 418 (Mar).

2 See *Re Tebbs, Redfern v Tebbs* [1976] 2 All ER 858, [1976] 1 WLR 924 (the test is whether the past conduct of the trustees gives rise to a reasonable prima facie inference that other breaches of trust not yet known to the plaintiff or the court have occurred); and EQUITABLE JURISDICTION vol 47 (2014) PARA 51.

3 See EQUITABLE JURISDICTION vol 47 (2014) PARA 51.

4 *Laming v Gee* (1878) 10 ChD 715. Permission may be given without requiring proof that the information on which the fresh claim is founded was not acquired in time to be utilised in the former claim: *Re Kurtz, Emerson v Henderson* (1904) 90 LT 12. See also *Re Hoghton, Hoghton v Fiddey* (1874) LR 18 Eq 573.

5 *Re Symons, Luke v Tonkin* (1882) 21 ChD 757. See also *Edmonds v Robinson* (1885) 29 ChD 170 at 175 per Kay J; and *Re Tebbs, Redfern v Tebbs* [1976] 2 All ER 858, [1976] 1 WLR 924.

6 See *Iliffe v Trafford* [2002] WTLR 507, [2002] NPC 3.

1184. Liability on a common account. Where the account directed by the order is what is called a common account, the personal representative[1] is bound not only to bring in an account of his receipts, but to discharge himself as regards those receipts, and show what he has done with the money received; and, in taking the account, disbursements made by him in breach of his fiduciary duties will be disallowed[2].

1 As to the meaning of 'personal representative' see PARA 608.

2 *Re Stuart, Smith v Stuart* (1896) 74 LT 546; *Re Newland, Bush v Summers* (1904) 49 Sol Jo 14. In taking an account, all just allowances are to be made without any direction to that effect: see CPR Pt 40; CPR PD 40A—*Accounts, Inquiries etc* para 4. See also EQUITABLE JURISDICTION vol 47 (2014) PARA 55; CIVIL PROCEDURE vol 12A (2015) PARA 1252.

1185. Right to claim limitation as defence. A personal representative who is entitled to set up the Limitation Act 1980[1] as a defence[2] must do so at the time the order for accounts is made, so that the order can be qualified by a reference to that Act, or the question directed to be reserved until further consideration; and if this is not done, the defence cannot be raised while the accounts are being vouched or at the hearing on further consideration[3].

1 See the Limitation Act 1980 s 22; and LIMITATION PERIODS vol 68 (2016) PARAS 916, 1159 et seq. For the necessity of pleading the Limitation Act 1980 see CPR Pt 16; CPR PD 16—*Statements of Case* (1999) para 13.1; and CIVIL PROCEDURE vol 11 (2015) PARA 340 et seq. As to the meaning of 'personal representative' see PARA 608.

2 But see *Re Loftus, Green v Gaul* [2006] EWCA Civ 1124, [2006] 4 All ER 1110, [2007] 1 WLR 591 (claims to an account held to fall within the Limitation Act 1980 21(1)(b) with the result that no period of limitation prescribed by the Act applied).

3 *Re Williams, Jones v Williams* [1916] 2 Ch 38.

1186. Order to lodge money in court. A personal representative[1], though not shown to be insolvent or to have abused his trust, may be ordered to lodge in court a sum of money found due from him on taking his accounts, or admitted to be in his hands[2] or in the hands of his firm[3], or to be due to the estate from him[4]. The money need not be in his possession at the date of the order; it is sufficient if he is proved to have received it and never to have discharged himself of it[5]. It must be shown, however, that the money is or has been in his actual, and not merely his constructive, possession or control; the master's certificate finding a balance due is not of itself sufficient evidence of the actual possession or control[6].

The court should not order a representative to pay money into court upon an interim application, except where it is made out to the court's satisfaction that he has the sum claimed in his hands[7] or under his control[8]; nor should the court, upon an administration claim[9] being made, order a representative to pay money into court unless it is actually in his hands. It is not sufficient that it has been in his hands and that he is responsible for it[10].

1 As to the meaning of 'personal representative' see PARA 608.
2 *Strange v Harris* (1791) 3 Bro CC 365.
3 *Johnson v Aston* (1822) 1 Sim & St 73.
4 *Rothwell v Rothwell* (1825) 2 Sim & St 217. A representative ordered to pay money into court is not as a result deprived of his lien on the fund for his costs: *Blenkinsop v Foster* (1838) 3 Y & C Ex 205.
5 *Middleton v Chichester* (1871) 6 Ch App 152.
6 *Re Fewster, Herdman v Fewster* [1901] 1 Ch 447; *Re Wilkins, Emsley v Wilkins* (1901) 46 Sol Jo 14.
7 *Neville v Matthewman* [1894] 3 Ch 345, CA, commenting upon *Freeman v Cox* (1878) 8 ChD 148; *Crompton and Evans' Union Bank v Burton* [1895] 2 Ch 711.
8 *Re Benson, Elletson v Pillers* [1899] 1 Ch 39.
9 See PARA 1166. As to the meaning of 'administration claim' see PARA 1162.
10 *Nutter v Holland* [1894] 3 Ch 408, CA, disapproving *Re Chapman, Fardell v Chapman* (1886) 54 LT 13.

1187. Interest on debts and legacies. Where an account of the debts[1] of a deceased person is directed by any judgment, then, unless the deceased's estate is insolvent, or the court otherwise orders, interest is allowed on any debt which carries interest at the rate it carries[2], and, on any other debt, from the date of judgment at the rate payable on judgment debts at that date[3] or, in relation to expenses incurred after judgment, the date when the expenses became payable[4]. A creditor who has established his debt in proceedings under the judgment and whose debt does not carry interest is entitled to interest from the date of the judgment at the rate payable on judgment debts at that time out of any assets which may remain after satisfying the costs of the proceedings, the debts which have been established and the interest on such of those debts as by law carry interest[5]. The payment of such interest is subject to the deduction of income tax at the standard rate by the representative[6].

Where an account of legacies is directed by any judgment, then, subject to any directions contained in the will or codicil in question, and to any order made by the court, interest is allowed on each legacy at the basic rate payable for the time being on funds in court or at such other rate as the court directs beginning one year after the testator's death[7].

1 For these purposes, 'debt' includes funeral, testamentary or administration expenses: CPR PD 40A—*Accounts, Inquiries etc* para 14(3)(a). As to debts incurred in running the deceased's business see PARA 1042.
2 CPR PD 40A—*Accounts, Inquiries etc* para 14(1)(a). As to interest in respect of County Court judgments or orders see the County Courts (Interest on Judgment Debts) Order 1991, SI 1991/1184 (amended by the SI 1996/2516; SI 1998/2400; and SI 2014/1773).
3 CPR PD 40A—*Accounts, Inquiries etc* para 14(1)(b). The current rate is 8%: see the Judgments Act 1838 s 17; and CIVIL PROCEDURE vol 12A (2015) PARA 1236.
4 CPR PD 40A—*Accounts, Inquiries etc* para 14(3)(b).
5 CPR PD 40A—*Accounts, Inquiries etc* para 14(2).
6 *Re Michelham, Michelham v Michelham* [1921] 1 Ch 705.
7 CPR PD 40A—*Accounts, Inquiries etc* para 15. See also PARA 1080.

1188. Enforcement of order for payment into court. An order for payment into court by a personal representative may be enforced by committal[1], but the court has a discretion to refuse the committal[2].

The order may also be enforced by a writ of sequestration against the personal representative's estate and effects but only with the consent of the court[3]. The person obtaining the writ is not a judgment creditor of the representative, and the court has no jurisdiction under the writ to direct a sale of the representative's real estate[4].

1 *Marshman v Brookes* (1863) 32 LJPM & A 95, 11 WR 549; *Baker v Baker* (1860) 2 Sw & Tr 380. As to the meaning of 'personal representative' see PARA 608.
2 See CONTEMPT OF COURT vol 22 (2012) PARA 112.
3 See CPR 83.2(3)(c), CPR 83.2A; and CIVIL PROCEDURE vol 12A (2015) PARA 1372.
4 *Johnson v Burgess* (1873) LR 15 Eq 398; *Pratt v Inman* (1889) 43 ChD 175 at 180. As to the effect of writs of sequestration see CIVIL PROCEDURE vol 12A (2015) PARA 1380.

1189. Order fixing time for payment. A judgment for the recovery from the defendant of a sum of money, as distinguished from an order to pay a sum of money into court, cannot be supplemented by an order fixing the time for the payment by him of the sum of money, even where the defendant stands in a fiduciary position[1].

1 *Re Oddy, Major v Harness* [1906] 1 Ch 93, CA; *Drewett v Edwards* (1877) 37 LT 622; *Hulbert and Crowe v Cathcart* [1894] 1 QB 244. See also CPR 83.5(1); and CIVIL PROCEDURE vol 12A (2015) PARA 1375.

1190. Effect of judgment on personal representative's powers. After a judgment has been given for general administration[1], the personal representative's[2] powers of selling the property, dealing with or distributing the assets and managing the estate cannot be exercised without the court's previous consent[3], notwithstanding that the judgment directs that none of the accounts and inquiries ordered is to be prosecuted except with the permission of the judge in person[4]. After judgment the personal representative is not entitled to do any act which affects the relative rights of creditors[5]. He cannot, accordingly, pay one creditor in preference to another[6], nor can he give a creditor a valid acknowledgement of a debt so as to prevent the creditor's right of action being statute-barred[7]. The judgment does not, however, determine the personal representative's right of retainer[8]; nor does it, where no receiver has been appointed or injunction granted, deprive him of his legal powers to deal with the assets so as to invalidate the title of persons without notice of the judgment claiming under a disposition made by him in exercise of his legal powers[9].

An order for an inquiry is not a decision on the question to which the inquiry relates where the question itself is by the same order directed to stand over[10].

1 Ie under CPR 64.2(b) (see PARA 1162).
2 As to the meaning of 'personal representative' see PARA 608.
3 *Re Furness, Wilson v Kenmare* [1943] Ch 415, [1944] 1 All ER 66; *Widdowson v Duck* (1817) 2 Mer 494 at 499; *Bethell v Abraham* (1873) LR 17 Eq 24; *Minors v Battison* (1876) 1 App Cas 428, HL. As to the effect upon the discretionary powers of executor-trustees of a judgment for the execution of the trusts of a will see TRUSTS AND POWERS vol 98 (2013) PARA 289.
4 *Re Furness, Wilson v Kenmare* [1943] Ch 415, [1944] 1 All ER 66.
5 *Shewen v Vanderhorst* (1830) 2 Russ & M 75; affd (1831) 1 Russ & M 347.
6 As to the abolition of the right to prefer see PARA 983 note 3. A creditor who has obtained payment of part of his debt, before the administration order, will not receive any further payment until all the other creditors are paid proportionately: *Mitchelson v Piper* (1836) 8 Sim 64.
7 *Phillips v Beal (No 2)* (1863) 32 Beav 26.
8 As to the abolition of the right to retain in cases of death after 1 January 1972 see PARA 983 note 3.
9 *Berry v Gibbons* (1873) 8 Ch App 747; *Re Hoban, Lonergan v Hoban* [1896] 1 IR 401; *Re Furness, Wilson v Kenmare* [1943] Ch 415 at 420–421, [1944] 1 All ER 66 at 69. See also *Halley v O'Brien* [1920] 1 IR 330, CA (where sale without consent of the court; consent given at the trial of an action for specific performance of the contract of sale, held sufficient).
10 See *Re Wright, Blizard v Lockhart* [1954] Ch 347 at 353, [1954] 1 All ER 864 at 867 per Roxburgh J; affd [1954] Ch 347 at 357–358, [1954] 2 All ER 98 at 101–102, CA, per Romer LJ. See also CIVIL PROCEDURE vol 12A (2015) PARA 1623.

1191. Effect of proceedings and judgment in creditors' claims. A judgment for administration prevents time from running against the claims of all creditors coming in under the judgment[1], but the mere institution of administration proceedings is not sufficient to effect this[2].

1 *Re Greaves, Bray v Tofield* (1881) 18 ChD 551.
2 *Re Greaves, Bray v Tofield* (1881) 18 ChD 551, commenting upon *Sterndale v Hankinson* (1827) 1 Sim 393.

(6) PROCEEDINGS UNDER JUDGMENT

1192. Directions by the court in relation to account or inquiry. Where the court orders any account to be taken or any inquiry to be made, it may give directions as to the manner in which the account is to be taken and verified or the inquiry is to be conducted[1]. The court may at any stage in the taking of an account or in the course of an inquiry direct a hearing in order to resolve an issue that has arisen and for that purpose may order that points of claim and points of defence be served and give any necessary directions[2].

For the purpose of considering a claim the court may: (1) direct it to be investigated in any manner; (2) direct the person making the claim to give further details of it; and (3) direct that person to file written evidence or attend court to give evidence, to support his claim[3].

1 See CPR PD 40A—*Accounts, Inquiries etc* para 1; and CIVIL PROCEDURE vol 12A (2015) PARA 1250. Such directions may be made by the same or subsequent order: see CPR PD 40A para 1.1. The court may direct any necessary advertisement and fix the time within which the advertisement should require a reply: CPR PD 40A para 10.
2 See CPR PD 40A—*Accounts, Inquiries etc* para 5; and CIVIL PROCEDURE vol 12A (2015) PARA 1251.
3 See CPR PD 40A—*Accounts, Inquiries etc* para 12; and CIVIL PROCEDURE vol 12A (2015) PARA 1252. A creditor who is not a party has no right to attend: see *Re Schwabacher, Stern v Schwabacher* [1907] 1 Ch 719.

1193. Examination of claims. Where the court orders an account of debts or other liabilities to be taken, it may direct[1] any party, within a specified time, to: (1) examine the claims of persons claiming to be owed money out of the estate or fund in question; (2) determine, so far as he is able, which of them are valid; and (3) file written evidence stating his findings and his reasons for them, and listing any other debts which are or may be owed out of the estate or fund[2]. If the personal representatives or trustees concerned are not the parties directed by the court to examine claims, the court may direct them to join with the party directed to examine claims in producing the written evidence required[3].

1 As to directions by the court see PARA 1192.
2 CPR PD 40A—*Accounts, Inquiries etc* para 11.1; and see CIVIL PROCEDURE vol 12A (2015) PARA 1252.
3 CPR PD 40A—*Accounts, Inquiries etc* para 11.3; and see CIVIL PROCEDURE vol 12A (2015) PARA 1252. As to the meaning of 'personal representative' see PARA 608.

1194. Kin inquiries. Among the inquiries which may be directed by the court[1] are inquiries as to relationships, generally called 'kin inquiries', which may arise both on intestacy and under the terms of a will. Where the court orders an inquiry for next of kin or other unascertained claimants to an estate or fund, it may direct any party, within a specified time, to: (1) examine the claims that are made; (2) determine, so far as he is able, which of them are valid; and (3) file written evidence stating his findings and his reasons for them[2].

If the personal representatives or trustees concerned are not the parties directed by the court to examine claims, the court may direct them to join with the party directed to examine claims in producing the written evidence required[3].

In complex cases a pedigree should be prepared, cross-referring to supporting witness statements or affidavits. The dates of relevant births, marriages and deaths, should be strictly proved so far as this can be done[4].

Where some of the persons entitled to a share in a fund are known but there is, or is likely to be, difficulty or delay in ascertaining other persons so entitled, the court may direct, or allow, immediate payment of their shares to the known persons without reserving any part of those shares to meet the subsequent costs of ascertaining the other persons[5]. Where a beneficiary is presumed dead, it is open to a personal representative to take out missing beneficiary insurance as an alternative to applying to court[6].

1 As to directions by the court see PARA 1192.
2 CPR PD 40A—*Accounts, Inquiries etc* para 11.2; and see CIVIL PROCEDURE vol 12A (2015) PARA 1252.
3 CPR PD 40A—*Accounts, Inquiries etc* para 11.3; and see CIVIL PROCEDURE vol 12A (2015) PARA 1252. As to the meaning of 'personal representative' see PARA 608.
4 As to proof of births, marriages and deaths by certified copies of register entries and as to the use of family papers and ancient documents see CIVIL PROCEDURE vol 12 (2015) PARAS 927 et seq, 1094–1095; and MATRIMONIAL AND CIVIL PARTNERSHIP LAW vol 72 (2015) PARA 23 et seq. As to registration of the person see generally REGISTRATION CONCERNING THE INDIVIDUAL vol 88 (2012) PARA 201 et seq. As to adopted and illegitimate children see PARA 1063; and CHILDREN AND YOUNG PERSONS vol 9 (2012) PARAS 98, 142–147.
5 CPR PD 40A—*Accounts, Inquiries etc* para 7; and see CIVIL PROCEDURE vol 12A (2015) PARA 1254.
6 *Re Evans, Evans v Westcombe* [1999] 2 All ER 777. The personal representative can do this notwithstanding that he is a beneficiary of the estate.

1195. Notice of decision. If the court has allowed or disallowed any claim or part of a claim and the person making the claim was not present when the decision was made, the court will serve on that person a notice informing him of its decision[1].

1 See CPR PD 40A—*Accounts, Inquiries etc* para 13; and CIVIL PROCEDURE vol 12A (2015) PARA 1252.

(7) COSTS

1196. General rule as to costs in relation to administration of estates. The general rule is that the costs of and incidental to all proceedings in both the High Court and the County Court, including proceedings relating to the administration of estates and trusts, are in the discretion of the court which has full power to determine by whom and to what extent the costs are to be paid[1]. This general rule is subject to the proviso that a personal representative[2] or trustee is entitled to an indemnity out of the relevant trust fund or estate for costs properly incurred, which may include costs awarded against the trustee or personal representative in favour of another party[3]. Whether costs were properly incurred depends on all the circumstances of the case, and may, for example, depend on:

(1) whether the trustee or personal representative obtained directions from the court before bringing or defending the proceedings;
(2) whether the trustee or personal representative acted in the interests of the fund or estate or in substance for a benefit other than that of the estate, including his own; and

(3) whether the trustee or personal representative acted in some way unreasonably in bringing or defending, or in the conduct of, the proceedings[4].

The trustee or personal representative is not to be taken to have acted for a benefit other than that of the fund by reason only that he has defended a claim in which relief is sought against him personally[5].

In administration proceedings[6] a personal representative who has acted properly is allowed his full costs of the proceedings as a matter of course, and in priority to the costs of all other parties[7]. He is entitled to be allowed all costs properly incurred on an indemnity basis[8]. This right to a full indemnity[9] may, however, be modified if he has failed to adopt the normal disinterested and independent attitude proper to a trustee. In such a case part of his costs may be disallowed[10]. His prior right to costs is not affected by the fact that the order on further consideration directs the costs of all parties to be paid out of the funds in court and the funds prove to be insufficient to meet all the costs[11].

Where trustees or personal representatives are parties the court may make an order deciding the incidence of costs in advance of the trial[12]. Trustees and personal representatives may, and probably should, seek directions even before the issue of proceedings by way of a 'Beddoes' application[13].

1 Senior Courts Act 1981 s 51 (substituted by the Courts and Legal Services Act 1990 s 4(1); and amended by the Crime and Courts Act 2013 Sch 9 para 29, Sch 10 para 61): see CIVIL PROCEDURE vol 12A (2015) PARA 1684. See also CPR 44.2. As to the costs provisions under the CPR see CPR Pts 44–48; and CIVIL PROCEDURE vol 12A (2015) PARA 1689. The court has very broad discretion as to costs. The former common law principles, although not generally adverted to in the CPR, may be of assistance to the court in exercising its discretion: see CIVIL PROCEDURE vol 12A (2015) PARA 1684.

2 As to the right to costs of a solicitor personal representative who or whose firm acts for the estate see PARA 653. As to the meaning of 'personal representative' see PARA 608.

3 See CPR 46.3; CPR PD 46—*Costs Special Cases* para 1.1.

4 CPR PD 46—*Costs Special Cases* para 1.1.

5 CPR PD 46—*Costs Special Cases* para 1.2.

6 The same practice applies to the costs of proceedings for the determination of questions without administration of the estate: *Re Medland, Eland v Medland* (1889) 41 ChD 476, CA. See also PARA 1197. As to the procedure see PARA 1166.

7 *Tanner v Dancey* (1846) 9 Beav 339; *Sanderson v Stoddart* (1863) 32 Beav 155; *Dodds v Tuke* (1884) 25 ChD 617; *Re Love, Hill v Spurgeon* (1885) 29 ChD 348, CA; *Re Barne, Lee v Barne* (1890) 62 LT 922. They are allowed in priority to a mortgagee plaintiff's costs of sale: *Re Spensley's Estate, Harrison v Spensley* (1872) 42 LJ Ch 21. A trustee who is accused of breach of duty not causing loss to the trust fund is prima facie entitled to an indemnity for his own costs, whether he is found to be in breach of duty or not, but will lose it if guilty of 'misconduct':*Turner v Hancock* (1882) 20 ChD 303; *Re Londonderry's Settlement, Peat v Walsh* [1965] Ch 918, [1964] 3 All ER 855, [1965] 2 WLR 229, CA; *Armitage v Nurse* [1998] Ch 241,]1997] 2 All ER 705, [1997] 3 WLR 1046. There is no reason in principle why such an indemnity could not extend to damages and costs awarded to a successful beneficiary in an action against a trustee who was able to show that the liability was properly incurred: see *Blades v Isaac* [2016] EWHC 601 (Ch) at [83]–[115], [2016] WTLR 589. See also *Radclyffe, Pearce v Radclyffe* (1881) 29 WR 420; *Re Wallett, Hayter v Wells* (1883) 32 WR 26; *Royal National Lifeboat Institution v Headley* [2016] EWHC 1948; and PARA 1200.

8 See CPR 46.3.

9 As to the right to indemnity see further PARA 1018.

10 *Re Dargie, Miller v Thornton-Jones* [1954] Ch 16, [1953] 2 All ER 577; *Holding and Management Ltd v Property Holding and Investment Trust plc* [1988] 2 All ER 702, [1988] 1 WLR 644.

11 *Re Griffith, Jones v Owen* [1904] 1 Ch 807, following *Gaunt v Taylor* (1843) 2 Hare 413, and not following *Swale v Milner* (1834) 6 Sim 572. As to the circumstances in which an order will be made under what is now the Solicitors Act 1974 s 73 (see LEGAL PROFESSIONS vol 66 (2015)

PARA 783 et seq), allowing the costs of the creditor's solicitor on the common fund basis in a creditor's action for administration see *Re Drew, Simmons and Simmons v Drew* (1913) 135 LT Jo 323.

12 *Re Westdock Realisations Ltd* [1988] BCLC 354; *McDonald v Horn* [1995] 1 All ER 961, CA. See the dicta of Park J in *Breadner v Granville Grossman* [2000] All ER (D) 996 quoted in *Raymond Saul & Co (a firm) v Holden (as personal representative of Hemmings)* [2008] EWHC 8565 (Ch) at [30]–[34], [2008] All ER (D) 168 (Dec) at [30]–[34].

13 *Re Beddoe* [1893] 1 Ch 547, CA. See also *Evans v Evans* [1985] 3 All ER 289, sub nom *Re Evans* [1986] 1 WLR 101; *McDonald v Horn* [1995] 1 All ER 961, CA; *Alsop Wilkinson (a firm) v Neary* [1995] 1 All ER 431, [1996] 1 WLR 1220; *Singh v Bhasin* (1998) Times, 21 August.

1197. Costs of administration proceedings generally. In the case of proceedings begun under the alternative procedure[1] for the determination of questions arising in the administration of the estate[2], the costs of all parties are allowed out of the estate where the application is made by the personal representative, or by a beneficiary or creditor[3] where there is some difficulty which would have justified an application by the personal representative[4]. If, however, a beneficiary applies to the court without real justification or takes advantage of the alternative procedure to have a question determined which, but for the procedure, should have been commenced using the normal procedure[5] or is otherwise properly described as hostile litigation, the court may apply the rule that the unsuccessful party should pay the costs of the successful party[6].

1 Ie under CPR Pt 8: see PARA 1166; and CIVIL PROCEDURE vol 11 (2015) PARA 150 et seq.

2 Ie under CPR Pt 64: see PARA 1172; and CIVIL PROCEDURE vol 11 (2015) PARA 188.

3 As to creditors' costs see PARAS 1203, 1205.

4 See *Re Buckton, Buckton v Buckton* [1907] 2 Ch 406; *Re Halston, Ewen v Halston* [1912] 1 Ch 435; *Re Flecher, King v King* (1918) 62 Sol Jo 740. The principle applied in *Re Buckton, Buckton v Buckton* of allowing a beneficiary's costs to be paid from the estate was extended in *Blades v Isaac* [2016] EWHC 601 (Ch), [2016] WTLR 589 to a beneficiary who succeeded in an action against trustees for breach of duty to disclose information about the terms of the trust. Although the trustees were unsuccessful, the court exercised its discretion under CPR 44.2(2) (see PARA 1210) not to order the trustees to pay the claimant's costs. The court acted on counsel's advice and out of genuine concern for the beneficiaries.

5 Ie under CPR Pt 7: see PARA 1166; and CIVIL PROCEDURE vol 11 (2015) PARA 135 et seq.

6 *Re Buckton, Buckton v Buckton* [1907] 2 Ch 406 at 415 per Kekewich J; *Re Halston, Ewen v Halston* [1912] 1 Ch 435 at 439; *Re Flecher, King v King* (1918) 62 Sol Jo 740; *Alsop Wilkinson (a firm) v Neary* [1995] 1 All ER 431, [1996] 1 WLR 1220.

1198. Prospective costs orders. Where trustees (including executors and administrators[1]) have power to agree to pay the costs of a party to such an application, and exercise such a power, an order is not required and the trustees are entitled to recover out of the trust fund any costs which they pay pursuant to the agreement made in the exercise of such power[2].

Where the trustees do not have, or decide not to exercise, a power to make such an agreement, the trustees or the party concerned may apply to the court at any stage of proceedings for an order that the costs of any party (including the costs of the trustees) are to be paid out of the fund (a 'prospective costs order')[3].

On an application for a prospective costs order the court may:

(1) in the case of the trustees' costs, authorise the trustees to meet such costs out of the fund[4];

(2) in the case of the costs of any other party, it may authorise or direct the trustees to pay such costs (or any part of them, or the costs incurred up to a particular time) out of the trust fund to be assessed, if not agreed by the trustees and to make payments from time to time on account of such costs[5].

1 References to trustees in CPR Pt 64 and CPR PD 64A—*Estates, Trusts and Charities* include executors and administrators: CPR 64.1(2).

2 CPR PD 64A—*Estates, Trusts and Charities* para 6.2.
3 CPR PD 64A—*Estates, Trusts and Charities* para 6.3.
4 CPR PD 64A—*Estates, Trusts and Charities* para 6.4(a). See note 5.
5 CPR PD 64A—*Estates, Trusts and Charities* para 6.4(b). Such an order will be for payment on the indemnity basis unless the court directs the standard basis. The court will normally expect to deal with such an application without a hearing: see CPR PD 64A para 6.5. As to the distinction between the indemnity and standard bases see CPR 44.4; and CIVIL PROCEDURE vol 12A (2015) PARA 1704.

1199. Fund for payment of costs. Such costs of a claim for administration as are properly payable out of the estate are to be treated as testamentary and administration expenses[1]. Accordingly, in the case of deaths after 1925, the costs are to be paid in due course of administration in accordance with the rules and principles considered earlier in this title[2].

1 *Miles v Harrison* (1874) 9 Ch App 316; *Harloe v Harloe* (1875) LR 20 Eq 471; *Penny v Penny* (1879) 11 ChD 440.
2 See PARA 993 et seq. As to the payment of costs in the case of death before 1926 see PARA 1012.

1200. When personal representative is liable for costs. Where administration proceedings are rendered necessary by the personal representative's gross and indefensible neglect to furnish accounts, he will be ordered to pay all the costs, including the costs of taking and vouching the accounts[1]. So, too, a representative who unnecessarily institutes administration proceedings will be ordered to pay the costs[2]. In a claim against a personal representative, where the court, after hearing the facts, makes an order for administration without any reservation of costs, it is not in accordance with the practice to entertain an application on further consideration that the representative should be ordered to pay costs down to the judgment; but this practice does not extend to a case where the order is made without evidence on both sides, or full discussion, either for the sake of convenience or to save expense, or otherwise in circumstances in which the court has not a sufficient knowledge of the facts[3].

1 *Heugh v Scard* (1875) 33 LT 659; *Re Skinner, Cooper v Skinner* [1904] 1 Ch 289, holding that *Hewett v Foster* (1844) 7 Beav 348 does not represent the modern practice. As to other cases where the personal representative has been ordered to pay the costs see *Eglin v Sanderson* (1862) 3 Giff 434; *Kemp v Burn* (1863) 4 Giff 348; *Gresham v Price* (1865) 35 Beav 47; *Re Bell's Estate, Bath v Bell* (1878) 39 LT 422; *Re Radclyffe, Pearce v Radclyffe* (1881) 29 WR 420; *Re Wallett, Hayter v Wells* (1883) 32 WR 26. See *Royal National Lifeboat Institution v Headley* [2016] EWHC 1948 (Ch) where a trustee who had failed to provide accounts over many years was ordered to pay the costs of the beneficiaries and refused an indemnity from the trust fund on the basis that the costs of the application were not 'properly incurred' by the trustee under CPR 46.3 (as to which see PARA 1196). As to cases where a trustee may be ordered to pay the costs of an action for account or for the execution of the trust brought by the beneficiary see TRUSTS AND POWERS vol 98 (2013) PARA 339. As to the meaning of 'personal representative' see PARA 608.
2 *Re Cabburn, Gage v Rutland* (1882) 46 LT 848.
3 *Re Gardner, Roberts v Fry* [1911] WN 155.

1201. Costs of personal representative in default. No costs are given to a personal representative who is in default to the estate, until the default is made good[1]. An executor not in default need not appear by the same solicitor as a defaulting co-executor; he is entitled to act by a separate solicitor, and if he does so he will be awarded his costs[2]. If he chooses to appear by the same solicitor as his defaulting co-executor he will be allowed only his proportion of the costs out of the estate[3]. A defaulting executor who becomes bankrupt is entitled to his costs subsequent to the bankruptcy, but the prior costs must be set off against the debt[4]. The personal representative of a defaulting executor, fairly accounting, is entitled to his costs out of the assets, even if the assets are insufficient to repair the breach of trust[5].

1 The personal representative's solicitor is in no better position: *Re O'Kean, Ferris v O'Kean* [1907] 1 IR 223, CA. As to the meaning of 'personal representative' see PARA 608.
2 *Smith v Dale* (1881) 18 ChD 516 at 518 per Jessel MR.
3 *Smith v Dale* (1881) 18 ChD 516, dissenting from *Watson v Row* (1874) LR 18 Eq 680. See also *McEwan v Crombie* (1883) 25 ChD 175.
4 *Samuel v Jones* (1843) 2 Hare 246; *Re Vowles, O'Donoghue v Vowles* (1886) 32 ChD 243, following *Re Basham, Hannay v Basham* (1883) 23 ChD 195, and *Lewis v Trask* (1882) 21 ChD 862, and dissenting from *Re Clare, Clare v Clare* (1882) 21 ChD 865.
5 *Haldenby v Spofforth* (1846) 9 Beav 195; *Palmer v Jones* (1874) 43 LJ Ch 349; *Re Kitto, Kitto v Luke* (1879) 28 WR 411.

1202. Mere delay or mistake no reason for depriving personal representatives of costs. Mere delay in rendering accounts is not of itself sufficient ground for visiting a personal representative with the payment of costs, or even for depriving him of his costs[1]; nor is the fact that he has made a mistake, or has endeavoured to charge in his accounts items which he is not legally entitled to charge, provided his claims are not dishonest claims, nor such as no reasonable man could say ought to have been put forward[2].

1 *Heighington v Grant* (1845) 1 Ph 600; *White v Jackson* (1852) 15 Beav 191. As to when the personal representative is liable for costs see PARA 1200. As to the meaning of 'personal representative' see PARA 608.
2 *Re Jones, Christmas v Jones* [1897] 2 Ch 190 at 197–198 per Kekewich J. See also *Turner v Hancock* (1882) 20 ChD 303, CA; *Travers v Townsend* (1828) 1 Mod 496; *Bennett v Attkins* (1835) 1 Y & C Ex 247; *Smith v Cremer* (1875) 24 WR 51.

1203. Costs of parties other than personal representatives. The costs of all parties other than the personal representative are entirely within the discretion of the court[1]; neither a claimant residuary legatee nor a creditor is entitled to his costs out of the estate as a matter of right[2]. A person unnecessarily added as a party has the right to attend, but is not required to appear or to brief counsel for the hearing. If he is satisfied that he has no claim, and still attends he will not be entitled to his costs[3]. A claimant who obtains judgment in an administration claim without any reservation as to costs is entitled to his costs of taking the accounts[4]; and as a general rule the court allows the costs of all necessary and proper parties to administration proceedings as a first charge upon the estate which is being administered[5]; but it will only allow them where the proceedings are in their origin directed, with some show of reason and a proper foundation, for the benefit of the estate, or have in their result conduced to that benefit[6]. Thus a legatee tenant for life who had received the whole of his income to date was disallowed the costs of administration proceedings instituted by him and made to pay personally the costs occasioned by his 'idle' insistence on an income account[7].

1 See the Senior Courts Act 1981 s 51; CPR 44.2; *Re McClellan, McClellan v McClellan* (1885) 29 ChD 495, CA; *Re Amory, Westminster Bank Ltd v British Sailors' Society Inc at Home and Abroad* [1951] 2 All ER 947n. See also CIVIL PROCEDURE vol 12A (2015) PARAS 1696–1701; COURTS AND TRIBUNALS vol 24 (2010) PARA 693. As to the meaning of 'personal representative' see PARA 608.
2 The costs of the next friend of a residuary legatee who is a minor are not the costs of the next friend but of the minor claimant, and cannot be set off against a debt which the next friend owes to the estate: *Re Barton, Holland v Kersley* (1912) 56 Sol Jo 380. A creditor's costs of establishing his debt will usually be allowed if he is successful unless the court otherwise directs. The judgment or order may have already provided for the costs of the claim without limiting the award to costs incurred to the date of the order so that all the proceedings in private properly conducted under the order are governed by it: see *Krehl v Park* (1875) 10 Ch App 334; *Quarrell v Beckford* (1816) 1 Madd 269 at 285–286.

3 *Re Amory, Westminster Bank Ltd v British Sailors' Society Inc at Home and Abroad* [1951] 2 All ER 947n.
4 *Re Roby, Sherbrooke v Taylor* (1916) 60 Sol Jo 291.
5 *Loomes v Stotherd* (1823) 1 Sim & St 458 at 461; *Ford v Earl of Chesterfield (No 3)* (1856) 21 Beav 426; *Larkins v Paxton* (1835) 2 My & K 320; *Barker v Wardle* (1835) 2 My & K 818.
6 *Bartlett v Wood* (1861) 9 WR 817 at 818 per Lord Westbury LC; *Turner v Frampton* (1846) 2 Coll 331.
7 *Croggan v Allen* (1882) 22 ChD 101.

1204. Personal representative's right to indemnity by creditor. A claimant creditor must, so far as the estate is insufficient to meet them, pay the personal representative's costs of the claim where it appears that there were no assets at the time the claim was brought sufficient to meet his claim, whether or not he had notice of the insufficiency of the assets[1]. Where there is a deficiency of assets any costs payable out of the estate are added to the debts and apportioned among them[2].

1 *Hibernian Bank v Lauder* [1898] 1 IR 262; *Bluett v Jessop* (1821) Jac 240; *Sullivan v Bevan* (1855) 20 Beav 399; *King v Bryant* (1841) 4 Beav 460; *Fuller v Green* (1857) 24 Beav 217. As to the meaning of 'personal representative' see PARA 608.
2 *Morshead v Reynolds* (1856) 21 Beav 638. As to interest on debts see PARA 1187.

1205. When creditor is entitled to costs on the indemnity basis. Where the estate was insufficient for payment of debts, the former rule was that a creditor was entitled to his costs on the indemnity basis both where he was the original claimant[1] and where he had obtained the conduct of the claim[2]; on the other hand, if the estate was not deficient, he obtained his costs only on the standard basis[3].

Similarly, the claimant in a legatee's action where the estate was insufficient to pay legacies[4] was entitled to his costs on the indemnity basis but only if the fund was sufficient to pay creditors[5].

However, the Civil Procedure Rules have introduced wholly new costs provisions[6].

1 *Tootal v Spicer* (1831) 4 Sim 510; *Hood v Wilson* (1831) 2 Russ & M 687; *Re Flynn, Guy v M'Carthy* (1886) 17 LR Ir 457; *Henderson v Dodds* (1866) LR 2 Eq 532. As to the distinction between the indemnity and standard bases see CPR 44.4; and CIVIL PROCEDURE vol 12A (2015) PARA 1704.
2 *Re Richardson, Richardson v Richardson* (1880) 14 ChD 611.
3 See the law on this subject reviewed by Stirling LJ in *Re New Zealand Midland Rly Co, Smith v Lubbock* [1901] 2 Ch 357, CA, explaining *Stanton v Hatfield* (1836) 1 Keen 358, and *Goldsmith v Russell* (1855) 5 De GM & G 547. Where the general estate was sufficient to pay separate creditors, but insufficient to pay joint creditors of a testator who was one of a firm of traders, the separate creditor claimant obtained costs on the solicitor and client basis: *Re McRea, Norden v McRea* (1886) 32 ChD 613.
4 *Cross v Kennington* (1848) 11 Beav 89; *Thomas v Jones* (1860) 1 Drew & Sm 134; *Re Harvey, Wright v Woods* (1884) 26 ChD 179.
5 *Weston v Clowes* (1847) 15 Sim 610, disapproving *Burkitt v Ransom* (1846) 2 Coll 536; *Wetenhall v Dennis* (1863) 33 Beav 285. See also *Re Richardson, Richardson v Richardson* (1880) 14 ChD 611 at 613 per Jessel MR, explaining that *Re Burrell, Burrell v Smith* (1870) LR 9 Eq 443, was not intended to alter the general rule; and *Re Wilkins, Wilkins v Rotherham* (1884) 27 ChD 703.
6 See PARA 1196 et seq; and CIVIL PROCEDURE vol 12A (2015) PARA 1697 et seq.

1206. Costs of overpaid beneficiary. As a rule a beneficiary who has been overpaid will not be paid his separate costs, even though the deficiency has arisen from the wasting of the estate subsequently to the payment to him[1].

1 *Re Winslow, Frere v Winslow* (1890) 45 ChD 249.

1207. Proceedings by unpaid residuary legatees. Where a portion of the estate has been distributed among certain residuary legatees, and the unpaid residuary legatees institute administration proceedings, the legatees who have received their shares cannot be ordered to contribute to the costs of the claim, but they will not get their costs without first bringing in their shares and contributing to the costs[1].

1 *Mackenzie v Taylor* (1844) 7 Beav 467; *Re Tann, Tann v Tann, Gravatt v Tann (No 2)* (1869) LR 7 Eq 436; *Hilliard v Fulford* (1876) 4 ChD 389.

1208. Costs of inquiries. Where some of the persons entitled to share in a fund are known but there is, or is likely to be, difficulty or delay in ascertaining other persons so entitled, the court may direct the cost of inquiries to fall on the share of the fund[1]. The costs of establishing a claim as next of kin of an intestate are allowed out of the estate[2].

In the case of legacies it is the duty of the personal representatives to ascertain who is entitled, but where inquiry is necessary the court may order that the costs fall on the legacy[3].

1 See CPR PD 40A—*Accounts, Inquiries etc* para 7; and PARA 1194.
2 *Bennett v Wood* (1837) 7 Sim 522; *Bakewell v Tagart* (1838) 3 Y & C Ex 173.
3 Older cases were decided when RSC Ord LXV R14B was in force which provided for payment in this way unless the court ordered otherwise: see *Re Whitaker, Denison-Pender v Evans* [1911] 1 Ch 214. Even then costs were directed to be paid out of the general residuary estate where the difficulty arose from the language the testator has employed: see *Re Groom, Booty v Groom* [1897] 2 Ch 407; *Re Hall-Dare, Le Marchant v Lee Warner* [1916] 1 Ch 272, or where the testator was taken to have contemplated that the payment of a legacy would involve some proceedings on behalf of the legatee or by the personal representative: *Re Parton, Parton v Parton* (1911) 131 LT Jo 106.

1209. Costs of improper litigation. The court will not permit costs occasioned by improper litigation, the representation of unnecessary parties[1], or by negligent conduct of administration proceedings, to be paid out of the estate under its care[2]. A beneficiary who sets up a case of misconduct against the representative which he fails to substantiate must, of course, pay the costs of the proceedings[3]. The costs of a successful claimant in an issue directed to be tried in administration proceedings will be ordered to be paid in full out of the assets[4].

1 *Re Amory, Westminster Bank Ltd v British Sailors' Society Incorporated at Home and Abroad* [1951] 2 All ER 947n. See also PARA 1203.
2 *Brown v Burdett* (1888) 40 ChD 244, CA; *Re Scowby, Scowby v Scowby* [1897] 1 Ch 741, CA. See also *Curteis v Candler* (1821) 6 Madd 123.
3 *Williams v Jones* (1886) 34 ChD 120, CA.
4 *Re Dunn, Brinklow v Singleton* (1902) 46 Sol Jo 432.

1210. Costs of unsuccessful claims and appeals. The general rule is that the costs occasioned by an unsuccessful claim, or unsuccessful resistance to any claim, to any property are not to be paid out of the estate unless the court otherwise directs[1]. The costs of a claimant, even though he fails to establish his claim, may, however, be allowed out of the estate where he has enabled the court to construe the will or to distribute the fund[2].

The costs of an unsuccessful appeal on a point of construction may be allowed in a proper case[3]. In such a case the trustees should always be represented, and their costs will come out of the estate, but the appellant should, where there are numerous respondents in the same interest, serve them with notice that the court will be asked to allow only one set of costs against him if his appeal fails[4]. However, a party who does not join in a successful appeal may remain bound by the order below[5].

1 See CPR 44.2(2); and CIVIL PROCEDURE vol 12A (2015) PARA 1698.
2 The court has a general discretion to allow an unsuccessful party his costs: see CPR 44.2(2)(b); and CIVIL PROCEDURE vol 12A (2015) PARA 1698. See eg *Thomason v Moses* (1842) 5 Beav 77;

Wedgwood v Adams (1844) 8 Beav 103; *Merlin v Blagrave* (1858) 25 Beav 125. For other instances see *Westcott v Culliford* (1844) 3 Hare 265 at 274; *Cooper v Pitcher* (1845) 4 Hare 485; *Johnston v Todd* (1845) 8 Beav 489; *Boreham v Bignall* (1850) 8 Hare 131; *Lee v Delane* (1850) 4 De G & Sm 1.

3 *Re Stuart, Johnson v Williams* [1940] 4 All ER 80, CA. Personal representatives should not themselves appeal where they are seeking only the court's protection. See *Re Londonderry's Settlement, Peat v Walsh* [1965] Ch 918, [1964] 3 All ER 855, [1965] 2 WLR 229, CA.

4 See note 3.

5 See *Elliot v Lord Joicey* [1935] AC 209 at 235, HL, per Lord Russell of Killowen.

1211. Appeal against order for costs. An appeal from a decision of a judge in the County Court or the High Court, generally requires permission from the trial judge or the Court of Appeal[1], and the same principle has been applied to an appeal from an order as to costs of a master (or district judge)[2]. In general, decisions as to costs are in the discretion of the court[3] which means that the appellate court will only interfere if the original decision was wrong in principle.

However, a personal representative[4] or trustee is entitled to an indemnity out of the relevant trust fund or estate for costs properly incurred[5]. Hence, an order depriving a personal representative of his costs is not at the judge's discretion but is made on the basis that the personal representative is guilty of misconduct. Permission to appeal may be more likely to be granted. On the other hand an order allowing him his costs must have been made either on the ground that he has been guilty of no misconduct and is therefore entitled to them, or that, although guilty of misconduct, the court has in its discretion allowed him his costs, and an appeal can only be made on the basis that the judge or master wrongfully exercised his discretion[6].

1 See CPR 52.3; and CIVIL PROCEDURE vol 12A (2015) PARAS 1517, 1538–1540. See also *Scherer v Counting Instruments Ltd* [1986] 2 All ER 529, [1986] 1 WLR 615n, CA.

2 *Hoddle v CCF Construction Ltd* [1992] 2 All ER 550.

3 See PARA 1196. A declaration that the court does not think fit to make any order as to costs amounts to a judicial decision that the trustee is not entitled to his costs, and that he cannot retain them out of the estate: *Re Hodgkinson, Hodgkinson v Hodgkinson* [1895] 2 Ch 190, CA.

4 As to the meaning of 'personal representative' see PARA 608. See also PARA 1196.

5 See PARA 1196.

6 *Charles v Jones* (1886) 33 ChD 80, CA.

15. PERSONAL REPRESENTATIVES' LIABILITIES

(1) LIABILITY FOR DECEASED'S OBLIGATIONS

1212. General rule as to liability for deceased's obligations. All claims founded upon any obligation under a contract, bond or covenant, or upon any debt or duty which might have been enforced by suing the deceased in his lifetime, are in like manner enforceable, to the extent of assets, against the personal representative[1], even though he is not named in the instrument creating the obligation[2]. The personal representative[3] can never be under a duty to commit a breach of a contract so enforceable, but if it is onerous he should take every opportunity to come to terms[4]. Nevertheless, disclaimer of a contract by the personal representative, before performance by the contractor, may not always suffice to defeat the entitlement of persons who would have benefited if the contract had been performed[5].

1 Bac Abr, Executors and Administrators (P) 1; Shep Touch (7th Edn) p 482; *Hambly v Trott* (1776) 1 Cowp 371 at 375; *Hyde v Skinner* (1723) 2 P Wms 196; *Kennewell v Dye* [1949] Ch 517, [1949] 1 All ER 881.

2 Went Off Ex (14th Edn) 239, 243. See further the Law Reform (Miscellaneous Provisions) Act 1934 s 1; and PARA 1277 et seq. As to the survival of causes of action in contract see CONTRACT vol 22 (2012) PARA 639. See also the Consumer Credit Act 1974 s 86; and CONSUMER CREDIT vol 21 (2016) PARA 231. See further the Matrimonial Causes Act 1973 s 36; and MATRIMONIAL AND CIVIL PARTNERSHIP LAW vol 72 (2015) PARA 336.

3 As to the meaning of 'personal representative' see PARA 608.

4 *Ahmed Angullia v Estate and Trust Agencies (1927) Ltd* [1938] AC 624, [1938] 3 All ER 106, PC. See also *Reid v Lord Tenterden* (1833) 4 Tyr 111 (prompt offer to surrender lease); *Wilkinson v Cawood* (1797) 3 Anstr 909; and Went Off Ex (14th Edn) 224, 290 (waiver of lease where value of land less than rent and insufficient assets).

5 See *Re Rushbrook's Will Trusts, Allwood v Norwich Diocesan Fund and Board of Finance (Incorporated)* [1948] Ch 421, [1948] 1 All ER 932 (disclaimer by executors of a contract to repair buildings did not defeat the entitlement of specific devisees of property to have the costs of repairs paid from the testator's personal estate); and see PARA 1215 text and note 1.

1213. Contract founded on personal considerations: effect of death. Where a contract is founded on personal considerations, the death of either party before breach of the contract[1] puts an end to the relationship[2]. Accordingly an agreement between an employer and employee or master and apprentice[3] is determined by the death of either party[4], and an agreement to write a book or to paint a picture is determined by the death of the author or artist[5]. On the death of a master no portion of the premium could be recovered by an apprentice[6], and a similar rule held in the case of a solicitor to whom a clerk had been articled[7]; but personal representatives[8] are entitled to sue for any money actually earned by the deceased during his lifetime[9], and even for remuneration accruing due after his death, if it appears to have been the intention of the parties that remuneration should continue payable after the termination of the contract[10].

Despite the general rule, some types of contractual right, closely based on personal considerations, are, by their nature and origin, capable of assignment and transmission after the death of either party[11].

1 A personal representative may be sued if the contract was broken in the deceased's lifetime: *Siboni v Kirkman* (1836) 1 M & W 418 at 423.

2 *Farrow v Wilson* (1869) LR 4 CP 744; *Graves v Cohen* (1929) 46 TLR 121. See also CONTRACT vol 22 (2012) PARAS 335, 475. The common law rule has been modified, however, in cases to which the Law Reform (Frustrated Contracts) Act 1943 applies, and permits the recovery of money paid upon a contract that has become frustrated even though there has not been a total failure of consideration: see CONTRACT vol 22 (2012) PARA 484 et seq.

3 As to apprentices see EMPLOYMENT vol 39 (2014) PARAS 112, 128–129.

4 *Farrow v Wilson* (1869) LR 4 CP 744; *R v Peck* (1698) 1 Salk 66; and see EMPLOYMENT vol 41 (2014) PARAS 722, 732.
5 *Hall v Wright* (1859) EB & E 765 at 794, Ex Ch, per Pollock CB; *Siboni v Kirkman* (1836) 1 M & W 418 at 423. See note 10.
6 *Whincup v Hughes* (1871) LR 6 CP 78. See also note 3.
7 *Ferns v Carr* (1885) 28 ChD 409, dissenting from *Hirst v Tolson* (1850) 2 Mac & G 134. See also RESTITUTION vol 88 (2012) PARA 494.
8 As to the meaning of 'personal representative' see PARA 608.
9 *Stubbs v Holywell Rly Co* (1867) LR 2 Exch 311.
10 *Wilson v Harper* [1908] 2 Ch 370. See also PARA 1279; and CONTRACT vol 22 (2012) PARA 336.
11 See *Experience Hendrix LLC v Purple Haze Records Ltd* [2007] EWCA Civ 501, [2008] EMLR 351, [2007] All ER (D) 430 (May), concerning the 'performer's property rights' under the Copyright, Designs and Patents Act 1988 Pt II (ss 180-212): see ss 191A–191C; and PARA 27 note 23 (the performer's non-property rights, are not assignable or transmissible except as set out in s 192A).

1214. Conveyance of land contracted to be sold: effect of death. The personal representatives[1] of a person at whose death there was subsisting an enforceable contract[2] for the sale of his freehold interest in any land[3] have power and are bound to convey the land for all their deceased's estate and interest in it[4]. Where a lease had been granted which contained an option to purchase the reversion to the lease and the option was validly exercised (but not accepted), an order for specific performance was made against the personal representative of the grantor[5].

1 As to the meaning of 'personal representative' see PARA 608.
2 Where a contractual option to purchase land was granted by the testator's will itself, the grantee was entitled to enforce his option against the executor: *Re Gray, Allardyce v Roebuck* [2004] EWHC 1538 (Ch), [2004] 3 All ER 754; normally, the same result will follow where the option is granted by the testator during his lifetime; see note 4 and see PARA 1281, for survival of contractual causes of action. Cf a mere right of pre-emption which, without more, does not create an interest in land: see *Pritchard v Briggs* [1980] Ch 338, [1980] 1 All ER 294, CA. To be an enforceable contract to sell land, compliance with the statutory formalities must be shown: *Firstpost Homes Ltd v Johnson* [1995] 4 All ER 355, [1995] 1 WLR 1567 (agreement failed to comply with Law of Property (Miscellaneous Provisions) Act 1989 s 2).
3 See *Kennewell v Dye* [1949] Ch 517, [1949] 1 All ER 881; and CONVEYANCING vol 23 (2016) PARA 35.
4 See the Administration of Estates Act 1925 s 2; and PARA 945. Where the vendor has received the entire purchase price before his death he becomes a bare trustee of the legal estate for the purchaser: see *Re Cuming* (1869) 5 Ch App 72; *Re Colling* (1886) 32 ChD 333, CA. As to sale of land generally see CONVEYANCING.
5 See *Taylor v Crotty* [2006] EWCA Civ 1364, 150 Sol Jo LB 1330, [2006] All ER (D) 32 (Oct), CA.

1215. Effect on building contract of employer's death. The personal representatives[1] of an employer are entitled to the benefit of the performance of a building contract, but, on the other hand, they are liable to the contractor for the price. If a building is being erected under a building contract made with the deceased upon land belonging to him at the time of his death, a devisee of the land is entitled, subject to the terms of the will, to require that the cost of completing the building in accordance with the contract be paid by the personal representatives out of the deceased's real and personal estate applicable to the discharge of his debts and liabilities[2].

1 As to the meaning of 'personal representative' see PARA 608.
2 *Re Rushbrook's Will Trusts, Allwood v Norwich Diocesan Fund and Board of Finance* [1948] Ch 421, [1948] 1 All ER 932; *Holt v Holt* (1694) 2 Vern 322; *Cooper v Jarman* (1866) LR 3 Eq 98; *Re Day, Sprake v Day* [1898] 2 Ch 510; but cf *Ahmed Angullia v Estate and Trust Agencies (1927) Ltd* [1938] AC 624, [1938] 3 All ER 106, PC. As to the liability of the deceased's real and personal estate for debts and liabilities see the Administration of Estates Act 1925 s 34(3); and PARA 998 et seq. As to joint contractors see PARA 1231. As to the incidence of benefit and liability on a building contract as between a specific devisee and residuary legatees see *Re Day's Will Trusts, Lloyds Bank Ltd v Shafe* [1962] 3 All ER 699, [1962] 1 WLR 1419 (where a further distinction was drawn between the cost of repairs required to be done under the testatrix's lifetime landlord's repairing covenant (ordered to be met from the residuary estate) and

undefined general repairs, which might or might not have been carried out by a builder, had the testatrix survived (not required to be borne by the estate)); and LANDLORD AND TENANT vol 63 (2012) PARA 743.

1216. Effect on building contract of contractor's death. On the death of a building contractor before he has completed his contract his personal representatives are bound to perform the contract[1] unless the contractor was employed owing to some special personal qualification[2], and are entitled to recover payment[3]. If the contractor's personal representative enters into a fresh or supplementary contract in his capacity as such he will be personally liable on the contract, but may bring an action on it in his representative capacity, and this right of action, if accrued, will pass to an administrator de bonis non on the death of the original personal representative[4].

Where one of several joint contractors dies, his personal representatives are entitled to share in the contract, and to have their rights as between themselves and their joint contractors ascertained on its completion, and cannot, without their consent, be bought out at a valuation[5].

1 Fitzherbert's La Graunde Abridgement, Barre, pl 60 (1453), cited by Coke CJ in *Quick and Harris v Ludborrow* (1615) 3 Bulst 29 at 30. As to the meaning of 'personal representative' see PARA 608.
2 *Siboni v Kirkman* (1836) 1 M & W 418 at 422–423. As to the termination on death of contracts founded on personal considerations see PARA 1213. As to non-assignability of obligations under personal building contracts see further BUILDING CONTRACTS vol 6 (2011) PARAS 256–257.
3 *Marshall v Broadhurst* (1831) 1 Cr & J 403.
4 *Moseley v Rendell* (1871) LR 6 QB 338. As to administration de bonis non see PARA 793.
5 *McClean v Kennard* (1874) 9 Ch App 336. See also *Ambler v Bolton* (1872) LR 14 Eq 427.

1217. Tax liabilities re person who dies. The personal representatives of a person who dies chargeable to tax are liable for the income tax[1] and any penalties already imposed[2], and for capital gains tax[3], charged on the deceased, and may deduct any payments made out of the deceased's assets and effects[4]. In addition to any tax assessed on the deceased and unpaid at the time of his death, the personal representatives may be assessed on income and chargeable gains arising prior to the death which have not been assessed at the date of death[5].

The assessments discussed above must be made within certain time limits[6].

Personal representatives are liable for inheritance tax on a chargeable transfer made on the deceased's death so far as the tax is attributable to property which was not comprised in a settlement immediately before his death, or was so comprised and consists of land in the United Kingdom which devolves upon or vests in them[7].

Where inheritance tax becomes payable on the value transferred by a potentially exempt transfer or lifetime chargeable transfer, the transferor's personal representatives will become liable where there is no person liable for the tax[8], or the tax remains unpaid 12 months after the end of the month of the death of the transferor[9]. Where property is treated as included in the estate because the gifted property is property subject to a reservation[10] the personal representatives will be liable for the inheritance tax attributable to that property if the tax remains unpaid 12 months after the end of the month of death[11].

On the death of a person who is a taxable person for the purposes of value added tax any person carrying on his business may be treated as a taxable person until some other person is registered in respect of it[12].

There are special statutory provisions for the taxation of estates in the course of administration[13].

1 See the Taxes Management Act 1970 s 74(1); and INCOME TAXATION vol 59 (2014) PARA 1763. As to the meaning of 'personal representative' see PARA 608.

2 The Crown's claim for penalties falls within the expression 'all causes of action' in the Law Reform (Miscellaneous Provisions) Act 1934 s 1(1) (see PARAS 1277–1278) and accordingly survives the taxpayer's death: *A-G v Canter* [1939] 1 KB 318, [1939] 1 All ER 13, CA. The power to impose a penalty on the personal representatives of a deceased person has been repealed and no similar provision now exists (even where it is clear that there were inaccuracies in returns submitted by that person before his death): see the Taxes Management Act 1970 s 100A(1) (repealed). Such provisions are likely to be incompatible with the Convention for the Protection of Human Rights and Fundamental Freedoms (Rome, 4 November 1950; TS 71 (1953); Cmnd 8969) art 6 (as set out in the Human Rights Act 1998 Sch 1: see RIGHTS AND FREEDOMS vol 88A (2013) PARA 14): see Application 19958/92 *AP v Switzerland* (1997) 26 EHRR 541, ECtHR.

3 See the Taxes Management Act 1970 ss 74(1), 77(1); and CAPITAL GAINS TAXATION vol 6 (2011) PARA 1052. See also the Taxation of Chargeable Gains Act 1992 s 65; and CAPITAL GAINS TAXATION vol 6 (2011) PARA 702.

4 See the Taxes Management Act 1970 s 74(1); and INCOME TAXATION vol 59 (2014) PARA 1763.

5 See the Taxes Management Act 1970 s 74; and INCOME TAXATION vol 59 (2014) PARA 1763. This may include adjustments to the liability of earlier years (eg as the result of the revision of liability in respect of trading income or discontinuance of a trade under the Income Tax (Trading and Other Income) Act 2005 s 202).

6 As from 1 April 2010 such an assessment must normally be made no later than four years after the end of the year of assessment in which death occurred: see the Taxes Management Act 1970 s 40(1) (amended by the Finance Act 2008 s 118(1), Sch 39 paras 1, 11(1), (2); and SI 2009/403). In a case involving a loss of tax brought about carelessly or deliberately by a person who has died (or another person acting on that person's behalf before that person's death) an assessment to tax can be made on personal representatives for any year of assessment ending not earlier than six years before his death: see the Taxes Management Act 1970 s 40(2) (amended by the Finance Act 2008 s 118(1), Sch 39 paras 1, 11(1), (3)). As to transitional provision specifying that these amendments do not come into force until 1 April 2012 for certain purposes see the Finance Act 2008, Schedule 39 (Appointed Day, Transitional Provision and Savings) Order 2009, SI 2009/403, art 10. See further INCOME TAXATION vol 59 (2014) PARAS 2228–2229.

7 See the Inheritance Tax Act 1984 s 200(1)(a); and INHERITANCE TAXATION vol 59A (2014) PARA 264. The personal representative's liability for inheritance tax is an original liability: *IRC v Stannard* [1984] 2 All ER 105, [1984] 1 WLR 1039.

8 Ie within the Inheritance Tax Act 1984 s 199(1)(b)–(d): see INHERITANCE TAXATION vol 59A (2014) PARAS 255, 264, 266, 267, 279.

9 See the Inheritance Tax Act 1984 s 204(8) (substituted by the Finance Act 1986 s 101, Sch 19 para 28(3), in relation to transfers of value made, and other events occurring, on or after 18 March 1986); and INHERITANCE TAXATION vol 59A (2014) PARAS 264, 270. Liability is limited to the extent of the assets mentioned in the Inheritance Tax Act 1984 s 204(1): see INHERITANCE TAXATION vol 59A (2014) PARA 264.

10 Ie within the meaning of the Finance Act 1986 s 102 (see INHERITANCE TAXATION vol 59A (2014) PARA 48 .

11 See the Inheritance Act 1984 s 204(9) (substituted by the Finance Act 1986 s 101, Sch 19 para 28(3), in relation to transfers of value made, and other events occurring, on or after 18 March 1986); and INHERITANCE TAXATION vol 59A (2014) PARA 264. Liability is limited to the extent of the assets mentioned in the Inheritance Act 1984 s 204(1): see INHERITANCE TAXATION vol 59A (2014) PARA 264. The personal representatives have a right to recover that amount from the person in whom the property to which the tax is attributable is vested: see the Inheritance Act 1984 s 211(3); and INHERITANCE TAXATION vol 59A (2014) PARA 271.

12 See the Value Added Tax Regulations 1995, SI 1995/2518, reg 9; and VALUE ADDED TAX vol 99 (2012) PARA 25. As to assessments after death see the Value Added Tax Act 1994 s 77(5); and VALUE ADDED TAX vol 99 (2012) PARA 386.

13 See the Income Tax (Trading and Other Income) Act 2005 Pt 5 (ss 649–689A); and INCOME TAXATION vol 59 (2014) PARA 2075 et seq.

1218. Personal statutory obligations: effect of death. A statutory obligation which is purely personal, and for the enforcement of which a statutory mode is provided, for example the liability of the putative father under an affiliation order, ceases when, by the person's death, the statutory mode of enforcing payment has ceased, and no claim can be maintained against his personal representatives either for arrears or for future payments[1]. Similarly, payments of arrears of alimony are not enforceable against the personal representative of a deceased husband[2]. Secured periodical payments under the Children Act 1989[3] which bind the payer's estate may be made[4]. Unsecured periodical payment orders cease to have effect on the death of the person liable to make payments under the order[5]. Arrears of child support maintenance for which a deceased person was liable immediately before death are a debt payable by the deceased's executor or administrator out of the deceased's estate to the Secretary of State[6]. Fines imposed for criminal convictions and other penalties imposed upon a living person which are due to the Crown will, despite their personal nature, normally survive the death of that person and fall upon his estate[7]; similarly, the bankruptcy of a testator or of a beneficiary is capable of affecting assets of the estate that may come within the hands of the personal representatives of the testator or of the personal representatives of the beneficiary, or of both[8].

1 *Re Harrington, Wilder v Turner* [1908] 2 Ch 687. Affiliation proceedings were abolished by the Family Law Reform Act 1987 s 17 but without prejudice to the operation of existing orders: see s 33(2), Sch 3 para 6. Orders for secured periodical payments which bind the payer's estate may now be made under the Children Act 1989 s 15, Sch 1 para 1(2)(b): see the text and notes 3–4.
2 *Re Hedderwick, Morton v Brinsley* [1933] Ch 669.
3 Ie under the Children Act 1989 s 15, Sch 1 (see CHILDREN AND YOUNG PERSONS vol 9 (2012) PARA 562 et seq).
4 See the Children Act 1989 Sch 1 para 1(2)(b); and CHILDREN AND YOUNG PERSONS vol 9 (2012) PARA 562. The personal representatives of a deceased parent liable to make payments under a secured periodical payments order may apply for the variation or discharge of the order: see Sch 1 para 7; CHILDREN AND YOUNG PERSONS vol 9 (2012) PARA 567.
5 See the Children Act 1989 Sch 1 para 3(3); and CHILDREN AND YOUNG PERSONS vol 9 (2012) PARA 563. There may also be a claim for family provision: see PARA 565 et seq.
6 See the Child Support Act 1991 s 43A; the Child Support (Management of Payments and Arrears) Regulations 2009, SI 2009/3151, reg 11; and CHILDREN AND YOUNG PERSONS vol 9 (2012) PARA 579. Where the deceased's estate is insolvent the arrears are a provable debt: see *Berry v Child Support Agency* [2016] EWHC 1418 (Ch).
7 See *HM Treasury v Harris* [1957] 2 QB 516, [1957] 2 All ER 455; and PARA 1217, text and note 2.
8 See *Re Hemming, Raymond Saul & Co (a firm) v Holden* [2008] EWHC 2731 (Ch), [2009] Ch 313, [2008] All ER (D) 176 (Nov); and see also PARAS 922, 981, 1219.

1219. Trustee in bankruptcy of testator, or third party, or legatee: effect of death. Although the personal representative[1] is not generally liable for the obligations in the bankruptcy of the testator, the property which formerly belonged to or was vested in the testator will have become, or in the case of after-acquired property, be liable to become, vested in the trustee in bankruptcy[2]. The personal representative's powers and rights to administer the estate may thereby become postponed and subordinated to those of a trustee in bankruptcy[3].

The position of a bankrupt testator is dealt with elsewhere in this title[4]. The personal representative and the estate may still be affected, even though the bankruptcy is not that of the testator, but rather of a third party; where a testator has benefited from a voidable preference made by a third party, the personal representative may be ordered to repay the preference to the trustee in bankruptcy of the third party[5].

In the case of a bankrupt legatee, any interest of the legatee in the estate, provided that it is of a species of property recognised by the insolvency legislation for that purpose, including the interest of a residuary legatee, will vest in or, in the case of after-acquired property, be liable to become vested in[6], the trustee in bankruptcy[7].

Where a legatee has become bankrupt in the testator's lifetime, payment of a legacy to him without notice of his bankruptcy before the trustee in bankruptcy has intervened has been held to be good[8]. However the cases were decided before the current legislation[9] and can probably no longer be relied upon.

The case of a legatee who becomes bankrupt subsequent to the death of the testator may raise different considerations from those involved where the legatee is already bankrupt by that date[10], but the court will be astute to avoid arbitrary results which might otherwise result from the relationship between the date of a legatee's bankruptcy and the date of the testator's death[11].

1 As to the meaning of 'personal representative' see PARA 608.
2 See *Rooney v Cardona* [1999] 1 WLR 1388, [1999] 2 FLR 1148, CA; the Insolvency Act 1986 ss 306, 307, 436; and BANKRUPTCY AND INDIVIDUAL INSOLVENCY vol 5 (2013) PARAS 398, 458. Under s 307, the bankrupt is under a duty to give notice to the trustee, within 21 days of his becoming aware of the devolution upon him of after-acquired property (such as legacy) (see s 333(2); and BANKRUPTCY AND INDIVIDUAL INSOLVENCY vol 5 (2013) PARA 415) and the trustee may then, by written notice to the bankrupt, claim the property for the bankrupt's estate (see s 307(1)–(3); and BANKRUPTCY AND INDIVIDUAL INSOLVENCY vol 5 (2013) PARA 458).
3 With a bankrupt testator, the vesting in the trustee occurs immediately upon his appointment (see the Insolvency Act 1986 s 306(1); and BANKRUPTCY AND INDIVIDUAL INSOLVENCY vol 5 (2013) PARA 398); with after-acquired property, such as with a bankrupt legatee, there is a statutory relation-back of the vesting in the trustee to the time at which the property was acquired by, or devolved upon the bankrupt (see s 307(3); and BANKRUPTCY AND INDIVIDUAL INSOLVENCY vol 5 (2013) PARA 459).
4 See PARAS 981, 982.
5 See *Cadlock v Aboagye* [2006] EWHC 3654 (Ch), [2006] All ER (D) 170 (Dec).
6 See note 2.
7 See *Re Hemming, Raymond Saul & Co (a firm) v Holden* [2008] EWHC 2731 (Ch), [2009] Ch 313, [2008] All ER (D) 176 (Nov) (held that the right of a residuary legatee was a composite right to have the residue (if any) paid to him as and when the administration was complete; that composite right was a chose in action which was transmissible and accordingly fell within the first limb of the definition of 'property' in the Insolvency Act 1986 s 436; that right vested in the trustee in bankruptcy and would not re-vest in the bankrupt unless and until his bankruptcy debts and costs were repaid; that right was capable of being asserted by the trustee against the executor).
8 *Re Ball* [1899] 2 IR 313. See also *Cohen v Mitchell* (1890) 25 QBD 262, 59 LJQB 409; *Re Bennett* [1907] 1 KB 149, 76 LJKB 134. The right of the trustee in bankruptcy to claim after-acquired property is contained in the Insolvency Act 1986 s 307 (see BANKRUPTCY AND INDIVIDUAL INSOLVENCY vol 5 (2013) PARA 459).
9 See the Insolvency Act 1986 s 307(4); and PARA 1065.
10 Where the legatee becomes bankrupt after the death of the testator, the chose in action comprising the legatee's interest in the unadministered estate, which arose at the death, cannot be after-acquired property and vests in the trustee on his appointment, by way of a statutory deemed assignment: see the Insolvency Act 1986 s 311(4); and BANKRUPTCY AND INDIVIDUAL INSOLVENCY vol 5 (2013) PARA 410. The representative's consequent liability towards the trustee, for dealing with any such property as is vested in the trustee, may, it seems, depend in some circumstances upon his having notice of the deemed assignment to the trustee of the legatee's interest: notice of the deemed assignment need not be given except in so far as it is necessary, in a case where the deemed assignment is from the bankrupt himself, for protecting the priority of the trustee: see s 311(4); and BANKRUPTCY AND INDIVIDUAL INSOLVENCY vol 5 (2013) PARA 410. In this context, notices required to be gazetted by the Insolvency Rules 1986, SI 1986/1925, are evidence of the facts contained within the notice but do not appear to provide constructive notice to the world of the bankruptcy: see the Insolvency Rules 1986, SI 1986/1925, r 12.20 (now revoked: see generally r 12A.37); *Rooney v Cardona* [1999] 1 WLR 1388, [1999] 2 FLR 1148, CA; and BANKRUPTCY AND INDIVIDUAL INSOLVENCY vol 5 (2013) PARA 778. The obligation to surrender control under the Insolvency Act 1986 s 312(3), which can apply to a personal representative's obligation, carries a 'reasonable excuse' defence under s 312(4): see BANKRUPTCY AND INDIVIDUAL INSOLVENCY vol 5 (2013) PARA 475. See also the duties owed by the bankrupt himself to the trustee under ss 312(3), (4), 333 (see BANKRUPTCY AND INDIVIDUAL INSOLVENCY vol 5 (2013) PARA 475). See also, generally, PARA 1064.
11 See *Re Hemming, Raymond Saul & Co (a firm) v Holden* [2008] EWHC 2731 (Ch), [2009] Ch 313, [2008] All ER (D) 176 (Nov).

1220. Incomplete gifts: effect of death. In general a gift which has been promised but is not secured by an instrument under seal or, in the case of a chattel, completed by delivery is unenforceable either against the promisor or against his personal representatives[1], but the circumstances may be such as to make the promisor or his personal representatives liable to implement his promise[2], and an imperfect gift may be perfected by the donor appointing the donee to be his executor[3]; the principle remains that there is no equity to perfect an imperfect gift[4]. The subject of incomplete gifts is considered elsewhere in this work[5].

1 As to the meaning of 'personal representative' see PARA 608.
2 See eg ESTOPPEL vol 47 (2014) PARAS 362, 385, 392.
3 See PARA 626.
4 See *Connell v Connell, Connell v Findlay* [2008] UKPC 44, [2009] All ER (D) 123 (Jan) (document, testamentary on its face but unwitnessed, was not effective to pass title to property or to constitute immediate and effective inter vivos declaration of trust). See also *Kaye v Zeital* [2010] EWCA Civ 159, [2010] All ER (D) 49 (Mar) (intestate deceased had purported to transfer shares to partner inter vivos; method used was in effective to divest deceased or the beneficial interest, which fell into the intestate estate).
5 See GIFTS vol 52 (2014) PARA 267 et seq.

1221. Contracts to leave property by will and other lifetime dispositions of assets. A person with whom a contract is made by a testator to leave property by will may, if the contract is made for consideration and is otherwise enforceable, have a maintainable claim against the testator's estate if he has not fulfilled his promise in his will[1], but the doctrine of part performance[2] will not be strained so as to give effect to an oral promise where there is no such memorandum in writing as is required by law[3].

It seems, however, that a lifetime voluntary conveyance by a person of his property in association with a leaseback arrangement to himself, if made with intent to defraud creditors, and which causes prejudice to a person who would otherwise be able to claim under the Inheritance (Provision for Family and Dependants) Act 1975, may be seen as an attempt at avoidance of obligation and set aside, even though the claimant could not properly be described as a creditor[4]. Such property will then become assets in the hands of the personal representatives of the person making the original disposition[5].

Where the deceased gave an assurance or promise to leave property by will to the promisee which is relied on to the detriment of the promisee, the court will order provision to be made from the estate if it would be unconscionable not to grant relief[6].

1 See *Schaefer v Schuhmann* [1972] AC 572, [1972] 1 All ER 621, PC; and PARAS 20, 21.
2 In relation to contracts for the sale or other disposition of an interest in land by will made on or after 27 September 1989 the doctrine of part performance is now abolished: see the Law of Property (Miscellaneous Provisions) Act 1989 s 2; PARAS 20, 21. As to the doctrine of part performance see CONTRACT vol 22 (2012) PARA 494; SPECIFIC PERFORMANCE vol 95 (2013) PARA 301 et seq.
3 See *Maddison v Alderson* (1883) 8 App Cas 467, HL (understanding between the testator and another, but no enforceable contract to leave by will a life estate in land). As to the court's power to order provision for dependants where the deceased has contracted to leave property by will see note 4 and PARA 588.
4 See *Cadogan v Cadogan* [1977] 3 All ER 831, [1977] 1 WLR 1041 (disposition of property with intention to avoid matrimonial provision caused prejudice to surviving spouse claimant under the Inheritance (Family Provision) Act 1938 and was able to be set aside under Law of Property Act 1925 s 172 (replaced now by the Insolvency Act 1986 s 423); this case may be relevant where the Inheritance (Provision for Family and Dependants) Act 1975 s 10 (dispositions intended to defeat applications for financial provision) and s 11 (contracts to leave property by will) do not apply on the facts). See also *Re Eichholz, Eichholz's Trustee v Eichholz* [1959] Ch 708, [1959] 1 All ER 166. Other transactions in fraud of creditors are dealt with under the Insolvency Act 1986 s 423 and it seems that the Revenue Authorities may qualify as 'victims' of voidable transactions within the Insolvency Act 1986 ss 423, 424: *Hill v Spread Trustee Co Ltd* [2006] EWCA Civ 542, [2007] 1 All ER 1106, [2007] 1 WLR 2404.
5 *Richardson v Smallwood* (1822) Jac 552.
6 See *Thorner v Major* [2009] UKHL 18, [2009] 1 WLR 776, [2009] 3 All ER 945; PARA 20; and ESTOPPEL vol 47 (2014) PARAS 392–393; SPECIFIC PERFORMANCE vol 95 (2013) PARA 305.

1222. Liability of personal representative of original lessee. The personal representative of an original lessee under a lease granted before 1 January 1996[1] is liable in his representative capacity, to the extent of assets, upon the covenants contained in the lease for the residue of the term, whether the term was assigned by the lessee in his lifetime[2] or by the representative after his death[3]. Upon a conveyance, however, he may avail himself of the benefit of statutory protection[4]. On the assignment of a lease granted on or after 1 January 1996 the original lessee or his personal representative will cease to be liable on the tenant's covenants (and cease to be entitled to enforce the landlord's covenants) on the assignment[5].

1 As to leases granted after 1 January 1996 see the text to note 5.

2 *Brett v Cumberland* (1619) Cro Jac 521; *Coghill v Freelove* (1690) 3 Mod Rep 325. As to a lessee's liability on covenants after assignment and the nature of that liability see *Re Downer Enterprises Ltd* [1974] 2 All ER 1074, [1974] 1 WLR 1460.

3 *Helier v Casebert* (1665) 1 Lev 127; *Pitcher v Tovey* (1692) 4 Mod Rep 71 at 76; *Youngmin v Heath* [1974] 1 All ER 461, [1974] 1 WLR 135, CA.

4 See PARA 990.

5 See the Landlord and Tenant (Covenants) Act 1995 ss 5, 31(1); the Landlord and Tenant (Covenants) Act 1995 (Commencement) Order 1995, SI 1995/2963; and LANDLORD AND TENANT vol 63 (2012) PARA 702 et seq.

1223. Personal representative of assignee of a term. Where the deceased was an assignee of the term, his estate remains liable upon the covenants so long as the term is vested in his personal representative. Where the lease is an onerous one, it will normally be the duty of the representative, as he cannot disclaim it[1], to offer to surrender it to the lessor, and, in the event of his refusal to accept a surrender, to find an assignee, even if he is without means[2]. There appears to be a distinction, in this situation, between the treatment of express covenants and those covenants implied by law, in that the personal representative of an implied covenantor will not usually be liable for breaches of the implied covenant that take place after the death of the implied covenantor[3].

1 See *Rubery v Stevens* (1832) 4 B & Ad 241.

2 *Reid v Lord Tenterden* (1833) 4 Tyr 111; *Rowley v Adams* (1839) 4 My & Cr 534. As to the right of an assignee to assign over to a person without means see *Taylor v Shum* (1797) 1 Bos & P 21; *Onslow v Corrie* (1817) 2 Madd 330; and LANDLORD AND TENANT vol 63 (2012) PARA 711.

3 *Adams v Gibney* (1830) 6 Bing 656; *Williams v Burrell* (1845) 1 CB 402.

1224. Entry a condition of personal liability under lease. A personal representative can only be sued in his personal capacity if he has entered upon the deceased's leasehold[1], but the entry by one of several personal representatives does not render his co-representatives liable to an action for use and occupation[2]. A covenant to enter is binding on the personal representative notwithstanding his fiduciary capacity[3]. Where the representative has entered upon the deceased's leasehold the lessor has the option to sue him either in his representative capacity or in his personal capacity as assignee of the lease; and in the latter case judgment goes against him de bonis propriis[4].

1 *Wollaston v Hakewill* (1841) 3 Man & G 297; *Rendall v Andreae* (1892) 61 LJQB 630; *Re Owers, Public Trustee v Death* [1941] Ch 389, [1941] 2 All ER 589. A person who enters on the deceased's leasehold may by his intermeddling with the estate become an executor de son tort, and by his conduct be estopped from denying that he is assignee of the term and liable accordingly on the covenants: see *Stratford-upon-Avon Corpn v Parker* [1914] 2 KB 562, DC; and ESTOPPEL vol 47 (2014) PARA 341. See also PARA 1263; and *Fielding v Cronin* (1885) 16 LR Ir 379, CA.

2 *Nation v Tozer* (1834) 1 Cr M & R 172. As to joint representation see PARA 926. As to the executor de son tort see PARA 1261.

3 *Lloyds Bank Ltd v Jones* [1955] 2 QB 298, [1955] 2 All ER 409, CA.

4 See the cases cited in note 1.

1225. Limitation of personal liability of personal representative in relation to leases. If the personal representative is sued as assignee of the lease for the rent accrued during the time he was in possession, he is entitled to set up by way of defence that he is only assignee as personal representative, and that the profits or yearly value of the property amount to a sum less than the rent[1]. In such a case the personal liability of the representative is limited to the profits or yearly value of the property; it is not confined to the actual profits he may have received, but extends to the profits which he might have received if he had used due diligence[2]. The representative cannot limit his personal liability where an action is brought against him as assignee of the lease for breach of a covenant to repair[3].

1 *Re Bowes, Earl of Strathmore v Vane, Norcliffe's Claim* (1887) 37 ChD 128 at 133; *Billinghurst v Speermen* (1695) 1 Salk 297; *Buckley v Pirk* (1710) 1 Salk 316.

2 *Re Bowes, Earl of Strathmore v Vane, Norcliffe's Claim* (1887) 37 ChD 128 at 133; *Whitehead v Palmer* [1908] 1 KB 151; *Rubery v Stevens* (1832) 4 B & Ad 241; *Hopwood v Whaley* (1848) 6 CB 744. It is submitted that *Remnant v Bremridge* (1818) 8 Taunt 191 is no longer good law.

3 *Tremeere v Morison* (1834) 1 Bing NC 89; *Sleap v Newman* (1862) 12 CBNS 116; *Rendall v Andreae* (1892) 61 LJQB 630.

1226. Remedy by distress. Where the lessee dies before the expiration of the term, and his personal representative continues in possession for the remainder, a distress may be taken for rent due for any part of the term, including arrears accrued due during the lessee's lifetime[1].

1 Went Off Ex (14th Edn) 291; *Braithwaite v Cooksey* (1790) 1 Hy Bl 465. As to distress generally see LANDLORD AND TENANT vol 62 (2012) PARA 288 et seq.

1227. Specific performance of agreement for a lease. Specific performance may be ordered against the personal representative of a person who has agreed to accept a lease[1], but only if the lease is so framed as not to impose a personal liability upon the representative[2].

1 *Phillips v Everard* (1831) 5 Sim 102. As to specific performance see generally SPECIFIC PERFORMANCE vol 95 (2013) PARA 301 et seq.

2 *Stephens v Hotham* (1855) 1 K & J 571.

1228. Settled leasehold. Where leasehold property is settled by will the tenant for life is bound as between himself and the testator's estate to perform the covenants and indemnify the estate[1], although he is not liable for repairs necessary at the commencement of his interest or in respect of breaches of covenant which had arisen before the testator's death[2]. Although as between himself and the testator's estate the tenant for life may be under an obligation to indemnify the estate, the remainderman cannot enforce that obligation after the death of the tenant for life against his estate[3].

1 *Re Kingham, Kingham v Kingham* [1897] 1 IR 170; *Re Betty, Betty v A-G* [1899] 1 Ch 821 (dissenting from *Re Baring, Jeune v Baring* [1893] 1 Ch 61; *Re Tomlinson, Tomlinson v Andrew* [1898] 1 Ch 232); *Re Gjers, Cooper v Gjers* [1899] 2 Ch 54. See also *Re Redding, Thompson v Redding* [1897] 1 Ch 876.

2 *Re Courtier, Coles v Courtier, Courtier v Coles* (1886) 34 ChD 136, CA, commenting upon *Re Fowler, Fowler v Odell* (1881) 16 ChD 723.

3 *Re Parry and Hopkin* [1900] 1 Ch 160. Where, however, an equitable tenant for life, after the death of the last surviving trustee, had entered into receipt of the rents, her estate was held liable for a failure to carry out an obligation to repair imposed by the trust instrument upon the trustees: *Re Field, Sanderson v Young* [1925] Ch 636. See further SETTLEMENTS vol 91 (2012) PARA 897.

1229. Settled freehold. Although the estate of a legal tenant for life of freehold land[1] was not liable at common law for waste, permissive or voluntary[2], yet where there is an express direction in the instrument creating the settlement that the property is to be kept in repair by the tenant for life, failure to comply with that obligation raises in equity a liability against the estate of the deceased tenant for life[3]. This liability is equitable, and not consequent upon a tort. Therefore the limitation of time within which an action had once to be brought against personal representatives for a tort[4] did not apply[5].

The estate of a tenant for life is liable to make good to the persons entitled under the settlement any damages occasioned by his default in complying with his statutory obligations to maintain and insure improvements[6].

1 New settlements cannot be created under the Settled Land Act 1925 after 1996 although there are savings in respect of settlements in existence at that date: see the Trusts of Land and Appointment of Trustees Act 1996 s 2(1); and SETTLEMENTS vol 91 (2012) PARA 576 et seq. See also PARA 821 note 2.
2 *Phillips v Homfray* (1883) 24 ChD 439 at 455, CA, per Bowen LJ (on appeal sub nom *Phillips v Fothergill* (1886) 11 App Cas 466, HL); *Re Cartwright, Avis v Newman* (1889) 41 ChD 532, following *Gibson v Wells* (1805) 1 Bos & PNR 290; *Herne v Bembow* (1813) 4 Taunt 764; *Powys v Blagrave* (1854) 4 De GM & G 448, explaining dicta in *Yellowly v Gower* (1855) 11 Exch 274; *Woodhouse v Walker* (1880) 5 QBD 404 at 407. As to waste see SETTLEMENTS vol 91 (2012) PARA 887 et seq.
3 *Re Williames, Andrew v Williames* (1885) 54 LT 105, CA; *Re Field, Sanderson v Young* [1925] Ch 636. See also *Messenger v Andrews* (1828) 4 Russ 478; *Gregg v Coates, Hodgson v Coates* (1856) 23 Beav 33. The equitable liability for permissive waste is confined to cases where there is an obligation to keep in repair: *Re Cartwright, Avis v Newman* (1889) 41 ChD 532.
4 See the Law Reform (Miscellaneous Provisions) Act 1934 s 1(3) (repealed).
5 *Jay v Jay* [1924] 1 KB 826.
6 See the Settled Land Act 1925 s 88(5); and SETTLEMENTS vol 91 (2012) PARA 865.

1230. Shares, underwriting agreements and contributories: effect of death. Although membership of a company ceases on death[1], the title to a persons' shares devolves upon his personal representatives[2], who, subject to any provisions in the articles of association, may transfer his shares without being registered as shareholders, or, in the absence of any right of veto conferred on the company by its articles, may have their names entered on the register[3]. The provisions of Part 30 of the Companies Act 2006[4] apply also to a person who is not a member of a company but to whom shares in a company have been transferred or transmitted by operation of law as they apply to a member of the company[5].

A contract to underwrite shares is not personal, and the legal personal representatives of the underwriter may be sued on it[6].

If, in the event of a company being wound up, a contributory dies, either before or after he has been placed on the list of contributories, his personal representatives are liable in a due course of administration to contribute to the company's assets in discharge of his liability, and are contributories accordingly[7].

1 See COMPANIES vol 14 (2016) PARA 389.
2 As to the meaning of 'personal representative' see PARA 608.
3 See COMPANIES vol 14 (2016) PARAS 409, 445.
4 Ie the Companies Act 2006 Pt 30 (ss 994–999) (petition by company members and others in respect of unfair prejudice): see COMPANIES vol 15 (2016) PARA 657 et seq.
5 See the Companies Act 2006 s 994; and COMPANIES vol 15 (2016) PARA 657 et seq.
6 See *Re Worthington, ex p Pathé Frères* [1914] 2 KB 299, CA; *Warner Engineering Co Ltd v Brennan* (1913) 30 TLR 191, DC; *Beardmore & Co Ltd v Barry* 1928 SC 101, Ct of Sess; and COMPANIES vol 15A (2016) PARA 1344.
7 See the Insolvency Act 1986 ss 79, 81(1); and COMPANIES vol 15 (2016) PARA 784.

1231. Joint contracts and other joint obligations: effect of death. The obligation upon a joint contract devolves upon the survivors, and the estate of a deceased joint contractor is under no primary liability[1]. Joint obligations may arise under statute rather than under contract but the devolution of a deceased person's obligation might still be determinable under the common law[2].

The question whether a particular promise is joint or several, or both joint and several, is one of construction[3]. A bond, though joint in form, and though it would be construed as creating a joint obligation only at law, may in equity, in the administration of the estate of a deceased obligor, be construed as joint and several, especially in the case of a bond given by partners, or in substitution for an antecedent joint and several liability[4].

As between the co-contractors, where the joint contract is for the benefit of all, there is an implied condition that each will contribute an aliquot part to the contractor who pays the debt, and an action for contribution will lie against the personal representative of a deceased co-contractor[5]. It cannot, however, be stated as a universal proposition that in all cases where two or more persons jointly employ a third there is an implied condition for all to contribute rateably among themselves so as to bind the personal representative of a deceased co-contractor; each case turns on its own facts[6].

1 See *Harrison (Inspector of Taxes) v Willis Bros (WH Willis and Executors of HH Willis)* [1966] Ch 619 at 645, [1965] 3 All ER 753 at 761, CA, per Winn LJ (income tax assessments made in partnership name were properly made and were effective against surviving partner but not against executor of deceased partner). See CONTRACT vol 22 (2012) PARA 646. The executor of a deceased joint contractor cannot, therefore, either by payment of interest (*Slater v Lawson* (1830) 1 B & Ad 396) or by acknowledgment (*Read v Price* [1909] 1 KB 577; affd [1909] 2 KB 724, CA) prevent the debt being statute-barred as against his co-contractors.

2 See *Harrison (Inspector of Taxes) v Willis Bros (WH Willis and Executors of HH Willis)* [1966] Ch 619, [1965] 3 All ER 753 (joint tax obligation, but note that for firms formed after April 6 1994, and all firms from tax year 1997–1998, each partner is only liable in respect of the income tax assessable on his share of the partnership profits, Income and Corporation Taxes Act 1998 s 111(1)-(3) (see now Income Tax (Trading and other Income) Act 2005, Pt IX (ss 846-863L)).

3 As to rules of construction in respect of joint and several promises see CONTRACT vol 22 (2012) PARA 644.

4 See DEEDS AND OTHER INSTRUMENTS vol 32 (2012) PARA 311.

5 *Ashby v Ashby* (1827) 7 B & C 444; *Batard v Hawes* (1853) 2 E & B 287. As to rights of contribution generally see EQUITABLE JURISDICTION vol 47 (2014) PARAS 58–59. See also FINANCIAL INSTRUMENTS AND TRANSACTIONS vol 49 (2015) PARA 790 et seq.

6 *Prior v Hembrow* (1841) 8 M & W 873 at 889 per Alderson B. As to the interest in the deceased's property of personal representatives under a joint representation see PARA 926.

1232. Partnership debts: effect of death. The separate estate of a deceased partner is severally liable in due course of administration for all debts and obligations of the firm incurred while he was a partner, so far as they remain unsatisfied, but subject to the prior payment of his separate debts[1]. Joint covenants by partners as lessees are not, however, construed as joint and several after the death of one partner so as to render his estate liable for breaches occurring after his death[2]. The partnership creditor is entitled to prove in the administration of the deceased partner's estate after the separate debts are paid without first proving that the surviving partner is insolvent, and without being obliged first to have recourse to the joint assets[3]; but it is necessary that the surviving partner should be present at the taking of the accounts of the deceased partner's estate[4]. Where there are no partnership assets, the joint creditors come in pari passu with the separate creditors[5].

Where a deceased partner has paid off an outstanding mortgage debt on assets owned by the partnership to prevent enforcement of the mortgagee's charge, in return for an assignment of the charge to the paying partner, the deceased's personal representative cannot assert entitlement to redemption of the charge as a condition precedent to sale of the property in dissolution proceedings, in the absence of evidence of the intentions of the deceased in paying off the outstanding sums[6]. There may, nevertheless, be cases where discharge of outstanding debts may give rise to the paying partner acquiring, by subrogation, the creditor's right to reimbursement, provided that the repayment was made with intention to keep the debt against the partnership alive[7].

1 Partnership Act 1890 s 9. See also PARTNERSHIP vol 79 (2014) PARA 68. The Partnership Act 1890 did not enlarge the liabilities for which, before the Act, the estate of a deceased partner was responsible: *Friend v Young* [1897] 2 Ch 421. The Partnership Act 1890 s 9 declares and settles the principle, which had long been acted upon in equity, that although partners were at law only jointly liable on contracts, a surviving partner could, in equity, obtain contribution from the estate of a deceased partner for liabilities to which he was subject as such survivor, and that unpaid creditors might avail themselves directly of the equity which the surviving partner could thus insist upon: *Kendall v Hamilton* (1879) 4 App Cas 504, HL. The fact that the remedy was enforced in equity at the instance of creditors of the firm has in some old cases been treated as an adoption by the former Court of Chancery of the rule of the lex mercatoria that partnership debts create a several as well as joint liability (see *Devaynes v Noble, Sleech's Case* (1816) 1 Mer 529 at 564), but this view was rejected by the House of Lords: see *Kendall v Hamilton* at 538. As to the circumstances which determine whether the remedy against the deceased partner's estate is or is not barred see *Vulliamy v Noble* (1817) 3 Mer 593 at 619; *Way v Bassett* (1845) 5 Hare 55; *Brown v Gordon* (1852) 16 Beav 302; *Devaynes v Noble, Clayton's Case* (1816) 1 Mer 529 at 572; *Wilkinson v Henderson* (1833) 1 My & K 582; *ex p Kendall* (1811) 17 Ves 514 at 525; *Thorpe v Jackson* (1837) 2 Y & C Ex 553 (which shows that the surviving partner is a necessary party to the action); *Braithwaite v Britain* (1836) 1 Keen 206; *Winter v Innes* (1838) 4 My & Cr 101; *Cowell v Sikes* (1827) 2 Russ 191; cf *Mills v Boyd* (1842) 6 Jur 943; and see EQUITABLE JURISDICTION vol 47 (2014) PARA 65. As regards the partners where there is in equity no survivorship of property there is no survivorship of the liability: see *Beresford v Browning* (1875) 1 ChD 30 at 34, CA, per James LJ; affg LR 20 Eq 564. Cf *Wilmer v Currey* (1848) 2 De G & Sm 347. See also *Patel v Patel* [2007] EWCA Civ 1520, [2007] All ER (D) 276 (Dec), (where deceased partner's debt to partnership accrued on his death and statutory dissolution of partnership; his personal representative began a new partnership with survivor of former partnership; debt devolved onto the deceased partner's estate rather than onto the new partnership, but had become time-barred).
2 *Clarke v Bickers* (1845) 14 Sim 639.
3 *Wilkinson v Henderson* (1833) 1 My & K 582; *Re Hodgson, Beckett v Ramsdale* (1885) 31 ChD 177, CA; *Re Doetsch, Matheson v Ludwig* [1896] 2 Ch 836 at 839, where it was held that this rule of procedure applied to the case of a foreign firm having a place of business here (one of the partners domiciled in England dying and leaving assets in England) notwithstanding that the law of the foreign country differed from that of England.
4 *Re Hodgson, Beckett v Ramsdale* (1885) 31 ChD 177, CA.
5 See COMPANY AND PARTNERSHIP INSOLVENCY vol 17 (2011) PARAS 1297–1298.
6 See *Zaman v Zoha* [2006] EWCA Civ 770, [2006] All ER (D) 350 (Mar).
7 See *M'Intyre v Miller* (1845) 13 M & W 725 and *Re Downer Enterprises* [1974] 2 All ER 1074 at 1082.

1233. Discharge of partnership liability. The estate of a deceased partner may be discharged by direct payments, or by dealings of the creditor with the continuing partners operating as payment of the joint debt[1]. It may also be discharged by the acceptance by the creditor of the security of the continuing partners in lieu of the original partnership liability[2], or by novation of the original contract with the continuing partners[3]. But the circumstance that the creditor continues his transactions with the survivors, and, at their request, forbears for some years to enforce payment[4], or receives interest on his debt from the surviving partners[5], or obtains judgment against them[6], is not of itself sufficient to discharge the deceased partner's estate.

1 *Winter v Innes* (1838) 4 My & Cr 101 at 110.
2 *Thompson v Percival* (1834) 5 B & Ad 925.
3 *Re Head, Head v Head (No 2)* [1894] 2 Ch 236, CA (distinguishing *Re Head, Head v Head* [1893] 3 Ch 426); *Bilborough v Holmes* (1876) 5 ChD 255.
4 *Winter v Innes* (1838) 4 My & Cr 101 at 110.
5 *Harris v Farwell* (1846) 13 Beav 403.
6 *Jacomb v Harwood* (1751) 2 Ves Sen 265 at 267; *Re Hodgson, Beckett v Ramsdale* (1885) 31 ChD 177, CA.

1234. Wrongful acts of co-partner. Where a firm becomes liable for the wrongful acts or omissions of a partner, or for the misapplication of money or property of a third person, every partner is liable both jointly and severally[1]. In such a case the liability of a deceased partner devolves upon his representatives. Where the wrongful act is committed after the death of a partner, no liability is imposed upon his estate[2].

1 See the Partnership Act 1890 ss 10–12; and PARTNERSHIP vol 79 (2014) PARA 69; *Erlanger v New Sombrero Phosphate Co* (1878) 3 App Cas 1218, HL. Cf *Re Bell's Indenture, Bell v Hickey* [1980] 3 All ER 425, [1980] 1 WLR 1217 (deceased partner's estate not liable for misapplication of trust money by co-partner, where deceased took no part in and had no knowledge of transactions).

2 *Devaynes v Noble, Houlton's Case* (1816) 1 Mer 529 at 616; *Friend v Young* [1897] 2 Ch 421.

1235. Partnership debts contracted after death. The estate of a deceased partner is not liable for debts of his late firm contracted after his death[1]; nor does the continued use of the old firm name, or of the deceased partner's name as part of it, of itself impose liability upon his representative or estate for such debts[2]. A debt which accrues between one partner and another on the occasion of the death of the debtor partner can fall upon the estate of the deceased partner[3].

1 See the Partnership Act 1890 s 36(3); and PARTNERSHIP vol 79 (2014) PARA 73.

2 See the Partnership Act 1890 s 14(2); and PARTNERSHIP vol 79 (2014) PARA 73. As to the liability of a person who holds himself out as a partner see PARTNERSHIP vol 79 (2014) PARAS 70–74. As to controls over business names see TRADE MARKS AND TRADE NAMES vol 97A (2014) PARA 476 et seq.

3 See *Patel v Patel* [2007] EWCA Civ 1520, [2007] All ER (D) 276 (Dec).

1236. Guarantors: effect of death. The effect of the death of the surety in a contract of guarantee depends on the nature and terms of the particular contract, but the general principle has been established that the guarantee will not be determined by the death of the surety of which the creditor has no notice[1]. Where a surety has died (or become bankrupt) and his personal representative (or trustee in bankruptcy) claims a share in a fund administered by executors or trustees, equity requires that what is owed under the guarantee (or a dividend, in the case of bankruptcy) must be brought into the fund before the share can be taken out[2].

1 See *Ashby v Day* (1885) 33 WR 631; affd (1886) 54 LT 408, CA. See also FINANCIAL INSTRUMENTS AND TRANSACTIONS vol 49 (2015) PARAS 827–829.

2 See *Cherry v Boultbee* (1839) 4 My & Cr 442 at 447–448 (as explained in *Re SSSL Realisations (2002) Ltd (formerly Save Service Stations Ltd) (in liq) v AIG Europe (UK) Ltd* [2006] EWCA Civ 7 at [107]–[108], [2006] Ch 610 per Chadwick LJ).

1237. Implied obligations upon death. It is not only where there is an express contract that an action grounded on some default of the person whose personal representative is sued can be maintained: if the position of the parties is such that the law would imply a contract from that position, then the representative may still be held liable[1]. There are many cases where an action can be brought upon an obligation implied by law in consequence of the position which the parties have undertaken one to another[2]. Familiar instances are those of common carriers and bailees[3], and those arising out of the relation of solicitor and client[4].

1 *Batthyany v Walford* (1887) 36 ChD 269 at 279, CA, per Cotton LJ.

2 *Batthyany v Walford* (1887) 36 ChD 269, CA. For implied obligations arising as between co-contractors in joint contracts see also PARA 1231 text and note 4.

3 *Morgan v Ravey* (1861) 6 H & N 265. As to bailees see BAILMENT AND PLEDGE vol 4 (2011) PARAS 101–102. As to common carriers see generally CARRIAGE AND CARRIERS vol 7 (2015) PARAS 1, 3 et seq.

4 *Wilson v Tucker* (1822) 3 Stark 154; *Blyth v Fladgate, Morgan v Blyth, Smith v Blyth* [1891] 1 Ch 337; *Davies v Hood* (1903) 88 LT 19; and see *Knights v Quarles* (1820) 2 Brod & Bing 102. As to the relationship between solicitor and client see LEGAL PROFESSIONS vol 66 (2015) PARA 561 et seq.

1238. Breach of trust: effect of death. The liability of a trustee for a breach of trust survives against his personal representative[1], whether the loss is occasioned by default on his part or by his act[2], and even though the consequences do not occur until after his death[3]. The personal representative's liability originates from and depends entirely on the deceased's liability, so the representative cannot rely upon any limitation period in answer to the claim which the deceased himself could not have set up[4]. An action for breach of trust may be brought against the surviving trustees without joining the representatives of a deceased trustee[5]. Where the action is brought against the representatives of the last surviving trustee, new trustees must be appointed so that the trust estate may be represented before the court[6].

1 *Adair v Shaw* (1803) 1 Sch & Lef 243 at 272; *Lord Montford v Lord Cadogan* (1810) 17 Ves 485 at 489; *Walsham v Stainton* (1863) 1 De GJ & Sm 678; *Concha v Murrieta, De Mora v Concha* (1889) 40 ChD 543, CA (revsd on the facts sub nom *Concha v Concha* [1892] AC 670, HL); *Re Wassell, Wassell v Leggatt* [1896] 1 Ch 554; *Re Franklyn, Franklyn v Franklyn* (1913) 30 TLR 187, CA. As to breach of trust see TRUSTS AND POWERS vol 98 (2013) PARA 665 et seq. See *Armitage v Nurse* [1998] Ch 241, [1997] 2 All ER 705 (defendant trustees and personal representatives of deceased trustees able to take advantage of trustee exemption clause where actual dishonesty not pleaded); and *Barnes v Tomlinson* [2006] EWHC 3115 (Ch), [2006] All ER (D) 95 (Dec) (claim against administratrix of deceased company director failed to show dishonesty by directors). See also *Spread Trustee Co Ltd v Hutcheson* [2011] UKPC 13, [2012] 2 AC 194, [2012] 1 All ER 251 (adopting *Armitage v Nurse* above, in holding that exclusion of liability of trustee for negligence is lawful under Guernsey law). As to the meaning of 'personal representative' see PARA 608.

2 *Devaynes v Robinson* (1857) 24 Beav 86 at 95.

3 *Grayburn v Clarkson* (1868) 3 Ch App 605.

4 *Brittlebank v Goodwin* (1868) LR 5 Eq 545, following dicta in *Baker v Martin* (1832) 5 Sim 380; *Story v Gape* (1856) 2 Jur NS 706; *Obee v Bishop* (1859) 1 De GF & J 137 at 141, and dissenting from *Dunne v Doran* (1844) 13 I Eq R 545; *Brereton v Hutchinson* (1853) 2 I Ch R 648; affd (1854) 3 I Ch R 361. As to limitation periods see LIMITATION PERIODS.

5 *Re Harrison, Smith v Allen* [1891] 2 Ch 349.

6 *Re Jordan, Hayward v Hamilton* [1904] 1 Ch 260.

(2) LIABILITY FOR PERSONAL REPRESENTATIVE'S OWN ACTS

(i) Liability to Third Parties

1239. Personal representative's own contracts and liability. A personal representative[1] is personally liable upon his own contracts[2] and cannot limit his liability to the extent of assets in his hands. Accordingly, upon counts for goods sold and delivered and work and labour done, he can only be charged personally, and the only possible judgment is de bonis propriis[3]. A claim can, however, be maintained against him in his representative character where the consideration for his promise is a contract or transaction with his testator[4].

Representatives of a deceased partner who are entitled to profits, but who never interfere in the business, are not liable as partners in the firm[5].

1 As to the meaning of 'personal representative' see PARA 608.

2 As to the liabilities of an executor de son tort see PARA 1267. As to the liability of a personal representative who employs an agent see PARA 1050.

3 *Farhall v Farhall* (1871) 7 Ch App 123 at 127; *Dowse v Coxe* (1825) 3 Bing 20 (revsd on other grounds sub nom *Biddell v Dowse* (1827) 6 B & C 255); *Powell v Graham* (1817) 7 Taunt 580 at 585.
4 *Corner v Shew* (1838) 3 M & W 350; *Farhall v Farhall* (1871) 7 Ch App 123 at 128. As to the liability of a representative in carrying on his testator's business see PARA 1038.
5 *Holme v Hammond* (1872) LR 7 Exch 218. As to the liability of persons holding themselves out as partners see PARTNERSHIP vol 79 (2014) PARAS 70–74.

1240. Consideration for promise to answer damages out of own estate. Like all other agreements not under seal[1], a promise by a personal representative to answer damages out of his own estate[2] is only enforceable in contract if given for valuable consideration[3], such as giving time for payment[4], or undertaking to pay interest on a debt not bearing interest[5]. Where the agreement is an instrument, such as a promissory note, which prima facie imports a consideration and may induce forbearance, it is not necessary to give evidence of consideration from elsewhere[6]. There can, of course, be no forbearance to sue a person who has not actually taken out administration[7].

1 See CONTRACT vol 22 (2012) PARA 308; DEEDS AND OTHER INSTRUMENTS.
2 There is no need for a note or memorandum in writing for such a promise: see the Statute of Frauds (1677) s 4; and PARA 975 note 2.
3 *Reech v Kennegal* (1748) 1 Ves Sen 123; *Rann v Hughes* (1778) 7 Term Rep 350n, HL; *Jones v Tanner* (1827) 7 B & C 542. As to consideration see CONTRACT vol 22 (2012) PARA 308 et seq.
4 *Davis v Rayner* (1671) 2 Lev 3; *Hawes v Smith* (1675) 2 Lev 122.
5 *Bradly v Heath* (1830) 3 Sim 543; *Jones v Ashburnham* (1804) 4 East 455; *Childs v Monins* (1821) 2 Brod & Bing 460.
6 *Ridout v Bristow* (1830) 1 Cr & J 231.
7 *Nelson v Serle* (1839) 4 M & W 795, Ex Ch.

1241. Indorsement of bills of exchange. A person who is under an obligation to indorse a bill of exchange in a representative capacity may indorse it in terms which negative personal liability[1]. If he fails to indorse it in such terms he is personally liable upon it[2].

1 Bills of Exchange Act 1882 s 31(5). See FINANCIAL INSTRUMENTS AND TRANSACTIONS vol 49 (2015) PARA 279.
2 *King v Thom* (1786) 1 Term Rep 487. See also *Alexander v Sizer* (1869) LR 4 Exch 102 (where a company official was held to have signed a promissory note in a representative capacity, so avoiding personal liability).

1242. Torts by personal representative. A personal representative[1] is, of course, personally responsible for all torts committed by him, but where the injury has been occasioned by him or by his agents in the reasonable management of the trust estate he is entitled to be indemnified out of the assets[2]; and the person injured has the right to be subrogated to the personal representative's indemnity[3]. The right of subrogation is co-extensive with the indemnity so that, in a case where the tort has resulted from the personal representative carrying on the deceased's business, the right will extend only to those assets properly applicable to the conduct of the business against which the indemnity would apply[4].

Where an administrator informally renounces his office, but does not complete the necessary formalities, he may be held to have breached his duty by neglect and default in failing to act thereafter in the administration of the estate to prevent maladministration by others, even though he took no active part in it[5].

1 As to the meaning of 'personal representative' see PARA 608.
2 *Benett v Wyndham* (1862) 4 De GF & J 259; *Re Raybould, Raybould v Turner* [1900] 1 Ch 199 (both referred to in *Barnett v Semenyuk* [2008] EWHC 2939 (Ch), [2008] BPIR 1427); *Flower v Prechtel* (1934) 150 LT 491, CA. As to the right of a personal representative to indemnity from the estate see PARA 1018. As to liability in tort generally see TORT vol 97 (2015) PARA 405 et seq.

3 *Re Raybould, Raybould v Turner* [1900] 1 Ch 199. As to the principles of subrogation see EQUITABLE JURISDICTION vol 47 (2014) PARA 207; and *Re Downer Enterprises Ltd* [1974] 2 All ER 1074 at 1084, [1974] 1 WLR 1460 at 1470 per Pennycuick V-C, where the ambiguity of the expression 'primary liability' is discussed. See also *Barnett v Semenyuk* [2008] EWHC 2939 (Ch), [2008] BPIR 1427 (a person who recovered damages and costs on behalf of the trust against a trustee was subrogated to the trustee's position and entitled to be indemnified against the trust property).

4 See *Ex p Garland* (1804) 10 Ves 110.

5 See *Segbedzi v Segbedzi* (13 May 1999, unreported), CA (the administrator's liability towards the beneficiary was relieved under the Trustee Act 1961 s 61 (see TRUSTS AND POWERS vol 98 (2013) PARA 707) but he remained under a contractual indemnity towards third-party sureties for the administration).

1243. Undue delay by deceased solicitor's personal representatives and powers of intervention. The extensive powers of the Solicitors Regulation Authority[1] to deal with the property of defaulting solicitors[2] are exercisable where the Authority considers that there has been undue delay on the part of the personal representatives of a deceased solicitor who immediately before his death was practising as a sole solicitor[3] in connection with that solicitor's practice or in connection with any trust[4]. Accordingly[5], on the application of the Authority, the High Court may order that no payment is to be made without the court's leave by any person (whether or not named in the order) of any money held by him (in whatever manner and whether it was received before or after the making of the order) on behalf of the representatives[6]; the Authority may resolve that all money held by or on behalf of the representatives is to vest in the Solicitors Regulation Authority on trust for the persons beneficially entitled to it[7]; the High Court may require a person whom it suspects of holding money on behalf of the representatives or has information which is relevant to identifying any money held by or on behalf of the representatives, to give information as to any such money and the accounts in which it is held to the Authority[8]; the Authority may require the representatives, and the High Court on its application may order a person other than the representatives it believes has possession or control of certain documents, to produce or deliver to any person appointed by the Authority all documents in their or his possession, or under their control, in connection with the solicitor's practice, or former practice, or any trusts and the court may authorise a person to enter any premises to search for documents and property[9]; and the High Court may, on the Authority's application, from time to time order that communications to the personal representative are to be directed to the Authority and authorise the Authority or a person appointed by it to take steps necessary to protect the public interest or interests of clients in relation to a website purporting to be maintained by the personal representative[10].

These provisions do not apply where there is a surviving partner, for in that case he is fully responsible.

1 The Solicitors Regulation Authority is the body currently responsible for the regulation of solicitors and to which the powers of the Law Society have been devolved and the Authority is the relevant body in practice: see LEGAL PROFESSIONS vol 65 (2015) PARA 454.

2 As to these powers, and the circumstances justifying their exercise, see the Solicitors Act 1974 s 35, Sch 1 Pts I, II; and LEGAL PROFESSIONS vol 66 (2015) PARA 666 et seq. As to solicitor-representatives see PARA 653. As to the meaning of 'personal representative' see PARA 608.

3 'Sole solicitor' means a solicitor who is the sole principal in a practice other than an incorporated practice: see the Solicitors Act 1974 s 87(1); and LEGAL PROFESSIONS vol 66 (2015) PARA 666.

4 See the Solicitors Act 1974 Sch 1 para 1(1)(b); and LEGAL PROFESSIONS vol 66 (2015) PARA 666.

5 The powers referred to are also exercisable in relation to the personal representatives of a deceased solicitor where the Solicitors Regulation Authority has reason to suspect dishonesty on their part in connection with that solicitor's practice or former practice or in connection with any trust of

which that solicitor is or was formerly a trustee or that an employee is or was a trustee in his capacity as such an employee: see the Solicitors Act 1974 Sch 1 para 1(1)(a)(iii); and LEGAL PROFESSIONS vol 66 (2015) PARA 666.

6 See the Solicitors Act 1974 Sch 1 paras 4(2), 5(1); and LEGAL PROFESSIONS vol 66 (2015) PARA 668.

7 See the Solicitors Act 1974 Sch 1 paras 4(2), 6(1), (2), 6A; and LEGAL PROFESSIONS vol 66 (2015) PARA 668. A copy of the resolution and a notice prohibiting the payment out of any such sums must be served on the representatives: see Sch 1 paras 4(2), 6(3); and LEGAL PROFESSIONS vol 66 (2015) PARA 668. As to the making of rules in relation to the treatment of sums vested in it, and in particular rules relating to where the Authority is unable to trace the person or persons beneficially entitled to any such sums, see Sch 1 para 6B; and LEGAL PROFESSIONS vol 66 (2015) PARA 668.

8 See the Solicitors Act 1974 Sch 1 paras 4(2), 8; and LEGAL PROFESSIONS vol 66 (2015) PARA 668.

9 See the Solicitors Act 1974 Sch 1 paras 4(2), 9(1)(a), (5), (6); and LEGAL PROFESSIONS vol 66 (2015) PARA 667.

10 See the Solicitors Act 1974 Sch 1 paras 4(2), 10(1), (2), (7); and LEGAL PROFESSIONS vol 66 (2015) PARA 669.

(ii) Liability to Beneficiaries on a Devastavit

1244. Nature of a devastavit. A personal representative[1] in accepting the office accepts the duties of the office, and becomes a trustee in the sense that he is personally liable in equity for all breaches of the ordinary trusts which in courts of equity are considered to arise from his office[2]. The violation of his duties of administration is termed a devastavit; this term is applicable not only to a misuse by the representative of the deceased's effects, as by spending or converting them to his own use, but also to acts of maladministration or negligence[3]. The failure of a personal representative properly and formally to renounce his office may cause him to become liable for breach of his duty and negligence in failing to prevent maladministration of the estate by other personal representatives after the date of his purported resignation[4].

Even where a devastavit can be established, it is still necessary to establish that the breach of duty caused actual loss to the estate, in line with ordinary principles of causation[5].

1 As to the meaning of 'personal representative' see PARA 608.

2 *Re Marsden, Bowden v Layland, Gibbs v Layland* (1884) 26 ChD 783 at 789 per Kay J. As to the duty or 'great use' of a trustee to commit judicious breaches of trust see *Perrins v Bellamy* [1899] 1 Ch 797 at 798, CA, per Lindley MR, as corrected in *National Trustees Co of Australasia Ltd v General Finance Co of Australasia Ltd* [1905] AC 373 at 376, PC. As to the liability of a trustee for breach of trust see TRUSTS AND POWERS vol 98 (2013) PARA 665 et seq.

3 Bac Abr, Executors and Administrator (L) 1.

4 See *Segbedzi v Segbedzi* (13 May 1999, unreported), CA; and PARA 1242 text and note 5.

5 See *Younger v Saner* [2002] EWCA Civ 1077, [2002] All ER (D) 372 (Jul).

1245. Maladministration under a devastavit. A personal representative commits a devastavit if he makes payments to legatees without providing for debts[1] or for calls upon shares which have not been fully paid up[2]; or if he applies the assets in payment of claims which he has no right to satisfy[3]. To avoid a devastavit, a personal representative may apply to the court for liberty to distribute to beneficiaries without further retention or security against the emergence of one or more unascertained or contingent claims against the estate; in some circumstances, the sanction of the court can properly be given, even where the provision for future creditors was not assuredly and in all possible events complete and, such liberty, in the absence of fraud, wilful concealment or misrepresentation will, if acted upon, give complete protection against a creditor's claim of devastavit[4]. The representative's duties to get in the estate and invest money in hand have already been considered[5]; a breach of such duties amounts to a devastavit. An executor is also liable for paying a legatee a sum greater than is warranted by the existing state of the assets, but he will not be disallowed a payment made to one of several residuary legatees, because through a subsequent decrease in the value of the assets such a residuary legatee may have received more than the other residuary legatees[6].

1 See eg *Taylor v Taylor* (1870) LR 10 Eq 477; *Re Bewley's Estate, Jefferys v Jefferys* (1871) 24 LT 177. For the statutory protection given to representatives who advertise for debts see PARA 965. Where the representative fails to advertise it would appear that he cannot rely on mere want of notice of the debt: see *Chelsea Waterworks Co v Cowper* (1795) 1 Esp 275; *Norman v Baldry* (1834) 6 Sim 621; *Smith v Day* (1837) 2 M & W 684; *Hill v Gomme* (1839) 1 Beav 540. As to statutory protection where the priority order for payment of debts in an insolvent estate is not observed see PARA 983.

2 See PARA 988.

3 Com Dig, Administration (1) 1; *Shallcross v Wright* (1850) 12 Beav 558; *Re Midgley, Midgley v Midgley* [1893] 3 Ch 282, CA; *Re Rosenthal, Schwarz v Bernstein* [1972] 3 All ER 552, [1972] 1 WLR 1273.

4 *Re Yorke, Stone v Chataway* [1997] 4 All ER 907. See also Practice Note [2001] 3 All ER 765. In cases where administrators apply to the court for sanction to distribute the deceased's estate without reference to the claim of potential creditors and the cause of action is a series of disputed and stale claims against the estate, the court should consider whether any, and if so what, protection should be afforded to the potential creditor whereby the court would take a practical view and might in an appropriate case conclude that no protection beyond the personal liability of the beneficiaries was needed: *Re K* [2007] EWHC 622 (Ch), 9 ITELR 759, [2007] All ER (D) 473 (Mar).

5 See PARA 959 et seq.

6 *Lloyd v Lloyd* (1875) 23 WR 787.

1246. Negligence under a devastavit. A personal representative is guilty of a devastavit where loss occurs to the estate owing to his negligence, as where by his delay in taking proceedings a debtor is enabled to plead the statutory limitations[1], or the debt is lost owing to the debtor's bankruptcy or inability to pay[2]; or if he allows debts bearing interest to run on when he has assets in hand sufficient to discharge them[3]. No liability, however, attaches to executors for delay in proving the will[4]. A simple failure properly and formally to renounce his appointment as personal representative, accompanied by a failure, thereafter, to discharge his duties may amount to negligence[5]. An executor, including the solicitor who drafted the will, may take advantage of an indemnity clause which protects him from his own negligence[6]. An indemnity clause which excludes liability for loss unless caused by actual fraud will exonerate a personal representative from liability for loss unless caused by his own dishonesty no matter how indolent, impudent, lacking in diligence, negligent or wilful his conduct may have been and is not void for repugnancy or on the grounds of public policy[7]. Similarly an indemnity clause which excludes liability for loss unless caused by wilful and individual fraud or wrongdoing on the part of the trustee requires a knowing and deliberate breach of duty or reckless indifference to the possibility of such breach not merely an intentional action[8].

1 *Hayward v Kinsey* (1701) 12 Mod Rep 568 at 573. As to genuine mistakes made upon legal advice see PARA 1256. As to negligence generally see NEGLIGENCE.

2 See PARA 959.

3 *Bate v Robins* (1863) 32 Beav 73; *Hall v Hallet* (1784) 1 Cox Eq Cas 134; *Dornford v Dornford* (1806) 12 Ves 127 at 130. A personal representative is not liable for loss arising from his payment of a non-interest-bearing debt before an interest-bearing debt: *Re Stevens, Cooke v Stevens* [1898] 1 Ch 162 at 174, CA, per Chitty LJ.

4 *Re Stevens, Cooke v Stevens* [1897] 1 Ch 422 (affd [1898] 1 Ch 162, CA); *Re Morris, Griffiths, Morris v Morris* (1908) 124 LT Jo 315.

5 *Segbedzi v Segbedzi* (13 May 1999, unreported), CA (although this case involved an administrator, rather than an executor). See also *Fountain Forestry Ltd v Edwards* [1975] Ch 1 at 14, [1974] 2 All ER 280 at 285 per Brightman J; and PARA 1253 note 9 on the similarity of approach to the two offices.
6 *Bogg v Raper* [1998] 1 ITELR 267, [1998] CLY 4592, CA.
7 *Armitage v Nurse* [1998] Ch 241, [1997] 2 All ER 705, CA. A trustee will be treated as acting dishonestly if he acts in a way which he does not honestly believe to be in the interests of the beneficiaries whether or not he stands to gain or thinks he stands to gain from his actions: *Armitage v Nurse* at 251 and 711 per Millett LJ. Although it is well established that the test of honesty in an express trustee is whether the trustee is conscious that he is committing a breach or not, it is for the court to determine what the normally acceptable standards of honest conduct are; the fact that a defendant genuinely believes that he has not fallen below those standards is irrelevant: *Barnes v Tomlinson* [2006] EWHC 3115 (Ch) at [78], [2006] All ER (D) 95 (Dec) per Kitchin J (applying *Armitage v Nurse*). See also *Spread Trustee Co Ltd v Hutcheson* [2011] UKPC 13, [2012] 2 AC 194, [2012] 1 All ER 251; and PARA 1238 note 1.
8 *Barnsley v Noble* [2016] EWCA Civ 799: it is the fraud or wrongdoing, not the doing, which must be wilful. See also *Bonham v Fishwick* [2007] EWHC 1859 (Ch).

1247. Unremunerated representative a gratuitous bailee. Where the testator's assets have come into the possession of an unremunerated personal representative[1] and are afterwards lost to the estate, the equitable rule that the representative stands in the position of a gratuitous bailee, and cannot therefore be charged without some wilful default[2], applies[3]. The person seeking to charge the representative must show that the loss was attributable to his wilful default; it does not rest upon the representative to show that it was not[4]. A personal representative enjoys the same protection as a trustee against losses incurred by the appointment of an agent, nominee or custodian[5].

A paid trustee[6] is expected to exercise a higher standard of diligence and knowledge than an unpaid trustee, and a bank which advertises itself largely in the public press as taking charge of administrations is under a special duty[7].

1 As to the meaning of 'personal representative' see PARA 608. For circumstances in which remuneration is available under the Trustee Act 2000 see PARAS 650, 651. Where a trustee becomes involved in additional services to enhance the value of the trust property, which were unforeseen at the time of the appointment, and applies to the court under its inherent jurisdiction for remuneration for such services, the jurisdiction is to be exercised by balancing, on the one hand, the fact that the office of trustee was essentially gratuitous and, on the other, that it was most important that the trust should be properly administered: see *Re Duke of Norfolk's Settlement Trusts* [1982] Ch 61, [1981] 3 All ER 220; and *Perotti v Watson* [2002] EWCA Civ 771, [2001] All ER (D) 73 (Jul).
2 *Job v Job* (1877) 6 ChD 562; *Jones v Lewis* (1751) 2 Ves Sen 240 at 241; *Little v Governors of County Down Infirmary* [1918] 1 IR 221. The old rule at common law was that the representative was liable for the loss of assets once they had come to his hands: see *Crosse v Smith* (1806) 7 East 246. As to gratuitous bailment see BAILMENT AND PLEDGE vol 4 (2011) PARA 111 et seq. See also *Perotti v Watson* [2002] EWCA Civ 771, [2001] All ER (D) 73 (Jul) (trustee (who was also a solicitor) of deceased's estate applied successfully to the court for remuneration, where none was expressly authorised, but reduction was ordered to reflect wilful default in administration).
3 See BAILMENT AND PLEDGE vol 4 (2011) PARA 121.
4 *Re Brier, Brier v Evison* (1884) 26 ChD 238, CA. See also *Hodges v Smith* [1950] WN 455. As to the measure of diligence demanded of a gratuitous bailee see BAILMENT AND PLEDGE vol 4 (2011) PARA 121.
5 See the Trustee Act 2000 ss 23, 35; and TRUSTS AND POWERS vol 98 (2013) PARAS 1, 437.
6 As to personal representatives' remuneration see PARA 648 et seq.
7 *Re Waterman's Will Trusts, Lloyds Bank Ltd v Sutton* [1952] 2 All ER 1054; *Bartlett v Barclays Bank Trust Co Ltd* [1980] Ch 515, [1980] 1 All ER 139. See also Mervyn Davies 'Liability of the Paid Trustee' 33 Conveyancer and Property Lawyer 179.

1248. Proof in personal representative's bankruptcy in respect of devastavit. Upon the bankruptcy of the personal representative the person injured by a devastavit may put in a proof[1]. Where the bankrupt representative is one of several representatives, the others may prove in his bankruptcy in respect of his devastavit[2].

1 Toller's Law of Executors (7th Edn) 429. See also *Re West, Ex p Turner* (1842) 2 Mont D & De G 613, 6 Jur 840.
2 *Re Davis, Ex p Courtenay* (1835) 2 Mont & A 227. See also BANKRUPTCY AND INDIVIDUAL INSOLVENCY vol 5 (2013) PARAS 539–540.

1249. Devolution of personal representative's liability. Where a person as personal representative[1] of a deceased person, including an executor de son tort[2], wastes or converts to his own use any part of the deceased's real or personal estate[3], and dies, his personal representative is, to the extent of the defaulter's available assets, liable and chargeable in respect of that waste or conversion in the same manner as the defaulter would have been if living[4].

1 As to the meaning of 'personal representative' see PARA 608.
2 As to the meaning of 'executor de son tort' see PARA 606.
3 As to the meaning of 'real estate' see PARA 607 note 1.
4 Administration of Estates Act 1925 s 29. See also *Coward v Gregory* (1866) LR 2 CP 153; *Re West, Ex p Turner* (1842) 2 Mont D & De G 613, 6 Jur 840 and cf *Wilson v Hodson* (1872) LR 7 Exch 84 (see PARA 1270 note 3).

1250. Effect of concurrence of party in devastavit. The concurrence in the act of devastavit of the party suing generally releases the personal representative from liability[1], even though the party concurring derived no benefit from it[2]. The question whether there is a genuine, informed concurrence is also relevant to whether a personal representative should be relieved from liability under certain provisions[3] of the Trustee Act 1925[4].

1 *Walker v Symonds* (1818) 3 Swan 1 at 64.
2 *Chillingworth v Chambers* [1896] 1 Ch 685 at 700, CA; *Re Somerset, Somerset v Earl Poulett* [1894] 1 Ch 231, CA; *Fletcher v Collis* [1905] 2 Ch 24, CA. As to the jurisdiction to impound the beneficiary's interest see PARA 1262.
3 Ie the Trustee Act 1925 s 61 (see TRUSTS AND POWERS vol 98 (2013) PARA 707).
4 See *Mitchell v Halliwell* [2005] EWHC 937 (Ch), [2005] All ER (D) 210 (May) (summary judgment application and cross-application based upon possibility of devastavit and concurrence by parties in agreeing to commutation of annuity to personal representative and payment to him of lump sum in lieu of the annuity, where parties did not have independent legal advice). See also *Re Pauling's Settlement Trusts, Younghusband v Coutts & Co* [1961] 3 All ER 713 at 730, [1962] 1 WLR 86 at 108.

(3) LIABILITY FOR ACTS OF THIRD PARTIES AND CO-EXECUTORS

1251. Liability for agents, nominees, custodians and co-executors. A personal representative[1] has the power to appoint custodians[2] and nominees[3] and to delegate certain functions to an agent[4]. The personal representative is not generally liable for any act or default of the agent, nominee or custodian appointed by him[5]. However he does have a duty of care when entering arrangements with custodians, nominees and custodians[6] and to keep such arrangements under review[7] and may be liable where he has failed to comply this duty[8].

1 As to the meaning of 'personal representative' see PARA 608.
2 See the Trustee Act 2000 ss 17, 18, 35; PARA 1048; and TRUSTS AND POWERS vol 98 (2013) PARA 432. As to the person who may be so nominated see s 19 and TRUSTS AND POWERS vol 98 (2013) PARA 433.

3 See the Trustee Act 2000 ss 16, 35; PARA 1049; and TRUSTS AND POWERS vol 98 (2013) PARA 432. As to the person who may be so nominated see s 19 and TRUSTS AND POWERS vol 98 (2013) PARA 433.
4 See the Trustee Act 2000 ss 11, 35; PARA 1049; and TRUSTS AND POWERS vol 98 (2013) PARA 430.
5 See the Trustee Act 2000 ss 23, 35; PARA 1049; and TRUSTS AND POWERS vol 98 (2013) PARA 437.
6 See the Trustee Act 2000 ss 23, 35, Sch 1 para 3(1)(a)–(d), (2); PARA 1049; and TRUSTS AND POWERS vol 98 (2013) PARA 437.
7 See the Trustee Act 2000 ss 22, 23, 35, Sch 1 para 3(1), (e); PARA 1049; and TRUSTS AND POWERS vol 98 (2013) PARA 436.
8 See the Trustee Act 2000 ss 23, 35; PARA 1049; and TRUSTS AND POWERS vol 98 (2013) PARA 437.

1252. Liability for co-executor's acts. In the absence of any provision to the contrary contained in the will, an executor is chargeable only for money and securities actually received by him, and is answerable and accountable only for his own acts, receipts, neglects or defaults, and not for those of any other executor[1]. This statement must be qualified by the proposition that where the neglect or default of the executor is such that he fails to prevent breaches committed by his co-executor, in circumstances where he should, and could, have done so, the executor may become liable[2]. Nevertheless, there is some authority to suggest that where there are only two trustees or personal representatives, a testator's misplaced confidence in his choice of one of them will not easily prejudice the position of the other[3].

1 See the Trustee Act 1925 s 30(1) (now repealed) which provided a wider statutory indemnity that applied to trustees, personal representatives and administrators. It also states the general effect of the very extensive case law found in notes 2, 3 and in PARA 1253, much of which predates the statute and earlier Trustee Acts. The repeal of s 30 appears to leave the general case law (which is to the same effect) as applicable; it has often been asserted that s 30 and earlier statutory measures in the same form did no more than place upon a statutory footing the equitable principles that govern this matter: see *Re Munton, Munton v West* [1927] 1 Ch 262, CA; and PARA 1253. The law may now be modified in an appropriate case by the effect of Trustee Act 2000 ss 1, 2, 11, 12(1), Sch 1, if the co-executor is used in an agency capacity. The main effect of the repeal of the Trustee Act 1925 s 30 may be that under the case law, the burden of proving that the executor has acted properly, as regards co-executors, appears to fall back upon him: see *Brice v Stokes* (1805) 11 Ves 319 and *Stiles v Guy* (1849) 1 H & Tw 523 at 532, sub nom *Styles v Guy* (1849) 1 Mac & G 422 at 433.
2 See *Re Munton, Munton v West* [1926] 1 Ch 262, CA and PARA 1253.
3 See *Hargthorpe v Milforth* (1594) Cro Eliz 318 at 319. See also *Re Lucking's Will Trust, Renwick v Lucking* [1967] 3 All ER 726, [1968] 1 WLR 866 (as to liability of trustee of a will trust in supervising the management of a company forming part of the trust estate).

1253. Executor's duty to take care. It is the duty of executors to watch over and, if necessary, to correct each other's conduct[1], and an executor who stands by and sees a breach of trust committed by his co-executor becomes himself responsible for that breach[2]. It seems that this may be the case even where a personal representative who had taken no part in an administration takes informal steps to vacate his office, but has not complied with the due formalities[3].

It is not incumbent on one executor by force to prevent money from getting into the hands of another executor[4]; but if he unnecessarily hands over assets to a co-executor[5], or unnecessarily does an act which enables his co-executor to obtain sole possession of the assets[6], he is liable for the loss incurred.

The test of his liability is the necessity of the act. If the act is one which is required by the regular course of business, it is not an unnecessary act[7]. Therefore if money is required for the payment of debts or legacies, one executor is safe in joining in the sale of assets and permitting another executor to receive the proceeds for that purpose; but if he joins in such a sale when the money is not required, and he has no reasonable grounds for believing that it is so required, he is liable for the money so received by his co-executor[8]; and it would appear that he cannot safely entrust his co-executor with the assets for the purpose of handing them over to the residuary legatee[9].

1 *Styles v Guy* (1849) 1 Mac & G 422 at 433. As to the right of one of several executors to draw on the estate's bank account see FINANCIAL INSTITUTIONS vol 48 (2015) PARA 153.
2 *Booth v Booth* (1838) 1 Beav 125; *Williams v Nixon* (1840) 2 Beav 472.
3 See *Segbedzi v Segbedzi* (13 May 1999, unreported), CA.
4 *Langford v Gascoyne* (1805) 11 Ves 333.
5 *Townsend v Barber* (1763) 1 Dick 356; *Lincoln v Wright* (1841) 4 Beav 427. See also *Lowe v Shields* [1902] 1 IR 320, CA.
6 *Candler v Tillett* (1855) 22 Beav 257 at 263; *Lewis v Nobbs* (1878) 8 ChD 591.
7 *Clough v Bond* (1838) 3 My & Cr 490 at 496; *Re Gasquoine, Gasquoine v Gasquoine* [1894] 1 Ch 470, CA.
8 *Terrell v Matthews* (1841) 1 Mac & G 433n. See also *Chambers v Minchin* (1802) 7 Ves 186 at 193; *Brice v Stokes* (1805) 11 Ves 319; *Lord Shipbrook v Lord Hinchinbrook* (1810) 16 Ves 477; *Underwood v Stevens* (1816) 1 Mer 712; *Lees v Sanderson* (1830) 4 Sim 28.
9 See *Moses v Levi* (1839) 3 Y & C Ex 359. It seems that the position of co-administrators is similar to that of co-executors despite the difference in the origins of the offices: see *Fountain Forestry Ltd v Edwards* [1975] Ch 1 at 14, [1974] 2 All ER 280 at 285 per Brightman J; and PARA 926.

(4) LIABILITY TO ACCOUNT

1254. Duty of personal representatives to keep accounts. It is the duty of personal representatives[1] to keep clear and accurate accounts, and always to be ready to render such accounts when called upon to do so[2]. It is no excuse that they are inexperienced in keeping accounts, for in that case it would be their duty to employ a competent accountant to keep them[3]. Where they are required by the beneficiaries to furnish accounts, they may demand to have the costs of doing so paid or guaranteed before complying with the request[4]. A legatee is not entitled to a copy of the accounts at the expense of the estate[5], but he is entitled to inspect the accounts kept by the representative.

A personal representative is liable to be ordered by the court to account either generally in proceedings for general administration of the estate[6] or under the court's jurisdiction to order specific accounts[7].

1 As to the meaning of 'personal representative' see PARA 608.
2 See the Administration of Estates Act 1925 s 25(b) (see PARA 957); *Freeman v Fairlie* (1812) 3 Mer 29 at 43–44; *Pearse v Green* (1819) 1 Jac & W 135 at 140; *Thompson v Dunn* (1870) 5 Ch App 573; *Read v Read* [2009] EWCA Civ 739 (where both interim and final inventory and accounts were ordered by the court); *Sutcliffe v Sutcliffe* [2005] EWHC 3058 (Ch) at [5], [2005] All ER (D) 116 (Jul). Where the will creates a continuing trust with income and reversionary interests, every beneficiary is entitled to see the trust accounts, whether his interest is in possession or not: see Millett LJ in Armitage v Nurse [1998] Ch 241 at 261, CA, [1997] 3 WLR 1046,]1997] 2 All ER 705 at 720. However each beneficiary is entitled to only the accounts which are relevant to their interests: see *Royal National Lifeboat Institution v Headley* [2016] EWHC 1948 (Ch) where charities with reversionary interests were held entitled to see capital but not income accounts. See also TRUSTS AND POWERS vol 98 (2013) PARA 401.
3 *Wroe v Seed* (1863) 4 Giff 425 at 429.
4 *Re Bosworth, Martin v Lamb* (1889) 58 LJ Ch 432.
5 *Ottley v Gilby* (1845) 8 Beav 602.
6 As regards accounts in administration proceedings see PARA 1181. As regards the jurisdictional question see *Read v Read* [2009] EWCA Civ 739.
7 See *Practice Direction—Accounts, Inquiries etc* PD 40A; and CIVIL PROCEDURE vol 12A (2015) PARA 1252. See also *Sutcliffe v Sutcliffe* [2005] EWHC 3058 (Ch), [2005] All ER (D) 116 (Jul) (judge dealt with question of accounts on summary basis in a small estate; order made to vest property in beneficiaries, subject to right of absentee beneficiary to apply to challenge summary

account and to vary or discharge the order made, provided the application be accompanied by vouched estate accounts). As to the remedy of account see EQUITABLE JURISDICTION vol 47 (2014) PARA 49 et seq.

1255. Liability of personal representatives to account for tax purposes. In addition to his general duty to keep accounts, the personal representative has a general duty to provide information and documents for tax purposes[1]. He is liable, for inheritance tax purposes, to deliver an account of all relevant property and its value[2] and to account for the tax payable in respect of such property to the extent of the assets which he has received as personal representative or ought to have received but for his own neglect or default[3].

1 See the Finance Act 2008 Sch 36 Pt 1; and INCOME TAXATION vol 59 (2014) PARA 2179. As to the personal representative's liability in respect of any income tax and capital gains tax chargeable on the deceased see the Taxes Management Act 1970 ss 74, 77(1); and CAPITAL GAINS TAXATION vol 6 (2011) PARA 1052; INCOME TAXATION vol 59 (2014) PARA 1763. As to the meaning of 'personal representative' see PARA 608.

2 See the Inheritance Tax Act 1984 s 216(1), (3); and INHERITANCE TAXATION vol 59A (2014) PARA 275.

3 See the Inheritance Tax Act 1984 ss 200(1)(a), 204(1); and INHERITANCE TAXATION vol 59A (2014) PARA 264.

1256. Unauthorised payments by personal representative. Where a personal representative has paid away money to the wrong party, even if in good faith by mistake, or has made unauthorised investments, he is to be treated as having the sum in hand and must replace the capital with interest[1]; it is no answer that he has acted on legal advice[2]. He will not be charged, however, with interest at the instance of a beneficiary who was in a position to ask for accounts long before the application[3] nor in respect of disbursements honestly made, but disallowed in taking his accounts[4].

1 *A-G v Köhler* (1861) 9 HL Cas 654; *Re Hulkes, Powell v Hulkes* (1886) 33 ChD 552, dissenting from *Saltmarsh v Barrett (No 2)* (1862) 31 Beav 349. For the interest payable in similar circumstances see *West v West* [2003] All ER (D) 17 (Jun) (see PARA 1257, note 2).

2 *Doyle v Blake* (1804) 2 Sch & Lef 231 at 243; *Boulton v Beard* (1853) 3 De GM & G 608; *National Trustees Co of Australasia Ltd v General Finance Co of Australasia Ltd* [1905] AC 373, PC; *Marsden v Regan* [1954] 1 All ER 475 at 481, [1954] 1 WLR 423 at 433, CA, per Sir R Evershed MR. However, the court has power to relieve a personal representative from personal liability for breach of trust: see the Trustee Act 1925 ss 61, 68(1) para (17); and PARA 1259. See also TRUSTS AND POWERS vol 98 (2013) PARA 665.

3 *Jones v Morrall* (1852) 2 Sim NS 241.

4 *Re Jones, Christmas v Jones* [1897] 2 Ch 190.

1257. Interest on balances due from personal representative. Upon balances found due from a personal representative on taking his accounts, simple interest is charged as a rule[1]. The rate at which interest is charged is in the discretion of the court. The current practice is to charge interest at the same rate as is allowed from time to time on money in court on special account (formerly the short-term investment account) though in special cases interest at a higher rate may be awarded in which case it may be appropriate to apportion part of the interest to the capital of the trust fund[2]. In some cases compound interest may be awarded[3]. Accordingly, where the will contains a trust for accumulation, compound interest will be charged[4]; and where the representative, without actually trading with the assets, had appropriated them for the payment of his own debts or made use of them for his own enjoyment, he was charged with interest at a higher rate[5]. The special case need not necessarily be made before the original judgment in the proceedings[6].

1 *Re Barclay, Barclay v Andrew* [1899] 1 Ch 674 at 682 per Stirling J.

2 *Bartlett v Barclays Bank Trust Co Ltd (No 2)* [1980] Ch 515 at 546–547, [1980] 2 All ER 92 at 97–98 per Brightman LJ; *Jaffray v Marshall* [1994] 1 All ER 143, [1993] 1 WLR 1285. See also *West v West* [2003] All ER (D) 17 (Jun) (in the absence of absolute guidance from the authorities, there was no order for compound interest but, in order to compensate adequately for substantial sums wrongly paid by the trustees, interest would be paid at 1% above the special account rate). As to the court's discretion in respect of the rate of interest see PARA 1126. As to interest on debts see the Senior Courts Act 1981 s 35A, the County Courts Act 1984 s 69; CPR Pt 40; *Practice Direction—Accounts, Inquiries etc* PD 40A paras 14, 15; PARA 1187; and COURTS AND TRIBUNALS vol 24 (2010) PARA 701.

In former years the rate was normally 4%: see *Re Beech, Saint v Beech* [1920] 1 Ch 40; *Re Parry, Brown v Parry* [1947] Ch 23, [1946] 2 All ER 412. The rate was for some time 3%: see *Re Barclay, Barclay v Andrew* [1899] 1 Ch 674. See also *Re Goodenough, Marland v Williams* [1895] 2 Ch 537; *Re Lambert, Middleton v Moore* [1897] 2 Ch 169; *Rowlls v Bebb, Re Rowlls, Walters v Treasury Solicitor* [1900] 2 Ch 107, CA; *Wyman v Paterson* [1900] AC 271 at 279, HL, per the Earl of Halsbury LC and at 289 per Lord Shand; *Re Whiteford, Inglis v Whiteford* [1903] 1 Ch 889.

3 *Rocke v Hart* (1805) 11 Ves 58; *Tebbs v Carpenter* (1816) 1 Madd 290 at 306.

4 *Raphael v Boehm* (1805) 11 Ves 92 at 107 (affd (1807) 13 Ves 407); *Dornford v Dornford* (1806) 12 Ves 127; *Knott v Cottee* (1852) 16 Beav 77; *Gilroy v Stephen* (1882) 30 WR 745; *Re Emmet's Estate, Emmet v Emmet* (1881) 17 ChD 142; *Re Barclay, Barclay v Andrew* [1899] 1 Ch 674. As to trusts for accumulation see TRUSTS AND POWERS vol 98 (2013) PARA 100.

5 *Piety v Stace* (1799) 4 Ves 620; *Mousley v Carr* (1841) 4 Beav 49; *Westover v Chapman* (1844) 1 Coll 177. See also *Treves v Townshend* (1783) 1 Bro CC 384; *Berwick-upon-Tweed Corpn v Murray* (1857) 7 De GM & G 497 at 519; *Re Jones, Jones v Searle* (1883) 49 LT 91.

6 *Re Barclay, Barclay v Andrew* [1899] 1 Ch 674.

1258. Interest on balances due to personal representative. A personal representative who discharges debts due from the estate out of his own money is entitled to be allowed the sums so paid on taking his accounts[1], together with interest[2]. The interest should only be calculated on balances found due to him on the master's certificate[3], but the balances may be struck annually[4], and interest allowed, even though the debts themselves did not carry interest[5]. The representative is not allowed interest on payments made out of his own money for costs[6].

1 *Spackman v Holbrook* (1860) 2 Giff 198.

2 *Small v Wing* (1730) 5 Bro Parl Cas 66 at 72, HL.

3 *Gordon v Trail* (1820) 8 Price 416. As to the master's certificate see CIVIL PROCEDURE.

4 *Finch v Pescott* (1874) LR 17 Eq 554.

5 *Biggar v Eastwood* (1884) 15 LR Ir 219 at 235–236.

6 *Gordon v Trail* (1820) 8 Price 416; *Lewis v Lewis* (1850) 13 Beav 82.

(5) RELIEF FROM LIABILITY

1259. Court's jurisdiction to grant relief to personal representative. The court has jurisdiction to relieve a personal representative[1] either wholly or partly from personal liability for a breach of trust where he has acted honestly and reasonably, and ought fairly[2] to be excused for the breach and for omitting to obtain the court's directions in the matter in which he committed the breach[3]. Each case must be decided on its own merits, but the court must be satisfied that the representative acted reasonably as well as honestly[4]. A personal representative may successfully obtain relief for his breach of trust but still incur personal contractual liability, arising from the same circumstances[5]. The genuine concurrence of beneficiaries in a devastavit may be relevant to whether the personal representative should be relieved from liability[6].

Accordingly, executors may in special circumstances be relieved from liability for failure to get in debts owing to the estate[7], for making payments to their solicitors in reliance upon their statement that the sums were required for purposes of administration[8], or for making payments to legatees where they have reason to believe that the estate is solvent[9].

The granting of this relief is essentially a matter within the discretion of the judge of first instance whose conclusions will not be disturbed on appeal unless it is shown that he misdirected himself or left out something which he ought to have taken into account[10]. The mere fact that the personal representative takes professional advice will not automatically result in relief being given[11] but acting on the basis of the generally held view of the law is a ground for relief[12]. The court will be very slow to grant relief to a paid trustee, such as a bank, which deliberately places itself in a position where its duty conflicts with its interests[13].

1 As to the meaning of 'personal representative' see PARA 608. A personal representative acting under directions given under the court's jurisdiction to determine questions or give other relief available in administration proceedings is, of course, pro tanto protected: see PARA 1168. As to concurrence by beneficiaries see PARA 1250. As to the statutory protection afforded to personal representatives see PARAS 965, 484. See also PARA 1297.

2 'Fairly' means in fairness to himself and the other persons affected: see *Marsden v Regan* [1954] 1 All ER 475 at 481, [1954] 1 WLR 423 at 434, CA, per Sir R Evershed MR. As to breach of trust see TRUSTS AND POWERS vol 98 (2013) PARA 665 et seq. As to the committal of judicious breaches of trust see PARA 1244 note 2.

3 See the Trustee Act 1925 ss 61, 68(1) para (17); *Re Allsop, Whittaker v Bamford* [1914] 1 Ch 1, CA. See also *Re Evans, Evans v Westcombe* [1999] 2 All ER 777; and TRUSTS AND POWERS vol 98 (2013) PARA 665. The county court has jurisdiction where the amount or value of the estate does not exceed the county court limit: see the Trustee Act 1925 s 63A(1); and TRUSTS AND POWERS vol 98 (2013) PARA 57. As to the county court limit see PARA 866 note 2. As to the statutory relief from liability in respect of the acts of co-representatives see PARA 1252. As to losses incurred by the employment of agents see PARA 1048. Since, for these purposes, 'trustee' includes a personal representative (see s 68(1) para (17); and PARA 609), there is power to relieve for devastavit. As to devastavit see PARA 1244. See also *Bergliter v Cohen* [2006] EWHC 123 (Ch), [2006] All ER (D) 88 (Jan) (relief refused to executors because it was not reasonable for them to fail to seek advice of counsel or directions from the court on proper construction of will; non-professional executor also refused relief as he would had his own remedy against co-trustees, had the point arisen).

4 *Re Turner, Barker v Ivimey* [1897] 1 Ch 536.

5 See *Segbedzi v Segbedzi* (13 May 1999, unreported), CA (personal representative granted relief but still liable under contract of indemnity towards sureties for the administration).

6 *Re Pauling's Settlement Trusts, Younghusband v Coutts & Co* [1961] 3 All ER 713 at 730, [1962] 1 WLR 86 at 108; *Mitchell v Halliwell* [2005] EWHC 937 (Ch), [2005] All ER (D) 210 (May).

7 *Re Roberts, Knight v Roberts* (1897) 76 LT 479, CA; *Re Grindey, Clews v Grindey* [1898] 2 Ch 593, CA.

8 *Re Lord De Clifford's Estate, Lord De Clifford v Quilter, Lord De Clifford v Marquis of Lansdowne* [1900] 2 Ch 707, following *Bacon v Bacon* (1800) 5 Ves 331.

9 *Re Kay, Mosley v Kay* [1897] 2 Ch 518.

10 *Marsden v Regan* [1954] 1 All ER 475 at 482, [1954] 1 WLR 423 at 435, CA, per Sir R Evershed MR.

11 *Marsden v Regan* [1954] 1 All ER 475 at 481, [1954] 1 WLR 423 at 434, CA, per Sir R Evershed MR; *Re Evans, Evans v Westcombe* [1999] 2 All ER 777 at 789 per Richard McCombe QC. See also *Green v Walkling* [2007] EWHC 3251 (Ch), [2008] 2 BCLC 332 (relief granted to company director under Companies Act 1985 s 727 where he had acted honestly and reasonably on professional advice in attempt to act consistently with requirements of the Proceeds of Crime Act 2002). See also TRUSTS AND POWERS vol 98 (2013) PARA 665.

12 *Re Wightwick's Will Trusts, Official Trustees of Charitable Funds v Fielding-Ould* [1950] Ch 260 at 266, [1950] 1 All ER 689 at 692 per Wynn-Parry J.

13 *Re Pauling's Settlement Trusts, Younghusband v Coutts & Co* [1964] Ch 303 at 328–329, [1963] 3 All ER 1 at 11, CA, per Willmer LJ.

1260. Indemnity to personal representative for beneficiary's interest. The court has jurisdiction where the personal representative commits a breach of trust at the instigation or request or with the consent in writing[1] of a beneficiary, to impound the beneficiary's interest in the trust estate by way of indemnity to the representative[2]. In order to impound this interest it must be shown that the beneficiary knew the facts which would make the act a breach of trust[3]. The statutory jurisdiction to impound does not operate to deprive the representative of the benefit of the general rule enabling him to offer a good defence to a claim by a party who has concurred in the breach[4].

1 The instigation or request need not be in writing: see *Griffith v Hughes* [1892] 3 Ch 105, a decision upon the same words in the Trustee Act 1888 s 6 (repealed).
2 See the Trustee Act 1925 ss 62, 68(1) para (17); and TRUSTS AND POWERS vol 98 (2013) PARA 715. As to county court jurisdiction see PARA 1259 note 3.
3 *Re Somerset, Somerset v Earl Poulett* [1894] 1 Ch 231, CA. See also TRUSTS AND POWERS vol 98 (2013) PARA 669.
4 *Fletcher v Collis* [1905] 2 Ch 24, CA. See PARA 1252.

(6) THE EXECUTOR DE SON TORT

(i) Intermeddling with the Estate

1261. Person fraudulently obtaining or retaining estate. Any person who, to the defrauding of creditors or without full valuable consideration, obtains, receives, or holds any real or personal estate[1] of a deceased person or effects the release of any debt or liability due to the estate of the deceased, is chargeable as executor de son tort[2] to the extent of the real and personal estate received or coming to his hands, or the debt or liability released, after deducting:

(1) any debt for valuable consideration and without fraud due to him from the deceased person at the time of his death; and
(2) any payment made by him which might properly be made by a personal representative[3].

Such a person also becomes liable for payment of inheritance tax[4]. It seems to be the case that concealing the death of a person from a beneficiary, with the intention and result of retaining or receiving property of the deceased, might constitute a person as executor de son tort[5], as might the continuation in possession of property belonging to the deceased, without the right to such possession[6].

1 As to the meaning of 'real estate' see PARA 607 note 1.
2 As to the meaning of 'executor de son tort' see PARA 606. The term is applicable to an intestacy: see PARA 606 text to note 7. As to the procedure to force an executor de son tort to obtain a grant see PARA 699; and as to administration proceedings see PARA 1166.
3 Administration of Estates Act 1925 s 28. As to the meaning of 'personal representative' see PARA 608. See also *Hawes v Leader* (1611) Yelv 196; *Nunn v Wilsmore* (1800) 8 Term Rep 521; *Seally v Powis* (1835) 1 Har & W 2. In *James v Williams* [2000] Ch 1, [1999] 3 All ER 309, CA (where expenditure on repairs and maintenance of estate property by an executor de son tort was held to be such a payment).
4 See PARA 1266.
5 See *Kay v Tibbs* [2007] All ER (D) 31 (Feb) (costs application, following discontinuance of claim based upon alleged concealment of death from beneficiary and further alleged acts as executor de son tort; court departing from usual discontinuance rule relating to costs).
6 See *Martin v Myers* [2004] EWHC 1947 (Ch), [2004] All ER (D) 396 (Jul) (intestacy situation and issues as to whether surviving occupant of family home had been spouse of deceased owner or not and, if not, whether she enjoyed a possessory title to defeat intestacy claimants; whether possessory claim would be defeated by existence of constructive trust); see PARA 1269 text and note 12. See also *Opanubi v Daley* [2002] EWHC 1596 (Ch) at [19], [2002] All ER (D) 411 (Jul).

1262. Slight acts of interference sufficient to be executor de son tort. The slightest circumstance may make a person executor de son tort if he intermeddles with the assets in such a way as to denote an assumption of the authority or an intention to exercise the functions of an executor[1] or administrator[2]. Demanding payment of debts due to the deceased, paying the deceased's debts[3], carrying on his business[4] or disposing of goods[5] may make a person executor de son tort; but setting up a colourable title to the deceased's goods is not enough[6]. A person who enters on or collects the rents of a deceased person's leasehold property and pays the ground rent may, by reason of privity of estate or estoppel, render himself liable to the landlord on the covenants of the lease as executor de son tort[7], but a person who takes over leasehold property from an executor de son tort does not[8]. Where a person who was entitled to a grant of administration neglected to obtain it, but occupied and dealt with estate property as an owner, he constituted himself executor de son tort[9]. An English company which transferred shares and paid dividends to the deceased's executors in America to the knowledge that the executors had not obtained and did not intend to obtain probate in England made itself an executor de son tort and was liable to pay penalties, deliver an account and pay such duty as would have been payable if probate had been obtained in England[10].

1 *Peters v Leeder* (1878) 47 LJQB 573.
2 As to the relation back of an administrator's title after grant see PARA 645.
3 Godolphin's Orphan's Legacy, Pt II, c 8 s 1. In *Serle v Waterworth* (1838) 4 M & W 9 (revsd on another point sub nom *Nelson v Serle* (1839) 4 M & W 795) the giving by the deceased's widow of a promissory note for a debt which was owing from the deceased was held not to constitute the widow executrix de son tort. As to executors de son tort see PARA 606.
4 *Hooper v Summersett* (1810) Wight 16.
5 *Read's Case* (1604) 5 Co Rep 33b; *Nulty v Fagan* (1888) 22 LR Ir 604.
6 *Femings v Jarrat* (1795) 1 Esp 335; Godolphin's Orphan's Legacy, Pt II, c 8 s 3.
7 *Williams v Heales* (1874) LR 9 CP 177; *Stratford-upon-Avon Corpn v Parker* [1914] 2 KB 562, DC.
8 *Paull v Simpson* (1846) 9 QB 365.
9 *James v Williams* [2000] Ch 1, [1999] 3 All ER 309, CA.
10 *New York Breweries Co Ltd* v A-G [1899] AC 62.

1263. Acts of charity or necessity will not make a person liable as executor de son tort. If necessity arises a person may give directions for the funeral of the deceased person[1], and may appropriate a reasonable sum for that purpose out of the deceased's money[2]. He may also place the deceased's goods in a place of safety[3], lock them up for preservation and make an inventory of them[4], may order necessaries for the household, provide for the deceased's horses and cattle, and pay any doctor's fees[5]. By so doing he will not make himself liable as an executor de son tort[6].

1 *Harrison v Rowley* (1798) 4 Ves 212 at 216.
2 Godolphin's Orphan's Legacy, Pt II c 8 s 6; *Camden v Fletcher* (1838) 4 M & W 378 at 381 per Parke B.
3 *Re Fitzpatrick* (1892) 29 LR Ir 328.
4 Godolphin's Orphan's Legacy, Pt II c 8 s 3.
5 Godolphin's Orphan's Legacy, Pt II c 8 ss 3, 6. However, if he advertises for creditors he will make himself liable: *Long and Feaver v Symes and Hannam* (1832) 3 Hag Ecc 771.
6 As to the analogous question whether or not an executor has by his conduct accepted his appointment as executor see PARA 627.

1264. Persons not liable as executor de son tort. A person who receives payment from the executor de son tort of a debt due from the deceased[1] or who takes over property of a deceased person from an executor de son tort does not himself become an executor de son tort[2] although, if he has taken the property with notice of a trust, it may be followed into his hands as trust property[3].

A person who takes possession of the foreign assets of a deceased person without taking possession of his English assets does not become executor de son tort[4]. A person who, as a nominee holder for the deceased's estate of assets in the United Kingdom, procures the transfer of the assets out of the United Kingdom is an executor de son tort[5].

A person who takes possession of the effects under the authority or as agent of a rightful executor, whether or not the will has been proved, cannot be charged as executor de son tort[6], and, although his authority may be revoked by the death of the rightful executor, so as to render him chargeable if, after his principal's death, he proceeds to act as an executor[7], yet the mere retention of the assets as a trustee for the person beneficially entitled will not render him chargeable as executor de son tort[8].

1 *Hursell v Bird* (1891) 65 LT 709.
2 *Paull v Simpson* (1846) 9 QB 365; *Hill v Curtis* (1865) LR 1 Eq 90 at 97 per Page Wood V-C. See also *James v Williams* [2000] Ch 1, [1999] 3 All ER 309, CA (where the defendant took the property under the will of her brother who was executor de son tort, it was held that she took it as constructive trustee for their sister). As to the meaning of 'executor de son tort' see PARA 606.
3 *Hill v Curtis* (1865) LR 1 Eq 90. See also EQUITABLE JURISDICTION vol 47 (2014) PARA 238.
4 *Beavan v Lord Hastings* (1856) 2 K & J 724.
5 *IRC v Stype Investments (Jersey) Ltd, Re Clore* [1982] Ch 456, [1982] 3 All ER 419, CA.
6 *Hall v Elliot* (1791) Peake 86; *Sykes v Sykes* (1870) LR 5 CP 113. It is otherwise if the person taking possession acts under the directions, and at the request of, another executor de son tort: *A-G v New York Breweries Co Ltd* [1898] 1 QB 205, CA; affd sub nom *New York Breweries Co Ltd v A-G* [1899] AC 62, HL.
7 *Cottle v Aldrich* (1815) 4 M & S 175.
8 *Tomlin v Beck* (1823) Turn & R 438.

1265. Determination of liability as executor de son tort. The question whether a person has intermeddled is one of fact: the result of that intermeddling, namely whether it constitutes the person an executor de son tort, is a matter of law[1].

1 *Padget v Priest* (1787) 2 Term Rep 97. Therefore the question whether a person has tortiously intermeddled with an estate could not normally be determined on an originating summons: *Re Chalmers, Chalmers v Chalmers* (1921) 65 Sol Jo 475. As to the current procedure see now CPR Pt 8; and CIVIL PROCEDURE vol 11 (2015) PARA 150 et seq. In *Younger v Saner* [2002] EWCA Civ 1077, [2002] All ER (D) 372 (Jul), a person's unauthorised use of a trust arrangement and an estate's interest in shares, where no estate property actually came into his hands, may not have constituted him executor de son tort but, instead, a sort of self-appointed fiduciary. The case also shows that causation of loss must be established. See also, in this regard, *Degazon v Barclays Bank International Ltd* [1988] 1 FTLR 17, CA.

(ii) Effect of Acts of Executor De Son Tort

1266. Lawful acts of executor de son tort bind the estate. Generally speaking, all lawful acts done in the professed administration of the estate by a person purporting to act as personal representative which a rightful executor would have been bound to perform in due course of administration, bind the estate[1]. To render an act binding, it must be shown that at the time when it was done the person who did it was acting in the character of executor; an isolated wrongful act consisting of the handing over of goods of the deceased to a creditor is not of itself binding on the estate[2].

The rule that lawful acts bind the estate will apply where an executor de son tort acts in obedience to a statutory duty which extends to such an executor. For example, an executor de son tort is within the meaning of 'personal representative'[3] for the purposes of liability[4] to inheritance tax[5], but not for the purposes of the Trustee Act 1925[6].

1 *Coulter's Case* (1598) 5 Co Rep 30a; *Parker v Kett* (1701) 1 Ld Raym 658 at 661; *Buckley v Barber* (1851) 6 Exch 164 at 183; *Thomson v Harding* (1853) 2 E & B 630.

2 *Mountford v Gibson* (1804) 4 East 441. Where a person who had formerly acted as agent of the deceased continued so to act after his death, leases granted by him were valid and bound the estate: see *Opanubi v Daley* [2002] EWHC 1596 (Ch) at [19], [2002] All ER (D) 411 (Jul).

3 See the Inheritance Tax Act 1984 s 272, by which 'personal representative' includes any such person as is mentioned in s 199(4)(a) (ie any person who takes possession of or intermeddles with, or otherwise acts in relation to, property so as to become liable as executor or trustee): see INHERITANCE TAXATION vol 59A (2014) PARAS 34, 253. See *New York Breweries Co Ltd v A-G* [1899] AC 62, HL; *IRC v Stype Investments (Jersey) Ltd, Re Clore* [1982] Ch 456, [1982] 3 All ER 419, CA.

4 As to the liability of personal representatives for inheritance tax see in particular the Inheritance Tax Act 1984 ss 200(1)(a), 204(1); and as to repayment of tax to personal representatives by the person in whom property is vested see s 211(3). See further INHERITANCE TAXATION vol 59A (2014) PARAS 256, 264.

5 As to the burden of inheritance tax on death see PARA 1128. See also generally INHERITANCE TAXATION vol 59A (2014) PARA 3.

A person who takes possession of or intermeddles with the property of a deceased person without the authority of the personal representatives or the court is, as regards any liability for payment of death duties, capital transfer tax, or inheritance tax, a 'personal representative' within the definition contained in the Administration of Estates Act 1925 s 55(1)(xi), the Law of Property Act 1925 s 205(1)(xviii): see notes 3, 4; and PARA 608. As to the abolition of capital transfer tax and its replacement by inheritance tax see PARA 1128 note 2; and INHERITANCE TAXATION vol 59A (2014) PARA 1 et seq.

Accordingly it seems that an executor de son tort has the statutory powers of a personal representative under the foregoing Acts so far as applicable for the purpose of paying inheritance tax, or, in the case of a death before 25 July 1986, capital transfer tax or estate duty. An executor de son tort also has power under the Inheritance Tax Act 1984 s 212 to sell or mortgage any property in respect of which he is liable for inheritance tax in order to pay the tax, interest on it, and costs properly incurred in respect of it: see INHERITANCE TAXATION vol 59A (2014) PARA 272.

6 See the Trustee Act 1925 s 68(1) para (9); and TRUSTS AND POWERS vol 98 (2013) PARA 430. Consequently an executor de son tort is not 'a personal representative' for the purposes of the definition of 'trustee' in that Act, which includes a personal representative, nor for the purposes of Trustee Act 2000 where s 39 applies the same definition: see PARA 609; and TRUSTS AND POWERS vol 98 (2013) PARA 3.

(iii) Liabilities and Rights of Executor De Son Tort

1267. Liability of executor de son tort to be sued. An executor de son tort is liable to be sued by the rightful personal representative[1], a creditor[2] or a beneficiary[3]. He is not liable for more than has come to his hands[4], and he may, as against the rightful representative, set up in mitigation of damages all payments made by him in due course of administration[5]; but it would appear that he cannot avail himself of any right of recoupment if the rightful representative is a creditor and there are insufficient assets left to pay his debt[6].

At one time an executor de son tort could rely on the law of limitation in the same manner and subject to the same considerations as could a properly appointed executor[7], but the position is now more complex[8]. A properly appointed executor cannot obtain title by long possession against those interested in the estate because he is a trustee for the purposes of the Limitation Act 1980[9], and by that Act no period of limitation applies to a claim by a beneficiary to recover trust property in the possession of a trustee[10]. An executor de son tort, however, is not as such a trustee for the purposes of that Act[11]; and consequently he may be able to establish a title by possession provided he is not shown in the particular circumstances of the case to be an express or constructive trustee[12]. Where an unmarried partner of the deceased simply remained in the family home after his death and there were no obvious factors to affect her conscience, no constructive trust arose to prevent her from acquiring a possessory title[13].

After judgment has been obtained by a creditor of the deceased against the executor de son tort, execution may issue against chattels real of which the executor de son tort has taken possession[14].

An executor de son tort may be liable for inheritance tax[15], and may also be liable to a penalty for administering without obtaining a grant of probate or letters of administration[16].

A minor who intermeddles with an estate cannot be made to account as an executor de son tort[17].

1 Godolphin's Orphan's Legacy, Pt II c 8 s 2. As to the meaning of 'executor de son tort' see PARA 606. As to the meaning of 'personal representative' see PARA 608.

2 *Kellow v Westcombe* (1673) Freem KB 122; 2 Bl Com (14th Edn) 506. As to administration proceedings see PARA 1168.

3 1 Roll Abr 919 (F 1).

4 *Stokes v Porter* (1558) 2 Dyer 166b; *Lowry v Fulton* (1839) 9 Sim 115; *Yardley v Arnold* (1842) Car & M 434.

5 *Padget v Priest* (1787) 2 Term Rep 97; *Fyson v Chambers* (1842) 9 M & W 460 at 468 per Lord Abinger CB. The decision in *Woolley v Clark* (1822) 5 B & Ald 744, disallowing recoupment, probably went on the ground that the executor de son tort had not acted in good faith: see *Thomson v Harding* (1853) 2 E & B 630 at 635 per Lord Campbell CJ. See *James v Williams* [2000] Ch 1, [1999] 3 All ER 309, CA (expenditure on repairs and maintenance of estate property). To bind the estate the payment must be made by a person who has become an executor de son tort; an isolated wrongful payment is not sufficient: see PARA 1266 note 2.

6 2 Bl Com (14th Edn) 507; *Mountford v Gibson* (1804) 4 East 441 at 453; *Elworthy v Sandford* (1864) 3 H & C 330. Under the old form of pleading the executor de son tort could not, as against the rightful representative, plead his payments in abatement of the action: *Whitehall v Squire* (1691) Carth 103.

7 *Webster v Webster* (1804) 10 Ves 93; *Doyle v Foley* [1903] 2 IR 95.

8 Ie since the Limitation Act 1939, subsequently re-enacted with amendments as the Limitation Act 1980.

9 In the Limitation Act 1980, 'trustee' has the same meaning as in the Trustee Act 1925 (see the Limitation Act 1980 s 38(1)), and consequently includes a properly appointed executor but not an executor de son tort: see the Trustee Act 1925 s 68(1) paras (9), (17). See also *James v Williams* [2000] Ch 1, [1999] 3 All ER 309, CA; and PARA 609. See also LIMITATION PERIODS vol 68 (2016) PARA 916; TRUSTS AND POWERS vol 98 (2013) PARA 4.

10 See the Limitation Act 1980 s 21(1); and LIMITATION PERIODS vol 68 (2016) PARA 1138.

11 See note 9.

12 For an example of an executor de son tort who was held to be a constructive trustee for this purpose see *James v Williams* [2000] Ch 1, [1999] 3 All ER 309, CA (beneficiary under an intestacy who occupied the deceased's land while there was no grant of letters of administration held to be a constructive trustee). Cf *Earnshaw v Hartley* [2000] Ch 155, [1999] 3 WLR 709, CA (limitation defence of beneficiary in occupation of land in an intestate's estate held to be defeated by virtue of Limitation Act 1980 s 15(6), Sch 1 para 9). See also the article by F Hinkes in 38 Conveyancer (NS) (May–June 1974) 177. See *Martin v Myers* [2004] EWHC 1947 (Ch), [2004] All ER (D) 396 (Jul); and *Opanubi v Daley* [2002] EWHC 1596 (Ch) at [19], [2002] All ER (D) 411 (Jul).

13 See *Martin v Myers* [2004] EWHC 1947 (Ch), [2004] All ER (D) 396 (Jul), where *James v Williams* [2000] Ch 1, [1999] 3 All ER 309, CA, was distinguished, in that the unmarrie d partner of a deceased, intestate person had no right to have the property vested in her or to take administration and there was no evidence from which it could be inferred that her conscience should have been affected, as she left the property to the beneficiaries of the deceased intestate in her will.

14 *Doherty v Nelson* [1895] 2 IR 90.

15 See PARA 1266. As to the liability to penalties for failure to deliver accounts etc in relation to inheritance tax see INHERITANCE TAXATION vol 59A (2014) PARA 328 et seq.

16 See PARA 668.

17 *Stott v Meanock* (1862) 31 LJ Ch 746. As to the appointment of minors see PARA 620.

1268. Answer by executor de son tort to creditor's action. As against a creditor an executor de son tort may plead that he has fully administered the estate[1], or that he has, before a claim has been brought, handed over all the assets in his hands to the rightful personal representative[2], or has settled accounts with him[3], or that there was no causative link between the purported wrongful act and the loss to the creditor[4]; but it is no answer to the creditor that he has done so after a claim has been brought[5], nor can he obtain a valid discharge by handing over the assets to another who has himself never become a rightful representative of the deceased[6].

1 *Oxenham v Clapp* (1831) 2 B & Ad 309 (where the executor de son tort paid a specialty debt after action brought by a simple contract debtor and successfully pleaded the payment in bar of action); *Yardley v Arnold* (1842) Car & M 434. As to the plea of full administration (plene administravit) see PARA 1290. As to the meaning of 'executor de son tort' see PARA 606.
2 *Padget v Priest* (1787) 2 Term Rep 97. As to the meaning of 'personal representative' see PARA 608.
3 *Hill v Curtis* (1865) LR 1 Eq 90 at 97, dissenting from dicta of Lord Cottenham LC in *Carmichael v Carmichael* (1846) 2 Ph 101 at 103.
4 *Degazon v Barclays Bank International Ltd* [1988] 1 FTLR 17, CA.
5 *Curtis v Vernon* (1790) 3 Term Rep 587 (affd sub nom *Vernon v Curtis* (1792) 2 Hy Bl 18); *Layfield v Layfield* (1834) 7 Sim 172; cf *Oxenham v Clapp* (1831) 2 B & Ad 309 (see note 1).
6 *Sharland v Mildon, Sharland v Loosemore* (1846) 5 Hare 469; *Hill v Curtis* (1865) LR 1 Eq 90 at 100.

1269. Other civil liabilities of executor de son tort. An executor de son tort is answerable for the acts of another when authorised and directed by him[1]. The executor de son tort of a rightful executor is also liable for the original testator's debts[2]. An executor de son tort may be required to submit a statement of the deceased's affairs after an insolvency administration order has been made in respect of the deceased's estate[3].

1 *Re Ryan, Kenny v Ryan* [1897] 1 IR 513. As to the meaning of 'executor de son tort' see PARA 606.
2 *Meyrick v Anderson* (1850) 14 QB 719.
3 See the Administration of Insolvent Estates of Deceased Persons Order 1986, SI 1986/1999, arts 3, 5, Sch 1 Pt II para 15, Sch 2 para 1 (under which, if there is no personal representative, a statement of affairs can be required from such person as the court may on the application of the official receiver direct); and BANKRUPTCY AND INDIVIDUAL INSOLVENCY vol 5 (2013) PARA 240.

1270. Liability of representative of executor de son tort. The executor or administrator of a defaulting executor de son tort[1], namely one who has wasted or converted to his own use any real or personal estate[2] of a deceased person, is, to the extent of the defaulter's available assets, liable and chargeable in respect of that waste or conversion in the same manner as the defaulter would have been if living[3]. However, in the absence of any allegation of waste or conversion by the executor de son tort, his representative is not liable for a breach of contract committed by the person with whose goods the executor de son tort has intermeddled[4].

The question of the application of a particular limitation period to the act of an executor de son tort, or raised by his personal representative in answer to the original wrong, may turn upon the question whether the circumstances are such as to give rise to a constructive trust[5].

1 As to the meanings of 'executor' and 'executor de son tort' see PARA 606. As to the meaning of 'administrator' see PARA 607.
2 As to the meaning of 'real estate' see PARA 607 note 1.
3 Administration of Estates Act 1925 s 29. This provision applies generally to the personal representative of a defaulting personal representative and not merely to the personal representative of a defaulting executor de son tort; cf PARA 1249.
4 *Wilson v Hodson* (1872) LR 7 Exch 84; cf *Coward v Gregory* (1866) LR 2 CP 153 (see PARA 1249 note 4).
5 See *Martin v Myers* [2004] EWHC 1947 (Ch), [2004] All ER (D) 396 (Jul) (no constructive trust applied so limitation period arose in favour of executor de son tort); cf *James v Williams* [2000]

Ch 1, [1999] 3 All ER 309, CA (constructive trust bound executor de son tort and her personal representative).

16. ACTIONS BY AND AGAINST PERSONAL REPRESENTATIVES

(1) PRACTICE AND PROCEDURE

1271. Indorsement on claim form; parties. Where a person claims or is claimed against in a representative capacity, a statement of that capacity must be indorsed on the claim form[1]. It has been held that where two or more personal representatives are claiming and one of them is debarred or estopped the other or others cannot maintain the claim[2]. However, there are many instances where the decision has been doubted[3].

Any proceedings[4] may be brought by or against trustees or personal representatives in their capacity as such without joining[5] any persons beneficially interested in the trust or estate[6]. Personal representatives may be substituted for a person mistakenly joined as a defendant after his death[7], and no cause or matter will be defeated by the misjoinder or non-joinder of parties, because the court has powers to add a new party or to order any person to cease to be a party; in either case, where it is desirable to exercise such power for the purpose of resolving issues and matters in dispute[8].

1 See CPR 16.2(3), (4). Regard should be had generally to the Chancery Guide (2016). As to beginning or maintaining proceedings by an executor before probate see PARA 635; as to beginning proceedings before a grant of administration see PARA 647. A party wishing to deny another party's right to claim in a representative capacity should do so specifically.

2 See *Brewer v Westminster Bank Ltd* [1952] 2 All ER 650; cf *Catlin v Cyprus Finance Corpn* (London) Ltd [1983] QB 759, [1983] 1 All ER 809 (where two executors opened a joint bank account to be operated by both signatures and one forged the other's signature, held, dismissing the bank's application, that the bank's obligation was a single obligation owed to the executors jointly which could only be enforced if both were parties).

3 See *Welch v Bank of England* [1955] Ch 508; *Jackson v White* [1967] 2 Lloyd's Rep 68; *Catlin v Cyprus Finance Corpn (London) Ltd* [1983] QB 759, [1983] 1 All ER 809, where Bingham J declined to follow *Brewer v Westminster Bank Ltd* [1952] 2 All ER 650, on the basis that the bank had made a separate agreement with each of the contractors severally that it would not honour any drawings unless each had authorised the withdrawal. As to the meaning of 'personal representative' see PARA 608. As to joint representation see PARA 926.

4 This includes proceedings to enforce a security by foreclosure or otherwise: see CPR Pt 19; and PARA 647.

5 Unless beneficiaries are necessary parties they ought not to be made parties and their costs will be disallowed: see *Re Cooper, Cooper v Vesey* (1882) 20 ChD 611 at 635, CA.

6 CPR 19.7A(1). However, any judgment or order made in the claim is binding upon the beneficiaries unless the court orders otherwise in the same or other proceedings: CPR 19.7A(2). This is without prejudice to the court's power to order any person having such an interest to be made a party, or to make a representation order under CPR Pt 19: see PARA 647 text and note 5.

7 See CPR 19.8; and PARA 818.

8 See CPR 19.2(2), (3); and CIVIL PROCEDURE vol 11 (2015) PARA 483 et seq.

1272. Notice of claim to non-parties. At any stage in a claim relating to the estate of a deceased person or property subject to a trust, or the sale of any property[1], the court may, on the application[2] of any party or of its own motion, direct that notice[3] of the claim be served[4] on any person who is not a party to the claim but who will or may be affected by a judgment in the proceedings[5]. A person served with such a notice may, by acknowledging service[6], become a party to the claim but if he does not do so he will be bound by any judgment given in the proceedings as if he was a party[7].

1 CPR 19.8A(2).

2 An application may be made without notice being served on any other party and must be supported by written evidence which includes the reasons why the person to be served should be bound by the judgment in the claim: CPR 19.8A(3).
3 The notice must be:
   (1) in the specified form required by the practice direction;
   (2) issued by the court; and
   (3) accompanied by a copy of the claim form and of all other statements of case, witness statements, or affidavits served in the claim, and by a form of acknowledgement of service with such modifications as may be necessary (CPR 19.8A(4)).
4 As to service generally see CPR Pt 6; and CIVIL PROCEDURE vol 11 (2015) PARA 244.
5 CPR 19.8A(2).
6 Acknowledgement must be made within 14 days of service: see CPR 19.8A(5).
7 CPR 19.8A(6); Administration of Justice Act 1985 s 47(1), (2). If, after service of a notice of a claim on a person, the claim form is amended so as substantially to alter the relief claimed, the court may direct that a judgment is not to bind that person unless a further notice, together with a copy of the amended claim form, is served on him: CPR 19.8A(7).

1273. Joinder of representative and personal claims. Subject to the court's power to order a separate trial of any issue[1] a claimant may claim in one action, relief against the same defendant in respect of more than one cause of action, if the claimant claims or the defendant is alleged to be liable in the capacity of personal representative of an estate in respect of one or more of the causes of action and in his personal capacity, but with reference to the same estate in respect of all the others[2]. Where the claims cannot be conveniently tried together the court may order separate trials or make such other order as may be expedient[3], for example an order confining the claim to those claims which can be conveniently disposed of together.

1 Ie under CPR 3.1(2)(i): see CIVIL PROCEDURE vol 12 (2015) PARA 1075.
2 See CPR 7.3. See also *Padwick v Scott, Re Scott's Estate, Scott v Padwick* (1876) 2 ChD 736 at 743. A claim by a claimant as personal representative of a tenant for life for rent accrued due in the deceased's lifetime cannot be joined with a claim for rent by the claimant in his own right as remainderman in respect of rent accruing due subsequently: *Lord Tredegar v Roberts* [1914] 1 KB 283, CA.
3 See CPR 3.1(2)(i).

1274. Permission to bring or defend proceedings. It is normally advisable for a personal representative[1] before bringing or defending a claim to obtain the consent of all the beneficiaries on whom the burden of costs would ultimately fall or, if for any reason this is not forthcoming, to seek the court's directions by issuing a claim form to that end[2]. If the beneficiaries' consent or the court's sanction is not obtained, the personal representative litigates at his own risk as to costs in the sense that he may be deprived of his right to be indemnified out of the estate if the court considers that he acted unreasonably in prosecuting or defending the claim[3]. Where an executor, or a solicitor acting for the executor, brings a claim for determination of a matter arising from the administration of the estate, or the trust, he must remain neutral in the conduct of the claim, or risk losing his right to an indemnity against costs[4].

1 As to the meaning of 'personal representative' see PARA 608.
2 See CPR 25.2(1), 64(2), (4). The application should be made by application notice in accordance with CPR 25.2(1): see *Re Beddoe, Downes v Cottam* [1893] 1 Ch 547, CA. The contents of a Beddoe application are not confidential and may be admitted in evidence: *Midland Bank Trust Co Ltd v Green* [1980] Ch 590, [1978] 3 All ER 555 (on appeal on another point [1981] AC 513, [1981] 1 All ER 153, HL). Accordingly, the Beddoe application should not be made in the claim to which the representatives are parties, and about the conduct of which they are seeking directions, but must be made by a separate claim: *Alsop Wilkinson v Neary* [1995] 1 All ER 431, [1996] 1 WLR 1220. See also *McDonald v Horn* [1995] 1 All ER 961, CA; *Singh v Bhasin* (1998) Times, 21 August; and PARA 1168 et seq.

3 *Re Beddoe, Downes v Cottam* [1893] 1 Ch 547, CA; *Re England's Settlement Trusts, Dobbs v England* [1918] 1 Ch 24. As to the personal representative's right to indemnity see PARA 1018.

4 See *Raymond Saul & Co (a firm) v Holden (as personal representative of Hemmings)* [2008] EWHC 8565 (Ch) at [29], [2008] All ER (D) 168 (Dec) at [29]. See also *Alsop Wilkinson (a firm) v Neary* [1995] 1 All ER 431, [1996] 1 WLR 1220; *Breadner v Granville Grossman* [2000] All ER (D) 996 quoted in *Raymond Saul & Co (a firm) v Holden (as personal representative of Hemmings)* [2008] EWHC 8565 (Ch) at [30]–[34], [2008] All ER (D) 168 (Dec) at [30]–[34]; and *Re Evans* [1986] 1 WLR 101.

1275. Legal aid for certain claims. Since 1 April 2013 there has been a new system of legal aid[1]. The Legal Aid Agency is a non-statutory executive agency of the Ministry of Justice, established by the Lord Chancellor for the purpose of providing civil and criminal legal aid and advice in England and Wales; the Agency has replaced the former Legal Services Commission[2].

1 See now the Legal Aid, Sentencing and Punishment of Offenders Act 2013 Pt 1 (ss 1–43); and LEGAL AID vol 65 (2015) PARA 2 et seq.

2 As to the Legal Aid Agency see LEGAL AID vol 65 (2015) PARA 156. As to the Lord Chancellor's powers see LEGAL AID vol 65 (2015) PARA 155.

1276. Costs claimed by personal representative. Subject to the court's discretion[1], in ordinary cases a personal representative[2] who claims as such and fails is personally liable for the costs of the claim[3], and, unless the defendant has been guilty of some misconduct inducing the claimant to bring the claim[4], the judgment against him will be that the defendant recover the costs to be levied de bonis propriis[5], but this will not preclude the personal representative from indemnifying himself out of the estate if he is entitled to such indemnity under the principles previously stated[6].

1 As to the court's discretion to award costs see CPR 44.3; and CIVIL PROCEDURE vol 12A (2015) PARA 1689. See also *Raymond Saul & Co (a firm) v Holden (as personal representative of Hemmings)* [2008] EWHC 8565 (Ch), [2008] All ER (D) 168 (Dec).

2 As to the meaning of 'personal representative' see PARA 608.

3 See *Boynton v Boynton* (1879) 4 App Cas 733, HL.

4 *Godson v Freeman* (1835) 2 Cr M & R 585; *Farley v Briant* (1836) 3 Ad & El 839; *Birkhead v North* (1847) 4 Dow & L 732; *Redmayne v Moore* (1856) 2 Jur NS 691.

5 *Ashton v Poynter* (1835) 1 Cr M & R 738; *Southgate v Crowley* (1835) 1 Bing NC 518.

6 See PARA 1018. See also *Re Ritchie (Costs), Ritchie v Joslin (Cost)* [2009] WTLR 885 (no indemnity for executor's costs in unsuccessfully defending challenge to will based on lack of capacity); and the cases cited in PARA 1274 note 3.

(2) ACCRUAL OF CAUSES OF ACTION

(i) Survival of Causes of Action

1277. Survival of causes of action for benefit of estate. On the death of a person on or after 25 July 1934[1], all causes of action vested in him survive for the benefit of the estate[2] except a cause of action for defamation[3] which continues to be governed by the maxim actio personalis moritur cum persona (a personal action dies with the person)[4]. The statutory right of a person to claim damages for bereavement does not survive for the benefit of his estate on his death[5]. Criminal proceedings are similarly of a personal nature and the court has formerly had no jurisdiction to allow a criminal appeal to continue after the death of the appellant even if the estate would benefit financially from a successful appeal[6]. That position appears to be changing and it seems that some circumstances may justify an appeal against a conviction being brought, effectively, by the estate of a deceased convicted person[7]. Compensation for miscarriages of justice may also be paid to the personal representative of a wrongly convicted person[8].

1 Ie the date of the passing of the Law Reform (Miscellaneous Provisions) Act 1934. As to deaths before this date, the Administration of Estates Act 1925 s 26(2) (repealed) (replacing the Civil Procedure Act 1833 s 2) enabled a personal representative to maintain, for any injury committed to the deceased's real estate and chattels real within six months before his death, any action which the deceased could have maintained, but the action had to be brought within a year after the death: see eg *Jones v Simes* (1890) 43 ChD 607 at 613. Apart from statute no action could be brought for injury to a deceased's real estate: *Phillips v Homfray* (1883) 24 ChD 439 at 463, CA; on appeal sub nom *Phillips v Fothergill* (1886) 11 App Cas 466, HL.

The Administration of Estates Act 1925 s 26(1) (repealed) (replacing, as to deaths after 1925, 13 Edw 1 (Statute of Westminster the Second) (1285) c 23; 25 Edw 3 stat 5 (1351–2) c 5; and 31 Edw 3 stat 1 c 11 (1357)) provided that for any debt due to a deceased person, and for any injury to or right in respect of his personal estate in his lifetime, his personal representative should have the same right of action as the deceased would have had if alive. These statutes applied to all torts except those relating to the testator's freehold and those where the injury done was of a personal nature: *Twycross v Grant* (1878) 4 CPD 40 at 45, CA, per Bramwell LJ.

2 Law Reform (Miscellaneous Provisions) Act 1934 s 1(1). The effect of this Act was to abolish the general application of the maxim actio personalis moritur cum persona: Law Revision Committee's Interim Report dated 7 March 1934 (see 77 L Jo 246).

3 Law Reform (Miscellaneous Provisions) Act 1934 s 1(1) proviso (amended by the Law Reform (Miscellaneous Provisions) Act 1970 s 7(2), Schedule; and the Administration of Justice Act 1982 s 75, Sch 9 Pt I). In the event of the insolvency of an estate against which proceedings are maintainable by virtue of the Law Reform (Miscellaneous Proceedings) Act 1934 s 1, any liability in respect of the cause of action in respect of which the proceedings are maintainable is deemed to be a debt provable in the administration of the estate, notwithstanding that it is a demand in the nature of unliquidated damages arising otherwise than by a contract, promise or breach of trust: s 1(6).

4 The general result of the application of the common law maxim actio personalis moritur cum persona was that a personal representative could not sue or be sued for a wrong committed against or by the deceased for which unliquidated damages only would be recoverable: *Kirk v Todd* (1882) 21 ChD 484 at 488, CA; *Pulling v Great Eastern Rly Co* (1882) 9 QBD 110, DC. The principle was applicable both at law and in equity: *Peek v Gurney* (1873) LR 6 HL 377. Accordingly, an action for deceit did not lie against the personal representatives of a person who had fraudulently induced another to take shares in a company, or even to purchase shares from the deceased himself: *Re Duncan, Terry v Sweeting* [1899] 1 Ch 387. It also applied to proceedings authorised by Act of Parliament against a person which were in the nature of an action for personal tort: *Story v Sheard* [1892] 2 QB 515.

The only cases in which, apart from questions of breach of contract express or implied, a remedy for a wrongful act could be pursued against the estate of a deceased person were where property or the proceeds or value of property belonging to another had been appropriated by the deceased person and added to his own estate or money. In such cases the action, although arising out of a wrongful act, did not die with the person; but where there was nothing among the deceased's assets which in law or in equity belonged to the plaintiff, and the damages which had been done to him were unliquidated and uncertain, the wrongdoers' personal representatives could not be sued merely because it was worth the wrongdoer's while to commit the act and an indirect benefit might have been reaped by it: *Phillips v Homfray* (1883) 24 ChD 439 at 454, CA, per Bowen LJ and Cotton LJ, and see at 457 et seq for observations upon the earlier authorities.

In such cases proceedings could not be pursued against the personal representative even though the death of the wrongdoer did not take place until after a judgment or order directing an inquiry as to damages: *Phillips v Homfray* (1883) 24 ChD 439, CA (on appeal sub nom *Phillips v Fothergill* (1886) 11 App Cas 466, HL); *Smith v Eyles* (1742) 2 Atk 385; *Davoren v Wootton* [1900] 1 IR 273, CA.

5 Since 1 January 1983, the right of a person to claim damages for bereavement under the Fatal Accidents Act 1976 s 1A (see NEGLIGENCE vol 78 (2010) PARA 25) does not survive for the benefit of his estate on his death: Law Reform (Miscellaneous Provisions) Act 1934 s 1(1A) (added by the Administration of Justice Act 1982 ss 4(1), 73(1)). See NEGLIGENCE vol 78 (2010) PARA 24 et seq.

6 See *R v Jefferies* [1969] 1 QB 120, [1968] 3 All ER 238, CA; *R v Kearley (No 2)* [1994] 2 AC 414, [1994] 3 All ER 246, HL; and CRIMINAL PROCEDURE vol 28 (2015) PARA 677. These decisions may, however, be narrowly interpreted in view of the statutory origins of the former Court of Criminal Appeal and the present Court of Appeal (Criminal Division), in criminal matters, and it

has been conceded that an appellant's executors have an interest in the recovery of a fine: see *Hodgson v Lakeman* [1943] KB 15, CA; *R v Rowe* [1955] 1 QB 573 at 574, [1955] 2 All ER 234 at 235, CCA, per Goddard CJ. As to criminal appeals see also PARA 1289.

7 See *R v Matthew, R v Warrington* [2010] EWCA Crim 29 (permission given for appeals against convictions for single murder involving both accused; one of convicted persons since deceased, but permission granted to relatives of deceased to bring appeal). See also *R v Bentley* [2001] Cr App R 307, CA (conviction for murder quashed posthumously).

8 See the Criminal Justice Act 1988 s 133(1); and CRIMINAL PROCEDURE vol 28 (2015) PARA 823.

1278. Survival of causes of action against estate. On the death of a person on or after 25 July 1934[1], all causes of action subsisting against him[2] survive against his estate[3] except causes of action for defamation[4]. The cause of action may survive but yet be difficult or unable to be prosecuted. Where the Official Solicitor agreed to act as personal representative for the limited purpose of accepting and acknowledging service of a writ for a debt owed by the deceased, the court was not prepared to enforce a judgment in default of appearance against assets of the estate, in the absence of any person recognised by law as the defendant to an action in personam[5].

1 See PARA 1277 note 1. As regards deaths before that date, the Administration of Estates Act 1925 s 26(5) (repealed), replacing the Civil Procedure Act 1833 s 2 (repealed), enabled an action to be brought against personal representatives for a wrong committed by the deceased to another person in respect of his property, provided the injury was committed within six months before the wrongdoer's death and proceedings were brought within six months after the representative had taken out representation: see eg *Re Williames, Andrew v Williames* (1884) 52 LT 41 (affd (1885) 54 LT 105, CA); Jay v Jay [1924] 1 KB 826.

2 Where damage has been suffered by reason of any act or omission in respect of which a cause of action would have subsisted against any person if that person had not died before or at the same time as the damage was suffered, there is deemed, for the purposes of the Law Reform (Miscellaneous Provisions) Act 1934, to have been subsisting against him before his death such cause of action in respect of that act or omission as would have subsisted if he had died after the damage was suffered: s 1(4).

3 See the Law Reform (Miscellaneous Provisions) Act 1934 s 1(1). As to the proof of liabilities in respect of which proceedings are maintainable under s 1 as debts in the administration of insolvent estates see PARA 981. As to the court's jurisdiction to dispense with representatives see PARA 818.

4 Law Reform (Miscellaneous Provisions) Act 1934 s 1(1) proviso (amended by the Law Reform (Miscellaneous Provisions) Act 1970 s 7(2), Schedule; and by the Administration of Justice Act 1982 s 75(1), Sch 9 Pt I), Law Reform (Miscellaneous Provisions) Act 1934 s 1(1A) (added by the Administration of Justice Act 1982 ss 4(1), 73(1)). See also the Fatal Accidents Act 1976 s 1A; and PARA 1277 note 5.

5 See *Re Amirteymour* [1978] 3 All ER 637, [1979] 1 WLR 63, CA; and *Piggott v Aulton* [2003] EWCA Civ 24, [2003] RTR 540, [2003] All ER (D) 271 (Jan). Where a person who had an interest in a claim has died and that person has no personal representative the court may order:

(1) a claim to proceed in the absence of a person representing the estate of the deceased; or
(2) a person to be appointed to represent the deceased (CPR 19.8(1)).

Where a defendant against whom a claim could have been made has died and a grant of probate or administration has been made, the claim must be brought against the personal representatives of the deceased. Where a grant of probate or administration has not been made:

(a) the claim must be brought against the estate of the deceased; and
(b) the claimant must apply to the court for an order appointing a person to represent the estate in the claim (CPR 19.8(2)).

1279. Examples of causes of action which survive death. The causes of action which survive for the benefit of or against the estate of the deceased[1] include rights of action founded on breaches of contractual obligations[2], rights of action for personal injuries to the deceased, including claims for damages for pain and suffering[3] and for loss of expectation of life[4], and rights of action founded on statutory duties or rights, if as a matter of construction the statute envisages this[5]. In addition, causes of action based upon a wide range of personal and moveable intellectual property and associated rights will survive for the benefit of the estate[6]. However, it has been held that the court should be cautious in extending the meaning of 'causes of action' to applications for financial relief in the Family Division which are essentially personal in nature arising between parties to a marriage or children of a marriage and deriving from no source other than the matrimonial legislation[7], although agreements made subsequent to such applications may be treated differently, in some circumstances[8]. A claim for provision under the Inheritance (Provision for Family and Dependants) Act 1975 does not survive for the benefit of the claimant's estate[9] and neither does the right to apply for secured maintenance after a decree absolute in matrimonial proceedings[10]. A claim for penalties for incorrect income tax returns is a cause of action which survives against a deceased person's estate[11].

No right or liability of a purely personal nature, dependent on the skill or qualification of one party, can be assigned by operation of law. Therefore the personal representatives may not sue or be sued on such a contract made by the deceased, and the contract is discharged by the death[12]. However, they may sue for any money earned by the deceased under the contract[13], or even for money accruing after death, if it appears that the parties intended that the remuneration should continue to be payable after the ending of the contract[14]. If a party to a contract assigns his rights in equity before he dies, his personal representatives continue to represent him for the purpose of joining or being joined with the assignee in suing the debtor[15].

1 See PARAS 1277–1278.

2 See *Beckham v Drake* (1849) 2 HL Cas 579 at 597 per Williams J. See also CONTRACT vol 22 (2012) PARA 639. As to the personal representative's liabilities for the deceased's obligations see PARA 1212 et seq. The damages recoverable are not limited to those which the deceased could have recovered in his own lifetime. The proper measure of damages is the loss to the deceased's estate: *Otter v Church, Adams, Tatham & Co* [1953] Ch 280, [1953] 1 All ER 168. As to the measure of damages see generally DAMAGES vol 29 (2014) PARA 499 et seq.

3 *Slater v Spreag* [1936] 1 KB 83. As to the limitation period for claims for personal injuries by the personal representatives or dependants of a deceased person see the Limitation Act 1980 s 11(5). The applicable periods are now three years from:

(1) the date at which the cause of action accrued; or

(2) the date of knowledge (if later) of the person injured (s 11(4)).

Where the person injured dies before the application of the periods mentioned in s 11(4), the period applicable as respects the cause of action surviving for the benefit of his estate by virtue of Law reform (Miscellaneous Provisions) Act 1934 s 1 is three years from:

(a) the date of death; or

(b) the date of the personal representative's knowledge; whichever is the later (s 11(5)).

Where there is more than one personal representative the applicable date is that of the earliest representative to gain knowledge: see s 11(7). See further LIMITATION PERIODS vol 68 (2016) PARA 998.

Fear of impending death felt by the victim of a fatal injury, before any actual injury occurs, cannot by itself give rise to a cause of action which survives for the benefit of the victim's estate. Claims based on pain and suffering which might have occurred for a few seconds prior to the impending death of crush victims failed in *Hicks v Chief Constable of the South Yorkshire Police* [1992] 2 All ER 65, 8 BMLR 70, HL, but, where a person's expectation of life has been reduced by his injuries, an award of damages for pain and suffering is to take account of any suffering caused or likely to be caused to him by the awareness that his expectation of life has been shortened: see the Administration of Justice Act 1982 s 1(1)(b). See also *Rothwell v Chemical and Insulating Co Ltd, Re Pleural Plaques Litigation* [2007] UKHL 39, [2007] 4 All ER 1047, [2007] 3 WLR 876 (in the absence of an actionable injury, other factors, including anxiety, did not constitute an actionable claim).

4 See DAMAGES vol 29 (2014) PARA 435et seq.

5 See *Peebles v Oswaldtwistle UDC* [1896] 2 QB 159, CA (action by executors to enforce public health duties); *Darlington v Roscoe & Sons* [1907] 1 KB 219, CA (enforcement by deceased dependant's personal representatives of workmen's compensation claim); *United Collieries Ltd v Simpson* [1909] AC 383, HL (similar case under the workmen's compensation legislation); *Post Office v Official Solicitor* [1951] 1 All ER 522 (employers of injured workman entitled to indemnity under workmen's compensation legislation against estate of deceased who had caused

the injury). See also *Sienkiewicz v Greif (UK) Ltd* [2009] EWCA Civ 1159, [2010] 2 WLR 951, [2009] All ER (D) 84 (Nov) (negligence and breach of statutory duty claim brought by administratrix, where deceased died from mesothelioma); *Dean v Wiesengrund* [1955] 2 QB 120, [1955] 2 All ER 432, CA (right of deceased tenant's personal representatives to recover overpayments of rent under the Rent Acts); *Harvey v RG O'Dell Ltd* [1958] 2 QB 78, [1958] 1 All ER 657 (statutory rights under the Law Reform (Married Women and Tortfeasors) Act 1935). As to statutory obligations of a purely personal nature which do not survive see PARA 1218.

6 See eg the Copyright, Designs and Patents Act 1988 ss 90(1), 93, 95 (copyright and moral rights), ss 191A, 191B (performers' property rights), s 222(1) (design right); the Copyright (Rights in Databases) Regulations 1997, SI 1997/3032, reg 23 (database right); and COPYRIGHT vol 23 (2016) PARAS 639, 653, 894; and INFORMATION TECHNOLOGY LAW. See also the Patents Act 1977 ss 30–33 (patents); the Registered Designs Act 1949 ss 2, 19 (registered designs) (see PATENTS AND REGISTERED DESIGNS vol 79 (2014) PARAS 677, 699); and the Trade Marks Act 1994 ss 2, 24 (trade marks) (see TRADE MARKS AND TRADE NAMES vol 97A (2014) PARAS 111, 113). A claim in passing off survives to the benefit of the estate: see *Sweeney v MacMillan Publishers Ltd* [2001] All ER (D) 332 (Nov) (passing off claim properly brought, but failed to be established by claimant); and *Oakley & Sons v Dalton* (1887) 35 Ch D 700, 56 LJ Ch 823. A claim for relief or damages based on breach of confidence probably devolves upon the estate, to the extent that equities have arisen: see *Morison v Moat* (1851) 9 Hare 241, 20 LJ Ch 513.

7 *D'Este v D'Este* [1973] Fam 55 at 59, sub nom *D (J) v D (S)* [1973] 1 All ER 349 at 352. See also *Thwaite v Thwaite* [1982] Fam 1, [1981] 2 All ER 789, CA; *Arthur J S Hall & Co v Simons* [1999] 1 FLR 536, CA; *Xydhias v Xydhias* [1999] 2 All ER 386, [1999] 1 FLR 683, CA; *Cox v Cox* [2006] EWHC 1077 (Ch), [2006] BCC 890, [2006] All ER (D) 256 (Apr).

8 See *Soulsbury v Soulsbury* [2007] EWCA Civ 969, [2008] Fam 1, [2007] All ER (D) 132 (Oct) (former husband agreed periodic payments to claimant under order by consent; later he made agreement to replace periodic payments by lump sum to claimant from his will, but his later marriage revoked the will. His personal representative refused to pay all or any of the promised sum to the claimant; held, that the later agreement between the former spouses had not been a compromise of a claim for ancillary relief and there was no contemplation of a return to court to approve the agreement, which was therefore valid and binding upon the estate).

9 *Whyte v Ticehurst* [1986] Fam 64, [1986] 2 All ER 158; *Re Bramwell* [1988] 2 FLR 263. As to provision under the Inheritance (Provision for Family and Dependants) Act 1975 see PARA 565 et seq.

10 See *Dipple v Dipple* [1942] P 65, [1942] 1 All ER 234. See also the general guidance in *Barder v Caluori* [1988] AC 20 at 37, [1987] 2 All ER 440 at 449 (proceedings where one party to the suit has died).

11 *A-G v Canter* [1939] 1 KB 318, [1939] 1 All ER 13, CA. The power to impose a penalty on the personal representatives of a deceased person has been repealed see PARA 1217.

12 *Chamberlain v Williamson* (1814) 2 M & S 408; *Phillips v Alhambra Palace Co* [1901] 1 KB 59 at 63; *Shipman v Thompson* (1738) Willes 103 at 104n; *Farrow v Wilson* (1869) LR 4 CP 744; *Phillips v Jones* (1888) 4 TLR 401; *Blades v Free* (1829) 9 B & C 167; *Foster v Bates* (1843) 12 M & W 226; *Campanari v Woodburn* (1854) 15 CB 400; *Friend v Young* [1897] 2 Ch 421; *Pool v Pool* (1889) 58 LJP 67; *Tasker v Shepherd* (1861) 6 H & N 575; *Graves v Cohen* (1929) 46 TLR 121. As to the principle that a personal contract is frustrated if the promisor becomes incapable of performing it see CONTRACT vol 22 (2012) PARA 475.

13 *Stubbs v Holywell Rly Co* (1867) LR 2 Exch 311.

14 *Wilson v Harper* [1908] 2 Ch 370. See also *Robey v Arnold* (1898) 14 TLR 220, CA; *Salomon v Brownfield and Brownfield Guild Pottery Society Ltd* (1896) 12 TLR 239; *Bilbee v Hasse* (1889) 5 TLR 677 (affd (1890) Times, 16 January, CA); and cf *Nayler v Yearsley* (1860) 2 F & F 41; *Boyd v Mathers* (1893) 9 TLR 443, CA; *Morris v Hunt & Co* (1896) 12 TLR 187; *Gerahty v Baines* (1903) 19 TLR 554; *Knight v Burgess* (1864) 33 LJ Ch 727; *Weare v Brimsdown Lead Co Ltd* (1910) 103 LT 429.

15 *Brandt v Heatig* (1818) 2 Moore CP 184.

1280. Act or omission causing death. At common law the death of a human being could not be complained of in a civil court as an injury. Accordingly a man's wife or child might suffer the greatest pecuniary loss by his death and would have no remedy against a person who, by an act of negligence, caused the death, even though the victim, if instead of being killed had been incapacitated for life, could have recovered substantial damages[1]. This common law rule has been abolished[2], but where the death has been caused by the act or omission which gives rise to the cause of action, the damages are to be calculated without reference to any loss or gain to his estate consequent on his death, except that a sum in respect of funeral expenses may be included[3].

Some common law rules on causation have been modified to accommodate particular fact situations where injustice may have been caused by their strict application, because damage would only be likely to occur to the immediate victim, or secondary victims, along with the consequent possibility of claims brought by the victims or their personal representatives, long after the original wrongful act[4].

1 *Baker v Bolton* (1808) 1 Camp 493; *Osborn v Gillett* (1873) LR 8 Exch 88; *Clark v London General Omnibus Co Ltd* [1906] 2 KB 648, CA; *Admiralty Comrs v SS Amerika* [1917] AC 38, HL; *Jackson v Watson & Sons* [1909] 2 KB 193, CA.

2 See the Law Reform (Miscellaneous Provisions) Act 1934 s 1(1); and PARA 1277. As to earlier statutes which ameliorated the effect of the common law rule see note 3.

3 Law Reform (Miscellaneous Provisions) Act 1934 s 1(2)(c). See also DAMAGES vol 29 (2014) PARA 496. The rights conferred by the Act for the benefit of the estates of deceased persons are in addition to and not in derogation of any rights conferred on the dependants of deceased persons by the Fatal Accidents Acts 1846 to 1959 (see now the Fatal Accidents Act 1976; and NEGLIGENCE vol 78 (2010) PARA 24 et seq): Law Reform (Miscellaneous Provisions) Act 1934 s 1(5) (amended by the Carriage by Air Act 1961 s 14(3), Sch 2). See also the Carriage by Air Act 1961; and CARRIAGE AND CARRIERS vol 7 (2015) PARA 121. As to the measure of damages under the Fatal Accidents Act 1976 see NEGLIGENCE vol 78 (2010) PARA 24 et seq. As to the limitation period for such claims see PARA 1279 note 3; and LIMITATION PERIODS vol 68 (2016) PARA 1000.

4 See *Fairchild v Glenhaven Funeral Services Ltd* [2002] UKHL 22, [2003] 1 AC 32, [2002] 3 All ER 305; *Sienkiewicz v Greif* (UK) Ltd [2009] EWCA Civ 1159, [2010] 2 WLR 951, [2009] All ER (D) 84 (Nov) (negligence and breach of statutory duty claim brought by administratrix, where deceased died from mesothelioma); and the Compensation Act 2006 s 3(1). But see the limits of such modification of the rules in *Rothwell v Chemical and Insulating Co Ltd, Re Pleural Plaques Litigation* [2007] UKHL 39, [2007] 4 All ER 1047, [2007] 3 WLR 876.

1281. No exemplary damages in cause of action by estate of deceased . Where a cause of action survives for the benefit of the estate of a deceased person, the damages recoverable for the benefit of the estate do not include any exemplary damages[1].

1 Law Reform (Miscellaneous Provisions) Act 1934 s 1(2)(a)(i) (substituted in respect of deaths occurring on or after 1 January 1983 by the Administration of Justice Act 1982 ss 4(2), 73). As to exemplary damages see DAMAGES vol 29 (2014) PARA 325.

1282. Covenants relating to land: cause of action by personal representative . Where the deceased person's real estate was not vested in his personal representative[1], the heir or devisee was the proper person to bring an action for breach of covenant relating to the estate, even though committed during the deceased's lifetime, if the ultimate damage accrued after the ancestor's death[2]. Such an action can now be brought by the personal representative or, in the case of a specific devise, by the devisee after assent. It would appear that any damages so recovered by the personal representative would be held by him on behalf of the specific devisee, if any, but otherwise they form part of the deceased's general estate. The personal representative can, without reference to the fact that the real estate is vested in him, maintain an action for breach of such a covenant, where damage accrued in the deceased's lifetime, whether the covenant is one that runs with the land[3] or is merely collateral[4], but in the latter case he can only sue the original covenantor, and not an assign of the latter[5]. Any damages so recovered would appear to be part of the deceased's residuary personal estate.

1 See PARA 945 note 1. As to the meaning of 'personal representative' see PARA 608.

2 *Kingdon v Nottle* (1813) 1 M & S 355; *King v Jones* (1814) 5 Taunt 418; affd sub nom *Jones v King* (1816) 4 M & S 188.

3 *Morley v Polhill* (1689) 2 Vent 56; *Smith v Simonds* (1687) Comb 64. As to covenants running with the land see CONVEYANCING vol 23 (2016) PARA 77 et seq; REAL PROPERTY AND REGISTRATION vol 87 (2012) PARA 1076 et seq.
4 *Raymond v Fitch* (1835) 2 Cr M & R 588; *Ives v Brown* [1919] 2 Ch 314.
5 *Formby v Barker* [1903] 2 Ch 539, CA; *Chambers v Randall* [1923] 1 Ch 149.

1283. Effect of death of party to claim. Where a party to a claim dies but the cause of action survives, the claim does not abate by reason of the death[1]. The court has power to make judgments or orders made in the claim binding upon non-parties as if they had been parties to the claim[2], and, whether the cause of action survives or not, where a party dies after the verdict or finding of the issues of fact and before judgment is given, judgment may be given notwithstanding the death[3]. The personal representatives of a deceased party may obtain an order without notice that they be made parties and the proceedings are then carried on as if they had been substituted for the deceased party[4], but they become personally liable for all the costs of the claim ab initio[5]. Where a sole claimant or defendant dies, but no order substituting a new party is made, the other party may, in the case of a cause of action which survives, apply for an order that unless the claim is proceeded with within a specified time the claim is to be struck out as against the party who has died[6]. The court has also power to appoint an interim receiver for the preservation of property, notwithstanding the death of a sole defendant[7].

Where a defendant against whom a claim could have been brought has died, and a grant of probate or administration has not been made, the claim must be brought against the estate of the deceased and the claimant must apply to the court for an order appointing a person to represent the estate of the deceased in the claim[8]. Where a person who had an interest in a claim has died and that person has no personal representative, the court may order a claim to proceed in the absence of a person representing the estate, or for a person to be appointed to represent the estate of the deceased[9].

1 See CPR 19.8(2), (4); and CIVIL PROCEDURE vol 11 (2015) PARAS 489–490. See also *Jones v Simes* (1890) 43 ChD 607.
2 See CPR 19.8A; and CIVIL PROCEDURE vol 11 (2015) PARA 495.
3 See CPR Pt 19; and CIVIL PROCEDURE vol 11 (2015) PARA 489.
4 As to the addition or substitution of parties see CPR 19.1–19.4. See also *Smith v Williams* [1922] 1 KB 158. As to the possible right of a representative to bring a fresh action see *Swindell v Bulkeley* (1886) 18 QBD 250 at 255, CA, per Lopes LJ. As to the procedure where there are multiple claimants see *Practice Direction—Group Litigation* PD 19B.
5 *Boynton v Boynton* (1879) 4 App Cas 733, HL.
6 See CPR Pt 3; and CIVIL PROCEDURE vol 11 (2015) PARA 489.
7 *Re Parker, Cash v Parker* (1879) 12 ChD 293; *Re Clark, Clark v Clark* (1910) 55 Sol Jo 64.
8 CPR 19.8(2)(b)(ii). Where it is sought to start proceedings against the estate of a deceased defendant where probate or letters of administration have not been granted, the claimant should issue the claim against 'the personal representatives of A.B. deceased'. The claimant should then, before the expiry of the period for service of the claim form, apply to the court for the appointment of a person to represent the estate of the deceased: *Practice Direction—How to Start Proceedings: The Claim Form* PD 7A para 5.5. See also PARA 1278 note 5.
9 CPR 19.8(1); and see PARA 1278 note 5.

1284. Payment out of court to representative of deceased claimant. The court has jurisdiction to order money paid into court in an action by a defendant to be paid out to the representative of a claimant who has died[1], or to the claimant when the defendant has died[2].

Accordingly, unless the court otherwise directs, any fund in court directed to be paid, transferred or delivered to a person entitled to it in his own right or as sole or sole surviving executor, is to be paid, transferred or delivered, if that person dies, to his legal personal representative[3] or, in the case of certain small estates on an intestacy where there has been no grant of administration, to the relative with the prior right to a grant[4].

Provision is also made for the payment of funeral expenses and inheritance tax out of funds of court. The Accountant General must make a payment from the fund in court of the deceased to a funeral director in respect of reasonable funeral expenses if provided with certain documents[5]. The Accountant General must make a payment from the fund in court of the deceased to Her Majesty's Revenue and Customs in respect of all or part of the inheritance tax due on the deceased's estate if provided with certain documents[6].

1 *Brown v Feeney* [1906] 1 KB 563, CA.

2 *Maxwell v Viscount Wolseley* [1907] 1 KB 274, CA.

3 See the Court Funds Rules 2011, SI 2011/1734, r 24; and COURTS AND TRIBUNALS. Where a grant of representation has been obtained, the Accountant General must pay out the fund in court to the personal representative of the deceased if provided with a written request; and a sealed copy of the grant of representation: see r 24(2). Where a grant of representation has been obtained by two or more persons, the Accountant General must only pay out the fund in court if provided with:
(1) the documents required under r 24(2) (see above);
(2) the written consent of each living person named as a personal representative in the grant of representation; and
(3) a copy of the death certificate of any deceased person who was named as a personal representative in the grant of representation (s 24(3)).

Rule 24 applies where a person entitled to a fund in court dies: r 24(1). As to the Accountant General see COURTS AND TRIBUNALS vol 24 (2010) PARA 751.

4 Where the value of the estate is less than £5,000 and the person dies testate, the Accountant General must pay out the fund in court to the person who claims to have the right to a grant of probate if provided with:
(1) a written request;
(2) a copy of the will of the deceased; and
(3) a copy of the death certificate of the deceased (Court Funds Rules 2011, SI 2011/1734, r 24(4)).

Where the value of the estate is less than £5,000 and two or more persons have a right to a grant of probate, the Accountant General must only pay out the fund in court if provided with:
(a) the documents required under r 24(4) (see above);
(b) the written consent of each living person who has been named as an executor in the deceased's will; and
(c) a copy of the death certificate of any deceased person who was named as an executor in the deceased's will (r 24(5)).

Where the value of the estate is less than £5,000 and the person dies intestate, the Accountant General must pay out the fund in court to the person who claims to have a prior right to a grant of letters of administration if provided with:
(i) a written request;
(ii) a written declaration of kinship; and
(iii) a copy of the death certificate of the deceased (r 24(6)).

Where the value of the estate is less than £5,000 and two or more persons claim to have a prior right to a grant of letters of administration, the Accountant General must only pay out the fund in court if provided with:
(A) the documents required under r 24(6) (see above);
(B) the written consent of each person who appears to have a prior right to a grant of letters of administration; and
(C) a written declaration of kinship of each such person (r 24(7)).

5 See the Court Funds Rules 2011, SI 2011/1734, r 25. The documents are:
(1) a funeral invoice; and
(2) a written request from an executor of the deceased's estate; or the person who arranged the funeral if the deceased died intestate (see s 25(2)).

Rule 25 applies where a person who is entitled to a fund in court and subject to an order of the Court of Protection dies: r 25(1).

6 See the Court Funds Rules 2011, SI 2011/1734, r 26. The documents are:
(1) the completed relevant form from Her Majesty's Revenue and Customs; and

(2) a written request from an executor of the deceased's estate; or a person who appears to have a prior right to a grant of letters of administration of the estate if the deceased died intestate (see r 26(2)).

Rule 26 applies where a person who is entitled to a fund in court and subject to an order of the Court of Protection dies: r 26(1).

1285. Divorce and dissolution of civil partnership proceedings: effect of death. Where one of the parties to a divorce or dissolution dies, whether proceedings may be taken after the death of either party depends on the circumstances in each case[1]. The personal representative[2] of a person who has obtained a decree nisi for the dissolution of his marriage cannot continue the suit for the purpose of making the decree absolute, for death itself ends the marriage or civil partnership[3], but there is no general rule that divorce or dissolution proceedings automatically abate when one of the parties dies[4]. Where, following a consent order for financial provision on divorce, a fundamental assumption (such as that the wife and children would need a home for a considerable period of time) has been invalidated by a supervening event, such as the death of the wife and children, the Court may order a change to the provision agreed[5].

1 See MATRIMONIAL AND CIVIL PARTNERSHIP LAW vol 73 (2015) PARAS 919–921.
2 As to the meaning of 'personal representative' see PARA 608.
3 See MATRIMONIAL AND CIVIL PARTNERSHIP LAW vol 72 (2015) PARAS 1–3.
4 *Purse v Purse* [1981] Fam 143, [1981] 2 All ER 465, CA; *Barder v Barder (Caluori intervening)* [1988] AC 20, [1987] 2 All ER 440, HL.
5 *Barder v Barder (Caluori intervening)* [1988] AC 20, [1987] 2 All ER 440, HL. See also *Wa v Executors of the Estate of Ha* [2015] EWHC 2233 (Fam), [2015] WTLR 1471.

1286. Criminal appeals: effect of death. In criminal matters the Court of Appeal is confined by the statute creating the jurisdiction[1]. This makes no provision for the survival, on the appellant's death, of appeals, whether against conviction or sentence[2], although it is open to personal representatives to petition the Secretary of State for relief, and he could if so minded seek the opinion of the court[3]. However, it has been held that personal representatives may continue an appeal where they have a pecuniary interest, such as a possible right to repayment of a fine[4], although this exception does not seem to extend to the recovery of costs where the only other surviving interest is the sentimental one of clearing the deceased's name[5].

1 See the Criminal Appeal Act 1968; and CRIMINAL PROCEDURE vol 28 (2015) PARA 734 et seq.
2 *R v Jefferies* [1969] 1 QB 120 at 124, [1968] 3 All ER 238 at 240, CA, per Widgery LJ.
3 See *R v Jefferies* [1969] 1 QB 120, [1968] 3 All ER 238, CA; *R v Kearley (No 2)* [1994] 2 AC 414, [1994] 3 All ER 246, HL; and PARA 1277. See eg *R v Bentley* [2001] 1 Cr App R 307, CA.
4 *Hodgson v Lakeman* [1943] KB 15, DC; R v Rowe [1955] 1 QB 573 at 575, [1955] 2 All ER 234 at 235, CCA, per Lord Goddard CJ.
5 *R v Rowe* [1955] 1 QB 573, [1955] 2 All ER 234, CCA; cf *R v Bentley* [2001] 1 Cr App R 307, CA (conviction for murder quashed posthumously). See also PARA 1277.

(ii) Causes of Action Arising after Death

1287. Injury to property after death of owner. As the legal personal representative[1] is in law the owner of the property of his testator or intestate, he may maintain claims in respect of injury done to that property after the death of the owner, whether he has been in actual possession of it or not[2]; and he may claim either in his individual capacity or in his representative character[3].

1 As to the meaning of 'personal representative' see PARA 608.
2 *Hollis v Smith* (1808) 10 East 293.
3 *Adams v Cheverel* (1606) Cro Jac 113.

1288. Contracts entered into by personal representative. In the case of contracts, the personal representative may claim in his representative character wherever the money, when recovered, would be assets of the deceased[1]. Accordingly he may claim in his representative character for money lent by him out of the estate[2], for work done by him as executor[3], for goods supplied by him in carrying on the testator's business[4] or for the deceased's money wrongfully paid away by the representative[5]. Where a personal representative had assigned copyright material created by the testator, he was able to assert reversionary rights to part of the material[6].

Where one of several executors has entered into a contract on his own account only, the others cannot join him in claiming on the contract, even when the money recovered would be assets; but they can join where the contract was entered into by the executor on account of himself and his co-executors, or generally on account of the estate[7]. Where solicitors instructed by the personal representative failed to progress the administration of the estate, and, as a result, properties forming part of the estate remained unlet during the administration, the personal representative had a cause of action in his own right[8].

1 *Abbott v Parfitt* (1871) LR 6 QB 346. This may involve the interposition of a corporate claimant, in some circumstances: see *Python (Monty) Pictures Limited v Paragon Entertainment Corpn* [1998] EMLR 640 (damages recovered by corporate claimant, owned by five surviving members and personal representatives of the deceased sixth member of famous comedy team, for breach of contract to finance and produce film based on work of the team). As to the meaning of 'personal representative' see PARA 608.

2 *Webster v Spencer* (1820) 3 B & Ald 360.

3 *Edwards v Grace* (1836) 2 M & W 190.

4 *Abbott v Parfitt* (1871) LR 6 QB 346. See also *Aspinall v Wake* (1833) 10 Bing 51. However, where the personal representative, being also the beneficiary, is carrying on the business in his own interest, he cannot claim in his representative character: *Bolingbroke v Kerr* (1866) LR 1 Exch 222, as explained in *Abbott v Parfitt*.

5 *Clark v Hougham* (1823) 2 B & C 149.

6 *Chappell & Co Ltd v Redwood Music Ltd* [1980] 2 All ER 817, HL, [1981] RPC 337; cf *Novello & Co Ltd v Keith Prowse Music Publishing Co Ltd* [2004] EWCA Civ 1776, [2005] RPC 578, [2004] All ER (D) 198 (Dec).

7 *Heath v Chilton* (1844) 12 M & W 632, explaining *Webster v Spencer* (1820) 3 B & Ald 360 on this point. The position of an administrator is similar to that of an executor: see PARAS 926, 1024.

8 *Chappell v Somers & Blake (a firm)* [2003] EWHC 1644 (Ch), [2004] Ch 19, [2003] 3 All ER 1076.

1289. Death of personal representative. Where the proceeds of a contract entered into by a personal representative would form part of the deceased's assets, the person entitled to claim on the contract on the representative's death is the personal representative of the original deceased, who will be the personal representative of the deceased representative where the chain of representation has not been broken[1] and the administrator de bonis non of the original deceased in other cases[2].

1 See the Administration of Estates Act 1925 s 7; and PARA 637. As to the chain of representation see PARA 637 et seq. As to the meaning of 'personal representative' see PARA 608.

2 *Moseley v Rendell* (1871) LR 6 QB 338. As to administration de bonis non see PARA 793.

(3) ACTIONS AGAINST PERSONAL REPRESENTATIVES

(i) Defences and Judgments

1290. Defences available to personal representatives. A person against whom a claim is made in the capacity of personal representative may in general plead in answer to a claim brought against him in his representative capacity any defence which would have been open to the deceased[1]. He may further rely upon the following defences:

(1) that he was never executor or administrator (ne unques executor);

(2) that he has fully administered (plene administravit), or fully administered with the exception of certain assets (plene administravit praeter)[2];

(3) the existence of debts of a higher nature and no assets ultra;

(4) the right to set off a debt[3]; and

(5) the expiration of the appropriate period of limitation[4].

If the defence of plene administravit or plene administravit praeter is pleaded, the burden of proving assets rests on the claimant[5], and the personal representative is only answerable to the amount of assets proved[6]. The amount of the duty paid by the executor on obtaining probate is admissible in evidence upon the issue of plene administravit[7], but is it not prima facie evidence of the amount of assets which have come to his hands[8].

1 In addition he may in certain instances have a defence by the cause of action not surviving against him: see PARA 1278 et seq. As to the meaning of 'personal representative' see PARA 608.

2 He may also pray in aid the court's discretion, to give liberty to distribute without further retention or security against contingent liabilities, in a proper case: see *Re Yorke, Stone v Chataway* [1997] 4 All ER 907, [1997] 33 LS Gaz R 26; *Re K (deceased)* [2007] EWHC 622 (Ch), 9 ITELR 759, [2007] All ER (D) 473 (Mar).

3 These defences should be specifically pleaded: see CPR 16.5; *Practice DirectionStatements of Case* PD 16 paras 10, 12, 13; and CIVIL PROCEDURE vol 11 (2015) PARA 355. The representative may plead both ne unques executor and plene administravit: *Tyson v Kendall* (1850) 19 LJQB 434. As to set-off see PARA 1296. See also *Ducker v Pulling* [2007] EWHC 2148 (Ch), [2007] All ER (D) 488 (Jul) (claimant executors entitled to set off tax liability of company, formerly owned by deceased, against sum payable to defendant under compromise of action agreement, containing defendant's warranty and indemnity of estate against sums owed by company). As to defences open to a person against whom a claim is brought as executor de son tort see PARA 1267.

4 See the Limitation Act 1980 ss 21, 22; PARA 1279; and LIMITATION PERIODS vol 68 (2016) PARA 1138 et seq.

5 *Giles v Dyson* (1815) 1 Stark 32.

6 *Erving v Peters* (1790) 3 Term Rep 685 at 688 per Lord Kenyon CJ.

7 *Mann v Lang* (1835) 3 Ad & El 699.

8 *Stearn v Mills* (1833) 4 B & Ad 657, dissenting from *Foster v Blakelock* (1826) 5 B & C 328; *Mann v Lang* (1835) 3 Ad & El 699; *Lazonby v Rawson* (1854) 4 De GM & G 556.

1291. Judgment against future assets. If the personal representative pleads plene administravit or plene administravit praeter[1] and no other defence, or no other defence except that of outstanding claims of a higher nature and no assets ultra, the claimant may either join issue, or, if he is willing to admit the truth of the plea, may apply for leave to sign judgment for his claim and costs against assets coming to the representative's hands after the date of the judgment, or judgment as to part of his claim against assets acknowledged, and as to the residue of his claim and costs against such future assets[2]. In the latter case costs are not awarded against the representative personally, nor does he get his costs[3].

If issue is joined upon the plea of plene administravit and the claimant fails upon that issue, he may enter judgment against future assets, but must pay the personal representative's general costs, even though the representative may have raised other defences in which he has not succeeded[4].

1 As to the meanings of 'plene administravit' and 'plene administravit praeter' see PARA 1290. As to the meaning of 'personal representative' see PARA 608.
2 As to judgment on admissions see CPR Pt 14; and CIVIL PROCEDURE vol 11 (2015) PARA 325 et seq.
3 *Cockle v Treacy* [1896] 2 IR 267 at 270, CA, per Walker C; *Smith v Tateham* (1848) 2 Exch 205; *De Tastet v Andrade* (1817) 1 Chit 629n.
4 *Millar & Co v Keane* (1889) 24 LR Ir 49; approved in *Cockle v Treacy* [1896] 2 IR 267, CA; *Iggulden v Terson* (1834) 2 Dowl 277; *Hogg v Graham* (1811) 4 Taunt 135; *Ragg v Wells* (1817) 8 Taunt 129; *Edwards v Bethel* (1818) 1 B & Ald 254; *Cockson v Drinkwater* (1783) 3 Doug KB 239; *Lucas v Jenner* (1833) 1 Cr & M 597.

1292. Judgment where plene administravit accepted or succeeds but personal representative unsuccessfully challenges claim. If the claimant admits the defence of plene administravit[1] and the claim goes to trial on the claim only and the claimant succeeds as to that, he will get judgment of assets coming to the personal representative's hands after judgment as to the debt, and as to the costs de bonis testatoris et si non de bonis propriis[2].

Where the personal representative pleads a denial of the claim and defences of both plene administravit and plene administravit praeter[3] and fails on the former defence, he must pay the general costs of the action of those two claims even though he succeeds on the latter plea, the costs of which were ordered to be paid by the claimant[4].

1 As to the meaning of 'plene administravit' see PARA 1290.
2 *Marshall v Willder* (1829) 9 B & C 655. As to the meaning of 'personal representative' see PARA 608.
3 As to the meaning of 'plene administravit praeter' see PARA 1290.
4 *Squire v Arnison* (1884) Cab & El 365.

1293. Judgment where personal representative fails upon issue of plene administravit. Where the personal representative fails upon the issue of plene administravit[1], the claimant obtains judgment for his debt and costs to be levied of the goods and chattels and all real and personal estate of the deceased, and in case of deficiency for his costs to be levied out of the proper goods and chattels of the representative[2]. If, upon the issue of plene administravit, it appears that the representative has been guilty of a devastavit, which has caused a failure of assets, it must be decided that he has assets to that amount, and not a devastavit[3]. Where the claim is brought against several representatives, all of whom plead plene administravit, and the claimant proves assets in the hands of some only of the defendants, judgment should be entered in favour of the other defendants[4].

1 As to the meaning of 'plene administravit' see PARA 1290. As to the meaning of 'personal representative' see PARA 608.
2 *Gorton v Gregory* (1862) 3 B & S 90, Ex Ch. In *Griffith v Killingley* (1931) unreported, the words 'all the real and personal estate within the meaning of the Administration of Estates Act 1925' were ordered to be inserted in the judgment.
3 Went Off Ex (14th Edn) 312. As to devastavit see PARA 1244 et seq.
4 *Parsons v Hancock* (1829) Mood & M 330; *Cousins v Paddon* (1835) 2 Cr M & R 547 at 558.

1294. Judgment by default against personal representative or failure to plead plene administravit. If the personal representative allows judgment to go against him by default, or fails to plead plene administravit[1], he admits the claim and that he has sufficient assets to satisfy the claim[2], but not necessarily that he has sufficient assets to meet costs unascertained at the date of the judgment[3]. The admission of the claim does not justify the claimant in signing a personal judgment against him[4].

1 As to the meaning of 'plene administravit' see PARA 1290. As to the meaning of 'personal representative' see PARA 608.
2 *Rock v Leighton* (1700) 1 Salk 310; *Ramsden v Jackson* (1737) 1 Atk 292 at 294; *Leonard v Simpson* (1835) 2 Bing NC 176 at 179; *Palmer v Waller* (1836) 1 M & W 689; *Thompson & Sons v Clarke* (1901) 17 TLR 455; *Re Marvin, Crawter v Marvin* [1905] 2 Ch 490; *Batchelar v Evans* [1939] Ch 1007 at 1010, [1939] 3 All ER 606 at 608–609. See also *Re a Debtor (No 87 of 1999), Debtor v Johnson* [2000] BPIR 589, [2000] TLR 95 (a debtor's cross demand against the statutory demand by executrix; held, executrix's failure to plead plene administravit raised a strong presumption that she had sufficient assets to meet his debt and cross demand and justified setting aside the statutory demand). As to amendment of the defence to plead plene administravit praeter after judgment by default but before inquiry as to damages see *Midland Bank Trust Co Ltd v Green (No 2)* [1979] 1 All ER 726, [1979] 1 WLR 460.
3 *Marsden v Regan* [1954] 1 All ER 475, [1954] 1 WLR 423, CA.
4 *Skelton v Hawling* (1749) 1 Wils 258; Erving v Peters (1790) 3 Term Rep 685; *Lacons v Warmoll* [1907] 2 KB 350 at 360, CA. The judgment in *Re Higgins' Trusts* (1861) 2 Giff 562, that the default judgment binds the representatives' own assets, cannot be supported except as to costs. As to the effect of judgments by default or consent see *Pople v Evans* [1969] 2 Ch 255, [1968] 2 All ER 743; and CIVIL PROCEDURE vol 12 (2015) PARA 535 et seq; CIVIL PROCEDURE vol 12A (2015) PARA 1223.

1295. Enforcement of judgment. Having obtained a judgment against a personal representative, the claimant may sue on a writ of control[1]. If the proceeds recovered by the enforcement agent are less than the amount outstanding[2] the claimant may bring an action against the representative alleging a devastavit[3] and, if successful, may obtain execution against the personal representative's own property[4].

1 As to writs of control (formerly writs of fieri facias) see CIVIL PROCEDURE vol 12A (2015) PARA 1334. As from 6 April 2014 most writs of fieri facias were renamed 'writs of control': see the Tribunals, Courts and Enforcement Act 2007 s 62(4)(a), Schs 12, 13.
2 As to information about the execution of writs see CIVIL PROCEDURE vol 12A (2015) PARA 1378.
3 As to devastavit see PARA 1244 et seq.
4 See CIVIL PROCEDURE vol 12A (2015) PARA 1311. Any rule of law requiring a writ of execution issued from the High Court to be directed to a sheriff has been abolished: see the Courts Act 2003 s 99(2). As to the enforcement of High Court writs of execution see Sch 7; and CIVIL PROCEDURE vol 12A (2015) PARA 1315.

1296. Set-off in claim by or against personal representative. The right of set-off extends to a claim by or against a personal representative where there are mutual debts between the testator or intestate and the other party[1]. A debt which has accrued due after the death of the testator or intestate cannot, however, be set off against a debt which accrued due during his life[2]; and, in general, a debt due to or from a personal representative in his personal capacity cannot be set off against a claim against, or debt due to, the estate[3]. Mutual debts arising as the result of an agreement by the personal representatives to compromise a claim for a declaration in favour of a later will can fall within the right of set-off[4].

1 See 2 Geo 2 c 22 (Insolvent Debtors Relief) (1728) s 13; 8 Geo 2 c 24 (Set-off) (1734). These Acts have been repealed, but the right of set-off is preserved: see CIVIL PROCEDURE vol 11 (2015) PARA 399. The right to set off existed in equity before the statutory right was given: see *Freeman v Lomas* (1851) 9 Hare 109 at 112–113; *Pope v Energem Resources Ltd* [2009] EWCA Civ 1086; and CIVIL PROCEDURE vol 11 (2015) PARA 406 et seq; EQUITABLE JURISDICTION vol 47 (2014) PARA 245. As to the meaning of 'personal representative' see PARA 608.
2 See eg *Re Gregson, Christison v Bolam* (1887) 36 ChD 223; and CIVIL PROCEDURE vol 11 (2015) PARA 436.

3 See eg *Bishop v Church* (1748) 3 Atk 691. See also *Re a Debtor (No 87 of 1999), Debtor v Johnson* [2000] BPIR 589, [2000] TLR 95 (demand brought, in form, against testatrix was, in the particular circumstances, treated as one made upon her personally); and CIVIL PROCEDURE vol 11 (2015) PARA 436 et seq.
4 *Ducker v Pulling* [2007] EWHC 2148 (Ch), [2007] All ER (D) 488 (Jul).

1297. Protection of personal representatives by the court or under statutory provisions. In addition to the relief which a personal representative[1] may obtain from the court at its discretion[2], he may be entitled to statutory protection where he has given adequate notice for claims by advertisement[3] or appropriated a sufficient fund to answer future claims in respect of leaseholds[4], where he has distributed the estate without ascertaining that no adoption order has been made[5], where he has distributed the estate and an application under the Inheritance (Provision for Family and Dependants) Act 1975[6] is allowed after the expiration of six months from the grant[7], or where the Limitation Act 1980 applies[8].

1 As to the meaning of 'personal representative' see PARA 608.
2 See PARA 1259.
3 See PARA 965.
4 See PARA 990.
5 See PARA 1063.
6 See PARA 565 et seq.
7 See PARA 1064.
8 See LIMITATION PERIODS vol 68 (2016) PARA 1148.

(ii) Admission of Assets

1298. What constitutes an admission of assets by personal representative. An admission of assets may be by express acknowledgement (whether made to the creditor or beneficiary or to another[1]) or by conduct. If a personal representative suffers judgment to go against him by confession or by default, or fails to plead plene administravit or no assets ultra[2], it is an admission of assets[3]. The admission by an executor of his indebtedness to the estate at the time of the testator's death is an admission of assets in his hands to the amount of the debt[4]. Payment of interest for a considerable period on a legacy, as distinguished from a single payment[5], amounts to an admission of assets to satisfy the legacy[6]. Payment of legacy duty also amounted to an admission[7], but not where the amount returned on the legacy duty account was returned merely as the estimated value of the legacy[8]. Crediting the legatee with the amount of his legacy in the books of a business in which the testator was a partner is a sufficient admission where the will contains no power to employ the assets in the business[9], but not where there is a direction that the legacies are to remain in the business[10]. Part payment of a legacy on account is not an admission of assets to pay in full[11].

1 *Holland v Clark* (1843) 2 Y & C Ch Cas 319, 7 Jur 213.
2 See PARA 1290. As to the meaning of 'personal representative' see PARA 608.
3 *Rock v Leighton* (1700) 1 Salk 310; *Skelton v Hawling* (1749) 1 Wils 258; *Re Marvin, Crawter v Marvin* [1905] 2 Ch 490; *Thompson & Sons v Clarke* (1901) 17 TLR 455; *Marsden v Regan* [1954] 1 All ER 475 at 478, [1954] 1 WLR 423 at 429, CA, per Sir R Evershed MR. See also *Re a Debtor (No 87 of 1999), Debtor v Johnson* [2000] BPIR 589, [2000] TLR 95 (failure to raise a plea of plene administravit; such a failure may be difficult to cure by seeking permission to amend the defence during the trial). See also PARA 1294. As to estoppel of the personal representative, who fails to raise in former proceedings defences available to him, from raising them in subsequent proceedings see CIVIL PROCEDURE vol 12A (2015) PARAS 1629 et seq, 1311.
4 *Rothwell v Rothwell* (1825) 2 Sim & St 217 at 218; *Richardson v Bank of England* (1838) 4 My & Cr 165 at 174.

5 *Corpn of Clergymen's Sons v Swainson* (1748) 1 Ves Sen 75; *A-G v Chapman* (1840) 3 Beav 255; *Whittle v Henning* (1840) 2 Beav 396; *A-G v Higham* (1843) 2 Y & C Ch Cas 634; *Brewster v Prior* (1886) 35 WR 251; *Parry v Huddleton* (1854) 18 Jur 992.
6 Payment of interest on a specific or demonstrative legacy does not amount to an admission of general assets: *Severs v Severs* (1853) 1 Sm & G 400.
7 *Lazonby v Rawson* (1854) 4 De GM & G 556; *Whittle v Henning* (1840) 2 Beav 396. Legacy duty was abolished by the Finance Act 1949 s 27 (repealed), as regards, among other events, the death of any person after 29 July 1949 and was finally abolished by the Finance Act 1975 s 50(1)(c). Payments of inheritance tax would probably be considered with these authorities in mind.
8 *Hutton v Rossiter* (1855) 7 De GM & G 9.
9 *Townend v Townend* (1859) 1 Giff 201. A personal representative will not be estopped from challenging a partnership balance sheet simply because the deceased had signed earlier balance sheets: *Re White, White v Minnis* [1999] 2 All ER 663, [1999] 1 WLR 2079.
10 *Hutton v Rossiter* (1855) 7 De GM & G 9.
11 *Smith v Stothard* (1837) 1 Jur 540.

1299. Agreement for arbitration of claim against estate. A reference to arbitration[1] of a claim against the estate is in general considered as a reference not only of the matters in dispute, but also of the question whether the personal representative has assets, and an award by the arbitrator that the representative is to pay a sum of money is equivalent to determining that he has assets to pay the amount[2] unless the award is that the payment is to be made out of assets[3]. An executor, by referring a cause to arbitration, does not preclude himself from availing himself of a defence that has arisen after the reference[4].

1 As to arbitration see generally ARBITRATION.
2 *Worthington v Barlow* (1797) 7 Term Rep 453; *Pearson v Henry* (1792) 5 Term Rep 6 (explaining *Barry v Rush* (1787) 1 Term Rep 691); *Re Wansborough, Wansborough v Dyer* (1815) 2 Chit 40. Cf *Robson v* (1813) 2 Rose 50; *Riddell v Sutton* (1828) 5 Bing 200; Davies v Ridge (1800) 3 Esp 101. As to the meaning of 'personal representative' see PARA 608.
3 *Love v Honeybourne* (1824) 4 Dow & Ry KB 814.
4 *Alder v Park* (1836) 5 Dowl 16, 2 Har & W 78. Nor, seemingly, would he have precluded himself, by referring a cause, from a plea of judgment recovered puis darrein continuance, while the reference was pending, although it appeared from affidavits that he had a certain amount of assets in his hands: *Alder v Park*. This matter would now be governed by the Administration of Estates Act 1971 s 10 (which abolished preference and retainer and substituted a partial defence for personal representatives: see PARA 983) and CPR Pt 16 (statements of case: see CIVIL PROCEDURE vol 11 (2015) PARA 340 et seq).

1300. Extent of admission by personal representative of assets. Although it is very old law that the payment of one legacy is an admission of assets for every other legatee[1] or creditor[2], the court endeavours to deal fairly with each case, and not by a mere unintentional admission of assets by executors to subject them to liabilities which they never contemplated or meant to undertake[3]. Therefore, if an executor should choose on his own responsibility, without reference to the state of the assets, to pay small legacies given to employees, it would be hard to say that he had conclusively bound himself to pay all the legacies given by the will[4], and an executor who had made a payment to one legatee which was warranted by the existing state of the assets would not be precluded from setting up against the other legatees a subsequent depreciation in value of the estate[5].

Even as against creditors, the payment of a legacy is not of itself such an admission of assets to pay debts as to disentitle the executor from explaining the circumstances under which the payment was made[6], nor will payment of interest on a debt amount to an admission of assets for payment of the principal[7]. It may be otherwise where all legacies have been paid or satisfied and the executor is a major beneficiary[8].

1 *Cook v Martyn* (1737) 2 Atk 2 at 3 per Lord Hardwicke. See also PARA 1096.

2 *Savage v Lane* (1847) 6 Hare 32; *Re a Debtor (No 87 of 1999), Debtor v Johnson* [2000] BPIR 589, [2000] TLR 95.
3 *Morewood v Currey* (1879) 28 WR 213 at 215 per Hall V-C; *Postlethwaite v Mounsey* (1842) 6 Hare 33n; *Cadbury v Smith* (1869) LR 9 Eq 37.
4 *Postlethwaite v Mounsey* (1842) 6 Hare 33n at 35 per Wigram V-C.
5 *Re Schneider, Kirby v Schneider* (1906) 22 TLR 223.
6 *Savage v Lane* (1847) 6 Hare 32.
7 *Cleverly v Brett* (1772) 5 Term Rep 8n.
8 See *Re a Debtor (No 87 of 1999), Debtor v Johnson* [2000] BPIR 589, [2000] TLR 95 (where the inference was that in an estate which had been fully wound up, and the administratrix had failed to raise a plea of plene administravit (see PARA 1290) and was also the main beneficiary, that raised a presumption of assets sufficient to meet a debtor's claim).

1301. Effect of admission by personal representative of assets. Although an admission cannot be retracted unless a case of mistake is clearly made out[1], it is susceptible of explanation[2], and must be taken to have reference to the circumstances with which the personal representative was at the time acquainted, and if the circumstances on which he based his admission fail, the admission fails also[3].

On an admission of assets an immediate personal judgment may be made against the personal representative[4], whether the claim is by a creditor or a legatee[5] and even though the creditor claims on behalf of himself and all other creditors[6], for in so far as the representative has no assets to meet the claim, a rebuttable presumption that he has committed a devastavit arises[7]. An admission of assets by one executor does not preclude a creditor from requiring the other executors to account[8]. An admission of assets to pay a debt covers the interest on the debt[9].

An admission of assets may, in some circumstances, justify the setting aside of a statutory demand made by the executor against a person who brings a cross-demand, even though the cross-demand is brought against the executor in his personal capacity[10].

An express admission of assets for payment of a legacy in an action for recovery of the legacy covers the costs of the action, if the court thinks fit to give them[11], but an implied admission of assets arising from a default judgment or failure to plead plene administravit[12] does not cover costs unascertained at the date of the judgment[13].

By admitting assets an executor of an executor renders himself liable to the same judgment as that to which the original executor would himself, if living, have been liable[14].

1 *Drewry v Thacker* (1819) 3 Swan 529 at 548.
2 *Payne v Tanner* (1886) 55 LJ Ch 611 at 613; *Brewster v Prior* (1886) 35 WR 251 at 252; *Inge v Kenny* (1845) 4 Hare 452.
3 *Horsley v Chaloner* (1750) 2 Ves Sen 83 at 85; *Payne v Little* (1856) 22 Beav 69; *Clark v Bates* (1848) 2 De G & Sm 203.
4 *Horsley v Chaloner* (1750) 2 Ves Sen 83; *Say v Creed* (1844) 3 Hare 455 at 459; *Barnard v Pumfrett* (1841) 5 My & Cr 63; *Rogers v Soutten* (1838) 7 LJ Ch 118; *Gordon v Scott* (1844) 3 Hare 459n; *Lincoln v Wright* (1841) 4 Beav 427 at 431. As to the meaning of 'personal representative' see PARA 608.
5 *Jeffs v Wood* (1723) 2 P Wms 128 at 131.
6 *Woodgate v Field* (1842) 2 Hare 211.
7 *Leonard v Simpson* (1835) 2 Bing NC 176; *Batchelar v Evans* [1939] Ch 1007, [1939] 3 All ER 606; *Marsden v Regan* [1954] 1 All ER 475, [1954] 1 WLR 423, CA. As to devastavit see PARA 1244 et seq.
8 *Norton v Turvill* (1723) 2 P Wms 144 at 145.
9 *Foster v Foster* (1789) 2 Bro CC 616; *Tew v Earl Winterton* (1792) 1 Ves 451 at 452, commented on in *Hovey v Blakeman* (1799) 4 Ves 596 at 606.
10 *Re a Debtor (No 87 of 1999), Debtor v Johnson* [2000] BPIR 589, [2000] TLR 95.

11 *Philanthropic Society v Hobson* (1833) 2 My & K 357.
12 See PARAS 1290, 1294.
13 *Marsden v Regan* [1954] 1 All ER 475, [1954] 1 WLR 423, CA.
14 *Davenport v Stafford* (1852) 2 De GM & G 901.

INDEX

Wills and Intestacy

Words and Phrases